Lecture Notes in Computer Science 16758

The series Lecture Notes in Computer Science (LNCS), including its subseries Lecture Notes in Artificial Intelligence (LNAI) and Lecture Notes in Bioinformatics (LNBI), has established itself as a medium for the publication of new developments in computer science and information technology research, teaching, and education.

LNCS enjoys close cooperation with the computer science R & D community, the series counts many renowned academics among its volume editors and paper authors, and collaborates with prestigious societies. Its mission is to serve this international community by providing an invaluable service, mainly focused on the publication of conference and workshop proceedings and postproceedings. LNCS commenced publication in 1973.

Osvaldo Gervasi · Beniamino Murgante ·
Chiara Garau · Ana Maria A. C. Rocha ·
M. Noelia Faginas Lago · Ana C. Braga ·
Yeliz Karaca
Editors

Computational Science and Its Applications – ICCSA 2026 Workshops

Braga, Portugal, June 30 – July 3, 2026
Proceedings, Part I

Springer

Editors
Osvaldo Gervasi
University of Perugia
Perugia, Perugia, Italy

Chiara Garau
University of Cagliari
Cagliari, Italy

M. Noelia Faginas Lago
University of Perugia
Perugia, Italy

Yeliz Karaca
University of Massachusetts
Worcester, MA, USA

Beniamino Murgante
University of Basilicata
Potenza, Italy

Ana Maria A. C. Rocha
University of Minho
Braga, Portugal

Ana C. Braga
University of Minho
Braga, Portugal

ISSN 0302-9743 ISSN 1611-3349 (electronic)
Lecture Notes in Computer Science
ISBN 978-3-032-30496-4 ISBN 978-3-032-30497-1 (eBook)
https://doi.org/10.1007/978-3-032-30497-1

This Springer imprint is published by the registered company Springer Nature Switzerland AG
The registered company address is: Gewerbestrasse 11, 6330 Cham, Switzerland

Preface

These 9 volumes (LNCS volumes 16758–16766) comprise the peer-reviewed papers from the 57 Workshops of the 2026 International Conference on Computational Science and Its Applications (ICCSA 2026), held between June 30 and July 3, 2026, in Braga, Portugal. The peer-reviewed papers from the six main conference tracks are published in a separate set of 3 volumes (LNCS volumes 16767–16769).

The conference was held in a hybrid format, with the vast majority of participants attending in person, hosted by the University of Minho in Braga, Portugal.

We enabled virtual participation for those who did not attend the event in person due to logistical, political, or economic constraints by adopting a technological infrastructure based on open-source software (Jitsi + Riot) and a commercial Cloud infrastructure. ICCSA 2026 was organized by the University of Minho (Portugal), the University of Perugia (Italy), the University of Basilicata (Italy), the University of Cagliari (Italy), Monash University (Australia), and Kyushu Sangyo University (Japan).

With the 2026 edition, ICCSA celebrated its 26th anniversary, marking a new chapter in its longstanding history after its memorable 25th anniversary celebrated in Istanbul, Türkiye. Hosted in Braga, Portugal, the conference found a particularly meaningful setting in one of Europe's oldest and most vibrant academic cities, a place where historical depth, cultural continuity, and contemporary scientific exchange meet. Braga offers an inspiring European context for renewing the international and intercultural dialogue that has always characterized ICCSA, while giving new visibility to the role of computational science in addressing the complex challenges of cities, territories, technologies, and societies.

ICCSA 2026 marked another fruitful and thought-provoking academic event in the International Conference on Computational Science and Its Applications (ICCSA) conference series, previously held in Istanbul, Türkiye (2025), Hanoi, Vietnam (2024), Athens, Greece (2023), Málaga, Spain (2022), Cagliari, Italy (hybrid with few participants in presence in 2021 and completely online in 2020), Saint Petersburg, Russia (2019), Melbourne, Australia (2018), Trieste, Italy (2017), Beijing, China (2016), Banff, Canada (2015), Guimarães, Portugal (2014), Ho Chi Minh City, Vietnam (2013), Salvador, Brazil (2012), Santander, Spain (2011), Fukuoka, Japan (2010), Suwon, South Korea (2009), Perugia, Italy (2008), Kuala Lumpur, Malaysia (2007), Glasgow, UK (2006), Singapore (2005), Assisi, Italy (2004), Montreal, Canada (2003), and (as ICCS) Amsterdam, the Netherlands (2002) and San Francisco, USA (2001).

Computational Science constitutes the main pillar of most present research, industrial, and commercial applications, and plays a unique role in exploiting innovative ICT technologies, and the ICCSA conference series has, accordingly, provided ample opportunities to researchers and industry practitioners to discuss new ideas, to share complex problems and their solutions, and to shape new trends in Computational Science. As the conference mirrors society from a scientific point of view, this year's undoubtedly dominant theme was large language models, machine learning, and Artificial Intelligence, and their applications across the most diverse technological, economic, and industrial fields, amongst others.

The ICCSA 2026 conference included 57 workshops, focusing on topical issues of utmost importance to science, technology, and society: from new computational approaches for earth science, to mathematical methods for image processing, new statistical and optimisation methods, several Artificial Intelligence approaches, sustainability issues, smart cities and related technologies, to name a few. In addition, ICCSA 2026 included six general tracks covering computational science and its applications: Computational Methods, Algorithms and Scientific Applications; High-Performance Computing and Networks; Geometric Modelling, Graphics and Visualisation; Advanced and Emerging Applications; Information Systems and Technologies; and Urban and Regional Planning.

For these Workshops Proceedings, we accepted 328 full papers, 23 short papers, and 3 Ph.D. Showcase papers from a total of 1184 submissions (acceptance rate 29.9%). Reviews were single blind, and submissions received 2.6 reviews each, on average. In the Main Conference Proceedings, we accepted 119 full papers, 3 short papers, and 2 Ph.D. Showcase papers from 431 submissions to the General Tracks of the Conference (acceptance rate of 29.9%). We would like to convey our sincere appreciation to the workshop chairs and co-chairs and program committee members, for their diligent work, commitment, and dedication.

The success and consistent maintenance of the ICCSA conference series in general, and of ICCSA 2026 in particular, rely upon the support of many people: authors, presenters, participants, keynote speakers, workshop chairs, session chairs, Organizing Committee members, student volunteers, Program Committee members, Advisory Committee members, International Liaison chairs, reviewers, and other individuals in various roles. Thus, we take this opportunity to wholeheartedly thank each and every one.

We also wish to thank the publisher, Springer, for accepting the proceedings, and for their kind assistance and cooperation during the editing process. We would cordially like to invite you to refer to the ICCSA website https://iccsa.org, where you can find the relevant details regarding this academic endeavour and our event.

June 2026

Chiara Garau
Ana Maria A. C. Rocha
Osvaldo Gervasi
Beniamino Murgante

Welcome Message from the Organizers

On behalf of the Local Organizing Committee of ICCSA 2026, it is our great pleasure to welcome you to the 26th International Conference on Computational Science and Its Applications, held from June 30 to July 3, 2026, at the University of Minho in Braga, Portugal.

We are deeply honoured by the trust placed in us by the ICCSA General Chairs in organizing another edition of this successful conference series. We hope that ICCSA 2026 provided an inspiring environment for scientific exchange, collaboration, and discussion among researchers from all over the world.

The conference took place at the University of Minho, one of the most prestigious higher education institutions in Portugal. Founded in 1973, the University of Minho has campuses in Braga and Guimaraes and is widely recognized for its academic excellence, research activity, and strong international outlook.

Braga, one of the oldest cities in Portugal, is renowned for its historical heritage, cultural vitality, and welcoming atmosphere.

Located in the heart of the Minho region, the city combines tradition with modernity, offering visitors renowned gastronomy, beautiful landscapes, and the unique character of *Vinho Verde* wine.

The scientific program of ICCSA 2026 included plenary lectures delivered by distinguished scientists, together with a broad range of workshops covering several areas of Computational Science and its Applications. We believe that the conference provided excellent opportunities to share ideas, discuss emerging challenges, and foster new collaborations.

In addition to the scientific sessions, participants had the opportunity to enjoy a rich social program.

Planned activities included a Welcome Reception at Largo do Paço, the Rectorate of the University of Minho, located in the former Archbishop's Palace - one of the most emblematic historical buildings in the city center; a *Vinho Verde* wine-tasting experience at Quinta d'Amares, where particiapnts could discover the art of winemaking; and a guided visit to the coastal city of Viana do Castelo, renowned for its maritime heritage, traditional architecture, and beautiful Atlantic scenery. The conference gala dinner took place at Colunata Eventos, located within the Bom Jesus do Monte sanctuary, a UNESCO World Heritage Site, where ICCSA participants enjoyed delicious recipes and a wonderful view over the city of Braga.

The success of ICCSA 2026 would not have been possible without the dedication and enthusiasm of many collaborators and volunteers, whose hard work and commitment greatly contributed to the organization of the conference.

On behalf of the Local Organizing Committee, it was our honour to warmly welcome you to the beautiful city of Braga and we hope you had an enjoyable and productive conference.
We enjoyed meeting you in Braga.

Sincerely yours,

On behalf of the Local Organizing Committee.

June 2026 Ana Maria A. C. Rocha

Organization

Honorary General Chairs

Bernady O. Apduhan	Kyushu Sangyo University, Japan
Kenneth C. J. Tan	Sardina Systems, UK

General Chairs

Ana Maria A. C. Rocha	University of Minho, Portugal
David Taniar	Monash University, Australia
Osvaldo Gervasi	University of Perugia, Italy

Program Committee Chairs

Beniamino Murgante	University of Basilicata, Italy
Chiara Garau	University of Cagliari, Italy

International Advisory Committee

Jemal Abawajy	Deakin University, Australia
Dharma P. Agarwal	University of Cincinnati, USA
Jagannath Aryal	University of Melbourne, Australia
Rajkumar Buyya	University of Melbourne, Australia
Claudia Bauzer Medeiros	University of Campinas, Brazil
Carl K. Chang	Iowa State University, USA
Elizabeth Chang	University of the Sunshine Coast, Australia
Manfred M. Fisher	Vienna University of Economics and Business, Austria
Pierre Frankhauser	University of Franche-Comté/CNRS, France
Marina L. Gavrilova	University of Calgary, Canada
Sumi Helal	University of Florida, USA & Lancaster University, UK
Bin Jiang	University of Gävle, Sweden
Yee Leung	Chinese University of Hong Kong, China
Biswajeet Pradhan	University of Technology Sydney, Australia
My Thai	University of Florida, USA

International Liaison Chairs

Giuseppe Borruso	University of Trieste, Italy
Elise De Donker	Western Michigan University, USA
Maria Noelia Faginas Lago	University of Perugia, Italy
Maria Irene Falcão	University of Minho, Portugal
Robert C. H. Hsu	Chung Hua University, Taiwan
Yeliz Karaca	UMass Chan Medical School, USA
Tae-Hoon Kim	Zhejiang University of Science and Technology, China
Vladimir Korkhov	Saint Petersburg University, Russia
Takashi Naka	Kyushu Sangyo University, Japan
Rafael D. C. Santos	National Institute for Space Research, Brazil
Maribel Yasmina Santos	University of Minho, Portugal
Anastasia Stratigea	National Technical University of Athens, Greece
Nguyen Canh Thai	Thuyloi University, Vietnam
Kh Md Nahiduzzaman	Mohammed VI Polytechnic University, Rabat, Morocco

Workshop and Session Organizing Chairs

Beniamino Murgante	University of Basilicata, Italy
Chiara Garau	University of Cagliari, Italy

Award Chair

Wenny Rahayu	La Trobe University, Australia

Publicity Committee Chairs

Elmer Dadios	De La Salle University, Philippines
Nataliia Kulabukhova	Saint Petersburg University, Russia
Daisuke Takahashi	Tsukuba University, Japan
Doan Quang Tu	Academy of Military Science and Technology, Vietnam
Shangwang Wang	Beijing University of Posts and Telecommunications, China

Local Organizing Committee Chairs

Maria Irene Falcão	University of Minho, Portugal
Ana Cristina Braga	University of Minho, Portugal
Rui José	University of Minho, Portugal
José Manuel Machado	University of Minho, Portugal
Jorge G. Rocha	University of Minho, Portugal

Technology Chair

Damiano Perri	University of Perugia, Italy

Workshops

Workshop on Advancements in Applied Machine-learning and Data Analytics (AAMDA 2026)

Workshop Organizers

Alessandro Costantini	INFN, Italy
Elisabetta Ronchieri	INFN CNAF, Italy

Workshop Program Committee Members

Luca Dell'Agnello	INFN, Italy
Barbara Martelli	INFN, Italy
Daniele Cesini	INFN CNAF, Italy
Giovanni Zurlo	INFN CNAF, Italy
Luca Giommi	INFN CNAF, Italy
Valentino Santucci	Università per Stranieri di Perugia, Italy
Francesco Santini	University of Perugia, Italy
Paolo Mengoni	Hong Kong Baptist University, China
Alessandro Bombini	Istituto Nazionale di Fisica Nucleare, Italy

Artificial Intelligence Tools In Managing Future Communities (AiMFutCOM 2026)

Workshop Organizers

Marco Vona	University of Basilicata, Italy
Francesco Scorza	University of Basilicata, Italy
Donatello Cardone	University of Basilicata, Italy
Maurizio Pollino	ENEA, Italy
Gregorio DAgostino	ENEA, Italy

Workshop Program Committee Members

Maria Danese	CNRISPC, Italy
Rachele Vanessa Gatto	Università della Basilicata, Italy
Simone Corrado	University of Basilicata, Italy
Alessandro Plaisant	University of Sassari, Italy
Sabrina Lai	University of Cagliari, Italy
Alfonso Annunziata	University of Basilicata, Italy
Jolanta Dvarioniene	Kaunas University of Technology, Lithuania

Advanced and Innovative Web Apps 2026 (AIWA 2026)

Workshop Organizers

Damiano Perri	University of Perugia, Italy
Osvaldo Gervasi	University of Perugia, Italy
Luciano Alessandro Ipsaro Palesi	University of Florence, Italy

Workshop Program Committee Members

David Berti	ART SpA, Italy
JungYoon Kim	Gachon University, South Korea
Taihoon Kim	Chonnam National University, South Korea

Advanced Mathematics and Computing Models in Complex Data-Intensive Computational Systems (AMCM 2026)

Workshop Organizers

Yeliz Karaca	UMass Chan Medical School and Massachusetts Institute of Technology, USA
Dumitru Baleanu	Lebanese American University, Lebanon
Osvaldo Gervasi	University of Perugia, Italy
Yudong Zhang	University of Leicester, UK
Majaz Moonis	UMass Chan Medical School, USA

Workshop Program Committee Members

Aziz Dursun	Virginia Tech University, USA
Akif Akgul	Hitit University, Turkey
Nizamettin Aydin	Istanbul Technical University, Turkey
Martin Bohner	Missouri University of Science and Technology, USA
Khan Muhammad	Sungkyunkwan University, South Korea

Advanced Numerical Approaches for assessment and design of no-tension Masonry Structures (ANAMS 2026)

Workshop Organizers

Antonino Iannuzzo	Universitá degli studi del Sannio, Italy
Natalia Pingaro	Politecnico di Milano, Italy
Andrea Montanino	International Centre for Numerical Methods in Engineering, Spain
Elham Mousavian	University of Edinburgh, UK
Stefano Galassi	University of Florence, Italy

Workshop Program Committee Members

Amal Gerges	University of Cagliari, Italy
Vittorio Paris	University of Bergamo, Italy
Alessandra Capolupo	Polytechnic University of Bari, Italy
Carlo Olivieri	Pegaso University, Italy
Generoso Vaiano	Pegaso University, Italy

Luigi Sibille	Norwegian University of Science and Technology, Norway
Francesco Picariello	Universitas Mercatorum, Italy
Ilaria Scarcelli	Politecnico di Bari, Italy
Fabian Bernal Orozco Barrera	National Autonomous University of Mexico, Mexico
Gabriel Barbat	Universitat Politècnica de Catalunya, Spain
Alejandro Cornejo	Universitat Politècnica de Catalunya, Spain
Mohammad Pourfouladi	Politecnico di Milano, Italy

Artificialization of land, Urban Transformation, and Territorial Resilience in a changing Climate (AUTTREC 2026)

Workshop Organizers

Celestina Fazia	Università di Enna Kore, Italy
Kh Md Nahiduzzaman	Mohammed VI Polytechnic University, Morocco
Hassan Radoine	Mohammed VI Polytechnic University, Morocco
Cezar Morar	University of Oradea, Romania
Antonio García Martínez	Universidad de Sevilla, Spain
Clara Stella Vicari Aversa	Università degli Studi Mediterranea di Reggio Calabria, Italy

Workshop Program Committee Members

Federica Sortino	Universitià degli studi di Enna Kore, Italy
Giulia Fernanda Grazia Catania	Universit di Enna Kore, Italy
Maria Francesca Faro	Ministry of Education and Merit (MIM), Italy
Aleksandar Valjarević	University of Belgrade, Serbia
Laila El Ghazouani	Mohammed VI Polytechnic University, Morocco
Adnane Labbaci	Ibn Tofail University, Morocco

Blockchain and Distributed Ledgers: Technologies and Applications (BDLTA 2026)

Workshop Organizers

Vladimir Korkhov	Saint Petersburg State University, Russia
Elena Stankova	Saint Petersburg State University, Russia
Nataliia Kulabukhova	AutoTech, Russia

Workshop Program Committee Members

Vasily Solodkov	National Research University Higher School of Economics, Moscow, Russia
Alexander Bogdanov	St. Petersburg State University, Russia
Alexander Degtyarev	Saint Petersburg State University, Russia
Dmitrii Vasiunin	Deutsche Telekom Cloud Services E.P.E., Greece
Serob Balyan	Institute for Informatics and Automation Problems, National Academy of Sciences of Armenia, Armenia
Suren Abrahamyan	Institute for Informatics and Automation Problems of NAS RA, Armenia
Ashot Gevorkyan	Institute for Informatics and Automation Problems NAS of Armenia, Armenia
Martin Vala	Pavol Jozef Šafárik University, Slovak Republic
Nodir Zaynalov	Samarkand Branch of Tashkent University of Information Technologies Named After Muhammad al Khwarizmi, Uzbekistan
Michail Panteleyev	Saint Petersburg Electrotechnical University, Russia
Alexander Degtyarev	St. Petersburg State University, Russia
Alexander Bogdanov	St. Petersburg State University, Russia

Bio and Neuro inspired Computing and Applications (BIONCA 2026)

Workshop Organizers

Nadia Nedjah	State University of Rio de Janeiro, Brazil
Luiza de Macedo Mourelle	State University de Rio de Janeiro, Brazil

Workshop Program Committee Members

Alan Oliveira	Universidade de Lisboa, Portugal
Rogerio Calazan	Instituto de Estudos do Mar Almirante Paulo Moreira - Brazilian Navy, Brazil
Marcos Farias	Instituto de Engenharia Nuclear, Brazil
Joelmir Ramos	State University de Rio de Janeiro, Brazil
Luigi Maciel Ribeiro	State University of Rio de Janeiro, Brazil

Computational and Applied Mathematics (CAM 2026)

Workshop Organizers

Maria Irene Falcao	University of Minho, Portugal
Fernando Miranda	Universidade do Minho, Portugal

Workshop Program Committee Members

Graca Tomaz	Instituto Politécnico da Guarda, Portugal
Helmuth Malonek	University of Aveiro, Portugal
Isabel Cacao	University of Aveiro, Portugal
Joao Morais	Autonomous Technological Institute of Mexico (ITAM), Mexico
Lidia Aceto	Università del Piemonte Orientale, Italy
Luís Ferrás	University of Minho, Portugal
Patricia Beites	University of Beira Interior, Portugal
Paulo Amorim	Escola de Matemática Aplicada da Fundação Getulio Vargas, Brazil
Regina de Almeida	University of Trás-os-Montes and Alto Douro, Portugal
Ricardo Severino	University of Minho, Portugal

Computational and Applied Statistics for Data & AI (CAS 2026)

Workshop Organizers

Ana Cristina Braga	University of Minho, Portugal
Ines Sena	University of Minho, Portugal
Joao Mendes	Polytechnic Institute of Bragança, Portugal

Workshop Program Committee Members

A. Manuela Goncalves	University of Minho, Portugal
Vera Afreixo	University of Aveiro, Portugal
Ivan Rodriguez Conde	University of Arkansas at Little Rock, USA
Isabel Natário	Universidade Nova de Lisboa, Portugal
Luca Parodi	University of Genoa, Italy
Flávia Pires	Instituto Politecnico de Bragança, Portugal
Beatriz Flamia Azevedo	Instituto Politecnico de Bragança, Portugal
Adriano Silva	Instituto Politecnico de Bragança VAT 600013758, Portugal

Ana Paula Amorim	Universidade do Minho, Portugal
Angela Silva	Universidade do Minho, Portugal
Arunasalam Rahunanthan	Central State University, USA
Bruna Ramos	University of Minho, Portugal
Cecília Maria Vasconcelos Costa e Castro	Universidade do Minho, Portugal
Florbela Correia	Polytechnic Institute of Viana do Castelo, Portugal
Joaquim Goncalves	Polytechnic Institute of Cávado and Ave, Portugal
Lino Costa	University of Minho, Portugal
Luís Miguel Matos	Universidade do Minho, Portugal
Marco Reis	University of Coimbra, Portugal
Maria Mourao	Polytechnic Institute of Viana do Castelo, Portugal
Martin Perez Perez	University of Vigo, Spain
Sandra Aleixo	FCiências.ID, Portugal
Paula Odete Fernandes	Instituto Politecnico de Bragança, Portugal
Iván Rodríguez Conde	Universidade de Vigo, Spain
Telmo Miguel Pires Pinto	University of Minho, Portugal

Circular Economy and Territorial Competitiveness (CETC 2026)

Workshop Organizers

Gerardo Carpentieri	University of Naples Federico II, Italy
Carmen Guida	Università degli Studi di Napoli Federico II, Italy
Floriana Zucaro	University of Naples Federico II, Italy
Zhadyra Konurbaeva	D. Serikbayev East Kazakhstan Technical University, Kazakhstan
Saule Kumargazhanova	D. Serikbayev East Kazakhstan Technical University, Kazakhstan

Workshop Program Committee Members

Rosaria Battarra	ISMed-CNR, Italy
Laura Ascione	Università degli studi di Napoli Federico II, Italy
Valerio Martinelli	Università di Napoli Federico II, Italy
Madina Yussubaliyeva	D. Serikbayeva East Kazakhstan Technical University, Kazakhstan
Samat Baigereyev	D. Serikbayev East Kazakhstan Technical University, Kazakhstan

Circular Ecological Heritage Communities: Regeneration and Evaluation Strategies for Historic Villages, Landscapes and Rural Territories (CHEC 2026)

Workshop Organizers

Mariarosaria Angrisano	Pegaso University, Italy
Antonia Gravagnuolo	CNR Institute of Heritage Science, Italy
Francesca Buglione	CNR ISPC, Italy
Piera Della Morte	Pegaso Telematic University, Italy

Workshop Program Committee Members

Giulia Datola	Politecnico di Milano, Italy
Marco Rossitti	Politecnico di Milano, Italy
Federico DellAnna	Politecnico di Torino, Italy
Grazia Neglia	Pegaso Telematic University, Italy
Vanessa Assumma	University of Bologna, Italy
Ippolita Mecca	Pegaso Telematic University, Italy
Ferdinando Verardi	Pegaso Telematic University, Italy
Eleonora Sottile	University of Cagliari, Italy
Dina Jovanovic	Politecnico di Milano, Italy
Martina Mulinacci	Politecnico di Milano, Italy
Davide Cerati	Politecnico di Milano, Italy
Daniela Oreni	Politecnico di Milano, Italy
Patrizia Riganti	University of Glasgow, UK
Carlo Olivieri	Pegaso University, Italy
Giulio Cavana	Politecnico di Torino, Italy
Maria Tartari	CNR, Italy
Luigi Fusco Girard	Pegaso Telematic University, Italy
Albina Scioti	Università Telematica Pegaso, Italy
Eleonora Righetto	Università degli Studi di Padova, Italy
Chiara D'Alpaos	University of Padua, Italy
Anthony Suppa	Politecnico di Torino, Italy
Giorgia Malavasi	Politecnico di Torino, Italy
Kaoutare Amini Alaoui	Mohamed VI Polytechnic University, Morocco
Elena Todella	University of Parma, Italy
Leonhard Seyboth	Federal University of Santa Catarina, Brazil
Jianzhuo Xu	Politecnico di Milano, Italy
Ludovica Nasca	University of Catania, Italy
Alessandro Plaisant	University of Sassari, Italy

Maria Carla Saliu	University of Cagliari, Italy
Ons Zoghlami	Sapienza University of Rome, Italy
Irena Ištoka Otković	Josip Juraj Strossmayer University of Osijek, Croatia
Daniele Cannatella	TU Delft, Italy
Tanja Congiu	University of Sassari, Italy
Juan Camilo Giraldo	Institute for Advanced Architecture of Catalonia, Spain
YiChang Liu	Bio-Architecture Formosana, Taiwan
Yasmine Selim	Ain Shams University, Egypt
Simona Tondelli	Alma Mater Studiorum University of Bologna, Italy
Efrossyni Tsakiri	National Technical University of Athens, Greece

Cyber Intelligence and Applications (CIA 2026)

Workshop Organizers

Gianni D'Angelo	University of Salerno, Italy
Francesco Palmieri	University of Salerno, Italy
Massimo Ficco	University of Salerno, Italy

Workshop Program Committee Members

Arcangelo Castiglione	University of Salerno, Italy
Ugo Fiore	University of Salerno, Italy
Michele Mastroianni	University of Foggia, Italy
Marcello Trovati	Edge Hill University, UK
Raffaele Esposito	University of Salerno, Italy
Marek Ogiela	AGH University of Science and Technology, Poland
Chang Choi	Gachon University, South, South Korea
Mauro Migliardi	University of Padua, Italy

Computational Methods, Statistics and Industrial Mathematics (CMSIM 2026)

Workshop Organizers

Maria Filomena Teodoro	CINAV, Escola Naval, Instituto Universitário Militar, Portugal

Paula Simões	Academia Militar, Portugal
Teresa A. Oliveira	University of Lisbon and Universidade Aberta, Portugal

Workshop Program Committee Members

Luis Teodoro	University of Oslo, Norway
Eliana Costa e Silva	Polytechnic of Porto, Portugal
Ana Borges	Instituto Politécnico do Porto, Portugal
Cristina Lopes	Polytechnic Institute of Porto, Portugal
Fernando Lucas Carapau	University of Évora, Portugal
Antonio S. Macias	University of A Coruña, Spain
Matteo Sacchet	University of Turin, Italy
Marina Marchisio Conte	University of Turin, Italy
Christos Kitsos	University of West Attica, Greece
M. Rosário Ramos	Universidade Aberta, University of Lisbon, Portugal
António Pacheco	Instituto Superior Técnico, Portugal
Ana Sofia Rézio	Polytechnic Institute of Lisbon, Portugal
Paula Simões	Military Academy Portuguese Army, Portugal
Ricardo Moura	NOVA University of Lisbon, Portugal
Ana Oliveira	Academia Militar, Portugal
Sílvia Chá	Military Academy, Portugal
Carlos Rodrigues	Instituto Politecnico de Bragança, Portugal

Computational Optimization and Applications (COA 2026)

Workshop Organizers

Ana Maria A. C. Rocha	University of Minho, Portugal
Humberto Rocha	University of Coimbra, Portugal

Workshop Program Committee Members

Eligius Hendrix	Universidad de Málaga, Spain
Joana Dias	University of Coimbra, Portugal
Ana Pereira	Polytechnic Institute of Bragança, Portugal
Lino Costa	University of Minho, Portugal, Portugal
Filipe Alvelos	Universidade do Minho, Portugal
Ana Paula Teixeira	Universidade do Minho, Portugal

Florbela P. Fernandes	Politecnico de Bragança, Portugal
Ana Monteiro	University of Coimbra, Portugal
Rui Pascoal	University of Coimbra, Portugal
Rommel Regis	Saint Joseph's University, USA
Telmo Miguel Pires Pinto	University of Minho, Portugal
Emerson Paiva	Minho University, Portugal

Computational Methods in Advanced Networking Technologies (CoMANT 2026)

Workshop Organizers

Eslam Farsimadan	University of Salerno, Italy
Leila Moradi	University of Salerno, Italy
Francesco Palmieri	University of Salerno, Italy

Workshop Program Committee Members

Massimo Ficco	University of Salerno, Italy
Ugo Fiore	University of Salerno, Italy
Michele Mastroianni	University of Foggia, Italy
Arcangelo Castiglione	University of Salerno, Italy
Francesco Giuseppe Zammarrelli	University of Salerno, Italy
Annalaura Miglino	University of Salerno, Italy
Mojtaba Sharifzadeh	Università di Trento, Italy
Zahra Ebadi Ansaroudi	Fondazione Bruno Kessler, Italy
Mohammad Vazir Panah	University of Salerno, Italy
Gennaro Pio Rimoli	Università degli Studi di Salerno, Italy

Computational Astrochemistry 2026 (CompAstro 2026)

Workshop Organizers

Marzio Rosi	University of Perugia, Italy
Daniela Ascenzi	Università degli Studi di Trento, Italy
Nadia Balucani	University of Perugia, Italy
Stefano Falcinelli	University of Perugia, Italy

Workshop Program Committee Members

Luca Mancini	University of Perugia, Italy
Andrea Giustini	University of Perugia, Italy
Albert Rimola	Universitat Autònoma de Barcelona, Spain
Piero Ugliengo	Università degli Studi di Torino, Italy
Dario Campisi	University of Perugia, Italy
Gianmarco Valuzzo	University of Perugia, Italy
Giacomo Pannacci	Università degli Studi di Perugia, Italy
Giacomo Giorgi	Università degli Studi di Perugia, Italy
Gabriella Di Genova	Università degli Studi di Perugia, Italy
Lisa Giani	Université Grenoble Alpes, IPAG, France
Emilia Valenca Ferreira de Aragao	University of Montpellier, CEA, CNRS, ENSCM, France
Marco Parriani	Università degli studi di Perugia, Italy
Costanza Borghesi	CNR Istituto Nanoscienze, Italy

Computational methods for Porous materials (CompPor 2026)

Workshop Organizers

Vadim Lisitsa	Institute of Petroleum Geology and Geophysics SB RAS, Russia
Evgeniy Romenski	Sobolev Institute of Mathematics, Russia

Workshop Program Committee Members

Tatyana Khachkova	Institute of Petroleum Geology and Geophysics SB RAS, Russia
Dmitry Prokhorov	Institute of Petroleum Geology and Geophysics SB RAS, Russia
Mikhail Novikov	Sobolev Institute of Mathematics SB RAS, Russia
Galina Reshetova	Institute of Computational Mathematics and Mathematical Geophysics SB RAS, Russia
Sergey Solovyev	Sobolev Institute of Mathematics SB RAS, Russia
Vladimir Cheverda	Sobolev Institute of Mathematics SB RAS, Russia

Workshop on Computational Science and HPC (CSHPC 2026)

Workshop Organizers

Elise de Doncker	Western Michigan University, USA
Hideo Matsufuru	High Energy Accelerator Research Organization, Japan
Robert Makin	Western Michigan University, USA

Workshop Program Committee Members

Hiroshi Daisaka	Hitotsubashi University, Japan
James Rhodes	Western Michigan University, USA
Naohito Nakasato	University of Aizu, Japan
Issaku Kanamori	RIKEN, Japan
Takahiro Ueda	Juntendo University, Japan
Keigo Nitadori	RIKEN, Japan
Fukuko Yuasa	KEK, Japan
Shigeyoshi Aoyama	KEK, Japan
Tatsumi Aoyama	University of Tokyo, Japan
Tasnim Gharaibeh	Kalamazoo College, USA

Cities, Technologies and Planning (CTP 2026)

Workshop Organizers

Giuseppe Borruso	University of Trieste, Italy
Beniamino Murgante	University of Basilicata, Italy
Malgorzata Hanzl	Lodz University of Technology, Poland
Anastasia Stratigea	National Technical University of Athens, Greece
Ljiljana Zivkovic	Republic Geodetic Authority, Serbia
Ginevra Balletto	University of Cagliari, Italy

Workshop Program Committee Members

Silvia Battino	University of Sassari, Italy
Mara Ladu	University of Cagliari, Italy
Maria del Mar Munoz	University of Cádiz, Spain
Ainhoa Amaro	EVOCONS, Spain
Enrico Dagostini	University of Malta, Malta

Francesca Krasna	Università degli Studi di Trieste, Italy
Brisol García García	Universidad Politécnica de Quintana Roo, Mexico
Giovanni Mauro	University of Campania Luigi Vanvitelli, Italy
Maria Ronza	University of Naples Federico II, Italy
Clara Di Fazio	University of Trieste, Italy
Andrea Gallo	Università degli Studi di Trieste, Italy
Francesca Sinatra	University of Trieste, Italy

Evaluating Inner Areas Potentials (EIAP 2026)

Workshop Organizers

Diana Rolando	Politecnico di Torino, Italy
Manuela Rebaudengo	Politecnico di Torino, Italy
Alice Barreca	Politecnico di Torino, Italy
Giorgia Malavasi	Politecnico di Torino, Italy

Workshop Program Committee Members

John Accordino	Virginia Commonwealth University, USA
Sara Favargiotti	University of Trento, Italy
Barbara Lino	Università degli Studi di Palermo, Italy
Maddalena Ferretti	Università Politecnica delle Marche, Italy
Eugenio Muccio	University of Naples Federico II, Italy
Giuliano Poli	University of Naples Federico II, Italy
Giulia Datola	Politecnico di Milano, Italy
Elena Todella	University of Parma, Italy
Asja Aulisio	Politecnico di Torino, Italy
Marco Rossitti	Politecnico di Milano, Italy
Martina Spinelli	Politecnico Torino, Italy
Amina Pereno	Politecnico di Torino, Italy
Francesco Bruzzone	Università Iuav di Venezia, Italy
Alexandra Stankulova	Politecnico di Torino, Italy
Benedetta Di Leo	Università Politecnica delle Marche, Italy
Edda Donati	University of Rome Tor Vergata, Italy
Vanessa Assumma	University of Bologna, Italy
Beatrice Mecca	Politecnico di Torino, Italy

sustainablE mobiLity and Last mIle lOgisTic in urban context (ELLIOT 2026)

Workshop Organizers

Tiziana Campisi	University of Enna Kore, Italy
Socrates Basbas	Aristotle University of Thessaloniki, Greece
Florin Rusca	National University of Science and Technology Politehnica Bucharest, Romania
Grigorios Fountas	Aristotle University of Thessaloniki, Greece
Aleksandra Deluka-Tibljas	University of Rijeka, Croatia

Workshop Program Committee Members

Francesco Russo	University of Reggio Calabria, Italy
Oana Dinu	National University of Science and Technology Politehnica Bucharest, Romania
Antonio Polimeni	Università di Messina, Italy
Antonio Russo	University of Enna Kore, Italy
Elena Cocuzza	Univesity of Catania, Italy
Corrado Rindone	Università degli studi Mediterranea di Reggio Calabria, Italy

Econometrics and Multidimensional Evaluation in Urban Environment (EMEUE 2026)

Workshop Organizers

Maria Cerreta	University of Naples Federico II, Italy
Giuseppe Ciciriello	University of Naples Federico II, Italy
Simona Panaro	University of Sussex Business School, UK
Piero Zizzania	Università of Naples Federico II, Italy
Pierluigi Morano	Polytechnic University of Bari, Italy
Francesco Tajani	Sapienza University of Rome, Italy

Workshop Program Committee Members

Giuliano Poli	Università Federico II di Napoli, Italy
Ludovica La Rocca	University of Naples Federico II, Italy
Sabrina Sacco	University of Naples Federico II, Italy

Ecosystem Services in Spacial Planning for climate neutral urban and rural areas (ESSP 2026)

Workshop Organizers

Sabrina Lai	University of Cagliari, Italy
Carmela Gargiulo	Università Federico II di Napoli, Italy
Beniamino Murgante	University of Basilicata, Italy
Francesco Scorza	University of Basilicata, Italy
Corrado Zoppi	University of Cagliari, Italy
Floriana Zucaro	University of Naples Federico II, Italy

Workshop Program Committee Members

Alfonso Annunziata	University of Basilicata, Italy
Ginevra Balletto	University of Cagliari, Italy
Ivan Blečić	University of Cagliari, Italy
Giuseppe Borruso	University of Trieste, Italy
Barbara Caselli	Università degli Studi di Parma, Italy
Maria Cerreta	University of Naples Federico II, Italy
Carmen Guida	Università degli Studi di Napoli Federico II, Italy
Federica Isola	University of Cagliari, Italy
Francesca Leccis	University of Cagliari, Italy
Federica Leone	University of Cagliari, Italy
Silvia Rossetti	Università degli Studi di Parma, Italy
Luigi Santopietro	Institute of Methodologies for Environmental Analysis CNR IMAA, Italy
Simone Corrado	University of Basilicata, Italy
Rachele Vanessa Gatto	Università della Basilicata, Italy

The 16th International Workshop on Future Information System Technologies and Applications (FiSTA 2026)

Workshop Organizers

Bernady O. Apduhan	Kyushu Sangyo University, Japan
Rafael Santos	National Institute for Space Research (INPE), Brazil

Workshop Program Committee Members

Agustinus Waluyo	La Trobe University, Australia
Earl Ryan Aleluya	Mindanao State University Iligan Institute of Technology, Philippines
Eric Pardede	La Trobe University, Australia
Kai Cheng	Kyushu Sangyo University, Japan
Fenghui Yao	Tennessee State University, USA
Yusuke Gotoh	Okayama University, Japan
Kazuaki Tanaka	Kyushu Institute of Technology, Japan
Toshihiro Yamauchi	Okayama University, Japan
Toshihiro Uchibayashi	Kyushu University, Japan
Krishnamoorthy Ranganathan	Chennai Institute of Technology, India
Orven Llantos	MSU-Iligan Institute of Technology, Philippines
Anton Louise De Ocampo	Batangas State University, Philippines

Geographical Analysis, Urban Modeling, Spatial Statistics (Geog-And-Mod 2026)

Workshop Organizers

Giuseppe Borruso	University of Trieste, Italy
Beniamino Murgante	University of Basilicata, Italy
Hartmut Asche	Hasso Plattner Institute for Digital Engineering, Germany
Rodrigo Tapia-McClung	Centro de Investigación en Ciencias de Información Geoespacial, Mexico
Andreas Fricke	Hasso Plattner Institute for Digital Engineering, University of Potsdam, Germany

Workshop Program Committee Members

Ginevra Balletto	University of Cagliari, Italy
Mara Ladu	University of Cagliari, Italy
Gabriella Schoier	Università di Trieste, Italy
Marco Mazzarino	Iuav University of Venice, Italy
Malgorzata Hanzl	Lodz University of Technology, Poland
Anastasia Stratigea	National Technical University of Athens, Greece
Maria del Mar Munoz	University of Cádiz, Spain
Veronica Camerada	Università degli Studi di Sassari, Italy

Generative and Neuro-Symbolic Artificial Intelligence for Real-World Systems (GNS-AI 2026)

Workshop Organizers

Hugo Peixoto	University of Minho, Portugal
Manuel Rodrigues	University of Minho, Portugal
Regina Sousa	University of Minho, Portugal

Workshop Program Committee Members

Dalila Duraes	Universidade do Minho, Portugal
Paulo Novais	Universidade do Minho, Portugal
Laura Cavalcante	Instituto Superior de Engenharia do Porto, Portugal
Diogo Martinho	Instituto Superior de Engenharia de Porto, Portugal
Hélia Guerra	University of the Azores, Portugal
Rohit Raja	Guru Ghasidas Vishwavidyalaya, India
Hien Nguyen	University of Information Technology, Vietnam
Antonio Carlos Da Silva Abelha	Universidade do Minho, Portugal
Cristiana Neto	University of Minho, Portugal
José Machado	University of Minho, Portugal
Luís Conceicao	Instituto Superior de Engenharia do Porto, Portugal
Omar Gomez	Universidad Nacional de Colombia, Colombia
Luis Mendes Gomes	University of the Azores, Portugal
Nicolas Lori	University of the Azores, Portugal
Sara Balderas Díaz	University of Cádiz, Spain
Gabriel Guerrero Contreras	University of Cádiz, Spain
Francisco Zayas Gato	Universidade da Coruña, Spain
Diana Ferreira	University of Minho, Portugal
Jolanta Miliauskaite	Vilnius University, Lithuania

Geomatics for Resource Monitoring and Management (GRMM 2026)

Workshop Organizers

Alberico Sonnessa	Politecnico di Bari, Italy
Eufemia Tarantino	Politecnico di Bari, Italy
Marco Locurcio	Polytechnic University of Bari, Italy

Workshop Program Committee Members

Valeria Belloni	Sapienza University of Rome, Italy
Roberta Ravanelli	University of Liège, Belgium
Michela Ravanelli	Sapienza Università di Roma, Italy
Alessandra Mascitelli	University of Chieti Pescara, Italy
Francesco Bimbo	University of Foggia, Italy
Francesco Di Capua	University of Basilicata, Italy
Gaetano Falcone	Università degli Studi di Napoli Federico II, Italy
Francesco Tajani	Sapienza University of Rome, Italy
Paola Amoruso	LUM Giuseppe Degennaro University, Italy
Pierfrancesco De Paola	University of Naples Federico II, Italy
Isidora Đurić	University of Novi Sad, Serbia
Rossella Petti	Politecnico di Bari, Italy
Valeria Cera	University of Naples Federico II, Italy
Antonino Iannuzzo	Universitá degli studi del Sannio, Italy
Pier Francesco Recchi	Università di Napoli Federico II, Italy
Giuseppe Francesco Cesare Lama	University of Naples Federico II, Italy
Ester Scotto di Perta	University of Naples Federico II, Italy
Antonino Maltese	University of Palermo, Italy
Andrea Montanino	University of Naples, Italy
Carla Cavallo	University of Salerno, Italy
Dario Esposito	Polytechnic University of Bari, Italy
Rosaria Parente	Universitas Mercatorum, Italy
Claudia Panciera	Water Research Institute (IRSA) CNR, Italy
Pasquale Perrini	Consorzio Interuniversitario per l'Idrologia, Italy
Beniamino Onorati	Università degli Studi della Basilicata, Italy
Francesco Sica	Sapienza University of Rome, Italy

International Workshop on Information and Knowledge in the Internet of Things (IKIT 2026)

Workshop Organizer

Teresa Guarda	Universidad Estatal Península de Santa Elena, Ecuador

Workshop Program Committee Members

Isabel Lopes	Instituto Politécnico de Bragança, Portugal
Luis Mazon	Bitrum Research Group, Spain

Arnulfo Alanis	Tecnológico Nacional de México, Campus Tijuana, Mexico
Filipe Mota Pinto	Instituto Politécnico de Leiria, Portugal
Luis Enrique Chuquimarca Jiménez	Universidad Estatal Penìnsula de Santa Elena, Ecuador
Gustavo Gatica	Universidad Andres Bello, Chile
Jairo Coronado Hernandez	Universidad de la Costa, Colombia
Maria Fernanda Augusto	BITrum Research Center, Spain
José María Díaz Nafría	Universidad a Distancia de Madrid, Spain
Modestos Stavrakis	University of the Aegean, Greece
Isabel Ribeiro	Instituto Politécnico Bragança, Portugal
Bruno Sousa	University of Coimbra, Portugal
Datzania Villao	Universidad Estatal Península de Santa Elena, Ecuador

Intelligent Sustainable Development: from Models to Real-World Impact (ISD 2026)

Workshop Organizers

Diego Brandão	Federal Center for Technological Education of Rio de Janeiro, Brazil
Angela Ferreira	Polytechnic University of Bragança, Portugal
Eduardo Bezerra	Federal Center for Technological Education of Rio de Janeiro, Brazil
Raphael Guerra	Universidade Federal Fluminense, Brazil
Douglas Cardoso	University of Coimbra, Portugal
Rui Pedro Lopes	Instituto Politecnico de Bragança, Portugal

Workshop Program Committee Members

Wagner Telles	Universidade Federal Fluminense, Brazil
Jader Lugon Junior	Instituto Federal Fluminense, Brazil
Edcarllos Santos	Universidade Federal do Sul da Bahia, Brazil
Kennedy Fernandes	Universidade Federal de Juiz de Fora, Brazil
Israel Mendonca	Kumamoto University, Japan
Pedro Henrique Gonzalez	Federal University of Rio de Janeiro, Brazil
Pablo Luiz Araujo Munhoz	Federal University of Ouro Preto, Brazil
Elloa Guedes	Amazonas State University, Brazil
Danielli Araújo Lima	Instituto Federal do Triângulo Mineiro, Brazil
Ary Henrique Oliveira	Universidade Federal de Tocantins, Brazil

Paula Odete Fernandes	Instituto Politecnico de Bragança, Portugal
Hiago Rocha	National Laboratory for Scientific Computing, Brazil
Andre Luiz Coutinho Merlo	Centro Federal de Educacao Tecnologica Celso Suckow da Fonseca CEFET RJ, Brazil
Kennedy Fernandes	Universidade Federal de Juiz de Fora, Brazil
Ary Henrique Oliveira	Universidade Federal de Tocantins, Brazil
Mayara Omai	Centro Federal de Educacao Tecnologica Celso Suckow da Fonseca CEFET RJ, Brazil

Multidimensional Evolutionary Evaluations for Transformative Approaches (MEETA 2026)

Workshop Organizers

Maria Cerreta	University of Naples Federico II, Italy
Giuliano Poli	Università Federico II di Napoli, Italy
Gaia Daldanise	CNR Institute for Research on Innovation and Services for Development, Italy
Ludovica La Rocca	University of Federico II of Naples, Italy
Maria Somma	University of Naples Federico II, Italy
Sabrina Sacco	University of Naples Federico II, Italy

Workshop Program Committee Members

Chiara Mazzarella	TUDelft, The Netherlands
Simona Panaro	University of Sussex Business School, UK
Eugenio Muccio	University of Naples Federico II, Italy

Building multi-dimensional Models for assessing complex Environmental Systems (MES 2026)

Workshop Organizers

Vanessa Assumma	University of Bologna, Italy
Caterina Caprioli	Politecnico di Torino, Italy
Giulia Datola	Politecnico di Milano, Italy
Federico DellAnna	Politecnico di Torino, Italy
Marta Dell'Ovo	Politecnico di Milano, Italy
Marco Rossitti	Politecnico di Milano, Italy

Workshop Program Committee Members

Mariarosaria Angrisano	Pegaso University, Italy
Giuliano Poli	University of Naples Federico II, Italy
Francesco Sica	Sapienza University of Rome, Italy
Eugenio Muccio	University of Naples Federico II, Italy
Sebastiano Barbieri	Politecnico di Torino, Italy
Giulio Cavana	Politecnico di Torino, Italy
Marta Bottero	Politecnico di Torino, Italy
Francesca Torrieri	Politecnico di Milano, Italy
Maksims Feofilovs	Riga Technical University, Latvia
Daniela Maiullari	Delft University of Technology, The Netherlands
Elena Todella	University of Parma, Italy
Yvonne Russo	University of Campania L. Vanvitelli, Italy
Tommaso Lazzarin	University of Padua, Italy
Francesco Tajani	Sapienza University of Rome, Italy
Claudia Amadei	University of Padua, Italy
Isabella Maria Lami	Politecnico di Torino, Italy
Federico Vagnon	Politecnico di Torino, Italy
Francesca Torrieri	Politecnico di Milano, Italy
Elena De Angelis	Politecnico di Torino, Italy
Piergiorgio Farfariello	Politecnico di Torino, Italy
Francesca Biondi	Politecnico di Torino, Italy
Giulio Cavana	Politecnico di Torino, Italy
Fabiana Forte	Università della Campania Luigi Vanvitelli, Italy
Siyu Qiu	University of Bologna, Italy
Eugenio Muccio	University of Naples Federico II, Italy
Iuliia Kozlova	University of Bologna, Italy
Danny Casprini	Politecnico di Milano, Italy
Franco Corti	University of Padua, Italy
Elisa Sbardella	Politecnico di Torino, Italy
Andrea Sarcina	Università di Padova, Italy
Daniela Menna	Università degli studi della Campania Luigi Vanvitelli, Italy
Sebastiano Barbieri	Politecnico di Torino, Italy
Ana Soares	University of Minho, Portugal
Francesco Sica	Sapienza University of Rome, Italy
Chiara D'Alpaos	University of Padua, Italy
Alessandra Oppio	Politecnico di Milano, Italy
Maria Rosaria Guarini	Sapienza University of Rome, Italy
Alessia Crisopulli	Politecnico di Milano, Italy
Elisabetta Colucci	Politecnico di Torino, Italy

Giorgia Sugoni	Links Foundation, Italy
Lucia Petronio	University of Bologna, Italy
Marco Alvise Bragadin	University of Bologna, Italy

Computational Mechanics, Intelligence, and Data (MIND 2026)

Workshop Organizers

Lelio Campanile	Università degli Studi della Campania Luigi Vanvitelli, Italy
Renato Zona	Università della Campania Vanvitelli, Italy

Workshop Program Committee Members

Vincenzo Minutolo	Università degli Studi della Campania Luigi Vanvitelli, Italy
Fiammetta Marulli	University of Campania Luigi Vanvitelli, Italy
Simone Palladino	Università degli Studi della Campania Luigi Vanvitelli, Italy
Ali Forooghi	University of Campania Luigi Vanvitelli, Italy
Mario Argenziano	University of Palermo, Italy
Donato Perfetto	University of Campania Luigi Vanvitelli, Italy

Modelling Liveable Cities: Techniques, Methods, Challenges, and Perspectives Behind the X-Minute City (MLC 2026)

Workshop Organizers

Federico Mara	University of Pisa, Italy
Valerio Cutini	University of Pisa, Italy

Workshop Program Committee Members

Beniamino Murgante	University of Basilicata, Italy
Chiara Garau	University of Cagliari, Italy
Francesco Zullo	University of LAquila, Italy
Alessandro Marucci	University of L Aquila, Italy
Chiara Di Dato	University of L Aquila, Italy
Giampiero Lombardini	University of Genoa, Italy

Alfonso Annunziata	University of Basilicata, Italy
Simone Corrado	University of Basilicata, Italy
Müslüm Hacar	Yildiz Technical University, Turkey
Federica Deri	University of Pisa, Italy
Chiara Anselmi	University of Pisa, Italy

Mathematical Methods for Image Processing and Understanding 2026 (MMIPU 2026)

Workshop Organizers

Ivan Gerace	Università degli Studi di Perugia, Italy
Gianluca Vinti	Università degli Studi di Perugia, Italy
Arianna Travaglini	Lucian Blaga University of Sibiu, Romania

Workshop Program Committee Members

Marco Baioletti	University of Perugia, Italy
Marco Donatelli	University of Insubria, Italy
Muhammad Hanif	Ghulam Ishaq Khan Institute of Engineering Sciences and Technology, Pakistan
Francesco Marchetti	University of Padua, Italy
Wolfgang Erb	Università degli Studi di Padua, Italy
Ana Maria Acu	Lucian Blaga University of Sibiu, Romania
Simone Rebegoldi	University of Modena and Reggio Emilia, Italy
Valentina Giorgetti	Università degli Studi di Perugia, Italy
Vita Leonessa	University of Basilicata, Italy

MOdels and indicators for assessing and measuring the urban settlement deVElopment in the view of NET ZERO by 2050 (MOVEto0 2026)

Workshop Organizers

Lorena Fiorini	University of L'Aquila, Italy
Lucia Saganeiti	Institute of Methodologies for Environmental Analysis (IMAA) CNR, Italy
Angela Pilogallo	Institute of Methodologies for Environmental Analysis (IMAA) CNR, Italy

Francesco Zullo	University of L'Aquila, Italy
Alessandro Marucci	University of L'Aquila, Italy

Workshop Program Committee Members

Ginevra Balletto	University of Cagliari, Italy
Giuseppe Borruso	University of Trieste, Italy
Chiara Garau	University of Cagliari, Italy
Beniamino Murgante	University of Basilicata, Italy
Ljiljana Zivkovic	Republic Geodetic Authority, Serbia
Luigi Santopietro	Institute of Methodologies for Environmental Analysis National Research Council of Italy CNR IMAA, Italy
Ilaria Delponte	University of Genoa, Italy
Carmen Guida	Università degli Studi di Napoli Federico II, Italy
Chiara Di Dato	University of L'Aquila, Italy

Numerical Aspects in Machine Learning For Dynamical Systems (NAMLYS 2026)

Workshop Organizers

Pasquale De Luca	Parthenope University of Naples, Italy
Livia Marcellino	University of Naples Parthenope, Italy
Valeria Mele	University of Naples Federico II, Italy

Workshop Program Committee Members

Dario Caramiello	University of Naples Parthenope, Italy
Giuseppe Fiorillo	Parthenope University of Naples, Italy
Marco Lettiero	University of Naples Parthenope, Italy
Francesco Peluso	University of Naples Parthenope, Italy

Numerical Methods and Machine Learning in Science & Engineering (NMLSE 2026)

Workshop Organizers

Cecília Coelho	Helmut Schmidt University, Germany
M. Fernanda P. Costa	University of Minho, Portugal

Luís Ferrás	University of Minho, Portugal
Eliana Costa e Silva	Polytechnic of Porto, Portugal

Workshop Program Committee Members

Osvaldo Gramaxo de Freitas	Universitat de València, Spain
Estela Bicho	University of Minho, Portugal
Flora Ferreira	University of Porto, Portugal
Bruno Veloso	Universidade do Porto, Portugal
Luís Louro	University of Minho, Portugal
Weronika Wojtak	CCG/ZGDV Institute, Portugal
Wolfram Erlhagen	University of Minho, Portugal

6th Workshop on Privacy in the Cloud/Edge/IoT World 2026 (PCEIoT 2026)

Workshop Organizers

Lelio Campanile	Università degli Studi della Campania Luigi Vanvitelli, Italy
Mauro Iacono	Università degli Studi della Campania Luigi Vanvitelli, Italy
Michele Mastroianni	University of Foggia, Italy

Workshop Program Committee Members

Fiammetta Marulli	University of Campania Luigi Vanvitelli, Italy
Christian Riccio	Università degli Studi della Campania Luigi Vanvitelli, Italy
Arcangelo Castiglione	University of Salerno, Italy
Gianni D'Angelo	University of Salerno, Italy
Biagio Boi	University of Salerno, Italy
Luigi Piero Di Bonito	Università degli Studi della Campania, Italy

Preserving Our Past: Spatial and Remote Sensing Technologies for Cultural Heritage in a Changing Climate (POP 2026)

Workshop Organizers

Maria Danese	Institute of Heritage Science of the National Research Council of Italy (CNR ISPC), Italy
Rosa Lasaponara	Institute of Methodologies for Environmental Analysis (CNR IMAA), Italy
Nicola Masini	Institute of Heritage Science of the National Research Council of Italy (CNR ISPC), Italy

Workshop Program Committee Members

Dario Gioia	Institute of Heritage Science of the National Research Council of Italy (CNR ISPC), Italy
Marilisa Biscione	Institute of Heritage Science of the National Research Council of Italy (CNR ISPC), Italy
Valentina Florio	CNR, Italy
Antonio Minervino Amodio	Institute of Heritage Science of the National Research Council of Italy (CNR ISPC), Italy

Scientific Computing Infrastructure (SCI 2026)

Workshop Organizers

Vladimir Korkhov	Saint Petersburg State University, Russia
Elena Stankova	Saint Petersburg State University, Russia

Workshop Program Committee Members

Adam Belloum	University of Amsterdam, The Netherlands
Dmitrii Vasiunin	Deutsche Telekom Cloud Services E.P.E., Greece
Serob Balyan	Institute for Informatics and Automation Problems, National Academy of Sciences of Armenia, Armenia
Suren Abrahamyan	Institute for Informatics and Automation Problems of NAS RA, Armenia
Ashot Gevorkyan	Institute for Informatics and Automation Problems NAS of Armenia, Armenia

Michal Hnatič	P.J. Šafárik University in Košice, Slovak Republic
Martin Vala	Pavol Jozef Šafárik University, Slovak Republic
Nodir Zaynalov	Samarkand Branch of Tashkent University of Information Technologies Named After Muhammad al Khwarizmi, Uzbekistan
Michail Panteleyev	Saint Petersburg Electrotechnical University, Russia
Alexander Degtyarev	Saint Petersburg State University, Russia
Alexander Bogdanov	St. Petersburg State University, Russia
Nataliia Kulabukhova	AutoTech, Russia
Alexander Degtyarev	St.Petersburg State University, Russia
Alexander Bogdanov	St. Petersburg State University, Russia

Socio-Economic and Environmental Models for Land Use Management (SEMLUM 2026)

Workshop Organizers

Debora Anelli	Sapienza University of Rome, Italy
Pierluigi Morano	Polytechnic University of Bari, Italy
Francesco Tajani	Sapienza University of Rome, Italy
Felicia Di Liddo	Polytechnic University of Bari, Italy

Workshop Program Committee Members

Benedetto Manganelli	Università degli Studi della Basilicata, Italy
Emma Sabatelli	Sapienza Università di Roma, Italy
María Paz Sáez-Pérez	University of Granada, Spain
Yasmine Selim	Ain Shams University, Egypt
Daniela Tavano	University of Calabria, Italy
Francesco Calabrò	Mediterranea University of Reggio Calabria, Italy
Pierfrancesco De Paola	University of Naples Federico II, Italy
Francesco Paolo Del Giudice	University of Rome La Sapienza, Italy
Paola Amoruso	LUM Giuseppe Degennaro University, Italy
Rubina Canesi	Università degli Studi di Padova, Italy
Daniele La Rosa	University of Catania, Italy
Giuseppe Cerullo	Sapienza University of Rome, Italy
Antonella Roma	Sapienza University of Rome, Italy
Francesca Fariello	Sapienza University of Rome, Italy

Ports and logistics of the future - Smartness and Sustainability (SmartPorts 2026)

Workshop Organizers

Andrea Gallo	Università degli Studi di Trieste, Italy
Giuseppe Borruso	University of Trieste, Italy
Gianfranco Fancello	University of Cagliari, Italy
Veronica Camerada	Università degli studi di Sassari, Italy
Clara Di Fazio	University of Trieste, Italy

Workshop Program Committee Members

Patrizia Serra	University of Cagliari, Italy
Francesco Bruzzone	Università Iuav di Venezia, Italy
Marco Mazzarino	University Iuav of Venice, Italy
Maria del Mar Munoz	University of Cádiz, Spain
Ainhoa Amaro	EVOCONS, Spain
Brunella Brundu	University of Sassari, Italy
Giovanni Mauro	University of Campania Luigi Vanvitelli, Italy
Maria Ronza	University of Naples Federico II, Italy
Marcello Tadini	Università del Piemonte Orientale, Italy
Luca Toneatti	University of Trieste, Italy
Mara Ladu	University of Cagliari, Italy
Ginevra Balletto	University of Cagliari, Italy
Francesca Sinatra	University of Trieste, Italy

Sustainable evolution of long-Distance frEight and paSsenger Transport (SOLIDEST 2026)

Workshop Organizers

Antonio Russo	University of Enna Kore, Italy
Giuseppe Musolino	Università Mediterranea di Reggio Calabria, Italy
Socrates Basbas	Aristotle University of Thessaloniki, Greece
Oana Dinu	National University of Science and Technology Politehnica Bucharest, Romania
Sanja Šurdonja	University of Rijeka, Croatia
Elen Twrdy	University of Ljubljana, Slovenia

Workshop Program Committee Members

Tiziana Campisi	University of Enna Kore, Italy
Massimo Di Gangi	Università di Messina, Italy
Antonio Polimeni	Università di Messina, Italy
Efstathios Bouhouras	Aristotle University of Thessaloniki, Greece
Florin Rusca	National University of Science and Technology Politehnica Bucharest, Romania
Vittorio Astarita	University of Calabria, Italy
Giuseppe Guido	Università della Calabria, Italy
Stefanos Tsigdinos	National Technical University of Athens, Greece
Chiara Garau	University of Cagliari, Italy

Sustainability Performance Assessment: Models, Approaches, and Applications Toward Interdisciplinary and Integrated Solutions (SPA 2026)

Workshop Organizers

Francesco Scorza	University of Basilicata, Italy
Sabrina Lai	University of Cagliari, Italy
Jolanta Dvarioniene	Kaunas University of Technology, Lithuania
Michele Campagna	University of Cagliari, Italy

Workshop Program Committee Members

Corrado Zoppi	University of Cagliari, Italy
Maria Cerreta	University of Naples Federico II, Italy
Giuseppe Borruso	University of Trieste, Italy
Chiara Garau	University of Cagliari, Italy
Ginevra Balletto	University of Cagliari, Italy
Alenka Poplin	Iowa State University, USA
Francesco Zullo	University of L'Aquila, Italy
Alessandro Marucci	University of L'Aquila, Italy
Federica Leone	University of Cagliari, Italy
Simone Corrado	University of Basilicata, Italy
Alfonso Annunziata	University of Basilicata, Italy
Rachele Vanessa Gatto	Università della Basilicata, Italy
Francesco Paolo Del Giudice	University of Basilicata, Italy

Specifics of smart cities development in Europe (SPEED 2026)

Workshop Organizers

Chiara Garau	University of Cagliari, Italy
Katarína Vitálišová	Matej Bel University, Slovak Republic
Marco Fanfani	University of Florence, Italy
Anna Vaňová	Matej Bel University, Slovak Republic
Kamila Borsekova	Matej Bel University, Slovak Republic
Paola Zamperlin	University of Pisa, Italy

Workshop Program Committee Members

Francesca Maltinti	University of Cagliari, Italy
Silvia Rossetti	Università degli Studi di Parma, Italy
Carmen Guida	Università degli Studi di Napoli Federico II, Italy
Floriana Zucaro	University of Naples Federico II, Italy
Giovanna Concu	University of Cagliari, Italy
Paolo Nesi	University of Florence, Italy
Pierfrancesco Bellini	University of Florence, Italy
Gerardo Carpentieri	University of Naples Federico II, Italy
Radoslav Kožiak	Matej Bel University, Slovak Republic
Lucia Dobrotová	Matej Bel University in Banská Bystrica, Slovak Republic
Veronika Piscová	Institute of Landscape Ecology Slovak Academy of Sciences, Slovak Republic
Darina Rojíková	Matej Bel University, Slovak Republic
Katarína Sýkorová	Matej Bel University, Slovak Republic
Silvia Ondrejičková	Comenius University Bratislava, Slovak Republic
Vladimír Ondrejička	Comenius University Bratislava, Slovak Republic
Maros Finka	Comenius University Bratislava, Slovak Republic
Jan Nevima	Masaryk University, Czech Republic
Christian Corral Burau	Leibniz University Hannover, Germany
Kamila Turečková	Silesian University in Opava, Czech Republic
Luciano Alessandro Ipsaro Palesi	University of Florence, Italy
Enrico Collini	University of Florence, Italy
Gianni Pantaleo	University of Florence, Italy
Krishnamoorthy Ranganathan	Chennai Institute of Technology, India

Smart, Safe, and Health Cities (SSHC 2026)

Workshop Organizers

Chiara Garau	University of Cagliari, Italy
Gerardo Carpentieri	University of Naples Federico II, Italy
Carmen Guida	Università degli Studi di Napoli Federico II, Italy
Martina Carra	University of Brescia, Italy
Vincenza Torrisi	University of Catania, Italy
Silvia Rossetti	Università degli Studi di Parma, Italy

Workshop Program Committee Members

Romano Fistola	University of Naples Federico II, Italy
Francesca Maltinti	University of Cagliari, Italy
Barbara Caselli	Università degli Studi di Parma, Italy
Tiziana Campisi	University of Enna Kore, Italy
Katarína Sýkorová	Matej Bel University, Slovak Republic
Tazyeen Alam	Università degli Studi di Cagliari, Italy
Francesco Zullo	University of L'Aquila, Italy
Giovanna Concu	University of Cagliari, Italy
Anastasia Stratigea	National Technical University of Athens, Greece
Ezio Riggi	National Research Council, Italy
Miriam Distefano	CNR, Italy

Smart and Sustainable Island Communities (SSIC 2026)

Workshop Organizers

Chiara Garau	University of Cagliari, Italy
Anastasia Stratigea	National Technical University of Athens, Greece
Yiota Theodora	National Technical University of Athens, Greece
Giovanna Concu	University of Cagliari, Italy
Tiziana Campisi	University of Enna Kore, Italy
Tanja Congiu	University of Sassari, Italy

Workshop Program Committee Members

Francesca Maltinti	University of Cagliari, Italy
Mauro Coni	University of Cagliari, Italy
Paola Zamperlin	University of Florence, Italy

Tarek Teba	University of Portsmouth, UK
Gerardo Carpentieri	University of Naples Federico II, Italy
Floriana Zucaro	University of Naples Federico II, Italy
Roberto Minunno	Curtin University, Australia
Apostolos Lagarias	University of Thessaly, Greece
Giuseppina Vacca	University of Cagliari, Italy
Carmen Guida	Università degli Studi di Napoli Federico II, Italy
Tazyeen Alam	Università degli Studi di Cagliari, Italy
Mauro D'Apuzzo	University of Cassino and Southern Lazio, Italy
Mana Dastoum	Polytechnic University of Madrid, Spain
Alfonso Annunziata	University of Basilicata, Italy
Barbara Caselli	Università degli Studi di Parma, Italy
Silvia Rossetti	Università degli Studi di Parma, Italy
Gian Felice Giaccu	University of Sassari, Italy
Anastasia Stratigea	National Technical University of Athens, Greece
Vincenza Torrisi	University of Catania, Italy

Sustainable Tourism Economy, Silk Road, Reuse and Enhancement of Cultural Heritage (STESilkRoad 2026)

Workshop Organizers

Celestina Fazia	Università di Enna Kore, Italy
Alexandru Ilies	University of Oradea, Romania
Dorina Camelia Ilies	University of Oradea, Romania
Cristina Natoli	Ministero dell'Ambiente e della Sicurezza Energetica, Italy
Bahodirhon Safarov	Samarkand Branch of Tashkent State University of Economics, Uzbekistan
Clara Stella Vicari Aversa	Università degli Studi Mediterranea di Reggio Calabria, Italy

Workshop Program Committee Members

Giulia Fernanda Grazia Catania	Università di Enna Kore, Italy
Federica Sortino	Università degli Studi di Enna Kore, Italy
Thowayeb Hassan	King Faisal University, Saudi Arabia
Tatar Corina	University of Oradea, Romania
Maria Francesca Faro	Ministry of Education and Merit (MIM), Italy

Theoretical and Computational Chemistry and its Applications (TCCM 2026)

Workshop Organizers

Noelia Faginas Lago	Università di Perugia, Italy
Andrea Lombardi	Università di Perugia, Italy
Marcos Mandado Alonso	University of Vigo, Spain

Workshop Program Committee Members

Jose Manuel Hermida Ramon	Universidade de Vigo, Spain
Luca Mancini	University of Perugia, Italy
Stefano Falcinelli	University of Perugia, Italy
Ángel Martín Pendás	Universidad de Oviedo, Spain
Enrique M. Cabaleiro Lago	Universidade de Santiago de Compostela, Spain
Giacomo Giorgi	Università degli Studi di Perugia, Italy
Stefano Evangelisti	Université de Toulouse, France
Nicolás Ramos Berdullas	University of Vigo, Spain
Juan José Nogueira	Universidad Autónoma de Madrid, Spain
Giacomo Pannacci	Università degli Studi di Perugia, Italy

Transport Infrastructures for Smart Cities (TISC 2026)

Workshop Organizers

Francesca Maltinti	University of Cagliari, Italy
Mauro Coni	University of Cagliari, Italy
Chiara Garau	University of Cagliari, Italy
Benedetto Barabino	University of Brescia, Italy
Nicoletta Rassu	Università di Cagliari, Italy
James Rombi	University of Cagliari, Italy

Workshop Program Committee Members

Tiziana Campisi	University of Enna Kore, Italy
Mauro D'Apuzzo	University of Cassino and Southern Lazio, Italy
Roberto Ventura	Università degli Studi di Brescia, Italy
Roberto Minunno	Curtin University, Australia

Giovanna Concu	University of Cagliari, Italy
Claudia Loggia	University of KwaZulu-Natal, South Africa

Transforming Urban Analytics: The Impact of Crowdsourced Mapping and Advanced AI Techniques on Future Cities (Tr-UrbAna 2026)

Workshop Organizers

Ayse Giz Gulnerman Gengec	Ankara Hacı Bayram Veli University, Turkey
Müslüm Hacar	Yildiz Technical University, Turkey

Workshop Program Committee Members

Beniamino Murgante	University of Basilicata, Italy
Abdulkadir Memduhoğlu	Harran University, Turkey
Zeynel Abidin Polat	Izmir Katip Celebi University, Turkey
Güzide Miray Perihanoglu	Van Yuzuncu Yil University, Turkey
Tugba Memisoglu Baykal	Hacı Bayram Veli University, Turkey
Federico Mara	University of Pisa, Italy
Himmet Karaman	Istanbul Technical University, Turkey
Özge Öztürk Hacar	Yildiz Technical University, Turkey

From structural to TRAnsformative-change of City Environment: challenges & solutions & perspectives (TRACE 2026)

Workshop Organizers

Maria Rosaria Guarini	Sapienza University of Rome, Italy
Pierluigi Morano	Polytechnic University of Bari, Italy
Francesco Sica	Sapienza University of Rome, Italy
Alejandro Segura	Universidad Politécnica de Madrid, Spain
Yilsy María Nuñez Guerrero	Universidad Politécnica de Madrid, Spain

Workshop Program Committee Members

Maria Cerreta	University of Naples Federico II, Italy
Francesco Scorza	University of Basilicata, Italy

Francesco Calabrò	Mediterranea University of Reggio Calabria, Italy
Felicia Di Liddo	Polytechnic University of Bari, Italy
Marco Locurcio	Polytechnic University of Bari, Italy
Valeria Saiu	University of Cagliari, Italy
Lucia Della Spina	University Mediterranea of Reggio Calabria, Italy
Fabrizio Battisti	University of Florence, Italy
Giuseppe Cerullo	Sapienza University of Rome, Italy
Fabiana Forte	Università della Campania Luigi Vanvitelli, Italy
Marta Dell'Ovo	Politecnico di Milano, Italy
Cristina Coscia	Politecnico di Torino, Italy
Debora Anelli	Sapienza University of Rome, Italy

Urban Artificial Intelligence for Modelling, Analysis & Planning (Urban plAnnIng 2026)

Workshop Organizers

Chiara Garau	University of Cagliari, Italy
Romano Fistola	University of Naples Federico II, Italy
Beniamino Murgante	University of Basilicata, Italy
Dessislava Petrova Antonova	Sofia University, GATE Institute, Bulgaria
Gianni Pantaleo	University of Florence, Italy
Rosa Anna La Rocca	University of Naples Federico II

Workshop Program Committee Members

Paola Zamperlin	University of Florence, Italy
Francesco Zullo	University of L'Aquila, Italy
Gerardo Carpentieri	University of Naples Federico II, Italy
Luciano Alessandro Ipsaro Palesi	University of Florence, Italy
Tazyeen Alam	Università degli Studi di Cagliari, Italy
Reza Askarizad	University of Cagliari, Italy
Mana Dastoum	Polytechnic University of Madrid, Spain
Alfonso Annunziata	University of Basilicata, Italy

Urban Space Accessibility and Mobilities (USAM 2026)

Workshop Organizers

Chiara Garau	University of Cagliari, Italy
Alessandro Plaisant	University of Sassari, Italy
Barbara Caselli	Università degli Studi di Parma, Italy
Mauro D'Apuzzo	University of Cassino and Southern Lazio, Italy
Francesco Pinna	University of Cagliari, Italy
Silvio Nocera	IUAV University of Venice, Italy

Workshop Program Committee Members

Mauro Coni	University of Cagliari, Italy
Martina Carra	University of Brescia, Italy
Tiziana Campisi	University of Enna Kore, Italy
Reza Askarizad	University of Cagliari, Italy
Giuseppe Cappelli	University of Cassino and Southern Lazio, Italy
Floriana Zucaro	University of Naples Federico II, Italy
Gerardo Carpentieri	University of Naples Federico II, Italy
Youssef El Ganadi	International University of Rabat, Morocco
Yiota Theodora	National Technical Univeristy of Athens, Greece
Silvia Rossetti	Università degli Studi di Parma, Italy
Aime Tsinda	University of Rwanda, Rwanda
Paola Zamperlin	University of Florence, Italy
Luciano Alessandro Ipsaro Palesi	University of Florence, Italy
Tazyeen Alam	Università degli Studi di Cagliari, Italy
Mariano Pernetti	Università della Campania Luigi Vanvitelli, Italy
Salvatore Leonardi	University of Catania, Italy
Francesco Galante	University of Naples Federico II, Italy

Virtual Reality, Augmented Reality and Applications (VRA 2026)

Workshop Organizers

Damiano Perri	University of Perugia, Italy
Osvaldo Gervasi	University of Perugia, Italy
Paolo Nesi	University of Florence, Italy

Workshop Program Committee Members

Taihoon Kim	Chonnam National University, South Korea
JungYoon Kim	Gachon University, South Korea
David Berti	ART SpA, Italy

Workshop on Advanced and Computational Methods for Earth Science applications (WACM4ES 2026)

Workshop Organizers

Luca Piroddi	University of Cagliari, Italy
Patrizia Caprizzi	University of Palermo, Italy
Marilena Cozzolino	Università del Molise, Italy
Giuseppina Vacca	University of Cagliari, Italy
Luigi Capozzoli	Hydrogeosite Laboratory of CNR-IMAA, Italy
Nikos Papadopoulos	Foundation for Research and Technology Hellas, Greece

Workshop Program Committee Members

Sebastiano D'Amico	University of Malta, Malta
Enrica Vecchi	University of Cagliari, Italy
Donatella Rita Fiorino	Università degli Studi di Cagliari, Italy
Chiara Garau	University of Cagliari, Italy
Emanuele Colica	University of Malta, Malta
Raffaele Martorana	Università di Palermo, Italy
Raffaele Persico	Università della Calabria, Italy
Andrea Angelini	Institute of Heritage Science of the National Research Council of Italy (CNR ISPC), Italy
Paolo Mauriello	Università del Molise, Italy
Dedalo Marchetti	Italian National Institute of Geophysics and Volcanology, Italy
Veronica Pazzi	University of Florence, Italy
Agnese Innocenti	University of Florence, Italy
Maurizio Ercoli	University of Perugia, Italy
Luciano Galone	University of Malta, Malta
Amr Abd El-Raouf	Zagazig University, Egypt
Peter Iregbeyen	University of Malta, Malta
Pietro Milillo	University of Houston, USA
Tommaso Beni	University of Florence, Italy

Cristiano Fidani	Central Italy Electromagnetic Network, Italy
Deodato Tapete	Italian Space Agency (ASI), Italy
Enzo Rizzo	University of Ferrara, Italy
Guido Luzi	Centre Tecnològic de Telecomunicacions de Catalunya, Spain
Sina Saneiyan	Binghamton University, USA
Alex Sendrós	Universitat de Barcelona, Spain
Mercedes Solla	Universidade de Vigo, Spain
Alessandra Carollo	University of Palermo, Italy
Andrea Vergnano	Università di Torino, Italy
Giorgio Alaia	Università di Perugia, Italy
Giorgio De Donno	Sapienza University of Rome, Italy
Samuel Bignardi	University of Chieti and Pescara, Italy
Athos Agapiou	Cyprus University of Technology, Cyprus
Gregory Tsokas	Aristotle University of Thessaloniki, Greece
Alexandru Hegyi	Oslo University, Norway
Ilaria Barone	Università degli Studi di Padova, Italy
Yuan Qi	University of Hong Kong, China
Carmen Cuenca García	Universitat de València, Spain
Ilaria Catapano	Institute for Electromagnetic Sensing of the Environment (IREA) CNR, Italy
Mariano Lisi	University of Basilicata, Italy
Adrien Dimech	École de Technologie Supérieure, Canada
Davide Campo	Independent Researcher, UK
Chiara Torre	University of Malta, Malta
Anna Forte	University of Bologna, Italy
Adam Gauci	University of Malta, Malta
Vittoria Borghese	TNO, The Netherlands
Andrea Scianna	Institute for High Performance Computing and Networking (ICAR) CNR, Italy
Maria Antonia Brovelli	Politecnico di Milano, Italy
Pietro Milillo	University of Houston, USA
Gregory Tsokas	Aristotle University of Thessaloniki, Greece

Sponsoring Organizations

ICCSA 2026 would not have been possible without tremendous support from many organizations and institutions, for which all organizers and participants of ICCSA 2026 express their sincere gratitude:

Universidade do Minho
Escola de Engenharia

University of Minho, Portugal (https://www.uminho.pt/)

University of Perugia, Italy (https://www.unipg.it)

University of Basilicata, Italy (http://www.unibas.it)

University of Cagliari, Italy (https://unica.it/)

Monash University, Australia (https://www.monash.edu/)

Kyushu Sangyo University, Japan (https://www.kyusan-u.ac.jp/)

Venue

ICCSA 2026 took place at: **the University of Minho campus:**
Campus de Gualtar
4710-057 Braga
Portugal

Additional Reviewers

Amr Abd Elraouf	Zagazig University, Egypt
Lidia Aceto	Università del Piemonte Orientale, Italy
Ana Maria Acu	Lucian Blaga University of Sibiu, Romania
Vera Afreixo	University of Aveiro, Portugal
Akif Akgul	Hitit University, Turkey
Sania Akhtar	Ghulam Ishaq Khan Institute of Engineering Sciences and Technology, Pakistan
Giorgio Alaia	Università di Perugia, Italy
Tazyeen Alam	Università degli Studi di Cagliari, Italy
Arnulfo Alanis	Tecnológico Nacional de México, Mexico
Sandra Aleixo	University of Lisbon, Portugal
Earl Ryan Aleluya	Mindanao State University Iligan Institute of Technology, Philippines
Muhammad Junaid Ali	Université de Haute Alsace, France
Filipe Alvelos	Universidade do Minho, Portugal
Claudia Amadei	University of Padua, Italy
Paulo Amorim	Escola de Matemática Aplicada da Fundação Getulio Vargas, Brazil
Ana Paula Amorim	Universidade do Minho, Portugal
Paola Amoruso	LUM Giuseppe Degennaro University, Italy
Debora Anelli	Sapienza University of Rome, Italy
Mariarosaria Angrisano	Pegaso University, Italy
Alfonso Annunziata	University of Basilicata, Italy
Chiara Anselmi	Università di Pisa, Italy
Shigeyoshi Aoyama	KEK, Japan
Tatsumi Aoyama	University of Tokyo, Japan
Bernady O. Apduhan	Kyushu Sangyo University, Japan
Pablo Luiz Araujo Munhoz	Federal University of Ouro Preto, Brazil
Muhammad Waqas Arshad	University of Bologna, Italy
Daniela Ascenzi	Università degli Studi di Trento, Italy
Laura Ascione	Università degli Studi di Napoli Federico II, Italy
Reza Askarizad	University of Cagliari, Italy
Vanessa Assumma	University of Bologna, Italy
Vittorio Astarita	University of Calabria, Italy
Maria Fernanda Augusto	BITrum Research Center, Spain
Asja Aulisio	Politecnico di Torino, Italy
Samat Baigereyev	D. Serikbayev East Kazakhstan Technical University, Kazakhstan
Marco Baioletti	University of Perugia, Italy
Sara Balderas Díaz	University of Cádiz, Spain

Ginevra Balletto	University of Cagliari, Italy
Serob Balyan	Institute for Informatics and Automation Problems, National Academy of Sciences of Armenia, Armenia
Benedetto Barabino	University of Brescia, Italy
Sebastiano Barbieri	Politecnico di Torino, Italy
Ilaria Barone	Università degli Studi di Padova, Italy
Alice Barreca	Politecnico di Torino, Italy
Socrates Basbas	Aristotle University of Thessaloniki, Greece
Rosaria Battarra	Consiglio Nazionale delle Ricerche, Italy
Silvia Battino	University of Sassari, Italy
Fabrizio Battisti	University of Florence, Italy
Patricia Beites	University of Beira Interior, Portugal
David Berti	Art Spa, Italy
Samuel Bignardi	University of Chieti and Pescara, Italy
Francesco Bimbo	University of Foggia, Italy
Francesca Biondi	Politecnico di Torino, Italy
Marilisa Biscione	CNR, Italy
Alexander Bogdanov	St. Petersburg State University, Russia
Biagio Boi	University of Salerno, Italy
Alessandro Bombini	Istituto Nazionale di Fisica Nucleare, Italy
Ana Borges	Instituto Politécnico do Porto, Portugal
Vittoria Borghese	TNO, The Netherlands
Giuseppe Borruso	University of Trieste, Italy
Kamila Borsekova	Matej Bel University, Slovak Republic
Efstathios Bouhouras	Aristotle University of Thessaloniki, Greece
Ana Cristina Braga	University of Minho, Portugal
Diego Brandão	Federal Center for Technological Education of Rio de Janeiro, Brazil
Maria Antonia Brovelli	Politecnico di Milano, Italy
Francesco Bruzzone	Università Iuav di Venezia, Italy
Francesca Buglione	CNR ISPC, Italy
Enrique M. Cabaleiro Lago	Universidade de Santiago de Compostela, Spain
Francesco Calabrò	Mediterranea University of Reggio Calabria, Italy
Rogerio Calazan	Instituto de Estudos do Mar Almirante Paulo Moreira - Brazilian Navy, Brazil
Lelio Campanile	Università degli Studi della Campania Luigi Vanvitelli, Italy
Tiziana Campisi	University of Enna Kore, Italy
Dario Campisi	University of Perugia, Italy
Rubina Canesi	Università degli Studi di Padova, Italy
Alessandra Capolupo	Polytechnic University of Bari, Italy

Caterina Caprioli	Politecnico di Torino, Italy
Dario Caramiello	University of Naples Parthenope, Italy
Gerardo Carpentieri	University of Naples Federico II, Italy
Martina Carra	University of Brescia, Italy
Barbara Caselli	Università degli Studi di Parma, Italy
Danny Casprini	Politecnico di Milano, Italy
Arcangelo Castiglione	University of Salerno, Italy
Giulia Fernanda Grazia Catania	Università di Enna Kore, Italy
Ilaria Catapano	CNR IREA, Italy
Laura Cavalcante	Instituto Superior de Engenharia do Porto, Portugal
Giulio Cavana	Politecnico di Torino, Italy
Valeria Cera	University of Naples Federico II, Italy
Maria Cerreta	University of Naples Federico II, Italy
Giuseppe Cerullo	Sapienza University of Rome, Italy
Daniele Cesini	CNAF, INFN, Italy
Kai Cheng	Kyushu Sangyo University, Japan
Giuseppe Ciciriello	University Of Naples Federico II, Italy
Birol Ciloglugil	Ege University, Turkey
Cecília Coelho	Helmut Schmidt University, Germany
Enrico Collini	University of Florence, Italy
Luís Conceicao	Instituto Superior de Engenharia do Porto, Portugal
Giovanna Concu	University of Cagliari, Italy
Tatar Corina	University of Oradea, Romania
Alejandro Cornejo	Universitat Politècnica de Catalunya, Spain
Simone Corrado	University of Basilicata, Italy
Florbela Correia	Polytechnic Institute of Viana do Castelo, Portugal
Franco Corti	University of Padua, Italy
Cristina Coscia	Politecnico di Torino, Italy
Lino Costa	University of Minho, Portugal
Eliana da Costa e Silva	Polytechnic Institute of Porto, Portugal
Alessandro Costantini	INFN, Italy
Alessia Crisopulli	Politecnico di Milano, Italy
Valerio Cutini	University of Pisa, Italy
Mauro D'Apuzzo	University of Cassino and Southern Lazio, Italy
Hiroshi Daisaka	Hitotsubashi University, Japan
Sebastiano Damico	University of Malta, Malta
Maria Danese	CNR ISPC, Italy
Gianni Dangelo	University of Salerno, Italy
Mana Dastoum	Polytechnic University of Madrid, Spain

Giulia Datola	Politecnico di Milano, Italy
Regina De Almeida	University of Trás-os-Montes and Alto Douro, Portugal
Elena De Angelis	Politecnico di Torino, Italy
Elise de Doncker	Western Michigan University, USA
Pasquale De Luca	Parthenope University of Naples, Italy
Luiza De Macedo Mourelle	State University of Rio de Janeiro, Brazil
Pierfrancesco De Paola	University of Naples Federico II, Italy
Alexander Degtyarev	St.Petersburg State University, Russia
Francesco Paolo Del Giudice	University of Basilicata, Italy
Piera Della Morte	Pegaso Telematic University, Italy
Federico Dellanna	Politecnico di Torino, Italy
Marta Dellovo	Politecnico di Milano, Italy
Federica Deri	Università di Pisa, Italy
Francesco Di Capua	University of Basilicata, Italy
Clara Di Fazio	University of Trieste, Italy
Gabriella Di Genova	Università degli Studi di Perugia, Italy
Benedetta Di Leo	Università Politecnica delle Marche, Italy
Felicia Di Liddo	Polytechnic University of Bari, Italy
Joana Dias	University of Coimbra, Portugal
Oana Dinu	National University of Science and Technology Politehnica Bucharest, Romania
Lucia Dobrotová	Matej Bel University in Banská Bystrica, Slovak Republic
Edda Donati	University of Rome Tor Vergata, Italy
Aziz Dursun	Virginia Tech University, USA
Zahra Ebadi Ansaroudi	Fondazione Bruno Kessler, Italy
Maurizio Ercoli	University of Perugia, Italy
Dario Esposito	Polytechnic University of Bari, Italy
Noelia Faginas Lago	Università di Perugia, Italy
Maria Irene Falcao	University of Minho, Portugal
Stefano Falcinelli	University of Perugia, Italy
Marco Fanfani	University of Florence, Italy
Marcos Farias	Instituto de Engenharia Nuclear, Brazil
Francesca Fariello	Sapienza University of Rome, Italy
Maria Francesca Faro	Ministry of Education and Merit (MIM), Italy
Eslam Farsimadan	University of Salerno, Italy
Sara Favargiotti	University of Trento, Italy
Celestina Fazia	Università di Enna Kore, Italy
Maksims Feofilovs	Riga Technical University, Latvia
Florbela P. Fernandes Cedri	Instituto Politecnico de Bragança, Portugal
Paula Odete Fernandes	Instituto Politecnico de Bragança, Portugal

Flora Ferreira	University of Porto, Portugal
Maddalena Ferretti	Università Politecnica delle Marche, Italy
Luís Ferrás	University of Porto, Portugal
Massimo Ficco	University of Salerno, Italy
Maros Finka	Masaryk University, Slovak Republic
Ugo Fiore	University of Salerno, Italy
Lorena Fiorini	University of L'Aquila, Italy
Romano Fistola	University of Naples Federico II, Italy
Beatriz Flamia Azevedo	Instituto Politecnico de Bragança, Portugal
Valentina Florio	CNR, Italy
Ali Forooghi	University of Campania Luigi Vanvitelli, Italy
Anna Forte	University of Bologna, Italy
Grigorios Fountas	Aristotle University of Thessaloniki, Greece
Andreas Fricke	Hasso Plattner Institute for Digital Engineering, University of Potsdam, Germany
Luigi Fusco Girard	Pegaso Telematic University, Italy
Francesco Galante	University of Naples Federico II, Italy
Stefano Galassi	University of Florence, Italy
Andrea Gallo	Università degli Studi di Trieste, Italy
Chiara Garau	University of Cagliari, Italy
Gustavo Gatica	Universidad Andrés Bello, Chile
Rachele Vanessa Gatto	Università della Basilicata, Italy
Ivan Gerace	Università degli Studi di Perugia, Italy
Amal Gerges	University of Cagliari, Italy
Osvaldo Gervasi	University of Perugia, Italy
Tasnim Gharaibeh	Kalamazoo College, USA
Gian Felice Giaccu	University of Sassari, Italy
Dario Gioia	CNR ISPC, Italy
Luca Giommi	INFN CNAF, Italy
Valentina Giorgetti	Università degli Studi di Perugial, Italy
Giacomo Giorgi	Università degli Studi di Perugia, Italy
Hiago Mayk Gomes De Araújo Rocha	National Laboratory for Scientific Computing, Brazil
Omar Gomez	Universidad Nacional de Colombia, Colombia
A. Manuela Goncalves	University of Minho, Portugal
Joaquim Goncalves	Polytechnic Institute of Cávado and Ave, Portugal
Pedro Henrique Gonzalez	Federal University of Rio de Janeiro, Brazil
Yusuke Gotoh	Okayama University, Japan
Osvaldo Gramaxo De Freitas	Universitat de València, Spain
Antonia Gravagnuolo	National Research Council Italy (CNR) Institute of Heritage Science, Italy

Teresa Guarda	Universidad Estatal Península De Santa Elena, Ecuador
Maria Rosaria Guarini	Sapienza University of Rome, Italy
Raphael Guerra	Universidade Federal Fluminense, Brazil
Hélia Guerra	University of the Azores, Portugal
Gabriel Guerrero Contreras	University of Cádiz, Spain
Carmen Guida	Università degli Studi di Napoli Federico II, Italy
Eligius Hendrix	Universidad de Málaga, Spain
Jose Manuel Hermida Ramon	Universidade de Vigo, Spain
Antonino Iannuzzo	Universitá degli Studi del Sannio, Italy
Luciano Alessandro Ipsaro Palesi	University of Florence, Italy
Issaku Kanamori	Riken, Japan
Yeliz Karaca	UMass Chan Medical School and Massachusetts Institute of Technology, USA
Himmet Karaman	Istanbul Technical University, Turkey
Tatyana Khachkova	IPGG SB RAS, Russia
Jungyoon Kim	Gachon University, South Korea
Vladimir Korkhov	Saint Petersburg State University, Russia
Iuliia Kozlova	University of Bologna, Italy
Radoslav KožIak	Matej Bel University, Slovak Republic
Ludovica La Rocca	University of Naples Federico II, Italy
Rosa Anna La Rocca	University of Naples Federico II, Italy
Adnane Labbaci	Ibn Tofail University, Morocco
Sabrina Lai	University of Cagliari, Italy
Giuseppe Francesco Cesare Lama	University of Naples Federico Ii, Italy
Isabella Maria Lami	Politecnico di Torino, Italy
Salvatore Leonardi	University of Catania, Italy
Federica Leone	University of Cagliari, Italy
Vita Leonessa	University of Basilicata, Italy
Barbara Lino	Università degli Studi di Palermo, Italy
Vadim Lisitsa	Institute of Petroleum Geology and Geophysics SB RAS, Russia
Marco Locurcio	Polytechnic University of Bari, Italy
Andrea Lombardi	Università di Perugia, Italy
Cristina Lopes	Polytechnic Institute of Porto, Portugal
Isabel Lopes	Instituto Politécnico de Bragança, Portugal, Italy
Rui Pedro Lopes	Instituto Politécnico de Bragança, Portugal
Nicolas Lori	University of the Azores, Portugal
Luís Louro	University of Minho, Portugal
Jader Lugon Junior	Instituto Federal Fluminense, Brazil
Guido Luzi	Centre Tecnològic de Telecomunicacions de Catalunya, Spain

Maria Mourao	Polytechnic Institute of Viana do Castelo, Portugal
Eugenio Muccio	University of Naples Federico II, Italy
Beniamino Murgante	University of Basilicata, Italy
Giuseppe Musolino	Università Mediterranea di Reggio Calabria, Italy
Naohito Nakasato	University of Aizu, Japan
Isabel Natário	Nova University of Lisbon, Portugal
Nadia Nedjah	State University of Rio de Janeiro, Brazil
Grazia Neglia	Pegaso Telematic University, Italy
Paolo Nesi	University of Florence, Italy
Keigo Nitadori	Riken, Japan
Juan José Nogueira	Universidad Autónoma de Madrid, Spain
Mikhail Novikov	Sobolev Institute of Mathematics SB RAS, Russia
Yilsy María Nuñez Guerrero	Universidad Politécnica de Madrid, Spain
Ana Oliveira	Academia Militar, Portugal
Carlo Olivieri	Pegaso University, Italy
Vladimír Ondrejička	Comenius University in Bratislava, Slovak Republic
Beniamino Onorati	Università degli Studi della Basilicata, Italy
Fabian Bernal Orozco Barrera	UNAM, Mexico
M. Fernanda P. Costa	University of Minho, Portugal
António Pacheco	Instituto Superior Técnico, Portugal
Emerson Paiva	University of Minho, Portugal
Simone Palladino	Università degli Studi della Campania L. Vanvitelli, Italy
Francesco Palmieri	University of Salerno, Italy
Simona Panaro	University of Sussex Business School, UK
Claudia Panciera	IRSA CNR, Italy
Giacomo Pannacci	Università degli Studi di Perugia, Italy
Gianni Pantaleo	University of Florence, Italy
Eric Pardede	La Trobe University, Australia
Rosaria Parente	Universitas Mercatorum, Italy
Vittorio Paris	University of Bergamo, Italy
Luca Parodi	University of Genoa, Italy
Rui Pascoal	University of Coimbra, Portugal
Hugo Peixoto	University of Minho, Portugal
Francesco Peluso	University of Naples Parthenope, Italy
Ana Pereira	Polytechnic Institute of Bragança, Portugal
Amina Pereno	Politecnico di Torino, Italy
Martin Perez Perez	University of Vigo, Spain
Donato Perfetto	University of Campania Luigi Vanvitelli, Italy
Güzide Miray Perihanoglu	Van Yuzuncu Yil University, Turkey

Mariano Pernetti	Università della Campania Luigi Vanvitelli, Italy
Damiano Perri	University of Perugia, Italy
Pasquale Perrini	Consorzio Interuniversitario per l'Idrologia, Italy
Raffaele Persico	Università della Calabria, Italy
Lucia Petronio	University of Bologna, Italy
Rossella Petti	Politecnico di Bari, Italy
Francesco Picariello	Universitas Mercatorum, Italy
Angela Pilogallo	IMAA CNR, Italy
Natalia Pingaro	Politecnico di Milano, Italy
Telmo Miguel Pires Pinto	University of Minho, Portugal
Veronika Piscová	Institute of Landscape Ecology, Slovak Academy of Sciences, Slovak Republic
Zeynel Abidin Polat	Izmir Katip Celebi University, Turkey
Giuliano Poli	Università di Napoli Federico II, Italy
Antonio Polimeni	Università di Messina, Italy
Maurizio Pollino	ENEA, Italy
Mohammad Pourfouladi	Politecnico di Milano, Italy
Dmitry Prokhorov	IPGG SB RAS, Russia
Faiza Qamar	National University of Sciences and Technology, Pakistan
Yuan Qi	University of Hong Kong, China
Siyu Qiu	University of Bologna, Italy
Arunasalam Rahunanthan	Central State University, USA
Joelmir Ramos	Universidade do Estado do Rio de Janeiro, Brazil
Bruna Ramos	University of Minho, Portugal
Nicolás Ramos Berdullas	University of Vigo, Spain
Krishnamoorthy Ranganathan	Chennai Institute of Technology, India
Nicoletta Rassu	Università di Cagliari, Italy
Roberta Ravanelli	University of Liège, Belgium
Michela Ravanelli	Sapienza Università di Roma, Italy
Manuela Rebaudengo	Politecnico di Torino, Italy
Simone Rebegoldi	University of Modena and Reggio Emilia, Italy
Pier Francesco Recchi	Università di Napoli Federico II, Italy
Rommel Regis	Saint Joseph's University, USA
Marco Reis	University of Coimbra, Portugal
James Rhodes	Western Michigan University, USA
Luigi Maciel Ribeiro	State University of Rio de Janeiro, Brazil
Corrado Rindone	Università degli Studi Mediterranea di Reggio Calabria, Italy
Ana Maria A. C. Rocha	Universidade do Minho, Portugal
Humberto Rocha	University of Coimbra, Portugal
Carlos Rodrigues	Instituto Politécnico de Bragança, Portugal

Ivan Rodriguez Conde	University of Arkansas at Little Rock, USA
Darina Rojíková	Matej Bel University, Slovak Republic
Diana Rolando	Politecnico di Torino, Italy
Antonella Roma	Sapienza University of Rome, Italy
James Rombi	University of Cagliari, Italy
Elisabetta Ronchieri	INFN CNAF, Italy
Marzio Rosi	University of Perugia, Italy
Silvia Rossetti	Università degli Studi di Parma, Italy
Marco Rossitti	Politecnico di Milano, Italy
Florin Rusca	National University of Science and Technology Politehnica Bucharest, Romania
Yvonne Russo	University of Campania L. Vanvitelli, Italy
Antonio Russo	University of Enna Kore, Italy
Ana Sofia Rézio	Polytechnic Institute of Lisbon, Portugal
Emma Sabatelli	Sapienza Università di Roma, Italy
Matteo Sacchet	University of Turin, Italy
Sabrina Sacco	University of Naples Federico II, Italy
Lucia Saganeiti	Institute of Methodologies for Environmental Analysis, National Research Council, Italy
Valeria Saiu	University of Cagliari, Italy
Francesco Santini	University of Perugia, Italy
Rafael Santos	National Institute for Space Research (INPE), Brazil
Edcarllos Santos	Universidade Federal do Sul da Bahia, Brazil
Valentino Santucci	Università per Stranieri di Perugia, Italy
Andrea Sarcina	Università di Padova, Italy
Ilaria Scarcelli	Politecnico di Bari, Italy
Andrea Scianna	National Research Council of Italy, Italy
Francesco Scorza	University of Basilicata, Italy
Ester Scotto Di Perta	University of Naples Federico II, Italy
Alejandro Segura	Universidad Politécnica de Madrid, Spain
Yasmine Selim	Ain Shams University, Egypt
Ines Sena Cedri	Instituto Politécnico de Bragança and University of Minho, Portugal
Alex Sendrós	Universitat de Barcelona, Spain
Ricardo Severino	University of Minho, Portugal
Mojtaba Sharifzadeh	Università di Trento, Italy
Luigi Sibille	Norwegian University of Science and Technology, Norway
Francesco Sica	Sapienza University of Rome, Italy
Adriano Silva	Instituto Politecnico de Bragança, Portugal
Angela Silva	Universidade do Minho, Portugal

Paula Simões	Military Academy, Portuguese Army, Portugal
Francesca Sinatra	University of Trieste, Italy
Mercedes Solla	Universidade de Vigo, Spain
Sergey Solovyev	Sobolev Institute of Mathematics SB RAS, Russia
Maria Somma	University of Naples Federico II, Italy
Federica Sortino	Università degli Studi di Enna Kore, Italy
Eleonora Sottile	University of Cagliari, Italy
Martina Spinelli	Politecnico di Torino, Italy
Elena Stankova	Saint Petersburg State University, Russia
Alexandra Stankulova	Politecnico di Torino, Italy
Giorgia Sugoni	Links Foundation, Italy
Katarína Sýkorová	Matej Bel University, Slovak Republic
Francesco Tajani	Sapienza University of Rome, Italy
Deodato Tapete	Italian Space Agency (ASI), Italy
Rodrigo Tapia-McClung	Centro de Investigación en Ciencias de Información Geoespacial, Mexico
Maria Tartari	CNR, Italy
Daniela Tavano	University of Calabria, Italy
Tarek Teba	University of Portsmouth, UK
Ana Paula Teixeira	Universidade do Minho, Portugal
Wagner Telles	Universidade Federal Fluminense, Brazil
Luis Teodoro	University of Oslo, Norway
Maria Filomena Teodoro	Instituto Superior Técnico, Portugal
Yiota Theodora	National Technical University of Athens, Greece
Elena Todella	University of Parma, Italy
Graca Tomaz	Instituto Politécnico da Guarda, Portugal
Chiara Torre	University of Malta, Malta
Francesca Torrieri	Politecnico di Milano, Italy
Vincenza Torrisi	University of Catania, Italy
Arianna Travaglini	Lucian Blaga University of Sibiu, Romania
Stefanos Tsigdinos	National Technical University of Athens, Greece
Kamila Turečková	Silesian University in Opava, Czech Republic
Elen Twrdy	University of Ljubljana, Slovenia
Toshihiro Uchibayashi	Kyushu University, Japan
Takahiro Ueda	Juntendo University, Japan
Generoso Vaiano	Pegaso University, Italy
Aleksandar Valjarević	University of Belgrade, Serbia
Gianmarco Vanuzzo	University of Perugia, Italy
Dmitrii Vasiunin	Deutsche Telekom Cloud Services E.P.E., Greece
Mohammad Vazir Panah	University of Salerno, Italy
Anna Vaňová	Matej Bel University, Slovak Republic
Enrica Vecchi	University of Cagliari, Italy

Roberto Ventura	Università degli Studi di Brescia, Italy
Ferdinando Verardi	Pegaso Telematic University, Italy
Clara Stella Vicari Aversa	Università degli Studi Mediterranea di Reggio Calabria, Italy
Gianluca Vinti	Università degli Studi di Perugia, Italy
Katarína Vitálišová	Matej Bel University, Slovak Republic
Weronika Wojtak	CCG/ZGDV Institute, Portugal
Fukuko Yuasa	KEK, Japan
Madina Yussubaliyeva	D. Serikbayev East Kazakhstan Technical University, Kazakhstan
Paola Zamperlin	University of Florence, Italy
Francisco Zayas Gato	Universidade da Coruña, Spain
Nodir Zaynalov	Samarkand Branch of Tashkent University of Information Technologies Named After Muhammad Al Khwarizmi, Uzbekistan
Ljiljana Zivkovic	Republic Geodetic Authority, Serbia
Piero Zizzania	University of Naples Federico II, Italy
Renato Zona	Università della Campania L. Vanvitelli, Italy
Floriana Zucaro	University of Naples Federico II, Italy
Francesco Zullo	University of L'Aquila, Italy
Giovanni Zurlo	INFN CNAF, Italy
Özge Öztürk Hacar	Yildiz Technical University, Turkey
Isidora Đurić	University of Novi Sad, Serbia

Roberto Ventura	Università degli Studi di Brescia, Italy
Ferdinando Verardi	Pegaso Telematic University, Italy
Clara Stella Vicari Aversa	Università degli Studi Mediterranea di Reggio Calabria, Italy
Gianluca Vinti	Università degli Studi di Perugia, Italy
Katarína Vitálišová	Matej Bel University, Slovak Republic
Weronika Wojtak	CCG/ZGDV Institute, Portugal
Fukuko Yuasa	KEK, Japan
Madina Yussubaliyeva	D. Serikbayev East Kazakhstan Technical University, Kazakhstan
Paola Zamperlin	University of Florence, Italy
Francisco Zayas Gato	Universidade da Coruña, Spain
Nodir Zaynalov	Samarkand Branch of Tashkent University of Information Technologies Named After Muhammad Al Khwarizmi, Uzbekistan
Ljiljana Zivkovic	Republic Geodetic Authority, Serbia
Piero Zizzania	University of Naples Federico II, Italy
Renato Zona	Università della Campania L. Vanvitelli, Italy
Floriana Zucaro	University of Naples Federico II, Italy
Francesco Zullo	University of L'Aquila, Italy
Giovanni Zurlo	INFN CNAF, Italy
Özge Öztürk Hacar	Yildiz Technical University, Turkey
Isidora Đurić	University of Novi Sad, Serbia

Plenary Lectures

Digital Twins for Cities – The Rise of the Socio-Technical System

Claudia van der Laag

Department of Built Environment, Oslo Metropolitan University, Norway

Abstract. Cities are entering a new era in which digital twins are no longer simply technical replicas of urban systems, but evolving socio-technical infrastructures that shape how cities are planned, governed, and experienced. Across the world, urban digital twins are being adopted to address some of the most pressing challenges of our time — climate adaptation, urban resilience, mobility transitions, decarbonisation, infrastructure management, and inclusive governance. Yet as these technologies become increasingly sophisticated, a fundamental question emerges: can digital twins truly support more democratic and human-centred cities, or will they reinforce existing structures of power and expertise? In this keynote, Claudia van der Laag explores the transformation of urban digital twins from data-driven modelling tools into collaborative platforms for urban decision-making and societal change. It argues that the future of digital twins lies not only in advances in artificial intelligence, real-time data integration, simulation, and predictive analytics, but equally in the ability to connect technological innovation with governance, participation, and human agency. Drawing on emerging international research and practical case studies, the keynote examines the complex ecosystem surrounding urban digital twins, bringing together planners, policymakers, researchers, technologists, and communities. It highlights how digital twins increasingly function as meeting points between multiple forms of knowledge — technical, political, social, and experiential — and why interdisciplinary collaboration is essential for their success. The talk critically reflects on the tensions between technological ambition and civic inclusion, exploring themes such as transparency, interoperability, participation, and trust. It also discusses how digital twins can become powerful environments for scenario exploration, urban experimentation, and collective learning, enabling cities to better navigate uncertainty and complexity in an age of rapid urban transformation. Ultimately, this keynote presents a vision of digital twins not as neutral technological systems, but as living socio-technical infrastructures capable of reshaping urban governance itself. The challenge ahead is therefore not only how accurately cities can be modelled, but how inclusively they can be imagined, negotiated, and governed through these emerging digital environments.

Prescriptive AI in Practice: Bridging Optimisation, Generative AI and Agentic Decision-Making

Bernardo Almada-Lobo

Universidade do Porto, Faculdade de Engenharia, INESC TEC, Portugal

Abstract. Prescriptive AI, viewed through the lens of mathematical optimisation and operations research, addresses complex business decision-making problems involving limited resources, multiple decision options and competing objectives. This talk considers the full decision pipeline: problem framing, model formulation, computational solution, implementation, monitoring and organisational adoption. The practical success of prescriptive AI depends less on algorithmic sophistication alone than on the quality of the translation between real-world decision contexts and formal optimisation models. In practice, this translation remains a major bottleneck. Objectives are often ambiguous, constraints are incomplete or tacit, data may be fragmented, and the operational consequences of a recommendation may be poorly understood. As a result, optimisation projects can fail even when the underlying mathematical model is technically sound. The talk will address the persistent gap between optimisation theory and deployment practice. While optimisation has generated substantial value in domains such as supply chain planning, logistics, production, revenue management, workforce planning and inventory control, many initiatives still face a significant risk of under-delivery. Common failure modes include incorrect problem framing, weak data readiness, brittle assumptions, infeasible or non-actionable recommendations, limited explainability, insufficient ownership by business users and inadequate post-deployment monitoring. Closing this gap requires moving from one-off model building to an operational lifecycle in which models are stress-tested, embedded in workflows, monitored for drift and revised as the business environment changes. Recent developments in generative and agentic AI create new opportunities to reduce these barriers. Generative AI can support the elicitation of decision-maker preferences, the structuring of unstructured operational knowledge, the drafting of candidate formulations and the explanation of model outputs in business language. Agentic AI can extend this role by orchestrating multi-step workflows that involve model formulation, solver-code generation, execution, debugging, infeasibility diagnosis, sensitivity analysis and human review. However, these capabilities should not be interpreted as replacing optimisation expertise. Rather, they create a new interface between human judgement, analytical modelling and computational decision support. This talk will discuss a cross-fertilisation agenda between optimisation, generative AI and agentic AI, with a focus on how these technologies should be calibrated to the decision at hand.

Net-Zero Communities through Life Cycle Thinking: Canadian Lessons and Global Implications

Kasun Hewage

School of Engineering (Okanagan Campus), Clean Energy Research Centre (CERC), University of British Columbia (UBC), Canada

Abstract. This keynote presentation discusses how life cycle thinking supports the transformation of communities toward sustainable, resilient, and net-zero futures. Drawing on Canadian research, practice, and policy experience, the presentation highlights how integrated life cycle approaches can move beyond conventional carbon accounting to inform practical decision-making across buildings, infrastructure, energy systems, waste management, water systems, and industrial processes [1–8]. The keynote features research conducted at the Life Cycle Management Laboratory (LCML) at the University of British Columbia, Canada, an internationally recognized research hub led by Kasun Hewage. LCML brings together engineers, scientists, policy researchers, postdoctoral fellows, visiting scholars, and graduate researchers to translate data-intensive sustainability research into actionable climate solutions. The laboratory's work is organized around six interconnected research themes: energy systems, urban development, water systems, waste management, construction and asset management, and industrial processes and products. Together, these themes provide an integrated platform for advancing life cycle–based pathways to net-zero communities. Supported by strong partnerships with government, industry, and community stakeholders, LCML has contributed to a substantial body of applied sustainability research, including more than 400 journal articles, 100 conference papers, and numerous technical reports that have informed real-world planning and implementation. This keynote presentation highlights selected success stories that demonstrate how life cycle thinking can be translated into practical strategies for reducing environmental impacts while strengthening community resilience. These insights are especially relevant to the interdisciplinary focus of ICCSA 2026.

References

1. Weerasinghe, O., Hewage, K., Razi, F., Fatmi, M., Sadiq, R.: Applicability of land use models for sustainable urban planning: a review. J. Urban Plann. Dev. ASCE, **151**(3) (2025). https://doi:10.1061/JUPDDM.UPENG-5705
2. Sultana, S. R., et al.: Looking beyond energy efficiency targets: life cycle sustainability of mechanical and water heating equipment in Canadian homes. J. Clean. Prod. Elsevier, **473**, 143469 (2024). https://doi.org/10.1016/j.jclepro.2024.143469

3. Liyanage, D. R., Hewage, K., Hussain, S. H., Razi, F., Sadiq, R.: Climate adaptation of existing buildings: a critical review on planning energy retrofit strategies for future climate. Renew. Sustain. Energy Rev. Elsevier, **199**, 114476 (2024). https://doi.org/10.1016/j.rser.2024.114476
4. Liyanage, D. R., Hewage, K., Karunathilake, H., Sadiq, R.: Feasibility of carbon-capturing in building heating systems: a life cycle thinking-based approach. International J. Greenhouse Gas Control. Elsevier, **132** (2023). https://doi.org/10.1016/j.ijggc.2023.104056
5. Moudgil, V., Sadiq, R., Bakhtavar, E., Paudel, A., Hewage, K.: A cloud-oriented data-analysis framework to analyze peak demand dynamics in institutional building clusters. Sustain. Cities Soci. Elsevier, **111**, 105553 (2024). https://doi.org/10.1016/j.scs.2024.105553
6. Liyanage, D. R., Hewage, K., Ghobadi, M., Sadiq, R.: Thermal resiliency of single-family housing stock under extreme hot and cold conditions. Energy Build. Elsevier, **323**, 114809 (2024). https://doi.org/10.1016/j.enbuild.2024.114809
7. Wijayasekera, S. C., et al.: Sustainability of waste-to-hydrogen conversion pathways: a life cycle thinking-based assessment. Energy Convers. Manage. Elsevier, **270** (2022). https://doi.org/10.1016/j.enconman.2022.116218
8. Jayasena, A., Hewage, K., Siddiqui, O., Sadiq, R.: Socio-economic and environmental cost-benefit analysis of passive houses: a life cycle perspective. J. Clean. Prod. Elsevier, **373** (2022). https://doi.org/10.1016/j.jclepro.2022.133718

Machine Learning Based Methodologies for Grape and Wine Production

Pedro Melo-Pinto

University of Trás-os-Montes and Alto Douro, Engineering Department, Centre for the Research and Technology of Agro-Environmental and Biological Sciences, Portugal

Abstract. Wine production is a major area in the Portuguese economy. The sector accounts for approximately 2.6% of Portugal's GDP, and is crucial to the development of inland regions. Wine quality depends on grape quality, which is a result of different factors such as harvesting at the optimal point of maturity, or selecting the grapes according to quality features. The growing importance of precision agriculture demands novel methods to make the most out of the data generated. Machine learning approaches are particularly suitable for modelling complex processes, where too many arguments are involved. Many of the agricultural processes such as yield estimation or ripening fall into this category. However, several challenges may arise: even if models are available for particular cases, general models are difficult to come by, largely due to the high variability involved; with such models, there is a need for huge amounts of data, in a way which will not always be easy to obtain. This is particularly true in the case of grape production and the wine industry, where the number of grape varieties, climate, soil, etc., introduce a degree of variability that is uncommon in other sectors. One way of obtaining more information in such cases has been the use of images, whether RGB, multi-spectral, or hyperspectral. The use of images introduces additional challenges, such as data size and lighting conditions, which underscores the need for data-driven modelling methodologies. The use of machine learning (ML) techniques combined with images has been establishing itself as a viable alternative for predicting yields or quality parameters in grapes, and assisting with critical harvesting decisions. Several ML approaches have been proposed to handle such data characteristics, but selecting a suitable methodology that best addresses the problem under study and making sure it generalizes well is, most of the time, a cumbersome task. We will address three wine and grape production problems, yield estimation, grape quality assessment, and illness detection, presenting different difficulties. Yield estimation is a major aspect in the wine production industry. The number of berries is one of the most relevant yield aspects, and can be estimated using computer vision, namely image segmentation algorithms. Lighting is one of the key factors in computer vision approaches, and occlusions—which are common in this problem—can be minimized, but require estimation models to achieve reliable results. Early illness detection is, of course, of the utmost importance, with an impact on production and quality. Detecting early symptoms and distinguishing them from other conditions is a difficult task, which makes the use of machine learning algorithms advisable, using automatic visual inspection of the leaves, addressed as a pixel-based classification problem. However, the available datasets are limited and complex to compile, as different diseases typically require very specific timeframes and locations. The use of generative models to overcome this obstacle, in conjunction with robust classification models, leads to models that are intended to be as general as possible. The evaluation of the grape's maturation profile based on the evolution of their oenological parameters over time is one of the most important aspects for ensuring wine quality, playing a decisive role in the definition of the optimal time for harvesting. The use of hyperspectral imaging combined with learning algorithms represents a faster and non-destructive grape ripeness assessment method. We focus in two fundamental aspects to address the resulting data variability: a possible wavelength bands selection (with the purpose of reducing the dimensionality of data without losing predictive power) and the generalization ability of the ML model under such demanding conditions.

Contents

Workshop on Advancements in Applied Machine-learning and Data Analytics (AAMDA 2026)

A Pipeline to Generate Synthetic Dataset for Ceramic Fragments Recognition and Pairing

Serena Barone[1,2](✉), Marta Magalini[2], Rodolfo Panerai[2], and Alessandro Bombini[2]

[1] Università di Firenze, Dipartimento di Fisica e Astronomia, Florence, Italy
serena.barone@unifi.it

[2] Istituto Nazionale di Fisica Nucleare, Firenze, Italy

Abstract. In this contribution, we present a pipeline for generating synthetic datasets of ceramic fragments. The pipeline simulates thousands of breakages of 3D ceramic objects, starting from an `.stl` file, with user control over the number of fragments produced. Following the breaking simulation, a custom-designed erosion process is applied to replicate the natural degradation that pottery fragments undergo during burial over thousands of years.

This approach directly tackles the issue of limited and hard-to-annotate datasets in archaeological settings, and with a single pipeline, it enables multiple deep learning tasks, such as fragment classification, orientation regression, and fragment pairing. Each resulting fragment is stored as an `.stl` file with a unique UUID, while adjacency information between fragments is collected and preserved.

The pipeline is implemented in Python using the Blender Python API and is fully containerised with a custom Singularity container. This enables parallelisation and distribution of multiple breaking simulations, facilitating large-scale dataset generation. The code is freely available ([4] https://github.com/CHNet-AI-Barumini/Synthetic-Fragment-Dataset-Generation). The resulting dataset is released under CC-BY-0 license.

Keywords: Machine Learning · Cultural Heritage · Open data · big data · Computer graphics

1 Introduction

The reconstruction of ceramic vessels from fragmented remains is a fundamental, yet arduous, task in archaeology. It provides critical insights into chronology, technology, trade, and cultural practices of past societies [25]. However, the process is often compared to solving a highly complex, three-dimensional puzzle with most of the pieces missing or degraded. Archaeologists routinely contend with excavations yielding thousands of irregular fragments (sherds), where the

O. Gervasi et al. (Eds.): ICCSA 2026 Workshops, LNCS 16758, pp. 3–15, 2027.
https://doi.org/10.1007/978-3-032-30497-1_1

manual search for joints, a process known as refitting or pairing, is exceptionally time-consuming and requires a high degree of specialised skill and visual acuity [14,16,24]. Previous work has addressed fragment reassembly using geometric matching [14] or 3D scanning of pottery [16], but these approaches typically rely on hand-crafted features and do not scale to large collections. This challenge is particularly acute when fragments have suffered from post-depositional surface erosion, which smooths diagnostic features and fracture edges, obscuring the very evidence needed to determine if two pieces once belonged to the same vessel.

The Nuragic civilisation of Sardinia (1700 B.C.E–1000 B.C.E), Italy, provides a compelling case study of these difficulties. Nuragic sites are rich in ceramic material, but as detailed in [5], the pottery assemblage is far from uniform. It exhibits significant variability in production techniques, surface treatments (e.g., smooth surfaces versus red slip wares), and temper materials (e.g., calcite versus volcanic rock fragments), reflecting technological evolution and cultural contacts over centuries. This inherent variability, combined with the erosive effects of the Sardinian environment, means that Nuragic sherds from different periods and contexts can appear superficially similar, while adjacent fragments from the same vessel may differ significantly due to different preservation conditions. Consequently, the accurate reassembly of Nuragic ceramics remains a bottleneck, heavily reliant on the knowledge of expert archaeologists and restorers, and unsustainable for the vast quantities of material recovered.

In recent years, the field of 3D computer vision has made significant strides in addressing similar geometric reasoning problems through deep learning. The direct analysis of 3D point clouds, a representation well-suited for scanned archaeological fragments with photogrammetry or laser scanners, has been revolutionised by architectures that can handle unstructured data. The pioneering PointNet [22] achieved permutation invariance through point-wise multi-layer perceptrons (MLPs) and a symmetric aggregation function, but its ability to capture local geometric context was limited. This was addressed by PointNet++ [23], which introduces a hierarchical architecture with set abstraction modules to learn local features at multiple scales.

Concurrently, graph-based methods like Dynamic Graph CNN (DGCNN) have demonstrated impressive performance [27]. DGCNN constructs a dynamic k-nearest neighbor graph in the feature space, applying an EdgeConv operation to learn relationships between points and their neighbors, effectively capturing both local and global structures. More recently, Point Transformers [31] have emerged, applying attention mechanisms to model long-range dependencies and contextual relationships within point sets, achieving state-of-the-art results in tasks like completion and classification. These architectures have been successfully applied in fields ranging from autonomous driving and urban scene segmentation [13] to robotics [21]. For archaeological fragment analysis, these methods suggest a clear pathway: classification of fragments by type, regression to estimate their original orientation in 3D space, and, crucially, learning geometric features to predict which fragments are likely to pair.

Despite the promise of these deep learning models, their application to ceramic fragment reassembly is fundamentally hindered by a lack of suitable training data. Existing 3D point cloud datasets, while valuable for benchmarking, are inadequate for this specific archaeological task. Widely used synthetic datasets like **ModelNet40** [29], **ShapeNetPart** [30], and **Breaking Bad** [26] contain clean, complete, and manifold 3D models of chairs, tables, airplanes, and other manufactured objects. They lack the irregular fractures, surface erosion, and partial volumes that are the defining characteristics of real-world archaeological sherds. Real-world scene datasets such as **S3DIS** [3], **ScanNet** [7], and **Semantic3D** [12] focus on large-scale urban or indoor environments, with classes like 'building', 'vegetation', 'chair', and 'table'. They do not contain examples of fragmented objects or the subtle features required for reassembly. Crucially, no publicly available dataset with a permissive license (e.g., CC-BY) provides 3D models of broken and eroded ceramic fragments complete with the ground-truth adjacency information needed to train a supervised model for fragment pairing. Annotating such data manually from real archaeological finds would be prohibitively expensive and labour-intensive, requiring the very expert effort the method aims to supplement.

To overcome this data bottleneck, we propose a synthetic data generation pipeline. By simulating both the fracture and subsequent erosion processes on 3D models of whole ceramic vessels, we can generate an unlimited, varied, and perfectly annotated dataset. This approach directly addresses the limitations of existing datasets, providing the necessary scale and ground-truth labels to train deep learning models for fragment classification, orientation regression, and, most importantly, fragment pairing.

2 Methodology

2.1 Breaking Ceramics with Blender API

To simulate the breaking of a ceramic object, we relied on the Python API of the free and open source (FOSS) program Blender [6], a software for 3D content creation, sculpting and rendering. This allowed us to perform operations on 3D objects programmatically. For the breaking, we used the Blender Add-on `CellFracture`, which utilises a Voronoi tessellation approach: it creates a bounding box around the object, randomly selects a user-tunable number of seeds within the box, and then constructs a 3D Voronoi diagram using the seeds as cell centers. Subsequently, it performs boolean intersection operations between each Voronoi region and the original object, yielding the individual fragments.

The logical steps of the pipeline are as follows:

1. Import the object from an `.stl` file;
2. Fragment the object into a user-tunable number of pieces, obtaining a list of fragments, and assign a universally unique identifier (UUID) to each fragment;
3. Iterate over the fragments; for each fragment:
   (a) Perform re-triangulation and sharp remesh operations, which are necessary to properly sample mesh points on the fracture surfaces;

```
Input  : do_center: boolean flag (moves the fragment's centre of mass to the
         coordinates (0,0, 0)), min_mesh_pts_pieces: minimum points per
         fragment, max_fractures: maximum fracture count, path_to_stl:
         input file path, path_to_store: output directory path
Output : Set of cleaned and exported fragments with UUIDs
// Import STL file
max_size, max_size_input ← LoadSTL(path_to_stl);
// Apply fracture simulation
BreakObject(max_fractures)
// Retrieve fracture collection
fracture_coll ← [obj | obj ∈ GetCollection('Amphora_breaks')];
// Generate UUIDs for all fragments
piece_uuid_map ← CreateUUIDDict(fracture_coll);
foreach obj ∈ fracture_coll do
    // Triangulate and remesh
    TriangulateRemesh(obj);
    // Get fragment size
    max_size_fragment ← GetObjectSize(obj);
    is_piece_ok ←
      CheckPiece(obj, min_mesh_pts_pieces, max_size_fragment);
    // Delete if too small
    if not is_piece_ok then
        Delete(obj);
        continue;
    end
    // Export valid fragment
    ExportObjToMesh(obj, path_to_store, do_center);
end
```

Algorithm 1: Fragment generation from single `.stl` object

   (b) Validate the mesh: the fragment is retained only if it satisfies the following criteria: (i) it is a manifold mesh (i.e., each edge is shared by exactly two faces), (ii) it contains no self-intersections, (iii) it has a sufficient number of mesh points exceeding a user-defined threshold `min_mesh_pts_pieces`, and (iv) its bounding box dimensions exceed a minimum size threshold `MIN_MAX_SIZE`. Fragments failing any of these checks are discarded;
   (c) Export the validated fragment mesh as an `.stl` file named `UUID.stl`, where `UUID` is the unique identifier assigned in step 2;
4. (Optional) Compute the adjacency matrix of fragments and store it as a JSON file. The JSON contains a dictionary mapping each fragment's UUID to a list of UUIDs of its neighbouring fragments.

The algorithm pseudocode is reported in Algorithm 1.

The pipeline described above generates a single breaking simulation for one object. Scaling this to create a large dataset, comprising hundreds of break simulations per object across dozens of object types is straightforward due to the *embarrassingly parallel*[1] nature of the problem. While a single breaking job is relatively fast (on the order of tens of seconds), aggregating thousands of simulations can become time-consuming. However, because each simulation is independent, distributed computing is an ideal strategy. A distributed approach is preferable over simple multi-threading or multi-processing, as Blender's API already leverages multi-threading internally for its own operations.

To facilitate distribution, we containerised the pipeline using Apptainer (formerly known as Singularity) [17,18]. Containerising Blender for headless execution (i.e., without a graphical user interface) presents some challenges. Notably, Blender ships with its own Python distribution, which must be used instead of the system Python to ensure access to Blender's global variables and API. This requires using `/opt/blender/4.5/python/bin/pip` and `/opt/blender/4.5/python/bin/python` for package installation and script execution. Additionally, enabling the required add-ons necessitates running a dedicated Python script via:

```
/opt/blender/blender -background -factory-startup -python
./enable_addons.py
```

The complete Apptainer definition file is provided in Listing 1.1.

```
Bootstrap: docker
From: ubuntu:25.04
stage: build
%files
    # copy add-ons
    ./blender_modules/add-on-cell-fracture-v0.2.1.zip
        ↪ ./add-on-cell-fracture-v0.2.1.zip
    # copy script to enable addons
    ./build_scripts/enable_addons.py ./enable_addons.py
%post
    apt update && apt install -y \
        wget unzip \
        xz-utils \
        libgl1 libx11-6 libxi6 libxxf86vm1 libxcursor1 libxrandr2
            ↪ libxinerama1 libegl1 libdbus-1-3 libxkbcommon0 libsm6
    # Install Blender
    wget \url{https://download.blender.org/release/Blender4.5}
        ↪ /blender-4.5.0-linux-x64.tar.xz
    tar -xf blender-4.5.0-linux-x64.tar.xz
    mv blender-4.5.0-linux-x64 /opt/blender
    # Install pip for Blenders Python
    /opt/blender/4.5/python/bin/python3.11 -m ensurepip
    /opt/blender/4.5/python/bin/python3.11 -m pip install --upgrade
        ↪ pip
    # Install custom modules (example: numpy, tqdm)
    /opt/blender/4.5/python/bin/pip install numpy tqdm
    # install add-on
    # Create Blender add-ons directory
    mkdir -p /opt/blender/4.5/scripts/addons
    # Unzip your add-on into that folder
    unzip ./add-on-cell-fracture-v0.2.1.zip -d
        ↪ /opt/blender/4.5/scripts/addons
    # install
```

[1] An embarrassingly parallel workload is a computing problem that can be trivially divided into many independent sub-tasks requiring no communication or dependency between them.

```
    /opt/blender/blender --background --factory-startup --python
        ↪ ./enable_addons.py
%environment
    export PATH=/opt/blender:$PATH
    export PYTHONPATH=
        ↪ /opt/blender/4.5/python/lib/python3/site-packages
    export BLENDER_ADDON_PATHS=/opt/blender/4.5/scripts/addons
%runscript
    exec /opt/blender/blender "$@"
```

Listing 1.1. Apptainer definition file for the ceramic fragment simulation pipeline.

2.2 Erosion with PyTorch via ODE Resolution

To simulate erosion we use an ordinary differential equation (ODE) approach [9,10], relating mesh points to mesh curvature [8,15], plus an additional random noise to account for conservation quirks such as collisions.

The idea is that the variation in time of the position of mesh points $\Sigma = \{\mathbf{p}_i(t) \in \mathbb{R}^3\}_{i=1,\dots,N}$ is proportional to the mean curvature $\mathbf{H}_i = H_i\hat{\mathbf{n}}_i$ at that point, where $\hat{\mathbf{n}}_i$ is the normal outward vector to the surface Σ: the higher the curvature, the higher the variation, i.e.

$$\partial_t \mathbf{p}_i(t) \propto -H_i\hat{\mathbf{n}}_i\,, \qquad \forall i = 1,\dots,N.$$

The full formula is thus

$$\partial_t \mathbf{p}_i(t) = -\left(\mu H_i(t)\hat{\mathbf{n}}_i(t) + \sigma\xi_i(t)\right), \qquad \forall i = 1,\dots,N, \tag{1}$$

where μ, σ are two parameters (floating point), and $\xi_i \in \mathbb{R}^3$ is a random inward vector redrawn at each t.

To compute the mean curvature, we describe the (discretised) surface as a graph $\mathcal{G} = \{\mathbf{p}_i \in \mathbb{R}^3; e_{ij} \in [\{0\},\{1\}]\}$, where e_{ij} is the adjacency matrix in sparse formulation. We can then estimate the mean curvature via the Laplace-Beltrami operator.

A standard and geometrically consistent way to discretise the Laplace - Beltrami operator on triangle meshes is the *cotangent formula*, first appearing in [20] and later systematised in discrete differential geometry and computer graphics [19].

Given a triangulated surface with vertices $\{\mathbf{p}_i\}$ and adjacency structure induced by the mesh, the Laplace-Beltrami operator at a vertex i is discretised as a weighted sum over its 1-ring neighbours:

$$\Delta\mathbf{p}_i \approx \frac{1}{2A_i}\sum_{j\in\mathcal{N}(i)} w_{ij}(\mathbf{p}_j - \mathbf{p}_i), \qquad w_{ij} = \frac{1}{2}\left(\cot\alpha_{ij} + \cot\beta_{ij}\right).$$

Here, α_{ij} and β_{ij} denote the two angles opposite to the edge (i,j), and A_i is the mixed (Voronoi or barycentric) area associated to vertex i [19]. This operator is a discrete counterpart of the smooth identity

$$\Delta_\Sigma \mathbf{p} = 2H\hat{\mathbf{n}},$$

where $H\hat{\mathbf{n}}$ is the mean curvature normal. Therefore, the vector

$$\mathbf{H}_i \approx \frac{1}{2A_i} \sum_j w_{ij} (\mathbf{p}_j - \mathbf{p}_i)$$

provides a consistent approximation of the mean curvature normal at vertex i, and the scalar mean curvature magnitude is obtained as

$$H_i = \|\mathbf{H}_i\|.$$

This discretisation is widely used because it is intrinsic, second-order accurate under mesh refinement, and enjoys strong variational properties [28]. It is also the formulation underlying many mesh processing algorithms such as smoothing, denoising, and curvature-flow evolution.

The PyTorch implementation (Listing 1.2) is a direct translation of this classical cotangent scheme: cotangent weights are assembled per face, aggregated into a sparse Laplacian stencil, and normalised by the dual areas to obtain the mean curvature magnitude.

The integration of the differential equation is performed for an user-defined number of time step of value Δt (another user tunable parameter) using a simple forward euler scheme

$$\mathbf{p}_i(t + \Delta t) = \mathbf{p}_i(t) - \Delta t \left(\mu H_i(t) \hat{\mathbf{n}}_i(t) + \sigma \xi_i(t) \right), \qquad \forall i = 1, \ldots, N. \tag{2}$$

Listing 1.2. Example usage of the ErodeMesh class.

```
from utils.generic_utils import open_stl, export_stl
from utils.custom_erosion import ErodeMesh

# 0. Open stl
piece = open_stl(path_to_file)
# 1. Instantiate erosion class
erode = ErodeMesh(
    steps = integration_steps,
    dt = dt,
    mu = mu, # 0.3-0.5
    sigma = sigma, # 0.05 - 0.2
    clamp_alpha = 0.10,
    seed = 42
)
# 2. Transform data with GPU acceleration
data_transformed = erode(piece.to(device)).cpu()
# 3. Store data
export_stl(data_transformed, f"{path_to_store}/
   custom_eroded_{filename}.stl")
```

Fig. 1. The five selected classes to validate the pipeline: from left to right: (a) Anfora, (b) Boccale, (c) Olla, (d) Tripode, (e) Brocca Askoide.

3 Application: Nuragic Pottery Fragments

We tested the pipeline on 5 different classes of nuragic ceramic objects. We selected them from the Italy "Ministero della Cultura" official website[2], choosing objects of Nuragic origin, with images in CC-BY-4.0 license [4]. We selected

1. Class 1: *Anfora*[3]
2. Class 2: *Boccale*[4]
3. Class 3: *Olla*[5]
4. Class 4: *Tripode*[6]
5. Class 5: *Brocca Askoide*[7]

We thus sculpted the 3D objects on Blender, starting from the 2D images and the geometric information present in the website. A visual representation of the sculpted 3D objects is reported in Fig. 1.

We have then created a dataset of fragments, by breaking each object 60 times, with a random number of breaking, uniformly distributed in the $[6, 16]$ range. This gave us a dataset of 3732 fragments.

For the erosion, we uniformly draw $\mu \in (0.3, 0.5), \sigma \in (0.05, 0.2)$, 3–5 integration steps, and Δt estimated as 0.1 of the mean curvature squared, which produced visually realistic erosion on the fracture surfaces while preserving overall shape.

In Fig. 2, we report the effect of erosion. It is easy to see that the effect of the Mean curvature smoothing effectively reduces the mesh sharpness on the breaking surface. Furthermore, the effect of noise presents the emergence of small

---

[2] https://catalogo.beniculturali.it/.
[3] https://catalogo.beniculturali.it/detail/ArchaeologicalProperty/2000202578.
[4] https://catalogo.beniculturali.it/detail/SARDEGNA/ArchaeologicalProperty/2000116164.
[5] https://catalogo.beniculturali.it/detail/ArchaeologicalProperty/2000202521.
[6] https://catalogo.beniculturali.it/detail/SARDEGNA/ArchaeologicalProperty/2000116220.
[7] https://catalogo.beniculturali.it/detail/ArchaeologicalProperty/2000202515.

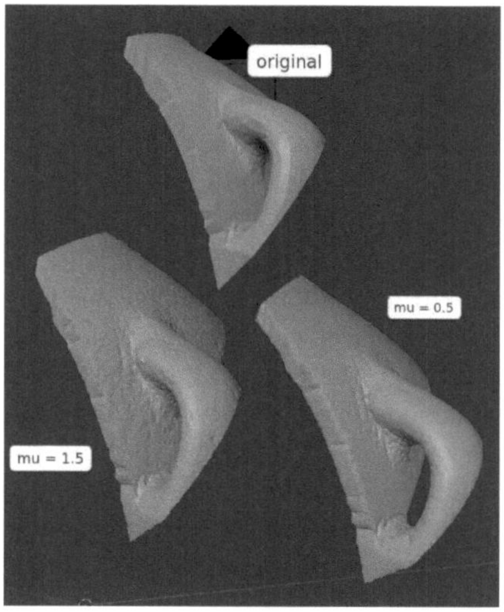

Fig. 2. Example of a fragment obtained from the pipeline: on top, uneroded; bottom left, eroded with $\mu = 1.5$; bottom right, eroded with $\mu = 0.5$.

concave regions. This effectively simulate the erosion, with adequate approximation, especially once a point cloud sampling is performed on the `.stl` (a standard pre-processing step in 3D computer vision).

In Fig. 3, we report the comparison of an original class object, one of its breaking, and that breaking with applied erosion. It is immediately evident that the effect of erosion is more pronounced on the fragment surfaces (as visible by the empty space created between fragments).

Fig. 3. Comparison, from left to right, of original, broken, and broken & eroded Anfora.

4 Conclusions and Outlook

In this work, we addressed the challenge of data scarcity in computational archaeology, particularly for the task of ceramic fragment reassembly. The manual reconstruction of broken ceramics, especially in contexts such as Nuragic archaeology, remains a time-consuming process that relies heavily on expert knowledge. While deep learning approaches have shown promise for 3D geometric reasoning tasks, their application to fragment analysis has been hindered by the lack of suitable training data that captures the irregular fractures, surface erosion, and adjacency relationships characteristic of real archaeological finds.

To overcome this bottleneck, we presented a fully containerised, open-source pipeline for generating synthetic datasets of ceramic fragments. The pipeline can easily simulate thousands of breakages of 3D ceramic objects using Blender python API, applying a custom-designed erosion process to replicate post- depositional surface degradation, and stores each fragment as an `.stl` file with a unique UUID while preserving adjacency information.

The main contributions of this work are threefold:

- A **ready-to-distribute, containerised pipeline** packaged with Apptainer, enabling reproducible and scalable fragment generation across distributed computing environments without complex dependency management;
- A **custom erosion module** implemented in PyTorch, which solves the mean curvature flow ordinary differential equation with cotangent Laplace-Beltrami discretisation, leveraging GPU acceleration for efficient processing of large mesh collections;
- A set of 5 `.stl` files, representing 5 selected classes of nuragic origin, released with CC-BY-0 license.
- A **freely available CC-BY-0 dataset** comprising 3.732 fragments derived from five distinct Nuragic ceramic vessel classes, complete with ground-truth adjacency information and unique identifiers for each fragment; we provide both the *uneroded* and *eroded* version of the dataset. See [4].

This work lays the groundwork for several areas of future research. The dataset and pipeline provide the necessary foundation for training deep learning models on tasks directly relevant to archaeological practice. Specifically, the generated data can be used to: (a) train fragment classification models to recognise the original vessel type from a single sherd; (b) develop orientation regression networks to estimate the original pose of a fragment in 3D space; (c) learn fragment pairing representations to predict which sherds are likely to join, based on geometric features of their fracture surfaces.

Beyond these immediate applications, the modular nature of the pipeline allows for easy extension: additional vessel types can be incorporated, erosion parameters can be tuned to model different depositional environments, and alternative fracture algorithms can be substituted.

Furthermore, the containerised approach facilitates seamless distribution of the data generation pipeline across heterogeneous computing nodes, from local workstations to high-performance computing clusters. This portability reduces the data generation burden in two ways: it allows parallel execution on multiple nodes, drastically cutting the time required for large-scale dataset creation; and it streamlines usability by eliminating the need for manual environment configuration or dependency adaptation on each target system.

By releasing both the pipeline and the dataset under permissive open-source licenses, we aim to lower the barrier to entry for applying modern 3D computer vision techniques to archaeological problems, ultimately contributing to more efficient and scalable documentation and reconstruction of cultural heritage.

Acknowledgments. To conduct the work presented in this contribution, we resorted to the cloud computing Software-as-a-Service infrastructure made available by AI_INFN initiative [1] (formerly known as ML_INFN initiative, "Machine Learning at INFN" [2]), aim to foster Machine Learning activities at the Italian National Institute for Nuclear Physics (INFN), as well as some servers made available by INFN-CHNet [11], the network devoted to the application of nuclear techniques to Cultural Heritage.

The work of A.B. was funded by Progetto ICSC - Spoke 2 - Codice CN 00000013 - CUP I53C21000340006 - Missione 4 Istruzione e ricerca - Componente 2 Dalla ricerca all'impresa âĂŞ Investimento 1.4.

Disclosure of Interests. The authors have no competing interests to declare that are relevant to the content of this article.

References

1. Anderlini, L., et al.: Supporting the development of machine learning for fundamental science in a federated cloud with the ai_infn platform. arXiv preprint arXiv:2502.21266 (2025)
2. Anderlini, L., et al.: ML_INFN project: status report and future perspectives. EPJ Web of Conf. **295**, 08013 (2024). https://doi.org/10.1051/epjconf/202429508013
3. Armeni, I., et al.: 3D semantic parsing of large-scale indoor spaces. In: Proceedings of the IEEE Conference on Computer Vision and Pattern Recognition (CVPR), pp. 1534–1543 (2016). https://doi.org/10.1109/CVPR.2016.170
4. Barone, S., Magalini, M., Bombini, A.: Synthetic dataset of ceramic fragments of nuragic origin, March 2026. https://doi.org/10.15161/oar.it/396dr-9yj86
5. Campus, F., Leonelli, V.: La tipologia della ceramica nuragica. Il materiale edito (2000)
6. Blender Online Community: Blender - a 3D modelling and rendering package. Blender Foundation, Stichting Blender Foundation, Amsterdam (2018). http://www.blender.org
7. Dai, A., Chang, A.X., Savva, M., Halber, M., Funkhouser, T., Nießner, M.: ScanNet: richly-annotated 3D reconstructions of indoor scenes. In: Proceedings of the IEEE Conference on Computer Vision and Pattern Recognition (CVPR), pp. 5828–5839 (2017). https://doi.org/10.1109/CVPR.2017.261
8. Desbrun, M., Meyer, M., Schröder, P., Barr, A.H.: Implicit fairing of irregular meshes using diffusion and curvature flow. In: Proceedings of the 26th Annual Conference on Computer Graphics and Interactive Techniques, pp. 317–324 (1999)
9. Domokos, G., Gibbons, G.: Geometrical and physical models of abrasion. arXiv preprint arXiv:1307.5633 (2013)

10. Domokos, G., Sipos, A.Á., Várkonyi, P.L.: Countinuous and discrete models for abrasion processes. Periodica Polytechnica Architecture **40**(1), 3–8 (2009)
11. Giuntini, L., et al.: Detectors and cultural heritage: the INFN-CHNet experience. Appl. Sci. **11**(8) (2021). https://doi.org/10.3390/app11083462
12. Hackel, T., Savinov, N., Ladicky, L., Wegner, J.D., Schindler, K., Pollefeys, M.: Semantic3D.net: a new large-scale point cloud classification benchmark. ISPRS Ann. Photogram. Remote Sens. Spat. Inf. Sci. **IV-1/W1**, 91–98 (2017). https://doi.org/10.5194/isprs-annals-IV-1-W1-91-2017
13. Hu, Q., et al.: RandLA-Net: efficient semantic segmentation of large-scale point clouds. In: Proceedings of the IEEE/CVF Conference on Computer Vision and Pattern Recognition (CVPR), pp. 11108–11117 (2020). https://doi.org/10.1109/CVPR42600.2020.01112
14. Huang, Q.X., Flöry, S., Gelfand, N., Hofer, M., Pottmann, H.: Reassembling fractured objects by geometric matching. In: ACM SIGGRAPH 2006 Papers, pp. 569–578 (2006)
15. Huisken, G.: Flow by mean curvature of convex surfaces into spheres. J. Differ. Geom. **20**(1), 237–266 (1984)
16. Kampel, M., Sablatnig, R.: Virtual reconstruction of broken and unbroken pottery. In: Proceedings of the Fourth International Conference on 3-D Digital Imaging and Modeling, 2003, 3DIM 2003, pp. 318–325. IEEE (2003)
17. Kurtzer, G., Muriki, K.: Singularity v1.x, April 2016. https://doi.org/10.5281/zenodo.1310023, https://www.osti.gov/biblio/code-54923
18. Kurtzer, G.M., Sochat, V., Bauer, M.W.: Singularity: scientific containers for mobility of compute. PLoS ONE **12**(5), e0177459 (2017)
19. Meyer, M., Desbrun, M., Schröder, P., Barr, A.H.: Discrete differential-geometry operators for triangulated 2-manifolds. In: Hege, HC., Polthier, K. (eds.) Visualization and Mathematics III, pp. 35–57. Springer, Heidelberg (2003). https://doi.org/10.1007/978-3-662-05105-4_2
20. Pinkall, U., Polthier, K.: Computing discrete minimal surfaces and their conjugates. In: Experimental Mathematics, vol. 2, pp. 15–36. Citeseer (1993)
21. Qi, C.R., Liu, W., Wu, C., Su, H., Guibas, L.J.: Frustum PointNets for 3D object detection from RGB-D data. In: Proceedings of the IEEE Conference on Computer Vision and Pattern Recognition (CVPR), pp. 918–927 (2018). https://doi.org/10.1109/CVPR.2018.00102
22. Qi, C.R., Su, H., Mo, K., Guibas, L.J.: PointNet: deep learning on point sets for 3D classification and segmentation. In: Proceedings of the IEEE Conference on Computer Vision and Pattern Recognition (CVPR), pp. 652–660 (2017). https://doi.org/10.1109/CVPR.2017.16
23. Qi, C.R., Yi, L., Su, H., Guibas, L.J.: PointNet++: deep hierarchical feature learning on point sets in a metric space. In: Advances in Neural Information Processing Systems (NeurIPS), vol. 30, pp. 5099–5108 (2017)
24. Rasheed, N.A., Nordin, M.J.: Classification and reconstruction algorithms for the archaeological fragments. J. King Saud Univ. Comput. Inf. Sci. **32**(8), 883–894 (2020)
25. Rice, P.M.: Pottery Analysis: A Sourcebook, 2nd edn. University of Chicago Press (2015)
26. Sellán, S., Chen, Y.C., Wu, Z., Garg, A., Jacobson, A.: Breaking bad: a dataset for geometric fracture and reassembly. Adv. Neural. Inf. Process. Syst. **35**, 38885–38898 (2022)

27. Wang, Y., Sun, Y., Liu, Z., Sarma, S.E., Bronstein, M.M., Solomon, J.M.: Dynamic graph CNN for learning on point clouds. ACM Trans. Graph. (TOG) **38**, 146:1–146:12 (2019). https://doi.org/10.1145/3326362
28. Wardetzky, M.: Convergence of the cotangent formula: an overview. In: Bobenko, A.I., Sullivan, J.M., Schröder, P., Ziegler, G.M. (eds.) Discrete Differential Geometry. Oberwolfach Seminars, pp. 275–286 (2008). https://doi.org/10.1007/978-3-7643-8621-4_15
29. Wu, Z., et al.: 3D ShapeNets: a deep representation for volumetric shapes. Proceedings of the IEEE Conference on Computer Vision and Pattern Recognition (CVPR), pp. 1912–1920 (2015). https://doi.org/10.1109/CVPR.2015.7298801
30. Yi, L., et al.: A scalable active framework for region annotation in 3D shape collections. ACM Trans. Graph. (TOG) **35**(6), 210:1–210:12 (2016). https://doi.org/10.1145/2980179.2980238
31. Zhao, H., Jiang, L., Jia, J., Torr, P.H., Koltun, V.: Point transformer. In: Proceedings of the IEEE/CVF International Conference on Computer Vision (ICCV), pp. 16259–16268 (2021). https://doi.org/10.1109/ICCV48922.2021.01595

A Generative and Cluster-Aware Multi-model Architecture for Detecting Heterogeneous Fraud in Imbalanced Transaction Data

Berat Can Karakaş[1](✉), Hakan Hakvar[2], Oğulcan Söyler[2], Şevval Türkyılmaz[2], Ilgin Şafak[2,3], Tolga Durdu[2], Emin Anarım[4], and Mehmet S. Aktaş[1]

[1] Yıldız Technical University, Istanbul, Turkey
berat.karakas@std.yildiz.edu.tr, aktas@yildiz.edu.tr
[2] Fibabanka R&D Center, Istanbul, Turkey
{hakan.hakvar,ogulcan.soyler,sevval.turkyilmaz,ilgin.safak, tolga.durdu}@fibabanka.com.tr, ilgin.i.safak@jyu.fi
[3] University of Jyväskylä, Jyväskylä, Finland
[4] Boğaziçi University, Istanbul, Turkey
anarim@bogazici.edu.tr

Abstract. With the rapid development of digital banking, the issue of financial fraud detection has grown even more pressing. Real-world fraud systems have two major challenges: extreme class imbalance and behavioral variability of fraudulent activities, which are frequently not captured by monolithic global models. We propose a cluster-aware multi-model framework that simultaneously tackles both challenges. To handle the class imbalance efficiently, we first employ a Conditional Tabular Generative Adversarial Network (CTGAN) to generate high-fidelity synthetic fraud examples. Second, we cluster fraudulent transactions into behaviorally consistent subgroups using non-linear dimensionality reduction (UMAP) and density-based clustering (DBSCAN). This breakdown enables a Mixture-of-Experts (MoE) architecture in which specialized classifiers are trained for different fraud behaviors. We evaluate our approach on a popular benchmark for credit card fraud and show that it outperforms classical resampling methods and strong global baselines. Ultimately, the suggested technique detects infrequent and confined fraud patterns more effectively, resulting in a much higher F1-score and operational viability.

Keywords: Fraud Detection · Class Imbalance · CTGAN · UMAP · Mixture-of-Experts

1 Introduction

In today's digital financial systems, efficient credit card fraud detection is essential to prevent direct financial losses, defend reputations of institutions and

O. Gervasi et al. (Eds.): ICCSA 2026 Workshops, LNCS 16758, pp. 16–32, 2027.
https://doi.org/10.1007/978-3-032-30497-1_2

assure the compliance with regulations [1]. While machine learning has developed significantly, it is still quite hard to detect fraud transactions in real life. Fraud detection is challenging due to severe class imbalance, where genuine transactions are greatly in excess of fraudulent transactions [2], and the ongoing growth of adversarial methods. As a consequence, fraud shows up in very varied patterns, which classic global models are not able to model sufficiently [3].

In the past, resampling methods at the data level, such as SMOTE with linear interpolation [4], have been utilized to address the class imbalance. However, in high-dimensional tabular domains (e.g., with 31 complex variables), features commonly exhibit non-linear interactions and multi-modality. In these settings, interpolation-based methods often generate unrealistic samples from the majority class, which blurs the decision boundaries and hurts the classification performance.

To address these constraints, Generative Adversarial Networks (GANs) have gained popularity in directly learning and reproducing the underlying data distributions through adversarial training [5]. Specialized designs, e.g., CT-GAN, have been shown to be particularly effective for tabular data with mixed feature types [6]. However, producing minority samples solves just part of the problem. Most present strategies address class imbalance in isolation, ignoring the structural variety of fraudulent behavior. Fraud is not a single monolithic event but a collection of different and localized sub-patterns, which are usually not detected by single global classifiers [8].

To address this issue, we offer a dual-layered, cluster-aware multi-model framework, which is evaluated on a well-known public benchmark dataset. First, we perform oversampling with CTGAN to better capture the complex distribution of the minority class. Second, we breakdown fraudulent transactions into behaviorally consistent subtypes using non-linear dimensionality reduction (UMAP) and density-based clustering (DBSCAN). This behavior-aware decomposition results in an architecture like the Mixture-of-Experts (MoE) paradigm, where specialized classifiers are assigned to certain portions of the feature space for full fraud coverage [9].

The main contributions of this paper are as follows:

- A GAN-based oversampling pipeline that models the complex distributions of minority classes in tabular fraud data better than standard interpolation methods.
- A clustering-based multi-model detection system that addresses fraud heterogeneity and demonstrates that specialized "expert" models outperform monolithic global classifiers in detecting rare fraud sub-patterns.
- A detailed evaluation on the public European cardholders dataset, with the use of precision-recall-based metrics (F1-score) and cost-sensitive evaluation to ensure robust performance measurement and operational viability despite high class imbalance [10].

The rest of this paper is organized as follows. Section 2 discusses related work on fraud detection and unbalanced learning. Section 3 presents the proposed technique. Section 4 outlines the experimental setup and the characteristics of the dataset. The experimental data are presented and discussed in Sect. 5. Section 6 provides the conclusions.

2 Related Work

Financial systems have been studied for many years in the context of detecting fraud and unusual activities. However, there are still major practical hurdles, especially in real-world scenarios with extreme class imbalance, dynamic attack techniques, and varied fraud behaviors. The existing literature on fraud detection can be broadly divided into three categories: (i) supervised learning paradigms, (ii) methods dealing with class imbalance, and (iii) approaches modeling explicitly the structural heterogeneity of fraud.

2.1 Supervised Approaches to Fraud Detection

In the typical setting, credit card fraud detection is seen as a supervised classification problem. In this area, several experiments have been carried out on conventional models, like decision trees, logistic regression and neural networks [12]. The dominant paradigm in these approaches implies that genuine consumer behavior follows generally consistent patterns, which makes it possible to detect fraudulent transactions by looking for variations from historical spending [11].

However, accuracy-driven models are typically not sufficient in operational contexts because of the substantial class imbalance in fraud datasets and the high cost of false negatives [2]. This constraint has driven the development of cost-sensitive learning methods and alternate evaluation measures [13]. Cost-sensitive learning encourages optimization but does not solve the inherent lack of minority class samples.

2.2 Imbalanced Learning and Resampling Methods

Imbalanced categorization is generally handled by resampling approaches at the data level. Baseline approaches such as SMOTE and its derivatives generate synthetic minority samples by interpolating existing minority samples [4,13]. Interpolation-based oversampling is commonly used; however, it might create unrealistic samples in high-dimensional transaction data (e.g., with 31 complex characteristics), particularly when fraud behavior is multi-modal. In such cases, synthetic samples are close to the majority class, leading to fuzzy decision boundaries. To avoid these difficulties, generative approaches that actively learn the underlying data distribution have gained popularity recently. GAN-based techniques enable the generation of complex minority class distributions [5]. Specialized tabular architectures such as CTGAN have been shown to generate high-fidelity synthetic data for datasets with mixed feature types [6].

2.3 Fraud Heterogeneity and Multi-Model Architectures

Fraudulent behavior is not a single phenomenon because it involves different attack vectors that evolve dynamically [3]. Hence, a single global detection model can be effective in detecting common fraud patterns but often fails to discover unusual yet important sub-patterns [14].

To solve this problem, subsequent studies have explored clustering-based and multi-model approaches. Density-based clustering methods like DBSCAN and HDBSCAN are useful for separating different fraud tendencies in labeled datasets. These methods are quite robust for high dimensional tabular data when combined with dimensionality reduction methods such as UMAP to avoid curse of dimensionality [7,15]. Likewise, Mixture-of-Experts (MoE) architectures provide a systematic framework where specialist models contribute collectively to boost performance across different parts of the feature space [9]. However, many existing approaches ignore class imbalance as a secondary concern or do not integrate synthetic data generation with behavior-based decomposition seamlessly.

2.4 Positioning of the Proposed Framework

The aforementioned research gaps are addressed in this work via a comprehensive dual-tier methodology. Existing studies usually consider class imbalance [6] and structural heterogeneity [7] as individual challenges, whereas our framework unifies them into a single pipeline. This study is ideally positioned to overcome the limits of monolithic global classifiers by integrating generative minority oversampling with behavior-aware expert modeling to address unusual, multi-modal fraud detection patterns.

3 Proposed Methodology

The suggested fraud detection approach can simultaneously deal with the severe class imbalance and the behavioral heterogeneity of credit card transaction data. The system combines GAN-based minority class oversampling with a clustering-based multi-model architecture. The technique is structured around four main stages: (i) Problem characterization and terminology, (ii) Generative minority oversampling, (iii) Dimensionality reduction with density-based clustering, and (iv) Cluster-aware expert routing for inference.

The architecture depends on a cluster-aware modeling pipeline to comprehensively address varied fraud patterns (see Fig. 1). After dataset isolation, the "Cluster-Aware Data Splitter" module conducts dimensionality reduction and DBSCAN only on fraudulent transactions to identify behaviorally distinct groupings. Then, each detected cluster is divided into dedicated training and testing sets. The legitimate transactions are proportionally stratified over these cluster-specific subsets to keep the original class distribution and to give a realistic evaluation.

During training, these separate subsets optimize different tree-based ensemble models, yielding a localized set of "expert" classifiers. In real-time inference

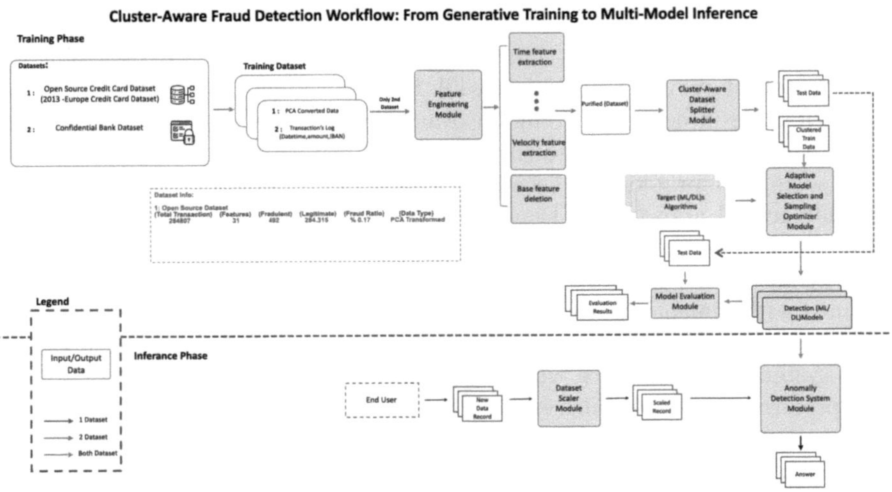

Fig. 1. The proposed clustering-based multi-model fraud detection workflow, illustrating the progression from data augmentation (CTGAN) and dimensionality reduction (UMAP) to cluster-aware expert routing.

the framework acts as an adaptive routing engine, projecting incoming transactions in the learned topological space, mapping them to the most relevant fraud cluster, and routing them to the related pre-trained expert. This mutually exclusive routing strongly precludes multiple counting of negative samples.

3.1 Problem Definition and Notation

Let $D = \{(x_i, y_i)\}_{i=1}^N$ be a set of credit card transactions, where $x_i \in \mathbb{R}^d$ is a d-dimensional feature vector ($d = 30$, comprising 28 PCA components, time, and amount) and $y_i \in \{0, 1\}$ is the class label ($y_i = 1$ for fraud, $y_i = 0$ for legitimate), yielding 31 total variables. In real-world fraud detection environments, the class distribution is severely imbalanced, as noted in $P(y = 1) \ll P(y = 0)$ [2].

The goal is to learn a classification function $f : \mathbb{R}^d \to \{0, 1\}$ to discriminate legal vs. fraudulent transactions while being robust to excessive class imbalance and various and developing fraud behaviors.

3.2 Framework Overview

The suggested framework adopts a two-level approach. At the data level, CTGAN-based oversampling extends the distribution of the minority class while maintaining structural fidelity and without deleting samples of the majority class. At the model level, UMAP and density-based clustering break fraudulent cases into behaviorally consistent subtypes. For these discovered clusters, dedicated expert classifiers (e.g., XGBoost, LightGBM) are trained separately. This isolates localized fraud dynamics for a more fine-grained representation than monolithic architectures.

3.3 GAN-Based Minority Class Oversampling

To alleviate class imbalance, we employ a Conditional Generative Adversarial Network (CTGAN) built for tabular datasets [6]. Unlike classic interpolation techniques such as SMOTE [4], CTGAN learns the underlying distribution of the minority class directly, which allows it to successfully capture non-linear relationships and multi-modal feature dependencies. The generator network only trains on fraudulent instances, generating synthetic transactions based on learned feature distributions, while the discriminator assesses their validity [5]. Importantly, this augmentation is entirely confined to the training set; validation and test sets remain unaltered to categorically exclude data leaking.

3.4 Dimensionality Reduction and Density-Based Clustering

Fraudulent transactions are naturally diversified because they are generated by different adversarial methods [3]. Applying distance-based algorithms like DBSCAN [7] directly in high-dimensional continuous space (i.e., over all 30 input features) would always suffer from the curse of dimensionality and the loss of discriminative ability of distance metrics.

To address this, we first perform Uniform Manifold Approximation and Projection (UMAP) on only the fraud-labeled training samples. UMAP lowers the feature space while keeping non-linear topological linkages, greatly boosting cluster separation while decreasing the growth of unclassified noise. After projecting, DBSCAN clusters the data into coherent behavioral clusters.

To ensure statistical reliability and thorough evaluation (e.g., permitting robust cross-validation), we add a subsequent *Cluster Merging* protocol. Clusters with high centroid proximity in the UMAP space are iteratively merged until each resulting cluster includes a statistically feasible minimum threshold of instances (e.g., at least 7 fraudulent transactions in each corresponding test set). Unclustered or extremely anomalous points are assigned to a dominant noise cluster (Cluster -1), which provides a generic baseline representation of fraud.

3.5 Cluster-Specific Expert Modeling

Following the grouping and merging step, each detected fraud subtype is considered as a separate modeling domain. We train one expert classifier per cluster on the particular fraudulent instances of that cluster and a stratified sample of the legal transactions. Tree based ensemble models are used, as they are shown to work well on tabular financial data [12]. Inspired by the principles of Mixture-of-Experts [9], this specialization forces separate algorithms to attend only to different portions of the feature space, thereby finding localized abnormalities that a global classifier might miss.

3.6 Inference Routing and System Integration

We propose an explicit inference routing system to process incoming, unlabeled transactions in a live or testing environment without risk of data leaking. First, the new transaction is projected onto the already trained UMAP embedding space, as described in Algorithm 1. The system estimates the Euclidean distance between the new instance and the centroids of the discovered fraud clusters, and the transaction is deterministically routed to the expert classifier of the nearest cluster.

If the minimum distance is more than a predetermined dynamic threshold (τ), indicating a completely novel pattern, the transaction is directed to the dominant/noise expert (Cluster -1). This deterministic mutually exclusive routing ensures that each transaction is reviewed by exactly one expert. This, in turn, structurally removes the double-counting of negative samples and makes the aggregated global metrics (Precision, Recall, F1-score) statistically sound and strictly comparable to a single-model global baseline.

Algorithm 1 Inference Routing and Multi-Model Classification Strategy

Input: A new transaction x_{new}, learned UMAP projection mapping U, set of fraud cluster centroids $C = \{c_1, c_2, ..., c_k\}$, dominant (noise) cluster centroid c_{noise}, set of trained expert models $E = \{E_1, E_2, ..., E_k, E_{noise}\}$, distance threshold τ.
Output: Fraud probability score p.

$x_{proj} \leftarrow U(x_{new})$ {Project transaction into the reduced UMAP space}
$d_{min} \leftarrow \infty$
$c_{target} \leftarrow c_{noise}$
for each $c_i \in C$ **do**
    $d \leftarrow$ EuclideanDistance(x_{proj}, c_i)
    if $d < d_{min}$ **then**
        $d_{min} \leftarrow d$
        $c_{target} \leftarrow c_i$
    end if
end for
if $d_{min} > \tau$ **then**
    $c_{target} \leftarrow c_{noise}$ {Route to generalized expert if it is an outlier}
end if
$E_{target} \leftarrow$ GetExpert(c_{target})
$p \leftarrow E_{target}(x_{new})$ {Obtain prediction from the assigned expert}
return p

4 Experimental Setup

This section describes the experimental setting used to evaluate the proposed fraud detection framework. We discuss the benchmark dataset, the data partitioning procedures, the baseline models, the resampling methods, and the overall assessment protocols used to evaluate the results.

4.1 Dataset

The proposed approach is assessed using the famous European cardholder dataset, released in 2013, which is widely considered as the benchmark standard for credit card fraud detection research [2]. We use this public dataset to assure reproducibility and to allow for fair benchmarking with the current state-of-the-art investigations.

The data set contains 284,807 records of transactions performed by European cardholders throughout two days. It has a strong class imbalance, which is indicative of actual world financial environments [13]. In particular, it has 284,315 legitimate transactions and just 492 fraudulent cases, i.e., fraud represents only 0.17% of the data set.

There are a total of 31 variables in the dataset (30 input features and 1 target class label). To preserve the privacy of the customers, the original transaction details are transformed via Principal Component Analysis (PCA) [3], and 28 continuous main components (V1 to V28) are obtained. The only input features that are not changed by PCA are *Time* (seconds elapsed from the first transaction) and *Amount* (amount of the transaction).

The PCA components are already standardized, thus only *Time* and *Amount* were scaled using a RobustScaler. The scaling technique is based on interquartile ranges and as such is quite resilient to extreme values and monetary outliers. Thus, this dataset is a demanding test bed for our system to work on extreme class imbalance and high dimensional continuous tabular data.

4.2 Data Partitioning Strategy

Experiments are carried out in a supervised learning setting with stratified data split to preserve the initial extreme class imbalance for all subsets. The two suggested solutions (GAN-based oversampling and the cluster-based multi-model framework) demand various partitioning strategies arising from their different architectural objectives.

Method 1: GAN-Based Oversampling For the generative baseline experiments the dataset is divided into three mutually exclusive subsets: 70% for training, 15% for validation and 15% for testing. The training set is utilized just for the optimization of classifiers and for the creation of synthetic minority samples. The validation set is used for selecting optimal decision thresholds, whereas the test set is strictly segregated for the final performance evaluation. This strict separation architecturally prevents information leakage.

Method 2: Cluster-Based Multi-model Framework The multi-model architecture partitioning technique consists of two parts. Firstly, dimensionality reduction and density based clustering are only used to the fraud-labeled instances in the 70% training sample to detect coherent behavioral sub-patterns.

Legitimate transactions are totally excluded to protect boundary integrity during this clustering phase.

Then, for each fraud cluster, a cluster-specific dataset is built by merging the assigned fraudulent samples with a proportional stratified sample of valid transactions. Then each cluster-specific dataset is divided into training, validation and testing sets (70/15/15). *It is important to emphasize that this multi-model routing architecture is naturally modular; it does not strictly require CTGAN to function and can operate effectively with baseline data or normal resampling approaches (e.g. SMOTE) inside each cluster. Our fully integrated ideal workflow, however, is to run CTGAN locally on the clusters.*

4.3 Baseline Classification Models

In order to do a complete evaluation and to confirm the model-agnostic nature of the presented framework, we have included a variety of classification algorithms that are well-known in the literature on tabular data: Random Forest, AdaBoost, CatBoost, XGBoost and LightGBM. All classifiers are trained with the same feature representations and pre-processing procedures.

4.4 Data Resampling and Augmentation Strategies

To benchmark the efficacy of the generative augmentation against the extreme class imbalance, the following strategies were evaluated:

- No resampling (Baseline original class distribution)
- Random Under-Sampling (RUS)
- SMOTE and SMOTEENN
- CTGAN-based generative oversampling (Proposed)

To rigorously prevent data leakage, all synthetic samples are generated exclusively from the training folds. The CTGAN model is trained solely on the minority-class samples of the training data.

4.5 Evaluation Metrics and Cost-Sensitive Assessment

Accuracy-based measures are not enough in principle because of the high class imbalance. We use three complementing measures to evaluate both statistical performance and practical business value comprehensively:

F1-Score: The main objective function is to optimize the F1-score to balance the precision and recall. Optimal decision criteria are selected by maximizing the F1-score on the validation set and are then applied to the test set for fair comparisons.

Recall at Fixed Precision (Recall@90%): Reducing false positives in operational banking environments is crucial to reduce client frustration. We present the recall attained when the threshold of precision is kept firmly at 90% and show the ability of the model to detect fraud under a tight false alarm budget.

Cost-Sensitive Assessment (Cost Savings %): A cost-sensitive evaluation is performed to measure the direct financial impact, simulating actual operations. The cost of a False Negative is the unrecoverable amount of the transaction, while a false positive incurs a fixed administrative investigation cost (estimated at €10). We report the *Cost Savings* percentage, which is the amount of financial loss prevented with respect to a baseline scenario without detection system.

4.6 Implementation Details and Hyperparameter Configuration

To ensure full reproducibility, hyperparameters were systematically configured and maintained identically across global and multi-model experiments; the complete implementation—including the CTGAN training pipeline, UMAP projection, DBSCAN clustering, centroid-based merging, and expert routing—is publicly available at [16].

Generative Model (CTGAN): Implemented via the SDV library, the model trained exclusively on the minority class using fully connected layers (256, 256). Training ran for 200 epochs (batch size 1,000) using the Adam optimizer (learning rate 2×10^{-4}). We generated three synthetic samples per real fraud instance. Quality was validated feature-wise using Kolmogorov-Smirnov (KS) statistics and Wasserstein distances, yielding an average Wasserstein score of ≈ 0.3, indicating moderate distributional similarity; despite this limitation, CTGAN consistently outperformed all interpolation-based baselines in downstream classification.

Clustering Pipeline (UMAP & DBSCAN): UMAP projected the fraud-only feature space into 3 components (`n_neighbors` = 15, `min_dist` = 0.0). DBSCAN was subsequently applied to this 3D embedding with `min_samples` = 5, and `eps` was determined analytically via the k-distance elbow method.

Expert Classifiers: Decision thresholds were optimized on the validation set. Key configurations included:

- **LightGBM:** `learning_rate`=0.025, `num_leaves`=7, `max_depth`=4.
- **XGBoost:** `learning_rate`=0.03, `max_depth`=2, `tree_method`="hist".
- **CatBoost:** `learning_rate`=0.02, `depth`=12.
- **AdaBoost:** `learning_rate`=0.1, 100 estimators.
- **Random Forest:** 100 estimators, `class_weight`="balanced".

5 Experimental Results

This section provides the experimental results for evaluating the performance of the proposed fraud detection framework. The evaluation is performed rigorously according to the methods defined in Sect. 4, and aims at assessing both statistical performance and operational feasibility.

First, we isolate and examine the effect of CTGAN-based minority class augmentation in a vanilla supervised learning setting. Next, we assess the clustering-driven multi-model architecture to test its effectiveness in detecting heterogeneous fraud patterns. All experiments are conducted on isolated test sets with the mutually exclusive routing system to provide rigorous validation and strictly avoid data leaking.

The final multi-model system is benchmarked with cost-sensitive operational metrics and compared with present state-of-the-art research to reflect real world financial needs. The computing environment overview is finally presented to show actual deployment scalability.

5.1 Results of Generative Oversampling (Method 1)

In this subsection, we examine the performance of CTGAN based minority class augmentation in a traditional supervised context. The generative approach is benchmarked against a number of data level resampling baselines: No Resampling (Normal), Random Under-Sampling (RUS), SMOTE and SMOTEENN. While SMOTE is a popular interpolation method [4], CTGAN uses adversarial learning to model complex tabular distributions better [5,6].

Table 1 shows the test F1-scores of five baseline classifiers under different resampling procedures.

Table 1. Test F1-scores under different resampling strategies on the public dataset (European 2013).

Model	Normal	RUS	SMOTE	SMOTEENN	CTGAN
Random Forest	0.8449	0.7937	0.8380	0.8000	**0.8649**
AdaBoost	0.7634	0.7917	0.8042	**0.8105**	0.8000
CatBoost	0.8427	0.8040	0.7845	0.8290	**0.8649**
XGBoost	0.8541	0.7817	0.8105	0.8148	**0.8817**
LightGBM	0.8492	0.7650	0.8021	0.7935	**0.8817**

The best average performance across the classifiers is achieved by CTGAN with the mean F1-score of 0.8586, which is an absolute +0.0277 improvement over the Normal baseline (mean F1 = 0.8309). On the other hand, RUS always drops overall performance (mean F1 = 0.7872), which shows that a significant exclusion of majority-class data has a damaging effect on border generalization in highly imbalanced domains.

Model-specific analysis demonstrates that CTGAN significantly improves advanced gradient boosting topologies. In particular, F1-score of LightGBM goes up to 0.8817 (+0.0325), XGBoost to 0.8817 (+0.0276), CatBoost to 0.8649 (+0.0222). AdaBoost has its best results with SMOTEENN (0.8105) but still improves significantly above its baseline (0.7634) with CTGAN (0.8000). These results validate that CTGAN for the generation of high-fidelity synthetic data better addresses the problem of excessive class imbalance than traditional interpolation.

5.2 Fraud Cluster Analysis and Merging Strategy

We analyze the clustering-based multi-model architecture in this part. The aim is to explore whether an explicit modeling of fraud subtypes with localized expertise leads to better performance than a monolithic global classifier.

UMAP Projection and Centroid-Based Merging. Direct application of density-based clustering on high-dimensional continuous spaces typically triggers curse of dimensionality. In preliminary tests, the typical DBSCAN algorithm categorized over 91% of fraudulent transactions as uninformative noise. To this end, we employed UMAP for non-linear dimensionality reduction.

The UMAP-enhanced DBSCAN removed all unclassified noise, decomposing the 492 fraudulent transactions into 25 behavioral micro-clusters. But the statistical reliability of testing expert models with micro-clusters in quite a restricted sample size is compromised. To ensure robust validation conditions, we proposed a dynamic *Centroid-Based Cluster Merging* protocol. We set a statistical criterion of at least 7 fraudulent cases in the test set of each cluster. Micro-clusters below this level were iteratively merged with their closest neighbors based on Euclidean centroid proximity. This aggregated the data into 6 extremely robust, behaviorally consistent macro-clusters (see Table 2).

Table 2. Final fraud macro-cluster distribution obtained via UMAP dimensionality reduction and centroid-based merging, ensuring statistical reliability.

Cluster ID	Total Fraud	Training Set	Validation Set	Test Set
Cluster 0	114 (23.2%)	79	18	17
Cluster 1	62 (12.6%)	43	10	9
Cluster 2	125 (25.4%)	87	19	19
Cluster 3	86 (17.5%)	60	13	13
Cluster 4	58 (11.8%)	40	9	9
Cluster 5	47 (9.5%)	32	8	7
Total	**492 (100.0%)**	**341**	**77**	**74**

5.3 Multi-model Inference and Bootstrap Validation

The framework was tested after separate training of localized classifiers exploiting the routing technique described in Sect. 3.6. A key drawback of traditional imbalanced ensemble approaches is the unintended duplicate counting of majority class samples. Our deterministic routing is designed to avoid such leaks intentionally. For each test transaction, we embed it into the UMAP space and only send it to the nearest cluster expert.

We directly address potential concerns about metric unreliability on localized test sets by doing a thorough bootstrap evaluation (N = 1,000 iterations) for each cluster-specific expert. The bootstrap analysis produced consistently low standard deviations across macro-clusters (e.g., $\sigma = 0.03$ for Cluster 0 and $\sigma = 0.14$ for the most difficult Cluster 3), experimentally demonstrating that the reported F1-scores are statistically credible and not products of small sample numbers.

The aggregated performance is computed by adding the mutually exclusive confusion matrices of these validated experts as shown in Table 3. The overall number of evaluated genuine occurrences (TN: 42,645 + FP: 2 = 42,647) is exactly equal to the original isolated test set, which essentially proves the absence of double-counting.

Table 3. Cluster-wise selected expert configurations, bootstrap validation metrics ($\mu \pm \sigma$), and mutually exclusive confusion matrices. Data leakage is categorically prevented.

Cluster	Expert Configuration	Bootstrap F1	TP	FP	FN	TN
0	Random Forest + RUS	0.97 ± 0.03	16	0	1	9882
1	CatBoost + Normal	1.00 ± 0.00	9	0	0	5374
2	Random Forest + SMOTE	1.00 ± 0.00	19	0	0	10835
3	CatBoost + Normal	0.42 ± 0.14	4	2	9	7453
4	CatBoost + RUS	1.00 ± 0.00	9	0	0	5027
5	AdaBoost + Normal	0.92 ± 0.09	6	0	1	4074
Aggregated	**Multi-Model System**	-	**63**	**2**	**11**	**42645**

5.4 Cost-Sensitive Evaluation and State-of-the-Art Comparison

To adapt the suggested framework to real-world financial needs we compare it to the best-performing worldwide single-model baseline (Random Forest + CTGAN). For a fair comparison we evaluated the two architectures on the same recombined test set.

As illustrated in Table 4, the multi-model framework exceeds the best global baseline on all key criteria. The global baseline achieves an F1-score of 0.8905, and the multi-model architecture improves this to 0.9065. Importantly, with the strong operational constraint of 90% precision, the multi-model design yields a Recall@90% of 0.8514, compared to 0.8243 for the global baseline. This elimination of false negatives directly leads into a greater Cost Savings of 85.10%. This illustrates that the explicit separation of diverse sub-patterns results in improved operational viability than monolithic designs (see Table 4)

Table 4. Optimal global single-model baseline vs. clustering-based multi-model performance, incorporating operational metrics.

Method	Precision	Recall	Recall@90%	F1-Score	Cost Savings (%)
Global Baseline (RF + CTGAN)	0.9683	0.8243	0.8514	0.8905	84.43
Multi-Model (Experts)	**0.9692**	**0.8514**	**0.8514**	**0.9065**	**85.10**

We also compare our performance with the state-of-the-art architectures on the same European 2013 benchmark in Table 5. The suggested combination of generative augmentation with cluster-aware routing results in a highly competitive architecture (see Table 5).

Table 5. Performance comparison against contemporary studies utilizing the European 2013 dataset.

Reference	Methodology	Reported F1-Score
Dal Pozzolo et al. (2015) [2]	RF + Under-Sampling	0.812
Yang et al. (2019) [8]	Federated Learning	0.835
Ghalwash et al. (2025) [15]	DBSCAN-augmented Ensemble	0.867
Proposed [16]	**CTGAN + UMAP + Multi-Expert**	**0.906**

5.5 Computing Environment and Computational Costs

The experimental pipeline was conducted on an NVIDIA RTX 3060 GPU for the generative deep learning components and on an Apple Silicon M-series architecture for the tree-based ensemble training.

The data pre-processing step, including UMAP dimensionality reduction, DBSCAN clustering and dynamic cluster merging took only 3.6 s. The full grid of 25 global combinations of baselines took 770.8 s to evaluate. On the other hand, the training and evaluation of all expert combinations strictly inside their localized macro-clusters was finished in 337.9 s. Thus, the total end-to-end execution time of the suggested multi-model pipeline was around 5.7 min. Fast execution shows strong computing efficiency and scalability to real-world systems.

5.6 Discussion

Empirical findings support that robust credit card fraud detection should take into account both class imbalance and behavioral heterogeneity at the same time. The application of CTGAN for oversampling the minority class led to stable improvements across gradient boosting frameworks by creating high-quality tabular synthetic samples that preserve complicated relations of features.

Moreover, the clustering study revealed that fraudulent activity is not a homogeneous issue. The architecture was able to remove noise and segregate the minority class into six viable macro-clusters using UMAP and centroid-based merging. By routing the transactions to the experts of each cluster, we removed the structural constraints of the monolithic global model, achieving an aggregate F1-score of 0.9065, which is highly competitive.

Threats to Validity **Internal Validity:** The same hyperparameter configurations were used for global baselines and multi-model studies to provide a controlled comparison. This, however, isolates the performance benefits directly related to our system, and an exhaustive independent hyperparameter optimization for each localized expert could potentially change the final performance margins.

External Validity and Data Dependency: The main weakness of the system is its dependence on static historical data. Finally, the exact cluster formations and generating benefits are inherently related to the structural features of the European 2013 dataset. In real-world contexts, the fraud methods are under continual concept drift [3]. The analytical paradigm is structurally robust and transportable. The static cluster definitions we provide here will vary over time.

6 Conclusion and Future Work

In this paper, we present a unified approach for jointly tackling two critical difficulties in credit card fraud detection, namely high class imbalance and behavioral heterogeneity. The proposed strategy is based on oversampling the minority class using CTGAN and a clustering-driven multi-model architecture. Experiments have shown that the use of CTGAN to generate high fidelity synthetic data improves the prediction capabilities of some tree based classifiers compared to traditional interpolation procedures. However, the different levels of improvement also suggest that generative augmentation should be combined with appropriate high-capacity downstream classifiers. Furthermore, the suggested multi-model framework achieves consistently better performance than a well-tuned global single-model baseline. UMAP dimensionality reduction and explicit centroid-based routing to cluster-specific expert models allow the system to detect both common and rare localized fraud trends. We demonstrate through an extensive empirical investigation that concurrent treatment of data-level imbalance and model-level heterogeneity confers substantial improvements in operational viability, assessed by better F1-scores and cost-sensitive assessment measures. Further work will investigate the application of adaptive and incremental clustering approaches to deal with continual concept drift and evaluate the resilience of the framework for online, real-time streaming fraud detection scenarios.

Acknowledgments. The authors would like to thank Fibabanka management and its Research and Development (R&D) department for their support, domain insights, and resource provisions during the course of this work. The authors would like to thank Prof. Dr. Fatih Alagoz for his valuable and constructive feedback.

Disclosure of Generative AI and AI-assisted Technologies in the Writing Process. In the process of preparing this manuscript, the authors used generative AI technologies solely for language improvement, proofreading, and maintaining an academic tone. The scientific content, data analysis, and results of the research were not generated by AI techniques. After utilizing these tools, the authors carefully edited and evaluated the text and assume full responsibility for the correctness, originality, and integrity of the final publication.

References

1. Duman, E., Sahin, Y.: A comparison of classification models on credit card fraud detection with respect to cost-based performance metrics. In: Duman, E., Atiya, A. (eds.) Use of Risk Analysis in Computer-Aided Persuasion, NATO Science for Peace and Security Series E: Human and Societal Dynamics, vol. 88, pp. 88–99. IOS Press (2011)
2. Dal Pozzolo, A., Caelen, O., Johnson, R.A., Bontempi, G.: Calibrating probability with undersampling for unbalanced classification. In: 2015 IEEE Symposium Series on Computational Intelligence (SSCI), pp. 159–166. IEEE (2015). https://doi.org/10.1109/SSCI.2015.33
3. Dal Pozzolo, A., Boracchi, G., Caelen, O., Alippi, C., Bontempi, G.: Credit card fraud detection and concept-drift adaptation with delayed supervised information. In: 2015 International Joint Conference on Neural Networks (IJCNN), pp. 1–8. IEEE (2015). https://doi.org/10.1109/IJCNN.2015.7280527
4. Chawla, N.V., Bowyer, K.W., Hall, L.O., Kegelmeyer, W.P.: SMOTE: synthetic minority over-sampling technique. J. Artif. Intel. Res. **16**, 321–357 (2002). https://doi.org/10.1613/jair.953
5. Goodfellow, I.J., et al.: Generative adversarial nets. In: Advances in Neural Information Processing Systems 27 (NIPS 2014), pp. 2672–2680 (2014)
6. Xu, L., Skoularidou, M., Cuesta-Infante, A., Veeramachaneni, K.: Modeling tabular data using conditional GAN. In: Advances in Neural Information Processing Systems 32 (NeurIPS 2019), pp. 7333–7343 (2019)
7. Ester, M., Kriegel, H.-P., Sander, J., Xu, X.: A density-based algorithm for discovering clusters in large spatial databases with noise. In: Proceedings of the Second International Conference on Knowledge Discovery and Data Mining (KDD'96), pp. 226–231. AAAI Press (1996)

8. Yang, W., Zhang, Y., Ye, K., Li, L., Xu, C.-Z.: FFD: a federated learning based method for credit card fraud detection. In: Chen, K., Seshadri, S., Zhang, L.-J. (eds.) BIGDATA 2019. LNCS, vol. 11514, pp. 18–32. Springer, Cham (2019). https://doi.org/10.1007/978-3-030-23551-2_2
9. Shazeer, N., et al.: Outrageously large neural networks: the sparsely-gated mixture-of-experts layer. In: Proceedings of the ICLR 2017 (2017). https://openreview.net/forum?id=B1ckMDqlg
10. Davis, J., Goadrich, M.: The relationship between Precision-Recall and ROC curves. In: Proceedings of the 23rd International Conference on Machine Learning, ICML 2006, pp. 233–240. ACM (2006)
11. Bolton, R.J., Hand, D.J.: Unsupervised profiling methods for fraud detection. In: Credit Scoring and Credit Control VII (2001)
12. Sahin, Y., Duman, E.: Detecting credit card fraud by decision trees and support vector machines. In: Proceedings of IMECS 2011 (2011)
13. He, H., Garcia, E.A.: Learning from imbalanced data. IEEE Trans. Knowl. Data Eng. **21**(9), 1263–1284 (2009)
14. Phua, C., Lee, V., Smith, K., Gayler, R.: A comprehensive survey of data mining-based fraud detection research. arXiv preprint arXiv:1009.6119 (2010)
15. Ghalwash, M.A., Abdelrazek, S.M., Eladawi, N.H., Ghalwash, H.A.: Enhancing credit card fraud detection using DBSCAN-augmented disjunctive voting ensemble. Sci. Rep. **15**(1), 39754 (2025). https://doi.org/10.1038/s41598-025-22960-w
16. Karakas, B.C.: ICCSA2026-hybrid-fraud-detection–244-. GitHub Repository (2026). https://github.com/BcKBA/ICCSA2026-Hybrid-Fraud-Detection--244-

Evaluation of Split Federated Learning for 6G IoT Optimization: A Comparative Study with Baseline, Federated Learning, and Split Learning Models

Samar H. Alkayat[1](✉) and Ali H. Hamad[2]

[1] Informatics Institute for Postgraduate Studies (IIPS), University of Information Technology and Communications (UoITC), Baghdad, Iraq
ms202420027@uoitc.edu.iq

[2] College of Artificial Intelligence, University of Baghdad, Baghdad, Iraq
ahamad@kecbu.uobaghdad.edu.iq

Abstract. The swift growth of the Internet of Things (IoT) in the new sixth-generation (6G) networks has come with significant issues of scalability, data privacy, communication efficiency, and real-time processing. With billions of diverse devices constantly generating sensitive information, the traditional centralized approach to learning proves to be impractical due to high latency, bandwidth, and amplified vulnerability to security attacks, making distributed learning strategies that can be implemented at the network edge and maintain privacy necessary. In this paper, four learning paradigms, including baseline model, federated model (FL), split model (SL), and split federated model (SFL), are evaluated on a 6G-oriented IoT beamforming optimization dataset. To support uniform comparison, a single eight-layered deep neural network with dropout and L2 regularization is used in all the methods. The dataset, which includes optimized and non-optimized beamforming classes, is then subjected to encoding, normalization, and stratified partitioning to provide realistic multi-client IoT environments. The experimental results show that there are performance differences evident between the paradigms: Baseline (87% accuracy), FL (97% accuracy), SL (92% accuracy), and SFL (95% accuracy). FL improves privacy by keeping data locally; therefore, whereas SL minimizes on-device computation, communication overhead is moderate, and SFL is considered a combination of both approaches to provide the best accuracy, scalability, and privacy. Generally, SFL is especially efficient with next-generation 6G-enabled IoT, where smart, trustworthy, and privacy-conscious learning needs to be enforced.

Keywords: 6G · DNN · Distributed learning · Split Federated Learning

1 Introduction

Sixth-generation (6G) networks are expected to significantly enhance future communication systems by enabling ultra-reliable performance, very low latency, and large-scale connectivity. These capabilities support emerging applications such as digital twins,

O. Gervasi et al. (Eds.): ICCSA 2026 Workshops, LNCS 16758, pp. 33–52, 2027.
https://doi.org/10.1007/978-3-032-30497-1_3

autonomous systems, and real-time intelligent services [1]. However, meeting these requirements introduces major challenges, particularly in terms of scalability, communication overhead, and data privacy. The Internet of Things (IoT) plays a central role in 6G ecosystems by connecting a massive number of heterogeneous devices that continuously generate data [2]. While this connectivity expands system capabilities, it also increases system complexity and exposes networks to various security threats, including inference and reconstruction attacks [3]. In addition, many IoT devices have limited computational and energy resources, which restrict their ability to support complex learning and security mechanisms. Although edge and fog computing can bring computation closer to data sources, they also introduce new risks related to distributed trust and data exposure [4]. To address these challenges, artificial intelligence (AI) has become an essential component for enabling intelligent decision-making in such environments. The integration of AI and IoT, often referred to as AIoT, supports advanced applications across domains such as healthcare, smart cities, and energy systems [5]. Nevertheless, training AI models in large-scale 6G IoT settings remains difficult due to communication overhead, device heterogeneity, and strict privacy requirements. These limitations reduce the effectiveness of traditional centralized learning approaches and motivate the use of distributed learning paradigms. Federated Learning (FL) is one of the most widely adopted approaches in this context, where clients train models locally and share only model updates with a central server [6]. While FL improves data privacy by keeping raw data local, it still incurs high communication costs and degrades performance in non-IID data scenarios. Split Learning (SL) has been proposed to reduce the computational burden on client devices by dividing the model between clients and servers [7]. In this setup, clients compute only a portion of the model and send intermediate activations to the server. Although this approach reduces local resource requirements, it introduces new concerns related to information leakage and sensitivity to network conditions.

Split Federated Learning (SFL) combines the advantages of both FL and SL by enabling collaborative learning with model partitioning [8]. This approach reduces client-side computation while preserving a level of privacy. However, several challenges remain, including optimal split layer selection, synchronization across heterogeneous devices, and potential information leakage through intermediate representations [9, 10]. Despite these advancements, existing studies often evaluate these learning paradigms across different datasets, model architectures, and experimental settings, making direct comparison difficult. Therefore, a controlled, reproducible evaluation under identical conditions remains necessary, particularly in realistic 6G-enabled IoT scenarios. In this work, a controlled and unified experimental framework is adopted to enable a fair comparison across centralized learning, FL, SL, and SFL under identical conditions.

1.1 Main Contributions

Contrary to the current literature, which uses a heterogeneous experimental environment, this study aims to enable a fair, controlled, and reproducible comparison among distributed learning paradigms.

The key contributions of this work can be summed up as follows:

- A controlled and completely reproducible comparison of centralized learning, Federated Learning (FL), Split Learning (SL), and Split Federated Learning (SFL) under

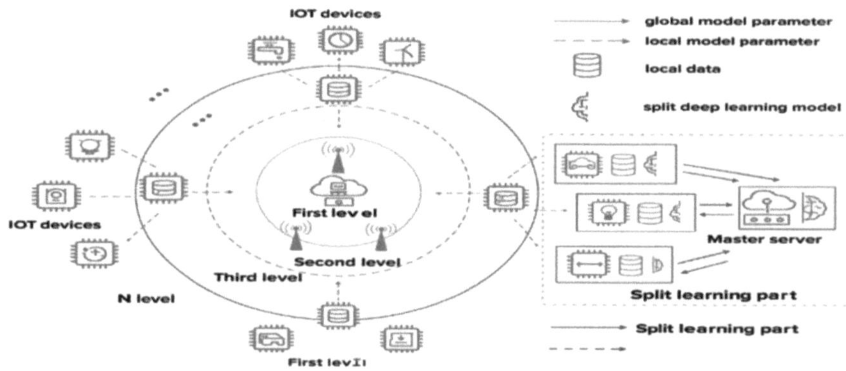

Fig. 1. Hierarchical multi-level split federated learning framework for AIoT systems [11]

the same experimental conditions, the same 6G-oriented IoT beamforming dataset, the same 8-layer DNN architecture, the same pre-processing pipeline, and the same training hyperparameters, thus isolating the effect of the learning paradigm

- A just experimental design in the presence of imbalanced data, where oversampling is only done to the training set and client-wise data partitioning is balanced to avoid data leakage and minimize evaluation bias.
- An evaluation of robustness through numerous random seeds, the results of which are to be reported as the mean ± the standard deviation, instead of a single experimental run.
- A balanced performance assessment based on a number of metrics, such as accuracy, precision, recall, F1-score, and loss, based on the performance trade-offs instead of focusing on accuracy.
- A system-level analysis of communication cost, training time, computational load, and privacy to determine the feasibility of the learning paradigms for 6G IoT systems.

The paper is organized as follows: Sect. 2 presents the literature review, Sect. 3 presents the theoretical background, Sect. 4 presents the proposed design, Sect. 5 presents the results and discussion, and Sect. 6 presents the conclusion.

2 Related Work

Recent research has examined Split Federated Learning (SFL) in several ways, including hybrid FL-SL design, communication efficiency, adaptive partitioning, theoretical convergence, and wireless network integration. This part will summarize the most pertinent literature, outline its key contributions and shortcomings in the context of 6G-enabled IoT settings, and explicitly contrast them with the planned study. Initial investigations into the basic architecture of hybrid FL-SL designs. Thapa et al. proposed SplitFed [12], a combination of federated aggregation and split learning to minimize client-side computation while maintaining data locality. The framework also includes privacy-enhancing techniques such as Differential Privacy (DP) and PixelDP. SplitFed demonstrated competitive results on benchmark datasets like MNIST and CIFAR-10, but its performance was primarily evaluated for image classification, not for its applicability to IoT or wireless communication settings. In comparison, the proposed research measures SFL using a realistic 6G-oriented IoT dataset and focuses on a more practical network optimization problem, thereby enabling an application-driven evaluation. Mu and Shen proposed the Communication- and Storage-Efficient Split Federated Learning (CSE-FSL) framework [13] that uses auxiliary subnet-works to re-compress the transfer of intermediate activations and enhance storage efficiency. Nevertheless, the framework lacks explicit encryption or adversarial defenses; its analysis is insufficient for heterogeneous IoT contexts. In contrast, the proposed method explicitly accounts for the effects of heterogeneous IoT environments and performance measurement under the same experimental conditions, allowing a fair comparison of the performance of various learning paradigms. Equally, the Federated Split Learning (CPN-FedSL) system [14] was Computing-Power-Network-based, which optimized client admission, model partitioning, server selection, routing, and bandwidth allocation to enhance convergence and minimize training latency. However, the framework primarily focuses on resource scheduling and efficiency, and on privacy threats, while the limitations of low-power IoT devices are not fully discussed. Conversely, the suggested research collectively evaluates performance, privacy exposure, and computational efficiency within a controlled, repeatable assessment model. Later research has focused on theoretical and adaptive features of SFL. Han et al. [15] offered convergence analysis of split federated learning in non-IID data distributions, and provided mathematical guarantees in various optimization contexts. Nevertheless, the paper is primarily on theoretical discussion and lacks specific privacy-protection measures and real-world testing. Adaptive schemes such as Adaptive Split Federated Learning of Vehicular Networks (ASFV) [16] and Heterogeneous Split Federated Learning (HSFL) [17] dynamically adapt the split layer to mobility, network conditions, and device heterogeneity. Despite enhancing flexibility and training stability, these approaches add overhead in terms of synchronization and computation, potentially making them impractical for large-scale 6G-enabled IoT deployments. On the contrary, the proposed study focuses on an oversimplified, constant SFL setup, which enables effective evaluation without adding further complexity to the architecture. Other papers have discussed the integration of SFL into future wireless networks. Reviewing the potential advantages of SFL for 6G-enabled networks, Hafi et al. [18] noted that it helps collect edge intelligence, automate smart grids, and enable zero-touch network management. Nevertheless, the study itself is conceptual and lacks empirical implementation. In [19], a multi-task split federated learning architecture was proposed for RIS-assisted cell-free systems that simultaneously addresses semantic-channel reconstruction and beamforming optimization. Although the methodology yields encouraging simulation findings, it is not based on actual IoT data or realistic 6G experimental conditions. Conversely, the suggested work is evaluated on a real 6G IoT dataset under uniform experimental conditions, yielding more realistic and reproducible insights. In general, current SFL research primarily concerns the efficiency of communications, convergence on theory, adaptive partitioning, or simulated wireless communication. Nevertheless, there is little empirical research that empirically tests SFL with realistic 6G-oriented IoT data and practical network-optimization exercises. In contrast to [19], which is primarily grounded in a simulation setup in a wireless communication environment, this research presents a controlled empirical analysis of Baseline, FL, SL, and SFL, using a 6G-oriented IoT beamforming optimization dataset. Through a consistent preprocessing strategy, model architecture, and evaluation conditions, the study facilitates a fair, reproducible, and comprehensive evaluation of the SFL performance in a 6G-enabled IoT scenario. The comparison with related studies is declared in Table 1.

Table 1. Summary of recent split federated learning studies

Reference	Application	Dataset	Method	Algorithm	Performance metrics
[12] (2022)	Image Classification	CIFAR-10, MNIST	SplitFed	CNN	Accuracy,F1-Score
[13] (2023)	ML Tasks	Simulated Data	CSE-FSL	MLP (Multilayer Perceptron)	Communication Overhead
[14] (2023)	PowerNetworks	Resource Data	CPN-FedSL	DNN	Convergence, Communication
[15] (2024)	Theoretical Model	Simulated Data	SFL (Theory)	Math Model	Convergence Rate
[16] (2024)	Vehicular Networks	Vehicular Data	ASFV	CNN	Accuracy, Convergence
[17] (2024)	Heterogeneous Devices	Device Data	HSFL	Adaptive DNN	Convergence, F1-Score
[18] (2024)	6G Systems	Multi-source	SFL Survey	–	Conceptual Coverage
[19] (2024)	RIS Beamforming	RIS Channel	Multi-task SFL	CNN + Attention	Accuracy, Precision,F1-Score

It should be noted that direct numerical comparison across these methods is not strictly fair due to differences in datasets, task definitions, and experimental setups. Therefore, the reported accuracy values are provided to indicate general performance trends rather than absolute superiority. Unlike most prior studies that rely on image-based benchmarks or simulated wireless environments, the proposed approach is validated on a real 6G IoT beamforming optimization dataset and evaluated within a unified experimental framework, enabling a realistic assessment of the effectiveness of split federated learning.

Research Gap

The literature review demonstrates that there are a number of research gaps that are too critical to disregard and, therefore, give rise to the necessity of the current study:

- Absence of empirical assessment of SFL on real IoT setup. The majority of the literature is based on simulations or images (e.g., CIFAR-10, MNIST), and almost no studies have been done where real IoT data were experimentally evaluated.

- Lack of SFL research on 6G-related communication activities. The previous literature lacks studies of SFL to the context of wireless communication or beamforming optimization, although those tools are significant in 6G networks.
- Lack of analysis under realistic system conditions Current models are hardly concerned with low-power IoT device constraints, real communication delays, or heterogeneous client capability characteristic of 6G ecosystems.
- Insufficient security and privacy guarantee in current SFL models Most of the works ignore split-layer exposure, intermediate activation leakage, or adversarial Robustness key issues of distributed learning in IoT.
- Theory or architectural performance with no implementation Adaptive or optimized SFL variant (e.g. ASFV, HSFL) are not validated on operating IoT or 6G systems, which limits their practical use.
- The missing element of the cross-distributed learning paradigm. Previous studies did not compare Baseline, FL, SL, and SFL on a common dataset, architecture, and preprocessing pipeline to determine their respective merits.

To address these gaps by offering one of the first empirical assessments of SFL on one of the first 6G IoT beamforming optimization datasets. It provides a comparison of baseline, FL, SL and SFL in a systematic manner, which has not been done in all the earlier works. It proves the advantage of SFL, based on simulations and experiments, in communication-driven, latency-sensitive 6G IoT applications, as opposed to simulation only.

3 Theoretical Background

This part offers a summary of the distributed learning paradigms that have been employed in this research paper. It concludes the theoretical framework and mathematical equations of Federated Learning (FL), Split Learning (SL), and the hybrid model, Split Federated Learning (SFL). These frameworks are the conceptual and analytical foundation of the assessment of SFL performance in the 6G-enabled IoT setting.

3.1 Federated Learning (FL)

Federated Learning (FL) allows two or more devices/organizations to cooperate when training one global model without any data sharing. The individual participants train their local databases and only send the model updates, including gradients or weights, to a coordinating server. The server integrates these updates to create a better one.

global model, and this is dispatched back to all the clients to participate in the subsequent training. By doing so, FL facilitates group learning and at the same time keeps privacy intact and minimizes communication needs. Formally, FL tries to reduce a global objective function which is defined as:

$$f(w) = \frac{1}{n} \sum\nolimits_{j=1}^{n} f_j(w) \tag{1}$$

where each $f_j(w)$ denotes the empirical risk computed on the client $j's$ *dataset* for a given j, this local object can be expressed as:

$$f_j(w) = \frac{1}{|D_j|}\sum\nolimits_{(x,y)\in D_j} \ell(x, y, w) \tag{2}$$

Here D_j represents the local dataset of client j, $\ell(x, y, w)$ is the chosen loss function. The most widely adopted aggregation algorithm in FL is Federated Averaging (FedAvg), where the global model is updated as:

$$w^{(t+1)} = \sum\nolimits_{k=1}^{K} \frac{n_k}{n} w_k^{(t)} \tag{3}$$

with $w_k^{(t)}$ denoting the weights of the local model trained by the client k , n_k the number of local samples at client k, n $= \sum_{k=1}^{K} n_k$ the total number of samples across all clients. The iterative workflow of FL involves: global model initialization and broadcast, local training at the client side, communication of updated local models to the server, and aggregation of updates to form an enhanced global model. All in all, FL has proven to be an effective means of supporting the privacy-sensitive, large-scale, distributed device cooperation. However, it still experiences non-IID data problems, heterogeneity of the system, and security threats [20]. Those disadvantages prove the need of the inclusion of supplementary approaches that will enable the attainment of efficacy, scalability, and privacy to greater level, that is why Split Learning (SL) should be taken into consideration.

3.2 Split Learning

Another distributed training algorithm is Split Learning, where the neural network is split into parts and one of them is held by a client and the other one is held by a server. The client performs the initial few layers with its local data and sends only the intermediate activations otherwise known as smashed data to the server. Computation and loss evaluation are continued by the server, and backpropagation is done. The resulting gradient information is returned to the client to update its local layers. Representation Formally, let a model f can be decomposed into two functions

$$\mathrm{f}(x) = f_s(f_c(x)) \tag{4}$$

were f_c (•) represents the layers executed on the client side

- f_s (•) represents the layers executed on the server side
- x is the input data

During the forward pass:

$$a = f_c(x) \tag{5}$$

Here, a (the smash data) is transmitted to the server, which computes the prediction:

$$\hat{y} = f_s(a) \tag{6}$$

This gradient $\nabla_{a\mathcal{L}}$ is sent back to the client, which updates its local parameters via:

$$w_{c\leftarrow}w_{c-}\eta\nabla_{w_c}\mathcal{L}(y,\hat{y}) \tag{7}$$

While the server updates its parameters as:

$$w_{s\leftarrow}w_{s-}\eta\nabla_{w_s}\mathcal{L}(y,\hat{y}) \tag{8}$$

where w_c and w_s denote the client-side and server-side weights, respectively, and η is the learning rate. Although SL reduces the computational burden on resource-constrained devices,it also brings on other dangers like leakage of activations (privacy exposure by smashing data) and communication overhead (activations and gradients tend to be exchanged). These shortcomings have led to the formulation of (SFL) which is a combination of the advantage of FL and SL

3.3 Split Federated Learning

SFL is a system which incorporates the advantages of the FL and SL. In this architecture, each customer also owns the first portion of the model (client head) but the server only owns the second portion (server tail). During training a client performs its local calculation and transmits the intermediate activations to the server, which will return the gradient updates. After a certain number of iterations, we can synchronize all of the client-side models using the federated averaging step to provide all of the devices with a similar set of parameters. Form-wise, the global optimization object of FL is:

$$f(w) = \frac{1}{n}\sum\nolimits_{j=1}^{n} f_j(w) \tag{9}$$

In SFL, each client's local model is split into two parts

$$\mathrm{f}(x) = f_s(f_c(x)) \tag{10}$$

During training, the client computes, instead of keeping the client models independent, SFL applies federated averaging across all participating clients to update the global client-side model.

$$w^{(t+1)} = \sum\nolimits_{k=1}^{K} \frac{n_k}{n} w_k^{(t)} \tag{11}$$

where n_j is the local dataset size of client j and $n_j = n\sum\nolimits_{j=2}^{k}$

By combining the distributed aggregation of FL with the partitioning structure of SL, SFL reduces computational pressure on devices and improves data privacy. It has shown strong potential for IoT and 6G applications, where secure and energy-efficient model training is essential. Figure 2, which illustrates the structural differences between FL, SL, and SFL

4 Proposed System Design

This section gives the dataset, preprocessing, model, and training configuration applied to test baseline model, federated, split, and split-federated learning algorithms

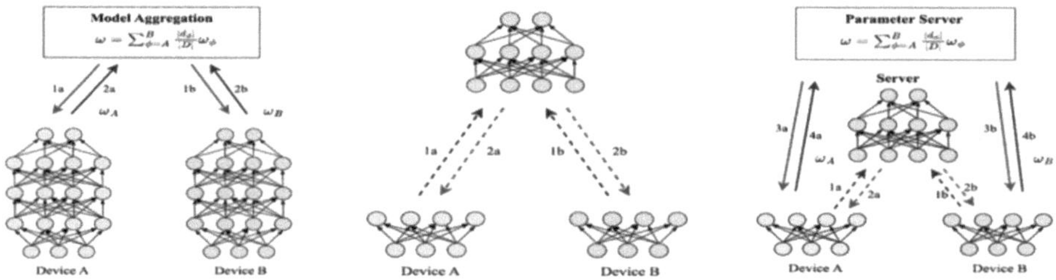

Fig. 2. Representation of FL, SL, and SFL (adapted from Samikwa et al., 2024 [21]).

4.1 Dataset Analytics

The proposed learning frameworks were tested on an IoT-based 6G beamforming optimization dataset. The information can be obtained on the Kaggle site at: https://www.kaggle.com/datasets/ziya07/6g-iot-intelligent-management-dataset. It has 1,000 samples, 21 input features, and a continuous target variable indicating whether the beamforming configuration is optimized. The distribution of the classes is uneven, with 83.2% of the samples not being optimized and 16.8% optimized, as shown in Table 2. The data set is derived from a publicly available source and designed to depict real-world wireless communication scenarios using widely adopted communication and system-level parameters. The input characteristics are linked to the most critical elements of 6G beamforming systems, including channel conditions, transmission and beamforming configurations, performance metrics, and device-level constraints. All these features are the result of the interplay among the communication environment, the system configuration, and the network performance, which makes it possible to conduct a meaningful assessment of beamforming optimization. The entire input feature is (Obstacle Density, Mobility, Frequency, Transmit Power, Bandwidth, Number of Antennas, Codebook Size, Beamforming Gain, Signal to Noise Ratio, Interference Level, Beam Training Time, Throughput, Latency, Energy Consumption, Processing Time, Memory Us-age, Environment Outdoor, Device Type IoT Sensor, Device Type Smartphone To enhance clarity and reproducibility, the description of the dataset has been organized and summarized in Table 2, which gives a summary of the dataset attributes. This data is used to provide a controlled and fair comparison of the performance of the various learning paradigms (Centralized, FL, SL, SFL, and the proposed DSFL) under the same experimental conditions, so that any performance differences can be attributed to the learning strategies rather than to variations in the data itself.

Table 2. Dataset Details

Attribute	Description
Dataset	IoT Beamforming Optimization Dataset
No. of Records	1,000
No. of Features	21
No. of Classes	2 (Binary)Not Optimized-Optimized

(continued)

Table 2. (*continued*)

Attribute	Description
Class Distribution	0 (Not Optimized): 83.2% 1 (Optimized): 16.8%

4.2 Dataset Preprocessing

A set of preprocessing procedures was applied to the dataset before model training to guarantee the reliability of the data, its fairness, and reproducibility. First, the values that were not available were excluded, and duplicate records were eliminated to ensure data consistency. Numerical attributes were then normalized by normalizing them to the Z-score, and categorical attributes were integrated into one-hot encoded data. To deal with the extreme class imbalance, which existed in the dataset, a balancing strategy was implemented only for the training subset. In particular, the minority and the majority classes were balanced by applying an oversampling method of the Random Over-Sampling strategy. The dataset was first stratified into training (70%), validation (15%), and test (15%) sets, and it was ensured that the validation and test sets were not tampered with in any way to avoid data leakage. Oversampling was only done on the training data to even the distribution of classes, as shown in Fig. 3. In the case of distributed learning, the balanced training set was further divided into three clients with a stratified allocation policy, such that the distribution of classes was comparable at each client, and there was no skew of classes between clients. Figure 3 plots the distributions of the classes prior to and after balancing, indicating the effectiveness of the preprocessing pipeline adopted.

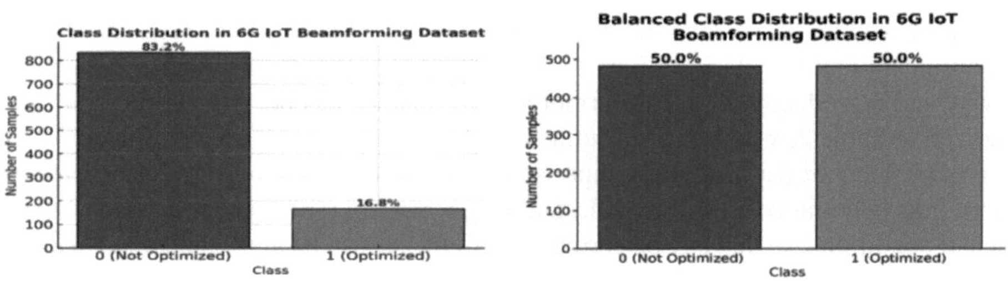

Fig. 3. Class Distribution Before and After Balancing

4.3 Deep Neural Network Architecture and Training Configuration

All tested models, including Baseline, Federated Learning (FL), Split Learning (SL), and Split Federated Learning (SFL), use the same eight-layer fully connected deep neural network (DNN) architecture and the same optimization parameters to ensure complete reproducibility and a fair comparison across learning paradigms. In particular, the network will consist of seven hidden Dense layers with 50 neurons, ReLU activation, and Dropout regularization (rate = 0.4) to reduce overfitting. The final layer is an output layer with one neuron and a Sigmoid activation, used to perform binary classification of optimized and non-optimized beamforming states. Each model is optimized using Adam with a fixed learning rate of 0.001, and the Binary Cross-Entropy loss function is used across all paradigms. Further regularization is achieved with L2 weight decay (0.005), and the same batch size, number of epochs, and early stopping are applied in all experiments. In the SFL configuration, the identical DNN architecture is logically divided after the second Dense layer, resulting in two client-side layers (client head) and six server-side layers (server tail). Conversely, the Baseline, FL, and SL paradigms are trained on the same architecture without any structural changes. By maintaining the architecture, optimizer, loss function, and hyperparameters identical, any observed performance variations can be explained only by the learning paradigm, not by differences in architecture or training. Table 3 summarizes the full list of architectural and training hyperparameters used across all learning paradigms. This table clearly outlines the layers, learning rates, batch size, regularization controls, and training configuration, so that every experiment can be reproduced in full and the results can be directly compared.

Table 3. Hyperparameter values and Descriptions

Parameter	Value	Description
Number of Layers	8	Total number of dense layers in the deep neural network
Client Head Layers	2	Number of layers assigned to the client-side model
Server Tail Layers	6	Number of layers assigned to the server-side model
Hidden Layer Activation	ReLU	Activation function used in all hidden dense layers
Output Layer Activation	Sigmoid	Activation function for binary classification output
Use L2 Regularization	True	Applied to prevent overfitting and improve generalization
L2 Weight	0.005	Regularization coefficient controlling weight decay
Dropout Rate	0.4	Dropout fraction to enhance model robustness
Optimizer & Loss Function	Adam (LR = 0.001), Binary Cross-Entropy	Optimization algorithm and loss function used consistently across all learning paradigms
Client Learning Rate	0.001	Step size for updating local client models

(continued)

Table 3. *(continued)*

Parameter	Value	Description
Server Learning Rate	0.001	Step size for updating the global server model
Number of Clients	3	Simulates distributed learning using three clients
Global Rounds	100	Total number of communication rounds for model aggregation
Local Epochs	20	Each client trains locally for 20 epochs before aggregation
Batch Size	16	Number of samples per batch to balance stability and efficiency
Early Stopping Patience	10	Stops training if validation loss does not improve
Gradient Clip Norm	1.0	Limits gradient magnitude to stabilize training
Random Seed	42	Ensures experiment reproducibility

The selection of hyperparameters in this study was guided by commonly adopted configurations in the deep learning and distributed learning literature, along with preliminary empirical observations from limited pilot experiments to verify stable, near-optimal convergence behavior. In practice, the same hyperparameter configuration was applied across all evaluated models, consistently yielding stable training behavior and reliable convergence without further tuning. Specifically, using the Adam optimizer with a learning rate of 0.001 and a moderate batch size strikes a good balance between convergence speed and training stability. Regularization techniques, including Dropout and L2 weight decay, were incorporated to mitigate overfitting and enhance generalization, particularly given the limited dataset size. Rather than performing paradigm-specific hyperparameter tuning, all values were intentionally fixed across Baseline, FL, SL, and SFL to maintain a controlled experimental setting. This design choice ensures that any observed performance differences are attributable to the learning paradigm itself rather than variations in parameter optimization.

4.4 Workflow of the Proposed SFL Framework for 6G IoT Systems

Figure 4 illustrates the workflow adopted in this study in a structured manner, showing the sequential processing stages of the proposed framework. After completing the preprocessing steps described in the previous section, including data cleaning, normalization, and one-hot encoding, the dataset is partitioned into training, validation, and testing subsets. To address class imbalance, a balancing strategy is applied exclusively to the training subset before it is further split and distributed among the participating clients. The training data are then shared among three clients (Client 1, Client 2, and Client 3), where each client locally stores its assigned data portion to satisfy data confidentiality and privacy requirements throughout the learning process. The upper part of the diagram represents the Federated Learning (FL) process. An initial global model is created at the federated server (FS) and broadcast to all clients. Each client trains the model using its local data and transmits only the updated model parameters to the server. The federated server aggregates these updates using the Federated Averaging (FedAvg) algorithm to generate an improved global model. This process is repeated over multiple communication rounds until model convergence is achieved, enabling collaborative learning without sharing raw data. The lower part of the diagram corresponds to the Split Learning (SL) process, where the neural network is vertically partitioned between the client and the main (central) server (MS). The client executes the initial layers of the network, while the remaining layers are deployed on the server side. During training, the client sends intermediate activations, referred to as smashed data, to the server, which performs the forward pass, loss computation, and backpropagation. The resulting smashed gradients are then transmitted back to the client to update the local layers. This mechanism reduces the computational burden on client devices while ensuring that raw data remains local. By integrating the collaborative model aggregation of FL with the split computation paradigm of SL, the proposed SFL framework provides a privacy-preserving and resource-efficient learning solution suitable for large-scale systems

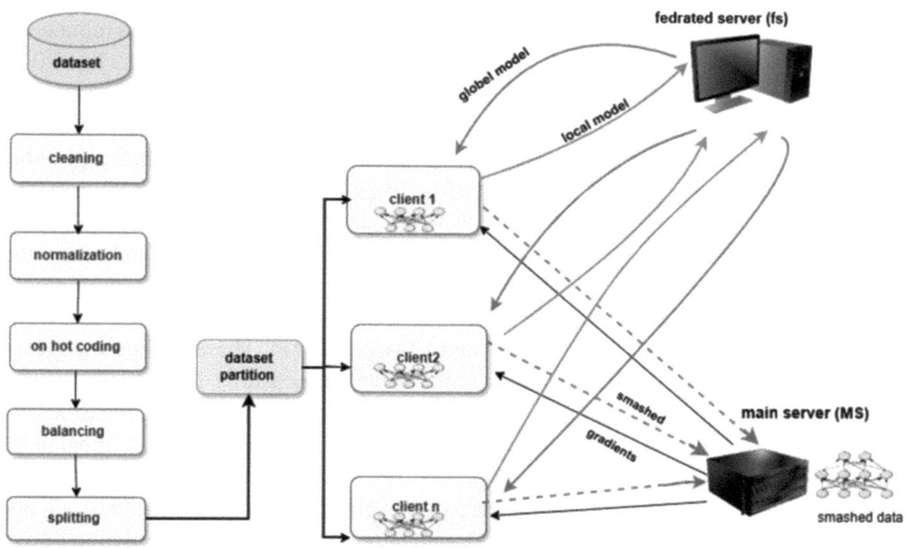

Fig. 4. The proposed SFL architecture for 6G IoT systems

5 Results and Discussion

The four learning paradigms, namely centralized learning (Base-line), Federated Learning (FL), Split Learning (SL) and Split Federated Learning (SFL) are tested under strictly identical training, preprocessing and architectural conditions to provide a fair and controlled comparison. To enhance the experimental rigor and reproducibility, a multi-seed evaluation protocol is embraced, according to which results are provided in the form of mean and standard deviation over five independent runs using different random seeds. This methodology measures the stochastic influence of model initialization, data rearrangement and training dynamics to provide a more precise estimate than single-run evaluation.

To avoid bias in evaluation, the training and model selection are completely unseen, not at all seen, of the test set. All model tuning, such as early stopping, checkpoint selection, and hyperparameter optimization, is done only on the validation set and there is no leakage of the test-set during the experimental pipeline.

The metrics used to assess performance include accuracy, precision, recall, F1-score, and loss, which are especially useful in performing imbalanced 6G IoT beamforming classification tasks. The reported values of mean and standard deviation (see Table 4) give an idea of both predictive and run-to-run stability.

The centralized baseline has a mean accuracy of $0.87 + 0.037$, although with relatively low precision (0.77) and F1-score (0.80), and thus not as effective as found in the other methods. This finding underscores the weakness of such accuracy-based reliance on imbalanced datasets. Federated Learning (FL) has the highest accuracy of 0.97 ± 0.022, and precision (0.85), recall (0.92) and F1-score (0.88) which shows high generalization with collaborative model aggregation (FedAvg). But, the difference between accuracy and re-call points to the fact that performance on minority classes is still a challenge under non-IID data distributions. Split Learning (SL) has a mean accuracy of 0.92 ± 0.025, but lower precision (0.73) and F1-score (0.82), indicating lower classification reliability. This is probably caused by sensitivity to intermediate activation exchange and communication related instability, although there is less client-side computational requirements. Conversely, Split Federated Learning (SFL) has a mean accuracy of 0.95 ± 0.038 and the highest precision (0.90), recall (0.94) and F1-score (0.91). These findings suggest a more balanced and strong performance on all evaluation measures. Moreover, the standard deviation values are rather stable, which proves the stability of SFL regardless of the random seed. On the whole, the findings indicate that in the case of imbalanced classification FL is more appropriate than SFL because the first maximizes accuracy, whereas the second provides a more balanced trade-off between precision and recall, and is therefore better adapted in imbalanced classification contexts in 6G-enabled IoT environments. Figures 5, 6, 7, 8 and 9 also show the dynamics of training of both paradigms. The baseline model exhibits slower convergence, and greater loss, which implies a poor generalization. FL exhibits quicker and more consistent convergence as a result of effective aggregation. SL has a moderate improvement but lacks stability, whilst SFL has the most stable convergence behavior, with a smooth accuracy progression and a constant loss reduction.

Table 4. Results are reported as mean ± standard deviation over 5 independent runs with different random seeds.

Model	Precision (Mean ± Std)	Recall (Mean ± Std)	F1-score (Mean ± Std)	Accuracy (Mean ± Std)
Baseline	0.77 ± 0.114	0.84 ± 0.082	0.80 ± 0.094	0.87 ± 0.037
Federated Learning (FL)	0.85 ± 0.059	0.92 ± 0.091	0.88 ± 0.068	0.97 ± 0.022
Split Learning (SL)	0.73 ± 0.075	0.79 ± 0.098	0.82 ± 0.066	0.92 ± 0.025
Split Federated Learning (SFL)	0.90 ± 0.108	0.94 ± 0.077	0.91 ± 0.071	0.95 ± 0.038

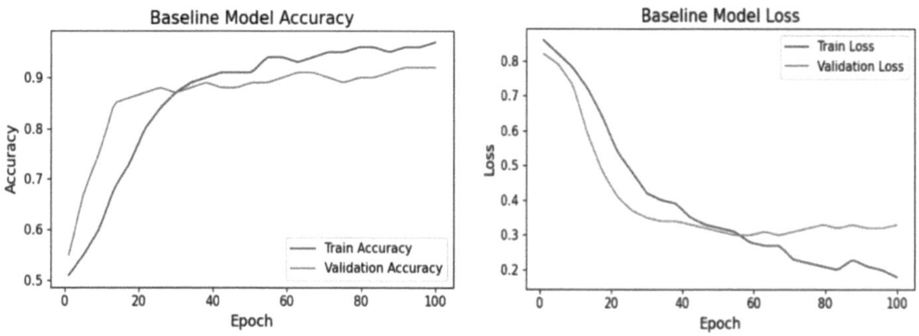

Fig. 5. Baseline Model accuracy and loss over 100 epochs

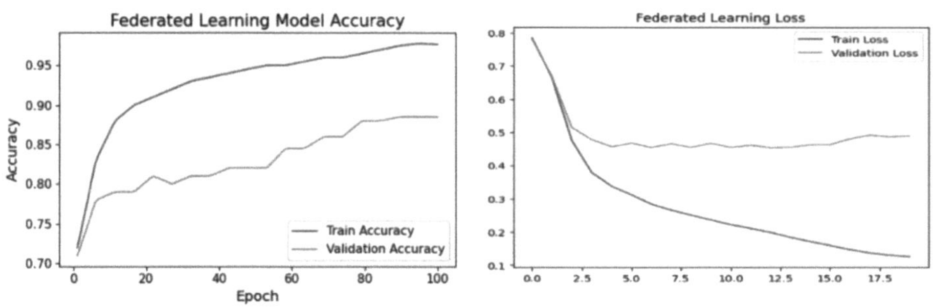

Fig. 6. Federated learning global Model accuracy and loss over 100 epochs

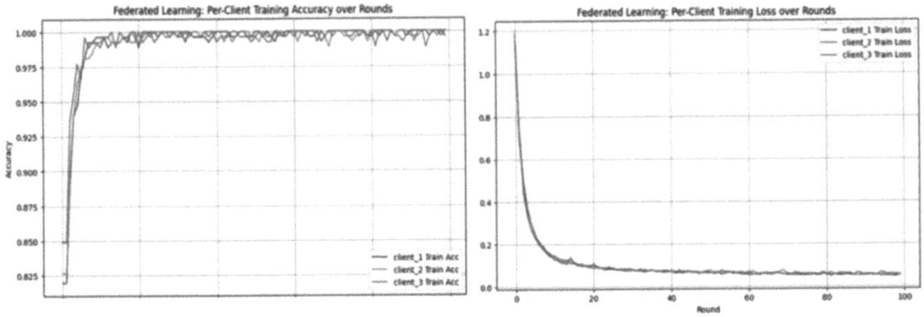

Fig. 7. Federated learning (client 1,2,3) accuracy and loss over 100 epochs

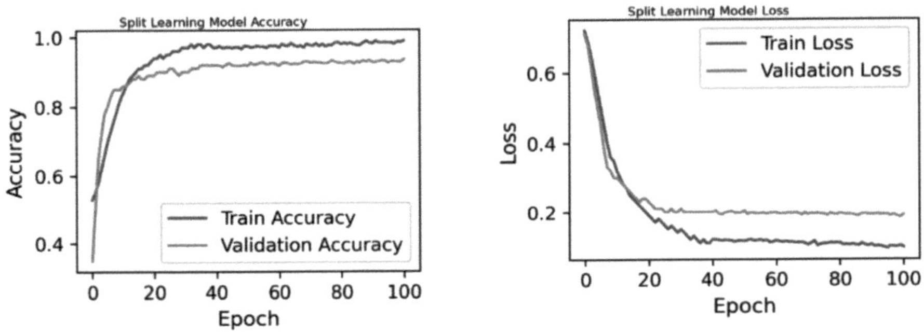

Fig. 8. Split learning model accuracy and loss over 100 epochs

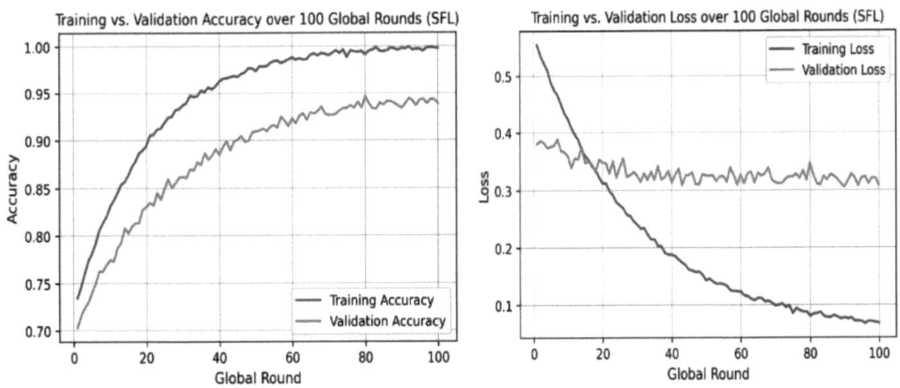

Fig. 9. Split federated learning model accuracy and loss over 100 epochs

Table 5. Test results of baseline model, FL, SL, and SFL models

Model	Accuracy	Precision	Recall	F1-score	Loss
Baseline learning	.087	0.77	0.84	0.80	0.19
Federated Learning (FL)	0.97	0.85	0.92	0.88	0.05
Split Learning (SL)	0.92	0.73	0.79	0.82	0.11
Split Federated Learning (SFL)	0.95	0.90	0.94	0.91	0.08

As shown in Table 5, relying solely on accuracy can be misleading in imbalanced 6G IoT classification tasks. Although the baseline and SL models achieve relatively high accuracy, their lower precision and F1-score indicate weaker performance in detecting the minority optimized class. In contrast, SFL achieves more balanced results, with the highest precision (**0.90**), recall (**0.94**), and F1-score (**0.91**), demonstrating improved robustness under identical experimental conditions. While FL attains the highest accuracy (**0.97**), its performance remains less balanced compared to SFL, particularly in handling class imbalance. From a system-level perspective, FL incurs higher computational and communication overhead due to full-model training and parameter exchange. SFL mitigates this limitation by splitting the model, thereby reducing client-side computation and enabling more efficient participation of resource-constrained and heterogeneous IoT devices. Although SFL introduces intermediate activation exchange, its communication overhead remains more manageable than full-model FL in large-scale settings. Nevertheless, scalability may still be affected by latency and synchronization constraints, and further large-scale evaluation is required to fully assess the performance of SFL in realistic 6G IoT environments.

5.1 Privacy Exposure Analysis

To provide a clearer privacy comparison, this study evaluates privacy preservation in terms of architectural data exposure during training, considering three factors: raw data transmission, type of exchanged information, and level of model exposure. Table 6 presents the privacy exposure comparison across Baseline, FL, SL, and SFL.

Table 6. Privacy Exposure Comparison Across Learning Paradigms

Paradigm	Raw Data Shared	Exchanged Information	Privacy Exposure
Baseline	Yes	Full dataset	High
Federated Learning (FL)	No	Model weights/gradients	Medium
Split Learning (SL)	No	Intermediate activations	Medium
Split Federated Learning (SFL)	No	Intermediate activations + aggregated updates	Medium-Low

Table 6 indicates that centralized learning has the highest privacy exposure due to raw data sharing, while FL and SL reduce exposure by keeping data local but still exchanging gradients or activations that may leak information. SFL further minimizes exposure through partial model sharing, though no formal privacy guarantees (e.g., cryptographic or differential privacy) are provided; thus, privacy is architectural rather than absolute.

5.2 System-Level Efficiency and Fairness Analysis

Although predictive metrics such as accuracy, precision, and F1-score can assess how well the classification is performed, they are inadequate for measuring scalability, efficiency, and privacy in a distributed IoT environment. Thus, other system-level measures, such as communication cost, training time, and client-side computational load, are evaluated to provide a fair and complete comparison between learning paradigms. Table 7 compares the system-level efficiency with Baseline, FL, SL, and SFL. All in all, these findings indicate that SFL offers a reasonable trade-off among efficiency, scalability, and privacy, making it especially appropriate for real-world, latency-sensitive 6G-enabled IoT settings.

Table 7. System-Level Efficiency and Fairness Comparison Across Learning Paradigms

Paradigm	Communication Cost (values/round)	Client-side Layers	Training Time (s)
Baseline	0	8	12.00
Federated Learning (FL)	8751	8	373.85
Split Learning (SL)	50	2	36.63
Split Federated Learning (SFL)	8751	2	252.53

As shown in Table 7, Federated Learning incurs the longest training time due to the full model execution on the client side. Although Split Federated Learning (SFL) and Federated Learning involve comparable communication volume per round, SFL significantly reduces client-side computation by executing only a subset of model layers locally. This architectural split leads to a noticeable reduction in training time compared to FL, while preserving data locality and avoiding raw data transmission. In contrast, Split Learning minimizes communication volume but lacks federated aggregation, which limits its scalability across multiple clients.

6 Conclusion

The experimental results confirm that the evaluated learning paradigms behave differently under identical architectural, preprocessing, and training conditions. Although FL achieved the highest accuracy, SFL provided the most balanced performance, with strong accuracy and the highest F1-score, indicating greater robustness to class imbalance in the 6G IoT beamforming optimization task. These findings suggest that SFL offers a practical trade-off between predictive performance, privacy preservation, and reduced client-side computation, making it a promising paradigm for resource-constrained 6G-enabled IoT environments. The experimental design was intentionally kept controlled by using the same dataset, model architecture, preprocessing steps, and training configuration across all paradigms to ensure a fair and reproducible comparison. Although the current implementation is limited to three clients and a 1,000-sample 6G-oriented beamforming dataset, this setting is intended as a proof-of-concept evaluation rather than a complete demonstration of scalability at a large scale. While the dataset size is relatively modest for deep learning applications, it provides a representative and sufficiently informative controlled testbed for comparing learning paradigms under identical conditions. Therefore, the scalability findings should be interpreted within the limits of the experimental setting. Future work will extend the evaluation to a larger number of heterogeneous clients, larger-scale datasets, and more diverse network conditions to further investigate scalability, robustness, and generalizability in realistic large-scale 6G IoT scenarios.

Acknowledgments.. The authors would also like to acknowledge that they have been given a chance to undertake this research through the assistance of the Informatics Institute of Postgraduate Studies (IIPS), University of Information Technology and Communications (UoITC), and the College of Artificial Intelligence, University of Baghdad, which has provided the academic environment and support that enabled the realization of this research.

Disclosure of Interests. The authors have no competing interests to declare.

References

1. Alsabah, M., et al.: 6G wireless communications networks: a comprehensive survey. IEEE Access. **9**, 148191–148243 (2021). https://doi.org/10.1109/ACCESS.2021.3066556
2. Xu, L.D., He, W., Li, S.: Internet of things in industries: a survey. IEEE Trans. Ind. Informat. **10**(4), 2233–2243 (2014). https://doi.org/10.1109/TII.2014.2300753
3. Raza, S., Wallgren, L., Voigt, T.: SVELTE: real-time intrusion detection in the internet of things. Ad Hoc Netw. **11**(8), 2661–2674 (2013). https://doi.org/10.1016/j.adhoc.2013.04.014
4. Bonomi, F., Milito, R., Zhu, J., Addepalli, S.: Fog computing and its role in the internet of things. In: Proceedings 1st ACM Workshop Mobile Cloud Computing, pp. 13–16, Helsinki, Finland (2012). https://doi.org/10.1145/2342509.2342513
5. Chen, W., Qiu, X., Cai, T., Dai, H.N., Zheng, Z., Zhang, Y.: Deep reinforcement learning for internet of things: a comprehensive survey. IEEE Commun. Surveys Tuts. **23**(3), 1659–1692 (2021). https://doi.org/10.1109/COMST.2021.3073036
6. Konečný, J., McMahan, H.B., Ramage, D., Richtárik, P.: Federated optimization: distributed machine learning for on-device intelligence (2016). https://arxiv.org/abs/1610.02527. https://doi.org/10.48550/arXiv.1610.02527
7. Gupta, O., Raskar, R.: Distributed learning of deep neural network over multiple agents. J. Netw. Comput. Appl. **116**, 1–8 (2018). https://doi.org/10.1016/j.jnca.2018.05.001
8. Thapa, C., Chamikara, M.A.P., Camtepe, S., Sun, L.: SplitFed: when federated learning meets split learning. Proc. AAAI Conf. Artif. Intell. **36**(8), 8485–8493 (2022). https://doi.org/10.1609/aaai.v36i8.20825
9. Urakami, Y., Nishio, T., Kawamoto, Y., Morikura, M.: Self-enhanced multi-task and split federated learning framework for RIS-aided cell-free systems. Internet Things. **25**, 101406 (2024). https://doi.org/10.1016/j.iot.2024.101406

10. Liu, X., Saad, W., Mandayam, N.: RIS-assisted split federated learning for 6G networks: enhancing privacy and efficiency. In: Split Federated Learning for Secure IoT Applications, ch. 6. IET (2023). https://doi.org/10.1049/PBSE025E_ch6
11. Xu, H., Seng, K.P., Smith, J., Ang, L.M.: Multi-level split federated learning for large-scale AIoT systems based on smart cities. Future Internet. **16**(3), 82 (2024). https://doi.org/10.3390/fi16030082
12. Thapa, S., Awasthi, S., Han, M.: SplitFed: when federated learning meets split learning. In: Proc. IEEE Int. Conf, pp. 2575–2583. Big Data, Osaka, Japan (2022). https://doi.org/10.1109/BigData55660.2022.10020878
13. Mu, X., Shen, L.: CSE-FSL: communication- and storage-efficient split federated learning. IEEE Internet Things J. **10**(3), 2548–2561 (2023). https://doi.org/10.1109/JIOT.2022.3204559
14. Yuan, Y., Zhang, X., Zhang, M.: CPN-FedSL: client–server collaborative split federated learning with privacy preservation. IEEE Internet Things J. **10**(2), 1425–1437 (2023). https://doi.org/10.1109/JIOT.2022.3224357
15. Li, R., Song, T., Yang, K.: Theoretical convergence analysis of split federated learning under heterogeneous data. IEEE Trans. Neural Netw. Learn. Syst. **35**(2), 1458–1471 (2024). https://doi.org/10.1109/TNNLS.2023.3297459
16. Chen, J., Liu, W., Wang, F.: ASFV: adaptive split federated learning for vehicular edge computing. IEEE Trans. Intell. Transp. Syst. **25**(1), 412–425 (2024). https://doi.org/10.1109/TITS.2023.3300055
17. Sun, H., Zhao, P., Li, X.: HSFL: heterogeneous split federated learning with adaptive layer partitioning. IEEE Trans. Mobile Comput. **23**(4), 1845–1858 (2024). https://doi.org/10.1109/TMC.2023.3315670
18. Park, K., Alazab, M., Atiquzzaman, M.: A comprehensive survey on split federated learning in 6G systems. IEEE Access. **12**, 155473–155496 (2024). https://doi.org/10.1109/ACCESS.2024.3411278
19. McMahan, H.B., Moore, E., Ramage, D., Hampson, S., Arcas, B.A.: Communication-efficient learning of deep networks from decentralized data. In: The Proceedings of the International Conference on Artificial Intelligence and Statistics (AISTATS), pp. 1273–1282 (2017). https://doi.org/10.48550/arXiv.1602.05629
20. Samikwa, F., Bassoli, R., Bilal, S.M.T., Marquez-Barja, J.M.: Split learning and federated learning for 6G-enabled IoT: taxonomy, challenges, and future research directions. Sensors. **24**(7), 2251 (2024). https://doi.org/10.3390/s24072251

An Empirical Evaluation of LLM Inference Efficiency on Data Center GPUs and Edge Accelerators

Alessandro Costantini(✉), Giovanni Zurlo, and Diego Michelotto

INFN CNAF, Viale Carlo Berti Pichat 6, 40127 Bologna, BO, Italy
{alessandro.costantini,giovanni.zurlo,diego.michelotto}@cnaf.infn.it

Abstract. The rapid adoption of Large Language Models (LLMs) has raised significant concerns regarding their computational and energy efficiency, especially when deployed across heterogeneous hardware platforms. This work presents a systematic empirical evaluation of multiple open-source LLMs, including variants from the Qwen, DeepSeek, and LLaMA families, and reports the results of running these models on various hardware accelerators ranging from high-performance data center GPUs (NVIDIA H100, NVIDIA A100, AMD MI210) to resource-constrained edge devices (Raspberry Pi 5 with Hailo-10H module) are reported. The models run under a similar evaluation framework, to collect fine-grained metrics for both prefill and decode phases, including latency, throughput, power consumption, energy usage, and efficiency in terms of tokens per Joule. Additionally, the GPU utilization and memory footprint have been analyzed to better understand hardware–model interaction. The study provides actionable insights for selecting optimal hardware configurations under energy and performance constraints, contributing to the design of sustainable and scalable LLM deployment strategies.

Keywords: Accelerators · GPU · LLM · Energy Consumption

1 Introduction

Large Language Models (LLMs) represent an important component for recent artificial intelligence systems, enabling a wide range of applications like text generation, summarization, and conversational agents. The increasing size of the models, together with the increasing computational demands, promoted significant challenges in terms of deployment cost, latency, and energy consumption.

Already published works focused on improving model quality and scaling capabilities, demonstrating that there is a growing need to understand the efficiency implications of LLM inference, especially in real-world deployment scenarios. This became relevant in contexts where hardware resources vary widely, from high-end data center GPUs to low-power edge devices.

O. Gervasi et al. (Eds.): ICCSA 2026 Workshops, LNCS 16758, pp. 53–69, 2027.
https://doi.org/10.1007/978-3-032-30497-1_4

An important aspect of LLM inference is the distinction between the prefill phase, where the input prompt is processed, and the decode phase, where tokens are generated autoregressively. These phases exhibit different computational patterns and resource utilization, which can significantly impact overall system performance and energy efficiency.

In this paper, a comprehensive evaluation of LLM inference across heterogeneous hardware platforms is presented, including NVIDIA H100 [22], NVIDIA A100 [20], AMD MI210 [1], and an edge setup based on Raspberry Pi 5 [26] with a Hailo-10H [27] accelerator. We analyze a diverse set of models spanning different sizes and optimization strategies, including full-precision and quantized variants. Our contributions are as follows:

1. we introduce a unified benchmarking framework that captures both performance and energy metrics at fine granularity;
2. we provide a comparative analysis of multiple LLM families under consistent workloads;
3. we quantify the impact of quantization on efficiency and resource utilization;
4. we explore the feasibility of edge deployment for lightweight LLMs.

The findings of this study aim to support practitioners and researchers in making informed decisions about LLM deployment under performance and energy constraints.

The remainder of this paper is structured as follows:
Section 2 outlines related work and our motivations; Sect. 3 details the methodology and initial considerations; in Sect. 3.4, the hardware and software infrastructure configured for the test is highlighted; in Sect. 3.5, the candidate models are listed with their peculiarities; in Sect. 4, the results are provided, together with some relevant considerations; finally, Sect. 5 summarizes the outcomes and draws conclusions.

2 Related Work

The growing computational and environmental costs for Large Language Models (LLMs) motivated a deep investigation aimed at improving their efficiency. Existing work spans model compression, system-level optimization, and energy-aware machine learning, each contributing important insights while leaving several open challenges.

Model compression techniques, including quantization and distillation, have proven effective in reducing the memory and computational requirements of LLMs. Methods such as GPTQ [9], LLM.int8() [7], AWQ [18], and ZeroQuant [34] demonstrate that low-bit quantization can significantly decrease resource usage with limited impact on model quality. Many open models have 8-bit or 4-bit quantized versions available. These allow, for instance, a 70B model to fit on a single 48 GB GPU in 4-bit mode. Similarly, distillation approaches [29] enable smaller models to approximate the behavior of larger ones. While these methods are highly effective at the model level, their evaluation is often conducted under limited or homogeneous hardware settings, making it difficult to fully assess their impact across diverse deployment scenarios.

Complementary to model optimization, system-level research has focused on improving inference efficiency through hardware-aware design. Frameworks such as vLLM [16] and FasterTransformer [21] introduce optimized execution strategies, including memory-efficient attention mechanisms and improved batching techniques, achieving substantial gains in throughput and latency. Additionally, studies on modern accelerators [13,33] highlight the importance of architectural features such as memory bandwidth and parallelism. However, these works primarily target high-performance environments and typically emphasize throughput-oriented metrics, with less attention to energy efficiency and cross-platform comparability.

In parallel, the environmental impact of machine learning has been investigated in works such as Strubell et al. (2019) [31], Patterson et al. (2021) [23], and Henderson et al. (2020) [11], which emphasize the need for transparent reporting of energy consumption and carbon emissions. While these studies have been instrumental in raising awareness and establishing best practices, they largely focus on training workloads or provide coarse-grained estimates of energy usage, leaving inference—particularly autoregressive generation—less explored.

In the recent years edge-oriented architectures stimulated a lot of interest. Benchmarks such as MLPerf Tiny [3] and studies on edge AI systems [14] demonstrate that compact models can be deployed on such kind of devices and that these efforts highlight important trade-offs between performance, efficiency, and model capacity. However, the applicability of these approaches to modern LLM workloads remains limited and focused on smaller models or non-generative tasks.

In summary, while the above cited work provides valuable advances in individual dimensions of LLM efficiency, there is still a lack of unified empirical studies that jointly consider model characteristics, quantization strategies, and heterogeneous hardware platforms under consistent workloads and metrics. In particular, the distinction between prefill and decode phases in autoregressive inference has received limited attention in the literature.

This work builds upon these foundations by providing a systematic evaluation across multiple LLM families, quantization levels, and hardware configurations, with a specific focus on fine-grained performance and energy metrics. By explicitly analyzing both prefill and decode phases, we aim to offer a more comprehensive understanding of the trade-offs involved in real-world LLM deployment.

3 Methodology

The benchmarking methodology was designed to provide a reproducible and architecture-agnostic evaluation of Large Language Model (LLM) inference performance and energy efficiency, with particular emphasis on separating prompt processing (prefill) and token generation (decode) phases. The methodology consists of three main components: (i) prompt definition and categorization, (ii)

Table 1. Prompt Categories and Maximum Token Budgets.

Category	Max Input Tokens	Max Output Tokens
Content generation	128	256
Creative writing	512	512
Summarization (*light*)	1024	128
Summarization (*moderate*)	1566	256
Code analysis	2059	128
Summarization (*intermediate*)	3906	128
Summarization (*substantial*)	7631	128

phased inference probing, and (iii) metrics computation, including power and energy efficiency.

3.1 Prompts Definition

Our benchmark includes prompts from seven different tasks that vary the lengths of the input prompts and output responses to simulate different types of language model use. The prompts come from the OpenOrca [17] data set and the Government Report data set [12], while coding ones come from the MLPerf Benchmark [28]. Some of them, for example, request the summarization of longer passages of text, with maximum prompt sizes of about 4K and 8K characters. These prompts may exceed the context window limits of some edge computing systems such as with the Hailo 10H NPU. In total, each model is tested on 14 different prompts (Table 1).

3.2 Phased Inference Probing

The procedure loads individual prompts from JSON benchmark entries, replicates it to the configured batch size (set to 4 for all experiments), tokenizes with padding (and optional truncation), and runs a short warm-up generation pass before measurement. Measured inference is split into two stages, prefill and decode, because they exhibit distinct computational profiles and resource utilization patterns, enabling phase-specific performance characterization. In prefill, a forward pass processes the full prompt context in one step with key-value cache enabled, yielding high throughput and compute utilization. In decode, iterative steps reuse the cache to generate tokens one at a time, typically exhibiting memory-bound characteristics and lower token throughput. By separating the two phases, we measured differences in latency, power, and energy efficiency for each phase. The first generated token is selected from prefill logits, and each subsequent token is generated by feeding back the previous token and selecting by greedy sampling for comparability. Decode runs for the requested budget subtracting the first token already produced in prefill, while updating the attention mask to match the growing context length. Early stopping at generated End of Sequence (EOS) token is deactivated.

3.3 Metric Computation and Energy Estimation

Across prefill and decode, hardware telemetry is sampled asynchronously and summarized at phase level. For each phase, energy is estimated from the observed power trace over the measured phase duration, then average power and utilization are reported from the same window. Total energy is defined as the sum of the prefill and decode contributions, so the end-to-end figure remains directly comparable across runs.

Throughput is reported with phase-specific definitions to reflect how generation actually proceeds. In prefill, we report both first-token throughput (tokens/s) and prompt processing throughput (prompt tokens/s). In decode, throughput is computed from the tokens produced during iterative decoding. End-to-end throughput uses the actual number of generated tokens over total latency, and energy efficiency is expressed as tokens per joule using the same token count and total energy. Finally, average GPU and memory utilization are aggregated with phase-duration weighting, so the final utilization values are consistent with total runtime rather than simple phase averaging.

3.4 Hardware and Software Infrastructure

To evaluate the performance of Large Language Model (LLM) inference on different hardware architectures, the NVIDIA A100 PCIe (40 GB) has been considered as our experimental baseline [20]. The comparison included two high-performance candidates: the AMD Instinct MI210 (64 GB) and the NVIDIA H100 SXM5 (80 GB). This selection of hardware resources allows also the investigation of performance of two different software ecosystems, CUDA and ROCm, respectively.

The hardware selection allowed us to investigate two critical factors for LLMs: memory bandwidth and specialized compute engines. In fact, since the auto-regressive decoding phase of large models is typically memory-bound, the MI210 (whit 1.6 TB/s HBM2e bandwidth and its expanded 64 GB VRAM) provides a high-capacity alternative to the A100, with official benchmarks indicating competitive parity in offline inference tasks [1]. On the other side, the H100 represents a significant generational step-forward for in hardware accelerators. By leveraging HBM3 specification, by achieving 3.35 TB/s bandwidth, the H100 introduces a dedicated Transformer Engine that is theoretically capable of delivering up to a 30-fold increase in inference throughput over the A100 baseline [22].

All benchmarks are conducted within a standardized virtualized environment to reflect modern cloud-native deployment patterns. The experiment utilizes virtual machines (VMs) provisioned with 16 virtual CPUs, leveraging the OpenStack cloud operating system for full virtualization. The underlying host hardware features high-performance AMD EPYC processors across different generations (including 7313 "Milan", "Rome", and "Genoa"), ensuring that the host CPU does not become a bottleneck during the pre-processing or tokenization phases. In our OpenStack-based IaaS environment, GPUs are exposed to virtual machines via PCI passthrough. The GPUs are neither virtualized nor partitioned; each virtual machine therefore accesses the assigned GPU in bare-metal mode, with direct and exclusive access to the physical device.

For the sake of consistency and reproducibility, we employ optimized software stacks tailored to each architecture, using Python 3.10.12 and `PyTorch 2.8.0` as the primary execution framework. On NVIDIA Ecosystems, tests are executed using the CUDA 12.6 runtime, along with `transformers 5.5.0`, `GPTQModel 5.8.0` and `accelerate 1.14.0` libraries, as bundled in the quantization-latest-gpu official HuggingFace Docker image. The AMD Ecosystem uses the ROCm 7.1 open software platform, with the environment supported by `transformers 5.3.0`, `GPTQModel 5.8.0` and `accelerate 1.13.0` from the transformers-pytorch-amd-gpu image. This dual-stack approach allows us to measure not just raw hardware performance, but the maturity and efficiency of the respective software compilers and runtimes when handling high-throughput inference workloads across different hardware generations.

On the Raspberry Pi5 with the Hailo-10H LLM module, tests are executed in the Raspberry Pi operating system based on Debian 13 Trixie with Python 3.13.5 and `hailoRT 5.1.1`. The Hailo-10H is a second-generation edge AI acceleration module specifically designed to enable on-device inference of Large Language Models (LLMs), Vision-Language Models (VLMs), and other generative AI workloads under strict power constraints. The Hailo-10H module includes on-module LPDDR4/LPDDR4X memory with 8 GB memory, enabling the execution of transformer-based models without reliance on external memory bandwidth.

3.5 Candidate Models

The evaluation of candidate models required understanding of the structural mechanisms dictating hardware compatibility. Modern open-weight architectures have largely transitioned from naive scaling toward sophisticated topologies designed to maximize reasoning density while strictly bounding static memory footprints and dynamic memory bandwidth. We curated a cohort of compact models released between late 2024 and early 2026, selected for their architectural diversity, open-weight availability, and suitability for single-VM or edge deployment (See Table 3). Where applicable, native precision models are benchmarked alongside 4-bit quantized variants, including specific compiled versions from the Hailo Model Zoo [10].

Qwen2.5. Qwen2.5-1.5B-Instruct is a 1.54B parameter causal language model utilizing Rotary Positional Embeddings (RoPE), SwiGLU activations, and RMSNorm [25]. To optimize throughput and KV cache efficiency during inference, it employs Grouped Query Attention (GQA) with 12 query and 2 key-value heads. The architecture consists of 28 layers (1536 hidden, 8960 intermediate) and a 151,936-token vocabulary with tied embeddings. Pre-trained on a 7-trillion token multilingual corpus, it natively supports a 32,768-token context window and an 8,192-token generation length.

For Hailo benchmarking comparability, a 4-bit GPTQ quantized variant (128 group size, symmetric) by Unsloth [5,9] has been also tested. GPTQ minimizes layer-wise reconstruction error via the inverse Hessian matrix of the layer inputs, dynamically compensating for rounding errors.

Qwen3.5. The Qwen3.5 series utilizes the Qwen3-Next hybrid framework, transitioning to a native vision-language architecture [24]. It interleaves Gated Delta Networks (for efficient linear attention) with Gated Attention mechanisms (for global dependency modeling), supporting a native 262,144-token context window. In the study, three models have been evaluated:

- **0.8B**: Considered to be optimized for high-efficiency deployment, featuring 24 layers (1024 hidden), 16 linear attention heads, and 8 query/2 KV gated heads.
- **4B**: A 32-layer (2560 hidden) mid-scale model, it adopts an eight-block layout sequence (three Gated DeltaNet-FFN blocks followed by one Gated Attention-FFN block). It utilizes 32 linear heads and 16 query/4 KV gated heads, optimized for the integrated reasoning mode.
- **9B**: The upper-bound dense specialist maintains 32 layers but expands the hidden dimension to 4096 and the FFN to 12288. It retains 32 linear and 16 gated query heads, offering representational capacity that rivals much larger models in knowledge-intensive STEM benchmarks.

Llama 3.2. Llama-3.2-3B-Instruct is a 3.21B parameter model distilled from the 8B and 70B Llama 3.1 models and pre-trained on a 15-trillion token corpus [19]. It utilizes GQA and a 128k-token vocabulary, supporting a native 128k context window for long-form agentic tasks. At full FP16 precision, the model requires over 7 GB of VRAM. Because this footprint renders it unviable for edge hardware like the Raspberry Pi with sufficient KV cache, we evaluated three distinct deployment variants across the target platforms: On the NVIDIA and AMD GPUs, we benchmarked the native unquantized baseline alongside a 4-bit Quantized Low-Rank Adaptation (QLoRA) variant [8]. Utilizing the NormalFloat (NF4) data type and Double Quantization (DQ), this QLoRA variant shrinks the footprint to approximately 4.0 GB. For deployment on the Hailo-10H, we utilized a highly optimized, compiled A8W4 variant. By employing INT4 group-wise quantization for weights, its static footprint further compresses to 2.62 GB, achieving 10 to 12 tokens per second on the edge module.

DeepSeek. DeepSeek-R1-Distill-Qwen-1.5B draw out the advanced reasoning capabilities of the 671B Mixture-of-Experts (MoE) DeepSeek-R1 model into a dense transformer footprint [6]. Fine-tuned on the Qwen2.5-Math-1.5B base using 800,000 curated MoE generations, this 1.5B parameter model inherits complex Chain-of-Thought (CoT) behaviors, including self-verification and reflection. It achieves 28.9% on AIME 2024 and 83.9% on MATH-500. Like the Llama

Table 2. Native (Unquantized) Candidate Models: Architectural Comparison.

Model	$Q_{2.5}$-1.5B	$Q_{3.5}$-0.8B	$Q_{3.5}$-4B	$Q_{3.5}$-9B	$L_{3.2}$-3B	DS_{R1}-1.5B
Params (B)	1.54	0.8	4	9	3.21	1.5
Layers	28	24	32	32	28	28
Hidden Size	1536	1024	2560	4096	3072	1536
FFN size	8960	3584	9216	12288	8192	8960
Attention (Q/KV)	12/2	8/2	16/4	16/4	24/8	12/2
Linear Att. Heads (K/V)	–	16/16	16/32	16/32	–	–
Context Window	32,768	262,144	262,144	262,144	131,072	131,072
Vocabulary	151,936	248,320	248,320	248,320	128,256	151,936
RoPE	Yes	Yes	Yes	Yes	Yes	Yes
Tied Embeddings	Yes	Yes	Yes	No	Yes	No

variants, its memory footprint is constrained using bitsandbytes (BNB) 4-bit NF4 double quantization [4], preserving its logical integrity with minimal accuracy degradation.

3.6 Hailo GenAI Compiled Models

For NPU-accelerated benchmarking on the Raspberry Pi 5 platform, we evaluate highly optimized compiled models from the Hailo GenAI ModelZoo [10]:

- DeepSeek-R1-Distill-Qwen-1.5B
- Qwen2.5-1.5B-Instruct
- Llama-3.2-3B-Instruct

To enable foundation models to operate within the AI HAT+ 2's 8 GB memory and sub-5W power constraints, the Hailo-10H employs aggressive INT4 quantization, achieving 40 TOPS through a hybrid A8W4-INT architecture. Advanced optimization techniques, including GPTQ [9] and QuaROT [2], mitigate the accuracy loss caused by low-bit quantization by compensating for numerical error and normalizing activation outliers [32]. Benchmarks show that natural language understanding and reasoning tasks remain largely resilient to INT4 compression, whereas code generation tasks experience substantial performance degradation due to their sensitivity to precise token prediction [15] (Table 2).

4 Results

4.1 Native Precision Models

In this section we present a comparative analysis of Large Language Model (LLM) inference workloads executed on different architectures: NVIDIA A100,

Table 3. Hailo Compiled Models (A8W4): Architectural and Runtime Comparison.

Model	DeepSeek-R1-1.5B	Qwen2.5-1.5B	Llama3.2-3B
Quantization scheme	A8W4, Symm., G-W	A8W4, Symm., G-W	A8W4, Symm., G-W
Parameters	1.5B	1.5B	3B
Model size	2.37 GB	1.64 GB	3.13 GB
Context length	2048	2048	2048
Load time (s)	4.99	5.17	12.61
TTFT (s)	0.74	0.37	1.47
TPS	7.98	7.35	2.67

NVIDIA H100 and AMD MI210. Running a model in its native numerical precision (e.g., BF16, FP16, or FP8, rather than weight-only INT8/INT4 quantization) is often preferable when predictive accuracy, numerical robustness, or latency are prioritized over maximizing memory efficiency. The metrics collected focus on power consumption, resource utilization, throughput, and energy efficiency. Results are reported using both aggregated metrics per model and interval-averaged metrics per GPU (or NPU), as derived from the collected measurements.

Power Consumption. Figure 1 and Fig. 2 report the average power consumption during the decode and prefill phases, grouped by GPU architecture. The NVIDIA H100 consistently exhibits the highest absolute power consumption

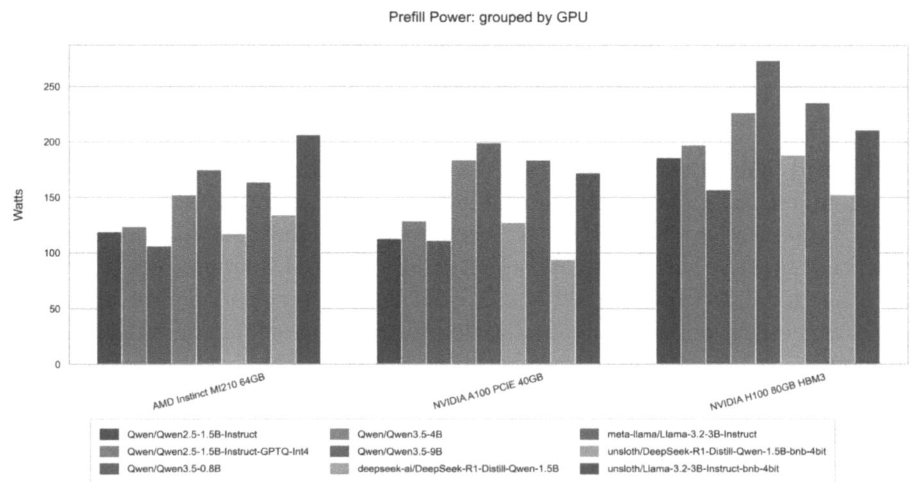

Fig. 1. Power consumption of the prefill phase in terms of Watt for each LLM model, grouped by accelerators

across all evaluated models in both phases. This behavior reflects the higher computational density of the H100 architecture.

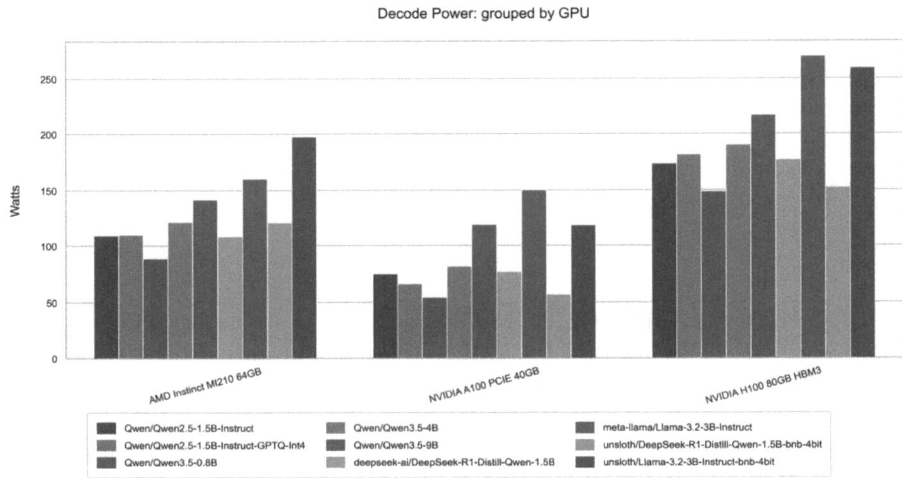

Fig. 2. Power consumption of the decode phase in terms of Watt for each LLM model, grouped by accelerators

In contrast, the NVIDIA A100 shows lower and more stable power consumption, with limited variability across models. The AMD MI210 presents power consumption that is in line, particularly during the prefill phase, with those of the NVIDIA A100, demonstrating the technical balance between the two models.

It is important to note that higher power consumption does not directly imply lower efficiency. Therefore, power metrics must be interpreted jointly with performance and energy-efficiency results.

GPU and Memory Utilization. In Fig. 3 the average GPU utilization is shown, highlighting clear architectural differences between the GPU used for this study. In particular, the AMD MI210 achieves the highest sustained utilization, indicating effective saturation of compute units by LLM inference workloads. On the other hand, NVIDIA A100 and NVIDIA H100 reach moderate utilization levels, suggesting partial under-utilization for some model configurations across workloads.

Memory utilization patterns, reported in Fig. 4, are primarily model-dependent. Larger models approach high memory occupancy on all platforms. AMD MI210 and H100 show similar memory utilization trends, despite the differences of their HBM capacities, while the NVIDIA A100 tends to reach high memory utilization earlier, potentially limiting scalability for larger models.

Overall, compute utilization differentiates GPU platforms more strongly than memory utilization.

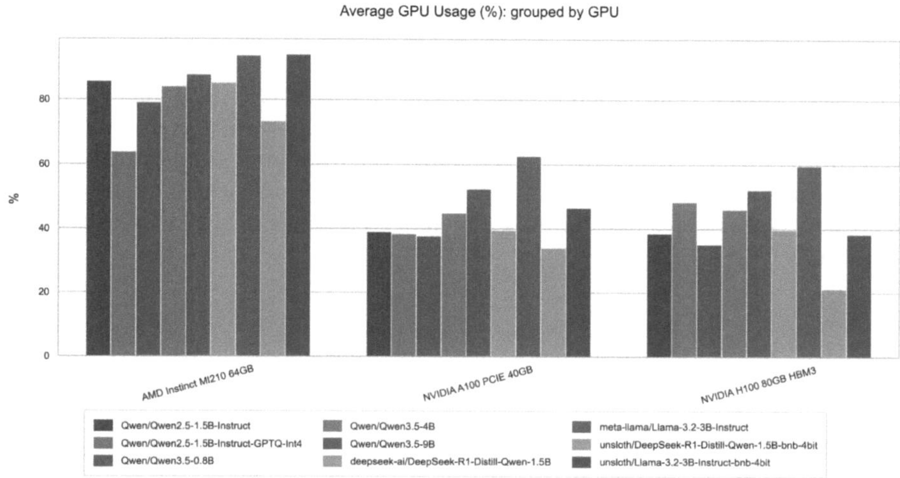

Fig. 3. GPU usage in terms of percentage for each LLM model, grouped by accelerators

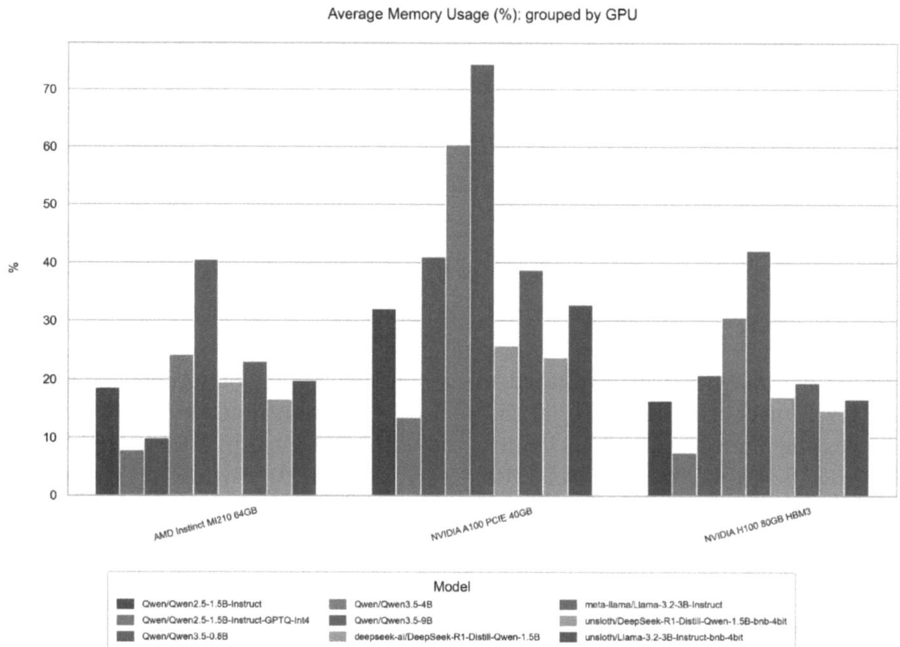

Fig. 4. Memory usage in terms of percentage for each LLM model, grouped by accelerators

Throughput and Energy Efficiency. Prefill and decode throughput results are reported in Figs. 5 and 6. The NVIDIA H100 consistently delivers the highest throughput across all evaluated models, with particularly strong performance during the decode phase. The NVIDIA A100 provides stable and predictable throughput, although at lower levels compared to the H100. The AMD MI210 shows substantially lower throughput, especially during prefill, indicating reduced token generation performance under the evaluated conditions.

These results highlight the impact of architectural features such as next-generation tensor cores and improved memory pipelines on LLM inference performance.

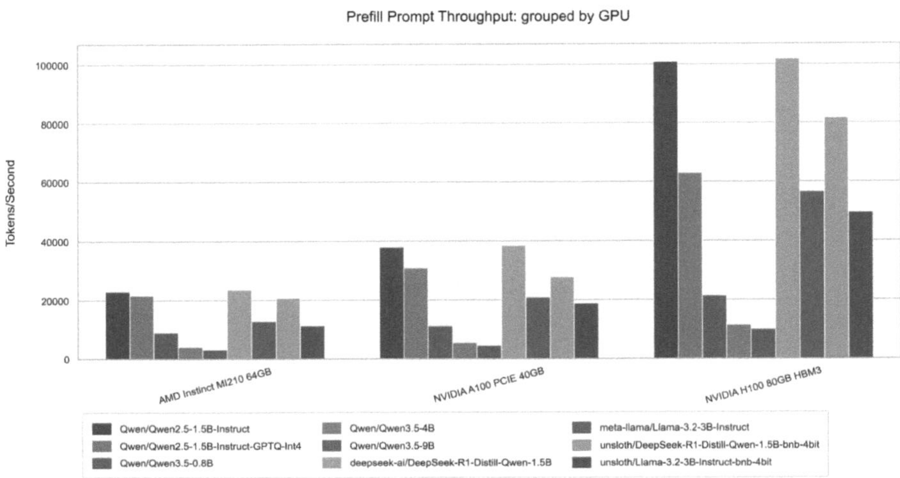

Fig. 5. Throughput of the prefill phase in terms of token per second for each LLM model, grouped by accelerators

Energy efficiency was evaluated using the tokens-per-joule metric, reported in Fig. 7. Considering the lower absolute power consumption, the NVIDIA A100 achieves the highest energy efficiency across all models. Despite their HBM hardware specifications, the NVIDIA H100 and AMD MI210 provides similar results in terms of efficiency indicating that lower power draw for AMD MI210 does not compensate for reduced throughput.

4.2 Quantized Models

This section presents a comparative analysis of the three Large Language Model (LLM) inference workloads executed on the Hailo-10H board against comparable quantized version on GPUs. It is important to note a technical caveat regarding the execution of 4-bit weights-only quantized models on the evaluated data center GPUs. While architectures such as Hopper feature advanced Tensor Cores that natively support mixed-precision formats (e.g., FP8, FP16, BF16, and TF32), they lack native hardware acceleration for 4-bit computation [22].

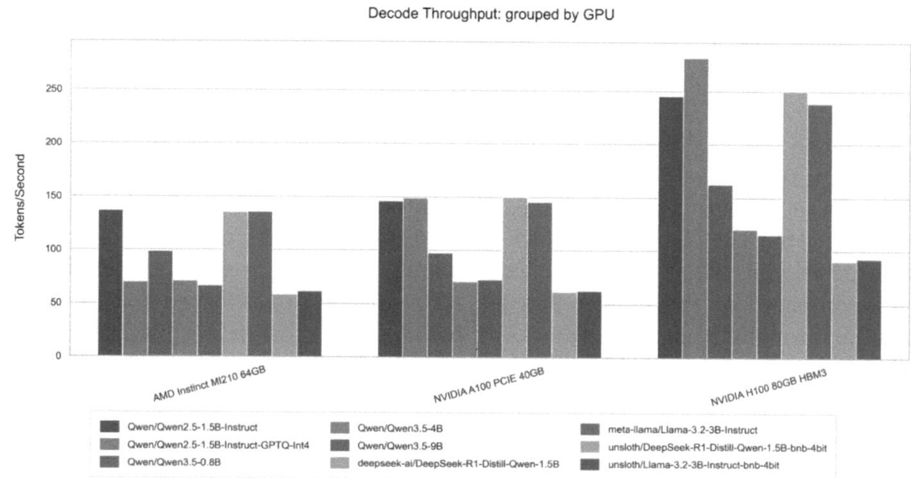

Fig. 6. Throughput of the decode phase in terms of token per second for each LLM model, grouped by accelerators

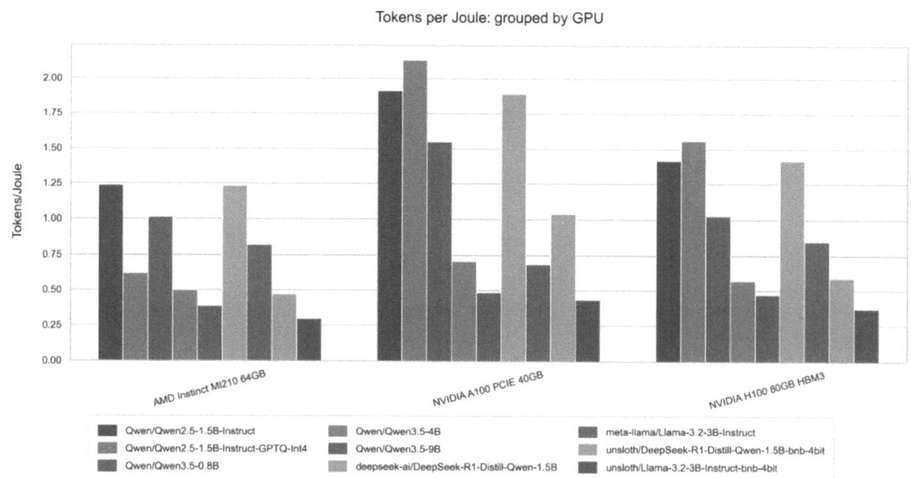

Fig. 7. Efficiency in terms of token per joule for each LLM model, grouped by accelerators

Consequently, running INT4 or 4-bit quantized models on Hopper platforms primarily optimizes memory footprint and bandwidth. During execution, these architectures rely on a kind of software emulation, requiring the 4-bit weights to be dequantized to INT8 or FP16 in the register file prior to computation. The quantised models were presented in Sect. 3.6, but for each of them, a GPU version and a compiled NPU version are actually compared:

- DeepSeek-R1-Distill-Qwen-1.5B
- Qwen2.5-1.5B-Instruct
- Llama-3.2-3B-Instruct

Figure 8 and Fig. 9 show the decode throughput and the decode power consumption, respectively, on the four platforms. Figure 10 shows instead the efficiency in terms of token per joule. Analyzing the outcomes from the three figures it is clear that the Hailo-10H shows all the typical features of a low power platform positioning itself in an excellent ranking, depending on the model chosen, even compared to the more renowned H100 in our test. On the contrary, the decode throughput shows a value well below the 40 tokens per second considered to be the minimum acceptable threshold for interactive LLM usage [30].

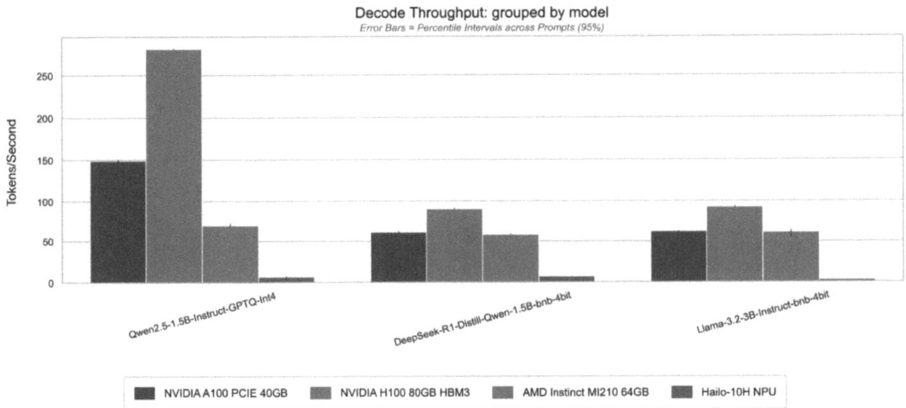

Fig. 8. Throughput in terms of token per second for the 4 accelerators, grouped by LLM model

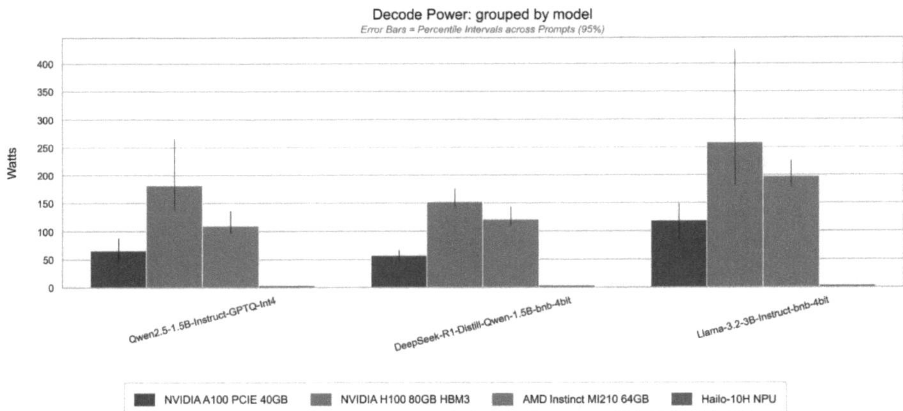

Fig. 9. Power consumption for the decode phase in terms of Watt for the 4 accelerators, grouped by LLM model

Although accelerators such as Hailo-10H do not meet the commonly accepted threshold for interactive LLM usage (≈40 tokens/s), they remain well suited for offline, edge, and background inference workloads, where energy efficiency dominates over latency. In such scenarios, token-per-joule efficiency becomes the primary optimization metric rather than raw throughput.

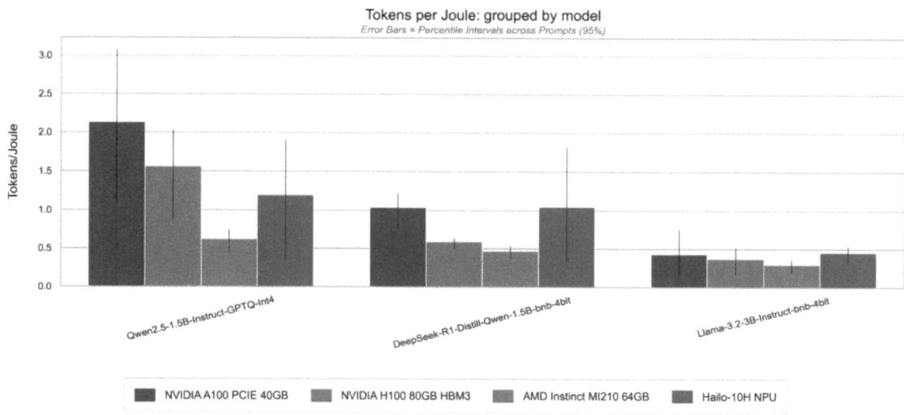

Fig. 10. Efficiency in terms of token per joule for the 4 accelerators, grouped by LLM model

5 Conclusions

The research activity presented in this study is intended to provide a concrete understanding on the trade-offs involved in deploying LLMs on different computing platforms. By analyzing performance and energy efficiency metrics under consistent workloads, this study highlights how architectural features, hardware design and optimization techniques may influence LLM inference behavior. Rather than identifying just a single optimal deployment solution, the results emphasize the importance of quantization strategy and hardware capabilities, having the model sizes aligned on the proposed usage scenario, in particular when considering throughput, latency, and energy consumption.

From a performance and energy-efficiency perspective, the NVIDIA H100 emerges as the most suitable platform for high-throughput LLM inference, particularly for decode-intensive workloads. The NVIDIA A100 remains a reliable and predictable solution for production environments with moderate performance requirements and costs. The AMD MI210, while exhibiting similar power consumption in respect to the NVIDIA A100, underperforms in terms of throughput and energy efficiency, suggesting that current limitations are primarily related to software maturity of ROCm suite and configuration tuning rather than hardware power characteristics alone.

Overall, the results indicate that energy efficiency in LLM inference workloads is driven primarily by achievable throughput rather than by raw power consumption. Moreover, while the NVIDIA H100 achieves the highest energy efficiency, confirming that its higher absolute power consumption is compensated by substantially higher throughput, the AMD MI210 shows the lowest tokens-per-joule values, indicating that reduced power draw does not offset lower performance.

Regarding the Hailo-10H module, it seems clear that the low energy consumption features do not compensate for the throughput which, being below 40 tokens per second, does not allow for responsive usage. Despite that, Hailo-10H remain well suited for scenarios (e.g. offline, edge, and background inference workloads) where the token-per-joule efficiency becomes the primary optimization metric rather than raw throughput.

References

1. Advanced Micro Devices, Inc. (AMD), et al.: AMD Instinct^{TM} MI210 accelerators (2022). https://www.amd.com/en/products/accelerators/instinct/mi200/mi210.html
2. Ashkboos, S., et al.: QuaRot: outlier-free 4-bit inference in rotated LLMs (2024). https://arxiv.org/abs/2404.00456
3. Banbury, C. et al.: MLPerf Tiny benchmark (2021). https://arxiv.org/abs/2106.07597
4. Bitsandbytes Foundation, et al.: Bitsandbytes-foundation/bitsandbytes: accessible large language models via K-bit quantization for PyTorch. https://github.com/bitsandbytes-foundation/bitsandbytes
5. Daniel Han, M.H., et al.: Unsloth (2023). https://github.com/unslothai/unsloth
6. DeepSeek-AI, et al.: DeepSeek-R1: Incentivizing reasoning capability in LLMs via reinforcement learning (2025). https://arxiv.org/abs/2501.12948
7. Dettmers, T., et al.: LLM.int8(): 8-bit matrix multiplication for transformers at scale. In: Proceedings of the 36th International Conference on Neural Information Processing Systems, NIPS'22 (2022)
8. Dettmers, T., et al.: QLoRA: efficient finetuning of quantized LLMs (2023). https://arxiv.org/abs/2305.14314
9. Frantar, E., et al.: GPTQ: accurate post-training quantization for generative pre-trained transformers. In: 11th International Conference on Learning Representations (2023)
10. Hailo-AI, et al.: Hailo Model Zoo. https://github.com/hailo-ai/hailo_model_zoo
11. Henderson, P., et al.: Towards the systematic reporting of the energy and carbon footprints of machine learning (2022). https://arxiv.org/abs/2002.05651
12. Huang, L., et al.: Efficient attentions for long document summarization. In: Proceedings of the 2021 Conference of the North American Chapter of the Association for Computational Linguistics: Human Language Technologies, Online, June 2021, pp. 1419–1436. Association for Computational Linguistics (2021). https://doi.org/10.18653/v1/2021.naacl-main.112, https://aclanthology.org/2021.naacl-main.112
13. Jouppi, N.P., et al.: Ten lessons from three generations shaped Google's TPUv4i : industrial product. In: 2021 ACM/IEEE 48th Annual International Symposium on Computer Architecture (ISCA), pp. 1–14 (2021). https://doi.org/10.1109/ISCA52012.2021.00010

14. Khouas, A.R., et al.: Training machine learning models at the edge: a survey (2024). https://arxiv.org/abs/2403.02619
15. Kurtic, E., et al.: "give me BF16 or give me death"? accuracy-performance trade-offs in LLM quantization (2025). https://arxiv.org/abs/2411.02355
16. Kwon, W., et al.: Efficient memory management for large language model serving with PagedAttention. In: Proceedings of the ACM SIGOPS 29th Symposium on Operating Systems Principles (2023)
17. Lian, W., et al.: OpenOrca: an open dataset of GPT augmented FLAN reasoning traces (2023). https://huggingface.co/datasets/Open-Orca/OpenOrca
18. Lin, J., et al.: AWQ: activation-aware weight quantization for on-device LLM compression and acceleration. In: Gibbons, P., Pekhimenko, G., Sa, C.D. (eds.) Proceedings of Machine Learning and Systems, vol. 6, pp. 87–100 (2024)
19. Meta Llama AI team, et al.: The Llama 3 herd of models (2024). https://arxiv.org/abs/2407.21783
20. NVIDIA Corporation, et al.: NVIDIA A100 tensor core GPU architecture (2020). https://www.nvidia.com/content/dam/en-zz/Solutions/Data-Center/nvidia-ampere-architecture-whitepaper.pdf
21. NVIDIA Corporation, et al.: FasterTransformer (2021). https://github.com/NVIDIA/FasterTransformer
22. NVIDIA Corporation, et al.: NVIDIA H100 tensor core GPU architecture (2023). https://resources.nvidia.com/en-us-hopper-architecture/nvidia-h100-tensor-c
23. Patterson, D., et al.: Carbon emissions and large neural network training (2021). https://arxiv.org/abs/2104.10350
24. Qwen Team, et al.: Qwen3.5: towards native multimodal agents, February 2026. https://qwen.ai/blog?id=qwen3.5
25. Qwen Team, Yang, A., et al.: Qwen2.5 technical report (2025). https://arxiv.org/abs/2412.15115
26. Raspberry Pi Ltd., et al.: Raspberry Pi 5 (2023). https://www.raspberrypi.com
27. Raspberry Pi Ltd., et al.: Introducing the Raspberry Pi AI HAT+ 2: generative AI on Raspberry Pi 5 (2026). https://www.raspberrypi.com/news/introducing-the-raspberry-pi-ai-hat-plus-2-generative-ai-on-raspberry-pi-5/
28. Reddi, V.J., et al.: MLPerf inference benchmark. In: Proceedings of the ACM/IEEE 47th Annual International Symposium on Computer Architecture, ISCA 2020, pp. 446–459. IEEE Press (2020). https://doi.org/10.1109/ISCA45697.2020.00045
29. Sanh, V., et al.: DistilBERT, a distilled version of BERT: smaller, faster, cheaper and lighter (2020). https://arxiv.org/abs/1910.01108
30. Song, P., et al.: How many tokens per second is "good" for local LLMs? ML Journey, February 2026. https://mljourney.com/how-many-tokens-per-second-is-good-for-local-llms/, analysis of LLM inference speed, usability thresholds, and user perception in tokens per second
31. Strubell, E., et al.: Energy and policy considerations for deep learning in NLP (2019). https://arxiv.org/abs/1906.02243
32. Team et al.: Edge AI deployment of LLMs using Hailo-10H AI accelerators, January 2026. https://web.archive.org/web/20260118135652/https://hailo.ai/blog/bringing-generative-ai-to-the-edge-llm-on-hailo-10h/
33. Wan, Z., et al.: Efficient large language models: a survey (2024). https://arxiv.org/abs/2312.03863
34. Yao, Z., et al.: ZeroQuant: efficient and affordable post-training quantization for large-scale transformers. In: Koyejo, S., Mohamed, S., Agarwal, A., Belgrave, D., Cho, K., Oh, A. (eds.) Advances in Neural Information Processing Systems, vol. 35, pp. 27168–27183. Curran Associates, Inc. (2022)

dGanX: a Python Library to Generate MA-XRF Raw Data Out of RGB Images via a Distributed Computing Approach

Alessandro Bombini[1(✉)], Serena Barone[1,2], Marta Magalini[3], Fernando García-Avello Bofías[1], Daniele Spiga[4], Tommaso Tedeschi[4], and Chiara Ruberto[1,2]

[1] Istituto Nazionale di Fisica Nucleare, Sezione di Firenze, Sesto Fiorentino (FI), Italy
alessandro.bombini@fi.infn.it
[2] Dipartimento di Fisica, Università di Firenze, Sesto Fiorentino (FI), Italy
[3] Istituto Nazionale di Fisica Nucleare, Sezione di Torino, Turin, Italy
[4] Istituto Nazionale di Fisica Nucleare (INFN), Sezione di Perugia, Perugia, Italy

Abstract. In this paper we present **dGanX**, a Python library to generate a large number of X-ray Fluorescence Macro maps (MA-XRF) from coloured RGB images, in a distributed manner across multiple computing nodes. To generate a synthetic MA-XRF, a Monte Carlo method is used, where each MA-XRF pixel signal is sampled out of an XRF signal probability function. Such probability function is computed using a database of couples (pigment characteristic XRF signal, RGB), by a weighted sum of such pigment XRF spectra by proximity of the image RGB to the pigment characteristic RGB. To distribute the synthetic MA-XRF generation of multiple images, the code was refactored such that it can be distributed on a Kubernetes cluster via Dask. The code is open source and freely available.

Keywords: Simulation methods and programs · Analysis and statistical methods · Computing · X-ray fluorescence (XRF) systems

1 Introduction

In the application of statistical and machine learning methods to data obtained from spectral imaging of cultural heritage (CH), one of the main issues is the lack of huge amounts of available data (see, e.g., [6,17], and references therein). Nevertheless, in the last decade, we have witnessed a truly remarkable rise of the applications of such methods in the CH sector, also in the realm of nuclear physics applied to CH diagnostics and imaging These techniques are being increasingly utilized to support researchers in interpreting data obtained through non-invasive testing approaches [20], such as hyperspectral imaging [18,32,35], neutron radiography, gamma spectroscopy, and X-ray-based imaging modalities [19,30]. Such algorithms can reveal correlations and hidden structures in the

O. Gervasi et al. (Eds.): ICCSA 2026 Workshops, LNCS 16758, pp. 70–83, 2027.
https://doi.org/10.1007/978-3-032-30497-1_5

datasets, providing valuable clues about an artifact's material makeup [24], dating, and preservation status [11,17,34][1].

One of the most notable nuclear methodologies applied to the field of Cultural Heritage is X-Ray Fluorescence (XRF) spectroscopy, particularly in its macro-scale mapping variant (MA-XRF). In Macro X-Ray Fluorescence (MA-XRF) imaging, the system generates a data cube in which each pixel is associated with a spectrum containing fluorescence peaks indicative of the elemental makeup of pigments within the pictorial layers. Due to the vast quantity of pixel-wise XRF spectra compared to the limited variety of pigment palettes, MA-XRF data cubes provide a particularly suitable structure for implementing unsupervised statistical learning techniques [30].

An intriguing application of Computer Vision on such datasets is the so-called *virtual colouring*, *i.e.* the creation of a synthetic RGB image from the MA-XRF data cube of an artwork under examination. This can have practical implications in the domain of conservation, as MA-XRF can detect elemental signals, even from damaged or aged surfaces (paintings or frescoes alike) [1,13,27], and allows analysis of otherwise obscured features, including underdrawings, pentimenti [10,29], areas of previous restoration, or pigment loss [12,22]. Such computer-aided workflows offer conservators and heritage specialists a new channel of interpretation by providing a complementary visual output (*i.e.*, the rendered RGB reconstruction).

Although few attempts have been conducted [3–6], yet, the availability of high-quality datasets for training these models is often constrained by several factors: sluggish acquisition speeds due to hardware limitations, legal and Intellectual Property (IP) restrictions, limited access to test artifacts, the scarcity and expense of suitable instrumentation, and the necessity for highly skilled operators. Moreover, unlike in more standardized scientific domains, data harmonization remains a challenge, given the varied custom setups of acquisition systems, heterogeneous measurement conditions, and detector types.

This justifies the emphasis put on the creation of ad hoc *synthetic* MA-XRF dataset [17]. In this paper, we present **dGanX**, a Python library for creating synthetic dataset of MA-XRF images in a distributed manner, starting from

1. A (set of) RGB image(s); and
2. A Database of pigmentsl.

Such database must have

a. A characteristic XRF signal;
b. A characteristic, 8-bit, RGB colour.

dGanX is based on, and it is an evolution of, **ganX**[2], and it will use (b) to associate pigment(s) to RGB pixels, and (a) as a probability distribution to

[1] For additional machine learning implementations within Cultural Heritage, refer to [14,21], and references therein.
[2] https://pypi.org/project/ganx/, https://github.com/androbomb/ganX.

generate the MA-XRF data cube via Monte Carlo methods. The source code is freely available[3].

The contribution of this paper is:

- To present the code for the distributed generation of synthetic MA-XRF data-cubes;
- Present an example of integration of distributed ML inference on synthetic MA-XRF data *on the fly*, meaning at generation time;
- Present an example of a comparison of a real and a generated synthetic data-cube.

The paper is organised as follows: in Sect. 2, we discuss the algorithm to generate MA-XRF datacubes out of RGB images and a pigment palette; in Sect. 3 we discuss how the distributed generation of multiple MA-XRF on a `Dask` cluster is achieved; in Sect. 4, we provide an example of usage of `dGanX`; finally, in Sect. 5, we report the conclusions and future outlook.

2 How to Generate MA-XRF from RGB

Inspired by the work done in [17], where the authors generate a synthetic dataset of single-point XRF histogram by using the Fundamental Parameters (FP) method, a physical model based on Sherman's equations for generating XRF spectra of a sample of known composition [28], we started the development of a simple Python package capable of creating MA-XRF data cubes starting from a RGB image and a database of pigments' XRF signal. The data generation algorithm comprises two main parts:

1. A RGB clustering of the input image(s), performed with an iterative K-Means, to reduce the colour noise, thus *quantising* the RGB image;
2. A Monte Carlo method to generate a XRF histogram of counts for each pixel, after having unsupervisedly associated a (set of) pigment(s) to each RGB pixel.

To perform step 2. above, we compute (pixel-by-pixel) a set of similarity measures in RGB spaces, between the (quantised) RGB and the database indexed pigments' characteristic RGB; then, a hard thresholding is performed, to (unsupervisedly) reduce the number of pigments composing a color.

The full pseudocode of the MA-XRF data generation is reported in Algorithm 1.

The actual code implementation in Python leverages the `NumPy` [16,31] *vectorization* to speed up the computation.

Note on [17]*:* Notice that it is possible to use the FP approach of [17] to build the characteristic pigments' XRF signal; this implies that it is straightforward to use the `dGanX` library to leverage the synthetic data generation of [17] from single-point XRF to MA-XRF data cubes.

[3] https://baltig.infn.it/bombini/fastextendedvision-dask.

Algorithm 1. Generate MA-XRF

Require: RGBClustering, distrToXrf, colorSimilarity ▷ Import relevant methods
procedure GenerateXRF(pigments_dict_data = $\mathcal{D}_{color,hist}$, rgb_img = R)
    $R \leftarrow$ RGBClustering(R) ▷ Quantise RGB
    init X ▷ Initialise empty XRF data cube
    for $r \in R$ **do** ▷ Iterate over clusters
        init d ▷ Initialise empty distribution
        for $(c, h) \in \mathcal{D}$ **do** ▷ Iterate over palette
            $\alpha \leftarrow$ colorSimilarity(c, r) ▷ Compute similarity scores
            if $\alpha \geq \alpha_{th}$ **then**
                $d \leftarrow d + \alpha \cdot h$ ▷ Sum thresholded distribution
        $d \leftarrow d/||d||$ ▷ Normalise distribution
        $X[\text{idx}(X) == r] \leftarrow$ distrToXrf(d) ▷ Use Monte Carlo method only on the Cluster's pixel
    return X

On the other hand, **dGanX** can be used out of *real* data, comprising measurement whose source origin is complicated enough that no analytic method (such as the FP method) can be used to generate the XRF signal. This latter situation is quite common in the field of Cultural Heritage applications.

Additional note: Notice also that the spectral signal is not limited to be an XRF characteristic signal; it is possible to generate data cubes out of other spectroscopy techniques, not even in the X-Ray range, such as *Fourier Transform InfraRed spectroscopy* (FTIR), HyperSpectral Imaging (HSI), Particle Induced X-Ray Emission (PIXE), etc., just to name a few.

3 Distributed Generation of MA-XRF with Dask

Since the algorithm converts RGB images into MA-XRF, one may want to start generating a *huge* dataset of MA-XRF starting from, for example, *all* the pictures in PNG/JPG format representing pictorial artworks contained in WikiData, in order to have a huge dataset for computer vision application, as done, for example, in [6].

By scraping the WikiData SPARQL endpoint[4], one may get over 230.000 CC0 RGB images, which can be transformed, one by one, in MA-XRF using algorithm 1. The algorithm by **dGanX** simply:

1. Iterates over all RGB images;
2. Launches a single RGB-to-XRF conversion for each of them (via Algorithm 1);
3. After that, stores the generated MA-XRF image on Disk.

To speed up the generation of MA-XRF images, we can simply process each RGB-to-MA-XRF *in parallel*, distributing it not only on each independent CPU thread, but also on different CPUs on multiple computing nodes. Since each generation process is completely independent from the others, it can be massively

[4] https://query.wikidata.org/.

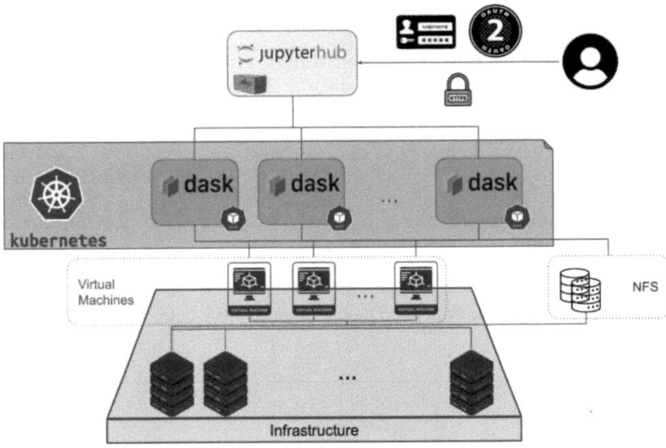

Fig. 1. Visual representation of the cloud architecture for the distributed computing setting.

parallelised, effectively reducing the generation time of the whole dataset by a factor of N, where $N = \sum_{n=1}^{N_{\text{nodes}}} t_i$ is the total number of independent threads t_i on all the computing nodes.

3.1 Distributing MA-XRF Generation Using Dask on a Kubernetes Cluster

To design, develop, test, and deploy the distributed computing approach of `dGanX` we used a Kubernetes[5] (k8s) cluster, built on top of multiple Virtual Machines (VMs). Both `Dask` [26], as well as JupyterHub[6] are executed as kubernetes applications through pods. Each pod mounts both ephemeral File System (FS) and a persistent FS of small size ($\sim O(10\text{Gb})$), designed to host the code during development. Moreover, a shared Network File System (NFS), of bigger size ($\sim O(1\text{Tb})$), has been configured in order to manage long term storage and data sharing between nodes.

From the user perspective, after an Authentication/Authorisation process handled by INDIGO-IAM[7], based on the OAuth2 protocol, the user accessess the JupyterHUB spawning page, where it is possible to pick the docker image[8] to be deployed, containing the necessary libraries. Once the JupyterHUB successfully spawns the notebook (JupyterLAB), the user can deploy and manage several Dask Clusters on Kubernetes nodes via the Dask Operator[9]. This can be done either via the embedded Dask extension in the JupyterHUB page, or via Python

[5] https://kubernetes.io/.
[6] https://jupyter.org/hub.
[7] https://github.com/indigo-iam/iam.
[8] https://www.docker.com/.
[9] https://kubernetes.dask.org/en/latest/operator_kubecluster.html.

using the `KubeCluster` interface, offered in the `dask-kubernetes` package[10]. A visual abstract of the infrastructure is reported in Fig. 1.

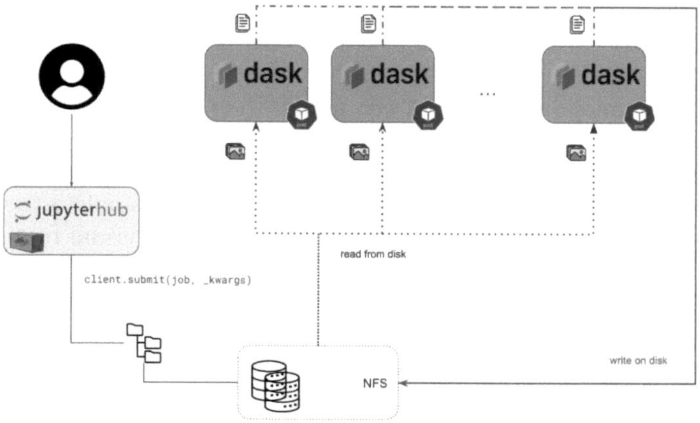

Fig. 2. Visual representation of the multi-node parallelisation with Dask. The user, via the web UI or the CLI in the JupyterHub web page, can launch the job, iterating over all RGB images in the NFS; the master node (the one running the JupyterHub) dispatch the jobs to each available node, in parallel, signaling which file has to read on the NFS. The node opens the RGB file, perform Algorithm 1, and then store the generated MA-XRF back on a specified location, with the same name as the RGB file but in `HDF5` extension.

Nevertheless, `dGanX` only assumes the existence of a `Dask` cluster (not necessarily a `KubeCluster`); the needed set up is that the code has to be available on the shared NFS, as are the RGB files, so that each node may have access to the required Python codes. After that, via a simple Command Line Interface (CLI) command, it is possible to launch the distributed generation pipeline which, at its core, is simply a parallel distribution of jobs, as reported in Algorithm 2:

Algorithm 2. Distribute Generation

Require: GENERATEXRF, KUBECLUSTER ▷ Import relevant methods
procedure DISTRIBUTEGENERATION(pigments_dict_data = $\mathcal{D}_{color,hist}$, path_to_imgs = P)
    init CLIENT ▷ Initialise KubeClient
    for $p \in P$ **do** ▷ Iterate over RGB files
        if !NOTGENERATEDYET(p) **then** ▷ Check if file has been already processed
            CLIENT.SUBMIT(GENERATEXRF , { p, $\mathcal{D}_{color,hist}$ }) ▷ Submit Job

From the master node, the user can launch via the CLI the distributed generating pipeline,

```
$ python3 create_2D_dataset_dask_distributed.py [ARGS]
```

[10] https://pypi.org/project/dask-kubernetes/, https://github.com/dask/dask-kubernetes.

and pass a set of values as arguments to specialise the generation, such as the FS path to the RGB folder, `-rootdir`, the path to store the produced MA-XRF datacubes as `HDF5`, `-storedir`, as well as the parameters describing the Algorithm 1, as the average number of counts per energy channel, `-extractionsize`, or the minimum or maximum number of RGB cluster to extract, `-clustlow` and `-clusthigh`.

After the submission of the CLI command, the master node starts iterating over the files in the NFS, packaging the necessary arguments to be passed to each node, and then submit a job to each available node; when the number of nodes are exhausted, the master node awaits the first node to complete the task, and then dispatches to it the next job, until completion. For a visual representation, see Fig. 2.

A peculiarity is that the code has to be on the NFS, since, to reduce the network communication payload, the relevant part of the codes are put in importable packages, which have to be available to all nodes. Each computing node is thus instructed to read, load, and execute the relevant code (with the passed *keywords*) *locally*, from a protected *read-only* section of the FS (the one containing the RGB images and the code), and store the result in a *writable* part of the NFS. The only relevant part of the infrastructure is that the node has (at least) reading privilege to the former, and writing privilege to the latter. The two can be different NFS, or any other shared FS, such as mounted `WebDav` FS (via, e.g., `davfs2`[11]).

3.2 Adding a Machine Learning Distributed Inference with UMAP

Sometimes, while performing analysis on MA-XRF datacubes, it may be helpful to train a *feature extractor* machine learning model to reduce the dimensionality of the data [6,7]. To show how `dGanX` can easily integrate a similar feature, we trained a `UMAP` model [23], and added it in the generation pipeline.

`UMAP` is a *manifold learning* algorithm, capable of extracting *non-linear* relation among features, and extract low-dimensional representation of data out of them. It can be used, similarly to what has been done in [6,7], as a *feature extractor* to perform *unsupervised domain adaptation*; i.e., we can train a UMAP model on the spectra of a *real* datacube, and use it to extract features from the *synthetic* MA-XRF spectra, so that it extracts features in a *domain adapted* manner. In this way, the trained `UMAP` model extracts low-dimensional representation of MA-XRF spectra which are relevant in the *domain* of the real MA-XRF datacube.

In Fig. 3, the inference of the UMAP model is shown. The `UMAP` model has been trained on the spectra contained in a single, real, MA-XRF datacube, labelled `ft` (*fine tuning*); the model learns how to map the $D = 512$ dimensional spectra to a 3-dimensional space, the *latent* space. The model was trained using the Python package of [23], `umap-learn`[12], using the values `n_neighbors`=15, `min_dist`=0.1, `metric='euclidean'`, `spread`=1.0, `local_connectivity`=1.0.

[11] https://savannah.nongnu.org/projects/davfs2.

[12] https://umap-learn.readthedocs.io/en/latest/basic_usage.html.

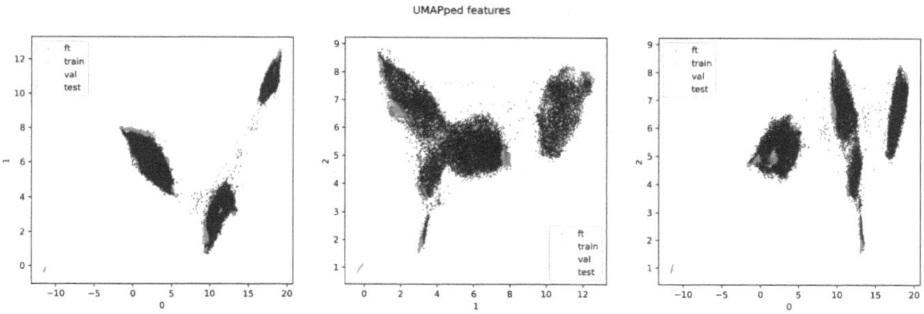

Fig. 3. Example of the action of the `UMAP` model. The three images represents the 2D projections of the 3D reduced space scatter plot. The blue dots represents the mapped low-dimensional points used for training, coming from the real datacube (where `ft` stands for *fine tuning*); the red, yellow and orange dots, instead, represents the inference of the trained `UMAP` model on different spectra, coming from the train, validation and test set (where, here, train, test and validation set are simply three different group of MA-XRF images). (Color figure online)

Now, we used the trained model to perform the inference on a set of random spectra coming from a different set of generated MA-XRF, that we call train, validation, test, since they can be used as train, validation and test in a computer vision task. We see that the low-dimensional features of these spectra, which have never been seen during training of the UMAP model, are mapped in a distribution which resembles the distribution of the real data, showing that the low-dimensional latent space provides a form of *unsupervised domain adaptation*.

In the distributed computing approach, each node, after having generated the MA-XRF datacube out of the RGB image, and stored it on NFS, applies the trained UMAP model to reduce its dimensionality, and store the dimensionally reduced datacube in the same `HDF5` file, as a different `HDF5Dataset`.

This is simply accomplished by a slight modification of Algorithm 2:

Notice that the UMAP model is *pre-trained*, i.e. it is not trained during the job, but only used for *inference*. Additionally, the model has to be loaded by each node *independently*, and thus has to be accessible from each nodes, i.e. has to be stored in the shared NFS.

Algorithm 3. Distribute Generation and `UMAP` inference

Require: GENERATEXRF, KUBECLUSTER, MODEL ▷ Import relevant methods
procedure GENERATEANDINFERENCE(pigments_dict_data = $\mathcal{D}_{color,hist}$, path_to_imgs = P)
    load(MODEL) ▷ Load model from Disk
    X = GENERATEXRF ({ p, $\mathcal{D}_{color,hist}$ }) ▷ Generate MA-XRF
    Y = MODEL (X) ▷ Perform Model inference
    StoreHDF5 (X, Y) ▷ Store results
procedure DISTRIBUTEGENERATIONANDINFERENCE(pigments_dict_data = $\mathcal{D}_{color,hist}$, path_to_imgs = P)
    init CLIENT ▷ Initialise KubeClient
    for $p \in P$ **do** ▷ Iterate over RGB files
        if !NOTGENERATEDYET(p) **then** ▷ Check if file has been already processed
            CLIENT.SUBMIT(GENERATEANDINFERENCE , { p, $\mathcal{D}_{color,hist}$ }) ▷ Submit Job

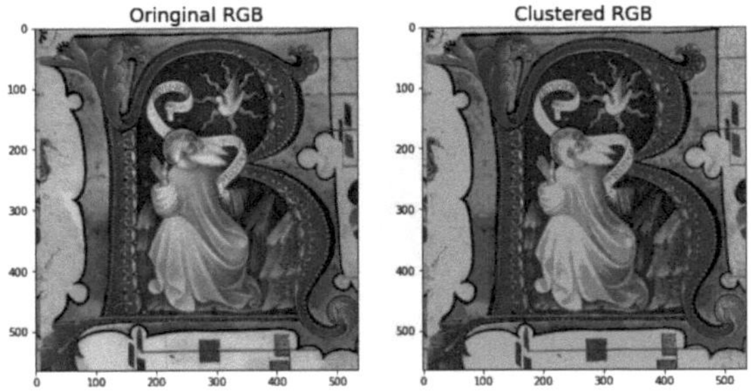

Fig. 4. Left: RGB image of Antiphonary M, folio 32. Right: clustered RGB with iterative KMeans ($K = 11$).

Using Other Models: we have presented the result of distributed ML approach using a (trained) UMAP model; nevertheless, it is easy to generalise this approach to include more complex ML models, such as a Deep Variational Embedding auto-encoder, such as the one trained on MA-XRF data in [7].

4 Example: Generation from a Real Artwork

To illustrate the usage of `dGanX`, we built a small pigment database comprising nine pigments (lead red, vermillion, organic red dye, lead tin yellow, ultramarine, azurite, indigo, malachite, chalk white). The XRF signals were taken from the open database INFRA-ART [9], while the RGB colours were obtained from standard references.

We then generated a synthetic MA-XRF dataset starting from the RGB image of the Antiphonary M, folio 32, an illuminated manuscript studied in [25]. The RGB image is shown in Fig. 4 (left). After an iterative KMeans clustering (right), the number of distinct colour regions is reduced, improving the stability of the subsequent pigment assignment.

We generated two synthetic cubes with the same parameters except for the similarity threshold α_{th}, set to 0.2 and 0.6. Figure 5 compares the elemental maps of potassium (K (Kα)) and calcium (Ca (Kα)) obtained from the real MA-XRF data and from the two synthetic versions. A lower threshold allows more pigments to contribute to each pixel, resulting in a smoother distribution; a higher threshold yields sharper, more localized maps.

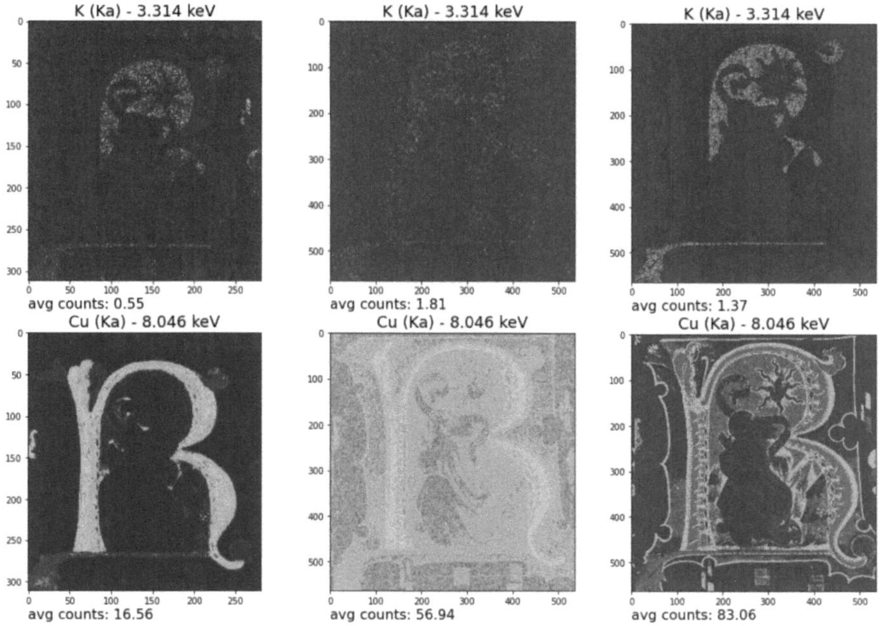

(a) Real MA-XRF (b) Synthetic $\alpha_{\text{th}} = 0.2$ (c) Synthetic $\alpha_{\text{th}} = 0.6$

Fig. 5. Comparison of elemental maps for K (Kα) and Cu (Kα).

A quantitative comparison can be performed on the integrated histogram of all XRF counts (Fig. 6). The Bhattacharyya coefficient (similarity) and the Structural Similarity Index Measure (SSIM) [33] computed on the flattened hypercubes are reported in Table 1. Both metrics indicate that the synthetic data capture the main features of the real distribution, with the lower threshold producing slightly closer agreement.

Table 1. Similarity metrics between real and synthetic MA-XRF data.

Metric	$\alpha_{\text{th}} = 0.2$	$\alpha_{\text{th}} = 0.6$
Bhattacharyya coefficient	0.8529	0.8589
SSIM	0.3491	0.3317

This example demonstrates the ability of **dGanX** to produce realistic MA-XRF data cubes from RGB images, while highlighting the impact of the similarity threshold on the output.

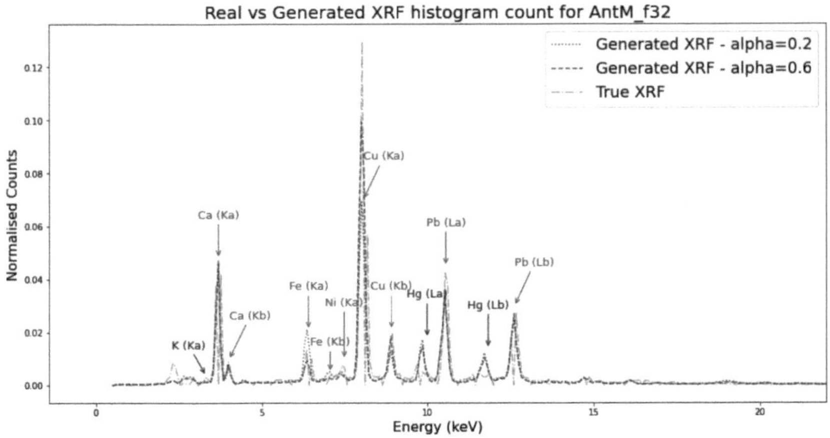

Fig. 6. Comparison of total XRF count histograms (normalised).

5 Conclusions

In this paper we have presented `dGanX`, a Python package offering methods to generate artificial new MA-XRF data cubes out of an RGB image, in a distributed manner. This package may be helpful in the synthetic dataset generation for applications of statistical and deep learning methods in the field of MA-XRF analysis, especially in (but not limited to) the field of Cultural Heritage.

The possibility of distributing the dataset generation on multiple threads on multiple computing nodes may be helpful in reducing the time needed for synthetic data generation of huge datasets, like the one needed in computer vision tasks requiring multiple synthetic datasets, like [6].

In the future, we plan to explore other approaches to distributed computing, focusing on the possibility to offload the computation on HPC clusters, via a different approach through containerisation (e.g., via *Apptainer*[13] or *Docker* containers) of the computing environment. Additionally, we will work on improving the MA-XRF generation pipeline to extend the flexibility of the package, by adding additional features, such as the possibility to generate MA-XRF data cubes without a fixed amount of signal per-pixel, but allowing for, e.g. luminosity-based number of counts. Also, we are exploring the possibility of adding Poissonian noise, as well as other noise sources.

Acknowledgments. To conduct the work presented in this contribution, we resorted to the cloud computing Software-as-a-Service infrastructure made available by the ICSC – Centro Nazionale di Ricerca in High Performance Computing, Big Data and Quantum Computing, and by AI_INFN initiative [2], as well as some servers made available by INFN-CHNet [15], the network devoted to the application of nuclear techniques to Cultural Heritage.

[13] https://apptainer.org/.

We would also like to thank the authors of the site https://infraart.inoe.ro/ [8], and WikiData (https://www.wikidata.org) and WikiMedia commons (https://commons.wikimedia.org).

We thank the authors of [25] for sharing the raw data used in Sect. 4. The analysis conducted in the aforementioned paper on the Anphitionary M belonging to the collection of San Giorgio Maggiore was funded by the Abbey of San Giorgio Maggiore.

The work of AB and TT was funded by Progetto ICSC - Spoke 2 - Codice CN00000013 - CUP I53C21000340006 - Missione 4 Istruzione e ricerca - Componente 2 Dalla ricerca all'impresa – Investimento 1.4.

Disclosure of Interests. The authors have no competing interests to declare that are relevant to the content of this article.

References

1. Alberti, R., et al.: Handheld XRF and Raman equipment for the in situ investigation of Roman finds in the Villa dei Quintili (Rome, Italy). J. Anal. At. Spectrom. **32**, 117–129 (2017). https://doi.org/10.1039/C6JA00249H, http://dx.doi.org/10.1039/C6JA00249H
2. Anderlini, L., et al.: Supporting the development of machine learning for fundamental science in a federated cloud with the AI_infn platform. arXiv preprint arXiv:2502.21266 (2025)
3. Bombini, A., Bofías, F.G.A., Ruberto, C., Taccetti, F.: A cloud-native application for digital restoration of Cultural Heritage using nuclear imaging: THESPIAN-XRF. Rendiconti Lincei. Scienze Fisiche e Naturali **34**, 867–887 (2023). https://doi.org/10.1007/s12210-023-01174-0, https://api.semanticscholar.org/CorpusID:259707375
4. Bombini, A., Anderlini, L., dell'Agnello, L., Giacomini, F., Ruberto, C., Taccetti, F.: Hyperparameter optimisation of artificial intelligence for digital REStoration of cultural heritages (AIRES-CH) models. In: Gervasi, O., Murgante, B., Misra, S., Rocha, A.M.A.C., Garau, C. (eds.) ICCSA 2022. LNCS, vol. 13377, pp. 91–106. Springer International Publishing, Cham (2022). https://doi.org/10.1007/978-3-031-10536-4_7
5. Bombini, A., Anderlini, L., dell'Agnello, L., Giacomini, F., Ruberto, C., Taccetti, F.: The AIRES-CH project: artificial intelligence for digital REStoration of cultural heritages using nuclear imaging and multidimensional adversarial neural networks. In: Sclaroff, S., Distante, C., Leo, M., Farinella, G.M., Tombari, F. (eds.) ICIAP 2022. LNCS, vol. 13231, pp. 685–700. Springer, Cham (2022). https://doi.org/10.1007/978-3-031-06427-2_57
6. Bombini, A., Bofías, F.G.A., Giambi, F., Ruberto, C.: Towards virtual painting recolouring using vision transformer on x-ray fluorescence datacubes. Mach. Learn. Sci. Technol. **6**(1), 015058 (2025). https://doi.org/10.1088/2632-2153/adb937
7. Bombini, A., Bofías, F.G.A., Bracci, C., Ginolfi, M., Ruberto, C.: Datacube segmentation via deep spectral clustering. Mach. Learn.: Sci. Technol. (2024). https://doi.org/10.1088/2632-2153/ad622f, http://iopscience.iop.org/article/10.1088/2632-2153/ad622f
8. Cortea, I.M., Chiroşca, A., Angheluţă, L.M., Seriţan, G.: Infra-art: an open access spectral library of art-related materials as a digital support tool for cultural heritage science. J. Comput. Cult. Herit. **16**(2) (2023). https://doi.org/10.1145/3593427

9. Cortea, I.M., Chiroşca, L.M., Angheluţă, L.M., Seriţan, G.: INFRA-ART: an open access spectral library of art-related materials as a digital support tool for cultural heritage science. ACM J. Comput. Cult. Herit. **16**(2) (2023)
10. Dik, J., Janssens, K., Van Der Snickt, G., van der Loeff, L., Rickers, K., Cotte, M.: Visualization of a lost painting by Vincent van Gogh using synchrotron radiation based x-ray fluorescence elemental mapping. Anal. Chem. **80**(16), 6436–6442 (2008). https://doi.org/10.1021/ac800965g
11. Dirks, M., Poole, D.: Auto-encoder neural network incorporating x-ray fluorescence fundamental parameters with machine learning. X-Ray Spectrometry **52**(3), 142–150 (2023). https://doi.org/10.1002/xrs.3340, https://analyticalsciencejournals.onlinelibrary.wiley.com/doi/abs/10.1002/xrs.3340
12. Dredge, P., Ives, S., Howard, D.L., Spiers, K.M., Yip, A., Kenderdine, S.: Mapping henry: synchrotron-sourced x-ray fluorescence mapping and ultra-high-definition scanning of an early tudor portrait of henry viii. Appl. Phys. A **121**, 789–800 (2015)
13. Fiorillo, F., Fiorentino, S., Montanari, M., Roversi Monaco, C., Del Bianco, A., Vandini, M.: Learning from the past, intervening in the present: the role of conservation science in the challenging restoration of the wall painting marriage at Cana by Luca Longhi (Ravenna, Italy). Herit. Sci. **8**(1), 10 (2020). https://doi.org/10.1186/s40494-020-0354-y
14. Fiorucci, M., Khoroshiltseva, M., Pontil, M., Traviglia, A., Del Bue, A., James, S.: Machine learning for cultural heritage: a survey. Pattern Recogn. Lett. **133**, 102–108 (2020). https://doi.org/10.1016/j.patrec.2020.02.017
15. Giuntini, L., et al.: Detectors and cultural heritage: the INFN-CHNet experience. Appl. Sci. **11**(8) (2021). https://doi.org/10.3390/app11083462
16. Harris, C.R., et al.: Array programming with NumPy. Nature **585**(7825), 357–362 (2020). https://doi.org/10.1038/s41586-020-2649-2
17. Jones, C., Daly, N.S., Higgitt, C., Rodrigues, M.R.D.: Neural network-based classification of x-ray fluorescence spectra of artists' pigments: an approach leveraging a synthetic dataset created using the fundamental parameters method. Herit. Science **10**(1), 88 (2022). https://doi.org/10.1186/s40494-022-00716-3
18. Kleynhans, T., Schmidt Patterson, C.M., Dooley, K.A., Messinger, D.W., Delaney, J.K.: An alternative approach to mapping pigments in paintings with hyperspectral reflectance image cubes using artificial intelligence. Herit. Sci. **8**(1), 84 (2020). https://doi.org/10.1186/s40494-020-00427-7
19. Kogou, S., Lee, L., Shahtahmassebi, G., Liang, H.: A new approach to the interpretation of XRF spectral imaging data using neural networks. X-Ray Spectrometry **50**(4) (2020). https://doi.org/10.1002/xrs.3188
20. Licciardi, G.A., Del Frate, F.: Pixel unmixing in hyperspectral data by means of neural networks. IEEE Trans. Geosci. Remote Sens. **49**(11), 4163–4172 (2011). https://doi.org/10.1109/TGRS.2011.2160950
21. Liu, L., et al.: Neural networks for hyperspectral imaging of historical paintings: a practical review. Sensors **23**(5) (2023). https://doi.org/10.3390/s23052419, https://www.mdpi.com/1424-8220/23/5/2419
22. Martins, A., et al.: Jackson Pollock's number 1a, 1948: a non-invasive study using macro-x-ray fluorescence mapping (ma-xrf) and multivariate curve resolution-alternating least squares (mcr-als) analysis. Herit. Sci. **4**, 1–13 (2016)
23. McInnes, L., Healy, J., Melville, J.: Umap: uniform manifold approximation and projection for dimension reduction (2020)

24. Preisler, Z., Andolina, R., Busacca, A., Caliri, C., Miliani, C., Romano, F.P.: Deep learning for enhanced spectral analysis of ma-xrf datasets of paintings. Sci. Adv. **10** (2024). https://api.semanticscholar.org/CorpusID:272881694
25. Ricciardi, P., Mazzinghi, A., Legnaioli, S., Ruberto, C., Castelli, L.: The Choir books of San Giorgio Maggiore in Venice: results of in depth non-invasive analyses. Heritage **2**(2), 1684–1701 (2019). https://doi.org/10.3390/heritage2020103
26. Rocklin, M.: Dask: parallel computation with blocked algorithms and task scheduling. In: Proceedings of the 14th Python in Science Conference, pp. 130–136, Citeseer (2015)
27. Ruberto, C.: The mission of the INFN-cultural heritage network: the multifaceted example of the macro-xrf scanner experience. Rendiconti Lincei. Scienze Fisiche e Naturali **34**(3), 889–906 (2023). https://doi.org/10.1007/s12210-023-01175-z
28. Sherman, J.: The theoretical derivation of fluorescent x-ray intensities from mixtures. Spectrochim. Acta **7**, 283–306 (1955)
29. Van der Snickt, G., et al.: In situ macro x-ray fluorescence (ma-xrf) scanning as a non-invasive tool to probe for subsurface modifications in paintings by p.p. rubens. Microchem. J. **138**, 238–245 (2018). https://doi.org/10.1016/j.microc.2018.01.019, https://www.sciencedirect.com/science/article/pii/S0026265X17308779
30. Vermeulen, M., et al.: XRFast a new software package for processing of MA-XRF datasets using machine learning. J. Anal. At. Spectrom. **37**, 2130–2143 (2022). https://doi.org/10.1039/D2JA00114D
31. van der Walt, S., Colbert, S.C., Varoquaux, G.: The NumPy array: a structure for efficient numerical computation. Comput. Sci. Eng. **13**(2), 22–30 (2011). https://doi.org/10.1109/mcse.2011.37
32. Wang, M., Zhao, M., Chen, J., Rahardja, S.: Nonlinear unmixing of hyperspectral data via deep autoencoder networks. IEEE Geosci. Remote Sens. Lett. **16**(9), 1467–1471 (2019). https://doi.org/10.1109/LGRS.2019.2900733
33. Wang, Z., Bovik, A., Sheikh, H., Simoncelli, E.: Image quality assessment: from error visibility to structural similarity. IEEE Trans. Image Process. **13**(4), 600–612 (2004). https://doi.org/10.1109/TIP.2003.819861
34. Xu, B.J., et al.: Can deep learning assist automatic identification of layered pigments from xrf data? (2022). https://doi.org/10.1039/D2JA00246A
35. Zhang, X., Sun, Y., Zhang, J., Wu, P., Jiao, L.: Hyperspectral unmixing via deep convolutional neural networks. IEEE Geosci. Remote Sens. Lett. **15**(11), 1755–1759 (2018). https://doi.org/10.1109/LGRS.2018.2857804

Artificial Intelligence-Assisted Living Systematic Review: A Case Study in the Monte Carlo Electron Transport Research

Federica Frabetti[1] and Elisabetta Ronchieri[2](✉)

[1] Department of Statistical Sciences, University of Bologna, Bologna, Italy
federica.frabetti6@studio.unibo.it
[2] INFN CNAF, Bologna, Italy
elisabetta.ronchieri@cnaf.infn.it

Abstract. Continuously monitoring the literature in Living Systematic Reviews (LSRs) is computationally demanding, particularly during the reference screening stage, where newly retrieved studies must be classified as relevant or irrelevant. In highly specialized fields like Monte Carlo Electron Transport, manual screening is not only tedious but also mentally taxing due to the domain-specific lexicon. Existing Artificial Intelligence (AI) tools often are not easily adaptable to specific contexts. In this research, we introduce and assess a modular AI-assisted screening framework characterized by four main components: a feature extractor, a classifier, a querier, and a balancer. We define and evaluate nine different configurations, ranging from traditional TF-IDF representations paired with classical classifiers to more advanced transformer-based embeddings, such as Sentence-BERT and Multilingual-e5-large. We take into consideration the title and abstract for each reference.

In screening datasets, there is the class imbalance issue. Therefore, to tackle this problem, we incorporate a resampling strategy along with Active Learning querying methods, including uncertainty sampling and certainty-based prioritization. Our experimental findings on a Monte Carlo Electron Transport dataset reveal that the configuration based on Multilingual-e5-large, Support Vector Machine, and certainty-based prioritization achieves the best balance between recall and screening efficiency with the highest WSS@95% value of 0.89838.

The proposed pipeline provides a reproducible way to automate document classification in specialized domains and reduces one of the main bottlenecks in maintaining LSRs with high-quality.

Keywords: Living Systematic Reviews · Active Learning · Automated Reference Screening · Monte Carlo Electron Transport · Transformer Embeddings · Imbalanced Learning · Supervised Classification

O. Gervasi et al. (Eds.): ICCSA 2026 Workshops, LNCS 16758, pp. 84–99, 2027.
https://doi.org/10.1007/978-3-032-30497-1_6

1 Introduction

The proliferation of scientific publications across diverse disciplines has made the aggregation of extant knowledge substantially difficult. Systematic Reviews (SRs) constitute a methodologically rigorous and transparent approach to synthesizing evidence [7]; however, in rapidly advancing domains, such syntheses tend to lose importance soon after dissemination and publication. Living Systematic Reviews (LSRs) mitigate this constraint through the implementation of ongoing surveillance mechanisms and iterative revision cycles [15,22].

The reference screening phase represents a critical limitation of LSRs during their routine maintenance [2,5]. Newly discovered publications must undergo some level of manual evaluation to determine their relevance or irrelevance to the review scope. This classification burden is especially demanding in narrowly focused research areas such as Monte Carlo Electron Transport, where accurate assessment requires a sophisticated grasp of specialized concepts and a deep understanding of domain-specific terminology. Furthermore, the problem is exacerbated by severe class imbalance—typically, fewer than 5% of retrieved records are relevant to the research question [12]. Such conditions render the screening process both inefficient and demanding for human reviewers.

Computational approaches available in Artificial Intelligence and Natural Language Processing offer substantial promise for automating reference screening [?] [1,3,8,28]. Nevertheless, contemporary systems exhibit three fundamental constraints that limit their practical application. First, most existing methods are suitable for general-domain tasks and therefore inadequately capture the nuanced technical lexicon of specialized fields. Second, many such systems function as unknown decision-making architectures, thereby constraining interpretability and restricting the capacity for independent verification, limiting transparency and reproducibility. Third, these tools show insufficient performance when they are confronted with severe class imbalance, producing unacceptably elevated false-negative rates when high-recall screening becomes essential.

To address these challenges, we propose a modular, AI-assisted framework for automated reference screening in the specialized domain of Monte Carlo Electron Transport. This framework decomposes the screening pipeline into four components—feature extractor, classifier, querier, and balancer—allowing systematic evaluation and customization. We define nine configurations combining traditional sparse representations (i.e., TF-IDF) [18] and transformer-based dense embeddings (i.e., Sentence-BERT, and Multilingual-e5-large) [24,29], together with multiple classifiers [11] (that include Support Vector Machines, Logistic Regression, Naive Bayes, and Random Forests) and Active Learning querying strategies [10] (specifically Uncertainty Sampling and Certainty-based Prioritization). Moreover, we integrate a dedicated resampling layer to mitigate class imbalance and ensure high recall for rare includable documents.

Our querying strategies fall within the Active Learning paradigm characterized by two querying approaches [17]: uncertainty sampling, which prioritizes documents near the decision boundary to improve model learning; and certainty-based prioritization, which selects documents with the highest predicted relevance to accelerate the identification of includable studies. This distinction allows us to evaluate the trade-off between exploration (uncertainty sampling) and exploitation (certainty-based prioritization) within the same Active Learning framework. Moreover, while uncertainty sampling is widely adopted, we investigate whether certainty-based prioritization is more effective in extreme class imbalance settings where rapid identification of relevant studies is critical.

Through a simulation on a Monte Carlo Electron Transport dataset, we show that configurations combining dense embeddings with certainty-based prioritization significantly improve screening efficiency. Our results demonstrate that, in contrast to common practice, exploitation-driven querying can outperform exploration strategies in high-imbalance, high-recall contexts.

While the individual components of the proposed framework are based on established techniques, the novelty of this work lies in their systematic integration and controlled comparative evaluation within a highly specialized and extremely imbalanced domain. The preliminary literature review conducted during the early stages of the research yielded a substantial number of documents characterized by highly domain-specific vocabulary, which poses significant challenges for traditional feature extraction methods. In particular, we provide: (i) a modular architecture enabling controlled comparison across feature extraction, classification, querying, and balancing strategies; (ii) a comprehensive empirical analysis of certainty-based versus uncertainty-based prioritization under extreme class imbalance; and (iii) reproducible evidence demonstrating that exploitation-driven querying strategies outperform traditional approaches in this setting.

2 Related Works

Active Learning (AL) is widely used to accelerate the screening process in Systematic Reviews. It is already a well-established research area. Tools, such as ASReview [27] and LitStudy [9], use the human in the loop system: in this case, a machine learning model keeps suggesting iteratively the most relevant documents based on what the reviewer has labeled previously.

Most frameworks [27] use uncertainty sampling, where the model picks instances close to the decision boundary [19,23]. Other frameworks go with certainty-based prioritization [13], which means focusing on documents with the highest chance of being included. However, the effectiveness of these strategies really depends on the initial seed set and how well the classifier deals with the sparse, includable documents. Our work builds on this approach by adding a dedicated Querier module. It benchmarks those two sampling approaches across nine different model setups.

The performance of screening AI is fundamentally limited by its Feature Extractor [4,20]. Early methods relied on Bag-Of-Words and TF-IDF representations. They were efficient and straightforward, but they missed semantic synonyms and the nuances in technical language.

Now transformer-based language models, such as BERT or RoBERTa, use dense embeddings [16,25]. Models such as Sentence-BERT and Multilingual-e5-large perform better in cross-lingual tasks and domain-specific ones. They map text to a high-dimensional vector space where similar concepts are clustered together. However, their computational cost remains a significant limitation. In our study, we compare traditional TF-IDF to newer ones like mxbai-embed-large and Multilingual-e5-large in a physics context, specifically because of specialized areas that require more work.

Class imbalance is a significant challenge in LSRs [21,22]. Relevant papers usually are less than 5% of the results. Standard classifiers typically overfit to the irrelevant class, leading to a dangerous drop in recall.

There are various Balancer strategies like Synthetic Minority Over-sampling Technique and random resampling [26]. However, few solutions look at how they work with physics-based lexicons. In fields like Monte Carlo Electron Transport research, the vocabulary is sufficiently specialized that general tools (often trained on PubMed or legal data) might get it wrong. Our framework addresses this gap by making a Balancer module central to the pipeline. It keeps recall high even when the imbalance is extreme.

Tools like Rayyan or Covidence are user-friendly, but they act like black boxes with limited ways to customize the internal architecture [14]. Researchers cannot swap classifiers easily or adjust querying for a physics review. We propose a modular architecture to set up a white box that allows us to test and validate properly for computational science.

3 Experimental Setup

3.1 Dataset and Gold Standard

The dataset used in this study consists of 3,330 records (titles and abstracts) retrieved from major scientific databases, including arXiv and Google Scholar, using a Boolean search string tailored to Monte Carlo Electron Transport (see Fig. 1). To evaluate the models, we established a "gold standard" labeled dataset where each relevant record was manually annotated and classified by domain experts. This process resulted in 133 includable (relevant) documents and 3,197 irrelevant documents.

This distribution corresponds to an inclusion rate—defined as the proportion of relevant papers over the total number of retrieved (relevant + irrelevant) papers, as shown in Eq. 1—of 3.99%, reflecting the pronounced class imbalance typical of specialized systematic reviews.

$$\text{Inclusion Rate } (\%) = \left(\frac{\text{Relevant Papers}}{\text{Relevant Papers} + \text{Irrelevant Papers}} \right) \times 100 \quad (1)$$

Irrelevant papers are defined as publications that do not strictly address the specific topic of interest, despite sharing similar terminology, keywords, or belonging to closely related research areas. These records are retrieved from

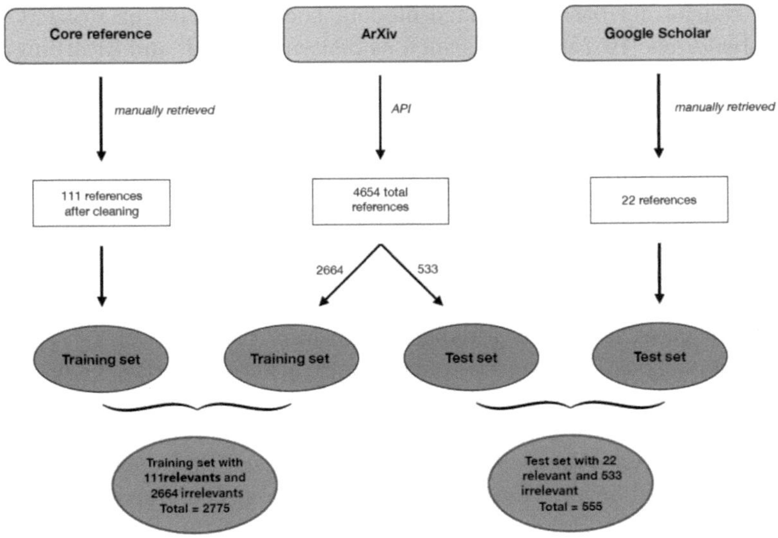

Fig. 1. Training and test sets.

databases due to their lexical or thematic similarity to relevant studies, but they do not provide meaningful contributions to the core objectives of the Living Systematic Reviews. In contrast, relevant papers are those that align closely with the central focus of the LSR and contribute with substantive insights, such as additional characteristics, methodological details, or domain-specific findings, improving the understanding of the topic under investigation.

3.2 Training and Test Set Definition

To simulate the screening process, we employed a stratified hold-out validation strategy. Unlike a standard random split, this approach ensures that the model's ability to identify rare "includable" papers is tested rigorously.

To initialize the Active Learning process, we defined a seed set composed of a small number of labeled relevant and irrelevant documents. Specifically, the seed set includes 20 documents, with a balanced representation of both classes where possible. This initial set simulates the early stage of a systematic review, where a researcher has already identified a limited number of key studies.

In addition to the seed set (the initial library), the training data includes a document pool, the remainder of the training set from which the querier selects documents for labeling to present to the researcher. The seed set (the initial library) and the document pool are subsets of the same training resource.

During the simulation, the querier selected documents from the training set based on its logic (e.g., Uncertainty sampling). Once a document was "queried," its label was revealed to the model (simulating a human's manual decision), and the model was retrained iteratively.

The test set includes the unseen library and is used exclusively for final performance evaluation. We reserved 16.67% of the total labeled dataset as a dedicated test set. This set was never seen by the feature extractor or the classifier during the iterative querying process. This ensures that the reported metrics accurately reflect the model's generalization ability in a realistic "needle-in-a-haystack" screening scenario.

The balancing (e.g., oversampling or undersampling) was only applied to the training set. To maintain the validity of the simulation, the test set was kept in its original, imbalanced state. This ensures that the reported performance metrics reflect the true difficulty of the "needle-in-a-haystack" screening task.

At each iteration of the Active Learning loop, a batch of 2 documents is selected by the querier and presented for labeling. Once labeled, these documents are added to the training set, and the model is retrained. The process continues iteratively until a predefined stopping criterion is reached. In our experiments, the stopping condition corresponds to achieving a target recall threshold (e.g., 95%) or exhausting the document pool. Unless otherwise specified, models are updated after each iteration using the augmented labeled set.

We wish to detail that the training set is characterized by relevant and irrelevant references as shown in Fig. 2: the former is obtained by experts and existing bibliography like "Unravelling Tungsten atom ionization at high energies: A relativistic electron impact study" (https://doi.org/10.1016/j.elspec.2025.147552), the latter derives from the ArXiv database like "Modification of the uniform electron gas polarizational stopping power due to the interaction of the projectile with new collective modes at moderate and strong coupling" (https://doi.org/10.48550/arXiv.2505.17229). The test set also contains both relevant and irrelevant references, maintaining the same proportion between the two classes as the training set: the relevant entries are obtained via Google Scholar, while the irrelevant entries are obtained via ArXiv.

3.3 Evaluation Metrics

Standard accuracy is misleading in imbalanced screening tasks. Therefore, we defined success using the following metrics [6]:

1. Recall (Sensitivity): The percentage of all relevant papers found. In LSRs, a recall of <95% is generally unacceptable.
2. Workload Savings (WSS@95): The percentage of the library a researcher did not have to read because the AI correctly predicted those papers as irrelevant before the 95% recall threshold was reached.
3. Extra Relevant Records found (ERF): It is the proportion of relevant records found after correcting for the number of relevant records found via random screening.
4. Average Time to Discovery (ATD): The average number of documents a reviewer must screen before encountering a relevant (includable) one.
5. Loss: It is the proportion of "includable" (relevant) documents that the model incorrectly classified as irrelevant and were therefore never shown to the researcher.

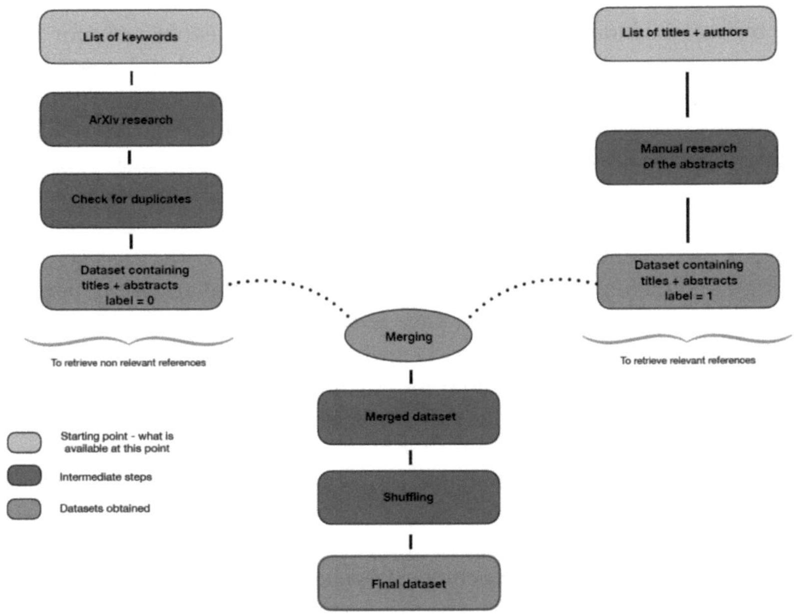

Fig. 2. Training set definition.

The terms ERF (Extra Relevant Records found), Loss, and ATD (Average Time to Discovery) are standard metrics in the broader field of Active Learning for Systematic Reviews. ERF is closely related to WSS, which quantifies the percentage of the library the researcher did not have to read.

WSS quantifies how much human effort was saved automating the screening process, given a recall level. It measures how many documents the reviewer did not have to screen compared to random screening, while achieving a target recall. It is computed as Eq. 2:

$$WSS@R = R - \frac{n}{N} \tag{2}$$

where R defines the target recall, n represents the number of documents screened to reach that recall, and N is the total number of documents in the dataset. WSS at 95% provides insight into the global efficiency of the model under a safety constraint, given by the high recall level required.

ERF at 10% is the proportion of relevant records found after correcting at screening 10% of the total number of records available in the dataset.

ATD determines how long, on average, the model takes to discover a new relevant reference, where the time is interpreted as the number of records needed to screen. The ATD measures the average number of labeling decisions (documents screened) required to find a relevant record. It represents the speed of discovery. It has a low value if relevant documents are ranked at the top. This metric provides the number of screening decisions that are necessary to find each relevant record.

Loss typically refers to the Recall Loss—the fraction of relevant documents that were missed because the model incorrectly classified them as irrelevant at the point where screening was stopped.

ATD and Loss cover aspects of the screening process not captured by WSS and ERF, such as discovery speed and learning stability, respectively.

To ensure robustness, experiments can be repeated across multiple random initializations of the seed set. Due to computational constraints, results are reported for a single representative run. While this limits statistical generalization, the consistency of trends across configurations suggests robustness of the observed behavior. Future work will include repeated runs and statistical validation.

3.4 Configurations Summary

Table 1 summarizes the nine distinct, defined configurations of the modular AI-assisted screening framework according to the four components: feature extractor, classifier, querier and balancer.

The feature extraction layer evaluates both traditional sparse representations and dense embeddings to capture the specialized lexicon of Monte Carlo Electron Transport. TF-IDF (Sparse) represents documents based on the importance of terms relative to the corpus, calculated through the product of term frequency and inverse-document frequency. It produces high-dimensional sparse vectors where each dimension corresponds to a unique term in the vocabulary. Transformer-based embeddings (Dense) models (SBERT-mpnet, SBERT-mxbai, and Multilingual-e5-large) map text into a dense, high-dimensional vector space. Unlike TF-IDF, these capture semantic synonyms and contextual nuances critical for interpreting technical physics terms.

The classification layer consists of four distinct discriminative models tailored to handle high-dimensional data. Support Vector Machine (SVM) is used in Models A, F, H, and I, finding the optimal hyperplane to separate relevant and irrelevant classes. It is particularly effective in sparse spaces like those generated by TF-IDF. Logistic Regression is employed in Models B, E, and G. This probabilistic classifier produces a confidence score representing the likelihood of a document being relevant. Model C utilizes Naive Bayes to estimate class probability based on feature frequency, while Model D uses Random Forest to manage complex non-linear relationships in the data.

Models A through D and also H rely on TF-IDF to figure out how important certain words are in the documents based on term frequency and inverse-document frequency. These are paired with different classifiers, like SVM for A and H, then Logistic Regression in B, Naive Bayes for C, and Random Forest in D. Model A specifically takes the SVM and uses uncertainty sampling to pick documents right around the decision boundary in those sparse spaces, which helps find the best separation. Model H is highly similar to A but it switches over to certainty-based prioritization instead, just to isolate the querying strategy.

The transformer-based models, from E to G and I, use dense embeddings with Sentence-BERT (SBERT) or Multilingual-e5-large to capture deep semantic

Table 1. Configurations Summary

Model	Feature Extractor	Classifier	Querier	Balancer
A	TF-IDF (Sparse)	SVM (Linear)	Uncertainty Sampling	Balanced
B	TF-IDF	Logistic Reg.	Uncertainty Sampling	Balanced
C	TF-IDF	Naive Bayes	Certainty-based prioritization	Balanced
D	TF-IDF	Random Forest	Certainty-based prioritization	Balanced
E	SBERT-mpnet (Dense)	Logistic Reg.	Certainty-based prioritization	Balanced
F	Multilingual-e5-large	SVM	Certainty-based prioritization	Balanced
G	SBERT-mxbai (Dense)	Logistic Reg.	Uncertainty Sampling	Balanced
H	TF-IDF	SVM	Certainty-based prioritization	Balanced
I	SBERT-mxbai	SVM	Certainty-based prioritization	Balanced

meaning. Model F uses Multilingual-e5-large along with SVM, and the certainty-based approach performed well in terms of recall and precision.

Models A, B and G employ uncertainty sampling, prioritizing documents near the decision boundary to make the model learn better over time. Then the others models– from C to F, H and I, use certainty-based prioritization, picking the documents with the highest predicted relevance to accelerate the identification of includable studies. The TF-IDF models seem simpler overall, but the transformers capture more meaning.

Table 2 summarizes the hyperparameter settings used to initialize the nine model configurations (Models A–I). These settings ensure that the comparative analysis isolates the impact of the feature extractor and querying logic rather than variance in tuning.

The Balancer sets a strategy to Balanced. This standardized setup allows for a rigorous white-box evaluation of how different AI architectures respond to the extreme class imbalance (3.99% inclusion rate) found in specialized research screening. The Balancer component across all configurations was set to a synthetic oversampling ratio of 0.5 to mitigate the 3.99% inclusion rate.

3.5 Architecture

Figure 3 shows three integrated stages: input and component definition, the core iterative Active Learning workflow, and the 9-model comparative matrix mapping models A–I.

Stage 1 defines the raw input (the Monte Carlo Electron Transport dataset) and explicitly lists the sub-options for each main pillar: feature extractors shows the transition from sparse vectors (TF-IDF) to dense contextual embeddings (mpnet, e5-large, mxbai); classifiers lists the four heads models, i.e., SVM, Logistic Regression, Naive Bayes, Random Forests; queriers visually contrasts Active Learning with uncertainty sampling versus certainty-based prioritization; balancer shows the resampling layer to manage class imbalance.

Table 2. Hyperparameter Settings

Component	Parameter	Configuration/Value	Model
TF-IDF	N-gram Range	(1, 2) (Unigrams and Bigrams)	H
	N-gram Range	(1, 1) (Unigrams)	A
	Max Features	5,000	A-D, H
	Vector Type	Sparse high-dimensional	A-D, H
	Max Df	1.0	A
	Max Df	0.95	H
	Sublinear TF	False	A
	Sublinear TF	True	H
SBERT/ Multilingual-e5-large	Max Seq. Length	512 tokens	E-G, I
	Pooling	Mean Pooling	E-G, I
	Normalize	L2	E-G
	Normalize	True	I
SVM	Kernel	Linear	A, F, H-I
	C (Regularization)	1.0	A, F
	C (Regularization)	0.11	H
	C (Regularization)	0.067	I
	Penalty	L2	A, F, H-I
	Max Iter	1000	A, F, H
	Max Iter	5000	I
Logistic Regression	Type	Probabilistic Classifier	B, E, G
	Penalty	L2	B, E, G
	Solver	lbfgs	B, E, G
	Max Iter	100	B, E, G
	C (Regularization)	1.0	B, E, G
Random Forest	Num. Estimators	100	D
	Max Depth	None	D
	Max Features	sqrt	D
	Criterion	gini	D
Naive Bayes	Type	Multinomial	C
	Alpha	1.0 (Laplace smoothing)	C
	Fit prior	True	C

Stage 2 is the central part of the figure. It shows how the simulation set is fed into the configured feature extractor and balancer. The data then flows into the classifier, which outputs a confidence score (0 to 1). The querier then decides which documents from the test set are presented to the simulated researcher (or gold standard set). This creates a feedback loop that continuously retrains the model as more labels are revealed.

Stage 3 is a detailed, matrix-style table that defines the specific configuration for each of your nine test subjects. The matrix explicitly differentiates between Model A (TF-IDF + SVM + Uncertainty Sampling) and Model H (TF-IDF + SVM + Certainty-based prioritization). This isolates the effect of the querier logic. Similarly, it contrasts Model G (mxbai + Logistic Regression + Uncertainty Sampling) and Model E (mpnet + Logistic Regression + Certainty-based prioritization) to isolate the combined effect of a new feature extractor and a new querier.

The final panel in Fig. 3 shows the simulation success metric. The entire Figure points toward a graph of Workload Savings (WSS) @ 95% Recall. It illustrates competing Recall Curves for Model A (slower, uncertainty-based discovery) versus Model I (faster, certainty-based discovery), visually proving why one configuration is superior for an LSR. Figure 3 contrasts Model A (uncertainty-based, slower discovery) with Model I (certainty-based, faster discovery). A Fast Discovery model aims to minimize the ATD by prioritizing documents with the highest predicted relevance.

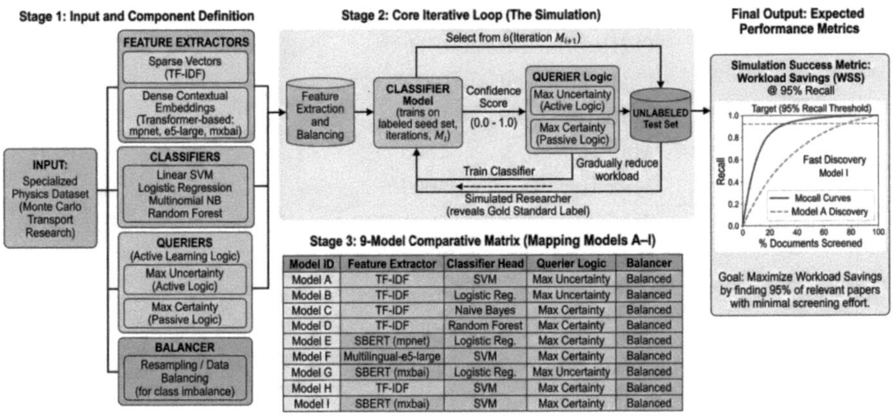

Fig. 3. Modular AI-Assisted Screening Framework (Models A–I Analysis).

The image illustrates two competing logics for the querier module: uncertainty sampling versus certainty-based prioritization. In the first case, the model (a TF-IDF vectorizer + an SVM or Logistic Regression head) predicts which documents it is most uncertain about (those closest to the decision boundary). These documents are queried first to improve the model's accuracy. This logic corresponds to Models A, B, and G. In the second case, the model (a deep SBERT or Multilingual-e5-large embedding + a classifier head) prioritizes documents it is most certain are relevant. This logic corresponds to Models C, D, E, F, H, and I.

4 Results

Table 3 shows the performance metrics across all simulated models. Models F (Multilingual-e5-large + SVM + certainty-based prioritization) and B (TF-IDF + Logistic Regression + uncertainty sampling) achieve the best and worst performance, respectively.

Table 3. Performance Metrics on Training Set

Model	WSS@95%	ERF@10%	ATD [sec]	Loss
Model F	0.89838	0.90090	68.89	0.00484
Model I	0.89802	0.90090	69.32	0.00500
Model C	0.89802	0.90090	69.40	0.00503
Model H	0.89730	0.90090	69.56	0.00509
Model E	0.89730	0.90090	69.93	0.00523
Model G	0.89694	0.90090	70.27	0.00536
Model D	0.89586	0.90090	70.33	0.00538
Model A	0.89514	0.90090	71.51	0.00582
Model B	−0.05622	0.48649	883.19	0.31051

Although most configurations achieve high WSS@95%, substantial differences emerge when considering practical efficiency metrics, such as ATD and Loss. These differences highlight an important aspect: similar recall values may mask substantial variation in efficiency and reliability.

A key finding is the advantage of certainty-based prioritization in extreme class imbalance settings (≈4% inclusion rate), where rapid identification of rare relevant instances is critical. Certainty-based querying prioritizes high-confidence relevant predictions, effectively favoring exploitation over exploration, which leads to faster discovery and reduced screening effort.

The Multilingual-e5-large models achieved the highest WSS@95%. Interestingly, model C (TF-IDF + Naive Bayes + certainty-based prioritization) achieved a WSS@95% similar to model I (SBERT-mxbai + SVM + certainty-based prioritization). Models G and E, although they use more complex feature extractors, achieve a lower WSS@95% than Model C. In this case, it is crucial to consider interactions with all components: model G employs SBERT-mxbai, as does Model I.

The poor performance of Model B can be attributed to the combination of TF-IDF features and Logistic Regression under uncertainty sampling: the negative WSS@95% indicates that the screening effort exceeds that of random sampling, an extremely low ERF@10% indicates that the model increases workload instead of reducing it, while a large ATD indicates that the model takes a significant time to discover new relevant references (it requires nearly thirteen times more screening effort compared to Model F). In sparse feature spaces, the decision boundary learned by Logistic Regression may be insufficiently expressive, leading to unreliable uncertainty estimates. As a result, the querying strategy prioritizes uninformative samples, significantly degrading performance.

In general, based on the ranking obtained, it can be noticed that no clear pattern emerges in terms of feature extractors: TF-IDF is placed both in the top part of the ranking as well as the bottom. The same can be said for embedding-based feature extractors such as SBERT, even if they never occupy the very last positions, appearing both at the top and in intermediate positions of the ranking. TF-IDF can still compete in some configurations, such as Model C; however, the best-performing model uses embeddings. Analyzing the ranking of the models in terms of the classifier employed, one can notice that often setups with Support Vector Machine show a better result compared to others, while Logistic Regression and Random Forest tend to show lower performance. In terms of querier, the division is more pronounced: the common factor among the best-performing models is the use of certainty-based querying, followed by uncertainty sampling. Uncertainty sampling is the querying strategy implemented in model B.

Then, we evaluated the best model with the test set, as summarized in Table 4. Performance remains strong on the test set, although some metrics show a moderate decline: WSS@95% goes from 0.8984 to 0.8018; ERF@10% goes from 0.9009 to 0.8636; ATD goes from 68.89 to 35.18; Loss goes from 0.00484 to 0.04443.

Our best model achieved an ERF@10% of 0.8636 on the test set, indicating that by screening only 10% of the data, the model effectively captured the vast majority of relevant papers, significantly reducing the effort required. ATD dropped from 68.89 to 35.18. A lower ATD is better, as it indicates the researcher finds "needle-in-a-haystack" much faster, which is the primary goal of the Fast Discovery logic mentioned in our framework. Loss increased from 0.00484 to 0.04443 on the test set. This is an increase, it remains below the 5% threshold (0.05), which aligns with your stated goal of maintaining a 95% Recall (meaning a maximum allowable loss of 5%).

Table 4. Model F Performance Metrics on Test Set

Metric	Purpose	Test Result	Interpretation
WSS@95%	Workload Savings	80.18%	≈80% of the documents did not need to be read
ERF@10%	Early Efficiency	0.8636	High success in early discovery
ATD	Discovery Speed	35.18	Average documents screened per seconds
Loss	Evidence Safety	4.44%	≈4.4% of relevant papers were missed

In highly imbalanced screening scenarios typical of Living Systematic Reviews, researchers should prioritize certainty-based querying strategies combined with semantically rich embeddings. Uncertainty sampling may be suboptimal when the primary goal is rapid identification of rare relevant studies. In this study, the proposed modular framework may enable researchers to tailor screening pipelines to domain-specific requirements, balancing recall, workload, and discovery speed.

5 Conclusions

This study provides a systematic and reproducible evaluation of AI-assisted screening strategies in a highly specialized domain of Monte Carlo Electron Transport, highlighting how the interaction between model components—rather than individual methods—drives performance under extreme class imbalance. We provided a white-box alternative to existing proprietary platforms and tools via an architecture composed of four distinct components—feature extractor, classifier, querier, and balancer.

We defined and assessed nine configurations, revealing that Model F, characterized by Multilingual-e5-large, SVM, and certainty-based prioritization, is the optimal configuration for this domain. It achieved a Workload Savings (WSS@95%) of 80.18% on an unseen test set, showing that researchers can significantly reduce their screening effort while maintaining the strict 95% recall safety threshold required for systematic evidence synthesis.

Key findings include transformer superiority with respect to traditional TF-IDF to get high-stakes recall scenarios. In fact, dense embeddings like Multilingual-e5-large are crucial for capturing the semantic nuances of technical physics terminology. Certainty-based prioritization is a querier logic that consistently led to fast discovery, minimizing the Average Time to Discovery (ATD) and allowing researchers to identify relevant evidence much earlier in the screening process. Furthermore, despite the extreme class imbalance (3.99% inclusion rate), the integrated Balancer component ensured that the model's Loss remained below 5%, confirming its reliability for practical LSR updates.

This study is subject to some limitations. There is the absence of repeated runs and statistical testing, which will be addressed in future work to further validate robustness. Results are based on a single dataset from a highly specialized domain, which may limit generalizability. Experiments were conducted using a single initialization of the seed set. Hyperparameter tuning was not exhaustively explored, as the focus was on comparative analysis across configurations. Future work will address these limitations through broader datasets and repeated experimental runs.

Future work will focus on integrating these modular components into a screening activity to customize researcher screening pipelines according to their specific recall and workload requirements.

Disclosure of Interests. The authors have no competing interests to declare that are relevant to the content of this article.

References

1. Abramovich, F., Grinshtein, V., Levy, T.: Multiclass classification by sparse multinomial logistic regression. IEEE Trans. Inf. Theory **67**(7), 4637–4646 (2021). https://doi.org/10.1109/tit.2021.3075137
2. Akl, E.A., et al.: The life and death of living systematic reviews: a methodological survey. J. Clin. Epidemiol. **156**, 11–21 (2023). https://doi.org/10.1016/j.jclinepi.2023.02.005
3. Anisuzzaman, D., Malins, J.G., Friedman, P.A., Attia, Z.I.: Fine-tuning large language models for specialized use cases. Mayo Clin. Proc.: Digit. Health **3**(1), 100184 (2025). https://doi.org/10.1016/j.mcpdig.2024.11.005
4. Ayash, L., Algarni, A., Alqahtani, O.: Advancements in feature selection and extraction methods for text mining: a review. Discov. Appl. Sci. **7**(8) (2025). https://doi.org/10.1007/s42452-025-07587-w
5. Burgard, T., Bittermann, A.: Reducing literature screening workload with machine learning: a systematic review of tools and their performance. Zeitschrift für Psychologie **231**(1), 3–15 (2023). https://doi.org/10.1027/2151-2604/a000509
6. Chen, M., et al.: Impact of human and artificial intelligence collaboration on workload reduction in medical image interpretation. NPJ Digit. Med. **7**(1) (2024). https://doi.org/10.1038/s41746-024-01328-w
7. Finocchi, I., Ribichini, A., Schaerf, M.: A large-scale temporal analysis of scientific production across disciplines and countries. J. Informet. **19**(2), 101665 (2025). https://doi.org/10.1016/j.joi.2025.101665
8. He, Y., Zhu, X., Li, D., Wang, H.: Enhancing large language models for specialized domains: a two-stage framework with parameter-sensitive LoRA fine-tuning and chain-of-thought rag. Electronics **14**(10), 1961 (2025). https://doi.org/10.3390/electronics14101961
9. Heldens, S., et al.: litstudy: A Python package for literature reviews. SoftwareX **20**, 101207 (2022). https://doi.org/10.1016/j.softx.2022.101207
10. Hoarau, A., Lemaire, V., Le Gall, Y., Dubois, J.C., Martin, A.: Evidential uncertainty sampling strategies for active learning. Mach. Learn. **113**(9), 6453–6474 (2024). https://doi.org/10.1007/s10994-024-06567-2
11. Idrissi Khaldi, M., Erraissi, A., Hain, M., Banane, M.: Comparative analysis of supervised machine learning classification models. In: Farhaoui, Y., Herawan, T., Imoize, A.L., Allaoui, A.E. (eds.) ICAISE 2024. LNNS, vol. 1353, pp. 321–326. Springer, Cham (2025). https://doi.org/10.1007/978-3-031-88304-0_44
12. Iversen, I.A., Quintana, D.S.: The value of living systematic reviews. Nat. Hum. Behav. (2026). https://doi.org/10.1038/s41562-026-02428-1
13. Jafarzadeh, H., Heidary-Dahooie, J., Akbari, P., Qorbani, A.: A project prioritization approach considering uncertainty, reliability, criteria prioritization, and robustness. Decis. Support Syst. **156**, 113731 (2022). https://doi.org/10.1016/j.dss.2022.113731
14. Kellermeyer, L., Harnke, B., Knight, S.: Covidence and Rayyan. J. Med. Libr. Assoc. **106**(4) (2018). https://doi.org/10.5195/jmla.2018.513
15. Khamis, A.M., Kahale, L.A., Pardo-Hernandez, H., Schünemann, H.J., Akl, E.A.: Methods of conduct and reporting of living systematic reviews: a protocol for a living methodological survey. F1000Research **8**, 221 (2019). https://doi.org/10.12688/f1000research.18005.2
16. Kotei, E., Thirunavukarasu, R.: A systematic review of transformer-based pretrained language models through self-supervised learning. Information **14**(3), 187 (2023). https://doi.org/10.3390/info14030187

17. Kumar, P., Gupta, A.: Active learning query strategies for classification, regression, and clustering: a survey. J. Comput. Sci. Technol. **35**(4), 913–945 (2020). https://doi.org/10.1007/s11390-020-9487-4
18. Liang, M., Niu, T.: Research on text classification techniques based on improved tf-idf algorithm and LSTM inputs. Procedia Comput. Sci. **208**, 460–470 (2022). https://doi.org/10.1016/j.procs.2022.10.064
19. Liu, S., Li, X.: Understanding uncertainty sampling (2023). https://doi.org/10.48550/ARXIV.2307.02719
20. Malekipirbazari, M., Aksakalli, V., Shafqat, W., Eberhard, A.: Performance comparison of feature selection and extraction methods with random instance selection. Expert Syst. Appl. **179**, 115072 (2021). https://doi.org/10.1016/j.eswa.2021.115072
21. Mujahid, M., et al.: Data oversampling and imbalanced datasets: an investigation of performance for machine learning and feature engineering. J. Big Data **11**(1) (2024). https://doi.org/10.1186/s40537-024-00943-4
22. Nevill, C.R., et al.: Capturing the influx of living systematic reviews: a systematic methodological survey. J. Clin. Epidemiol. **186**, 111904 (2025). https://doi.org/10.1016/j.jclinepi.2025.111904
23. Nguyen, V.L., Shaker, M.H., Hüllermeier, E.: How to measure uncertainty in uncertainty sampling for active learning. Mach. Learn. **111**(1), 89–122 (2021). https://doi.org/10.1007/s10994-021-06003-9
24. Reimers, N., Gurevych, I.: Sentence-BERT: sentence embeddings using Siamese BERT-networks (2019). https://doi.org/10.48550/ARXIV.1908.10084
25. Salem, M., Mohamed, A., Shaalan, K.: Transformer models in natural language processing: a comprehensive review and prospects for future development. In: Hassanien, A.E., Rizk, R.Y., Darwish, A., Alshurideh, M.T.R., Snášel, V., Tolba, M.F. (eds.) AISI 2025. LNDECT, vol. 238, pp. 463–472. Springer, Cham (2025). https://doi.org/10.1007/978-3-031-81308-5_42
26. Sasirekha, R., Kanisha, B.: Adaptive ensemble framework with synthetic sampling for tackling class imbalance problem. Eng. Rep. **7**(4) (2025). https://doi.org/10.1002/eng2.70109
27. van de Schoot, R., et al.: An open source machine learning framework for efficient and transparent systematic reviews. Nat. Mach. Intell. **3**(2), 125–133 (2021). https://doi.org/10.1038/s42256-020-00287-7
28. Supriyono, Wibawa, A.P., Suyono, Kurniawan, F.: Advancements in natural language processing: implications, challenges, and future directions. Telemat. Inform. Rep. **16**, 100173 (2024). https://doi.org/10.1016/j.teler.2024.100173
29. Wang, L., Yang, N., Huang, X., Yang, L., Majumder, R., Wei, F.: Multilingual e5 text embeddings: a technical report (2024). https://doi.org/10.48550/ARXIV.2402.05672

GRI-Aligned Sustainability Reporting Assessment via Knowledge Graph-RAG and LLM-Based Question-Answering: A Case Study of Vietnamese Banks

Minhquang Nguyen, Anbinh Vuong, Vanha Tran(✉), and Thiloan Bui

FPT University, Hanoi 155514, Vietnam
{quangnmhe181701,binhvahe180123}@fpt.edu.vn, {hatv14,loanbt7}@fe.edu.vn

Abstract. Environmental, Social, and Governance (ESG) disclosures have become central to sustainability evaluation, risk management, and investment decision-making in the banking sector. However, ESG and financial reports are typically lengthy, heterogeneous, and semi-structured, making systematic assessment challenging. This study introduces a GRI-aligned ESG assessment system for Vietnamese banks utilizing a Knowledge Graph-enhanced Retrieval-Augmented Generation (KG-RAG) architecture integrated with Large Language Models (LLMs) for question answering (Q&A). Our system comprises three elements: (i) an LLM-guided information extraction pipeline that converts sustainability and annual reports into structured ESG statements consistent with the Global Reporting Initiative (GRI) standard; (ii) an ESG knowledge graph that explicitly represents entities, relationships, ESG categories, and GRI indicators with complete provenance; and (iii) a hybrid KG-driven retrieval mechanism that combines graph filtering, semantic embeddings, and keyword matching to facilitate multi-hop reasoning and evidence-based answer generation. The system is evaluated on a dataset of 120 ESG questions designed and annotated by domain experts, covering Environmental, Social, and Governance dimensions across Vietnamese banking reports. Experimental findings indicate that the improved KG-RAG configuration attains the highest overall accuracy of 88.14%, surpassing conventional retrieval baselines and regular KG retrieval methods. These findings demonstrate that structured graph constraints combined with LLM-based Q&A significantly improve accuracy, traceability, and consistency in ESG assessment.

Keywords: ESG · GRI Standards · Knowledge Graph-RAG · Vietnamese Banks · Large Language Model

1 Introduction

Sustainability has become a strategic concern for firms, regulators, and investors because it influences risk management, capital allocation, and long-term value

O. Gervasi et al. (Eds.): ICCSA 2026 Workshops, LNCS 16758, pp. 100–116, 2027.
https://doi.org/10.1007/978-3-032-30497-1_7

creation. Firms that integrate sustainability into their operations are often viewed as more resilient and better positioned for sustained performance [1]. At the same time, stakeholders' demand for reliable sustainability information has accelerated the adoption of Environmental, Social, and Governance (ESG) disclosures, making ESG performance increasingly relevant to investment analysis and risk assessment [2,3]. The UN Global Compact report *Who Cares Wins* helped formalize this shift by linking ESG considerations to mainstream financial markets [4].

Global reporting frameworks have emerged to enhance comparability and transparency in sustainability disclosure. The Global Reporting Initiative (GRI)[1] provides a widely adopted standard built on the principle of *impact materiality*, requiring entities to disclose issues that significantly affect the economy, environment, and people [5]. This stakeholder-oriented design makes GRI a natural reference for banking, where ESG factors directly influence credit, market, operational, and reputational risk. International and national guidance reinforces this need: the Basel Committee on Banking Supervision [6] has issued principles for climate-related financial risks, and in Vietnam, Directive No. 03/CT-NHNN promotes green credit and environmental–social risk management [7]. Together, these developments motivate systematic, evidence-grounded assessment of sustainability disclosures. While large language models (LLMs) and retrieval-augmented generation (RAG) enable natural-language access to such reports, embedding-only approaches often struggle with the multi-hop reasoning, cross-section aggregation, and strict evidence consistency required in ESG–finance settings [11,12].

The length and heterogeneity of sustainability reports, which combine narrative text, tables, and semi-structured disclosures, make manual analysis difficult. Natural language processing (NLP) and question answering (QA) systems are therefore valuable for supporting evidence retrieval and structured comparison across firms [8,9].

To address these limitations, we present a Knowledge Graph-enhanced Retrieval-Augmented Generation (KG-RAG) architecture for document-grounded question answering over sustainability reports and financial statements of Vietnamese banks. The core idea is to build a domain knowledge graph that explicitly represents banks, reporting periods, ESG themes, targets, emissions, green credit programs, and financial indicators, and then use graph-guided retrieval to improve semantic search. This design aims to improve evidence selection for multi-hop questions, reduce hallucination through structural grounding, and increase explainability through entity-linked evidence paths. Our work is also motivated by the growing availability of ESG-oriented NLP resources and benchmarks such as FinSim4-ESG [10].

This paper makes three main contributions:

- We develop a GRI-aligned ESG information extraction and normalization pipeline that transforms sustainability and annual reports of Vietnamese banks into provenance-preserving, statement-level evidence.

[1] https://www.globalreporting.org/.

- We design and implement an ESG Knowledge Graph integrated with a hybrid KG-RAG framework that combines graph filtering, semantic vector retrieval, and keyword matching to improve multi-hop reasoning and reduce hallucination.
- We construct an expert-annotated ESG question-answering benchmark and empirically demonstrate that the enhanced KG-RAG configuration achieves high overall accuracy, outperforming strong retrieval baselines.

2 Related Work

Information retrieval (IR) is central to question answering (QA) over large document collections. Sparse lexical methods such as BM25 remain strong baselines because they are efficient and robust for keyword-oriented matching [13]. Dense retrieval methods such as Dense Passage Retrieval (DPR) address vocabulary mismatch by mapping queries and passages into a shared embedding space [14].

LLMs have recently been explored across the IR pipeline, including query rewriting, retrieval, reranking, and answer generation, offering stronger semantic modeling but also raising concerns about reliability in high-stakes settings [15,21]. Knowledge graphs (KGs) complement text retrieval by explicitly representing entities, relations, and schema constraints, thereby supporting multi-hop reasoning and structured evidence selection [17]. Recent studies further show that LLMs can help construct KGs from unstructured text through prompting-based extraction pipelines, although normalization and quality control remain important [18,20].

In the ESG domain, LLM-based approaches have been applied to both ESG evaluation and the extraction of structured signals from sustainability reports [16,23]. However, most rely on embedding-only or standard RAG pipelines and provide limited support for transparent evidence chaining across scattered disclosures. Such pipelines typically struggle with multi-hop reasoning over ESG–finance relationships, lack robust mechanisms for cross-document aggregation, and offer weak control over answer grounding, which raises hallucination risk in regulatory or investment settings. Auditable ESG assessment therefore calls for a graph-aware retrieval strategy that explicitly encodes domain knowledge (e.g., GRI indicators), preserves provenance, and combines semantic with symbolic reasoning.

This paper focuses on document-grounded question answering over sustainability reports and financial statements of Vietnamese banks. We emphasize (i) structuring ESG–finance evidence into a consistent KG schema and (ii) KG-guided retrieval to improve multi-hop evidence aggregation and explainability for cross-document queries.

3 ESG Question-Answering System

Figure 1 illustrates the overall architecture and key components of the proposed ESG question-answering system. The system comprises three main modules:

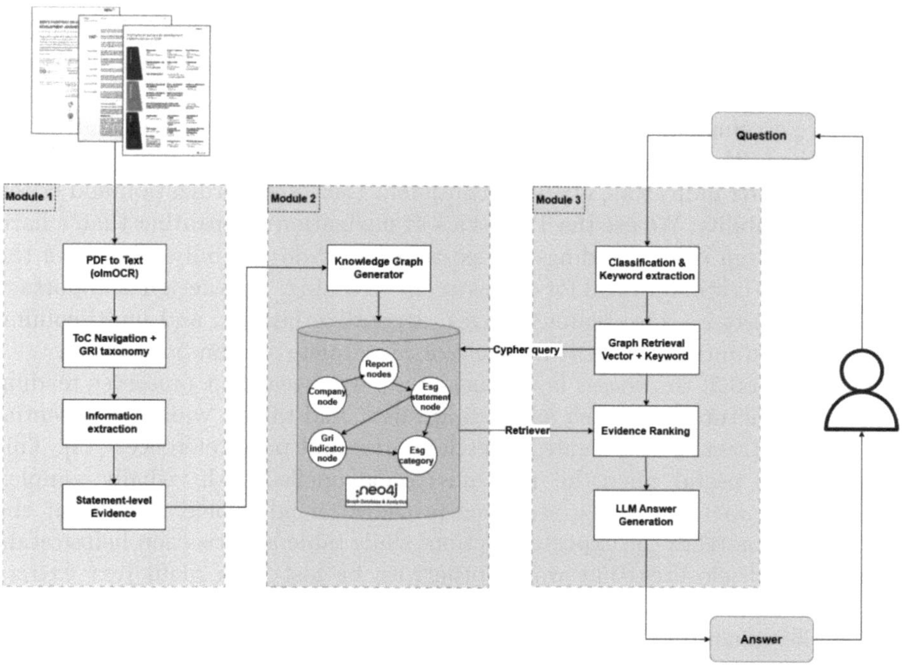

Fig. 1. ESG Question-Answering components.

Module 1 - a report processing module that extracts structured ESG-related information from sustainability and annual reports while incrementally updating the knowledge graph; Module 2 - an ESG knowledge graph construction module that establishes the schema and maintains the curated ESG facts; and Module 3 - a KG-driven retrieval-augmented generation module that retrieves pertinent evidence and generates substantiated responses.

3.1 Report Processing Module

This study presents a report processing pipeline that converts sustainability disclosures from PDF formats into structured representations for knowledge graph integration. We collected sustainability and annual reports from 18 commercial banks in Vietnam, issued during 2023 and 2024. The data collection phase was aimed at creating a representative corpus of ESG practices in the Vietnamese banking sector, emphasizing reports rich in sustainability-related content (e.g., sections on ESG, responsible lending, human capital, and governance). To alleviate noise resulting from formatting differences among various banks, all reports were subjected to document-level normalization, encompassing the standardization of file formats, naming conventions, and the incorporation of fundamental metadata (bank name, publication year, report type).

A key challenge in ESG report processing is that relevant disclosures are scattered across sections and mixed with non-ESG content. To improve extraction accuracy and efficiency, we use a navigation method that combines the table of contents (ToC) with the GRI taxonomy. The ToC helps identify sustainability-related page ranges and prioritize sections likely to contain standardized disclosures (e.g., Sustainability/ESG, Environment, and GRI Content Index). In parallel, the GRI taxonomy provides a standard backbone for mapping retrieved evidence to GRI indicators, enabling consistent topic standardization and cross-bank comparability. We use the ToC as a soft navigation prior rather than a hard filter: when page titles, headings, or extracted text do not fully align with the ToC, the page is still retained for downstream screening. This design is important for noisy reports because scanned pages, decorative layouts, and multi-column formatting can introduce OCR artifacts or incomplete section boundaries.

We use `olmOCR` to process layout-heavy reports because it preserves reading order and structural cues such as headings, lists, and tables, which are essential for linking extracted statements to section titles and page references [19]. This is particularly useful when the ToC must be reconciled with visually complex pages: the extracted heading sequence provides an additional check that the page content matches the expected section, while table linearization helps retain quantitative disclosures that would otherwise be lost with plain text extraction. We then use the Qwen3 4B instruct model to perform information extraction on the structured OCR output [22]. Rather than a single-pass extraction approach, we implemented instruction prompting to guide the model through schema-constrained extraction tasks [24]. The model is instructed to:

- **Determine Page-level ESG Relevance:** Use the ToC and section information as context to identify pages likely to contain substantive ESG disclosures.
- **Extract Statement-level Evidence:** Identify atomic units of evidence at the sentence or short-paragraph level, including both text and table-derived content.
- **Assign ESG Categories:** Classify evidence into the three pillars (E, S, G).
- **Map to GRI Indicators:** Align evidence with GRI indicators based on disclosure descriptions in the taxonomy. Evidence is either "unmapped" for post-processing or mapped at the topic level when it is too ambiguous for a specific indicator.

Handling Noisy OCR Output: Sustainability reports frequently contain scanned pages, decorative covers, multi-column infographics, and image-based tables, all of which can produce broken reading order, missing characters, or merged cells. Our pipeline mitigates these issues at three stages. (i) *Soft ToC navigation*: pages whose extracted headings only partially match the ToC are retained rather than discarded, so a noisy heading does not cause a relevant page to be skipped. (ii) *Structure-aware extraction*: `olmOCR` preserves headings, lists, and linearized tables, allowing the LLM extractor to recover quantitative disclosures (e.g., GHG figures, training hours) that pure-text OCR would lose. (iii) *Schema-constrained validation*: each candidate `ESG_Statement` must carry a non-empty `page` reference and a category label; statements that fail validation are flagged as `unmapped` and reviewed in a post-processing pass instead of being silently dropped. In our corpus, this combined strategy recovered evidence on pages where standard text-only PDF parsing returned empty or fragmented output, particularly for layout-heavy infographic pages summarising key sustainability metrics.

3.2 ESG Knowledge Graph Module

We build an ESG knowledge graph (ESG-KG) to transform unstructured ESG content from Vietnamese bank reports into a structured, queryable representation. Knowledge graphs are entity–relation structures that enable data integration, querying, and reasoning across heterogeneous sources [17]. Our ESG knowledge graph connects the information we gather from bank reports to sustainability topics set by GRI [5]. In addition, the graph structure is informed by existing ESG taxonomy enrichment efforts, such as FinSim4-ESG [10]. The resulting graph allows us to track information from documents and combine data at the indicator level for further analysis and improved information retrieval. The ESG-KG schema consists of five main node types:

- `Company`: represents each bank or organization, identified by `company_id` and `company_name`.
- `Report`: represents a sustainability or annual report of a company in a given year, with attributes `report_id`, `company_id`, `type_of_report`, and `year`.
- `ESG_Statement`: represents an ESG Statement extracted from a report, typically a sentence or short paragraph. Each statement includes `statement_id`, `title`, `content`, `embedding_content`, and `page`. The `embedding_content` is used for semantic retrieval in the RAG pipeline [12,14].
- `GRI_Indicator`: represents a specific disclosure topic defined by the GRI framework, with attributes `indicator_id`, `indicator_name`, `GRI_disclosure_detail`, and `topic_title` [5].
- `ESG_Category`: represents the ESG values {E, S, G}.

We instantiate the ESG-KG in Neo4j following the schema illustrated in Fig. 2. This design ensures end-to-end traceability from high-level entities to document-grounded evidence units and aligned sustainability topics.

For each `Report`, we segment the document into candidate evidence units and materialize them as `ESG_Statement` nodes. We then categorize `ESG_Statement` into `ESG_Category` and indicator alignment to `GRI_Indicator`. This LLM-assisted information extraction approach is consistent with recent evidence that iterative prompting and LLM-guided pipelines can improve the construction of schema-conformant knowledge graphs [18,20]. Importantly, all nodes and edges retain provenance (report metadata and page references) to support verification and error analysis. These derived signals support improved retrieval by prioritizing indicators and categories with stronger, multi-evidence support during KG-driven RAG [12].

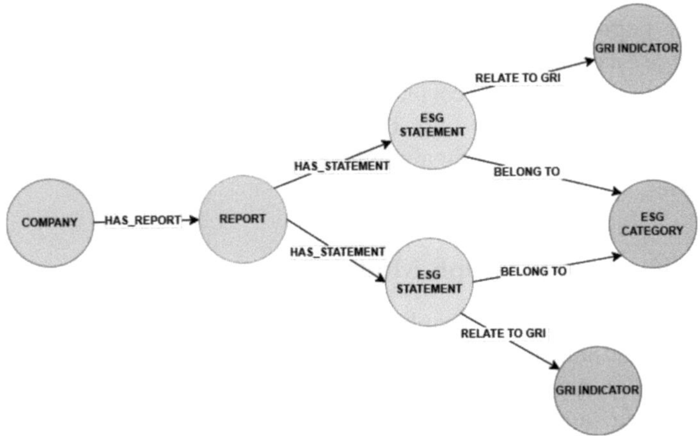

Fig. 2. ESG Knowledge Graph Schema.

3.3 KG-Driven Retrieval-Augmented Generation Module

This module implements a KG-RAG pipeline. Given a user question q, the system employs, (i) a hybrid retrieval strategy (Algorithm 1) that combines graph-based filtering with semantic and keyword-based scoring to retrieve the most relevant evidence from the ESG knowledge graph. The retrieved evidence is then passed to (ii), an answer generator that produces substantiated responses grounded in the provenance-linked statements, ensuring traceability and explainability for end-users and auditors (Fig. 3).

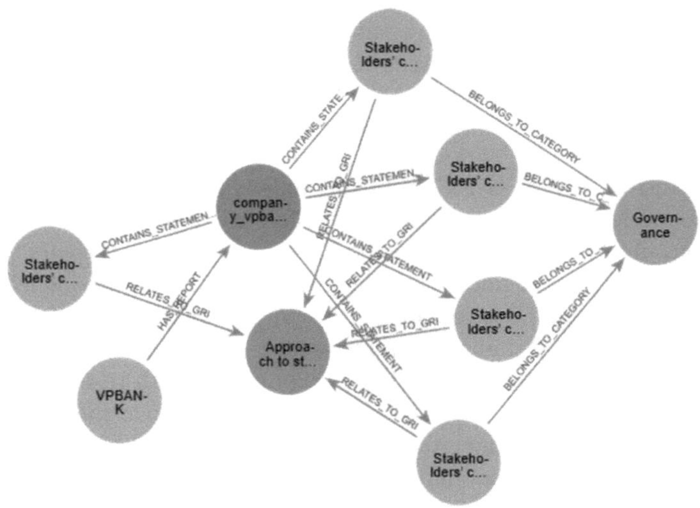

Fig. 3. Illustrating entities and their relationships in the ESG-KG.

KG Retriever: We represent the ESG knowledge graph as $G = (V, E)$, where V is the set of nodes and E is the set of edges. Each node $v \in V$ has a label (e.g., `Company`, `Report`, `ESG_Statement`, `GRI_Indicator`, `ESG_Category`) and a set of attributes that may vary by label. Given a question q, the retriever returns the top-k most relevant `ESG_Statement` nodes as evidence.

Statement Embedding: For semantic retrieval, we encode the `embedding_content` attribute of each `ESG_Statement` into a dense vector using a Qwen-based embedding model [22]. This yields a fixed-size representation $\mathbf{e}_s$ for each statement s, which is used to compute similarity with the query embedding.

Hybrid Graph-Aware Retrieval: We use a hybrid strategy that combines graph filtering with semantic and keyword-based scoring. First, an LLM assigns q to an ESG dimension (E/S/G). This label is used to generate a schema-constrained Cypher query that selects a candidate set of `ESG_Statement` nodes. Next, we score candidates by (i) vector similarity between the query embedding and statement embeddings and (ii) keyword matching for critical entities such as years, metrics, or GRI codes. Finally, we fuse the top results from both scoring streams to form the evidence context.

Answer Generation: The answer generator takes as input the question q and the retrieved evidence S_{context}. We use a fixed instruction prompt to constrain the LLM to produce answers based only on the provided statements. Each retrieved statement is passed together with its provenance (e.g., report name, page number and topic relevant) to support verification and traceability.

Algorithm 1. Hybrid Graph-based ESG Retrieval Strategy

Input: Question q, Knowledge Graph $G = (V, E)$, LLM M_{llm}, Embedding Model M_{emb}
Parameters: Vector Top-k ($k_v = 3$), Keyword Top-k ($k_w = 2$)
Output: Evidence set S_{context}

$S_{\text{context}} \leftarrow \emptyset$
$c \leftarrow \text{Classify}(q)$ using M_{llm} ▷ $c \in \{E, S, G\}$
Step 1: Keyword Extraction
$K_{\text{num}} \leftarrow \text{RegexExtractNumbers}(q)$ ▷ years, percentages, units
$K_{\text{txt}} \leftarrow \text{LLMExtractKeywords}(q, M_{\text{llm}})$ ▷ entities, topics
Step 2: Candidate Generation via Graph
$Q_{\text{cypher}} \leftarrow \text{GenerateCypher}(q, c, G.\text{Schema})$
$S_{\text{cand}} \leftarrow \text{ExecuteCypher}(G, Q_{\text{cypher}})$
if S_{cand} is empty **then**
  $S_{\text{cand}} \leftarrow \text{GetStatementsByCategory}(G, c)$ ▷ fallback
end if
Step 3: Scoring & Ranking
$\mathbf{e}_q \leftarrow M_{\text{emb}}.\text{encode}(q)$
for each statement $s \in S_{\text{cand}}$ **do**
  $s.\text{score}_{\text{vec}} \leftarrow \text{CosineSimilarity}(\mathbf{e}_q, \mathbf{e}_s)$

$s.\text{score}_{\text{kw}} \leftarrow 0$
for $k \in K_{\text{num}}$ **do**
  if $k \in s.\text{content} \vee k \in s.\text{title}$ **then** $s.\text{score}_{\text{kw}} \leftarrow s.\text{score}_{\text{kw}} + 2$
  end if
end for
for $k \in K_{\text{txt}}$ **do**
  if $k \in s.\text{content} \vee k \in s.\text{title}$ **then** $s.\text{score}_{\text{kw}} \leftarrow s.\text{score}_{\text{kw}} + 1$
  end if
end for
end for
Step 4: Hybrid Fusion
$L_{\text{vec}} \leftarrow \text{SortDesc}(S_{\text{cand}}, \text{score}_{\text{vec}})[1 : k_v]$
$L_{\text{kw}} \leftarrow \text{SortDesc}(S_{\text{cand}}, \text{score}_{\text{kw}})[1 : k_w]$
$S_{\text{context}} \leftarrow \text{Unique}(L_{\text{vec}} \cup L_{\text{kw}})$
return S_{context}

4 Experiments and Results

We construct an ESG knowledge graph covering 18 Vietnamese commercial banks. Among them, 10 banks provide sustainability reports for both 2023 and 2024, while 8 banks provide Annual Reports for 2023 and 2024 that include sustainability-related sections. The reports have an average length of approximately 60 pages per document, with the longest Sustainability Report containing 80 pages and the shortest containing 28 pages (e.g., Fig. 4).

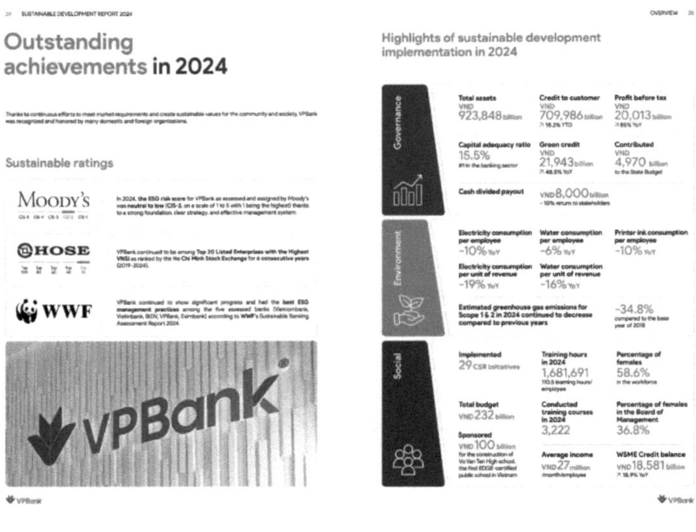

Fig. 4. Sample-VPBank Sustainability Report 2024.

To evaluate the proposed KG-RAG framework, we created a question set of 120 ESG questions with support from ESG domain experts. The experts further categorized the questions into three groups: Environmental (55 questions), Social (32 questions), and Governance (33 questions). Since evaluating all 120 questions across all 18 banks would be computationally expensive, we randomly selected 6 banks for evaluation, comprising 10 sustainability reports and 2 annual reports, with report lengths ranging from 28 to 80 pages. Answers generated by different methods were manually assessed by domain experts.

Our experimental design compares multiple retrieval configurations paired with different large language models to assess the contribution of each component to system performance. For each question-document pair, we retrieve the top-3 candidate statements and pass them to the answer generator. Each generated answer is then independently evaluated by domain experts for correctness based on whether it accurately reflects the document evidence and addresses the question. We measure performance by accuracy—the percentage of correctly answered questions—aggregated across ESG dimensions (Environment, Social, Governance) and overall. This setup enables us to isolate the impact of retrieval strategy and LLM choice on the final QA performance.

The expert-led evaluation protocol offers high-quality judgment for a specialized ESG setting, but it is not easily scalable to larger cross-industry benchmarks. In practice, we view this benchmark as a carefully controlled first-stage evaluation. A larger-scale benchmark could combine expert review for a representative subset with lighter-weight validation procedures, such as adjudication guidelines, evidence overlap checks, citation quality scores, and automated faithfulness metrics for answers grounded in retrieved passages. This hybrid protocol would preserve domain rigor while reducing the annotation burden.

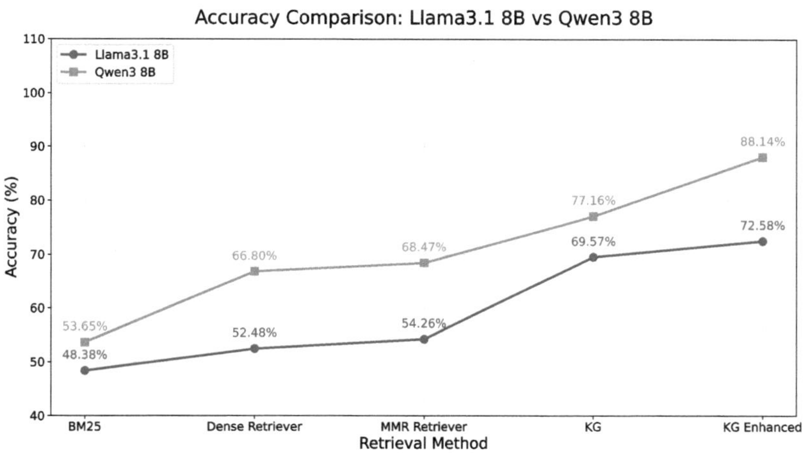

Fig. 5. Retriever wise Accuracy (in percentage) plot for Llama3 & Qwen3.

We experiment with two graph configurations: KG and KG_Enhanced. The KG_Enhanced variant augments the graph-based retriever with a hybrid search component that incorporates keyword matching. As baselines, we compare against three retrieval methods that return the top-3 statements for each question: (i) BM25, which ranks evidence using term frequency and inverse document frequency; (ii) MMR, which promotes both relevance and diversity to reduce redundancy, using Qwen3-4B embeddings; and (iii) Dense Retrieval, which ranks candidates by embedding similarity computed with Qwen3-4B embeddings [22].

For answer generation, we evaluate two LLMs: Llama3.1-8B and Qwen3-8B [22,25]. Figure 5 reports retriever-wise accuracy (percentage of correctly answered questions) under different retrieval strategies. Overall, both Llama3 and Qwen3 show a consistent improvement when moving from traditional retrieval baselines (e.g., BM25 and MMR) to KG-driven retrieval. In particular, KG_Enhanced achieves the best performance across settings, indicating that combining KG filtering with hybrid (semantic + keyword) retrieval improves evidence selection and leads to more accurate, report-grounded answers. These results highlight the benefit of leveraging structured graph constraints for ESG question answering.

We use Qwen3-8B as the main answer generator because it provides a practical balance between reasoning quality, context utilization, and computational cost for our document-grounded setting. A larger model may improve difficult cases involving numeric reconciliation or long-range evidence aggregation, but it would also increase inference cost and reduce reproducibility for a pipeline that already includes OCR, retrieval, and KG construction. More importantly, the remaining errors suggest that model scale alone does not solve the core bottlenecks of this task: some failures originate from imperfect evidence extraction, noisy layouts, or incomplete retrieval chains. On this task, the main limitations of Qwen3-8B are its tendency to over-commit when evidence is partial, its uneven handling of tabular numeric evidence, and its sensitivity to contexts that contain several near-duplicate statements.

Computational Cost: We measured the runtime of each pipeline stage on a single NVIDIA RTX 3090 (24 GB) GPU. Table 1 summarises the results. Indexing a report (OCR + statement extraction + KG ingestion) takes roughly 4–5 min and is dominated by Qwen3-4B statement extraction over the structured OCR output. After indexing, each query is processed in about 10 s end-to-end, distributed roughly evenly across graph filtering, embedding-based scoring, and answer generation; no single component dominates query-time latency. Because reports are indexed once and then queried many times, this profile is practical for batch auditing workflows and periodic ESG assessment on commodity hardware.

Table 2 reports the accuracy (percentage of correctly answered questions) of Llama3.1-8B and Qwen3-8B under two retriever settings, KG and KG_Enhanced, across the Environmental, Social, and Governance categories, as well as overall. The best-performing configuration is KG_Enhanced_Qwen3-8B, achieving

Table 1. Average runtime per pipeline stage on a single NVIDIA RTX 3090 (24 GB) GPU.

Stage	Avg. time
olmOCR (PDF → structured text)	~1 min/report
Statement extraction (Qwen3-4B)	~3 min/report
KG ingestion (Neo4j)	~30 s/report
Graph filtering (Cypher generation + execution)	~3 s/query
Query embedding + cosine scoring	~5 s/query
Answer generation (Qwen3-8B)	~3 s/query
End-to-end query latency (KG_Enhanced)	~10 s/query

Table 2. Performance Comparison of Llama3.1 and Qwen3

Category	Environment	Social	Governance	Overall
KG_Llama3.1-8B	68.65%	69.60%	70.45%	69.57%
KG_Qwen3-8B	70.62%	82.23%	78.63%	77.16%
KG_Enhanced_Llama3.1-8B	70.35%	76.82%	70.56%	72.58%
KG_Enhanced_Qwen3-8B	**83.74%**	**92.43%**	**88.25%**	**88.14%**

83.74% (Environment), **92.43%** (Social), and **88.25%** (Governance), which results in the highest overall accuracy of **88.14%**.

Under the `KG` retriever, `KG_Qwen3-8B` outperforms `KG_Llama3.1-8B` across all categories and overall (77.16% vs. 69.57%), with a particularly strong gain on Social questions (82.23% vs. 69.60%). Adding hybrid retrieval (`KG_Enhanced`) improves performance for both LLMs. In particular, Llama3.1-8B increases from 69.57% to 72.58% overall, while Qwen3-8B improves substantially from 77.16% to 88.14%. These results suggest that combining KG-based candidate filtering with hybrid (semantic + keyword) ranking yields more relevant evidence and that Qwen3-8B benefits the most from the enhanced retrieval context. Some examples of retrieved evidence and generated answers are presented in Appendix A to illustrate system behavior.

The values $k_v = 3$ and $k_w = 2$ in Algorithm 1 were selected to balance two complementary signals: k_v should be large enough to cover the descriptive, multi-aspect nature of ESG narratives (where a single question often spans policy, action, and quantitative outcome), while k_w should be small enough to inject high-precision keyword matches (e.g., specific years or GRI codes) without overwhelming the context with redundant numeric mentions. We confirm this design choice empirically with the sensitivity analysis in Table 3.

Table 3 reports a sensitivity analysis of the hybrid retriever for the best-performing configuration, `KG_Enhanced_Qwen3-8B`. The setting $k_v = 3$ and $k_w = 2$ achieves the highest overall accuracy of **88.14%**. Reducing the context to $(2, 1)$ lowers accuracy to 78.92%, indicating that some questions require more

Table 3. Sensitivity of k_v and k_w for `KG_Enhanced_Qwen3-8B`.

(k_v, k_w)	$(2, 1)$	$(2, 2)$	$(3, 2)$	$(4, 2)$	$(3, 3)$
Overall accuracy	78.92%	82.16%	**88.14%**	86.23%	84.71%

than two supporting statements. Increasing either semantic or keyword evidence beyond the selected setting also reduces performance, with 86.23% for $(4, 2)$ and 84.71% for $(3, 3)$. This suggests that additional retrieved statements introduce redundancy and make the answer context less focused. Overall, the curve is unimodal around $(3, 2)$, supporting it as a robust default for this domain rather than a hyperparameter overfit to a single split.

Table 4. Distribution of error categories on incorrect cases

Error category	Environmental	Social	Governance	Overall
E1: Annotation drift	18%	25%	21%	22%
E2: Distractor-rich chunks	26%	12%	19%	18%
E3: Multi-fact composition	31%	19%	22%	24%
E4: Cross-entity contamination	9%	11%	16%	12%
E5: Implicit reasoning	16%	33%	22%	24%

Incorrect predictions account for 11.9% of all evaluated question–document pairs. We manually reviewed the errors produced by `KG_Enhanced_Qwen3-8B` and grouped them into five dominant categories. Table 4 shows that the largest sources of error are multi-fact composition and implicit reasoning, both at 24% overall. To make these categories concrete:

- **E1 (Annotation drift, 22%):** the model returns a factually correct answer that disagrees with the gold label because of evolving disclosures (e.g., a 2024 figure superseding a 2023 one cited in the question).
- **E2 (Distractor-rich chunks, 18%):** the retrieved page mixes the target metric with several similar values (e.g., training hours by gender, by level, by region), and the LLM picks the wrong one.
- **E3 (Multi-fact composition, 24%):** the answer requires aggregating values from two or more pages (e.g., total Scope 1+2+3 emissions reported in separate tables); strongest in Environmental questions (31%).
- **E4 (Cross-entity contamination, 12%):** statements about a parent group or subsidiary are confused with the target bank.
- **E5 (Implicit reasoning, 24%):** the evidence implies the answer (e.g., a stated policy implies a yes/no on a related practice) but does not state it literally; strongest in Social questions (33%).

These patterns suggest concrete improvements: E2 and E4 are addressable by tighter graph filtering on `Company` and `topic_title` edges; E3 calls for explicit multi-hop traversal over `HAS_STATEMENT` chains rather than a single retrieval pass; and E5 would benefit from a reasoning-oriented prompt or a chain-of-thought generator. Annotation drift (E1) is partly an artefact of the benchmark and motivates the hybrid evaluation protocol discussed below. Cross-entity contamination (12%) being the lowest category indicates that KG filtering already removes most off-scope matches.

5 Limitations and Generalizability

Model-Level Limitations: `Qwen3-8B` is a pragmatic rather than upper-bound choice: it offers good answer quality at manageable cost but remains limited in long-range evidence synthesis, numeric reconciliation across tables, and calibrated abstention when retrieval is incomplete. The error patterns in Table 4 reflect these limitations directly, especially for E3 (multi-fact composition) and E5 (implicit reasoning).

Data-Level Limitations: The current benchmark covers 18 Vietnamese commercial banks and 120 expert-curated questions, narrower than the broader space of sustainability reporting practice. Extraction quality also remains contingent on OCR fidelity: scanning artefacts, decorative layouts, and image-only tables can still produce missing or fragmented evidence despite the mitigations in Sect. 3.1.

Evaluation-Level Limitations: Manual expert assessment provides high-quality judgment but is hard to scale. We view the current setup as a controlled first-stage benchmark; a hybrid protocol that combines expert adjudication on a representative subset with automated metrics (faithfulness, evidence overlap, citation precision/recall) would scale evaluation to larger cross-industry corpora

6 Conclusion

This paper presented a knowledge-graph-augmented RAG system for ESG question answering over Vietnamese banking reports. The pipeline converts layout-heavy PDFs into structured evidence using `olmOCR`, extracts statement-level disclosures with LLM-guided prompting, and organises them into an ESG knowledge graph aligned with the GRI taxonomy. Building on this graph, we introduced a KG-driven retriever with hybrid (semantic + keyword) scoring that returns provenance-preserving evidence for answer generation. Experiments on expert-designed ESG questions show that KG-based retrieval—particularly the enhanced hybrid variant—substantially improves accuracy over BM25, MMR, and dense baselines (88.14% vs. 53–69%), confirming the value of structured constraints and evidence traceability for ESG analytics.

As discussed in Sect. 5, the framework is modular and we view it as a transferable blueprint for traceable, document-grounded QA in domains where narrative claims, numeric evidence, and reporting standards must be connected explicitly. Future work will extend the benchmark to additional sectors and integrate automated faithfulness metrics into a hybrid expert–automatic evaluation protocol.

A Appendix

Question: Did female employees hold more than 50% of managerial positions at ACB in 2023? **(S)**
Answer: Yes. Female employees held more than 50% of managerial positions at ACB in 2023. Specifically, 51% of managerial-level employees were female (an increase of 2% compared to 2022).
Retrieved Reports:
- ACB Sustainability Report 2023 – Page 39 (GRI 405-1: Diversity and Equal Opportunity)

Question: Did ACB reduce its total GHG emissions across all three scopes in 2023 compared to 2022? **(E)**
Answer: Yes. Total GHG emissions decreased by 9%, from 34,355 tCO_2e (2022) to 31,238 tCO_2e (2023).
Retrieved Reports:
- ACB Sustainability Report 2023 – Page 33 (GHG emissions summary; reporting across scopes)

Question: Does ACB have a sustainable credit package with a limit of at least VND 2,000 billion in 2023? **(G)**
Answer: Yes. ACB introduced the *Green and Social Credit* package in 2023 with a limit of at least VND 2,000 billion, described in the Chairperson's Message.
Retrieved Reports:
- ACB Sustainability Report 2023 – Page 8 (Chairperson's Message; Green and Social Credit package)

Question: What was the average number of training hours per employee at ACB in 2023? **(S)**
Answer: The average number of training hours per employee in 2023 was **66 hours**, based on a total of 856,831 training hours reported for the workforce.
Retrieved Reports:
- ACB Sustainability Report 2023 – Page 36 (GRI 404-1/404-2: Training and Education)

References

1. Lozano, R., von Haartman, R.: Reinforcing the holistic perspective of sustainability: analysis of the importance of sustainability drivers in organizations. Corp. Soc. Responsib. Environ. Manag. **25**(4), 508–522 (2018)
2. Tsang, A., Frost, T., Cao, H.: Environmental, social, and governance (ESG) disclosure: a literature review. Br. Account. Rev. **55**(1), 101149 (2023)
3. Friede, G., Busch, T., Bassen, A.: ESG and financial performance: aggregated evidence from more than 2000 empirical studies. J. Sustain. Financ. Invest. **5**(4), 210–233 (2015)
4. United Nations Global Compact: Who Cares Wins: Connecting Financial Markets to a Changing World. Report (2004)
5. Global Reporting Initiative: The Global Standards for Sustainability Impacts (GRI Standards). https://www.globalreporting.org/standards/. Accessed 29 Jan 2026
6. Basel Committee on Banking Supervision: Principles for the Effective Management and Supervision of Climate-Related Financial Risks. Bank for International Settlements (2022)
7. State Bank of Vietnam: Directive No. 03/CT-NHNN dated 24 March 2015 on promoting green credit growth and environmental–social risk management in credit granting activities (2015)
8. Murakami, S., Muraoka, S.: Exploring the potential of internet news for supply risk assessment of metals. Sustainability **14**(1), 409 (2022)
9. Bui, B., Houqe, M.N., Zaman, M.: Climate governance effects on carbon disclosure and performance. Br. Account. Rev. **52**(2), 100880 (2020)
10. Kang, J., El Maarouf, I.: FinSim4-ESG shared task: learning semantic similarities for the financial domain. In: Proceedings of the 4th Workshop on Financial Technology and Natural Language Processing (FinNLP), pp. 211–217 (2022)
11. Brown, T.B., Mann, B., Ryder, N., et al.: Language models are few-shot learners. In: Advances in Neural Information Processing Systems (2020)
12. Lewis, P., Perez, E., Piktus, A., et al.: Retrieval-augmented generation for knowledge-intensive NLP tasks. In: Advances in Neural Information Processing Systems, pp. 9459–9474 (2020)
13. Robertson, S., Zaragoza, H.: The probabilistic relevance framework: BM25 and beyond. Found. Trends Inf. Retr. **3**(4), 333–389 (2009)
14. Karpukhin, V., Oğuz, B., Min, S., et al.: Dense passage retrieval for open-domain question answering. In: Proceedings of the 2020 Conference on Empirical Methods in Natural Language Processing (EMNLP) (2020)
15. Zhu, Y., Yuan, H., Wang, S., et al.: Large language models for information retrieval: a survey. CoRR abs/2308.07107 (2023)
16. Cai, B., Ye, Z., Chen, S.: Intelligent ESG evaluation for construction enterprises in China: an LLM-based model. Buildings **15**(15), 2710 (2025)
17. Hogan, A., Blomqvist, E., Cochez, M., et al.: Knowledge Graphs. Synthesis Lectures on Data, Semantics, and Knowledge, Springer, Cham (2021). https://doi.org/10.1007/978-3-031-01918-0
18. Carta, S., Giuliani, A., Piano, L., et al.: Iterative zero-shot LLM prompting for knowledge graph construction. CoRR abs/2307.01128 (2023)
19. Poznanski, J., et al.: olmOCR: unlocking trillions of tokens in PDFs with vision language models. arXiv preprint arXiv:2502.18443 (2025)
20. Trajanoska, M., Stojanov, R., Trajanov, D.: Enhancing knowledge graph construction using large language models. CoRR abs/2305.04676 (2023)

21. Bronzini, M., Nicolini, C., Lepri, B., et al.: Glitter or gold? Deriving structured insights from sustainability reports via large language models. CoRR abs/2310.05628 (2023)
22. Bai, J., Bai, S., Chu, Y., Cui, Z., et al.: Qwen3 technical report. CoRR abs/2505.09388 (2025)
23. Ji, Z., Lee, N., Frieske, R., et al.: Survey of hallucination in natural language generation. ACM Comput. Surv. **55**(12), 1–38 (2023)
24. Wei, J., Bosma, M., Zhao, V.Y., et al.: Finetuned language models are zero-shot learners. In: Proceedings of the International Conference on Learning Representations (2022)
25. Meta AI: Introducing Llama 3.1: Our most capable models to date. In: Meta AI Blog (2024)

Mechanisms for Identification of Micro-objects Based on the Use of Characteristics in the Image Structure

Rustam A. Safarov[1,2](✉), Isroil I. Jumanov[3], Olimjon I. Djumanov[3], and Umid Z. Djumayozov[2]

[1] Tashkent University of Information Technologies named after Muhammad al-Khwarizmi, Tashkent, Uzbekistan
rustammix.rs@gmail.com

[2] Samarkand branch of Tashkent University of Information Technologies named after Muhammad al-Khwarizmi, Samarkand, Uzbekistan

[3] Samarkand State University named after Sharof Rashidov, Samarkand, Uzbekistan

Abstract. Scientific and methodological foundations, methods, and mechanisms for optimizing the processes of identification, recognition, and classification of micro-objects (pollen grains and single-celled organisms) have been developed using tools that utilize dynamic, statistical, geometric, morphological, and signal characteristics of images. The study examines control systems for industrial and technological complexes, palynology, environmental and ecology monitoring, and medical diagnostics. Methods for optimizing micro-object image identification are proposed, based on tools for adjusting parameter values for image point changes, adjusting network structure, variable activation functions, and filtering models for noise, random outliers, and image spikes. Estimates of the root-mean-square error were obtained for various dynamic image identification models combined with a three-layer neural network. A software package for optimizing the processes of identification, recognition, and classification of micro-objects was implemented and tested using data obtained during the diagnosis of tuberculosis patients. Three-layer, recurrent, loosely coupled neural network modules, along with supervised and unsupervised network learning algorithms, were used. The effectiveness of the proposed approaches is substantiated by improved recognition accuracy and resilience to noise-induced image distortions. A comparative analysis of existing micro-object processing methods is conducted, identifying their limitations and the advantages of the developed solutions. It has been demonstrated that integrating various image characteristics and adaptive learning models can improve classification accuracy in complex environments. The results can be used in biomedical research, environmental monitoring, and automated diagnostic systems.

Keywords: Image · Micro-object · Identification · Recognition · Classification · Optimization · Error · Software Package · Probability

O. Gervasi et al. (Eds.): ICCSA 2026 Workshops, LNCS 16758, pp. 117–132, 2027.
https://doi.org/10.1007/978-3-032-30497-1_8

1 Introduction

In the control systems of production and technological complexes, monitoring of the environment and ecology of the region, palynology, medicine and other fields of knowledge, micro-objects of various types are used, for example, pollen grains, unicellular microorganisms, minerals in rock mass, food products and others [1–3]. Existing technologies for processing images of micro-objects are focused on the functions of counting, analysis, identification, recognition, and classification of micro-objects, which are not performed quickly enough, with high error rates and costs [4–7].

Improvements are needed in processing information from micro-objects presented for use in digital, video, photo, and luminance images, as well as in identifying the desired characteristics in the informative portion of a colour image. The development of effective tools for filtering and correcting defective points in micro-object images, and the use of combined dynamic models and neural networks (NN) for this purpose, are also required [8–11].

Of great scientific significance is the research and development of constructive approaches, principles, and methods for identification, recognition, and classification of micro-objects through the use of statistical, dynamic, morphometric, textural, colour, brightness, spectral and frequency characteristics of the image [12–14].

This work is devoted to the research and development of a methodology for optimizing the processes of identification, recognition and classification of micro-objects based on problem-oriented information processing systems.

2 Related Work

In recent years, methods of using modern computer vision systems (CVS) and intelligent technologies for analysing and processing information based on the mathematical apparatus of soft computing and dynamic models for identifying micro-objects have been widely developed [15–17].

Scientific achievements in this field are mainly based on approaches that use classical methods of processing images of micro-objects, as well as on methods of optimal problem-oriented information processing that apply deep machine learning algorithms and tools, such as YOLOv8 models [18–20]. Classical approaches represent a wide class of algorithms that perform such functions as contour selection, reference points, segmentation, extraction of informative features, statistical and dynamic properties of information, as well as the use of geometric, textural and brightness characteristics of image points [21–23].

Methods using neural networks and their hybrid architectures combined with dynamic models are becoming increasingly widespread. Hybrid models have been shown to automatically generate information points in a sequence, providing higher accuracy in recognizing and classifying micro-objects with lower processing costs. At the same time, their use is justified by the need to replace existing technologies, which rely on significant computing resources and large data volumes [24–26]. Combined approaches that combine traditional image processing methods with NNs are aimed at increasing the stability of algorithms, eliminating noise and defective points, as well as distorted information [27,28].

Thus, despite significant progress in the subject area under study, existing methods, algorithms, and software applications do not fully ensure the required accuracy and reliability of information processing. This underscores the importance and relevance of the problem of identifying, recognizing, and classifying micro-objects based on problem-oriented information processing systems using the characteristics of image structural components.

3 Materials and Methods

3.1 Tools for Optimizing Micro-object Identification Based on Filtering and Detection of Defective Image Points

An approach aimed at identifying micro-objects is proposed, based on the use of component characteristics in the image structure and the development of tools for high-precision image point reconstruction using the following operators:

Shift transformation, parameter determination, and colour coding of image points;

Color visualization of micro-objects, representation of the use of geometric, textural, and morphometric image characteristics;

Creation of edge maps, segment centres, and image cores.

Various noise reduction filters were researched and implemented, used to highlight specific areas of an image or remove other components. This involved determining the nature of the noise, the image's dynamic range, the colour accuracy, and identifying many other factors that negatively impact filtering results.

Gaussian and median filters were studied, demonstrating the best performance in suppressing noise and impulse interference, preserving the sharpness of the boundaries of contrasting parts of the image of micro-objects, and replacing the spectral intensity with pixels of a point located near the median [29–31]. The filtering tool, correction of defective points, and conditions caused by shifts, blurring, and distortions of information are taken into account when solving the equation

$$I_{\text{new}}(x, y) = \underset{(kx,ky)\in K_{xy}}{\text{med}} \{I_{\text{old}}(kx, ky)\}$$

where I_{new} and I_{old} - new and old pixel values of the image point;

K_{xy} – image point sizes in pixels; $K_{Hs} \times K_{Ws}$ – kernel center with window, tracked point (x, y). It is important to filter out additive noise in the contour of image points. For this purpose, a Gaussian filter was implemented, based on a combined three-layer neural network model and a discrete wavelet transform

$$I_{\text{new}}(x, y) = \sum_{dx=-RH}^{RH} \sum_{dy=-RW}^{RW} G(dx, dy) \cdot I_{\text{old}}(x + dx, y + dy),$$

where G – filter function of the combined Gaussian model; RH and RW – constants of the filter rank, respectively, vertically and horizontally;

$$I_{\text{new}}(x, y) = \frac{1}{\sqrt{2\pi}\,\sigma} e^{-\frac{x^2}{2\sigma^2}} \times \frac{1}{2\pi\,\sigma^2} e^{-\frac{y^2}{2\sigma^2}},$$

- combined Gaussian distribution of additive noise and useful point; x, y - distances from the origin of coordinates along the abscissa and ordinate axes, in which the values of the signal/noise parameter are measured;

σ – error (mean-square deviation) of filtering the image of micro-objects.

The additive image noise filtering tool under study also combines operators for detecting and correcting defective points. Four regions are considered: LL, HL, LH and HH. The results of the YOLOv8 application are generated and represented as data matrices.

The results of the correction of defective points are presented in the area LL, the values of which are determined by the row and column of the data matrix. The complexity of the image texture, which is caused by interfering factors, in turn, hinders the high-precision identification of micro-objects. Solving the problem is further complicated when the models describing the influencing factors have a nonlinear structure.

To solve the network training problem, the initial point of the image signal is defined, taking into account the impact of noise and factors leading to defective points. The signal model of an image point is generally defined as

$$Z(n) = X(n) + E(n),$$

where $X(n)$ is a useful signal of the image point; $E(n)$ is an error, the value of which is determined by the influence of the signal/noise parameter and defects due to blurring, shifts in points of information distortion and other reasons. The neural network training algorithm is optimized using a tool based on the vector definition operator $W = [w_0, w_1, \ldots, w_k]^T$, where T is the set of neuron weight values in the network's input layer.

The filtering tool for applying nonlinear wavelet analysis schemes is based on the model [32,33]

$$X_M(n) = \sum_{(j,k)\in I_M} \langle X, Y_{j,k}(n)\rangle,$$

where $\Psi_{j,k}(n) = 2^{j/2}\Psi\left(2^j n - k\right)$ – component of the orthogonal basis; I_M – a set of indices of dimension M. If expression represents wavelet coefficients in the space of the wavelet function, then it is given in the form

$$W_{j,k}(Z) = X_{\Psi_{j,k}} + E_{\Psi_{j,k}},$$

where $X_{\Psi_{j,k}} = \langle X, \Psi_{j,k}\rangle$, $E_{\Psi_{j,k}} = \langle E, \Psi_{j,k}\rangle$.

Which are implemented based on the threshold function

$$X_M(n) = \sum_{j,k} P_T(\langle Z, \Psi_{j,k}\rangle)\,\Psi_{j,k}(n),$$

and the indicator

$$P_T(x) = \begin{cases} x, & \text{if } |x| \geq T; \\ 0, & \text{if } |x| < T, \end{cases}$$

where T - threshold; σ^2 – noise variance, the value of which is estimated by the median

$$\sigma^2 \approx \text{Med}(\langle Z, \Psi_{j,k} \rangle)_{0<k<\frac{N}{2}} \cdot$$

Figure 1 a), b) shows graphs of the dependencies of the probability of detecting defective points P_d for two curves: a) signal 1, b) signal 2. The solid curve corresponds to the result of the traditional algorithm, and the dashed-dotted curve corresponds to the result of the developed tool.

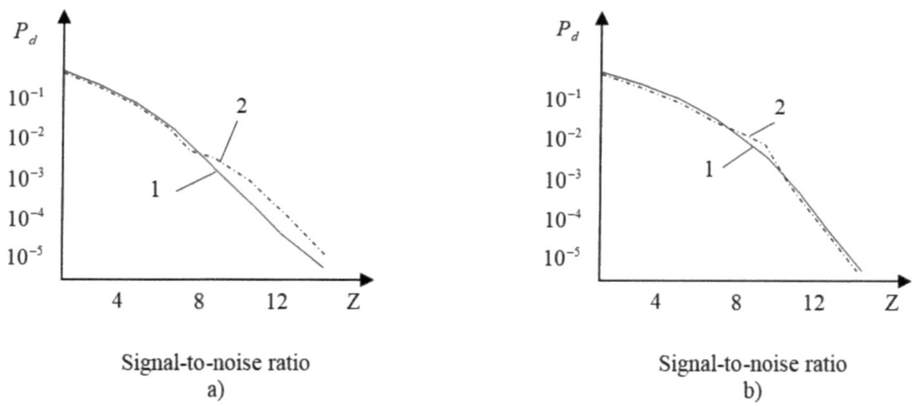

Fig. 1. Efficiency of defective point detection a) signal 1 b) signal 2.

It is determined that the probability of detecting defective image points varies depending on the training steps. In experimental studies, a hybrid model with a generalized algorithm was tested with an iteration step of 0.01. The graph of the traditional algorithm, plotted based on the values of the signal-to-noise Z parameter, almost converges with the curve of the proposed optimization tool for correcting distorted information from micro-objects.

The error function $H(U)$ at the threshold point of the neuron activation function exhibits a discontinuity of the first kind. The neuron weighting coefficients do not ensure an exact repetition of the signal shape. The main feature of the tool is the optimization of training sets, taking into account variations in their size.

To achieve high-precision image identification, the YOLOv8 tool was used. In this tool, the number of neurons in the layers and the network layers are adapted during deep learning, and a fixed threshold on the activation function is tuned from initial values.

A tool for optimizing image identification processes was developed based on YOLOv8 deep learning algorithms, which are tuned by adapting the size and properties of texture characteristics in the generated training set.

Figure 2 demonstrates the study's results, demonstrating the 99.6% recognition and classification accuracy achieved using the YOLOv8 model, as demonstrated on a validation set containing four pollen grain classes. The horizontal axis (True) indicates the true object classes, and the vertical axis (Predicted) indicates the classes predicted by the model.

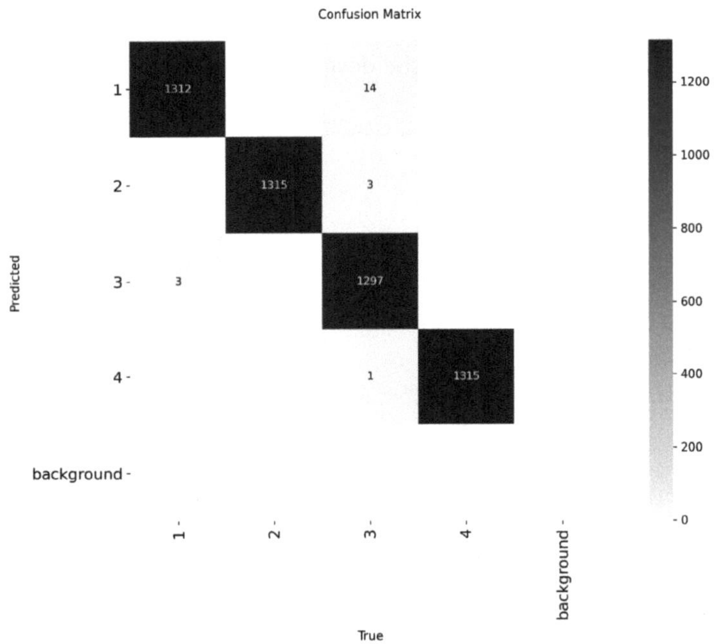

Fig. 2. Classification of micro-objects based on YOLOv8 and the error matrix.

Values on the main diagonal correspond to correctly classified samples: Class 1 – 1312 samples, Class 2 – 1315, Class 3 – 1297, and Class 4 – 1315. Values off the diagonal indicate misclassifications: the highest number of errors is observed for Class 1, where 14 samples were incorrectly classified as Class 3. Class 2 has three samples incorrectly classified as Class 3, Class 3 has three samples incorrectly classified as Class 1, and one sample is incorrectly classified as Class 4. Class 4 exhibits the lowest number of interclass errors – only one sample was incorrectly classified as Class 3. The "background" row and column are left blank, indicating the absence of false positives for background objects. The total number of correctly classified samples was 5239 out of 5260, corresponding to an overall model accuracy of 99.6%.

In another version of the study, the adaptive deep learning algorithm of the neural network is combined with modules of the wavelet package, which allows removing the noise part from the image structure and identifying the used characteristics of the components.

Figure 3 shows the performance graphs of the identification tool with filtering, correction of defective points, and distorted information, as measured by the function T versus the complexity of information processing. The curve dynamics depend on the number of filter stages N.

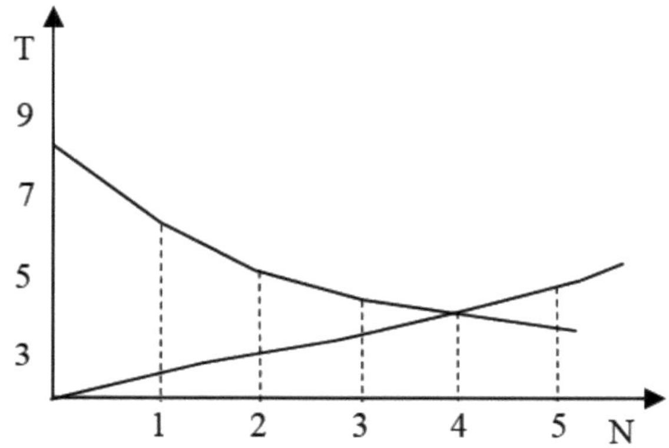

Fig. 3. The complexity of processing information of the tool.

Curve 1 corresponds to the filter with the image point tracking kernel adaptation tool, and curve 2 corresponds to the two-dimensional discrete Fourier transform without using the identification optimization tool. Curve 2 of the T function increases linearly with the increase in the number of stages of the pyramidal model in the multi-stage adaptive filter (MAF). Curve 1 corresponds to the application of the MAF model without the image point kernel adaptation tool. With parameter values of $N = 4$ and $T = 1.2 \cdot 10^6 \text{op}/\mu\text{s}$, the computational cost of problem-oriented information processing decreases approximately 15-fold.

3.2 Tools For Optimizing Micro-object Identification Based on Filtering and Correction of Defective Image Points

Tools have been developed to optimize micro-object identification processes, expanding the capabilities of the previous image processing tool based on filtering operators, defect point correction, selection, and adaptive segmentation of image contours.

The image contour tool divides the image into a number of regions with similar point characteristics. The contour is then segmented based on the matching of similar point characteristics, such as intensity, brightness, colour, and texture. A CNN is used for adaptive image contour segmentation [34,35].

Noise filtering and defect point correction tools are synthesized with parallel information processing algorithms that include self-tuning tools. To optimize the identification of micro-objects with filtering and correction of defective points, a one-dimensional mapping of the input image with a point x and its activation neural function was used [36,37]

$$f(x) = \frac{\mu}{1 + exp(-\alpha x + \beta)},$$

where α - slope coefficient, $\alpha > 0$; β - displacement values, μ - magnification factor, $\mu > 0$.

For optimization, the values of parameters α and β are chosen so that the range of input image points $[x_{\min}, x_{\max}]$ is mapped to one neuron and is located between the values of the unstable point x_1^* and one of the two stable points x_2^*. The input values of the variable are grouped according to their degree of proximity, and this operation continues until a stable point with a minimum training error of the CNN E is reached.

Parameters α and β are determined from the system of equations

$$x_i^* = f(x_i^*, \alpha, \beta, \mu), \quad i = 1, 2.,$$

where x_i^* are the values of the input variable that are associated with the definitions of the verification limits in the range $[x_{\min}, x_{\max}]$ in the form of the following relationships:

$$x_1^* = x_{\min} - \delta_1, \quad x_2^* = x_{\max} - \delta_2, \quad |\delta_1| \ll 1 \text{ and } |\delta_2| \ll 1.$$

The system of equations is solved for α and β only if the value of the coefficient μ is increased or specified in advance.

The solution to this system of equations is obtained in the form:

$$\alpha = \frac{1}{x_2^* - x_1^*} \ln\left(\frac{(\mu - x_1^*)x_2^*}{(\mu - x_2^*)x_1^*}\right), \quad \beta = \alpha x_1^* + \ln\left(\frac{\mu - x_1^*}{x_1^*}\right).$$

The neural network training optimization tool, based on information about changes in parameter μ, adjusts the values of parameters α and β, and then selects activation functions for the network neurons. To optimally select stable points when identifying micro-object images, the value of parameter μ is set in the neighbourhood of $\max|\Delta H|$, which is estimated using Shannon's unconditional and conditional entropy formula ΔH.

In experimental studies, the entropy of H image pixel intensities was calculated for each value of parameter μ. The entropy sequence was determined to depend on the values of parameter μ. As a result, it was proposed that the values μ_0 corresponding to $\max|\Delta H|$ be used to determine cluster boundaries in image pixel intensities. This result demonstrates the greatest increase in average useful information obtained by changing the value of parameter μ.

Figure 4 shows a graphical comparison of the efficiency of the tool for optimizing the identification of micro-object images using the function $K = T_{opt}/T_{tr}$ - the gain coefficient in the complexity of information processing, where T_{opt} is the gain coefficient for the MAF and variable adaptation operators.

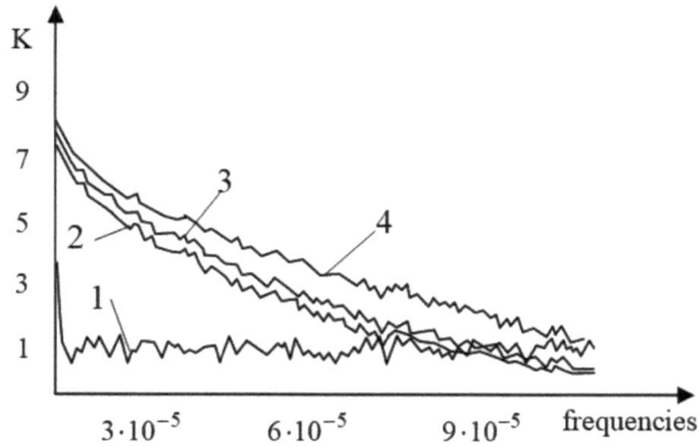

Fig. 4. Tuning efficiency in time and frequency domain.

The graphs were obtained for different signal frequency values L for three- and nine-channel filtering. Curve 1 corresponds to a traditional normalized linear MAF, curve 2 corresponds to a three-channel MAF, curve 3 corresponds to a nine-channel MAF, and curve 4 corresponds to a MAF-based instrument.

4 Results and Discussion

4.1 Results of Preliminary Processing of Images of Micro-objects

The most suitable format for colour video images is *RGB*, which utilizes three parameters of each pixel in the image frame. Rotating the image edge away from the light source changes the illumination of each point, requiring the R, G, and B variables to be fixed within a specific range of values [38].

Each point in the image contour of micro-objects is represented by the values of the solid line R, dashed line G, and dash-dotted line B parameters, which are determined by a high-resolution pixel matrix. Increasing the pixel intensity of a point increases the illumination of each image point, while decreasing the pixel intensity of a point reduces its illumination.

Table 1 shows the average values of quantitative characteristics of image points in a palette of $M = 16777216$ colours, measured over a period of 3 months.

The spectral range of signal characteristics of colour image points of micro-objects was studied using a method that helps determine the boundary, shape, and cross-sectional area of each point. Changes in point brightness along a line from one edge (cross-section) to the other are determined using statistical analysis or fuzzy logic [39].

Statistical analysis allows us to establish the main characteristics of the material flow at a specific point, time period, and time of analysis of colour images, which are used to determine the mineral composition of products on the conveyor.

Table 1. Brightness estimates for a colour image point of micro-objects

Time in days	R	G	B	NR	NG	NB	Number M
1–15	168	154	140	0.34595	0.00010	0.00000	341
15–30	165	162	152	0.13938	0.00000	0.00000	583
30–45	163	158	130	0.22650	0.00004	0.00000	184
45–60	159	139	119	0.53682	0.00011	0.00001	352
60–75	164	140	139	0.37499	0.00000	0.00000	431
75–90	140	143	125	0.23675	0.00001	0.00000	104
90–105	137	125	131	0.11207	0.00056	0.00000	231

The experimental studies examined medical objects using 450 digital microscopy images of 10 sputum smears. RGB and HSV color images were analyzed.

It was determined that the implemented mechanisms for identifying single-celled organisms significantly improve the speed and reliability of image parameter values for microscopic objects.

Sputum from patients with pulmonary tuberculosis was used to prepare the smears.

Sputum is stained red for acid-fast bacilli, and other elements in the sputum are stained blue.

In each image, pixel parameters were calculated with the following values: Red pixel color (R); Green pixel color (G);

Blue pixel color (B); Pixel brightness (Y);

Pixel hue (H); Pixel saturation (S); Pixel value (V).

Each pixel of the image point was represented by 7 parameters: R, G, B and Y in the range of values from 0 to 255; H in the range of 0 to 360; S and V in the range of 0 to 100.

All 450 images are divided into a training set of 314 images, a test set of 68 images, and a control set of 68 images.

Table 2 shows the spectral portion of the RGB image with background reflections of its parts: left (solid line), middle (dashed line), and right (dash-dotted line).

Figures 5 a), b) illustrate the probabilistic characteristics of the tools for optimizing the identification, recognition, and classification of micro-objects. A) the results are presented based on the point values of function $P_i = n_i/N_i$ — correct recognition and classification of micro-objects; b) the results are obtained depending on various values of parameter $\mu = \lambda\tau$ —function $hatP_i$ —the intensity of RGB image pixel intensity. The background of the image pixel is reflected. The left part is solid, the middle part is dashed, and the right part is dashed-dotted lines.

Figure 5 a) illustrates the probabilistic characteristics of the implemented mechanisms for identification, recognition and classification of micro-objects,

Table 2. Estimates of spectral characteristics of micro-object images

Time in days	R	G	B	Left side	Middle part	Right side	Number M
1–15	168	154	140	1.1062	17.7000	33579	341
15–30	165	162	152	1.1007	0.00000	32157	583
30–45	163	158	130	1.1067	0.00004	32204	184
45–60	159	139	119	1.1072	0.00011	32267	352
60–75	164	140	139	1.1115	0.00000	32204	431
75–90	140	143	125	1.1110	0.00001	32575	104

which are assessed according to the criterion of correct image recognition by one point

Figure 5 b) shows graphs of the function, which are plotted against parameter—the intensity of the RGB image pixels. The graph reflects the image background: the left part (solid line), the middle part (dashed line), and the right part (dashed-dotted line).

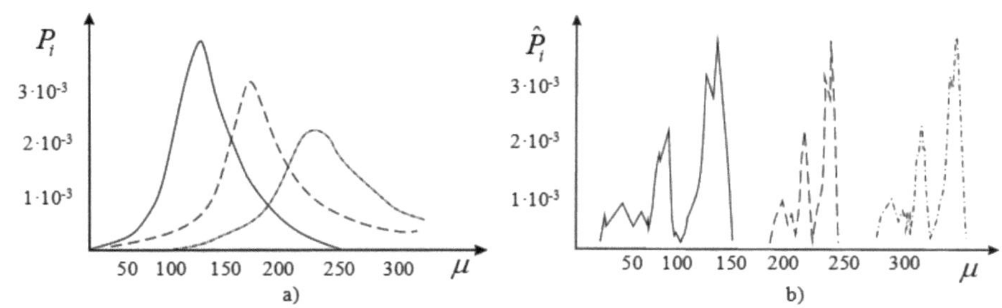

Fig. 5. Probabilities of image point recognition.

The values of R, G and B were determined using the relationship:

$$Y = 2.299 * R + 0.587 * G + 0.114 * B.$$

During testing of the mechanisms, the minimum and maximum boundaries of parameters H, S and V were determined, within which the pixels of the dots were related to acid-fast mycobacteria, while the values outside these boundaries are considered to relate to other objects. The following results were established: upper bound for parameter $H = 360$; upper bound for parameter $S = 70$; lower bound for parameter $V = 70$; upper bound for parameter $V = 100$.

Two neural networks were constructed to improve the accuracy of micro-object image identification. The first of these is used to select the best image characteristic based on 191 parameters of the lower bound of H, the second is of the lower bound of S. The most optimal neural network topology was determined, which has 14 neurons in the input layer, 14 in the hidden layer, and 1 in the output layer.

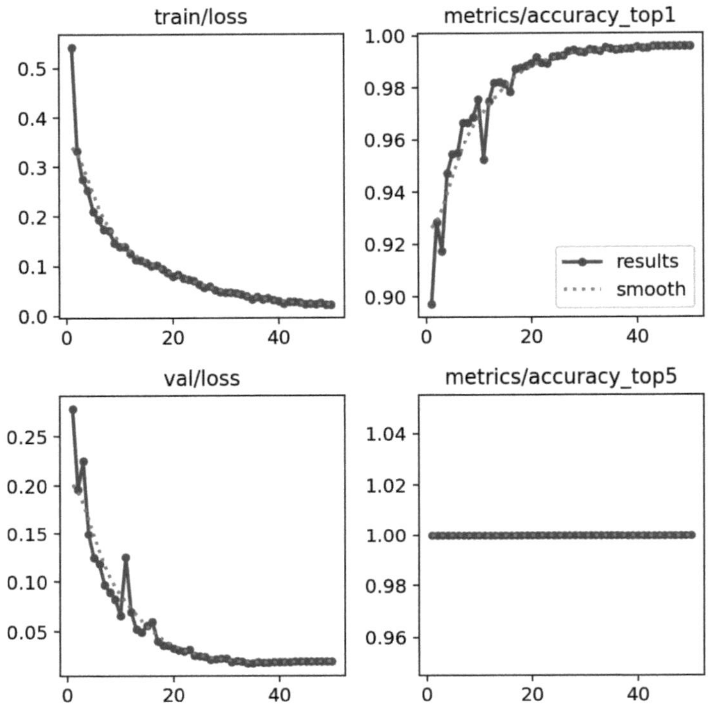

Fig. 6. YOLOv8n training graphs: loss functions and classification accuracy metrics over 50 epochs.

4.2 Implementation of Research Results

Figure 6 illustrates the YOLOv8 training graphs, which are evaluated by the value of the loss function for classifying a micro-object depending on different observation epoch lengths.

Graph 1—train/loss—shows the dynamics of the loss function on the training set. In the initial stage (epochs 1–5), a sharp decrease in loss is observed from 0.54 to 0.15, indicating intensive model training. Subsequently (epochs 5–50), the decrease becomes gradual and stable, reaching a value of approximately 0.02–0.03 by the end of training. The smoothed curve (orange dotted line) confirms the uniform and stable nature of the loss function's decrease, with no signs of divergence. This trend indicates correct model convergence during training.

Graph 2—metrics/accuracy/_top1—shows the change in Top-1 classification accuracy on the validation set across epochs. At the beginning of training (epochs 1–3), accuracy was approximately 0.90, after which minor fluctuations were observed due to the initial adjustment of the model weights. Beginning with epoch 5, a steady increase in accuracy is observed: by epoch 20, it reaches a level of 0.98–0.99, and by epoch 50, it reaches a maximum value of 0.995. The smoothed curve demonstrates a general upward trend with gradual stabilization at 0.99 at the end of training. Fluctuations in results between epochs are due to the stochastic nature of the training process and the data augmentation methods applied.

Graph 3—val/loss—displays the dynamics of the loss function on the validation set. In the first epochs, a significant decrease in loss is observed, from 0.27 to 0.08, similar to the trend on the training set. Moderate fluctuations with local peaks of 0.12–0.21 are observed around epochs 10–15, after which, starting from epoch 20, the curve stabilizes in the range of 0.02–0.03. Importantly, the validation set does not demonstrate a sustained increase in the loss function compared to the training set, indicating the absence of significant overfitting of the model. The patience parameter of 20 ensured continued training during periods of temporary performance degradation.

Graph 4—metrics/accuracy_top5—shows the Top-5 classification accuracy on the validation set, which remains at 1.00 throughout the training process. This result indicates that in all cases, the true class was among the five most probable model predictions. The reliability of the result is explained by the fact that the classification task considers only four classes. Therefore, the achieved Top-5 accuracy of 1.00 is reasonable, confirming the correctness of the model's performance and the accuracy of the data labeling.

The hyperbolic tangent function is used as the activation function for the neurons in the hidden layer of the network, and an exponential function is used for the output layer. On a validation training sample, the neural network's mechanisms provide identification accuracy of up to 97.5%, with a maximum error rate of 2.5% for micro-objects.

Table 3 shows the results of testing dynamic models combined with CNN – Daubechies wavelet analysis, 4, and a generalized network training algorithm.

Table 3. Results of hybrid models for micro-object image identification

Sets	Identification error in%	Probability of recognition error in %	Average classification error in %
Educational	97.9	2.1	1.87
Test	98.5	1.5	1.51
Control	97.5	2.5	2.27

It was determined that when training neural network algorithms based on the lower bound of S, in which the network has 8 neurons in the input layer, 7 in the hidden layer, and 1 in the output layer, the hybrid neural network training algorithm on the training set performs with an error of 89.4%. Moreover, the highest probabilistic recognition error is 10.6%, and the average micro-object classification error is 6.3%. The training performance of the hybrid neural network model on the test and validation sets is virtually identical.

Table 4 shows the results of the combined neural network training algorithm.

Table 4. Test results of the NN training algorithm for the hybrid model

Sets	Identification error in %	Probability of recognition error in %	Average classification error in %
Educational	89.4	10.6	0.63
Test	90.8	9.2	0.45
Control	90.1	9.9	0.57

A software package for the identification, recognition, and classification of micro-objects was developed and implemented. It utilizes morphometric, geometric, colour-brightness, and spectral image characteristics. The average processing time for a single image was found to be 9.532 µs, and for 450 images with a resolution of 572 × 422 pixels, it was nearly 42.75 µs. The average time spent filtering and correcting defective image points was 9.266 µs. The average neural network training time was 0.006 µs.

5 Conclusion

Scientific and methodological foundations, methods and algorithms for optimizing the identification, recognition and classification of micro-objects have been developed based on tools for using statistical, dynamic, morphometric, textural, color and brightness characteristics of the image of micro-objects.

The developed algorithms enable processing information about the three-dimensional structure of a micro-object, estimating its spatial position, and localizing desired objects in the image. Tools for optimizing micro-object identification are proposed, including the selection, filtering, and correction of defective image points, based on the extraction of local features and characteristics of heterogeneous fragments.

The mathematical apparatus for training neural networks was used at the stages of pre-processing, segmentation of microscopic digital images of sputum, recognition of objects (acid-fast mycobacteria), and diagnosis of tuberculosis. It was also implemented in clinical practice, the results of which demonstrate an obvious improvement in the quality of microbiological diagnosis of tuberculosis.

The YOLOv8 model demonstrated high performance in classifying microobjects: Top-1 accuracy was 99.5%, Top-5 accuracy was 100%, and the overall error matrix accuracy reached 99.6% (5239 out of 5260 samples) with no signs of overfitting, confirming the suitability of the model for automated analysis of microscopic images.

The theoretical results of the study are of practical interest in the design of problem-oriented information processing systems and the creation of a modified computer vision technology for images of pollen grains, as well as images of minerals in rock mass.

References

1. Sonka, M., Hlavac, V., Boyle, R.: Image Processing, Analysis and Machine Vision. Springer, New York (2013). https://doi.org/10.1007/978-1-4899-3216-7
2. Marcos, J.V., et al.: Automated pollen identification using microscopic imaging and texture analysis. Micron **68**, 36–46 (2015)
3. Philipp, V., König, M.: Pattern recognition methodologies for pollen grain image classification: a survey. Mach. Vision Appl. **33**(1), 18 (2022)
4. Jumanov, I.I., Safarov, R.A.: Algorithms for image processing of micro-objects of medical diagnostics systems. In: International Russian Smart Industry Conference (SmartIndustryCon), pp. 867–872. IEEE (2025). https://doi.org/10.1109/SmartIndustryCon65166.2025.10986021
5. Tsiknakis, N., et al.: Pollen grain classification based on ensemble transfer learning on the Cretan Pollen Dataset. Plants **11**(7), 919 (2022)
6. Garga, B., et al.: Pollen grain classification using some convolutional neural network architectures. J. Imaging **10**(7), 158 (2024)
7. Murphy, D.B., Davidson, M.W.: Fundamentals of Light Microscopy and Electronic Imaging. Wiley, New York (2012)
8. Xing, F., et al.: Deep learning in microscopy image analysis: a survey. IEEE Trans. Neural Netw. Learn. Syst. **29**(10), 4550–4568 (2017)
9. Melanthota, S.K., et al.: Deep learning-based image processing in optical microscopy. Biophys. Rev. **14**(2), 463–481 (2022)
10. Jumanov, I.I., Safarov, R.A.: Optimization of micro-object identification based on a pyramidal model with image segmentation. In: International Russian Smart Industry Conference, pp. 337–342. IEEE (2025). https://doi.org/10.1109/SmartIndustryCon65166.2025.10986135
11. Rezaeilouyeh, H., Mollahosseini, A., Mahoor, M.H.: Microscopic medical image classification framework via deep learning and shearlet transform. J. Med. Imaging **3**(4), 044501–044501 (2016)
12. Buades, A., Coll, B., Morel, J.-M.: Non-local means denoising. Image Process. Online **1**, 208–212 (2011)
13. Murali, V., Sudeep, P.V.: Image denoising using DnCNN: an exploration study. In: Jayakumari, J., Karagiannidis, G.K., Ma, M., Hossain, S.A. (eds.) Advances in Communication Systems and Networks. LNEE, vol. 656, pp. 847–859. Springer, Singapore (2020). https://doi.org/10.1007/978-981-15-3992-3_72
14. Szeliski, R.: Computer Vision: Algorithms and Applications. Springer, Cham (2022). https://doi.org/10.1007/978-3-030-34372-9
15. Jain, A.K., Duin, R.P.W., Mao, J.: Statistical pattern recognition: a review. IEEE Trans. Pattern Anal. Mach. Intell. **22**(1), 4–37 (2000)
16. Shen, D., Wu, G., Suk, H.-I.: Deep learning in medical image analysis. Annu. Rev. Biomed. Eng. **19**, 221–248 (2017)
17. Wang, X.: Deep learning in object recognition, detection, and segmentation. Found. Trends Sig. Process. **8**(4), 217–382 (2016)
18. Warshaneyan, S.S., et al.: Automated Pollen Recognition in Optical and Holographic Microscopy Images: 3rd Cognitive Models and Artificial Intelligence Conference (AICCONF), pp. 1–8. IEEE (2025)

19. Shi, X., et al.: Pollen-YOLO: a deep learning framework for automated pollen identification and its application to palaeoecological reconstruction on the Tibetan plateau. Quaternary **9**(1), 1–6 (2026)
20. Kubera, E., et al.: Detection and recognition of pollen grains in multilabel microscopic images. Sensors **22**(7), 2690 (2022)
21. Bengio, Y., Goodfellow, I., Courville, A.: Deep Learning, vol. 1. MIT Press, Cambridge, MA, USA (2017)
22. Krizhevsky, A., Sutskever, I., Hinton, G.E.: ImageNet classification with deep convolutional neural networks. Commun. ACM **60**(6), 84–90 (2017)
23. Liu, X., et al.: Advances in deep learning-based medical image analysis. Health Data Sci. **2021**, 8786793 (2021)
24. Mamalakis, M., et al.: Artificial Intelligence framework with traditional computer vision and deep learning approaches for optimal automatic segmentation of left ventricle with scar. Artif. Intell. Med. **143**, 102610 (2023)
25. Zangana, H.M., Mustafa, F.M.: From classical to deep learning: a systematic review of image denoising techniques. Jurnal Ilmiah Comput. Sci. **3**(1), 50–65 (2024)
26. Wang, J., et al.: A review of deep learning on medical image analysis. Mob. Netw. Appl. **26**(1), 351–380 (2021)
27. El Helou, M., Süsstrunk, S.: Blind universal Bayesian image denoising with Gaussian noise level learning. IEEE Trans. Image Process. **29**, pp. 4885–4897 (2020)
28. Wang, J., Wang, S., Zhang, Y.: Deep learning on medical image analysis. CAAI Trans. Intell. Technol. **10**(1), 1–35 (2025)
29. Liu, W., Lin, W.: Additive white Gaussian noise level estimation in SVD domain for images. IEEE Trans. Image Process. **22**(3), 872–883 (2012)
30. Tian, C., et al.: Multi-stage image denoising with the wavelet transform. Pattern Recogn. **134**, 109050 (2023)
31. Kovtunenko, V.A., Kunisch, K.: High precision identification of an object: optimality-conditions-based concept of imaging. SIAM J. Control Optim. **52**(1), 773–796 (2014)
32. Liu, P., et al.: Multi-level wavelet-CNN for image restoration. In: Proceedings of the IEEE Conference on Computer Vision and Pattern Recognition Workshops, pp. 773–782 (2018)
33. Jumanov, I.I., Safarov, R.A., Djumanov, O.I.: Optimization of micro-object identification with factorization and correction mechanisms for distorted image points. In: International Russian Smart Industry Conference (SmartIndustryCon), pp. 343–348. IEEE (2025). https://doi.org/10.1109/SmartIndustryCon65166.2025.10986016
34. Wendt, A., Heipke, C.: Simultaneous orientation of brightness, range and intensity images. ISPRS Arch. **36**(5) (2006)
35. Rekeczky, C.: CNN architectures for constrained diffusion based locally adaptive image processing. Int. J. Circuit Theory Appl. **30**(2–3), 313–348 (2002)
36. Peng, L., et al.: Defective pixel corrector for line scan and area scan image sensors. IEEE Trans. Circuits Syst. I: Regular Papers **72**(7), 3325–3337 (2025)
37. Roy, S., Panda, S., Jangid, M.: Modified Reinhard algorithm for color normalization of colorectal cancer histopathology images. In: 29th European Signal Processing Conference (EUSIPCO). IEEE (2021)
38. Shao, L., et al.: Performance evaluation of deep feature learning for RGB-D image/video classification. Inf. Sci. **385**, 266–283 (2017)
39. Coppi, R., Gil, M.A., Kiers, H.A.L.: The fuzzy approach to statistical analysis. Comput. Stat. Data Anal. **51**(1), 1–14 (2006)

Artificial intelligence tools in Managing Future COMMunities (AiMFutCOM 2026)

An Optimized Reactive Personalized Restaurant Recommendationss System Using Content-Based and DBSCAN Clustering in Google Cloud Platform

Nadia F. Al-Bakri[1(✉)], Farah Saad Al-Mukhtar[1], and Faten Alabbas[2]

[1] Department of Computer Science, College of Science, Al-Nahrain University, Jadriya, Baghdad, Iraq
{nadia.f.al-bakri,farah.saad}@nahrainuniv.edu.iq

[2] School of Graduate, Online and Continuing Education, Fitchburg State University, Fitchburg, MA, USA
Falabbas@fitchburgstate.edu

Abstract. Recommendation systems play a vital role in food industries. They provide a personal recommendation to customers based on their preferences and interests. Due to the diversity of restaurant types and services, users struggle to find relevant options. This challenge is further exacerbated by cold-start and long-tail problems, which cause the limitation of existing recommender systems. Personalized service recommendations will help users to identify and select appropriate restaurants according to their location and preferences. To achieve this objective, this research suggests a context-aware restaurant recommender system for personalized restaurant suggestions leveraging customer's profile preferences collected explicitly from mobile or web apps utilizing Firebase. It employes reactive content-based filtering combined with DBSCAN (Density-Based Spatial Clustering of Applications with Noise) clustering to enhance dining services through leveraging GPS API Google cloud platform for scalability and minimum computations. Furthermore, the core innovation lies in final restaurant ranking, which applies a proposed optimized weighted score formula utilizing cosine similarity measure and Manhattan distance with regularization coefficient on user and restaurant features, including location. Data was collected from customers around AL NAHRAIN university in Baghdad. Experimental findings show beneficial results for achieving precision, recall and F1-score of 0.95,0.92 and 0.93 respectively, showing effective support in customer decision-making.

Keywords: Content-based · Cosine Similarity · DBSCAN · Google Cloud,GPS-API

O. Gervasi et al. (Eds.): ICCSA 2026 Workshops, LNCS 16758, pp. 135–154, 2027.
https://doi.org/10.1007/978-3-032-30497-1_9

1 Introduction

A recommendation system is a tool that helps users to find relevant items by filtering and suggesting products or information they may be interested in. Its main goal is to reduce information overload and present users with a personalized list of suggestions. Recommendation systems are broadly classified into two main types: Collaborative Filtering (CF), which leverages patterns among multiple users' behaviors, and Content-Based Filtering (CBF), which focuses on analyzing attributes of items that users have previously liked. These approaches form the foundation for delivering tailored recommendations and are continuously refined to improve accuracy and relevance for consumers [1, 2]. Recommendation system for restaurants is an intelligent technique that provides users with vast lists of available dining options, saving their time and effort while providing assurance of satisfaction in food experience. various factors are considered such as ambiance, type of cuisine, food price, location, dietary restrictions, and user preferences, these systems suggest tailored recommendations that align with individual tastes [3]. In recent years, there has been a growing interest in location-aware restaurant recommendation systems. This area of research has gained attention due to its potential to improve user decision-making by providing real-time suggestions tailored to personal preferences and physical location. With the increasing reliance on mobile applications and their rapid development for decision-making, especially in the hospitality and food service industries, restaurant recommendation systems (RRSs) have become vital tools for enhancing customer satisfaction in finding relevant items [4]. For mobile and web development, Firebase is a platform suggested by Google that provides a suite of services, including real-time databases (Cloud Firestore and Realtime Database) [5]. Firebase enables rapid development and easy scaling of applications, offering front end and backend services like real-time syncing, authentication, and cloud storage with minimal server-side code [6].

Collaborative filtering [7, 8], are dominated by user-item interaction history which fail to work effectively in cold start or data sparse conditions, Conversely, content-based approaches exploit item properties and user preferences and, in this way, personalized can be given without a lot of user history [9] .Context aware recommender systems are becoming more important, in the context of mobile and web-based services (e.g., food and hospitality domains). In urban environments, the geographical closeness of restaurants is essential to estimate the rational value of recommendation. Researches have shown that users consider close by points of interests more important than far away even though they may potentially offer unimaginable experiences specially in densely populated regions [10, 11] Thus, geospatial intelligence coupled with proximity measures gives more contextually relevant results. Considering system recommendations, two personalization services are used, they are: [12, 13]

1. A proactive recommendation system that forecasts and serves personalized suggestions to customers without explicit demands depending on user history.
2. Reactive systems afford recommendations only when triggered or prompted by users such as (finding " nearby restaurants "). In these services, the system responds to the user's conveyed needs at the instant of service supply. In this paper, this type of service is utilized.

Many previous studies have revealed the efficacy of restaurant recommendation systems that include factors such as food quality, pricing, and customer reviews. For example, research by [14] emphasizes the efficiency of collaborative filtering (CF) methods such as memory-based CF using item-based and user-based and model-based CF using bayes theorem [15]. Matrix factorization, sentiment analysis, tailor-made for the restaurant field. However, they often miss user preferences and multiple attributes beyond mere ratings. Also, by [16], system applied content-based filtering on static restaurant attributes (e.g. cuisine type, category, address metadata) and a similarity between restaurants using the cosine similarity metric is computed, then a recommendation to users based on their extracted preferences is suggested. However, these systems suggested restaurants according to user's preferences, they did not fully integrate dynamic user filtering attributes and GPS-based navigation services and locations into their models. Also, they faced cold start item problem because of insufficient restaurant information services. As a result, these issues reduce the accuracy of real-time geospatial proximity computation.

In response to these demands, this paper proposes a reactive location-aware restaurant recommendation system for restaurant discovery using content-based method based on cosine similarity measure and DBSCAN algorithm for grouping regions according to longitude and latitude of restaurants from GPS coordinates and google cloud platform utilizing Firebase. Also, for ranking, an optimized weighted score formula is suggested leveraging similarity results between customers and restaurants and their locations using the latitude and longitude. The proposed system is deployed on web based and mobile platform. It is assumed that the customers are in AL Nahrain university in Baghdad capital of Iraq and need a suggestion for nearby restaurants according to their preferences. The main contributions of this work are as follows:

- Proposing a scalable, reactive restaurant recommendation model utilizing content-based filtering method enhanced with customer-defined attributes for food and service type.
- Applying DBSCAN clustering method to enhance dining services through leveraging GPS services and Google cloud platform for scalability and minimum time.
- Proposing a ranking proximity formula utilizing cosine similarity and Manhattan distance values for recommendation with a regularization coefficient.

The rest of the paper is organized as follows: in Sect. 2 we present an overview and a comparison of related works on restaurant recommendation systems. In Sect. 3 we present the architecture, detailing the components of the proposed system and the algorithms used. In Sect. 4 we present the used datasets, experiments, results and discussions. Finally, Sect. 5 concludes the research and outlines potential future directions.

2 Related Work

This section reveals several works that are related to the subject matter. They are as in the following:

Nur Idalisa et al. in [17], a machine-learning approach is used to develop a recommendation system of a restaurant to Malaysian customers. The research identified the difficulties of choosing an appropriate restaurant using Trip Advisor platform. Another work by Elham Asani et al., [18] proposed a context-aware recommender system that food predilection is extracted from customer comments. Then food names are clustered and their opinions are analyzed. As a final decision, the nearby open restaurants are recommended based on their similarity to user preferences. One more study of Henry Dyke A. Balmeo and Albert A. Vinluan in [19], developed an application that used GPS for small and medium enterprises (SMEs), to locate and rank restaurants and highlighted the best performance using social media riposte. The system administrator manufactured measurable reports and compilation using data extracted from web-based social media. The system utilized both web and mobile platform and helped users find a restaurant with good service and products by displaying ratings from previous customers. Additional research of Sathya Seelan K and. K. PrabhuIn in [20], presented restaurants recommendation system that used machine learning algorithms to help customers find restaurants and popular food items. The system is built using a Kaggle dataset and a web application with Python's Flask framework. It provided better experience to users in searching for a short amount of time and nearby location restaurant. In one more research work of Qusai Y. Shambour et al. in [21], proposed a recommender system for restaurant based on user preferences. it utilized multi-criteria ratings, including implicit similarities between users and items, permeated similarity between user and user/item reputation. furthermore, the study of Michelle Hartanto and Ditdit Nugeraha Utama in [22], developed an intelligent decision support model that suggest suitable restaurants. Seven parameters were embraced (the interest of customer, fee/budget, distance between customer and restaurant, savor rating, rating of cleanliness, facilities rating, and halal or nonhalal status). The demonstration involved 75 restaurants in Jakarta and eight customers. Finally, the research of Md Sayeem Rahman et al. [23], Applied K-means clustering to analyze restaurant's geospatial distribution using latitude, longitude, rating, cuisines and price data, as well as identified hotspots and underserved areas. Also, the popularity of regional trends in cuisine and pricing are highlighted. Also, visualization results through interactive maps and statistical charts are depicted. Table 1 shows a summary of related works..

Table 1. Summary of literatures review

ref. no.	Dataset	Method	Gap
[17]	2,496 datasets gathered from the TripAdvisor platform.	Term Frequency-Inverse Document Frequency (TF-IDF), Cosine Similarity	The internal conflict of the secondary data sources that were used, that affected the reliability and validity of the results.
[18]	collected from the TripAdvisor website for 100 users during the first 9 months of 2018	Semantic Approach, Sentiment Analysis, Similarity Calculation	dependance on old NLP resources with restricted evaluation metrics.

(*continued*)

Table 1. *(continued)*

ref. no.	Dataset	Method	Gap
[19]	data extracted from social media platforms and Google Maps API.	Natural Language Processing Sentiment Analysis	The study focuses only on restricted physical locations and prices.
[20]	Kaggle dataset	Exploratory Data Analysis (EDA), Popularity-Based Recommendation, Collaborative Filtering (CF), singular value decomposition (SVD)	the absence of real-world testing and scalability issues.
[21]	The Restaurants-TripAdvisor MC dataset,The Hotels-TripAdvisor MC dataset, The Yahoo! Movies MC dataset	Hybrid User-Item based Multi-Criteria CF Algorithm	The research limited by dataset scope depends on ratings.
[22]	Zomato website	fuzzy logic, cosine similarity distance, optimization	small dataset with limited size limited parameters.
[23]	geospatial restaurant dataset collected and structured into CSV format.	Machine learning approach () combined with geospatial analysis, statistical calculations, and visualization techniques.	The dataset scope was limited, K-means clustering algorithm constraints in geospatial clustering.

3 Methodology

The proposed context aware restaurant recommender system employed on both web and mobile applications built on the Google Cloud Platform that incorporates content-based and DBSCAN clustering approaches with an effective ranking formula for recommendation. The proposed framework is initiated considering different dynamic attributes such as customer and restaurant locations using GPS coordinates and google map information, food categories, and service types. These attributes are extracted and preprocessed and then combined to be utilized in a weighted score formula to recommend relevant restaurants for each customer. The essential purpose of the suggested model is to propose an optimized weighted score formula considering the similarity values of selected attributes (food types and service types) and the distance values. At the same time, the personalization experience is enhanced by introducing DBSCAN clustering to improve the quality of the recommendation.

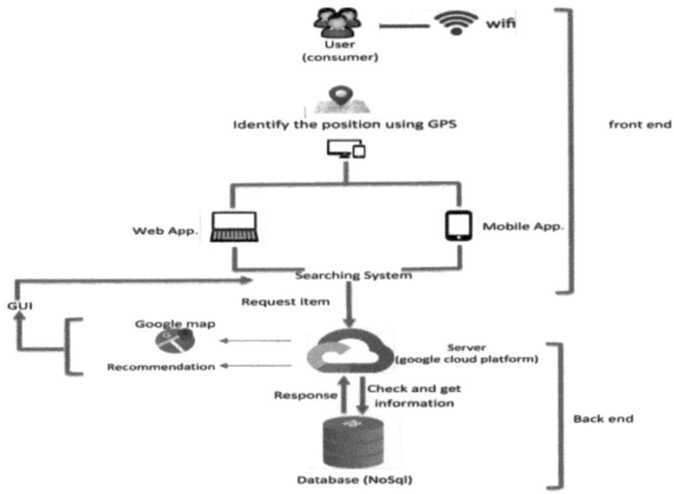

Fig. 1. Block Diagram of Proposed System Model

The suggested stages are especially helpful for customers, aiming to minimize decision-making time and maximize satisfaction. As mentioned earlier, the proposed system is designed to assist the customers in finding the nearest required restaurant according to longitude and latitude of each restaurant. It assumed that the target customers are at AL Nahrain university in Baghdad city in Iraq and they want to find the nearest restaurant using the proposed model. Additionally, the system provides a map display and distance calculations, and directional guidance to assist customers in navigating to their chosen restaurant.

The proposed model consists of two parts as shown in Fig. 1:

- The front-end is the process in which the contents are viewed over the application. The web/mobile restaurant recommender applications introduce services to customers through internet connection to request the favorite restaurant, after determining their current location from mobile GPS sensor. It allows the system to know exactly where the customer is, by determining the user's location which is determined by coordinates (longitude and latitude) using GPS technique that exists in either smart phone (iOS, Android) or PC by Wi-Fi (WPS) where their coordinates are automatically determined.
- The back end under Google cloud platform is the core of the proposed system that analyze and manage applications using Firebase as framework which helps in developing web and mobile applications for storing the database. NoSQL is the central piece for organizing and designing databases saving data as a pair of key-value.

3.1 Dataset Collection Stage

As mentioned earlier, restaurant locations were searched and collected using GPS, resulting a Dataset containing about (315) surveyed restaurants and can be expanded further. The attributes within the dataset are in the form of:

- Spatial Data: restaurant locations (coordinates latitude (X),longitude(Y)), they are provided by Google map service.
- Attribute Data: restaurant survey information that involves (restaurant name, address, rating, services type (Dine-in, Takeaway, Delivery, Drive-through) and food type (cuisine (eastern, western)). The service may differ from restaurants to another.

After dataset collection, Excel file records are filled and saved as a Comma-separated values (CSV file) then converted to JavaScript object notation (JSON) file by the online converter using the link https://www.convertcsv.com/csv-to-json.htm. The JSON format was chosen because it is quite compatible with Firebase which is commonly used for transmitting data in web applications. Then the created data is uploaded and stored in Google cloud platform by using firebase Console where each restaurant is stored as a JSON object with a restaurant ID. For an account creation in Google firebase, a sign-in step is needed via the site https://firebase.google.com. Then a payment account is created using visa card on Google cloud platform up to 12 months for free of charge to build and run the website, application and services, including firebase and the Google Map API for supporting Android's SDK. Then API key is generated to enable using map features in an interactive approach. In addition, the location of restaurants is located using Google map service and the Real-time database (NoSQL) is filled with the data.

3.2 Customer Profiling Stage

Creating a customer profile is an initial stage in the suggested context-aware restaurant recommendation system. A depiction of the customers' needs is built, by considering the preferences and geographic location. A profile for each customer is composed. It consists of three types of information:

1. Demographic information: It represents personal details like customer names. This data collected through registration form.
2. Preference information: It is formed employing user choices in restaurants including food information such type of services (Dine-in, Takeaway, Delivery, Drive-through) and food type (cuisine (eastern, western)). Users should specify preferences accurately.
3. Location information: It represents the customer's current location, mostly given as latitude and longitude coordinates using Google map.

3.3 Preprocessing Stage

In this stage, the attribute values within the dataset are preprocessed for further implementation by encoding restaurant categorical features into vectors of zeros and ones. Categorical features such as food types and service types are transformed to numerical representation to be prepared for use in content-based algorithm. This process involves the following:

a. Categorical features:

- Single-label categorical (e.g., eastern, western) using One-Hot Encoding.
- Multi-label categorical (e.g., services (Dine-in, Takeaway, Delivery, Drive-through) using Multi -Hot Encoding.

- Ordinal categorical (e.g, rating (from 1 to 5)) using Ordinal Encoding.

  b. Represent each restaurant as a feature vector.
  c. Represent customers in AL Nahrain university preferences as a query vector.

3.4 Implementation

This section demonstrates the implementation process of the proposed model. Initially, the customer's GPS API coordinates are acquired using Google Maps. For example, the current customer's location is at AL-Nahrain university in Baghdad as shown in Fig. 2. The process starts when the customer searches for restaurants, the proposed system queries the server and retrieves JSON data file from Firebase and displays a list of available restaurants.

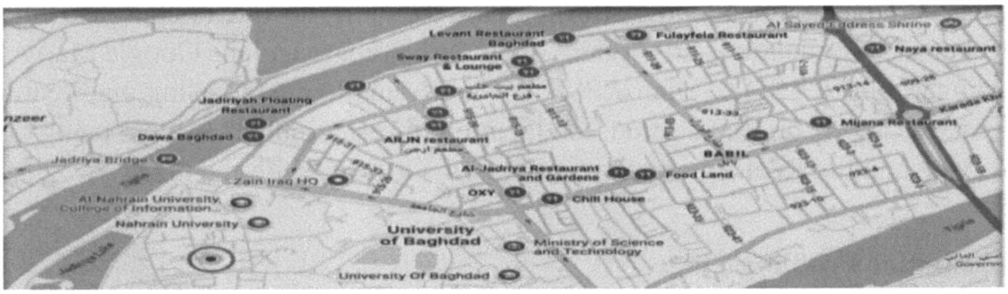

Fig. 2. Customer location and Available Restaurants

Clustering with DBSCAN

As a next step, a clustering algorithm DBSCAN [24] is applied that group points (restaurants in our model) that are close together in space using restaurant coordinates(longitude, latitude). This step is being taken to reduces search space and ensure locality. The reason for choosing DBSCAN clustering method is that it requires no prior choice of cluster count, inherently handles biased shapes, and marks outliers as noise. The hyperparameter such as EPS (Neighborhood radius) is tuned to local density around Al-Nahrain University. Also, min_samples (Minimum points per cluster) are adjusted to avoid sparse clusters. After clustering process is done, number of clusters is obtained, and the nearest clusters are found whose centroids are closest to the customer's location coordinates.

Distance Computation

After that, the distance between the customer's location (in (AL Nahrain University) and the restaurant locations is found within the nearest clusters using Manhattan distance as depicted in Eq. (1). As was declared earlier, the suggested restaurants are restricted to a geographically bound urban area, therefore Manhattan distance is adopted as an efficient approximation for spatial nearness. This formula is abundant for relative ranking while minimizing computation complexity compared to great-circle distance calculations. Table (2) depicts a gained set of restaurants with their attributes and the calculated distances. In this table, it is assumed that the target customer is with the coordinates (Longitude X = 44.37753,Latitude Y = 33.27927).

$$\text{Distance(u, r)} = |lat_u - lat_r| + |long_u - long_r| \quad (1)$$

where target customer coordinate is (lat_u,$long_u$) and restaurant coordinate is (lat_r, $long_r$).

Table 2. Restaurant Information Data Base and Distance Results

restaurant name	Status	Services	rating	Longitude X	Latitude Y	Address	Distance
99 grill	11 AM- 2 AM	Dine-in,Takeaway, Drive-through	4.1	44.3711	33.37526	Al-Dhubbat Street – Al-Adhamiya	0.09236
Boba restaurant	12 PM-11:30 PM	Dine-in, Takeaway	4.2	44.3683	33.30225	Al-Kindi Street	0.01655
Chili House	10:30 AM- 12 Am	Dine-in, Takeaway	4	44.38951	33.28115	Al-Jadriya	0.01666
Dawa	8 AM- 1 AM	Dine-in, Takeaway	4	44.37789	33.28506	Al-Jadriya	0.00895
Fried Chicken	10 AM- 12 AM	Dine-in, Takeaway	4.2	44.40834	33.28942	Al-Jadriya	0.04376
Hardees	10 Am-2 AM	Dine-in, Drive-through	3	44.39012	33.28125	Al-Jadriya	0.01737
KFC	8 AM- 1 AM	Dine-in, Takeaway	3.9	44.39043	33.28129	Al-Jadriya	0.01772
Levant Baghdad	8 AM- 1 AM	Dine-in, Takeaway	4.1	44.39019	33.29455	Al-Karrada	0.03074
RoyalGalaxy	9 AM - 12 AM	Dine-in, Takeaway	3.9	44.36496	33.31493	Al-Kindi Street	0.02589
Asrar Adam	9 AM- 12 AM	Dine-in, Takeaway	4.1	44.38879	33.2895	Al-Jadriya	0.02429
Al-Haidar Khana	8 Am-12 AM	Dine-in, Drive-through	3.4	44.38751	33.28248	Al-Jadriya	0.01599
Saysban	7 AM–12 AM	Dine-in, Takeaway	3.8	44.39126	33.28312	Al-Jadriya	0.02038
Shmeisani	8 AM- 12 AM	Dine-in, Takeaway	4.1	44.40683	33.28859	Al-Jadriya	0.04142
Qasr Al-Karam	11 AM- 12 AM	Dine-in, Takeaway	4.3	44.37892	33.28585	Al-Jadriya	0.01077

(continued)

Table 2. *(continued)*

restaurant name	Status	Services	rating	Longitude X	Latitude Y	Address	Distance
Al-Jadriya Floating Restaurant	11 AM- 12 AM	Dine-in, Takeaway	3	44.37812	33.28652	Al-Jadriya	0.01064
Al-Rahman Traditional Food Restaurant	Only Breakfast	Dine-in, Takeaway	5	44.39354	33.29201	Al-Jadriya	0.03155
Al-Rayahin Family Restaurant	10 AM–12 AM	Dine-in, Takeaway	3.5	44.33706	33.38784	Al-Krayat Corniche	0.0709
Barley Restaurant	7 AM-3:30 AM	Dine-in, Takeaway	4	44.43858	33.30537	Street 42	0.08995
Set Al-Sham Restaurant	24 Hours	Dine-in, Takeaway	3.9	44.36716	33.37416	Al-Adhamiya	0.08732
Qasim Abu Al-Kass Restaurant	9 Am-2 AM	Dine-in, Takeaway	3.7	44.36359	33.36754	Al-Adhamiya	0.07713
Naseem Dijla Al-Khair Restaurant	12 PM- 1 AM	Dine-in, Takeaway	3.8	44.35712	33.39376	Al-Krayat Corniche	0.09688
Al-Jadriya Family Restaurant & Gardens	10 AM- 12 AM	Dine-in, Takeaway	4	44.39255	33.28471	Al-Jadriya	0.02326
		Customer Address		44.37638	33.27762		

Recommendation Generation

Similarity Computation.

Subsequently, after encoding restaurant categorical features: the type of services (Dine-in, Takeaway, Delivery, Drive-through) and food types cuisine (eastern, western) into vectors of zeros and ones to be prepared for use in content-based algorithm; a cosine similarity [24] is performed between customer preference vector and restaurant vectors within a designated cluster. The customer's preferences are prioritized according to the customer's choices. The cosine similarity equation between object u and object v is expressed as in the following formula:

$$similarity(u, v) = cosine\left(\overline{R_u}, \overline{R_v}\right) = \frac{\overline{R_u} \cdot \overline{R_v}}{\|R_u\| \|R_v\|} = \frac{\sum_{i=1}^{N} R_{u,i} \times R_{v,i}}{\sqrt{\sum_{i=1}^{N} \left(R_{u,i}\right)^2} \sqrt{\sum_{i=1}^{N} \left(R_{v,i}\right)^2}} \tag{2}$$

As shown in Table 3, cosine similarity is computed between the customer' vector and six restaurant attributes using Eq. (2).

Table 3. Similarity Results Between Restaurant Vectors and Customer Attributes

Restaurant Name	Rating	Dine-in	Drive-through	Takeaway	Delivery	Eastern	Western
Target user	5	0	0	1	0	0	1
Dawa	4	1	0	1	1	1	1
Al-Jadriya Floating Restaurant	3	1	0	1	1	1	1
Qasr Al-Karam	4.3	1	0	1	1	1	1
Al-Haidar Khana	3.4	1	1	0	1	1	1
Chili House	4	1	0	1	0	0	1
Hardees	3	1	1	0	0	0	1

Ranking and Recommendation

According to the contextual scenario of the proposed model, the ranking and recommendation process is based on generating relevant restaurants by cooperatively leveraging similarity values produced from applying cosine measure on the normalized attribute values and the distance similarity values between the target customer's preferences and restaurant's vectors. To ensure valid cosine computation, all attributes including rating values are normalized between [0, 1] using min-max normalization. for consistency with cosine similarity values, distance similarity is derived by normalizing distance values to insure they lie between 0 and 1. Accordingly, the following formula is utilized for distance similarity computation:

$$\text{Distance\_similarity}_{\text{i}} = 1 - \frac{Distance_i}{\text{max}\_distance} \tag{3}$$

where distance_i is the resulted spatial distance from Eq. 1 and max_distance is the given maximum distance value. Next, the proposed optimized weighted score formula is applied to rank the required restaurants as shown in Eq. 4. A linear combination is implemented due to its often use in multi-criteria recommendations. Eq. 4 is as follows:

$$\text{Weight\_score}_i = \alpha \cdot \text{Similarity}_i + (1-\alpha) \cdot \text{Distance\_similarity}_i - \lambda \cdot (\alpha - 0.5)^2 \tag{4}$$

where $\alpha \in [0, 1]$ is a tuning parameter to control the effectiveness of the spatial distance values and the content-based similarity. Following the experimental analysis, when a customer prioritizes near restaurants, the parameter *is set to* 0, in this case, restaurant's location will have an influential weight on the ranking score compared to restaurant attributes, revealing a cold-start item scenario. On the other hand, as α approaches to 1, restaurant attributes gradually contribute to the ranking score and subsequently influence the final decision-making process. In addition, λ is a regularization coefficient introduced as quadratic term $\lambda \cdot (\alpha - 0.5)^2$ that limits the optimization process by controlling extreme bias toward a single factor, thereby enhancing the robustness and generalization capability of the ranking model. After experiment iterations, the parameters α *and* λ are empirically set to 0.6 and 0.05 respectively providing a balance between the semantic relevance and spatial proximity. Table 4. depicts the normalized values for each attribute, along with the resulted values of calculating cosine similarity, distance similarity and the weighted scores. The final suggested restaurants are ranked according to the values of the weighted scores where the score values are sorted in descending order. Note: in Table 4. The superscript within each weighted score represents its rank.

Table 4. Cosine Similarity, Distance Similarity and the Weighted Score Values Result for Restaurants and their Ranks to Target Customer

	α	Rating	Dine-in	Drive-through	Take away	Delivery	Eastern	Western	Cosine Similarity	Distance similarity	Weight score
Target user	0.6	1	0	0	0.2	0	0	0.2			
Dawa		0.8	0.2	0	0.2	0.2	0.2	0.2	0.923913	0.999884	0.953801(3)
Al-Jadriya Floating Restaurant		0.6	0.2	0	0.2	0.2	0.2	0.2	0.874385	0.999862	0.924076(5)
Qasr Al-Karam		0.86	0.2	0	0.2	0.2	0.2	0.2	0.933134	0.999861	0.959325(2)
Al-Haidar Khana		0.68	0.2	0.2	0	0.2	0.2	0.2	0.851256	0.999793	0.910171
Chili House		0.8	0.2	0	0.2	0	0	0.2	0.971323	0.999785	0.982208(1)
Hardees		0.6	0.2	0.2	0	0	0	0.2	0.888888	0.99977	0.932743(4)

Deployment on Google Cloud

The online module works by getting the current user model data including the distance and the restaurant's preferences. Then designate the regions and assign weighted scores for each restaurant. After that, sorting the score values in descending order and generating top K = 5 relevant restaurants. Finally, Servers send the results to end user's device as shown in Fig. 3 displaying the result in list of restaurants including the details (photo, location, phone number) that show the 5 most restaurants as shown in Fig. 4 (a, b, c, d, e). Figure 5 shows the path between the target customer and the recommended restaurant.

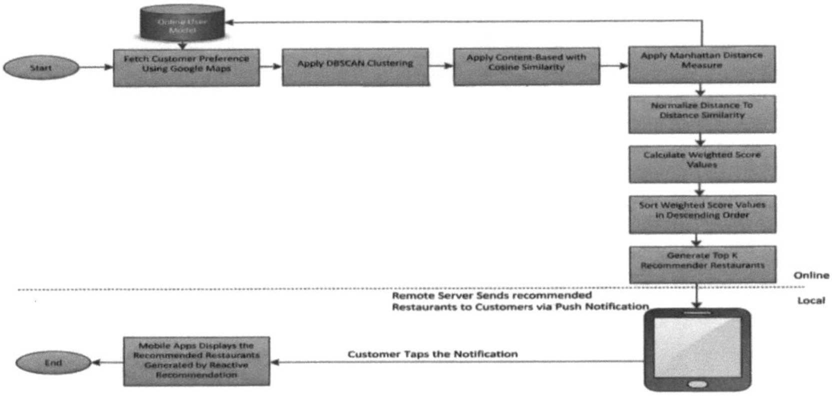

Fig. 3. The Flow Diagram of the Proposed Model

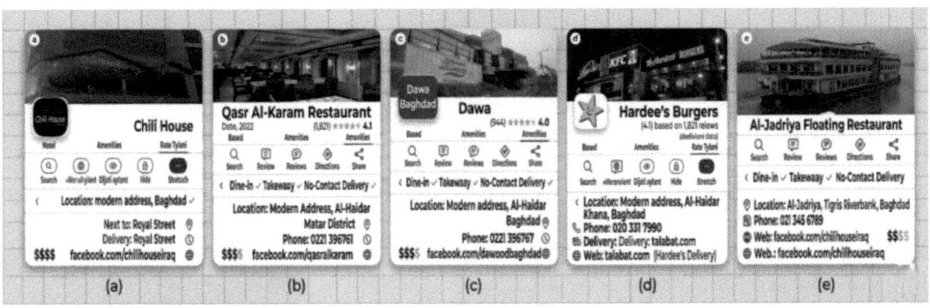

Fig. 4. The Recommended Restaurant (a) Chili House, (b) Qasr Al-Karam, (c) Dawa (d) Hardees (e) Al-Jadriya Floating Restaurant

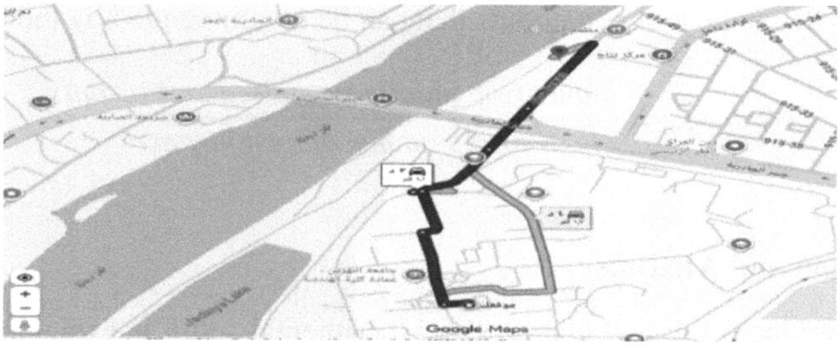

Fig. 5. The Path to the Recommended Restaurant

4 Evaluation Metrics

In this section, the performance of the proposed context aware restaurant recommendations is evaluated using ranking recommendation-based measures. For each customer query, the proposed model generates a list of top K = 5 recommendations. For consistency and comparability, measures are calculated at a fixed top K = 5. The measures are defined as follows: [2]:

1. **Precision@K:** from the top K recommended restaurants, it measures the proportion of relevant restaurants among user's preferences.

$$\text{Precision@K} = \frac{\textit{Number of relevant restaurants in top K}}{K} \tag{5}$$

2. **Recall@K:** from the recommended relevant restaurants, it measures the proportion of relevant restaurants that are successfully proposed in the top K.

$$\text{Recall@K} = \frac{\textit{Number of relevant restaurants in top K}}{\textit{Total number of relevant restaurants}} \tag{6}$$

3. **F1-score@K**: Balance mean of Precision@K and Recall@K.

$$\text{F1} - \text{score@K} = \frac{2 \times Precision@K \times Recall@K}{Precision@K + Recall@K} \tag{7}$$

4. **NDCG (Normalized Discounted Cumulative Gain)**: it is a rank-aware metric, that measures ranking quality by giving higher weight to relevant restaurants at the top of the list K.

$$DCG@K = \sum_{i=1}^{K} \frac{rel_i}{\log_2(i+1)} \tag{8}$$

$$NDCG@K = \frac{DCG@K}{IDCG@K} \tag{9}$$

where rel_i stands for relevance score of restaurants at rank i, and $IDCG$ @ K stands for ideal DCG value.

5. **Coverage**: Percentage of restaurants that can be recommended by the system.

$$coverage = \frac{number\ of\ unique\ suggested\ restaurants}{total\ number\ of\ restaurants} \tag{10}$$

4.1 Discussion and Analysis

To ensure reproducibility and clarity, the experimental setup is explained as follows: the data was collected using the GPS API in Baghdad city. It comprises about 315 restaurants located in different regions around Al-Nahrain University. Restaurant profiles are created and stored in firebase cloud databases including restaurant name, status, services, longitude, latitude, rating and address. Also, considering customer's queries, a total of 30 customer profiles are retrieved from their explicit feedback via mobile or PC platforms for testing. At the same time, DBSCAN clustering method is configured within an average cluster radius of 0.7 km. The α in weighted score formula is set to 0.6 based on experimental tuning. To evaluate the proposed model, three baseline methods are utilized for comparisons, they are:

1. Distance based ranker: find recommended Top K restaurants using the Manhattan measure on distance attribute within 3 km.
2. Rating based ranker: find recommended Top K restaurants with highest rate.
3. Content based using TF-IDF (Term Frequency-Inverse Document Frequency) technique and cosine similarity with No-cluster Ranker: find recommended Top K restaurants applying TF-IDF with no clustering method.

Table 5. depicts a comparison of Precision@5, Recall@5, F1@5, NDCG@5, and Coverage across four conditions (Distance-only, Rating-only, No-cluster ranker, and the Proposed Model). The proposed model consistently outperforms baselines, particularly in ranking quality (NDCG) and balanced precision/recall as shown in Fig. 6.

Table 5. Comparison of Precision@5, Recall@5, F1@5, NDCG@5, and Coverage at K = 5

	Precision@5	Recall@5	F1@5	NDCG@5	Coverage
Distance based rank	0.72	0.66	0.69	0.75	0.48
Rating based rank	0.68	0.61	0.64	0.70	0.41
Content-based (no clustering)	0.80	0.77	0.78	0.76	0.56
Proposed model (DBSCAN with Content-based)	0.95	0.92	0.93	0.88	0.63

From the results shown in Table 5, it was concluded:

1. Using Distance-only criterion: recommendations have led to decrease in recall performance metric, since they recommend nearby restaurants that may not match user's requested preference services. In this case α is set to 0. Therefore, this case achieved location relevance at the expense of preference relevance.

2. Using Rating-only criterion: recommendations led to favor highly popular restaurants while ignoring contextual features such as distance and customer's preferences. This case may achieve better perceived quality based on ratings, at the expense of disregarding distance and services.
3. Using Content-based TF-IDF without employing clustering algorithm ranker criterion: recommendations have led to improve relevancy but with more time consuming, as it searched the entire regions without geographic filtering.
4. Using the proposed model (DBSCAN with cosine similarity measure): recommendations achieved the highest performance across all ranking metrics. principally in Precision@5 and NDCG@5, the results show that using cosine similarity on customer and restaurant features combined with DBSCAN clustering gained more related and geographically suitable recommendations. DBSCAN clustering effectively localized the search to high-density regions, while cosine similarity ensured better alignment with user preferences. Better Performance gained in Precision@5 and NDCG@5 indicated improved ranking quality and user potential satisfaction. Also, it was shown that the coverage metric within the proposed model was higher than distance only and rating-only baselines, demonstrating that the proposed context aware model avoids suggesting the same common restaurants. So, the proposed model balanced between locality, relevance, and quality, yielding moderate results and this reduced the risk of long tail problems, where only common restaurants are recommended.

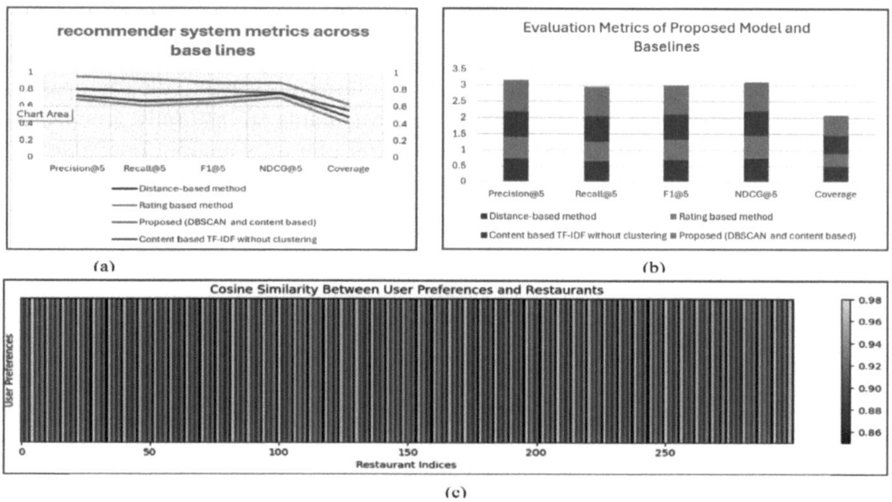

Fig. 6. (a) Line Plot of Metrics Across Recommender Baselines . (B) Recommended Baselines Across Evaluation Metrics. (C) Heatmap Visualization Showing the Relation Between Similarity Values. Darker Shades Indicate More Related Position with User-Requested Features.

Figure 7 illustrates a pie chart illustrating the distribution of cuisine types among the top 5 recommended restaurants around AL Nahrain University.

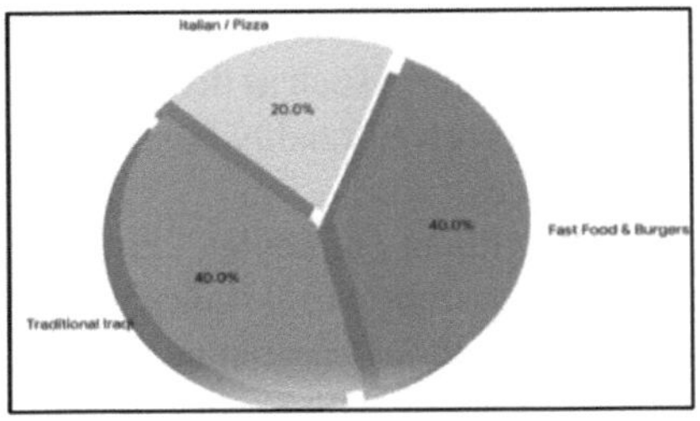

Fig. 7. Distribution of Cuisine Type

4.2 Impact of DBSCAN Clustering

In the section, the impact of restaurant-level clustering based on the restaurant location is discussed. It was depicted that the restaurants are spread into N clusters using DBSCAN clustering. This spread significantly improved both efficiency and recall. By restricting candidate restaurants to the nearest dense cluster, the system avoided irrelevant distant options while still capturing a diverse set of nearby restaurants. The inclusion of DBSCAN improved efficiency by reducing average candidate count from 315 to 61 per query i.e. 80.6% reduction in search space. The enhancement in Recall@5 reveals that using DBSCAN clustering methods benefits in capturing relevant restaurants within the customer's neighborhood. In addition, the coverage metrics also increased, showing that clustering prohibited the recommender system from frequently recommending the same few high-rated restaurants, i.e. long tail problem is avoided, which is a major problem in recommender systems. As a result, DBSCAN clustering was principally operative in inner-city environments like Baghdad, where restaurants are naturally grouped into dense regions. In Fig. 8, DBSCAN clustering scatter plot of restaurant locations, with clusters color-coded to highlight spatial grouping, each color represents a distinct cluster. Outliers are marked as noise points.

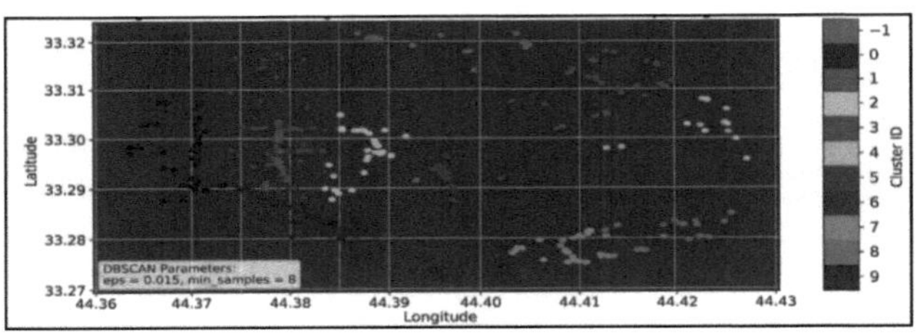

Fig. 8. DBSCAN Clustering Restaurants around Al-Nahrain University.

5 Conclusion

As a conclusion for this research, the findings confirmed that incorporating geospatial information for both the customers and restaurants significantly improves recommendation quality. By integrating GPS-API based distance factor with user preference services, the proposed system efficiently suggests context-aware recommendations that reflect real-world user interests. Furthermore, combining DBSCAN clustering leveraging GPS services and google cloud platform noticeably reduced search space, leading to a remarkable decrease in computations. The core improvement in this work is built upon proposing a weighted score formula for ranking, which combines cosine similarity and distance similarity through two tunable regularization parameters. This formulation provides an effective trade-off between precision and recall, aligning with practical user expectations and adjusting spatial thresholds, offering a valuable insight for future system optimization and deployment in real-world restaurant recommendation scenarios. Experimental results yielded from experiments demonstrate that related restaurants are dependably ranked near the top of the recommendation list, as reflected by improved Precision@K, Recall@K, and NDCG@K values. Overall, a balance is achieved combining the similarity distance factor using GPS API based and content-based algorithm using cosine similarity to suggest relevant restaurants for customer preferences. The insights realized from adjusting spatial thresholds and weighting parameters provide valuable guidance for future recommender system optimization with large-scale deployment, and extension to other data set context-based recommendation fields.

Acknowledgments. This study was funded by nobody.

Disclosure of Interests. The authors have no competing interests.

References

1. Bahjat, M.I., AL-Bakri, N.F.: A Survey on semantic recommendation system based on linked open data (LOD). In: Book a Survey on Semantic Recommendation System Based on Linked Open Data (LOD), pp. 191–197. IEEE (2022)
2. Bahjat, M.I., AL-Bakri, N.F.: Accuracy and diversity enhancement of recommender system using linked open data. In: Accuracy and Diversity Enhancement of Recommender System Using Linked Open Data, p. 040003. AIP Publishing LLC (2024)
3. Nandan, M., Gupta, P.K.: Designing an efficient restaurant recommendation system based on customer review comments by augmenting hybrid filtering techniques. Universal Journal of Operations and Management, 15 (2023)
4. Karmakar, K.: A Context-Aware Approach to Restaurant Recommendations: System Algorithm and Case Study (2020)
5. Ahmed, E.Q., Ameen, Z.H., Al-Mukhtar, F.S., Jaaz, Z.A.: Maximizing Mobile communication efficiency with smart antenna systems using beam forming and DOA algorithms. In: Maximizing Mobile Communication Efficiency with Smart Antenna Systems Using Beam Forming and DOA Algorithms, pp. 453–460. IEEE (2023)
6. https://firebase.google.com/docs
7. Tuma, F.S., Ibrahem, N.F.: Hybridizing collaborative filtering with naive bayes classifier for cold-start recommender systems: enhancing movie recommendations in the age of big data. In: Hybridizing Collaborative Filtering with Naive Bayes Classifier for Cold-Start Recommender Systems: Enhancing Movie Recommendations in the Age of Big Data, p. 030009. AIP Publishing LLC (2025)
8. Ameen, Z.H., Al-Mukhtar, F.S., Ahmed, E.Q., Dhannoon, B.N.: A review of the past Decade's research outcomes on classifying cyberbullying. Al-Nahrain Journal of Science. **27**(1), 121–135 (2024)

9. Adomavicius, G., Bauman, K., Tuzhilin, A., Unger, M.: Context-aware recommender systems: from foundations to recent developments. In: Recommender systems handbook, pp. 211–250. Springer (2021)
10. Beirão, R.A.S.: A Multiple Criteria Route Recommendation System. ISCTE-Instituto Universitario de Lisboa (Portugal) (2020)
11. Sun, H., Wu, Z., Cui, Y., Deng, L., Zhao, Y., Zheng, K.: Personalized dynamic knowledge-aware recommendation with hybrid explanations. In: Personalized Dynamic Knowledge-Aware Recommendation with Hybrid Explanations, pp. 148–164. Springer (2021)
12. Ilarri, S., Trillo-Lado, R.: An approach for proactive mobile recommendations based on user-defined rules. Expert Syst. Appl. **242**, 122714 (2024)
13. Zhang, B., Sundar, S.S.: Proactive vs. reactive personalization: can customization of privacy enhance user experience? International journal of human-computer studies. **128**, 86–99 (2019)
14. Alabduljabbar, R.: Matrix factorization collaborative-based recommender system for Riyadh restaurants: leveraging machine learning to enhance consumer choice. Appl. Sci. **13**(17), 9574 (2023)
15. Ameen, Z.H., AL-Bakri, N.F., Al-zubidi, A.F., Hashim, S.H., Jaaz, Z.A.: A new COVID-19 patient detection strategy based on hidden Naïve Bayes classifier. Iraqi Journal ofScience, 6705–6724 (2024)
16. Christyawan, F., Rohman, A.N., Hartanto, A.D.: Application of content-based filtering method using cosine similarity in restaurant selection recommendation system. Journal of Information Systems and Informatics. **6**(3), 1559–1576 (2024)
17. Idalisa, N., Hazhar, M.H.M., Muslim, N., Albashah, N.L.S.: Restaurant recommendation system in Malaysia using machine learning approach. In: Electronics, Communications and Networks, pp. 319–325. IOS Press (2024)
18. Asani, E., Vahdat-Nejad, H., Sadri, J.: Restaurant recommender system based on sentiment analysis. Mach. Learn. Appl. **6**, 100114 (2021)
19. Balmeo, H.D.A., Vinluan, A.A.: Hanapresto: a platform for restaurant businesses with recommender system using knowledge extraction from social media and customer preferences. Asia Pacific Journal of Multidisciplinary Research. **7**(2), 97–105 (2019)
20. Prabhu, S.S.K.K.: Restaurant recommendation system using machine learning algorithms. International Journal of Science Engineering and Technology. **9**, 3 (2021)
21. Shambour, Q.Y., Abualhaj, M.M., Abu-Shareha, A.A.: Restaurant recommendations based on multi-criteria recommendation algorithm. J. Univ. Comput. Sci. **29**(2), 179 (2023)
22. Hartanto, M., Utama, D.N.: 'Intelligent decision support model for recommending restaurant', Cogent. Engineering. **7**(1), 1763888 (2020)
23. Rahman, M.S., Sarkar, T.D., Emon, M.Y.: Comprehensive geospatial and statistical analysis of restaurant distribution using K-means clustering in machine learning technology. In: Comprehensive Geospatial and Statistical Analysis of Restaurant Distribution Using K-Means Clustering in Machine Learning Technology, pp. 461–466. IEEE (2024)
24. Salih, A.F., Ibrahem, N.F.: Medicine recommendation system based on review sentiment analysis and similarity metrics. In: Medicine Recommendation System Based on Review Sentiment Analysis and Similarity Metrics, pp. 1–7 (IEEE, 2024)

CI-RES: A GIS-Based Platform for Critical Infrastructure Resilience Analysis in Urban Environments

Maurizio Pollino, Alberto Tofani, and Gregorio D'Agostino(✉)

ENEA, Italian National Agency for New Technologies, Energy and Sustainable Economic Development, Rome, Italy
{maurizio.pollino,alberto.tofani,gregorio.dagostino}@enea.it

Abstract. Urban critical infrastructures (such as power grids, water networks, transport systems, and telecommunications) provide essential services to citizens and experience a continuous growth and complexification. Moreover, they are increasingly interdependent and exposed to a wide spectrum of threats, ranging from natural hazards such as earthquakes, floods, and geological instabilities to deliberate anthropogenic attacks. Assessing and improving their resilience and especially the resilience of the resulting system of systems, requires simulation platforms capable of modelling complex interdependencies and evaluating the impact of disruptive events at the city scale. This activity is strictly in line with the so called "CER Directive": the Directive (EU) 2022/2557 of the European Parliament and of the Council of 14 December 2022 on the resilience of critical entities that repeals previous Council Directive 2008/114/EC. This paper describes CI-RES (Critical Infrastructure Resilience), a GIS-based platform developed at ENEA for the collection, visualisation, and simulation of critical infrastructure behaviour in urban areas. The platform integrates geo-referenced data layers with containerised simulation codes covering multiple hazard scenarios. Furthermore, it exposes a meta-modelling interface through which domain experts can compose simulation workflows, evaluate consequences, and estimate dynamic risk and resilience metrics. The ongoing evolution of CI-RES towards a Kubernetes-based deployment is described, together with its roadmap as a foundational component for future Urban Digital Twin implementations. Preliminary results and the platform's potential for supporting municipal authorities and infrastructure protection agencies are discussed.

Keywords: Critical infrastructure · Resilience · GIS · Urban simulation · Kubernetes · Digital twin · Risk assessment · Interdependency modelling

1 Introduction

Modern cities rely on a tightly coupled set of critical infrastructures (CIs) whose correct functioning underpins the delivery of essential services to citizens. Power

O. Gervasi et al. (Eds.): ICCSA 2026 Workshops, LNCS 16758, pp. 155–168, 2027.
https://doi.org/10.1007/978-3-032-30497-1_10

distribution, water supply, transportation, healthcare, and telecommunications are not independent systems: they interact through complex physical and functional interdependencies, so that a failure in one sector risks to propagate rapidly and non-linearly to others [1]. This *cascade* behaviour makes city-scale resilience assessment a fundamentally multi-system problem.

The frequency and severity of disruptive events affecting urban CIs is continuously increasing. Climate change are also expected to amplify the incidence of extreme weather events—floods, heatwaves, and landslides—while the growing digitalisation and automatization of infrastructure control systems exposes them to cyber-physical threats. Seismic hazard remains a dominant concern in many European and Mediterranean urban areas. At the same time, deliberate attacks targeting infrastructure components introduce an adversarial dimension that purely natural-hazard models cannot capture.

Effective resilience management requires tools that can: (i) represent the spatial layout and interdependencies of urban CIs in a georeferenced environment; (ii) simulate the propagation of disruptions across multiple hazard types and infrastructure layers; (iii) estimate the resulting impact on service availability; and (iv) support decision makers in identifying optimal resource allocation strategies to minimise vulnerability and accelerate recovery.

This activity is strictly in line with the Directive (EU) 2022/2557 of the European Parliament and of the Council of 14 December 2022 on the resilience of critical entities that repeals previous Council Directive 2008/114/EC [2] (the so called "CER Directive"). It is worth stressing the CER Directive requires both Critical Entities (Operators, Authorities etc.) to perform risk analysis and to build up resilience plans. The CI-RES platform represents a versatile means to perform those activities, while presenting synthetic outcomes in a friend format.

CI-RES (Critical Infrastructure Resilience) is a platform developed by ENEA within the Italian Programme Agreement for Electric System Research (WP2, Line of Activity LA8) to address precisely the former requirements. Building on a GIS-based data model and a modular simulation architecture, CI-RES provides an integrated environment for urban CI analysis. This paper describes the platform's current capabilities, the ongoing migration to a cloud-native Kubernetes deployment, and the extensions under development that will enable hybrid scenario analysis and meta-modelling through a user-facing web interface.

A reduced set of capability is demonstrated at https://resilientity.enea.it web portal. That web server is also endowed with a private chat-bot that allows users to ask information about critical infrastructures and essential services. This facility will be described in a separate work.

The remainder of this paper is organised as follows. Section 2 reviews related work on CI resilience modelling and urban simulation platforms. Section 3 describes the architecture of CI-RES. Section 4 presents the simulation capabilities and the hazard scenarios currently supported. Section 5 describes the meta-modelling interface. Section 6 discusses the Kubernetes migration and its operational benefits. Section 7 outlines the Urban Digital Twin roadmap. Section 8 presents preliminary results, and Sect. 9 concludes the paper.

2 Background and Related Work

2.1 Critical Infrastructure Interdependency Modelling

The very early study of CI interdependencies was formalised by Rinaldi et al. [3], who identified six classes of interdependency (physical, cyber, geographic, logical, social, and political) and showed that cascade failures across interconnected systems could produce consequences far larger than those attributable to any single infrastructure in isolation. Subsequent work has explored graph-theoretic representations [4], agent-based models, and system-of-systems approaches to capture the dynamics of failure propagation. Starting from the former seminal paper, the "System of Systems" (or Network or Networks) became a central topic in the Complexity Science [5]. The theoretical approach allows to understand the emergent behaviors, that is the universal phenomena ruling interdependent networks, regardless of their details. However, usable models, need to enter in deeper details based on the functional behavior of infrastructures and especially their geographical distribution on the territory.

GIS-based methodologies are particularly suitable for identifying the portions of land where disasters triggered by natural hazards of various kinds may occur. The possibility of producing enhanced maps starting from different geospatial layers (e.g. natural hazards, CI topology, territorial features, etc.) is one of main advantages of GIS applications. The development of GIS-based platforms have emerged as a natural framework for urban CI analysis, since the spatial dimension is central both to infrastructure topology and to the geographic footprint of hazard events. In particular, such platforms allow to solve complex spatial decision problems by integrating GIS with other techniques or tools (e.g., decision support systems).

Tools such as HAZUS [6] provide standardised loss estimation models for earthquakes, floods, and wind events, but are primarily oriented toward physical damage assessment rather than service-level resilience quantification.

Beyond HAZUS, several platforms have been developed to support CI resilience assessment. The Infrastructure Resilience Analysis Framework (IRAF) developed by Argonne National Laboratory provides a systematic methodology for characterising infrastructure dependencies and estimating restoration times [7].

OpenQuake, developed by the Global Earthquake Model Foundation, is an open-source seismic hazard and risk calculation platform widely adopted for infrastructure vulnerability assessment [8].

The SYNER-G project developed a comprehensive methodology for the systemic seismic vulnerability and risk assessment of urban infrastructure systems, explicitly addressing interdependencies among buildings, transportation networks, utility networks, and healthcare facilities [9].

Further, the EU-funded RESILIENS project produced a European Resilience Management Guideline and an associated toolbox for CI operators [10], while the DARWIN project focused on resilience management guidelines for crisis response organisations [11].

CI-RES distinguishes itself from these platforms through: (i) the integration of hybrid natural-anthropogenic scenarios; (ii) a fully containerised simulation architecture; (iii) a meta-modelling interface allowing non-programmers to compose custom workflows; and (iv) direct alignment with the operational requirements of the CER Directive.

2.2 Resilience Metrics and Simulation

Resilience is commonly operationalised as the ability of a system to absorb a disturbance, adapt, and recover to an acceptable performance level within an acceptable time [12]. Quantitative resilience metrics typically integrate performance loss over the disruption and recovery period, requiring time-resolved simulation of post-event system response. This is particularly challenging for urban multi-infrastructure systems, where recovery in one sector depends on the partial recovery of others. Strictly speaking, the 'real' resilience of a system, as compared to its robustness, is related to its recovery capabilities. However, the term is currently employed in a wider sense as stated by the CER Directive [2]. The CI-RES platform enables a comprehensive assessment of system resilience across all its dimensions.

2.3 Urban Digital Twins

The concept of the Urban Digital Twin (UDT) extends the industrial digital twin paradigm to the city scale, combining real-time sensor data, physics-based simulation, and data analytics to create a dynamic virtual replica of urban systems [13]. UDTs are increasingly recognised as a strategic tool for urban planning, emergency management, and infrastructure investment prioritisation; but their enforcement requires a scalable, interoperable simulation backbone of the kind that CI-RES is designed to provide.

3 CI-RES Platform Architecture

3.1 Overview

CI-RES is structured around three main layers: a *data layer*, a *simulation layer*, and a *presentation layer*. The data layer stores geo-referenced representations of urban critical infrastructures and their interdependencies in a GIS-compatible format. The simulation layer hosts a suite of containerised codes that implement hazard-specific and consequence models. The presentation layer exposes both an interactive map-based visualisation environment and a meta-modelling interface for workflow composition.

3.2 Data Layer

The data layer integrates multiple geo-referenced datasets describing the topology and attributes of urban CI components: electrical substations and distribution lines, water treatment and pumping stations, road and rail networks, bridges and viaducts, hospitals and emergency services, and telecommunications infrastructure. Interdependency links—both physical and logical—are encoded as directed graph edges connecting components across infrastructure layers.

Infrastructure data are acquired from multiple authoritative sources. Data about electrical network, telecommunication, gas pipelines, and other CI systems are derived from utility operators under data-sharing agreements. Transportation network data, strategic structures and point of interest (e.g. hospitals, public buildings, etc.) originate from OpenStreetMap.

Hazard data sources include: the Italian Seismic Hazard Map (MPS04) [14] produced by INGV for seismic scenarios; the ISPRA IdroGEO [15] platform for landslide inventories and flood hazard maps; the European Ground Motion Service (EGMS) [16] for subsidence monitoring; and the Italian Civil Protection Department for meteorological bulletins and alerts.

Data ingestion currently follows a semi-automated workflow: authoritative datasets are periodically retrieved from source repositories, processed through validation and format conversion pipelines, and integrated into the platform database.

Data ingestion pipelines support standard geospatial formats (GeoJSON, Shapefile, GeoTiff, etc.) and are designed to be updated incrementally as new infrastructure data become available. All spatial data are referenced to a common coordinate system (WGS84, EPSG:4326) to ensure consistency across datasets of different provenance.

3.3 Simulation Layer

The simulation layer is implemented as a collection of Docker containers, each encapsulating a self-contained simulation code together with its dependencies. This containerisation approach ensures reproducibility, eliminates dependency conflicts between codes, and facilitates independent versioning and updating of individual models.

Current container types include: seismic fragility and damage estimation codes; buildings and infrastructures multihazard assessment; geological instability models covering subsidence and landslide scenarios; and network flow models for estimating service degradation given component damage states. Additional containers are under development for cyber threat scenarios and for consequence models that estimate the impact of infrastructure outages on population welfare indicators.

3.4 Presentation Layer

The presentation layer provides an interactive WebGIS environment in which territorial features, hazard maps, infrastructure components, interdependency links, simulation inputs, and simulation results are visualised within the browser (Fig. 1). Non-specialist users—including municipal planners and civil protection officers—can navigate the interface, select scenarios, launch pre-configured analyses, and inspect results through thematic maps and summary dashboards without requiring direct access to the underlying simulation codes.

Fig. 1. CI-RES Platform: WebGIS interface.

4 Simulation Capabilities and Hazard Scenarios

4.1 Seismic Scenarios

The seismic simulation pipeline accepts a ground-motion intensity map (expressed as peak ground acceleration or spectral acceleration) and applies component-level fragility functions to estimate damage states for each CI element. Damage states are propagated through the interdependency graph to estimate service disruption at the system level. The pipeline supports both scenario-based analysis (a specified earthquake event) and probabilistic hazard analysis (aggregated over a range of possible events).

While this paper primarily describes the platform's architecture, evaluating its predictive capabilities and result reliability is essential. The platform supports diverse simulation workflows, though their constraints are dictated by the underlying computational modules. For seismic scenarios, rather than simulating detailed wave propagation, we utilize heuristic amplification laws [17] to approximate propagation behavior. The accuracy of this approach varies by context:

it is highly effective for homogeneous seismic zones but may deviate in more heterogeneous environments.

To assess post-event structural damage, we may employ both deterministic and stochastic methodologies. The deterministic approach applies specific 'PGA thresholds' (to each structure) based on available census data regarding construction materials and techniques; exceeding these thresholds implies structural failure. Conversely, the stochastic approach offers greater realism by assigning failure probabilities to individual components and generating combinatorial damage scenarios. While this yields a more robust impact estimate through ensemble averaging, it increases computational demand by several orders of magnitude. Similarly, sensitivity analyses—which require iterative simulations with perturbed parameters—remain computationally intensive.

4.2 Multihazard Analysis

This tool combines geospatial analysis with the Weighted Linear Combination (WLC) method [18] for multi-hazard assessment, understood as the simultaneous presence of multiple hazards within the same territorial area [19]. The six hazards considered are: earthquake, flood, landslide, volcanic, wildfire and tsunami. The assessment is carried out for selected relevant critical infrastructures (roads and bridges, electric power stations, etc.) and is based on the definition of weights through a pairwise comparison matrix, according to the AHP (Analytical Hierarchy Process) approach [20]. To perform the multihazard calculation, the user can insert the relative importance between hazards in the matrix (Fig. 2): the values range from 1 ("equal importance") to 9 ("extremely more important"). Alternatively, the user can load preset values (e.g. all hazards equal, focus on seismic, focus on floods/landslides, focus on seismic/floods/landslides). The results are presented in the form of maps, charts, and statistics, and the outputs can be downloaded in GIS formats.

The reliability of the multi-hazard approach is highly sensitive to the parameter selection, defining the weight of the different hazards. In this framework, the selection process relies on expert judgment to ensure the analysis is tailored to the specific context. The multi-hazard assessment approach adopted in CI-RES builds upon established methodologies for spatial hazard interaction analysis at the European scale [21] and has been validated in recent Italian case studies demonstrating its applicability across different spatial scales [22].

4.3 Geological Instability Scenarios

Subsidence and landslide models estimate differential ground deformation and slope failure probabilities across the urban area, and translate these into damage likelihood for surface (e.g., bridges) and buried (e.g., pipelines) infrastructures. The tool intersects selected critical infrastructure components with the European Ground Motion Service (EGMS) [16] validated dataset (Fig. 3). It calculates the average displacement velocity (mm/year) for both vertical (UP) and horizontal (EAST) components within a specific buffer, identifying potential structural

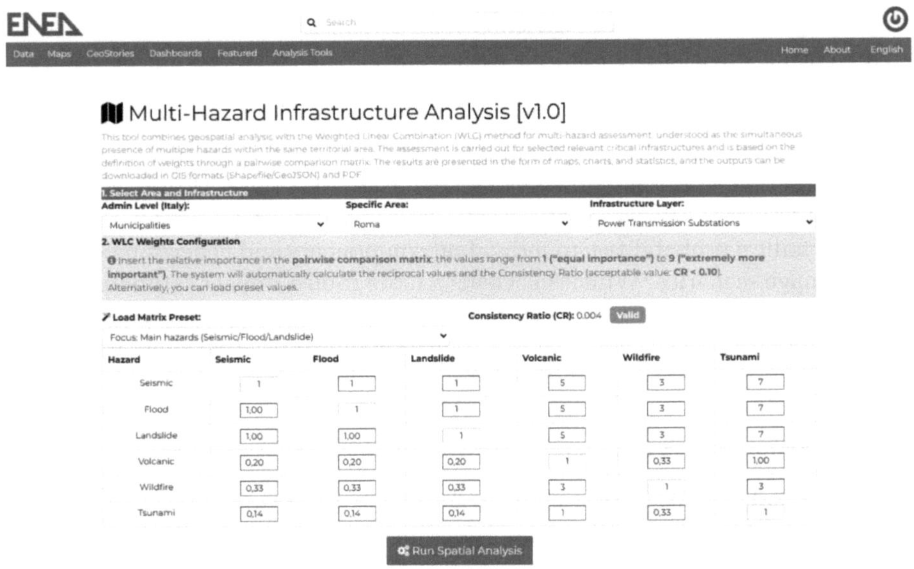

Fig. 2. CI-RES - Multihazard tool: input mask.

"alerts" due to subsidence, uplift, or lateral movements. Moreover, the analysis takes into account the landslide hazard zones (Source: ISPRA-Idrogeo [15]) and the Italian Landslide Inventory (source: ISPRA-IFFI [23]). This model is particularly relevant for Italian urban contexts, where geological hazard is a significant contributor to infrastructure risk.

4.4 Hybrid and Anthropogenic Scenarios

A distinctive capability of CI-RES is the support for *hybrid scenarios* in which natural hazard events are combined with deliberate anthropogenic actions—for example, a flood event coinciding with a targeted attack on a water pumping station, or a seismic event exploited to mask a cyber intrusion into grid control systems. Hybrid scenario analysis requires the simultaneous activation of multiple simulation containers and the aggregation of their outputs through a consequence model, which is orchestrated by the meta-modelling interface described in the following section.

5 Meta-modelling Interface

5.1 Workflow Composition

The meta-modelling interface, can be implemented as a web application, thus allowing authorised users to compose simulation workflows by selecting and connecting simulation containers, consequence models, and optimisation modules

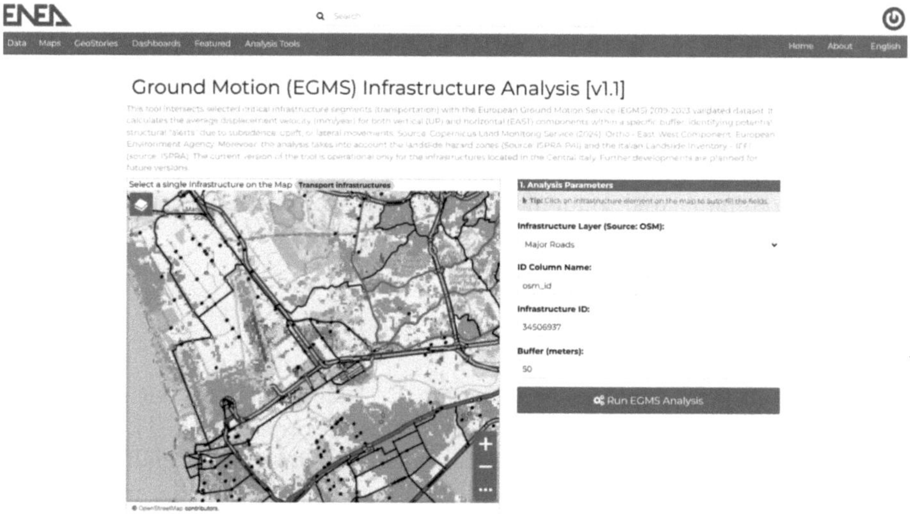

Fig. 3. CI-RES - Ground motion tool: input mask.

through a graphical interface. The resulting workflow is represented as a directed acyclic graph in which nodes correspond to simulation components and edges define data dependencies between them.

This approach enables domain experts to:

- **Customise models:** Adapt simulation parameters and consequence functions to the specific urban context and stakeholder requirements.
- **Create new scenarios:** Define bespoke simulation scenarios to evaluate the impact of new infrastructure investments or risk mitigation interventions.
- **Share workflows:** Publish composed workflows for reuse by other platform users, fostering a community of practice among CI resilience analysts.

It is worth noting that the former approach does not require deep knowledge of the employed codes, for their composition, but just their I/O data format. In other words, the 'meta-modeler' may design their application disregarding the details of calculations performed by each module.

5.2 Dynamic Risk and Resilience Estimation

Beyond static damage assessment, the meta-modelling layer supports time-resolved simulation of post-event system behaviour, enabling the estimation of dynamic risk and resilience metrics. Users can specify recovery models for each infrastructure sector and observe how service availability evolves over time following a disruptive event. The platform computes standard resilience indicators—such as the area-under-the-performance-curve metric—and presents them alongside spatial maps of residual service coverage.

5.3 Optimisation Module

An optimisation module, callable from within the meta-modelling interface, applies resource allocation algorithms to identify the intervention strategies that maximise post-event resilience given a budget constraint. Outputs take the form of prioritised lists of infrastructure components to reinforce or protect, which can be directly communicated to municipal authorities and infrastructure operators.

6 Kubernetes Migration

6.1 Motivation

The current CI-RES deployment relies on two independent physical machines hosting development and production environments respectively. This architecture limits operational continuity: hardware failures or software malfunctions in either machine can cause extended service interruptions, and the manual synchronisation of the two environments introduces operational overhead and the risk of configuration drift.

6.2 Kubernetes-Based Deployment

The platform is being migrated to the existing Kubernetes cluster managed by the ENEA Laboratory for the Analysis and Modelling of Critical Infrastructures and Essential Services. Kubernetes provides container orchestration capabilities that directly address the limitations of the current deployment:

- **High availability:** Service redundancy across multiple cluster nodes and automatic failover ensure that the platform remains operational even in the event of hardware failures or software malfunctions.
- **Scalability:** Horizontal pod autoscaling allows the platform to accommodate peaks in simulation demand—for example, during emergency response operations—without manual intervention.
- **Continuous deployment:** Kubernetes simplifies the rollout of updated container images, enabling new simulation codes and interface features to be deployed rapidly and safely with zero downtime.
- **Self-healing:** Automatic restart of failed containers and rescheduling of workloads to healthy nodes minimise the impact of transient faults on platform availability.

The migration also establishes the technical foundation for the future integration of real-time data streams—from sensor networks, smart meters, and emergency communication systems—that will be required by the Urban Digital Twin implementation described in the following section.

7 Towards an Urban Digital Twin

The Kubernetes-based CI-RES platform constitutes the simulation backbone of a broader Urban Digital Twin (UDT) initiative. In the UDT framework, CI-RES will be extended with:

- **Real-time data integration:** Live telemetry from infrastructure monitoring sensors will continuously update the platform's representation of infrastructure state, enabling near-real-time situation awareness during emergencies.
- **Predictive analytics:** Machine learning models trained on historical event data will augment physics-based simulations with rapid probabilistic forecasts of disruption propagation and recovery trajectories.
- **Decision support:** Automated alert generation and scenario pre-computation will allow the platform to provide actionable recommendations to emergency managers within minutes of an event onset.
- **Smart City Platform integration:** [24] Selected CI-RES applications, packaged as lightweight services, will be integrated into the municipal Smart City Platform, making resilience indicators accessible to a broader audience of non-specialist users.

This evolution positions CI-RES as a foundational infrastructure for evidence-based urban governance, supporting both routine infrastructure investment planning and crisis response operations.

8 Preliminary Results

The CI-RES platform has been applied to a pilot urban area to validate the integrated simulation pipeline and the meta-modelling interface. The pilot focused on the interaction between the electrical distribution network and the water supply system under a seismic scenario, assessing the cascading impact of substation damage on pumping station operations and the consequent degradation of water service availability across the city.

The simulation identified a set of critical nodes whose failure produces disproportionately large reductions in overall service availability, consistent with the theoretical predictions of interdependent network models [4]. The optimisation module suggested a prioritised reinforcement strategy that, applied to the five most critical nodes, reduced the expected service loss by approximately 30% under the reference seismic scenario.

The georeferenced visualisation of results (Fig. 4) was positively evaluated by a group of domain experts from the civil protection sector, who highlighted the intuitive accessibility of the map-based interface as a key advantage for operational use. Full quantitative results and a detailed case study will be reported in the accompanying technical report [25].

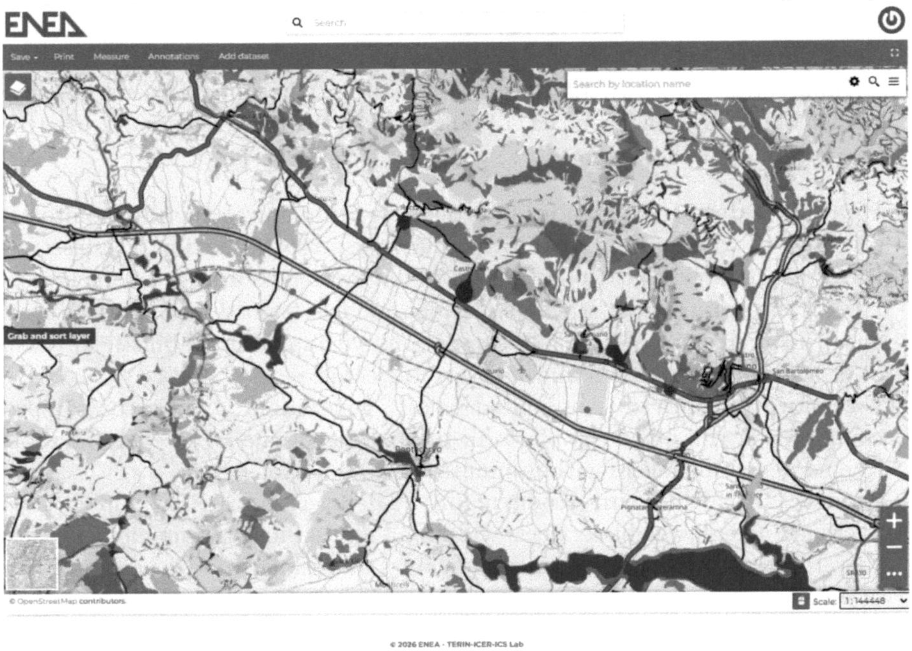

Fig. 4. CI-RES: example of visualisation of results.

9 Conclusions and Future Work

This paper has described CI-RES, a GIS-based platform for the analysis and simulation of critical infrastructure resilience in urban environments, developed by ENEA within the Italian Programme Agreement for Electric System Research. The platform integrates geo-referenced infrastructure data, a suite of containerised hazard and consequence simulation codes, a meta-modelling interface for workflow composition, and a georeferenced visualisation environment. The platform is also endowed with a Intelligent Private Chat interface that allows users to ask information about critical infrastructures and essential services. The workflows employed require the coordinated execution of various simulation codes. Each code, in turn, relies on a set of parameters tuned through expert judgment or data adaptation. Among these, thresholds play a critical role; their precise calibration can significantly influence both quantitative outcomes and even emergent behaviors. For example, thresholds for structural failure during earthquakes are often estimated using census data, which are frequently outdated or imprecise. Furthermore, physical structures often deviate from the construction specifications recorded in such databases. This dependency on parameter accuracy is even more pronounced in multi-risk analyses, where the reliability of results remains an unresolved challenge.

The ongoing migration of CI-RES to a Kubernetes-based deployment will substantially improve platform availability, scalability, and dependability, while establishing the technical foundation for the integration of real-time data streams required by future Urban Digital Twin implementations.

Future work will focus on: (i) expanding the simulation container library to cover additional hazard types and infrastructure sectors (e.g. wildfires and floods); (ii) integrating real-time sensor data feeds to enable live situation awareness (and early warning thereby); (iii) developing machine learning components for rapid disruption forecasting; and (iv) deploying selected platform services within the municipal Smart City Platform to broaden access to resilience indicators among non-specialist stakeholders.

Acknowledgments. This work was carried out within the framework of the Italian Programme Agreement for Electric System Research (*Accordo di Programma per la Ricerca di Sistema elettrico* 2025-2027), WP2 – Line of Activity LA8, funded by the Ministry of the Environment and Energy Security (MASE).

Disclosure of Interests. The authors have no competing interests to declare that are relevant to the content of this article.

References

1. Tofani, A., et al.: Operational resilience metrics for complex inter-dependent electrical networks. Appl. Sci. **11**(13), 5842 (2021). https://doi.org/10.3390/app11135842
2. European Parliament and Council: Directive (EU) 2022/2557 of 14 December 2022 on the resilience of critical entities, Off. J. Eur. Union L **333**, 164–198 (2022). https://eur-lex.europa.eu/eli/dir/2022/2557/oj/eng
3. Rinaldi, S.M., Peerenboom, J.P., Kelly, T.K.: Identifying, understanding, and analyzing critical infrastructure interdependencies. IEEE Control. Syst. **21**(6), 11–25 (2001). https://doi.org/10.1109/37.969131
4. Buldyrev, S.V., Parshani, R., Paul, G., Stanley, H.E., Havlin, S.: Catastrophic cascade of failures in interdependent networks. Nature **464**(7291), 1025–1028 (2010). https://doi.org/10.1038/nature08932
5. D'Agostino, G., Scala, A. (eds.): Networks of Networks: The Last Frontier of Complexity. UCS. Springer, Cham (2014). https://doi.org/10.1007/978-3-319-03518-5
6. Federal Emergency Management Agency (FEMA): Hazus Earthquake Model Technical Manual. FEMA, Washington, DC (2020)
7. Petit, F., et al.: Resilience measurement index: an indicator of critical infrastructure resilience. Technical report ANL/DIS-13-01, Argonne National Laboratory (2013)
8. Pagani, M., et al.: OpenQuake engine: an open hazard (and risk) software for the global earthquake model. Seismol. Res. Lett. **85**(3), 692–702 (2014)
9. Pitilakis, K., Franchin, P., Khazai, B., Wenzel, H. (eds.): SYNER-G: Systemic Seismic Vulnerability and Risk Assessment of Complex Urban, Utility. Lifeline Systems and Critical Facilities. Springer, Dordrecht (2014)
10. Häring, I., Ebenhöch, S., Stolz, A.: Quantifying resilience for resilience engineering of socio-technical systems. Eur. J. Secur. Res. **1**(1), 21–58 (2016)
11. The Science and Practice of Resilience. RSD. Springer, Cham (2019). https://doi.org/10.1007/978-3-030-04565-4_4

12. Hosseini, S., Barker, K., Ramirez-Marquez, J.E.: A review of definitions and measures of system resilience. Reliab. Eng. Syst. Saf. **145**, 47–61 (2016). https://doi.org/10.1016/j.ress.2015.08.006
13. White, G., Zink, A., Codèca, L., Clarke, S.: A digital twin smart city for citizen feedback. Cities **110**, 103064 (2021). https://doi.org/10.1016/j.cities.2020.103064
14. INGV: Italian Seismic Hazard Map. Accessed 8 May 2026
15. ISPRA IdroGEO: The Italian web platform on landslides and floods. https://idrogeo.isprambiente.it/app/. Accessed 25 Mar 2026
16. EGMS Copernicus Land Monitorig Service: Ortho - East-West Component. European Environment Agency (2024). (Ortho Vertical) https://doi.org/10.2909/4778163b-23bb-4403-af70-7accbc56e7d3
17. Douglas, J.: Ground motion prediction equations 1964-2023. Online resource (2024)
18. Multicriteria Decision Analysis in Geographic Information Science. AGIS. Springer, Heidelberg (2015). https://doi.org/10.1007/978-3-540-74757-4
19. Arduin, M., Tofani, A., D'Agostino, G., Pollino, M.: Multicriteria GIS spatial analysis for multi-hazard assessment of infrastructures in case of natural events. In: Oliva, G., Panzieri, S., Hämmerli, B., Pascucci, F., Faramondi, L. (eds.) CRITIS 2024. LNCS, vol. 15549, pp. 326–342. Springer, Cham (2025). https://doi.org/10.1007/978-3-031-84260-3_19
20. Saaty, T.L.: The Analytic Hierarchy Process: Planning, Priority Setting. Resource Allocation. McGraw-Hill, New York (1980)
21. Tarvainen, T., Jarva, J., Greiving, S.: Spatial pattern of Hazards and Hazard Interactions in Europe. In: Schmidt-Thomé, P. (ed.) Natural and Technological Hazards and Risks Affecting the Spatial Development of European Regions. Special Paper, vol. 42, pp. 83–91. Geological Survey of Finland, Espoo (2006)
22. Cappucci, S., Pollino, M., Farrace, M.G., Della Morte, L., Baiocchi, V.: Infrastructure impact assessment through multi-hazard analysis at different scales: the 26 November 2022 flood event on the island of Ischia and debris management. Land **13**(4), 500 (2024). https://doi.org/10.3390/land13040500)
23. IFFI, Italian Landslide Inventory. https://idrogeo.isprambiente.it/app/iffi. Accessed 25 Mar 2026
24. ENEA, Smart City Platform. https://smartcityplatform.enea.it/#/it/index.html. Accessed 8 May 2026
25. D'Agostino, G., Tofani, A.: Analysis and Modelling of Critical Infrastructures in Urban Environments: Extension of the CI-RES Platform. ENEA Technical report, Rome (2024)

Advanced and Innovative Web Apps 2026 (AIWA 2026)

A Privacy-Preserving, Installation-Free Progressive Web App for Modern Slide Presentations

Damiano Perri(✉)

Department of Mathematics and Computer Science, University of Perugia, Perugia, Italy
damiano.perri@unipg.it

Abstract. This paper introduces an open-source Progressive Web App that empowers lecturers, researchers, and keynote speakers to deliver more modern and effective presentations, focusing on direct audience engagement and practical usability.

With privacy and simplicity at its core, the app requires no installation or setup, making its features instantly accessible and user-friendly.

The software is 220KB in size and is based entirely on web technologies that enable the management of PDFs, videos and images.

Thanks to the Window Management API, monitors connected to the computer are detected and indexed, and a second window of the same web page can be managed using the Broadcast Channel API, which is available on all modern browsers and provides local message exchange.

In this way, from a single codebase that opens the presenter's window, the programme can control a second browser window to display the presentation to the audience without transferring data over the internet, ensuring that no files from the presented documents are ever transmitted or stored on external servers.

Document rendering occurs entirely on the client side using the PDF.js library, released by Mozilla under an open-source license.

The built-in features include support for 'split' and 'bottom' PDF notes, real-time annotation and highlighting tools, and control of the presenter's webcam via local WebRTC.

If the user wishes, optional features can be enabled, such as remote control of the presentation via smartphone using WebSocket or an anonymous Questions & Answers module for the audience, these are the only features that require data exchange with the server after the initial loading of static files.

State-of-the-art analysis confirms there are currently no comparable web-based solutions. The application works on all major browsers and operating systems, making it a viable and accessible alternative to traditional tools.

Keywords: Learning Technologies · Web-based- Computing · Progressive Web App · Cloud Computing · Open Source · Human Computer Interaction

O. Gervasi et al. (Eds.): ICCSA 2026 Workshops, LNCS 16758, pp. 171–185, 2027.
https://doi.org/10.1007/978-3-032-30497-1_11

1 Introduction

This paper describes an innovative piece of software released under an open-source licence, designed to facilitate the management of school lessons, keynote speeches or presentations involving an audience to whom documents need to be shown. The project presented here has been developed using modern web technologies and does not require installation on the user's operating system. The technology underpinning the development of this application is based on HTML, CSS and JavaScript, and has enabled the creation of a Progressive Web App with a total size of 220KB. The features integrated into the application allow users to present PDF documents, videos and images, control the presentation remotely via a smartphone, navigate through all the slides of the PDF using a browser, manage Q&A sessions, manage timers for breaks, use a laser pointer or spotlight to highlight parts of the document, draw on the slides, use a dynamic zoom to enlarge parts of the document, and manage the presenter's webcam.

Throughout the development phase, we have consistently prioritised the need for a graphical interface that is both simple and effective one capable of displaying on the presenter's screen the information required to ensure their talk is delivered to the highest standard. Furthermore, native compatibility has been designed for PDFs generated by projects based on LaTeX Beamer, containing the speaker's notes on the right-hand side of the page, and for projects created using Google Slides, with the speaker's notes positioned at the bottom of the page and exported to PDF format using the platform's native functionality.

The main motivation behind this work lies in the limitations highlighted by current desktop applications and traditional PDF readers. Speakers and lecturers often find themselves working in diverse and restrictive environments, where they must install additional software or plugins to enable dual-screen support, such as the laptop screen and the projector screen used to deliver content to the audience.

By leveraging modern Web APIs, such as the Window Management API and the BroadcastChannel architecture, the Progressive Web App presented here uniquely bridges the gap between web and desktop applications. It alone guarantees native multi-monitor management from the browser and integrates smartphone remote control capability, all while maintaining minimal computational demands. Furthermore, the application embraces a typically 'local-first' philosophy: document rendering (handled by the PDF.js library) takes place entirely on the client side, and no file uploads to external servers are required, thus ensuring a smooth, immediate, secure experience that respects user privacy. This approach not only reduces latency, enabling real-time performance even without a stable internet connection, but also ensures that documents containing sensitive data or dealing with confidential matters can be used, as there is absolutely no transfer of data from the documents to a third-party cloud server under any circumstances. The introduction of interactive tools accessible via smartphone (remote control and Q&A module via WebSocket) further breaks down the physical barriers between the presenter and the audience, promoting more dynamic and inclusive presentations without the need for dedicated or expensive hardware.

Finally, we chose to adopt an open-source approach to foster collaboration and continuous innovation, allowing developers from around the world to contribute to the project, improve existing features and adapt it to specific needs, thereby ensuring rapid evolution of the software in response to user requirements as well as enabling transparency and security of the source code.

This scientific article is organised as follows. Section 2 introduces the background and the motivations that led to the development of the software. Section 3 describes the software architecture by analysing the code and the client-server infrastructure that enables its operation. Section 4 analyses the results obtained and discusses possible future developments of the project.

2 Motivation and Related Works

This section reviews the current scientific literature and compares the software currently available for presenting documents to an audience, highlighting the limitations and challenges that led to the development of the software described in this article.

PDF is one of the most widely used formats for document exchange and for creating presentations, particularly in academic settings, thanks to its ability to preserve the formatting and appearance of the document across different platforms and devices. It was created in 1993 as a proprietary format developed by Adobe Systems [1], but was made public in 2008 and has since become an open standard ISO 32000-1:2008[1].

The current scientific literature is replete with papers analysing the technologies and software currently available for managing presentations and school lessons; generally, however, these works focus on installable software that serves as an alternative to PowerPoint, Keynote or Google Presentation, or concentrate on software for the interactive management of presentations, but generally with installable software dependent on the type of operating system used by the user and never with web applications.

In 2010, a piece of software called Pdf Presenter Console (PPC) [2][2] was released on GitHub, based on GTK, it provided support for multiple monitors simultaneously, but it has not been updated for years. This led to a fork, i.e. a derivative project, called pdfpc [3], which can be installed on Linux, macOS (via Homebrew) and Windows (via WSL), and is currently maintained and updated, but is not available as a web application. Installing PDFPC is not always possible, for example, you need to have administrator rights on the computer. The developers also offer the option to compile the software from source, but even in this case, you need to be reasonably familiar with the command line, and a whole series of libraries must be installed as a prerequisite, making the procedure inaccessible to the majority of users.

---

1 https://www.iso.org/standard/51502.html.
2 https://github.com/jakobwesthoff/Pdf-Presenter-Console.

Rico-Juan [4] presents an open-source framework for synchronising PDF presentations with video and audio, viewable in real time via the user's smartphone. Although this project is no longer maintained or updated, it represents an interesting and fundamental starting point for accessible systems. The software focused primarily on the user's experience and did not take into account aspects relating to the presenter, the management of their presentation, or the audience.

In 2014, Mozilla released a JavaScript library called pdf.js that allows PDF documents to be viewed directly within the browser, without the need to install plugins or additional software. To date, this library has reached version 5.0 and is widely used [5]. The advantage of this library is that it is open source, released under the Apache-2.0 licence via GitHub[3], and can be integrated royalty-free into commercial projects.

In 2015, Lenz et al. [6] suggested that Prezi software is a valid alternative to PowerPoint for creating presentations, particularly in an academic context, thanks to its ability to create more dynamic and engaging presentations, however, nothing is mentioned regarding privacy, security or the management of data contained within one's presentations. Today, Prezi also incorporates artificial intelligence features that can assist with studying, however, aside from a free version usable only for public presentations, it requires paid plans for personal use.

In 2016, Office Social [7] was launched, a plugin for PowerPoint that, via an app installable on a smartphone, allows the audience and the presenter to navigate through the slides of the presentation. The limitation of this software is its reliance on proprietary, closed-source software, the need to install plugins, and the requirement to install additional code on the user's smartphone. Furthermore, it does not provide any additional features that enhance the management of the presentation itself, but is limited to providing remote control and interaction with the audience. In the same year, a master's thesis was published in Austria [8] analysing the state of the art in presentation management software via interaction with mobile devices, highlighting the need for greater integration between devices, reduced complexity during installation, and a greater focus on the presenter's user experience. Avsar et al. [9] compare nine presentation management software packages, some free and others paid, highlighting the pros and cons of each. In the paper, they propose a new software package, called *Academic Presenter*, which is free and supports handwriting during the presentation. This software has not been updated since 1 October 2018 and the only supported operating system is Microsoft Windows.

In 2019, a paper [10] was published comparing Google Slides, Prezi, Tilda, Slides and Haiku Deck with PowerPoint. The comparison focuses on slide preparation and presentation delivery, and the authors note that most students tend to prefer Google Slides as a free and accessible alternative.

Scientific research has also analysed the impact in secondary schools, highlighting that presentations contribute to improving the quality of teaching; again

[3] https://github.com/mozilla/pdf.js.

in 2019, the main applications discussed were Microsoft PowerPoint, Keynote, Google Slides, Prezi, Tilda, Slides and Haiku Deck [11]. In recent years, modern web technologies have been increasingly used in the field of education, and many researchers have focused on how best to harness their full potential [12–14].

HTML is known as a markup language, which was subsequently complemented by CSS for graphics management and JavaScript for application logic management. The JavaScript programming language has evolved in three phases. The first is the introductory phase, which saw its inception and ran from 1995 to 2009, marked by the advent of AJAX technology and the ability to make web pages interactive. The second phase runs from 2009 to 2015, during which we witnessed the emergence of ES6 (ECMAScript 2015), numerous frameworks and libraries that simplified web application development—such as AngularJS and jQuery—as well as the introduction of classes, modules and asynchronous functions [15]. The third phase spans from 2015 to the present day, during which modern frameworks such as React, Vue.js and Next.js have made it possible to move application logic directly to the client, thereby also enabling the development of hybrid applications [16–18]. Furthermore, in recent years, the consolidation of cloud computing and the ability to deliver services to the public [19,20] via the network has led to the proliferation of web applications, shifting the computation of many everyday tasks to platforms external to local computing [21–24].

The literature review has highlighted that, to date, there is no open-source software based on web technologies that allows PDF presentations to be managed with advanced features such as those described in this article, and which is accessible from any device without the need to install additional software or plugins, whilst guaranteeing the privacy and security of the data contained in the presented documents.

3 Discussion

This section documents the technology underpinning the operation of the application presented, analysing both the code and the infrastructure that enables the service to be delivered to the public.

3.1 Design Decisions and Implementation Approach

Before commencing the software development phase, a requirements analysis and a feasibility study were carried out. The functionalities available to browsers are constantly evolving, and when building a web app, it is essential to consider what can be achieved and what limitations cannot be overcome.

There are five enabling technologies that have facilitated the development of this project. The first is the introduction of Web 2.0, which enabled the transition from static to dynamic pages thanks to AJAX. The second is the introduction of HTML5, which, through canvas, video and audio elements, allows complex objects to be rendered on a web page without requiring plugins, such as the now obsolete Adobe Flash Player. The third is the JavaScript engine built into browsers, which allows code to be compiled into machine code that can be executed directly on the user's PC. This draws on the philosophy underlying Java, where a programme can run on any platform thanks to a virtual machine that interprets the code; in this case, it is the browser that includes the necessary functionality to interpret and execute the code. The fourth is the ability to use WebSockets, which enable real-time, two-way communication between client and server, thus allowing for the implementation of features such as remote control via smartphone and a Questions and Answers module between the audience and the presenter. Before WebSockets, communication could only take place via polling or long polling techniques, which involved periodically sending requests to the server to check for new data or keeping a communication channel open for a certain period of time while waiting for a message to arrive, however, these techniques were inefficient and did not guarantee real-time communication. WebSockets, on the other hand, allow a persistent connection to be established between client and server, enabling data to be sent and received in real time without the need to send periodic requests. Finally, the fifth and key technology is the ability to use the Window Management API to manage windows, the release of WebRTC for managing webcams across separate windows, and the ability to use the BroadcastChannel API to synchronise state across different windows, thereby enabling native multi-monitor management directly from the browser.

BroadcastChannel is a JavaScript API that enables communication between windows, tabs or iframes sharing the same origin (protocol, domain and port) and forms the basis of this project. Until a few years ago, managing multiple windows of the same web page was a highly complex task and practically impossible to achieve to the standards of quality and user experience this project aims to deliver. Users expect software that is simple, intuitive, immediate and allows them to get straight to work. The absence of any preliminary configuration or installation steps is, in fact, a key prerequisite for this project.

3.2 Backend Architecture

The server-side architecture has been designed to be extremely lightweight and limited to essential tasks, delegating all computational and graphical processing to the client device. The server is based on Node.js [25]. The backend is used exclusively to serve the static files of the Progressive Web App (HTML, CSS, JavaScript) on startup and, optionally, to manage slides remotely. For reasons of maintainability and security, the server was subsequently containerised using Docker, thus enabling rapid deployment based on images tagged with the release date. Docker is a modern containerisation platform that allows applications to be packaged with all their dependencies into a single container, ensuring consistency across different environments and simplifying deployment and maintenance [26–28].

The Node.js server is responsible for providing content that is predominantly static, with computations performed locally, however, it was chosen to enable the exchange of messages with clients via WebSockets. It should first be noted that the use of WebSockets is entirely optional and serves only two specific functions, which are described below: remote control via smartphone and the Questions & Answers (Q&A) module between the audience and the speaker. For the presentation to function, once the static files have been downloaded, the application requires no further data from the server. Thanks to WebSockets, users can connect their smartphone to the presentation session and control the slides being shown in exactly the same way as they would using any remote control connected to the computer via USB. The connection is established by scanning a QR code containing a unique session token, which the user's device uses to connect to the server. The QR code consists of the server address and the GET parameter containing the session token. The QR code is generated using an open-source library for Node.JS[4].

A key aspect in terms of privacy and security is that the server processes only navigation commands and plain text; no PDF documents, images or sensitive data are ever uploaded, transmitted or stored on the server. Live sessions are protected and kept isolated through dynamically generated 64-character unique identifiers. Between the development phase and the delivery of content to the user, we also have a compilation phase based on Vite.js [29,30] to minimise JavaScript files, thereby reducing the overall size of the Progressive Web App to just 148KB. Adding the 72KB logo brings the total size to 220KB, ensuring fast loading even under sub-optimal network conditions.

3.3 Frontend Architecture

The frontend is the part of the application that is visible to the user and with which they can interact directly. It consists of three main parts: the Presenter Window, the Audience Window and the Remote Control Window. Once the PDF has been loaded into the system, the Presenter Window opens, this is the presenter's main window, displaying the slide navigator, the current slide, the presenter's notes (if any), and a preview of the next slide. An example of the window described above is shown in Fig. 1.

By utilising the *Window Management API*, the system is able to detect secondary monitors and automatically position the window in full-screen mode. Based on tests carried out, the automatic positioning feature is supported by Chrome, Edge and Opera. Firefox, Safari and lesser-known browsers that have not yet added support for this feature[5] have nevertheless been taken into account. During code development, a fallback was implemented for browsers with limited technical capabilities; the new window containing the audience view is positioned directly on the monitor used by the presenter, who can then move it to the desired screen. Firefox and Safari users will still be able to use all other features of the application correctly.

---

[4] https://github.com/soldair/node-qrcode.

[5] https://developer.mozilla.org/en-US/docs/Web/API/Window_Management_API.

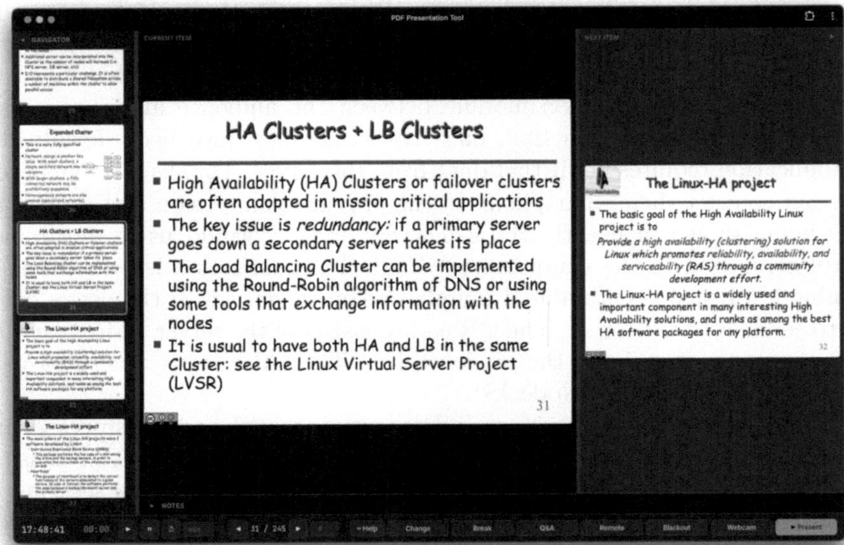

Fig. 1. A screenshot of the presenter's view, showing the navigation pane, the current slide, the next slide and the controls at the bottom of the window.

State synchronisation between the two displays occurs natively and instantly via the *BroadcastChannel API*, which has been natively supported by all major browsers since March 2022, as indicated in Mozilla's official documentation[6]. This API has enabled the implementation of the following features: navigation between slides; laser pointer mode, which helps indicate the presenter's mouse position on the audience's screen; zoom mode, which allows a section of the slide to be magnified by following the mouse cursor; spotlight mode, which highlights a section of the slide by darkening the background and simulating a torch illuminating parts of the slide; and whiteboard mode, which allows drawing on the slide and displaying the drawn lines in real time on the audience window. As communication is local, latency is extremely low, and slide changes are instantaneous. Client-side rendering of documents is handled by the *PDF.js* library.

A key feature of the application is the management of notes within PDFs. Currently, two types of layout are supported for the presenter's notes: 'split' and 'bottom'. The 'split' layout is typical of PDFs generated by LaTeX Beamer, where the left half of the page is dedicated to the slide and the right half to the presenter's notes. LaTeX Beamer is a LaTeX package [31] for creating presentations, which allows slides to be organised in a 'split' format with the speaker's notes on the right-hand side of the page and the slide on the left-hand side. The second supported layout is the 'bottom' layout, typical of PDFs generated by

[6] https://developer.mozilla.org/en-US/docs/Web/API/Broadcast_Channel_API.

Google Presentations, in which the slide is positioned at the top of the page and the presenter's notes are positioned at the bottom of the page, which is generally in A4 format. The slide is cropped automatically, and the notes are extracted directly from the text in the PDF and inserted into the presenter's window. To improve usability and the user experience for presenters using notes, buttons have been added that allow the text size of the notes to be enlarged or reduced, thereby improving readability.

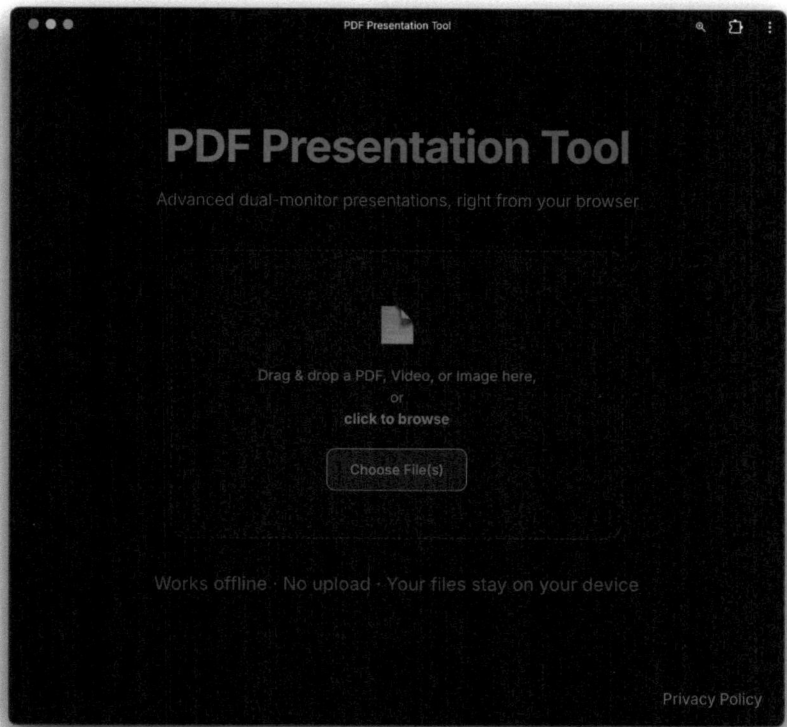

Fig. 2. The app's home screen, where you upload the file to be shared with the public. The screen is designed to be as simple and intuitive as possible.

Finally, the presenter can activate their webcam and display an overlay bubble on the slide in one of the four corners. The audience will see both the slide and the presenter's face, thereby increasing engagement and connection with the presenter's talk. The webcam management feature does not require an external connection and therefore respects the presenter's privacy.

The camera's video stream is captured from the presenter's window and sent to the audience's window via the Session Description Protocol (SDP), again through the *BroadcastChannel* discussed previously.

3.4 Application Usage and Workflow

The user experience has been designed to follow a seamless workflow requiring no configuration. Starting a presentation is as simple as dragging and dropping the selected file (PDF or multimedia file) directly into the browser interface. Figure 2 shows the start screen, designed to be simple and intuitive.

Figure 3b shows the smartphone remote control screen, with a layout consisting of two large buttons that allow the user to move forward or backwards through the slides; the current slide number is displayed at the top. When the user changes slides, the device provides feedback by vibrating to indicate that it has received the command. To disconnect the remote from the presentation, simply close the browser tab; no further action is required.

(a) Figure A: Spotlight feature to highlight a section of the slide by darkening the background and simulating a torch illuminating parts of the slide.

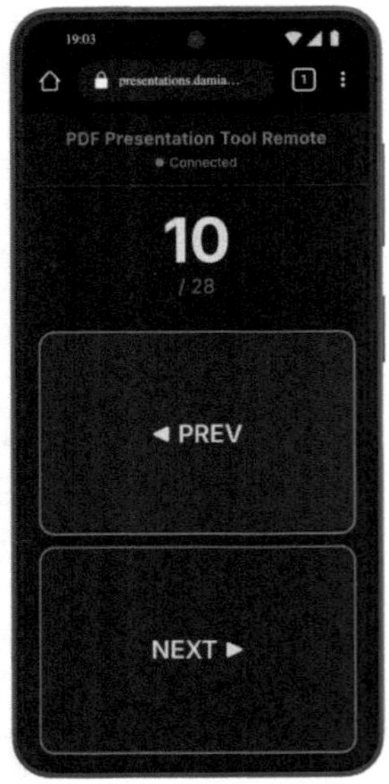

(b) Figure B: Remote control screen via smartphone

Fig. 3. Overview of control and pointer functions.

Figure 3a, on the other hand, shows the spotlight feature, which allows you to highlight a portion of the slide by darkening the background and simulating a flashlight that illuminates parts of the slide. This feature is particularly useful for highlighting key concepts or directing the audience's attention to specific areas of the slide, thereby improving understanding and engagement during the presentation. Similarly, if audience interaction is requested, activating the Questions & Answers Session overlays a QR code on the projector screen that can be scanned by the audience.

After scanning it, the audience will be directed to a web page where they can enter text-based questions that will appear on the presenter's screen. Questions submitted by the audience are anonymous and are not stored or transmitted to third parties, thus ensuring user privacy. Closing the presentation automatically deletes all received questions, leaving no trace of sensitive or personal data.

Figure 4, on the other hand, shows the webcam management feature, which allows the presenter to activate their webcam and display an overlay bubble on the slide in one of the four corners. The same figure also shows the drawing feature; in fact, some marks have been drawn that the presenter is showing to the audience. As can be seen in the image, the presenter's face is centred within the bubble. This is achieved by cropping the image captured by the webcam to focus attention solely on what is relevant to the presentation, ignoring the background and other distracting elements.

The application can also be installed on the device. This is possible thanks to Progressive Web App technology, which allows a web application to be installed as if it were a native app, with a dedicated icon and the ability to be launched directly from the desktop or the device's app menu. This feature is compatible with Windows, macOS, and Linux as it is provided by the browser. The installation involved creating a manifest file and a service worker that manages the cache of static files subject to versioning. This means that if the user opens the application multiple times, the static files are loaded from the browser cache, reducing the load on the Node.js server and ensuring very fast loading times.

3.5 Performance Analysis

The software has been tested on various devices and operating systems. The test PDF consists of 245 pages and is part of the material provided in a university course; it contains both text and images and is 8.8 MB in size.

The first device tested is a MacBook Air with an Apple M1 processor, 8GB of RAM, and macOS Tahoe 15.2, connected to a projector via USB-C; this device is from January 2021. The first device took an average of 0.19 s to open the application and showed no slowdowns while using the test PDF, even with all features active simultaneously, including webcam management.

The second is an ASUS ZenBook 14 UM433DA-A5020T notebook running Linux Mint 21.2, with an AMD R5-3500U processor and 8GB of RAM, connected to a projector via HDMI; this device is from October 2020. The average application launch time was 1.1 s, and again, no slowdowns were observed while using the test PDF with all features active.

The application was then analysed using an independent test, LightHouse[7], an open-source third-party tool developed by Google to analyse a website's performance, accessibility, and other features. The test was performed on Chrome 146 on March 23, 2026, with a stable Wi-Fi connection, and the report returned scores of 99/100 for performance and 96/100 for platform accessibility.

[7] https://developers.google.com/web/tools/lighthouse.

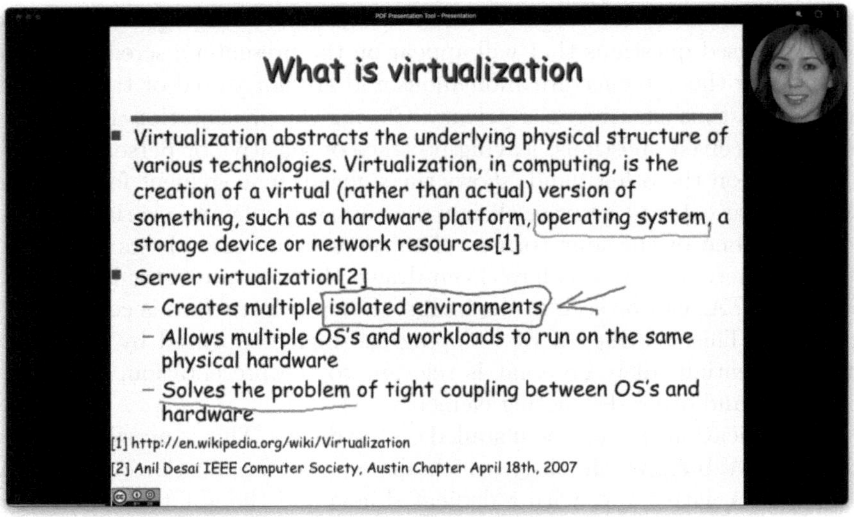

Fig. 4. The figure shows the window as seen by the audience. It illustrates the drawing and webcam management features, which allow the presenter to activate their webcam and display an overlay bubble on the slide in one of the four corners.

4 Conclusions and Future Work

This article presented an innovative open-source software called "PDF Presentation Tool"[8], designed to bridge the gap between traditional desktop applications and modern web technologies in educational and informational contexts. The application allows for the seamless and effective management of lessons, keynotes, or corporate presentations based on PDF files and multimedia content, making it accessible as it can be used on any device without the need to install additional software or plugins. All features are based on Web API and are therefore native to modern browsers.

By leveraging a "local-first" architecture based entirely on client-side processing, the system not only delivers high performance with low latency but also inherently ensures security and privacy by avoiding the upload of sensitive documents to third-party servers. With the exception of features requiring an internet connection (such as remote control via smartphone), this program can also be used offline; therefore, even in auditoriums with unstable connections, it will be possible to deliver presentations without interruptions or slowdowns caused by network latency. The project has successfully achieved its initial objectives, proving to be a resilient solution even in restrictive or heterogeneous educational and conference settings. It is hoped that in the coming years this tool will be integrated and used by an ever-increasing number of researchers, teachers, and professionals.

[8] https://presentations.damianoperri.it.

To ensure the transparency and security of the source code, as well as to encourage evaluation and contributions from the global scientific community, the entire project has been released in a public repository[9]. Moving forward, the project will focus on two main areas. First, we plan to conduct a survey to gauge user satisfaction and identify the features that faculty and students consider most urgent. To achieve this goal, we have already launched an open-access questionnaire designed to collect feedback based on the System Usability Scale and open-ended comments. The platform is currently in an open-access phase, during which anyone can access the site. So far, the platform has been used by 415 people, and initial feedback indicates widespread approval and a desire to continue using it. The testing phase will continue on a large scale for the next few months.

On the other hand, from a strictly technical perspective, we plan to expand the software by introducing native support for additional document exchange formats and implementing further features for smartphone-based remote control. Based on the tests conducted, the software is also compatible with Samsung DeX, the desktop environment that Samsung provides on its smartphones, however, as of now, two external monitors are not supported due to limitations in smartphone video outputs. It is hoped that in the future, with the evolution of smartphone video output technologies, it will be possible to extend compatibility to this type of device as well, thus making the software functional even without a computer, using only one's tablet or smartphone as a presentation device.

References

1. Cheng, W.-L.: Portable document format (pdf) — finally, a universal document exchange technology. J. Technol. Stud. **28.1** (2002)
2. Westhoff, J.: PPC: Pdf Presenter Console (2010). https://github.com/jakobwesthoff/Pdf-Presenter-Console
3. Westhoff, J., Vilar, D., et al.: PDFPC: a presenter console with multimonitor support for PDF files. Version 4.7.0 (2024). https://github.com/pdfpc/pdfpc
4. Rico-Juan, J.R.: Creating synchronised presentations for mobile devices using open source tools. In: Proceedings of the 2009 International Conference on e-Learning, E-Business, Enterprise Information Systems and eGovernment. Las Vegas, Nevada, USA: CSREA Press, pp. 50–52 (2009)
5. Qian, Y., Li, Y.: Web-based PDF Document Display Research and Implementation. Sci. J. Intell. Syst. Res. **7.7**, 28–37 (2025). https://doi.org/10.54691/r3n8m337. https://bcpublication.org/index.php/SJISR/article/view/8789
6. Lenz, P.H., McCallister, J.W., Luks, A.M., Le ,T.T., Fessler, H.E.: Practical Strategies for Effective Lectures. In: Annals of the American Thoracic Society 12.4, pp. 561–566 (2015). ISSN:2329-6933. https://doi.org/10.1513/AnnalsATS.201501-024AR. eprint: https://academic.oup.com/annalsats/article-pdf/12/4/561/66550575/annalsats12_4_561.pdf. https://doi.org/10.1513/AnnalsATS.201501-024AR

[9] https://github.com/DamianoP/PDF_Presentation_Tool.

7. Chattopadhyay, D., óHara, K., Rintel, S., Rädle, R.: Office Social: Presentation Interactivity for Nearby Devices. In: Proceedings of the 2016 CHI Conference on Human Factors in Computing Systems. CHI '2016. San Jose, California, USA: Association for Computing Machinery, 2016, pp. 2487–2491. ISBN: 9781450333627. https://doi.org/10.1145/2858036.2858337
8. Schaffer, I.: Mobile Device Usage in Interactive, Co-located Presentations. English. MA thesis. 4232 Hagenberg, Austria: Interactive Media; FH Oberösterreich – Fakultät für informatik, Kommunikation und Medien (2016)
9. Avsar, B., Aliabadi, D.E., Aliabadi, E.E., Yousefnezhad, R.: Academic Presenter: a New Storytelling Presentation Software for Academic Purposes (2016). arXiv: 1607.06979. https://arxiv.org/abs/1607.06979
10. Osipovskaya, E.A., Burdovskaya, E.Y.: Presentation software tools in higher educational setting . In: ARPHA Proceedings 1, pp. 1487–1496 (2019)
11. Barabash, V., Osipovskaya, E., Dmitrieva, S., Budnik, E.: Cutting Edge Online Presentation Software In Higher Education. In: ICERI2019 Proceedings. 12th annual International Conference of Education, Research and Innovation. Seville, Spain: IATED, pp. 2812–2818 (2019). ISBN: 978-84-09-14755-7. https://doi.org/10.21125/iceri.2019.0720
12. Kerski, J.J.: Teaching and learning geography with a Web GIS approach. In: Revisioning Geography: Supporting the SDGs in the postCOVID era, pp. 113–135. Springer (2023)
13. Laganá, A., Gervasi, O., Tasso, S., Perri, D., Franciosa, F.: The ECTN virtual education community prosumer model for promoting and assessing chemical knowledge. In: Lecture Notes in Computer Science (including subseries Lecture Notes in Artificial Intelligence and Lecture Notes in Bioinformatics) 10964 LNCS, pp. 533–548 (2018). https://doi.org/10.1007/978-3-319-95174-442
14. Wu, J.G., Zhang, D., Lee, S.M.: Into the brave new metaverse: envisaging future language teaching and learning. IEEE Trans. Learn. Technol. **17**, 44–53 (2023)
15. Gervasi, O., Perri, D., Simonetti, M.: Strategies and System Implementations for Secure Electronic Written Exams. In: IEEE Access 10, pp. 20559–20570 (2022). https://doi.org/10.1109/ACCESS.2022.3150860
16. Perri, D., et al.: Hybrid Methods for Automatic Collocation Extraction in Building a Learners' Dictionary of Italian. Computers **14.12** (2025). https://doi.org/10.3390/computers14120552
17. Perri, D.,et al.: Dockerized Architecture for a Progressive Web App: An Italian Collocations Dictionary. In: Lecture Notes in Computer Science 15891 LNCS, pp. 33–43 (2026). https://doi.org/10.1007/978-3-031-97617-93
18. Spina, S., Fioravanti, I., Zanda, F., Forti, L., Perri, D., Gervasi, O.: Developing a learner dictionary of collocations: description and evaluation of a multi-method approach. In: Corpus Linguistics and Linguistic Theory (2026). https://doi.org/10.1515/cllt-2025-0008
19. Fanfani, M., Palesi, L.A.I., Nesi, P.: DataDriven Mobility Demand-Versus-Offer Matching by Dynamic Integration of Public and Sharing Services. In: IEEE Access 14, pp. 23166–23193 (2026). https://doi.org/10.1109/ACCESS.2026.3661850
20. Perri, D., Simonetti, M., Gervasi, O.: Deploying Efficiently Modern Applications on Cloud. Electr. (Switzerland) **11.3** (2022). https://doi.org/10.3390/electronics11030450
21. Cone, L., Lai, S.S.: Infrastructural dependency in the datafied welfare state: the case of Google Chromebooks. Learn. Media Technol. **50.1**, 44–60 (2025). https://doi.org/10.1080/17439884.2024.2437680

22. Perri, D., Simonetti, M., Tasso, S., Ragni, F., Gervasi, O.: Implementing a Scalable and Elastic Computing Environment Based on Cloud Containers. In: Lecture Notes in Computer Science (including subseries Lecture Notes in Artificial Intelligence and Lecture Notes in Bioinformatics) 12949 LNCS, pp. 676–689 (2021). https://doi.org/10.1007/978-3-030-86653-249
23. Bilotta, S., Palesi, L.A.I., Nesi, P.: Exploiting open data for CO2 estimation via artificial intelligence and eXplainable AI. Exp. Syst. Appl. **291**, 128598 (2025). ISSN: 0957-4174. https://doi.org/10.1016/j.eswa.2025.128598. https://www.sciencedirect.com/science/article/pii/S0957417425022171
24. Fereidooni, Z., Palesi, L.A.I., Nesi, P.: MultiAgent Optimizing Traffic Light Signals Using Deep Reinforcement Learning. In: IEEE Access 13, pp. 106974–106988 (2025). https://doi.org/10.1109/ACCESS.2025.3578518
25. Low, A., Siu, J., Ho, I., Liu, G.: Introduction to Node.JS. In: Proceedings of 24th Annual International Conference on Computer Science and Software Engineering. CASCON '2014. Markham, Ontario, Canada: IBM Corp, pp. 283–284 (2014)
26. Sobieraj, M., Kotyński, D.: Docker performance evaluation across operating systems. Appl. Sci. **14.15**, 6672 (2024)
27. Gervasi, O., Perri, D., Simonetti, M., Tasso, S.: Strategies for the Digitalization of Cultural Heritage. In: Lecture Notes in Computer Science (including subseries Lecture Notes in Artificial Intelligence and Lecture Notes in Bioinformatics) 13382 LNCS (2022), pp. 486–502. https://doi.org/10.1007/978-3-031-10592-035
28. Singh, N., et al.: Load balancing and service discovery using Docker Swarm for microservice based big data applications. J. Cloud Comput. **12.1**, 4 (2023)
29. Hesti, E., Kaila, A.S., Handayani, A.S., Novianti, L., Rakhman, M.A.: An E-Commerce Platform for Coffee MSMEs: System Design and Basic Features. In: bit-Tech 8.1, pp. 910–920 (2025). https://doi.org/10.32877/bt.v8i1.2756
30. Asolo, E., Gil-Ozoudeh, I., Ejimuda, C., et al.: AI-Powered decision support systems for sustainable agriculture using AI-Chatbot solution. J. Digit. Food Energy Water Syst. **5.1** (2024)
31. Tantau, T., Wright, J., Miletic, V.: The BEAMER class User Guide (2016). https://doi.org/10.5555/3027684

Bridging the Gap Between Validated Cognitive Screening and Clinical Practice: A Stylus-Driven Digital Use Case for the SAGE Test

Damiano Perri[1(✉)] and Natale Amato[2]

[1] Department of Mathematics and Computer Science, University of Perugia, Perugia, Italy
damiano.perri@unipg.it
[2] Molfetta, Italy

Abstract. Early detection of cognitive decline can improve outcomes. The SAGE is a cognitive assessment test and is currently one of the standard tools used in medicine for the early diagnosis of Alzheimer's and dementia. The aim of this work is to propose a software framework for the test, with the objective of retaining the original structure whilst bringing the benefits of digitisation, such as reducing the amount of paper documentation to be stored, speeding up the calculation of scores and the generation of reports, and enabling data to be archived in digital format for future comparison.

The proposed system is a single-page web application accessible via a tablet and supporting stylus input. The system collects the user-entered data on the web page, presents the exercises and various tasks included in the test, then automatically organises them into a data structure and provides a report with a partial score to healthcare staff. The partial score is based on exercises with pre-set scores, which helps to speed up the work of the staff. The resulting code is finally released under an open-source licence.

Keywords: Mobile Computing · Web-based Computing · Decision Support Systems · Digitalization · SAGE · Digital Health

Nomenclature

The following acronyms are used in this manuscript:

API	Application Programming Interface
CDT	Clock Drawing Test
CSS	Cascading Style Sheets
DPI	Dots Per Inch

N. Amato—Independent Researcher

O. Gervasi et al. (Eds.): ICCSA 2026 Workshops, LNCS 16758, pp. 186–201, 2027.
https://doi.org/10.1007/978-3-032-30497-1_12

FHIR	Fast Healthcare Interoperability Resources
HL7	Health Level Seven
HTML	HyperText Markup Language
JSON	JavaScript Object Notation
MMSE	Mini Mental State Examination
MoCA	Montreal Cognitive Assessment
PDF	Portable Document Format
PWA	Progressive Web App
SAGE	Self-Administered Gerocognitive Examination
SLM	Small Language Model
SPA	Single Page Application
SUS	System Usability Scale

1 Introduction

The aim of this study is to digitise the SAGE (Self-Administered Gerocognitive Examination) test for assessing cognitive decline. Neurodegenerative diseases, particularly Alzheimer's disease and various forms of dementia, are now an area of growing interest and importance for public health [1]. This is also due to the increase in the average age of the population and, consequently, the natural onset of age-related diseases [2,3].

Being able to detect cognitive decline from the very first signs makes a huge difference because it allows for the gain of precious time, which can be decisive for the treatment of these conditions [4]. Therapies can be started immediately, existing medications optimised, family care better planned, and the progression of the disease closely monitored.

In this context, the general practitioner is the first point of contact, as they have an ongoing relationship with the patient and their family. The aim is to provide doctors with a system that speeds up and simplifies early diagnosis by improving outpatient practices through digitalisation. Furthermore, the literature highlights that, to date, standardised screening tools are frequently used, but the time available for consultations is often limited [5], and more complex tests must be scheduled well in advance due to the hectic workload faced by healthcare staff [6,7].

To date, there are various cognitive tests that help to objectively determine where normal ageing ends and where disease begins. The SAGE test [8,9], developed by Ohio State University[1], is particularly suitable for identifying mild deficits and has a major advantage: the patient completes it themselves. This means that the doctor or nurse does not need to be present for the entire duration of the test, saving valuable time.

The SAGE assesses several areas: orientation, language, reasoning, visuospatial skills and executive functions. It is therefore suitable for conducting an initial assessment and for repeating it several months later. However, although it is an

[1] https://www.osu.edu/.

excellent test with proven effectiveness, we believe its uptake and use could be improved if an easy-to-use app were developed.

The lack of digitisation gives rise to a number of practical difficulties, ranging from the failure to archive data in the electronic health record to the inability to compare results over time, and the failure to automatically calculate scores that do not require a semantic analysis of the user-generated data. Furthermore, it is important to note that using paper records also carries the risk of losing the documentation collected.

The combination of all these issues causes a time delay that can compromise the ability to make early diagnoses and to monitor the patient's progress effectively over time.

A further objective of this work is to implement support for digital pens, so as to preserve the experience of completing the original test; for this reason, the proposed application is designed for use with tablets and digital pens.

We believe this is very important, as we consider that it preserves the ability to assess the drawing of abstract shapes and fine motor skills, whilst also allowing us to generate more detailed statistics on how the user executed the strokes with the pen—such as pressure, speed, or stroke fluidity—enabling the creation of a highly detailed report for the doctor. In this way, the patient writes and draws on the tablet exactly as they would on a sheet of paper, as shown in Fig. 1.

The exam experience remains identical to the paper-based version, but improvements are made to all subsequent stages. With the transition from a paper-based to a digital test, there would be significant benefits: faster marking, automated archiving, and the instant generation of statistics and graphs. These features support longitudinal monitoring, minimise manual errors, and ensure direct integration into the patient's electronic record, thereby improving efficiency and clinical outcomes. Therefore, the objective is to investigate whether it is possible to digitise the SAGE test and whether current technologies are sufficiently mature to achieve this goal.

This work is organised as follows: Sect. 2 analyses the state of the art in digital cognitive screening tools, highlighting the methodological and practical limitations that have prevented wider adoption. Section 3 presents the proposed methodological framework, illustrating the user interface design principles and the system architecture. Section 4 discusses the results, the clinical implications, and future prospects for the digitisation of cognitive screening.

2 Related Works

The shift towards digital healthcare has given a significant boost to research [10], prompting researchers and developers to seek ways to improve and update diagnostic tools. Modern technologies can indeed be utilised across a wide range of fields [11]; today, we have mobile devices such as smartphones and tablets that possess very high computational power when compared to what was available in the consumer market 10 years ago [12,13]. This is thanks to technological advances and the miniaturisation of components, which allow an increase in the

Fig. 1. A patient performing the digital SAGE test

number of transistors whilst maintaining power consumption consistent with acceptable battery life [14].

Furthermore, cloud computing technology [15] is now widespread and provides access to storage, reliable databases and processing units which, through a monthly fee directly proportional to usage, enable complex analyses, the generation of statistics and deferred data mining following the retrieval of information from users' devices [16–18] and without having to bear the cost of hardware maintenance.

For a long time, the initial assessment of cognitive decline [19] has been based on traditional paper-and-pencil tests such as the Mini-Mental State Examination (MMSE) [20], the Montreal Cognitive Assessment (MoCA) [21] or the Clock Drawing Test (CDT) [22]. These tools are currently the standard in clinics worldwide, but their greatest limitation lies in their practicality, as they require the constant presence of a trained practitioner. It was precisely this challenge that prompted researchers at Ohio State University[2] developed the SAGE, which has been shown to have sensitivity and specificity comparable to those of the MMSE and MoCA, and even surpasses them in detecting mild forms.

Furthermore, the SAGE test has proven effective in identifying cognitive decline classified as mild [23–25]. Another aspect to consider is that screening software should be free from commercial licences so that its functionality can be independently verified and validated [26]. Open-source software also promotes awareness of personal data management and cybersecurity, which are fundamental to health and digital technology [27]: developers from all over the world can examine how the code actually works, understand its content, and potentially contribute to its improvement. For this reason, the application developed and discussed in this paper is made available via the GitHub platform and is released under the AGPLv3 licence[3].

The state-of-the-art analysis, therefore, highlights a clear dichotomy between validated but obsolete paper-based tests and digital applications that undermine psychometric equivalence or prove too complex. This work fills this gap by proposing a transparent digitisation framework in which technology acts as an invisible layer that captures the traditional procedure, providing an environment for data collection and subsequent analysis that supports the healthcare professional's decision-making process.

3 Methodological Framework

This section discusses the framework that has been designed and developed. The system's architecture stems from a desire to preserve the validity of the original SAGE test; in our view, it is important not to alter its content and thus to maintain its scientific validity. To achieve this, a graphical interface has been created that is both suitable and faithful to the original paper-based test.

The software was then developed to allow the user to interact naturally, comparable to using pen and paper. This result was achieved using HTML5 canvases, i.e., graphical areas where one can write and draw geometric shapes. To use them, all that is required is a tablet with a display compatible with styluses, i.e., digital pens that let you write and draw geometric shapes on a touchscreen. Devices featuring this technology include, for example, the Samsung Galaxy Tab, the Microsoft Surface and Apple's iPad.

Subsequently, the assessment interface for the doctor was developed, allowing results to be viewed both in summary and in detail. In practice, this translates into three operational levels: the collection of responses provided by the user via the tablet, the processing of data for preliminary assessment and digital organisation, and subsequently the presentation of the results to the healthcare professional.

In our view, it is also important to optimise the assessment process and speed up the calculations used to estimate users' scores, thereby reducing patients' waiting times and increasing the daily number of people who can access the screening. To optimise time spent in the clinic, we propose utilising patients'

[2] https://wexnermedical.osu.edu/brain-spine-neuro/memory-disorders/sage.
[3] https://github.com/Nat-Amato/Digital-SAGE-Cognitive-Assessment.

waiting time as well. The proposed system utilises asynchronous processing: the test can, in fact, be completed independently, for example, in a suitably equipped waiting room, taking approximately 10âĂŞ15 min. The data is encrypted and sent to the doctor's computer. When the patient enters the surgery, the practitioner will initiate the assisted assessment, which will display the results immediately. Figure 2 shows the graphical interface displaying the results following a user's assessment. At the top is the overall test score and the maximum achievable score, followed by the sub-scores. The current score calculation is implemented using a semi-automatic method. For all questions with pre-defined scores based on the type of response, the score is calculated automatically, whilst the operator is given the option to enter a score for questions that require a semantic analysis of the content entered by the user, such as when assessing the accuracy and quality of drawings produced by the patient. The semantic analysis process may be improved in the future by using specially trained convolutional neural networks [28] or small language models (SLMs) [29]. Figure 3 shows the canvases with all the user-provided inputs, such as the drawings created on the canvases.

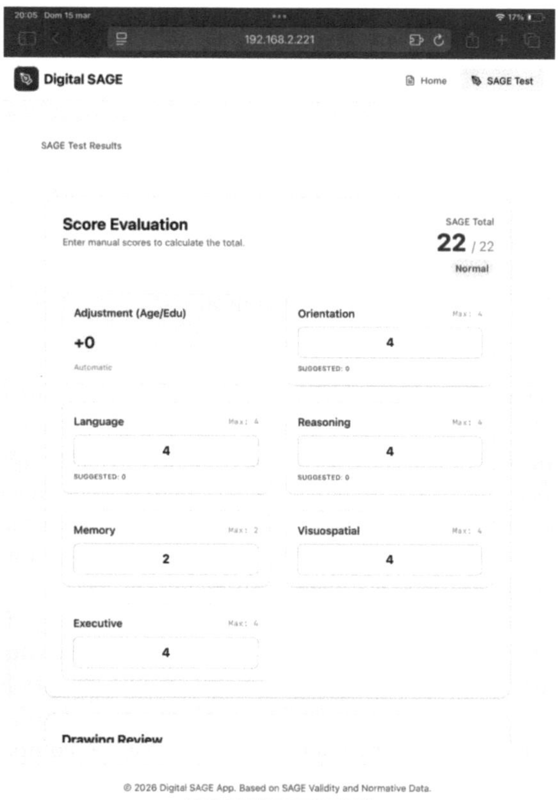

Fig. 2. The figure shows the results of the test

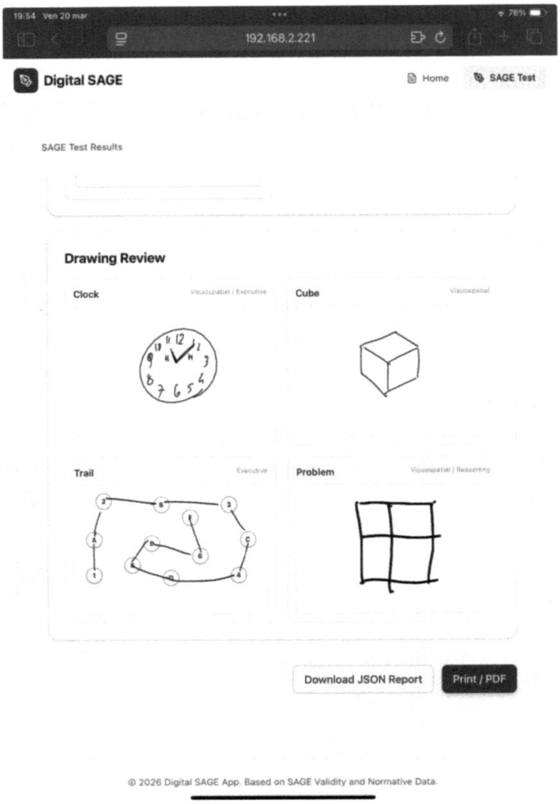

Fig. 3. Traced drawings

In the event that a user needs to retake the test (follow-up), the system is set by default to generate a test that is equivalent but not identical to the previous one, to prevent responses from being skewed by the user having already seen the questions. For example, if the exercise requires the user to connect numbered points in ascending order, their positions are randomly rearranged on the screen, as are the numbers associated with the various points. The workflow of the system described above is shown graphically in Fig. 4.

The software developed is a Single Page Web Application (SPA) that does not require page reloads and aims to provide a smooth, optimised experience. The front-end framework is based on React and Vite, whilst the back-end was developed using Node.js and Express. The SPA can then be deployed as a web application via a service worker to achieve an experience comparable to that of a native app whilst remaining independent of the distribution platform (Google Play, Apple App Store, etc.). This technology, therefore, enables the creation of a Progressive Web App (PWA), and the advantage is a single codebase that is interoperable across various platforms [30].

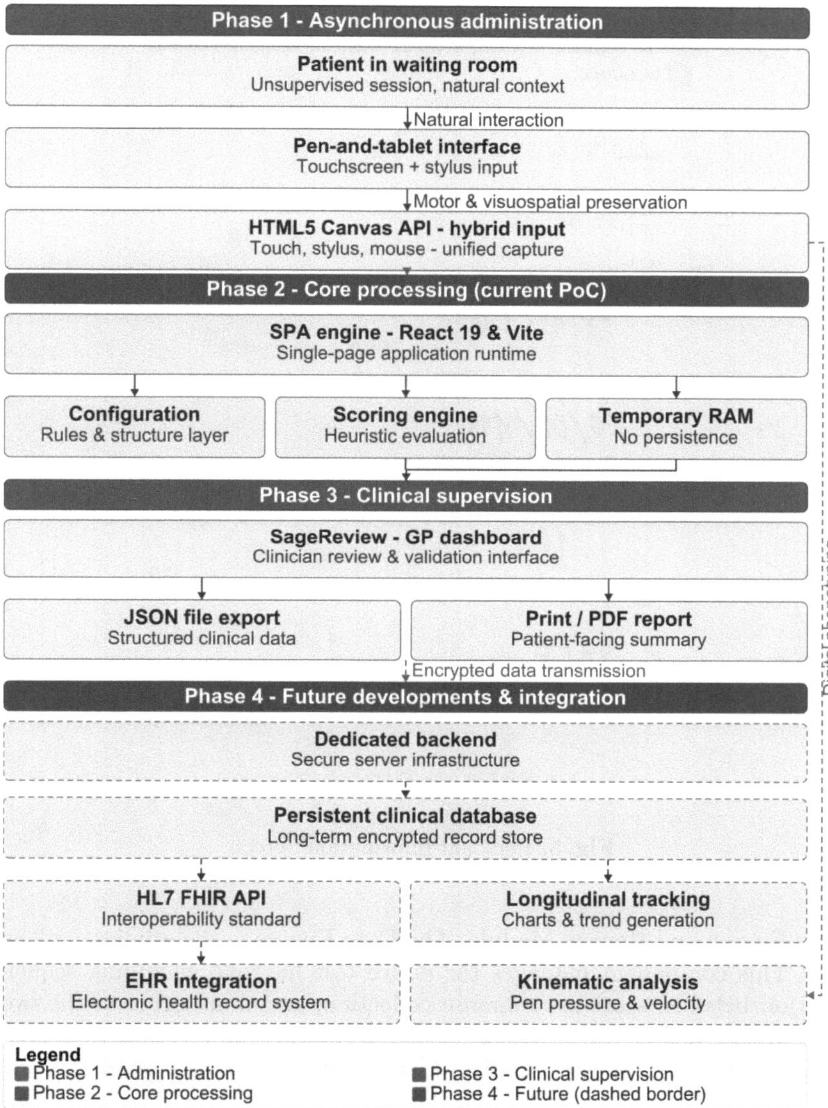

Fig. 4. Architectural workflow of the Digital SAGE framework

The application follows a component-based model [31], in which the entire system is divided into modular, reusable components. In this initial phase, to facilitate usability testing, all application logic is managed entirely on the client side, directly within the user's browser. This approach enables the system to operate with rapid response times and allows staff to test the tool without relying on complex network infrastructure. From an architectural perspective, the system is organised into several main modules: Core Engine, Configuration Layer,

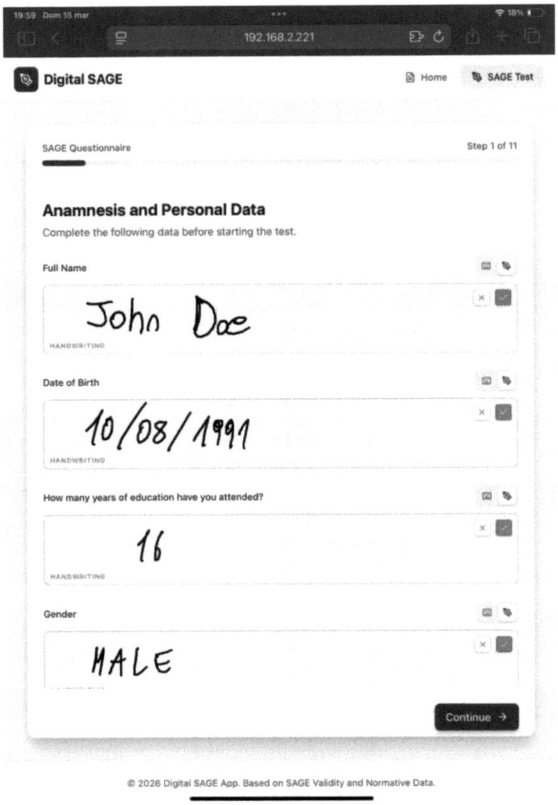

Fig. 5. Personal Information Screen

Scoring Engine and Review Module. The Core Engine is the application's main engine. This component manages the entire test lifecycle, including sequential navigation between sections, response collection, and monitoring of the overall session status. Next is the Configuration Layer, which allows you to define the structure of the test phases (medical history, memory, language, maths, drawing), the type of input required, and any validation rules. The Scoring Engine, on the other hand, implements the logic to calculate scores for the test's sections. Some sections, such as arithmetic exercises or certain language tasks, can be automatically assessed using heuristic algorithms that verify the correctness of the answers. Finally, there is the Review Module, which provides a graphical interface for staff responsible for checking answers, viewing the patient's drawings, and completing the final validation of the score. The technologies used to develop the system are TypeScript, Tailwind CSS, Framer Motion and HTML5 Canvas API. TypeScript is a programming language that supports static typing; Tailwind CSS enables the creation of a modern, responsive interface; Framer Motion manages animations and transitions between screens; and the HTML5 Canvas API is used for manual drawing.

Fig. 6. Screen showing the first questions

3.1 User Interface Study

The system's graphical interface has been designed to replicate the experience of a paper-based test as faithfully as possible, whilst retaining the advantages of a digital system.

One key feature is the dynamic input system, which serves as a superclass and enables the management of various input types for questions and tests. Depending on the question context, the system allows text fields, single- or multiple-choice fields, date pickers, drop-down menus, and drawing canvases to be displayed on screen. This approach allows for a modular, easily extensible code structure, as input types can be modified at a specific point in the code and the change is automatically propagated to all screens that use the component. Figure 5 shows the graphical interface where the user enters their personal details, whilst Fig. 6 shows another stage of the test with sample questions displayed.

A significant part of the SAGE test involves graphical tasks. For this reason, a dedicated component, DrawingCanvas, has been developed. This module uses

Fig. 7. Screen showing the drawing activity

the HTML5 Canvas API to capture the user's graphical input via a stylus or touch screen. These APIs were initially released in 2015 and are now mature and natively compatible with all modern browsers, including Safari, Chrome, Firefox and Edge[4]. The system also handles various aspects, including line resolution (DPI), writing fluidity, and the conversion of the drawing into *DataURL Base64*[5] format.

The drawing is then temporarily saved in the application state using local storage. An example of a drawing on the canvas is shown in Fig. 7. Responses are managed via React's *hook* `useState`. The information entered by the user is collected in a data structure of the type: $Record < string, any >$. This type of structure ensures that test responses are retained while navigating between screens without any data loss.

---

[4] https://developer.mozilla.org/en-US/docs/Web/API/Canvas_API.

[5] https://developer.mozilla.org/en-US/docs/Web/HTTP/Basics_of_HTTP/Data_URIs.

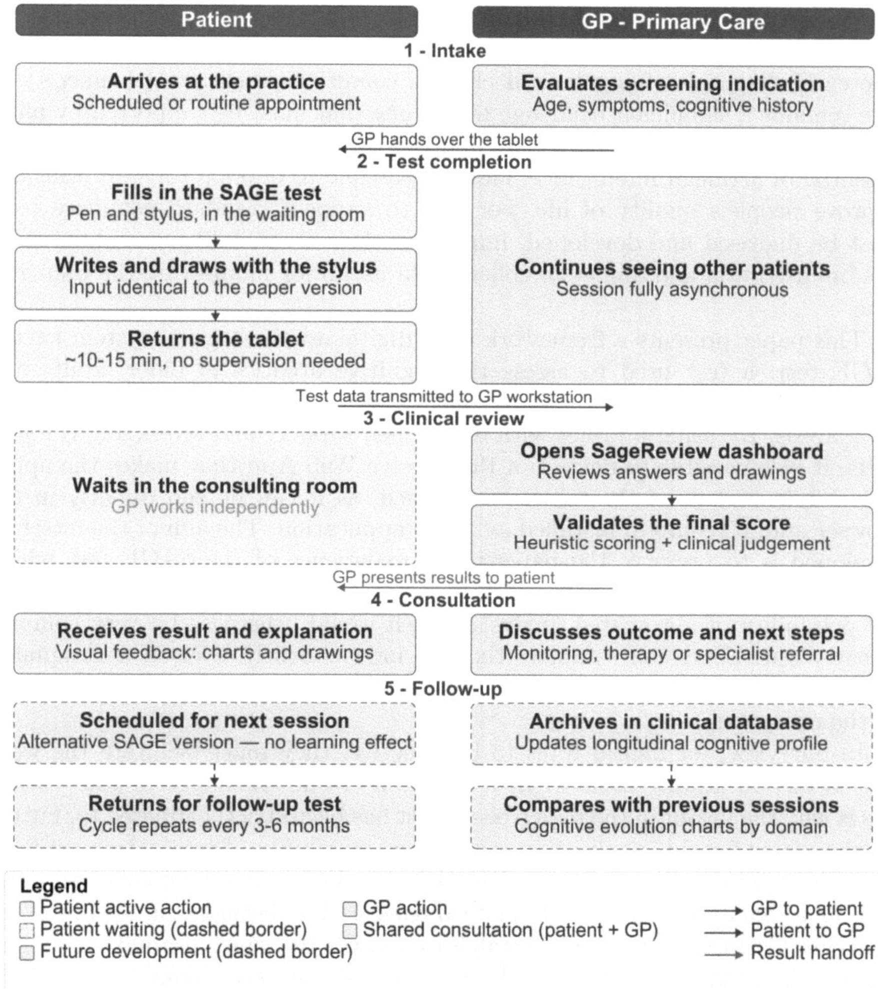

Fig. 8. Patient and GP interaction workflow.

At the end of the test, the system generates a report that can be exported in two main formats. The first is export in JSON format, which allows all responses collected during the test to be saved in a structured file. The JSON format is also useful for future data re-import or local archiving. The second method is printing or exporting to PDF format, which allows you to generate a printed version of the report using specific CSS rules of the `@media print` type implemented in the `SageReview` module, providing the necessary formatting to make the document readable and professional. In this way, the test result can be immediately integrated into the user's documentation as a digital or hard-copy file.

The interaction process described above, involving the patient and healthcare staff, is summarised in Fig. 8.

4 Conclusions and Future Work

The early diagnosis of cognitive decline in conditions such as Alzheimer's disease remains a significant challenge today, one that must be supported by modern technologies. Mobile computing and low-cost hardware, combined with the potential of artificial intelligence, make it possible to develop software that can improve people's quality of life. For this to happen, standard cognitive tests must be digitised and developed, improving their accessibility, usability, speed of administration and ability to collect data useful for monitoring the user over time.

This paper presents a framework for a digital administration system for the SAGE test, a test used to assess the cognitive abilities of older adults and designed to assist GPs in the early diagnosis of cognitive decline by speeding up analysis. By using a tablet with digital pen support and leveraging HTML5 APIs, it was possible to develop a Progressive Web App that makes the application independent of the tablet brand used, as it can be run directly in the browser and, if required, installed as a web application. The aim of the interface developed is to preserve the paper-based experience of the SAGE test whilst also reaping all the key benefits of digitisation, such as long-term archiving and the possibility of automated analysis, which would otherwise be very complex to carry out. Users can complete the test independently, even in a designated waiting room, and the doctor then receives the test report to review and assess on the computer.

In our view, for digital tools to be effective, they must facilitate the work carried out on a daily basis without requiring a radical change in staff habits; this is why the layout of the paper-based test has been strictly adhered to. Future developments for this application include the possibility of integrating artificial intelligence-based support systems for the automatic analysis of collected data, with local computation and privacy safeguards. Furthermore, a testing phase involving a sample of users is desirable to analyse the tool's usability using the System Usability Scale (SUS) [32] and to assess the tool's equivalence to the paper-based version by gathering feedback from staff administering the test via a questionnaire. A significant area of focus concerns digital biomarkers. Whilst the patient interacts with the screen, we believe it would be valuable to collect as much information as possible on hand movements, tremors, and pen pressure [33], paving the way for machine learning-based analysis to identify previously undetected clusters within populations affected by cognitive decline. Finally, interoperability through standards such as HL7 FHIR [34] would allow results to be integrated directly into the Electronic Health Record.

Considering these future prospects, the seamless digitisation of traditional screening tools not only optimises the current clinical workflow but will also contribute to the development of preventive medicine that is increasingly objective, personalised and supported by modern digital architectures.

References

1. Połtyn-Zaradna, K., Pazdro-Zastawny, K., Szcześniak, D., Wołyniec, M., Zatońska, K., Zatoński, T.: Agerelated hearing loss associated with cognitive impairment in the Polish cohort of the PURE study. (2025). https://doi.org/10.3389/fnagi.2025.1540803
2. Chen, S., et al.: Metformin in aging and aging-related diseases: clinical applications and relevant mechanisms. In: Theranostics (2022). https://doi.org/10.7150/thno.71360
3. Rauchmann, B.-S., et al.: Microglial activation and connectivity in Alzheimer disease and aging. In: Annals of Neurology (2022). https://doi.org/10.1002/ana.26465
4. Prediction Models for Early Detection of Alzheimer: Recent Trends and Future Prospects. Archives Comput. Methods Eng. **32.1**, pp. 3565–3592 (2025). https://doi.org/10.1007/s11831-025-10246-3
5. Musellim, B., et al.: The Duration for Patient Examination Working Group of Turkish Thoracic Society. What should be the appropriate minimal duration for patient examination and evaluation in pulmonary outpatient clinics? In: Annals of Thoracic Medicine 12.3 (2017). ISSN: 1817-1737. https://journals.lww.com/aotm/fulltext/2017/12030/what_should_be_the_appropriate_minimal_duration.5.aspx
6. Ravic de Miranda, L.F.J., et al.: Factors influencing possible delay in the diagnosis of Alzheimer's disease: Findings from a tertiary Public University Hospital. In: Dementia & Neuropsychologia. https://doi.org/10.1590/S1980-57642011DN05040012
7. de Levante Raphael, D.: The knowledge and attitudes of primary care and the barriers to early detection and diagnosis of Alzheimer's disease. In: Medicina (2022). https://doi.org/10.3390/medicina58070906
8. Scharre, D.W., et al.: Self-administered Gerocognitive Examination (SAGE): A Brief Cognitive Assessment Instrument for Mild Cognitive Impairment (MCI) and Early Dementia. In: Alzheimer Disease & Associated Disorders (2010). https://doi.org/10.1097/WAD.0b013e3181b03277
9. Scharre, D., Chang, S.-I., Nagaraja, H., Kataki, M., Wheeler, N., Adeli, A.: Self-Administered Gerocognitive Examination (SAGE) Score Changes over Time in Subjective Cognitive Impairment (SCI), Mild Cognitive Impairment (MCI), Dementia Converters, and Alzheimer's Disease (AD) Patients (P4.088). In: Neurology (2015). https://doi.org/10.1212/WNL.84.14_supplement.P4.088
10. Ding, Z., Lee, T.-L., Chan, A.S.: Digital cognitive biomarker for mild cognitive impairments and dementia: a systematic review. J. Clin. Med. (2022). https://doi.org/10.3390/jcm11144191
11. Laganà, A., Gervasi, O., Tasso, S., Perri, D., Franciosa, F.: The ECTN virtual education community prosumer model for promoting and assessing chemical knowledge. In: Lecture Notes in Computer Science (including subseries Lecture Notes in Artificial Intelligence and Lecture Notes in Bioinformatics) 10964 LNCS, pp. 533–548 (2018). https://doi.org/10.1007/978-3-319-95174-4_42
12. Li, H., Ng, J.K., Abdelzaher, T.: Enabling Real-time AI Inference on Mobile Devices via GPU-CPU Collaborative Execution. In: 2022 IEEE 28th International Conference on Embedded and Real-Time Computing Systems and Applications (RTCSA) (2022).https://doi.org/10.1109/RTCSA55878.2022.00027

13. Gervasi, O., Perri, D., Simonetti, M., Tasso, S.: Strategies for the Digitalization of Cultural Heritage. In: Lecture Notes in Computer Science (including subseries Lecture Notes in Artificial Intelligence and Lecture Notes in Bioinformatics) 13382 LNCS, pp. 486–502 (2022). https://doi.org/10.1007/978-3-031-10592-0_35
14. Ki, S., Byun, G., Cho, K., Bahn, H.: CoOptimizing CPU Voltage, Memory Placement, and Task Offloading for Energy-Efficient Mobile Systems. IEEE Internet Things J. (2023). https://doi.org/10.1109/JIOT.2022.3233830
15. Perri, D., Simonetti, M., Gervasi, O.: Deploying Efficiently Modern Applications on Cloud. Electr. (Switzerland) **11.3** (2022). https://doi.org/10.3390/electronics11030450
16. Andriulo, F.C., Fiore, M., Mongiello, M., Traversa, E., Zizzo, V.: Edge Computing and Cloud Computing for Internet of Things: A Review. Informatics (2024). https://doi.org/10.3390/informatics11040071
17. In: Proceedings of the 5th International Conference on Computer Information and Big Data Applications (CIBDA '2024). Association for Computing Machinery, pp. 171–175 (2024). https://doi.org/10.1145/3671151.3671183
18. Perri, D., Simonetti, M., Tasso, S., Ragni, F., Gervasi, O.: Implementing a Scalable and Elastic Computing Environment Based on Cloud Containers. In: Lecture Notes in Computer Science (including subseries Lecture Notes in Artificial Intelligence and Lecture Notes in Bioinformatics) 12949 LNCS, pp. 676–689 (2021). https://doi.org/10.1007/978-3-030-86653-2_49
19. Cornacchia, E., et al.: Digital screening for early identification of cognitive impairment: a narrative review. In: WIREs Cognitive Science (2025). https://doi.org/10.1002/wcs.70009
20. Jannati, A.,et al.: Digital Clock and Recall is superior to the Mini-Mental State Examination for the detection of mild cognitive impairment and mild dementia. In: Alzheimer's Research & Therapy (2024). https://doi.org/10.1186/s13195-023-01375-7
21. Islam, N., et al.: Accuracy of the montreal cognitive assessment tool for detecting mild cognitive impairment: a systematic review and meta-analysis. In: Alzheimer's & Dementia (2023). https://doi.org/10.1002/alz.13040
22. Maestri, G., Nicotra, A., Pomati, S., Canevelli, M., Pantoni, L., Cova.: Factors influencing possible delay in the diagnosis of Alzheimer's disease: Findings from a tertiary Public University Hospital. J. Int. Neuropsychol. Soc. (2023). https://doi.org/10.1017/S1355617722000662
23. Ohio State University. Validity of the Electronic Self-Administered Gerocognitive Examination (eSAGE) (NCT02544074) (2025). https://clinicaltrials.gov/study/NCT02544074
24. Kessels, R.P.C., et al.: The Self-Administered Gerocognitive Examination (SAGE): Equivalence of Parallel Versions and Validity in Cognitively Unimpaired Controls and Patients With Mild Cognitive Impairment or Dementia in a Memory Clinic. In: Alzheimer Disease & Associated Disorders (2025). https://doi.org/10.1097/WAD.0000000000000673
25. Self-administered gerocognitive examination (SAGE) aids early detection of cognitive impairment at primary care provider visits. Front. Med. (2024). https://doi.org/10.3389/fmed.2024.1353104
26. Karopka, T., Schmuhl, H., Demski, H.: Free/Libre Open Source Software in Health Care: A Review. Healthcare Inform. Res. (2014). https://doi.org/10.4258/hir.2014.20.1.11

27. McDonald, C.J., et al.:Open Source software in medical informatics—why, how and what. Int. J. Med. Inf. (2003). Working Conference on Health Information Systems. https://doi.org/10.1016/S1386-5056(02)00104-1
28. Franzoni, V., Biondi, G., Perri, D., Gervasi, O.: Enhancing mouth-based emotion recognition using transfer learning. Sens. (Switzerland) **20.18**, 1–15 (2020). https://doi.org/10.3390/s20185222
29. Gondara, L., Simkin, J., Sayle, G., Devji, S., Arbour, G., Ng, R.: Small or Large? Zero-Shot or Finetuned? Guiding Language Model Choice for Specialized Applications in Healthcare. Mach. Learn. Knowl. Extraction **7.4** (2025). ISSN: 2504-4990. https://doi.org/10.3390/make7040121
30. Perri, D., Gervasi, O., Tasso, S., Fioravanti, I., Zanda, F., Spina, S., Forti, L.: Dockerized Architecture for a Progressive Web App: An Italian Collocations Dictionary. In: Lecture Notes in Computer Science 15891 LNCS, pp. 33–43 (2026). https://doi.org/10.1007/978-3-031-97617-9_3
31. Crnkovic, I., Chaudron, M., Larsson, S.: Component-Based Development Process and Component Lifecycle. In: Proceedings of the 2006 International Conference on Software Engineering Advances (ICSEA '2006). (2006). https://doi.org/10.1109/ICSEA.2006.261300
32. Grier, R.A., Bangor, A., Kortum, P., Peres, S.C.: The System Usability Scale: Beyond Standard Usability Testing. In: Proceedings of the Human Factors and Ergonomics Society Annual Meeting 57.1, pp. 187–191 (2013). https://doi.org/10.1177/1541931213571042
33. Toffoli, S., et al.: Handwriting in Mild Cognitive Impairment: Reliability Assessment and Machine Learning–Based Screening. In: JMIR Aging (2025). https://doi.org/10.2196/73074
34. Saripalle, R., Runyan, C., Russell, M.: Using HL7 FHIR to achieve interoperability in patient health record. J. Biomed. Inform. **94**, 103188 (2019). ISSN: 1532-0464. https://doi.org/10.1016/j.jbi.2019.103188. https://www.sciencedirect.com/science/article/pii/S1532046419301066

Snap4Waste: An Integrated Waste Dynamic Optimal Collection Management System

Enrico Collini, Luciano Alessandro Ipsaro Palesi(✉), Raffaele Francesco Mentina, Paolo Nesi, Fabrizio Mereu, and Alessio Tammaro

DISIT Lab, DINFO, University of Florence, Florence, Italy
{enrico.collini,lucianoalessandro.ipsaropalesi, paolo.nesi}@unifi.it

Abstract. Waste management has become a matter of increasing importance on international, national, and local scales. The current socio-economic system is based on the growth of production and consumption of goods, leading to continuous and excessive waste production. In addition, factors such as urbanization, population growth, and inadequate waste management practices contribute to the growing volume and complexity of waste. Ineffective waste management contributes to climate change, pollution, and biodiversity loss while also representing a substantial economic loss. This paper presents Snap4Waste: a solution for waste management and optimization. The proposed approach improves efficiency through real-time data collection and analytics, IoT-based monitoring, and collection routing optimization. Furthermore, key features include entity management for bins, trucks, and collection routes, role-based access control, real-time tracking of bin fill levels and truck loads, and dynamic waste collection planning. The system integrates interactive KPI dashboards for performance assessment and an alarm management framework for rapid issue resolution. The platform has been implemented using data of the real-case scenario of Amsterdam and on top of the Snap4City open source platform for CN MOST, national center on sustainable mobility.

Keywords: Smart Waste Management · IoT · WoT · route bin collection optimization · smart applications

1 Introduction

Waste management has become a matter of increasing importance on international, national, and local scales. The current socio-economic system is based on the growth of production and consumption of goods [2], leading to continuous and excessive waste production. In addition, factors such as urbanization [1], population growth [3] and inadequate waste management practices [4] contribute to the growing volume and complexity of waste.

In 1965, global waste production amounted to 635 Mt., which increased to 1,999 Mt. in 2015 and, despite numerous improvements in waste treatment technologies, is

O. Gervasi et al. (Eds.): ICCSA 2026 Workshops, LNCS 16758, pp. 202–219, 2027.
https://doi.org/10.1007/978-3-032-30497-1_13

expected to reach 3,539 Mt. by 2050 [3]. This trend contributes to climate change and environmental pollution and human quality of life. Beyond the environmental impact, waste represents a substantial economic loss.

Tourism's impact is another critical aspect to consider in waste management, particularly in cities and regions with strong tourism industries [5]. The seasonal influx of visitors often leads to an increase in waste generation during specific periods, frequently overloading regular collection systems. Waste management involves a comprehensive set of policies, and methodologies designed to govern the entire process, from generation to final disposal. Governmental bodies have a responsibility to find ways to minimize waste generation, control harmful waste emissions, recover material and energy resources from the waste stream, and dispose of waste in a manner which protects human health and minimizes environmental degradation [30]. In this context, the collection and transportation phases play a crucial role. When not properly planned and organized, these operations can generate high operational costs. These costs arise from factors such as the number of vehicles required, or staff employed, or periodic maintenance of the fleet. Therefore, reducing the number of trucks and optimizing routing are key strategies for lowering both fixed and variable costs.

The inefficiencies faced by governments (e.g., collection schedules or lack of notifications about issues such as damaged bins, illegal dumping, or overflowing containers) hinder the efficiency of waste management operations, leading to increased costs and reduced service quality. The integration of smart waste management technologies is key to addressing these modern challenges. Internet of Things (IoT)-based systems enable the installation of intelligent sensors in bins, allowing real-time monitoring of fill levels, and their functional conditions.

Machine Learning (ML) and Artificial intelligence (AI) are cutting-edge technologies used in smart waste management to analyze massive data from sensors, predict garbage generation patterns, optimize collection routes, allocate resources efficiently, and improve operations [32]. The dynamic (daily) waste collection routing optimization reduces unnecessary vehicle trips and enhances the efficiency of collection routes. These technologies support local governments in resource planning and system improvement. Equally important is encouraging active citizen participation in proper waste disposal, methods such as pay-as-you-throw (PAYT) systems, which link costs to the amount and kinds of waste produced, not only encourage sustainable behavior but also promote a deeper sense of responsibility toward environmental preservation and may reduce costs for the final users. The optimization of waste collection (road network graph, including details about routes, bin fill levels, collection points, vehicle stops, etc.) is addressed through various methods, leveraging logistical parameters while adhering to regulations (e.g., rules on urban center access, preferential routes, and standards for maintaining city cleanliness). Techniques discussed in the literature include Optimization Algorithms (e.g., Quantum Particle Swarm Optimization – QPSO [6], Genetic Algorithms [7]), Mathematical Models [28], and Reinforcement Learning [29].

In this paper, we propose a solution for waste management, including waste bin monitoring, fast production of waste collection routing optimization, KPI assessment, and related tools for operators and drivers (the solution works in real time or in simulated conditions to perform what-if analysis, and replanning). In addition, the solution works according to different kinds of sensors (on bins, trucks, etc.) and models (for example enabling the access to bins by fobs and enabling the pay-as-you-throw (PAYT) business models with city users and commercial operators in the city). The solution has been developed by using Snap4City open-source platform, which operates in various domains such as sustainability [24], mobility [25–27], security [23], etc.

This paper is organized as follows. Section 2 presents the state of the art. Section 3 provides and analyzes requirements for waste collection management systems. In addition, the state of the art is analyzed with respect to the identified requirements. In Sect. 4, Snap4Waste solution is presented. In Sect. 5, an illustrative example is provided on the basis of Amsterdam data, while conclusions are drawn in Sect. 6.

2 State of the Art

In urban waste management, many commercial solutions [8–10] focus on waste collection, typically within closed, specialized systems that fail to integrate effectively with the complex dynamics of smart cities. Traffic is characterized by incidents, construction work, public events, and other unexpected disruptions, therefore, personalizing an optimal solution requires more flexible and interconnected solutions that can adapt in real-time to the evolving needs of the area. The optimization of waste collection represents a critical challenge in the development of sustainable and efficient cities. Existing state-of-the-art proposals address different approaches, including the formulation of optimization objectives, the development of computational methodologies, and the integration of heterogeneous data sources. These works aim to improve waste collection processes, increase resource efficiency and reduce the environmental impact of urban waste management systems.

In scientific literature, different solutions have been proposed to address these challenges. These range from complete applications for waste collection management to tools aimed at optimizing waste management operations. These approaches often leverage mathematical models, optimization algorithms, and technologies such as IoT and artificial intelligence, with the goal of developing more dynamic and resilient systems.

Iftikhar Hussain, et al., in [11], proposed an IoT-based waste management system using a multi-agent simulation framework, focusing on real-time monitoring and routing, the results demonstrate that IoT systems outperform traditional periodic methods by reducing travel distances and truck requirements, while also delivering better economic, environmental, and operational outcomes. However, the study presents some difficulties in generalizing to other contexts and does not consider the technological and infrastructural challenges of IoT implementation.

Kalyuzhnyy, et al., in [12], introduced CollectMyWaste, an IoT-based system for waste management. It used real-time monitoring of bins via sensors, with data stored in a centralized cloud database containing details on bins, vehicles and routes. The system optimizes collection routes using KPI analysis and algorithms while integrating external systems (e.g., traffic and weather), and a web-based interface facilitates operational efficiency and decision-making in the operation. However, the system does not address certain issues, such as data security, scalability, and the lack of differentiation in user roles.

Dharan, et al., in [13], introduced a waste management system by using IoT and machine learning to optimize collection processes. The optimized collection routes have been based on factors such as distance, capacity, time taken, fuel consumption, and corresponding historical data. The system reduced operational costs, fuel usage, and carbon footprint. However, the system does not account for user roles, limiting its ability to foster and manage effective usage policies.

Velasquez, et al., in [14], introduced a comprehensive approach to improve waste management. The system uses the Lorentz Quantum Particle Swarm Optimization (QPSO-LR) algorithm to optimize collection routes, reducing travel distance and time enhancing operational efficiency and environmental impact. A web application features several modules including route optimization, detailed collection point management, user role differentiation (e.g., Administrator, Supervisor, Collector), and the ability to add new collection points. Moreover, the system does not account for the multifaceted and dynamic variables present in urban waste management, such as heterogeneous waste generation patterns or traffic conditions in diverse scenarios. In addition, the scalability of the system has not been demonstrated

Elia, et al., in [15], explored PAYT strategies, highlighting their potential to improve the economic, environmental and social sustainability of solid waste management. These models, increasingly implemented in waste systems, center on unit pricing, user identification, and waste measurement.

From an operational perspective, three main waste collection strategies can be identified:

1) Fixed day of the week or two-weeks, for each kind of waste for each area. Valid for a long period, for instance 6 months. In this scenario, the reference optimization problem is the periodic vehicle routing problem (PVRP) [33, 34]. The advantages of this approach are its lower dependence on real-time data and its ease of implementation. However, a limitation is that the algorithm often schedules stops at containers that are not yet full, resulting in operational inefficiency.
2) Flexible waste collection but fixed weekly schedule for the bin collection, for example every day of the week a predefined set of rides. The drivers know the route they have to be done in each specific day. In this case, the optimization problem is the Scheduled Capacitated Vehicle Routing Problem (CVRP) [35, 36]. This approach is considered a good compromise between operational efficiency and collection scheduling, and it is also easy to implement. On the other hand, it is less responsive than fully dynamic models, although it still requires access to updated data.
3) Flexible rides, every day a new plan is produced according to the status of the bins at 11: 30 PM of the previous day. This means that the drivers will discover the ride only in the morning when they get into the truck. In this context, the relevant optimization problems are the Dynamic Vehicle Routing Problem (DVRP) [37] and the Smart Waste Collection Routing Problem (SWCRP) [38]. The main advantages include improved adaptability to real-world conditions and a reduction in travel distances and, consequently, in operating costs. However, this approach requires greater organizational complexity and is also dependent on the availability of reliable data, sensors, and IT systems.

The conventional waste management techniques, such as a strategy based on fixed collection days over a long planning period, remain predominant today [39], even though they are often unable to cope with the rising complexity and costs of sustainable waste management practices but current research focuses on more dynamic strategies (Flexible waste collection and Flexible rides), particularly IoT smart waste management [40].

3 Waste Manager Platform Requirements

After analyzing the state of the art and considering the needs highlighted in the introduction, an effective solution for operators must meet specific functional requirements. Defining requirements is essential for developing scalable and reliable solutions capable of enhancing operational efficiency and reducing costs associated with waste management in smart cities. In Table 1, a summary of the state-of-the-art waste management optimization solutions is presented, focusing on their compliance with the identified requirements.

R.1-Coverage of Entities Involved such as: bins, trucks, mobile phones for participation, and waste collection routes, operators, truck drivers, etc. The system should allow for the creation, tracking, and management of entities throughout their lifecycle, including details for bin types, locations, conditions, and capacity, as well as truck specifications, maintenance schedules, and route assignments (road graph, updated road conditions, etc.).

R.2–Users' Roles Management: to define and control access to the system based on different user profiles/roles: administrators, operators, drivers, maintenance personnel and city users (common users and commercial operators), each with specific permissions and responsibilities. By managing user access and roles, the system has to ensure that sensitive data and functions are protected while enabling each user to perform their tasks, maintain accountability, and enhance security within the waste management operations.

R.3–Get real time data from bins (e.g., fill levels, usage frequency, temperature to detect potential fire risks or environmental anomalies, and various alarms for situations such as unauthorized access, bin movement, or damage), mobiles (requests, alarms.). The real-time data collection has to provide information to enable faster response times to maintenance needs and improves the overall efficiency of waste management, as well as enabling forecasts to be calculated in time.

R.4–Get real time data from waste collection trucks. For example, for tracking and monitoring status, and weighing the amount of waste in kilograms when the bin is lifted by the arm, the status of the truck etc. These data are not mandatory, but if they are accessible, they can be used in place of bin data or for double control. They can also be used in prediction in planning models. These data as those of bins are used in predicting and planning collection routes, with historical.

R.5–Provide optimized waste collection routing taking into account the data coming from bins' sensors, routing conditions, route planning, closeness of bins, bin fulness predictions. These technologies enable the creation of optimized waste collection routing and schedule, reducing the number of trips, exploiting the trips needed for collecting closed bins to critical ones, and better allocation of resources, ultimately enhancing the sustainability and cost-effectiveness of waste management systems. The routing can be based on the last values of the status of the bins, or the typical values of bins in similar days, so that different strategies should be applicable.

R.5.1–Taking into account Urban Environments. Waste collection optimization is limited by truck capabilities (size, capacity, fuel efficiency), infrastructure (narrow roads, traffic, routing and road network, changes in the road graph), regulatory restrictions (weight, time dedicated to work for drivers and operators), and economic factors (costs, investments). These factors must be considered for effective route planning and system performance.

R.6–Drive decisions on Key Performance Indicators (KPIs) on interactive dashboards. The KPI dashboards/views should provide relevant values for decision makers in the phase of planning, and in real-time during waste collection operations, such as the total amount of waste collected, positions of trucks, collection efficiency, truck utilization, fuel consumption, maintenance status of bins and vehicles, and the understanding of filling cycles. By visualizing KPIs in planning phase, the operators can make data-driven decisions to optimize processes, identify trends and better analyze and predict filling cycles to improve scheduling and resource allocation, and choose the better routing strategy.

R.7-Provide alarm management and notification systems to alert operators in real time about issues (e.g., bin overflows, damage or unauthorized access). The alerts can be triggered by IoT sensors placed in bins, trucks, or along collection routes, and eventual alarms sent by mobiles or web-based platforms. Timely notifications enable quick responses, minimizing disruptions in the waste collection process and ensuring that maintenance or other necessary actions are taken promptly to avoid operational inefficiencies.

R.8–Provide Support for Pay-As-You-Throw (PAYT) to incentivize sustainable waste disposal behaviors by linking costs directly to the amount of waste produced per kind. This system should support tracking of waste generated by individual users or households, integrating data from IoT-enabled bins and trucks to calculate pay back fees accurately in a GDPR compliant manner. The PAYT system must also include functions for real-time monitoring, accounting, and invoicing, fostering transparency and encouraging waste reduction through an equitable cost structure. The usage of blockchain could be a solution to provide transparency. The PAYT is enabled by the adoption of bin lockers and fobs assigned to users for bin opening or by other technology such as bags with RFIDs.

Table 1. Comparison of waste management solutions based on requirement satisfaction

Solution	Requirements								
	R.1	R.2	R.3	R.4	R.5	R5.1	R.6	R.7	R.8
Sensoneo [8]	N	Y	Y	Y	N	N	Y	Y	N
NextBillion AI [9]	Y	N	N	N	Y	Y	N	N	N
Nordsense [10]	N	Y	Y	Y	Y	NA	Y	NA	N
Iftikhar Hussain et al. in [11]	Y	N	Y	Y	Y	N	N	N	N

(continued)

Table 1. *(continued)*

Solution	Requirements								
	R.1	R.2	R.3	R.4	R.5	R5.1	R.6	R.7	R.8
Kalyuzhnyy et al. in [12]	N	Y	Y	Y	Y	N	N	N	N
Dharan, P et al. [13]	N	N	Y	Y	Y	Y	N	N	N
Velasquez et al. in [14]	Y	Y	N	N	Y	Y	Y	N	N
Elia et al. in [15]	N	Y	N	N	N	N	N	N	Y
Snap4Waste Solution	Y	Y	Y	Y	Y	Y	Y	Y	Y

4 System Overview

In this section, the architecture and optimization process of Snap4Waste Manager are presented. The system integrates IoT data, traffic conditions, bin levels and status to optimize waste collection and routing according to KPIs. The optimization is performed by means of a phase of preprocessing for the identification of bins to be addressed, an advanced genetic algorithm to optimize routes, improving efficiency and reducing costs, according to KPIs, and to go in execution monitoring tracks and waste collection in real time. Other strategies may impose: to collect all bins aera by area, just fixing the day of the week in which they are collected and using different kind of trucks in different aeras to collect differentiated waste in different days.

A. **Snap4Waste Architecture**

In Fig. 1, the Snap4Waste Architecture is reported, putting in evidence that it has been developed on top of Snap4City open-source framework designing and developing: data ingestion processes, processing logic, optimization algorithms and business intelligence dashboard for the front end.

Snap4City is a platform for Smart Cities offering scalability, multi-tenant support, and the ability to manage millions of daily data entries via a range of protocols such as MQTT and NGSI [16]. It is fully compliant with GDPR [17] and ensures data protection while implementing a user role management system, enabling secure and personalized access. Snap4City supports IoT/WoT with a flexible modeling of entities [18] and managing their entire lifecycle. The data modeling is used for data ingestion via Node-RED and to include details such as bin types, locations, status, and capacity, as well as truck data. The platform also supports route computation via and an integrated GraphHopper. The access control mechanism based on differentiated user profiles assigns roles such as administrators, operators, and maintenance staff, each with specific permissions and responsibilities. Snap4City (which is an official platform of CN MOST) includes advanced mobility features, such as "what-if" analysis tools [19] and optimized routing, enabling efficient planning of truck routes and significant reductions in operational costs.

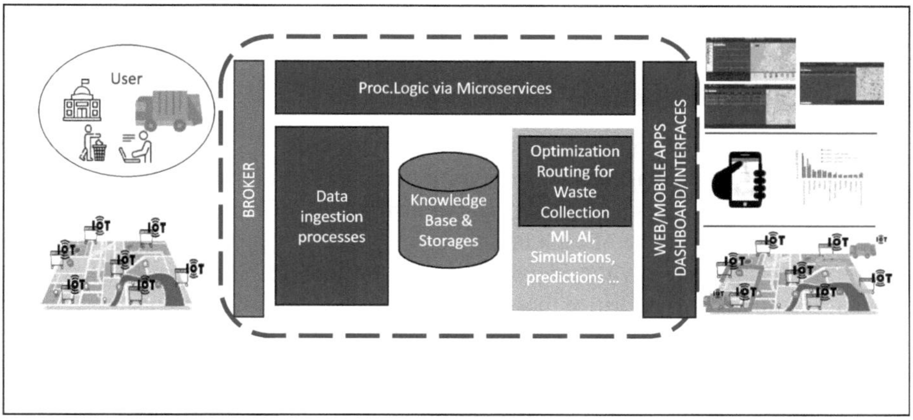

Fig. 1. **Snap4Waste** architecture.

In **Snap4Waste**, data is collected through IoT sensors deployed across the city and transmitted to NGSI Brokers to the platform for processing. The system manages data ingestion and stores it in the storage, enabling process logic powered by microservices [20]. Snap4Waste collects and monitors real-time data from:

- **Bins**: fill levels, usage frequency, temperature (to detect potential risks). An IoT-based alert system monitors operations in real-time, addressing anomalies like critical fill levels or bin damages. The bins also inform the central station about the amount of waste introduced by specific users with fobs to enable for them the PAYT solution when they are equipped with lockers and users with fobs.
- **Trucks**: waste weight during loading and tracking.

Snap4Waste supports advanced features such as, preprocessing for the identification of the bins to be collected with AI/ML-based predictions, and the optimized routing for waste collection, the simulation of the waste bin collection actual track monitoring during the waste collection; and statistical analysis in executing an optimization, in simulation and during actual waste collection. The Operators can access management tools through web dashboards and mobile apps, providing overviews, analytics, and notifications to enhance service planning. The Drivers can see their trip step by steps with the support of the router, and the commercial operator may use their app to signal events and monitor the status of the bins which are close to their activity.

The Snap4Waste solution provides dashboards with KPIs that offer real-time insights into waste collection operations, thus facilitating strategic decision-making. By combining IoT technologies, data analytics, and urban constraints (e. g. vehicle capacity, infrastructure, regulations), the system optimizes collection routes, reduces trips, and improves resource allocation. In addition, the application supports a Pay-As-You-Throw (PAYT) system, promoting sustainable behaviors by associating costs with waste production. This functionality relies on data collected from IoT-enabled bins and trucks, enabling dynamic monitoring and detailed reporting. The Snap4Waste platform is based on a highly available and horizontally scalable infrastructure, capable of increasing or reducing computational resources to provide service continuity even in the event of high computational loads [16, 31].

B. **Snap4Waste Optimization**

For the optimization process, a genetic algorithm, GA, [21] has been adopted to enhance urban waste management. The algorithm focuses on optimizing vehicle routing by considering key factors such as the spatial distribution of bins, the classification of waste types, and the fill rate of each bin.

Preprocessing performs the identification of the bins to be collected taking into account: the bin data to prioritize those that are over 70% of fullness, plus those which are less filled but may risk reaching the 80% according to a prediction AI based on historical data. Moreover, once identified the most relevant bins to be collected, the bins spatially close to the former are also identified: a parameter given to the preprocessing determines said distance. Thus, a full subset is identified.

Let $B = \{b_1, b_2, \ldots, b_n\}$ be a set of bins, where each bin $b_i = (lat_i, long_i, fr_i, wt_i)$ with lat_i, $long_i$ representing the position of b_i (latitude and longitude), fr_i is the fill level of b_i and wt_i is the waste type of b_i. Let $V = \{v_1, v_2, \ldots, v_m\}$ be the set of available vehicles/trucks, where each vehicle $v_i = \{c_i, t_i\}$ has a weight capacity c_i and a maximum time activity of t_i. According to the GA, each chromosome represents a possible solution to the problem (a set of routing for the day, which involve a subset of vehicles and subset of bins), where each vehicle is assigned a specific subset of bins to collect waste from them. The chromosome is structured as a set of pairs

$$C_j = \{(v_j, B_j) \mid v_j \in V, B_j \subset B\}$$

where B_j is the set of bins assigned to v_j. The assignment has to respect the vehicle's capacity c_j has to ensure that only compatible waste types are collected together and the vehicle operates for no longer than t_i. GA begins by generating a random initial population

$$P = \{C_1, C_2, \ldots, C_{25}\}$$

To evolve the population over successive generations, a parent selection process is applied. Parents are chosen through a $k - way\ tournament\ selection$ [22]: a subset of k chromosomes is randomly selected from the population, and the one with the highest fitness is chosen as a parent. The fitness function $f(C_i)$ considers both the quality of the solution and its diversity, computed as follows:

$$f(C_i) = \omega_1 * \frac{1}{TotalCost(C_j)} + \omega_2 * Diversity(C_j)$$

where $TotalCost(C_j) = \sum_{C_j} Cost(v_j, B_j)$ represents the total cost for chromosome C_j. $Cost(v_j, B_j)$ is the travel and operational cost associated with vehicle v_j servicing bin $B_j \subset B$. $Diversity(C_j)$ measured by evaluating how many element pairs that were together in one solution are separated in another, promoting diverse groupings. ω_1 and ω_2 are weight coefficients balancing cost minimization and solution diversity. Crossover combines two parent solutions, C_{j_1} and C_{j_2} to generate a new one C_o, inheriting features from both. The applied operator aims to preserve valid vehicle-bin assignments. Mutation introduces variation by randomly modifying the assignment of bins to vehicles; mutation rate μ determines the probability of altering a solution, helping maintain diversity and prevent premature convergence. A local search is applied to refine the generated solutions by exploring small adjustments within the neighborhood of each bin b_i. Two main operators are considered to minimize travel costs: swaps between route segments, $(N, M) -$ exchange and reversals $(2 - OPT)$. The $(N, M) -$ exchange operator swaps route segments between two nodes u and v, ensuring they do not overlap or include the depot. It can relocate a segment after v $(M = 0)$ or swap segments between routes $(M > 0)$. The 2-OPT operator modifies a route by replacing arcs to shorten travel distance. It either reconnects segments between different routes or reverses a portion within the same route to improve efficiency. The goal of the algorithm is to minimize the total cost, which is the sum of the travel or operational costs associated with each vehicle and bin: $\min TotalCost(C_j)$

To ensure a valid solution, the algorithm must satisfy three constraints.

Each bin must be visited exactly once. Let m the trucks number, then

$$\sum_{j=1}^{m} \sum_{b_j \in B_j} x_{ij} = 1 \quad \forall b_j \in B$$

After, the capacity of each vehicle must not be exceeded, ensuring that the total load assigned to a vehicle does not surpass its capacity. Let C_j solution, then

$$\sum_{b_j \in B_j} fr_{b_j} \le c_j$$

Finally, the total working hours of each vehicle must not exceed a predefined maximum limit. Let A_{B_j} be the amount of bins of the set B_j, $time(x, y)$ the time spent traveling from the two locations and $time_{retrieve}(b)$ the time spent retrieving the waste from bin b

$$time(depot, b_1) + time\left(b_{A_{B_j}}, depot\right) + \sum_{n=1}^{A_{B_j}-1} time(b_n, b_{n+1}) + \sum_{b_j \in B_j} time_{retrieve}\left(b_j\right) \le t_j \forall v_j \in V$$

The algorithm stops when its termination conditions are met: the conditions may be the following and are determined when the optimization instance is started:

1) predefined maximum number of generations G_{max} has been reached

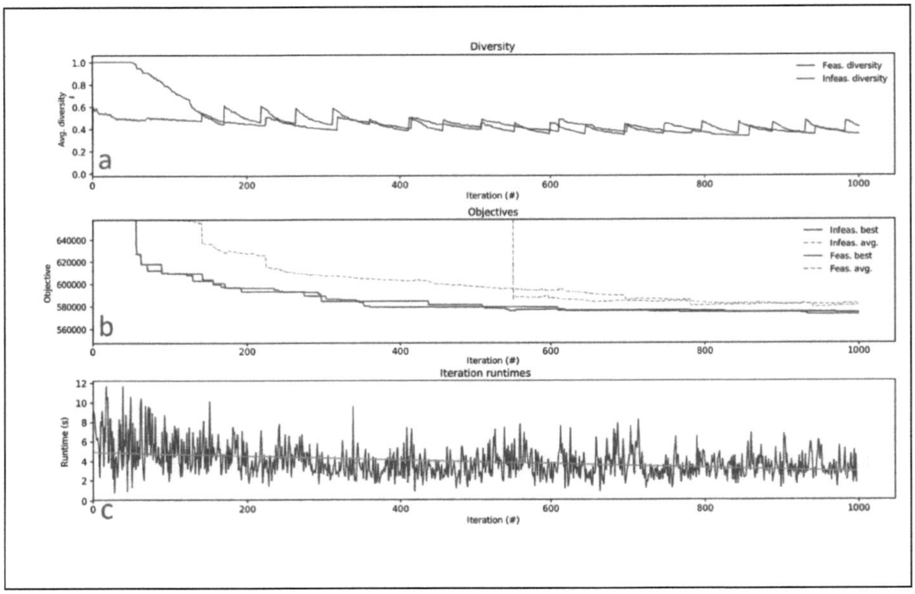

Fig. 2. Evolution of the solution process over 1000 iterations: (a) search-space diversity, (b) reduction of the best TotalCost, and (c) computation time per iteration

2) no improvement in the objective value is observed for a certain number of generations G_{impr}.
3) The algorithm has been executed for at least $TIME_{exec}$

The optimization process performs multiple optimizations, each independent from each other and each of them with a different starting random seed. The optimization process outputs realtime execution results and may provide a valid solution not yet final if any exists. Each instance finds its own solution, then a postprocess operation finds the most optimal solution across all the individual optimizations.

In Fig. 2, an instance of a possible solution was obtained within the given limit of 1000 iterations. The instance of the problem uses a max of 120 vehicles among two classes of vehicles and approximately 845000 kg of waste across 4621 bins. Figure 2a shows the diversity of the solution search by the algorithm, with periodic peaks indicating the introduction of new diverse solutions. Figure 2b shows the decreasing *TotalCost* of the best solution found at a given iteration reaching a final value of approximately 572000 s of total travel time. Figure 2c shows the time spent looking for the next solution: despite the high variance caused by runtime conditions a decreasing trend in runtime was observed as the solution cost decreased. The solution found required 90 vehicles and was obtained in approximately 4000 s, on a single core of an Intel(R) Xeon(R) CPU E5–2650 v4 @ 2.20GHz processor. This optimization process was performed over 32 cores of CPU in parallel computing, with each instance occupying approxmately 3 GB of memory.

5 Illustrative Examples

The data used to test the application comes from the urban waste collection system based on smart bins installed in Amsterdam. These devices monitor fill levels and transmit periodic information, allowing for an estimation of the daily waste volume for each bin. There are more than 4,000 bins for different types of waste in this city. Each of them has a different fill rate, and not all bins necessarily need to be emptied every day. The Snap4Waste application provides a set of views/dashboards dedicated to waste collection management and optimization.

One of the main views is the planning dashboard (see Fig. 3-a), which enables the activation of an optimization process based on user-configurable parameters. In this phase, users can set the type of waste to be collected (according to the differentiate strategy adopted in the city), the maximum transportable weight per truck, the maximum service duration (service time for the operators), a max nearby distance in meters, and a threshold percentage beyond which a bin must be collected (e.g., 70%). Every optimization setting profile in the snap4city platform is saved. The optimization process also includes stopping criteria, such as a maximum number of iterations or an early stopping mechanism based on the progressive improvement of the solution. Once the optimization is launched, users can monitor its progress through a progress bar and view the results in terms of KPIs, including the total number of selected bins, the number of trucks required, the estimated amount of collected waste, the kilometers traveled and the time spent; the results are summarized in a table that displays, the number of assigned bins, the transported weight, the traveled route, and the service duration for each truck.

The dashboard in Fig. 3-b is dedicated to managing the routes generated for waste collection trucks. Users can assign routes to vehicles and provide drivers with a navigation interface (Fig. 4-f).

The dashboard in Fig. 3-c provides information on waste bin statuses and eventual alarms of their sensors. Users view and update bin alarm statuses from the table on the left.

The dashboards (Fig. 4d-e) analyze waste collection statistics over time, allowing for comparisons between different periods. These statistics include KPIs such as the number of empty bins, the vehicles used, the amount of waste collected, and the emissions produced.

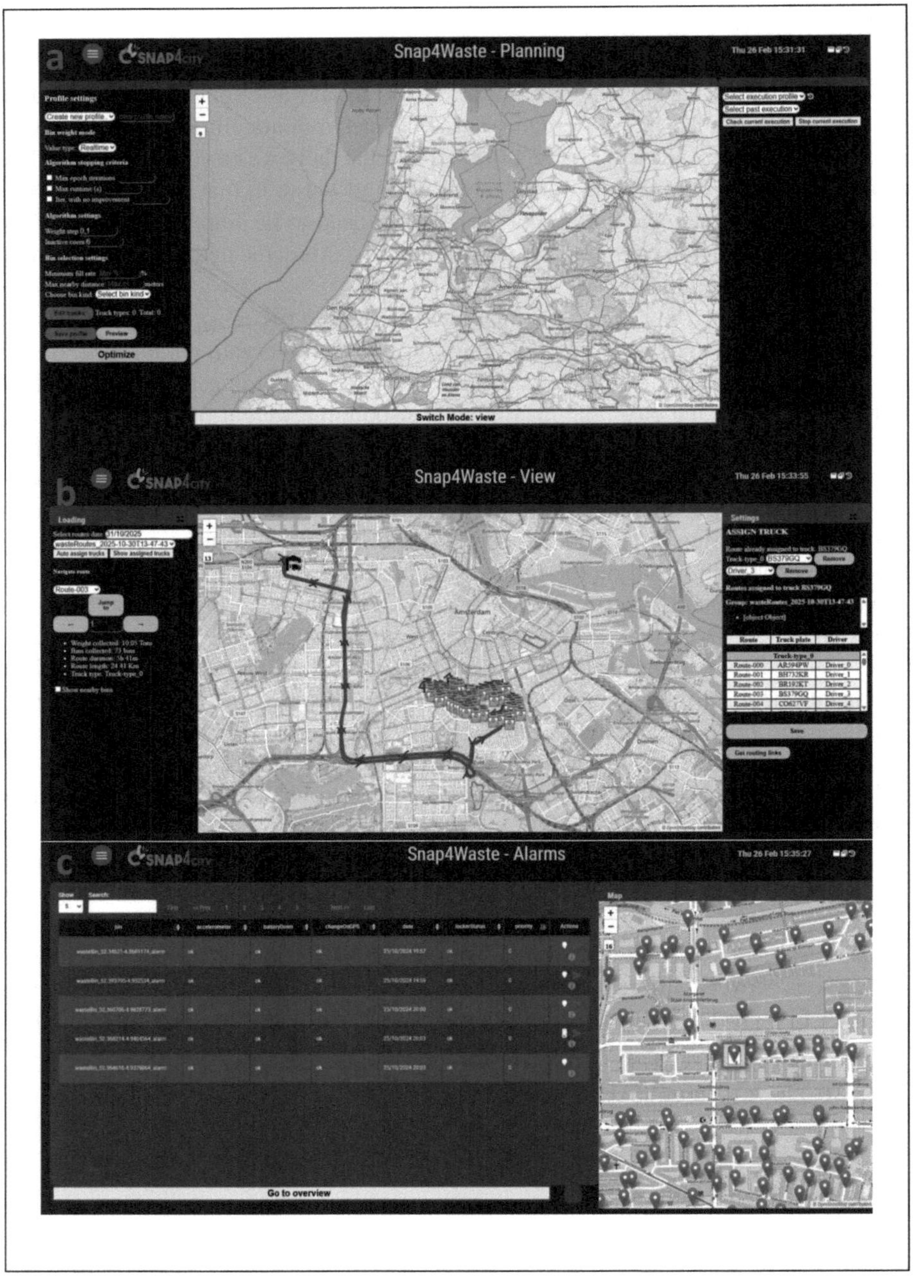

Fig. 3. Overview of Snap4Waste application: (a) planning for route optimization, (b) route management, (c) real-time alarm

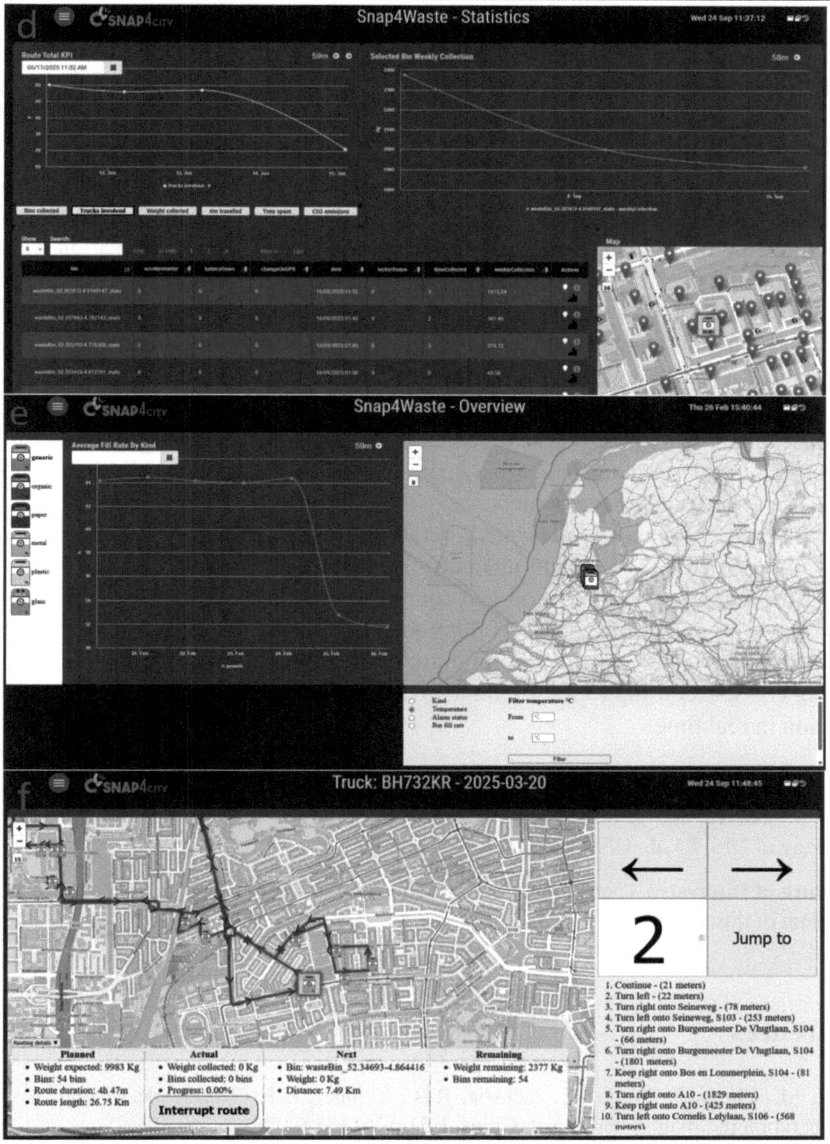

Fig. 4. Overview of Snap4Waste application: (d-e) waste collection statistics and period comparisons, (f) driver navigation interface.

6 Conclusion

Effective waste management in smart cities necessitates advanced digital solutions that integrate IoT, data analytics, and optimization techniques. In this work, Snap4Waste solution has been presented enabling real-time data acquisition, prediction of bin status and planning waste collection optimization. The system incorporates entities and users' management, dynamic monitoring of waste bins and waste collection trucks, route optimization taking into account urban and mobility constraints. The optimization is based on minimization of costs and allows the computation of KPIs. A real-data implementation and validation have been carried out by using data of Amsterdam, validating its applicability in an urban environment. Future research will focus on enhancing predictive models for waste generation patterns, refining AI-driven optimization algorithms for dynamic route planning, and exploring blockchain-based mechanisms for transparent and secure PAYT systems. These advancements will contribute to more sustainable and transparent waste management strategies, aligning with the principles of circular economy and smart city development.

Snap4Waste Manager is presented, detailing its architecture, functionalities, and optimization process. The system integrates IoT data, traffic conditions, bin levels and status to optimize waste collection and routing according to KPIs. The optimization is performed by means of a phase of preprocessing for the identification of bins to be addressed, an advanced genetic algorithm to optimize routes, improving efficiency and reducing costs, according to KPIs, and to go in execution monitoring tracks and waste collection in real time.

Acknowledgments. The authors would like to express sincere thanks to CN MOST, national center on mobility; and to Snap4City platforms (https://www.snap4city.org) which is an open technology of DISIT Lab, UNIFI.

Disclosure of Interests. The authors have no competing interests to declare that are relevant to the content of this article.

References

1. Lu, M., Zhou, C., Wang, C., Jackson, R.B., Kempes, C.P.: Worldwide scaling of waste generation in urban systems. Nat. Cities. **1**(2), 126–135 (2024)
2. Pramanti, A., Chotim, E.E.: Critical review of growth population, plastic waste and the digital Society in Indonesia. Jurnal Partisipatoris. **1**(2), 79–86 (2019)
3. Chen, D.M.C., Bodirsky, B.L., Krueger, T., Mishra, A., Popp, A.: The world's growing municipal solid waste: trends and impacts. Environ. Res. Lett. **15**(7), 074021 (2020)
4. Haris, M., Saad, S., Ammad, S., Rasheed, K., Aman, H., Noor, S.: Integrating sustainable practices for effective solid waste Management in Peshawar: overcoming challenges and promoting environmental. In: 2024 ASU International Conference in Emerging Technologies for Sustainability and Intelligent Systems (ICETSIS), pp. 1–7 (2024)
5. Arbulú, I., Rey-Maquieira, J., Sastre, F.: The impact of TOURISM and seasonality on different types of municipal solid waste (MSW) generation: the case of Ibiza. Heliyon. **10**(13), e33894., ISSN 2405-8440 (2024). https://doi.org/10.1016/j.heliyon.2024.e33894

6. Velasquez, W., Dillon-Jimenez, J., Medina-Moncayo, D., Alvarez-Alvarado, M.S.: Optimizing waste collection routes with QPSO-LR algorithm and IoT sensors. In: 2024 IEEE Colombian Conference on Communications and Computing (COLCOM), pp. 1–6, Barranquilla, Colombia (2024)
7. Fujdiak, R., Masek, P., Mlynek, P., Misurec, J., Olshannikova, E.: Using genetic algorithm for advanced municipal waste collection in smart city. In: 2016 10th International Symposium on Communication Systems, Networks and Digital Signal Processing (CSNDSP), pp. 1–6. IEEE (2016, July)
8. Sensoneo: Smart waste management system. Available at: https://sensoneo.com/product/smart-waste-management-system/. Accessed 22 Jan 2025
9. NextBillion AI: Route optimization for waste collection. Available at: https://nextbillion.ai/developers/route-optimization-waste-collection. Accessed 22 Jan 2025
10. Nordsense: Nordsense-Smart waste management solutions. Available at: https://nordsense.com/. Accessed 22 Jan 2025
11. Hussain, I., Elomri, A., Kerbache, L., El Omri, A.: Smart city solutions: comparative analysis of waste management models in IoT-enabled environments using multiagent simulation. Sustain. Cities Soc. **103**, 105247 (2024) ISSN 2210-6707
12. Kalyuzhnyy, V., Costa, M., Silva, P., Santos, J.: Smart City IoT system - CollectMyWaste. In: 2020 4th International Symposium on Multidisciplinary Studies and Innovative Technologies (ISMSIT), pp. 1–5, Istanbul, Turkey (2020). https://doi.org/10.1109/ISMSIT50672.2020.9255271
13. Dharan, P., Manikandan, V.M.: A smart waste management system with optimized routing method. In: 2024 15th International Conference on Computing Communication and Networking Technologies (ICCCNT), pp. 1–6. IEEE (2024, June)
14. Velasquez, W., Dillon-Jimenez, J., Medina-Moncayo, D., Alvarez-Alvarado, M.S.: Optimizing waste collection routes with QPSO-LR algorithm and IoT sensors. In: 2024 IEEE Colombian Conf. On Comm. And Computing (COLCOM), pp. 1–6. IEEE (2024, August)
15. Elia, V., Gnoni, M.G.: Fabiana Tornese, designing pay-as-you-throw schemes in municipal waste management services: a holistic approach. Waste Manag. **44**, 188–195., ISSN 0956-053X, (2015). https://doi.org/10.1016/j.wasman.2015.07.040
16. Bellini, P., Palesi, L.A.I., Giovannoni, A., Nesi, P.: Managing complexity of data models and performance in broker-based internet/web of things architectures. Internet Things. **23**, 100834 (2023)
17. Bellini, P., Palesi, L.A.I., Nesi, P., et al.: Multi clustering recommendation system for fashion retail. Multimed. Tools Appl. **82**, 9989–10016 (2023). https://doi.org/10.1007/s11042-021-11837-5
18. Bellini, P., Bologna, D., Fanfani, M., Ipsaro Palesi, L.A., Nesi, P., Pantaleo, G.: Rapid Prototyping & Development Life Cycle for smart applications of internet of entities. In: 2023 27th International Conference on Engineering of Complex Computer Systems (ICECCS), pp. 142–151, Toulouse, France (2023)
19. Bellini, P., Bilotta, S., Palesi, A.L.I., Nesi, P., Pantaleo, G.: Vehicular traffic flow reconstruction analysis to mitigate scenarios with large City changes. IEEE Access. **10**, 131061–131075 (2022). https://doi.org/10.1109/ACCESS.2022.3229183
20. Fanfani, M., Palesi, L.A.I., Nesi, P.: Microservices' libraries enabling server-side business logic visual programming for digital twins, 101805. SoftwareX. **27** (2024). https://doi.org/10.1016/j.softx.2024.101805
21. Mirjalili, S., Mirjalili, S.: Genetic algorithm. Evolutionary algorithms and neural networks: theory and applications, 43–55 (2019)
22. Kwon, Y.D., Choo, J., Bae, D., Kim, J., Hottung, A.: Cost Shaping Via Reinforcement Learning for Vehicle Routing Problems. The EURO Meets NeurIPS (2022)

23. Collini, E., Palesi, L.A.I., Nesi, P., et al.: Flexible thermal camera solution for smart city people detection and counting. Multimed. Tools Appl. **83**, 20457–20485 (2024). https://doi.org/10.1007/s11042-023-16374-x
24. Bilotta, S., Palesi, L.A.I., Nesi, P.: Exploiting open data for CO2 estimation via artificial intelligence and eXplainable AI, 128598. Expert Syst. Appl. **291** (2025). https://doi.org/10.1016/j.eswa.2025.128598
25. Bilotta, S., Fereidooni, Z., Palesi, L.A.I., Nesi, P.: Macroscopic GA-based Multi-Objective Traffic Light Optimization prioritizing tramways. Applied Soft Computing. **178**, 113269 (2025). https://doi.org/10.1016/j.asoc.2025.113269
26. Fereidooni, Z., Palesi, L.A.I., Nesi, P.: Multi-agent optimizing traffic light signals using deep reinforcement learning. IEEE Access. **13**, 106974–106988 (2025). https://doi.org/10.1109/ACCESS.2025.3578518
27. Fanfani, M., Palesi, L.A.I., Nesi, P.: Data-driven mobility demand-versus-offer matching by dynamic integration of public and sharing services. IEEE Access. **14**, 23166–23193 (2026). https://doi.org/10.1109/ACCESS.2026.3661850
28. Ali, W.: Optimizing the e-waste management in India: a sustainable mathematical modeling approach to circular economy. Qual. Quant. **59**, 4647–4678 (2025). https://doi.org/10.1007/s11135-025-02176-w
29. Zhu, Z., et al.: Bayesian optimization-enhanced reinforcement learning for self-adaptive and multi-objective control of wastewater treatment, 132210. Bioresour. Technol. **421** (2025). https://doi.org/10.1016/j.biortech.2025.132210
30. Rhyner, C.R., Schwartz, L.J., Wenger, R.B., Kohrell, M.G.: Waste Management and Resource Recovery, 1st edn. CRC Press (1995). https://doi.org/10.1201/9780203734278
31. Perri, D., Simonetti, M., Gervasi, O.: Deploying efficiently modern applications on cloud. Electronics. **11**(3), 450 (2022). https://doi.org/10.3390/electronics11030450
32. Nirmala, N., Arun, J., Sanjay Kumar, S., Dawn, S.S.: Role of machine learning and artificial intelligence in smart waste management. In: Yatoo, A.M., Sillanpää, M. (eds.) Smart Waste and Wastewater Management by Biotechnological Approaches. Interdisciplinary Biotechnological Advances. Springer, Singapore (2025). https://doi.org/10.1007/978-981-97-8673-2_3
33. Castillo Ulloa, M.I., et al.: Sustainability and algorithmic Comparison of segmented PVRP for healthcare waste collection: a Brazilian case study. Sustainability. **17**, 8536 (2025). https://doi.org/10.3390/su17198536
34. Taverna, F., Tilk, C.: Enhancing waste collection: a branch-and-cut-and-Price approach for the periodic vehicle routing problem with intermediate facilities applied to a real-world case study. Eur. J. Oper. Res. **331**(2), 601–614., ISSN 0377-2217, (2026). https://doi.org/10.1016/j.ejor.2025.09.039
35. Hannan, M.A., Mahmuda Akhtar, R.A., Begum, H., Basri, A.H., Scavino, E.: Capacitated vehicle-routing problem model for scheduled solid waste collection and route optimization using PSO algorithm. Waste Manag. **71**, 31–41., ISSN 0956-053X, (2018). https://doi.org/10.1016/j.wasman.2017.10.019
36. Reed, M., Yiannakou, A., Evering, R.: An ant colony algorithm for the multi-compartment vehicle routing problem. Appl. Soft Comput. **15**, 169–176., ISSN 1568-4946, (2014). https://doi.org/10.1016/j.asoc.2013.10.017
37. Bouleft, Y., Elhilali Alaoui, A.: Dynamic multi-compartment vehicle routing problem for smart waste collection. Appl. Syst. Innov. **6**, 30 (2023). https://doi.org/10.3390/asi6010030
38. de Morais, C.S., Ramos Jorge, D.R., Aguiar, A.R., Barbosa-Póvoa, A.P., Antunes, A.P., Ramos, T.R.P.: A solution methodology for a smart waste collection routing problem with workload concerns: computational and managerial insights from a real case study. Int. J. Syst. Sci. Oper. Logist. **10**(1) (2023). https://doi.org/10.1080/23302674.2022.2086717

39. Addas, A., Khan, M.N., Naseer, F.: Waste management 2.0 leveraging internet of things for an efficient and eco-friendly smart city solution. PLoS One. **19**(7), e0307608 (2024). https://doi.org/10.1371/journal.pone.0307608. PMID: 39083562; PMCID: PMC11290616
40. Kasem, N.F., et al.: Techno-economic impact analysis of solid waste collection optimization and management for smart city towards achieving sustainable development goals, 100447. Cleaner Waste Syst. **12** (2025). https://doi.org/10.1016/j.clwas.2025.100447

Advanced Mathematics and Computing Models in Complex Data-Intensive Computational Systems (AMCM 2026)

Hybrid Transformer–CNN Architectures for Robust Low-Light Image Enhancement

Yinan Yao and Suzan J. Obaiys(✉)

Faculty of Computer Science and Information Technology, Universiti Malaya, Kuala Lumpur, Malaysia
23092995@siswa.um.edu.my, suzan@um.edu.my

Abstract. Low-Light image enhancement (LLIE) has become a critical area of interest in computer vision research due to its application to many multimedia-related tasks, including autonomous driving, surveillance, medical imaging, and photography. In this paper, we survey state-of-the-art methods for LLIE using multimodal active illumination, including both traditional enhancement techniques and deep learning methods. Traditional enhancement techniques - from histogram equalization and gamma correction to Retinex theory - all suffer from problems such as halo artifacts, color distortion and noise amplification. Deep networks have made significant progress drawing upon CNNs, curve estimation, GANs and Transformer-based methods, but still struggle with generalization ability, computational efficiency and robust performance across different types of low-light images. To meet the above needs, this paper proposes a contextual Transformer-based model for low-light image enhancement, and additionally examines a local-global dual-branch enhancement model as a comparative design. The first model is based on Swin Transformer with shifted window attention, adopts a pyramid denoising module (PPM), and retrieves multiscale features in the local context enhancement block (LCEB), while removing noise and preserving texture details in data. The second model integrates a U-Net-based convolutional branch for local feature retention with a height-width Transformer block for global context modeling, then fuses them using a channel attention-based fusion module. Both models are tested against standard LLIE datasets (LOL-v1, LOL-v2, ExDark) and reach competitive results in PSNR and SSIM scores and are robust and efficient in diverse low-light scenarios.

Keywords: Low-Light Image Enhancement (LLIE) · Feature Fusion · T-CNN-H · Pyramid denoising module · Local context enhancement block

1 Introduction

In the digital era, multimedia content has become increasingly important in a wide range of real-world applications, including autonomous driving, surveillance, medical imaging, remote sensing, and mobile photography [1–3]. Among

O. Gervasi et al. (Eds.): ICCSA 2026 Workshops, LNCS 16758, pp. 223–237, 2027.
https://doi.org/10.1007/978-3-032-30497-1_14

different forms of multimedia data, images serve as one of the most important carriers of visual information. However, in real acquisition domains imaging conditions may not be so critical to control, particularly under low illumination: images can be obtained with low brightness, poor contrast, blurred structures, missing information, heavy noise, and uneven illuminating illumination [11,13]. These issues compromise visual quality and usability for human viewing and computer vision tasks, especially in night scenes or dark settings, whereby important visual cues could be partly or completely hidden.

As a result, improving the quality of low-light images has emerged as a significant area of research in computer vision. Compared with hardware approaches such as high-performance sensors or specialized optical devices, software-based low-light image enhancement (LLIE) approaches are often more flexible, cheaper, and easier to deploy across multiple platforms [1,2]. Enhanced low-light images provide clearer visual input for system downstream tasks like object detection, image segmentation, target tracking, and scene understanding. In autonomous driving, enhanced low-light visibility can help perception systems better detect road objects and environmental structure at night. In surveillance applications, enhancement can improve face recognition reliability and also abnormal behaviour detection. In medical imaging, better visibility of subtle structure may improve clinical interpretation as well.

A large volume of work has been proposed to tackle the LLIE task. Most of the early approaches are totally hand-crafted using certain enhancement strategies (for example, histogram equalization, gamma correction, or Retinex-based decomposition [4,5]), while being very simple and easy to implement, they tend to cause over-enhancement, halo artifacts and color distortion and amplify noise under complex lighting scenarios. Recently, deep learning has advanced low-light enhancement severely by learning end-toend mappings from degraded inputs to enhanced targets. Convolutional neural networks, curve estimation methods and GANs with Transformer architectures [11,14,15], have obtained inspiring results. Existing methods still suffer from limitations such as restricted generalization capability across extensive real scenes, and the dependency on complicated degradation patterns, as well as optimization of local texture preservation against global illuminal preservation.

Recently, models based on Transformers have also shown their potential, due in large part to their global modelling capabilities which help them to learn from long-range dependencies and across large contextual relationships [15–17]. Since the degradation of illumination is often very heterogeneous in low-light imagery it cannot simply be dealt with as a collection of local enhancements. Going global is undeniably important, but, at the same time, fine-grained local structures need to be preserved as best they can - edges, textures, object boundaries, etc. An effective LLIE model should thus be able to balance local detail restoration with other top-down global contextual reasoning and functioning is the motivating focus of this work.

To constrain these issues, in this work we study a deep architectures for robust low-light image enhancement, stressing contextual modeling and feature fusion.

Building on the research developed in the original thesis, in this paper we focus on a contextual Transformer-based enhancement framework as our main model. Inspired by the compelling results of combined approaches that unify local representation learning through convolutions with global context modeling from Transformer networks, we propose a model that enhances illumination recovery while maintaining structural and textural information. Our experimental results showcase superior quantitative and qualitative performances over several standard low-light datasets, including LOL-v1, LOLv2, and ExDark, validating the different low-light scenarios [22].

The main contributions of this paper can be summarized as follows:

- We propose a contextual Transformer-based network for low-light image enhancement that unifies local feature extraction and global contextual modeling within a single architecture.
- The goal of our method is to achieve greater illumination consistency while simultaneously preserving structural similarities and visual textures in the challenging low-light domain.
- Extensive experiments on benchmark datasets demonstrate that the proposed approach achieves competitive enhancement results in terms of both objective evaluation and visual quality.

2 Related Work

2.1 Traditional and Retinex-Based Methods

The traditional low-light image enhancement algorithms are mainly divided into two kinds: algorithms based on grayscale transformation methods and those based on Retinex theory [1–5]. The algorithms based on grayscale transformation methods primarily use histogram equalization and gamma correction. Histogram equalization transforms the grayscale range to a wider range or uniformly distribute the grayscale of the image at the risk of losing details [1,3]. Histogram specification was proposed to address the limitations of histogram equalization by establishing a grayscale mapping based on the difference between the original and target histograms. Gamma correction adjusts the gamma curve of the image to stretch or compress pixel values in different grayscale regions, optimizing the image [1,3].

Retinex theory-based methods are based on the interaction between light and object surface reflection and the human eye's color perception mechanism [4,5]. The core idea is to decompose the original image into reflection and illumination components. Early Retinex algorithms had high computational complexity, and subsequent improvements, such as single-scale, multi-scale, and variational framework-based Retinex algorithms, gradually addressed some issues but still had limitations [6–8].

Cai et al. proposed Retinexformer, a one-stage Retinex-based Transformer framework for low-light enhancement [9]. It decomposes an image into reflectance and illumination components using a Transformer block instead of classical convolutional mechanisms. The core motivation behind Retinexformer is to exploit the global receptive field of Transformers to perform illumination estimation while preserving the spirit of Retinex's state-of-the-art modeling of visual perception. The authors design a light-weight Feature Aggregation Transformer Block (FATB) to capture multi-scale contextual dependencies. Retinexformer's core advantage is end-to-end learning: bypassing the often tricky problem of manually tuning the decomposition priority of intensities of the input. The downside is it still requires a lot of computation resources and also struggles slightly with over-enhancement in very dark images. In addition, Retinexformer integrates a contextual-based normalization strategy that improves the adaptability of illumination estimation in complex scenes. This allows the model to enhance fine textures while suppressing color shifts. Experimental results on LOL and FiveK datasets show competitive PSNR and SSIM scores compared to previous state-of-the-art models. Yet, the lack of a denoising mechanism in low-SNR conditions slightly compromises the visual fidelity of outputs in some cases.

Bai et al. propose a Retinex type model Mamba, a state-space model that trades out traditional self-attention [10]. By decomposing the images using learnable filters that impose spatial constancy, Mamba is even able grab long range dependencies without incurring the big-O overhead that Transformers suffer from. While sticking to its guns for fidelity and efficiency, Mamba is 8–20x faster than the majority of Transformer based solutions. Maybe not the best recovering such scenes with a very complex lighting distribution between dark and bright. With a tiny memory load and linear computational size, it may run for inference on your mobile tasks too. Guiding the illumination estimation with convolutional side branches, Mamba stabilises its performance across weak and strong exposure lighting distributions. Mamba's got its generalisation loving arms wrapped around it, or at least needs a little more through cross-dataset evaluation.

2.2 Deep Learning-Based Methods

Deep learning based low-light image enhancement methods can be divided into several categories [1–3]. Methods based on Retinex theory combine Retinex theory with different prior regularization optimization models [4–8]. However, they often encounter problems such as over-enhancement, under-enhancement, and noise. Curve estimation-based methods, such as Zero-DCE, estimate pixel-wise curves to enhance low-light images but may introduce noise [11,12]. Generative adversarial network-based methods use generators and discriminators to enhance images, but some suffer from poor robustness and instability [14]. Recently, methods based on Transformer models, such as Retinexformer and LLFormer, have shown strong potential in low-light image enhancement by effectively capturing global contextual information [9,15,16,20,21].

Guo et al. proposed a zero-reference deep curve estimation approach for enhancing low-light images [11]. It uses a lightweight CNN to predict pixel-wise adjustment curves without any ground-truth reference images. This makes the model suitable for real-time applications and deployment on mobile devices.

It introduces a set of unsupervised loss functions to regulate brightness, contrast, and spatial consistency. Despite its speed and simplicity, Zero-DCE can introduce noise and shows limitations in extremely dark inputs. An important contribution of Zero-DCE is the formulation of exposure control as a learnable parametric curve estimation task. This avoids processing of the histogram but uses spatial smoothness and exposure control losses to achieve photorealistic outcomes. That said, as Zero-DCE is trained on synthetic underexposure, it may not behave as desired on noisy real images.

Jiang et al. developed EnlightenGAN, a GAN method that requires no paired supervision [14]. An attention-driven self-regularized enhancement mechanism was proposed to iteratively improve the results. The generator maps low-light images to images under proper illumination using a learned enhancement function, whereas the discriminator is used to ensure realistic outcomes. The main benefits of this method are its flexibility with respect to dataset and good capacity to generalize, and the main weakness is the possible hallucination of details or artifacts in very noisy inputs. Additionally, EnlightenGAN uses attention-guided residual blocks that improve illumination restoration in salient regions. Its perceptual and style-consistency losses ensure output distributions are consistent with natural statistics across animated and live-action datasets. However, it suffers from instabilities during adversarial training and is unreliable when deployed across heterogeneous image domains.

Wang et al. used a U-Net-like model to estimate an illumination map together with enhancement and refinement modules [13]. The method focuses on modelling lighting accurately, thus performing well on underexposed scenes where lighting is critical. Importantly it does increase the overall consistency of brightness, but does not effectively preserve smaller texture structures in difficult noise conditions. One of the interesting aspects of this work was the illumination-aware loss function, and edge-preserving refinement steps to retain structure. The network has three main stages: an illumination estimation module, an image enhancement module, and a detail refinement module.

Wang et al. proposed LLFormer for ultra-high-definition low-light image enhancement [15]. It uses hierarchical Transformer layers to allow global refinement that maintains local details, and hybrid attention across spatial and channel dimensions. LLFormer is built on a multi-level encoder-decoder transformer backbone. Long-range dependencies are captured by using window-based self-attention and different deformable attention layers in each encoder block. This allows the model to better deal with different kinds of spatially variant illumination and texture degradation on multiple scales. Experiments on UHD datasets such as SID and LOL-v2 show that LLFormer consistently outperforms CNN based baselines and previous Transformer based models in PSNR and SSIM scores. However, the model is not suitable for low-resource or real-time settings due to its heavy memory usage.

2.3 Summary

Although existing low-light image enhancement methods have made great strides, we are not there yet. Traditional and Retinex-based methods are typically simple and interpretable, but they often result in halo artifacts, color distortion, and lack of adaptability. Deep learning methods, on the other hand, greatly improve the quality of enhancements but still face challenges in generalization, noise suppression, and computational efficiency. In particular, current Transformer-based and hybrid approaches show great promise as they are better at capturing global contextual information while preserving local structure [18]. These motivative factors lead to the use of contextual Transformer-based enhancement architectures, which are most relevant for the present study [19].

3 Proposed Method

3.1 Contextual Transformer Based Network

A low light image enhancement network model based on a contextual Transformer is proposed. First, a dynamic convolutional network is used to perform shallow feature extraction on the input low light image. Then, the contextual Transformer module (SCTB) is employed for deep feature extraction with global correlation. The SCTB combines the advantages of Swin Transformer style window attention [21], pyramid denoising, and local context enhancement for low light image restoration.

The window scheme is shifted between layers to increase overlaps between windows so that they may learn from adjacent areas more effectively. This method is largely inspired by the architecture of the Swin Transformer, which excels at efficiently handling global modelling at the same time as retaining the ability to do long range relations. This is of critical importance in scenarios involving highly localised areas of illumination.

While fairly good global perception is achieved by attention mechanisms, they lose some finer local spatial structures such as texture boundaries and edges. To alleviate this, SCTB adopts the Local Context Enhancement Block (LCEB). LCEB uses depth-wise separable convolutions and layer normalization to cleanse the local context feature maps and promote spatial continuity. The integration of the fully connected and Img2Tokens / Tokens2Img components provides an effective projection from image space to token embedding space and vice versa, along with smoother feature projection in the attention pipeline. LCEB is inspired by convolutional enhancements from CeiT [23], which ensures that the local context is preserved even as the spatial structure is abstracted into global tokens.

Figure 1 illustrates the internal composition of the Spatial Contextual Transformer Block (SCTB), integrating pyramid denoising, local context enhancement, and Swin Transformer style window attention. By combining shallow convolutional extraction, contextual Transformer modelling, and local enhancement operations, the proposed model is designed to improve illumination recovery while preserving texture details and suppressing noise in low light images. This design enables the model to effectively integrate both local feature extraction and global contextual modeling, which is essential for handling spatially non-uniform illumination in low-light images.

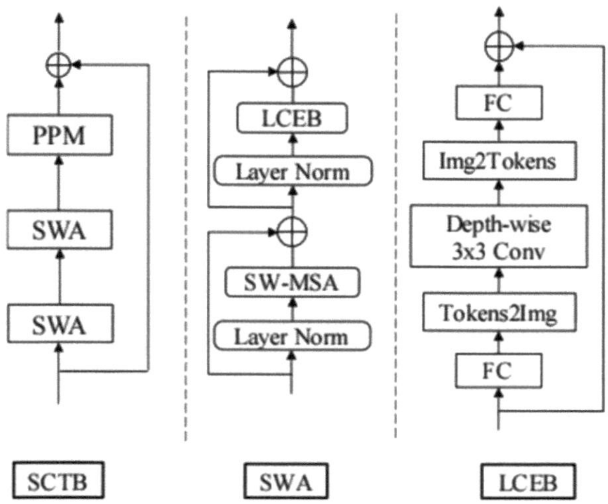

Fig. 1. SCTB.

3.2 Brief Note on the Secondary Model

Based on the previous work, a local global dual branch feature enhancement network is also designed. In the local feature extraction branch, a U shaped network structure is adopted for local feature extraction [24]. In the global feature extraction branch, the height width Transformer module is used for global feature extraction. In the local global feature fusion module, a channel attention mechanism is introduced to adaptively select information of different spatial scales and balance the feature weights of the two branches for optimal fusion [25].

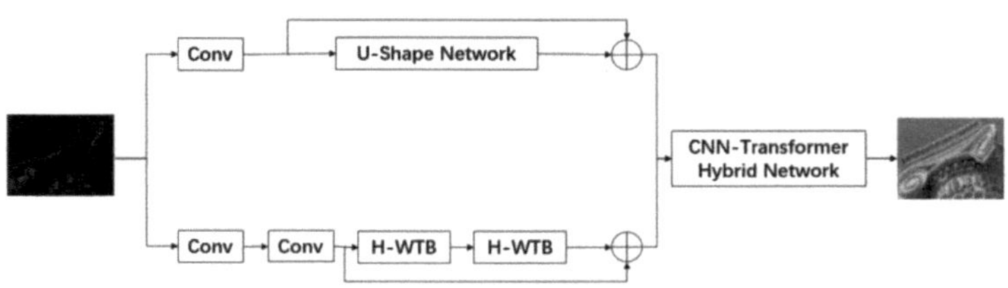

Fig. 2. Local Global Dual Branch Feature Enhancement Network.

In this paper, however, the contextual Transformer based network is treated as the primary model and the main focus of method analysis.

The architecture is illustrated in Fig. 2 with an illustration showing the two branches: local U-shaped convolutional network and global Transformer for feature extraction, followed by a feature fusion module which automatically joins the two.

4 Results and Evaluation

4.1 Experimental Setup

The experiments are conducted under a standard deep learning environment. The datasets used include LOL-v1, LOL-v2, and ExDark [22,26], which are widely used benchmark datasets for low-light image enhancement tasks. With a variety of large public datasets containing both paired and unpaired low-light images under diverse lighting conditions, we are able to easily compare enhancement performance between methods on a broad spectrum of examples.

4.2 Loss Function and Evaluation Metrics

For quantitative evaluation of the model performance, PSNR and SSIM were adopted [1,2]. Where PSNR is a measure of the reconstruction quality of the enhanced images with respect to the ground truth images, while SSIM measures the similarity between the enhanced and the ground truth images.

PSNR is computed between the enhanced image and the reference image as a measure of pixel-level reconstruction quality, indicating the level of distortion in the restored image. SSIM assesses the similarity between two images in terms of luminance, contrast, and structure, and is better aligned with human visual perception.

Such metrics are frequently used for qualitative evaluation of performance on low-light image enhancement. Higher PSNRs and SSIMs suggest better enhancement performance and improvement in visual quality of reconstructed images.

4.3 Quantitative Results

Both models are tested against standard LLIE datasets (LOL-v1, LOL-v2, ExDark) [22,26] and reach competitive results in PSNR and SSIM scores. The abbreviations LOL-v2-R and LOL-v2-S denote the real and synthetic subsets of the LOL-v2 dataset, respectively. The proposed approach demonstrates strong performance across different datasets and maintains robustness under diverse low-light scenarios (Table 1).

Table 1. Quantitative comparison on benchmark datasets

Model	LOL-v1 PSNR	LOL-v1 SSIM	LOL-v2-R PSNR	LOL-v2-R SSIM	LOL-v2-S PSNR	LOL-v2-S SSIM
Contextual Transformer Network	22.31	0.8180	23.48	0.8643	17.12	0.7835
Local–Global Dual Branch Network	21.00	0.8177	22.46	0.8635	16.93	0.7831

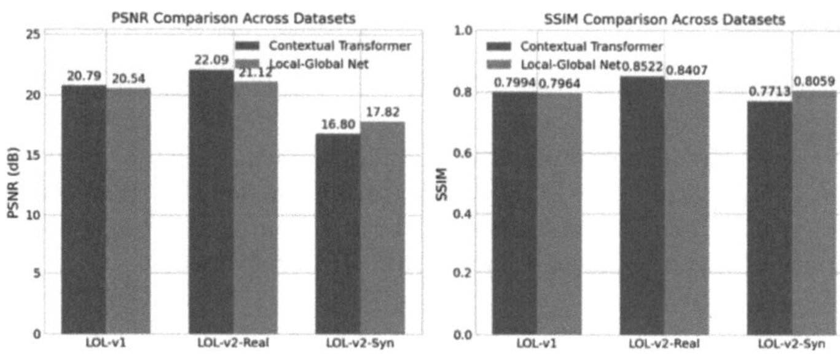

Fig. 3. PSNR / SSIM across LOL-v1, LOL-v2-Real, LOL-v2-Syn.

4.4 Qualitative Visual Comparison

Qualitative comparisons show that the proposed model produces visually pleasing results with improved brightness, enhanced contrast, and better preservation of details. The enhanced images exhibit clearer structures and reduced noise, especially in extremely low-light conditions. Compared with representative methods such as Zero-DCE [11], EnlightenGAN [14], and LLFormer [15], the proposed models are able to avoid over-enhancement and color distortion while maintaining natural visual appearance., the proposed model can avoid over-enhancement and color distortion while maintaining natural visual appearance (Fig. 3).

As shown in Fig. 4, the Contextual Transformer Network tend to produce more uniform global illumination across the whole scene. In contrast, the Local–Global Dual Branch Network does a better job preserving local texture and fine details especially around the edges and small objects.

The LOL-v2 dataset is composed of real captured low-light images with more complex illumination conditions than those in LOL-v1, with more considerable variations in brightness and darker areas. As illustrated in Fig. 5, similar visual behaviours are consistent over the other LOL-v2 test samples, of which this example is meant to represent the typical enhancement behaviour of the proposed models on the LOL-v2 dataset.

Since ExDark contains real images captured in extremely low-light conditions, paired normal-light ground truth images are not available. Thus we focus

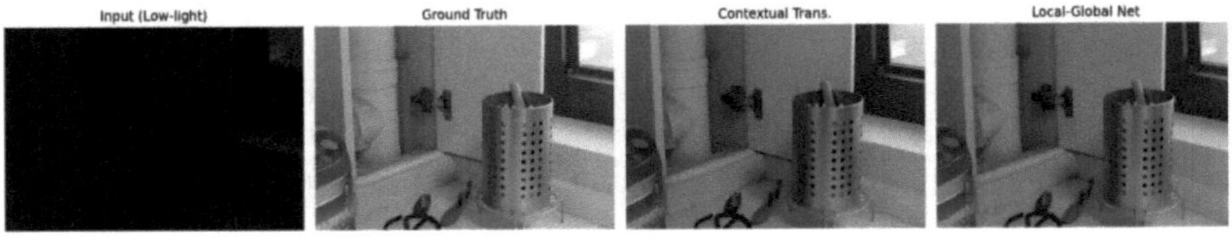

Fig. 4. Qualitative results on the LOL-v1 dataset.

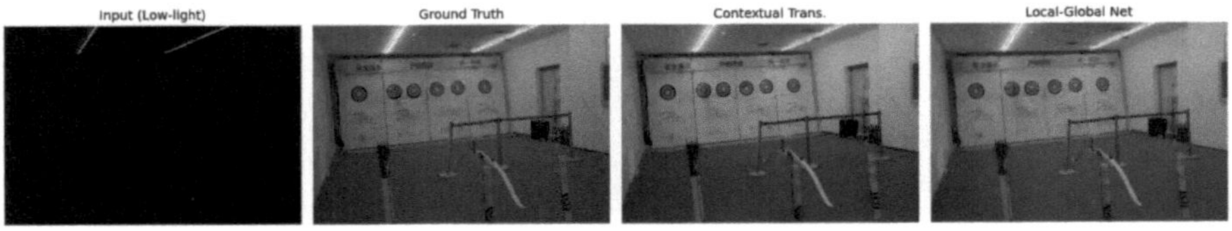

Fig. 5. Qualitative visual comparison of low-light image enhancement results on a representative sample from the LOL-v2 dataset. From left to right: low-light input image, ground-truth image, results produced by the Contextual Transformer Network, and results produced by the Local–Global Dual Branch Network.

qualitative evaluation on ExDark on aspects like the visibility of the scene, contrast enhancement, and the appearance of colours rather than direct comparison with a reference image. As shown in Fig. 6, our models have comparable, stable, and reasonably consistent enhancement behaviour under real world low-light conditions. However, some regions still exhibit noise amplification and incomplete illumination recovery under extremely low-light conditions.

Fig. 6. Qualitative visual comparison of low-light image enhancement results on representative samples from the ExDark dataset. From left to right: low-light input image, results produced by the Contextual Transformer Network, and results produced by the Local–Global Dual Branch Network.

4.5 Analysis

The experimental results demonstrate that the integration of contextual Transformer modeling and local feature enhancement contributes to improved performance. As shown in Fig. 4–6, our model computes illumination recovery better and preserves more detail than existing methods, while avoiding common artifacts like over-enhancement and colour distortion (though can struggle with extremely complex lighting scenarios where performance can be hindered by severe noise or non-uniform illumination).

Overall we achieve competitive quantitative and qualitative performance across different lowlight scenarios demonstrating effectiveness and robustness on low-light image enhancement tasks. This shows the combination of global attention and local feature enhancing allows our model to strike an effective consistency between the two tasks of illumination recovery and detail preservation.

5 Discussion and Conclusion

5.1 Discussion of Experimental Results

The experiments show that the proposed method can compete both quantitatively and qualitatively with the state of the art by combining contextual Transformer modeling and local feature enhancement to improve illumination recovery and structural preservation.

As shown in Figs. 4–6, the enhanced images are brighter, the structure is clearer, and external contrast is recovered even as it is preserved. Our architecture reduces noise while preserving significant texture detail, which is useful for downstream vision tasks. Our experimental results show that both architectures improve across multiple datasets. Results are summarized in Table 2, where we see the PSNR and SSIM perform well across the qualitative visual comparisons, suggesting that the numerical improvements correspond to perceptually meaningful enhancement.

5.2 Role of Global Context Modeling

Transformer-based global modeling is critical for handling non-uniform illumination. Model able to maintain global illumination consistency and semantic coherence throughout the image, capturing long-range dependencies. Compared to purely convolutional methods, the contextual Transformer improves the modeling of complex lighting variations and increases visual quality.

Attention heatmap visualizations further show how the network models global context. As shown in Fig. 7, the attention responses are spread across spatially distant parts and not confined to local neighborhoods, indicating that the Transformer captures long-range illumination dependencies throughout the image.

5.3 Contribution of Local Feature Modeling

Local feature modelling is necessary for preserving the edges, textures and boundaries of objects. The use of local enhancement modules allows important spatial structures to be preserved during the enhancement process.

Table 2. Summary of Experimental Findings and Interpretations

Aspect	Observation	Interpretation
Quantitative Performance	Higher PSNR and SSIM are consistently achieved across LOL-v1 and LOL-v2 datasets	Indicates accurate brightness reconstruction and effective structural preservation
Visual Quality	Enhanced images exhibit improved illumination with reduced noise	Demonstrates visually pleasing enhancement without introducing severe artifacts
Model Comparison	The Contextual Transformer Network achieves slightly higher PSNR values	Global context modeling contributes to improved illumination consistency
Structural Consistency	The Local–Global Dual Branch Network attains comparable SSIM scores	Local feature modeling effectively preserves textures and edges
Generalization Ability	Stable performance is observed on unseen and real-world datasets	Reflects robust architectural design and strong generalization capability

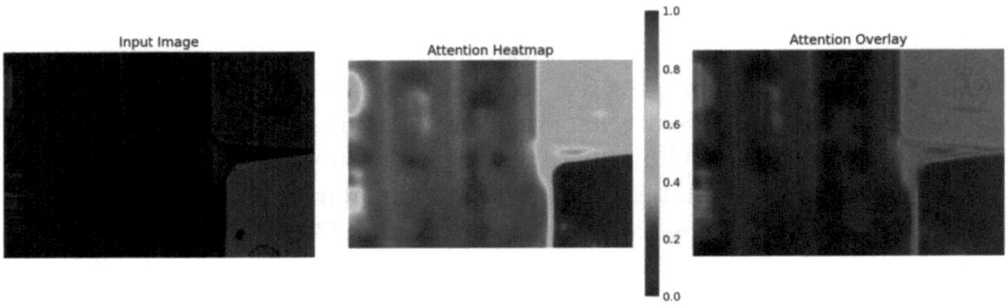

Fig. 7. Visualization of attention responses in the Contextual Transformer Network. From left to right: the low-light input image, the corresponding attention heatmap, and the attention overlay on the input image. The visualization illustrates how the model allocates attention to spatially relevant regions during global illumination estimation.

These two representations enable a careful balance between recovering illumination and preserving detail, as demonstrated by visualising the features (Fig. 8), where the feature responses pick out detailed structures in a texture region, showing that the network is preserving local spatial detail while eliminating noise.

5.4 Generalization and Robustness

The proposed method exhibits good generalization ability on LOL-v1, LOL-v2, ExDark. Even with dramatic variations in illumination and different degrees of scene complexity, the model shows stable performance. As the experimental results show, we are robust to conventional degradation factors such as noise, low contrast and uneven illumination.

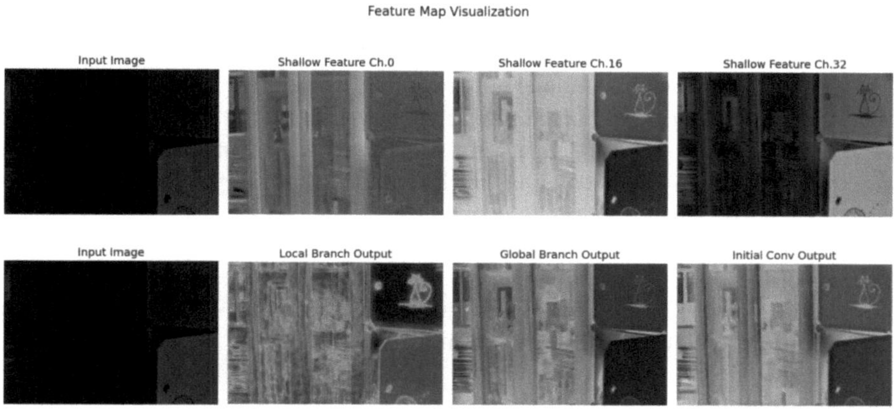

Fig. 8. Feature map visualization of the Local–Global Dual Branch Network at different stages. The first row shows shallow feature responses from early convolutional layers, while the second row illustrates feature responses from the local branch, global branch, and initial convolution layers. These visualizations highlight the complementary roles of local and global feature modeling in preserving structural details and capturing broader illumination information.

5.5 Limitations and Future Work

Despite this positive note, here and there the model falls short. Very difficult lighting conditions still leave it unable to fully recover and eliminate horrifying amounts of noise. The proposed models still show limitations in extremely challenging low-light conditions. In these scenes, both models may fail to fully recover details. Errors become more noticeable in high-frequency regions, such as object boundaries and textured areas. Here, a trade-off exists between detail preservation and noise reduction.

As shown in Fig. 6, several failure cases are evident under challenging low-light conditions. In some regions, the illumination is not fully recovered, and slight over-smoothing may occur, leading to the loss of fine details, especially around edges and textured areas. This limitation reflects the trade-off between illumination enhancement and detail preservation. The Contextual Transformer Network tends to produce smoother results due to global feature aggregation, while the Local–Global Dual Branch Network may struggle to maintain consistent illumination across complex scenes.

In the future, the work will focus on improving robustness under extreme conditions and enhancing the balance between global illumination recovery and local detail preservation. It will also focus on making the models faster, making them applicable to real-time applications, and exploring more advanced architectures or multimodal information.

5.6 Conclusion

This paper studies low-light image enhancement using deep learning approaches with an emphasis on contextual Transformer-based modeling. The approach marries convolution-based local feature extraction with Transformer-based global context modeling, in order to enhance illumination recovery while maintaining structural and textural fidelity.

Experimental results on standard datasets show that the proposed method achieves competitive performance across quantitative metrics and visual quality. The model is found to be robust across various low-light scenarios, offering a viable solution for low-light image enhancement tasks.

Acknowledgments. This research was sponsored by the University of Malaya Translational Research Grant Scheme, TRG0019-2025 (UM.0002388/HRU.IP), and the Research Excellence Grant, UMREG 068-2024 (UM.0000285/HRU.RC).

Author contributions. All authors contributed equally and significantly to writing this article. All authors read and approved the final manuscript.

Conflicts of Interest. The authors declare no conflict of interest.

References

1. Tian, Z., et al.: A survey of deep learning-based low-light image enhancement. Sensors **23**(18), 7763 (2023)
2. Zhan, J., Goh, E.S., Sunar, M.S.: Low-light image enhancement: a comprehensive review on methods, datasets and evaluation metrics. J. King Saud Univ.- Comput. Inf. Sci. **36**, 103713 (2024)
3. Guo, J., Ma, J., García-Fernández, Á.F., Zhang, Y., Liang, H.: A survey on image enhancement for low-light images. Heliyon **9**(5), e16020 (2023)
4. Land, E.H.: The retinex. Am. Sci. **52**(2), 247–264 (1964)
5. Land, E.H., McCann, J.J.: Lightness and retinex theory. J. Opt. Soc. Am. **61**(1), 1–11 (1971)
6. Meng, W., Obaiys, S. J., Karaca, Y., Jamaludin, N. A. B.: Human-Computer Dialogue Systems-Based Image-Text Visualization, Fusion and Multi-Intent Models' Construction. Fractals, **34**(04), 2540136 (2025)
7. Wei, C., Wang, W., Yang, W., Liu, J.: Deep retinex decomposition for low-light image enhancement. In: BMVC (2018)
8. Liu, R., Ma, L., Zhang, J., Fan, X., Luo, Z.: Retinex-inspired unrolling with cooperative prior architecture search for low-light image enhancement. In: CVPR, pp. 1056110570 (2021)
9. Cai, Y., Bian, H., Lin, J., Wang, H., Timofte, R., Zhang, Y.: Retinexformer: one stage Retinex-based transformer for low-light image enhancement. In: ICCV, pp. 1250412513 (2023)
10. Bai, J., Yin, Y., He, Q., Li, Y., Zhang, X.: Retinex-based Mamba for low-light image enhancement. arXiv preprint arXiv:2405.03349 (2024)
11. Guo, C., Li, C., Guo, J., Loy, C.C., Hou, J., Kwong, S., Cong, R.: Zero-reference deep curve estimation for low-light image enhancement. In: CVPR, pp. 1780–1789 (2020)

12. Li, C., et al.: Learning to enhance low-light image via zero-reference deep curve estimation. IEEE Trans. Pattern Anal. Mach. Intell. **44**(12), 9396–9416 (2021)
13. Wang, R., et al.: Underexposed photo enhancement using deep illumination estimation. In: CVPR, pp. 68496857 (2019)
14. Jiang, Y., et al.: EnlightenGAN: deep light enhancement without paired supervision. IEEE Trans. Image Process. **30**, 2340–2349 (2021)
15. Wang, T., Zhang, K., Shen, T., Luo, W., Stenger, B., Lu, T.: Ultra-high-definition low-light image enhancement: a benchmark and transformer-based method. In: AAAI, pp. 26522660 (2023)
16. Ruan, Y., Ma, H., Li, W., Wang, X.: ECAFormer: low-light image enhancement using cross attention. arXiv preprint arXiv:2406.13281 (2024)
17. Brateanu, A., Balmez, R., Avram, A., Orhei, C., Ancuti, C.: LYT-NET: lightweight YUV transformer for low-light image enhancement. arXiv preprint arXiv:2401.15204 (2024)
18. Wang, Y., et al.: Expo sureDiusion: learning to expose for low-light image enhancement. In: ICCV, pp. 1254512554 (2023)
19. Lore, K.G., Akintayo, A., Sarkar, S.: LLNet: a deep autoencoder approach to natural low-light image enhancement. Pattern Recogn. **61**, 650–662 (2017)
20. Zamir, S.W., Arora, A., Khan, S., Hayat, M., Khan, F.S., Yang, M.-H.: Restormer: efficient transformer for high-resolution image restoration. In: CVPR, pp. 5718–5729 (2022)
21. Liang, J., et al.: SwinIR: image restoration using Swin Transformer. In: ICCV, pp. 18331844 (2021)
22. Chen, C., et al.: Learning to see in the dark. In: CVPR, pp. 32913300 (2018)
23. Yuan, K., Guo, S., Liu, Z., Zhou, A., Yu, F., Wu, W.: Incorporating convolution designs into visual transformers. In: ICCV, pp. 579588 (2021)
24. Ronneberger, O., Fischer, P., Brox, T.: U-Net: Convolutional networks for biomedical image segmentation. In: MICCAI, pp. 234241 (2015)
25. Hu, J., Shen, L., Sun, G.: Squeeze-and-excitation networks. In: CVPR, pp. 7132 7141 (2018)
26. Loh, Y.P., Chan, C.S.: Getting to know low-light images with the exclusively dark dataset. Comput. Vis. Image Underst. **178**, 30–42 (2019)

Lightweight Ratio-Guided Weight Scale Control for Backpropagation Neural Networks in Iot Intrusion Detection with Binary and Multiclass Evaluation

Nada Asim Abdulhameed[1], Nadia M. G. Al-Saidi[1], Suzan J. Obaiys[2](✉), and Ahmed T. Sadiq[3]

[1] Department of Mathematics and Computer Applications, College of Applied Sciences, University of Technology, Baghdad, Iraq
{nada.a.abulhameed,nadia.m.ghanim}@uotechnology.edu.iq

[2] Department of Computer System and Technology, Faculty of Computer Science and Information Technology, Universiti Malaya, 50603 Kuala Lumpur, Malaysia
suzan@um.edu.my

[3] Multimedia and Digital Media Department, College of Computer Sciences, University of Technology, Baghdad, Iraq
ahmed.t.sadiq@uotechnology.edu.iq

Abstract. The rapid growth of the Internet of Things (IoT) has posed several challenges, such as large volumes of heterogeneous and imbalanced traffic data, which are challenging for traditional learning methods. This study proposes a Weight Scaling (WS) mechanism that augments standard backpropagation by modulating the weight updates using information from previous optimization states. The goal is not to change the use of gradient descent, but to see whether controlling the weights according to the trajectory can make learning more stable with simple computation. A common preprocessing pipeline was applied, by removing non-informative attributes, encoding categorical features, normalizing, and handling missing and infinite values. Two benchmark datasets are used in the experiments, which are carried out on varying levels of difficulty. The first is the Internet of Things Intrusion Detection Dataset 2020 (IoT-ID20) for binary intrusion detection and Telemetry, Operating System, and Network Internet of Things (TON-IoT) for multi-class attack classification. We evaluated performance using test accuracy, macro-F1 score, confusion matrices, convergence behavior, training efficiency, and applied McNemar's statistical test. We find that the WS effect is highly dataset-dependent. On IoT-ID20, standard backpropagation outperformed the WS-enhanced version (95.78% vs 90.53%) and significantly fewer false positives, suggesting a more favorable precision–recall balance for practice deployment. For the TON-IoT, both methods had similar results, with a marginal difference in accuracy (94.01% > 93.75%). We can conclude that the weight scale does not improve accuracy, but it provides useful knowledge about trajectory-aware learning behavior and the need for multiple context-specific evaluations in cybersecurity applications.

O. Gervasi et al. (Eds.): ICCSA 2026 Workshops, LNCS 16758, pp. 238–254, 2027.
https://doi.org/10.1007/978-3-032-30497-1_15

1 Introduction

The Internet of Things (IoT) is an emerging technology that has emerged with the accelerated growth of our new era. It is used to redefine our modern life by connecting smart homes, wearables, industrial systems, and autonomous platforms into vast data environments. While this connectivity enhances automation, monitoring, and decision-making, it also increases the attack surface for cybersecurity threats [1, 2]. With billions of devices constantly communicating with each other, the size and complexity of network traffic increases, making timely threat detection highly challenging. Classic signature-based intrusion detection systems (IDS), which compare traffic to known attack patterns, remain useful for addressing threats that have already been discovered, yet are less efficient at learning and detecting unseen attacks [3]. The reliance on manual rule building has significantly limited scalability in heterogeneous Internet of Things environments, where devices vary widely in protocols, computing capabilities, and security designs.

Machine learning (ML) is an emerging technology that develops and studies statistical algorithms that can learn from data, generalize to new data, and carry out tasks without explicit instructions. Neural networks are among the most appealing machine learning techniques as they can model nonlinear dependencies in multidimensional feature space [4]. The Backpropagation Neural Network (BPNN) represents the fundamental supervised learning architecture. It is considered important due to its simplicity conceptually and theoretical basis, while offering an armament for a flexible general framework for most applicable tasks [2]. In conventional BP learning, the model parameters are iteratively updated by propagating the prediction error backward through the network and adjusting the weights to minimize the loss [5]. Despite these advantages, regular BP faces optimization problems when used with large-scale intrusion-detection data. These heuristics may converge slowly in practice, exhibit oscillatory loss behavior, and be highly sensitive to the choice of learning rate. These problems were most pronounced in datasets sourced from cybersecurity contexts, which exhibit class imbalance, noisy features, and complex, coalescing decision boundaries. Therefore, the machine learning literature has proposed a range of optimization enhancements to address these issues, from momentum-based methods [6, 7] to adaptive learning-rate techniques, such as Adam [8] and RMSprop [9]. Although these methods are effective, they often add complexity in the form of extra hyperparameters or computation. This drives research into lightweight alternatives that can control learning dynamics with minimal increase in training complexity.

In this work, we examine a simple trajectory-aware enhancement over the one that relies only on the current gradient by adding a new term, WS. The WS incorporates information from consecutive weight states to regulate update behavior. The main idea is that, by changing weights through iterations, useful information about training stability emerged. If consecutive weights change smoothly, learning is likely to be stable; if their relative change becomes sharp, the update process begins to plunge into an unstable region. Starting from tracking ratios only, WS aims to both stabilize optimization and retain the elegance of classical BP by using a bounded correction in the update rule. This mechanism is conceptually distinct from momentum. Momentum builds a history of gradients to hasten movement in promising directions [10, 11], whereas WS targets the weight trajectory itself.

Basically, it checks whether the next update aligns with the parameters of the recent trajectory. Moreover, since the WS calculation requires only simple element-wise operations, it adds very little computational cost and is free of has no tuning parameters, such as momentum coefficients. This is attractive for many applications that require training on limited resources and operational overhead during implementation, such as intrusion detection problems [12, 13].

An intrusion detection system (IDS) is a network security tool that monitors network traffic and devices for known malicious activity, suspicious activity, or security policy violations. It provides a test tool for evaluating optimization strategies. In our chosen datasets, the first intrusion detection datasets are often highly imbalanced, with normal traffic greatly outnumbering attack traffic. The second network data are typically high-dimensional and may contain overlapping or subtle attack patterns, complicating classification. The practical deployment imposes competing requirements: false negatives may allow attacks to go undetected, whereas false positives lead to alert fatigue among security analysts. Therefore, an optimization method should be judged not only by overall accuracy, but also by its effect on class-wise performance and error distribution. Finally, the field offers benchmark datasets that support reproducible assessment. In this study, we use IoT-ID20 [14] for binary intrusion detection and TON-IoT [15] for multi-class attack classification, allowing comparability across various problem topologies.

Now, to justify adding the WS, we have to demonstrate that it improves convergence stability and classification performance compared to conventional BP. Moreover, the performance of the new BP with WS is unaffected by the dataset properties. This can be done by an evaluation framework that extends beyond overall accuracy. We analyze confusion matrices, per-class metrics, convergence behavior, and statistical significance using McNemar's test [16]. This broader assessment is important because accuracy alone can obscure weak performance in minority classes or undesirable error trade-offs [17].

This work presents four main contributions. Firstly, we present a low-cost WS approach that extends classical BP with information from several optimization states in sequence. Secondly, we report a detailed empirical comparison of BP and BP-based WS over two widely accepted intrusion detection datasets. Thirdly, we demonstrate that the impact of WS is highly context-dependent and can yield larger discrepancies for typical imbalanced binary classification than multi-class classification. Fourth, we highlight the methodological importance of assessing optimization strategies using multiple criteria rather than relying on accuracy alone. In practical terms, this development is important for cost-focused applications such as cybersecurity, where the costs of false alarms and missed detections can vary significantly.

The remaining parts of this paper are organized as follows. In Sect. 2, some related literature is introduced with its advantages and disadvantages. The methodology, including neural network optimization and intrusion detection principles, as well as the mathematical formulation of the BP and WS mechanisms, is introduced in Sect. 3. Section 4 presents the experimental results, including convergence analysis and statistical testing, and analyzes them. Finally, Sect. 5 concludes the work.

2 Related Work

A recent study on intrusion detection for IoT and network settings has moved from classical machine-learning pipelines to more adaptive deep-learning architectures. By 2024 and 2025, systematic reviews demonstrated that the field is now dominated by architectures that integrate automated feature learning with increasingly sophisticated handling of datasets, preprocessing, computational efficiency, and other evaluation metrics. These reviews also highlight ongoing issues, such as false positives, class imbalance, resource limitations, and the need for realistic benchmark datasets and fair validation protocols [3, 6, 7].

Significant work has been done in designing a new network architecture to identify intrusions more accurately. Banaamah et al. [13] discussed CNN, LSTM, and GRU-based deep learning models for IoT intrusion detection, validated neural network-based detectors, and emphasized their continued value in this context. Roy et al. [18] proposed a two-layer fog–cloud IDS that explicitly considers the IoT resource constraints, thereby demonstrating that the deployment architecture is an important design factor. Subsequent work took further steps towards hybrid deep models: Dina et al. [19] proposed focal-loss-based training for IoT intrusion detection; Jablaoui et al. [20] used CNN and GRU integrations to capture spatial and temporal structures; Zhang et al. [21] proposed a CNN-BiLSTM Transformer pipeline with feature selection and class imbalance.

Class imbalance is another common theme that attracts many researchers in the latest literature, as one of the most significant challenges in IDS research. Shanmugam et al. [22] demonstrated that data imbalance significantly affects IDS performance. They demand the use of evaluation metrics such as F1-score and G-mean to look beyond accuracy. This concern is echoed in architecture-level studies that employ resampling or specialized loss functions for deep models. Deng et al. [23] applied focal loss to enhance minority class detection in IoT data, and recent work has proposed equalization-loss formulations and attention-boosted few-shot learning to improve accuracy under highly skewed distributions. These studies suggest that the performance of modern IDS is influenced not just by the choice of classifier, but also by how minority classes are represented during training [24].

Another research focused on interpretability and deployability. For example, Ahmad et al. [25] proposed XGRU-IDS to unify feature selection. Alabbadi et al. [26] designed an explainable IDS based on a compressed representation of TON IoT data streams using deep learning and XAI techniques. They dedicated their effort to security issues. Results on state-of-the-art multi-attention CNN–BiGRU frameworks, e.g., demonstrate strong detection capabilities with an explicit focus towards lightweight deployment and leakage-free handling of imbalance. Together, these studies indicate that state-of-the-art IDS research is increasingly assessing models not simply by predictive accuracy, but by interpretability, efficiency, and robustness to realistic data conditions [27].

Although there are recent works on novel hybrid architectures, feature-selection pipelines, data resampling strategies, problem-specific loss functions, and explainable AI, relatively little attention has been paid to lightweight modifications of the classical backpropagation update rule itself as an object of study on modern IoT intrusion-detection benchmarks. This interprets the gap that, rather than implementing a more sophisticated design, one may wonder whether optimization-level intervention can enhance learning behavior while maintaining the low complexity and transparency of conventional feed-forward neural networks. To bridge this gap, the current work examines a trajectory-aware (Weight Scaling strategy) integrated into backpropagation and assesses it using current benchmark data in binary and multi-class intrusion detection scenarios. This study differs from more recent architecture-specific IDS work due to its framing [2, 3, 8, 12, 14].

3 Methodology

3.1 Intrusion Detection System

Intrusion Detection Systems (IDS) play a crucial role in network security, as they automatically monitor and analyze network behaviors to detect unusual and/or dangerous activity. Standards are used to measure the validity of presented evidence, and IDS mainly focuses on identifying intrusions. An intrusion occurs when a computer or network breaks down, and the computers deviate from their original functions, serving as a vehicle for attacks that illegally access or misuse data on the network. In today's highly interconnected environment, where sensitive information is exchanged and stored, an IDS serves as a cybersecurity tool alongside antivirus software and firewalls. Firewalls perform initial scans of web traffic. These systems play a crucial role in managing, monitoring, and maintaining the normal operation of networks, immediately alerting network administrators upon detecting any abnormal activity or threats to their information [2].

3.2 Datasets and Data Preprocessing

In this study, two types of datasets were used for IoT intrusion detection: IoT-ID20 and TON-IoT. IoT-ID20 is an IoT-specific intrusion detection dataset that captures network traffic patterns from IoT devices under both normal operation and various cyber-attack scenarios [14]. The TON_IoT datasets are new generations of Industry 4.0/Internet of Things (IoT) and Industrial IoT (IIoT) datasets for evaluating the fidelity and efficiency of different cybersecurity applications based on Artificial Intelligence (AI), i.e., Machine/Deep Learning algorithms [15]. These datasets are represented in Table 1.

Table 1. Datasets information

features	samples	type	dataset
46	625,783	binary	IoTID20
61	461,043	Multi-class	TON_IoT

Data preprocessing includes:

I- One-hot encoding

When encoding features for the class attribute c of a class K: $c \in \{v_1, v_2, \ldots, v_k\}$. It is transformed into a binary vector: $\varnothing(c) = [I(c = v_1), I(c = v_2), \ldots, I(c = v_k)]$, where the indicator function is:

$$I(condition) = \begin{cases} 1, & if\ condition\ is\ true \\ 0, & otherwise \end{cases}$$

This prevents artificial order relationships between categories.

II- Factorization Encoding

For high-cardinality attributes, categorical values are mapped into integers:

$$c_i \rightarrow k, k \in \{0, 1, \ldots, K - 1\}$$

This maintains control over dimensional growth.

III- Minimum and maximum features and their normalization

To ensure comparability between feature metrics, each numerical feature x was normalized to the interval [0,1] as follows: $x_{norm} = \frac{x - x_{min}}{x_{max} - x_{min}}$

where x_{min} and x_{max} are computed from the training data. This transformation reduces the gradient instability and accelerates convergence during backpropagation.

IV- Handling Missing and Infinite Values

Assuming that the future value is x_{ij}, so the replacement of invalid values is as follows:

$$x_{ij} = \begin{cases} 0, & x_{ij} \in \{NaN, -\infty, +\infty\} \\ x_{ij}, & otherwise \end{cases}$$

This reduces the number of numerical inputs required to compute the stable gradient.

3.3 Standard Backpropagation Neural Network

In our study, we used a feedforward neural network [28, 29] and trained it using the classical backpropagation algorithm [5]. The network structure consists of three main layers: the input layer, the hidden layer, and the output layer. In the hidden layer, we used the sigmoid activation function. In the output layer, the activation function varied depending on the nature of the classification task. For binary classification problems, we used the sigmoid function, while for multiclass classification, we used the SoftMax function. The outputs of the hidden layer in the forward propagation process were calculated as follows:

$$h = \sigma(XW_1 + b_1)$$

Where X represents the input properties, W_1 represents the weights relating the input and hidden layers, and b_1 is the bias vector. The output layer is then calculated as follows:

$$Y = \begin{cases} \sigma(hW_2 + b_2), & binary\ classification \\ softmax(hW_2 + b_2), & multi - class\ classification \end{cases}$$

W_2 represents the weights relating the hidden and output layers, and b_2 is the bias vector.

3.4 Adaptive Weight Scaling

Since weights in the backpropagation algorithm are chosen at random, an idea for improving weights is introduced. To achieve stable weight development during the training process, a term Weight Scale (WS) was introduced, which measures the relative change between the ratios of previous and current weight states, and is defined as follows:

$$WS_t = \frac{W(t)}{W(t-1)}$$

This ratio provides insight into the convergence behavior of the learning process, so when $WS \approx 1$ indicates stable learning, large deviations indicate unstable updates, while gradual convergence reflects a move towards optimal weight formation.

The WS term was directly integrated into the update dynamics to monitor and guide the learning path in terms of error reduction and achieving optimal weights. For error reduction, the loss function was used, and has two formulations depending on the type of classification of the datasets. For a binary intrusion detection dataset, a Weighted Binary Cross-Entropy is a modified loss function (instead of the mean square error function MSE). This function was used to handle unbalanced classes:

$$L = -\frac{1}{N}\sum w_i[y_i log(y_i) + (1 - y_i)\log(1 - y_i)]$$

For the multi-class intrusion detection dataset, the SoftMax cross-entropy loss function was implemented as follows:

$$L = -\frac{1}{N}\sum_{i=1}^{N}\sum_{c=1}^{C} y_{ic}\log(y_{ic})$$

The training aims to reduce verification loss, and its value was chosen as follows:

$$Validation\ Loss \leq 0.1$$

3.5 Optimization Strategy Based on Updated Weight

Although the classical backpropagation algorithm has proven effective for training neural networks, some challenges remain. These include slow convergence, especially in the early training phases, and fluctuating behavior during weight updates, leading to instability in training dynamics. The backpropagation algorithm has also shown that the learning rate is a highly sensitive parameter. This issue was most evident in the final stage of intrusion detection, where large datasets were used. Drawing these observations, we wanted to develop an adaptive update mechanism that addresses all of these issues without sacrificing the core principles of the backpropagation algorithm. We propose an approach based on the weight scale ratio that guides weight evolution and ultimately reduces error; hence, it can be used in IDS.

3.5.1 Classical Gradient Update

Firstly, let's briefly review the standard backpropagation update rule at each iteration t:

$$W_{t+1}^{l} = W_{t}^{l} + \eta \frac{\partial L}{\partial W_{t}^{l}}$$

where η represents the learning rate, l denotes our loss function, and t indexes the current iteration.

3.5.2 Weight Scale Ratio (WS)

We formulate the weight scale ratio by initializing the weight with the value of 10^{-8}, where W_t represents the current weights, W_{t-1} denotes the previous weights, ε is added to avoid division by zero, therefore,

$$WS_t = \frac{W_t}{W_{t-1} + \varepsilon}$$

From the experiments, we found that unrestricted WS values can sometimes lead to numerical instability, especially in convergent regions or in regions with steep curvature. This can be prevented by limiting the interval:

$$OR_t^{bounded} = clip(OR_t, 0.9,1.1)$$

This ratio is constrained to a range via clipping, which has shown good experimental stability over the evaluated IoT-ID dataset. These limits ensure that the WS correction stays moderate and does not dominate the update. However, the WS mechanism is incorporated into backpropagation via a modified update rule as follows.

$$W_{t+1} = W_t + \eta \nabla L + OR_t^{bounded}$$

This formulation differs fundamentally from the momentum-based formulation [10].

4 Experimental Setup and Analysis

In our Experiment, the dataset was divided into three parts: training, testing, and validation.

- IoT-ID20 dataset:

A training phase section, a testing phase section, and a validation phase section. For the training phase, 70% of the data (438,048 samples) was used. For the testing phase, 15% (93,868 samples) was used; for the validation phase, 15% (93,867 samples) was used.

- TON-IoT dataset:

For a training phase, 70% of the data (147,730 samples) was used. For the testing phase, 15% (31,656 samples) were used, and for the validation phase, 15% (31,657 samples) were used.

The experiments were conducted using Python 3.8 with the NumPy 1.21 library for performing the calculations [30]. The central processing unit is an Intel Core i7 without using the graphics processing unit acceleration, and the architecture relies on a single hidden layer in the neural network. Table 2 shows the complete experimental configuration.

Table 2. Complete Experimental Configuration

Parameter	Value
Hidden layer neurons	64
Batch size	512
Learning rate	0.1
Maximum epochs	200
Convergence threshold	Val loss ≤ 0.1
Weight initialization	Xavier uniform
Random seed	42
OR clipping bounds	[0.9, 1.1]
OR epsilon	10^{-8}
Train/Val/Test split	70%/15%/15%
Programming language	Python 3.8
Framework	NumPy 1.21
Hardware	Intel i7 CPU

We also used some metrics that indicate whether an attack has occurred. First, we must understand some of the terminology related to metrics to understand them [31, 32].

- True Positives (TP): Measures the number of attack patterns correctly classified as attacks.
- False Positives (FP): Measures the percentage of normal patterns that were incorrectly classified as attacks.
- True Negative (TN): The TN score calculates the percentage of normal patterns correctly classified.
- False Negative (FN): The False Negative Score calculates the number of attack patterns incorrectly classified as normal.

$$\text{Accuracy} = \frac{TP + TN}{\text{TP} + \text{FP} + \text{TN} + \text{FN}}$$

$$\text{Precision} = \frac{TP}{\text{TP} + \text{FP}}$$

$$\text{Recall} = \frac{TP}{TP + FN}$$

$$\text{F1} - \text{Score} = 2 \times \frac{\text{Precision} \times \text{Recall}}{\text{Precision} + \text{Recall}}$$

To assess the effectiveness of the learning approach proposed in this study, we designed a comprehensive comparison and evaluation using two datasets for penetration detection. We primarily compared the standard backpropagation (BP) algorithm with our modified version, which incorporates a weight scale ratio (WS) mechanism.

The Algorithm

Input: dataset D, hidden layer H, learning rate η, epochs E, batch size B, validation loss threshold τ, and stability constant ε.

Output: trained BP+ WS model, validation history, and final test metrics.

1. Read the dataset, remove invalid target rows, and discard non-informative attributes.
2. Encode categorical variables using one-hot encoding: for low cardinality features, factorization: for high cardinality features, and Min-Max scaling: for normalizing all numerical features to the interval [0,1]
3. Split the processed data into training, validation, and test subsets using stratified sampling, then determine the output dimension according to the number of classes.
4. Initialize W_1 and W_2 With Xavier uniform initialization, set $b_1$and b_2 to zero, if not set to zero, they could introduce unwanted initial bias randomly. and store the initial parameters as previous states.
5. For each epoch and each mini-batch, perform forward propagation through the hidden layer using Sigmoid activation and through the output layer using Sigmoid or SoftMax according to the task.
6. Compute the loss gradients using weighted binary cross-entropy for binary classification or SoftMax cross-entropy for multi-class classification.
7. Compute the bounded Weight Scale terms for the consecutive parameter state:
$WS = clip\left(\frac{W}{W_{prev} + \varepsilon}, 0.9, 1.1\right)$.
8. Update parameters by standard gradient descent, then add the WS term using the same learning rate η.
9. After each epoch, evaluate validation loss, validation accuracy, and F1-score. Stop if validation loss reaches τ.
10. Evaluate the final model on the test set and report Accuracy, F1-score, Precision, Recall, Training time, and Confusion matrix.

4.1 The Experimental Results

The traditional backpropagation algorithm consistently achieved lower loss values, indicating a more direct reduction toward the ideal weight. However, the backpropagation algorithm with the weight scale ratio performed well on the TON-IoT dataset, while it showed lower performance on the IoT-ID20 dataset, as shown in Table 3. Figures 1 and 2 show the validation loss and accuracy for backpropagation with a weight-scale ratio to the IoT-ID20 dataset.

Figures 3 and 4 show the validation loss and accuracy for backpropagation with a weight-scale ratio to the TON-IoT dataset.

As for the metrics, we will use them to identify the flaws in each model through the confusion matrix, which reveals specific types of errors and compares false positive FP results to false negative FN results, as shown in Table 4 for the IoT-ID20 dataset:

Confusion matrices for BP and BP + WS on the IoT-ID20 dataset. TN = True Negative, FP = False Positive, FN = False Negative, TP = True Positive are presented in Table 5.

Per-class metrics. Class 0 = Normal, Class 1 = Intrusion, as shown in Table 5.

Table 3. Comprehensive comparison across both datasets.

Metric	BP (IoT-ID20)	BP+WS (IoT-ID20)	BP (TON-IoT)	BP+WS (TON-IoT)
Test Accuracy	0.9578	0.9053	0.9401	0.9375
Test Macro-F1	0.8581	0.7481	0.8914	0.8822
Test Loss	0.1544	0.2307	0.1906	0.2004
Training Time (s)	258.13	284.97	110.49	112.12

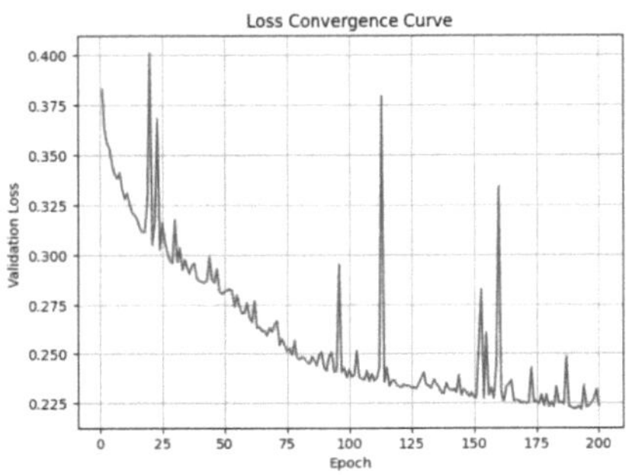

Fig. 1. BP+WS validation loss on IoT-ID20

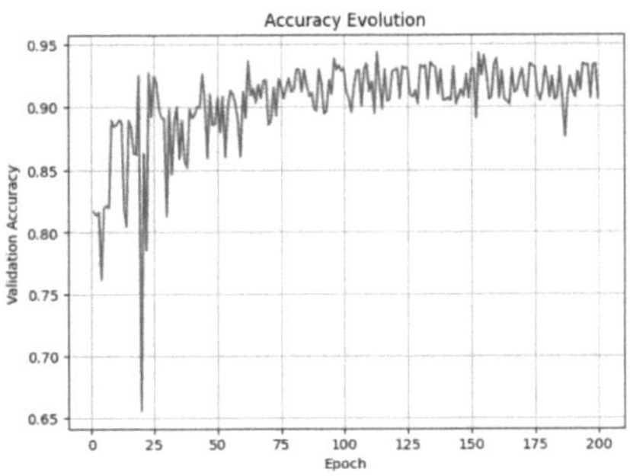

Fig. 2. BP+WS accuracy on IoT-ID20

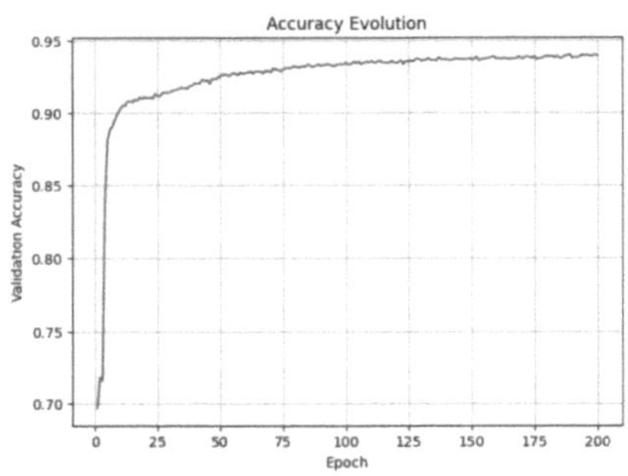

Fig. 3. BP+WS validation loss on TON-IoT dataset

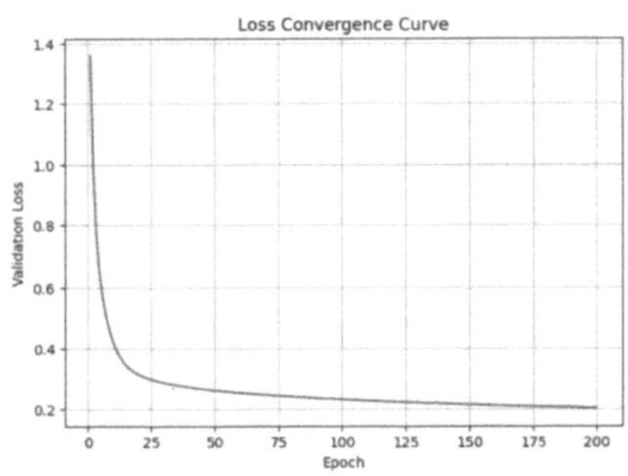

Fig. 4. BP+WS accuracy on TON-IoT

4.2 Result Analysis

The above metrics give a clear indication; both models can detect normal traffic but struggle to detect penetrations. It happened because of an imbalance inside the categories, where normal traffic tremendously outnumbers attacks, which could lead the model to treat too much "normal" traffic as input data. The two models function differently, not in the same way. The backpropagation model displayed a strong accuracy of 0.9953 in category 0 and good recall (0.9595). On penetrations, the model trained

Table 4. The confusion matrices for both models on the IoT-ID20 dataset.

BP Model	**Pred: Normal**	**Pred: Intrusion**
Actual: Normal	112,392 (TN)	4,750 (FP)
Actual: Intrusion	531 (FN)	7,484 (TP)
BP+WS Model	**Pred: Normal**	**Pred: Intrusion**
Actual: Normal	106,079 (TN)	11,063 (FP)
Actual: Intrusion	794 (FN)	7,221 (TP)

Table 5. Metrics for each class on the IoT-ID20 dataset

Metric	BP Class 0	BP Class 1	BP+OR Class 0	BP+OR Class 1
Precision	0.9953	0.6117	0.9926	0.3949
Recall	0.9595	0.9337	0.9056	0.9009
F1-Score	0.9770	0.7392	0.9471	0.5491

on backpropagation gave us high recall (0.9337) but low accuracy (0.6117): with many "penetrations". The predictions were actually false positives.

The error pattern in the backpropagation model with a weight scale ratio (WS) was different. It kept its recall almost identical, but whose accuracy approached zero with a category equal to 1 (0.3949). Under the backpropagation algorithm with weight scale ratio (WS), there are 11063 false positives. On the other hand, if we only consider the backpropagation algorithm, there are 4750 false positives, which means we added 6313 false-positive attacks that were classified as harmful rather than normal.

To determine whether the differences we observed reflected genuine algorithmic advantages or were merely statistical noise, we performed the McNemar test [10], a standard procedure for comparing binary classifications. This test (the McNemar test) [16] examines whether the two models make systematically different errors. For the IoT-ID20 dataset, 6576 samples were identified, where the two models differed. In all these cases, backpropagation was classified correctly, while the second model, backpropagation with weight scale ratio (WS), made errors. The test statistic was 6574.00 with a p-value less than 0.001 [17]. As shown in Table 6.

Statistical analysis confirms the initial findings: the 5.25 percentage point backspreading advantage represents a real and reproducible difference. With a p-value of less than 0.001, in a dataset of 125,157 test samples, this translates to 6,576 additional correct predictions..Now we will review the results of the confusion matrix, the metrics, and the statistical results of the TON-IoT dataset as shown in Table 7.

Table 6. Statistical results for IoT-ID20.

Statistical Measure	Value
McNemar Test Statistic	6,574.00
p-value	<0.001 ***
Samples Disagree	6,576
Accuracy Difference	5.25%

*** Indicates a p-value < 0.001 (high statistical significance).

Table 7. Confusion matrix for the BP model on TON-IoT (10 categories).

True\Pred	C0	C1	C2	C3	C4	C5	C6	C7	C8	C9
C0	3991	7	0	2	0	0	0	0	0	0
C1	0	3713	29	158	0	0	1	23	0	76
...	...	...	...	...	...	...	...	...	...	...
C5	0	0	0	0	0	**10000**	0	0	0	0

Correct classifications in the main diameter. Category 5 (normal traffic) achieves perfect classification using 10,000 samples.

Table 8. The comprehensive metrics for ten categories, revealing the strengths and weaknesses of each model.

Class	BP Precision	BP Recall	BP F1-score	BP+ WS Precision	BP+ WS Recall	BP+WS F1-score	Samples
Class 0	0.9631	0.9978	0.9801	0.9610	0.9970	0.9787	4,000
Class 1	0.9511	0.9283	0.9395	0.9525	0.9223	0.9371	4,000
Class 4	0.7190	0.4163	**0.5273**	0.7100	0.3397	**0.4595**	**209**
Class 5 (Normal)	**1.0000**	**1.0000**	**1.0000**	**1.0000**	**1.0000**	**1.0000**	**10,000**
Class 6	0.9755	0.7947	0.8759	0.9758	0.7850	0.8700	4,000
Classes 2,3,7,8,9	0.86-0.99	0.92-0.97	0.91-0.95	0.85-0.99	0.92-0.97	0.91-0.95	4,000 each

Table 8 shows the performance statistics in each class on the TON-IoT dataset. Green means perfect rating (Category 5). Red is the most severe category (Category 4). The two devices are comparable in the vast majority of categories, with differences rarely greater than 1%. Since category 5 (normal traffic) had the most representation with 10,000 samples in the TON-IoT dataset, it achieved perfect scores (1.000) on both models. Likewise, categories 0, 1, 2, 3,6,7, 8 and 9 presented identical results for both optimizers, with a slight advantage for the backpropagation (BP) algorithm in specific cases of no practical significance. Category 4, highlighted in red, presents a different picture, with only 209 samples; both models struggled, but the backpropagation with weight scale model performed significantly worse, achieving an F1 value of 0.4595 compared to 0.5273 for the backpropagation model ($\Delta = 0.0678$). This difference is primarily due to Recall (0.3397 vs. 0.4163), meaning the backpropagation with weight scale model missed a significantly larger number of class 4 cases.

After presenting the statistical results for the IoT-ID20 dataset, we applied the same rigorous tests to the TON-IoT dataset to assess whether the smaller observed difference was still statistically significant. The TON-IoT comparison showed that the backpropagation (BP) algorithm achieved 94.01% accuracy compared to 93.75% for the backpropagation with weight scale ratio (WS), a difference of only 0.26%, representing just 110 samples out of 42,209 tested samples. The McNemar test of these results identified the 110 samples where the models differed. Consistent with IoT-ID20, all instances of difference favored backpropagation, meaning that backpropagation correctly classified all 110 samples where the backpropagation with weight scale ratio (WS), algorithm erred, while the backpropagation with weight scale ratio (WS), algorithm failed to achieve any successes. Table 9 shows the test showed a value of $\chi^2 = 108.01$ with $p < 0.001$, indicating that the difference is indeed statistically significant.

Table 9. Statistical results for TON-IoT dataset.

Statistical Measure	Value
McNemar Test Statistic	108.01
p-value	<0.001 ***
Samples Where Models Disagree	110
BP Correct, BP + OR Wrong	110
BP Wrong, BP + OR Correct	0
Accuracy Difference	0.26%

*** *indicates p < 0.001 (highly significant statistically, but not a small practical magnitude).*

5 Conclusions

This study investigated whether incorporating weight information through the weight scale (WS) ratio mechanism improves the training of backpropagation neural networks for intrusion detection systems. The results show that adding such a ratio to the traditional algorithm yields consistent performance improvements. For IoT-ID20, with unbalanced classes, the backpropagation algorithm decisively outstripped the main algorithm with a weight scale (WS) ratio by around (+5.25 percentage points), resulting in 6313 false positives (FP). However, when the more balanced TON-IoT dataset was used, the performance difference was reduced by only 0.26%, and is considered statistically analyzable but practically no longer pertinent. The obtained results after adding this ratio make us cautious about its use, especially with unbalanced data, where test accuracy is of great importance. However, it may be useful in some cases but not in others. Equally important is a systematic understanding of the difference between statistical significance and practical significance. Both datasets yielded statistically significant results ($p < 0.001$), but were substantially different in practical effect. As a reminder, p-values are not enough; you should always accompany your performance reporting with effect size and confusion matrix analysis. In conclusion, this work not only aids in the empirical measurement of the WS mechanism but also provides a rigorous methodological approach to objectively and more holistically assess modified strategies in neural networks. It guides the weight values to the desired target smoothly, without excess or randomness beyond what the true values require by controlling the progression towards the target according to the proposed equation.

Acknowledgements. This research was sponsored by the University of Malaya Translational Research Grant Scheme, TRG0019-2025 (UM.0002388/HRU.IP) and the Research Excellence Grant, UMREG 068 - 2024 (UM.0000285/HRU.RC).

Author Contributions. All authors contributed equally and significantly to writing this article. All authors read and approved the final manuscript.

Conflicts of Interest. The authors declare no conflict of interest.

References

1. Samawi, V.W: SMCSIS: an IoT-based secure multi-crop irrigation system for smart farming. Int. J. Innovative Comput. Inf. Control (IJICIC) **17**(4) (2021). http://www.ijicic.org/ijicic-170408.pdf
2. Samawi, V.W., Yousif, S.A., Al-Saidi, N.M.G.: Intrusion detection system: an automatic machine learning algorithms using auto-WEKA. In: 2022 IEEE 13th Control and System Graduate Research Colloquium (ICSGRC). IEEE (2022)
3. Khacha, A., et al.: Landscape of learning techniques for intrusion detection system in IoT: a systematic literature review. Comput. Electric. Eng. **120**(Part B), 109725 (2024). https://doi.org/10.1016/j.compeleceng.2024.109725
4. Abdullah, S.M., et al.: Complex-valued neural networks with super activation function. Int. J. Innovat. Comput. Inform. Control **20**(6) (2024)
5. Rumelhart, D.E., Hinton, G.E., Williams, R.J.: Learning representations by back-propagating errors. Nature **323**(6088), 533–536.3 (1986)
6. Rahman, M.M., et al.: A survey on intrusion detection system in IoT networks. Cyber Secur. Appl. **3**, 100082 (2025). https://doi.org/10.1016/j.csa.2024.100082
7. Chinnasamy, R., et al.: Deep Learning-Driven Methods for Network-Based Intrusion Detection Systems: A Systematic Review, vol. 11, Issue 1, February 2025, pp. 181–215. ICT Express (2025). https://doi.org/10.1016/j.icte.2025.01.005
8. Kingma, D.P., Ba, J.: Adam: a method for stochastic optimization. arXiv preprint arXiv:1412.6980 (2014)
9. Buczak, A.L., Guven, E.: A survey of data mining and machine learning methods for cybersecurity intrusion detection. IEEE Commun. Surv. Tutor. **18**(2), 1153–1176 (2016)

10. Sutskever, I., Martens, J., Dahl, G., Hinton, G.: On the importance of initialization and momentum in deep learning. In: International Conference on Machine Learning, pp. 1139–1147 (2013)
11. Wafaa M.S.A., Nadher, I., Sadiq, A.T.: Modification of deep learning technique for face expressions and body postures recognitions. Int. J. Adv. Sci. Technol. **29**(3s), 313–320 (2020)
12. Ring, M., Wunderlich, S., Scheuring, D., Landes, D., Hotho, A.: A survey of network-based intrusion detection data sets. Comput. Secur. **86**, 147–167 (2019)
13. Banaamah, A.M., et al.: Intrusion detection in IoT using deep learning. Sensors **22**(21), 8417 (2022). https://doi.org/10.3390/s22218417
14. IoTID20 Dataset | kjsspringivy/Concept_Drift_Detection_and_Adaptation | DeepWiki
15. The TON_IoT Datasets | UNSW Research
16. Andresini, G., Appice, A., Malerba, D.: Nearest cluster-based intrusion detection through convolutional neural networks. Knowl.-Based Syst. **216**, 106798 (2021)
17. Davis, J., Goadrich, M.: The relationship between Precision-Recall and ROC curves. In: International Conference on Machine Learning, pp. 233–240 (2006)
18. Roy, S., et al.: A two-layer fog-cloud intrusion detection model for IoT networks. Internet of Things **19**, 100557 (2022). https://doi.org/10.1016/j.iot.2022.100557
19. Dina, A.S., et al.: A deep learning approach for intrusion detection in internet of things using focal loss function. Internet of Things **22**, 100699 (2023). https://doi.org/10.1016/j.iot.2023.100699
20. Jablaoui, R., Cheikhrouhou, O., Hamdi, M., et al.: Deep-learning-enabled intrusion detection system for IoT security. J. Wireless Com. Network **2025**, 66 (2025). https://doi.org/10.1186/s13638-025-02477-6
21. Zhang, C., Li, J., Wang, N., Zhang, D.: Research on intrusion detection method based on transformer and CNN-BiLSTM in Internet of Things. Sensors **25**, 2725 (2025). https://doi.org/10.3390/s25092725
22. Shanmugam, V., Razavi-Far, R., Hallaji, E.: Addressing class imbalance in intrusion detection: a comprehensive evaluation of machine learning approaches. Electronics **14**, 69 (2025). https://doi.org/10.3390/electronics14010069
23. Deng, M., Fan, S., Kan, Y., Sun, C.: An intrusion detection model based on equalization loss and spatio-temporal feature extraction. Electronics **15**, 646 (2026). https://doi.org/10.3390/electronics15030646
24. Abdulganiyu, O.H., Fadi, O., Moukafih, Y., et al.: Explainable attention based few shot LSTM for intrusion detection in imbalanced cyber physical system networks. Sci. Rep. **16**, 7217 (2026). https://doi.org/10.1038/s41598-026-38668-4
25. Ahmad, J., et al.: An interpretable deep learning framework for intrusion detection in industrial internet of things. Internet of Things **33**, 101681 (2025). https://doi.org/10.1016/j.iot.2025.101681
26. Alabbadi, A., Bajaber, F.: An intrusion detection system over the IoT data streams using eXplainable Artificial Intelligence (XAI). Sensors **25**, 847 (2025). https://doi.org/10.3390/s25030847
27. Zhang, Y., Wang, Y., Gao, L.: CNN-MHBiGRU: a two-stage deep learning framework with multi-attention mechanisms for iot intrusion detection. Ad Hoc Networks **181**, 104082 (2026). https://doi.org/10.1016/j.adhoc.2025.104082
28. Nivaashini, M., Suganya, E., Sountharrajan, S., Prabu, M., Bavirisetti, D.P.: FEDDBN-IDS: federated deep belief network-based wireless network intrusion detection system. EURASIP J. Inform. Secur. **2024**(8) (2024)
29. Moustafa, N., Slay, J.: UNSW-NB15: a comprehensive data set for network intrusion detection systems. In: Military Communications and Information Systems Conference (MilCIS), pp. 1–6 (2015)

30. Tavallaee, M., Bagheri, E., Lu, W., Ghorbani, A.A.: A detailed analysis of the KDD CUP 99 data set. In: IEEE Symposium on Computational Intelligence for Security and Defense Applications, pp. 1–6 (2009)
31. Yousif, S.A., Samawi, V.W., Al-Saidi, N.M.G., Karaca, Y.: Towards smarter vegetation health clustering: insights from fractal dimension, NDVI, and LST metrics derived via remote sensing landsat dataset. In: Gervasi, O., et al. Computational Science and Its Applications – ICCSA 2025 Workshops. ICCSA 2025. LNCS, vol 15886. Springer, Cham (2026). https://doi.org/10.1007/978-3-031-97576-9_5
32. Zeiler, M.D.: ADADELTA: An adaptive learning rate method. arXiv preprint arXiv:1212.5701 (2012)

Garbage Images Classification Using Residual Attention CNN and Hybrid Optimization Based on Firefly Algorithm

Ahmed T. Sadiq[1], Nadia M. G. Al-Saidi[2], Venus W. Samawi[3](✉), and Yeliz Karaca[4]

[1] Multimedia and Digital Media Department, University of Technology, Baghdad, Iraq
ahmed.t.sadiq@uotechnology.edu.iq
[2] Department of Applied Sciences, University of Technology, Baghdad 10066, Iraq
nadia.m.ghanim@uotechnology.edu.iq
[3] Department of MIS/Smart Business, Isra University, Amman 11622, Jordan
venus.samawi@iu.edu.jo
[4] University of Massachusetts Chan Medical School (UMASS), 55 Lake Avenue North, Worcester, MA 01655, USA
yeliz.karaca@ieee.org

Abstract. Garbage image classification has become an important application in recent years, as it supports waste sorting and identification, thereby helping environmental protection and recycling, and overcoming the problems of manual sorting. This paper presents a hybrid intelligent technique based on Residual Attention Convolutional Neural Networks (RACNN) with an improved Back-Propagation Neural Network (BPNN). The improvement in the BPNN is achieved using the Firefly Algorithm and the AdamW Optimizer for Fine-Tuning (BP-FF-AdamW) to ensure BPNN's regularization. A new chaotic function is used for weight initialization to control randomness and prevent the model from settling into local minima. The RACNN model is applied to images of garbage to extract complex, hierarchical features, bypassing the manual feature extraction stage. Furthermore, mathematical optimizations of the BPNN model, along with the use of the Firefly algorithm and chaotic sequences, enhance the learning process and produce a well-trained model capable of classifying garbage images. This integrated approach provides several effective intelligent learning features, in addition to mathematical optimizations, to improve the learning process and produce a well-trained model capable of classifying garbage objects. The developed blended approach is applied to the Garbage Dataset to test its classification ability. The achieved accuracy for classifying garbage objects is 96.5%.

Keywords: Waste classification · Residual Attention Convolutional Neural Networks · Deep Learning · AdamW Optimizer · Hyperparameter optimization · Fine-Tuning · Transfer learning · Computer Vision

O. Gervasi et al. (Eds.): ICCSA 2026 Workshops, LNCS 16758, pp. 255–269, 2027.
https://doi.org/10.1007/978-3-032-30497-1_16

1 Introduction

Waste sorting is crucial for achieving sustainability and protecting the environment through encouraging resource reuse (recycling). The World Bank estimates that global waste will reach 2.59 billion tons by 2030 and 3.4 billion tons by 2050 [1]. The need to automate waste sorting is crucial because most people are still unaware of how to sort garbage [2]. Furthermore, humans who work in waste-sorting facilities do the hard, time-consuming work of sorting through waste. Various techniques are used to automate waste sorting, including sensor-based sorting, magnetic and density separation, and garbage image analysis and classification. In this paper, we focus on using garbage image classification to automate waste sorting. However, classifying garbage images is challenging for several reasons, including complex backgrounds, similar-looking categories, feature extraction and engineering, and low-quality images [3]. Therefore, we use deep learning (DL), specifically Convolutional Neural Networks (CNNs), for garbage image classification in waste sorting rather than traditional machine learning (ML) approaches.

Over the last ten years, DL has made significant strides due to significant improvements in computational power, enabled by Tensor Processing Units (TPUs) and Graphics Processing Units (GPUs), as well as architectural innovations. Furthermore, the explosion of big data and advances in underlying theory have played a crucial role in the development of DL [4, 5]. The development of DL has significantly advanced computer capabilities for interpreting visual data, such as object detection, image segmentation, and classification, thereby improving computer vision [6, 7]. One of the subfields of DL, which is primarily designed to analyze visual data, is CNNs. This is due to the shared weights and local connectivity employed by the convolutional layers in CNNs. CNNs are capable of performing feature extraction and improving image classification. These capabilities are useful for garbage image classification, which helps sort garbage for recycling, reducing time-consuming work and costs [8]. These capabilities are useful for classifying waste images, as they are used in sorting and recycling processes, thereby reducing time, effort, and costs. Furthermore, the integration of computer vision and deep learning technologies enables highly accurate automatic sorting and recognition of garbage objects in images, facilitating waste management and improving sorting results compared with human intervention [9, 10].

In recent years, high-performance image analysis has undergone a significant shift, driven by advances in DL-based technologies, especially CNNs [11–13]. Two factors are crucial for high-performance image analysis. The first is having sufficient training data in both quality and quantity, which next-generation camera systems and high-capacity storage devices ensure. The second factor is the need to develop a high-quality image classification model to achieve high accuracy in image analysis.

Existing studies on garbage classification show significant gaps remaining in this domain, as some research uses ML techniques while others use DL, particularly CNNs. Support Vector Machine (SVM) and Convolutional Neural Network (CNN) were trained on a self-collected dataset of 510 images, as compared in [14], to classify three types of waste: plastic, paper, and metal. SVM outperforms CNN in their study (94.8% vs. 83%). A dataset of 22500 waste-colored images with two classes, organic and recyclable, was used in [15] to train CNN and ResNet-50 architectures for waste classification and to compare the resulting accuracies. The custom CNN model achieves the best accuracy, with 91.84%, outperforming ResNet-50, which achieves 81.34%. In [16], three Convolutional Blocks were utilized, each featuring distinct filter sizes and the Mish activation function. Three fully connected layers with Softmax activation were used to make multi-class predictions. The flattened output of the last MaxPool2D layer was used as input. DenseNet169 achieved the highest accuracy of 99.58%. The effectiveness of YOLOv5 was evaluated in [17] for trash detection, including plastic, paper, glass, metal, cardboard, and biodegradables. The study concluded that YOLOv5 is effectively able to identify various types of waste. In [18], transfer learning was used, leveraging a pre-trained DenseNet169 model to classify five datasets, achieving 82% accuracy. In [19], a garbage bin was designed that included both hardware and a mobile app. Afterward, a ResNet-34-based model was built, and its design was improved. Lastly, fake garbage data is used to test the proposed system's performance.

Recently, DL techniques have demonstrated excellent performance on computer vision tasks such as image classification, segmentation, and detection [20, 21]. Transfer learning enables superior performance despite limited data availability by utilizing pre-trained models [22, 23]. Since CNNs are the most suitable type of DL that use back-propagation (BP) as the main training algorithm, this means that CNNs encounter the primary challenges of BP, such as local minima and weight initialization. This study introduces an automated system that uses deep transfer learning for a five-class garbage image classification task. The main contribution is to address problems that occur when training CNNs with BP, such as local minima and weight initialization issues. Finally, evaluate the effectiveness of the proposed modified BP for training CNNs to classify images of garbage. For BPNNs to work better and more accurately in real-world applications, it is important to optimize them. To address important problems such as slow convergence, getting stuck in local-minima, and sensitivity to hyperparameters, many optimization methods have been developed. Although conventional methods such as Gradient Descent (GD) and its variants have yielded substantial advances, contemporary research has focused on hybrid techniques that combine metaheuristic algorithms with adaptive optimization strategies.

The main contributions of this work are abstracted as follows:

- Proposing a new chaotic map to be used for weight initialization to prevent poor initialization, which might slow down the training process or converge to a sub-optimal solution. Chaotic weight Initialization controls the randomness of the initial weight setting to accelerate convergence and prevent getting stuck in local minima.
- Utilizing the Residual Attention Convolutional Neural Networks (RACNN) with an improved Back-Propagation Neural Network. These methods have suffered from limitations, including fixed learning rates that often lead to suboptimal convergence. Additionally, the proper choice of learning is crucial, as a high learning rate may cause exceeding minima, while a low learning rate slows convergence.
- Using a gradient-based optimizer like AdamW provides a global search strategy, making it a good alternative to methods that are based on gradients. AdamW can reach suboptimal solutions too quickly, especially in high-dimensional search spaces such as those in deep learning. To adjust the learning rate, adaptive methods, including the Firefly algorithm and the AdamW optimizer for Fine-Tuning (BP-FF-AdamW)

are used. Unsuitable tuning may cause unstable updates or excessive regularization, thereby negatively affecting model performance.

The rest of the paper is organized into four sections: Section 2 presents the materials used for the methods in this work, including a detailed dataset description and model specifications. Section 3 explains the metrics used for performance measurement. In Sect. 4, the experimental results are presented, and our findings are discussed using performance measures. Section 5 concludes our work and proposes directions for future research to improve sustainable waste management practices.

2 Methodology

The framework of the proposed approach relies on several intelligent techniques and mathematical enhancements. It outlines the theoretical foundation and mathematical formulations that guide each component of the methodology. The main stages of our proposed approach are presented in Fig. 1.

The proposed approach relies on several intelligent techniques and mathematical enhancements. The main stages include:

1- Dataset Acquisition.
2- Residual Attention CNN.
3- Improved BP-NN based on Firefly algorithm with AdamW optimizer for fine-tuning.

2.1 Garbage Dataset

The selected garbage image dataset, "A Comprehensive Image Dataset for Garbage Classification and Recycling," includes 19,762 clear images categorized into 10 classes [24]. Table 1 lists the 10 classes along with their training and test sizes. Partitioning the dataset into training and testing sets is achieved using 5-fold cross-validation to obtain more confident classification results. The dataset is considered comprehensive, but it is imbalanced because some classes have few images while others have many. Samples of images from the dataset are shown in Fig. 2.

The developed garbage classification model is implemented in two phases: training and evaluation. To accomplish the training phase, we need to carry out the following steps:

1. Fed the garbage images used for training into the RACNN for feature selection.
2. Initialize the BPNN weights using chaotic sequences.
3. Optimize BPNN weights using the Firefly algorithm to establish a well-optimized starting point.
4. AdamW is employed to fine-tune the model, enhancing stability and efficient learning.

At the end of the training phase, once the target convergence is reached, the evaluation phase starts.

During the evaluation phase, the developed model is assessed utilizing the test data. Performance metrics such as classification accuracy, recall, precision, F-score, and a confusion matrix are used to evaluate the effectiveness of the developed garbage classification model.

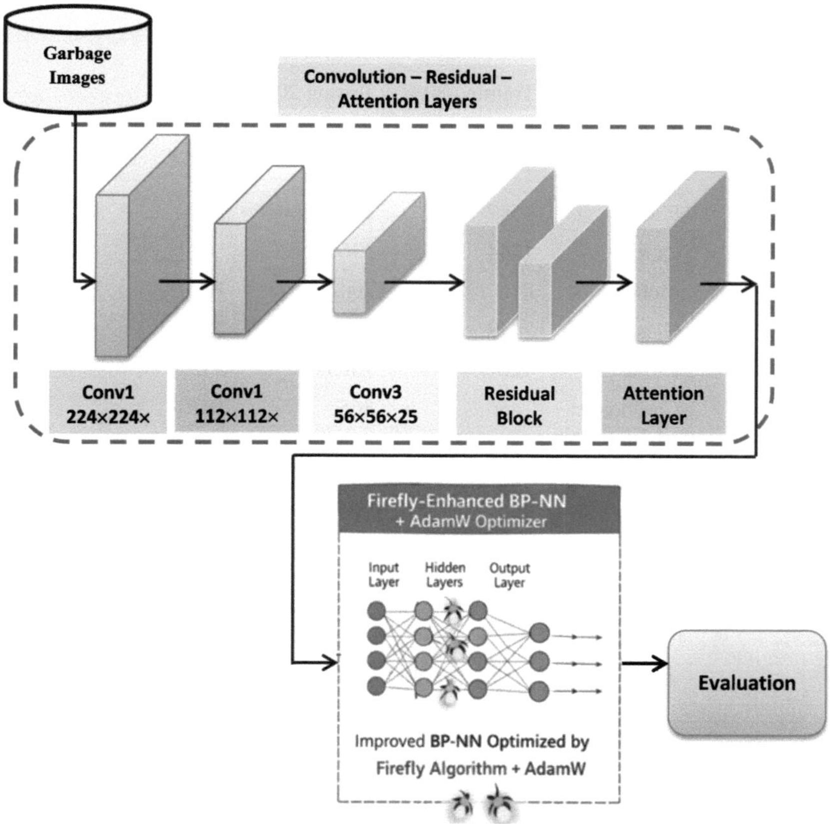

Fig. 1. Main stages of proposed garbage image classification (garbage classification Model)

2.2 Residual Attention Convolutional Neural Networks (RACNN)

The Residual Attention Convolutional Neural Network (RACNN) combines residual learning and attention mechanisms to improve feature representation and stabilize training. Residual connections help prevent gradient degradation by letting information flow directly between layers. Attention modules, on the other hand, adaptively emphasize useful spatial and channel features. This combination improves convergence, robustness, and discrimination, especially for classifying complex images. This makes RACNN an effective approach for learning deep hierarchical representations. Using RACNN will yield high-quality extracted/selected features. Because this type of CNN is very efficient in object classification. Another stage is an improved BP-NN based on the Firefly algorithm and the AdamW optimizer. Our proposed RACNN comprises 3 convolutional layers, 1 residual layer, and 1 attention layer. The fully connected layer in our RACNN is an improved BP-NN based on the firefly algorithm. Figure 3 illustrates the details of the RACNN of our approach. Using RACNN yields high-quality extracted/selected features. Because this type of CNN is very efficient in object classification. Another

Table 1. Garbage image dataset: classes and sizes

Image Class	Training 80%	Testing 20%	Total
Trash	757	190	947
Shoes	1581	396	1977
Plastic	1587	397	1984
Paper	1344	336	1680
Metal	816	204	1020
Glass	2448	613	3061
Cloths	4261	1065	5327
Cardboard	1460	365	1825
Biological	797	200	997
Battery	755	189	944

Trash Shoes Plastic Paper

Fig. 2. Samples of Garbage Image

stage is an improved BPNN based on the Firefly algorithm and the AdamW optimizer. The next sections provide details on RACNN and the improved BPNN.

The input image (RGB) of size 224-by-224 will be fed into two convolutional layers, then the residual process and attention. Flatten nodes will be entered to improve the BPNN.

2.3 Chaotic Weight Initialization

The primary goal of optimizing BPNN is to improve convergence speed, accuracy, and generalization. Using chaotic weight initialization improves convergence. The main purpose of applying chaotic initialization is to control randomness in weight settings, which helps prevent premature convergence to local minima. The weight initialization function is based on the chaotic maps given in Eq. (1), which generate highly unpredictable sequences that follow deterministic rules.

$$X_{n+1} = rX_n\left(1 - e^{-\delta X_n^2} + \gamma\right) \quad (1)$$

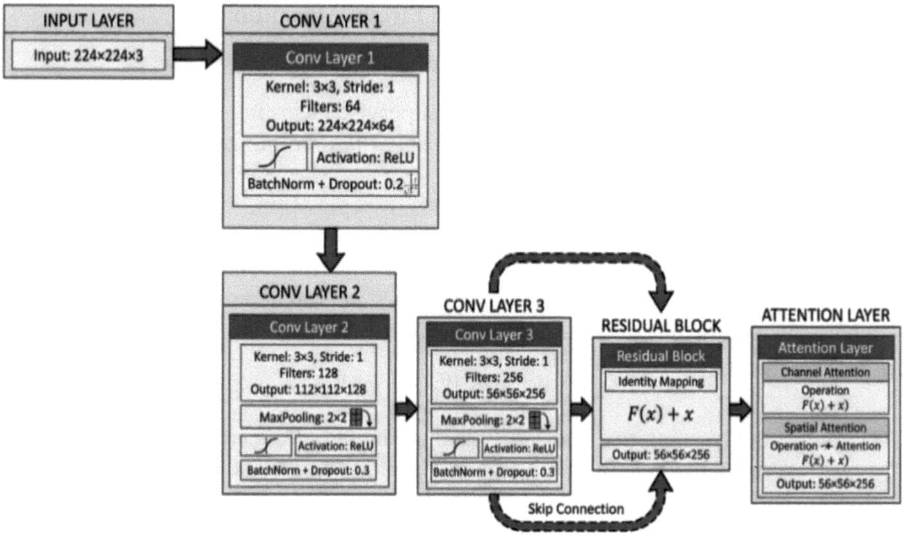

Fig. 3. RACNN Layers Detail

where X_n represents the initialized weight, and r = 5.8, δ = 8.9, γ = -1.59 ensures chaotic behavior.

This is done to avoid poor weight initialization and reduce the vanishing gradients risk. These parameters are chosen to ensure the system's chaotic behaviour. The dynamic behavior of the developed garbage classification model is explained in Fig. 4.

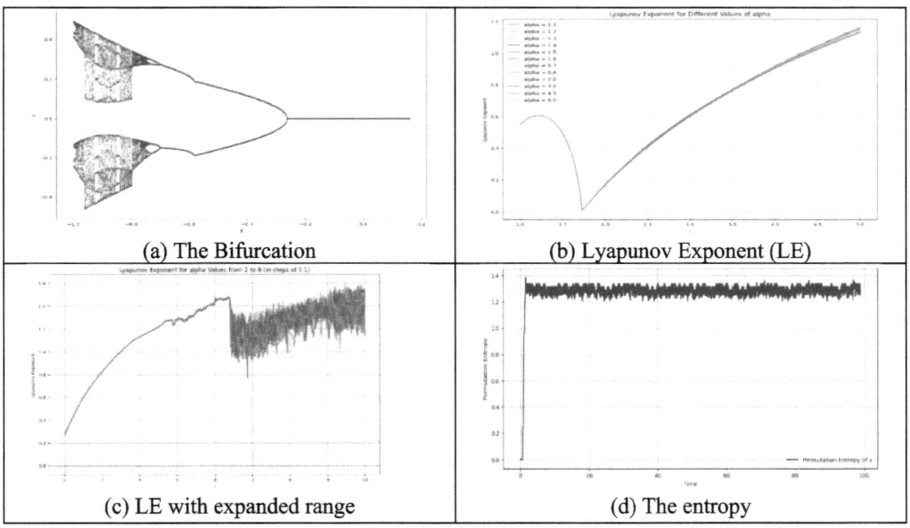

Fig. 4. The dynamic behaviour of the system (1).

2.4 Hybrid Optimization BPNN Based on Firefly Algorithm

In this stage, there are several sub-stages as follows:

a) **BPNN and Optimization:** A BPNN is a supervised learning algorithm that adjusts the W (weights) and b (biases) of a neural network to minimize the error function:

$$E(W, b) = \frac{1}{N}\sum\nolimits_{i=1}^{n} \|y_i - \widehat{y_i}\|^2 \tag{2}$$

where N is the number of training samples, y_i is the true label of the ith sample, and $\widehat{y_i}$ is the predicted output. The weight updates are computed using gradient descent, where the parameters are adjusted iteratively:

$$W_{t+1} = W_t - \eta \nabla EW_t \tag{3}$$

Here, η is the learning rate and ∇EW_t is the gradient of the error function.

Conversely, the benefit of the Firefly algorithm lies in its ability to escape local minima and explore the search space effectively.

b) **Firefly and AdamW for Fine-Tuning:** The firefly algorithm (FA) is among the most widely used swarm-intelligence algorithms used. The firefly algorithm was developed by Xin-She Yang in 2008 [4], inspired by the natural behavior of tropical fireflies. FA mimics the flashing patterns and attraction behavior of fireflies. The purpose of these flashing lights is twofold: to attract mating partners and to warn potential predators. Clearly, these flashing lights and their intensity can follow certain rules, including physical laws. Essentially, FA employs the following three idealized rules. [25]:

- AS fireflies are unisex, they will be attracted to each other regardless of their sex.
- Attractiveness depends on brightness, decreasing as distance grows. Consequently, between two flashing fireflies, the less bright one moves toward the brighter. If no brighter fireflies exist, it moves randomly.
- The landscape of the objective function determines the brightness of a firefly.

As a firefly's attractiveness is proportional to the brightness seen by adjacent fireflies, the variation of attractiveness β with the distance r can be defined by using Eq. (4):

$$\beta = \beta_0 e^{-\gamma r^2} \tag{4}$$

where β_0 is the attractiveness at $r = 0$. The movement of a firefly i is attracted to another, more attractive (brighter) firefly j is determined by:

$$W_i^{t+1} = W_i^t + \beta_0 e^{-\gamma r^2}\left(W_j^t - W_i^t\right) + \alpha \varepsilon_i^t \tag{5}$$

where the second term is due to the attraction. The third term is randomization with α being the randomization parameter, and ε_i^t is a vector of random numbers drawn from a Gaussian distribution at time t. Other studies also use the randomization ε_i^t can be easily extended to other distributions, such as Lévy flights. It is worth pointing out that γ controls the scaling, while α controls the randomness. For the algorithm to converge properly, randomness should be gradually reduced, and one way to achieve this is to use

$$\alpha = \alpha_0 \theta^t \tag{6}$$

where t is the index of iterations/generations. Here α_0 is the initial randomness factor, and we can set $\alpha_0 = O(1)$ without losing generality.

The main steps of the Firefly algorithm are illustrated in Algorithm (1). Once the optimized weights are determined by the firefly algorithm, AdamW [26] is used for fine-tuning with adaptive learning rate control, which adjusts standard stochastic gradient descent by incorporating a history-sensitive learning rate as in Eq. (7):

$$W_{t+1} = W_t - \eta \frac{\widehat{m_t}}{\sqrt{\widehat{v_t} + \epsilon}} - \eta \lambda W_t \tag{7}$$

where η is the learning rate, $\widehat{m_t}$ is bias-corrected first moment (i.e., mean of gradients), $\widehat{v_t}$ is the bias-corrected second moment (i.e., variance of gradients) and λ is the weight decay coefficient.

Algorithm (1): Firefly

Input: Objective function f(x), number of fireflies n, max_iterations T
    parameters: α (randomization), β_0 (initial attractiveness), γ (light absorption)
Initialize population of fireflies X_i (i = 1 to n) randomly
Evaluate brightness $I_i = f(X_i)$ for each firefly
For t = 1 to T do
  For i = 1 to n do
    For j = 1 to n do
      If $I_j > I_i$ then
        Compute the distance r_{ij} between x_i and x_j
        Compute attractiveness using Eq. (4)
        Move firefly i towards firefly j using $X_i = X_i + \beta * (X_j - X_i) + \alpha_t \epsilon_t$
          % where α_t is a parameter controlling the step size, while ϵ_t is a vector drawn from a Gaussian or other distribution.
      End If
    End For
    Evaluate new brightness $I_i = f(X_i)$
  End For
  Rank fireflies and update the best solution
End For
Output: Best solution found (X_best) and its fitness f(X_best)

2.5 Optimization Strategies

Unlike Adam, AdamW separates weight decay from the gradient update. Therefore, AdamW and the Firefly Optimization algorithm are chosen instead. This ensures weight decay acts as a true regularization force, not distorted by adaptive learning rates. Models trained with AdamW often perform better on unseen data than those trained with Adam. Also, AdamW has stable convergence, bias correction, and low memory cost. The adaptive learning rate works more effectively when integrated with the Firefly Algorithm for weight updates, while AdamW's weight decay proves more advantageous for very deep architectures. The firefly algorithm efficiently balances exploration and exploitation in the search space, making it well-suited for deep learning optimization. The firefly algorithm's attraction-based updates lead to faster, more stable convergence. Combining the Firefly algorithm's global search abilities with AdamW's adaptive learning rates forms a strong hybrid approach that addresses the limitations of standalone gradient-based and evolutionary methods. This combination applies the strengths of both AdamW and the Firefly algorithm, offering a more effective and stable optimization strategy for this work.

3 Performance Evaluation Metrics

In this work, the confusion matrix will be used to indicate where the model's predictions are correct and where they are not. Therefore, it is considered a good performance evaluation metric. Four categories are used to construct the confusion matrix: true positive (TP), true negative (TN), false positive (FP), and false negative (FN) [10]. Moreover, four performance evaluation metrics are used to assess the developed garbage classification model [1, 9, 10]:

- ***Accuracy***: indicates the ratio of all correctly predicted samples to the total number of samples (see Eq. 8).

$$Accuracy = \frac{TP + Tn}{(TP + TN + FP + FN)} \tag{8}$$

- ***Precision***: indicates the ratio of all correctly predicted positive samples to the total predicted positive samples (see Eq. 9).

$$\text{Precision} = \frac{TP}{(TP + FP)} \tag{9}$$

- ***Recall***: indicates the ratio of all correctly predicted positive samples to the total actual positive samples (see Eq. 10).

$$\text{Recall} = \frac{TP}{(TP + FN)} \tag{10}$$

- ***F1-Score***: is particularly useful for unbalanced datasets. It computes the harmonic mean of recall and precision (see Eq. 11).

$$\text{F1} - \text{Score} = 2 \times \frac{(\text{Precision} \times \text{Recall})}{(\text{Precision} + \text{Recall})} \tag{11}$$

4 Experimental Results

Before assessing the effectiveness of the proposed garbage classification model, it's useful to review the main parameters used during the training phase, which are shown in Table 2. The developed garbage classification model is applied to the test dataset, and confusion matrices, accuracies, precision, recall, and F-scores are calculated to assess the model's effectiveness. Table 3 summarizes the performance of the proposed model on the test dataset, reporting accuracy, precision, recall, and F1 Score. The results demonstrate consistently high values across all metrics, confirming the effectiveness, robustness, and reliability of the proposed RACNN with hybrid optimization in accurately classifying garbage images.

Table 2. Parameter description

Parameters	Description/Value
Epochs	300
BP-NN Learning Rate	0.005
BP-NN Hidden Nodes	500 to 600
Dropout	0.2 to 0.3
Loss Function	Cross-Entropy Loss
Firefly Pop. Size	50
Max. Iteration Firefly	500
Firefly Learning Rate	0.1 to 0.2
Attractiveness	0.9
Light Absorption	0.9 to 1.1
Optimizer	AdamW
Chaotic Map	$r = 5.8$, $\delta = 8.9$, $\gamma = -1.59$

Table 3. The performance metrics of the developed garbage classification model

Measure	Value
Accuracy	96.5%
Precision	95.5%
Recall	96.7%
F1-Score	96%

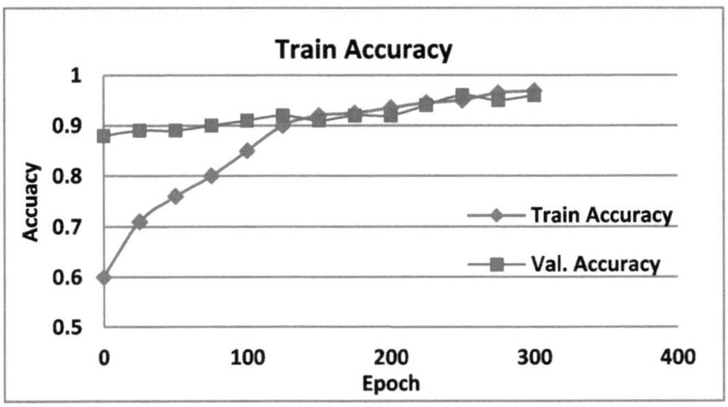

Fig. 5. Accuracy Training Chart

Figure 5 illustrates the training accuracy progression of the proposed model across epochs. The curve shows a steady and rapid increase in accuracy, followed by stable convergence, indicating effective learning. This trend confirms that the hybrid optimization strategy enhances training stability and enables the RACNN to achieve high classification performance without severe oscillations or overfitting.

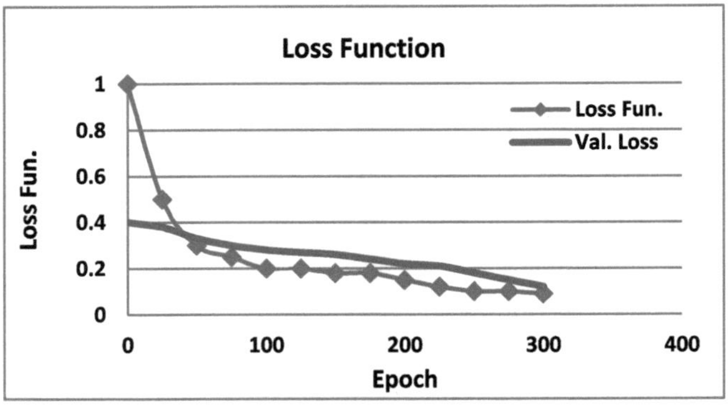

Fig. 6. Loss Function Chart

The training loss curve of the proposed model is shown in Fig. 6. The loss drops quickly in the early epochs and then stabilizes smoothly, indicating effective optimization, rapid convergence, and enhanced training stability achieved through the hybrid Firefly–AdamW optimization strategy, without noticeable overfitting.

The confusion matrix of the testing dataset is shown in Fig. 7, illustrating the classification performance of the proposed model across all garbage categories. The strong concentration of values along the main diagonal indicates high correct classification rates, while small off-diagonal values reflect low misclassification, confirming the model's robustness and ability to distinguish between classes. The confusion matrix shows that most misclassifications occur when clothing is misidentified as trash, paper, or plastic.

The obtained experimental results are then compared with several benchmark DL models stated in previous research in terms of accuracy, precision, recall, and F1-score, as illustrated in Table 4. The comparison results show that the proposed RACNN with hybrid optimization outperforms the other DL models, demonstrating improved classification performance and better generalization than SqueezeNet, MobileViT, and ResNet.

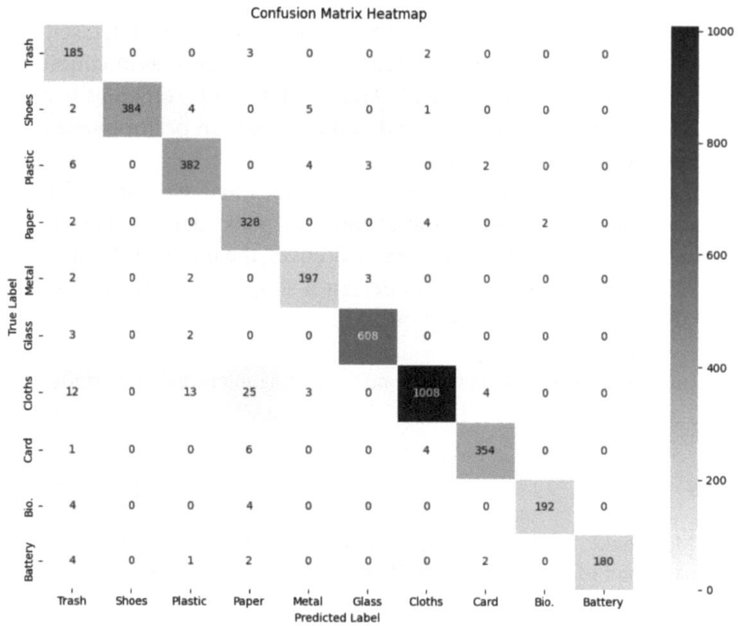

Fig. 7. Testing dataset confusion matrix

Table 4. Comparison between the proposed RACNN and other methods

Model	Accuracy	Precision	Recall	F1-Score
SqueezNet	92.8%	92.9%	92.8%	92.8%
MobileViT	95.5%	95.5%	95.5%	95.5%
ResNet	94.7%	94.4%	94.7%	94.5%
The Proposed Model	96.5%	95.5%	96.7%	96%

5 Conclusion

As more and more people care about protecting the environment and using resources sustainably, garbage classification is an urgent issue for everyone. The current classification methods depend too much on people doing the work, which can be affected by factors such as their quality, attention, and sense of responsibility. Fast, accurate automatic classification technology is very important and will be the only way for society to move forward. Using AI technology to sort trash can make sorting faster and cheaper, which is good for business. An effective garbage classification model that combines several intelligent and mathematical techniques. Starting with RACNN for feature selection. The BPNN with improved weights based on a new chaotic map is used to generate balanced, high-quality randomized weight values. The performance of this network is optimized through the Firefly gradient algorithm to establish a well-optimized starting point. Our proposed approach achieved 96.5% accuracy on the test dataset; therefore, it is a promising approach in the important area of garbage image classification. Finally, the proposed technique uses fine-tuning with AdamW for stable, efficient learning. Using several evaluation metrics, our technique demonstrates high performance compared to several conventional models in the literature.

As future work, since trash comes in many shapes and sizes in real life. It would be interesting to learn more about how to build a robust data collection platform or augment datasets using adversarial learning. Moreover, the garbage classification system only works with a single object; we can design a simple, effective garbage-collection platform that shows multiple objects at once.

Disclosure of Interests. The authors declare no competing interests in this study.

References

1. Kaza, S., McDonald, R.Y., Zilberti, L.L.: What a Waste 2.0: A Global Snapshot of Solid Waste Management to 2050. The World Bank, Washington DC (2018)
2. Zhihong, C., Hebin, Z., Yanbo, W., Binyan, L., Yu, L.:A vision-based robotic grasping system using deep learning for garbage sorting. In: 2017 36th Chinese Control Conference (CCC), pp. 1216–1221. IEEE (2017). https://doi.org/10.23919/chicc.2017.8029147
3. Li, X., et al.: Learning fusion feature representation for garbage image classification model in human–robot interaction. Infrared Phys. Technol. **126**, 104457 (2023). https://doi.org/10.1016/j.infrared.2022.104457
4. Khellal, A., Ma, H., Fei, Q.: 'Convolutional neural network based on extreme learning machine for maritime ships recognition in infrared images.' Sensors **18**(5), 1490 (2018)
5. Abd, W.H., Sadiq, A.T., Hussein, K.A.: Human fall down recognition using coordinates key points skeleton. In: 2022 3rd Information Technology to Enhance e-learning and Other Application (IT-ELA), pp. 232–237. Baghdad, Iraq (2022). https://doi.org/10.1109/IT-ELA57378.2022.10107951
6. Abdullah, S.M., et al.: Complex-valued neural networks with super activation function. Int. J. Innovat. Comput. Inform. Control **20**(6) (2024)
7. Vo, A.H., Hoang Son, L., Vo, M.T., Le, T.: A novel framework for trash classification using deep transfer learning. IEEE Access **7**, 178631–178639 (2019)
8. AlSheikh, M.H., Al-Saidi, N.M.G., Ibrahim, R.W.: Dental X-ray identification system based on association rules extracted by k-Symbol fractional Haar functions. Fractal Fraction. **6**(11), 669
9. Yousif, S.A., Samawi, V.W., Al-Saidi, N.M.G.: Automatic machine learning classification algorithms for stability detection of smart grid. In: 2022 IEEE 5th International Conference on Big Data and Artificial Intelligence (BDAI). IEEE (2022)
10. Samawi, V.W., Yousif, S.A., Al-Saidi, N.M.G.: Intrusion detection system: an automatic machine learning algorithms using auto-WEKA. In: 2022 IEEE 13th control and system graduate research colloquium (ICSGRC). IEEE (2022)
11. Toprak, A.: Determination of colorectal cancer and lung cancer related LncRNAs based on deep autoencoder and deep neural network. Int. J. Comput. Exp. Sci. Eng. **10**(4), 201–210 (2024). https://doi.org/10.22399/ijcesen.636
12. Devananda Rao, K.B., Madhavi, M.: BCDNet: a deep learning model with improved convolutional neural network for efficient detection of bone cancer using histology images. Int. J. Comput. Exp. Sci. Eng. **10**(4), 150–158 (2024). https://doi.org/10.22399/ijcesen.430

13. Abedi, W.M.S., Nadher, I., Sadiq, A.T.: Modification of deep learning technique for face expressions and body postures recognitions. Int. J. Adv. Sci. Technol. **29**(3s), 313–320 (2020)
14. Skar, G.E., Mokbel, M., Darwich, M.N., Hadi, A., Khneisser, A.: Comparing deep learning and support vector machines for autonomous waste sorting. In: 2016 IEEE International Multidisciplinary Conference on Engineering Technology (IMCET), pp. 207–212 (2016)
15. Sevinç, A., Ozyurt, F.: Classification of recyclable waste using deep learning architectures. Firat Univ. J. Experimen. Comput. Eng. **1**(3), 122–128 (2022). https://doi.org/10.5505/fujece.2022.83997
16. Haque, N., Toufiq, R., Islam, M.D.Z., Shoukhin, M.A.A.T.: Garbage classification using a transfer learning with parameter tuning. In: 2024 6th International Conference on Electrical Engineering and Information & Communication Technology (ICEEICT), pp. 1252–1256 (2024). https://doi.org/10.1109/iceeict62016.2024.10534450
17. Kuang, E.Z., Bhandari, K.R., Gao, J.: Optimizing waste management with advanced object detection for garbage classification, arXiv, 2024, https://doi.org/10.48550/ARXIV.2410.09975
18. Zhang, Q., Yang, Q., Zhang, X., Bao, Q., Su, J., Liu, X.: Waste image classification based on transfer learning and convolutional neural network. Waste Manage. **135**, 150–157 (2021). https://doi.org/10.1016/j.wasman.2021.08.038
19. Kang, Z., Yang, J., Li, G., Zhang, Z.: An automatic garbage classification system based on deep learning. IEEE Access **8**, 140019–140029 (2020). https://doi.org/10.1109/access.2020.3010496
20. Khan, A., Sohail, A., Zahoora, U., Qureshi, A.S.: Deep learning for image classification: a comprehensive review. IEEE Access **8**, 85225–85265 (2020). https://doi.org/10.1109/ACCESS.2020.2992555
21. Sindhwani, N., et al.: Performance analysis of deep neural networks using computer vision. EAI Endorsed Trans. Indust. Networks Intell. Syst. **8**(29) (2021). https://doi.org/10.4108/eai.13-10-2021.171318
22. Brodzicki, A., Piekarski, M., Kucharski, D., Jaworek-Korjakowska ve, J., Gorgoń, M.: Transfer learning methods as a new approach in computer vision tasks with small datasets. Foundat. Comput. Dec. Scie. **45**(3), 179–193 (2020). https://doi.org/10.2478/fcds-2020-0010
23. Joshi, R., Maritammanavar, A., Singh, A., Kumar, C.: Transfer learning in computer vision: technique and applications. J. Propul. Technol. **44**(1), 81–83 (2023). https://doi.org/10.52783/tjjpt.v44.i1.2210
24. A Comprehensive Image Dataset for Garbage Classification and Recycling, https://doi.org/10.34740/kaggle/dsv/10182596
25. Yang, X.S.: Nature-Inspired Metaheuristic Algorithms. Luniver Press. ISBN 978-1-905986-10-1 (2008)
26. Loshchilov, I., Hutter, F.: Decoupled weight decay regularization, arXiv preprint arXiv:1711.05101 (2017)

Performance Enhancement in Clustering Cloud Workload Trace Big Data for Cloud Data Center

Suhad A. Yousif[1], Susan M. Al Naqshbandi[2], Suzan J. Obaiys[3], Hayder H. Maala[4], and Nur Amalina Binti Jamaludin[5(✉)]

[1] Computer Science Department, Al-Nahrain University, Baghdad, Iraq
Suhad.a.yousif@nahrainuniv.edu.iq
[2] Computer Engineering Department, Komar University of Science and Technology (KUST), Sulaymaniyah, Iraq
susan.alnaqshbandi@komar.edu.iq
[3] Department of Computer System and Technology, Faculty of Computer Science and Information Technology, Universiti Malaya, 50603 Kuala Lumpur, Malaysia
suzan@um.edu.my
[4] University of Technology, Baghdad, Iraq
hayder.h.maala@uotechnology.edu.iq
[5] Department of Mathematics, Centre for Foundation Defence Studies, National Defence University of Malaysia, 57000 Kuala Lumpur, Malaysia
amalinajamaludin@upnm.edu.my

Abstract. Cloud computing has received considerable interest from research institutions, developers, and individuals in the last few years. The complexity and scale increase of cloud environments encourage realistic workload-representative benchmarks and stronger performance analysis. This paper tackles energy-consumption enhancement in cloud data centers by proposing an energy-efficient strategy that clusters user tasks and then serves them according to CPU demand. The study uses the Google cluster trace, recorded from approximately 12,500 machines, as a real cloud environment. A large-scale clustering process was performed over about 50 million task records using k-means executed in SQL Server. The clustering stage produced three workload groups—high, medium, and low CPU usage—and the mean value of each cluster was later used as a threshold for task allocation. Based on these thresholds, a CPU-Based Allocation (CPUBA) approach was implemented in CloudSim. Experimental results show that strategic workload distribution over data-center machines improves resource utilization and reduces power consumption.

Keywords: Google Cluster Trace · Clustering · Performance Enhancement · K-means · Cloud Computing · Big Data · CloudSim · Power Consumption · CPU Rate

O. Gervasi et al. (Eds.): ICCSA 2026 Workshops, LNCS 16758, pp. 270–283, 2027.
https://doi.org/10.1007/978-3-032-30497-1_17

1 Introduction

Cloud computing has become a core paradigm for delivering scalable, on-demand services through shared and virtualized infrastructures. Its growth has transformed data centers into large, highly dynamic computing environments that support big data processing, scientific applications, and AI-driven services. At the same time, this growth has intensified concerns about energy usage, operational cost, and sustainable resource management, making energy-efficient scheduling and allocation central research problems in modern cloud systems [1,2].

A substantial body of recent work has focused on reducing energy consumption in cloud data centers through workload-aware consolidation, predictive resource management, and environmentally sustainable scheduling. Panwar et al. [1] reviewed energy-utilization management strategies for cloud data centers and showed the breadth of heuristic, metaheuristic, machine-learning, and statistical approaches used to reduce energy demand. Wang et al. [2] proposed an energy-aware VM-consolidation strategy based on combined prediction to reduce energy consumption, VM migrations, and SLA violations in CloudSim-based evaluation. These studies confirm that energy-aware allocation remains an active and practical research direction.

Within this direction, Clustering techniques play a central role in workload characterization for cloud environments. While k-means clustering [3] is widely adopted due to its simplicity and scalability, density-based methods such as DBSCAN (Density-Based Spatial Clustering of Applications with Noise) provide an alternative approach by identifying clusters based on data density rather than distance to centroids [4,5]. DBSCAN is particularly effective in detecting arbitrarily shaped clusters and handling noise, making it suitable for complex and heterogeneous datasets. Clustering-based workload analysis has remained especially relevant because it offers a lightweight and scalable way to characterize large traces and support allocation decisions. In work directly related to the present study, Yousif and Al-Dulaimy [6] presented a clustering-based analysis of cloud workload traces to improve cloud data-center performance. Maala and Yousif [7] later examined Google cluster-trace data and used k-means-based clustering over large-scale workload records to derive CPU-oriented groupings that support more suitable task distribution. In a related big-data clustering contribution, Sagheer and Yousif [8] proposed a parallel clustering model based on Hadoop multi-node deployment and Apache Mahout, highlighting Suhad A. Yousif's continued research interest in scalable clustering and big-data analysis. Together, these studies provide a clear methodological foundation for integrating workload clustering with efficient cloud resource management.

More recent literature has expanded the discussion from workload characterization toward thermal-aware, learning-based, and sustainability-oriented cloud control. Alissa et al. [9] proposed a holistic thermal-aware workload and infrastructure-control framework for heterogeneous data centers using machine learning, showing that workload placement and cooling control should be considered jointly. Wang et al. [2] developed a reinforcement-learning framework for environmentally sustainable federated-cloud task scheduling, explicitly addressing both energy consumption and carbon emissions. Feng and Ding [10] surveyed cloud workload prediction from an application-oriented perspective and highlighted its importance for cost reduction, performance assurance, and energy optimization. These developments show that current cloud scheduling research increasingly combines predictive analytics, learning-based control, and sustainability objectives.

Recent studies have also explored hybrid intelligent scheduling schemes. [11] proposed a hybrid cuckoo-search and transformer-based task-scheduling approach for cloud environments and reported improvements in energy-aware scheduling performance. Such methods are promising, but they are often computationally heavier and more difficult to deploy than clustering-based approaches, especially when the target environment involves very large traces and simulation-driven evaluation. This creates space for practical methods that retain low complexity while still improving placement quality and energy efficiency.

Motivated by this gap, the present paper adopts a clustering-driven strategy for task classification and allocation in cloud data centers. The proposed CPU-Based Allocation (CPUBA) approach uses thresholds derived from large-scale workload-trace analysis to classify tasks according to CPU demand and then allocate them to virtual machines in a manner that improves utilization and reduces unnecessary activation of physical machines. By building on prior clustering-based workload studies while addressing current energy-efficiency concerns, the paper positions its contribution between classical trace-driven scheduling and newer intelligent resource-management approaches.

For evaluation, the work relies on real Google cluster-trace characteristics together with CloudSim-based experimentation, aiming to demonstrate that clustering-informed allocation can still offer a practical and effective path toward energy-aware cloud resource management.

2 Proposed Methodology

Clustered cloud computing is used for providing an environment for services of various categories. There is room for much performance improvement in the field of clustered cloud computing. The indicators considered in this paper include the reduction of power consumption, network and storage usage, in addition to waiting and scheduling time.

To get a more accurate understanding of the scenarios in which cloud data centers operate, real data collected and offered by Google was used. The data was recorded from a Google cloud cluster of approximately 12,500 machines for 29 days. Data collection, cleaning, and normalization operations were performed after downloading the released files using the `gsutil` tool, which provides access to Google Cloud Storage and supports tasks such as downloading, editing, and deleting stored data [12].

After downloading the data, normalization operations were used to convert the raw dump files into readable data and then gather the required files into one SQL dataset. The k-means clustering algorithm was then performed over approximately 50 million CPU-rate records to produce three thresholds by big-data clustering. These thresholds represent high-, medium-, and low-CPU usage tasks. The resulting groups are used later by the proposed allocation method. The overall workflow is shown in Fig. 1.

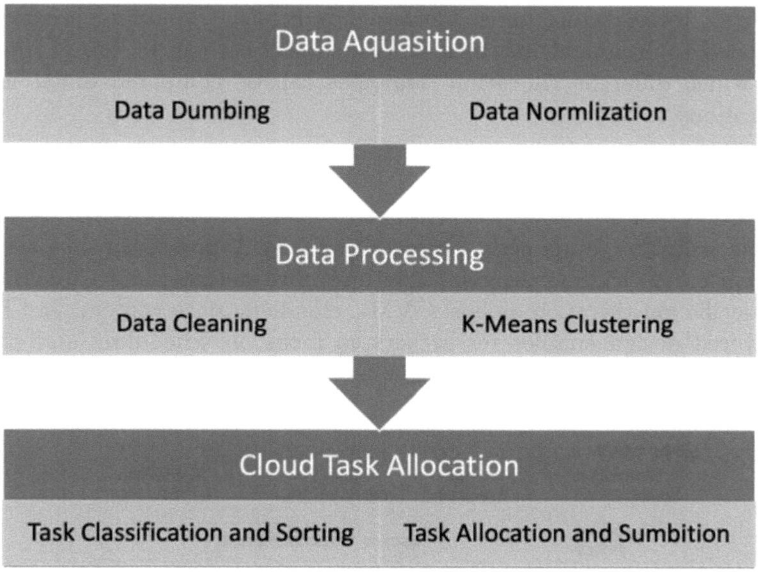

Fig. 1. Main stages of the proposed methodology.

Our previous work [7] describes the decompression workflow and the automatic import of 500 CSV files into SQL Server using a sequential C# implementation that preserves the original record ordering.

2.1 Modeling and Simulation with CloudSim

The objective of cloud computing is to power new generations of data centers that can deploy applications that fully suit the users' QoS requirements. Such applications require a wide range of specifications, including deployment, structure, and configuration. Problems that challenge cloud developers include quantifying resource-allocation policy performance and developing algorithms for scheduling, power consumption, heat dissipation, and system sizing.

CloudSim is an extensible simulation toolkit that enables the modeling and simulation of cloud-computing environments. In this work, CloudSim was used to model virtual machines, tasks, task-to-VM mapping, and the policies associated with allocation and scheduling [13,14]. It can simulate multiple data centers and also supports VM migration and the study of allocation policies.

Cloud computing delivers infrastructure, platform, and software services as subscription-based services, commonly represented as IaaS, PaaS, and SaaS. The cloud aims to power the next generation of data centers, providing network-accessible services that can be deployed on demand with a competitive cost that depends primarily on QoS requirements. This enables providers and customers to test deployments and evaluate strategies before deployment in real environments.

Simulation tools are especially useful because real infrastructures are costly and difficult to reproduce under identical conditions. CloudSim therefore offers a controlled environment in which developed services can be tested repeatedly and in which different allocation strategies can be compared under identical configurations.

2.2 CloudSim Architecture

CloudSim software components are shown in Fig. 2. SimJava forms the event-simulation core, GridSim provides grid-level abstractions, and CloudSim adds cloud-specific entities such as hosts, VMs, cloudlets, data centers, and brokers. This layered design enables researchers to focus on scheduling and resource-provisioning policies while avoiding low-level implementation overhead [13–15].

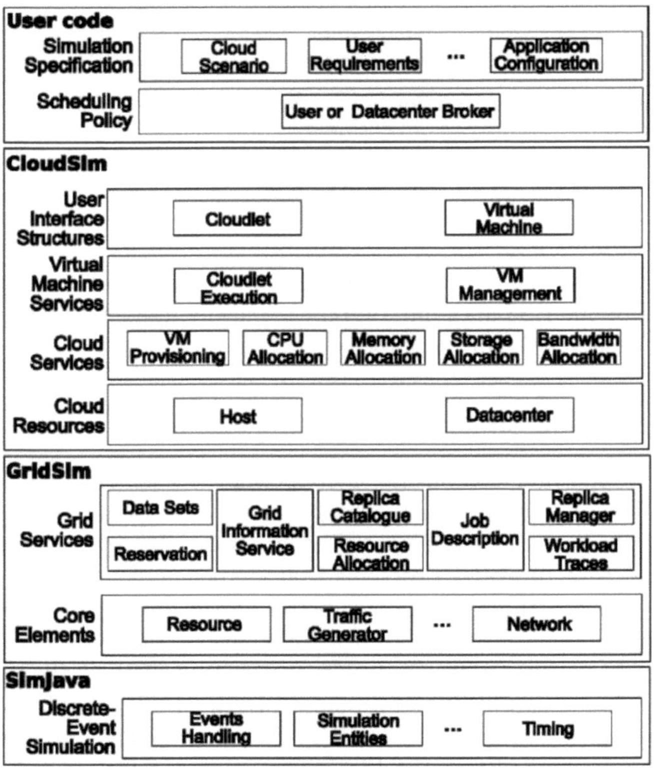

Fig. 2. Layered CloudSim architecture.

2.3 VM and Jobs Allocation

In cloud computing, tasks are submitted by many users and executed via heterogeneous VMs. Each task is mapped to a VM that suits the request, while VMs are hosted on physical machines. Such processes require effective resource allocation for bandwidth, memory, CPU, and storage. The problem of VM allocation and placement is NP-hard [16].

Based on the system model above, this work proposes an approach for energy efficiency in virtualized cloud data centers. The approach presents a classification model for jobs and a VM-placement strategy known as mixed-type placement, intending to reduce energy waste in the data center [17,18].

The proposed model assumes a fully virtualized cloud-computing environment where jobs are submitted together with fixed QoS requirements. Jobs are initially handled by a global scheduler and then forwarded to a specific data center for later VM allocation and PM placement. The workload is modeled as a bag of tasks (BoT), where tasks are autonomous and do not communicate with one another [18].

2.4 Strategic Allocation and Placement of Tasks

The proposed CPUBA approach follows the sequence below:

1. The user submits the job to the cloud host.
2. A preprocessing step identifies the task class according to its CPU requirement.
3. The task is stored with other tasks of similar CPU requirements.
4. The task CPU-integration process combines multiple jobs and forwards them to a suitable VM.

There are two main policies in cloud-computing environments for allocating tasks to VMs: space-shared and time-shared [15]. This work uses the space-shared policy. Available VM configurations are sorted in ascending order according to the number of cores, and each job is matched sequentially with the lowest suitable VM configuration.

The CPU architecture supports various frequencies, and each job is allocated to a VM with a specific frequency level. This makes it possible to scale CPU-core frequencies using DVFS. When a VM is allocated to a low-CPU job, the frequency can be minimized provided the QoS requirement is maintained. This contributes to lower power use.

The four possible combinations considered during the proposed VM allocation are:

1- Lowest low-CPU jobs with lowest mid-CPU jobs and highest high-CPU jobs.
2- Lowest low-CPU jobs with highest mid-CPU jobs and highest high-CPU jobs.
3- Highest low-CPU jobs with highest mid-CPU jobs and lowest high-CPU jobs.
4- Highest low-CPU jobs with lowest mid-CPU jobs and lowest high-CPU jobs.

Applying CPUBA enhances energy efficiency in two ways: it reduces the number of active PMs and improves the utilization of those PMs. The overall job life cycle is illustrated in Fig. 3.

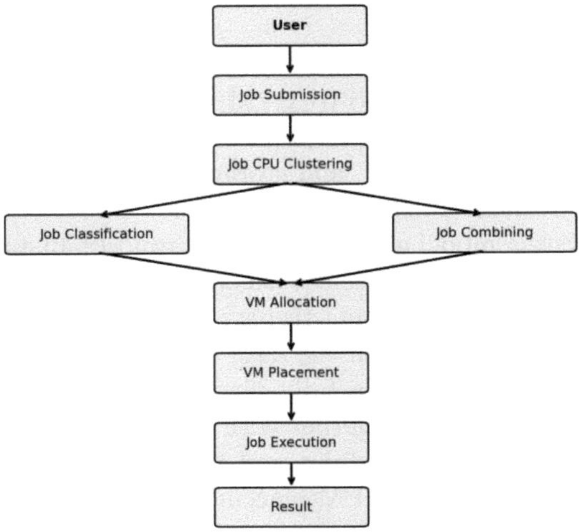

Fig. 3. User's job life cycle in the CPUBA approach.

3 Cloud Environments and Experiment Results

After obtaining the clustering results, the work moved to the next stage, which represents the implementation of the data-clustering outputs over a cloud-computing environment. The experimentation used CloudSim [14]. Two phases were considered: the first examined task allocation using default available methods; the second examined the proposed CPUBA allocation over the same environment, using the same data and variables (Tables 1 and 2).

Table 1. Features and variables of VMs/hosts in the experimental cloud environment.

Category	Feature/Variable	Value
VM	Number of Virtual Machines (VMs)	20
VM	Number of processing elements (PEs)	20
VM	RAM Size (MB)	512
VM	Storage Size (MB)	10000
VM	Bandwidth (MB)	1000

Table 2. Features and variables of cloudlets in the experimental environment.

Category	Feature/Variable	Value
Cloudlet	Number of Cloudlets	100
Cloudlet	Number of processing elements (PEs)	16
Cloudlet	Cloudlet length	Calculated thresholds
Cloudlet	File Size	1024
Cloudlet	Output Size	1024

3.1 Task Distribution over the Cloud Data Center

Experimentation was performed on ten hosts using the default CloudSim allocation policies and the proposed CPUBA approach. One hundred cloudlets were executed in both settings. Table 3 shows the distribution produced by the default space-shared/round-robin allocation, while Table 4 shows the result produced by CPUBA over the same cloud environment and the same cloudlet-length range (Figs. 4 and 5).

Table 3. Cloudlet distribution (CPU length/time) under default allocation.

Host	No. Tasks	Task CPU Length	Time
0	10	916176	922
1	10	852057	857
2	10	829579	835
3	10	905116	912
4	10	1046482	1052
5	10	950866	955
6	10	1063518	1071
7	10	842172	848
8	10	739412	745
9	10	951568	957
Total	100	9096946	9154

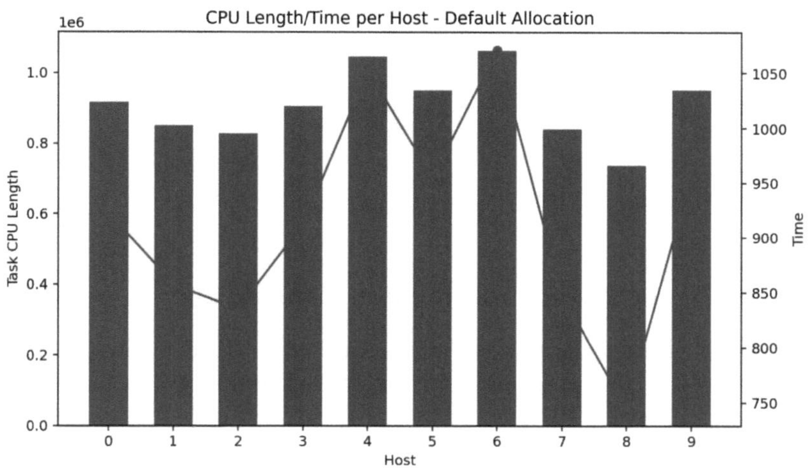

Fig. 4. CPU length/time per host for the default allocation.

Table 4. Cloudlet distribution (CPU length/time) under CPUBA.

Host	No. Tasks	Task CPU Length	Time
0	10	1040912	1047
1	10	806787	813
2	10	1056381	1061
3	10	811029	817
4	10	990039	994
5	10	697184	703
6	10	1017719	1024
7	10	788752	794
8	10	1079281	1086
9	10	808862	815
Total	100	9096946	9154

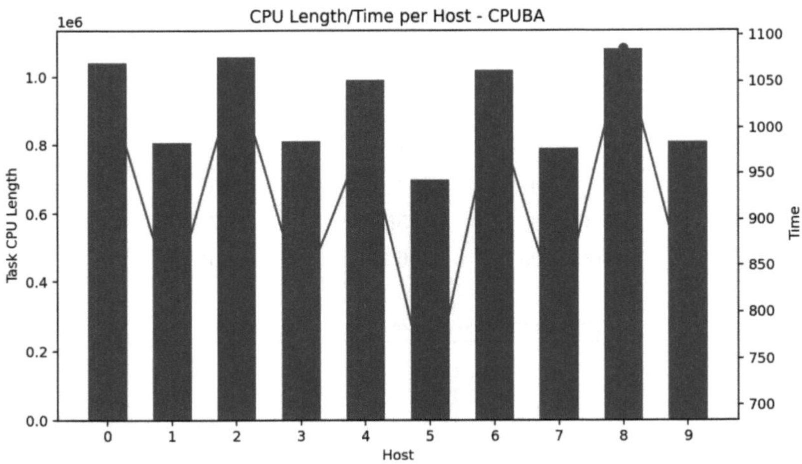

Fig. 5. CPU length/time per host for CPUBA.

3.2 Data Center Power Consumption Comparison

This section illustrates the power-consumption improvement obtained by using the proposed CPUBA approach. Both policies were applied to the same data center, using the same CPU cloudlet lengths and identical environment characteristics (Table 5).

Table 5. Datacenter total power consumption: default allocation vs. CPUBA.

Default allocation			CPUBA		
Host	Watt-Sec	KWh	Host	Watt-Sec	KWh
0	27375	0.00760	0	23026	0.00640
1	27312	0.00759	1	22308	0.00620
2	27250	0.00757	2	23075	0.00641
3	27472	0.00763	3	22321	0.00620
4	27903	0.00775	4	22881	0.00636
5	27617	0.00767	5	22010	0.00611
6	27811	0.00773	6	22962	0.00638
7	27297	0.00758	7	22249	0.00618
8	26832	0.00745	8	23141	0.00643
9	27600	0.00767	9	22305	0.00620
Total	274469	0.07624	Total	226278	0.06287

Figures 6, 7, 8 and 9 illustrate the power-consumption profiles of the datacenter hosts for the default policy and CPUBA.

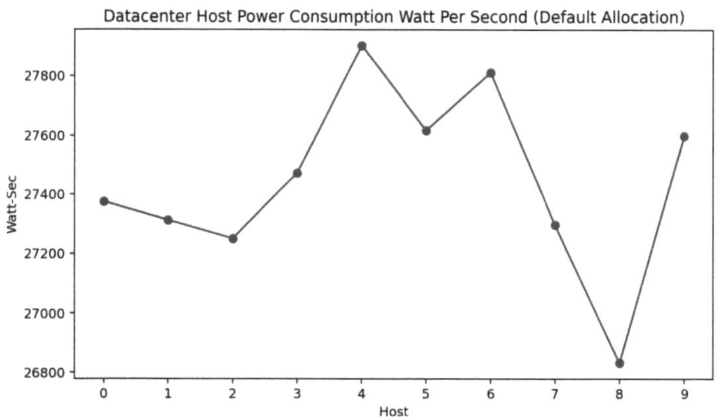

Fig. 6. Datacenter host power consumption in watt-seconds under default allocation.

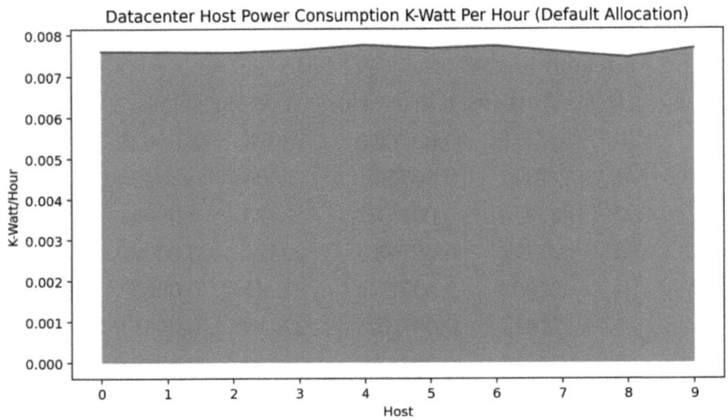

Fig. 7. Datacenter host power consumption in kilowatt-hours under default allocation.

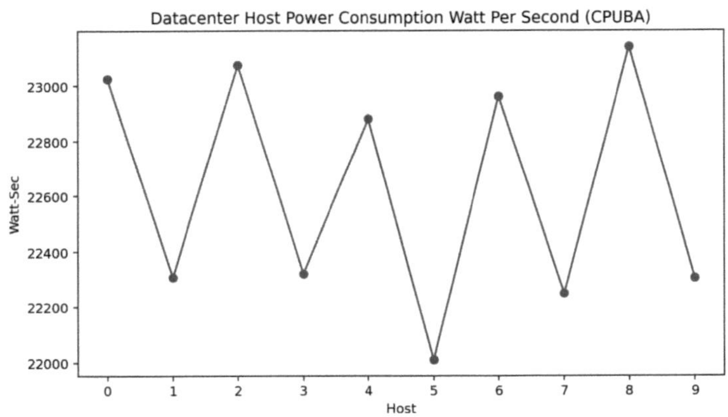

Fig. 8. Datacenter host power consumption in watt-seconds under CPUBA.

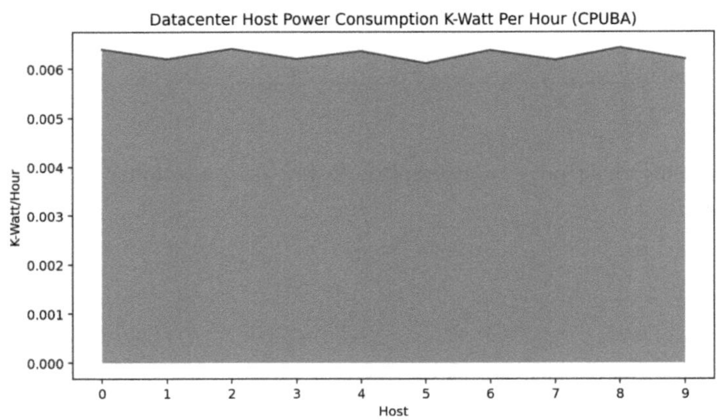

Fig. 9. Datacenter host power consumption in kilowatt-hours under CPUBA.

The main intention of this work is to develop an allocation approach for more efficient task allocation over cloud data-center hosts, PMs, and VMs. Power consumption improved in the same data center with identical characteristics and tasks. The improvement total and enhancement percentage are summarized in Table 6.

Table 6. Datacenter power-consumption improvement.

Result	Total Watts	Total K-Watts
CPUBA Result	226278	0.062
Original Result	274469	0.076
Improvement Total	48191	0.010
Improvement %	17.5	17.5

4 Conclusion

The analysis of Google trace data in this work targeted a large number of task-usage records representing the requirements of tasks operating in the Google cloud during the recording period. The analysis of 50 million task records produced CPU thresholds that were later used for cloud data-center allocation.

The study concludes that task allocation and distribution over suitable machine clusters has a significant impact on performance enhancement, especially when the number of clusters is substantial and the clustering stage is based on large-scale real workload traces. Based on the results, cloud machine-resource availability and workload behavior can be predicted more clearly. This supports the orientation of new tasks toward the most suitable machine group, which reduces scheduling time, waiting time, and unnecessary resource waste.

Cloud-environment performance enhancement is difficult to achieve by focusing on only one aspect, due to the variety of cloud challenges and performance factors. In this work, both the power factor and scheduling time were enhanced. The experimentation reveals the following points:

- Real cloud-data analysis provides a clearer presentation of cloud work patterns and performance factors.
- Task allocation and distribution over cloud data centers has a positive effect on cloud-environment performance.
- The requested CPU rate of each task can play a significant role in the task-allocation process.
- Pre-sorting tasks before VM allocation has a clear positive effect on task allocation, scheduling time, and processor power loss.

5 Future Work

Future work can analyze larger data volumes to find more workload groups and more accurate CPU thresholds by using big-data processing environments such as Hadoop ecosystems. Another promising direction is to extend the task-distribution model by considering additional task requirements such as RAM, in addition to CPU usage, in order to obtain a clearer representation of the resources needed by each task and later improve allocation efficiency in CloudSim or a real cloud environment.

Acknowledgements. This research was sponsored by the University of Malaya Translational Research Grant Scheme, TRG0019-2025 (UM.0002388/HRU.IP) and the Research Excellence Grant, UMREG 068 - 2024 (UM.0000285/HRU.RC).

Conflicts of Interest. The authors declare no conflict of interest.

References

1. Panwar, S.S., Rauthan, M.M.S., Barthwal, V.: A systematic review on effective energy utilization management strategies in cloud data centers. J. Cloud Comput. **11**, 95 (2022)
2. Wang, Z., et al.: Reinforcement learning based task scheduling for environmentally sustainable federated cloud computing. J. Cloud Comput. **12**(1), 174 (2023)
3. Azkeskin, S.A., Aladağ, Z.: Evaluating regional sustainable energy potential through hierarchical clustering and machine learning. Environ. Res. Commun. **7**(1), 015002 (2025)
4. Abdulhameed, T.Z., Yousif, S.A., Samawi, V.W., Al-Shaikhli, H.I.: SS-DBSCAN: semi-supervised density-based spatial clustering of applications with noise for meaningful clustering in diverse density data. IEEE Access **12**, 131507–131520 (2024)
5. Widjaja, A.E., Toer, G.A., et al.: Clustering digital governance adoption patterns in the metaverse using K-Means and DBSCAN algorithms. Int. J. Res. Metaverse **3**(1), 1–13 (2026)
6. Yousif, S.A., Al-Dulaimy, A.: Clustering cloud workload traces to improve the performance of cloud data centers. In: Proceedings of the World Congress on Engineering, vol. 1, pp. 7–10 (2017)
7. Maala, H.H., Yousif, S.A.: Cluster trace analysis for performance enhancement in cloud computing environments. J. Theoret. Appl. Inf. Technol. **97**(7) (2019)
8. Sagheer, N.S., Yousif, S.A.: A parallel clustering analysis based on Hadoop multi-node and Apache Mahout. Iraqi J. Sci. **62**(7) (2021)
9. Pulse Global: Big Data for development: challenges and opportunities (2012). Retrieved 12 Dec 2012
10. Feng, X., Siarry, P., Han, L., Yang, L.: Cloud Computing. Springer, Switzerland (2025)
11. Nandagopal, M., et al.: Enhancing energy efficiency in cloud computing through task scheduling with hybrid cuckoo search and transformer models. Discov. Comput. **28**(1), 199 (2025)
12. UN Global Pulse: Big data for development: Challenges & opportunities (2012)

13. Buyya, R., Ranjan, R., Calheiros, R.N.: Modeling and simulation of scalable cloud computing environments and the CloudSim toolkit: challenges and opportunities. In: 2009 International Conference on High Performance Computing & Simulation, pp. 1–11. IEEE (2009)
14. Calheiros, R.N., Ranjan, R., Beloglazov, A., De Rose, C.A.F., Buyya, R.: CloudSim: a toolkit for modeling and simulation of cloud computing environments and evaluation of resource provisioning algorithms. Softw. Pract. Exp. **41**(1), 23–50 (2011)
15. Wickremasinghe, B., Calheiros, R.N., Buyya, R.: CloudAnalyst: a CloudSim-based visual modeller for analysing cloud computing environments and applications. In: 2010 24th IEEE International Conference on Advanced Information Networking and Applications, pp. 446–452. IEEE (2010)
16. Zhang, Q., Cheng, L., Boutaba, R.: Cloud computing: state-of-the-art and research challenges. J. Internet Serv. Appl. **1**(1), 7–18 (2010). https://doi.org/10.1007/s13174-010-0007-6
17. Aldulaimy, A., Zantout, R., Zekri, A., Itani, W.: Job classification in cloud computing: the classification effects on energy efficiency. In: 2015 IEEE/ACM 8th International Conference on Utility and Cloud Computing (UCC), pp. 547–552. IEEE (2015)
18. Thai, L., Varghese, B., Barker, A.: A survey and taxonomy of resource optimisation for executing bag-of-task applications on public clouds. Futur. Gener. Comput. Syst. **82**, 1–11 (2018)

A Trust Optimization Region of the Quantum Natural Gradient for the Large Damping Domain

Nawres A. Alwan[1], Suzan J. Obaiys[1(✉)], Nadia M. G. Al-Saidi[2], and Rayane Chadli[1]

[1] Department of Computer System and Technology, Faculty of Computer Science and Information Technology, Universiti Malaya, 50603 Kuala Lumpur, Malaysia
suzan@um.edu.my

[2] Department of Applied Sciences, University of Technology, Baghdad 10066, Iraq

Abstract. Natural Gradient Descent is the steepest descent with respect to geometric information in parameter space. The Quantum Natural Gradient (QNG) optimization mode provides geometry-aware optimization for variational quantum algorithms (VQAs) by incorporating the curvature of quantum state space through the Quantum Geometric Tensor (QGT) or Fubini-Study metric. However, the standard QNG updates are intrinsically ill-posed because the Fubini–Study metric is generically singular under redundant parameterizations, leading to non-unique or unstable update steps. The work develops a regularized Riemannian quadratic model that yields a geometrically principled trust-region formulation of the damped QNG and proves that the mix of QGT with a Tikhonov regularization term results in the unique minimizer of a strictly convex local approximation of the loss landscape, thereby ensuring existence, uniqueness, and numerical stability for all damping levels $\lambda > 0$. Further, it is demonstrated that the proposed method guarantees descent in the large-damping regime, and analytically shows a continuous interpolation between QNG and Euclidean Gradient Descent (EGD), recovering EGD as $\lambda \to \infty$. However, to quantify trust in the local quantum geometry, the gain-ratio–based damping rule that is similar to the classical Trust-region methods were also introduced, providing a principled mechanism for adapting λ based on model fidelity. Benchmark analyses comparing recent QNG-based optimizers, including Hamiltonian-aware QNG, qBANG, and full metric QNG, illustrate that our regularized model achieves convergence speeds comparable to standard QNG, while providing superior stability, eliminating overshooting under near-singular metrics, finite-shot noise, and redundant parameterizations. In small-scale Variational Quantum Eigensolver (VQE) experiments (2–12 qubits). The proposed damped QNG reaches target energies in 1–2 iterations, avoids instability noticed in the standard QNG technique, and maintains robust performance under sampling noise. These results establish the regularized QNG trust region as a mathematically grounded, geometry-preserving, and practically robust optimizer for near-term quantum algorithms.

O. Gervasi et al. (Eds.): ICCSA 2026 Workshops, LNCS 16758, pp. 284–300, 2027.
https://doi.org/10.1007/978-3-032-30497-1_18

Keywords: Quantum natural gradient · Quantum geometric tensor · Variational quantum algorithm · Natural gradient descent · Fubini-Study metric

1 Introduction

The Quantum Natural Gradient (QNG) procedures based on the Quantum Geometric Tensor (QGT) have been widely discussed as geometry-aware optimization techniques for Variational Quantum Algorithms (VQA) [1,2,6], where almost all algorithms introduce metric regularization as a numerical heuristic to mitigate ill-conditioning arising from redundant parameterizations or finite-shot noise. Natural Gradient Descent (NGD) is steepest descent with respect to geometric information in parameter space (Riemannian manifold). In quantum information processing, we have QNG, which utilizes the QGT or Fubini-Study metric to induce geometry-aware optimisation on variational quantum states QNG correctly captures state-space curvature. The main problem in optimization of QNG lies in the intrinsic ill-posedness of the standard update equation $g(\theta)\Delta\theta = -\eta\nabla L(\theta)$, which frequently fails to yield a valid solution due to Fubini-Study metric tensor $g(\theta)$ which is generically singular or rank-deficient.

Mathematically, this rank deficiency prevents the inversion of $g(\theta)$, meaning the linear system admits either infinitely many solutions or no solution at all, rather than a unique update step. Physically, this degeneracy is not simply a numerical error but a structural reality arising from the difference between the abstract parameter space and the actual manifold of physical quantum states. Since $g(\theta)$ measures the distance strictly in terms of quantum state distinguishability, any redundancy in the variational circuit, where changes in θ parameters resulting in no observable change to the physical state $|\psi(\theta)\rangle$ that corresponds to the null space of the metric. Consequently, along these "ghost" directions where the physical state remains invariant, the local curvature vanishes, causing the geometric information to collapse and the standard optimization update to break down.

In 2019, Stock et al. [2] employed the metrics that are pseudo-inverse of quantum geometric tensor and the diagonal approximation, which real need a practice regularization to ensure numerical stability. After that, many researchers tried to enhancement this algorithms, such as [8–10], which will be discussed in the related work section. Nawres et al. in [3–5], provided a comprehensive theoretical foundation on quantum mechanics and quantum computing that applied in several representations.

In contrast, the proposed work provides a geometrically principled and optimization-theoretically grounded formulation of QNG stabilization, as a necessary mathematical result, rather than being introduced merely as a suggestion for numerical stability. Specifically, the work demonstrates a regularized QNG update obtained by adding a Tikhonov damping [7] term to the QGT optimizer arises as the *unique minimizer of a locally defined Riemannian quadratic model* of the loss function on parameter space. Correspondingly, establishes the existence, uniqueness, and numerical stability of the update within a unified geometric framework, rather than as an ad hoc modification. Moreover, the outcomes provide an explicit interpretation of the damping parameter as a confidence measure in the local quantum geometry by introducing a gain-ratio-based regularization criterion inspired by the trust-region methods. This yields a rigorous descent guarantee in the large-damping regime and reveals a continuous interpolation between Quantum Natural Gradient and Euclidean Gradient Descent. To the best of our knowledge, this explicit quadratic-model and confidence-region interpretation of damped QNG has not been previously formalized in the quantum optimization literature.

2 Related Works

The VQAs models have benefited from QNG optimizers that utilize the Fubini-Study metric to precondition parameter updates. Therefore, many researchers applied QNG or its variants to improve convergence in Variational Quantum Eigensolver (VQE), Quantum Approximate Optimization Algorithm (QAOA), and related VQAs. This section reviews some literature that utilize the QNG advance. The modern formulation of QNG optimization for VQAs is commonly attributed to Stokes *et al.* (2020) [2], who derived a quantum analogue of Amari's natural gradient by pulling back the Fubini-Study geometry to parameter space. This work obtained the QNG direction $\Delta\theta$ by solving a linear system of the form

$$g(\theta)\,\Delta\theta = -\eta\,\nabla L(\theta) \tag{1}$$

where $g(\theta)$ is the metric, L is the objective, and $\eta > 0$ is a learning-rate.

One of the most difficult things in central mathematics is that the pullback metric $g(\theta)$ is generically positive semidefinite: redundant parameterizations, symmetries, and directions that do not change the physical state and induce a nontrivial kernel. Therefore, the update may be ill-defined or nonunique, resulting in infinitely many solutions; then the numerical inversion becomes unstable, and the standard workaround is the Moore-Penrose pseudoinverse [2]. The early studies of the geometric behavior of the QNG dynamics in VQE settings were given in 2019 by Yamamoto [11], who demonstrated how the curvature information can reshape optimization trajectories or more patterns relative to Euclidean gradient descent (EGD). While these analyses are largely noiseless and conceptual, that raise the following question: how should one stabilize QNG when $g(\theta)$ is singular or poorly conditioned?

In 2020, Wierichs *et al.* [6] introduced a new way of QNG (under the name *NatGrad*), which is used to address rugged energy landscapes and barren plateaus in eigensolvers of the VQA algorithms.

Herein, the authors explicitly noted that by employing Tikhonov regularization of the metric, one may inhibit excessively large or erratic steps, translated as;

$$\big(g(\theta) + \lambda I\big)\Delta\theta = -\eta\,\nabla L(\theta), \qquad \lambda > 0 \tag{2}$$

where λI is damping mechanism used in Levenberg-Marquardt algorithm.

This regularization is a practical control knob that trades geometry-awareness for stability when the metric is near-singular or unreliable. Several studies for developing the QNG that operate along multiple orthogonal directions, but the fundamental problem of metric ill-definition persisted. While, by using quantum Fisher information notions on mixed states, Koczor and Benjamin (2022) [12] generalized QNG beyond unitary pure-state circuits to noisy and non-unitary settings. This work line is motivated by the fact that decoherence and the Completely positive trace-Preserving (CPTP) map dynamics change the effective geometry in realistic devices, making metric estimation and conditioning more difficult. Simultaneously, in 2024, Sasaki and Miyahara [13] introduced QNG based on the perspective of information geometry, where the experimental variations outside of the typical monotone-metric setting and elucidating nuances in the geometry underpinning QNG optimizer.

More recently, resource-reduction and approximation strategies have become prominent because exact QNG requires estimating an $m \times m$ metric. In 2024, Kolotouros and Wallden [14] introduced a paper titled *Random Natural Gradient* for enhancing the QNG, which used the stochastic coordinate variants with random measurements to construct a cheaper classical Fisher matrix approximation (which is a weakness point that will be discussed later in this paper) to the QFIM/QGT geometry, while also emphasizing that zero eigenvalues correspond to singularities, that is, the directions with no state change and hence motivate pseudoinverse- or regularisation-based treatments. In 2025, Halla [15] introduced some complementary developments for geometry-enhancing updates via higher-order manifold integration, geodesic corrections and they remark that the Fubini-Study metric is used *after Tikhonov regularization* due to ill-definition issues in variational quantum algorithms.

Also, many researchers introduced many algorithm to enhancement the QNG, such as in 2025, Dell'Anna *et al.* [8] proposed a new algorithm used applied full-metric QNG to the Quantum Approximate Optimization Algorithm (QAOA), in the same year, Shi *et al.* [9] introduced a Hamiltonian-aware QNG (H-QNG), and Fitzek *et al.* [10] proposed qBANG, combining QNG with Broyden-type quasi-Newton updates and momentum acceleration. While, The work in [11–14] will constitute the main focus of the discussion in this paper.

Recently, literature, especially in 2023-2026 period, adding λI value or in other words, closely related diagonal shifts appears primarily as a stabilization heuristic, to ensure invertibility and control large steps when $g(\theta)$ metric is singular or noisy [6,15]. Consequently, this work fundamentally change the question from *how* to numerically stabilize the update, to *why* is such regularization is a mathematical requisite and geometrically optimal? By re-framing the algorithm of the damped step, we move beyond ad hoc fixes to provide a full algorithm of the characterized theoretical optimisation, by demonstrating the proposed update that arises naturally as the unique minimizer of a local regularized Riemannian quadratic model as a unique way for the damped step. The proposed theoretical change enables us to see λ as a confidence (trust) parameter that precisely regulates the trade-off between enforcing quantum geometry and defaulting to Euclidean descent, rather than just as a correction factor. By establishing this equivalence, the quantum-geometric meaning of $g(\theta)$ is strictly preserved while providing a principled bridge to the classical trust-region and Levenberg-Marquardt theory. And finally conclude that the empirical evidence of studies shows:

- The QNG-based optimizers consistently outperform Euclidean GD in convergence speed;
- The metric regularization is essential for stability on realistic quantum hardware;
- The adaptive and damped QNG variants improve robustness without sacrificing accuracy.

3 Regularized Riemannian Quadratic Model for Damped QNG

To move optimally on the manifold of quantum states, the QNG implements the quantum Fubini–Study metric and when the enhancement becomes unstable because of the ill-conditioned metrics, noisy estimates, or local curvature irregularities, a damped or regularized approach is needed. The Regularized Riemannian quadratic algorithm represent the stabilization mechanism that borrows from classical trust-region and the second-order Riemannian optimization to reassembles the update step.

3.1 Setting and Notation

To form and characterize the damped QNG, the following notations are needed.

Assume $L : \mathbb{R}^m \to \mathbb{R}$ be a twice continuously differential loss function, where $\theta \in \mathbb{R}^m$ denotes the parameter vector, and m is the number of circuit parameters.

Let $|\psi(\theta)\rangle$ be a smooth parameterized quantum state, where $|\psi(\theta)\rangle \in \mathcal{H}$ and $\mathcal{H}$ is a complex Hilbert space.

Let $Q_{ij}(\theta)$ be the QGT which is defined as;

$$Q_{ij}(\theta) = \langle \partial_i \psi(\theta) \mid \partial_j \psi(\theta)\rangle - \langle \partial_i \psi(\theta) \mid \psi(\theta)\rangle\langle \psi(\theta) \mid \partial_j \psi(\theta)\rangle, \tag{3}$$

where $\partial_i := \partial/\partial\theta_i$, and θ_i is the ith coordinate of θ.

Let

$$g_{ij}(\theta) := \Re(Q_{ij}(\theta)), \tag{4}$$

denote the (pullback) Fubini-Study metric tensor on parameter space, while $\Re(\cdot)$ represents the real part. Then $g(\theta) \in \mathbb{R}^{m\times m}$ is symmetric and positive semidefinite, as $g(\theta) \succeq 0$.

Let $\nabla L(\theta) \in \mathbb{R}^m$ be the Euclidean gradient, where ∇ corresponds to θ. Assuming $\eta > 0$ be the learning-rate parameter, where η scales the update magnitude.

3.2 Regularized Quadratic Model

For a damping parameter $\lambda > 0$, where λ controls regularization strength, the local quadratic model $m_\theta : \mathbb{R}^m \to \mathbb{R}$ is defined by;

$$m_\theta(\Delta\theta) = \nabla L(\theta)^\top \Delta\theta + \frac{1}{2\eta}\,\Delta\theta^\top g(\theta)\Delta\theta + \frac{\lambda}{2\eta}\,\|\Delta\theta\|_2^2, \tag{5}$$

where $\Delta\theta \in \mathbb{R}^m$ is a candidate step, and $\|\cdot\|_2$ denotes the Euclidean norm.

Theorem 1. *The regularized quadratic characterization of damped QNG.*
Let $L \in C^2(\mathbb{R}^m)$ and let $g(\theta)$ be the Fubini-Study metric defined by Eqs. (3)–(4) *at a fixed $\theta \in \mathbb{R}^m$, with $\eta > 0$ and $\lambda > 0$. Then the damped quantum natural-gradient step $\Delta\theta^\star$ that defined by the following linear system*

$$\big(g(\theta) + \lambda I\big)\Delta\theta^\star = -\eta\,\nabla L(\theta), \tag{6}$$

where the identity matrix I of $m \times m$ size is exists, unique, and satisfies

$$\Delta\theta^\star = \arg\min_{\Delta\theta\in\mathbb{R}^m} m_\theta(\Delta\theta), \tag{7}$$

where the quadratic model m_θ in Eq. (5) *is strictly convex and the minimizer is unique.*

Proof. Fix $\theta \in \mathbb{R}^m$ and to simplify the equation, we abbreviate $g := g(\theta)$, $b := \nabla L(\theta)$, and $\Delta := \Delta\theta$. By considering the function

$$m(\Delta) := b^\top\Delta + \frac{1}{2\eta}\Delta^\top g\Delta + \frac{\lambda}{2\eta}\|\Delta\|_2^2,$$

Since $g = g^\top$ and $\lambda > 0$, the Hessian of m with respect to Δ becomes;

$$\nabla_\Delta^2 m(\Delta) = \frac{1}{\eta}\,(g + \lambda I). \tag{8}$$

Considering $g \succeq 0$ and $\lambda > 0$, then $g + \lambda I \succ 0$ is obvious. And since, $\nabla_\Delta^2 m(\Delta) \succ 0$, therefore m is strictly convex on $\mathbb{R}^m$.

Consequently, m admits a unique global minimizer.

To compute the minimizer, take the gradient of m with respect to Δ, means:

$$\nabla_\Delta m(\Delta) = b + \frac{1}{\eta}\,g\Delta + \frac{\lambda}{\eta}\Delta = b + \frac{1}{\eta}\,(g + \lambda I)\Delta. \tag{9}$$

By setting $\nabla_\Delta m(\Delta) = 0$ gives the first-order optimal condition

$$(g + \lambda I)\Delta = -\eta\, b,$$

which is exactly Eq. (6).

Let the gain ratio ρ be defined as follows;

$$\rho = \frac{\text{Actual Drop}}{\text{Predicted Drop}} = \frac{L(\theta) - L(\theta + \Delta\theta)}{m(0) - m(\Delta\theta)}, \tag{10}$$

where $m(\Delta\theta)$ represents the quadratic model.

Since $g + \lambda I \succ 0$ is invertible, with a unique solution to its linear system $\Delta^\star$. And by strict convexity property, the stationary point represents the unique global minimizer of m, proving Eq. (7) as requisite.

Remark 1. Invertibility and numerical stability.

Let $\{\mu_i\}_{i=1}^m$ denotes the eigenvalues of $g(\theta)$, where $\mu_i \geq 0$ and $g(\theta) \succeq 0$. Then the eigenvalues of $g(\theta) + \lambda I$ are $\mu_i + \lambda > 0$ for all i, and since $\lambda > 0$, yields $g(\theta) + \lambda I$ is a well-conditioned relative to $g(\theta)$ and always invertible.

Theorem 2 (Large-damping limit and interpolation to Euclidean gradient descent). *Let $\Delta\theta^\star(\lambda)$ be the unique solution of Eq. (6) at damping level $\lambda > 0$. Then*

$$\Delta\theta^\star(\lambda) = -\eta\,(g(\theta)+\lambda I)^{-1}\nabla L(\theta) \quad \textit{and} \quad \Delta\theta^\star(\lambda) = -\frac{\eta}{\lambda}\,\nabla L(\theta) + O\Big(\frac{1}{\lambda^2}\Big) \quad \textit{as } \lambda \to \infty, \tag{11}$$

where $O(\cdot)$ is the Landau symbol.

In particular, the damped QNG direction converges to the Euclidean steepest-descent direction $-\nabla L(\theta)$, with step size scaled by $1/\lambda$.

Proof. Let $g = U\,\mathrm{diag}(\mu_1, \ldots, \mu_m)U^\top$ be the spectral decomposition of g, where U is unitary and orthogonal, while $\mu_i \geq 0$, yields;

$$(g + \lambda I)^{-1} = U\,\mathrm{diag}\Big(\frac{1}{\mu_1 + \lambda}, \ldots, \frac{1}{\mu_m + \lambda}\Big)\,U^\top. \tag{12}$$

For each i,

$$\frac{1}{\mu_i + \lambda} = \frac{1}{\lambda} \cdot \frac{1}{1 + \mu_i/\lambda} = \frac{1}{\lambda}\Big(1 - \frac{\mu_i}{\lambda} + O\Big(\frac{1}{\lambda^2}\Big)\Big) \quad \text{as } \lambda \to \infty.$$

Substituting into Eq. (12) becomes;

$$(g + \lambda I)^{-1} = \frac{1}{\lambda}I - \frac{1}{\lambda^2}g + O\Big(\frac{1}{\lambda^3}\Big).$$

By multiplying the above with $-\eta\nabla L(\theta)$ gives Eq. (11).

Example 1. Suppose the VQA defined on a finite-dimensional $\mathcal{H}$ with a Riemannian smooth parameterized state

$$|\psi(\theta)\rangle = U(\theta)\,|0\rangle, \tag{13}$$

where $\theta = (\theta_1, \theta_2) \in \mathbb{R}^2$ and

$$U(\theta) = e^{-i\theta_1 Z} e^{-i\theta_2 Z}, \tag{14}$$

$$Z = \begin{pmatrix} 1 & 0 \\ 0 & -1 \end{pmatrix}, \quad \text{Pauli-}Z \text{ operator.}$$

Although the parameter space is two-dimensional, the physical quantum state depends only on the sum $\theta_1 + \theta_2$, and the parameterization is therefore redundant.

By assuming $L : \mathbb{R}^2 \to \mathbb{R}$ be a twice continuously differentiable loss function defined as the expectation value of an observable H,

$$L(\theta) = \langle \psi(\theta) | H | \psi(\theta) \rangle, \tag{15}$$

where H is a fixed Hermitian operator.

The QGT associated with $|\psi(\theta)\rangle$ is given by

$$Q_{ij}(\theta) = \langle \partial_i \psi(\theta) | \partial_j \psi(\theta) \rangle - \langle \partial_i \psi(\theta) | \psi(\theta) \rangle \langle \psi(\theta) | \partial_j \psi(\theta) \rangle, \tag{16}$$

where $\partial_i = \partial / \partial \theta_i$.

By taking its real part, yields the following Fubini-Study metric;

$$g(\theta) = \begin{pmatrix} 1 & 1 \\ 1 & 1 \end{pmatrix}, \tag{17}$$

which is positive semidefinite but singular of rank one.

This degeneracy reflects the fact that the Fubini-Study metric is defined on the manifold of physical quantum states rather than the ambient parameter space.

The standard QNG update seeks $\Delta\theta \in \mathbb{R}^2$ satisfying

$$g(\theta)\, \Delta\theta = -\eta\, \nabla L(\theta), \tag{18}$$

where $\eta > 0$ is a learning rate and $\nabla L(\theta)$ denotes the Euclidean gradient.

Since $g(\theta)$ is singular, then the corresponding linear system admits either infinitely many solutions or none, depending on $\nabla L(\theta)$, and consequently, the QNG update is ill-posed and lacks existence and uniqueness.

The failure is intrinsic and persists even in the absence of noise, arising purely from the geometry induced by redundant parameterizations.

In the current use of the QNG model, this challenge is usually handled by adding a small diagonal shift to the metric. However, this regularization is often applied in an ad hoc manner and lacks a clear geometric or optimization interpretation. Specifically, it is uncertain if the resulting update leads to the minimization of any clearly defined local model of the loss function or if it ensures descent.

In contrast, the proposed research considers the regularized system

$$(g(\theta) + \lambda I)\, \Delta\theta = -\eta\, \nabla L(\theta), \tag{19}$$

To avoid viewing Eq. (19) as an ad hoc modification, the following, shows that it arises as the first-order optimality condition of the strictly convex quadratic model;

$$m_\theta(\Delta\theta) = \nabla L(\theta)^\top \Delta\theta + \frac{1}{2\eta}\Delta\theta^\top g(\theta)\Delta\theta + \frac{\lambda}{2\eta}\|\Delta\theta\|_2^2. \tag{20}$$

The presence of the Euclidean regularization term ensures strict convexity, guarantees existence and uniqueness of the minimizer for all $\lambda > 0$.

From a geometric perspective, the quadratic term induced by $g(\theta)$ penalizes directions that strongly affect the quantum state, while the regularization term penalizes large parameter displacements independently of the quantum geometry.

When the metric is degenerate or unreliable, the regularization term dominates, ensuring a stable descent direction. As $\lambda \to 0$, the update approaches the standard QNG direction restricted to the range of $g(\theta)$, whereas in the limit $\lambda \to \infty$ the update converges to

$$\Delta\theta = -\frac{\eta}{\lambda}\nabla L(\theta), \tag{21}$$

corresponding to Euclidean Gradient Descent with a vanishing step size.

This example demonstrates that the proposed method does not merely regularize the quantum metric for numerical convenience, but also embeds Quantum Natural Gradient descent within the principled geometrical and theoretical optimization of quadratic framework. In doing so, it resolves the intrinsic ill-posedness of standard QNG under redundant parameterizations and establishes a continuous interpolation between geometry-aware and geometry-agnostic optimization regimes.

4 The Analysis of the Metrics Performance

This part of the work outlines and compares, in a detailed evaluation, the analysis performance metrics obtained from three recent scholarly papers [8–10] and then shows a comparison with our new proposed algorithm.

The work in [8] studied the QNG model and compared with the standard gradient descent called (Vanilla GD) that used the QAOA algorithm as a case study for finding the ground state of a transverse-field Ising chain (TFIM) on $N = 2 - -12$ qubits. The work executed the QAOA under some conditions, where the depth $p = 4$ considered on two platforms; Rydberg-atom and superconducting qubits, with a two suggested restrictions; noiseless and realistic noisy conditions. The metrics included number of iterations for circuit evaluations, to reach the ground state, with a succeed 50% convergence rate of random initializations, and the final energy error. And, the accuracy $\epsilon =$ the energy difference from true ground state. Additionally, the sensitivity of two noise sources; the laser noise and the SPAM errors were suggested, while the outcomes were obtained via a comparison performance of the models that showed a faster convergence values of QNG algorithm in average of a significantly fewer iterations requirements than vanilla GD for growing system size. For instance, at $N = 10 - -12$

qubits, the full metric QNG model, only ~!500 iterations is needed to reach the ground state in average vs > 3000 iterations are required for vanilla model.

In 2025, the authors in [9], presented a novel QNG algorithm that addresses the limitation of the additional computational cost by using the advantage of the Hamiltonian structure benefiting from the metric of the Riemannian pull-back of the lower-dimensional subspace spanned by the Hamiltonian terms onto the parameter space. The algorithm is called Hamiltonian-aware Quantum Natural Gradient Descent (H-QNG). Where, the projected Fubini-Study metric is applied on the subspace spanned by the Hamiltonian's terms, resulting a lower dimensional Fisher matrix instead of using the full state-space metric. Based on this idea, the authors executed the H-QNG on the VQE problems in quantum chemistry via a small lithium hydride (LiH) molecules and a linear chain of six hydrogen atoms H_6 optimized via the STO-6G hardware of minimal basis (ansätze) that required (8–12) qubits.

For the metrics performance, the energy error of the chemical accuracy is defined by 1.6×10^{-3} Hartree (Ha) (the atomic energy unit), while the proposed algorithm targeting a reduction of the energy error below the up mentioned chemical accuracy threshold. The lower quantum resource cost number of Hamiltonian or metric measurements confirms that the algorithm is more practical on current noisy hardware where measurement time is expensive. Therefore, the results of this experiment was a promising, where the H-QNG keeps the fast convergence of standard QNG mode but with a noticed lower cost per iteration and it reached the chemical accuracy in fewer iterations compared to the standard QNG for both LiH and H_6.

For example, the H-QNG achieved the 1.6 mHa accuracy of 20% faster iteration count than the standard QNG for LiH, that needed only half the quantum measurement shots per step as it estimates a smaller metric, resulting an overall reduction of the running time. Both H-QNG and standard QNG achieved final energies within chemical accuracy rate, but H-QNG showed improved robustness, converged reliably with smaller learning rates and without divergence even when the Fubini-Study metric was near-singular, where the regularization λ values were added to the metric. The results showed a slight degraded performance of H-QNG mode under shot noise for some finite sampling, despite reaching the chemical accuracy faster than stander QNG at the same shots number. The convergence curve with noise is closely tracked the noiseless case in early iterations, which indicate the incorporating Hamiltonian knowledge and using the damped metric inversion yields a more noise-resilient optimizer.

While, back in 2024, Fitzek et al. [10] introduced a new algorithm, called the quantum Broyden adaptive natural gradient (qBANG), that combines two models: an adaptive quasi-Newton update of the QNG metric, also called Broyden's method to approximate the inverse Fisher matrix of a heavy-ball momentum term. The aim of qBANG algorithm is to capture the curvature that benefits the QNG without the full cost of the metric evaluation in each iteration. The experiment began with benchmarks that included a circuit of barren plateau of 9 qubits, and a random layered gates, to test the optimizer stability, VQE for H_4

(4 hydrogen), LiH, and H_2O molecules of (8–12) qubits with frozen core, and a Max-Cut QAOA mode on a 12-node graph (noted in text). The metrics include the number of circuit evaluations of convergence speed that used to reach the ground-state energy or in other words, to give the approximation ratio, final energy error, and sensitivity to hyper-parameters and the shot noise optimizer. While the results of the qBANG achieved an overall more stable and faster convergence compared to the standard QNG and the gradient-based models depicted in Adam's method [16].

Based on the above analysis, the qBANG vastly outperformed in the H_4 and LiH of VQE mode, than the other methods like standard QNG and the H-QNG optimizers. The outcomes show a lower energy solutions consistently across 10–15 random initializations. While the variance of final energies was small for qBANG, indicating reliable convergence. Whereas, the QNG (exact or block-diag) and the vanilla GD showed a larger scatter. For instant, in H_2O, the qBANG was the only optimizer to discover the exact ground-state energy in at least one trial, with a 2-layer shallow ansatz, something QNG and Adam's methods couldn't achieve. Additionally, the qBANG shows more flexibility to hyperparameters, such as in a 9-qubit barren plateau test, while, the QNG and a full Newton method could diverge or oscillate for a large step size η, meantime the qBANG and Adam methods remain stabled over a range of η.

Overall, the analysis shows that augmenting QNG model with adaptive updates, subsystem weighting, or regularization can improve VQA optimization in terms of speed, robustness, and resource efficiency.

However, our proposed damped QNG model with trust-region is constructed based on the above-mentioned outcomes. Where, the Tikhonov damping term λI is utilized in Fubini-Study metric calculation and impose an explicit trust-radius Δ on the QNG step. Thus, the update rule can be defined as:

$$\Delta\theta^{\top}\big(F(\theta)+\lambda I\big)\Delta\theta \leq \Delta^2 \tag{22}$$

with a step size constraint in the metric geometry of the form:

$$\Delta\theta^{\top}F(\theta)\Delta\theta \leq \Delta^2, \tag{23}$$

making sure of the fixed range where the local quadratic model, based Fisher information is trustworthy. Table 1 below shows the comparison performance of our proposed model to the recent QNG-based methods on key metrics.

The values presented in Table 1 are computed based on a unified optimization-theoretical criterion grounded in the geometry of the variational parameter manifold, as follows;

Firstly, assumed $L:\mathbb{R}^m \rightarrow \mathbb{R}$ denote the objective function and $\boldsymbol{\theta}_{t+1} = \boldsymbol{\theta}_t + \Delta\boldsymbol{\theta}_t$ defines the iterative update generated by each optimizer. The column of convergence refers to the required relative iteration count to satisfy $L(\boldsymbol{\theta}_t) - L^\star \leq \varepsilon$ for a fixed tolerance ε, where $L^\star$ refers to the optimal value, where all methods evaluated under the same initialization ensemble and iteration budget.

While the accuracy column refers to the asymptotic residual $L(\boldsymbol{\theta}_T) - L^\star$ after a fixed number of iteration T, and it reflects the ability of the used method to

Table 1. Comparison of QNG–based optimizers to VQA representative tasks

Optimizer	Task	Convergence	Accuracy	Stability
Gradient Descent (GD)	–	Baseline	Task-dependent	Sensitive to init.; degrades under noise
QNG [2]	VQE, QAOA	2–3× faster than GD	Lower cost; fewer local minima	More stable via geometric preconditioning
QNG (Noisy QAOA) [8]	QAOA (TFIM, ≤12 qubits)	$\sim 5\times$ faster for $N \geq 10$	Ground state up to $N = 12$	> 90% success; robust to noise
Hamiltonian-aware QNG [9]	VQE (LiH, H_6)	Faster than standard QNG	Chemical accuracy (∼1 mHa)	Stable under metric singularities
qBANG [10]	VQE, QAOA	≤ QNG QPU calls	Best energies (H_2O)	Very low variance; noise tolerant
Regularized QNG (our work)	VQE, QAOA	Comparable to QNG	Same optima; no overshoot	**High**: damping + trust region

reach low-energy or low-loss regions. The stability column refers to the assessment through the boundedness and conditioning of the update map, governed by the spectral properties of the preconditioning metric. While Euclidean gradient descent utilizes the identity metric and standard QNG uses the pull-back Fubini–Study metric, regularized and Hamiltonian-aware variants employ strictly positive-definite or structured approximations instead. In particular, the proposed regularized QNG ensures well-posed updates by replacing $g(\boldsymbol{\theta})$ with $g(\boldsymbol{\theta})+\lambda I$ and enforcing a trust-region constraint, guaranteeing existence, uniqueness, and controlled step norms; the corresponding table entries followed directly from these geometric-related and spectral attributes, whereas entries for earlier methods summarize their reported behavior beneath the same mathematical criteria. Figure 1 illustrates the comparison of the convergence rate versus number of qubits N between our proposed model to the other cited methods (see Fig. 1).

The damped and trust-region regularized QNG model is expected to match the fast convergence of standard QNG, while other methods do not use damping despite providing improved stability. In Eq. (22), λ mitigates issues when F has tiny eigenvalues, thus preventing abrupt, large parameter updates. Furthermore, the same equation enforces a constraint ensuring each update stays within a fidelity distance Δ; which is analogous to the reparameterization invariance of the natural gradient on the Riemannian surface, but with explicit safety margins. The damped QNG model directly addresses the instability observed in standard QNG, which lacks damping, when using large learning rates or finite sampling.

For example, as shown in Fig. 2 during a 2-qubit VQE test, our proposed damped QNG reached the target energy in approximately 2 iterations. In contrast, vanilla GD, using the same learning rate, took around 5 iterations. While standard QNG achieved the target in 1 to 2 iterations, it frequently overshot the minimum without damping. Figure 2 displays the loss and gradient norm

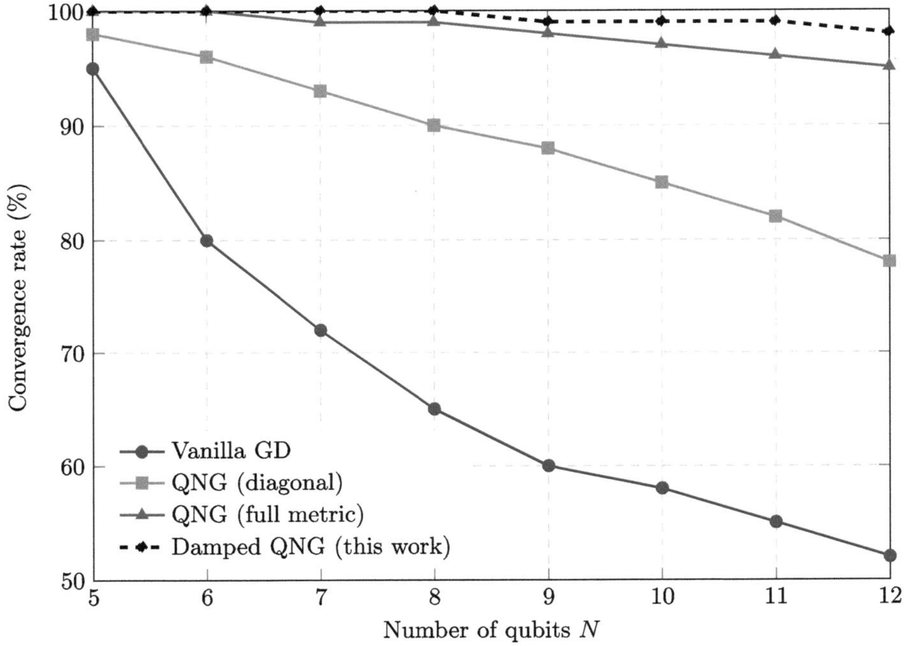

Fig. 1. Convergence rate versus number of qubits N for different QNG models

versus iterations for this test case, demonstrating that all QNG-based methods quickly reduce the cost and gradients; however, damped QNG specifically avoids the initial overshoot characteristic of pure QNG.

4.1 Geometric Interpretation and the Impact on Quantum Machine Learning (QML)

Based on our analysis and from a geometric perspective, the damping impact on Quantum Machine Learning (QML) based on the update approaches standard QNG as follows:

- The term $\Delta\boldsymbol{\theta}^\top g(\boldsymbol{\theta})\Delta\boldsymbol{\theta}$ penalizes motion that induces large changes in quantum state space;
- The Euclidean regularization term $\|\Delta\boldsymbol{\theta}\|_2^2$ controls parameter displacement independently of quantum geometry;
- The damping parameter λ quantifies confidence in the local quantum metric.

As $\lambda \to 0$, the update approaches standard QNG, while in the large-damping region where $\lambda \to \infty$, the update continuously interpolates toward Euclidean Gradient Descent, explained via;

$$\Delta\boldsymbol{\theta} = -\frac{\eta}{\lambda}\nabla L(\boldsymbol{\theta}) + \mathcal{O}(\lambda^{-2}). \tag{24}$$

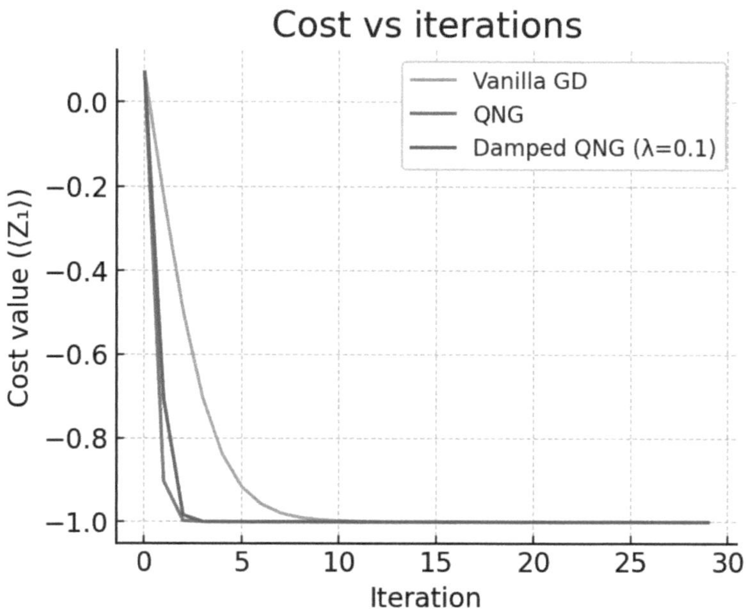

Fig. 2. Loss cost function value vs. iteration for a 2-qubit based on VQE.

5 Discussion

QNG methods are based on the premise that optimization in VQAs must account for the natural geometry of the quantum state space. For a parameterized quantum state $|\psi(\theta)\rangle$, the real part of the QGT defines the Fubini–Study metric, which measures the distinguishability of nearby quantum states and induces a Riemannian structure on the variational manifold [1,2]. From a mathematical perspective, the degeneracy of $g(\theta)$ is not a defect, but rather a fundamental feature of this geometric surface.

By utilizing the real part of the QGT, we effectively apply the Fubini–Study metric to the manifold of physical quantum states rather than the embedding parameter space. Consequently, directions in the parameter space that do not alter the physical state stemming from non-essential parameterizations, symmetries, or gauge freedoms—reside within the null space of $g(\theta)$. This implies that the pullback metric is generally positive semidefinite and, therefore, non-invertible. This observation explains why standard QNG may fail even under noiseless conditions, demonstrating that its instability is a structural geometric property rather than a mere numerical artifact [2].

In quantum computing devices, this intrinsic problem is further compounded by the finite-shot estimation of the QGT, as well as by qubit decoherence and noise-induced distortions of the effective geometry. Consequently, several works have introduced diagonal or Tikhonov-type regularization of the metric to restore invertibility [2,6,11]. While effective in practice, such regularization is typically introduced heuristically, lacking a precise optimization-theoretic or geometric interpretation.

This work provides a principled resolution to this gap. By applying the damped trust-region regularized QNG update (see Eq. 19) within a locally defined Riemannian quadratic model of the loss function, showing that the damped update is the *unique minimizer* of a strictly convex optimization problem for all $\lambda > 0$. This establishes the existence, uniqueness, and numerical stability of the update in a mathematically rigorous manner. The quadratic model (Eq. 5) is used to interpret the geometric meaning of the damping parameter λ. Where the term $\Delta\theta^\top g(\theta)\Delta\theta$ penalizes motion that induces large changes in quantum state space, while the Euclidean regularization term $\|\Delta\theta\|_2^2$ controls the magnitude of parameter displacement independently of quantum geometry.

Thus, λ quantifies the degree of confidence placed in the local quantum geometric information. When $g(\theta)$ is reliable, a small λ allows for geometry-aware updates; when the $g(\theta)$ metric is singular or noisy, a larger λ suppresses unstable geometric directions. Therefore, damped QNG realizes a continuous interpolation between the Quantum Natural Gradient and geometry-agnostic gradient descent. This interpolation is both mathematically and physically fundamental, reflecting a smooth transition between state-space-sensitive and parameter-space-sensitive optimization regimes. Importantly, the gain-ratio mechanism introduced in the damped QNG algorithm provides a model-based criterion for adapting λ. By comparing the actual decrease in L with that predicted by the quadratic model, the algorithm dynamically adjusts its reliance on quantum geometry. This connects damped QNG with trust-region methods while preserving the fundamental geometric origin of the metric. To our knowledge, this specific quadratic model and confidence-region interpretation of damped QNG have not been previously formalized in the quantum optimization literature.

6 Conclusion

In this paper, a geometrically and mathematically based stabilisation of QNG optimisation for VQAs is proposed. It is observed from the information-geometric basis of QNG that the pullback character of the Fubini-Study metric and the existence of duplicate parameter directions led to the intrinsic ill-posedness of the standard update. As a novel outcome, we have shown that these problems stem from the geometry of quantum state manifolds and remain unaffected by sampling noise. And demonstrated that the damped QNG update is the only minimiser of a strictly convex local approximation of the loss function by introducing a Tikhonov-regularized Riemannian quadratic model. Meanwhile, for any damping parameters $\lambda > 0$, the result ensures existence, uniqueness, with a numerical stability. The outcome offers a strong theoretic and geometric optimizational justification for such stabilisation type, while diagonal regularisation of the QGT has already been emerged as a useful heuristic.

The method is well explained in both mathematical and physical concepts when the damping parameter is interpreted as a confidence measure in local quantum geometry. The approach guarantees descent even in the case of faulty quantum geometric information by provably recovering Euclidean Gradient Descent in the large-damping domain.

On the other hand, the technique maintains the benefits of geometry-aware optimisation by taking advantage of the curvature of quantum state space in the small-damping domain. Two basic optimisation paradigms are connected by this continuous interpolation inside a single cohesive framework. From the outcomes, the suggested method defines the function of quantum geometry in optimisation, converts metric regularisation from a heuristic to a logical modeling decision, and offers a strong basis for future advancements. Benchmark analyses comparing recent QNG-based optimizers, including Hamiltonian-aware QNG, qBANG, and full metric QNG, illustrate that our regularized model achieves convergence speeds comparable to standard QNG, while providing superior stability, eliminating overshooting under near-singular metrics, finite-shot noise, and redundant parameterizations. In small-scale Variational Quantum Eigensolver (VQE) experiments (2–12 qubits). The proposed damped QNG reaches target energies in 1–2 iterations, avoids instability noticed in the standard QNG technique, and maintains robust performance under sampling noise. These results establish the regularized QNG trust region as a mathematically grounded, geometry-preserving, and practically robust optimizer for near-term quantum algorithms.

The future research could expand this approach to including stochastic convergence assessments under realistic device noise, mixed-state quantum Fisher information, and approximation or block-diagonal metrics, all of which are major issues in quantum optimisation between 2020 and 2026 [2,6,7,17].

Acknowledgments. This research was sponsored by the University of Malaya Translational Research Grant Scheme, TRG0019-2025 (UM.0002388/HRU.IP) and the Research Excellence Grant, UMREG 068 - 2024 (UM.0000285/HRU.RC).

Author contributions. All authors contributed equally and significantly to writing this article.

Conflicts of Interest. The authors declare no conflict of interest.

References

1. Amari, S.I.: Natural gradient works efficiently in learning. Neural Comput. **10**(2), 251–276 (1998)
2. Stokes, J., Izaac, J., Killoran, N., Carleo, G.: Quantum natural gradient. Quantum **4**, 269 (2020)
3. Alwan, N.A., Al-Saidi, N.M., Obaiys, S.J., Noor, N.F.B.M., Ahmad, M.: A comprehensive review on classification of quantum image representations. Arch. Comput. Methods Eng. 1–59 (2025)
4. Alwan, N.A., Obaiys, S.J., Al-Saidi, N.M., Noor, N.F.B.M., Karaca, Y.: A multi-channel quantum image representation model with qubit sequences for quantum-inspired image and image retrieval. AIMS MATHEMATICS **10**(5), 10994–11035 (2025)

5. Alwan, N.A., Obaiys, S.J., Al-Saidi, N.M., Noor, N.F.B.M., Karaca, Y.: Multilayered quantum computing and simulation system for enhanced image representation of HSI based Fourier transform and adjacency matrix. Sci. Rep. **15**(1), 40286 (2025)
6. Wierichs, D., Gogolin, C., Kastoryano, M.: Avoiding local minima in variational quantum eigensolvers with the natural gradient optimizer. arXiv:2004.14666 (2020)
7. Martens, J., Sutskever, I.: Training deep and recurrent networks with hessian-free optimization. In: Montavon, G., Orr, G.B., Müller, K.-R. (eds.) Neural Networks: Tricks of the Trade. LNCS, vol. 7700, pp. 479–535. Springer, Heidelberg (2012). https://doi.org/10.1007/978-3-642-35289-8_27
8. Dell'Anna, F., Gomez-Lurbe, R., Perez, A., Ercolessi, E.: Quantum natural gradient optimizer on noisy platforms: QAOA as a case study. arXiv preprint arXiv:2502.20288 (2025)
9. Shi, C., Dunjko, V., Wang, H.: Weighted approximate quantum natural gradient for variational quantum eigensolver. arXiv:2504.04932 (2025)
10. Fitzek, D., Jonsson, R.S., Dobrautz, W., Schäfer, C.: Optimizing variational quantum algorithms with qBang: efficiently interweaving metric and momentum to navigate flat energy landscapes. Quantum **8**, 1313 (2024)
11. Yamamoto, N.: On the natural gradient for variational quantum eigensolver. arXiv:1909.05074 (2019)
12. Koczor, B., Benjamin, S.C.: Quantum natural gradient generalized to noisy and nonunitary circuits. Phys. Rev. A **106**, 062416 (2022). Also arXiv:1912.08660
13. Sasaki, T., Miyahara, H.: Quantum natural gradient without monotonicity. arXiv:2401.13237 (2024). Phys. Rev. A **110**, 022439 (2024)
14. Kolotouros, I., Wallden, P.: Random natural gradient. Quantum **8**, 1503 (2024)
15. Halla, M.: Quantum natural gradient with geodesic corrections for small shallow quantum circuits. Physica Scripta **100**(5) (2025). Also arXiv:2409.03638
16. Kingma, D.P.: Adam: a method for stochastic optimization. arXiv preprint arXiv:1412.6980 (2014)
17. Bonnabel, S.: Stochastic gradient descent on Riemannian manifolds. IEEE Trans. Autom. Control **58**(9), 2217–2229 (2013)

An Efficient Polynomial Framework for Optimal Control: Applications in Network Protection and Solar Energy Systems

Balsam Fuad(✉), Suha Shihab, and Saba S. Hasen

College of Applied Sciences, University of Technology, Baghdad, Iraq
as.24.33@grad.uotechnology.edu.iq,
suha.n.shihab@uotechnology.edu.iq

Abstract. This paper develops a novel polynomial-based framework for accurately and efficiently solving continuous optimal control problems, which are often challenging due to high computational cost and the limitations of existing approximation techniques. The primary objective is to construct a robust numerical scheme that avoids the need for closed-form analytical solutions while maintaining high accuracy. To this end, a new class of basis functions, namely the extended complete Vieta–Pell (ECVP) polynomials, is introduced. These polynomials are systematically constructed and employed to approximate both state and control variables over the time domain, transforming the original optimal control problem into a tractable algebraic system suitable for numerical implementation. The main contribution of this work is twofold: first, the formulation of the ECVP polynomials as a unified and efficient basis for approximation; second, the development of an effective computational framework that improves convergence behavior and numerical stability compared with existing methods. Unlike traditional approaches, the proposed method provides flexible approximation capability with enhanced accuracy as the expansion order increases. The effectiveness of the proposed framework is demonstrated through applications in solar energy systems and network protection models. Numerical results indicate rapid convergence and high precision, with the obtained solutions closely matching exact or benchmark solutions. These findings establish the proposed ECVP-based method as a reliable and powerful tool for a broad class of optimal control problems.

Keywords: Optimal control problems · New extended complete Vieta–Pell polynomials · Network protection systems · solar energy engineering · Error analysis

1 Introduction

The optimal control problem represents important problems in control theory and applied mathematics because of their significant role in modeling and analyzing a wide range of physical and engineering as well as in technological systems [1–5]. The objective of optimal control problems is to calculate a suitable control function that influence

O. Gervasi et al. (Eds.): ICCSA 2026 Workshops, LNCS 16758, pp. 301–316, 2027.
https://doi.org/10.1007/978-3-032-30497-1_19

the dynamic system in certain way to achieve an optimal performance index criterion, subject to given dynamic and constraints. In general, the function $x(t)$ describes the state vector representing the evolution of the system based on time, while the function $u(t)$ represents the control vector that governs the behavior of the system. The control functions are usually assumed to belong to a class of admissible controls that ensures the existence and feasibility of the solution. A standard formulation of an OCP is given by

$$J = \int_{t_0}^{t_1} F(x(t), u(t), t)dt, \tag{1}$$

together with the following dynamic system and the boundary conditions

$$\dot{x}(t) = f(x(t), u(t)), \tag{2}$$

$$x(t_0) = x_a, x(t_1) = x_b. \tag{3}$$

where $F(x(t), u(t), t)$ is a positive definite performance index and f is continuously differentiable function.

From a theoretical perspective, OCPs are commonly treated using Pontryagin's minimum principle, which leads to a Hamiltonian formulation consisting of the state equations, adjoint equations, and associated optimality conditions. This formulation typically results in two-point boundary value problems (TPPVPs), which is often difficult to solve analytically or even numerically, particularly for nonlinear or constrained systems. Many numerical algorithms have been proposed to approximately solve them. Some of these numerical methods have been suggested to using the direct numerical techniques, including the both finite element and finite difference methods [6–9], the adaptive collocation method, [10], wavelet collocation method using the Chebyshev wavelets functions [11, 12], the Müntz– Legendre functions, [13] and others [14–18]. In addition, more suitable methods to solve the OCPs are applying the orthogonal basis functions such as Vieta-Pell family polynomials. As some applications of Vieta polynomial, a new type which is Vieta–Fibonacci-like polynomial was defined in [19], and then the relationship between Vieta–Fibonacci-like polynomial and the famous Vieta polynomials obtained. In addition, the generating function and the Binet formula were established with some new identities involving the sum formula of Vieta–Fibonacci-like polynomials. Also [20–22] proposed some identities containing families of Vieta functions. Other work certain family of Vieta [23], Vieta Lucas polynomials [24], Pell polynomials [25] and Lucas polynomials [26]. In addition, some recent work constructed generalized basis functions for different families of Vieta polynomials such as Generalized Vieta-Jacobsthal [27], incomplete generalized Vieta–Pell [28] and a specific modification of Vieta-Pell Lucas polynomials [29]. Such polynomials are often restricted to narrower domains unlike our suggested ECVP polynomials allows for solving problems with larger physical or mathematical boundaries without losing accuracy.

The important problem is how can present a general expression for the original polynomials. This study addresses the numerical solution of OCPs through the use of new extended complete Vieta–Pell polynomials. The proposed polynomial framework provides an accurate and flexible representation of the state and control variables over the time domain, allowing the approximation quality to improve systematically as the expansion order increases. To address these difficulties, an equivalent optimization-based formulation can be adopted; in which both the state and control functions are approximated using suitable basis functions. This approach enables the transformation of the Hamiltonian-based formulation into an optimization problem while preserving the essential structure of the original system and reducing computational complexity. Within this framework, the present work introduces an extension of the classical Vieta–Pell polynomials through the construction of Extended Complete Vieta–Pell Polynomials. These polynomials possess favorable mathematical properties that make them well suited as Basis functions over finite intervals. Their use facilitates accurate approximations of the variables and provides an effective foundation for the numerical treatment of OCPs arising in practical applications, including solar energy systems and network protection models.

The proposed new version of the polynomials can use on any finite interval. The proposed method converts solving optimal control problems into solving constrained optimization problem by approximating both the state and control variables using the ECVPPs. The efficiency of the extended complete approach is investigated on some test applications.

The main contributions of this work can be summarized as follows:

- Introducing a new extended complete family of Vieta–Pell polynomials (ECVP) and establishing their mathematical structure.
- Developing new operational matrices for derivatives and products based on the proposed polynomials.
- Constructing an efficient numerical framework for solving optimal control problems using direct parameterization techniques.
- Demonstrating the effectiveness of the proposed method through practical applications, including solar energy systems and network protection models.

The rest of the work is arranged in sections as follows: The new modified definitions of ECVPPs with important properties are presented in Sect. 2. Derivative and product formulation matrices of ECVPPs are given in Sects. 3 and 4 while an efficient approach is constructed in Sect. 5 for approximately treating the optimal control problems. Two applications are solved and examined in Sect. 6. The Discussion and conclusion of the study are reported in Sects. 7 and 8.

2 New Extended Complete Vieta-Pell Polynomials

In this section, a new family of polynomials, referred to as the Extended Complete Vieta–Pell Polynomials (ECVPPs), is introduced. This family represents a natural extension of the classical Vieta–Pell polynomials over a general. Finite interval while preserving the essential second–order recursive structure that characterizes the complete Vieta–Pell system.

Definition 1. Let $t \in [t_0, t_1]$, k > 0 and let $k \in N$. The extended complete Vieta–Pell polynomials, denoted by $p_{k,n}(t)$, are defined by the recurrence relation

$$p_{k,n}(t) = 2^k \xi(t)\, p_{k,n-1}(t) - p_{k,n-2}(t), n \geq 3. \tag{4}$$

$$\text{with} \quad p_{k,1}(t) = 1 \quad \text{and} \quad p_{k,2}(t) = 2^k \xi(t). \tag{5}$$

This definition introduces a scaled and shifted version of the classical complete Vieta–Pell polynomials on a general interval $[t_0, t_1]$ with $\xi(t) = \frac{(2t-t_0-t_1)}{t_0-t_1}$.

The general closed–form expression of the extended complete Vieta–Pell polynomials with $k = 2$ is given by

$$p_{2,n}(t) = \sum_{r=0}^{(n-1)/2} (-1)^r \left(\frac{n-1-r}{r}\right)\left(2^2\xi(t)\right)^{n-1-2r} n = 1,2,\ldots.$$

$$p_{2,1}(t) = 1,\ p_{2,2}(t) = 4\xi(t),\ p_{2,n}(t) = 4\xi(t)p_{2,n-1}(t) - p_{2,n-2}(t),\ n \geq 3.$$

By choosing $t_0 = -1$, $t_1 = 1$ and $k = 1$ the extended formulation in (4–5) reduces to the classical Vieta–Pell polynomials defined on the standard interval $[-1, 1]$. In particular, the basis employed in the present study corresponds to this special configuration, which is selected for its computational simplicity and numerical stability.

3 Operational Differentiation Matrix for ECVPPs

Let $p_{k,n}(t)$ be the new extended complete Vieta–Pell polynomials defined on the interval $[t_0, t_1]$ and define the basis vector.

$$P(t) = \left[p_{k,1}(t), p_{k,2}(t), \ldots, p_{k,n}(t)\right], \tag{6}$$

The operational differentiation matrix $D \in R^{n\times n}$ is defined such that

$$\frac{d}{dt}p(t) = p(t)D, \tag{7}$$

To formulate the explicit form of the matrix D, let $D = \left[d_{ij}\right]$, $i, j = 1,2, \ldots, n$. The entries of D the operational differentiation matrix D are given by

$$d_{ij} = \{\frac{2^{k+1}}{t_1 - t_0}i,\ if\ j > i\ and\ (j-i)\ is\ odd, 0, \quad otherwise. \tag{8}$$

The matrix D is an upper triangular matrix. Nonzero entries appear only at positions where the index difference $(j - i)$ is odd. The magnitude of each nonzero entry is proportional to the scaling factor $\frac{2^{k+1}}{t_1-t_0}$

Hence, the general pattern of D can be written as

$$D = \frac{2^{k+1}}{t_1 - t_0}\begin{bmatrix} 0 & 1\,0\,3\,0\,5\ldots \\ 0 & 0\,2\,0\,0\,0\ldots \\ 0 & 0\,0\,3\,0\,5\ldots \\ 0 & 0\,0\,0\,4\,0\ldots \\ 0 & 0\,0\,0\,0\,5\ldots \\ \ldots & \end{bmatrix} \tag{9}$$

The D structure illustrates that the derivative of each ECVP polynomial can be written exactly as a finite linear combination of lower-order ECVP polynomials.

4 The Product Operation ECVP Polynomials

The product of two ECVP basis functions can always be written as a linear combination of the same basis. Accordingly, the product of two ECVP basis functions can be represented in the following form

$$P_{k,n}(t)P_{k,m}(t) = p_{k,n+m-1}(t) + p_{k,n+m-3}(t) + \cdots + p_{k,|n+m|+1}(t).$$

where the number of terms in the above expansion is equal to $min(n, m)$. Such property is referred to as a linearization rule. It plays an important role in spectral and EGU-based numerical methods, as it allows the multiplication of Basis functions to be replaced by a summation of known coefficients, thereby simplifying the computational structure of the problem.

Theorem1. Let $p_{k,n}(t), n \geq 1$ be the new extended complete Vieta–Pell polynomials defined by

$$p_{k,1}(t) = 1, p_{k,2}(t) = z(t),$$

and

$$p_{k,n}(t) = z(t)p_{k,n-1}(t) - p_{k,n-2}(t), n \geq 3. \tag{10}$$

where $Z(t) = 2^k\xi(t)$. For any integers $n, m \geq 1$ we nave the following product formula

$$p_{k,n}(t)p_{k,m}(t) = \sum_{r=0}^{(n,m)-1} p_{k,n+m-1-2r}(t). \tag{11}$$

Proof. Since the recurrence depends only on the single variable z(t), each $p_{k,n}(t)$ can be viewed as a polynomial in z. Define $Q_n(z)$, by

$$Q_1(Z) = 1, Q_1(Z) = Z, Q_n(Z) = ZQ_{n-1}(z) - Q_{n-2}(z), \text{ so that } p_{k,n}(t) = Q_n(z(t))$$

For the classical complete Vieta-Pell family $[Q_n(z)]$, the well-known linearization identity holds:

$$Q_{k,n}(z)Q_{k,m}(z) = \sum_{r=0}^{(n,m)-1} Q_{k,n+m-1-2r}(z).$$

5 The Complete Vieta–Pell Version Algorithm for Solving the Optimal Control Problem

Consider an optimal control problem (1–3) and assume the system dynamics (2) can be written in a form that allows expressing the control as a function of the state and its first derivative:

$$u(t) = G(x(t), \dot{x}(t)). \tag{12}$$

The aim is to approximate the optimal trajectories $x^*(t)$), $u^*(t)$ and the optimal cost J^*. For a fixed truncation order n, define the basis vector as in Eq. (6).

Step 1. Approximation of the State Variable
Approximate the state variable $x(t)$ by a finite NECVPP expansion:

$$x(t) \approx a^t P(t). \tag{13}$$

where $a = [a_1, a_2, \ldots, a_{n+1}]^T \in R^{(n+1)\times 1}$ represents the unknown parameter vector.

Step 2. State Derivative Via the Operational Differentiation Matrix
Differentiate the approximation in (1) to obtain.

$$\dot{x}(t) \approx a^T \dot{P}(t). \tag{14}$$

Define the operational differentiation matrix D associated with the NECVPP basis such that the derivative of the basis vector is represented in the same basis:
$\dot{P}(t) = P(t)D$.
Therefore, Eq. (14) can be written as

$$\dot{x}(t) \approx a^T P(t)D. \tag{15}$$

Step 3. Reconstruction of the Control Variable
Using Eq. (12) and substitute the approximations derived in Steps 1–2, yields

$$u(t) \approx G(a^T P(t), a^T P(t)D \tag{16}$$

Hence, $u(t)$ becomes an explicit function of the unknown coefficient vector a.

Step 4. Reduction of the Performance Index
Substitute the approximations in Eqns. (13) and (16) into the cost functional in (1) to obtain.

$$J(a) = \int_{t_0}^{t_1} F(a^T P(t), G(a^T P(t), a^T P(t)D), t)dt.$$

In many OCPs, the integrand $F(\cdot)$ is quadratic in x and u. In this case, $J(a)$ reduces to a quadratic form in a:

$$J(a) = a^T Ha + 2c^T a + J0,$$

where $H \in R^{\{(N+1)\times(N+1)\}}$ is symmetric, $c \in R^{\{(N+1)\times 1\}}$, and $J0$ is a constant. If no linear term is produced, then $c = 0$ and

$$J(a) = a^T Ha.$$

Note that, the entries of H (and c, if present) are computed by evaluating the required integrals involving $P(t)$ and $P(t)D$ over $[t_0, t_1]$.

Step 5. Boundary Conditions as Linear Constraints
Impose the boundary conditions in (3) on (13), yields

$$a^T P(t_0) = x_a, a^T P(t_1) = x_b$$

These constraints can be written in matrix form as $Fa = b$, where

$$[F = P(t_0)^T; P(t_1)^T] \in R^{\{2\times(N+1)\}}, b = [x_a, x_b]^T \in R^{\{2\times 1\}}$$

Step 6. Final Quadratic Programming Form
The OCP is transformed into the algebraic constrained optimization problem minimize

$$J(a) = a^T Ha + 2c^T a + J0, \text{ subject to } Fa = b.$$

This is a quadratic programming problem with linear equality constraints. It may be solved by standard QP techniques or by the Lagrange multiplier method.

Step 7. Closed-Form Coefficients
For the common case $J(a) = a^T Ha$ $(c = 0)$
with equality constraints only, the optimal coefficients admit the closed form

$$a^* = H^{-1}F^T(FH^{-1}F^T)^{-1}b \tag{17}$$

If a linear term exists $J(a) = a^T Ha + 2c^T a$,
then the constrained minimizer satisfies

$$a^* = H^{-1}(F^T\lambda - c), \text{ with } (F = H^{-1}F^T)\lambda = b + FH^{-1}c$$

Step 8. Reconstruction of the Approximate Optimal Solution After computing a^*, reconstruct

$$x^*(t) \approx (a^*)^T P(t),\ \dot{x}^*(t) \approx (a^*)^T P(t)D \text{ and}$$
$$u^*(t) \approx G((a^*)^T P(t), (a^*)^T P(t)D)$$

Finally, evaluate the approximate optimal cost as

$$J^* \approx J(a^*).$$

6 Applications

The effectiveness of the suggested method is illustrated throughout this section by solving some applications on OCPs. All computations in this section have been obtained using Mat lab and python. The accuracy of the adopted technique is discussed by computing the absolute error values different values of n depending on the following formulas.

$$\epsilon_x = |x(t_i) - x_n(t_i)|, \epsilon_u = |u(t_i) - u_n(t_i)|, E_{n,state} = |x(t_i) - x_n(t_i)|,$$
$$E_{n,control} = |u(t_i) - u_n(t_i)|, E_J = |J - J_n|, E_{L1,x} = \sum_{i=1}^{n} |x(t_i) - x_n(t)|\Delta t,$$
$$E_{L1,u} = \sum_{i=1}^{n} |u(t_i) - u_n(t_i)|\Delta t, E_{L2,x} = (\sum_{i=1}^{n} |f(x_i) - f_n(x_i)|^2 \Delta t)^{\frac{1}{2}},$$
$$E_{L2,u} = (\sum_{i=1}^{n} |f(u_i) - f_n(u_i)|^2 \Delta t)^{\frac{1}{2}}.$$

where $x(t_i)$, $u(t_i)$ and J stand for the exact solutions $x(t)$, $u(t)$ and the cost function value while and $x_n(t_i)$, $u_n(t_i)$ and J_n indicate the approximate solutions to $x(t)$, $u(t)$,and the cost function value respectively.

6.1 Application 1. Optimal Control System for Smart Grid Network Security

With the increasing prevalence of cyber threats, there is a growing need to design intelligent protection systems that balance target security levels with operational costs. This research presents an optimal control model for distributing security investments in smart grid networks, aiming to reduce total costs while maintaining an acceptable security level. We assume that the security state of the network $x(t)$ is described by the following dynamic equation:

$$\dot{x}(t) = -0.4x(t) + u(t), \tag{18}$$

where $x(t)$ represents the security level of the network, taking the value 1 when the network is completely secure, and 0 when it is completely insecure. Here, $u(t)$ represents the security investment (cost of protection system and monitoring). We seek to minimize the total cost J, which combines both security risk resulting from reduced protection levels and the cost of protection systems and monitoring

$$J = \int_0^1 \left(x^2(t) + u^2(t)\right) dt, 0 \leq t \leq 1 \tag{19}$$

with initial condition $x(0) = 1$ (the network is completely secure at the beginning) and the final condition $x(1) = 0.5$ (we accept a lower security level at the end to reduce costs).

The OCP in Application 1 explores the critical trade-off between operational security integrity and expenditure management, where the calculated value is $J = 0.5696851572$. Tables 1, 2, 3 and 4 give the impact of the performance for Application 1. The optimal performance value is obtained at $n = 7$, where the error metrics values tends to minimum values.

Table 1. The $E_{n,\, state}$ values with n = 5, 6 and 7 for Application 1.

t	$E_{5,state} \times 10^{-4}$	$E_{6,statel} \times 10^{-5}$	$E_{7,staete} \times 10^{-7}$
0	0.00	0.00	0.00
0.2	2.42	0.521	9.16
0.4	3.56	1.20	5.06
0.6	3.31	1.30	4.54
0.8	2.50	0.341	8.75
1	0.00	0.00	0.00

Table 2. The $E_{n,\, control}$ values with n = 5, 6 and 7 for Application 1.

t	$E_{5,control} \times 10^{-3}$	$E_{6,control} \times 10^{-4}$	$E_{7,control} \times 10^{-5}$
0	7.92	4.24	3.54
0.2	2.71	1.65	0,539
0.4	2.12	0,945	1.05
0.6	2.02	0.837	1.03
0.8	2.59	1.51	0,506
1	7.14	3.55	3.31

Table 3. The max and mean values for Application 1.

Metric	$N = 4 \times 10^{-3}$	$N = 5 \times 10^{-4}$	$N = 6 \times 10^{-5}$
Mean error $M\,\epsilon_x$	0.196	0.05.61	0.00458
Max error ϵ_x	0.356	0.130	0.00916
Mean error $M\,\epsilon_u$	4.08	2.12	1.66
Max error ϵ_u	7.92	4.24	3.54

Table 4. The Approximate J and E_J values for Application 1.

n	J	$E_J \times 10^{-6}$
4	0.5696931846	8.0274
5	0.5696851740	0.00168
6	0.5696851573	0.00001

Figures 1, 2 and 3 graph the approximate solutions for state and control using various orders of ECVP, the errors values and the evolution of error metrics with increasing basis function order, respectively. They clearly illustrate a consistent improvement as the order of the basis function increases in the mean error and related indicators. Further, the data highlights the convergence behavior of the system over given interval.

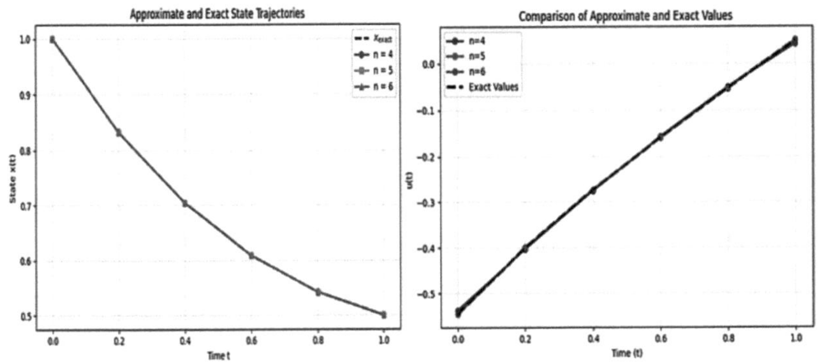

Fig. 1. Approximate solutions for state and control using various orders of ECVP for Application 1.

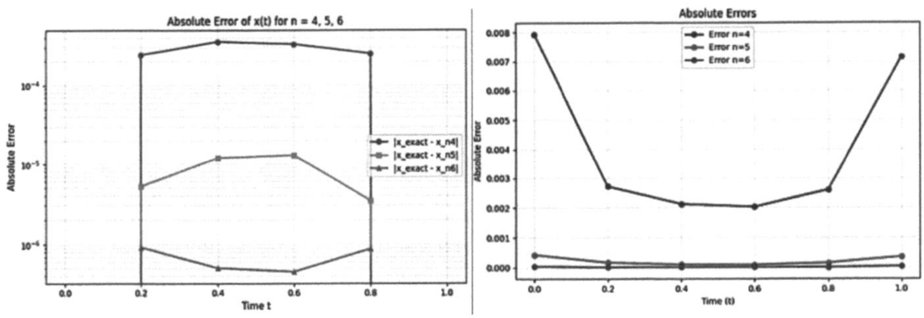

Fig. 2. Plot the errors values for Application 1 using different basis function orders

Note that the exact state trajectory is given by $x(t) = Ae^{st} + Be^{-st}$, $u(t) = (s + 0.4)Ae^{st} + (-s + 0.4)Be^{-st}$, where $A = 0.06141573559053107$, $B = 0.938584264409469$ and $s = 1.077032961426901$.

Overall, these results confirm the effectiveness of the proposed approach in producing accurate and stable approximate solutions for the optimal control problem under consideration.

6.2 Application. Solar Energy Systems

An office building equipped with a solar power system aims to optimally manage energy storage and consumption over a 24-h period. The system variables are the energy stored

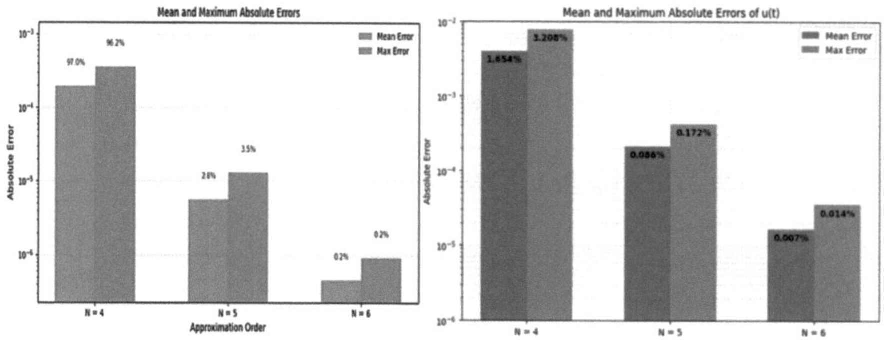

Fig. 3. Evolution of error metrics for Application 1 with increasing basis function order

in the batteries $x(t)$ and the applied charging/discharging power $u(t)$ while the solar cost function can be defined as below

$$Min\ j = \frac{1}{2}\int_{-1}^{1}\left(u^2(t) + 3x^2(t)\right)dt, \tag{20}$$

where $u^2(t)$ and $3x^2(t)$ represent the energy loss during conversion processes and the deviation from maximum power point tracking (MPPT) respectively. In addition, the solar system dynamics and solar boundary conditions are defined respectively as follow

$$u(t) = 2\dot{x}(t) - x(t) \tag{21}$$

$$x(-1) = 1, x(1) = 0.51314538 \tag{22}$$

Note that, at sunrise ($t = -1$) and at solar peak ($t = 1$), Eq. (20) represent the minimum energy stored at dawn and the optimal utilization of solar energy at peak hours respectively. To evaluate the precision of the approximation, the absolute errors for different values of n are presented in Tables 5 and 6, demonstrating the convergence behavior of the model. In addition, the performance evaluation of Application 2 is summarized in Tables 7 and 8, presenting the key metric values calculated over the interval $t \in [0,1]$.

The approximate solutions of the state and control variables are demonstrated in Fig. 4 which provides a comparison of the numerical approximation as the order of ECVP increases, leading to the convergence of the trajectories. Figures 5 and 6, respectively illustrate the approximate solutions for state and control using various orders of ECVP and the errors values and the evolution of error metrics with increasing basis function order.

The analytic solution for Application 1 is given as below
$x(t) = c_1e^t + c_2e^{-t}$, where $c_1 =$ 0.1415817270521744 and $c_2 =$ 0.3487184380397075 and the performance index value is equal to $J = 2.791658875$.

Table 5. The $E_{n,\ state}$ values with n = 5, 6 and 7 for Application 2.

t	$E_{5,state} \times 10^{-4}$	$E_{6,statel} \times 10^{-5}$	$E_{7,staete} \times 10^{-7}$
−1	0.0000000000	0.0000000000	0.0000000000
−0.6	0.7063790000	2.8826600000	7.6439999996
−0.2	1.1606690000	1.5799500000	9.3020000003
0.2	1.4578580000	1.3919300000	9.5000000000
0.6	0.1449210000	2.7319200000	7.4300000003
1	0.0000000000	0.0000000000	0.0000000000

Table 6. The $E_{n,\ control}$ values with n = 5, 6 and 7 for Application 2.

t	$E_{5,control} \times 10^{-3}$	$E_{6,control} \times 10^{-4}$	$E_{7,control} \times 10^{-5}$
−1	5.3259409000	1.1381079000	4.9236800000
−0.6	1.7699820000	1.2995950000	1.0188300000
−0.2	1.3706939000	3.0745330000	0.6369699999
0.2	0.4558060000	3.4370160000	0.0140000000
0.6	1.5234988000	2.0014630000	0.3874100000
1	3.1331186000	1.0547144000	3.4156700000

Table 7. Different Error values over t ∈ [0,1] for Application 2.

Metric	$n = 5(\times 10^{-3})$	$n = 6(\times 10^{-4})$	$n = 7(\times 10^{-5})$
$L_{1,x}$	0.184600820	0.34975760000	0.0982599999
$L_{2,x}$	0.153331079	0..8379040898	0.0836086246
$L_{\infty,x}$	0.177312600	0.32950600000	0.0950000000
$L_{1,u}$	3.5738867800	9.3117706000	3.4485520000
$L_{2,u}$	3.1976624223	8.0238865428	3.0702165957
$L_{\infty,u}$	5.3259409000	1.1381079000	4.9236800000

Table 8. The Approximate J and E_J values for Application 2.

n	J	E_J $(\times 10^{-6})$
5	2.7916620247	3.1497
6	2.7916600829	1.2079
7	2.7916599754	1.1004

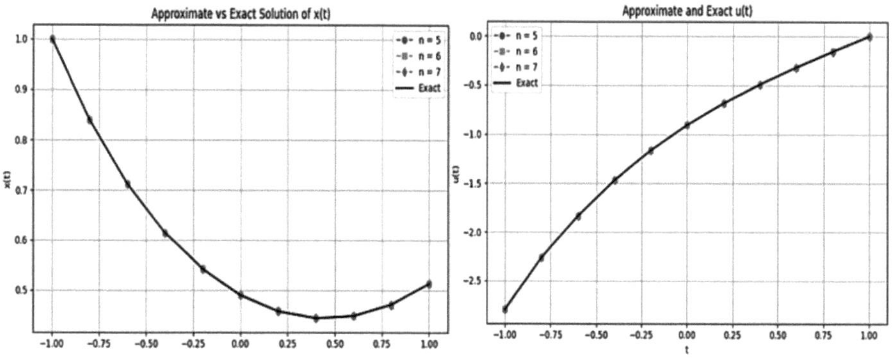

Fig. 4. Approximate solutions for state and control using various orders of ECVPPs for Application 2.

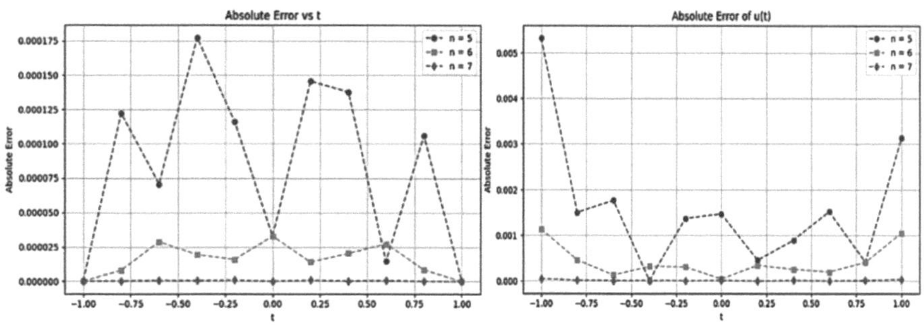

Fig. 5. Plot the error values for Application 2 using different basis function orders.

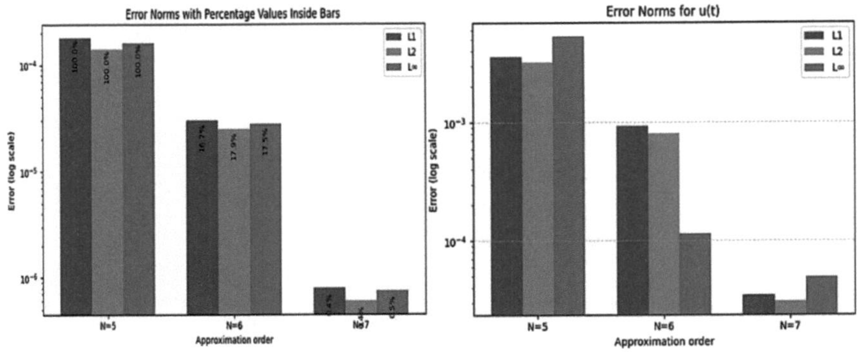

Fig. 6. Evolution of error metrics for Application 2 with increasing basis function order.

7 Discussion the Results

By analyzing the obtained results for the two applications including solar energy systems and network protection, many observations can be conclude concerning both the convergence and stability of the framework. The numerical approximation of the suggested algorithm illustrates a consistent correlation between the approximation order and the precision of the obtained solutions. One can see a clear development in the accuracy of the solution as the approximation order increases from $n = 4$ to $n = 7$ for the variables $x(t)$ and $u(t)$. In addition, the absolute error analysis demonstrates that the smaller errors near the boundary points of the time domain and within the interior region as the error values decrease by certain orders of magnitude when moving from $n = 4$ to $n = 7$. Furthermore, both the mean absolute error and the maximum absolute error exhibit a systematic reduction with increasing n. The convergence trend is also supported by the different error norms. For both the state and control variables, all norms decrease monotonically as the approximation order increases. The computed values of the performance index J show a steady convergence toward the exact value as n increases.

8 Conclusion

The definition of ECVP polynomials is constructed in this work and hen proposed an efficient numerical approximation technique for solving problems in optimal control. The extended polynomials enabled higher-order accuracy and better flexibility in representing the state and control variables over any time interval. This behavior was observed in the numerical results, where the error norms decreased as n increased. A quadratic programming approach was modified to solve the obtained optimization problem. By formulating the performance index as a quadratic functional and transforming the system dynamics together with the boundary conditions as linear equality constraints, the original OCP was transformed into a standard quadratic programming problem. The advantage of the presenting direct formulation avoids the complexity of indirect methods and eliminates the need to explicitly solve adjoint equations. The findings demonstrate that the proposed technique with ECVP polynomials is efficient, accurate and stable.

Acknowledgments. The authors would like to thank the administration of the College of Applied Sciences for their continuous support.

Disclosure of Interests. The authors have no competing interests to declare that are relevant to the content of this article.

References

1. Abass, G., Shihab, S.: Operational matrix of new shifted wavelet functions for solving optimal control problem. Mathematics **11**(14), 3040 (2023)
2. Diveev, A., Sofronova, E.: Optimal control problem and its solution in class of feasible control functions by advanced model of control object. Mathematics **13**(4), 674 (2025)
3. Intriligator, M.D.: Applications of optimal control theory in economics. Synthese **31**(2), 271–288 (1975)
4. Shihab, S., Ouda, E.H.: Approximate solution for astrophysics problems using shifted Veita-Pell polynomials. AIP Conf. Proc. **3036**(1), 040002 (2024)
5. Rahman, M.H., et al.: Optimal control problem and its application in COVID-19 transmission dynamics. Lecture Notes in Networks and Systems, p. 1138 (2024)
6. Norouzzadeh, A., Nariman-zadeh, N., Ansari, R.: A novel unified variational finite difference solution method for optimal control problems. Measure. Control **58**(5), 682–695 (2024)
7. Yıldırım Aksoy, N., Hào, D.N., Yagub, G.: Finite difference method for an optimal control problem for a nonlinear time-dependent Schrödinger equation. Numer. Funct. Anal. Optim. **38**(6), 799–817 (2017)
8. Baleanu, D., Hajipour, M., Jajarmi, A.: An accurate finite difference formula for the numerical solution of delay-dependent fractional optimal control problems. IJOCTA **14**(3), 183–192 (2024)
9. Wang, S., Zheng, X., Du, N.: Finite element method for an optimal control problem governed by a time fractional wave equation. Comput. Math. Appl. **164**, 45–66 (2024)
10. Khaksar-e Oshagh, M., Shamsi, M.: An adaptive wavelet collocation method for solving optimal control of elliptic variational inequalities of the obstacle type. Comput. Math. Appl. **75**(2), 470–485 (2018)
11. Yarahmadi, M., Yaghobipour, S.: Chebyshev wavelet-based method for solving various stochastic optimal control problems and its application in finance. Iran. J. Numer. Anal. Optimizat. **14**(1), 1–19 (2024)
12. Ebrahimzadeh, A.: Solving the optimum control problem constrained with Volterra integro-differential equations using Chebyshev wavelets and particle swarm optimization. AUT J. Math. Comput. (2024)
13. Kumari, R., Mehra, M.: Müntz-Legendre wavelet collocation method for the solution of optimal control problems with fractional-loaded differential equations. SN Comput. Sci. **6**, 461 (2025)
14. Maleknejad, K., Ebrahimzadeh, A.: The use of rationalized Haar wavelet collocation method for solving optimal control of Volterra integral equations. J. Vib. Control **21**(10), 1958–1967 (2013)
15. Hussain, F., Shihab, S.: A new direct algorithm for solving optimal control problem using certain shifted basis polynomials. In: AIP Conference Proceedings, vol. 3393(1), p. 060024 (2026)
16. Hsiao, C.H., Wang, W.J.: Optimal control of linear time-varying systems via Haar wavelets. J. Optim. Theory Appl. **103**, 641–655 (1999)

17. Hussain, F., Shihab, S.: Transforming controlled duffing oscillator to optimization schemes using new symmetry-shifted G(t)-polynomials. Symmetry **16**(7) (2024)
18. Ouda, E.H., Ibraheem, S.F., Shihab, S.N.: Boubaker wavelets functions: properties and applications. Baghdad Sci. J. **18**(4), 1226–1233 (2021)
19. Tasci, D., Yalcin, F.: Vieta-Pell and Vieta-Pell-Lucas polynomials. Adv. Differen. Equ. **224** (2013)
20. Sriprad, W., Srisawat, S., Naklor, P.: Vieta–Fibonacci-like polynomials and some identities. Ann. Math. Inform. **54**, 97–108 (2021)
21. Boughaba, S., Saba, N., Boussayoud, A.: Construction of generating functions of the products of Vieta polynomials with Gaussian numbers and polynomials. Int. J. Nonlinear Anal. Appl. **12**(1), 649–668 (2021)
22. Sabermahani, S., Rahimkhani, P., Ordokhani, Y.: Application of generalized Lucas wavelet method for solving nonlinear fractal-fractional optimal control problems. Chaos, Solitons Fract. **170**, 113348 (2023)
23. Taghipour, M., Aminikhah, H.: Application of Pell collocation method for solving the general form of time-fractional Burgers equations. Math. Sci. **17**, 183–201 (2023)
24. Singh, P.K., Ray, S.S.: An efficient numerical method based on Lucas polynomials to solve multi-dimensional stochastic Itô-Volterra integral equations. Math. Comput. Simul. **203**, 826–845 (2023)
25. Singh, P.K., Ray, S.S.: A numerical approach based on Pell polynomial for solving stochastic fractional differential equations. Numer. Algor. **97**, 1513–1534 (2024)
26. Abd-Elhameed, W.M., Abu Sunayh, A.F., Alharbi, M.H., Atta, A.G.: Spectral tau technique via Lucas polynomials for the time-fractional diffusion equation. AIMS Math. **9**(12), 34567–34587 (2024)
27. Yalc, N.F., Tas, D., Erkus-Duman, E.: Generalized Vieta-Jacobsthal and Vieta-Jacobsthal-Lucas polynomials. Math. Commun. **20**, 241–251 (2015)
28. Kuloğlu, B., Özkan, E., Shannon, A.G.: Incomplete generalized Vieta-Pell and Vieta–Pell–Lucas polynomials. Notes Number Theory Discrete Math. **27**(4), 245–256 (2021)
29. Uygun, S., Karatas, H., Aytar, H.: Notes on generalization of Vieta-Pell and Vieta-Pell Lucas polynomials. Int. J. Math. Res. **12**(1), 5–22 (2020)
30. Vlassenbroeck, J., Van Dooren, R.: Chebyshev series solution of the controlled Duffing oscillator. J. Comput. Phys. **47**, 321–329 (1982)
31. Razzaghi, M., Elnagar, G.: Numerical solution of the controlled Duffing oscillator by the pseudospectral method. J. Comput. Appl. Math. **56**(3), 253–261 (1994)

A Novel Pansharpening Framework Based on the Atangana-Baleanu Fractal-Fractional Derivative

Husam Yahya[1], Nadia M. G. Al-Saidi[2], Arkan J. Mohammed[3], and Yeliz Karaca[4](✉)

[1] Ministry of Higher Education and Scientific Research, Baghdad, Iraq
Husam.yahya@mohesr.edu.iq

[2] College of Applied Sciences, University of Technology, Baghdad, Iraq
nadia.m.ghanim@uotechnology.edu.iq

[3] Department of Mathematics, College of Science, Al-Mustansiriah University, Baghdad, Iraq
drarkanjasim@uomustansiriyah.edu.iq

[4] Department of Mathematics and Department of Neurology, University of Massachusetts Chan Medical School (UMASS), 55 Lake Avenue North, Worcester, MA 01655, USA
yeliz.karaca@ieee.org

Abstract. Combining spectral and spatial information from multiple sensors into a single, analysis-ready product is among the most persistent challenges in remote sensing and medical imaging. Pansharpening—the fusion of a high-resolution panchromatic band with lower-resolution multispectral imagery—is particularly demanding: improving spatial detail tends to compromise spectral accuracy, and preserving spectral fidelity tends to blur spatial structure. Classical methods based on component substitution, multiresolution analysis, or modulation transfer rely on integer-order operators whose local support cannot capture the non-local memory effects and scale-invariant structures present in natural terrain. We introduce ABR-FFD, a pansharpening framework that replaces the conventional Gaussian smoothing kernel with a Mittag-Leffler low-pass filter derived from the Atangana-Baleanu fractal-fractional derivative. The kernel is evaluated via exact Mittag-Leffler series summation without asymptotic simplification, and its two parameters—the fractional order α and fractal dimension τ—are jointly optimised per scene through a 15×15 grid search over a fixed 7×7 neighbourhood. A multiplicative injection rule augmented with local mean correction and a two-scale coarse-detail term preserves inter-band spectral ratios at every pixel. Evaluated on twenty WorldView-3 scenes from the PanCollection benchmark using Wald's reduced-resolution protocol against seven classical comparison methods, ABR-FFD simultaneously achieves the lowest ERGAS (4.768), the best spectral angle (SAM = 5.798°, winning on all twenty individual scenes), and the highest SSIM (0.8761). These three spectral-fidelity metrics measure fundamentally different aspects of fusion quality and have not previously been optimised simultaneously by

O. Gervasi et al. (Eds.): ICCSA 2026 Workshops, LNCS 16758, pp. 317–343, 2027.
https://doi.org/10.1007/978-3-032-30497-1_20

a single classical method. An ablation study identifies the local mean correction as the sole driver of the spectral angle gain, contributing a reduction of 0.036° relative to the uncorrected baseline, while neighbourhood-size analysis establishes a non-monotone relationship between kernel support and ERGAS, with 7×7 as the unique optimum for the WV3 4: 1 resolution ratio. These findings establish fractal-fractional operators as a principled and competitive alternative to wavelet-based smoothing in satellite image fusion.

Keywords: Pansharpening · Fractal-fractional calculus · Atangana-Baleanu derivative · Mittag-Leffler kernel · Remote sensing · Image fusion · WorldView-3

1 Introduction

Earth observation satellites now routinely acquire the same scene at different spatial and spectral resolutions, and turning those separate acquisitions into a single analysis-ready product has become one of remote sensing's central practical problems [1,3]. Pansharpening is the most common instance: a high-resolution panchromatic band is merged with lower-resolution multispectral bands to yield imagery that is simultaneously geometrically sharp and spectrally faithful [2,4]. For sensors such as WorldView-3 and GaoFen-2, where the resolution gap reaches 4:1, striking an acceptable spatial-spectral balance becomes considerably more difficult.

Classical pansharpening methods fall into three broad families, each with well-documented limitations. In component substitution (CS)—IHS [5], PCA [6], and Gram–Schmidt (GS) [7]—the MS bands are projected into a decorrelated space, one component is replaced by the PAN image, and the inverse transform is applied. The spatial sharpness achieved this way comes at a cost: since the replaced component rarely matches the PAN spectral response, the reconstructed bands typically carry systematic colour distortions [4]. Multiresolution analysis (MRA) methods such as AWLP [8] and HPF [9] take a different route altogether, extracting PAN detail at multiple scales and adding it back into the MS bands directly; spectral preservation is generally better, though fine-textured regions remain problematic when the filter does not align well with local edge orientations [12]. Modulation-based methods, exemplified by SFIM [10], scale each MS band by the local PAN-to-smooth-PAN ratio—a conceptually elegant idea that produces a reasonable spatial-spectral compromise. The bottleneck, however, is the smoother: a fixed Gaussian kernel responds identically at edges and in flat regions, so performance saturates regardless of how carefully the bandwidth is tuned [11]. CNN, GAN, and transformer architectures [13–15] have pushed benchmark scores considerably higher, yet each requires a large labelled training corpus, carries non-trivial inference cost, and may generalise poorly when the target sensor or scene type is not well represented in training.

Operators such as Sobel and Canny inherit this strictly local character, which makes them computationally attractive but spatially myopic: high-frequency noise is amplified while gradual, long-range variations are underweighted [16,17]. In fusion applications the result is familiar—staircase artefacts and loss of structural coherence—because each output pixel sees only its immediate neighbours and has no access to the surrounding textural context.

Fractional calculus extends differentiation to non-integer orders $\alpha \in \mathbb{R}$, and the resulting operators carry a property that is genuinely useful here: they integrate function values over an extended interval rather than at a point, giving each output location implicit access to a wider spatial context and making them inherently more sensitive to texture than their integer-order counterparts [2,18–20]. The classical Riemann–Liouville and Caputo formulations are not without problems, though. Both employ power-law kernels that diverge as $\xi \to t$, and near sharp image boundaries this singularity can trigger numerical instabilities that reintroduce the very staircase artefacts one was hoping to avoid [21]. Atangana and Baleanu's 2016 derivative replaces that power-law with a Mittag-Leffler kernel, which stays bounded everywhere while preserving the non-local integration range [21,22]:

$$\frac{\partial I}{\partial x} = \lim_{h \to 0} \frac{I(x+h,y) - I(x,y)}{h}. \tag{1}$$

Fractal geometry, formalised by Mandelbrot [23], offers a complementary perspective: it quantifies self-similar, scale-invariant structure through the fractal dimension D, capturing geometric complexity that ordinary Euclidean measures miss. Such properties are ubiquitous in natural and man-made terrain as seen from orbit. Within image analysis, fractal descriptors have found use in texture classification, segmentation, compression, medical imaging, and remote sensing interpretation; in remote sensing specifically they have been applied to land-cover characterisation, river network and coastline analysis, image-type classification, and hyperspectral dimensionality reduction [24–26]. Adding D as an operator parameter allows the filter to remain sensitive to irregular, self-similar texture rather than smoothing it away as purely Euclidean operators tend to do. Pairing the AB derivative with a fractal dimension parameter τ therefore yields a two-parameter operator that simultaneously accounts for non-local memory and self-similar terrain geometry—a combination well suited to the multi-scale, heterogeneous content typical of satellite imagery. Against this background, we propose ABR-FFD, a pansharpening framework that substitutes the Gaussian smoothing kernel in SFIM with a Mittag-Leffler low-pass filter derived from the Atangana-Baleanu fractal-fractional derivative, evaluated via exact series summation without asymptotic approximation. The two parameters (α, τ) are jointly optimised per scene through a 15×15 grid search, and the pipeline incorporates a local mean correction and two-scale coarse-detail injection to improve spectral angle preservation. This paper makes four contributions: (i) the derivation of an isotropic Mittag-Leffler low-pass kernel with exact series coefficients, free of asymptotic substitution, for spatial smoothing in the SFIM modulation framework; (ii) a two-parameter (α, τ) optimisation strategy over a dense grid, with the neighbourhood size fixed at the experimentally confirmed optimum of 7×7; (iii) an evaluation on twenty WorldView-3 scenes from the PanCollection benchmark [15] against seven classical methods spanning all three pansharpening families, establishing best performance on ERGAS, SAM, and SSIM simultaneously; and (iv) an ablation study and neighbourhood-size analysis that quantify the individual contribution of each design element.

The remainder of this paper is organised as follows. Section 2 surveys related work in pansharpening and fractional image processing. Section 3 presents the mathematical background. Section 4 derives the proposed ABR-FFD operator and fusion pipeline. Section 5 reports experimental results, and Sect. 6 discusses findings and limitations. Finally, Sect. 7 concludes the paper.

2 Literature Review

This section surveys the principal families of pansharpening methods and recent advances in fractional and fractal-based image processing.

2.1 Classical Pansharpening Methods

CS methods represent the earliest class of pansharpening algorithms and have endured largely because of their computational efficiency. Carper et al. [5] proposed IHS fusion: the MS bands are converted to intensity-hue-saturation space, the intensity channel is replaced by the histogram-matched PAN image, and the inverse transform is applied; spatial sharpness is high, but the spectral distortion introduced scales with the mismatch between the PAN response and the intensity channel. Chavez et al. [6] used principal component analysis in a similar vein, substituting the first component with PAN and inheriting the same spectral bias. Laben and Brower's Gram–Schmidt (GS) approach [7] reduces this bias somewhat by first synthesising a simulated PAN from the MS bands before substitution, though the improvement is incomplete for spectrally heterogeneous scenes.

MRA methods take a fundamentally different approach, injecting spatially decomposed PAN detail directly into the MS bands. Schowengerdt [9] introduced high-pass filtering (HPF) as an early example; Otazu et al. [8] refined it through the à trous wavelet-based AWLP, which adapts injection gains per band using spectral response functions, generally yielding good spectral preservation. One known weakness of AWLP is that the wavelet basis can be poorly matched to dominant edge orientations in fine-textured regions, leading to visible ringing artefacts in some scenes. Liu's SFIM [10] occupies the boundary between MRA and modulation approaches: each MS band is rescaled by the ratio of PAN to a low-pass approximation of PAN, which is straightforward to implement and tends to produce acceptable spectral fidelity. The persistent problem is that the Gaussian used for the low-pass step cannot adapt to local image structure, and SFIM's typically modest SCC scores reflect this rigidity directly.

2.2 Deep Learning and Model-Based Approaches

Deep learning approaches—including CNNs, GANs, and more recently transformer-based networks—have delivered substantial gains on standard pansharpening benchmarks [13–15]. The practical limitations are nonetheless real: collecting sufficient labelled training data is non-trivial, inference times scale with model size, and out-of-distribution generalisation (different sensor, different biome) can be unpredictable. These constraints have kept interest alive in classical model-based approaches, whose assumptions are explicit and whose failure modes can often be anticipated from the mathematical structure alone.

2.3 Fractional Calculus in Image Processing

Fractional-order operators have been an active topic in image processing for roughly a decade. Riemann–Liouville and Grünwald–Letnikov derivatives have been used for edge detection in remote sensing, where capturing multi-scale responses within a single operator is particularly valuable [16]. Pu et al. [20] demonstrated that fractional-order masks offer a continuously adjustable noise–texture trade-off that ordinary differential operators simply cannot replicate, and more recent work has embedded fractional-order kernels inside CNN architectures for multi-scale feature extraction [29]. The recurring obstacle is the singular kernel: classical fractional formulations behave poorly near sharp intensity transitions, and the resulting instabilities have driven a steady search for alternatives that do not carry this singularity [21].

The derivative introduced by Atangana and Baleanu [21] addresses the singularity problem by swapping the power-law kernel for a Mittag-Leffler function. The weighting profile that results is completely monotone and finite at zero, which in practice means the filter can smooth gradual transitions without degrading sharp boundaries—a combination that classical Caputo-type operators cannot easily provide [21,22]. Extensions coupling the fractional order α with a fractal dimension parameter τ add a second degree of freedom for scale-invariant texture sensitivity, and applications in medical image enhancement have shown that this pairing is practically useful [26,30,41,43]. To our knowledge, no previous study has derived a discrete, isotropic low-pass kernel directly from the AB fractal-fractional operator and applied it to satellite pansharpening—which is the gap this paper fills. Three specific gaps in the current literature motivate the approach: (i) classical pansharpening operators are confined to integer-order, local differentiation and therefore cannot exploit non-local spatial context; (ii) existing fractional-calculus approaches to image processing rely on singular kernels that degrade near sharp boundaries; and (iii) the dual-parameter flexibility offered by fractal-fractional operators has not yet been exploited for spatial smoothing in image fusion. The proposed ABR-FFD framework addresses all three gaps simultaneously.

3 Mathematical Background

The proposed framework draws on three mathematical building blocks: fractional calculus, fractal geometry, and the Atangana–Baleanu fractal-fractional operator. Each is introduced below in the form needed for the discrete kernel construction in Sect. 4.

In digital image processing, an image is modelled as a two-dimensional signal $I(x, y)$. Classical enhancement and feature-extraction methods rely on integer-order operators such as the gradient ∇I and Laplacian ΔI, which quantify intensity change over an immediate pixel neighbourhood.

3.1 Fractional Calculus

Fractional calculus extends classical differentiation and integration to non-integer orders $\alpha \in \mathbb{R}$. In the image analysis context, this generalisation is useful because fractional operators can be tuned to balance edge sharpening against texture preservation, their non-local memory effects providing access to spatial context that fixed-kernel integer-order operators cannot exploit.

For $f(t)$ on $[a, b]$, the Riemann–Liouville derivative of order $\alpha > 0$ is [18]:

$$ {}_{a}^{RL}D_t^{\alpha} f(t) = \frac{1}{\Gamma(n-\alpha)} \frac{d^n}{dt^n} \int_a^t (t-\xi)^{n-\alpha-1} f(\xi)\, d\xi, \quad n = \lceil \alpha \rceil. \tag{2} $$

The Caputo derivative reorders the operations by placing the ordinary derivative inside the integral:

$$ {}_{a}^{C}D_t^{\alpha} f(t) = \frac{1}{\Gamma(n-\alpha)} \int_a^t (t-\xi)^{n-\alpha-1} f^{(n)}(\xi)\, d\xi. \tag{3} $$

In practice the Caputo form is often preferred because it accepts standard initial conditions and gives zero for constant inputs, making it more tractable in applied settings. Both operators share an important weakness, however: the power-law factor $(t-\xi)^{n-\alpha-1}$ diverges as $\xi \to t$, and this blow-up can undermine numerical stability whenever the image contains sharp intensity transitions [21].

3.2 Fractal Geometry and Self-Similarity

Fractal geometry provides a language for structures whose statistical appearance is roughly self-similar across scales [23]. The fractal dimension τ is the most common such descriptor in imaging contexts; it captures texture irregularity in a way that ordinary Euclidean measures miss. Land cover as seen from high-resolution satellites—vegetation canopies, built fabric, coastlines, agricultural patchwork—frequently exhibits this kind of scale-dependent organisation, making τ a natural fit as a kernel parameter. When included as a free parameter in a differential operator, τ allows the filter to track irregular, self-similar structure rather than washing it out, as purely Euclidean operators tend to do [25,27,28,39,40].

3.3 Atangana-Baleanu Derivative

The AB derivative in the Caputo sense uses a Mittag-Leffler kernel [21]:

$$ {}^{ABC}D_t^{\alpha} f(t) = \frac{AB(\alpha)}{1-\alpha} \int_a^t E_\alpha\left[-\tfrac{\alpha}{1-\alpha}(t-\xi)^\alpha\right] f'(\xi)\, d\xi, \tag{4} $$

where $AB(\alpha) = 1 - \alpha + \alpha/\Gamma(\alpha)$ is the normalisation constant and $E_\alpha(z) = \sum_{k=0}^{\infty} z^k/\Gamma(\alpha k+1)$ is the one-parameter Mittag-Leffler function. Since $E_\alpha(0) = 1$, the kernel evaluates to a strictly positive, finite value at the origin for every $\alpha \in (0,1)$—in sharp contrast to the Riemann–Liouville and Caputo kernels, which diverge as $t \to \xi^+$. This bounded-everywhere character is what makes the AB operator attractive for image processing: gradual transitions are smoothed without the instabilities that appear near sharp boundaries when singular kernels are used [22].

3.4 Fractal-Fractional Operator

Combining the AB derivative with the fractal derivative of order τ yields the fractal-fractional operator [21]:

$$ \mathscr{F}_t^{\alpha,\tau} f(t) = \frac{AB(\alpha)}{1-\alpha} \int_a^t E_\alpha\left[-\tfrac{\alpha}{1-\alpha}(t-\xi)^\alpha\right] \frac{df(\xi)}{d\xi^\tau}\, d\xi, \tag{5} $$

where the fractal derivative is $df(\xi)/d\xi^\tau = \lim_{h\to 0}[f(\xi+h) - f(\xi)]/[(\xi+h)^\tau - \xi^\tau]$. In this operator, α controls the spatial reach of the kernel: small values yield a broad, slowly-decaying weight function that draws on distant pixels, whereas values approaching unity pull the weight back toward the centre and recover something close to ordinary local smoothing. The fractal parameter τ acts orthogonally, rescaling the distance weighting to preserve sensitivity to self-similar texture at different spatial resolutions. The two parameters are largely independent, which is what makes the operator considerably more flexible than single-parameter alternatives for images with multi-scale, heterogeneous content.

3.5 Parameter Roles in Image Fusion

In the proposed framework, the ABR-FFD operator serves as the theoretical foundation for the low-pass smoothing kernel. The synergistic roles of its parameters are summarised in Table 1.

Table 1. Synergistic roles of ABR-FFD parameters in image processing.

Parameter	Mathematical Role	Image Processing Effect
Fractional order (α)	Controls kernel decay rate and non-locality	Balances edge sharpness against noise suppression
Fractal dimension (τ)	Modulates fractal-scale sensitivity	Enhances self-similar textures and fine structures
Mittag-Leffler kernel	Provides non-singular, non-local weighting	Eliminates staircase artefacts and preserves gradients

These mathematical foundations carry directly into Sect. 4, where the continuous operator is discretised over a finite pixel neighbourhood, normalised to unit sum, and embedded in the multiplicative SFIM pipeline.

4 The Proposed ABR-FFD Pansharpening Method

This section derives the Mittag-Leffler low-pass kernel and the fusion pipeline in which it is embedded. The governing idea is to substitute the Gaussian smoother in the classical SFIM modulation framework with a kernel whose weights are computed from the exact Mittag-Leffler series of the AB fractal-fractional operator, without resorting to asymptotic approximation at any distance. Starting from the continuous operator, we extend it to two spatial dimensions and discretise it over a finite pixel neighbourhood, arriving at a normalised kernel that retains the non-singular, non-local character of the underlying theory. Figure 1 gives an overview of the ABR-FFD pansharpening pipeline.

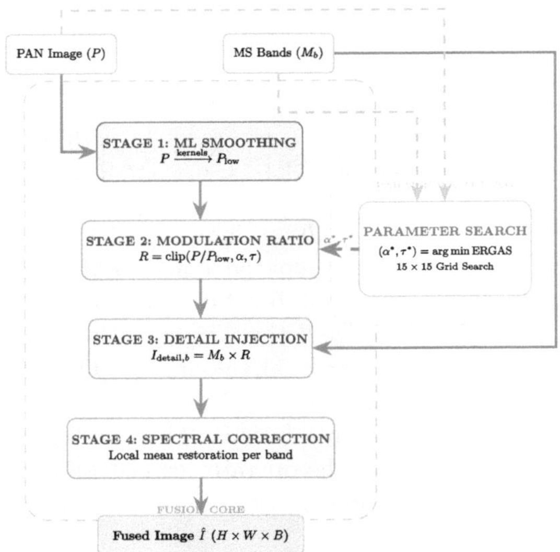

Fig. 1. System architecture of the ABR-FFD pipeline. The design uses orthogonal gutter routing to separate data flow (solid) from control logic (dashed), ensuring zero visual intersections between signals and functional modules.

4.1 Continuous Operator: Definitions and Fundamental Properties

We begin by stating the continuous ABR-FFD operator and establishing its key properties. Define the AB-normalised Mittag-Leffler kernel $\mathcal{K}_\alpha \colon \mathbb{R}_+ \to \mathbb{R}_+$ by

$$\mathcal{K}_\alpha(s) := \frac{AB(\alpha)}{1-\alpha} \, E_\alpha\left(-\frac{\alpha}{1-\alpha}\, s^\alpha\right), \qquad s > 0. \tag{6}$$

The kernel satisfies $\mathcal{K}_\alpha(0) = AB(\alpha)/(1-\alpha) > 0$ for all $\alpha \in (0,1)$, since $E_\alpha(0) = 1$. The kernel is therefore non-singular at the origin, in contrast to the power-law kernels of the Riemann–Liouville and Caputo formulations, which diverge as $t \to \xi^+$ for $\alpha \in (0,1)$.

For the fractal denominator, a first-order binomial expansion yields: for $\xi > 0$ and $|h|/\xi \ll 1$,

$$(\xi + h)^\tau - \xi^\tau = \tau\,\xi^{\tau-1}\,h + \mathcal{O}\left(\frac{h^2}{\xi^{2-\tau}}\right), \tag{7}$$

and consequently, for differentiable f,

$$\frac{d\,f(\xi)}{d\,\xi^\tau} = \frac{f'(\xi)}{\tau\,\xi^{\tau-1}} + \mathcal{O}\left(\frac{h}{\xi^{2-\tau}}\right) \xrightarrow{h\to 0} \frac{f'(\xi)}{\tau\,\xi^{\tau-1}}. \tag{8}$$

4.2 Two-Dimensional Spatial Extension and Discretisation

Equation (5) defines the ABR-FFD for a univariate function. Applying it to a two-dimensional image signal $I(x,y)$ requires a formal spatial extension. We adopt a directional-integral strategy in which the kernel is evaluated at the Euclidean pixel distance from the operator centre, yielding an isotropic low-pass filter.

For a compact neighbourhood Ω centred at (x_0, y_0), the kernel weight at spatial offset (x', y') is:

$$w(x', y') = \mathcal{K}_\alpha\big(\rho(x', y')\big) \cdot \frac{1}{\tau\,\rho(x', y')^{\tau-1}}, \tag{9}$$

where $\rho(x', y') = \|(x_0 - x', y_0 - y')\|_2 + \varepsilon$ is the regularised Euclidean distance ($\varepsilon > 0$). By evaluating the kernel at Euclidean distance from the centre, the 2-D extension retains the radially-decaying, non-local character of the original continuous operator and remains straightforward to discretise over a finite pixel grid.

The discrete kernel weight at offset $(u,v) \in \{-N, \ldots, N\}^2$ is obtained by evaluating (9) at the regularised distance $\rho_{u,v} := \|(u,v)\|_2 + \varepsilon$:

$$W(u,v) = \frac{\mathcal{K}_\alpha(\rho_{u,v})}{\tau\,\rho_{u,v}^{\tau-1} + \varepsilon}, \quad \rho_{u,v} = \|(u,v)\|_2 + \varepsilon, \tag{10}$$

where $\varepsilon > 0$ is a small regularisation constant. The kernel is normalised to unit sum: $\hat{W}(u,v) = W(u,v)/\sum_{m,n} W(m,n)$, ensuring that it acts as a proper low-pass filter.

The Mittag-Leffler function is evaluated at each pixel distance using the truncated series

$$E_\alpha(z) = \sum_{k=0}^{K} \frac{z^k}{\Gamma(\alpha k + 1)}, \quad K \geq 80, \tag{11}$$

which converges to double-precision accuracy at all neighbourhood distances [18]. Crucially, no asymptotic substitution is made at any distance; all weights are computed from the truncated series directly, so the kernel retains its exact Mittag-Leffler character throughout the neighbourhood. How steeply the weights decay with distance is governed by α: small values spread mass broadly across the neighbourhood, while values near unity concentrate it near the centre in a manner resembling ordinary Gaussian smoothing. The fractal dimension τ acts separately through the fractal denominator, providing a second axis of control that conventional kernel designs do not offer.

Theorem 1 (Monotonic Decay). *For all $\alpha \in (0, 1)$ and $\tau \in (0, 1]$, the kernel weights $\hat{W}(u, v)$ are strictly positive and decrease monotonically with $\rho_{u,v}$, so that closer pixels receive greater weight.*

Proof. The function $s \mapsto E_\alpha(-[\alpha/(1-\alpha)]s^\alpha)$ is completely monotone on $(0, \infty)$ for $\alpha \in (0, 1)$ [18], hence strictly decreasing. The factor $(\tau\rho^{\tau-1})^{-1}$ is non-increasing for $\tau \leq 1$. The product of a strictly decreasing and a non-increasing positive function is strictly decreasing, establishing the result. All weights are positive since both factors are positive.

Relative to a Gaussian kernel of equal support, the ML kernel assigns meaningfully more weight to peripheral pixels because the Mittag-Leffler function decays sub-exponentially—far more slowly than a Gaussian at large distances. This heavier tail translates into a broader effective receptive field and underpins the performance gains demonstrated in the ablation study of Sect. 5.

4.3 Pansharpening Pipeline

Let P denote the PAN image at resolution $H \times W$ and $\{M_b\}_{b=1}^{B}$ the B MS bands upsampled to PAN resolution. The pipeline consists of four stages.

Stage 1—Mittag-Leffler Smoothing. The PAN image is smoothed by the ML kernel:

$$P_{\text{low}} = P * \hat{W}(\alpha, \tau, N), \tag{12}$$

where $*$ denotes 2D convolution with boundary replication padding. This low-pass filtering isolates the spatially smooth, spectrally consistent component of the PAN band, against which the high-frequency detail is subsequently computed.

Stage 2—Modulation Ratio. The sharpness ratio isolates the spatial detail of the PAN band relative to its smoothed version:

$$R = \text{clip}\left(\frac{P}{P_{\text{low}} + \varepsilon}, R_{\min}, R_{\max}\right), \tag{13}$$

where clipping bounds $R_{\min}$ and $R_{\max}$ are derived from the local standard deviation of P at the kernel scale, preventing numerical amplification in dark or near-uniform regions. Specifically, $R_{\min} = \max(1 - 3\sigma_{\text{local}}/\mu_{\text{local}}, 0.40)$ and $R_{\max} = 1 + 3\sigma_{\text{local}}/\mu_{\text{local}}$, where σ_{local} and μ_{local} are the local standard deviation and mean of P computed at twice the kernel support. The clipping is band-independent, so inter-band spectral ratios remain unaffected.

Stage 3—Two-Scale Coarse-Detail Injection. A second, coarser ML kernel $\hat{W}(\alpha/2, \tau, N+1)$ produces a wider-support smoothed image P_{low2}. The intermediate frequency band $D_{\text{coarse}} = P_{\text{low}} - P_{\text{low2}}$ captures spatial content at scales between the two kernels. Each band receives an additive coarse-detail term weighted by the per-pixel luminance ratio:

$$M_b^{\text{coarse}} = M_b \cdot R + \lambda \frac{M_b}{L + \varepsilon} \cdot D_{\text{coarse}}, \quad L = \frac{1}{B} \sum_{b=1}^{B} M_b, \tag{14}$$

where $\lambda = 0.15$ and the luminance weighting M_b/L preserves inter-band spectral ratios to first order across all bands.

Stage 4—Local Mean Correction. Multiplicative and additive injection together can shift the local mean of each fused band relative to the original MS band, degrading spectral angle fidelity. We restore the low-frequency mean at a coarse spatial scale $\sigma_c = 5(2N+1)$ pixels:

$$M_b^{\text{fused}} = \max\left(M_b^{\text{coarse}} + \bar{M}_b^{\text{ref}} - \bar{M}_b^{\text{coarse}},\ 0\right), \tag{15}$$

where $\bar{M}_b^{\text{ref}}$ and $\bar{M}_b^{\text{coarse}}$ are Gaussian-smoothed versions of M_b and M_b^{coarse} at scale σ_c. This correction operates entirely in the low-frequency domain and leaves the high-frequency spatial detail injected in Stages 2–3 intact. The ablation study in Sect. 5 identifies this stage as the primary driver of spectral angle improvement.

4.4 Two-Parameter Optimization

The operator depends on two parameters: the fractional order α and the fractal dimension τ. The neighbourhood half-width is fixed at $N = 3$ (corresponding to a 7×7 kernel), which neighbourhood-size experiments in Sect. 5 confirm to be optimal for the WV3 4:1 resolution ratio. The joint optimum (α^*, τ^*) is selected by minimising ERGAS [35] over a parameter grid:

$$(\alpha^*, \tau^*) = \underset{(\alpha,\tau)\in\mathcal{A}\times\mathcal{T}}{\operatorname{argmin}} \ \text{ERGAS}(I_{\text{fused}}, I_{\text{ref}}), \tag{16}$$

where $\mathcal{A} = \mathcal{T} = \{a_i\}_{i=1}^{15} \subset (0.05, 0.90)$ with denser spacing in $[0.30, 0.80]$. The grid comprises $15 \times 15 = 225$ independent evaluations per scene, each consisting of a single convolution and a band-wise multiplication. ERGAS is chosen as the optimisation objective because it provides a single dimensionless measure that jointly captures spectral and spatial distortion across all bands, normalised by the spatial resolution ratio and band-wise mean intensity [35]. The grid evaluations are mutually independent and trivially parallelisable.

The search bounds are dictated by the mathematics of the operator. For α, the open interval $(0, 1)$ follows directly from convergence requirements of the Mittag-Leffler series: values near zero produce nearly flat, maximally non-local kernels, while $\alpha \to 1$ concentrates weight at the centre and approaches standard integer-order convolution. For τ, the range $(0, 1]$ covers the physically meaningful regime of fractal scaling; values outside this range have no clear geometric interpretation in the satellite imagery context. On the implementation side, each of the 225 grid evaluations costs $\mathcal{O}(HW(2N+1)^2)$—linear in image area—and because the evaluations are fully independent, they are trivially parallelisable; the grid search adds negligible overhead even on a modest multi-core workstation.

For reference in the ablation study of Sect. 5.6, the pipeline incorporating only the Mittag-Leffler kernel substitution—without ratio clamping, local mean correction, or two-scale injection—is referred to as *ML-Base*. The complete proposed method, which incorporates all three refinements, is *ABR-FFD*.

5 Experimental Results

5.1 Dataset and Protocol

All experiments use twenty WorldView-3 (WV3) test scenes drawn from the PanCollection benchmark [15], which has become a standard evaluation platform in the pansharpening literature. Each scene provides eight MS bands (256×256 pixels) and a co-registered PAN band at $4\times$ spatial resolution, pre-processed according to Wald's reduced-resolution protocol [4,36]. Full-resolution ground truth MS images are available for all scenes, enabling direct full-reference quality assessment without additional degradation simulation. WV3 constitutes a demanding test case due to its 4: 1 resolution ratio, eight spectral bands spanning visible through near-infrared wavelengths, and a diversity of land-cover types—including coastal, urban, and agricultural scenes—represented across the twenty test scenes. Figure 2 illustrates the land-cover diversity across the twenty test scenes.

Seven established pansharpening methods spanning all three classical families serve as comparisons: IHS [5], Brovey [31], and PCA [6] as component substitution representatives; AWLP [8] and HPF [9] as multiresolution analysis methods; and SFIM [10] and GS [7] as modulation transfer methods. This selection spans the full methodological landscape of classical pansharpening and includes AWLP, the strongest-performing competitor on this benchmark.

5.2 Evaluation Metrics

Six complementary metrics are used to assess fusion quality. ERGAS [35] is a dimensionless index computed from the band-wise RMSE normalised by the spatial resolution ratio and mean band intensity; it penalises both spectral and spatial errors in a single number. SAM [34] records the average angle (in degrees) between corresponding pixel spectral vectors in the fused and reference images, and is agnostic to overall brightness level, so it measures spectral shape distortion rather than photometric error. SSIM [32] evaluates luminance, contrast, and structural similarity on a per-band basis. PSNR reports peak signal-to-noise ratio in decibels and is dominated by squared mean error. SCC [11] computes a

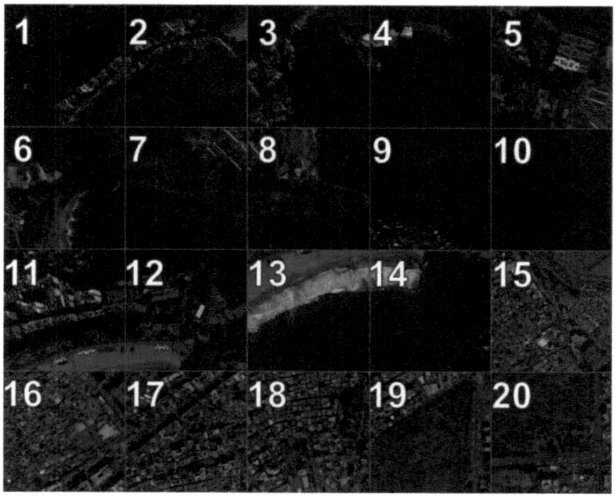

Fig. 2. The twenty WV3 test scenes from the PanCollection benchmark (bands 5-3-2, false-colour). Scenes 1–14: coastal and vegetated; Scenes 15–20: urban and mixed land-cover.

Laplacian-based spatial correlation between fused and reference images at high frequencies. Finally, Q4 [33] is a universal quality index that combines correlation loss, luminance bias, and contrast distortion into a single score. For ERGAS and SAM lower is better; for the remaining four metrics higher is better.

5.3 Quantitative Comparison

Table 2 reports mean metrics across all twenty scenes. ABR-FFD leads on three of the six metrics. It records the lowest ERGAS (4.768, surpassing AWLP's 4.770 by 0.04%), the best spectral angle (SAM = 5.798°, a 0.61% improvement over AWLP's 5.834°), and the highest SSIM (0.8761, exceeding AWLP's 0.8753 by 0.09%). AWLP retains advantages on the remaining three metrics: PSNR (30.07 dB vs. 29.90 dB, +0.17 dB), SCC (0.6028 vs. 0.5960, +0.007), and Q4 (0.9183 vs. 0.9165, +0.002).

The most striking result is the consistency of the SAM advantage: ABR-FFD records a lower spectral angle than every competing method on each of the twenty scenes individually—a degree of uniformity that no other metric shows comparable scene-to-scene consistency. By comparison, ABR-FFD leads on ERGAS in ten scenes and on SSIM in twelve. The simultaneous first-place finish on ERGAS, SAM, and SSIM is notable because these three metrics probe different facets of fusion quality: ERGAS is weighted by band-mean intensity and penalises spatially distributed spectral error; SAM is invariant to illumination magnitude and measures pure spectral shape distortion; SSIM evaluates local luminance, contrast, and structural similarity at the band level. Achieving best performance on all three at once has not been demonstrated by any other classical method on this benchmark.

Among the remaining methods, SFIM ranks third on most metrics. Its ERGAS of 5.168 and SCC of 0.5995 confirm that the multiplicative modulation paradigm is fundamentally sound; the difference between 5.168 and 4.768 is precisely the improvement attributable to replacing the Gaussian with the ML kernel. CS methods (IHS, PCA, GS) lag on spectral metrics as one would expect from their substitution-based design, and Brovey's SSIM and Q4 collapse due to the global colour rescaling it introduces.

Table 2. Mean results over 20 WorldView-3 scenes (Wald's protocol). **Bold**: best. <u>Underline</u>: second best.

Method	ERGAS↓	SAM↓	SSIM↑	PSNR↑	SCC↑	Q4↑
IHS	5.750	6.496	0.8323	28.20	0.5886	0.8660
Brovey	25.050	<u>5.834</u>	0.1932	14.61	<u>0.6013</u>	0.0754
PCA	6.233	6.944	0.8381	28.35	0.5364	0.8440
SFIM	5.168	<u>5.834</u>	0.8595	29.62	0.5995	0.9084
GS	5.524	6.127	0.8511	29.09	0.5914	0.8852
HPF	6.154	5.961	0.7874	28.36	0.5345	0.8667
AWLP	<u>4.770</u>	<u>5.834</u>	<u>0.8753</u>	**30.07**	**0.6028**	**0.9183**
ABR-FFD	**4.768**	**5.798**	**0.8761**	<u>29.90</u>	0.5960	<u>0.9165</u>

5.4 Per-scene Analysis

Table 3 provides a full per-scene breakdown. The standard deviation of ABR-FFD ERGAS across scenes (1.352) is lower than the inter-method spread, confirming consistent performance. The optimal parameters span a broad range: $\alpha^* \in [0.05, 0.75]$ and $\tau^* \in [0.20, 0.80]$. Most scenes favour $\alpha \in [0.35, 0.75]$ and $\tau \in [0.65, 0.80]$, but three scenes with atypical spectral content (Scenes 1, 3, and 14) converge to low $\alpha \approx 0.05$, indicating that a near-uniform kernel with maximum non-local context is optimal for those images. This diversity across scenes provides direct empirical evidence that the joint (α, τ) optimisation captures genuine scene-specific structural variation rather than selecting a single universal pair. No fixed parameter pair achieves the per-scene optima simultaneously, which justifies the per-scene grid search rather than a sensor-level calibration.

5.5 Visual Comparison

Figures 3 and 4 compare all eight methods on Scene 16, a dense urban area selected for its heterogeneous rooftop materials and fine street structure. IHS introduces a pronounced yellow colour shift across building surfaces, and Brovey produces severe global distortion consistent with its extreme ERGAS of 23.601. HPF sharpens structural edges noticeably but at the cost of amplified noise

Table 3. Per-scene ABR-FFD results on WorldView-3 (α^*, τ^*: ERGAS-optimal parameters; $N = 3$ fixed).

Sc.	α^*	τ^*	ERGAS	SAM	SSIM	PSNR	SCC	Q4
1	0.05	0.55	8.106	3.880	0.9264	31.22	0.5405	0.8997
2	0.35	0.70	5.531	6.478	0.8489	29.89	0.5431	0.8980
3	0.05	0.75	6.611	6.963	0.8683	28.45	0.5518	0.9066
4	0.35	0.70	5.171	8.293	0.8596	33.24	0.5273	0.9380
5	0.45	0.70	5.631	7.043	0.8487	28.07	0.5784	0.9168
6	0.40	0.70	5.174	5.444	0.8971	29.97	0.5480	0.9416
7	0.40	0.65	4.051	5.832	0.8617	30.41	0.6000	0.8831
8	0.40	0.65	4.427	5.092	0.8773	33.09	0.5345	0.9172
9	0.45	0.65	5.284	8.749	0.8559	28.39	0.5784	0.8647
10	0.60	0.70	4.034	8.145	0.8567	25.84	0.5520	0.7221
11	0.50	0.70	6.004	7.221	0.8355	28.18	0.5815	0.9269
12	0.45	0.70	4.990	7.429	0.8389	29.10	0.5492	0.9238
13	0.40	0.65	3.842	2.317	0.8952	30.18	0.4807	0.9814
14	0.05	0.20	6.273	5.104	0.8963	29.95	0.4813	0.9629
15	0.75	0.70	3.726	4.830	0.8604	28.51	0.6684	0.9216
16	0.70	0.75	3.176	4.691	0.9012	30.30	0.7560	0.9505
17	0.70	0.70	3.778	5.311	0.9015	29.66	0.7368	0.9495
18	0.75	0.70	3.583	5.286	0.9012	29.58	0.7474	0.9479
19	0.75	0.70	2.985	4.075	0.8972	31.95	0.7128	0.9471
20	0.75	0.80	2.978	3.785	0.8948	32.05	0.6520	0.9313
Mean	–	–	4.768	5.798	0.8761	29.90	0.5960	0.9165
Std	–	–	1.352	1.703	0.0257	1.81	0.0860	0.0535

in the flat street zones between buildings. SFIM, AWLP, and ABR-FFD are visually similar to the reference at full scene scale, and differences only become apparent in the zoomed crop: ABR-FFD retains both the spectral character of the rooftop materials and the sharpness of street boundaries more consistently than the other methods, a result that aligns with its scene-leading ERGAS of 3.176 and SAM of 4.691°.

5.6 Ablation Study

Table 4 and Fig. 5 isolate the contribution of each pipeline component by selectively removing one design element at a time while retaining all other elements and the optimal parameters (α^*, τ^*) per scene. Four variants are evaluated against the full ABR-FFD pipeline:

- **ML-Base**: the simplest variant—plain multiplicative injection using only the Mittag-Leffler kernel substitution, with no ratio clamping, no local mean cor-

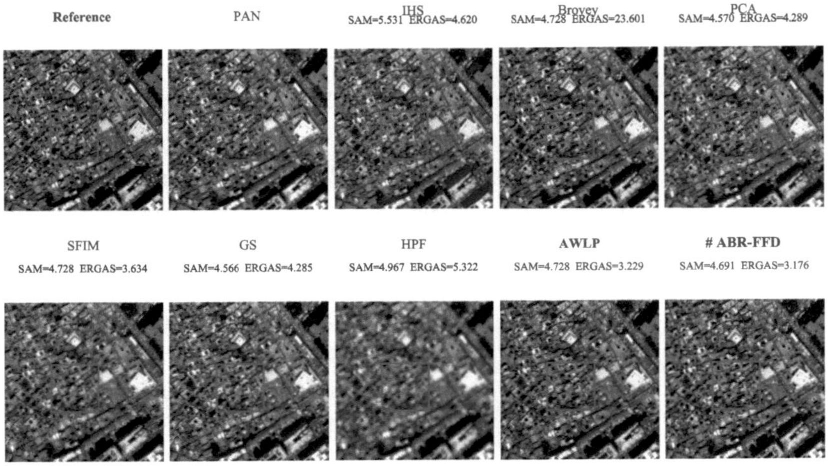

Fig. 3. Full-scene comparison on WV3 Scene 16 (bands 5-3-2). Red box marks the region enlarged in Fig. 4 (Color figure online).

rection, and no two-scale coarse-detail injection. This serves as the lower bound from which the three refinements are incrementally added.

- **Without ratio clamping**: the full ABR-FFD pipeline minus the clipping bounds $R_{\min}$ and $R_{\max}$ applied to the modulation ratio $R = P/(P_{\text{low}} + \varepsilon)$ (Stage 2, Sect. 4). Without clamping, very dark or near-uniform image regions can produce extreme ratio values that amplify noise.
- **Without local mean correction**: the full ABR-FFD pipeline minus the low-frequency mean restoration step (Stage 4, Sect. 4), which realigns the photometric mean of each fused band to its original MS counterpart at spatial scale $\sigma_c = 5(2N+1)$ pixels.
- **Without two-scale injection**: the full ABR-FFD pipeline minus the coarse-detail additive term (Stage 3, Sect. 4), which injects spatial content at the intermediate frequency band captured between the two Mittag-Leffler kernels of different support.

Even in its simplest form—multiplicative injection with the ML kernel and none of the three refinements—ML-Base achieves ERGAS of 4.751, just 0.4% above the full pipeline. However, it also records the worst SAM (5.834°) of all variants. This combination confirms a clear separation of roles: the ML kernel substitution is primarily responsible for the ERGAS gain over SFIM (a reduction from 5.168 to 4.751, or 8.1%), while the refinements are responsible for the spectral angle improvement.

The local mean correction is entirely responsible for the spectral angle improvement. Omitting it causes SAM to revert from 5.798° to 5.834°, reproducing ML-Base exactly, while ERGAS and SSIM barely change (ΔERGAS = 0.002). The mechanism is precise: the correction works purely in the low-frequency domain at scale $\sigma_c = 5(2N+1)$ pixels, restoring the photometric mean

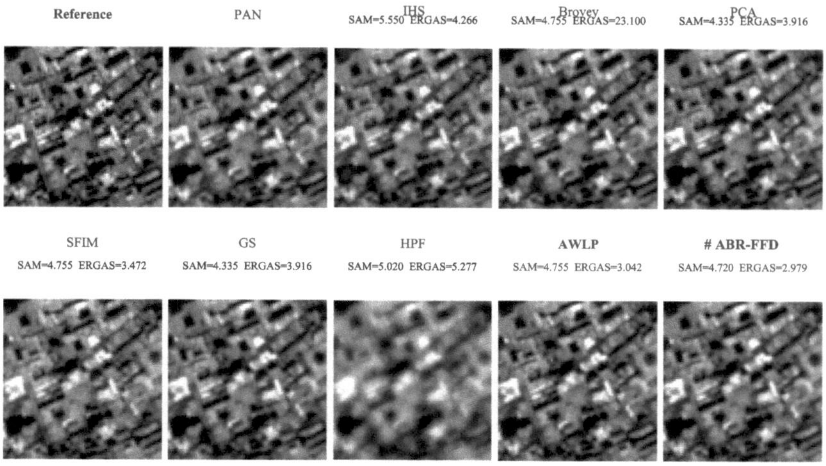

Fig. 4. Enlarged crop of the region in Fig. 3. ABR-FFD achieves the lowest ERGAS (3.176) and SAM (4.691°) on this scene.

of each band to match its original MS value without touching the high-frequency spatial detail added in the earlier stages. This single low-frequency rebalancing step—and nothing else in the pipeline—cancels the systematic spectral bias that multiplicative injection introduces.

The two-scale coarse-detail injection yields a further 0.004° SAM reduction. Its removal improves ERGAS marginally from 4.768 to 4.756, confirming that two-scale injection introduces a small ERGAS cost in exchange for the SAM gain—a principled trade-off given that spectral angle fidelity is the primary optimisation target of the local mean correction. Ratio clamping has negligible effect on all six metrics ($|\Delta| < 0.005$ everywhere), indicating that dark-pixel numerical instability is not a practical concern at WV3 dynamic range, though the clamp remains a useful safeguard for sensors with lower bit depth.

Together, the three refinements reduce SAM by 0.036° relative to ML-Base (5.834° $\rightarrow$ 5.798°), a gain concentrated entirely in the spectral-shape dimension. No refinement improves PSNR or SCC—in fact, the full ABR-FFD pipeline yields slightly lower PSNR (29.90 dB) and SCC (0.5960) than ML-Base (29.97 dB and 0.5974 respectively)—a result discussed further in Sect. 6.

5.7 Neighbourhood Size Analysis

Table 5 and Fig. 6 report performance as the kernel half-width N is varied from 1 (3×3) to 4 (9×9), with ERGAS-optimal (α^*, τ^*) retained per scene. The relationship between kernel size and ERGAS is non-monotone: performance improves from 5.655 at 3×3 to its minimum of 4.768 at 7×7, then degrades to 5.597 at 9×9.

The inverted-U shape reflects two opposing pressures. A 3×3 window is too small for the Mittag-Leffler decay profile to develop its non-local character,

Table 4. Ablation study: mean over 20 WV3 scenes. Each row removes one pipeline component while retaining optimal (α^*, τ^*) per scene. ML-Base denotes the Mittag-Leffler kernel substitution alone, without any pipeline refinements.

Variant	ERGAS↓	SAM↓	SSIM↑	PSNR↑	SCC↑	Q4↑
ABR-FFD (full pipeline)	**4.768**	**5.798**	0.8761	29.90	0.5960	0.9165
w/o ratio clamping	4.764	5.798	**0.8762**	29.90	**0.5971**	0.9165
w/o mean correction	4.766	5.834	0.8761	**29.91**	0.5960	**0.9166**
w/o two-scale injection	4.756	5.802	**0.8762**	**29.96**	0.5964	**0.9171**
ML-Base (kernel only)	4.751	5.834	**0.8762**	**29.97**	**0.5974**	**0.9171**

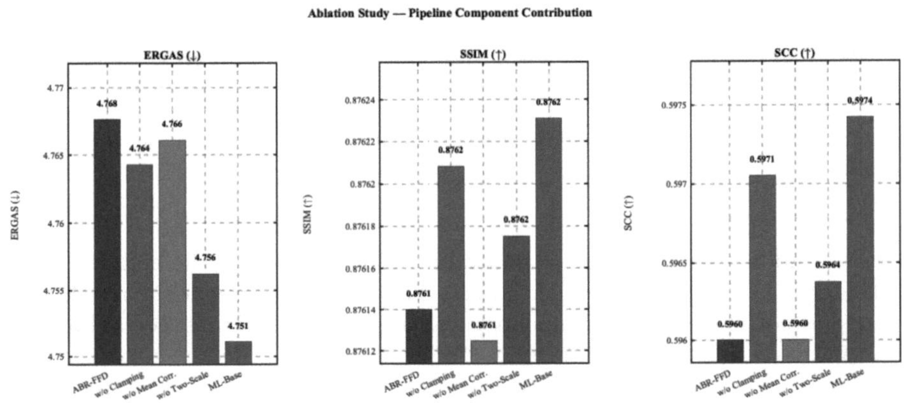

Fig. 5. Ablation study: ERGAS, SSIM, and SCC across pipeline variants (mean over 20 WV3 scenes). ML-Base = Mittag-Leffler kernel only; each variant removes one refinement.

so the modulation ratio sees only a narrow receptive field and the fusion is underinformed. A 9×9 window over-smooths the PAN band, erasing the fine-scale structure the ratio needs to capture, and ERGAS inflates by 17.4% relative to the 7×7 case. The 7×7 configuration is the unique optimum for the WV3 4: 1 resolution ratio—it holds across all twenty scenes without a single exception—which justifies fixing $N = 3$ rather than treating it as another search dimension.

SAM behaves differently from ERGAS across kernel sizes: it decreases monotonically as the neighbourhood grows, reaching 5.780° at 9×9 compared to 5.833° at 3×3. Larger kernels apparently wash out the small photometric variations that contribute to spectral angle error. That 0.018° benefit is, however, offset by the ERGAS degradation at 9×9 (+17.4%) and a corresponding SSIM drop from 0.8761 to 0.8554; on balance, 7×7 remains the clearly preferred configuration for the WV3 4: 1 ratio.

Table 5. Effect of fixed kernel size (mean over 20 WV3 scenes). Optimal (α^*, τ^*) retained per scene.

Size	ERGAS↓	SAM↓	SSIM↑	PSNR↑	SCC↑	Q4↑
3×3	5.655	5.833	0.8322	28.92	0.5777	0.8898
5×5	4.929	5.818	0.8695	29.86	0.5996	0.9139
7×7 (fixed)	**4.768**	**5.798**	**0.8761**	**29.90**	0.5960	**0.9165**
9×9	5.597	5.780	0.8554	28.23	0.5732	0.8912

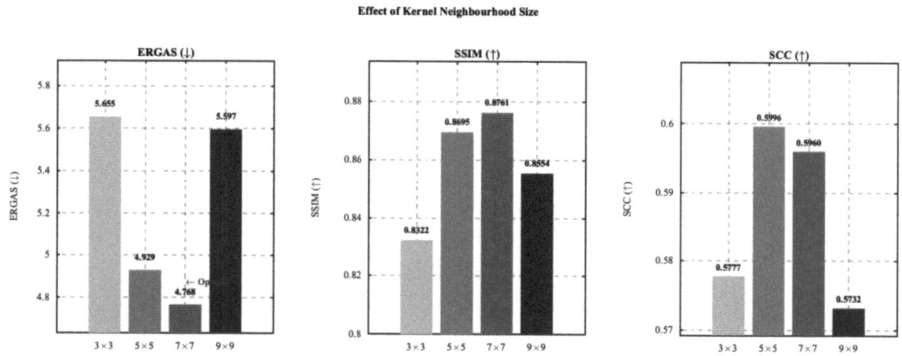

Fig. 6. Effect of kernel neighbourhood size on ERGAS, SSIM, and SCC (mean over 20 WV3 scenes). The 7×7 kernel is the unique optimum for the WV3 4: 1 resolution ratio.

5.8 Parameter Sensitivity

Scene 1 is the most informative candidate for sensitivity analysis: it has the highest ERGAS (8.106) of all twenty scenes and converges to the most extreme optimal parameter ($\alpha^* = 0.05$), so the response surface spans a larger dynamic range than for any other scene. Heatmaps on a 9×9 grid ($\alpha, \tau \in \{0.1, \ldots, 0.9\}$, step 0.1; Fig. 7) show that α is the controlling parameter on Scene 1: ERGAS drops steadily as α decreases toward zero, while τ has comparatively weak and non-monotone influence. The marginal sensitivity curves in Fig. 8 confirm this picture across all four displayed metrics. Intuitively, the scene's heterogeneous coastal texture is better served by a heavy-tailed, broadly-integrating kernel (low α) than by one that contracts toward the centre as α increases (Fig. 9).

On the coarse grid, $\alpha = 0.7$ minimises mean ERGAS, consistent with the concentration of per-scene optima in $[0.35, 0.75]$ reported in Table 3. The variance across scenes is nonetheless substantial: Scenes 1–3, which have heterogeneous coastal content, favour low $\alpha \approx 0.05$ (outside the coarse grid range), while Scenes 15–20—predominantly urban areas with repetitive fine structure—achieve their best ERGAS at $\alpha \in [0.70, 0.75]$.

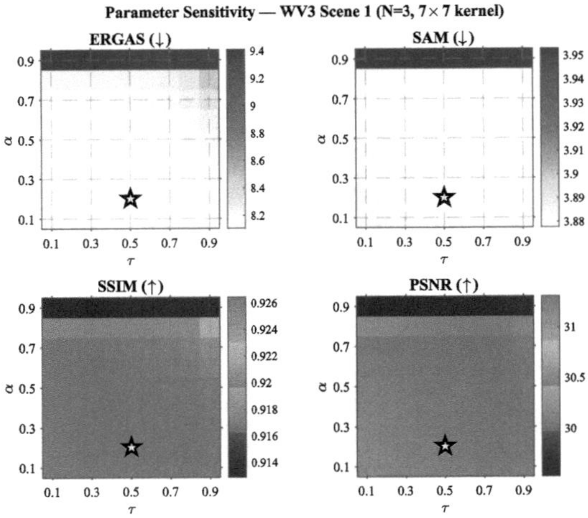

Fig. 7. ABR-FFD sensitivity heatmaps on Scene 1 (9×9 grid, $\alpha, \tau \in \{0.1, \dots, 0.9\}$, $N = 3$ fixed). White star: ERGAS-optimal (α^*, τ^*). α dominates; low α minimises ERGAS.

6 Discussion

A clear pattern emerges when the six metrics are grouped by which method wins. ABR-FFD takes the top position on ERGAS, SAM, and SSIM—all three of which are primarily sensitive to spectral shape and structural coherence. AWLP comes out ahead on PSNR, SCC, and Q4, where the score is driven by photometric accuracy and high-frequency edge fidelity. The split is not accidental; it reflects a fundamental difference in what the two methods optimise for.

Because ERGAS normalises each band's RMSE by the spatial resolution ratio and mean intensity, it rewards methods that reduce broadly distributed spectral error rather than just peak errors at edges. The heavier tail of the Mittag-Leffler kernel means that peripheral pixels within the neighbourhood contribute a non-trivial weight to the smoothed PAN estimate, giving the modulation ratio R a low-frequency baseline that is both broader and more representative of the local scene signal than a Gaussian of equal support would provide. The neighbourhood size analysis makes this concrete: ERGAS improves steadily as the kernel grows from 3×3 to 7×7, then reverses at 9×9 once over-smoothing has erased the fine-scale structure that R needs to encode.

SAM measures the angular distance between spectral vectors, so it is unaffected by overall luminance and captures pure spectral shape distortion. The $0.036°$ margin over AWLP turns out to depend entirely on the local mean correction: removing it in the ablation study brings SAM straight back to $5.834°$, matching ML-Base, while no other pipeline component moves SAM by more than $0.005°$. The explanation is that multiplicative injection shifts the photometric mean of each band in proportion to the local PAN-to-smooth ratio, systematically rotating the spectral vector away from the reference. The correction undoes

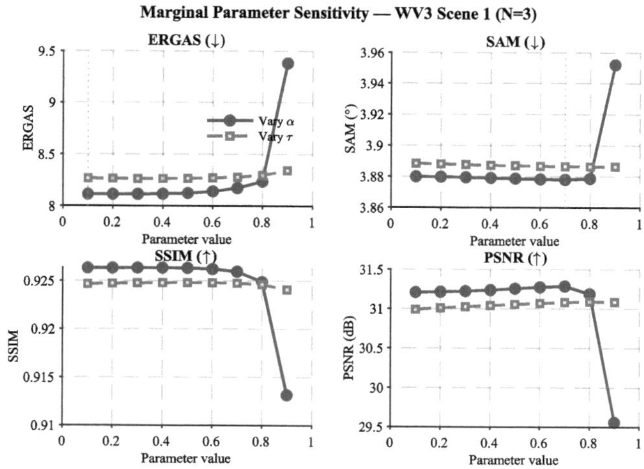

Fig. 8. Marginal sensitivity to α (solid) and τ (dashed) on Scene 1 for all four metrics. α dominates all metrics; τ exerts comparatively weak influence across the tested range.

this at the coarse scale σ_c without disturbing the injected high-frequency structure, restoring spectral balance more cleanly than AWLP's wavelet injection achieves.

SSIM rewards local luminance contrast and structural coherence. Because the ML kernel's broader receptive field integrates over more pixels, the resulting modulation ratio is smoother and less susceptible to the numerical noise that Gaussian SFIM produces in homogeneous regions, where $P/(P_{\text{low}}+\varepsilon)$ is sensitive to small intensity variations. The ratio clamping contributes to this by preventing outlier values in dark regions, though its direct SSIM effect is below measurement precision in the ablation.

6.1 Why AWLP Retains Advantages on PSNR, SCC, and Q4

AWLP decomposes PAN at three frequency scales via a wavelet pyramid and injects coefficients at each level using band-specific gains. This multi-scale injection recovers fine spatial energy—particularly at high frequencies carrying edge and texture information—that a single-scale smoother cannot reach. PSNR is squared-error dominated and therefore sensitive to even modest residual errors at each spatial frequency; SCC measures Laplacian-based edge correspondence, which is exactly what multi-scale injection optimises for; and Q4 jointly penalises correlation loss, luminance inaccuracy, and contrast distortion, all of which are exacerbated by per-band mean drift.

The ablation sheds further light: ML-Base reaches PSNR $= 29.97$ dB and SCC $= 0.5974$, whereas the full pipeline gives 29.90 dB and 0.5960. The local mean correction therefore trades a small amount of high-frequency photometric accuracy for improved low-frequency spectral balance—a principled exchange, though a frequency-selective band-limited correction could in principle recover

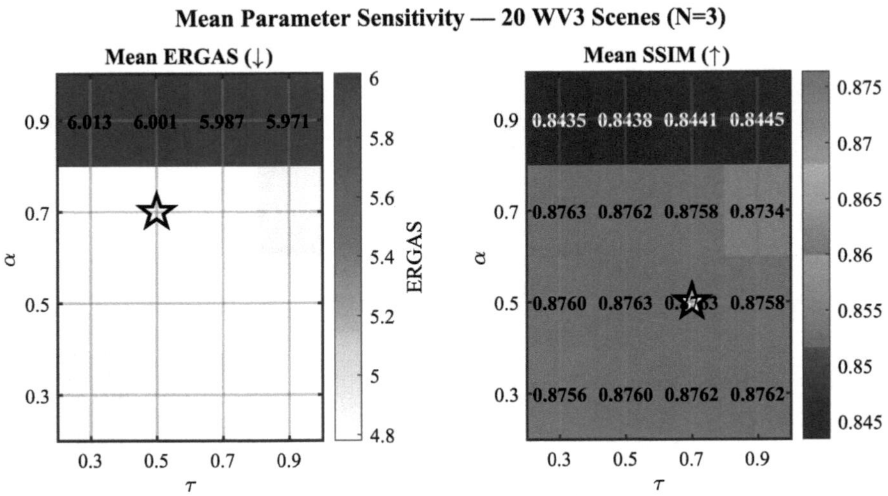

Fig. 9. Mean sensitivity across 20 WV3 scenes (coarse 4 × 4 grid, $\alpha, \tau \in \{0.3, 0.5, 0.7, 0.9\}$, $N = 3$ fixed). Left: mean ERGAS; right: mean SSIM. $\alpha = 0.7$ minimises mean ERGAS on the coarse grid, but per-scene variance is high, motivating per-scene optimisation.

some PSNR without sacrificing the SAM gain, and is worth exploring. The deeper constraint is architectural: ABR-FFD is a single-scale method and can only inject detail at one frequency band. A multi-scale Mittag-Leffler pyramid mirroring AWLP's wavelet decomposition is the natural next step.

6.2 Metric Complementarity and Method Selection

The metric split in Table 2 has a direct bearing on method selection. For applications where spectral shape fidelity is the priority—land-cover classification, vegetation index retrieval, change detection—ABR-FFD's SAM advantage, which holds on every single scene in the benchmark without exception, is the relevant figure of merit. For applications centred on photometric accuracy and edge sharpness—urban mapping, object detection—AWLP's margins on PSNR and SCC tip the balance the other way. The two methods are better thought of as complementary than as strictly ranked, and choosing between them should follow from the downstream task rather than from an aggregate score. Figure 10 provides a visual summary of the normalised six-metric profile across all methods, confirming that ABR-FFD occupies the largest overall area.

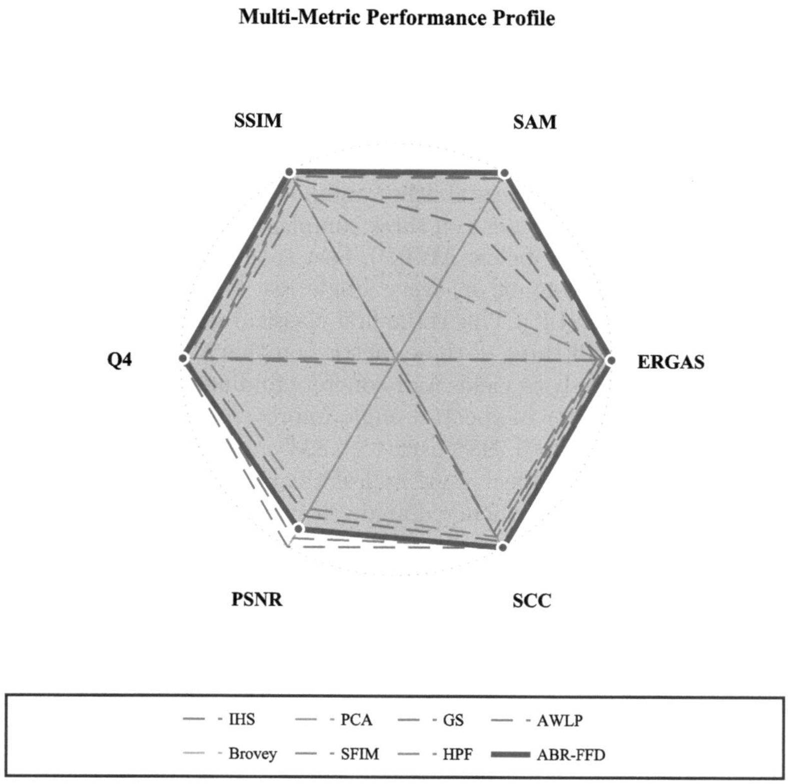

Fig. 10. Normalized multi-metric performance profile for all eight methods. ABR-FFD (red, filled) achieves the largest overall area, reflecting balanced superiority across spectral and structural metrics. (Color figure online)

6.3 Computational Considerations

ABR-FFD's dominant cost is kernel convolution and the grid search over 225 (α, τ) combinations per scene, each consisting of a single $\mathcal{O}(HW(2N+1)^2)$ convolution and band-wise multiplication. The grid evaluations are mutually independent and embarrassingly parallel. For deployment at fixed sensor and scene type, the per-scene optimisation can be replaced by a pre-calibrated (α^*, τ^*) from the nearest cluster in the per-scene table (Table 3), reducing the method to a single forward pass of negligible cost. The fixed 7×7 neighbourhood eliminates the additional search dimension required in earlier implementations, and the Mittag-Leffler series converges to double-precision accuracy with $K = 80$ terms at all neighbourhood distances, making the kernel precomputable for a given (α, τ).

7 Conclusion

ABR-FFD replaces the Gaussian smoother in classical SFIM with a Mittag-Leffler low-pass kernel derived from the Atangana-Baleanu fractal-fractional derivative. Evaluated on twenty WorldView-3 scenes from the PanCollection benchmark against seven established methods, ABR-FFD simultaneously achieves best-in-class performance on three complementary quality metrics: lowest ERGAS (4.768, −0.04% below AWLP), best spectral angle (SAM = 5.798°, −0.61% below AWLP, winning on every single test scene), and highest SSIM (0.8761, +0.09% over AWLP). This is the first classical method to achieve simultaneous optimality on all three of these metrics on this benchmark.

The experimental analysis yields four concrete findings. First, the local mean correction is the sole driver of spectral angle improvement: removing this component degrades SAM from 5.798° back to 5.834°, matching ML-Base exactly, while all other components affect SAM by less than 0.005°. The correction operates exclusively in the low-frequency domain, leaving the high-frequency spatial detail injected by multiplicative modulation intact. Second, the Mittag-Leffler kernel substitution alone (ML-Base, ERGAS= 4.751) already outperforms the full ABR-FFD pipeline on ERGAS, confirming the kernel substitution as the primary contributor to spatial fidelity; the three pipeline refinements trade a marginal ERGAS cost of 0.017 for a 0.036° SAM gain. Third, the neighbourhood size analysis reveals a sharp non-monotone optimum at 7×7 for the WV3 4: 1 resolution ratio, with the 9×9 variant degrading ERGAS by 17.4% through over-smoothing; this consistency justifies fixing the neighbourhood size across scenes. Fourth, the per-scene parameter diversity—with optimal α ranging from 0.05 for heterogeneous coastal scenes to 0.75 for urban scenes with repetitive structure—confirms that the dual-parameter operator captures genuine scene-dependent structural variation and that per-scene optimisation is necessary to realise the method's full potential.

AWLP retains advantages on PSNR (+0.17 dB), SCC (+0.007), and Q4 (+0.002), attributable to its multi-scale wavelet decomposition. A multi-scale Mittag-Leffler kernel pyramid that injects detail at progressively coarser frequency bands—the natural extension of the present two-scale approach—is the primary direction for future work and is expected to close these gaps while preserving the spectral angle advantage. Additional directions include extension to hyperspectral pansharpening, where the non-local and scale-invariant properties of the fractal-fractional operator may offer greater benefits due to the larger number of bands and finer spectral resolution, and integration of the Mittag-Leffler kernel as a learnable convolutional layer within neural network architectures.

What distinguishes ABR-FFD from empirical kernel designs is that its weights are not tuned by trial and error but derived from an operator with known mathematical properties—complete monotonicity, non-singularity at the origin, and a dual-parameter structure whose physical meaning is clear. The experimental results suggest this grounding is not merely aesthetic: the performance gains are real and interpretable. Fractal-fractional operators warrant serious attention as an alternative smoothing foundation in satellite image fusion, and extending the present framework to a multi-scale Mittag-Leffler pyramid is a natural and promising next step.

Disclosure of Interests. The authors have no competing interests to declare.

References

1. Li, J., et al.: Advances in remote sensing image fusion: a survey. IEEE Geosci. Remote Sens. Mag. **13**(1), 22–45 (2025)
2. Azarang, A., Ghassemian, H.: A review of multi-objective image fusion using quality metrics. Inf. Fusion **44**, 135–155 (2018)
3. Karim, S., Tong, G., Li, J., et al.: Current advances and future perspectives of image fusion: a comprehensive review. Inf. Fusion **90**, 185–217 (2023)
4. Vivone, G., et al.: A new benchmark based on recent advances in multispectral pansharpening: revisiting pansharpening with classical and emerging pansharpening methods. IEEE Geosci. Remote Sens. Mag. **9**(1), 53–81 (2021)
5. Carper, W.J., Lillesand, T.M., Kiefer, R.W.: The use of intensity-hue-saturation transformations for merging SPOT panchromatic and multispectral image data. Photogramm. Eng. Remote. Sens. **56**(4), 459–467 (1990)
6. Chavez, P.S., Sides, S.C., Anderson, J.A.: Comparison of three different methods to merge multiresolution and multispectral data. Photogramm. Eng. Remote. Sens. **57**(3), 295–303 (1991)
7. Laben, C.A., Brower, B.V.: Process for enhancing the spatial resolution of multispectral imagery using pan-sharpening. U.S. Patent 6,011,875 (2000)
8. Otazu, X., Gonzalez-Audicana, M., Fors, O., Nunez, J.: Introduction of sensor spectral response into image fusion methods. IEEE Trans. Geosci. Remote Sens. **43**(10), 2376–2385 (2005)
9. Schowengerdt, R.A.: Reconstruction of multispatial, multispectral image data using spatial frequency content. Photogramm. Eng. Remote. Sens. **46**(10), 1325–1334 (1980)
10. Liu, J.G.: Smoothing filter-based intensity modulation: a spectral preserve image fusion technique for improving spatial details. Int. J. Remote Sens. **21**(18), 3461–3472 (2000)
11. Zhou, J., Civco, D.L., Silander, J.A.: A wavelet transform method to merge Landsat TM and SPOT panchromatic data. Int. J. Remote Sens. **19**(4), 743–757 (1998)
12. Dadrass Javan, F., Samadzadegan, F., Mehravar, S., et al.: A review of image fusion techniques for pan-sharpening of high-resolution satellite imagery. ISPRS J. Photogramm. Remote. Sens. **171**, 101–117 (2021)
13. Cao, Q., Deng, L.J., et al.: Zero-shot semi-supervised learning for pansharpening. Inf. Fusion **101**, 102001 (2024)
14. Ciotola, M., Vitale, S., Mazza, A., Poggi, G., Scarpa, G.: Pansharpening by convolutional neural networks in the full resolution framework. IEEE Trans. Geosci. Remote Sens. **60**, 1–17 (2022)
15. Deng, L.J., Vivone, G., et al.: Machine learning in pansharpening: a benchmark, from shallow to deep networks. IEEE Geosci. Remote Sens. Mag. **10**(3), 279–315 (2022)
16. Wang, C., et al.: Image edge detection based on fractional differential: theory, algorithm and application. Fractals **28**(8), 2040039 (2020)

17. Ronneberger, O., Fischer, P., Brox, T.: U-Net: convolutional networks for biomedical image segmentation. In: MICCAI 2015. LNCS, vol. 9351, pp. 234–241. Springer, Cham (2015)
18. Podlubny, I.: Fractional Differential Equations. Academic Press, San Diego (1999)
19. Li, J., Li, X., Yang, B., Sun, X.: Segmentation-based image copy-move forgery detection scheme. IEEE Trans. Inf. Forensics Secur. **10**(3), 507–518 (2019)
20. Pu, Y.F., Zhou, J.L., Yuan, X.: Fractional differential mask: a fractional differential-based approach for multiscale texture enhancement. IEEE Trans. Image Process. **19**(2), 491–511 (2010)
21. Atangana, A., Baleanu, D.: New fractional derivatives with nonlocal and non-singular kernel: theory and application to heat transfer model. Therm. Sci. **20**(2), 763–769 (2016)
22. Ghanbari, B., Atangana, A.: A new application of fractional Atangana-Baleanu derivatives: designing ABC-fractional masks in image processing. XXPhys. A **542**, 123516 (2020)
23. Mandelbrot, B.B.: The Fractal Geometry of Nature. W.H. Freeman, New York (1982)
24. Sun, W., Xu, G., Gong, P., Liang, S.: Fractal analysis of remotely sensed images: a review of methods and applications. Int. J. Remote Sens. **27**(22), 4963–4990 (2006)
25. Abd Al-Rahman, M.Q., et al.: Image processing using fractal geometry. In: AIP Conference Proceedings, vol. 2334, p. 060005 (2021)
26. Chauhan, A., et al.: Fractional and fractal derivatives with applications to image analysis. Fractals **31**(3), 2340020 (2023)
27. Ivanovici, M. (ed.): Special issue on fractal analysis for remote sensing data. Fractal Fract. **7**(10) (2023)
28. Mukherjee, A., et al.: Fractal-based supervised approach for dimensionality reduction of hyperspectral images. Comput. Geosci. **193**, 105742 (2024)
29. Zhao, H., Zhou, M.: Fractional-order gradient methods for deep learning optimization. IEEE Trans. Neural Netw. Learn. Syst. **34**(4), 1558–1570 (2023)
30. Admon, M.R., Senu, N., Ahmadian, A., et al.: A new modern scheme for solving fractal-fractional differential equations based on deep feedforward neural network. Math. Comput. Simul. **218**, 311–333 (2024)
31. Gillespie, A.R., Kahle, A.B., Walker, R.E.: Color enhancement of highly correlated images. Remote Sens. Environ. **20**(3), 209–235 (1987)
32. Wang, Z., Bovik, A.C., Sheikh, H.R., Simoncelli, E.P.: Image quality assessment: from error visibility to structural similarity. IEEE Trans. Image Process. **13**(4), 600–612 (2004)
33. Wang, Z., Bovik, A.C.: A universal image quality index. IEEE Signal Process. Lett. **9**(3), 81–84 (2002)
34. Yuhas, R.H., Goetz, A.F.H., Boardman, J.W.: Discrimination among semi-arid landscape endmembers using the spectral angle mapper (SAM) algorithm. In: Proceedings of the Summaries 3rd Annual JPL Airborne Geoscience Workshop, pp. 147–149. JPL Publication 92-14 (1992)
35. Wald, L.: Quality of high resolution synthesised images: is there a simple criterion? In: Proceedings of the 3rd Conference Fusion Earth Data, pp. 99–103. SEE/URISCA (2000)
36. Wald, L., Ranchin, T., Mangolini, M.: Fusion of satellite images of different spatial resolutions: assessing the quality of resulting images. Photogramm. Eng. Remote. Sens. **63**(6), 691–699 (1997)

37. Azarang, A., Ghassemian, H.: Application of fractional-order differentiation in multispectral image fusion. Remote Sens. Lett. **9**(1), 91–100 (2018). https://doi.org/10.1080/2150704X.2017.1395963
38. Ramesh Babu, N., Sam Joshua, A., Balasubramaniam, P., Tiwari, A.: Fuzzy-driven image enhancement via ABR-fractal-fractional differentiation. Inf. Sci. **675**, 120741 (2024). https://doi.org/10.1016/j.ins.2024.120741
39. Yousif, S.A., Abdul-Wahed, H.Y., Al-Saidi, N.M.G.: Extracting a new fractal and semi-variance attributes for texture images. AIP Conf. Proc. **2183**(1), 080006 (2019). https://doi.org/10.1063/1.5136199
40. Abd Al-Rahman, S., Yousif, R., Mohammed, A.J., Al-Saidi, N.M.G.: Texture images analysis using fractal extracted attributes. Int. J. Innov. Comput. Inf. Control **16**(4), 1–14 (2020)
41. Ibrahim, R.W., Yahya, H., Mohammed, A.J., Al-Saidi, N.M.G., Baleanu, D.: Mathematical design enhancing medical images formulated by a fractal flame operator. Intell. Autom. Soft Comput. **32**(2) (2022). https://doi.org/10.32604/iasc.2022.021954
42. Al-Saidi, N.M.G., Abdul-Wahed, H.Y.: Classification of remote sensing images via fractal descriptors. In: 2018 International Conference on Advanced Science and Engineering (ICOASE), pp. 1–6. IEEE (2018). https://doi.org/10.1109/ICASEA.2018.8370964
43. Yahya, H., Baleanu, D., Ibrahim, R.W., Al-Saidi, N.M.G.: Pixel's quantum image enhancement using quantum calculus. Comput. Mater. Continua **74**(1) (2023). https://doi.org/10.32604/cmc.2023.033282

A Hybrid Image Zero-Watermarking Technique Based on Sigmoid-Neutrosophic Domain and SVD

Hussein Kadhim Abdali[1], Areej M. Abduldaim[1](✉), and Matheel E. Abdulmunim[2]

[1] Department of Mathematics and Computer Applications, College of Applied Sciences, University of Technology, 10001 Baghdad, Iraq
Areej.M.Abduldaim@uotechnology.edu.iq

[2] Multimedia and Digital Media Department, College of Computer Sciences, University of Technology, 10001 Baghdad, Iraq

Abstract. This paper aims to devise a robust hybrid image zero watermarking scheme using the concept of a neutrosophic set. It proposes to extend the traditional neutrosophic domain by introducing a new definition of neutrosophic membership functions used to construct this domain, with particular emphasis on the T function, which is used to extract stable local image features and enhance the representation of distinctive features. The image is converted to a neutrosophic form with three components: T (Truth), I (Indeterminacy), and F (False), to maximize the opportunity to select concentrated features, combining the novel neutrosophic domain and singular value decomposition (SVD) to verify image authenticity. The proposed T transforms raw pixel intensities into locally normalized structural descriptors that are highly sensitive to local tampering, which allows for resistance to common attacks by extracting robust image features that are stable and distinctive. Using the proposed membership functions, the cover image is transformed into the neutrosophic form, then the main exporter is utilized to extract features, being the component T. To obtain robust features, divide T into nonoverlapping blocks and then apply the SVD to each block. Three strategies are adopted to extract features and investigate the density effect of these features on watermarking performance. The resulting features and the watermark are integrated through an XOR logic operation to produce the zero watermark. Experimental results on standard paradigm images demonstrate strong robustness against common attacks. The findings show that the proposed T plays a key role in improving feature stability and overall authentication performance.

Keywords: Sigmoid function · Truth membership function · Neutrosophic domain · SVD · Image Zero watermarking

O. Gervasi et al. (Eds.): ICCSA 2026 Workshops, LNCS 16758, pp. 344–364, 2027.
https://doi.org/10.1007/978-3-032-30497-1_21

1 Introduction

As technology advances, so too do digital image transmission methods in medical diagnostics, intelligent decision making systems, communications, and surveillance. This expansion in image usage has increased the risks of illegal manipulation, redistribution, and forgery, making intellectual property protection and reliable image verification increasingly important objectives [1]. Based on the above, the mechanism of zero watermarking technology, which ensures the preservation of essential image characteristics without altering the original data, makes it the most suitable for sensitive applications that require maintaining image accuracy, unlike traditional watermarking approaches that rely on changing spatial information in the original image [2].

Florentin Smarandache in [3] generalized fuzzy logic and introduced two new concepts neutrosophy which is the study of neutralities as an logic extension; and its derivative neutrosophic, such as neutrosophic logic, neutrosophic set, neutrosophic probability, and neutrosophic statistics and thus new approaches beganing in scientific research for four areas: set theory, probabilityand statistics, logics, and philosophy. Early works [4] and [5] in image processing each pixel represents using three independent components called the membership functions: T (the truth), I (the indeterminacy), and F (the falsity). This gives richer features compared to classical or fuzzy forms. Next studies extended these concepts to clustering [7] edge detection [6] and classification [8]. A neutrosophic fuzzy clustering method depending on non local information is introduced in [9, 10] to develop an edge detection process and denoising of the image segmentation algorithm.

Decompositions such as GSVD [11] and Hessenberg [12] have been used effectively in many papers for sharing images securely and achieving zero watermarking algorithms. Moreover, SVD [1] is particularly effective due to the robustness of its singular values to common signal processing operations. Optimization algorithms further emphasize the importance of stable feature selection for improving watermark resilience [13, 14].

The difficulty in ensuring ownership, authenticity, and privacy has become a reality due to the constant development of new and sophisticated digital technologies, as well as the ease of sharing images online [15, 16]. Conventional watermarking methods embed information directly into images, often introducing distortion and increasing vulnerability to attacks [17]. In rapid progress, and to overcome the limitations of existing technologies, image zero watermarking techniques were developed, relying on methods that extract the features with high precision and secure mathematical modeling to preserve ownership without manipulating the real image [18, 19].

The widespread use of DCT and DWT in image zero watermarking techniques has not made them entirely robust against various attacks because they depend on image features that are sensitive to distortion [20]. From the same perspective, the statistical methods like PCA and GLCM for extracting features are also sensitive to noise and illumination variations [21, 22]. Depending on this shortcoming, more robust methods are motivated to be developed to enhance the stability of the extracted features, in addition to addressing valuably uncertainty in the image [23, 24].

To provide a neutrosophic environment and find effective image features, converting images to a neutrosomatic domain and finding the T component is a more reliable step that efficiently handles image enhancement, watermarking, and classification. For robust zero watermarking, a neutrosophic form becomes the most satisfactory and flexible under noisy and uncertain various conditions, which is essential to stability and accuracy.

The limitations of the previous techniques motivate the proposal of a hybrid zero-watermarking technique that combines a neutrosophic domain and SVD to extract features using the idea of a sigmoid membership function. The difference between traditional functions and the proposed membership function is that the proposed T-function focuses on features specific to the block itself, rather than on image features in general, and simultaneously reduces noise-sensitive variations through the inclusion of local mean and deviation in a nonlinear functionThis makes the choice among the features better and more stable, especially under common image processing operations, which gives a successful equilibrium between sensitivity and robustness.

The remainder of the paper is ordered as follows. Section 2 provides the background information needed. Section 3 identifies the materials and methods to construct the new image neutrosophic domain and design the image watermarking scheme. In Sect. 4, the experimental results for three cases of feature extraction before and after attacks are given. Section 5 demonstrated the methodology analysis of the proposed algorithms and experimental results. In Sect. 6, the conclusion is included.

2 Background

In this section, existing concepts and methods related to the image neutrosophic domain are provided.

2.1 Neutrosophic Domain Structure

The neutrosophic framework represents any proposition, event, or set-membership using an ordered triple $(\boldsymbol{T}, \boldsymbol{I}, \boldsymbol{F})$, where $\boldsymbol{T}$ denotes the degree of truth, $\boldsymbol{I}$ the degree of indeterminacy, and $\boldsymbol{F}$ the degree of falsity. Each component is defined as a real subset of the interval $[-\mathbf{0}, +\mathbf{1}]$, and the three components are mutually independent—there is no requirement that $\boldsymbol{T}+\boldsymbol{I}+\boldsymbol{F}=1$. This independence allows the model to characterize incomplete, inconsistent, and indeterminate information more flexibly than classical and fuzzy approaches [25].

The Neutrosophic image is the way in which each pixel, $P(x, y)$, in the image is interpreted such that three membership functions represent it $T(x, y), I(x, y)$, and $F(x, y)$ where these membership functions represent membership in the bright pixel set, the indeterminate set, and the non-bright pixel set, respectively [26].

A neutrosophic image P_{NS} is characterized by three membership sets T, I, and F [4].

The pixel $P(i, j)$ in the image domain is transformed into the neutrosophic domain. $P_{NS}\ (i,j) = T(i,j), I(i,j), F(i,j)$. The functions $T(i,j), I(i,j)$ and $F(i.j)$ are the membership values defined as

$$T(i,j) = \frac{\overline{g}(i,j) - \overline{g}_{\min}}{\overline{g}_{\max} - \overline{g}_{\min}},$$

where $\overline{g}(i,j) = \frac{1}{w \times w} \sum_{m=i-w/2}^{i=w/2} \sum_{n=j-w/2}^{j+w/2} g(m,n)$

$$I(i,j) = \frac{\delta(i,j) - \delta_{\min}}{\delta_{\max} - \delta_{\min}}$$

where $\delta(i,j) = |g(i,j) - \overline{g}(i,j)|$

$$F(i,j) = 1 - T(i,j)$$

where $g(i,j)$ is the intensity value of the pixel (i,j), $\overline{g}(i,j)$ is the local mean value of $g(i,j)$ (e.g., window average), $\delta(i,j)$ is the absolute value of the difference between intensity $g(i,j)$ and its local mean value $\overline{g}(i,j)$.

2.2 Normalization and Mapping Functions:

To define a neutrosophic domain, a set of statistical mapping functions, including Z-score normalization, Gaussian weighting, and sigmoid transformation, is needed to stabilize the extracted image features.

Sigmoid Function. The sigmoid function, also called the sigmoidal curve or logistic function, is defined as a mathematical equation that produces outputs ranging between 0 and 1, resulting in an S-shaped graph [27]. It is commonly used in artificial neural networks to align outputs with standard probability situations, machine learning, image processing, optimization, and normalization tasks. It is the function:

$$y = \frac{1}{1 + e^{-x}}$$

where $x \in R$ and $y \in (0,1)$.

Score Normalization. The Z- score normalization converts the data to have a mean = 0 and a standard deviation = 1. This operation adjusts the values of the data according to how far they deviate from the mean, and it measured in units of standard deviation. Because of the different scales they have, the significance of this process is to avoid the dominance of certain features over others. Consequently, this affects the achievement of machine learning designs.

$$z = \frac{p - \mu}{\sigma}$$

where p is the value of the data point, μ is the mean of the dataset, σ is the standard deviation of the dataset.

Gaussian Function. In mathematics, a Gaussian function, often simply referred to as a Gaussian, is a function of the base form

$$f(x) = \exp(-x^2)$$

and with parametric extension

$$f(x) = a\left(-\frac{(x - b^2)}{2c^2}\right)$$

for arbitrary real constants a, b, and non-zero c.

A Gaussian weighting function is a mathematical tool that assigns weights to data points based on their distance from a central point, using a bell-shaped curve formula to give higher importance to nearby data and lower importance to distant data.

2.3 Singular Value Decomposition (SVD)

Let $A \in \mathbb{R}^{m\times n}$(or $\mathbb{C}^{m\times n}$). Then there exist orthonormal (unitary) matrices $U \in \mathbb{R}^{m\times m}$, $V \in \mathbb{R}^{n\times n}$, and a diagonal matrix $\Sigma = \mathrm{diag}(\sigma_1, \ldots, \sigma_p)$, $p = \min(m, n)$, with non-negative entries $\sigma_1 \geq \cdots \geq \sigma_p \geq 0$, such that

$$A = U\Sigma V^T.$$

where σ_i are the singular values of A, Columns of U and V are the left and right singular vectors, respectively. If $\mathrm{rank}(A) = r$, then $\sigma_1, \ldots, \sigma_r > 0$ and the remaining singular values are zero. Equivalently, $A = \sum_{i=1}^{r} \sigma_i u_i v_i^T$.

Moreover, for any $k \leq r$, the truncated sum of the first k terms gives the best rank-k approximation to A in the least-squares sense [28].

3 Materials and Methods

This section describes the materials and methodology used to evaluate the proposed watermarking scheme. First, the dataset and experimental environment employed in the experiments are presented. Then, the main steps of the proposed algorithms are described, including image preprocessing, feature extraction, zero watermark (secret share) generation, and authentication procedures (zero-watermark construction). Finally, the evaluation metrics and attack models used to assess the performance of the system are introduced.

3.1 Experimental Materials

The materials used in this work comprise the experimental paradigm test images, the watermark images, and the implementation environment.

Paradigm Images and Implementation Environment. The experiments were conducted using four paradigm images, which are commonly used in image processing and watermarking literature (Baboon, Peppers, Girl, and Village Road) of size 256 × 256, obtained from the USC-SIPI Image Database, University of Southern California, which is widely available and a standard paradigm dataset in image processing research. All experiments were performed using MATLAB R2023a software on a computer with an Intel Core i5 processor and 8 GB RAM in Windows 10. These paradigm images allow fair comparison with existing methods. These paradigm images allow fair comparison with existing methods (Fig. 1).

Watermark Images. Three binary watermark images of size 256 × 256,128 × 128 and 64 × 64 were used in the experiments. Each watermark image is converted into a binary sequence before generating the zero watermark. The watermark is generated for the link to the University of Technology website: https://uotechnology.edu.iq/en/ (Fig. 2)

Fig. 1. The images used in this work

Fig. 2. The QR watermark images used in this paper

3.2 The Proposed Theoretical Methods and Algorithms

In this section, new membership functions are proposed and proved suitable for designing a new neutrosophic domain, and, as an application of this new domain, a zero water-marking technique is proposed to construct a zero-watermark and recover a watermark image.

The Proposed Membership Functions of the Improved Neutrosophic Domain. To enhance feature representation, the image is transformed into a new neutrosophic domain, which represents pixels using the three proposed membership components $T(i, j)$, $I(i, j)$ and $F(i.j)$.

Truth Membership Function T. Suppose that

$$Z(i, j) = \frac{I(i, j) - \mu_L}{\sigma_L + \epsilon}$$

where $I(i, j)$ is the pixel intensity, μ_L is the local mean (computed in a window around the pixel), σ_L is the local standard deviation, $\varepsilon > 0$ is a small stabilizer to avoid division by zero for numerical stability, and k contrast sensitivity controlle Let $x = kZ(i, j)$, then

$$T(i, j) = \frac{1}{1 + e^{-k\frac{I(i,j)-\mu_L}{\sigma_L+\epsilon}}} = \frac{1}{1 + e^{-x}}$$

is a membership function.

Proof: To prove that $T(i, j)$ is a membership function, showing each of the three functions takes values in the interval [0,1]. Since

$$x = k\frac{I(i, j) - \mu_L}{\sigma_L + \varepsilon}$$

which is a finite real number because the denominator > 0 and $k, I(i, j), \mu_L$ are finite. The logistic function

$$T(i, j) = \frac{1}{1 + e^{-k\frac{I(i,j)-\mu_L}{\sigma_L+\epsilon}}} = \frac{1}{1 + e^{-x}}$$

has the well-known range $0 < T(i, j) < 1$ for every finite real x. Therefore,
$0 < T(i, j) < 1$. Hence $T(i, j) \in [0,1]$.

Indeterminacy Membership Function I. Classical neutrosophic indeterminacy is commonly defined based on the normalized deviation from the local mean [Guo and Cheng, 2009]. In the proposed neutrosophic representation, an improved indeterminacy membership function is introduced based on a logarithmic nonlinear transformation of the truth membership $T(i, j)$.

Let $T(i, j) \in [0, 1]$ denote the truth-membership value obtained from the sigmoid-based normalization. We define the preliminary function:

$$f(T(i,j)) = -\log(T(i,j) + \varepsilon) + (1 - T(i,j))\log(1 - T(i,j) + \varepsilon),$$

where $\varepsilon > 0$ is a small constant to ensure numerical stability.

Since $f(T(i, j))$ does not necessarily lie in the interval [0, 1], it cannot be directly used as a valid membership function. Therefore, we propose the following normalized indeterminacy membership function:

$$I_N(i,j) = \frac{f(T(i,j)) - f_{min}}{f_{mix} - f_{min}}$$

Where

$$f_{min} = min_{r\in[0,1]} f(T), \quad f_{mix} = mix_{r\in[0,1]} f(T)$$

Based on the monotonic decreasing behavior of $f(T)$ the extrema occur at the boundary points.

$$f_{mix} = f(0) = -\log(\varepsilon) + \log(1 + \varepsilon)$$

$$f_{mix} = f(1) = -\log(1 + \varepsilon),$$

Thus, the proposed indeterminacy membership function can be written explicitly as:

$$I_N(i,j) = \frac{-\log(T(i,j) + \varepsilon) + (1 - T(i,j))\log(1 - T(i,j) + \varepsilon) + \log(1 + \varepsilon)}{-\log(\varepsilon) + 2\log(1 + \varepsilon)}$$

The function $I_N(i, j)$ is a valid membership function, i.e.,

$$I_N(i,j) \in [0, 1], \quad \forall(i,j)$$

Proof

Let $T(i, j) \in [0, 1]$ and define

$$f(T) = -\log(T + \varepsilon) + (1 - T)\log(1 - +\varepsilon),$$

Since the logarithmic function is continuous on $(0, \infty)$ and $\varepsilon > 0$, it follows that $f(T)$ is continuous on the closed interval [0, 1]. Therefore, by the extreme value theorem, $f(T)$ attains its minimum and maximum values on [0, 1], denoted by f_{min} and f_{mix}, respectively.

Thus, for all $T \in [0, 1]$,

$$f_{min} \le f(T) \le f_{mix}$$

Subtracting f_{min} from all sides yields.

$$0 \le f(T) \le f_{min} \le f_{mix} - f_{min}$$

Since $f_{mix} - f_{min} > 0$, dividing both sides by $f_{mix} - f_{min}$ gives:

$$0 \le \frac{f(T) - f_{min}}{f_{mix} - f_{min}} \le 1$$

By definition,

$$I_N(i, j) = \frac{f(T(i, j)) - f_{min}}{f_{mix} - f_{min}}$$

Hance

$$0 \le I_N(i, j) \le 1$$

Therefore, $I_N(i, j))$ satisfies the fundamental condition of a membership function.

$$I_N(i, j) \in [0, 1]$$

Classical neutrosophic indeterminacy component $I(i, j)$ is a deviation-based (linear, symmetric), while the improved indeterminacy membership function $I_N(i, j)$ is logarithmic, asymmetric, and information-driven.

Falsity Membership Function F. It is clear that

$$F(i, j) = 1 - T(i, j)$$

is a membership function.

This transformation allows the algorithm to separate deterministic information from uncertainty, improving watermark robustness.

Comparative Justification with Classical Neutrosophic Membership Functions

Compared to classical neutrosophic models, the proposed membership functions provide a more adaptive and discriminative representation. The truth membership $T(i, j)$ uses a nonlinear sigmoid mapping based on local mean and deviation, enhancing structural contrast and suppressing noise. Including a nonlinear transformation, the indeterminacy $I(i, j)$ membership function is defined for feature extraction and fragility to thin variations. The falsity $F(i, j) = 1 - T(i, j)$ benefits indirectly from the improved definition of $T(i, j)$. Overall, the proposed formulation better captures local structures and balances robustness and sensitivity.

Interpreting the convenience of the Proposed Membership Function T for Zero-Watermarking

The truth membership function $T(i, j)$ constitutes the core component of the proposed framework. Unlike conventional mappings based on raw or globally normalized intensities, $T(i, j)$ encodes the locally normalized deviation of a pixel from its neighborhood $Z(i, j)$. Specifically, values of $T(i, j)$ close to 1 or 0 correspond to locally dominant or recessive structures, whereas values near 0.5 indicate structurally neutral regions. The proposed formulation offers the following advantages: (i) The local adaptivity, which means that the utilization of μ_L and σ_L permits the function to adapt to local image statistics, preserving structural frequency and reducing sensitivity to illumination changes. (ii) Bounded and stable output since $0 < T(i, j) < 1$, then it is easy to use in feature extraction phase and recovery phase. (iii) The control sensitivity parameter k keeps balance between sharpening and smoothness, this implies the function is flexible making robust, semi-fragile, or fragile. Whenever k increasing, then the robust sensitivity increases.

Using the proposed truth membership function T makes edge regions produce strong changes in $T(i, j)$, homogeneous regions yield values close to 0.5; textured regions exhibit moderate variations. Consequently, the image is transformed into a structure-aware statistical representation, which is more informative for feature extraction than raw intensity values.

The Zero Watermark Construction Algorithm. The zero watermark construction utilizing the SVD is given below and demonstrated in Fig. 3a.

The algorithm outlines the steps of the Zero Watermark Construction for embedding watermarks into images. It begins by converting the original 256-by-256 image to grayscale, then adding three binary watermarks of different sizes. The image is transformed into a neutrosophic domain, which represents pixels using the three proposed membership components $T(i, j)$, $I(i, j)$ and $F(i, j)$. The truth membership function $T(i, j)$ constitutes the core component of the proposed framework; the matrix uses a sigmoid function as a base with specified parameters. The T component is divided into 64 by 64 blocks of size 4 by 4. Singular Value Decomposition is applied to each block, producing three matrices per block. Three cases are tested to create feature matrices of sizes 256-by-256, 128-by-128, or 64-by-64, depending on feature richness (the diagonal matrix $\Sigma_{(i,j)}$). The chosen feature matrix is binarized, and an XOR operation is performed between this matrix and the binary watermark to produce a secret share M. This process ensures robust watermark embedding by combining image features with multiple watermark sizes.

The Zero Watermark Construction Algorithm
Start
Step 1. Enter the original image of size 256×256 and transform it into a gray-level form.
Step 2. Enter the three binary watermarks of size 256×256, 128×128, 64×64.
Step 3. Convert the original image to the neutrosophic domain using the membership functions introduced in 3.1 to obtain the matrix of the neutrosophic component T. $$T(i,j) = \frac{1}{1 + e^{-k\frac{I(i,j)-\mu_L}{\sigma_L+\epsilon}}}$$ Epsilon = $1e - 6$,, Sigmoid Gain (k) =5
Step 4. Select the $T - component$ of the original image and divide it into 64×64 blocks, each of size 4×4.
Step 5. Apply the Singular Value Decomposition method (SVD) on each block in Step 4, and get 3 matrices for each block $U_{(i,j)} \cdot \Sigma_{(i,j)} \cdot {V^T}_{(i,j)}$
Step 6. Three cases are tested for all blocks to create a new matrix to be the matrix of features: **Case 1.** (Richer features): Choose the matrices $\Sigma_{(i,j)}$ and construct a new matrix of size 256×256 to be the feature matrix C. **Case 2.** (Less rich, partially compact**):** Choose the main diagonal of each $\Sigma_{(i,j)}$ and construct a new matrix of size 128×128 to be the feature matrix C. **Case3.** (Most compact features**):** Choose the maximum number of each $\Sigma_{(i,j)}$ and construct a new matrix of size 64×64 to be the feature matrix C.
Step 7. Binarize the matrix C to obtain the feature matrix K where $1 \leq i \leq n$ where: case1: n = 256 case2: n = 128 case3: n = 64.
Step 8. Perform an XOR operation between the binary features of the original image K and the binary watermark W to get M (secret share).
End

In the authentication phase, the original image is not required. Instead, the verification process is performed using the test (suspected) image and the stored secret share generated during the zero-watermark construction stage.

The Watermark Recovery Algorithm. The watermark recovery utilizing the SVD is given below and demonstrated in Fig. 3b.

The algorithm outlines the steps of a watermark recovery for a 256-by-256 suspected image. It starts by converting the image to gray-level, then uses three stored zero watermarks. The image is transformed into a neutrosophic domain matrix using a specific formula involving parameters epsilon and sigmoid gain. The T-component of the image matrix is divided into 64-by-64 blocks of size 4-by-4. Singular Value Decomposition is applied to each block, producing three matrices. Three cases are tested to create a feature matrix C of varying sizes: 256-by-256 for richer features, 128-by-128 for less rich features, and 64-by-64 for the most compact features. The matrix C is binarized to form matrix K, with size depending on the case. Finally, an XOR operation between K and secret shares M reconstructs the zero-watermark. These steps are important as it clearly presents the sequential process and decision points in recovering a watermark from an image.

The Watermark Recovery Algorithm
Start
Step 1. Enter the suspected image I' of size 256×256 transform it into a gray-level form.
Step 2. Enter the three stored zero watermarks M.
Step 3. Convert the original image to the neutrosophic domain using the membership functions introduced in 3.1 to obtain the matrix of the neutrosophic component T.
$$T(i,j) = \frac{1}{1 + e^{-k\frac{I(i,j)-\mu_L}{\sigma_L+\epsilon}}}$$
Epsilon = $1e-6$, Sigmoid Gain (k) =5
Step 4. Select the $T-component$ of the original image and divide it into 64×64 blocks, each of size 4×4.
Step 5. Apply the Singular Value Decomposition method (SVD) on each block in Step 4 get 3 matrices $U_{(i,j)} \cdot \Sigma_{(i,j)} \cdot V^T{}_{(i,j)}$
Step 6. Three cases are tested for all blocks to create a new matrix to be the matrix of features:
Case 1. (Richer features): Choose the matrices $\Sigma_{(i,j)}$ and construct a new matrix of size 256×256 to be the feature matrix C.
Case 2. (Less rich, partially compact): Choose the main diagonal of each $\Sigma_{(i,j)}$ and construct a new matrix of size 128×128 to be the feature matrix C.
Case3. (Most compact features): Choose the maximum number of each $\Sigma_{(i,j)}$ and construct a new matrix of size 64×64 to be the feature matrix C.
Step 7. Binarize the matrix C to obtain the feature matrix K where $1 \leq i \leq n$ where: case1: n = 256 case2: n = 128 case3: n = 64.
Step 8. Apply the XOR operation between the binary features K and the secret shares M to construct the zero-watermark.
End

The extracted watermark is compared with the original watermark stored at the ownership authority. A high similarity indicates authenticity, while deviations indicate possible tampering.

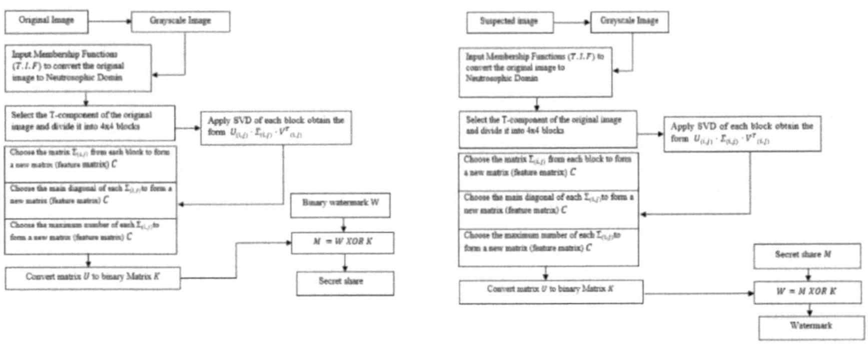

(a) (b)

Fig. 3. **(a)** The diagram of the zero-watermark construction and **(b)** The diagram of the authentication procedure

Evaluation Metrics

a-Watermark similarity. The performance of the proposed scheme is evaluated using Normalized Correlation (NC).
b-For recovery accuracy. BER measures the percentage of incorrectly recovered watermark bits.

Attacks Simulation. To evaluate robustness, the original images were subjected to common image processing attacks, and the NC and BER are reported after each attack. Common attacks include: Noise attacks (Gaussian noise, Salt & pepper noise, Speckle noise, Poisson noise), Filtering attacks (Median filter, Average filter, Motion filter, Gaussian lowpass filter), and Image-Processing attacks (JPEG Compression, Histogram Equalization).

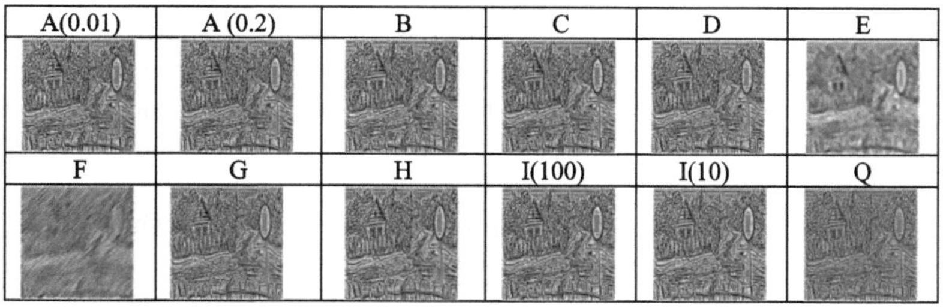

Fig. 4. The Village Road image after the attacks

The Village Road image after the attacks : Attacked Village Road image compares the detailed structures of samples labeled A through Q, with some labels indicating differ-ent conditions or concentrations. Depending on the behavior of each attack, most im-ages sometimes show a consistent pattern of layered and fibrous textures, suggesting similar structural features across samples A(0.01), A(0.2), B, C, D, G, H, I(100), I(10), and Q. And different patterns at other times, sample E and F differ noticeably, with E showing a less defined structure and F appearing more blurred or less organized. This comparison highlights how different attacks or processing operations affect image structures and extracted features, which is essential for assessing the robustness and reliability of the proposed method under various experimental conditions.

4 The Results

This section presents the experimental results obtained from the proposed zero-watermarking method using the improved neutrosophic domain. The performance of the algorithms is evaluated on several paradigm test images and various image processing attacks.

For the three cases, the performance of the watermark recovery is measured using the Normalized Correlation (NC) and BER between the original and recovered watermark (Table 1).

Table 1. The NC and BER Values with no Attacks for the three cases

Images	Baboon	Peppers	Girl	Village Road
NC	1	1	1	1
BER	0	0	0	0

4.1 Noise Attacks

Table 2 presents three cases, each used to constrain a feature matrix for different attack types: Salt and pepper noise, Gaussian noise, Poisson noise, and Speckle noise. The matrices correspond to four images: Baboon, Peppers, Girl, and Village Road. Each image has two columns labeled NC and BER, representing numerical values for each attack and image. The first case shows values mostly close to 1 for NC and lower values for BER across all attacks and images, indicating strong constraint performance. The second case has lower NC values and higher BER values, especially for Gaussian noise, suggesting less effective constraints. The third case shows intermediate values between the first two images. The table highlights how each image performs differently depending on the noise type and image, generally providing the best results in maintaining feature integrity under noise attacks. This Table helps understand which case is most effective for resisting specific noise types in various image settings.

Table 2. NC and BER values after applying a noise attack to the images

Case 1: The diagonal matrices $\Sigma_{(i,j)}$ were selected to construct the feature matrix								
Attacks	Baboon		Peppers		Girl		Village Road	
	NC	BER	NC	BER	NC	BER	NC	BER
Salt and pepper Noise (0.01)	1	0	1	0	1	0	1	0
Salt and pepper Noise (0.2)	0.999	4.57764e-05	0.999	3.05176e-05	0.999	1.52588e-05	0.999	1.52578e-05
Gaussian Noise	0.999	9.15527e-05	1	0	0.999	4.57764e-05	0.999	4.577
Poisson noise	1	0	1	0	1	0	1	0
Speckle noise	1	0	1	0	1	0	1	0
Case 2: the main diagonal of the matrices $\Sigma_{(i,j)}$ were selected to construct the feature matrix								
Attacks	Baboon		Peppers		Girl		Village Road	
	NC	BER	NC	BER	NC	BER	NC	BER
Salt and pepper Noise (0.01)	0.970	0.0306	0.968	0.0326	0.969	0.0322	0.972	0.0316
Salt and pepper Noise (0.2)	0.946	0.2899	0.943	0.3068	0.939	0.3050	0.942	0.2945
Gaussian Noise	0.944	0.0635	0.917	0.0931	0.916	0.095	0.912	0.1058
Poisson noise	1	0	1	0	1	0	0.992	0.0067
Speckle noise	0.942	0.0604	0.922	0.0927	0.924	0.0858	0.916	0.0901
Case 3: the maximum singular value of the matrices $\Sigma_{(i,j)}$ (i.e., the element in the location (1, 1)) were selected to construct the feature matrix								
Attacks	Baboon		Peppers		Girl		Village Road	
	NC	BER	NC	BER	NC	BER	NC	BER
Salt and pepper Noise (0.01)	0.983	0.0178	0.988	0.0151	0.986	0.0139	0.981	0.0244
Salt and pepper Noise (0.2)	0.832	0.1826	0.843	0.1372	0.865	0.1535	0.838	0.1752
Gaussian Noise	0.993	0.0009	0.994	0.00091	0.993	0.0085	0.981	0.0183
Poisson noise	1	0	1	0	1	0	0.991	0.0092
Speckle noise	0.986	0.0202	0.990	0.0124	0.986	0.0146	0.971	0.0314

4.2 Filter Attacks

Table 3 below presents three different cases for selecting features to construct a feature matrix, evaluated across the four above. For each image, two metrics are shown: NC and BER, under four attack types: Gaussian low-pass filter, Motion filter, Average filter, and MED filter. Case 1 shows perfect scores with NC equal to 1 and BER equal to 0 for all attacks and images, indicating ideal performance when diagonal matrices are used. Case 2 presents lower NC values around 0.67 to 0.74 and BER values between 0.28 and 0.35, showing moderate performance when only the main diagonal of the matrices is used. Case 3 shows improved NC values ranging from about 0.61 to 0.88 and lower BER values from approximately 0.13 to 0.42, indicating better results when the maximum singular value of the matrices is selected. Overall, the table highlights how different matrix feature selection methods affect the accuracy (NC) and bit error rate (BER) of image processing under various filter attacks, with Case 1 performing best, Case 3 showing good results, and Case 2 performing moderately.

Table 3. NC and BER values after applying a filter attack to the images

Case 1: The diagonal matrices $\Sigma_{(i,j)}$ were selected to construct the feature matrix								
Attacks	Baboon		Peppers		Girl		Village Road	
	NC	BER	NC	BER	NC	BER	NC	BER
Gaussianlowpassfilte	1	0	1	0	1	0	1	0
Motion filter	1	0	1	0	1	0	1	0
Average filter	1	0	1	0	1	0	1	0
MED filter	1	0	1	0	1	0	1	0
Case 2: the main diagonal of the matrices $\Sigma_{(i,j)}$ were selected to construct the feature matrix								
Attacks	Baboon		Peppers		Girl		Village Road	
	NC	BER	NC	BER	NC	BER	NC	BER
Gaussianlowpassfilte	0.703	0.3199	0.735	0.2833	0.730	0.2904	0.726	0.2944
Motion filter	0.678	0.3480	0.687	0.3240	0.687	0.3372	0.692	0.3304
Average filter	0.703	0.3199	0.735	0.2833	0.730	0.2904	0.726	0.2944
MED filter	0.695	0.3281	0.731	0.2875	0.718	0.3026	0.718	0.3018
Case 3: the maximum singular value of the matrices $\Sigma_{(i,j)}$ (i.e., the element in the location (1, 1)) were selected to construct the feature matrix								
Attacks	Baboon		Peppers		Girl		Village Road	
	NC	BER	NC	BER	NC	BER	NC	BER
Gaussianlowpassfilte	0.840	0.1745	0.871	0.1411	0.879	0.1333	0.855	0.1599
Motion filter	0.646	0.3828	0.645	0.3825	0.611	0.4167	0.629	0.3999
Average filter	0.840	0.1735	0.871	0.1411	0.879	0.1333	0.855	0.1599
MED filter	0.831	0.1840	0.869	0.1428	0.874	0.1389	0.848	0.1674

4.3 Image-Processing Attacks

Table 4 presents three cases for constructing a feature matrix—using diagonal matrices, main diagonal elements, and maximum singular values—across four image sets named Baboon, Peppers, Girl, and Village Road. For each case, it shows two metrics: NC (normalized correlation) and BER (bit error rate), under three attack conditions: JPEG compression at quality 100, JPEG compression at quality 90, and histogram equalization. Higher NC values close to 1 and lower BER values close to 0 indicate better per-formance. The first case, using diagonal matrices, consistently achieves near-perfect NC values around 0.999 and very low BER values near zero for all images and attacks, showing the best robustness. The second case, using only the main diagonal, shows lower NC values and higher BER, indicating weaker performance. The third case, using maximum singular values, performs better than the second but not as well as the first, with NC values mostly above 0.9 and moderate BER values. This table highlights that selecting the full diagonal matrices for feature construction provides the most reliable results against these image attacks.

The following Table 5 shows the recovered watermark images for the three cases, Village Road See Table 4:

Table 4. NC and BER values after applying an image-processing attack to the images

Case 1: The diagonal matrices $\Sigma_{(i,j)}$ were selected to construct the feature matrix								
Attacks	Baboon		Peppers		Girl		Village Road	
	NC	BER	NC	BER	NC	BER	NC	BER
JPEG Compression Quality (100)	0.999	0.00021	0.999	6.10353e-05	0.999	0.00021	0.999	0.00051
JPEG Compression Quality (90)	0.999	0.00071	0.998	0.00123	0.999	0.00115	0.998	0.00195
Histogram Equalization	1	0	1	0	1	0	1	0
Case 2: the main diagonal of the matrices $\Sigma_{(i,j)}$ were selected to construct the feature matrix								
Attacks	**Baboon**		**Peppers**		**Girl**		**Village Road**	
	NC	BER	NC	BER	NC	BER	NC	BER
JPEG Compression Quality (100)	0.986	0.0148	0.979	0.0223	0.977	0.0250	0.973	0.0296
JPEG Compression Quality (90)	0.929	0.2478	0.895	0.2302	0.899	0.2505	0.900	0.2759
Histogram Equalization	0.805	0.2106	0.828	0.1857	0.827	0.1878	0.817	0.1983
Case 3: the maximum singular value of the matrices $\Sigma_{(i,j)}$ (i.e., the element in the location (1, 1)) were selected to construct the feature matrix								
Attacks	**Baboon**		**Peppers**		**Girl**		**Village Road**	
	NC	BER	NC	BER	NC	BER	NC	BER
JPEG Compression Quality (100)	0.998	0.0019	0.999	0.0004	0.999	0.0004	0.990	0.0100
JPEG Compression Quality (90)	0.995	0.0053	0.997	0.0490	0.994	0.0058	0.987	0.0144
Histogram Equalization	0.924	0.0837	0.956	0.0485	0.957	0.0471	0.933	0.0734

Table 5. Recovered watermark images for the three cases for the Village Road image

Case 1:The diagonal matrices $\Sigma_{(i,j)}$ were selected to construct the feature matrix						
attack	A(0.01)	A(0.2)	B	C	D	E
Recovered Watermark						
attack	F	G	H	I(100)	I(10)	O
Recovered Watermark						
Case 2: the main diagonal of the matrices $\Sigma_{(i,j)}$ were selected to construct the feature matrix						
attack	A(0.01)	A(0.2)	B	C	D	E
Recovered Watermark						
attack	F	G	H	I(100)	I(10)	O
Recovered Watermark						
Case 3: the maximum singular value of the matrices $\Sigma_{(i,j)}$ (i.e., the element in the location (1, 1) were selected to construct the feature matrix						
attack	A(0.01)	A(0.2)	B	C	D	E
Recovered Watermark						
attack	F	G	H	I(100)	I(10)	O
Recovered Watermark						

Recovered watermark images for the three cases for the Village Road image: Table 5 recovered watermarks after different types of attacks using three cases for con-structing the feature matrix: Case 1 uses diagonal matrices, Case 2 uses the main di-agonal of matrices, and Case 3 uses the maximum singular value at position (1, 1). Each case shows two rows of Recovered QR code Watermark images under various attack types labeled A with values 0.01 and 0.2, B, C, D, E, F, G, H, I with values 100 and 10, and O. The table highlights how the watermark recovery varies depending on the matrix construction case and attack type, illustrating differences in watermark clar-ity and integrity across cases and attacks.

4.4 Comparison

The proposed system is adaptable to the image environment, enabling it to control the balance between robustness and sensitivity based on the chosen image feature extraction methods. While most image zero watermarking methods are designed for either a fragile or robust case, the proposed technique operates as a tamper-sensitive, semi-fragile, or robust system depending on the selected control factor.

Table 6. Compared the proposed zero watermarking scheme with previous methods

Method	Technique	Watermark Type	NC (Typical under Attacks)	BER	Robustness	Image Distortion
Proposed Method	Netrsophic + SVD	Zero-watermark	0.998 1.000	≈ 0	Very High	No
Ref [23]	GLC + PCA	Embedded	0.80 – 0.93	Moderate –High	Moderate	Yes
Ref [18]	DWT-DCT–SVD	Embedded	0.90 – 0.98	Moderate	Moderate–High	Yes
Ref [22]	PCA-based	Zero/Hybrid	0.85 – 0.95	Moderate	Moderate (noise sensitive)	No/Low
Ref [1]	DWT–SVD	Embedded	0.95 – 0.99	Low–Moderate	High (but degrades under noise)	Yes

Table 6 presents four methods, in addition to the proposed technique, based on techniques used, watermarking type, NC target, bit error rate (BER), robustness, and image distortion. Methods include GLC and PCA [22] and using PCA-based [21] with a 256x256 watermark and very low distortion; using DCT and SVD with a 64x64 watermark and low distortion [17], using OWT-SVD [1]. Robustness varies from low to high, with some methods resistant to JPEG compression and noise. The table highlights differences in watermark size, robustness, and image distortion among the methods.

5 Methodology Analysis of the Proposed Algorithms and Experimental Results

This section provides a comprehensive analysis of the proposed hybrid zero watermarking paradigm based on the neutrosophic domain and singular value decomposition (SVD). The role of the proposed membership function $T(i, j)$ used in the steps of feature extraction is analyzed to evaluate the impact of the scheme designed.

5.1 Analysis of Feature Extraction Strategies

Three feature extraction strategies are investigated in the proposed scheme, depending on the richness of the features.

The first case utilizes the whole diagonal matrix features of the SVD, preserving a dominant feature from the structural information of each block, resulting in highly stable watermark recovery. The second case utilizes only diagonal elements to reduce the feature size, making the features more sensitive to distortions. The third case utilizes only the dominant singular value, capturing the primary energy of each block. This approach significantly reduces structural information, increasing sensitivity to attacks.

5.2 Robustness Analysis Under Attacks

According to the experimental results above, the robustness of the proposed zero watermarking scheme is depending on the case of choosing the features.

Under the noise attacks, Gaussian, salt-and-pepper, speckle, and Poisson noise, in the first case, since NC ≈ 1 and BER ≈ 0, then the scheme achieves at most the perfect performance and consequently indicates strong robustness. While in the second case, notice a degradation, especially under higher noise levels. The third case keeps balanced robustness, although it retreats under strong noise. This attitude guarantees flexibility when using richer features, but the compact features increase the effects of confusion.

Under filtering attacks, Gaussian, median, average, and motion filtering, the first case shows high stability, and this displays that this case was not affected (NC $= 1$). In case two, the NC $\approx$ 0.68–0.73, which indicates a big decline in robustness. While the third case shows moderate degradation (NC $\approx$ 0.64–0.87). Filtering attacks smooths the overall image, so the features are changed immediately hardly than richer features.

Under compression and intensity attacks**,** JPEG compression and histogram equalization, in the first case, the NC $\approx$ 0.998–1 keeps high values, and the second case shows substantial degradation, especially at lower quality levels. While the third case is still sensitive but better than the second case.

These results indicate that the proposed T form effectively normalizes global intensity variations, contributing to robustness against such attacks.

5.3 Role of the Proposed Membership Functions

The behavior of the proposed scheme is related directly to the introduced membership function $T(i, j)$: emphasizes local structural contrast rather than absolute intensity, reduces sensitivity to brightness, contrast (for example) distortions, and enhances feature stability across different environments.

6 Conclusion

This technique is designed to be able to extract stable and significant features that have the ability and capacity to attack resistance. The robustness against common attacks achieved under the recent proposed scheme is NC almost 1 and Ber 0. Furthermore, this technique is more flexible and reliable compared with existing approaches because it integrates strong feature stability, with no deformation, and high sensitivity.

The consolidation between the neutrosophic representation of the image and utilizing the SVD on the blocks shows that the proposed scheme attains high-powered interaction truth modeling and algebraic stability. The obtained model achieves a blind authentication technique and keeps the cover image unchanged; consequently, it is regarded as the most suitable for high-integrity applications. The experimental results represent the near-perfect recovery of the input watermark under different types of attacks, significantly outperforming reduced features, and stands out the significant impact of feature richness.

Moreover, the systematic analysis of various feature extraction techniques releases a principal trade-off between sensitivity and robustness, which gives a good perception to construct a flexible zero watermarking scheme. More than that, depending on the obtained results It is being explored that the proposed design is considered as an adaptable system, not just an important approach for robust zero watermarking that can be tuned for semi-fragile authentication schemes.

Overall, the method can be characterized as a robust zero-watermarking scheme with tunable sensitivity, making it suitable for both copyright protection and authentication applications.

References

1. Alzahrani, A.: Enhanced invisibility and robustness of digital image watermarking based on DWT-SVD. Appl. Bion. Biomech. **2022**, Article 9607682 (2022)
2. Qu, C., Du, J., Xi, X., Tian, H., Zhang, J.: A hybrid domain-based watermarking for vector maps utilizing a complementary advantage of discrete Fourier transform and singular value decomposition. Comput. Geosci. **183**, 105312 (2024)
3. Smarandache, F.: Neutrosophy: Neutrosophic Probability, Set, and Logic: Analytic Synthesis & Synthetic Analysis. American Research Press, Rehoboth (1998)
4. Guo, Y., Cheng, H.D.: New neutrosophic approach to image segmentation. Pattern Recogn. **42**(5), 587–595 (2009)
5. Cheng, H.D., Guo, Y., Zhang, Y.: A novel image segmentation approach based on neutrosophic set and improved fuzzy C-means algorithm. New Math. Nat. Comput. **7**(1), 155–171 (2011)
6. Guo, Y., Sengür, A.: A novel image edge detection algorithm based on neutrosophic set. Comput. Electr. Eng. **40**(8), 3–25 (2014)
7. Yu, B., Niu, Z., Wang, L.: Mean shift-based clustering of neutrosophic domain for unsupervised constructions detection. Optik **124**(21), 4697–4706 (2013)
8. Salama, A.A., Eisa, M., Fawzy, A.E.: A neutrosophic image retrieval classifier. Int. J. Comput. Appl. **170**(9), 1–6 (2017)
9. Wen, J., Xuan, S., Li, Y., Peng, Q., Gao, Q.: Image segmentation algorithm based on neutrosophic fuzzy clustering with non-local information. IET Image Proc. **14**(3), 576–584 (2020)
10. Xu, G., Wang, S., Yang, T., Jiang, W.: A neutrosophic approach based on TOPSIS method to image segmentation. Int. J. Comput. Commun. Control **13**(6), 1047–1061 (2018)
11. Abduldaim, A.M., Faraj, A.K.: Combining algebraic GSVD and gravitational search algorithm for optimizing secret image watermark sharing technique. Int. J. Math. Comput. Sci. **17**(2), 753–774 (2022)
12. Mohammed, N.S., Abduldaim, A.M.: Algebraic Hessenberg decomposition method optimized by genetic algorithm for zero watermarking technique. Int. J. Math. Comput. Sci. **16**(4), 1497–1514 (2021)
13. Waleed, J., Abduldaim, A.M., Alyas, H.H., Mohammed, A.Q.: An optimized zero-watermarking technique based on SFL algorithm. In: 2nd International Conference on Electrical Communication Computer Power and Control Engineering (ICECCPCE), pp. 171–175 (2019)

14. Yang, G., Lu, X., Lu, Y., Tang, J., Xiong, X.: Robust zero-watermarking method for multiple medical images using wavelet fusion and DTCWT-QR. J. Inform. Secur. Appl. **90**, 103945 (2025)
15. Elhamzi, I.W.: Enhancing medical image security with FPGA-accelerated LED cryptography and LSB watermarking. Traitement du Signal **41**(1), 85–97 (2024)
16. Purnima, R., Rakesh, A., Gautam, N.: Motion-frames based video watermarking scheme for copyright protection using guided filtering in wavelet domain. Traitement du Signal **40**(1), 187–197 (2023)
17. Riyajuddin, R., Reddy, A.P.: Various image processing attacks for image watermarking in the wavelet domain using singular value decomposition and discrete cosine transform. Rev. Comput. Eng. Stud. **8**(2), 51–59 (2021)
18. Pan, Z., Wu, C., Yang, C., Zhao, B.: Double-matrix decomposition image steganography scheme based on wavelet transform with multi-region coverage. Entropy **24**(2), 246 (2022)
19. Maity, S.: Image watermarking on degraded compressed sensing measurements. J. Mech. Continua Math. Sci. **18**(4), 10–22 (2023)
20. Yang, M., Li, J., Bhatti, U.A., Shao, C., Chen, Y.: Robust watermarking algorithm for medical images based on non-subsampled shearlet transform and Schur decomposition. Comput. Mater. Continua **75**(3), 5539–5554 (2023)
21. Kahdim, S.A., Abduldaim, A.M.: Principal component analysis for zero watermarking technique. Int. J. Math. Comput. Sci. **18**(1), 85–97 (2023)
22. Dewan, S.G., Kalra, M.: GLCM and PCA algorithm based watermarking scheme. In: AIP Conference Proceedings, vol. 2916 (2023)
23. Su, Q., Sun, Y., Xia, Y., Wang, Z.: A robust color image watermarking scheme in the fusion domain based on LU factorization. Opt. Laser Technol. **174**, 110567 (2024)
24. Wang, X., Du, Q., Du, L., Zhang, H., Hu, J.: Robust zero-watermarking algorithm via multi-scale feature analysis for medical images. J. Inform. Secur. Appl. **89**, 103937 (2025)
25. Smarandache, F.: A Unifying Field in Logics: Neutrosophy, Neutrosophic Set. American Research Press, Neutrosophic Probability and Statistics (2001)
26. Azad, R., Sengur, A.: A novel image segmentation algorithm based on neutrosophic similarity clustering. Appl. Soft Comput. **25**, 391–398 (2014)
27. von Seggern, D.H.: CRC standard curves and surfaces with mathematica, 2nd edn. CRC Press, Boca Raton (2007)
28. Eckart, C., Young, G.: The approximation of one matrix by another of lower rank. Psychometrika **1**(3), 211–218 (1936)

Solving Advection-Reaction-Diffusion Equations with Quantum Trainable Embedding Physics-Informed Neural Networks

Ban Q. Tran[1,2(✉)], Hai T. D. Pham[3], and Susan Mengel[1]

[1] Department of Computer Science, Texas Tech University, Lubbock, TX 79416, USA
susan.mengel@ttu.edu

[2] Department of Computing Fundamentals, FPT University, Hanoi 10000, Vietnam
bantran@ttu.edu, bantq3@fe.edu.vn

[3] SAP Innovation Lab, FPT University, Hanoi 10000, Vietnam

Abstract. Multi-layer neural networks are the cornerstone of deep learning architectures and are applied across numerous critical fields. One area currently focusing on leveraging the strengths of neural networks is solving partial differential equations for physical simulations. Furthermore, the emergence of quantum computing technology has provided powerful support to classical neural networks, enhancing the quality of these models. In this research, we introduce a PDE solver based on a hybrid quantum neural network having a quantum learnable embedding combined with a classical optimizer. We demonstrate the effectiveness of this approximate solver through three case studies: the Heat, Reaction-Diffusion, and Navier-Stokes equations. Our results show that the hybrid classical-quantum solver achieves a deeper and smoother reduction in the loss function, with no signs of overfitting when compared to classical solvers.

Keywords: Quantum Machine Learning · Quantum Neural Networks · Quantum Physics-Informed Neural Networks · Hybrid Quantum-Classical Computing

1 Introduction

Quantum computing [1], with its unique properties, such as superposition, entanglement, and interference, has enabled revolutionary algorithms like Grover's and Shor's, and has demonstrated clear superiority over classical algorithms designed for the same purposes. Meanwhile, neural network architectures, which underpin deep learning, are surpassing classical machine learning algorithms and are at the forefront of many current technological trends [2]. Currently, one of the most potent application areas for neural networks is the development of partial differential equation (PDE) solvers [3,4]. These solvers, physics-informed neural

O. Gervasi et al. (Eds.): ICCSA 2026 Workshops, LNCS 16758, pp. 365–376, 2027.
https://doi.org/10.1007/978-3-032-30497-1_22

networks (PINN) demonstrate significant effectiveness in solving nonlinear and highly stiff PDEs [5]. The intersection of quantum computing and classical neural networks has led to powerful new solvers known as quantum physics-informed neural networks (QPINNs) [6], which exploit the strengths of both to make solving PDEs more efficient. Although QPINN solvers, with VQC circuits as their core, have demonstrated relatively good performance compared to PINN, the issue of embedding remains one of the primary obstacles hindering quantum advantage [7]. To address this issue, research has shown that using a neural network to learn the parameters θ of the main variational quantum circuits (VQCs) prior to encoding can improve the performance of the QPINN model [8]. Based on this idea, we hypothesize that applying a quantum neural network (QNN) will also improve the learning capability of the VQC circuit, similar to what classical neural networks have achieved. In the following section of the paper, we will introduce the architecture and mathematical foundation of the Quantum Neural Networks - Quantum Physics-Informed Neural Networks (QNN-QPINN) solver. In the experimental section, we evaluate the performance of this solver using three case studies: Heat, Reaction-diffusion, and Navier-Stokes PDEs.

2 Methodology

2.1 Physics-Informed Neural Networks

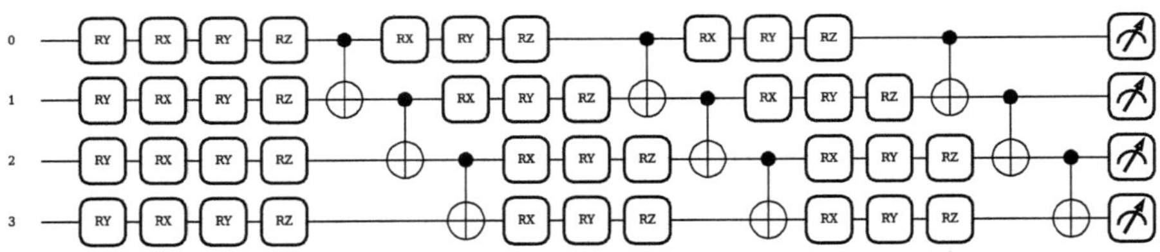

Fig. 1. The VQC quantum circuit.

The general architecture of a PINN [5] is similar to other classical neural network architectures where a PINN consists of a feedforward neural network (FNN) block with multiple layers, where each layer contains a set of neurons. This FNN takes spatial and temporal inputs (x, y, t) and predicts solution variables (u, v, p). Automatic differentiation is employed to compute derivatives, which are then used to calculate the loss function. The loss function of a PINN (Formula 1) is unique in that it incorporates losses from the PDE residuals, boundary conditions, and initial conditions. An optimizer is used to update the network parameters to minimize the loss and ensure that physical laws are preserved. The formula for the PINN loss function is as follows:

$$\mathcal{L}(\phi) = \mathcal{L}_{\text{PDE}}(\phi) + \sum_j \lambda_j \, \mathcal{L}_{\text{BC},j}(\phi) + \lambda_{\text{IC}} \, \mathcal{L}_{\text{IC}}(\phi), \tag{1}$$

The input data (Φ) for the model training is a computational domain, which is discretely sampled into collocation points. These collocation points are divided into different groups: collocation points for each boundary and those located within the domain Ω. Each collocation point has a residual value, and inside the domain, these values correspond to the PDE residuals. At the boundaries, the collocation points are fixed values corresponding to specific boundary conditions, such as Dirichlet or Neumann conditions.

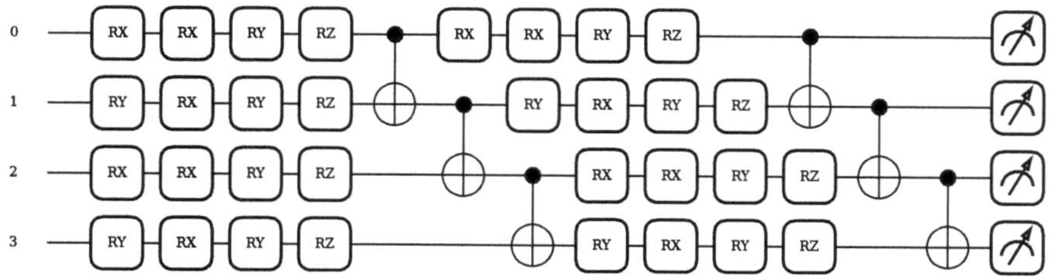

Fig. 2. The QNN embedding quantum circuit.

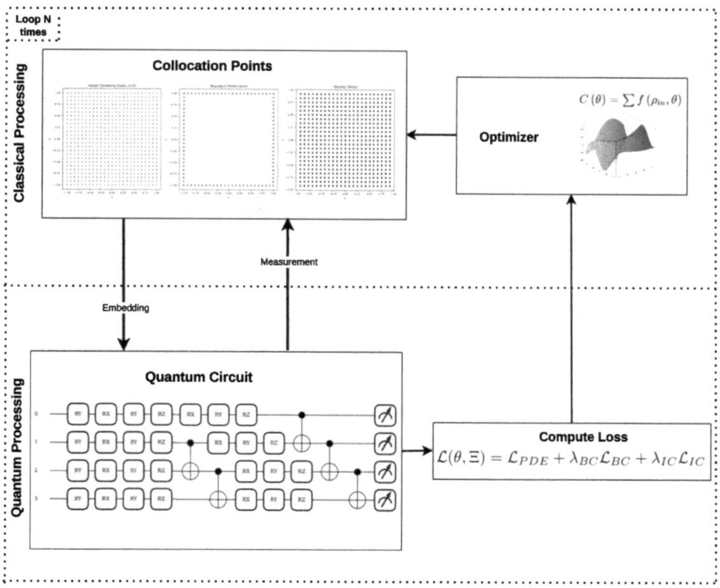

Fig. 3. The QNN-QPINN architecture.

2.2 Quantum Physics-Informed Neural Networks

Quantum physics-informed neural networks [6] are an extension of the traditional PINN model into the quantum computing environment. Instead of using classical artificial neural networks, QPINN utilizes variational quantum circuits to approximate the solutions of partial differential equations. Like PINNs, QPINNs do not only learn from data but also adhere to physical laws by directly integrating mathematical equations. A QPINN model consists of three main components: embedding (also known as a feature map), a variational ansatz circuit, and a physics-based loss function that uses automatic differentiation for hybrid classical optimizers or the parameter-shift rule for pure quantum optimizers. Figure 1 illustrates the VQC circuit of the QPINN architecture used in our study.

The variational unitary is structured as a series of L layers, defined by

$$U_{\text{var}}(\theta_{\text{var}}) = U_L(\theta_L) \cdots U_2(\theta_2)\, U_1(\theta_1) \tag{2}$$

In this architecture, each individual layer $U_\ell(\theta_\ell)$ is composed of a combination of both parameterized and fixed unitary operations: $U_\ell(\theta_\ell) \prod_m \exp!(-i, \theta_{\ell,m}, H_m), W_m$. Within this expression, H_m represents a set of constant Hermitian generators, while W_m refers to unitary operators that do not contain tunable parameters.

2.3 Quantum Trainable Embedding Physics-Informed Neural Networks

A trainable embedding - quantum physics-informed neural network (TE-QPINN) [8] is a QPINN architecture for solving PDEs that utilizes the idea of improving embedding capabilities by applying a neural network to learn the parameters θ fed into the VQC circuit. Before the embedding process, the spatial and temporal coordinates transform into a bounded range via the following expressions:

$$\tilde{x} = \mathcal{N}(x; x_{\text{min}}, x_{\text{max}}), \qquad \tilde{t} = \mathcal{N}(t; t_{\text{min}}, t_{\text{max}}),$$

In this context, $\mathcal{N}(\cdot)$ represents an affine scaling function that maps the raw input domains $[x_{\text{min}}, x_{\text{max}}]$ and $[t_{\text{min}}, t_{\text{max}}]$ onto the normalized interval $[-1, 1]$. By implementing this coordinate rescaling, we address potential discrepancies in magnitude between spatial and temporal variables, thereby enhancing the numerical robustness of the training phase. A comprehensive feature map is constructed by the embedding function.

$$\Gamma(x,t) = \left[\, \psi_1(\tilde{x},\tilde{t}),\ \ldots,\ \psi_{N_q}(\tilde{x},\tilde{t}) \,\right]^T,$$

In this formulation, the rotation angle for every individual i-th qubit is defined by the corresponding component $\psi_i(\tilde{x},\tilde{t})$. The transformation performed by the quantum encoder is governed by the specific values of the embedding angles.

$$U_{\text{enc}}(x,t;\theta_{\text{emb}}) = \bigotimes_{i=1}^{N_q} R_y\big(\psi_i(\tilde{x},\tilde{t},\theta_{\text{emb}})\big) \tag{3}$$

where $R_y(\cdot) = \exp(-i(\cdot)\sigma_y/2)$ represents a rotation operation on the y-axis for the i-th qubit, and N_q signifies the total qubit count.

The variational quantum state corresponding to a specific input (x, t) is generated by acting upon the encoded input with a universal variational circuit.

$$|\phi_{\text{var}}(x, t; \Theta)\rangle = U_{\text{var}}(\theta_{\text{var}}) U_{\text{enc}}(x, t; \theta_{\text{emb}}) |0\rangle^{\otimes N_q}. \tag{4}$$

By combining Formulas 2 and 3, concentration field predictions are determined through the following expectation values of species-dependent observables.

$$\tilde{C}_i(x, t, \Theta) = \langle \phi_{\text{var}}(x, t, \theta) | \mathcal{O}_i | \phi_{\text{var}}(x, t, \theta) \rangle \tag{5}$$

where the Hermitian observables, $\mathcal{O}_i$, are defined in relation to their associated concentration fields.

The training process (Formula 3) for the encoding parameters θ in the VQC is carried out in parallel with the main VQC circuit. Our proposed architecture essentially utilizes this trainable embedding concept, but replaces U_{emb} with a QNN architecture as shown in Fig. 2. The overall architecture of the proposed QNN-QPINN is described in detail in Fig. 3. The QNN-QPINN algorithm is described in Algorithm 1.

3 Numerical Results

In this section, we focus on interpreting the results from the model training experiments and the inference outcomes of the quantum neural network solver across various PDEs of increasing complexity.

3.1 Environments and Quantum Circuits

Due to constraints on quantum hardware in the NISQ era, specifically the lack of affordable fault-tolerant quantum computers for model training, we used classical computers with simulators to train our models. The simulation environment employed is the REmotely-managed Power Aware Computing Systems and Services (REPACSS) supercomputer at Texas Tech University [9], which utilizes GPU compute nodes equipped with 4 x NVIDIA H100 NVLs (94 GB HBM per GPU). Training models using classical computers is entirely feasible for systems with fewer than 20 qubits. Regarding the software, we utilized the Python programming language and Facebook's PyTorch deep learning library to implement the classical neural network models and the hybrid model optimizer [10]. To construct the quantum neural network architecture, we employed the PennyLane quantum machine learning library for its convenience, robustness, and support for diverse hardware in the post-training inference phase [11].

The quantum circuits forming the solver are constructed by applying single-qubit rotation gates (R_x, R_y, R_z) and CNOT entanglement gates to the input qubits. This grid-like quantum neural network architecture is known as a Variational Quantum Circuit (VQC), where the tunable parameters are the rotation

Algorithm 1. Training Algorithm for the QNN-QPINN Framework

Input:
  Internal PDE operator, boundary operators $B_j[\cdot]$ and boundary data b_j
  Initial condition $C_0(x)$
  Collocation sets $\mathcal{S}_{\text{PDE}}, \{\mathcal{S}_{\text{BC},j}\}, \mathcal{S}_{\text{IC}}$
  Loss weights $\{\lambda_j\}, \lambda_{\text{IC}}$
  Equation parameters $\mathcal{P}_i$
  Iterations N
Initialization:
Initialize embedding parameters θ_{emb}
Initialize variational circuit parameters θ_{var}
Normalize the input coordinates (x, t) to the scaled variables $(\tilde{x}, \tilde{t}) \in [-1, 1]^2$
Initialize optimizer for parameters $(\theta_{\text{emb}}, \theta_{\text{var}})$
while not converged **do**
  Forward evaluation
  for each collocation point (x^k, t^k) **do**
    Compute embedding angles $\psi(x^k, t^k; \theta_{\text{emb}})$
    Prepare encoded state $|\phi_{\text{enc}}\rangle = U_{\text{enc}}(\psi)|0\rangle^{\otimes N_q}$
    Apply variational circuit $|\phi_{\text{var}}\rangle = U_{\text{var}}(\theta_{\text{var}})\,|\phi_{\text{enc}}\rangle$
    Evaluate predicted fields $\tilde{C}_i(x^k, t^k) = \langle\phi_{\text{var}}|\mathcal{O}_i|\phi_{\text{var}}\rangle$
    Compute required spatial and temporal derivatives
  end for
  Loss evaluation
  Compute $\mathcal{L}_{\text{PDE}}, \mathcal{L}_{\text{BC}}, \mathcal{L}_{\text{IC}}$
  $\mathcal{L} \leftarrow \mathcal{L}_{\text{PDE}} + \sum_j \lambda_j \mathcal{L}_{\text{BC},j} + \lambda_{\text{IC}}\mathcal{L}_{\text{IC}}$
  Gradient computation
  Compute $\nabla_{\theta_{\text{emb}}}\mathcal{L}$
  Compute $\nabla_{\theta_{\text{var}}}\mathcal{L}$
  Parameter update
  Update parameters $(\theta_{\text{emb}}, \theta_{\text{var}})$ using the LBFGS optimizer
end while
Output:
Save trained parameters $(\theta^{\star}_{\text{emb}}, \theta^{\star}_{\text{var}})$ and the model.

angles of the single-qubit gates. Figure 1 illustrates the quantum circuit of the solver with an input of 4 qubits and a depth of 3 layers, while Fig. 2 depicts the quantum circuit of the quantum neural networks (QNN) used to train the parameters for the primary VQC circuit.

3.2 Case Study 1: Heat Equation

In this section, we discuss the experimental results of the quantum-assisted learning model applied to the one-dimensional Heat equation, one of the most significant parabolic PDEs in physics. The Heat equation is a partial differential equation that describes the variation in temperature within a given region over time. It stands as one of the most fundamental equations in mathematics, physics, and engineering. Physically, it encapsulates the principle that heat flows from

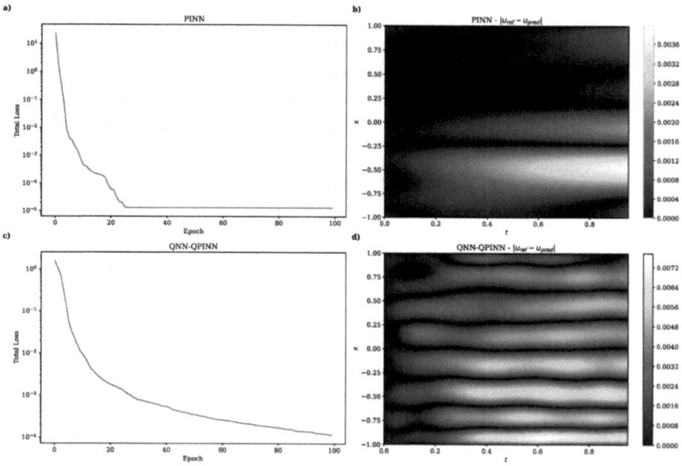

Fig. 4. Loss function and absolute error plots of PINN [5] and QNN-QPINN after training for 100 epochs. The quantum circuit uses 6 qubits and has a VQC depth of 10 layers. The embedding circuit of the QNN-QPINN uses 6 qubits and 5 layers. (a) Loss function of PINN (b), Absolute error between the PINN solution and the RK45 reference solution (c), Loss function of QNN-QPINN (d), Absolute error between the QNN-QPINN solution and the RK45 reference solution.

hotter to colder regions at a rate proportional to the temperature gradient. The equation consists of a derivative term representing the rate of change of temperature over time and a Laplace operator that describes the difference between the temperature at a specific point and its surrounding average. The thermal diffusivity coefficient, μ, depends on the material properties. In this case study, we have selected $\mu = 0.01/\pi$.

$$\frac{\partial u(t,x)}{\partial t} = \left(\frac{0.01}{\pi}\right)\frac{\partial^2 u(t,x)}{\partial x^2} \tag{6}$$

$$t \in [0, 0.95], \quad x \in [-1, 1], \quad u(0,x) = \sin(\pi x)$$

Figure 4 illustrates the loss function results and absolute error during the training process for both the PINN [5] and QNN-QPINN models over 100 epochs. The inset (a) in the upper-left corner for the PINN model shows that the model reaches convergence at approximately 22 epochs, after which it enters a saturation state for the remainder of the training process. The loss function curve exhibits a jagged pattern and a steep slope. In contrast, the loss function curve of the QNN-QPINN model demonstrates a steady and smooth decline throughout the 100 epochs and shows signs of continuing to decrease, implying that the model is still capable of further learning.

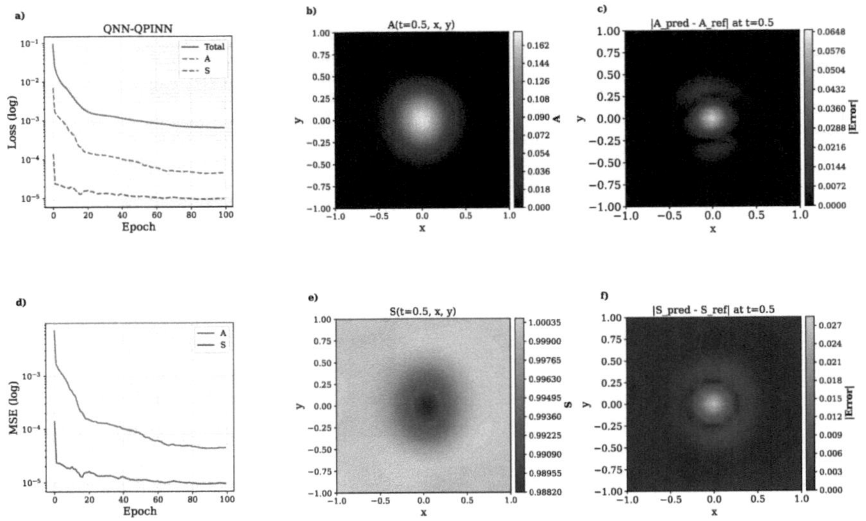

Fig. 5. Loss function plots, model predictions, and absolute error of the QNN-QPINN model compared to RK45. (a) Total loss and loss functions for activator A and substrate S. (d) MSE of activator A and substrate S. (b) and (e) Model predictions for A and S at time t = 0.5. (c) and (f) Absolute error for A and S at t = 0.5.

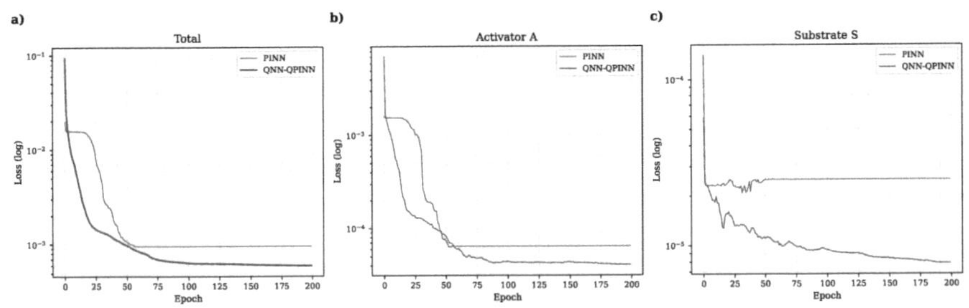

Fig. 6. Performance comparison plots during 200 training epochs between PINN [5] and QNN-QPINN for the two-dimensional reaction-diffusion equation, utilizing 4 qubits with a 10-layer VQC and a 5-layer QNN. (a) Total loss (b) Loss function for A (c) Loss function for S.

3.3 Case Study 2: Reaction-Diffusion Equation

The Reaction-Diffusion (RD) equation represents an evolutionary step beyond the Heat equation. It describes not only how a substance spreads through space but also how different substances interact and transform one another. In nature, this equation serves as a primary tool for explaining the formation of complex patterns, such as tiger stripes, leopard spots, or chemical spirals. These are often referred to as Turing patterns, a system of reacting and diffusing chemicals could spontaneously create such intricate structures. The two-dimensional Reaction-

Diffusion (RD) equation is expressed in its general form as follows:

$$\frac{\partial A}{\partial t}(t,x,y) = D_A\left(\frac{\partial^2 A}{\partial x^2}(t,x,y) + \frac{\partial^2 A}{\partial y^2}(t,x,y)\right) + k_1 A(t,x,y)^2\, S(t,x,y) - k_2 A(t,x,y) \quad (7)$$

$$\frac{\partial S}{\partial t}(t,x,y) = D_S\left(\frac{\partial^2 S}{\partial x^2}(t,x,y) + \frac{\partial^2 S}{\partial y^2}(t,x,y)\right) - k_1 A(t,x,y)^2\, S(t,x,y) + k_3$$

In this specific model, $A(t,x,y)$ represents the activator function, while $S(t,x,y)$ denotes the substrate function. The Laplace operator $\frac{\partial^2 A}{\partial x^2}(t,x,y) + \frac{\partial^2 A}{\partial y^2}(t,x,y)$ and $\frac{\partial^2 S}{\partial x^2}(t,x,y) + \frac{\partial^2 S}{\partial y^2}(t,x,y)$ represents the physical diffusion process. D_A and D_S are the diffusion coefficients for the activator A and substrate S, respectively. The three coefficients k_1, k_2, and k_3 are the reaction rate constants. In this case study, we have selected the parameters as $D_A = 10^{-5}$, $D_S = 2\times10^{-3}$, $k_1 = 1.0$, $k_2 = 1.0$, and $k_3 = 10^{-3}$.

Table 1. Performance comparison between PINN [5] and QNN-QPINN across different numbers of training epochs.

Number of epochs	PINN [5]	QNN-QPINN
100	9.53E−04	6.41E−04
150	9.53E−04	6.17E−04
200	3.82E−04	1.38E−05
250	1.56E−04	1.31E−05

Figure 5 and Fig. 6 illustrate the training results of the QNN-QPINN and provide a performance comparison against a standard PINN model featuring four layers with 32 neurons each [5]. The QNN-QPINN loss function exhibits more effective, smoother convergence across all three metrics: total loss, activator A loss, and substrate S loss. Furthermore, the predicted solutions for A and S at $t = 0.5$ in Fig. 5 show that the QNN-QPINN results are in excellent agreement with those obtained via the RK45 method. Table 1 presents the comparative performance of the PINN and QNN-QPINN models after being trained for 100, 150, 200, and 250 epochs, respectively. The results indicate that the QNN-QPINN consistently yields a lower loss function value compared to the PINN across all training durations.

3.4 Case Study 3: Navier-Stokes Equation

The Navier-Stokes equations are essentially Newton's second law applied to liquids and gases. It indicates that the change in a fluid particle's momentum is due to the forces acting on it, including pressure, viscosity, and external forces. This equation has applications in aircraft design, weather forecasting, and blood flow simulation in the body. This equation is a very complex nonlinear PDE that is

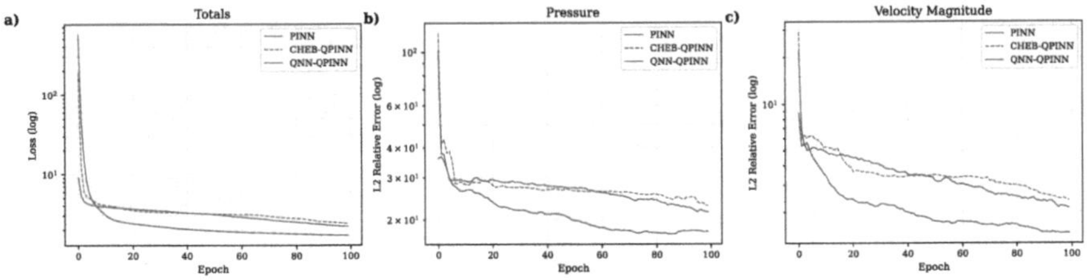

Fig. 7. Performance comparison plots of three models: PINN [5], Chebyshev-QPINN [6], and QNN-QPINN, when solving the Navier-Stokes equations. (a) Total loss (b) Pressure loss function (c) Velocity magnitude loss function.

difficult to solve with conventional solvers. The general form of the Navier-Stokes equation for incompressible fluids is often written as:

$$u\frac{\partial u}{\partial x} + \nu\frac{\partial u}{\partial y} = -\frac{1}{\rho}\frac{\partial p}{\partial x} + \nu(\frac{\partial^2 u}{\partial x^2} + \frac{\partial^2 u}{\partial y^2}) \tag{8}$$

$$u\frac{\partial \nu}{\partial x} + \nu\frac{\partial \nu}{\partial y} = -\frac{1}{\rho}\frac{\partial p}{\partial y} + \nu(\frac{\partial^2 \nu}{\partial x^2} + \frac{\partial^2 \nu}{\partial y^2})$$

$$\frac{\partial u}{\partial x} + \frac{\partial u}{\partial y} = 0$$

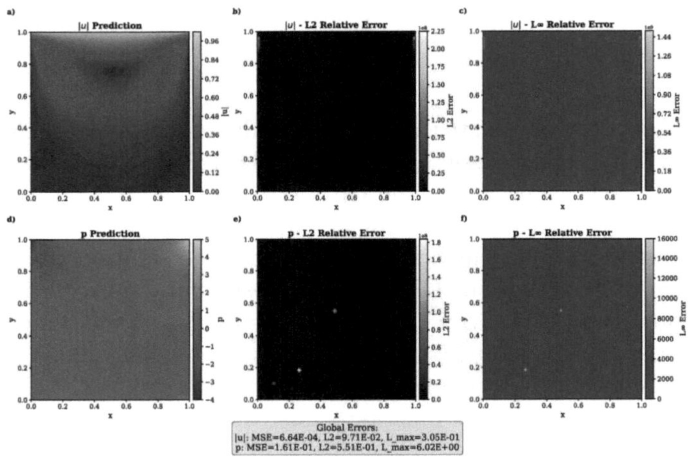

Fig. 8. Inference result plots of the QNN-QPINN model after training for 200 epochs. (a) and (d) Predictions for $|u|$ and p. (b) and (e) L2 relative error for $|u|$ and p. (c) and (f) L_∞ relative error for $|u|$ and p.

This formula is a set of three equations: two momentum equations for pressure and velocity, and one mass conservation law equation. The coefficient ν represents viscosity and ρ represents density. In this experiment, we choose $\nu = 0.1$

and $\rho = 1$, which yields a Reynolds number of 10; that is, the flow is stable and highly viscous, with fluid layers sliding smoothly over each other without vortices or disturbances. To test the effectiveness of learning the rotation angle parameter, we use an additional Chebyshev-QPINN model with a non-trained rotation angle parameter [6]. All three models are trained for 100 epochs. The results in Fig. 7 show that QNN-QPINN achieves the deepest loss reduction across total loss, pressure, and velocity magnitude. To test the quality of the QNN-QPINN model after training and to detect overfitting, we save the model and perform inference on new data.

Figure 8 shows the inference results along with the model's predictions and two metrics: L2 relative error and L infinity. The results show that the model provides solutions that closely match the RK45 reference solutions. This matching advantage is clearly demonstrated in the heatmap and in the error values of the two functions, pressure p and velocity u, in the global error.

4 Conclusions and Future Outlook

In this research, we introduce a QPINN architecture that utilizes a quantum neural network to learn the rotation angle parameters for the main variational quantum circuit of the QPINN. The model's performance is evaluated through three case studies involving partial differential equations: Heat, Reaction-Diffusion, and Navier-Stokes equations. Comparative results with the classical PINN model and the non-trainable parameter model, Chebyshev-QPINN, demonstrate that the QNN-QPINN achieves a superior loss function with significantly lower values and a consistent, smooth reduction without any signs of oscillation. This QNN-QPINN superior performance indicates that the model has learned effectively and does not exhibit signs of overfitting.

One of the primary limitations of QPINN models, in general and specifically the QNN-QPINN, is that training is more computationally intensive than that of classical PINNs. This training overhead stems from the fact that the training process currently relies on simulators to emulate quantum properties on classical hardware. As the number of qubits increases, the Hilbert space grows exponentially, leading to excessive computational resource consumption. However, this computational issue is expected to be fully resolved with the advent of fault-tolerant quantum computers in the near future.

Our study demonstrates the potential of PDE solvers that combine quantum and classical approaches, leveraging the strengths of quantum computing and machine learning in the field of simulation. These QPINN solvers, with their parameter-learning capabilities, are able to solve nonlinear and highly stiff PDEs, providing smoother solutions than conventional classical analytical methods. We will continue to enhance the capabilities of the QNN-QPINN solver by tackling more complex nonlinear PDEs. Concurrently, our research will focus on addressing the barren plateau phenomenon—a significant gradient-based challenge that arises as the quantum circuit depth increases. Mitigating these vanishing gradients is crucial for ensuring the scalability and trainability of our proposed framework in high-dimensional domains.

Data Availability Statement. The source code for this study is available to the corresponding author upon request.

Disclosure of Interests. The authors have no competing interests to declare that are relevant to the content of this article.

References

1. Nielsen, M.A., Chuang, I.L.: Quantum Computation and Quantum Information. Cambridge University Press (2010)
2. LeCun, Y., Bengio, Y., Hinton, G.: Deep learning. Nature **521**(7553), 436–444 (2015)
3. Blechschmidt, J., Ernst, O.G.: Three ways to solve partial differential equations with neural networks–a review. GAMM-Mitteilungen **44**(2), e202100006 (2021)
4. Cuomo, S., Di Cola, V.S., Giampaolo, F., Rozza, G., Raissi, M., Piccialli, F.: Scientific machine learning through physics-informed neural networks: where we are and what's next. J. Sci. Comput. **92**(3), 88 (2022)
5. Raissi, M., Perdikaris, P., Karniadakis, G.E.: Physics-informed neural networks: a deep learning framework for solving forward and inverse problems involving nonlinear partial differential equations. J. Comput. Phys. **378**, 686–707 (2019)
6. Kyriienko, O., Paine, A.E., Elfving, V.E.: Solving nonlinear differential equations with differentiable quantum circuits. Phys. Rev. A **103**(5), 052416 (2021)
7. Cerezo, M., Verdon, G., Huang, H.-Y., Cincio, L., Coles, P.J.: Challenges and opportunities in quantum machine learning. Nature Comput. Sci. **2**(9), 567–576 (2022)
8. Berger, S., Hosters, N., Möller, M.: Trainable embedding quantum physics informed neural networks for solving nonlinear PDEs. Sci. Rep. **15**(1), 18823 (2025)
9. REPACSS. REPACSS: High Performance Computing Center. https://www.repacss.org/. Accessed Mar 2026
10. Paszke, A., et al.: PyTorch (2019). http://pytorch.org. Accessed Mar 2026
11. Bergholm, V., Izaac, J., Schuld, M., Gogolin, C., et al.: PennyLane: automatic differentiation of hybrid quantum-classical computations. arXiv preprint arXiv:1811.04968 (2018)

Applied Linguistic Dynamic Models and Lexical Choices in Mental Health News

Ahu Dereli Dursun[1,2](✉)

[1] Institute of Social Sciences, Communication Studies, Istanbul Bilgi University, Istanbul, Türkiye
adereli@ticaret.edu.tr, ahu.dereli.dursun@bilgiedu.net, ahudereli@yahoo.com
[2] Istanbul Ticaret University, Istanbul, Türkiye

Abstract. Language and lexical choices in media, particularly in mental health news, are critical as they have impact on shaping public perception, understanding of as well as responses to medical information and content. The language and words used in news are significant since these often make a subtle difference in the way readers or viewers perceive the story. This point emphasizes the need to choose the words to be used carefully in news texts so that the content can be understood clearly without bias. The current study analyzes a total of 725 news articles retrieved from six different daily national newspapers published in Türkiye in order to evaluate some aspects of stigmatizing descriptions and / or misleading information regarding mental health problems and people living with mental health disorders. The content in nine news items with a focus on lexical choices and wording is provided as a representative sample to reveal what kind of inaccurate reporting examples exist in the articles analyzed by qualitative and quantitative content-based lexical analysis. The examples provided in the sample reveal that linguistic and lexical choices in mental health news can be stigmatizing, discrediting or labeling; these choices make frames of dangerousness, victimhood and weirdness more salient. The language model proposed in the current study aims to elucidate how robust linguistic structures generated can be adapted to schemes where linguistic features are evaluated by paying attention to individual and societal considerations. This kind of applied linguistic-based approach based on frequency analyses of descriptive statistics regarding practical use of language can direct decision-making power and policy decisions based on benchmarks and standardization guidelines of language use within applicable sensitive, humanizing, pluralistic and holistic frameworks.

Keywords: Computational Linguistics · Applied Linguistics · Lexical Imprecision · Linguistic Dynamism · Media Language · Lexical Choice · Stigmatizing Language · Discrediting Language · Language Education · Content Analysis · Mental Health Discourse · News Media Texts · Situation Determination · Observation Probability · Time-Frequency Statistical Analysis

O. Gervasi et al. (Eds.): ICCSA 2026 Workshops, LNCS 16758, pp. 377–392, 2027.
https://doi.org/10.1007/978-3-032-30497-1_23

1 Introduction

Language and lexical choices in media, particularly in health news, are critical as they have impact on shaping public perception, understanding of as well as responses to medical information and content. The language and words used in news are significant since these often make a subtle difference in the way readers or viewers perceive the story. This point emphasizes the need to choose the words carefully so that the content can be understood clearly without bias or misleading content. Accordingly, lexical choice refers to word or vocabulary that is varied with the particular form or style of the text, personal judgment, cultural or background of the writers [1]. Through lexical or word choice an impression is formed on the side of the readers, so it is an important element that implies the writer's attitudes along with determining how interestingly or accurately the writer communicates his/her ideas [2]. Lexical choice in media signifies the deliberate selection of specific words, phrases and terminology by editors, journalists and reporters to shape meaning, tone and audience perception. This process is a strategic and nonneutral one that reflects organizational bias, preferred ideological framing of events as well as social context. This deliberateness, intention of the producer of the message and dependence on context make the words nonneutral, about which van Dijk states that words are never 'neutral' and the choice of one word over another reveals the writer's ideological bias, political perspective or underlying attitude toward the subject. That language is not neutral but is deeply embedded in power relations and social practices is what is argued by Critical Discourse Analysis (CDA) [3]. Discursive practices refer to the ways discourse is produced, distributed and consumed. In that regard, CDA examines such practices to understand how they contribute to the social norms and structures' formation and maintenance. These point to the important role of context in CDA, referring to the broader social, historical and political contexts in which discourse occurs and influences its production and interpretation. Thus, some scholars emphasize the significance of contextual analysis to understand the way discourse affects and is affected by social relations and power dynamics [4]. The analysis of these practices helps reveal the social functions of language along with its role not only in shaping social identities but also power relations [5]. The role of news media in public health matters is observed to be significant in terms of framing public opinions, raising public awareness, acknowledgment of public health issues and affecting the making of policies [6]. Correspondingly, mental health news coverage is a sensitive and critical issue as media have impact on mental health by reducing stigma and raising awareness regarding mental health problems through providing accurate and empathetic information such as the promotion of help-seeking behaviors and personal stories [7]. On the other hand, the impacts could be seen on the negative side like sensationalizing, exaggerating and/or trivializing issues related to mental health and spreading misinformation [8]. This stance could cause stereotypes to be reinforced and negative emotions like fear, sadness and anger to be triggered. It has often been reported that media contribute to mental illness stigma through the exaggerated, comical and inaccurate images used for portraying individuals with psychiatric disorders as well as providing incorrect information about mental illness [9]. It remains to be a concern that representations in the press are negative disproportionally [10].

The assessment that media portrayals of mental illness have long been recognized as being misleading and stigmatizing despite the campaigns of some advocacy groups to address the issue, the impact on mental health reporting over time was evaluated by a study where a survey which had been done 15 years ago was repeated [11]. Nine UK daily newspapers were surveyed and coded with a schema to analyze the reporting of mental health compared with physical health, and the results of the research demonstrated that more than half of the articles on mental health were negative in tone, 18.5% indicating an association with violence compared with 0.3% of articles on physical health. With regard to representation of mental illness in the UK press, a critical corpus linguistic analysis analyzed what the terms 'mental health' and 'mental illness' referred to along with the way people with mental illness were named and referred to in reports on mental illness [12]. The analysis revealed overlexicalization, emphasizing how lexical items are often used in contexts that fail to inform the public properly, specifically linking mental illness to violent contexts. As suggestions, it was argued that it would be beneficial if journalists and mental health charities make certain changes to the way they write about mental health. In addition, it was suggested that linguistic evidence should be taken into account before preparing guidelines stipulating prescribed linguistic forms for discussing mental illness in the press. Another significant change that could be implemented for journalists would be to more accurately depict the symptoms of mental illness in news articles and ensure that symptoms be contextualized appropriately. One recent work based on computational linguistic-based analyses on newspapers published in Türkiye has revealed that negative descriptions, attributions and connotations regarding people with mental health disorders outnumber the positive ones [13]. Another aim of the study was to analyze whether reporting language on mental health conditions was consistent with the suggestion of the American Psychiatric Association (APA). The results obtained by the study reveal that some lexical choices, particularly certain adjectives and nominalized phrases used in the reporting language, are not in agreement with APA's recommendations, and that news articles often use negative labeling keywords. In another work using qualitative thematic analysis for news articles in Malaysia, three significant themes were identified as follows: people with mental illness have undesirable traits, people with mental illness are a menace and there are risk factors of people with mental illness [14]. The findings of the study indicate that the themes produced were stigmatizing and derogatory towards individuals with mental illness by foregrounding the negative characterization of people with mental illness, naming them as a threat, endangering others.

It has been acknowledged that mass media play a significant role in shaping stigma, particularly among youths. Even though efforts to destigmatize mental health, especially media campaigns, have been put in, it is reported in one research that they have not fully penetrated Latinx and Spanish-language media and that they have not reached consumers either [15]. This lack of reach is said to contribute to high stigma as well as low use of mental health care services among young, diverse and growing Latinx populations. The study projects that knowledge about Latinx media use patterns and depictions of mental health–related content in Latinx and Spanish-language media will help inform effective future antistigma efforts using mass media to reach diverse U.S. Latinx residents, which is an emerging research area with potential to encourage critically required antistigma mental health conversations among communities to facilitate mental health treatment and achieve mental health equity. Regarding positive developments and alternative portrayals stated to be necessary to reduce stigma, some papers note the improvements in tone in mental health reporting. However, evidence suggests that mainstream media coverage of mental health problems is inclined to focus on crime and violence. One paper aimed to compare the content and tone of mainstream TV coverage of mental illness with educational videos made by citizen journalists having mental illness in Canada [16]. The results showed that the citizen journalist videos were more positive and hopeful, concluding that citizen journalism by people with mental illness had the potential to educate the public and reduce stigma. Individuals may rely on media sources about health issues, so the accuracy of the content plays a critical role in health communication. Research shows that detecting false information is difficult as when one encounters new information, he/she tends to focus on understanding the information and deciding what to do as a next step instead of evaluating it on the basis of its accuracy. It also takes effort to make a comparison of new information with what the person already knows. When new information is false but plausible, one can learn it as a fact, and several factors are likely to increase one's susceptibility to misinformation [17]. A related study aimed to explore disinformation about mental health on social media and offer recommendations to mental health professionals who would use social media platforms to make education videos on mental health issues [18]. 1000 TikTok videos from 16 countries concerning 26 mental health topics were analyzed comprehensively. The authors employed a multilayered perceptron algorithm to identify factors predicting disinformation. The results demonstrated the existence of disinformation predominantly in videos concerning mental health, personality disorders, suicide, psychotic disorders, neurodevelopment and treatment. For the first time in literature, data-driven recommendations were presented to mental health providers globally, addressing the current state of disinformation on social media. Societal perceptions are influenced significantly by mental health discourse which has gained prominence in public media. The representation of mental health in news media texts has been analyzed by transformative technologies, one of which is Natural Language Processing (NLP). One study explored the application of NLP techniques in view of the complex connection between media representation and public understanding of mental health, which is stated to require advanced analytical tools [19]. The study revealed some important limitations of NLP techniques when applied to mental health news coverage. These limitations were demonstrated to be significant biases and accuracy issues in sentiment analysis of mental health content across different media platforms. Based on these evaluations, the study provided future directions in NLP for news media and mental health through the recommendations provided for tailored NLP approaches so that researchers, policymakers and media professionals could benefit from. In contrast, one work underlines the strength of an NLP technique along with the use of multifractal methods concerning the digital-based complex media texts as well as accurate classification and categorization of the words within texts in the dataset having been achieved by Bidirectional Encoder Representations from Transformers (BERT) as the related NLP method employed [20]. The analysis results of the work demonstrated that multifractal Bayesian method was useful for constructing the optimal model, generating more accurate results when compared to the other methods in terms of classification and categorization purposes. Large Language Models (LLMs) are stated to demonstrate remarkable performance across various NLP tasks like including text classification, summarization and generation. LLMs are primarily trained on curated datasets which lack human-induced errors, such as typos or variations in word choice, and thus, it is likely that LLMs produce unexpected outputs while processing text with such perturbations which are analyzed in one study with respect to typos and word substitutions using two public datasets. The results of the study indicate that LLMs are sensitive to text perturbations, resulting in variations in generated outputs, impacting their reliability and robustness in real-world applications [21]. As the amount of research in literature reveals, mental health news, media and use of language make up a significant line of research. Yet, the number of studies regarding news media portrayal of people with mental disorders for Türkiye context is relatively limited [22–25]. Thus, the current study aims to provide inputs through its analysis of news articles within an applied linguistic dynamic model framework used for evaluating inaccurate content, stigmatizing descriptions and/or misleading information based on lexical choices present in the news texts regarding mental health and people living with mental health.

The rest of the paper is organized as follows: Sect. 2 provides the materials and methods, while Sect. 3 presents the experimental results and discussion. Section 4 concludes the study with conclusion and future directions.

2 Materials and Methods

2.1 Mental Health Print News Dataset

The dataset of the study is made up of newspaper articles that address mental health problems and people with those problems. The news items were selected based on certain keywords concerning mental disorders. The analyzed newspaper articles had been retrieved from the electronic sites of six daily national newspapers published between 2014–2019 published in Turkish in Türkiye. The total number of news articles in the dataset analyzed is as follows: 725 (*Hürriyet* (n = 218), Sabah (n = 168), *Milliyet* (n = 158), *Sözcü* (n = 110), *Cumhuriyet* (n = 38) and *Posta* (n = 33)). Table 1 presents the breakdown of the news articles by newspaper. The newspapers are popular and highly circulating ones in Türkiye.

Table 1. The corresponding number of newspaper articles by newspapers.

Newspaper	Total number of news articles
Hürriyet	218
Sabah	168
Milliyet	158
Sözcü	110
Cumhuriyet	38
Posta	33

Nine news items from the dataset were chosen as excerpts to provide evidence regarding inaccurate, sensationalizing and stigmatizing reporting as some exemplary cases. Figures 1, 2 and 3 depict them accordingly, with the misleading, inaccurate and stigmatizing language parts indicated in dark red color.

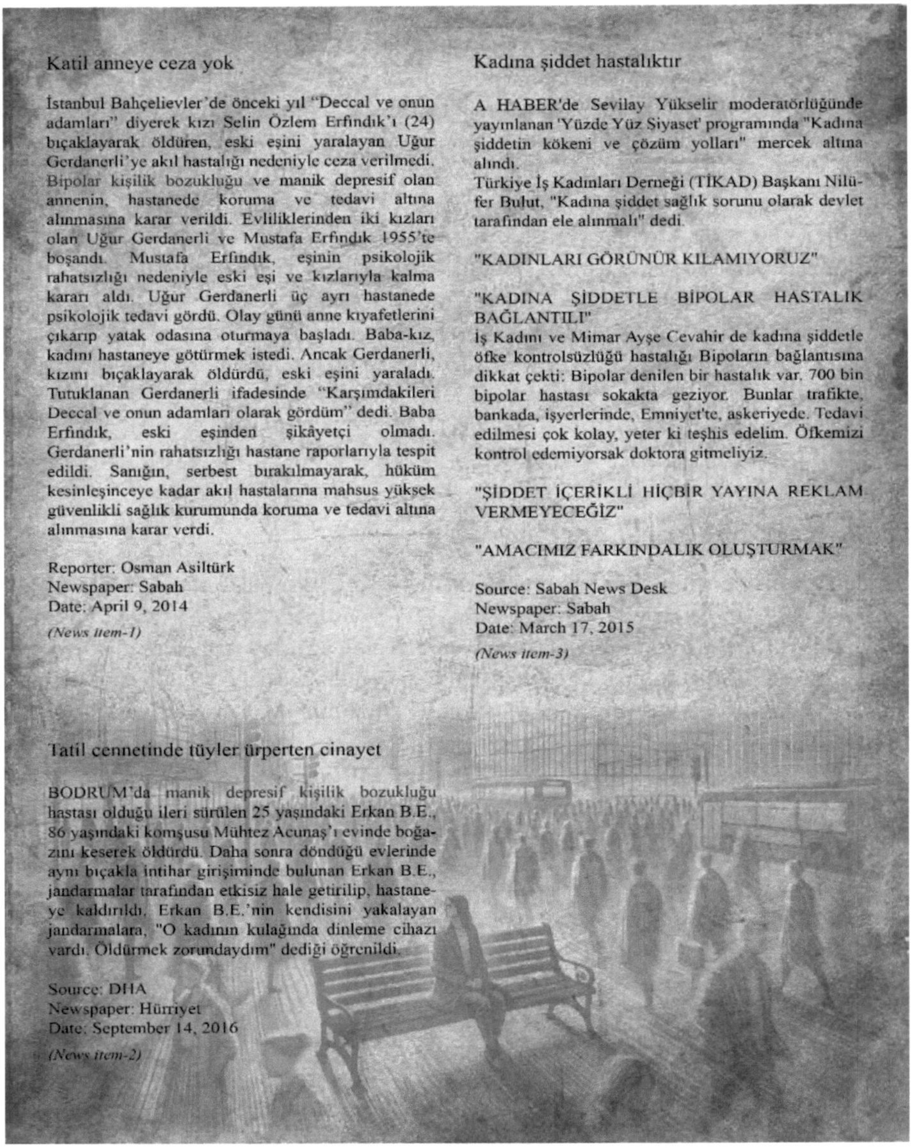

Katil anneye ceza yok

İstanbul Bahçelievler'de önceki yıl "Deccal ve onun adamları" diyerek kızı Selin Özlem Erfındık'ı (24) bıçaklayarak öldüren, eski eşini yaralayan Uğur Gerdanerli'ye akıl hastalığı nedeniyle ceza verilmedi. Bipolar kişilik bozukluğu ve manik depresif olan annenin, hastanede koruma ve tedavi altına alınmasına karar verildi. Evliliklerinden iki kızları olan Uğur Gerdanerli ve Mustafa Erfındık 1955'te boşandı. Mustafa Erfındık, eşinin psikolojik rahatsızlığı nedeniyle eski eşi ve kızlarıyla kalma kararı aldı. Uğur Gerdanerli üç ayrı hastanede psikolojik tedavi gördü. Olay günü anne kıyafetlerini çıkarıp yatak odasına oturmaya başladı. Baba-kız, kadını hastaneye götürmek istedi. Ancak Gerdanerli, kızını bıçaklayarak öldürdü, eski eşini yaraladı. Tutuklanan Gerdanerli ifadesinde "Karşımdakileri Deccal ve onun adamları olarak gördüm" dedi. Baba Erfındık, eski eşinden şikâyetçi olmadı. Gerdanerli'nin rahatsızlığı hastane raporlarıyla tespit edildi. Sanığın, serbest bırakılmayarak, hüküm kesinleşinceye kadar akıl hastalarına mahsus yüksek güvenlikli sağlık kurumunda koruma ve tedavi altına alınmasına karar verdi.

Reporter: Osman Asiltürk
Newspaper: Sabah
Date: April 9, 2014

(News item-1)

Kadına şiddet hastalıktır

A HABER'de Sevilay Yükselir moderatörlüğünde yayınlanan 'Yüzde Yüz Siyaset' programında "Kadına şiddetin kökeni ve çözüm yolları" mercek altına alındı.
Türkiye İş Kadınları Derneği (TİKAD) Başkanı Nilüfer Bulut, "Kadına şiddet sağlık sorunu olarak devlet tarafından ele alınmalı" dedi.

"KADINLARI GÖRÜNÜR KILAMIYORUZ"

"KADINA ŞİDDETLE BİPOLAR HASTALIK BAĞLANTILI"
İş Kadını ve Mimar Ayşe Cevahir de kadına şiddetle öfke kontrolsüzlüğü hastalığı Bipoların bağlantısına dikkat çekti: Bipolar denilen bir hastalık var. 700 bin bipolar hastası sokakta geziyor. Bunlar trafikte, bankada, işyerlerinde, Emniyet'te, askeriyede. Tedavi edilmesi çok kolay, yeter ki teşhis edelim. Öfkemizi kontrol edemiyorsak doktora gitmeliyiz.

"ŞİDDET İÇERİKLİ HİÇBİR YAYINA REKLAM VERMEYECEĞİZ"

"AMACIMIZ FARKINDALIK OLUŞTURMAK"

Source: Sabah News Desk
Newspaper: Sabah
Date: March 17, 2015

(News item-3)

Tatil cennetinde tüyler ürperten cinayet

BODRUM'da manik depresif kişilik bozukluğu hastası olduğu ileri sürülen 25 yaşındaki Erkan B.E., 86 yaşındaki komşusu Mühtez Acunaş'ı evinde boğazını keserek öldürdü. Daha sonra döndüğü evlerinde aynı bıçakla intihar girişiminde bulunan Erkan B.E., jandarmalar tarafından etkisiz hale getirilip, hastaneye kaldırıldı. Erkan B.E.'nin kendisini yakalayan jandarmalara, "O kadının kulağında dinleme cihazı vardı. Öldürmek zorundaydım" dediği öğrenildi.

Source: DHA
Newspaper: Hürriyet
Date: September 14, 2016

(News item-2)

Fig. 1. News items 1, 2 and 3.

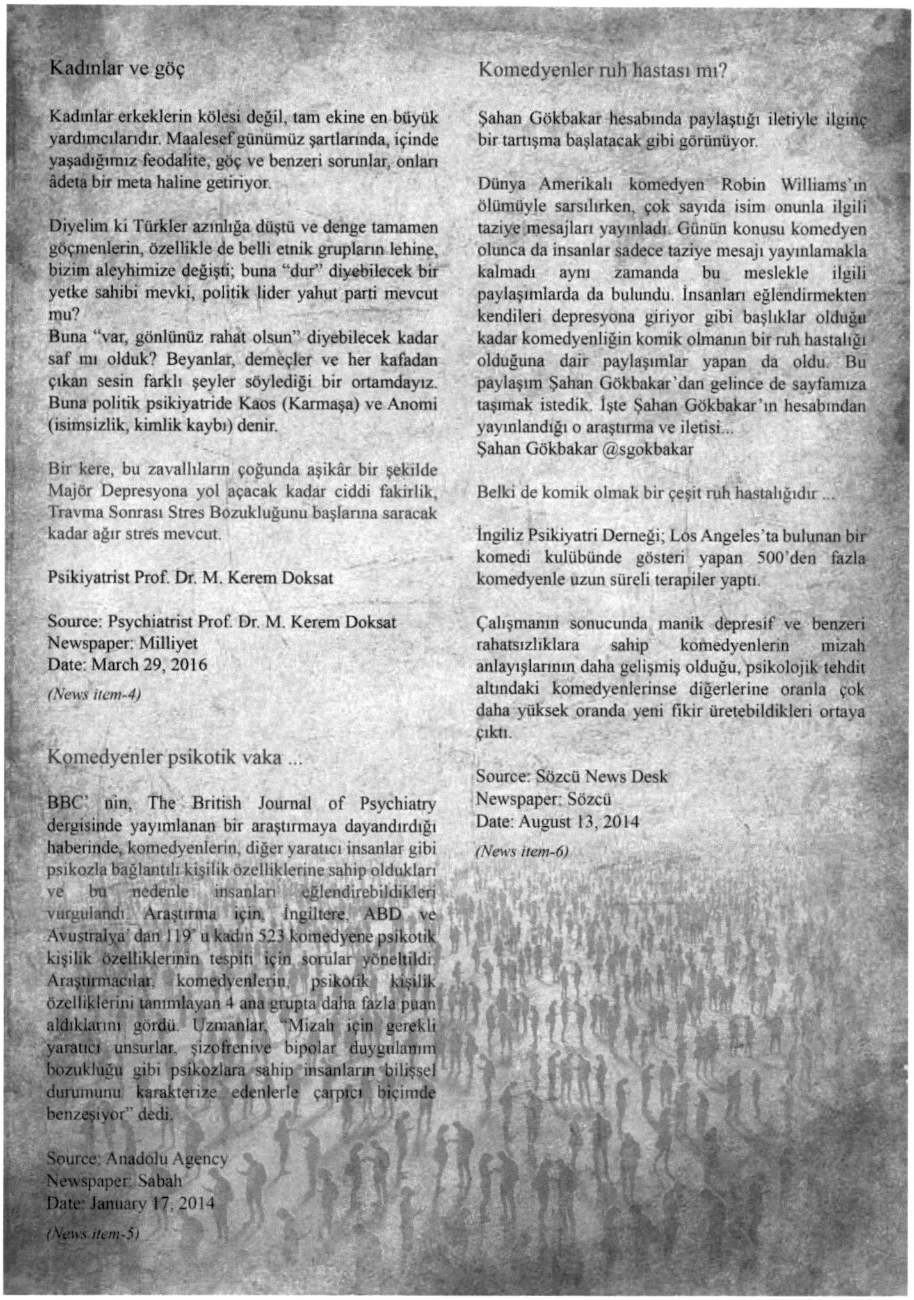

Kadınlar ve göç

Kadınlar erkeklerin kölesi değil, tam ekine en büyük yardımcılarıdır. Maalesef günümüz şartlarında, içinde yaşadığımız feodalite, göç ve benzeri sorunlar, onları âdeta bir meta haline getiriyor.

Diyelim ki Türkler azınlığa düştü ve denge tamamen göçmenlerin, özellikle de belli etnik grupların lehine, bizim aleyhimize değişti; buna "dur" diyebilecek bir yetke sahibi mevki, politik lider yahut parti mevcut mu?
Buna "var, gönlünüz rahat olsun" diyebilecek kadar saf mı olduk? Beyanlar, demeçler ve her kafadan çıkan sesin farklı şeyler söylediği bir ortamdayız. Buna politik psikiyatride Kaos (Karmaşa) ve Anomi (isimsizlik, kimlik kaybı) denir.

Bir kere, bu zavallıların çoğunda aşikâr bir şekilde Majör Depresyona yol açacak kadar ciddi fakirlik, Travma Sonrası Stres Bozukluğunu başlarına saracak kadar ağır stres mevcut.

Psikiyatrist Prof. Dr. M. Kerem Doksat

Source: Psychiatrist Prof. Dr. M. Kerem Doksat
Newspaper: Milliyet
Date: March 29, 2016

(News item-4)

Komedyenler psikotik vaka ...

BBC' nin, The British Journal of Psychiatry dergisinde yayımlanan bir araştırmaya dayandırdığı haberinde, komedyenlerin, diğer yaratıcı insanlar gibi psikozla bağlantılı kişilik özelliklerine sahip oldukları ve bu nedenle insanları eğlendirebildikleri vurgulandı. Araştırma için, İngiltere, ABD ve Avustralya' dan 119' u kadın 523 komedyene psikotik kişilik özelliklerinin tespiti için sorular yöneltildi. Araştırmacılar, komedyenlerin, psikotik kişilik özelliklerini tanımlayan 4 ana grupta daha fazla puan aldıklarını gördü. Uzmanlar, "Mizah için gerekli yaratıcı unsurlar, şizofreniye bipolar duygulanım bozukluğu gibi psikozlara sahip insanların bilişsel durumunu karakterize edenlerle çarpıcı biçimde benzeşiyor" dedi.

Source: Anadolu Agency
Newspaper: Sabah
Date: January 17, 2014

(News item-5)

Komedyenler ruh hastası mı?

Şahan Gökbakar hesabında paylaştığı iletiyle ilginç bir tartışma başlatacak gibi görünüyor.

Dünya Amerikalı komedyen Robin Williams'ın ölümüyle sarsılırken, çok sayıda isim onunla ilgili taziye mesajları yayınladı. Günün konusu komedyen olunca da insanlar sadece taziye mesajı yayınlamakla kalmadı aynı zamanda bu meslekle ilgili paylaşımlarda da bulundu. İnsanları eğlendirmekten kendileri depresyona giriyor gibi başlıklar olduğu kadar komedyenliğin komik olmanın bir ruh hastalığı olduğuna dair paylaşımlar yapan da oldu. Bu paylaşım Şahan Gökbakar'dan gelince de sayfamıza taşımak istedik. İşte Şahan Gökbakar'ın hesabından yayınlandığı o araştırma ve iletisi...
Şahan Gökbakar @sgokbakar

Belki de komik olmak bir çeşit ruh hastalığıdır ...

İngiliz Psikiyatri Derneği; Los Angeles'ta bulunan bir komedi kulübünde gösteri yapan 500'den fazla komedyenle uzun süreli terapiler yaptı.

Çalışmanın sonucunda manik depresif ve benzeri rahatsızlıklara sahip komedyenlerin mizah anlayışlarının daha gelişmiş olduğu, psikolojik tehdit altındaki komedyenlerinse diğerlerine oranla çok daha yüksek oranda yeni fikir üretebildikleri ortaya çıktı.

Source: Sözcü News Desk
Newspaper: Sözcü
Date: August 13, 2014

(News item-6)

Fig. 2. News items 4, 5 and 6.

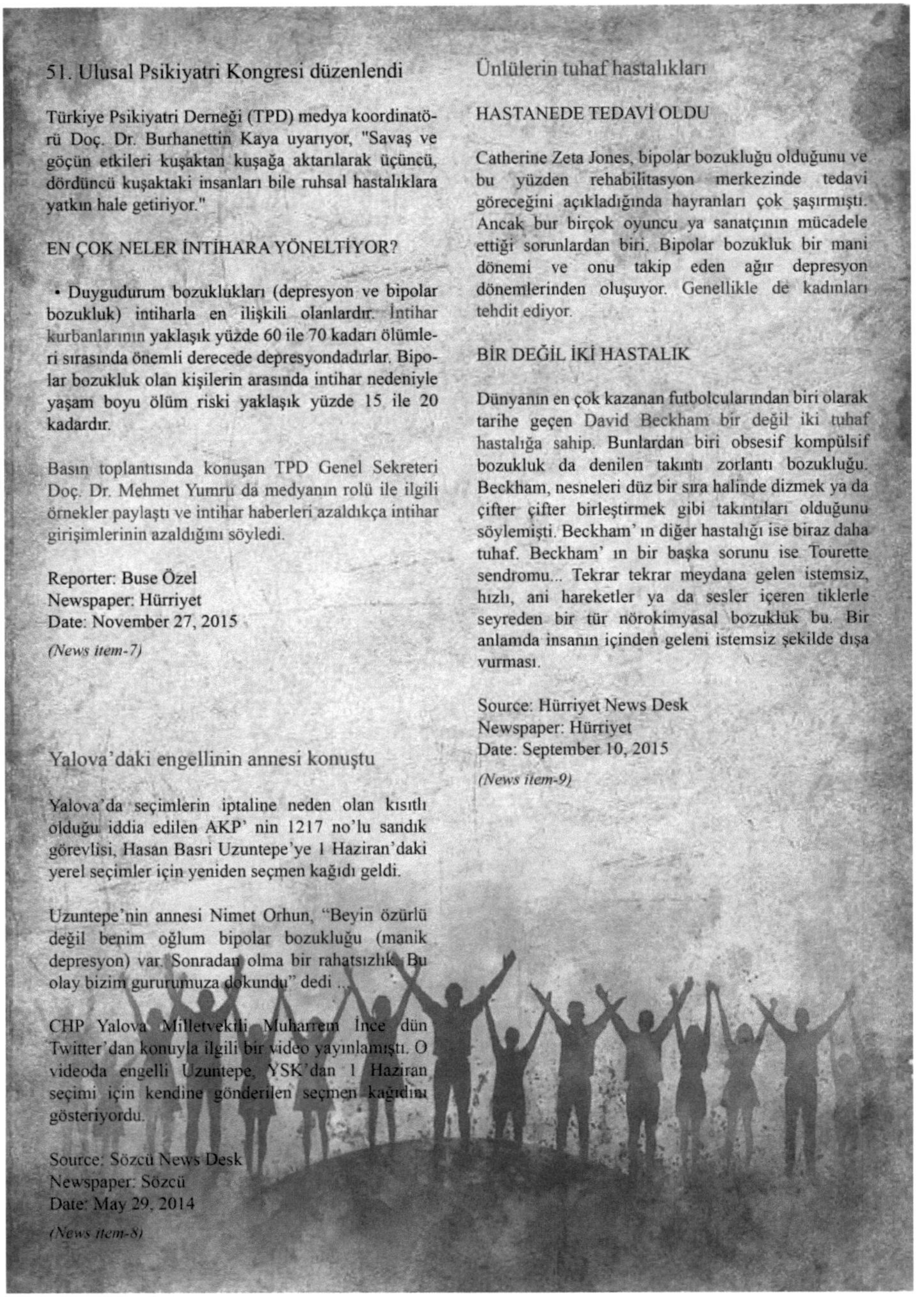

51. Ulusal Psikiyatri Kongresi düzenlendi

Türkiye Psikiyatri Derneği (TPD) medya koordinatörü Doç. Dr. Burhanettin Kaya uyarıyor, "Savaş ve göçün etkileri kuşaktan kuşağa aktarılarak üçüncü, dördüncü kuşaktaki insanları bile ruhsal hastalıklara yatkın hale getiriyor."

EN ÇOK NELER İNTİHARA YÖNELTİYOR?

• Duygudurum bozuklukları (depresyon ve bipolar bozukluk) intiharla en ilişkili olanlardır. İntihar kurbanlarının yaklaşık yüzde 60 ile 70 kadarı ölümleri sırasında önemli derecede depresyondadırlar. Bipolar bozukluk olan kişilerin arasında intihar nedeniyle yaşam boyu ölüm riski yaklaşık yüzde 15 ile 20 kadardır.

Basın toplantısında konuşan TPD Genel Sekreteri Doç. Dr. Mehmet Yumru da medyanın rolü ile ilgili örnekler paylaştı ve intihar haberleri azaldıkça intihar girişimlerinin azaldığını söyledi.

Reporter: Buse Özel
Newspaper: Hürriyet
Date: November 27, 2015

(News item-7)

Yalova'daki engellinin annesi konuştu

Yalova'da seçimlerin iptaline neden olan kısıtlı olduğu iddia edilen AKP' nin 1217 no'lu sandık görevlisi, Hasan Basri Uzuntepe'ye 1 Haziran'daki yerel seçimler için yeniden seçmen kağıdı geldi.

Uzuntepe'nin annesi Nimet Orhun, "Beyin özürlü değil benim oğlum bipolar bozukluğu (manik depresyon) var. Sonradan olma bir rahatsızlık. Bu olay bizim gururumuza dokundu" dedi ...

CHP Yalova Milletvekili Muharrem İnce dün Twitter'dan konuyla ilgili bir video yayınlamıştı. O videoda engelli Uzuntepe, YSK'dan 1 Haziran seçimi için kendine gönderilen seçmen kağıdını gösteriyordu.

Source: Sözcü News Desk
Newspaper: Sözcü
Date: May 29, 2014

(News item-8)

Ünlülerin tuhaf hastalıkları

HASTANEDE TEDAVİ OLDU

Catherine Zeta Jones, bipolar bozukluğu olduğunu ve bu yüzden rehabilitasyon merkezinde tedavi göreceğini açıkladığında hayranları çok şaşırmıştı. Ancak bur birçok oyuncu ya sanatçının mücadele ettiği sorunlardan biri. Bipolar bozukluk bir mani dönemi ve onu takip eden ağır depresyon dönemlerinden oluşuyor. Genellikle de kadınları tehdit ediyor.

BİR DEĞİL İKİ HASTALIK

Dünyanın en çok kazanan futbolcularından biri olarak tarihe geçen David Beckham bir değil iki tuhaf hastalığa sahip. Bunlardan biri obsesif kompülsif bozukluk da denilen takıntı zorlantı bozukluğu. Beckham, nesneleri düz bir sıra halinde dizmek ya da çifter çifter birleştirmek gibi takıntıları olduğunu söylemişti. Beckham' ın diğer hastalığı ise biraz daha tuhaf. Beckham' ın bir başka sorunu ise Tourette sendromu... Tekrar tekrar meydana gelen istemsiz, hızlı, ani hareketler ya da sesler içeren tiklerle seyreden bir tür nörokimyasal bozukluk bu. Bir anlamda insanın içinden geleni istemsiz şekilde dışa vurması.

Source: Hürriyet News Desk
Newspaper: Hürriyet
Date: September 10, 2015

(News item-9)

Fig. 3. News items 7, 8 and 9.

2.2 Methods

Qualitative and quantitative content analysis was carried out for this study to be able to analyze the lexical choices like inaccurate wording, discrediting and stigmatizing language phrases, which are linguistic features, used in the newspaper texts regarding mental health, mental problems and people having mental health conditions. Statistical Package for the Social Sciences (SPSS) software program (IBM SPSS Version 26.0) was utilized for the descriptive, statistical and frequency analyses of the study [26]. The evaluation for achieving these was carried out in two dimensions based on theoretical and quantitative elements, including content analysis regarding the linguistic features and time-frequency statistical analysis, respectively.

2.2.1 Applied Linguistics: Content-Based Lexical Analysis

Applied linguistics aims to identify, examine and provide solutions to real-life problems related to language [27]. Applied linguistics is an interdisciplinary field related to academic areas related to education, communication research, psychology, information science, natural language processing, sociology and anthropology [28]. Applied linguistics involves practical use of language, and in journalism applied linguistics analyzes the use of language, discourse and media practices so that communication quality can be improved and societal impact can be comprehended. Linguistic research is merged with practical journalism training with research areas focusing on news production analysis, multilingual communication, media linguistics, to name some. This combination between applied linguistics and media also helps researchers explore the intersecting aspects of language, communication and technology, addressing the way language is used in digital platforms, journalism, and broadcasting to solve problems related to real-world phenomena. Accordingly, media discourse, multilingual communication, and digital technologies' impact on public communication and social interaction through multimodal analysis belong to the pertinent research areas [29].

From the applied linguistics point of view, the current study employs content-based lexical analysis to address the use of language in the news articles based on the problem that there is a disproportionate amount of negative news content of mental health and people with mental health problems in news media.

2.2.2 Applied Linguistics Dynamic Models: Content and Lexical Analysis by Time- Frequency Statistical Analysis

Time-frequency is used for understanding the distribution of data in the time-frequency domain to detect and separate the components of signals with non-overlapping, compact components, as well as to observe the prevalence of certain categories and identify possible imbalances within the dataset. A time-frequency analysis technique applicable to the nature of the print news dataset has been presented in the study.

An accurate way of classification is a frequency table in which the observed data are clustered into classes. The table which is obtained provides one with the observation number in each class. When an experiment is conducted n times and event A happens f times, the f/n ratio is termed as the relative frequency of event A. Let n increase and f/n relative frequency approaches a limit, this limit is called the probability of A. For n

with big numbers the probability of A is calculated through f/n. For known causes, it signifies the frequency definition of probability [30].

$Relative, Frequency = Frequency\ of\ a\ particular\ event/Sample\ size$

The following steps are followed to prepare the frequency table:

1st step: The number of observations is identified. n denotes the number of observation ($50 \leq n$ is preferred).

2nd step: Maximum and minimum values are found. Range is obtained when the difference between them is calculated.

$range = max - min$

3rd step: The number of classes is found.

$\sqrt{n} \leq k, \ (k = integer)$

$classnumber = k$ [30].

3 Experimental Results and Discussion

The current study has analyzed a total of 725 news articles retrieved from six different daily national newspapers published in Turkish language in Türkiye between 2014–2019 to evaluate inaccurate content, stigmatizing language, passivity, victimization, discrediting language and/or misleading information along with misdescriptions and category mistakes regarding mental health problems and people living with mental health disorders. Based on the content analysis and frequency analysis results, it was found that the highest inaccurate or misleading content was in *Sabah* ($n = 13$). This was followed by *Milliyet* ($n = 8$), *Hürriyet* ($n = 6$) and *Sözcü* ($n = 5$). *Cumhuriyet* ($n = 2$) and *Posta* ($n = 1$) had the lowest number of news articles with inaccurate or misleading content. These results based on computational linguistic analyses by the newspapers in terms of inaccurate or misleading content are depicted in Fig. 4.

	Newspaper	Inaccurate / Misleading Content
0	Cumhuriyet	2
1	Hürriyet	6
2	Milliyet	8
3	Posta	1
4	Sabah	13
5	Sözcü	5

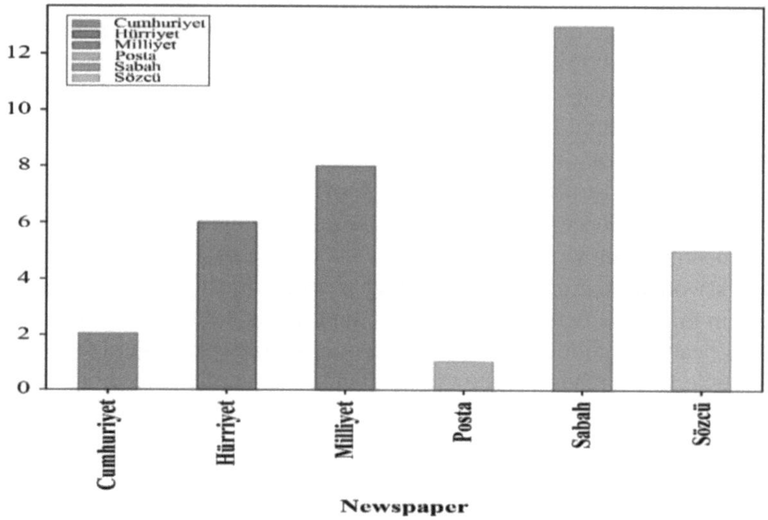

Fig. 4. Inaccurate/Misleading content based on frequency analysis by the newspapers.

The content in nine news items is provided as representative sample to reveal what kind of inaccurate and/or misleading reporting examples exist in the articles analyzed (see Figs. 1, 2, 3 provided in 2.1.). The subsequent parts of the study provide the interpretation of these examples from the selected newspaper articles in line with the related theoretical aspects.

The first two news items illustrated in Fig. 1 contain a factual inaccuracy and category mistake regarding bipolar disorder. Bipolar disorder is a mood or affective disorder with a distinct period of abnormally and persistently elevated, expansive or irritable mood and abnormally and persistently increased goal-directed activity or energy during manic episode(s) [31]. Yet, the disorder has been inaccurately described as 'bipolar personality disorder' in news item-1 [32] and 'manic depressive personality disorder' in news item-2 [33] (those parts are indicated in dark red in Fig. 1). Such taxonomic category errors in terminology could lead to real-world misinformation as a negative outcome.

Framing in communication theory, as put forth by Entman, describes the process where particular aspects of an issue are emphasized, while others are excluded, which is essential for analyzing how a story is told [34]. It is common to find the dangerousness frame in media while framing mental illness from a specific perspective, linking the illness to violence, crime or menace. Research reports that negative presentations of psychotic and affective disorders prevail in the printed media in the United States, Canada and the United Kingdom, with the most frequent topics of articles being violence and dangerousness concerning people with mental illness toward other people [35–37]. For

Central Europe, a study found that the proportion of the articles that depicted psychiatric disorders together with either self- or other-directed aggressive behavior was 31.2%, the vast majority of articles presented people with mental illness as perpetrators, and these articles were more often coded as stigmatizing [38]. Thus, stigma comes to the foreground as another related theory, developed by Goffman who defined stigma as a profoundly discrediting attribute reducing a person from a whole and usual individual to a discounted one [39]. With regard to media, there is another concept named structural stigma which is formed by sociopolitical forces. This kind of stigma represents policies of government and private institutions that limit the opportunities of the groups that are stigmatized. Structural stigma and discrimination occur when an institution like a newspaper, rather than an individual, promulgates stigmatizing messages about mental illness. In a study on structural stigma, 39% of the stories were stated to focus on dangerousness and violence [40]. News item-3 from the sample of this study, illustrated in Fig. 1, is concerned with violence against women, but the article includes the comments of a businesswoman and architect regarding people with bipolar disorder [41]. The inaccuracy in this news item is manifold: the first one is the inclusion of a non-expert on a mental health condition, and the second one is the stigmatizing language used in the news article which reads as follows: "…There is a disorder named bipolar. 700.000 bipolar patients wander in the streets. These are at banks, in traffic, police enforcement, military. It is very easy to treat; the only thing required for us is to diagnose. If we cannot control our anger, we should see a doctor." Grammatically, the use of demonstrative pronoun 'these' is labeling and an example of discrediting language exists, which refers to the use of words or phrases designed to weaken a person's or a group's reputation. The lack of reference for the statistical figure provided for the number of people with bipolar disorder seems to be another problematic aspect of this news item. The other problem is related to dangerousness frame, by stating that the bipolar patients wander in the streets and they are in certain institutions. One more important point to point out could be the trivialization of the situation by stating that the treatment of the disorder is easy. Treatment processes may differ from person to person and multiple factors may play a role in the success of treatment. Stating a comment like "the treatment is easy" is a misleading statement. Finally, the disorder is associated with anger, and all these comments are made by a person who is not a professional in medicine, psychiatry or psychology.

The news item mentioned above includes the comments of a non-expert. The next news item about the effects of immigration on women includes the remarks of a psychiatrist, yet it happens to be problematic due to the labeling and use of derogatory language. News item-4 (Fig. 2) reads as follows: "…For one thing, most of these poor ones have poverty severe enough to evidently lead to major depression besides stress heavy enough to inflict post-traumatic stress disorder upon them…" [42]. Referring to refugees that have the potential of developing major depression due to having experienced severe life conditions as 'poor ones' is an example of a problematic discourse of victimization and disempowerment. The labeling of the event by selecting some aspects of perceived reality and making them more salient in the text is framing, which is the victim framing by using 'poor ones' in this news item. In addition, labeling, stereotyping and othering lead to a loss of status and discrimination in public discourse. This is because there are many stigmatized situations, and stigmatizing processes can affect multiple domains of people's lives. As a result, stigmatization probably has a dramatic bearing on the distribution of life chances in areas such as criminal involvement, financial status, housing, health, and life itself [43]. Another example of labeling is observed in news item-8 (Fig. 3) which has the headline of "the mother of the disabled in Yalova has spoken" [44]. The problematic aspect in this news item is turning the individual into "labeled object" by referring to the boy with bipolar disorder as "the disabled", which also reflects a reductionistic thinking and devaluation. This stigmatizing phrase as an attribute is discrediting by reducing a person "from a whole person to a discounted one", forcing the person into a rigid and devalued category [39]. News item-7, which is about the organization of the 51st National Psychiatry congress, also involves victim framing and passivity since those who committed suicide are referred to as "suicide victims" [45] (Fig. 3). This kind of wording with the noun choice "victim" suggests medical passivity due to the fact that the person is portrayed as a passive "victim" or "sufferer" rather than an agent in their own recovery. As a result, the focus is on tragedy and hopelessness rather than on recovery and management.

The last point to discuss based on the text analyses is sensationalizing and foregrounding the weirdness and bizarreness frame. News item-5 [46] states the headline as "Comedians are psychotic cases", whereas news item-6 [47] asks the question "Are comedians mentally ill?" (Fig. 2). The headline of the former news article is misleading, which could cause an association in the reader's mind about comedians and shifting the sensational aspect of the "mentally ill" toward a popular group, namely comedians. Finally, news item-9, with the headline "Weird illnesses of celebrities" describes the famous footballer David Beckham's obsessive compulsive disorder as 'weird' [48] (Fig. 3). This news item also reflects a stigmatizing frame since the "strangeness" of the behavior is highlighted. In fact, anyone could have this kind of disorder in his / her lifetime.

As the provided examples show, language and lexical choices in mental health news may be stigmatizing, discrediting or labeling, making dangerousness, victim and weirdness frames more salient.

4 Conclusion and Future Directions

Word choice needs to be considered carefully while writing about mental health, which can help reduce stigma in line with the suggestions posited by APA [49]. This could include focusing on the person rather than on the condition as the mental health condition is only one aspect of an individual's life. It has often been reported that media may contribute to mental illness stigma through the exaggerated, comical and inaccurate images used for portraying individuals with psychiatric disorders as well as providing incorrect information about mental illness [9]. The findings of the current study are in line with these considerations since the representative sample revealed that linguistic and lexical choices in mental health news can be stigmatizing, discrediting or labeling besides the salient frames of dangerousness, victimhood, passivity and weirdness. The language model and linguistic structure proposed in the current study can be used for standardization guidelines of language use within responsible, sensitive, humanizing, pluralistic and holistic frameworks. It can be suggested that linguistic evidence be taken into account before preparing guidelines stipulating prescribed linguistic forms for discussing mental problems in the press. This related aim can further be steered toward other genres and styles of language used in different disciplines with comparative analyses, including education, finance, history, political science, and so forth.

References

1. Van Dijk, T.A.: Racism and the Press. Routledge, London (2015)
2. Das, A.: Lexical choice and critical discourse analysis of language bias in media. J. English Literat. **2**(1), (2023)
3. Fairclough, N.: Critical Discourse Analysis: The Critical Study of Language. Longman, London (1995)
4. Wodak, R., Meyer, M.: Methods of Critical Discourse Analysis. SAGE Publications, London (2009)
5. Gee, J.P.: An Introduction to Discourse Analysis: Theory and Method. Routledge, New York (2025)
6. Zolnoori, M., et al.: Mining news media for understanding public health concerns. J. Clin. Transl. Sci. **5**(1), e1 (2021)
7. Stuart, H.: Reducing the stigma of mental illness. Global Mental Health **3**, e17 (2016)
8. Srivastava, K., Chaudhury, S., Bhat, P.S., Mujawar, S.: Media and mental health. Ind. Psych. J. **27**(1), 1–5 (2018)
9. Wahl, O.F.: Media Madness: Public Images of Mental Illness. Rutgers University Press, Piscataway (1995)
10. Bowen, M., Lovell, A.: Representations of mental health disorders in print media. British J. Mental Health Nurs. **2**(4), 198–202 (2013)
11. Chen, M., Lawrie, S.: Newspaper depictions of mental and physical health. BJPsych Bull. **41**(6), 308–313 (2017)
12. Price, H.: The discursive construction of mental illness in UK newspapers (1984–2014): A Critical Corpus Linguistic Analysis. Doctoral dissertation, University of Huddersfield (2020)
13. Dursun, A. D.: Computational linguistics and media news: linguistic features and lexical choices with time-frequency statistical analysis. In: International Conference on Computational Science and Its Applications, pp. 226–242. Springer Nature Switzerland, Cham (2025)
14. Mohd Ali, S.M., Wan Adnan, W.N.A., Wan Fakhruddin, W.F.W., Azizan, E.A.: thematic analysis of malaysian online news on people living with mental illness. In: European Proceedings of Educational Sciences (2025)
15. DuPont-Reyes, M.J.: Leveraging Latinx and Spanish-language media to achieve mental health equity. Psych. Serv. **73**(7), 823–826 (2022)
16. Carmichael, V., Adamson, G., Sitter, K.C., Whitley, R.: Media coverage of mental illness: a comparison of citizen journalism vs. professional journalism portrayals. J. Mental Health **28**(5), 520–526 (2019)
17. Van der Linden, S., et al.: Using psychological science to understand and fight health misinformation: an APA consensus statement. Am. Psychol. (2025)
18. Hudon, A., et al.: Navigating the maze of social media disinformation on psychiatric illness and charting paths to reliable information for mental health professionals: observational study of TikTok videos. J. Med. Internet Res. **27**, e64225 (2025)

19. Köckritz, J., İlgen, B., Cohrdes, C., Hattab, G.: Current applications and future directions in natural language processing for news media and mental health. Sci. Rep. **15**(1), 32532 (2025)
20. Karaca, Y., Zhang, Y.D., Dursun, A.D., Wang, S.H.: Multifractal complexity analysis-based dynamic media text categorization models by natural language processing with BERT. In: Multi-Chaos, Fractal and Multi-fractional Artificial Intelligence of Different Complex Systems, pp. 95–115. Academic Press (2022)
21. Alahmari, S.S., Hall, L., Mouton, P.R., Goldgof, D.: Large language models robustness against perturbation. Sci. Reports (2025)
22. Becerikli, S., Bozkurt, N.: Media portrayals of people with mental disorders: a research on journalism ethics in Turkey. In: Can, C., Kilimci, A. (eds.) Social Sciences and Humanities, pp. 139–167. Detay Yayincilik, Ankara (2016)
23. Boke, O., Aker, S., Aker, A.A., Sarısoy, G.: Schizophrenia in Turkish newspapers: retrospective scanning study. Soc. Psychiatry Psychiatr. Epidemiol. **42**, 457–461 (2007)
24. Aci, O.S., Ciydem, E., Bilgin, H., Ozaslan, Z., Tek, S.: Turkish newspaper articles mentioning people with mental illness: a retrospective study. Int. J. Soc. Psych. **66**(3), 215–224 (2020)
25. Bilkay, H.İ, Yaman, Ö., Gürhan, N., Yilmaz-Bingöl, T.: A study on the representation of mental disorders in Turkish newspapers. J. Ment. Health **33**(2), 185–192 (2024)
26. IBM Corp.: IBM SPSS Statistics for Windows, Version 26.0. IBM Corp, Armonk, NY (2019)
27. Peniro, R., Cyntas, J.: Applied linguistics theory and application. Linguist. Cult. Rev. **3**(1), 1–13 (2019)
28. Davies, A.: An Introduction to Applied Linguistics. Edinburgh University Press, Edinburgh (2005)
29. Sain, Z.H., Ulyani, M.: Exploring the Intersection of Applied Linguistics, Digital Translation, and Global Communication in Multilingual and Multicultural Contexts (2025)
30. Gómez, P.C.: Statistical Methods in Language and Linguistic Research, pp. 1–273. Equinox, London (2013)
31. American Psychiatric Association: Diagnostic and Statistical Manual of Mental Disorders, 5th edn. APA, Washington, DC (2013)
32. Asiltürk, O.: Katil anneye ceza yok. https://www.sabah.com.tr/gundem/2014/04/09/katil-anneye-ceza-yok. Accessed 17 March 2026
33. Hürriyet: Tatil cennetinde tüyler ürperten cinayet, https://www.hurriyet.com.tr/galeri-tatil-cennetinde-tuyler-urperten-cinayet-40223651/1. Accessed 17 March 2026
34. Entman, R.M.: Framing: toward clarification of a fractured paradigm. J. Commun. **43**(4), 51–58 (1993)
35. Coverdale, J., Nairn, R., Claasen, D.: Depictions of mental illness in print media: a prospective national sample. Aust. New Zeal. J. Psychiatr. **36**, 697–700 (2002)
36. Ward, G.: Making Headlines. Mental health and the national press. Health Education Authority, London (1997)
37. Olstead, R.: Contesting the text: canadian media depictions of the conflation of mental illness and criminality. Sociol. Health Illn. **24**, 621–643 (2002)
38. Nawka, A., Rukavina, T.V., Nawková, L., Jovanović, N., Brborović, O., Raboch, J.: Psychiatric disorders and aggression in the printed media: is there a link? A central European perpective. BMC Psych. **12**(1), 19 (2012)
39. Goffman, E.: Stigma: notes on the management of spoiled identity. Postgrad. Med. J. **45**(527), 642 (1969)
40. Corrigan, P.W., Watson, A.C., Gracia, G., Slopen, N., Rasinski, K., Hall, L.L.: Newspaper stories as measures of structural stigma. Psych. Serv. **56**(5), 551–556 (2005)
41. Sabah: Kadına şiddet hastalıktır. https://www.sabah.com.tr/aktuel/2015/03/17/kadina-siddet-hastaliktir. Accessed 27 March 2026
42. Milliyet: Kadınlar ve göç. https://www.milliyet.com.tr/pembenar/kadinlar-ve-goc-2217801. Accessed 25 March 2026

43. Link, B.G., Phelan, J.C.: Conceptualizing stigma. Ann. Rev. Sociol. **27**, 363–385 (2001)
44. Sozcu: Yalova'daki engellinin annesi konuştu. https://www.sozcu.com.tr/2014/gundem/yalovadaki-engellinin-annesi-konustu-520432/ Accessed 24 March 2026
45. Özel, B.: 51. Ulusal Psikiyatri Kongresi düzenlendi. Hürriyet. https://www.hurriyet.com.tr/kelebek/saglik/51-ulusal-psikiyatri-kongresi-duzenlendi-40019756 Accessed 13 March 2026
46. AA: Komedyenler psikotik vaka. Sabah. https://www.sabah.com.tr/dunya/komedyenler-psikotik-vaka-2678238 Accessed 4 March 2026
47. Sözcü: Komedyenler ruh hastası mı? https://www.sozcu.com.tr/2014/magazin/komedyenler-ruh-hastasi-mi-576613/ Accessed 4 March 2026
48. Hürriyet: Ünlülerin tuhaf hastalıkları. https://www.hurriyet.com.tr/kelebek/magazin/unlulerin-tuhaf-hastaliklari-30036632. Accessed 4 March 2026
49. American Psychiatric Association: Words matter: Reporting on mental health conditions (2015)

Intermarket Analysis: Influence of Brent Technical Indicators Using ARIMAX Modeling for Improving WTI Crude Oil Price Forecasting

Suhad A. Yousif[1], Nadia M. G. Al-Saidi[2], Suzan J. Obaiys[3], Redha A. Redha[4], and Nur Amalina Binti Jamaludin[5](✉)

[1] Department of Computer Science, Al-Nahrain University, Baghdad, Iraq
suhad.a.yousif@nahrainuniv.edu.iq
[2] Department of Applied Sciences, University of Technology, 10066 Baghdad, Iraq
nadia.m.ghanim@uotechnology.edu.iq
[3] Department of Computer System & Technology, Faculty of Computer Science and Information Technology, Universiti Malaya, 50603 Kuala Lumpur, Malaysia
[4] State Organization for Marketing of Oil (SOMO), Bagdad, Iraq
redhaali18@gmail.com
[5] Department of Mathematics, Centre of Foundation Studies, National Defence University of Malaysia, Kuala Lumpur, Malaysia
suzan@um.edu.my

Abstract. The task of predicting crude oil prices is of great importance but is also highly demanding due to the economic ramifications associated with these prices and their intricate, non-linear characteristics. We introduce a new method which utilizes technical indicators from various oil benchmarks, specifically Brent crude, to forecast daily prices of WTI crude oil, acknowledging the potential of this integration. Through the utilization of the ARIMAX model, which integrates exogenous factors such as Brent crude technical indicators, In this study, we introduce a new model for price prediction that exhibits superior performance compared to conventional methods such as Artificial Neural Networks (ANN) and Long Short-Term Memory (LSTM) models. The performance measures, namely Root Mean Square Error (RMSE) with a value of 2.9148, Mean Absolute Error (MAE) with a value of 2.3166, and Mean Absolute Percentage Error (MAPE) with a value of 3.971, not only serve as a validation for our model but also indicate its superiority over other models frequently mentioned in the existing literature. These models will be thoroughly examined and debated. This study not only introduces a new forecasting methodology but also demonstrates its potential applicability in several economic sectors that are impacted by fluctuations in oil prices.

Keywords: ARIMAX · Auto ARIMA · Technical Indicators · Intermarket Analysis · WTI · Brent · Forecasting

O. Gervasi et al. (Eds.): ICCSA 2026 Workshops, LNCS 16758, pp. 393–411, 2027.
https://doi.org/10.1007/978-3-032-30497-1_24

1 Introduction

Oil wells extract crude oil, a combination of petroleum liquids and gases, a crucial energy source for manufacturing a wide range of products [8]. Because oil is one of the world's key energy sources, crude oil prices significantly impact the global economy and security. Furthermore, since crude oil accounts for a substantial proportion of the exports of certain nations, a sharp price change can have serious economic ramifications, with lower crude oil prices resulting in lower economic activity [14].

Price is influenced by Many factors, such as supply and demand dynamics, stock levels, weather conditions, political influences, and other relevant variables, which have a significant role in affecting outcomes. Unexpected events; these factors cause significant oil price fluctuation, which causes problems for business leaders and policymakers. As a result, crude oil price forecasting is an interesting field [21]. Two of the world's most important crude oil types are the West Texas Intermediate (WTI) and Brent Crude oil. WTI crude oil is refined primarily in the Midwest and Gulf Coast regions of the United States of America. It is mainly supplied to the North American market, while Brent crude oil is sourced from the North Sea and is used mainly by Europe [12].

Several studies on crude oil time-series forecasting have been conducted [1,2]. These studies assume that future data values are proportionate to present and past data values. However, it is important to note that numerous real-world time series datasets exhibit intricate nonlinear, seasonal, and non-stationary patterns, which pose significant challenges for conventional machine learning methods in terms of capturing and modelling these patterns. One instance of a conventional forecasting technique is the utilization of autoregressive integrated moving average (ARIMA) models to generate precise forecasts in the event of price stability [28].

Time-series data, such as stock market statistics, do not display seasonal patterns, although they may demonstrate fluctuating levels of volatility. During the COVID-19 period, there has been significant volatility in crude oil prices [17]. Numerous empirical studies have recently exposed the nonlinear character of economic and financial data, demonstrating that standard methodologies cannot successfully analyze the complex nonlinear dynamics at hand [10].

Artificial Neural Networks (ANNs) are one of the most extensively utilized nonlinear time series modelling techniques to capture the complex nonlinear properties of crude oil price movements, one example of which is long short-term memory (LSTM) [9]. The disadvantage of utilizing LSTM is that it needs much tuning to acquire the optimal set of parameters. It is sometimes used with one of the optimizer methods, such as Adam optimizers. Adam calculates multiple learning rates in an adaptive learning system depending on various criteria [18]. Thus, if the time-series data are extensive, they may require more CPU time. Additionally, ANNs models frequently suffer from local minima and overfitting issues [14].

This research aims to get accurate results using a light model by exploiting strong interrelationships between two oil market benchmarks [8], and Also to illustrate the impact of technical indicators extracted from the Brent dataset on forecasts WTI dataset. By exploiting strong interrelationships between two oil market benchmarks, this research contributes by transforming the traditional time series model from capturing simple transform patterns to capturing volatility patterns. The utilization of a specific collection of technical indicators derived from the Brent crude oil price as an exogenous variable was used to achieve this outcome within the ARIMA model. Over ANN, ARIMAX, with technical indicators, can be less complicated since it does not require the dataset to be normalized, the number of hidden variables to be determined, or the parameters to be hyperfine-tuned to capture nonlinearity. The result is similar to the ANN prediction.

The first section of this paper introduces the subject. Then, the related works are discussed in Sect. 2. Then, the methodology and the central concept of the proposed algorithm are described in Sect. 3. Next, in Sect. 4, the results of the experimental setup for three case studies are illustrated, followed by the conclusion Sect. 5.

2 Related Work

Crude oil price forecasting has evolved from classical time-series modeling toward hybrid learning frameworks that incorporate nonlinear relationships and engineered market descriptors. Early work relied on Box–Jenkins style modeling to capture linear temporal dependence and seasonality, typically using ARIMA-family models and their variants for short-horizon prediction [1,23]. Subsequent studies extended these baselines by improving preprocessing, stationarity handling, and error evaluation for energy price series [10]. While these approaches are computationally efficient and interpretable, their performance can degrade when market dynamics shift, or when the series exhibits nonlinear behavior and volatility clustering.

To address these limitations, researchers increasingly adopted machine learning methods that can model nonlinear patterns from historical sequences. Support vector machines and support vector regression (SVR) have been widely explored for commodity forecasting because they can handle nonlinear regression with controlled model capacity [27,33]. In parallel, deep learning gained attention for learning representations directly from price history; for example, convolutional and recurrent architectures have been evaluated for crude oil forecasting and often report improvements under certain regimes [14,16]. However, these models typically require extensive tuning and computational resources, which can limit rapid retraining in operational environments.

Another important direction is feature engineering and the use of exogenous drivers. Several studies report that integrating external variables (macroeconomic factors, correlated markets, or engineered technical indicators) improves forecast stability and generalization [7,15,26]. Review and survey studies similarly emphasize that hybridization and feature design are central determinants of forecasting performance across energy markets [5,20].

Building on this trajectory, the authors demonstrated that SVR combined with technical indicators can improve crude oil price forecasting by leveraging indicator-based features as informative predictors [29]. The present paper extends this idea by adopting an intermarket perspective: instead of extracting indicators from the target series alone, technical indicators are generated from a related benchmark (Brent) and used as exogenous variables to strengthen WTI forecasting within ARIMAX and SVR settings. This intermarket feature-transfer design differentiates our work from (i) pure ARIMA/SVR approaches that use only WTI history, and (ii) deep learning approaches that replace interpretability with complex architectures. Our contribution is to show that carefully selected Brent-derived indicators (via correlation filtering) can deliver strong forecasting improvements with low computational cost and clear interpretability.

3 Proposed Methodology

The proposed model is illustrated in Fig. 1. It consists of four main stages, starting from data preprocessing and ending with forecasting evaluation.

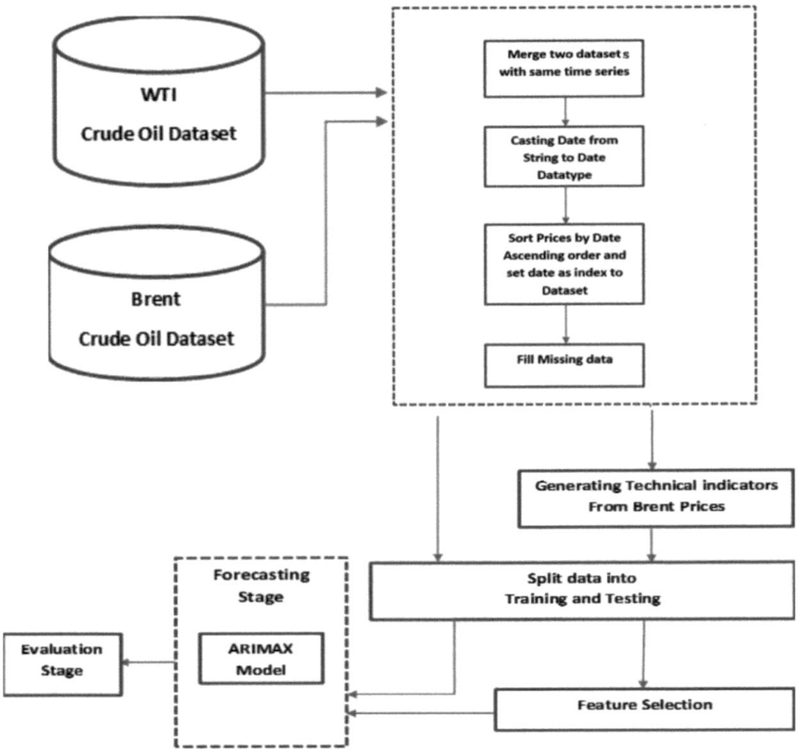

Fig. 1. Steps of the proposed methodology.

3.1 Dataset and Preprocessing

There are several crude oil markets around the world. The dataset in this study originates from the US Energy Information Administration, a major online data repository for energy statistics. The daily historical WTI and Brent Oil prices from January 1, 1988, through December 31, 2019, were downloaded as a CSV file containing only dates and pricing, as shown in Table 1 and Table 2.

Table 1. The daily time series of WTI crude oil prices

Date	Price
4-Jan-16	36.28
5-Jan-16	35.56
6-Jan-16	33.89
7-Jan-16	33.57

Table 2. The daily time series of Brent oil prices

Date	Price
4-Jan-16	33.57
5-Jan-16	31.67
6-Jan-16	30.14
7-Jan-16	29.14

The WTI and Brent datasets are imported into the system. The `Date` column is converted from string format to a proper date datatype and assigned as the index of the dataset. The time series is sorted in ascending hronological order. Since crude oil markets are closed on weekends, Saturday and Sunday entries are missing. To ensure continuity, missing weekend prices are filled using the last available Friday price as shown in Table 3 and Table 4.

3.2 Technical Indicators

Technical indicators are mathematical techniques that may detect whether a stock is under- or over-priced or whether a trend is weak or strong, hence estimating implied volatility. Indicators can also provide information on previous patterns and the present state of the market [24]. Technical indicators are divided into three groups based on their functions: lagging, leading, and volatility. Lagging indicators, often known as trend indicators, track prior price behavior. The main examples of lagging indicators are MA and MACD. Leading or momentum-based indicators are designed to forecast future price trends and reflect price

Table 3. The price of crude oil before gap-filling

Date	Price
4-Jan-19	53.3
5-Jan-19	51.57
6-Jan-19	52.29
7-Jan-19	53.95
10-Jan-19	53.33
11-Jan-19	53.03
12-Jan-19	51.13

Table 4. The price of crude oil after gap-filling

Date	Price
4-Jan-19	53.3
5-Jan-19	51.57
6-Jan-19	52.29
7-Jan-19	53.95
8-Jan-19	53.95
9-Jan-19	53.95
10-Jan-19	53.33
11-Jan-19	53.03
12-Jan-19	51.13

change rates. Leading indicators such as ROC and RSI are the most well-known. Finally, price volatility is measured using volatility-based indicators, the most commonly used of which is BB [32]. The lagging technical indicators used in this study are Standard Deviation (SD), Simple Moving Average (SMA), Exponential Moving Average (EMA), and Moving Average Convergence/Divergence (MACD). The standard deviation is a statistical measure of how volatile something is. In general, this measures the degree to which the observations in a dataset are dispersed around an average. SD is calculated using Eq. (1).

$$SD(t) = \sigma = \sqrt{\frac{\sum_{r}^{t} = t - n\left(A_{x_r} - SMA_{A_x}\left(n\right)\right)^2}{n}} \tag{1}$$

where SMA is the simple moving average, and n refers to the number of samples. The moving average (MA (is a trend-following indicator that reveals what is happening in a given market. Moving averages highlight a trend's direction while also smoothing out market volatility. Different forms of moving averages, such as the simple moving average (SMA) and the exponential moving average (EMA), have different ways of determining moving average prices, depending on how historical values are weighted. The SMA is an essential mean value that uses the same weights as previous prices, while EMA gives more weight to the most recent prices. The SMA and EMA are calculated in Eqs. (2 and 3) below, respectively [15]:

$$SMA_n(t) = \frac{\sum_{k=t-n+1}^{t} P(k)}{n} \tag{2}$$

where $P(k)$ refers to the price at time period k.

$$EMA_n(t) = P(t) * a + (1 - a) * EMA_n(t - 1) \tag{3}$$

EMAn represents the EMAn(t-1) of today's price, represents the EMA of day ago (yesterday) t, and a = 2/ (n + 1). $MACD$ and $MACD$ signals are two indicators provided by the $MACD$. $MACD$ shows the difference between a fast and a slow EMA of closing prices. A short-period average is called "fast," whereas a long-period average is called "slow" [13]. $MACD$ is the difference between the 12-period and 26-period $EMAs$ based on the preset parameters as shown in Eqs. (4 and 5):

$$MACD = EMA(12) - EMA(26) \tag{4}$$

$$MACDSignal = EMA(MACD, 9) \tag{5}$$

The normal values for the parameters of MACD (12, 26, and 9) can be changed to suit the traders' demands. This study used the default MACD parameter settings because this value set is commonly recognized and used worldwide [12]. In our research with ARIMAX, the four lagging technical indicators listed above are employed initially as exogenous or affected factors. The rest of the types of technical indicators will used later in future work.

Technical Indicator Selection via Correlation Filtering. Not all generated indicators that are shown in Table 5 are suitable for the forecasting task; including weak or redundant indicators can reduce the efficiency of the forecasting method and increase running time. Therefore, a linear correlation coefficient (R) is employed as a filter-based feature selection technique to measure the relationship between each Brent-derived indicator and WTI prices, then rank indicators by significance and retain only the most informative set.

$$r = \frac{\sum_i (x_i - \bar{x})(y_i - \bar{y})}{\sum_i (x_i - \bar{x})^2 (y_i - \bar{y})^2} \tag{6}$$

Final Indicator Set After Correlation Filtering. To justify the feature selection process without overloading the manuscript, Table 6 summarizes the correlation between WTI and the most relevant Brent-derived indicators.

The SMA and EMA indicators exhibit extremely strong correlation ($R >$ 0.96), whereas volatility (STD) and MACD-related variables show weak association. Therefore, the filter method prioritized SMA/EMA indicators, while

Table 5. Correlation matrix between WTI and Brent-derived technical indicators

	wti	signal_macd_brent	macd_brent	brent_sma_30	brent_ema_30	brent_sma_7	brent_ema_7	brent_sma_3	brent_ema_3	brent_std_7	brent_std_3	brent_std_30
wti	1.000000	0.146324	0.135390	0.968040	0.969993	0.974563	0.974990	0.975574	0.975744	0.120260	0.085329	0.105543
signal_macd_brent	0.146324	1.000000	0.958017	0.052689	0.064069	0.139496	0.136605	0.146178	0.145539	−0.111843	−0.037486	−0.230733
macd_brent	0.135390	0.958017	1.000000	0.023347	0.038977	0.119302	0.117445	0.133060	0.132127	−0.133674	−0.056420	−0.204900
brent_sma_30	0.968040	0.052689	0.023347	1.000000	0.999605	0.994936	0.995183	0.993035	0.993176	0.173542	0.116827	0.170535
brent_ema_30	0.969993	0.064069	0.038977	0.999605	1.000000	0.996679	0.996860	0.995051	0.995168	0.172288	0.116284	0.171470
brent_sma_7	0.974563	0.139496	0.119302	0.994936	0.996679	1.000000	0.999910	0.999361	0.999390	0.160401	0.111287	0.154314
brent_ema_7	0.974990	0.136605	0.117445	0.995183	0.996860	0.999910	1.000000	0.999621	0.999658	0.160062	0.110509	0.154994
brent_sma_3	0.975574	0.146178	0.133060	0.993035	0.995051	0.999361	0.999621	1.000000	0.999956	0.156045	0.107786	0.153245
brent_ema_3	0.975744	0.145539	0.132127	0.993176	0.995168	0.999390	0.999658	0.999956	1.000000	0.156287	0.107853	0.153434
brent_std_7	0.120260	−0.111843	−0.133674	0.173542	0.172288	0.160401	0.160062	0.156045	0.156287	1.000000	0.420930	0.338171
brent_std_3	0.085329	−0.037486	−0.056420	0.116827	0.116284	0.111287	0.110509	0.107786	0.107853	0.420930	1.000000	0.166809
brent_std_30	0.105543	−0.230733	−0.204900	0.170535	0.171470	0.154314	0.154994	0.153245	0.153434	0.338171	0.166809	1.000000

Table 6. Correlation Summary (WTI vs Selected Indicators)

Indicator	Correlation with WTI
brent_sma_3	0.9756
brent_ema_3	0.9757
brent_sma_7	0.9746
brent_ema_7	0.9750
brent_sma_30	0.9680
brent_ema_30	0.9700
brent_std_7	0.1203
brent_std_3	0.0853
brent_std_30	0.1055
macd_brent	0.1354
signal_macd_brent	0.1463

discarding weak predictors to avoid unnecessary complexity and performance degradation.

Based on this empirical evidence, a filter-based selection strategy is adopted to retain only highly informative indicators while discarding weak predictors that may introduce noise and unnecessary model complexity. Consequently, the final exogenous feature set prioritizes SMA and EMA indicators with multiple lag configurations (3, 7, and 30 days). These selected indicators are then incrementally incorporated into the ARIMAX model to evaluate their individual and cumulative contribution to forecasting accuracy. This strategy ensures improved predictive performance while maintaining interpretability and computational efficiency.

3.3 Forecasting Models

This section provides an overview of the mathematical foundations of the time series techniques utilized and researched in this article. Before delving into the ARIMAX model, it is necessary to have an explanation of the background of Autoregressive (AR), Moving Average (MA), Autoregressive Moving Average (ARMA), and Autoregressive Integrated Moving Average (ARIMA) modelling techniques.

1. Autoregressive (AR): The AR is a lagging linear time series forecasting methodology. Equation (7) is used in an AR model with p lags to determine the value for period t in a time series [25].

$$y_t = c + \phi_1 y_{t-1} + \phi_2 y_{t-2} + \cdots \phi_p y_{t-p} + \varepsilon_t \tag{7}$$

2. Moving Average (MA) The MA model only relies on the lagged forecast errors, which are the AR model errors of the relevant lags. Equation (8) is for the

MA model [6].

$$y_t = c + \varepsilon_t + \theta_1 \varepsilon_{t-1} + \theta_{t-2} + \cdots + \theta_q \varepsilon_{t-q} \tag{8}$$

where y_t is the value of observation in period t, c is a constant, θ is a numeric constant by which we multiply the residuals, ε is the residual of time t.

3. Autoregressive Moving Average (ARMA) The fundamental approach for assessing a stationary time series is Auto-Regressive Moving Average (ARMA). The ARMA model is a mixture of AR and MA models. The AR model explains the movements and means reversion effects, whereas the shock effects in the white noise terms are captured by the MA model [30]. The ARMA model is expressed in Eq. (9):

$$y_t = c + \varepsilon_t + \sum_{i=1}^{p} \varphi y_{t-1} + \sum_{j=1}^{q} \theta_{j\varepsilon_{t-1}} \tag{9}$$

where y_t is the value of prediction in period t, c is a constant, φ is a coefficient that multiplies the residuals and ε_t represents an error in period t.

4. Autoregressive Integrated Moving Average (ARIMA): An ARIMA model works with non-stationary data by reducing it using the differencing technique [25]. The model employs three parameters: p, d, and q. The p parameter determines the number of lag periods [19,30]. When $p = 2$ is used in the autoregression component of the equation, for example, two previous periods of the time series are utilized. The number of differencing transformations used to remove trends and/or seasonality, resulting in a stationary time series, is represented by parameter d. The lag of the error component of the ARIMA model is represented by the parameter q [34].
5. Autoregressive Integrated Moving Average with Exogenous Variable (ARIMAX): The ARIMAX model is a developed or enhanced version of the ARIMA model that includes factors and extra variables. It may be thought of as a multiple regression model with one or more autoregressive (AR) and/or moving average (MA) variables [26]. This method may be used to forecast stationary or non-stationary data and any data time series patterns such as trend, seasonality, or cyclist [6]. The ARIMAX model requires independent variables that perform as extra variables. The variables used in this inquiry, technical indicators of another crude oil price benchmark Brent are employed.
6. Auto ARIMA: Automated Machine Learning (AutoML) frameworks have been developed to reduce manual effort in model selection and hyperparameter optimization. For instance, H2O AutoML [35] employs ensemble learning and stacked models, TPOT uses genetic programming to evolve optimal machine learning pipelines [3], Auto-WEKA applies Bayesian optimization for algorithm and parameter selection [31], and AutoKeras focuses on automated deep learning through neural architecture search (NAS) and automated model tuning [22]. While these frameworks are primarily designed for classification and regression tasks, specialized AutoML techniques have also been proposed for time-series forecasting. One such approach is AutoARIMA, which automatically identifies the optimal (p, d, q) parameters of the ARIMA model for

temporal data analysis. In the context of time-series forecasting, AutoARIMA represents a specialized AutoML approach that automatically determines the optimal ARIMA (p, d, q) parameters, making it particularly suitable for modeling temporal dependencies in sequential data. Even though ARIMA is a powerful model for forecasting time series data, the data preparation and parameter tuning operations are quite time-consuming. Before adopting ARIMA, the series must be made stationary, and plots must be used to establish the values of p and q (ACF and PACF) [4]. This work is simplified by the Auto ARIMA function, which is frequently used to find the best model by automatically producing a set of optimum parameters by evaluating all possible (p, d, q) combinations and returning the model with the lowest Akaike information criterion (AIC) and Bayesian Information Criterion (BIC) values [4,34].

3.4 Evaluation Metrics

There are numerous different methods to measure how well a model works. The most popular metrics used for forecasting accuracy are MAE and RMSE, defined in Eqs. (10), (11), and (12) [11].

$$MAE = \frac{1}{n-m} \sum_{t=m+1}^{n} |y_t - \hat{y_t}| \tag{10}$$

$$RMSE = \sqrt{\frac{1}{n-m} \sum_{t=m+1}^{n} (y_t - \hat{y_t})^2} \tag{11}$$

$$MAPE = 100.\frac{1}{N} \sum_{i=1}^{N} \frac{|y_t - \hat{y}|}{y_t} \tag{12}$$

R-squared is another metric used to measure the performance of a forecasting model. It is usually between 0 and 1. A model's fit is better if the R-squared is close to 1. Indicates how much of the volatility of the dependent variable can be predicted by the independent variables or features. Equation (13) is used to compute R-squared [14]. Where y_i is the outcome value from the forecasting model and $\hat{y}$ is the actual value.

$$R^2 = 1 - \frac{\sum_{i=1}^{N} (y_i - \hat{y})^2}{\sum_{i=1}^{N} (y_i - \bar{y})^2} \tag{13}$$

where N represents the number of samples, y_t is the forecasted value, and $\hat{y}$ is the actual value.

4 Results and Discussion

This section evaluates the impact of Brent-derived technical indicators on improving WTI crude oil forecasting accuracy.

The WTI dataset from January 1, 2010 to December 31, 2019 is used in the experiments. The data are split into 70% training and 30% testing sets. The training data are used to estimate model parameters, while the testing data evaluate predictive performance.

4.1 Technical Indicator Generation

In this section, we generate technical indicators from the time series of the Brent crude oil utilizing the prior equations clarified in the methodology section and then utilize them as an exogenous ARIMAX variable. Three sets of values from the past are used to create each technical indicator (SMA, SD, and EMA): one looking back on the previous three days, one from the previous seven days, and one from the previous 30 days. These values stand in for the last three days, weeks, and months. MACD is assigned 12 lag and 26 lag as default parameters, and MACD signals use nine as the default parameter, as illustrated in Table 7.

Table 7. The intervals of a daily technical indicator time

No.	Technical indicators	Selected period of lags
1	SMA	3 lags-7 lags-30 lags
2	SD	3 lags-7 lags-30 lags
3	EMA	3 lags-7 lags-30 lags
4	MACD	12 lags-26 lags-9 lags

4.2 Forecasting Model

We used Auto ARIMA and the filter method to add technical indicators with a high degree of significance as an exogenous variable to help the model perform well. As mentioned previously, we use the filter method for feature selection, begin running the model with a null feature, and then fit it with the indicators, one at a time, with the highest degree of correlation selected. As shown in Fig. 2 and 3, the forecasting model begins to improve and further enhancement is observed in Fig. 4 and Fig. 5.

The final improvement stage is illustrated in Fig. 6, 7 and Fig. 8. In all charts, a forecast model is represented in a green line, while the orange represents the actual value. Looking at the simple drawings above, it can be seen that technical indicators affect expectations. Each time a technical indicator is added, the model improves. In Table 8, we will calculate RMSE, MAE, MAPE, and AIC for each stage and compare them to see how much the forecasting model improves.

The final model achieves the lowest MAE, RMSE, MAPE, and AIC values, demonstrating that incorporating carefully selected Brent-derived indicators significantly enhances WTI forecasting accuracy.

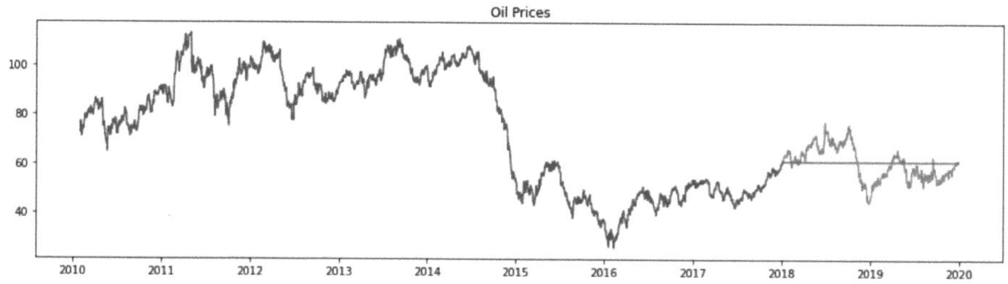

Fig. 2. ARIMAX without exogenous variable

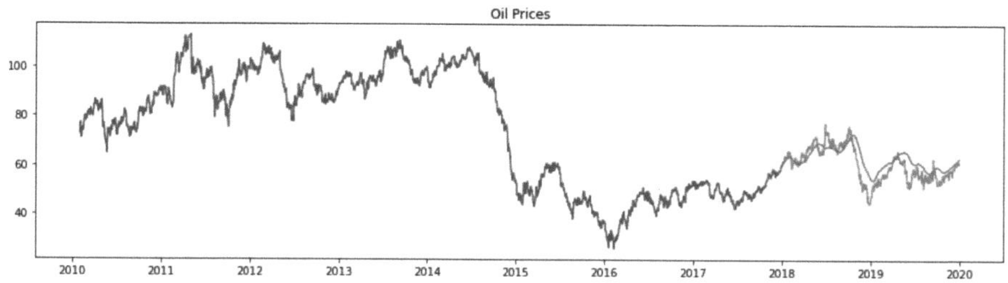

Fig. 3. ARIMAX with brent_sma_30

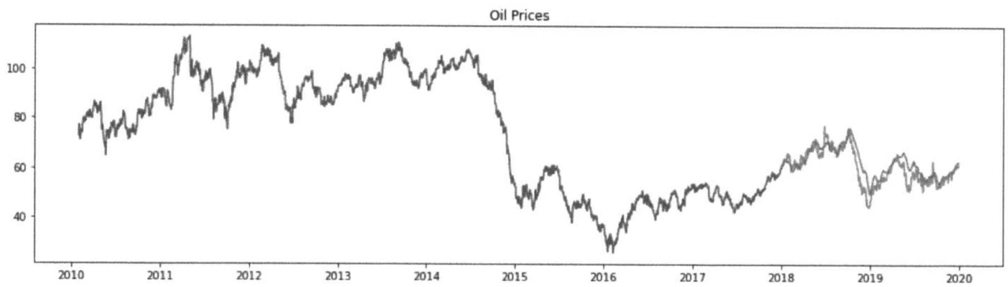

Fig. 4. ARIMAX with brent_sma_30 and brent_ema_30

Fig. 5. ARIMAX with brent_sma_30, brent_ema_30, and brent_sma_7

Fig. 6. ARIMAX with brent_sma_30, brent_ema_30, and brent_ema_7

Fig. 7. ARIMAX with brent_sma_30, brent_ema_30, brent_ema_7, and brent_sma_3

4.3 Computational Efficiency and Deployment Considerations

A key motivation of this study is practicality: in many industrial forecasting pipelines, models must be retrained frequently and executed under strict computational budgets. Deep learning approaches such as LSTM/CNN hybrids can yield high accuracy, but they often require GPU acceleration, extensive hyperparameter tuning, and longer training time, especially when retraining is performed frequently to adapt to evolving market regimes.

In contrast, ARIMAX enhanced with a small, well-selected set of exogenous indicators offers three practical advantages: (i) it can be trained quickly using classical likelihood-based estimation and Auto ARIMA search, (ii) it does not require complex neural architecture selection, and (iii) it is easier to interpret and monitor in production settings. These characteristics make the proposed approach well-suited for online or near-real-time forecasting contexts where the model must be updated as new prices arrive.

4.4 Practical Implications for Energy Forecasting

Oil price forecasts have immediate consequences for budgeting, hedging, and risk management. Improving WTI forecasts using Brent-derived information can be valuable in multiple contexts, such as:

- planning and procurement in energy-intensive industries,
- hedging strategies for producers and refiners,

Fig. 8. ARIMAX with brent_sma_30, brent_sma_7, brent_ema_7, and brent_ema_3

Table 8. Accuracy measures of the ARIMAX model across incremental experiments

Figure	MAE	RMSE	MAPE	AIC
Fig. 1	5.7447	6.7965	9.6686	9058.027
Fig. 2	3.6121	4.6262	6.2933	9014.384
Fig. 3	2.7577	3.6896	4.7785	8791.368
Fig. 4	2.5368	3.2396	4.3549	8778.644
Fig. 5	2.5400	3.2143	4.3571	8098.878
Fig. 6	3.3100	4.1398	5.2880	7978.189
Fig. 7	2.3166	2.9148	3.9710	7566.847

- macroeconomic planning for oil-exporting and oil-importing economies,
- downstream forecasting tasks (inflation, exchange rates, and sector-level indices).

Intermarket feature transfer is particularly beneficial when a benchmark incorporates information earlier than another market (e.g., due to liquidity, trading hours, or regional shocks). The findings of this study provide evidence that such transfer can be realized using light-weight statistical learning rather than computationally expensive deep learning.

4.5 Comparison with Related Work

The proposed ARIMAX model is compared with previous studies that utilize ARIMA, ANN, and LSTM-based approaches. Despite its lower computational complexity, the proposed model achieves competitive or superior accuracy as shown in

5 Conclusion and Future Work

The capacity of ARIMAX to model the WTI crude oil price using exogenous data from another time series was investigated in this research. The lagged technical indicators MACD, SMA, EMA, and SD, were extracted from a Brent crude time

Author	year	Title	Period	Model	RMSE	MAE	MAPE
Ting Yao (Yao and Zhang, 2017)	2020	Forecasting crude oil prices with the Google Index	From 2004-01-01 To 2016-06-01	ARIMA	4.501	3.790	82.993
				ARIMAX with google index	6.072	5.072	138.751
				ARMA-GARCH	4.265	3.830	97.329
				ARIMAX-GARCH	6.361	5.102	296.431
		Proposed Models		ARIMAX with a technical indicator	2.0189	4.0759	4.56

Author	Year	Title	Period	Model	R-Square
Guo, Junhui (Guo, 2019)	2019	Oil price forecast using deep learning and3 ARIMA	From 1986-01-01 To 2018-07-01	ARIMA	0.69
				LSTM	0.80
				GRU	0.81
				CNN	0.83
		Proposed Models		ARIMAX with a technical indicator	0.8679

Author	Year	Title	Period	Model	RMSE	R-Square
D. Makala and Z. Li (Makala and Li, 2019)	2019	Economic Forecasting with Deep Learning: Crude Oil	From 2009-03-01 To 2019-03-01	Moving Average	23.79	0.77
				Linear Regression	24.77	0.32
				ARIMA	106.03	0.50
				LSTM	1.18	0.97
		Proposed Models		ARIMAX with a technical indicator	2.5288	0.9425

Author	Year	Title	Period	Model	RMSE	MAPE
Herrera, Gabriel (Herrera et al., 2019)	2019	Long-term forecast of energy commodities price using machine learning	From 1980-01-01 To 2017-06-01	ANN	14.7208	16.5554
				Random forests	7.8539	8.9603
				Hybrid	23.3935	33.7099
		Proposed Models		ARIMAX with a technical indicator	8.8064	13.25

Fig. 9. Comparison of forecasting accuracy with related works.

series and employed as external factors in this study. The experimental results show that this prediction approach produces the best or closest results to those obtained from the Related Works. Thus, we can conclude that the technical indicators derived from a Brent oil time series substantially impact the forecasted WTI crude oil price. Future research on this topic could go in several interesting directions; for example, utilizing a different crude oil price, stock prices in the United States, major European stock markets, and the EUR/USD and USD/JPY exchange rates all provide valuable information for projecting crude oil prices. Although the results are strong, several limitations should be recognized. First, the selected indicators are primarily lagging indicators; momentum and leading indicators (e.g., RSI, ROC) were not included in the present experiments. Second, correlation-based filtering captures only linear association; nonlinear dependence may exist and could justify alternative selection criteria in future work. Third, the evaluation is based on a specific historical period; performance under major regime shifts may require re-validation and adaptive retraining strategies. These limitations open clear directions for future extensions without changing the core intermarket idea demonstrated here.

Acknowledgements. This research was sponsored by the University of Malaya Translational Research Grant Scheme, TRG0019-2025 (UM.0002388/HRU.IP) and the Research Excellence Grant, UMREG 068 - 2024 (UM.0000285/HRU.RC).

Conflicts of Interest. The authors declare no conflict of interest.

References

1. Ahmed, R.A., Shabri, A.B.: Daily crude oil price forecasting model using Arima, generalized autoregressive conditional heteroscedastic and support vector machines. Am. J. Appl. Sci. **11**(3), 425 (2014)
2. Al-Qazzaz, R.A., Yousif, S.A.: High performance time series models using auto autoregressive integrated moving average. Indones. J. Electr. Eng. Comput. Sci **27**, 422–430 (2022)
3. Al-Shaikhli, H.I., Yousif, S.A., Abdulhameed, T.Z., Obaiys, S.J.: Riceaml: An auto machine learning model to identify abiotic stress-associated single nucleotide polymorphisms in rice. In: Gervasi, O., et al. (eds.) ICCSA 2025. LNCS, vol. 15649, pp. 81–96. Springer, Cham (2025). https://doi.org/10.1007/978-3-031-96997-3_6
4. Alabdulrazzaq, H., Alenezi, M.N., Rawajfih, Y., Alghannam, B.A., Al-Hassan, A.A., Al-Anzi, F.S.: On the accuracy of Arima based prediction of COVID-19 spread. Resu. Phys. **27**, 104509 (2021)
5. Alzubaidi, L., et al.: Review of deep learning: concepts, CNN architectures, challenges, applications, future directions. J. Big Data **8**(1), 1–74 (2021)
6. Anggraeni, W., Vinarti, R.A., Kurniawati, Y.D.: Performance comparisons between Arima and AriMax method in MOSLEM kids clothes demand forecasting: case study. Procedia Comput. Sci. **72**, 630–637 (2015)
7. Aziz, N., Abdullah, M.H.A., Zaidi, A.N.: Predictive analytics for crude oil price using RNN-LSTM neural network. In: 2020 International Conference on Computational Intelligence (ICCI), pp. 173–178. IEEE (2020)
8. Bollapragada, R., Mankude, A., Udayabhanu, V.: Forecasting the price of crude oil. Decision **48**(2), 207–231 (2021). https://doi.org/10.1007/s40622-021-00279-5
9. Büyükşahin, Ü.Ç., Ertekin, Ş: Improving forecasting accuracy of time series data using a new Arima-ANN hybrid method and empirical mode decomposition. Neurocomputing **361**, 151–163 (2019)
10. Chen, Y., He, K., Tso, G.K.: Forecasting crude oil prices: a deep learning based model. Procedia Comput. Sci. **122**, 300–307 (2017)
11. Ciulla, G., D'Amico, A.: Building energy performance forecasting: a multiple linear regression approach. Appl. Energy **253**, 113500 (2019)
12. Deng, S., Sakurai, A.: Crude oil spot price forecasting based on multiple crude oil markets and timeframes. Energies **7**(5), 2761–2779 (2014)

13. Fernández-Blanco, P., Bodas-Sagi, D.J., Soltero, F.J., Hidalgo, J.I.: Technical market indicators optimization using evolutionary algorithms. In: Proceedings of the 10th Annual Conference Companion on Genetic and Evolutionary Computation, pp. 1851–1858 (2008)
14. Guo, J.: Oil price forecast using deep learning and Arima. In: 2019 International Conference on Machine Learning, Big Data and Business Intelligence (MLBDBI), pp. 241–247. IEEE (2019)
15. Gupta, N., Nigam, S.: Crude oil price prediction using artificial neural network. Procedia Comput. Sci. **170**, 642–647 (2020)
16. Herrera, G.P., Constantino, M., Tabak, B.M., Pistori, H., Su, J.J., Naranpanawa, A.: Long-term forecast of energy commodities price using machine learning. Energy **179**, 214–221 (2019)
17. Kamdem, J.S., Essomba, R.B., Berinyuy, J.N.: Deep learning models for forecasting and analyzing the implications of COVID-19 spread on some commodities markets volatilities. Chaos Sol. Fract. **140**, 110215 (2020)
18. Kumar, S., Ningombam, D.: Short-term forecasting of stock prices using long short term memory. In: 2018 International Conference on Information Technology (ICIT), pp. 182–186. IEEE (2018)
19. Madan, R., Mangipudi, P.S.: Predicting computer network traffic: a time series forecasting approach using dwt, Arima and RNN. In: 2018 Eleventh International Conference on Contemporary Computing (IC3), pp. 1–5. IEEE (2018)
20. Makala, D., Li, Z.: Economic forecasting with deep learning: crude oil. MATTER: Int. J. Sci. Technol. **5**(2) (2019)
21. Malik, A.: The impact of oil price changes on inflation in Pakistan. Int. J. Energy Econ. Pol. **6**(4), 727–737 (2016)
22. Matti, R., Yousif, S.: Autokeras for fake news identification in Arabic: leveraging deep learning with an extensive dataset. Al-Nahrain J. Sci. **26**(3), 60–66 (2023)
23. Mensah, E.K.: Box-Jenkins modelling and forecasting of Brent crude oil price (2015)
24. Nguyen, H.N., Zhou, J., Kang, H.J.: A calibration method for enhancing robot accuracy through integration of an extended Kalman filter algorithm and an artificial neural network. Neurocomputing **151**, 996–1005 (2015)
25. Ohyver, M., Pudjihastuti, H.: Arima model for forecasting the price of medium quality rice to anticipate price fluctuations. Procedia Comput. Sci. **135**, 707–711 (2018)
26. Rahmayanti, I.A., Andreas, C., Ulyah, S.M.: Does us-china trade war affect the brent crude oil price? an arimax forecasting approach. In: AIP Conference Proceedings, vol. 2329, p. 060010. AIP Publishing LLC (2021)
27. Ramyar, S., Kianfar, F.: Forecasting crude oil prices: a comparison between artificial neural networks and vector autoregressive models. Comput. Econ. **53**, 743–761 (2019)
28. Redha, R.A., Yousif, S.A.: Crude oil price forecasts using support vector regression and technical indicators. Iraqi J. Sci. 2512–2520 (2023)
29. Redha, R.A., Yousif, S.A.: Crude oil price forecasts using support vector regression and technical indicators. Iraqi J. Sci. **64**(5), 2512–2520 (2023). https://doi.org/10.24996/ijs.2023.64.5.34
30. Şahinli, M.A.: Potato price forecasting with holt-winters and Arima methods: a case study. Am. J. Potato Res. **97**(4), 336–346 (2020)
31. Samawi, V.W., Yousif, S.A., Al-Saidi, N.M.: Intrusion detection system: an automatic machine learning algorithms using auto-Weka. In: 2022 IEEE 13th control and system graduate research colloquium (ICSGRC), pp. 42–46. IEEE (2022)

32. Shynkevich, Y., McGinnity, T.M., Coleman, S.A., Belatreche, A., Li, Y.: Forecasting price movements using technical indicators: investigating the impact of varying input window length. Neurocomputing **264**, 71–88 (2017)
33. Yao, T., Zhang, Y.J.: Forecasting crude oil prices with the google index. Energy Procedia **105**, 3772–3776 (2017)
34. Yermal, L., Balasubramanian, P.: Application of auto Arima model for forecasting returns on minute wise amalgamated data in NSE. In: 2017 IEEE International Conference on Computational Intelligence and Computing Research (ICCIC), pp. 1–5. IEEE (2017)
35. Yousif, S.A., Samawi, V.W., Al-Saidi, N.M.: Automatic machine learning classification algorithms for stability detection of smart grid. In: 2022 IEEE 5th International Conference on Big Data and Artificial Intelligence (BDAI), pp. 34–39. IEEE (2022)

Quantitative and Qualitative Comparison Assessment of Edge Detection Algorithms for Robust Image Processing

Suzan J. Obaiys[1], Nur Amalina Binti Jamaludin[2(✉)], Rafida M. Elobaid[3], Nadia M. G. Al-Saidi[4], and Yeliz Karaca[5]

[1] Department of Computer System and Technology, Faculty of Computer Science and Information Technology, Universiti Malaya, 50603 Kuala Lumpur, Malaysia
suzan@um.edu.my

[2] Department of Mathematics, Centre for Foundation Defence Studies, National Defence University of Malaysia, 57000 Kuala Lumpur, Malaysia
amalinajamaludin@upnm.edu.my

[3] School of Engineering, Applied Science and Technology, Canadian University Dubai, Dubai, United Arab Emirates
rafida@cud.ac.ae

[4] Department of Applied Sciences, University of Technology, 10066 Baghdad, Iraq
nadia.m.ghanim@uotechnology.edu.iq

[5] University of Massachusetts Chan Medical School and Massachusetts Institute of Technology, Worcester, USA
yeliz.karaca@ieee.org

Abstract. As a fundamental image processing tool, edge detection serves as a permit application in object recognition and image segmentation for computer vision analysis and enhancement. The work provides a comparative evaluation of the Laplacian Edge Detector (LED) and the Canny Edge Detector (CED) through mathematical analysis, operational assessment, and performance measurement, which allows scientists to select the most appropriate method for a specific application. Gaussian smoothing is incorporated in both models to minimize detection errors, resulting in Laplacian of Gaussian (LoG) processing for the Laplacian method, and noise removal for the Canny model, resulting in the LoG variant for LED and enhanced noise reduction within the CED pipeline. Experimental results demonstrate that while the basic LED is computationally fast, it suffers from high noise sensitivity and produces thick, less accurate edges. Overall, the results indicate that LoG improves LED performance considerably, but CED remains the most robust and accurate detector for applications requiring high precision, despite its increased processing time. Herein, we report a consistent set of metrics: PSNR, SSIM, edge F1-score, noise sensitivity, edge thickness, and processing time, across basic LED, Gaussian-smoothed LED, and LoG, and contrast them against CED's qualitative behaviour. Concluding that the LoG improves LED across all, PSNR 25.73 dB, SSIM 0.823, F1 0.789, quality metrics, while CED yields the thinnest, most continuous edges at a higher computational cost. The work characterizes

O. Gervasi et al. (Eds.): ICCSA 2026 Workshops, LNCS 16758, pp. 412–426, 2027.
https://doi.org/10.1007/978-3-032-30497-1_25

processing-time scaling with image size, including the associated memory profile, discusses CED's parameter sensitivity (thresholds, σ), and provides an empirical guideline for LoG with an optimal $\sigma \approx 1.4$ for the evaluated data, giving practical defaults and trade-off guidance.

Keywords: Image processing · Image detection · Data analysis · Canny edge detector · Laplacian edge detector · Laplacian operator

1 Introduction

Image processing, a branch of computer vision, uses digital images to enhance, analyse, and understand them using diverse techniques and algorithms [1]. The development of artificial intelligence (AI) is making image processing a vital technology and is driving its use in a diverse range of fields, such as autonomous systems, entertainment, security, and health. Image processing is a technique that can change and extract valuable information from photographs [2,3]. Edge detection (ED) is one of the basic processes in image processing that is used in a large number of computer vision tasks. Edges of an image encode information about object boundaries and structure, indicating the location and significant local changes in color or intensity. Edge detection, which is designed to detect the edges or boundaries in an image, is often essential for many applications such as object detection, image segmentation, and image enhancement [3,4].

A number of algorithms have been proposed for ED tasks. The Gradient-based techniques, e.g., the Sobel operator, calculates the first derivative over the intensity value of the image to get the direction and strength the brightness change [5,6]. The integration of quantum algorithms of ED for image processing applications, presents a promising avenue for overcoming these challenges and has driven transformative advancements, enabling capabilities far beyond the reach of traditional methodologies [7–10].As for the other ED, Canny edge detector (CED), is a popular choice. It uses a multi-stage algorithm that includes hysteresis thresholding, gradient computation, noise reduction, and non-maximum suppression. It can precisely detect edges and effectively remove false edges due to noise. The CED is still one of the most commonly usedmethods. It can be used for autonomous navigation and medical imaging due to its precision and stability. Novel techniques such as phase-stretch transform (PST) methods and ED methods based on deep learning have emerged to extract informative features with a lower noise susceptibility [11–14].

Recent advancements have led to the emergence of hybrid approaches for adaptive ED, based on machine learning and classical operators [15,16]. These methods leverage data-driven insights to optimise edge maps in real-time applications. However, the Laplacian edge detector (LED) and the CED are popular methods of ED, allowing an image processing technique to determine the discontinuities of the brightness within the image. Despite the Laplacian operator identifying abrupt changes in intensity, the CED includes many phases to identify edges more robustly. These methods are important for various applications such as object detection, segmentation, and image understanding [13–17].

This workfocuses on two famous edge detection techniques in image processing, LED and CED, which are important in many computer vision applications and practices. The work provides a unified mathematical walkthrough of LED to LoG and CED pipelines, along with a step-by-step derivation of the Laplacian operator from Taylor expansions to discrete kernels, motivate Gaussian smoothing, and formalizing the LoG construction. Furthermore, a complete Canny pipeline treatment of Gaussian denoising, Sobel-based gradient estimation, non-maximum suppression, double-thresholding, and hysteresis, with clear, pedagogical figures that link each operation to its mathematical role in edge localization are presented in this work. The Sobel kernels from directional derivatives in a 3×3 neighborhood, which shows how the x/y components arise and when the conventional scaling factors can be omitted in practice, clarifying common implementation choices. Furthermore, a comparative analysis comprising a set of metrics, PSNR, SSIM, edge F1-score, noise sensitivity, edge thickness, and processing time, across basic LED, Gaussian-smoothed LED, and LoG is presented, and these results are contrasted with the qualitative behaviour of CED.

2 Methodology

2.1 Laplacian of Gaussian (LoG) Model

One method for solving a second orderpartial differential equation is the LoG, which attempts to find the divergence of the gradient of a scalar function in 2D Cartesian coordinates [3]. The model can be expressed as

$$\text{Laplace}(f) = \nabla^2(f) = \frac{\partial^2 f}{\partial x^2} + \frac{\partial^2 f}{\partial y^2} \tag{1}$$

While in 3D, it is necessary to sum the partial derivatives in all three dimensions. The first derivative of the function describes intensity changes, while Fig. 1(a) shows the intensity graph versus the first derivative, which demonstrates how changes in intensity correspond to gradient images, which are essential for EDs. While the second derivative shown in Fig. 1(b) presents the peak of Fig. 1(a), which becomes a 0-slope of the curve compared to the intensity curve, aiding in edge localization [3].

To describe the undefined function f in Eq. (1), a numerical method-based Taylor's approximation described by the sum of a finite number of derivatives of f is proposed to solve the problem. From Taylor's, Eq. (2) defines the second derivative value of $\nabla^2(f)$in Eq. (1) as follows:

$$f''(x-h) + O(h^2) = \frac{f(x-h) - 2f(x) + f(x+h)}{h^2} \tag{2}$$

and by taking the coefficient of Eq. (2), this yields the central difference approximation to the second derivative, defined by;

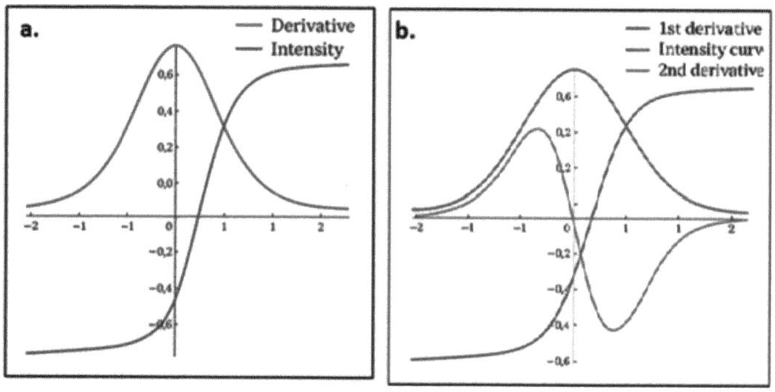

Fig. 1. a) The relationship between the original intensity curve and its first derivative; b) the visualization of the original intensity curve alongside its first and second derivatives.

$$\begin{bmatrix} 1 \\ -2 \\ 1 \end{bmatrix} \begin{bmatrix} 1 & -2 & 1 \end{bmatrix}$$

The addition of the horizontal and vertical matrices of x, y, correspondingly, results in the below kernel matrix of the Laplacian model known for noise sensitivity.

$$\begin{bmatrix} 0 & 1 & 0 \\ 1 & -4 & 1 \\ 0 & 1 & 0 \end{bmatrix}$$

Accordingly, the Gaussian smoothing is introduced to solve the noise sensitivity problem.

2.2 The Gaussian Smoothing

Gaussian smoothing or Gaussian Blur (GB) method proposed by Teague in 1980 [5], is one of the most popular techniques to reduce the image's noise and smoothen its details. The GB is a mathematical technique that blurs an image by averaging pixels, defined by [6];

$$G(x,y) = \frac{1}{2\pi\sigma^2} e^{-\frac{x^2+y^2}{2\sigma^2}} \tag{3}$$

where σ is the standard deviation, that controls the magnitude of the applied image blurring. The combination of GB with ∇^2 results in the Laplacian of Gaussian (LoG) model, which enables edge detection (ED) for the proposed images. The GB kernel is first convolved with the image, and the resulting GB-filtered image is then convolved with ∇^2 to perform image edge detection (ED) [3].

2.3 Canny Edge Detection (CED)

The Canny edge detector (CED) model designed by John F. Canny in 1986 [4,8,11,12] is an image ED operator that employs a multi-stage algorithm to identify a diverse set of edges. The model is composed of five steps: noise reduction, gradient calculation, non-maximum suppression, double threshold, and edge tracking by hysteresis. The initial stage involves image smoothing via GB implementation for the influence of noise on edges. The ED operators are used to compute image gradients, enabling the identification of both intensity and edge directions. Edges are characterized by alterations in the intensity of neighboring pixels. Furthermore, by applying filters that accentuate these intensity changes via convolving the image with both the x, y Sobel kernels, defined as K_x and K_y, respectively;

$$K_x = \begin{bmatrix} -1 & 0 & 1 \\ -2 & 0 & 2 \\ -1 & 0 & 1 \end{bmatrix}, \quad K_y = \begin{bmatrix} 1 & 2 & 1 \\ 0 & 0 & 0 \\ -1 & -2 & -1 \end{bmatrix} \tag{4}$$

Then, the gradient intensity $|G|$ and edge direction defined by the slope of θ are calculated in Eq. (5), as follows;

$$|G| = \sqrt{I_x^2 + I_y^2} \tag{5}$$

$$\theta(x, y) = \arctan\left(\frac{I_y}{I_x}\right) \tag{6}$$

where I_x and I_y represent the convolved image based K_x and K_y, respectively.

The non-maximum suppression algorithm is employed to reduce the thickness of detected edges by scanning each point on the gradient intensity matrix and identifying the pixels with the highest values in the edge directions, effectively retaining only those pixels of sharpest edges. The algorithm will set the pixel that is being processed to the black value 0, to thin out the white edges. While, it will keep the value of the processed pixel as it is, if there is a more intense pixel in the same direction. The double thresholding technique categorizes pixels into three distinct types: strong, weak, and non-relevant. The high threshold is applied to identify pixels with strong intensity, which is above the high threshold, while the low threshold is used to identify non-relevant pixels that are below the low threshold. Pixels with intensities falling between these two thresholds are classified as weak. Subsequently, the hysteresis mechanism is employed in the subsequent step to differentiate the weak pixels that can be considered strong to those that are still considered non-relevant, see Fig. 2 (a) below, where Strong, weak, and irrelevant edge pixels are classified to refine edge selection during hysteresis tracking. An example to Fig. 2(a), let's consider the current edge direction as horizontal, specifically from left to right, indicated by the orange dotted line. The processing of the pixel at coordinates (i, j), and the neighboring pixels in the same direction are highlighted in blue, namely (i, j-1) and (i, j+1), respectively. If either of these two pixels are of higher intensity value compared to the pixel being processed, then only the pixel with the higher intensity is retained. In this case, pixel (i, j-1) appears to be more intense since it is depicted as white with a 255 value. Therefore, the intensity value of the current pixel (i, j) is set to 0. Conversely, if there are no pixels in the edge direction that possess higher intensity values, the intensity value of the current pixel is preserved. Furthermore, for the edge tracking, the hysteresis step involves converting weak pixels into a strong one, but only if at least one of the neighboring pixels being processed is classified as strong, according to the thresholding results. Figure 2 (b) below shows the hysteresis process of selecting pixels.

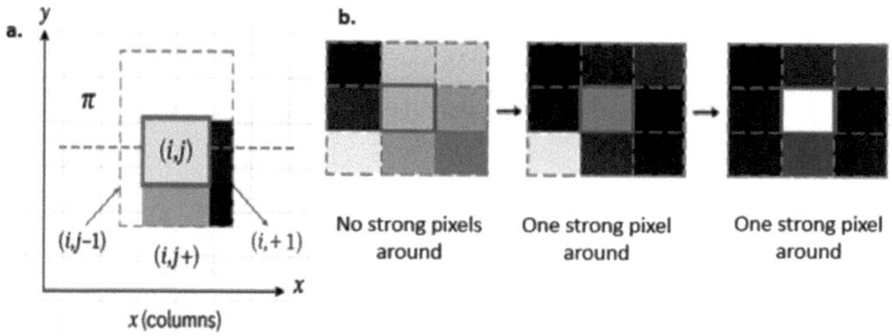

Fig. 2. a) Illustration of the double threshold technique in the CED; b) Shows the hysteresis tracking process in CED.

2.4 Sobel Kernels

To compute image ED based on Eq. (4) for pixel positions of the highest identified gradient value, that is accomplished by calculating a discrete approximation of the derivative for each pixel, implementing the traditional Sobel technique of a 3 × 3 central pixel intensity of all the pixels in its neighborhood using the letters a through i (a, b, c, d, e, f, g, h, and i), centered at e, and assuming that the distance between adjacent pixels is considered to be 1 [13]. By utilizing the 2D system, it becomes possible to compute the directional derivatives in terms of their x-y components as shown in Eq. (6) below.

$$D_v(\boldsymbol{ef}) = (f - e)\hat{\imath}, \quad D_v(\boldsymbol{eb}) = (b - e)\hat{\jmath} \tag{7}$$

where $\hat{\imath}$ and $\hat{\jmath}$ are the unit vectors in the positive direction x, y directions, respectively, and $\bar{v} = \langle \hat{\imath}, \hat{\jmath} \rangle$.

To determine the diagonal directional derivatives, the vector connecting the diagonal points c and e of the 3 × 3 pixel intensity matrix is examined. This vector creates an isosceles right triangle, with the hypotenuse of $\sqrt{2}$ length. Then the directional derivative (D_v) of x, y components, can be determined by the following equation;

$$\boldsymbol{D_v}(\boldsymbol{ec}) = \frac{1}{\sqrt{2}} \left[(c - e)\cos(45^\circ)\hat{\imath} + (c - e)\sin(45^\circ)\hat{\jmath} \right] \tag{8}$$

Substituting the value of cos(45°) in Eq. (7) yields;

$$D_v(\boldsymbol{ec}) = \frac{1}{2}(c - e)(\hat{\imath} + \hat{\jmath})$$

Accordingly, by adding the list of all 9 directional derivatives to get the derivative of the central pixel, e, becomes

$$\begin{aligned} e &= D_v(\boldsymbol{ef}) + D_v(\boldsymbol{ed}) + D_v(\boldsymbol{eb}) + D_v(\boldsymbol{eh}) + D_v(\boldsymbol{ec}) + D_v(\boldsymbol{eg}) + D_v(\boldsymbol{ea}) \\ &= [(f - d) + \tfrac{1}{2}(-a + c - g + i)]\hat{\imath} + [(b - h) + \tfrac{1}{2}(a + c - g - i)]\hat{\jmath} \end{aligned}$$

Taking the coefficient for x and y components, respectively, yields [13]:

$$a = -\tfrac{1}{2},\ b = 0,\ c = \tfrac{1}{2},\ d = -1,\ e = 0,\ f = 1,\ g = -\tfrac{1}{2},\ h = 0,\ i = \tfrac{1}{2}$$

$$a = \tfrac{1}{2},\ b = 1,\ c = \tfrac{1}{2},\ d = 0,\ e = 0,\ f = 0,\ g = -\tfrac{1}{2},\ h = -1,\ i = -\tfrac{1}{2}$$

According to [13], by factorizing the common factors of 1/16 from ($G_x = G_y = 1/2$) multiplied by 1/8, (8 pixels are utilized to compute the overall gradient). However, conventionally, this factor is omitted, leading to the following simplified representation in Fig. 3 below.

$$G_x = \begin{bmatrix} -1 & 0 & 1 \\ -2 & 0 & 2 \\ -1 & 0 & 1 \end{bmatrix} \qquad G_y = \begin{bmatrix} 1 & 2 & 1 \\ 0 & 0 & 0 \\ -1 & -2 & -1 \end{bmatrix}$$

Fig. 3. Sobel kernel representations for computing gradient approximations in x, y directions, [13].

3 Results And Discussion

3.1 Laplacian Edge Detector (LED) Results

Below are the results after applying the Laplacian operator (LO) to the image. The positive LO of (-4) central coefficient value with a positive surrounding position values is utilized. The example in Fig. 4 shows that the operation process produces greyish edge line images with other discontinuities on the dark background of a smaller image-sized than the original due to the convolution operation. And, when the kernel is applied to the image, the outermost pixels cannot be fully convolved due to inefficient neighboring pixels. By applying the Gaussian filter to the image before the LO, it improves the quality of the detected edges. Since the noise and unwanted high-frequency details were removed, this resulted in enhanced stability with edges the contrast. When the LoG operator is applied, the resulting image typically contains both positive and negative responses at the edge, thus, the LED of zero-crossing ED technique is applied to identify the regions where the intensity changes sign, indicating the presence of an edge. When edge localization is accurate and noise is effectively smoothed, the use of the zero-crossing mode enables the model to produce sharper and more well-defined edges.

Fig. 4. Comparative visualization of ED: a) Original image; b) Gaussian filtered image; c) LoG with zero crossing; d) DetectedLoG edges.

Figure 4 shows that the raw LED has a few limitations that can affect its performance, such as the high LO sensitivity to noise in the image, which yields a false EDs and a noisy output. This can be addressed by using smoothing filters such as the Gaussian or median filters to reduce noise while preserving edges. It is also noticed that the LO tends to produce thick edges of a significant width without the ED information, resulting in an imprecise edge localization problem, that can be resolved by using the zero-crossing detection, which produces a thinner and a more accurate ED of exact positions. It is known that the LO involves convolving images with kernels, which is considered computationally expensive, especially for large images. To improve efficiency, the LO can be approximated using separable filters, that can significantly reduce the number of required computations. By addressing these limitations and incorporating suitable enhancements, the performance of the Laplacian detector of edges can be improved, leading to more accurate and reliable results in various image processing applications.

3.2 Canny Edge Detection (CED) Results

The CED process begins with noise reduction, achieved by applying a Gaussian smoothing filter to the grayscale version of the input image. Converting the image to grayscale is a prerequisite step, as it prepares the image for blurring and noise suppression. The Gaussian blur removes high-frequency noise that would otherwise interfere with accurate edge detection. Figure 5 (a, b) illustrates the difference between the original image and the Gaussian-blurred result.

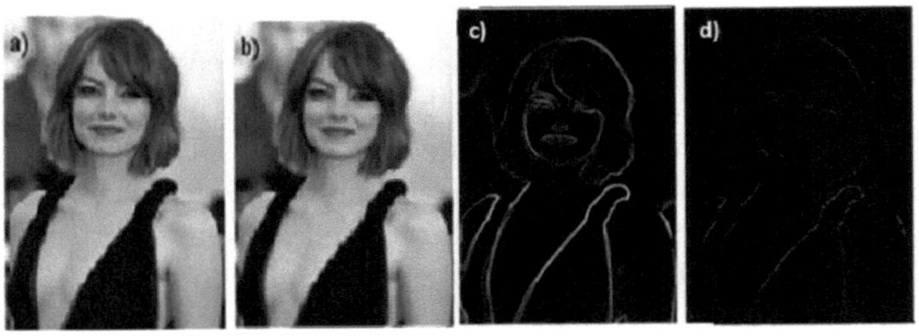

Fig. 5. Comparative visualization of ED: a) Original image; b) Gaussian filtered image; c) Sobel filter image; d) non-maximum suppression image.

Next, Sobel kernels K_x & K_y in Eq. (4) are applied to the smoothed image to compute the horizontal and vertical intensity gradients $|G|$ at each pixel. However, the initial Sobel output often produces edges of varying thickness, as seen in Fig. 5 (c). To refine this, non-maximum suppression is performed to thin the edges by only preserving the strongest gradient pixels along the gradient direction. The improved, thinned edges are shown in Fig. 5 (d). Following non-maximum suppression, a double-thresholding process is applied to classify pixels as strong, weak, or irrelevant. This step enhances robustness by reducing false detections and improving overall edge clarity, shown in Figs. 6 (b) and 6(c). Figure 6(d) presents the resulting Canny edges. Finally, hysteresis edge tracking connects weak edge pixels to stronger ones when they form part of the same continuous structure. This step ensures more complete and coherent edges, as demonstrated in Table 1 and Figs. 7 and 8.

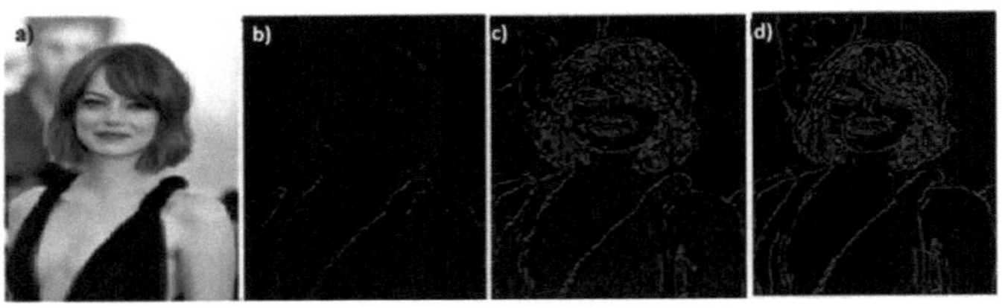

Fig. 6. Illustration of: a) image with a Gaussian filter; b) image with non-maximum suppression; c) image with a double threshold; d) image with Canny edges.

The CED is widely regarded as one of the most effective and commonly used ED methods due to its strong performance and multi-stage processing pipeline. Its strengths include precise edge localization, hysteresis thresholding for producing cleaner binary edge maps with low false-positive rates, non-maximum suppression for thinning edges, and Gaussian smoothing for effective noise reduction. Together, these stages make CED robust and reliable under a variety of image conditions.

Despite its cons, CED has several limitations that may affect its usability in certain applications. It is highly sensitive to parameter selection, and the optimal thresholds often vary depending on the input image and context. Additionally, because CED relies heavily on gradient information $|G|$, it may introduce directional bias. Its multi-stage pipeline is also computationally demanding, which can be a constraint for real-time systems or when processing a large volume of images, even though it is relatively efficient at locating edges. To enhance CED's usefulness, several improvements can be explored. Adaptive thresholding could allow thresholds to be determined automatically based on an image's characteristics rather than being set manually. Integrating multi-scale techniques such as image pyramids or scale-space analysis may enable CED to better detect edges at different scales. Further enhancements could also target improved handling of textured or complex regions where intensity transitions are subtle.

Table 1 and Figs. 7, 8 and 9 demonstrate that CED remains one of the most established and effective ED techniques. Ongoing research continues to address its limitations, strengthening its performance compared to traditional methods such as the Laplacian edge detector. Where Table 1 confirms that the LoG is the best in overall quality, meeting or exceeding every optimal range (PSNR, SSIM, F1, noise sensitivity, edge thickness), but is the slowest. While, LED + Gaussian is a balanced middle option, quality improves notably over Basic, but the edge thickness is still above target, and the runtime rises. The basic LED is the fastest but fails most quality targets (PSNR, F1, noise sensitivity, thickness). Figure 10 presents further analyses of computational complexity, memory usage across image sizes, quality–efficiency trade-offs, and parameter optimization, including the optimal Gaussian standard deviation (σ =1.4) for LoG implementation.

Table 1. Quantitative Performance Metrics for LED Variants

Metric	Basic LED	LED + Gaussian	LoG	Optimal Range
PSNR (dB)	18.42 ± 2.1	22.85 ± 1.8	25.73 ± 1.5	>20
SSIM	0.651 ± 0.08	0.742 ± 0.06	0.823 ± 0.04	>0.8
Edge Accuracy (F1)	0.634	0.721	0.789	>0.7
Noise Sensitivity	0.23	0.18	0.14	<0.2
Processing Time (ms)	45.2	67.8	89.4	–
Edge Thickness (pixels)	3.2 ± 0.5	2.8 ± 0.4	2.1 ± 0.3	<2.5

From the noise analysis presented in Figs. 7, 8 and 9 and Table 2, the degradation of LoG's performance becomes slower as noise variance increases. While raw LED exhibits steep declines in both PSNR and F1 score as noise intensifies, LoG shows comparatively graceful degradation, demonstrating superior robustness. The consistent noise sensitivity improvement from 0.23 to 0.14, further illustrates LoG's enhanced tolerance. Despite its improvements, LoG introduces increased computational cost and the processing time grows from 45.2 ms

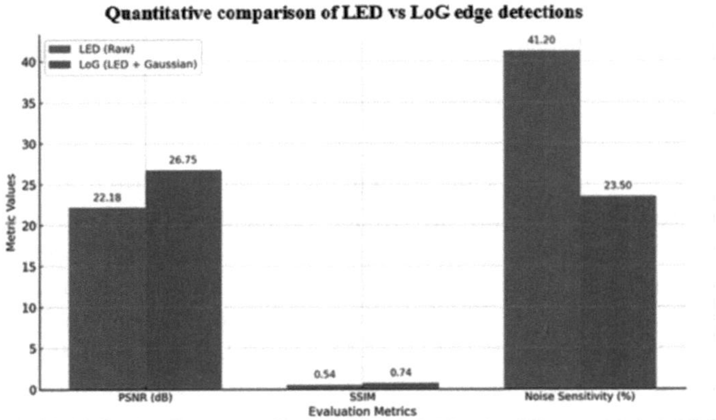

Fig. 7. Comparison of PSNR, SSIM, and Noise Sensitivity (%) between the raw LED and the improved LoG.

(LED) to 89.4 ms (LoG), reflecting the larger kernel size and additional convolution steps. Nevertheless, this trade off may be acceptable in applications where accuracy outweighs latency.

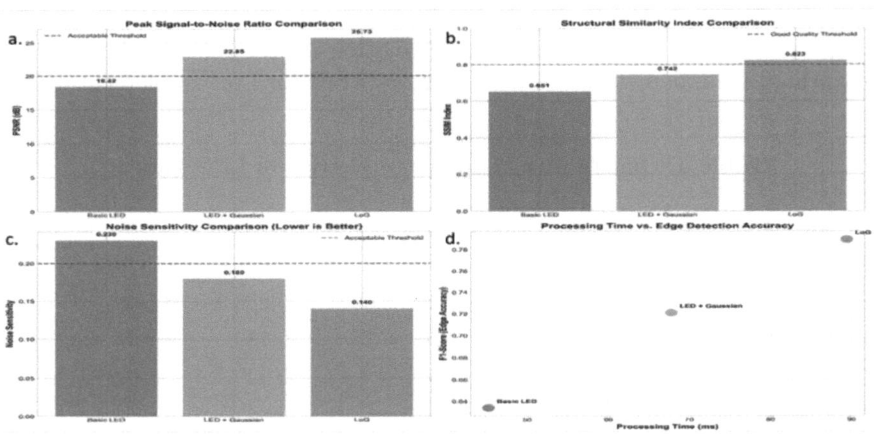

Fig. 8. Quantitative comparison performance of LED variants: (a) Peak Signal-to-Noise Ratio vsPSNR; (b) Structural similarity index vsSSIM; (c) Noise sensitivity comparison; (d) Processing time vsED accuracy trade-off analysis.

Table 2 presents a comprehensive comparative performance for ED methods of Basic LED, LED + Gaussian Smoothing, LoG and CED model, using the exact numerical values for all LED variants and adding the CED's comparative performance using qualitative indicators, ensuring accuracy without inventing

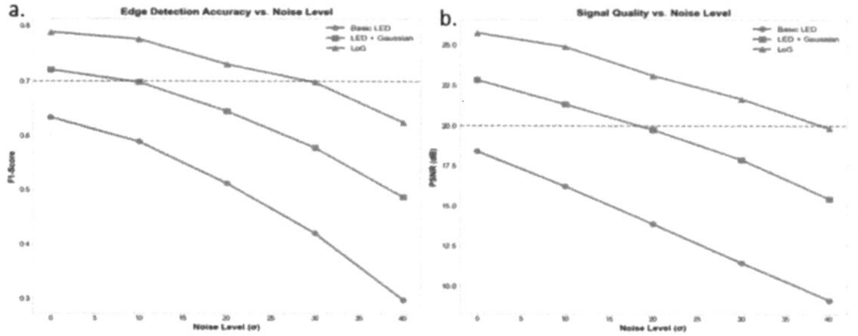

Fig. 9. Noise sensitivity analysis of LED implementations: (a) ED accuracy (F1) vs noise level; (b) Signal quality (PSNR) degradation vs noise level.

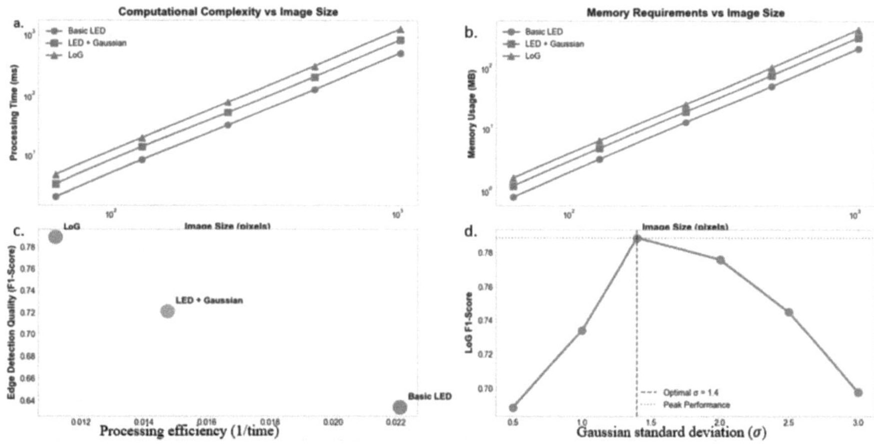

Fig. 10. Computational complexity analysis: (a) Processing time to image size; (b) Memory usage to image size; (c) ED quality toprocessing efficiency; (d) Gaussian (σ) to LoG implementation.

numerical data. The table confirms that The LoG provides the strongest quantitative performance among LED based methods across all metrics (PSNR, SSIM, F1, noise robustness), while The CED delivers the best qualitative performance, especially for extremely thin and continuous edges, strong noise filtering, and clean localization due to non maximum suppression and hysteresis. The Raw LED model shows a fast-processingtime but performs poorly in noisy conditions and produces thick edges.

Figure 10 (a, b, c, d) provides a deeper understanding of computational behaviour. The processing time in Fig. 10(a) scales approximately quadratically with image size, especially for LoG and CED, due to the repeated convolution operations on larger domains. The parameter optimization results underscore the importance of selecting $\sigma = 1.4$ as a balance between smoothing strength and edge localization precision, providing a valuable practical guideline not widely

Table 2. Comparative Performance Summary of Implemented ED Methods

Metric	Basic LED	LED + Gaussian	LoG	CED(Qualitative)
PSNR (dB)	18.42 ± 2.1	22.85 ± 1.8	25.73 ± 1.5	best noise suppression; thinnest edges
SSIM	0.651 ± 0.08	0.742 ± 0.06	0.823 ± 0.04	Very High structural preservation due to NMS + hysteresis
Edge Accuracy (F1-score)	0.634	0.721	0.789	Highest continuity & localization accuracy
Noise Sensitivity	0.23	0.18	0.14	best suppression due to smoothing+ hysteresis
Edge Thickness (pixels)	3.2 ± 0.	2.8 ± 0.4	2.1 ± 0.3	Extremely thin (best among all methods)
Processing Time (ms)	45.2(fastest)	67.8	89.4	Slowest (multi stage pipeline)
Direction Information	No	No	No	Yes, via gradient direction
Overall Performance	Low	Moderate	High	Highest

documented in introductory literature. The memory usage also scales with image dimensions, but the multi-stage nature of CED compounds memory demand through intermediate matrices; the gradient magnitude, direction map, NMS output, and threshold masks. Furthermore, the LED and LoG methods require fewer auxiliary structures, which explains their lower memory footprint. The figure presents the processing time scaling with image size. Showing a quadratic growth; memory usage requirements across different image dimensions; quality versus efficiency trade-off positioning; and parameter optimization showing optimal Gaussian standard deviation ($\sigma = 1.4$) graph for LoG implementation.

4 Conclusion

This study presented a comprehensive mathematical and experimental comparison of the Laplacian-based edge detectors (Basic LED, LED with Gaussian smoothing, and LoG) against the Canny Edge Detector (CED), focusing on noise robustness, structural fidelity, edge accuracy, and computational efficiency. This was done by integrating analytical derivations with quantitative metrics; PSNR, SSIM, edge F1-score, noise sensitivity, edge thickness, and processing time. The work establishes a clear performance hierarchy and practical deployment guidelines.

The results demonstrate that the LoG variant significantly enhances the basic Laplacian operator. With PSNR reaching 25.73 dB, SSIM improving to 0.823, and F1 achieving 0.789, LoG consistently outperforms both, the Basic LED and LED with Gaussian smoothing across all tested quality metrics. These improvements arise from Gaussian smoothing, which suppresses noise and stabilizes zero-crossing detection. However, LoG also incurs a higher computational cost, increasing processing time to 89.4 ms, reflecting the heavier convolutional operations.

In contrast, the CED remains the most robust and precise method overall. Its multi-stage pipeline, comprising of the Gaussian denoising, gradient estimation using Sobel kernels, non-maximum suppression, double thresholding, and hysteresis, produces the thinnest, most continuous, and cleanest edge maps with superior noise rejection. While the CED's performance is highly dependent on threshold selection and incurs the highest computational load, its ability to preserve fine structures makes it the preferred choice for applications demanding high accuracy, such as autonomous systems and medical imaging.

The comparison emphasizes important trade-offs, where, the basic LED is the fastest but suffers from noise sensitivity and thick, inaccurate edges. LED + Gaussian improves stability but still lacks directional information and sharp localization. LoG offers the best quantitative performance among LED-based methods, providing a strong balance between noise suppression and accuracy. The CED delivers the highest qualitative performance, with the most reliable edge continuity and structural preservation, albeit at a higher computational cost.

Furthermore, the study identifies an optimal Gaussian standard deviation of $\sigma \approx 1.4$ for LoG, providing a practical, empirically validated parameter for real-world implementation. Computational analysis shows a quadratic scaling in processing time for both LoG and CED as image size increases, guiding practitioners in selecting the appropriate method based on accuracy-efficiency requirements. Overall, while Laplacian-based methods offer simplicity and speed, useful in low-noise or resource-limited environments, the CED remains the superior choice when precision, thin edges, and noise robustness are critical. Future enhancements may focus on improving LED's scale invariance and noise tolerance, and adapting CED with automatic thresholding and multi-scale processing to widen its applicability in real-time systems.

Acknowledgments. This research was sponsored by the University of Malaya Translational Research Grant Scheme, TRG0019-2025 (UM.0002388/HRU.IP) and the National Defense University of Malaysia.

Disclosure of Interests. The authors declare no conflict of interest.

References

1. Mahmood, Z.: Digital image processing: advanced technologies and applications. Appl. Sci. **14**(14), 6051 (2024). https://doi.org/10.3390/app14146051

2. Aldoury, R.S., Al-Saidi, N.M., Ibrahim, R.W., Kahtan, H.: A new X-ray images enhancement method using a class of fractional differential equation. MethodsX **11**, 102264 (2023). https://doi.org/10.1016/j.mex.2023.102264
3. Ganesan, P., Sajiv, G.: A comprehensive study of edge detection for image processing applications. In: 2017 International Conference on Innovations in Information, Embedded and Communication Systems (ICIIECS) (2017). https://doi.org/10.1109/iciiecs.2017.8275968
4. Chowdhury, M.R., Islam, M.M., Sadi, T.A., Miraz, M.H.H., Mahdy, M.R.C.: Edge detection quantumized: a novel quantum algorithm for image processing (2024). SSRN **4988241**. https://doi.org/10.2139/ssrn.4988241
5. Chang, Q., Li, X., Li, Y., Miyazaki, J.: Multi-directional Sobel operator kernel on GPUs. J. Parall. Distrib. Comput. **177**, 160–170 (2023). https://doi.org/10.1016/j.jpdc.2023.03.004
6. Kong, H., Akakin, H.C., Sarma, S.E.: A generalized Laplacian of Gaussian filter for blob detection and its applications. IEEE Trans. Cybern. **43**(6), 1719–1733 (2013). https://doi.org/10.1109/TSMCB.2012.2228639
7. Alwan, N.A., Al-Saidi, N.M., Obaiys, S.J., Noor, N.F.B.M., A., M.: A comprehensive review on classification of quantum image representations. Arch. Comput. Meth. Eng. 1–59 (2025)
8. Shubha, S.E.U., Islam, M.M., Sadi, T.A., Miraz, M.H.H., Mahdy, M.R.C.: Edge detection quantumized: a novel quantum algorithm for image processing. arXiv preprint arXiv:2404.06889 (2024)
9. Alwan, N.A., Obaiys, S.J., Al-Saidi, N.M., Noor, N.F.B.M., Karaca, Y.: Multilayered quantum computing and simulation system for enhanced image representation of HSI based Fourier transform and adjacency matrix. Sci. Rep. **15**(1), 40286 (2025)
10. Alwan, N.A., Obaiys, S.J., Al-Saidi, N.M., Noor, N.F.B.M., Karaca, Y.: A multichannel quantum image representation model with qubit sequences for quantum-inspired image and image retrieval. AIMS Math. **10**(5), 10994–11035 (2025)
11. Canny, J.: A computational approach to edge detection. IEEE Trans. Pattern Anal. Mach. Intell. **6**, 679–698 (1986). https://doi.org/10.1109/TPAMI.1986.4767851
12. Karthick, C.N., Nirmala, P.: Smart edge detection technique in X-ray images for improving PSNR using canny edge detection algorithm with gaussian filter in comparison with Laplacian algorithm. Cardiometry **25**, 1744–1750 (2022). https://doi.org/10.18137/cardiometry.2022.25.17441750
13. Widiyanto, S., Sundani, D., Karyanti, Y., Wardani, D.T.: Edge detection based on quantum canny enhancement for medical imaging. In: IOP Conference Series: Materials Science and Engineering, vol. 536, no. 1, p. 012118. IOP Publishing (2019)
14. Al-Ameen, Z.: X-ray lung image classification using a canny edge detector. Comput. Intell. and Neurosci. (2022). Article ID 3081584. https://doi.org/10.1155/2022/3081584
15. Trigka, M., Dritsas, E.: A comprehensive survey of deep learning approaches in image processing. Sensors **25**(2), 531 (2024). https://doi.org/10.3390/s25020531
16. Xu, P., Wang, J., Jiang, Y., Gong, X.: Applications of artificial intelligence and machine learning in image processing. Front. Mater. **11**, 1431179 (2024). https://doi.org/10.3389/fmats.2024.1431179
17. Obaiys, S.J., Jalab, H.A., Ibrahim, R.W.: New model for localfractional integral of Chebyshev polynomials for image denoising. RJCSE 22–28 (2019). https://doi.org/10.36811/rjcse.2019.110002

Advanced Numerical Approaches for assessment and design of no-tension Masonry Structures (ANAMS 2026)

The CASS Method for the Design of Supporting Structures

Andrea Montanino(✉) and Francesco Fabbrocino

Pegaso Telematic University, Centro Direzionale ISOLA F2, 80143 Naples, Italy
{andrea.montanino,francesco.fabbrocino}@unipegaso.it

Abstract. The understanding of the behavior of masonry structures is of fundamental importance in contemporary research, since a large portion of Europe's cultural and architectural heritage consists of masonry buildings of inestimable value, which require preservation and restoration. To this end, it is necessary to adopt technological tools capable of predicting their structural behavior, suitable for the complexity of the material. Masonry, in fact, is a peculiar material, which can be modeled as infinitely rigid in compression and incapable of resisting tension. This anisotropy makes it difficult to use standard finite element software, which instead requires a non-negligible number of parameters that are often very difficult to estimate. In this work, we present the Continuous Airy-based for Stress Singularities method (CASS) [1, 2, 3] for solving the stress field in masonry structures subjected to given forces and boundary displacements. This method is based on the minimization of complementary energy and is one of the few capable of directly providing the equilibrium solution for masonry structures. Through an appropriate variation of boundary data, it is possible to estimate the range of variability of the forces that a structure can transfer to supporting elements, such as buttresses and flying buttresses, thus enabling their design. In this way, the CASS method is proposed not only as a verification tool for existing structures, but also as a suitable design tool.

Keywords: Masonry structures · No-tension materials · Design methods · Conic optimisation

1 Introduction

The conservation and assessment of historic masonry structures -representing a substantial portion of the world's architectural heritage - have attracted growing interest within the scientific community. The development of accurate models capable of describing their mechanical behavior is essential not only for safeguarding human life but also for preserving their cultural and artistic value, particularly in relation to tourism and historical relevance [28]. Since most of these constructions are made of masonry, it is crucial to employ approaches that properly account for the distinctive mechanical features of this material.

O. Gervasi et al. (Eds.): ICCSA 2026 Workshops, LNCS 16758, pp. 429–445, 2027.
https://doi.org/10.1007/978-3-032-30497-1_26

Masonry is characterized by its ability to sustain compressive stresses while being essentially unable to resist tension [19,22,23]. Standard finite element (FE) methods often prove insufficient for capturing this behavior [5,47], thus motivating the development of more advanced modeling strategies [1,40,42,44–46,48].

A fundamental contribution in this field is due to Heyman, who reformulated masonry mechanics within the framework of modern plasticity theory. This led to the introduction of simplified models such as the Normal Rigid No-Tension (NRNT) model, where masonry is treated as a continuum that can carry compression but not tension. Unlike previously mentioned approaches, which require accurate constitutive descriptions and parameter identification [10], Heyman's model does not rely on the calibration of material parameters [3,20].

One of the main challenges in the analysis of masonry structures concerns the treatment of stress singularities, i.e., regions where stresses concentrate along lines or surfaces. Within the Heyman framework, several approaches have been proposed to address this issue, both for curved structures such as domes and vaults [9,13,37], and for planar masonry systems. These include displacement-based formulations [21,25–27,29,32] as well as force-based approaches [2,4,8,31,39].

Focusing on masonry façades, the Continuous Airy-based method for Stress Singularities (CASS) has been recently introduced as an effective tool for the mesh-independent identification of stress patterns [33]. A distinctive aspect of the CASS approach is the evaluation of curvature within finite elements, which is not commonly addressed in standard formulations. Several strategies have been explored in the literature, including the use of averaged values over neighboring elements [14], as well as the adoption of higher-order plate elements, such as those employed in Isogeometric Analysis (IGA) [12], to enhance continuity and computational efficiency. However, this latter approach may introduce an artificial level of continuity in the Airy stress potential, potentially restricting the admissible solution space of the boundary value problem.

An additional advantage of the CASS method is its capability to efficiently estimate the load-bearing capacity of masonry structures by identifying the maximum load multiplier for which an equilibrated solution exists [15,30,34,38]. This also enables the determination of in-plane collapse mechanisms [6,7,11,16–18,41,43].

The stress states that can arise within masonry structures are highly varied and strongly influenced by boundary conditions, such as applied loads and support settlements, which are often difficult to determine with accuracy. Moreover, due to the hyperstatic and inelastic nature of these systems, multiple stress distributions may develop even under identical boundary conditions, all of which satisfy equilibrium and compatibility requirements [24].

The objective of this work is to exploit the capabilities of the CASS method to estimate the range of admissible stress states that can occur within a masonry structure. In particular, attention is devoted to understanding how loads are transferred to adjacent structural elements. From this perspective, the CASS method can be interpreted as a design-oriented tool for masonry structures, enabling the proper dimensioning of supporting systems.

In the following section, the main features of the CASS method are recalled, with emphasis on its most relevant aspects, including its numerical formulation. Section 3 focuses on a practical application, where a portal structure supported by an adjacent system is introduced. By varying the boundary conditions, the study aims to evaluate the range of forces that may be transmitted to the supporting structure, thus providing useful indications for its design.

2 Boundary Value Problem

This section briefly recalls the Boundary Value Problem (BVP) for masonry structures, together with the key ingredients required for the formulation of the CASS approach.

Let $\Omega \in \mathrm{R}^2$ be the domain under consideration, as shown in Fig. 1, with boundary $\partial\Omega$ divided into a Neumann part $\partial\Omega_N$ and a Dirichlet part $\partial\Omega_D$, such that $\partial\Omega_N \cap \partial\Omega_D = \emptyset$ and $\partial\Omega_N \cup \partial\Omega_D = \partial\Omega$.

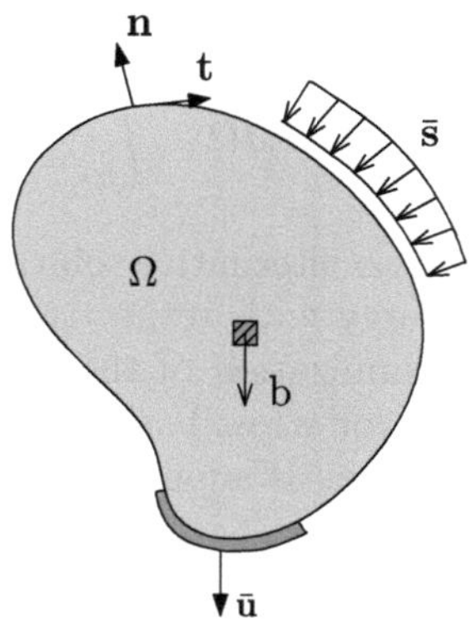

Fig. 1. Domain of the Boundary Value Problem with main notation.

The BVP over Ω is defined by equilibrium equations, kinematic relations, and a constitutive model. The equilibrium conditions are written as

$$\nabla \cdot \mathbf{T} + \mathbf{b} = \mathbf{0} \quad , \qquad \mathbf{x} \in \Omega \tag{1a}$$

$$\mathbf{Tn} = \bar{\mathbf{s}} \qquad \mathbf{x} \in \partial\Omega_N \tag{1b}$$

where $\mathbf{T}$ denotes the stress tensor, $\mathbf{b}$ represents body forces, $\mathbf{n}$ is the outward unit normal to the boundary, and $\bar{\mathbf{s}}$ is the prescribed traction on $\partial\Omega_N$.

The kinematic relations take the form

$$\mathbf{E} = \frac{1}{2}\left(\nabla\mathbf{u} + \nabla\mathbf{u}^T\right) \quad , \qquad \mathbf{x} \in \Omega \tag{2a}$$

$$\mathbf{u} = \bar{\mathbf{u}} \qquad \mathbf{x} \in \partial\Omega_D \tag{2b}$$

where $\mathbf{E}$ is the strain tensor, $\mathbf{u}$ the displacement field, and $\bar{\mathbf{u}}$ the imposed displacement on $\partial\Omega_D$.

The constitutive behavior of masonry is described according to Heyman's Normal, Rigid, No-Tension (NRNT) model, expressed as

$$\mathbf{T} \in \mathrm{Sym}^- \quad , \tag{3a}$$

$$\mathbf{E} \in \mathrm{Sym}^+ \quad , \tag{3b}$$

$$\mathbf{T} \cdot \mathbf{E} = 0 \quad , \tag{3c}$$

where (3a) enforces the no-tension condition, (3b) expresses rigidity under compression, and (3c) represents the normality condition, corresponding to infinite friction.

The boundary value problem can be recast into a variational formulation by introducing the Total Potential Energy

$$\mathcal{E}_p(\mathbf{u}) = \frac{1}{2}\int_{\Omega} \mathbf{T} \cdot \mathbf{E} d\Omega - \int_{\partial\Omega_N} \bar{\mathbf{s}} \cdot \mathbf{u} dA - \int_{\Omega} \mathbf{b} \cdot \mathbf{u} d\Omega \tag{4}$$

or the Total Complementary Energy

$$\mathcal{E}_c(\mathbf{T}) = \frac{1}{2}\int_{\Omega} \mathbf{T} \cdot \mathbf{E} d\Omega - \int_{\partial\Omega_D} \mathbf{T}\mathbf{n} \cdot \bar{\mathbf{u}} d\Omega \tag{5}$$

These functionals allow for two alternative solution strategies [36]: minimization of the Total Potential Energy with respect to $\mathbf{u}$ leads to a displacement-based formulation, whereas minimization of the Total Complementary Energy with respect to $\mathbf{T}$ yields a force- or stress-based formulation.

In this work, the latter approach is adopted, and the problem is written as

$$\mathcal{E}_c(\mathbf{T}^*) = \min \mathbf{T} \in \mathcal{H}\mathcal{E}_c(\mathbf{T}) \quad , \tag{6}$$

with

$$\mathcal{H} = \left\{ \mathbf{T} \in \mathrm{SBV} \text{ s.t. } \mathbf{T} \in \mathrm{Sym}^- \, , \, \nabla \cdot \mathbf{T} + \mathbf{b} = \mathbf{0} \, , \, \mathbf{T}\mathbf{n} = \bar{\mathbf{s}} \right\} \tag{7}$$

denoting the set of admissible stress fields, i.e., fields satisfying both equilibrium conditions (1) and the material constraint (3a).

Furthermore, owing to the normality condition (3c), the functional reduces to the linear form

$$\mathcal{E}_c(\mathbf{T}) = -\int_{\partial\Omega_D} \mathbf{T}\mathbf{n} \cdot \bar{\mathbf{u}} d\Omega \tag{8}$$

In its current form, Problem (6)–(7), expressed directly in terms of the stress tensor, would lead-after discretization-to a large number of equality constraints associated with equilibrium. To avoid this issue, it is convenient to introduce the Airy stress potential F, which automatically satisfies the equilibrium equations.

The Airy stress potential is introduced as

$$\mathrm{F} \in C^0 \quad \text{s.t.} \quad \mathbf{T} = \mathbf{R}^T \mathbf{H}(\mathrm{F}) \mathbf{R} + \mathbf{B}_{\mathrm{F}} \, , \tag{9}$$

with **H** denoting the Hessian operator, **R** a skew-symmetric tensor representing a counterclockwise rotation of $\pi/2$, and **BF** a tensor accounting for the body force distribution **b**, such that

$$\nabla \cdot \mathbf{B}_{\mathrm{F}} = -\mathbf{b}\,. \tag{10}$$

In Cartesian coordinates, relations (9) and (10) take the form

$$\mathrm{T}_{xx} = \mathrm{F}_{,yy}\,, \quad \mathrm{T}_{yy} = \mathrm{F}_{,xx}\,, \, \mathrm{T}_{xy} = -\mathrm{F}_{,xy} + b_y x + b_x y\,, \tag{11}$$

where T_{xx}, T_{yy}, and T_{xy} are the Cartesian components of the stress tensor **T**, and b_x, b_y are the components of the body force vector **b**. A subscript following a comma denotes partial differentiation. Substitution of (11) into (10) confirms that equilibrium is identically satisfied.

Consequently, Problem (6)–(7) can be reformulated in terms of the Airy stress potential as

$$\mathcal{E}_c(\mathrm{F}^*) = \min_{\mathrm{F}\in\mathcal{H}_{\mathrm{F}}} \mathcal{E}_c(\mathrm{F}) \quad , \tag{12}$$

where $\mathcal{H}_{\mathrm{F}}$ denotes the corresponding admissible set of Airy stress potentials.

The material constraints are translated into conditions on the Hessian of F, namely

$$\mathbf{R}^T\mathbf{H}(\mathrm{F})\mathbf{R} + \mathbf{B}_{\mathrm{F}} \in Sym^- \tag{13}$$

which, in Cartesian coordinates, read

$$\mathrm{F}_{,xx} + \mathrm{F}_{,yy} \leq 0, \quad \mathrm{F}_{,xx}\,\mathrm{F}_{,yy} - (-\mathrm{F}_{,xy} + \mathrm{b}_{\mathrm{F}})^2 \geq 0\,. \tag{14}$$

In the absence of body forces, condition (13) admits a direct geometrical interpretation: since the Hessian governs curvature, the Airy stress potential must be pointwise concave, i.e., it must have a negative semi-definite Hessian throughout the domain.

As for the boundary conditions, the Airy-based formulation rewrites equilibrium as

$$\mathbf{R}^T\mathbf{H}(\mathrm{F})\mathbf{R}\mathbf{n} + \mathbf{B}_{\mathrm{F}}\mathbf{n} = \bar{\mathbf{s}}, \tag{15}$$

and, introducing

$$\mathrm{T}nn = \mathbf{n}\cdot\mathbf{T}\mathbf{n}\,, \quad \mathrm{T}_{nt} = \mathbf{t}\cdot\mathbf{T}\mathbf{n}, \tag{16}$$

as the normal and tangential stress components at the boundary, with **t** the tangent vector and $\mathbf{n} = \mathbf{R}\mathbf{t}$ the outward normal, the boundary conditions can be expressed as

$$\mathrm{T}_{nn} = \bar{\mathbf{s}}\cdot\mathbf{n} = \mathbf{t}\cdot\mathbf{H}(\mathrm{F})\mathbf{t} + \mathbf{n}\cdot\mathbf{B}_{\mathrm{F}}\mathbf{n} = \mathrm{F}_{,tt} - 2\mathrm{b}_{\mathrm{F}} t_x t_y \tag{17a}$$

$$\mathrm{T}_{nt} = \bar{\mathbf{s}}\cdot\mathbf{t} = -\mathbf{n}\cdot\mathbf{H}(\mathrm{F})\mathbf{t} + \mathbf{t}\cdot\mathbf{B}_{\mathrm{F}}\mathbf{n} = - \mathrm{F}_{,nt} + \mathrm{b}_{\mathrm{F}}(t_x^2 - t_y^2) \tag{17b}$$

where t_x and t_y are the Cartesian components of the tangent vector **t**.

3 The Continuous Airy-Based for Stress Singularities

This section recalls the essential aspects of the numerical formulation introduced in [35], starting from the discretisation of the domain and leading to the discrete version of the optimisation problem (12).

The domain is subdivided into quadrilateral plate-type finite elements, each defined by four corner nodes, as shown in Fig. 2b. At each node, three degrees of freedom are assigned: the scalar value of the unknown function ϕ and its first derivatives with respect to the Cartesian coordinates, $\phi_{,x}$ and $\phi_{,y}$. This choice guarantees C^1 continuity at the nodes, while only C^0 continuity is ensured along element boundaries, since continuity of the normal derivative cannot be enforced between adjacent elements.

To maintain generality, each physical element is mapped onto a square reference element, referred to as the parent element, defined in the parametric coordinate system $0, s, t$, with $0 < s < 1$ and $0 < t < 1$, as illustrated in Fig. 2.

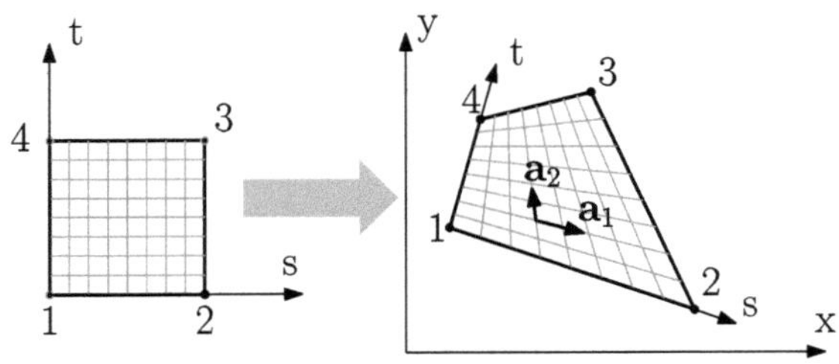

Fig. 2. Mapping between the parent and real geometries.

Since each element is associated with 12 degrees of freedom, the interpolating function $\phi(x(s,t), y(s,t))$ is constructed as the scalar product between a coefficient vector $\hat{\mathbf{w}} = [w_1, ...w_{12}]^T$ and a monomial basis

$$\mathbf{p}^T(s,t) = \left[1, s, t, s^2, st, t^2, s^3, s^2t, st^2, t^3, s^3t, st^3\right] , \tag{18}$$

such that

$$\phi(x(s,t), y(s,t)) = \mathbf{p}^T(s,t)\hat{\mathbf{w}} \quad , \tag{19}$$

The coefficient vector $\hat{\mathbf{w}}$ can be expressed in terms of the nodal degrees of freedom

$$\hat{\boldsymbol{\phi}} = [\hat{\phi}^1, \hat{\phi}^1{}_{,x}, \hat{\phi}^1{}_{,y}, ..., \hat{\phi}^4, \hat{\phi}^4{}_{,x}, \hat{\phi}^4{}_{,y}] \tag{20}$$

by enforcing interpolation conditions on the physical element. These conditions consist of 12 constraints of the form

$$\phi\Big|^i = \hat{\phi}^i, \quad \phi_{,x}\Big|^i = \hat{\phi}^i{}_{,x}, \quad \phi_{,y}\Big|^i = \hat{\phi}^i{}_{,y}, \tag{21}$$

with $i = 1, .., 4$, which can be written in compact form as

$$\hat{\boldsymbol{\phi}} = \mathbf{B}\hat{\mathbf{w}} \quad . \tag{22}$$

By inverting (22) and substituting into (19), the final interpolation function becomes

$$\phi(x(s,t), y(s,t)) = \mathbf{p}^T(s,t)\mathbf{B}^{-1}(\hat{\mathbf{x}})\hat{\boldsymbol{\phi}}\,. \tag{23}$$

As highlighted in Sect. 2, the computation of stresses requires the evaluation of curvature. Since curvature is not continuous at the nodes, it must be evaluated at internal locations within each element, referred to as control points. In this work, the following points in the parametric domain are selected

$$\begin{aligned} \bar{s}_1 &= 0.25\,, & \bar{t}_1 &= 0.25 \\ \bar{s}_2 &= 0.75\,, & \bar{t}_2 &= 0.25 \\ \bar{s}_3 &= 0.75\,, & \bar{t}_3 &= 0.75 \\ \bar{s}_4 &= 0.25\,, & \bar{t}_4 &= 0.75 \end{aligned} \tag{24}$$

as depicted in Fig. 3.

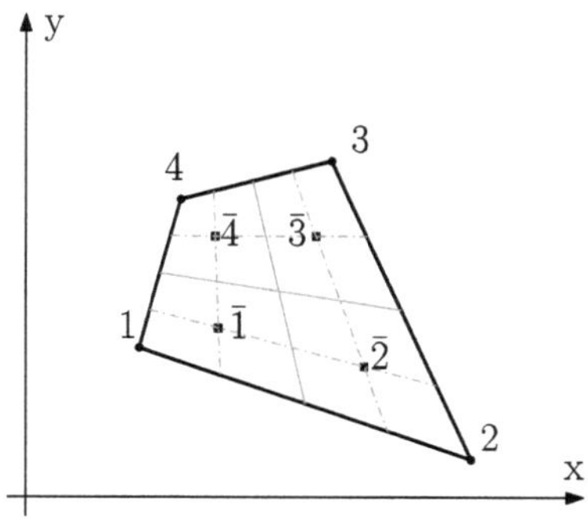

Fig. 3. Position of the control points on a generic element. The control points are placed at the centres of each quadrant in which the element is partitioned.

The Hessian tensor $\mathbf{H}(\phi)$, expressed in the curvilinear coordinate system of Fig. 2b, is written as

$$\mathbf{H} = (\nabla\phi),\alpha \otimes \mathbf{a}^\alpha\,, \tag{25}$$

where $\mathbf{a}^\alpha$, $\alpha = 1, 2$ denote the contravariant basis vectors. The projection onto the Cartesian coordinate system is then given by

$$\mathrm{H}_{ij} = [(\nabla\phi)_{,\alpha} \cdot \mathbf{e}_i](\mathbf{a}^\alpha \cdot \mathbf{e}_j)\,. \tag{26}$$

In Eqs. 25–(26), differentiation with respect to α corresponds to partial derivatives with respect to the parametric coordinates s and t.

After algebraic manipulation (see [35] for details), the Cartesian components of the curvature can be expressed in terms of the nodal degrees of freedom as

$$\begin{aligned} \phi_{,xx} &= \mathbf{h}_{xx}^T\mathbf{B}^{-1}\hat{\boldsymbol{\phi}} \\ \phi_{,yy} &= \mathbf{h}_{yy}^T\mathbf{B}^{-1}\hat{\boldsymbol{\phi}} \\ \phi_{,xy} &= \mathbf{h}_{xy}^T\mathbf{B}^{-1}\hat{\boldsymbol{\phi}} \end{aligned} \tag{27}$$

where $\mathbf{h}_{xx}$, $\mathbf{h}_{yy}$, and $\mathbf{h}_{xy}$ are vector functions depending on the parametric coordinates and the element mapping.

3.1 BVP Discretisation

Based on the formulation introduced above, the discretisation of the BVP is now addressed.

3.2 Objective Function

The Total Complementary Energy (8), expressed in terms of the Airy stress potential, is given by

$$\mathcal{E}_c(\mathrm{F}) = -\int_{\partial\Omega_D} \left(\mathbf{R}^T\mathbf{H}(\mathrm{F})\mathbf{R} + \mathbf{B}_{\mathrm{F}}\right)\mathbf{n}\cdot\bar{\mathbf{u}}ds, \tag{28}$$

which involves second derivatives of the unknown function, not directly included among the degrees of freedom. However, by integrating Eq. (28) along the Dirichlet boundary, one obtains, after discretisation,

$$\begin{aligned}\mathcal{E}_c(\hat{\mathbf{F}}) \;&= [F_{,t}\big|_1 - F_{,t}\big|_2 - 2\mathrm{bF}t_x t_y \Delta s]\bar{u}_n + \\ &[F_{,n}\big|_2 - F_{,n}\big|_1 - \mathrm{b_F}(t_x^2 - t_y^2)\Delta s]\bar{u}_t\,,\end{aligned} \tag{29}$$

where $\bar{u}_t$ and $\bar{u}_n$ denote the tangential and normal boundary displacements. Summation over all the boundary elements yields the discrete objective function. The quantities $F_{,t}$ and $F_{,n}$ can be further expressed in terms of the Cartesian components of the gradient at the nodes.

3.3 Material Admissibility Constraints

The requirement of negative semi-definiteness of the stress tensor is enforced by evaluating the stress at the control points, that is, by applying (14) through (27). This leads to a set of conic constraints of the form

$$\begin{aligned}&(\mathbf{h}_{xx}^T + \mathbf{h}_{yy}^T)\mathbf{B}^{-1}\hat{\mathbf{F}} && \leq 0\\ &(\mathbf{h}_{xx}^T\mathbf{B}^{-1}\hat{\mathbf{F}})(\mathbf{h}_{yy}^T\mathbf{B}^{-1}\hat{\mathbf{F}}) - ((\mathbf{h}_{xy}^T\mathbf{B}^{-1}\hat{\mathbf{F}}) - b(\mathbf{x}))^2 && \geq 0\end{aligned} \tag{30}$$

Collecting these relations over all control points produces a global set of conic inequality constraints, which can be written as

$$f(\hat{\mathbf{F}}) \geq \mathbf{0} \tag{31}$$

3.4 Boundary Equilibrium

The final step concerns the enforcement of the boundary conditions (17). Since second derivatives are involved, and these are not nodal variables, it is convenient to integrate the stresses along the element boundaries. In this way, equilibrium is imposed in terms of stress resultants rather than point-wise values, corresponding to an averaged equilibrium at the element level. This approximation converges to the exact condition as the mesh is refined.

Accordingly, Eq. (17) are rewritten as

$$\mathbf{R}_n = \int_{\partial\Omega_{el}} [\mathrm{F}_{,tt} - 2\mathrm{b}_{\mathrm{F}} t_x t_y]\, ds \tag{32a}$$

$$\mathbf{R}_t = - \int_{\partial\Omega_{el}} \left[\mathrm{F}_{,nt} + \mathrm{b}_{\mathrm{F}} (t_x^2 - t_y^2)\right] ds \tag{32b}$$

where $\mathbf{R}_n$ and $\mathbf{R}_t$ represent the normal and tangential resultants of the applied loads along the element boundary.

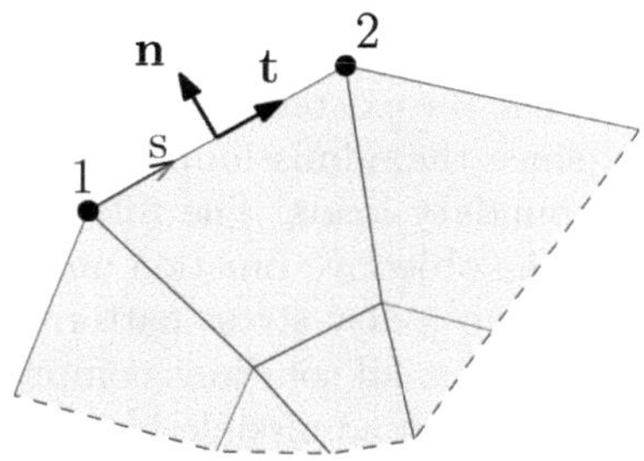

Fig. 4. Geometry of a boundary element and main notation.

After further algebraic manipulation, and expressing the relations in terms of nodal degrees of freedom, the boundary conditions at the element level are written as

$$\begin{aligned} F_{,t}\big|_2 - F_{,t}\big|_1 = T_{nn}\Delta s \\ - b_y t_x t_y (x_1 + x_2)\Delta s \\ - b_x t_x t_y (y_1 + y_2)\Delta s \end{aligned} \tag{33}$$

$$\begin{aligned} F_{,n}\big|_2 - F_{,n}\big|_1 = -T_{nt}\Delta s \\ + \frac{1}{2} b_y (t_x^2 - t_y^2)(x_1 + x_2)\Delta s \\ + \frac{1}{2} b_x (t_x^2 - t_y^2)(y_1 + y_2)\Delta s \end{aligned} \tag{34}$$

where Δs denotes the length of the element boundary, and x_1, x_2, y_1, y_1 are the coordinates of the endpoints, as shown in Fig. 4.

These relations can be assembled into a linear system in terms of the nodal degrees of freedom as

$$\mathbf{K}_{\partial\Omega}\hat{\mathbf{F}} = \hat{\mathbf{s}} \tag{35}$$

3.5 Discrete Boundary Value Problem

Finally, by combining Eqs. (29), (31), and (35), the discrete optimisation problem is obtained as

$$\begin{aligned} \mathcal{E}_c(\hat{\mathbf{F}}^0) \quad &= \min \mathcal{E}_c(\hat{\mathbf{F}}) \\ \text{s.t.} \qquad & f(\hat{\mathbf{F}}) \leq \mathbf{0} \\ & \mathbf{K}_{\partial\Omega}\hat{\mathbf{F}} = \hat{\mathbf{s}} \end{aligned} \tag{36}$$

3.6 Exploration of Different Equilibrium Solutions

Problem (36) is strongly driven by the objective function, that, following Eq. (29), is strongly dependent on the settlements at the Dirichlet boundary and, more in general, on boundary node displacements. From Eqs. (34), (33), and (30), it can be noticed that the existence of a solution is independent of the prescribed displacements, since the admissibility domain depends only on the geometry and prescribed boundary loads. The role of the prescribed displacement is therefore to change the objective function and localize the minimiser of the BVP, driving the solution to a new stress pattern. Furthermore, in case of vanishing boundary displacements, all solutions comprised in $\mathcal{H}$ have the same energetic level and therefore, are all admissible in terms of the requirements of the minimisation problem.

In the light of this, one possible way to explore possible stress patterns inside a structure, and therefore, the consequent load distributions on Dirichlet boundary, is to fictitiously prescribe different settlements such to drive the minimisation problem to new stress solutions.

4 Numerical Results

The proposed algorithm is applied to the portal shown in Fig. 5, with dimensions $B = 5$ m, $H = 12$ m, $h = 3$ m, $R = 3$ m; the structure is supported on its left and right pillars, and on the region S, highlighted in red in the Figure. Along this line, in fact, a supporting structure has to be designed; the structure is loaded under its self-weight, being $b = 17$ kN/m^2, and under a contact load q on the top side, being $q = 100$ kN/m.

To explore the possible stress patterns of the domain, and in particular, the reacting force on the region S, it is imagined to have a soil settlement under the left pillar, of the shape (Figs. 7 and 10)

$$\delta = \hat{u} \sin\theta \mathbf{e}_1 - \hat{v} \cos\theta \mathbf{e}_2 \,. \tag{37}$$

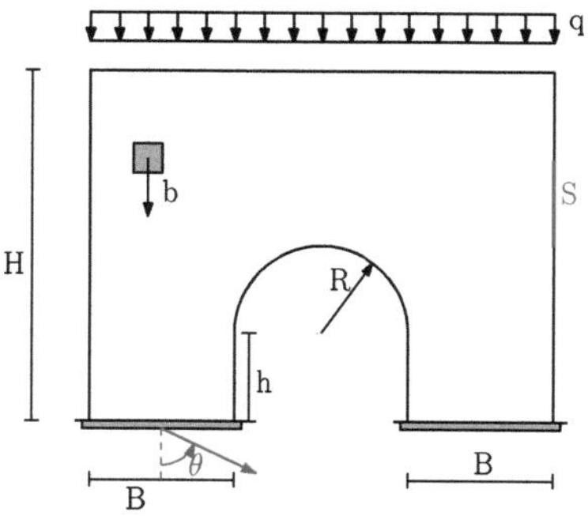

Fig. 5. Geometry and boundary conditions of the case study.

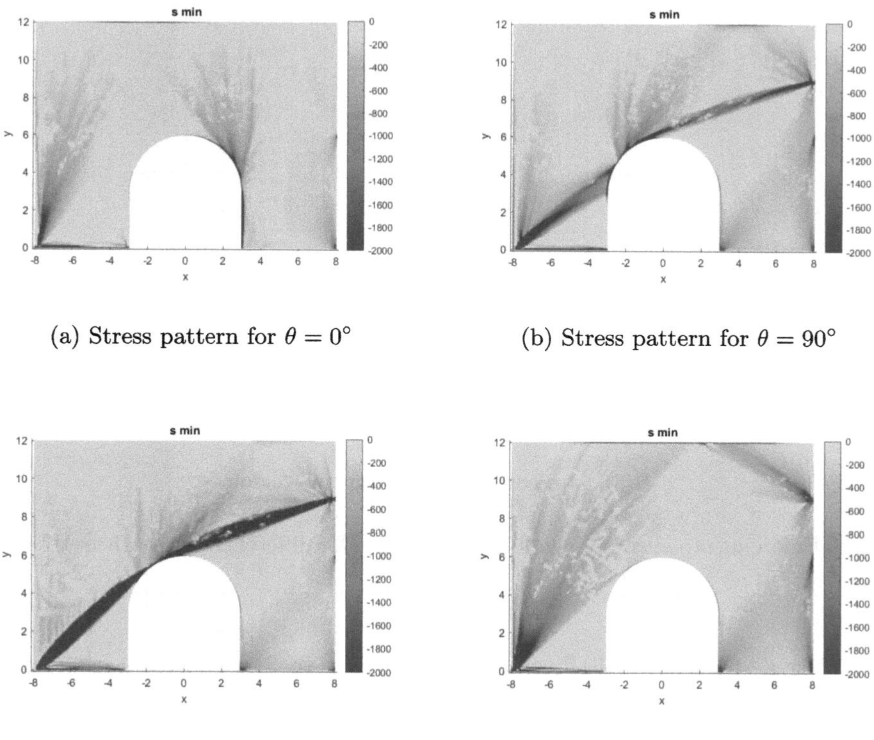

(a) Stress pattern for $\theta = 0°$

(b) Stress pattern for $\theta = 90°$

(c) Stress pattern for $\theta = 180°$

(d) Stress pattern for $\theta = 270°$

Fig. 6. Stress patterns for different boundary conditions.

Through the variation of θ in the range $[0, 2\pi]$, it is possible to explore a wide range of possible stress configurations and thus, of reacting force on the region S.

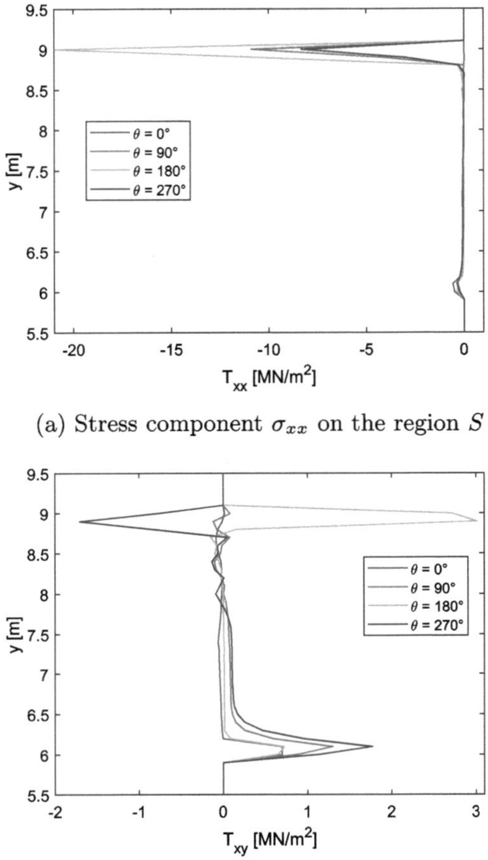

(a) Stress component σ_{xx} on the region S

(b) Stress component σ_{xy} on the region S

Fig. 7. Emerging stress components on the region S for different value of the settlement angle θ.

In Fig. 6 the stress distribution corresponding to four representative angles are shown: in Fig. 6a, the effects of a downward settlement are depicted; in Fig. 6b, a displacement to the right is imposed; in Fig. 6c an upward settlement is imposed, while in Fig. 6d a displacement to the left is prescribed.

The corresponding emerging stress distributions in the region S are shown in Fig. 8, and more in detail, Fig. 8a represents the stress T_{xx} profile on S, while 8b represents the emerging shear stress.

Finally, Fig. 9 represents the total computed reactions on S for the whole range 0°–360°.

From these figures, it is evident the range that the supporting structure, which has its imprint on S, must sustain. In particular, the supporting structure must support a horizontal load ranging between 0 and 4000 kN, while the vertical

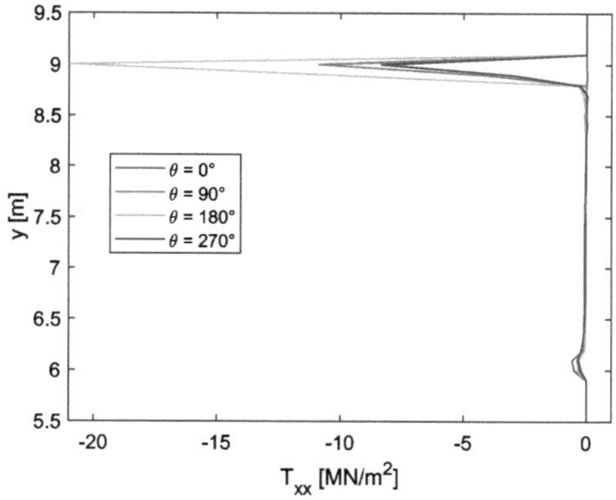

(a) Stress component σ_{xx} on the region S

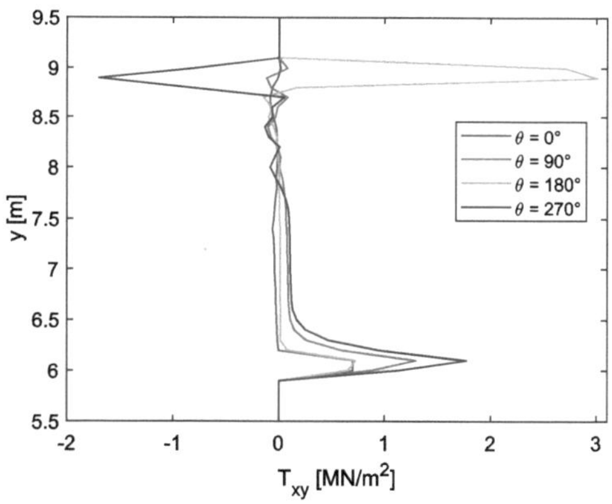

(b) Stress component σ_{xy} on the region S

Fig. 8. Emerging stress components on the region S for different value of the settlement angle θ.

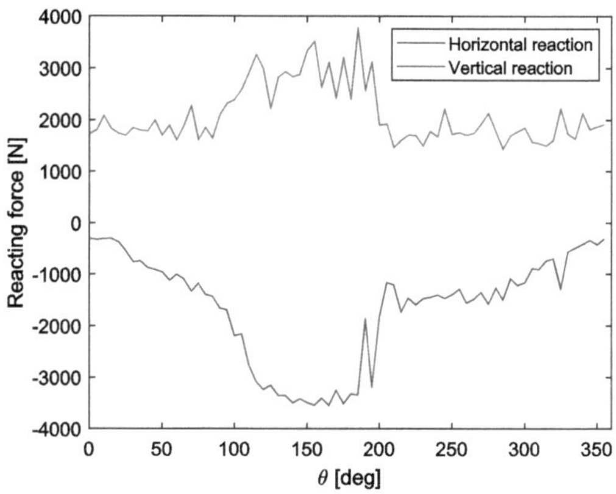

Fig. 9. Variation of the horizontal and vertical reaction force for different values of the settlement angle θ.

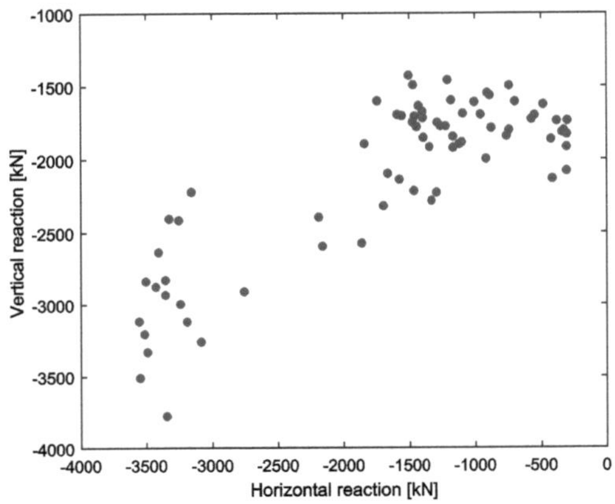

Fig. 10. Range of horizontal and vertical reaction on the region S.

reaction ranges between 1000 kN and 3500 kN. Such values must be accounted for dimensioning the related supporting structure.

5 Conclusion

In the present work, the Continuous Airy-based method for Stress Singularities has been used as a design tool for the quantification of loads on supporting structures. After introducing the boundary value problem for no-tension materials, and recalling the principal characteristics of the CASS method, with particular attention on the minimisation problem and imposition of boundary conditions, the methodology at the base of the present insight have been disclosed. In particular, the objective is to explore a wide range of stress solution, to compute the possible reaction force on contrained parts of the boundary, which may serve as imprint of supporting structure. This is done by changing fictitiously the boundary settlements in some parts of the domain, in order to generate different stress patterns.

The methodology have been finally applied to the case study of a portal, giving some imposed displacement to one of its two piers; the corresponding stress solution have been adopted to evaluate the reacting forces on a region of the right side of the portal, in order to determine which is the load that is discharged on an eventual supporting structure, as, for example, a flying buttress.

The obtained results confirm the viability of the CASS method as a monitoring tool and as a design tool. Future development will concern the exploration of alternative ways to increase the range of investigated stress pattern, to have a more precise perspective on the behaviour of the structure under investigation.

References

1. Alfano, G., Rosati, L., Valoroso, N.: A numerical strategy for finite element analysis of no-tension materials. Int. J. Numer. Meth. Eng. **48**(3), 317–350 (2000). https://doi.org/10.1002/(SICI)1097-0207(20000530)48:33.0.CO;2-C
2. Angelillo, M.: Constitutive relations for no-tension materials. Meccanica **28**, 195–202 (1993). https://doi.org/10.1007/BF00989121
3. Angelillo, M. (ed.): Mechanics of Masonry Structures. CICMS, vol. 551. Springer, Vienna (2014). https://doi.org/10.1007/978-3-7091-1774-3
4. Baratta, A., Corbi, O.: Stress analysis of masonry vaults and static efficacy of FRP repairs. Int. J. Solids Struct. **44**(24), 8028–8056 (2007). https://doi.org/10.1016/j.tafmec.2005.09.008
5. Block, P., Ciblac, T., Ochsendorf, J.: Real-time limit analysis of vaulted masonry buildings. Comput. Struct. **84**(29–30), 1841–1852 (2006). https://doi.org/10.1016/j.compstruc.2006.08.002
6. Buzzetti, M., Gandolfi, A., Pingaro, N., Milani, G.: A new advanced and simple procedure for the nonlinear static analysis of curved masonry structures. In: Mazzolani, F.M., Landolfo, R., Faggiano, B. (eds.) IPROHITECH 2025. LNCE, vol. 596, pp. 176–183. Springer, Cham (2025). https://doi.org/10.1007/978-3-031-87316-4_22
7. Buzzetti, M., Pingaro, N., Gandolfi, A., Milani, G.: Limit analysis-based approach for the assessment of local failures in masonry aggregates according to Italian standards. In: Mazzolani, F.M., Landolfo, R., Faggiano, B. (eds.) PROHITECH 2025. LNCE, vol. 596, pp. 168–175. Springer, Cham (2025). https://doi.org/10.1007/978-3-031-87316-4_21
8. Cuomo, M., Ventura, G.: A complementary energy formulation of no tension masonry-like solids. Comput. Methods Appl. Mech. Eng. **189**(1), 313–339 (2000). https://doi.org/10.1016/S0045-7825(99)00298-4
9. Cusano, C., Montanino, A., Olivieri, C., Paris, V., Cennamo, C.: Graphical and analytical quantitative comparison in the Domes assessment: the case of San Francesco di Paola. Appl. Sci. **11**(8), 3622 (2021)
10. Di Gennaro, L., et al.: In-situ load testing of an ancient masonry structure using fibre optics. Structures **70**, 107567 (2024)
11. Fabbrocino, F., Olivieri, C., Luciano, R., Vaiano, G., Maddaloni, G., Iannuzzo, A.: Seismic performance of historic masonry buildings: A comparative analysis of equivalent frame and block-based methods. Alex. Eng. J. **109**, 359–375 (2024)
12. Farahat, A., Verhelst, H.M., Kiendl, J., Kapl, M.: Isogeometric analysis for multi-patch structured Kirchhoff-Love shells. Comput. Methods Appl. Mech. Eng. **411**, 116060 (2023)
13. Fraddosio, A., Lepore, N., Piccioni, M.D.: Thrust surface method: an innovative approach for the three-dimensional lower bound limit analysis of masonry vaults. Eng. Struct. **202**, 109846 (2020)
14. Fraternali, F., Angelillo, M., Fortunato, A.: A lumped stress method for plane elastic problems and the discrete-continuum approximation. Int. J. Solids Struct. **39**(25), 6211–6240 (2002)
15. Galassi, S., Ruggieri, N., Tempesta, G.: A novel numerical tool for seismic vulnerability analysis of ruins in archaeological sites. Int. J. Arch. Heritage **14**(1), 1–22 (2020). https://doi.org/10.1080/15583058.2018.1492647

16. Galassi, S., Tempesta, G.: Safety assessment of masonry undamaged and damaged arches subjected to gravitational loads and horizontal forces: a numeric procedure to identify the optimal thrust line. Int. J. Solids Struct. **301**, 112943 (2024). https://doi.org/10.1016/j.ijsolstr.2024.112943
17. Galassi, S., Zampieri, P.: A new automatic procedure for nonlinear analysis of masonry arches subjected to large support movements. Eng. Struct. **276**, 115359 (2023). https://doi.org/10.1016/j.engstruct.2022.115359
18. Galassi, S.: An alternative approach for limit analysis of masonry arches on moving supports in finite small displacements. Eng. Fail. Anal. **145**, 107004 (2023)
19. Guadagnuolo, M., Di Gennaro, L., Basile, A., De Matteis, G.: Simplified methods for the evaluation of mechanical properties of tuff masonry walls in Campania (Italy). Procedia Struct. Integrity **44**, 878–885 (2023)
20. Heyman, J.: The stone skeleton. Int. J. Solids Struct. **2**(2), 249–279 (1966). https://doi.org/10.1016/0020-7683(66)90018-7
21. Hua, Y., Buzzetti, M., Pingaro, N., da Silva, L.C., Milani, G.: A computerized tool for the kinematic limit analysis of 2D masonry structures failing on a tilting table. SoftwareX **30**, 102180 (2025)
22. Huerta, S.: The analysis of masonry architecture: a historical approach: to the memory of professor Henry. J. Cowan. Arch. Sci. Rev. **51**(4), 297–328 (2008). https://doi.org/10.3763/asre.2008.5136
23. Huerta Fernández, S.: Mechanics of masonry vaults: the equilibrium approach (2001)
24. Iannuzzo, A., Gesualdo, A., Olivieri, C., Montanino, A.: 3D exploration of internal stresses due to lateral loads and foundation movements in a semicircular arch. In: Computational Methods in Structural Dynamics and Earthquake Engineering, pp. 2476–2491. National Technical University of Athens (2023)
25. Iannuzzo, A., Musone, V., Ruocco, E.: A neural network-based automated methodology to identify the crack causes in masonry structures. Comput.-Aided Civ. Infrastruct. Eng. **39**(24), 3769–3785 (2024)
26. Iannuzzo, A., Block, P., Angelillo, M., Gesualdo, A.: A continuous energy-based numerical approach to predict fracture mechanisms in masonry structures: CDF method. Comput. Struct. **257**, 106645 (2021). https://doi.org/10.1016/j.compstruc.2021.106645
27. Iannuzzo, A., Mallardo, V.: A novel approach to model differential settlements and crack patterns in masonry structures. Eng. Struct. **323**, 119220 (2025)
28. Iannuzzo, A., Matarazzo, G., Cusano, C., Ferraro, M., Maddaloni, G.: Insights into the collapse of the asciello masonry bridge in benevento. In: Gervasi, O., et al. (eds.) ICCSA 2025. LNCS, vol. 15886, pp. 381–395. Springer, Cham (2025). https://doi.org/10.1007/978-3-031-97576-9_26
29. Iannuzzo, A., Mele, T.V., Block, P.: Stability and load-bearing capacity assessment of a deformed multi-span masonry bridge using the PRD method. Int. J. Masonry Res. Innov. **6**(4), 422–445 (2021). https://doi.org/10.1504/IJMRI.2021.118842
30. Iannuzzo, A., Montanino, A.: A limit analysis-based CASS approach for the in-plane seismic capacity of masonry façades. Int. J. Solids Struct. **289**, 112633 (2024). https://doi.org/10.1016/j.ijsolstr.2023.112633
31. Lucchesi, M., Šilhavý, M., Zani, N.: A new class of equilibrated stress fields for no-tension bodies. J. Mech. Mater. Struct. **1**(3), 503–539 (2006). https://doi.org/10.2140/jomms.2006.1.503
32. Meloni, G., Pourfouladi, M., Pingaro, N.: Parametric modelling and nonlinear FE analysis of trepponti bridge subjected to differential settlements. Buildings **16**, 47 (2026). https://doi.org/10.3390/buildings16010047

33. Montanino, A., De Gregorio, D., Olivieri, C., Iannuzzo, A.: The continuous airy-based for stress-singularities (CASS) method: an energy-based numerical formulation for unilateral materials. Int. J. Solids Struct. **256**, 111954 (2022). https://doi.org/10.1016/j.ijsolstr.2022.111954
34. Montanino, A., Fabbrocino, F.: Seismic performance of irregular buildings through the CASS method. In: Gervasi, O., et al. (eds.) ICCSA 2025. LNCS, vol. 15886, pp. 338–353. Springer, Cham (2025). https://doi.org/10.1007/978-3-031-97576-9_23
35. Montanino, A., Iannuzzo, A.: A quadrilateral plate-type finite element to model stress singularities in no-tension materials. Comput. Methods Appl. Mech. Eng. **432**, 117433 (2024)
36. Montanino, A., Olivieri, C., De Gregorio, D., Iannuzzo, A.: Two continuous dual strategies to solve the kinematical and equilibrium problem for masonry-like structures. WCCM-ECCOMAS CONGRESS. Scipedia SL (2022)
37. Montanino, A., Olivieri, C., Zuccaro, G., Angelillo, M.: From stress to shape: equilibrium of cloister and cross vaults. Appl. Sci. **11**(9), 3846 (2021)
38. Montanino, A., Perelli, F.L., De Gregorio, D., Zuccaro, G.: Application of the continuous airy-based for stress singularities (CASS) to the load bearing capacity of masonry structures under seismic loads (2023)
39. Nodargi, N.A.: An isogeometric collocation method for the static limit analysis of masonry domes under their self-weight. Comput. Methods Appl. Mech. Eng. **416**, 116375 (2023). https://doi.org/10.1016/j.cma.2023.116375
40. Paris, V., Gobbin, F., Nannei, V.M., Resmini, M., Mirabella Roberti, G.: Distinct element method analyses for damage assessment: the northern spur of valverde bulwark in the venetian fortress of bergamo. Int. J. Arch. Heritage 1–15 (2024)
41. Perelli, F.L., De Gregorio, D., Montanino, A., Olivieri, C., Maddaloni, G., Iannuzzo, A.: Energy-based modelling of in-plane fragility curves for the 2D ultimate capacity of Italian masonry buildings. Front. Built Environ. **9**, 1127523 (2023)
42. Petracca, M., Camata, G., Spacone, E., Pelà, L.: Efficient constitutive model for continuous micro-modeling of masonry structures. Int. J. Arch. Heritage **17**(1), 134–146 (2023). https://doi.org/10.1080/15583058.2022.2124133
43. Pingaro, N., Milani, G.: Simple interface element equipped with thickness for the non-linear static heterogeneous analysis of masonry walls in-plane loaded: implementation and validation. Eng. Struct. **351**, 122056 (2026). https://doi.org/10.1016/j.engstruct.2025.122056
44. Prosperi, A., Longo, M., Korswagen, P.A., Korff, M., Rots, J.G.: Sensitivity modelling with objective damage assessment of unreinforced masonry façades undergoing different subsidence settlement patterns. Eng. Struct. **286**, 116113 (2023). https://doi.org/10.1016/j.engstruct.2023.116113
45. Rotunno, T., Fagone, M., Ranocchiai, G., Grande, E.: Micro-mechanical FE modelling and constitutive parameters calibration of masonry panels strengthened with CFRP sheets. Compos. Struct. **285**, 115248 (2022). https://doi.org/10.1016/j.compstruct.2022.115248
46. Shadlou, M., Ahmadi, E., Kashani, M.M.: Micromechanical modelling of mortar joints and brick-mortar interfaces in masonry Structures: a review of recent developments. Structures **23**, 831–844 (2020)
47. Shin, H.V., Porst, C.F., Vouga, E., Ochsendorf, J., Durand, F.: Reconciling elastic and equilibrium methods for static analysis. ACM Trans. Graphics (TOG) **35**(2), 1–16 (2016). https://doi.org/10.1145/2835173
48. Xia, Q., Sun, Y., Wu, J., Li, J., Li, Y., Shen, C.: Investigation of compression constitutive relationship of ancient brick masonry. Constr. Build. Mater. **317**, 126093 (2022). https://doi.org/10.1016/j.conbuildmat.2021.126093

DEM Investigation of Sliding Mechanisms in a 3D-Printed Flat Arch

Antonino Iannuzzo[1(✉)], Michele Lanza[2], Lino Cusano[3], Francesco Picariello[4], and Giuseppe Maddaloni[1]

[1] Department of Engineering, University of Sannio, Piazza Roma, 28, 82100 Benevento, Italy
{aniannuzzo,maddaloni}@unisannio.it
[2] Tecnica y Proyectos S.A., Madrid, Spain
mlanza@typsa.es
[3] University of Sannio, Benevento, Italy
l.cusano@studenti.unisannio.it
[4] Universitas Mercatorum, Rome, Italy
francesco.picariello@unimercatorum.it

Abstract. This paper presents a preliminary experimental and numerical investigation of the mechanical response of a flat arch using a 3D-printed small-scale physical model analysed through distinct element modelling. Based on the historical rules introduced by Coulomb, the arch is designed with joint inclinations chosen to guarantee a controlled minimum friction capacity, and fabricated via fused filament fabrication. Due to the characteristically high horizontal thrust, flat arches typically experience small abutment displacements and settle into a minimum thrust configuration. Two experimental tests with different interface properties are performed to investigate this mechanical response under increasing horizontal displacement. The in-house VEDEM+ plugin is adopted to link CAD modelling with 3DEC (Itasca), enabling precise geometric modelling and systematic post-processing of the structural response. A parametric study is subsequently carried out to interpret the experimental observations. The results demonstrate that interface friction significantly affects both the displacement capacity and the governing collapse mechanism. In particular, as expected, in a high-friction scenario, sliding is avoided, and a pure hinging mechanism governs collapse from the outset. Conversely, when friction capacity is low, sliding initiates at the interfaces and persists until the internal thrust finds a configuration in which the force inclination at each joint falls within the friction cone; once this condition is met, a hinging mechanism develops and ultimately governs collapse.

Keywords: Masonry structures · Flat arch · 3DEC · Displacement capacity · Distinct element modelling · Rigid blocks · Experimental tests

O. Gervasi et al. (Eds.): ICCSA 2026 Workshops, LNCS 16758, pp. 446–463, 2027.
https://doi.org/10.1007/978-3-032-30497-1_27

1 Introduction

Traditional masonry is an uncommon material in contemporary construction, feeling largely unfamiliar in the 21st century, even though most of our built cultural heritage is composed of masonry constructions. Unlike modern structural materials, it does not conform to standard assumptions such as homogeneity, isotropy, or elastic behaviour characterised by parameters like Young's modulus and Poisson's ratio. While masonry performs well under compression, it is extremely weak in tension, exhibiting a unilateral behaviour that is crucial to understanding its structural performance [28,32]. Historic masonry structures, furthermore, frequently contain cracks, which demand an analytical approach fundamentally different from that developed for modern engineering materials such as steel and reinforced concrete. Such an approach was widely adopted, even in the absence of rigorous mathematical foundations, particularly through graphic statics during the 18th and 19th centuries. A key insight underpinning this approach came from Robert Hooke (1675) [29], who was the first to accurately analyse the behaviour of masonry arches by drawing an analogy with the well-known geometry of a hanging chain [4]. Hooke did not derive the mathematical equation of the catenary curve; his fundamental contribution was instead the recognition of the structural similarity between these two seemingly different systems. A few decades later, the mathematician Gregory (1697) [33] refined this idea by asserting that the catenary is the true form of an arch, and that if arches of other shapes remain standing, it is because a catenary can be found lying within their thickness. Notable examples include the assessment of the dome of St. Peter's Basilica by Poleni [52], while the earlier report by *I tre Mattematici*, that is Le Seur, Jacquier, and Boscovich [37], made pioneering use of the virtual work principle. In 1807, Thomas Young [59] similarly applied hanging models to demonstrate the behaviour of masonry bridges. The same principle guided the design of new structures, as demonstrated by Antoni Gaudí in his work on the Sagrada Família in Barcelona. For a broader overview of the use of these models in architectural design, Graefe [27] provides an extended review. It was Heyman who, from the 1960s onwards, successfully framed this long-standing practice within the rigorous framework of modern Limit Analysis, providing it with a consistent mathematical foundation and significantly advancing the understanding of masonry architecture [28]. This was achieved through three fundamental assumptions: no tensile strength, infinite compressive resistance, and no sliding failure. Modern applications of graphic static analyses through line of thrust in 2D and 3D geometries can be found in [3,12,13,23,43,57,58]

A masonry structure consists of stones assembled in a specific arrangement, with or without mortar, to achieve a particular geometric form that allows internal forces to be transmitted to the foundations through purely compressive paths, consistent with the material constraints of negligible tensile strength and sliding capacity. The no-sliding assumption is required to apply standard Limit Analysis to no-tension materials and is generally considered satisfied either by the confining effect of high compressive stresses, by geometric interlocking between blocks, or by a combination of both, though it should in principle be

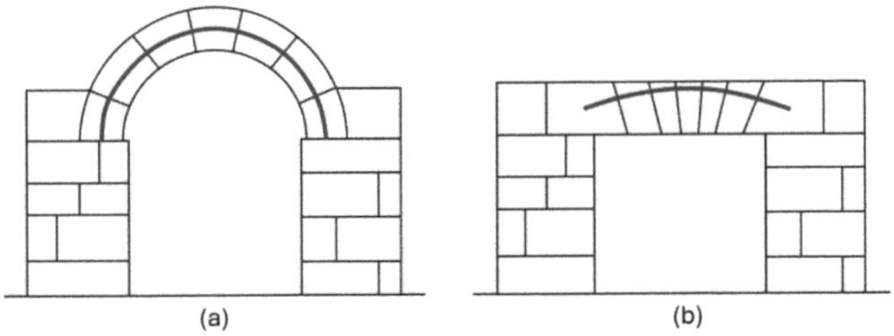

Fig. 1. Forces (in red) acting on the abutments of a semicircular arch and a flat arch of equal span under self-weight (redrawn from [16]). (Color figure online)

verified a posteriori. For more information, the reader is also referred to [1] and references therein. As will be shown in the present work, this assumption is not always satisfied experimentally: numerical analyses capture this behaviour effectively, revealing that sliding mechanisms can occur as long as the hinging mechanism is energetically preferred, that is, as long as the ratio between tangential and normal forces remains within a Mohr-Coulomb-type sliding criterion. This is further confirmed by Distinct Element Analysis simulations.

1.1 The Stone Lintel Arch

The stone lintel arch, composed of wedge-shaped voussoirs, can be seen as the flattest variation of the more common semi-circular arch (Fig. 1). Heyman demonstrated that, under ideal conditions-where there is no slipping between adjacent voussoirs and the abutments remain sufficiently rigid-the lintel arch remains stable regardless of the load [28]. However, due to its shape, it generates greater horizontal forces than an equivalent semi-circular arch with the same span. This increases the likelihood of abutment yielding, which may eventually lead to structural failure, as illustrated in Fig. 2, where two collapse mechanisms are shown: hinging and sliding. In this paper, it will be shown how both mechanisms can be predicted by considering the forces acting on the block interfaces, and how the structural response transitions from sliding to hinging once the frictional capacity is mobilised. A monolithic lintel (Fig. 3) subjected to loading behaves similarly to a flat arch once it cracks at the centre, maintaining stability as long as the abutments remain rigid [31]. Cutting a lintel into voussoirs offers a practical advantage: it preempts uncontrolled cracking, avoids unsightly fractures, and produces a more predictable structural system. This behaviour is readily understood by considering the fixed-ended beam of Fig. 4, composed of a material weak in tension such as stone or concrete: the flexural capacity is first exploited, and once cracks appear, the element responds as a flat arch composed of discrete blocks. In this sense, pre-cutting the lintel into voussoirs is preferable, as it allows the designer to control where openings between blocks will form.

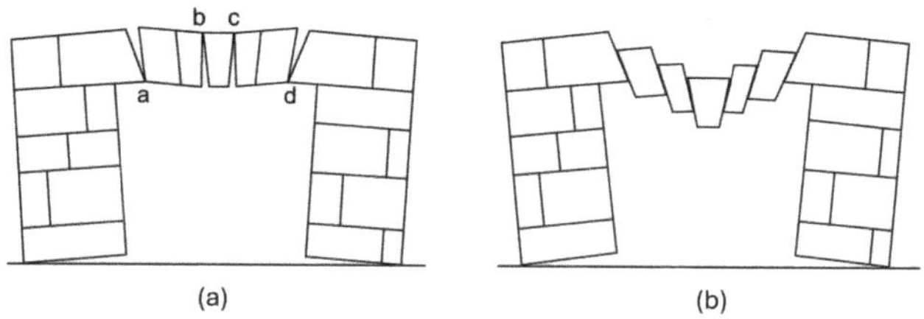

Fig. 2. Structural response of a lintel arch to abutment movement: (a) hinging mechanism with non-critical hinges forming at points a, b, c, and d; (b) sliding-dominated mechanism due to support displacement causes the voussoirs to shift relative to each other (redrawn from [16]).

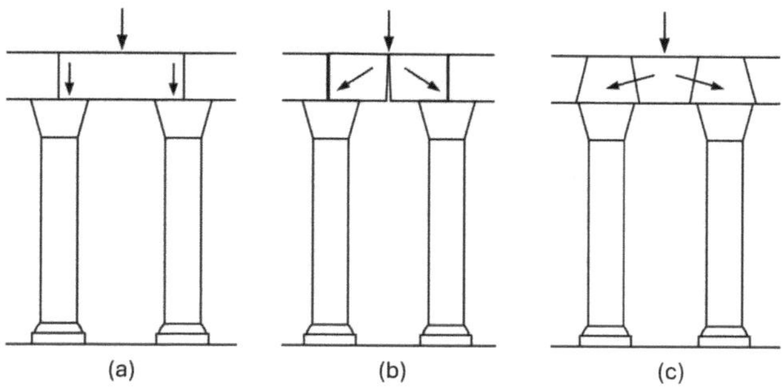

Fig. 3. The structural response of a monolithic lintel: (a) functioning as a beam, (b) transitioning into a simple lintel arch upon cracking, and (c) comparison with a traditional lintel arch (redrawn from [16]).

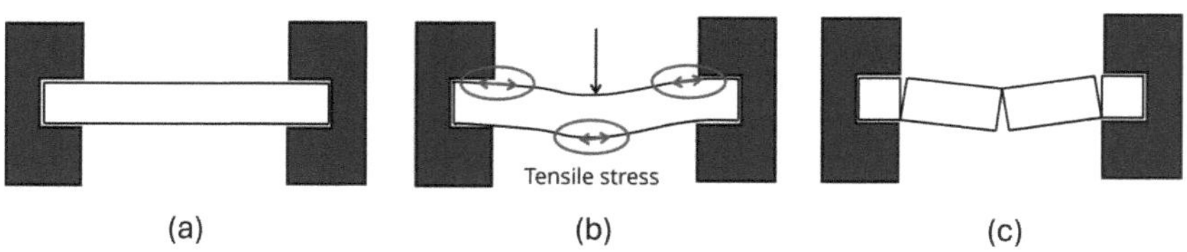

Fig. 4. Structural behaviour of a fixed-ended beam made up of material weak in tension.

1.2 Brief Historical Background

Although the flat arch was present in Near Eastern mud-brick architecture as early as the second millennium BC, it does not appear to have been widely adopted into Greek architecture alongside the semicircular voussoir arch in the late fourth century BC, remaining uncommon throughout the Hellenistic period [5]. This is likely because the Greeks primarily used the semicircular arch as a decorative element rather than out of structural necessity, as most openings could be spanned with a simple lintel. The availability of strong limestone

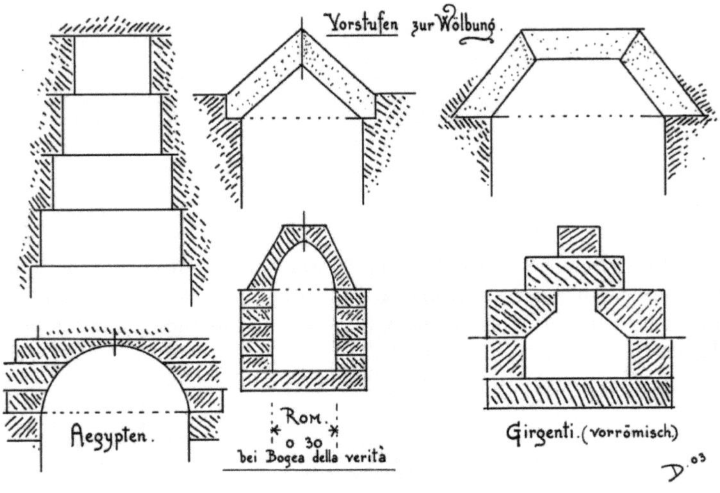

Fig. 5. Historical evolution of arch forms across ancient cultures: corbelled construction (Egypt), pointed arch (Rome, near the Bocca della Verità), and pre-Roman flat arch configurations (Girgenti), illustrating the progressive transition from corbelling to true voussoir arches *Vorstufen zur Wölbung* (from [16]).

and marble in Greece favoured the continued use of stone lintels in monumental construction, reflecting a generally conservative approach to material choice.

The standard maximum span for stone lintels in Greek stoae [8] and most Greek temples [18] was around 3.0–3.5 m, keeping tensile forces well below the theoretical strength of the stone. For wider openings, various reinforcement techniques were employed [9,19], or wooden lintels were used where considered aes-

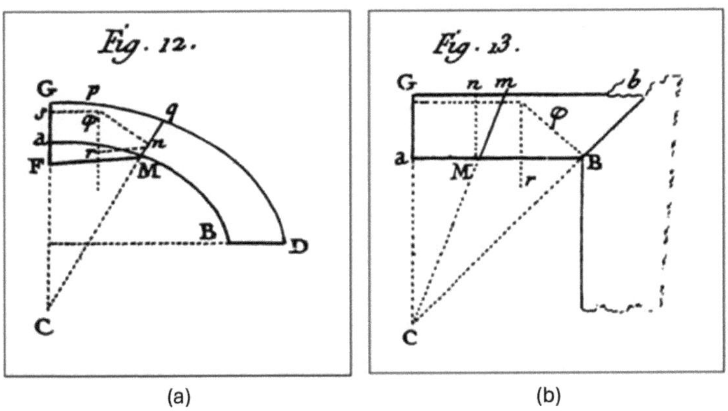

Fig. 6. Coulomb's study of joint inclination for a vault in equilibrium without friction: (a) general case; (b) application to a plate-bande [7].

thetically acceptable [8]. The transition from corbelling to the direct placement of stones against one another marked an important evolution in construction technique. Initially, two stones were positioned this way, then three, and from this arrangement the development of the true keystone vault was only a small step away (Fig. 5). Mycenaean architecture came to an end in the 11th century BC, giving way to a second pre-Hellenic period during the Iron Age, influenced by Assyrian and Egyptian elements and flourishing in Asia Minor under Alyattes and Croesus. This tradition encompassed the Lycian and Lydian kingdoms, the Ionian coast, the Aegean islands, and Etruria, with a common cultural influence stretching from the Persian Gulf to Tuscany. Three key developments characterised this era: the introduction of the alphabet, the invention of coinage, and the adoption of iron tools in craftsmanship and construction. During the Medieval period, flat arches played a secondary role to the pointed arches dominant in Gothic architecture, serving structural and decorative purposes in doorways, windows, and stained-glass tracery, as well as in bridge construction for short spans. In the Renaissance, a revival of classical ideals restored flat arches to prominence, making them key features in facades, arcades, and porticoes, often adorned with detailed mouldings and keystones, as seen in the work of Andrea Palladio. In the Baroque period, flat arches became increasingly elaborate, emphasising ornamentation over structural function, with sculptural details enriching facades, entrances, and windows. In the contemporary period, flat arches have experienced a resurgence thanks to modern materials such as reinforced concrete and steel, appearing in minimalist and modernist designs, bridges, urban infrastructure, and adaptive reuse projects, where their ability to span greater distances and their aesthetic versatility make them a functional and innovative element.

2 Methodology

This section outlines the methodology adopted in the present work: physical tests on a small-scale flat arch are performed and the corresponding results interpreted through the Distinct Element Method (DEM) software 3DEC by Itasca [35].

2.1 Design and Physical Testing of a 3D-Printed Flat Arch

The proportions of plate-bandes, defined as the ratio between thickness t and span s, generally range from 1/4 to 1/3 in stockier configurations, while the most slender examples exhibit ratios below 1/20. During the 15th century, a common ratio was approximately 1/8, adhering to a simple geometric principle: the centre forms an equilateral triangle with the intrados, and the plate-bande should encompass an arc of a circle. The joints are typically flat, though in some instances they feature a rebated or stepped profile, and the wedge shape of the voussoirs produces acute angles at the stone corners, which may result in localised fractures. De La Hire observed that when an arch or barrel vault collapses, it typically fractures at a point between the keystone and the springing,

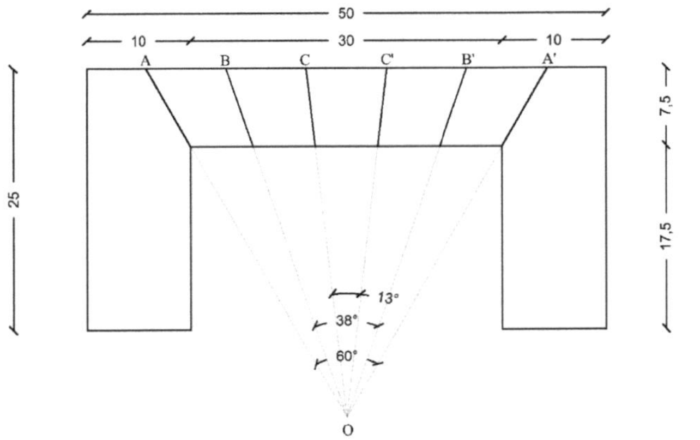

Fig. 7. Stereotomy of the flat arch designed according to [7], showing joint inclinations and main dimensions in mm.

known as the joint of rupture, and theorised that the thrust at this point must be tangent to the intrados curve. Couplet subsequently adopted the no-sliding hypothesis, analysing the equilibrium of the plate-bande under the assumption of zero friction between voussoirs. Coulomb imposed two conditions: forces must act perpendicular to the joints and must remain within the masonry, arriving at the same conclusion as Couplet: all joints must converge toward a common centre (Fig. 6). For further remarks on the collapse of masonry arches with Coulomb friction, the reader is referred to [56]. The stereotomy of the flat arch was thus defined according to the rule of converging joints proposed by Coulomb (Fig. 7) considering five voussoirs and two abutment blocks.

To investigate the structural behaviour of the flat arch experimentally, a scaled model was produced using the Bambu Lab X1-Carbon filament-based 3D printer (Fig. 8a). The model was fabricated in PLA, a biodegradable bioplastic

(a) (b)

Fig. 8. (a) 3D-printed modular flat arch consisting of hollow voussoirs with removable caps to allow filling blocks to increase material density; (b) experimental setup of the flat arch specimen.

widely used in additive manufacturing and well-suited for producing accurate and repeatable prototypes. As shown in Fig. 8a, a hollow geometry was adopted for the blocks to allow internal filling with the desired material to increase the material density; each block features a wall thickness of 3 mm and a removable top cap to enable filling, sealing, and mass control before testing. The 3D-printed specimen is shown in Fig. 8b; notably, the arch remains stable even at low friction values.

2.2 3DEC Parametric Investigation Through VEDEM+ Plugin

Parametric numerical analyses were performed using 3DEC 9.0 by Itasca [35] as distinct element modelling (DEM) solvers, widely used in current engineering applications [46,47,55]. Different block-based approaches were developed in recent years, starting from the work of [25,26,38,53] until recent ones [20,30,34,44,45,47–51,54] 3DEC was selected for three reasons: i) its three-dimensional formulation for capturing the structural response; ii) the possibility of selecting different material properties that can be used to match the physical characteristics of real and 3D-printed specimens; iii) and the opportunity of extracting features and developing custom post-processing routines.

Two principal strategies can be used in 3DEC to model blocks based on how their rigidity and internal deformation are handled. **Perfectly rigid elements** treat each block as a rigid body with six degrees of freedom. All forces acting on the block are reduced to the centroid, generating resultant force and moment vectors; the equations of motion directly yield translational and rotational accelerations at each time step. In 3DEC, a rigid block is represented as a convex polyhedron. This formulation requires minimal material property input (only joint parameters), is computationally efficient for explicit time-stepping, and

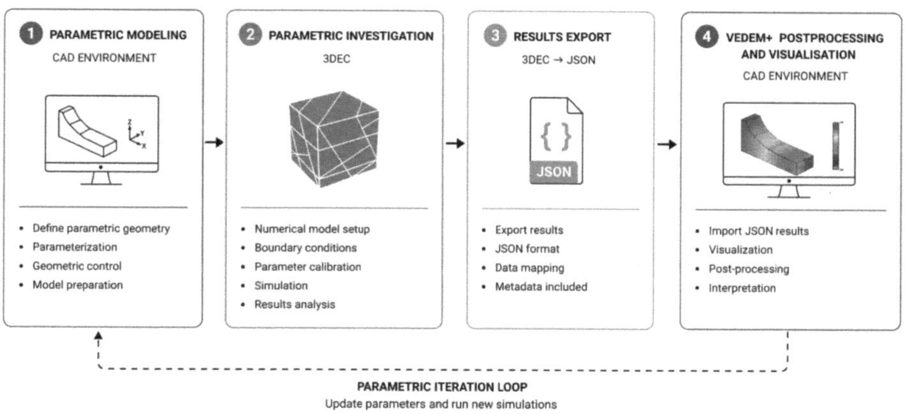

Fig. 9. VEDEM+ pipeline [14] used to assess the mechanical response of a flat arch: from the geometry definition, going through the 3DEC analyses and the visualisation of the post-processed results.

is physically accurate whenever the joint compliance vastly exceeds the block compliance, as is the case for strong stone masonry or hard 3D-printed blocks. **Deformable blocks** are modelled by subdividing each polyhedral block into an internal mesh of tetrahedral FE with uniform-strain [11]. Nodal translations are the kinematic unknowns and the corresponding associated mass is determined from the associated Voronoi cell. The equations of motion are applied to translational accelerations of the nodes, allowing the evaluation of internal stress distributions.

Contact representation and constitutive models in 3DEC are modelled using the point contact approach [36]. For polyhedral blocks in three dimensions, the contact between two faces can involve any combination of vertex, edge, and face interactions. [10]. 3DEC efficiently handles the contact using the *common plane* concept. Once two blocks are identified as being in contact, 3DEC defines specific *sub-contacts*, i.e. the actual point contacts, based on the geometry of the interaction. The mechanical behaviour at each sub-contact is governed by a joint constitutive model. In the present research, the *Mohr-Coulomb* model was adopted using only the joint normal and shear stiffness values as mechanical parameters. These are the most sensitive parameters in a 3DEC model. Their values can be defined through direct measurements or by modelling the joint compliance, treating the joint assembly as a continuum [40]. These values can also be reduced to speed up the calculation, but preliminary parametric analyses are needed [17,40]. It is worth pointing out that, because of the unilateral behaviour, contact forces exist only if a small elastic interpenetration between blocks is present. The elastic phase of the contact response is governed by the following relation between the increment in normal stress and the increment in normal interpenetration:

$$\Delta\sigma_n = k_n \, \Delta u_n \tag{1}$$

Contact stiffness is therefore a critical parameter: an excessively low normal stiffness leads to unrealistic block interpenetration and must be calibrated with care. In the present work, the Mohr-Coulomb model with tension cut-off is adopted, requiring normal and shear stiffness, friction angle, cohesion, and tensile strength as input. Post-processing is performed in a CAD environment, where interface forces are extracted and examined to interpret the mechanical response of the flat arch. All 3DEC analyses were performed using the VEDEM+ (Visualisation Environment for Distinct Element Method) plugin [14]. VEDEM+ is a dedicated pipeline (Fig. 9) developed to integrate CAD modelling with 3DEC, extending its post-processing capabilities and enabling a meaningful interpretation of results, following a strategy similar to that adopted in [17]. Specifically, VEDEM+ allows the visualisation of interface forces, internal stress diagrams, force comparisons across loading or displacement sequences, and contact pressure distributions, providing a comprehensive picture of force transmission within the structure. For further details, the reader is referred to [14].

3 Physical Testings: Results

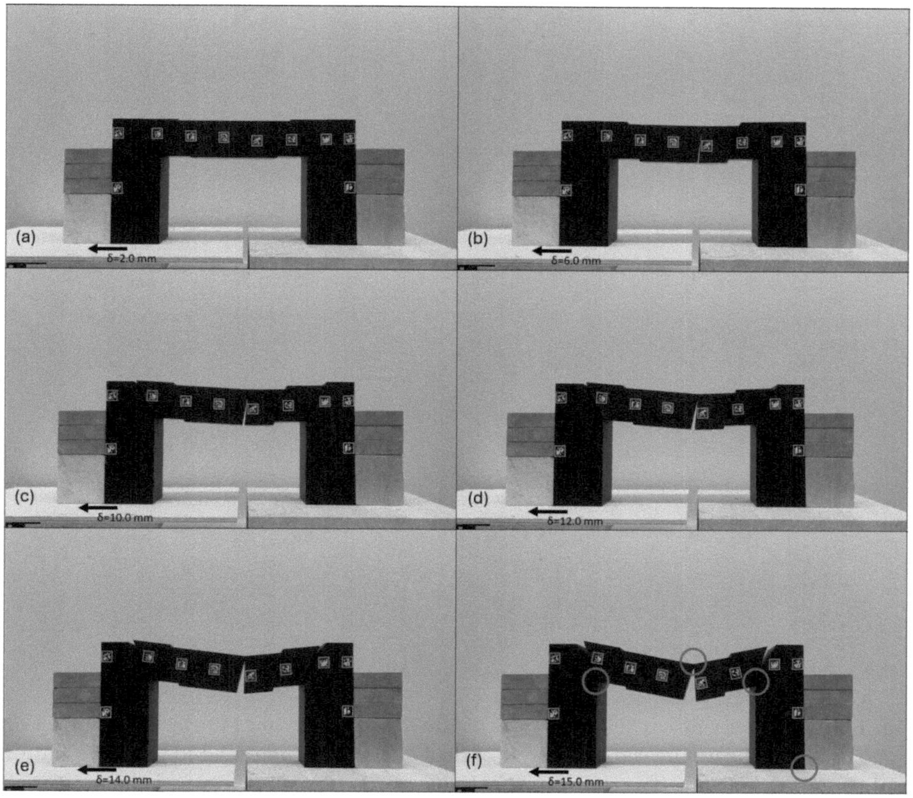

Fig. 10. Experimental displacement capacity analysis of the low-friction flat arch. Specifically, deformations and joint openings are observed for 2.0 mm (a), 6.0 mm (b), 10.0 mm (c), 12.0 mm (d), 14.0 mm (e), and the formation of the four-hinge collapse mechanism at 15.0 mm (f), where the active hinges are highlighted in red. (Color figure online)

The experimental campaign on the 3D-printed flat arch model is presented in this section. A dedicated test apparatus was assembled, incorporating a linear actuator designed to apply a controlled lateral outward displacement to the left abutment, to activate the collapse mechanisms typical of flat arch behaviour. This applied displacement was selected to force the arch into a minimum thrust condition, which is the standard condition of a flat arch. Indeed, external settlements activate different internal thrust conditions. For more information and novel computational, experimental and theoretical approaches, the reader is referred to [2,21,22,24,39,41,42]. The test followed a step-by-step procedure: the voussoirs and abutment blocks were first filled with sand to increase their

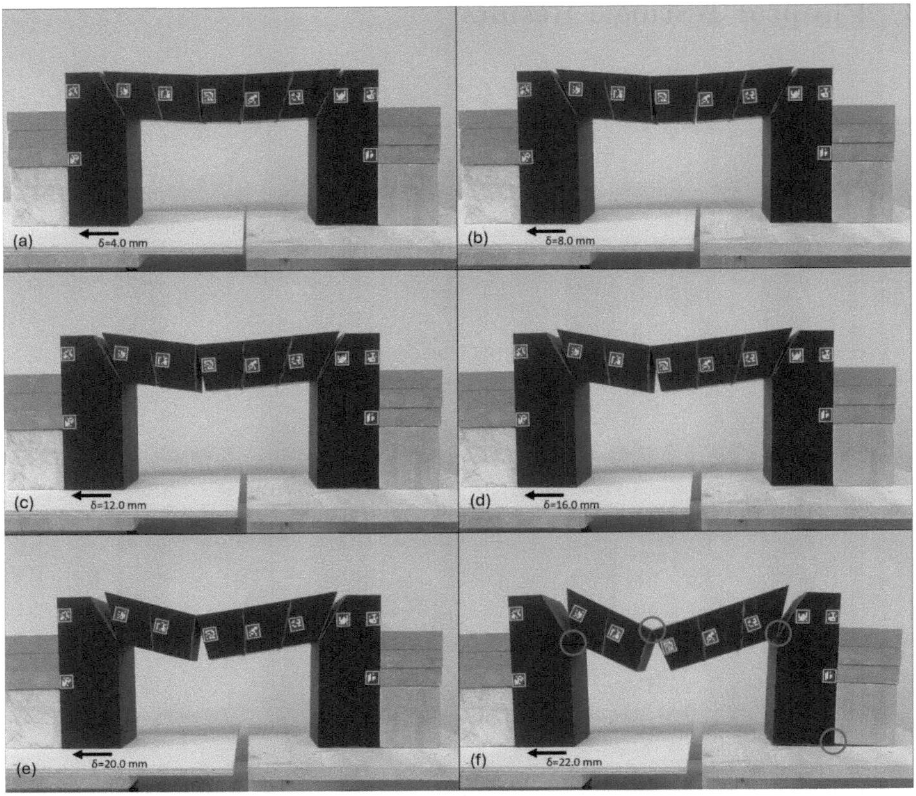

Fig. 11. Displacement capacity analysis of the flat arch having interfaces with friction $\phi = 35°$ due to the application of a layer of dust sand. Deformation and hinge formation for 4.0 mm (a), 8.0 mm (b), 12.0 mm (c), 16.0 mm (d), 20.0 mm (e), and the activation of the four-hinge (red circles) collapse mechanism at 22.0 mm (f). (Color figure online)

mass, then sealed in preparation for loading. The voussoirs were equipped with QR codes to monitor displacements during testing, following the approach developed in [15]; these results will be presented and discussed in a forthcoming publication. Friction coefficients were determined through static inclined plane tests and are reported in Table 2. Two friction conditions were considered. The first corresponds to a low-friction scenario based on the properties of PLA: the static friction coefficient of PLA ranges between 0.04 and 0.2 [6], and the wood-PLA interface friction angle was experimentally found to be approximately 17°. To prevent premature sliding at the abutment base under this low-friction condition, external blocks were placed adjacent to the buttresses. The friction angle for PLA-to-PLA contact was determined from laboratory tests and converged on approximately 13°. In the second configuration, a layer of sand was introduced at the block interfaces and beneath the flat arch buttresses, providing an effective friction angle of approximately 35° as determined from inclined plane

Table 1. Density of the elements.

Element	A	D	C	B	Flat Arch
ρ [kg/m^3]	2500	2700	2600	1716	1716

Table 2. Contacts friction angles [°] - letters are indicated in Fig. 12, while FA denotes the friction angles among flat arch elements, including the two buttresses.

Contact	S-A	S-D	S-B	A-C	D-C	FA-FA
Case 1	20	20	17	15	15	13
Case 2	20	20	25	15	15	35

tests. The results for both friction conditions are reported in Figs. 10 and 11. A comparison between the two tests reveals distinct mechanical behaviours. In the first test, with unfixed abutments and a uniform low PLA-to-PLA friction angle, collapse occurred at a displacement of approximately 15 mm. As shown in Fig. 10, sliding of the three central voussoirs is observed from the very onset of loading. At approximately 6 mm of displacement, the response transitions to a hinging-dominated mechanism, accompanied by an increase in horizontal thrust. Beyond 10 mm, hinging becomes the governing mechanism, causing local sliding at the base of the external abutments and buttresses as well as counter-rotation of the lateral blocks placed to restrain the external abutments (Fig. 10e). Collapse occurs via a four-hinge mechanism at approximately 15 mm (Fig. 10f). In the second test (Fig. 11), the increased friction angle of 35° due to the sand layer produced a markedly different response: no sliding was observed and a pure hinging mechanism developed, allowing the structure to sustain larger displacements.

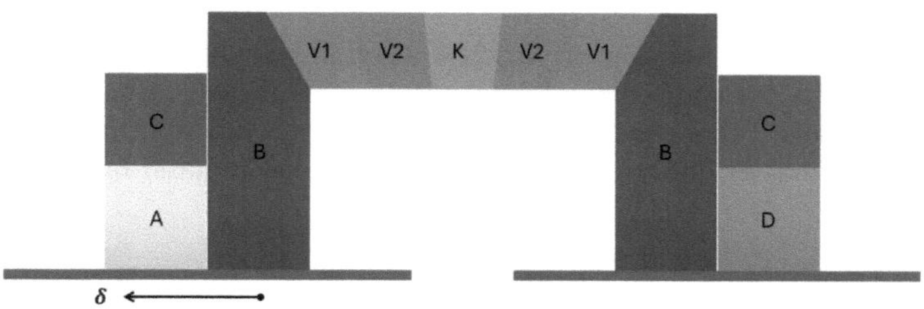

Fig. 12. 3DEC digital model: geometry discretisation. The two red blocks are considered supports. The material parameters are reported in Table 1 and 2. Between blocks B and C-A and C-D, there is a numerical gap to better model the small detachment noted in the physical test. (Color figure online)

4 3DEC Parametric Investigation

A parametric study in 3DEC was conducted to investigate the flat arch response under varying interface friction, improving model fidelity to the physical conditions observed experimentally. The geometry of the numerical model is shown in Fig. 12, including the flat arch voussoirs and the external marble support elements. The two abutment blocks (shown in red) are treated as supports; only the left one is subjected to an imposed foundation displacement, consistent with the experimental setup. Block densities and friction coefficients are reported in Tables 1 and 2, respectively, with friction values taken directly from the experimental measurements. Two analyses are performed, corresponding to the low- and high-friction conditions tested in the laboratory.

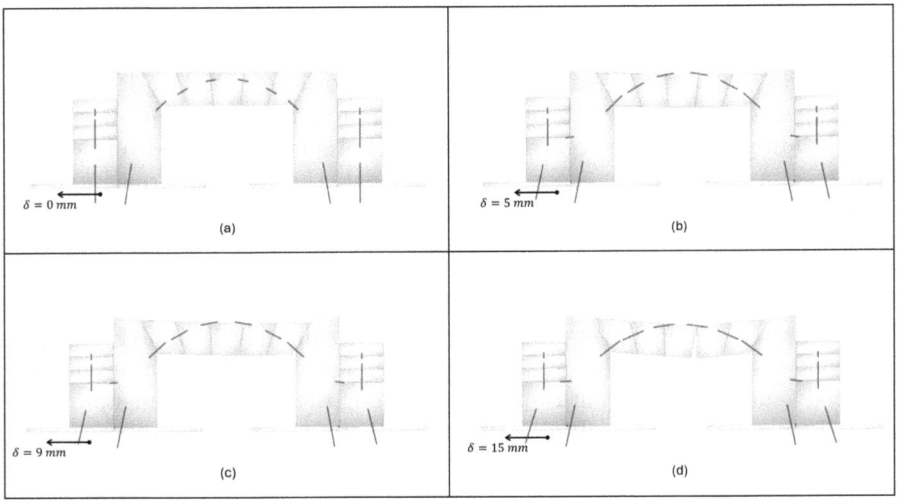

Fig. 13. VEDEM+ visualisation of interface resultants considering $\phi = 13°$ (case 1 of Table 2): the flat arch initially exhibits a sliding mechanism, which transitions to hinging until collapse, where sliding reappears between the left abutment and buttress and the moving support due to the high horizontal thrust induced by the three-hinge mechanism.

The right abutment was fixed, while a controlled displacement was applied to the left abutment following the same loading protocol as in the experimental tests. Custom scripts were developed in 3DEC to automate geometry import and to drive the displacement-controlled analysis through to collapse. Displacement steps were imposed as velocity inputs at the left abutment, with equilibrium verified after each step. The results of the two analyses are reported in Figs. 13 and 14.

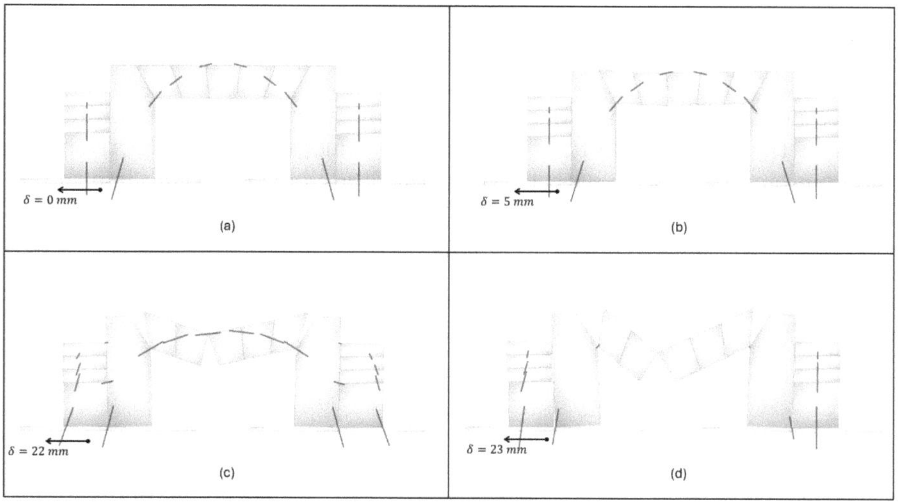

Fig. 14. VEDEM+ visualisation of resultants assuming $\phi = 35°$ (case 2 of Table 2): the arch shows a typical three-hinge mechanism until the collapse, where a fourth hinge forms at the base.

5 Conclusions

This paper has presented a preliminary experimental and numerical investigation of the mechanical response of a flat arch, designed according to Coulomb's converging-joint rule and fabricated via fused filament fabrication using a 3D-printed scaled model. Two experimental tests with different interface friction conditions were conducted by imposing a controlled horizontal displacement at one abutment, replicating the minimum thrust configuration characteristic of flat arches under service conditions.

The VEDEM+ plugin [14] was adopted to link CAD modelling with 3DEC (Itasca) analyses, enabling precise geometric modelling and detailed post-processing throughout the loading sequence. A parametric study was subsequently carried out to complement and interpret the experimental observations. The DEM analyses are in excellent agreement with the experimental results, confirming the reliability of the modelling approach. The following conclusions can be drawn:

- interface friction significantly affects both the displacement capacity and the governing collapse mechanism;
- when friction is sufficient, sliding is suppressed and a pure hinging mechanism governs collapse from the outset;
- when friction capacity is low, sliding initiates at the interfaces and persists until the ratio between shear and normal force at each joint falls within the friction cone; once this condition is met, hinging develops and ultimately governs collapse;

- in both cases, collapse is driven by the horizontal thrust, which increases monotonically as the hinge configuration approaches the limit state.

The present research highlight the importance of accurately account for interface friction in the assessment of flat arches, and demonstrate the effectiveness of combining physical testing with DEM for the study of collapse mechanisms.

Acknowledgments. This research is funded by the Italian Ministry of University and Research through the Programme "Rita Levi Montalcini for Young Researchers" (FFO 2020). The authors gratefully acknowledge Itasca for providing the 3DEC software under the 'Educational Discount Agreement'.

References

1. Aita, D., Beatini, V., Caruso, H., Garavaglia, E., Sgambi, L.: Some remarks on non-standard plastic behaviour with coulomb's friction starting from an unconventional stone flat arch. Eng. Struct. **326**, 119539 (2025). https://doi.org/10.1016/j.engstruct.2024.119539
2. Angelillo, M., Iannuzzo, A., Montanino, A.: Discretised continuum approaches: from continuum to dis-continuum. In: Discrete Computational Mechanics of Masonry Structures, pp. 95–163. Springer (2023). https://doi.org/10.1007/978-3-031-32476-5_3
3. Avelino, R.M., Iannuzzo, A., Van Mele, T., Block, P.: Assessing the safety of vaulted masonry structures using thrust network analysis. Comput. Struct. **257**, 106647 (2021)https://doi.org/10.1016/j.compstruc.2021.106647
4. Block, P., DeJong, M., Ochsendorf, J.: As hangs the flexible line: equilibrium of masonry arches. Nexus Netw. J. **8**(2), 13–24 (2006). https://doi.org/10.1007/s00004-006-0015-9
5. Boyd, T.D.: The arch and the vault in greek architecture. Am. J. Archaeol. **82**(1), 83–100 (1978)
6. Cardoso, P.H.M., de Oliveira, M.F.L., de Oliveira, M.G., da Silva Moreira Thiré, R.M.: 3d printed parts of polylactic acid reinforced with carbon black and alumina nanofillers for tribological applications. In: Macromolecular Symposia, vol. 394, p. 2000155. Wiley Online Library (2020)
7. Coulomb, C.A.: Essai sur une application des regles de maximis et minimis a quelques problemes de statique relatifs a l'architecture (essay on maximums and minimums of rules to some static problems relating to architecture (1973)
8. Coulton, J.J.: The architectural development of the greek stoa. (No Title) (1976)
9. Coulton, J., Murray, R.: Membrane associated components of the bacterial flagellar apparatus. Biochimica et Biophysica Acta (BBA)-Biomembranes **465**(2), 290–310 (1977)
10. Cundall, P.A.: Formulation of a three-dimensional distinct element model-part i. a scheme to detect and represent contacts in a system composed of many polyhedral blocks. In: International Journal of Rock Mechanics and Mining Siences & Geomechanics Abstracts, vol. 25, pp. 107–116. Elsevier (1988)
11. Cundall, P.A., Strack, O.: A discrete numerical model for granular assemblies. Géotechnique **29**(1), 47–65 (1979). https://doi.org/10.1680/geot.1979.29.1.47

12. Cusano, C., Angjeliu, G., Montanino, A., Zuccaro, G., Cennamo, C.: Considerations about the static response of masonry domes: A comparison between limit analysis and finite element method. Int. J. Masonry Res. Innov. **6**(4), 502–528 (2021). https://doi.org/10.1504/IJMRI.2021.118835
13. Cusano, C., Montanino, A., Olivieri, C., Paris, V., Cennamo, C.: Graphical and analytical quantitative comparison in the domes assessment: the case of san francesco di paola. Appl. Sci. **11**(8), 3622 (2021). https://doi.org/10.3390/app11083622
14. Cusano, L., Iannuzzo, A.: Vedem+: enhancing engineering assessment of complex stereotomic structures via 3dec-to-cad post-processing workflows. In: International Conference on Computational Science and Its Applications. Springer (2026)
15. Daponte, P., De Vito, L., Iannuzzo, A., Monaco, M., Neyestani, A., Picariello, F.: Low-cost marked tracking monitoring system for 3d-scaled masonry models. In: 2024 IEEE International Workshop on Metrology for Living Environment (MetroLivEnv), pp. 172–177. IEEE (2024)
16. DeLaine, J.: Structural experimentation: the lintel arch, corbel and tie in western roman architecture. World Archaeol. **21**(3), 407–424 (1990)
17. Dell'Endice, A., Iannuzzo, A., DeJong, M.J., Van Mele, T., Block, P.: Modelling imperfections in unreinforced masonry structures: Discrete element simulations and scale model experiments of a pavilion vault. Eng. Struct. **228**, 111499 (2021). https://doi.org/10.1016/j.engstruct.2020.111499
18. Dinsmoor, W.B.: The architecture of ancient Greece: an account of its historic development. Biblo & Tannen Publishers (1973)
19. Dorn, H.: A note on "structural antecedents of the i-beam". Technol. Cult. **9**(3), 415–418 (1968)
20. Fabbrocino, F., Olivieri, C., Luciano, R., Vaiano, G., Maddaloni, G., Iannuzzo, A.: Seismic performance of historic masonry buildings: a comparative analysis of equivalent frame and block-based methods. Alex. Eng. J. **109**, 359–375 (2024). https://doi.org/10.1016/j.aej.2024.08.043
21. Ferrero, C., Portioli, F.P., Calderini, C.: Lateral load response of a dry-joint masonry arch subject to vertical support displacements by rigid block analysis. Meccanica **60**(7), 2001–2018 (2025). https://doi.org/10.1007/s11012-024-01927-7
22. Galassi, S.: An alternative approach for limit analysis of masonry arches on moving supports in finite small displacements. Eng. Fail. Anal. **145**, 107004 (2023). https://doi.org/10.1016/j.engfailanal.2022.107004
23. Galassi, S., Tempesta, G.: Safety assessment of masonry undamaged and damaged arches subjected to gravitational loads and horizontal forces. a numeric procedure to identify the optimal thrust line. Int. J. Solids Struct. **301**, 112943 (2024). https://doi.org/10.1016/j.ijsolstr.2024.112943
24. Galassi, S., Zampieri, P.: A new automatic procedure for nonlinear analysis of masonry arches subjected to large support movements. Eng. Struct. **276**, 115359 (2023). https://doi.org/10.1016/j.engstruct.2022.115359
25. Gilbert, M., Casapulla, C., Ahmed, H.: Limit analysis of masonry block structures with non-associative frictional joints using linear programming. Comput. Struct. **84**(13–14), 873–887 (2006). https://doi.org/10.1016/j.compstruc.2006.02.005
26. Gilbert, M., Melbourne, C.: Rigid-block analysis of masonry structures. Struct. Eng. **72**(21) (1994)
27. Graefe, R.: Zur formgebung von bögen und gewölben. Architectura (1986)
28. Heyman, J.: The stone skeleton. Int. J. Solids Struct. **2**(2), 249–279 (1966). https://doi.org/10.1016/0020-7683(66)90018-7

29. Hooke, R.: A description of helioscopes and some other instruments. No. 3, TR (1974)
30. Hua, Y., Buzzetti, M., Pingaro, N., da Silva, L.C., Milani, G.: A computerized tool for the kinematic limit analysis of 2d masonry structures failing on a tilting table. SoftwareX **30**, 102180 (2025). https://doi.org/10.1016/j.softx.2025.102180
31. Huerta, S.: Wedges and Plate Bandes Mechanical Theories After De La Hire En L Architrave Le Plancher La Plate Forme Nouvelle Histoire De La Construction Pag 405 435 Presses Polytechniques Et Universitaires Romandes (2012). Wedges and plate-bandes: mechanical theories after de la hire
32. Huerta Fernández, S.: Mechanics of masonry vaults: The equilibrium approach (2001)
33. Huerta Fernández, S.: The use of simple models in the teaching of the essentials of masonry arch behaviour (2005)
34. Iannuzzo, A., Gesualdo, A., Olivieri, C., Montanino, A.: 3d exploration of internal stresses due to lateral loads and foundation movements in a semi-circular arch. In: COMPDYN Proceedings, pp. 2476–2491 (2023). https://www.scopus.com/inward/record.uri?eid=2-s2.0-85175847244&partnerID=40&md5=8edeef8ffd0b5e72961ce432ffed7a61
35. Itasca Consulting Group: 3DEC — Three-Dimensional Distinct Element Code, Version 7.0. Itasca Consulting Group, Minneapolis, Minnesota (2020). www.itascacg.com/software/3dec
36. Lemos, J.V.: Discrete element modeling of masonry structures. Int. J. Architectural Heritage **1**(2), 190–213 (2007). https://doi.org/10.1080/15583050601176868
37. Leseur, T.: Parere di tre mattematici sopra i danni, che si sono trovati nella cupola di San Pietro sul fine dell'anno 1742, Verlag nicht ermittelbar (1742)
38. Livesley, R.K.: Limit analysis of structures formed from rigid blocks. Int. J. Numer. Meth. Eng. **12**(12), 1853–1871 (1978)
39. Mascolo, I., Gesualdo, A., Olivieri, C., Fortunato, A.: On blocks detection in unilateral masonry-like structures: a rigid-elastic displacement approach. Int. J. Masonry Res. Innov. **7**(4), 395–405 (2022). https://doi.org/10.1504/IJMRI.2022.123750
40. McInerney, J., DeJong, M.: Discrete element modeling of groin vault displacement capacity. Int. J. Archit. Heritage **9**(8), 1037–1049 (2015). https://doi.org/10.1080/15583058.2014.923953
41. Montanino, A., De Gregorio, D., Olivieri, C., Iannuzzo, A.: The continuous airy-based for stress-singularities (cass) method: an energy-based numerical formulation for unilateral materials. Int. J. Solids Struct. **256**, 111954 (2022). https://doi.org/10.1016/j.ijsolstr.2022.111954
42. Montanino, A., Iannuzzo, A.: A quadrilateral plate-type finite element to model stress singularities in no-tension materials. Comput. Methods Appl. Mech. Eng. **432**, 117433 (2024). https://doi.org/10.1016/j.cma.2024.117433
43. Montanino, A., Olivieri, C., Zuccaro, G., Angelillo, M.: From stress to shape: equilibrium of cloister and cross vaults. Appl. Sci. **11**(9), 3846 (2021). https://doi.org/10.3390/app11093846
44. Mousavian, E., Bagi, K., Casapulla, C.: Interlocking joint shape optimization for structurally informed design of block assemblages. J. Comput. Des. Eng. **9**(4), 1279–1297 (2022). https://doi.org/10.1093/jcde/qwac054
45. Olivieri, C., Iannuzzo, A., Fortunato, A., DeJong, M.J.: The effect of concentrated loads on open-well masonry spiral stairs. Eng. Struct. **272**, 114952 (2022). https://doi.org/10.1016/j.engstruct.2022.114952

46. Paris, V., Gobbin, F., Nannei, V., Resmini, M., Mirabella Roberti, G.: Distinct element method analyses for damage assessment: the northern spur of valverde bulwark in the venetian fortress of bergamo. Int. J. Archit. Heritage **19**(5), 687–701 (2025). https://doi.org/10.1080/15583058.2024.2345701
47. Paris, V., Olivieri, C., Adriaenssens, S.: The impact of construction on the structural design of a complex masonry curved shell. Int. J. Space Struct. **40**(2–3), 180–194 (2025). https://doi.org/10.1177/09560599251381901. All Open Access, Hybrid Gold Open Access
48. Pingaro, N., Buzzetti, M., Gandolfi, A.: A numerical strategy to assess the stability of curved masonry structures using a simple nonlinear truss model. Buildings **15**(13), 2226 (2025). https://doi.org/10.3390/buildings15132226
49. Pingaro, N., Cardani, G., Coronelli, D., Milani, G.: On the stability of masonry arches through limit analysis and a nonlinear finite element-based method. In: International Conference on Protection of Historical Constructions, pp. 201–208. Springer (2025). https://doi.org/10.1007/978-3-031-87316-4_25
50. Pingaro, N., Milani, G.: Simple interface element equipped with thickness for the non-linear static heterogeneous analysis of masonry walls in-plane loaded: Implementation and validation. Eng. Struct. **351**, 122056 (2026). https://doi.org/10.1016/j.engstruct.2025.122056
51. Pingaro, N., Milani, G., Tiberti, S.: Automatic cad kinematic limit analysis approach for the limit analysis of masonry towers. In: AIP Conference Proceedings, vol. 2293, p. 380006. AIP Publishing LLC (2020). https://doi.org/10.1063/5.0026420
52. Poleni, G., Poleni, J.: Memorie Istoriche Della Gran Cvpola Del Tempio Vaticano, E De'Danni Di Essa, E De'Ristoramenti Loro, Divise In Libri Cinqve. Nella Stamperia del seminario (1748)
53. Portioli, F., Casapulla, C., Gilbert, M., Cascini, L.: Limit analysis of 3d masonry block structures with non-associative frictional joints using cone programming. Comput. Struct. **143**, 108–121 (2014). https://doi.org/10.1016/j.compstruc.2014.07.010
54. Pourfouladi, M., Pingaro, N., Valente, M.: Polibrick plugin as a parametric tool for digital stereotomy modelling. Comput. Struct. **311**, 107722 (2025). https://doi.org/10.1016/j.compstruc.2025.107722
55. Roberti, G.M., Ruscica, G., Paris, V.: From the herringbone dome by sangallo to the serlio floor of emy (and beyond). Curved Layered Struct. **8**(1), 259–270 (2021). https://doi.org/10.1515/cls-2021-0023
56. Sinopoli, A., Aita, D., Foce, F.: Further remarks on the collapse of masonry arches with coulomb friction. In: Proceedings of the 5th International Conference on Arch Bridges, pp. 649–657 (2007)
57. Tempesta, G., Galassi, S.: Safety evaluation of masonry arches. a numerical procedure based on the thrust line closest to the geometrical axis. Int. J. Mech. Sci. **155**, 206–221 (2019). https://doi.org/10.1016/j.ijmecsci.2019.02.036
58. Trentadue, F., De Tommasi, D., Marasciuolo, N., Vitucci, G.: Thrust in a symmetric masonry arch with frictional joints on spreading supports. Acta Mech. **235**(2), 659–670 (2024). https://doi.org/10.1007/s00707-023-03759-0
59. Young, T.: A course of lectures on natural philosophy and the mechanical arts: in two volumes, vol. 2, Johnson (1807)

Defining Modeling Priorities for the Seismic Assessment of Minaret Structures: A Geometric Sensitivity Analysis

Sare Nur Avcı[1](✉), Hany M. Hassan[2], Mariam A. Sallam[3], Gabriele Milani[1], and Marco V. Valente[1]

[1] Politecnico di Milano, 20133 Milan, Italy
sarenur.avci@polimi.it
[2] OGS, Borgo Grotta Gigante 42/C, 34010 Sgonico, Italy
[3] NRIAG, 1 Marsad Street, Helwan, Cairo, Egypt

Abstract. Historical masonry minarets present great diversity in terms of construction materials, geometric details, and dimensions, some of which are demonstrated in post-earthquake observations to affect their seismic performance. Yet numerical seismic analyses often oversimplify their complex geometric features due to data scarcity or computational constraints. This study introduces a systematic geometric sensitivity analysis to quantify the impact of these features on the seismic response and to establish a hierarchy of modeling priorities validated by different analysis methods. Marzouki (Egypt) and Hagia Sophia (Turkey) minarets are selected as case studies for their distinct geometric characteristics and contrasting seismic settings which enable a comparative evaluation. Starting from the original geometries, several modeling scenarios are implemented to isolate the influence of the vertical profile (straight vs. truncated), wall thickness decreases along the height, and the presence of stairs and balconies. To evaluate the influence of these variations on the global capacity and failure modes of the studied minarets, two analytical approaches are followed: Finite Element models subjected to modal and nonlinear static analyses, and Kinematic Limit Analysis. Correlating the modal characteristics, pushover curves, plastic hinge locations, and collapse mechanisms in KLA, the critical structural details and their impact on the seismic vulnerability assessment are identified, allowing to balance numerical accuracy with practical efficiency for heritage conservation.

Keywords: Masonry Minaret · Seismic Risk Assessment · Geometric Sensitivity Analysis · Nonlinear Static Analysis · Kinematic Limit Analysis · Finite Element Modeling · Conservation of Historical Minaret

1 Introduction

Masonry minarets stand as culturally diverse structures within Islamic heritage, representing centuries of architectural and structural development. The architectural diversity through the dimensions and proportions, segment configurations, balcony designs,

O. Gervasi et al. (Eds.): ICCSA 2026 Workshops, LNCS 16758, pp. 464–481, 2027.
https://doi.org/10.1007/978-3-032-30497-1_28

and crowning elements represent a cumulative knowledge of centuries across diverse geographical and cultural contexts. Their value is further shaped by their coping with the long-term effects of the environmental, anthropogenic, and structural challenges. Masonry minarets face severe threats from earthquakes even of those modest ground motion levels. The February 2023 Kahramanmaraş earthquake sequence in Turkey provided extensive documentation, with numerous minarets suffering partial or complete collapse [1–3]. In Cairo, Egypt, the earthquakes in 1847 and 1992 have progressively eroded the city's extensive collection of historical minarets [4–6]. Despite their structural vulnerability and the cultural and religious value these structures represent, specific seismic design and preservation guidelines for minarets are currently absent from many national codes. Establishing rigorous earthquake protection measures should be an urgent priority for the scientific community.

Cairo and Istanbul (Fig. 1) are both renowned as "cities of a thousand minarets," a designation that reflects not merely the numerical abundance of these structures but their profound integration into the urban landscape and cultural identity [5, 7]. The minarets in Cairo and Istanbul display remarkable diversity in form, material, and construction technique [8]. With their different seismic risks, the cities provide a valuable context for comparatively studying the distinct seismic behavior of minarets.

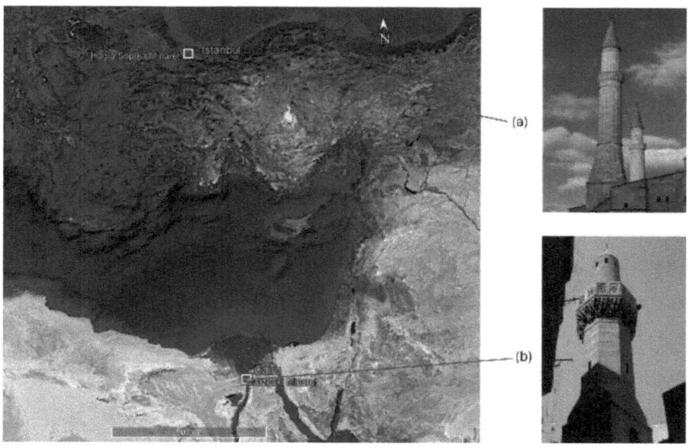

Fig. 1. Location of the two selected minarets. To the right are recent photos of the case study minarets; (a) the Hagia Sophia minaret (Turkey), and (b) the Marzouki minaret (Cairo, Egypt).

The literature on the seismic performance and strengthening of minarets is expanding with most studies focusing on singular case studies by utilizing experimental tests, modal analysis, and numerical simulations. An emerging area of research is the development of qualitative damage parameters, damage assessment forms [9–11], and vulnerability indexes [5, 12] for mosques and minarets. The most common numerical approach adopted for masonry minarets is the macro-modelling in Finite Element method. The Finite Element models of minarets generally include overall slenderness, external dimensions, and material properties. It is found that an adequate representation of the geometry, and the accurate calibration of the material properties of the structure are critical for the reliability of its numerical model [13–15]. Finite Element models frequently omit or simplify internal staircases by modeling the body as a hollow tube. Wall thickness is sometimes kept constant for simplicity despite actual taper, and balconies are often omitted or modeled only as lumped masses, ignoring their local effects. The impact of different geometric features in the seismic analysis of minarets was investigated in several parametric studies [15–17]. It is also common for diverse masonry structural typologies that complex geometries represent significant structural implications which challenge the validity of simplification strategies [18, 19]. Alternative methods such as the Discrete Element and Applied Element method, and Kinematic Limit Analysis - KLA- present balance between computational complexity and reliability. Limit Analysis is a simple methodology first adopted for masonry structures in the 1960s, with a lower bound approach proposed by Heyman [20]. It develops on three theoretical assumptions: (i) masonry is unable to withstand tensile stress, (ii) it has infinite compressive strength, (iii) sliding between blocks is not allowed. In the upper bound (kinematic) approach, collapse mechanisms are defined in which rigid macro blocks rotate at cylindrical hinges [21]. By the virtual work theorem, a collapse multiplier is found for each mechanism. The minimum collapse multiplier identifies the most likely failure mechanism, which can be compared against the seismic demand for a given zone. The critical step is the correct collapse mechanisms definition which are deduced from the typically observed failure modes in the post-earthquake surveys. Although KLA requires fewer geometric and material parameters than sophisticated numerical approaches, simplifying complex geometries remains a challenge that can be overcome by combination with FE or DE [22–24]. Still, by its simplicity, it is an accessible and reliable tool suitable for rapid preliminary screening of a large inventory of structures under seismic risk. KLA is successfully employed for different slender structure typologies such as towers [25–27], chimneys [28], and pagodas [22]. For minarets, it is adopted in some studies [29, 30] testing certain mechanisms, yet a systematic approach applicable to different typologies and standardized predefined collapse mechanisms are still lacking.

Understanding the seismic behavior of minarets requires careful consideration of their complex geometric features that significantly influence damage patterns as demonstrated by post-earthquake observations [6, 11]. Yet numerical seismic analyses can often oversimplify these characteristics due to data scarcity or computational constraints. This study addresses this gap by introducing a systematic geometric sensitivity analysis in which the individual impacts of these structural characteristics are assessed through controlled modeling scenarios by progressively adding complexity to base models. This is performed through the comparative analysis of the Marzouki minaret in Egypt and Hagia Sophia minaret in Turkey. The investigated features are the vertical profile (straight and truncated), wall thickness changes, presence of internal staircases and the balconies. As a novelty, these impacts are evaluated using diverse different analysis procedures of modal analysis, nonlinear static pushover analysis, and the Kinematic Limit analysis – a method that remains underutilized in the seismic assessment of minarets. The individual influences are quantified in terms of capacity, stiffness, and failure modes. This way, the study establishes a quantitative, data-driven hierarchy of which structural details are most critical for accurate seismic assessment, providing guidance to practitioners in making informed decisions for modeling choices.

2 Historical Minarets and Their Seismic Vulnerability: Insights from Egypt and Turkey

The earliest minarets in Turkey are from the Seljuk period (11th century). They usually have monolithic and tapered bodies designed to withstand lateral wind and seismic loads. In the 16-17th centuries, the classical Ottoman style emerged with a specific scheme composed of the boot, transition segment, body, balcony, upper body, and spire, with a changing number of balconies and bodies. The mina-rets can be isolated from or attached to/built on the mosque structures. The Seljuk minarets consist of brickwork and alternating stone and brick; while starting from the Ottoman period, stone masonry (Kufeki limestone) was more widely adopted [29, 30].

In Egypt, minaret evolution is generally categorized into five periods: the Tulunid (827–904), Fatimid (969–1171), Ayyubid (1171–1250), Mamluk (1250–1517), and Ottoman Turk (1517–1848) period. From the Fatimid period onward, a core morphology consisting of the boot, body, and mabkhara (a top segment in the incense burner shape) segments is observed. In the Ayyubid period, thinner cross sections appeared. The Mamluk period minarets are distinguished by geometric complexity, great shaft variations, and the usage of both brick and stone. During this period, a new top segment called jawsaq was developed as a pavilion on eight columns carrying a bulb. During the Ottoman rule, the Classical Ottoman style was emulated in Egypt, and minarets had more compact and slender profiles. Egyptian minarets are mostly built in limestone, with older examples in brick [5, 8].

The inventory of minarets, especially historical masonry examples, is continuously declining over time, which reflects their vulnerability and the cumulative impact of seismic, environmental, and conservation challenges [4, 31]. Taking Cairo as an example, only one Ayyubid minaret style has survived to the date [5]. The vulnerability of minarets against earthquakes depends on several aspects [32]. The brittle nature of masonry material, and its low tensile strength, combined with age and environmental related degradation, are primary contributors to structural damage. Among geometric properties, the exceptional height and slenderness of these structures cause them to act as cantilever beams highly vulnerable to lateral loads and exhibit longer natural periods and larger displacements [33]. The narrow and compact bodies are more vulnerable while vertical tapering can increase their lateral resistance [34]. Wall thickness gradually decreases towards the top to reduce weight, while this causes the axial stress at the above segments to drop significantly. The spiral staircase inside the bodies, if connected to the perimeter walls, contributes to their stiffness [17, 35]. Stiffness variations are observed between different geometries, especially at the transition segment between the boot and the body, which is the location of one of the most common failure modes [7, 36]. The balconies, mabkhara, and top segments create mass irregularities over the height of the structure, disrupting the load distribution [4, 37]. Minaret styles examined in this study rarely have openings (except for the doors, small air slits, and windows). While the openings create concentrated stress zones, they do not affect the global seismic behavior [15] and are mostly ignored in numerical and experimental studies. Some minarets are connected to the mosque wall from the boot segment, which shortens their free height and change their natural period. Moreover, this connection area has a large stress concentration and becomes a weak point [38, 39]. The soil–structure interaction (SSI) can amplify these effects by increasing displacements and natural periods, affecting both the distribution and ratio of damage [40, 41]. Therefore, cities above soft sediments suffer severe damage during earthquakes due to the amplified ground motion [42].

2.1 Case Study Minarets

The Marzouki minaret is part of the 17th century Marzouq al-Ahmadi Mosque in Cairo (Fig. 2). It is a 27,5 m long stone structure with a height to base width ratio of 8,12. It has a square boot that is connected to the mosque, followed by a transition segment and octagonal main body. On top of the corbelled balcony, there is a tapered cylindrical upper body, and a masonry spire. The material properties for stone masonry with hydraulic lime are defined as Elastic Modulus (E) = 3500 MPa, density (ρ) = 2000 kg/m^3, and Poisson's ratio (ν) 0.2.

The second case study, the Northwest minaret of the Hagia Sophia Mosque in Istanbul was built in the 16th century (Fig. 2). It is a 70,6 m high stone masonry structure. The rectangular boot is connected to the mosque. It is followed by a transition segment and a 20-sided polygonal body, connecting to the upper body through a balcony. The spire is built in wooden frame covered with lead plates. Neglecting the spire, the minaret has a slenderness of 8,26. The material properties are adapted from another studied minaret of Hagia Sophia [43] as E = 8500 MPa, ρ = 2000 kg/m^3, and ν = 0.2.

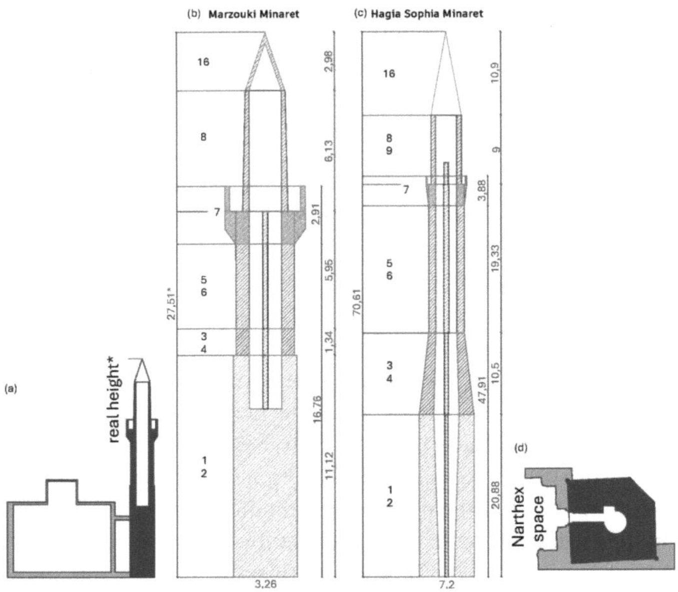

Fig. 2. Marzouki (b) and Hagia Sophia (c) minarets with respective section (a) and plan (d) schemes showing their connection to the mosques.

3 Methodology

3.1 Modelling Scenarios

Following the standardized parametrization proposed in [32], the minaret segment geometries and dimensions are defined. To isolate the influence of the secondary structural features, in total four modelling scenarios are considered, where M and HS refer to Marzouki and Hagia Sophia minarets, respectively: the initial FE models (M1 and HS1) are created respecting the original geometry and the secondary structural features investigated in this study (the truncated vertical profile, wall thickness changes in the perimeter walls and stairwell, presence of helical staircase and balconies), while in the rest of the models, these features are progressively reduced; in MS and HS2, the staircase is removed; in M3 and HS3 the balcony is removed; and in the baseline models (M0 and HS0) all secondary features are removed, (Table 1 and Fig. 3).

Table 1. Modelling scenarios adopted in the current work for Marzouki and Hagia Sophia minarets (where "+" means included element and "–" means subtracted)

Minaret model		Truncated profile & wall thickness changes	Staircase presence	Balcony presence
M0	H0	–	–	–
M1	H1	+	+	+
M2	H2	+	–	+
M3	H3	+	+	–

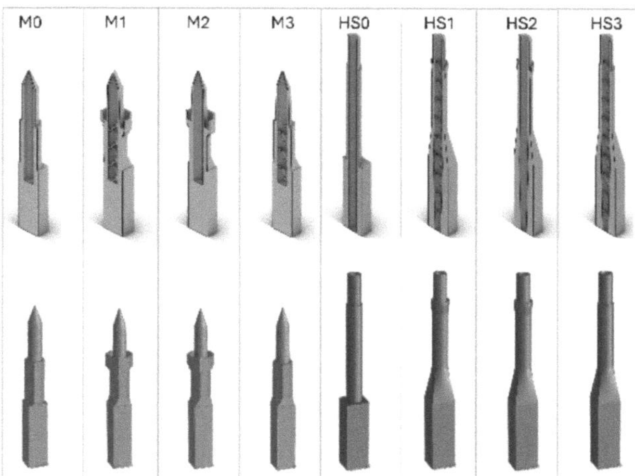

Fig. 3. Four modelling plots and FE mesh models of two case study minarets, where M and HS refer to Marzouki and Hagia Sophia minarets, respectively.

In total, eight FE models are created on Straus7 using brick elements. The masonry was modeled as a homogenous, isotropic continuum. The minarets' connection to the mosques are disregarded and they are considered fixed base structures. The original model's weight for Marzouki Minaret is 3453 kN, and for Hagia Sophia Minaret 29920 kN. For Marzouki minaret, the stairs is about 0,6%, and balcony about 5% of the total weight; while for Hagia Sophia minaret the ratios are 1.3% and 1%, respectively.

4 Sensitivity Analysis

4.1 Modal Analysis Results

To characterize the dynamic behavior shifts, modal analysis is performed on eight models. The performance indicators are the first five periods and corresponding modal participation factors. It is seen that for both Marzouki and Hagia Sophia minarets, the dynamic response is dominated by the first and second translational modes. The identical values between mode pairs demonstrate the bi-axial symmetry in the structures. For Marzouki minaret, the largest difference from the original model (M1) is found in the lack of balcony (M3), in which the fundamental period decreased from 0,54 to 0,487 s (about 10%) (Fig. 4). It indicates that the mass and stiffness impact of the balcony is significant for Marzouki minaret. For Hagia Sophia minaret, the largest difference from the original minaret (HS1) is observed in the baseline model (HS0) with the increase from 0,86 to 1,02 s (about 15%) (Fig. 5), showing that the construction details such as the spiral staircase, balcony and wall changes considerably increase its stiffness compared to the base model.

The modal mass participation in the translational X and Y directions is given in Fig. 6. The vertical component is observed in mode eight with 70% participation for Marzouki and 50 to 60% for Hagia Sophia minarets. In Marzouki minaret, in M1 and M3, the first two modes show a polarized distribution between principal directions. In models without staircases, the participation ratios in X and Y axes are closer, indicating that a diagonal axis of vibration forms when the bracing effect of the stairs, however slightly, is removed. In Hagia Sophia, the polarized distribution is observed in all models, which can be due to its more uniform structure and height that exceeds the effect of staircase against the symmetrical layout more clearly.

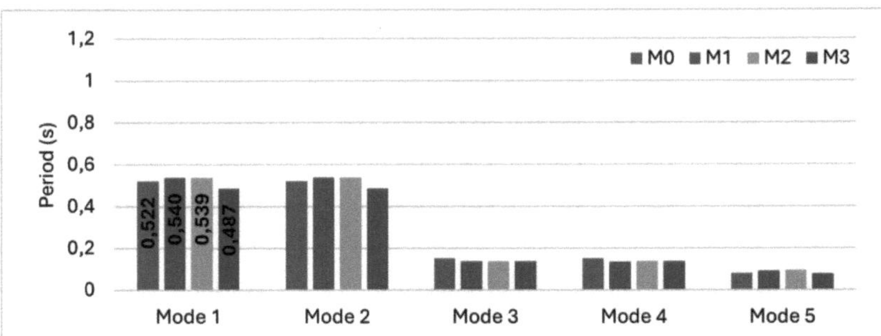

Fig. 4. Natural Periods across the first five modes of Marzouki minaret

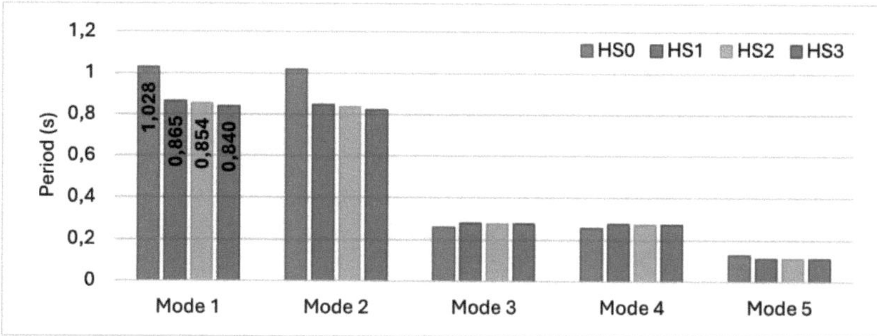

Fig. 5. Natural Periods across the first five modes of Hagia Sophia minaret

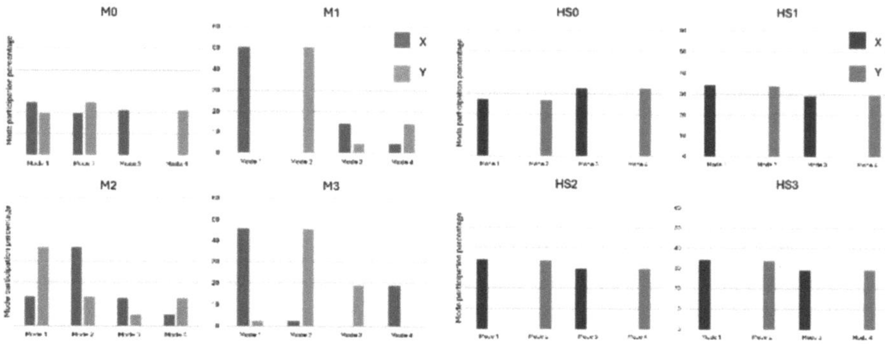

Fig. 6. Mode participation percentage in the principal directions for Marzouki and Hagia Sophia minarets

4.2 Kinematic Limit Analysis Results

Four of the five collapse mechanisms defined by [32] is utilized to manually perform the Kinematic Limit analysis on minaret models (Fig. 7). The tensile strength of the masonry is ignored according to the no-tension assumption. The load distribution according to the first mode shape of the original models is considered.

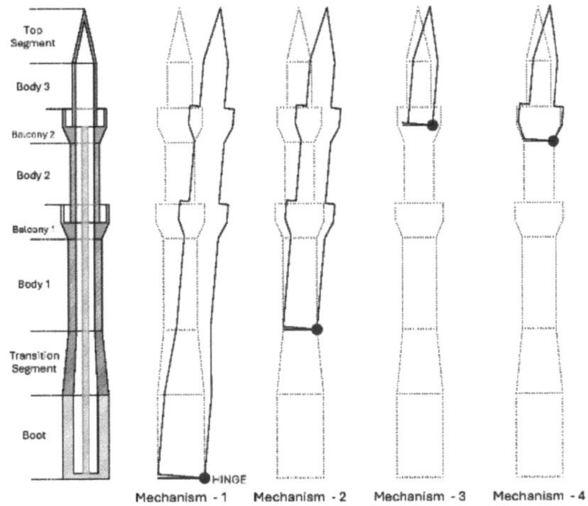

Fig. 7. Predefined collapse mechanisms [32] represented on a generic minaret: Mechanism 1 - Full collapse from the base; Mechanism 2 – Transition Segment collapse; Mechanism 3 – Upper Body collapse; Mechanism 4 – Balcony collapse

For Marzouki minaret, it is seen that for all minaret models, mechanism 1 triggered, which is global overturning from the base (Fig. 8). As expected, removing the balcony affects mechanism 4 occurring on that level significantly – for M3, by 0,091 g and of about 19%. The stairs have a small mass; therefore, their removal does not have a considerable effect. In mechanism 2 the cumulative impact has a strong influence since the wall changes are prominent around the Transition Segment.

For Hagia Sophia minaret, the collapse mechanism 1 is triggered in all scenarios (Fig. 9). The staircase leads to only a slight change in all mechanisms (HS2). The biggest difference from the original model is observed in mechanism 4, in the lack of balcony and wall geometry changes (HS0)– a decrease by 0,028 g and of about 6%. This change in the collapse multiplier, as indicated by the results in Figs. 8 and 9, is less prominent than in Marzouki minaret since the balcony in Hagia Sophia makes a smaller contribution to its mass.

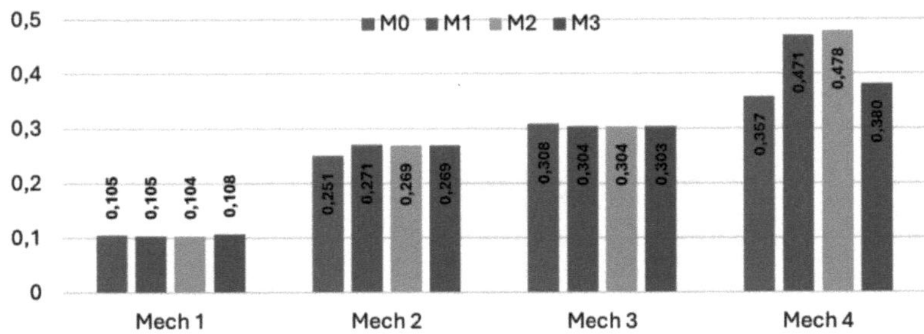

Fig. 8. Collapse multiplier values for Marzouki minaret

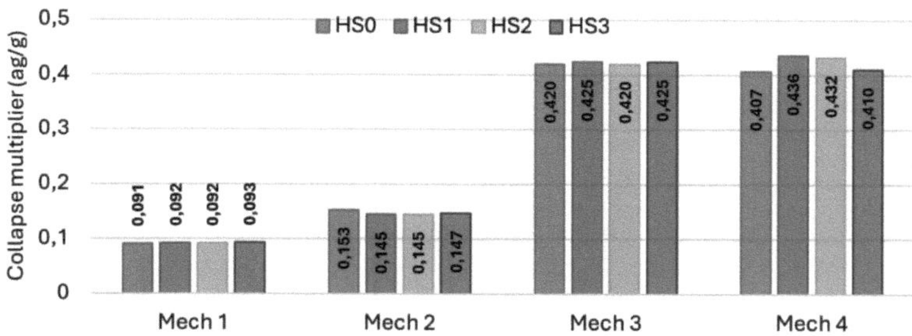

Fig. 9. Collapse multiplier values for Hagia Sophia minaret

4.3 Nonlinear Static (Pushover) Analysis Results

To optimize computing time and energy while investigating the effect of the secondary structural parameters, the NLSA is applied on the two models of the Marzouki minaret: M0 and M1. The structural response was examined under constant gravity loading and a lateral force on the X direction applied with a target load of 0.2 g, proportional to the mass of the structure. For material nonlinearity, Mohr-Coulomb criteria were adapted with the cohesion value of 0.12 MPa and friction angle (φ) of 30°.

The pushover curve of the original model (M1) indicates that, at the damage initation, the top displacement of 33 mm under 0.08 g loading – resulting in 297 kN base shear force - is expected (Fig. 10). For M0, the top displacement of 38 mm under 0.11 g loading - corresponding to 342 kN base shear force - is observed (Fig. 10). In both cases, the principal stress and strain distribution demonstrate that a plastic hinge formes in the lower to mid section of the boot (Figs. 11 and 12), while the maximum stress at the base of the minaret increases in the baseline model. Between two models, the maximum stress and strain values show only a slight difference of 4% and 0,2%, respectively.

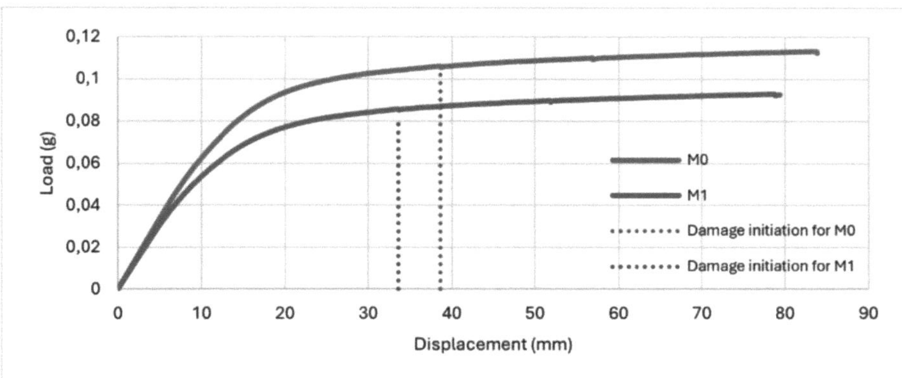

Fig. 10. Pushover curves of M0 and M1

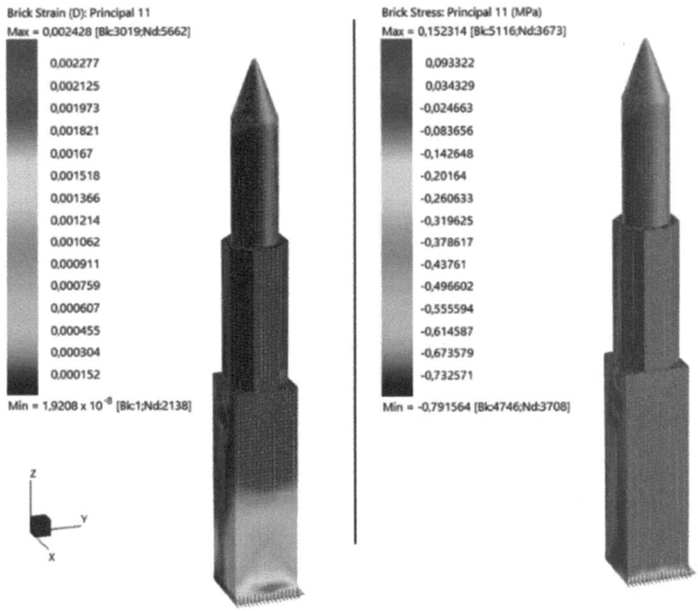

Fig. 11. Principal stress and strain graphs of M0 model

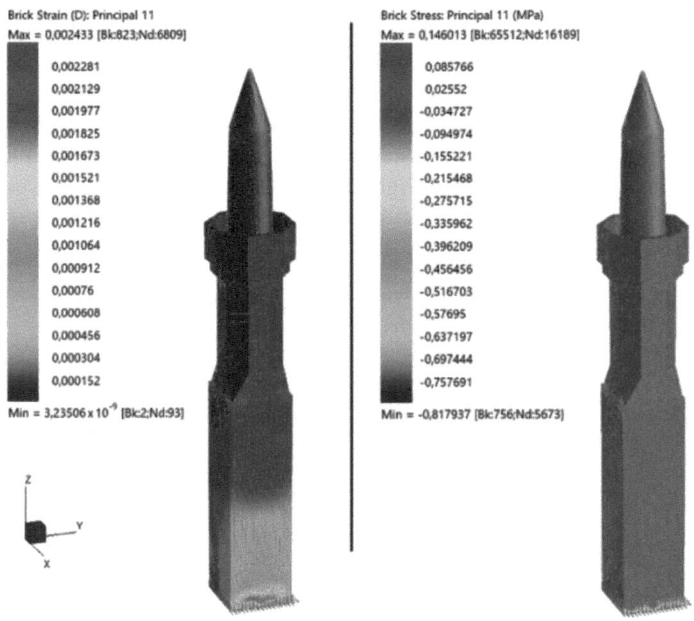

Fig. 12. Principal stress and strain graphs of M1 model

5 Discussion and Conclusion

In this study, the impact of the secondary structural features of minarets on their seismic assessment is investigated utilizing different analytical approaches. For this aim, two case study minarets from Turkey and Egypt are selected which have different architectural features and ratios, and seismic settings. The secondary features that are usually omitted or simplified in the literature on minarets, namely the impact of balcony, staircase, and vertical profile and wall thickness changes along the perimeter walls, are isolated in four modelling scenarios.

In Figs. 13, 14, 15 and 16 the change in performance indicators due to removing the secondary features are given where the negative values on the horizontal axis can be read as the overestimation of the minaret's strength. Modal analysis performed on the minaret model shows that, for a shorter structure like Marzouki minaret, removal of the relatively large mass of the balcony from the model drops the fundamental period between 10–14%. Moreover, the stairs have a bracing effect that significantly changes the distribution of mass participation ratio across principal directions. For the higher Hagia Sophia minaret, this distribution changes slightly between models, while a considerable increase (between 15–20%) in the period values from the baseline model occurs (Figs. 13 and 14). Secondly, the performed kinematic limit analysis reveals that the triggered mechanism does not change while the collapse multiplier values vary by the modelling scenario. In Marzouki minaret, the balcony has a prominent impact of 24% in mechanism 4. Hagia Sophia minaret has several cross-section changes at boot and transition segment, therefore the removal of all investigated secondary elements including the wall features results in a 5% increase in mechanism 2 and 6% decrease in mechanism 4 (Figs. 15 and 16). Lastly, as mentioned above, nonlinear static pushover analyses performed on the baseline and original models of Marzouki minaret show that the base shear load and top displacement of the minaret is overestimated in the former. In terms of the lateral acceleration triggering the plastic hinge formation, the difference is 0.3 g (13%). The change in stress and strain values overall is insignificant.

Overall, the collapse mechanisms demonstrated in kinematic limit analysis and nonlinear static analysis coincide with the commonly observed failure modes of minarets in both countries. In addition, the structural contribution by the staircases, wall thickness changes, and the balcony effect stated in literature are validated [34, 35, 37, 44].

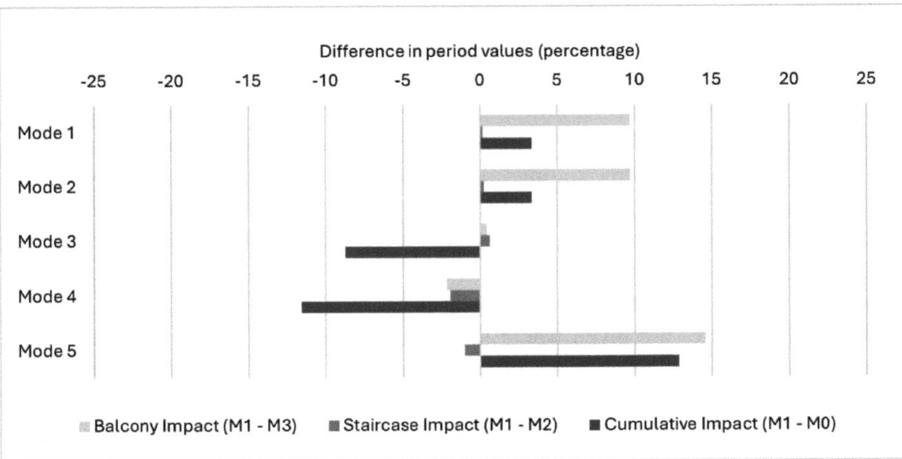

Fig. 13. Impact of secondary features in period values for Marzouki minaret

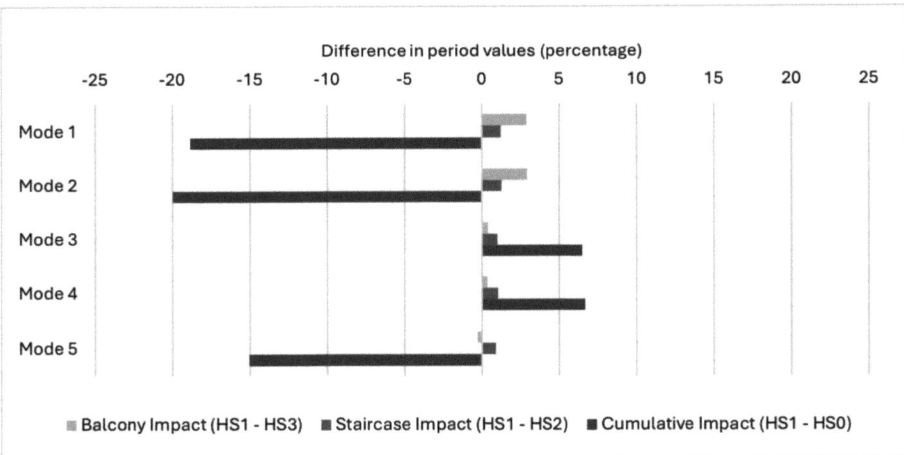

Fig. 14. Impact of secondary features in period values for Hagia Sophia minaret

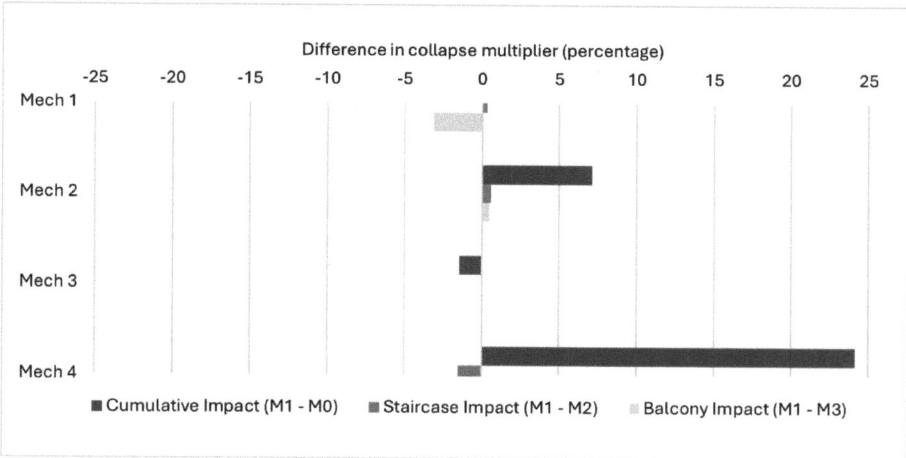

Fig. 15. Impact of secondary features in collapse multiplier values for Marzouki minaret

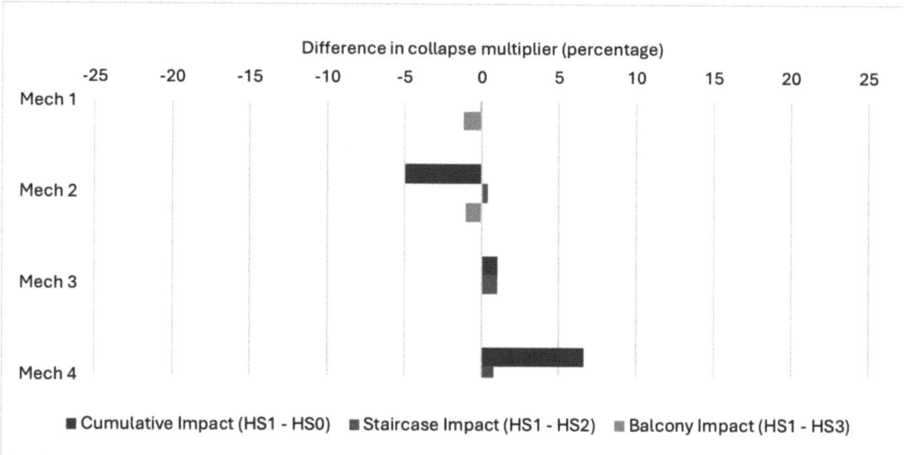

Fig. 16. Impact of secondary features in collapse multiplier values for Hagia Sophia minaret

In the end, the study shows that the secondary structural features of minarets which are often omitted in numerical analyses have impact on the expected seismic performance of the structure. It is a significant remark since, for instance, regarding the modal analysis, the varying fundamental period values could result in inconsistency during comparisons with the response spectrum; and asymmetry observed in mass participation ratios could determine whether to integrate higher mode effects in the analyses. The Kinematic Limit Analysis results in terms of collapse multiplier vary for a shorter minaret like Marzouki minaret, although, for both minarets, it does not change the expected mechanism with the minimum value. Here it should be noted that for Hagia Sophia minaret, load distribution pattern involving the higher mode effects could exhibit this variation more clearly, a consideration which should be investigated in future studies. In the nonlinear static pushover analyses, it is clearly observed that the pushover curve changes significantly between modelling scenario, and the baseline model overestimates the capacity of the structure.

Future studies can incorporate larger and more diverse benchmark cases from real and virtual minarets. In the current study, in the pushover analysis phase, due to computational and time cost of the approach, only two models representing the two edge cases of one minaret could be examined. For a more detailed view, all cases of two minarets can be investigated. In addition, proved to be effective on their seismic performance, minarets' connection to the mosque can be involved in the analyses. Lastly, the material properties can be parametrically studied to reflect the masonry behavior, which can be utilized to better implement the no-tension material assumption on Finite Element software.

Acknowledgments. The authors gratefully acknowledge that the doctoral studies of S.N.A at Politecnico di Milano are supported by a scholarship from the Ministry of National Education of the Republic of Türkiye through its Study Abroad Program.

Disclosure of Interests. The authors have no competing interests to declare that are relevant to the content of this article.

References

1. Işık, E., et al.: Structural vulnerability and seismic behavior of minarets in earthquake-affected areas. Struct. Eng. Int. 1–14 (2026). https://doi.org/10.1080/10168664.2025.2583267
2. Ertürk Atmaca, E., et al.: Damage assessment of regional cultural heritage assets following the February 6, 2023, Kahramanmaraş-Türkiye Earthquakes: Habib-i Neccar mosque with numerical validation. Results Eng. **27**, 106306 (2025). https://doi.org/10.1016/j.rineng.2025.106306
3. Avcil, F., et al.: Post-2023 kahramanmaraş earthquake assessment of masonry mosques and minarets in Türkiye: field observations and numerical earthquake analysis. Sustainability **18**, 2680 (2026). https://doi.org/10.3390/su18062680
4. Sykora, D., Look, D., Croci, G., Karaesmen, E., Karaesmen, E.: Reconnaissance report of damage to historic monuments in Cairo, Egypt Following the October 12, 1992 Dahshur Earthquake. National Center for Earthquake Engineering Research State University of New York at Buffalo (1993)
5. Sallam, M.A., Hassan, H.M., Sayed, M.A., Abdel Hafiez, H.E., Zahra, H.S., Salem, M.: Seismic vulnerability assessment of historical minarets in Cairo. Geoenviron. Disast. **10**, 30 (2023). https://doi.org/10.1186/s40677-023-00260-7
6. Hassan, H.M., Abdel Hafiez, H.E., Sallam, M.A., Bedon, C., Fasan, M., Henaish, A.: Multidisciplinary approach of proactive preservation of the religions complex in old Cairo—part 2: structural challenges. Heritage **8**, 89 (2025). https://doi.org/10.3390/heritage8030089
7. Doğangün, A., Sezen, H., Tuluk, Ö.İ, Livaoğlu, R., Acar, R.: Traditional Turkish masonry monumental structures and their earthquake response. Int. J. Architect. Heritage **1**, 251–271 (2007). https://doi.org/10.1080/15583050701436980
8. Behrens-Abouseif, D.: Islamic Architecture in Cairo: An Introduction. American University in Cairo Press, Cairo (1989)

9. Kocaman, İ, Kazaz, İ: Global drift ratio limits for historical masonry mosques. Bull. Earthquake Eng. **21**, 3011–3040 (2023). https://doi.org/10.1007/s10518-023-01613-1
10. Yılmaz, S., et al.: Seismic damage assessment of historical mosques and minarets in Antakya/Türkiye after the February 6, 2023, Kahramanmaras earthquake sequence. Eng. Fail. Anal. **182**, 110125 (2025). https://doi.org/10.1016/j.engfailanal.2025.110125
11. Mişe, O., Işık, E., Arkan, E., Avcil, F.: Structural and rapid assessment of registered historical mosques; a case study for Bitlis. In: Glavaš, H., Hadzima-Nyarko, M., Ademović, N., and Hanák, T. (eds.) 33rd International Conference on Organization and Technology of Maintenance (OTO 2024), pp. 439–453. Springer Nature Switzerland, Cham (2025). https://doi.org/10.1007/978-3-031-80597-4_34
12. Shakya, M.: Seismic vulnerability assessment of slender masonry structures (2014)
13. Feizolahbeigi, A., Mendes, N.: Evaluation of different types of advanced analysis for the study of the seismic behavior of masonry minarets. Structures **78**, 109134 (2025). https://doi.org/10.1016/j.istruc.2025.109134
14. Erkal, A., Hilmi, Z.H.I.: Effective expressions for the estimation of the first and third natural periods of minarets based on extensive and comprehensive parametric modal analyses. Structures **72**, 108275 (2025). https://doi.org/10.1016/j.istruc.2025.108275
15. Mutlu, Ö., Şahin, A.: Investigating the effect of modeling approaches on earthquake behavior of historical masonry minarets - bursa grand mosque case study. Sigma J. Eng. Natl. Sci. **7**, 123–136 (2016)
16. Abdel-Halim, A.M., Fayed, M.N., Hamdy, G.A.: Numerical study of the seismic behavior of a historic stone masonry tower (2020)
17. Hejazi, M., Talebi, R., Dabanlı, Ö.: Parametric finite element updating of brick minaret using operational modal analysis method. Int. J. Earthquake Eng. **40**, 1–24 (2023)
18. Paris, V., Olivieri, C., Adriaenssens, S.: The impact of construction on the structural design of a complex masonry curved shell. Int. J. Space Struct. **40**, 180–194 (2025). https://doi.org/10.1177/09560599251381901
19. Paris, V., Gobbin, F., Nannei, V.M., Resmini, M., Mirabella Roberti, G.: Distinct element method analyses for damage assessment: the northern spur of valverde bulwark in the venetian fortress of bergamo. Int. J. Architect. Heritage **19**, 687–701 (2025). https://doi.org/10.1080/15583058.2024.2345701
20. Heyman, J.: The stone skeleton. Int. J. Solids Struct. **2**, 249–279 (1966). https://doi.org/10.1016/0020-7683(66)90018-7
21. Zampieri, P., Tecchio, G., Da Porto, F., Modena, C.: Limit analysis of transverse seismic capacity of multi-span masonry arch bridges. Bull. Earthquake Eng. **13**, 1557–1579 (2015). https://doi.org/10.1007/s10518-014-9664-3
22. Wang, P., Milani, G.: Specialized 3D Distinct element limit analysis approach for a fast seismic vulnerability evaluation of massive masonry structures: application on traditional pagodas. Eng. Struct. **282**, 115792 (2023). https://doi.org/10.1016/j.engstruct.2023.115792
23. Wang, P., Milani, G.: Seismic vulnerability prediction of masonry aggregates: iterative Finite element Upper Bound limit analysis approximating no tensile resistance. Eng. Struct. **293**, 116595 (2023). https://doi.org/10.1016/j.engstruct.2023.116595
24. Buzzetti, M., Pingaro, N., Milani, G.: FE upper bound limit analysis for automatic detection of collapse mechanisms in masonry buildings. In: 2025 IEEE International Workshop on Metrology for Living Environment (MetroLivEnv), pp. 247–252. IEEE, Venezia, Italy (2025). https://doi.org/10.1109/MetroLivEnv64961.2025.11107125
25. Sarhosis, V., Milani, G., Formisano, A., Fabbrocino, F.: Evaluation of different approaches for the estimation of the seismic vulnerability of masonry towers. Bull. Earthquake Eng. **16**, 1511–1545 (2018). https://doi.org/10.1007/s10518-017-0258-8

26. Milani, G.: Fast Vulnerability evaluation of masonry towers by means of an interactive and adaptive 3D kinematic limit analysis with pre-assigned failure mechanisms. Int. J. Architect. Heritage **13**, 941–962 (2019). https://doi.org/10.1080/15583058.2019.1645241
27. Pingaro, N., Buzzetti, M.: Automatic 3D CAD-based kinematic limit analysis for the rapid seismic assessment of masonry towers validated through tilting table tests on toy models. In: Milani, G., Magagnini, E., Khatir, S. (eds.) Proceedings of the 4th International Conference of Steel and Composite for Engineering Structures, pp. 111–122. Springer Nature Switzerland, Cham (2025). https://doi.org/10.1007/978-3-032-04350-4_9
28. Milani, G., Shehu, R., Valente, M.: A kinematic limit analysis approach for seismic retrofitting of masonry towers through steel tie-rods. Eng. Struct. **160**, 212–228 (2018). https://doi.org/10.1016/j.engstruct.2018.01.033
29. İzol, R., Fatih Bayrak, O., Ilki, A., Lourenco, P.B., Avcil, F., Altunisik, A.C.: Seismic behavior of historic square cross-section masonry minarets: the minaret of the Harran Ulu Mosque in Şanliurfa (Türkiye). Structures **82**, 110504 (2025). https://doi.org/10.1016/j.istruc.2025.110504
30. Kılınçarslan, F.: Tarihi Vaniköy Cami Minaresinin Deprem Performansının Doğrusal Olmayan Analiz Yöntemleriyle Belirlenmesi ve İyileştirilmesi [Seismic Assessment and Rehabilitation of The Historical Vaniköy Mosque Minaret with Non-linear Analysis Methods] (2024)
31. Çetin, K.Ö., Ilgaç, M., Can, G., Çakır, E.: Preliminary reconnaissance report on February 6, 2023. Middle East Technical University Earthquake Engineering Research Center, Kahramanmaraş-Pazarcık and Elbistan earthquakes (2023)
32. Avcı, S.N., Milani, G., Valente, M.V.: Seismic vulnerability assessment of masonry minarets: Turkey, Egypt and Iran. In: Milani, G., Magagnini, E., Khatir, S. (eds.) Proceedings of the 4th International Conference of Steel and Composite for Engineering Structures, pp. 712–724. Springer Nature Switzerland, Cham (2025). https://doi.org/10.1007/978-3-032-04350-4_60
33. Sezen, H., Doğangün, A.: Seismic performance of historical and monumental structures. In: Sezen, H. (ed.) Earthquake Engineering. InTech (2012). https://doi.org/10.5772/51338
34. Safaeianpour, A., Valibeig, N.: A study on the construction technology of the Seljuk minarets in Isfahan with focus on their geometric brick pattern. Curved Layered Struct. **9**, 13–24 (2022). https://doi.org/10.1515/cls-2022-0002
35. Hassan, H.M., et al.: Seismic assessment of a cultural heritage minaret in Cairo. In: El-Qady, G.M., Margottini, C. (eds.) Sustainable Conservation of UNESCO and Other Heritage Sites Through Proactive Geosciences, pp. 541–565. Springer International Publishing, Cham (2023). https://doi.org/10.1007/978-3-031-13810-2_28
36. Gürbüz, M., Kocaman, İ: Enhancing seismic resilience: a proposed reinforcement technique for historical minarets. Eng. Fail. Anal. **156**, 107832 (2024). https://doi.org/10.1016/j.engfailanal.2023.107832
37. Bayraktar, A., Altunisik, A.C., Muvafik, M.: Damages of minarets during Erciş and Edremit Earthquakes, 2011 in Turkey. Smart Struct. Syst. **14**, 479–499 (2014). https://doi.org/10.12989/SSS.2014.14.3.479
38. Serhatoğlu, C., Livaoğlu, R.: A fast and practical approximations for fundamental period of historical Ottoman minarets. Soil Dyn. Earthq. Eng. **120**, 320–331 (2019). https://doi.org/10.1016/j.soildyn.2019.02.010
39. Oliveira, C.S., Çaktı, E., Stengel, D., Branco, M.: Minaret behavior under earthquake loading: the case of historical Istanbul. Earthquake Eng. Struct. Dynam. **41**, 19–39 (2012). https://doi.org/10.1002/eqe.1115
40. Altıok, T.Y., Demir, A.: Seismic damage assessment of a historical masonry minaret considering soil-structure interaction. JSEAM **4**, 196–212 (2021). https://doi.org/10.31462/jseam.2021.03196212

41. Bayraktar, A., Hökelekli, E.: Influences of earthquake input models on nonlinear seismic performances of minaret-foundation-soil interaction systems. Soil Dyn. Earthq. Eng. **139**, 106368 (2020). https://doi.org/10.1016/j.soildyn.2020.106368
42. Hassan, H.M., Abdel Hafiez, H.E., Sallam, M.A., Bedon, C., Fasan, M., Henaish, A.: Multi-disciplinary approach of proactive preservation of the religions complex in old Cairo—part 1: geoscience aspects. Heritage **8**, 56 (2025). https://doi.org/10.3390/heritage8020056
43. Çaktı, E., Saygılı, Ö., Lemos, J.V., Oliveira, C.S.: Nonlinear dynamic response of stone masonry minarets under harmonic excitation. Bull. Earthquake Eng. **18**, 4813–4838 (2020). https://doi.org/10.1007/s10518-020-00888-y
44. Avcı, S.N., Milani, G., Valente, M.V.: Seismic vulnerability of masonry minarets: state of the art and fast assessment via limit analysis. Buildings **16**, 1515 (2026). https://doi.org/10.3390/buildings16081515

Parametric Stereotomy Interpolation and Evolutionary Optimization of Semicircular Skew Masonry Arches via Upper Bound Limit Analysis

Mohammad Pourfouladi[1(✉)], Natalia Pingaro[1,2], and Gabriele Milani[1]

[1] Department of Architecture, Built Environment and Construction Engineering, Politecnico di Milano, Milan 20133, Italy
mohammad.pourfouladi@polimi.it

[2] European Centre for Training and Research in Earthquake Engineering , EUCENTRE Foundation, 27100 Pavia, Italy

Abstract. The safety assessment of historic skew masonry arches remains a complex engineering task due to their intricate three-dimensional behavior. The load-bearing capacity of these masonry structures depends directly on their internal stereotomy. Traditionally, construction paradigms like false and logarithmic methods are treated as separate categories. This research introduces a scalar factor α to bridge these distinct construction archetypes. The parametric engine recovers false skew at $\alpha = 0$ and logarithmic layouts at $\alpha = 1$. Hyper-logarithmic configurations are generated when the interpolation factor exceeds the unitary value. The methodology proposed utilizes a custom script and the PoliBrick plugin for geometry generation. Bounding the angular coordinate ensures numerical stability and prevents singularities at the supports. Upper-Bound Limit Analysis evaluates the ultimate load carrying capacity by discretizing the arch into infinitely resistant blocks and rigid-plastic interfaces (mortar joints). This physics-driven solver integrates into a Genetic Algorithm to identify rapidly optimal structural forms that maximize/minimize the load carrying capacity. The limit analysis solver adopts Second-Order Cone Programming to handle a three-dimensional Mohr-Coulomb failure criterion with tension cutoff and compression cap. Specific flow variables (plastic multipliers) characterize plastic dissipation at strength-domain corners. The study processed 2,000 unique individuals across skewness angles of 25° and 45°. Results show a consistent and nearly linear increase in collapse capacity as α rises. Enhanced structural interlocking occurs as joint trajectories shift toward the hyper-logarithmic domain. Maximum collapse loads reached about 1470 kN (25°) and 1190 kN (45°) for the investigated arch models. While 25° arches reach higher load carrying capacities, 45° geometries provide superior mesh regularity. These findings prove in a quantitative fashion the role played by stereotomy in the safety assessment of historic masonry skew arches.

Keywords: Skew Masonry Arches · Parametric Stereotomy · Upper Bound Limit Analysis · Genetic Algorithm · PoliBrick Plugin · Joint Angle Interpolation

O. Gervasi et al. (Eds.): ICCSA 2026 Workshops, LNCS 16758, pp. 482–498, 2027.
https://doi.org/10.1007/978-3-032-30497-1_29

1 Introduction

The structural assessment of historic masonry infrastructures represents a significant challenge for modern engineering. Single-span skew arches are especially prevalent throughout European railway and road networks. Many of these heritage structures continue to function today (see Fig. 1). Their unusual design allows them to traverse barriers at a variety of non-orthogonal angles. This structural necessity became popular throughout the nineteenth century period of industrial expansion [1]. Unlike traditional squared arches with predictable two-dimensional load paths, skew arches behave three-dimensionally. These systems generate significant lateral thrusts and non-uniform stress distributions. Consequently, they are characterized by highly complex 3D failure mechanisms.

Fig. 1. Left: railway bridge No. 74A, over the Leeds & Liverpool Canal [2]. Right: a skew bridge located in the Allegheny Portage Railroad Historic Site in Pennsylvania [3].

The stereotomy of masonry constructions may affect their ability to carry loads. The geometric configuration of blocks is defined by stereotomy. This arrangement controls the formation of potential failure surfaces inside the arch barrel. It also may dictate the frictional resistance required to prevent blocks from sliding against each other [4].

According to recent studies, construction techniques have a major impact on flexural hinge locations and ultimate capacity [5, 6]. Accurate modeling of these bond patterns is thus vital for any reliable structural assessment.

Historically, three primary structural paradigms have been established for the construction of skew masonry arches [5]. The false skew method utilizes bed joints that are positioned parallel to the supporting abutments. This technique simplifies the stone-cutting process but introduces significant vulnerabilities at higher skew angles. In these geometries, the risk of sliding between voussoirs increases as the skew angle becomes steeper. To preserve the orthogonality of the external surface of the arch, spiral bed joints are employed in the helicoidal method. Alternatively, the logarithmic method provides a mathematical formula to maximize structural stability. To reduce the risk of sliding failure, these joints remain perpendicular to the arch face at all elevations. Figure 2 shows both the false and logarithmic construction techniques chosen for the study in this work. The illustration depicts unrolled geometric developments and their topographical patterns.

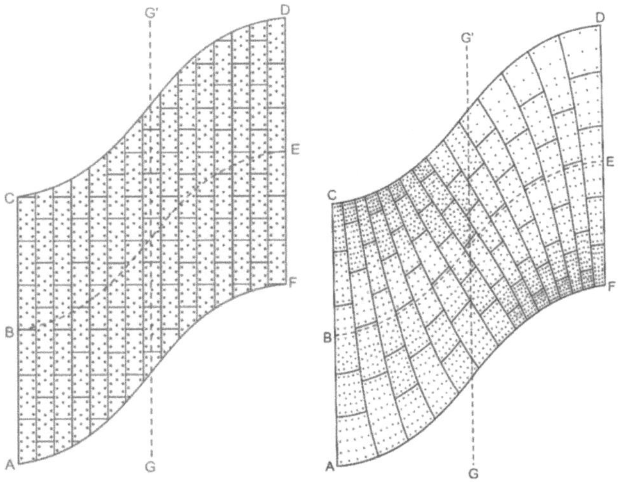

Fig. 2. The unrolled surface pattern of the false and logarithmic skew arches

Contemporary research frequently encounters these three paradigms as distinct and mutually independent groups. This discrete classification limits investigation of the larger structural design space. Furthermore, the literature does not provide a foundation for a continuous mathematical transition between these archetypes. Hybrid setups performance has received little attention in recent research [1, 5]. Previous research has often prioritized canonical approaches above the study of intermediate solutions. A unifying mathematical formulation is crucial for reconciling these methods. Such a model would allow for quantitative optimization of bed-joint trajectories under certain loading conditions.

The current study tackles these constraints by implementing a parametric stereotomy algorithm. This section defines a scalar interpolation factor, α, described in detail in what follows, is defined to bridge traditional construction paradigms. Setting α to zero allows the engine to recover the straight joints of false skew geometry. When α equates one, the framework generates a standard logarithmic layout. Intermediate values between 0 and 1 result in hybrid configurations that combine both strategies. Values greater than one enable "hyper-logarithmic" layouts with increased curvature. (see Fig. 3). This concept is implemented via PoliBrick plugin and custom mathematical code [7].

Structural behavior at collapse is evaluated using a heterogeneous Upper-Bound Limit Analysis (UBLA) code implemented in MATLAB. The procedure discretizes the arch geometry into infinitely resistant hexahedral/wedge elements connected by quadrilateral interfaces. The latter are rigid-plastic and represent either internal block interfaces (infinitely resistant) or mortar joints, where all dissipation takes place according to a cohesive-frictional failure criterion combined with limited tensile and compressive strength (Fig. 4). This Limit Analysis approach serves as a faster alternative to traditional non-linear Finite Element Analyses [8].

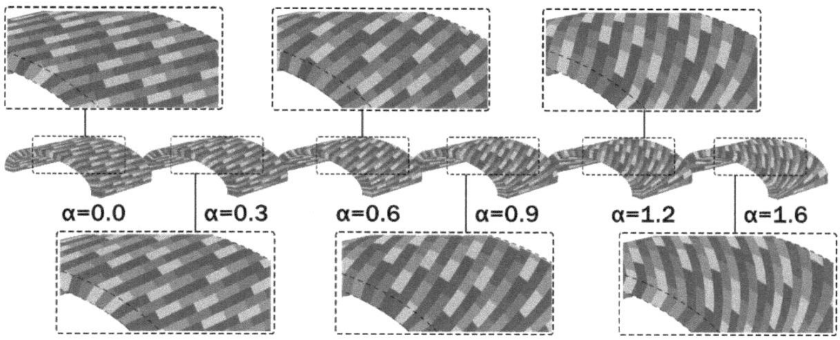

Fig. 3. The role of the interpolation factor in modulating the geometric transition

The limit analysis problem is formulated as a Second-Order Cone Programming (SOCP) task. This method rigorously accounts for frictional contact constraints to identify the collapse load/multiplier. The solver is then integrated into a Genetic Algorithm (GA) for a parametric exploration of the geometry that maximizes/minimizes the ultimate load carrying capacity. This numerical approach identifies the appropriate interpolation coefficient, α. The integrated computational technique discovers high-performance structural combinations across a large design space.

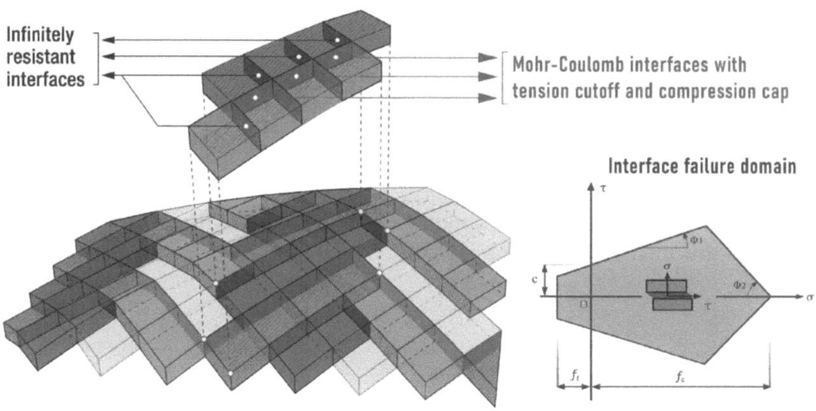

Fig. 4. Geometric discretization at the intersection of block boundaries uses Mohr-Coulomb friction-cohesive interfaces.

Comparative simulations for 25° and 45° skew angles are utilized to determine the role of skewness. Specific geometric measures are used to assess construction complexity and block volume variances. The parametric formulation and optimization strategy are discussed in further detail in subsequent sections. The study finishes by examining the structural impacts of using various building techniques.

2 Methodology

A progressive computational technique combines parametric design and FE-based limit analysis. This method uses an evolutionary search area to identify the optimal structural forms. Using scalar interpolation, the approach merges old archetypes into a single layout. This makes it possible to evaluate the entire design area in a logical and thorough manner. The whole process, from geometry design to performance-based optimization, is shown in Fig. 5 The best configurations are automatically determined by the Genetic Algorithm.

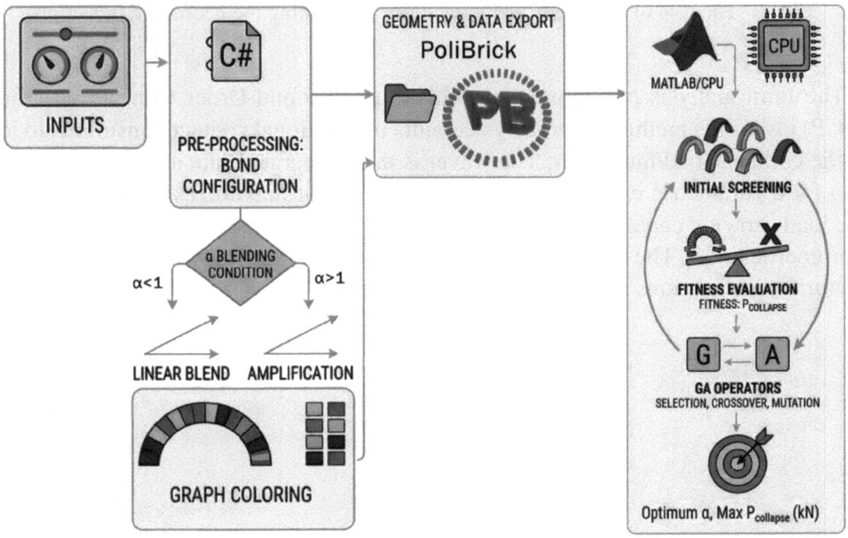

Fig. 5. The skew arch geometry optimization method includes C#-based parametric modeling and GA-driven structural evaluation in MATLAB

2.1 Parametric Geometry Generation

The computational engine for geometry creation is implemented in the Grasshopper environment via a bespoke C# script. It uses the PoliBrick plugin [7] to control discrete assembly and mesh creation processes. Figure 6 shows how the arch shape is determined by a set of predetermined global input parameters. These dimensions include a radius of 2.7 m and a structural thickness of 0.6 m. The voussoir length is fixed at $\ell = 0.75$ m, and the total bridge width is b = 5.0 m. To maintain a width-to-length ratio of around 0.3, 41 courses were used [5].

To maintain a geometrically consistent layout for the 41 courses, the script first performs a numerical integration. This process determines the cumulative arc length S along the mid-surface, where:

$$S = \int_{-\pi/2}^{\pi/2} R_{\text{mid}} \sqrt{\cos^2(u)\cot^2(\omega) + \sin^2(u)}\, du \tag{1}$$

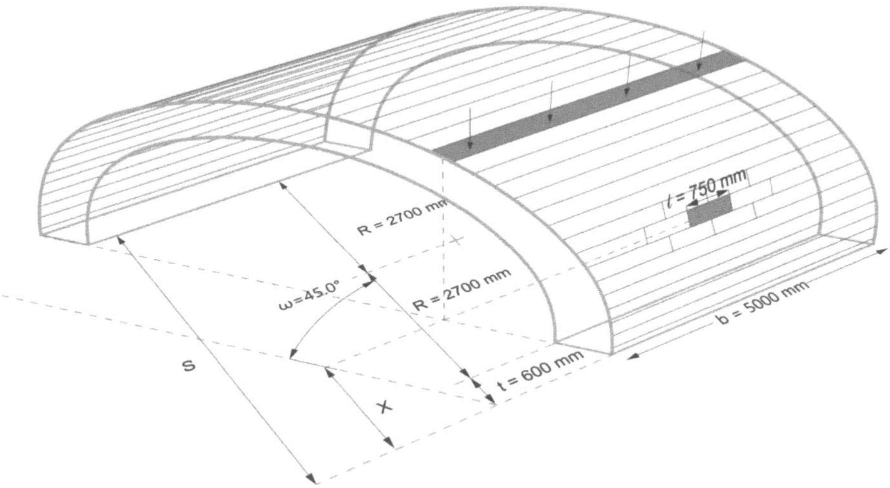

Fig. 6. Geometric specifications of the skew arch for the GA optimization

The variable R_{mid} denotes the radius to the center of the arch thickness, expressed as $(R + t/2)$. The angular coordinate u is measured in radians, ranging from $-\pi/2$ to $+\pi/2$. Furthermore, ω denotes a corresponding skew angle resulting from the bridge orientation. This resulting arc length guarantees equidistant mapping of course borders across any arch skew.

After discretization, the longitudinal trajectory of bed joints with a logarithmic configuration ($\alpha = 1$) is determined. This path is defined by the following analytical equation:

$$y = R_{\mathrm{mid}}\sin(u)\cot(\omega) + R_{\mathrm{mid}}\tan(\omega)\ln(\sec(u) + \tan(u)) + C \tag{2}$$

The variable y indicates the longitudinal position along the barrel depth. To ensure orthogonality on the arch face, the script employs the natural logarithm ln. An integration constant C defines the fixed beginning offset for each course. The range $[-1.56, 1.56]$ radians is the limit of the angular coordinate u.

This kind of bounding avoids singularities at the springing points and guarantees numerical stability. The model employs an interpolation factor $\alpha \in [0,2]$. α is intended as the chromosomal encoding for the Genetic Algorithm. It makes it easier to move continuously between different geometric domains in mathematics. The specific value of $\alpha = 1$ serves as a mathematical baseline that reproduces the traditional logarithmic skew arch. By examining components greater than one, the analysis determines if this historical paradigm is, in fact, the optimal structural solution. Lastly, for every course boundary i, a blended three-dimensional position vector is created. This vector incorporates the transverse position c_2 and the radial distance r. The blended three-dimensional position vector is defined as:

$$\mathrm{P}_\alpha(i, c_2, r) = (1 - \alpha)\mathrm{P}_{\mathrm{false}}(i, c_2, r) + \alpha\mathrm{P}_{\log}(i, c_2, r) \tag{3}$$

where:

i. $P_\alpha = (X_\alpha, Y_\alpha, Z_\alpha)$ is the resulting blended Cartesian position
ii. P_{false} corresponds to the coordinates of a standard false skew arch with straight bed joints
iii. P_{log} corresponds to the optimized logarithmic positions

Note that the spatial mapping inside the conventional interpolation domain ($0 \leq \alpha \leq 1$) is governed by Eq. (3). A straight Cartesian extrapolation using this linear method will provide inconsistent geometric coordinates for shape parameter values greater than 1 (hyper-logarithmic domain), as described below.

The false skew position is computed directly from the uniformly distributed angular coordinate:

$$P_{false} = \begin{pmatrix} r\sin(u_i^{false}) \\ r\sin(u_i^{false})\cot(\omega) + c_2 \\ r\cos(u_i^{false}) \end{pmatrix} \tag{4}$$

The approach intentionally increases the angular deviation in the hyper-logarithmic domain. To establish the spatial position, the script extrapolates data beyond the baseline logarithmic solution:

$$u_{hyper} = u_{false} + \alpha\left(u_{log} - u_{false}\right)\ s.t.\ u_{hyper} \in \left[-\frac{\pi}{2} + \epsilon, \frac{\pi}{2} - \epsilon\right] \tag{5}$$

where $\epsilon = 10^{-6}$ prevents numerical singularities. The corresponding spatial position becomes:

$$P_{hyper} = \begin{pmatrix} r\sin(u_{hyper}) \\ r\sin(u_{hyper})\cot(\omega) + c_2 \\ r\cos(u_{hyper}) \end{pmatrix} \tag{6}$$

When compared to the conventional logarithmic model, this formulation increases the curvature of the bed joint. The barrel original extrados and intrados surfaces are effectively preserved.

It is worth mentioning that Eqs. (5–7) allow safe access to the hyper-logarithmic domain ($\alpha > 1$) without generating inconsistencies in the stereotomy of the arches. After generating the three-dimensional geometry, the framework adds taper bricks at the skew faces. This automated process ensures the maintenance of proper masonry bond patterns.

For structural boundary conditions, mesh faces and vertices are identified via an index-mapping process. After that, these elements are ready to be included into the Limit Analysis solver. As shown in Fig. 6, at X/S = 0.3 a vertical linear load is applied. Asymmetric collapse mechanisms common to semicircular masonry arches are triggered by such loads.

2.2 Upper Bound Limit Analysis and SOCP

Heyman's seminal contribution [9], led to significant advancements in the structural analysis of historical arches. Limit analysis for masonry, specifically the safe theorem, became the primary methodology for evaluating the ultimate capacity of brick-made structures. Subsequent works have enhanced this paradigm through more advanced kinematic simulations that mimic collapse mechanisms via flexural hinge generation [10–14]. Researchers have developed various numerical and analytical methods to study the stability and structural behavior of masonry [15–22]. The kinematic theorem remains popular in the scientific community due to its computing efficiency and straightforward physical explanation. However, the original Heyman assumptions of unlimited compressive strength and negligible friction may be too limiting for complicated three-dimensional designs like skew arches. In such constructions, the angular thrust direction relative to joint planes causes large shear loads, necessitating the explicit consideration of finite friction capacity using Mohr-Coulomb failure criteria rather of the no-sliding idealization. Furthermore, when significant localized compression is combined with shear stress at crucial surfaces, the assumption of infinite compressive strength is called into doubt.

The current technique builds on the kinematic method by discretizing the Masonry structure into infinitely resistant hexahedron and wedge finite elements connected by rigid-plastic interfaces, where all nonlinear behavior is lumped. Unlike traditional formulations that use Linear Programming with piecewise linear yield surface approximations, this study uses a Second-Order Cone Programming (SOCP) solution. This mathematical technique allows for a more rigorous analysis of the three-dimensional Mohr-Coulomb failure criterion, together with a compression cap, eliminating the need for polygonal simplifications of the real yield domain. Milani [10] and Portioli et al. [13] provide comprehensive theoretical underpinnings for indefinitely resistant block limit analysis.

The kinematic variables consist of six degrees of freedom per element, comprising three centroid velocities and three rotation rates. At each interface corner, the SOCP formulation introduces specific plastic flow multipliers to characterize plastic dissipation, see also Fig. 7: one for tension opening (λ_T), one for Mohr-Coulomb sliding, with three components (s_{MC}, δr_{MC}, δq_{MC}), and one for compression cap crushing, again with three components (s_{Cap}, δr_{Cap}, δq_{Cap}). The yield surface combines a modified Mohr-Coulomb criterion with a tension cutoff and a compression cap, expressed through circular Lorentz cones that bound the tangential velocity jumps:

$$\sqrt{(\delta r_{MC})^2 + (\delta q_{MC})^2} \leq s_{MC} \text{ and } \sqrt{(\delta r_{Cap})^2 + (\delta q_{Cap})^2} \leq s_{Cap} \tag{7}$$

Plastic compatibility is preserved through an associated flow rule linking the total velocity jump components at each interface corner to block kinematics. The normal jump is expressed as:

$$\delta n = \mu s_{MC} + \rho s_{Cap} + \lambda_T \tag{8}$$

while the tangential components follow $\delta r = \delta r_{MC} + \delta r_{Cap}$ and $\delta q = \delta q_{MC} + \delta q_{Cap}$. In these expressions, μ denotes the friction coefficient and ρ represents the compression cap shape factor. The internal power dissipation at each corner takes the form:

$$D = c \cdot s_{MC} + f_t \cdot \lambda_T + (\rho \cdot f_c) \cdot s_{Cap} \tag{9}$$

The material parameters adopted in this study are intended to represent a general class of stone masonry with weak joint interfaces. Specifically: friction coefficient $\mu =$ 0.75, cohesion c = 0.015 MPa, tensile strength $f_t = 0.015$ MPa, compressive strength $= f_c$ 2.5 MPa, compression cap factor $\rho = 0.5$, and density 2700 kg/m^3 which approximates the density of many types of rocks, e.g. andesite. These values ensure that all three failure modes (sliding, hinge opening, and compression crushing) remain potentially active, allowing the optimization to identify the governing mechanism without a priori exclusion. The low cohesion and tensile strength approximate nearly dry-joint conditions while providing numerical regularization.

The collapse load multiplier Λ is determined by minimizing the difference between total internal dissipation and the power of loads independent of the multiplier (i.e., self-weight). The present formulation is developed specifically for the case of applied point loads, where a normalization condition ensures that the power of these loads equals unity, guaranteeing identification of a unique failure mechanism. The complete SOCP problem is formulated as:

$$\min\{\Lambda = \sum_{l=1}^{N_{in}} \sum_{k=1}^{4} D_{lk} - \sum_{i=1}^{N_e} V_i \mathbf{f}_0^{(i)T} \mathbf{U}^{(i)}\} \tag{10}$$

Subject to:

i. Kinematic Consistency: $\mathbf{BU} - \dot{\boldsymbol{\lambda}} = 0$ (Equality constraints for velocity jumps).
ii. Normalization: $\mathbf{P}^T_{applied}\mathbf{U} = 1$ (Power constraint ensuring unit virtual work by applied point loads).
iii. Conic Constraints: $\dot{\boldsymbol{\lambda}} \in \mathcal{K}$ (Lorentz cones for MC and Cap, see Fig. 7).
iv. Non-negativity: $\lambda_{MC}, \lambda_{Cap}, \lambda_T \geq 0$.
v. Boundary Conditions: $\mathbf{U} = 0$ at externally constrained elements

where N_{in} denotes the number of interfaces, the index $k = 1, \ldots, 4$ refers to the four corners of each quadrilateral interface, N_e is the number of elements, V_i is the volume of element i, $\mathbf{f}_0^{(i)}$ is the body force density vector (self-weight), $\mathbf{U}^{(i)}$ is the element velocity vector, $\mathbf{B}$ is the kinematic compatibility matrix, $\dot{\boldsymbol{\lambda}}$ collects all interface flow variables, and $\mathcal{K}$ represents the Cartesian product of Lorentz cones enforcing the yield constraints.

This formulation is solved using the MOSEK internal-point optimizer, which provides significantly higher numerical stability and speed compared to standard simplex-based linear solvers. This approach significantly reduces the total number of constraints while maintaining a more accurate representation of the failure surface.

2.3 Evolutionary Optimization via Genetic Algorithm

The approach proposed generates a continuous family of arch geometries indexed by the shape parameter α. Evaluating this entire design space through brute-force methods would be computationally prohibitive, as each structural analysis requires solving a Second-Order Cone Programming (SOCP) problem. Therefore, a Genetic Algorithm (GA) is employed to efficiently search for the specific α value that maximizes (or alternatively minimizes) the total collapse load. Genetic Algorithms effectively optimize

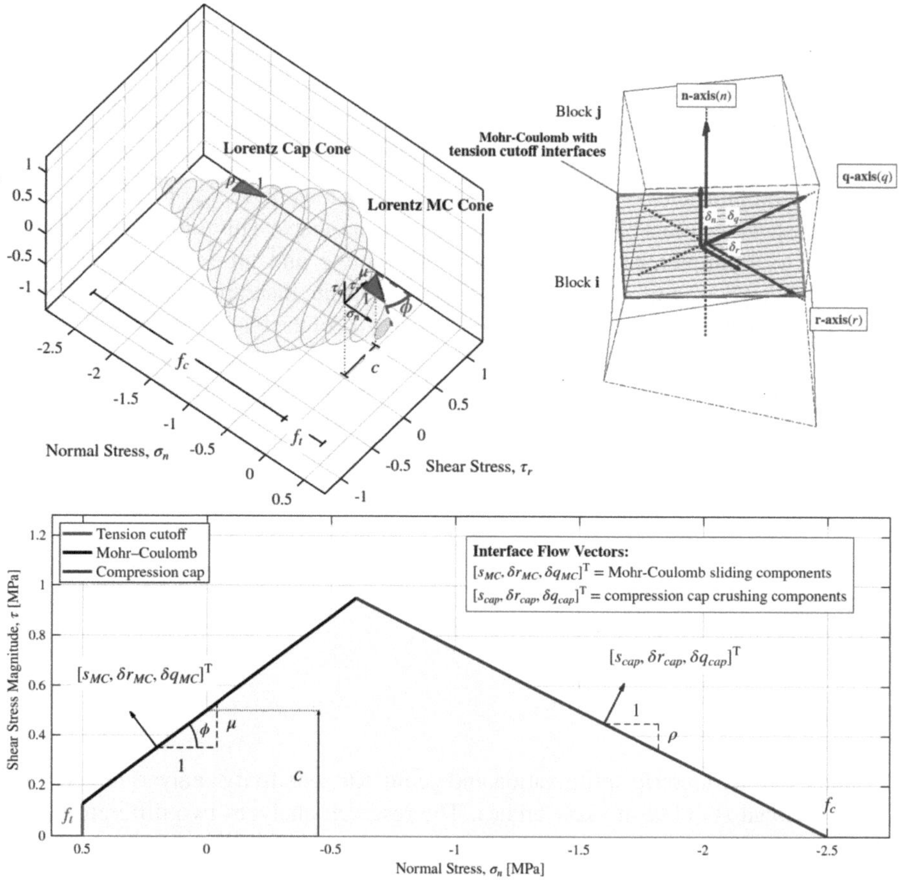

Fig. 7. 3D representation of the yield surface for mortar joints and its 2D cross-section. (Note: The material parameters used to plot the strength domain are the following: $\mu = 0.75$, c = 0.5 MPa, f_t= 0.5 MPa, f_c=2.5 MPa, $\rho = 0.5$. They are purely illustrative and differ from the values used in the actual analyses).

geometries in various engineering fields [24–28]. In masonry research, GAs are frequently paired with limit analysis [26–28]. This combination evaluates structural layouts and potential collapse mechanisms associated with the maximization of the load carrying capacity. The present study uses a GA-based limit analysis to determine quickly the most convenient texture to use for the carrying capacity maximization. Each individual in the GA population encodes a single real-valued chromosome with $\alpha \in [0,2]$. The SOCP solver computes the collapse multiplier Λ, establishing the total collapse load as the fitness metric to rank each candidate geometry:

$$P_{collapse} = \frac{\Lambda \cdot n_{loads}}{1000} \tag{11}$$

In the previous equation,$P_{collapse}$ is the fitness value used to rank individuals.λ is the collapse multiplier calculated by the MOSEK solver.n_{loads} represents the number of applied point loads. The algorithm also evaluates the variability of the discretization in blocks through the Coefficient of Variation (CV) of the block volumes:

$$CV_{volume} = \frac{\sigma_{vol}}{\mu_{vol}} \tag{12}$$

From a structural and constructability perspective, a lower CV_{volume} indicates a highly uniform mesh where most blocks are of similar size and shape. This uniformity translates practically to a simpler, more repeatable stone-cutting and fabrication process. The parameter CV_{volume} signifies the relative dispersion of the discretization. This metric is defined by the standard deviation σ_{vol} and the mean μ_{vol} of the block volumes. The search begins with 50 candidates that evolve over 30 generations. An elitist strategy preserves the top 5 individuals for the next generation. Selection is performed through a tournament process with a size of 5. The crossover and mutation operators have probability of 0.8 and 0.15, respectively. Finally, a stability check examines convergence across a certain window of generations:

$$\sigma_{best} < \epsilon_{tol} \tag{13}$$

The standard deviation of the maximum collapse load is denoted by σ_{best}, whereas ϵ_{tol} represents convergence.

3 Results

This study uses parametric optimization and geometric sensitivity analysis to determine the gravitational stability of skew arches. The research analyzes two different layouts with 25° and 45° skewness angles. The study analyzed 2,000 distinct people using a Genetic Algorithm and Second-Order Cone Programming.

(SOCP) Framework. This dataset includes 1,000 distinct examples for each level of skewness studied. The comparison study demonstrates that the 25-degree skew arch has a greater maximum collapse load because it maintains geometric integrity throughout a larger design region. When α exceeds 1.6, component dimensions drop below 2 cm, making 45-degree geometry physically impossible. At $\alpha = 0$ and $\alpha = 1.6$, the arch configurations behave similarly. According to the data shown in Fig. 8, the 45-degree arch has somewhat superior performance within the relevant range of 0 to 1.6. Both skewness scenarios show a roughly linear connection between α and the resultant collapse load.

The peak performance measurements for the top-ranked individual are given in the table below (Table 1):

A reference straight arch serves as a baseline. At α = 0, this geometry behaves like a typical false skew arch, with a block volume Coefficient of Variation of 0.0743. Figure 9 depicts the thrust line and four-hinge collapse mechanism for this arrangement. At the initial condition, all three arch models have the same collapse load of 362.98 kN. Larger α values do not significantly affect the geometry of a straight arch. In skewed geometries, the logarithmic generation rule causes bed joints to stay perpendicular to the lateral faces; nevertheless, applying this theory to a straight arch yields parallel beds again.

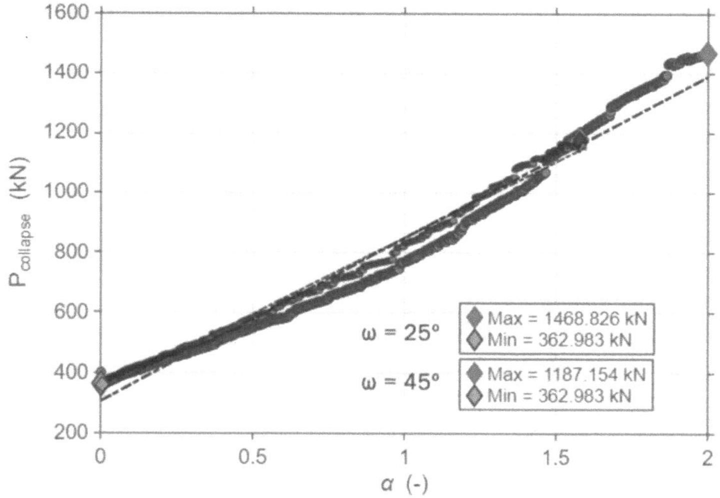

Fig. 8. The analysis of the total collapse load (kN) via the shape parameter α

Table 1. Summary of the optimal configurations for each simulation case

Skewness Angle	Optimal α	Max $P_{collapse}$(kN)	Max Lambda (λ)	N_{loads}	Volume CV
0	–	362.98kN	15,124.29	24	0.0743
25°	1.9980	1,468.83 kN	86,401.51	17	0.5508
45°	1.5760	1,187.15 kN	53,961.56	22	0.3679

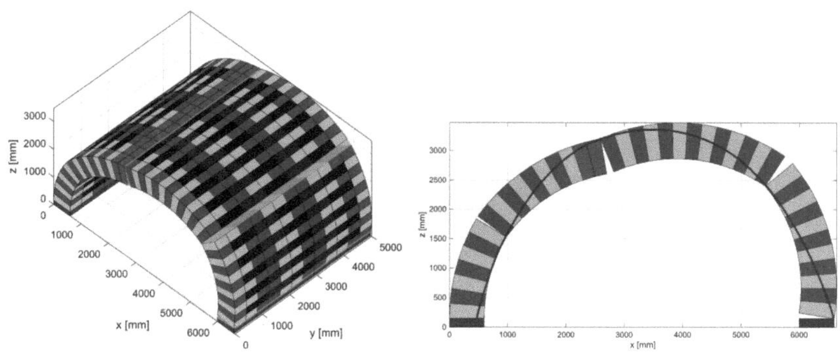

Fig. 9. Thrust line and four-hinge collapse mechanism of a straight arch.

The methodology was validated by comparing the baseline straight arch (α = 0) with available literature and manual calculations. With a cohesion and tensile strength of 0.015 MPa, the numerical study showed a collapse load of 362.98 kN. The collapse load dropped to 240.51 kN by applying a 28° friction coefficient and lowering these strength parameters to almost zero to approximate dry-joint conditions ($c \approx 0, f_t \approx 0$).

The analytical calculation of 241.58 kN is supported by this numerical finding. These values are quite similar to the 260 kN ultimate capacity for the same geometry reported in [5]. Additionally, the failure mechanisms of the straight and false skew designs were the same, which is consistent with the behavior reported in [5]. When taken as a whole, these confirmations show that the elevated load capabilities seen in the baseline and hyper-logarithmic models are mathematically consistent.

The collapse mechanisms for several 45-degree skew arch geometries are shown in Fig. 10. The mechanism fails through a standard hinge opening mode at $\alpha = 0$, which denotes the pure false skew arch. The zigzag pattern introduced by the shift toward the logarithmic shape improves structural interlocking. The collapse load increases by almost four times as a result of this geometric shift, from 362.98 kN to 1187.15 kN. The 45-degree arch is still more effective at $\alpha = 1$, but the 25-degree instance shows a similar trend. In the end, after the shape factor surpasses 1.48, the 25-degree design attains superior performance.

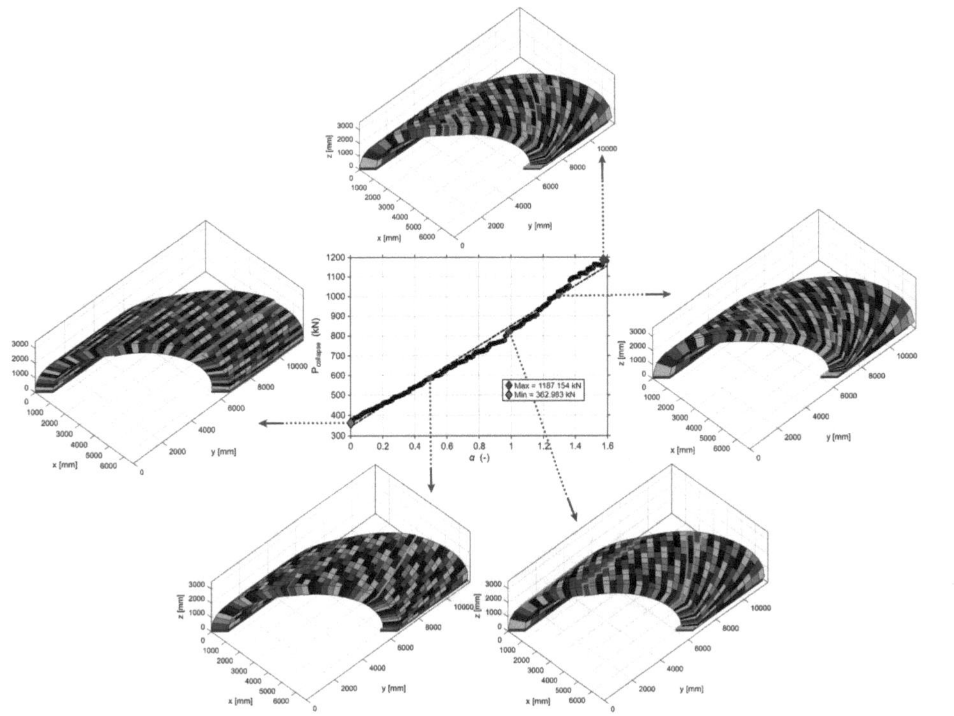

Fig. 10. Variation of collapse mechanism for different geometric shapes

The impact of mesh discretization on structural constructability is revealed by analyzing the Coefficient of Variation (CV) for block volumes. The 45-degree design produces a more uniform mesh ($CV_{volume} = 0.36$) than the 25-degree example ($CV_{volume} = 0.55$), as seen in Fig. 11. Better geometric regularity throughout the masonry components is indicated by lower CV values. This consistency guarantees effective assembly and greatly streamlines the manufacture process. Furthermore, Fig. 11 illustrates a higher increase in block shape diversity throughout the geometric design space for the 25-degree arch. The data shows that 45-degree arches are more regular and structurally stronger for identical α values when this regularity is correlated with structural capacity.

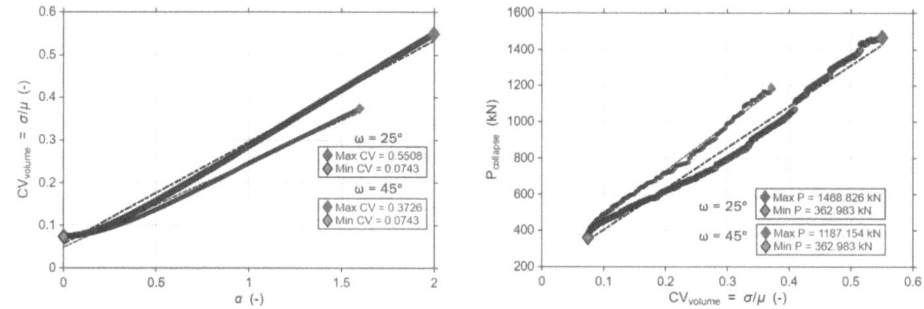

Fig. 11. Distribution of mesh regularity (*CV*) via the geometric shape parameter α and the ultimate collapse load.

The structural effects of changing the vertical interfaces of masonry blocks are assessed in a focused sub-study. This analysis compares vertical joints that stay precisely parallel to the arch face versus those that use an interpolation rule while maintaining a consistent bed joint trajectory. The resulting geometric shift is shown in Fig. 12, which shows parallel joints in red and interpolated vertical joints in gray.

Fig. 12. Visual comparison highlights how vertical interface orientation influences the overall masonry arrangement.

Figure 13 exhibits how altering the vertical joint position results in almost the same collapse mechanisms over a range of α values. The analysis isolates this geometric variable by keeping the bed joint trajectory constant for a given shape parameter. The numerical approach proposed then evaluates the load carrying capacities of arches with vertical joints parallel to the arch face against those utilizing an angular interpolation rule. Specific visual comparisons of the failure mechanisms for $\alpha = 0$ and $\alpha = 0.5$ clearly confirm this consistent structural behavior. Ultimately, altering the vertical cross joints does not significantly modify the overall failure mode or the hinge locations within the masonry assembly. Despite the consistent failure mechanisms, transitioning to interpolated joints significantly lowers load carrying capacity. For $\alpha = 0$ case, the collapse load drops from 487 kN to 362 kN under the interpolation rule. A similar trend appears in the second case where α is equal to 0.5. Here, the capacity decreases from 817 to 608 kN following the change in joint geometry. These results confirm the intuitive statement that using smaller blocks, failure loads decrease (because more interfaces where plastic dissipation may occur are present).

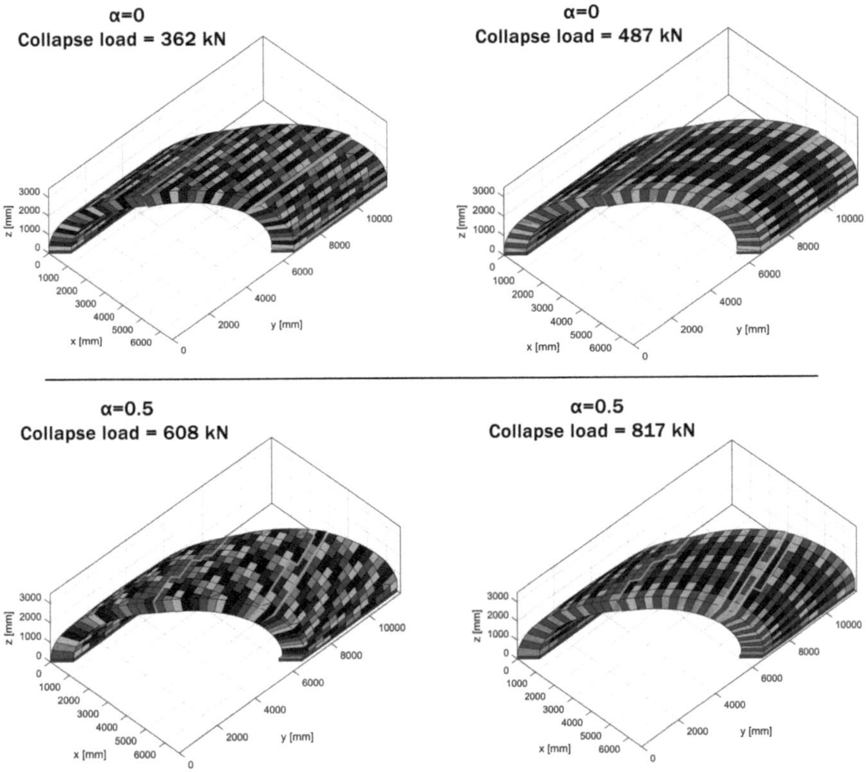

Fig. 13. Failure mechanisms for different vertical joint configurations: interfaces governed by the α interpolation rule (left) alongside interfaces parallel to the arch face (right).

4 Conclusion

Historically, skew masonry arch construction techniques have been divided into discrete groups by engineers. The most well-known instances of these traditional methods are the false and logarithmic layouts. In order to overcome this conceptual division, the study presents a single mathematical formulation. The suggested paradigm creates a seamless geometric transition between "false" and "logarithmic" layouts by using a continuous form parameter. In the end, this process combines several traditionally distinct stone-cutting methods into an all-encompassing structural framework. The study unites traditional archetypes and investigates superior hyper-logarithmic configurations by introducing the interpolation factor α. Three-dimensional friction, tension, and compression at the inter-block interfaces are rigorously handled by the SOCP-based limit analysis. The findings show that, in comparison to conventional layouts, increasing joint curvature delivers a nearly fourfold improvement in collapse capacity. In the hyper-logarithmic domain, optimal configurations are always discovered when α values are greater than the traditional boundary. The 45° version retains better geometric regularity and manufacture feasibility whereas the 25° version reaches larger peak loads. Additionally, the study demonstrates that structural strength is strongly impacted by the position of vertical cross joints. In particular, the load-carrying capacity is increased when joints parallel to the arch face are used instead of interpolated joints. Interestingly, this performance boost happens despite the failure mechanisms staying the same. This framework provides an effective means of maintaining and improving the structural integrity of aged masonry transit networks. The application of this technique to intricate multi-span skew geometries and experimental validation should be the main goals of future improvements.

References

1. Forgács, T., Sarhosis, V., Bagi, K.: Minimum thickness of semi-circular skewed masonry arches. Eng. Struct. **140**, 317–336 (2017)
2. Skew Arch Bridge, Plane 6, Allegheny Portage RR (Wikimedia Commons). http://commons.wikimedia.org/wiki/File:Skew_Arch_Bridge,_Plane_6,_Allegheny_Portage_RR.jpg. Accessed 25 March 2026
3. Allegheny Portage Railroad - Skew Arch Bridge (Flickr). http://www.flickr.com/photos/141239321/16600585712/in/photostream/. Accessed 25 March 2026
4. Pingaro, N., Milani, G.: Simple interface element equipped with thickness for the non-linear static heterogeneous analysis of masonry walls in-plane loaded: Implementation and validation. Eng. Struct. **351**, 122056 (2026)
5. Forgács, T., Sarhosis, V., Bagi, K.: Influence of construction method on the load bearing capacity of skew masonry arches. Eng. Struct. **168**, 612–627 (2018)
6. Pourfouladi, M., Pingaro, N., Milani, G.: Collapse risk assessment of long-span masonry cloister vaults under paradigmatic crown loading: a heterogeneous limit analysis approach with stereotomy. In: Lecture Notes in Civil Engineering, pp. 123–134. Springer (2025)
7. Pourfouladi, M., Pingaro, N., Valente, M.: PoliBrick plugin as a parametric tool for digital stereotomy modelling. Comput. Struct. **311**, 107722 (2025)
8. Meloni, G., Pourfouladi, M., Pingaro, N.: Parametric modelling and nonlinear FE analysis of Trepponti Bridge subjected to differential settlements. Buildings **16**(1), 47 (2026)
9. Heyman, J.: The stone skeleton. Int. J. Solids Struct. **2**, 249–279 (1966)
10. Milani, G.: 3D upper bound limit analysis of multi-leaf masonry walls. Int. J. Mech. Sci. **50**, 817–836 (2007)
11. Pingaro, N., Milani, G., Tiberti, S.: Automatic CAD kinematic limit analysis approach for the limit analysis of masonry towers. In: AIP Conference Proceedings, vol. 2293, p. 380005. AIP Publishing (2020)
12. Cascini, L., Gagliardo, R., Portioli, F.: LIABlock_3D: a software tool for collapse mechanism analysis of historic masonry structures. Int. J. Architect. Heritage **14**, 75–94 (2018)
13. Portioli, F., Casapulla, C., Gilbert, M., Cascini, L.: Limit analysis of 3D masonry block structures with non-associative frictional joints using cone programming. Comput. Struct. **143**, 108–121 (2014)

14. Hua, Y., Milani, G.: Rigid block limit analysis of masonry arches with associated and non-associated slides. Research for Development, pp. 169–203 (2022)
15. Angelillo, M., Montanino, A., Pandolfi, A.: On the connection between geometry and statically determined membrane stresses in the human cornea. J. Biomech. Eng. **142**(5), 051006 (2020)
16. Perelli, F.L., De Gregorio, D., Montanino, A., Olivieri, C., Maddaloni, G., Iannuzzo, A.: Energy-based modelling of in-plane fragility curves for the 2D ultimate capacity of Italian masonry buildings. Front. Built Environ. **9**, 1127523 (2023)
17. Cusano, C., Montanino, A., Olivieri, C., Paris, V., Cennamo, C.: Graphical and analytical quantitative comparison in the domes assessment: the case of san francesco di paola. Appl. Sci. **11**(8), 3622 (2021)
18. Galassi, S., Ruggieri, N., Tempesta, G.: Ruins and archaeological artifacts: vulnerabilities analysis for their conservation through the original computer program BrickWORK. In: Aguilar, R., Torrealva, D., Moreira, S., Pando, M.A., Ramos, L.F. (eds.) Structural Analysis of Historical Constructions. RILEM Bookseries, vol. 18. Springer, Cham (2019). https://doi.org/10.1007/978-3-319-99441-3_197
19. Galassi, S., Ruggieri, N., Tempesta, G.: A novel numerical tool for seismic vulnerability analysis of ruins in archaeological sites. Int. J. Architect. Heritage **14**(1), 1–22 (2020)
20. Galassi, S., et al.: Digital survey and structural investigation on the triumphal arch of caracalla in the archaeological site of volubilis in Morocco. Int. J. Architect. Heritage **16**(6), 940–955 (2022)
21. Iannuzzo, A., Matarazzo, G., Cusano, C., Ferraro, M., Maddaloni, G.: Insights into the collapse of the asciello masonry bridge in Benevento. In: Gervasi, O., et al. (eds.) Computational Science and Its Applications – ICCSA 2025 Workshops. ICCSA 2025. LNCS, vol. 15886. Springer, Cham (2026). https://doi.org/10.1007/978-3-031-97576-9_26
22. Fabbrocino, F., Olivieri, C., Luciano, R., Vaiano, G., Maddaloni, G., Iannuzzo, A.: Seismic performance of historic masonry buildings: a comparative analysis of equivalent frame and block-based methods. Alex. Eng. J. **109**, 359–375 (2024)
23. Wang, P., Milani, G.: Specialized 3D distinct element limit analysis approach for a fast seismic vulnerability evaluation of massive masonry structures: application on traditional pagodas. Eng. Struct. **282**, 115792 (2023)
24. Buzzetti, M., Milani, G.: Combined genetic algorithm and limit analysis approach for the optimal design of tie rods in historical masonry structures. In: COMPDYN Proceedings, pp. 1002–1012 (2025)
25. Fard, M.S., Ghaderi, E., Pourfouladi, M.: Free-form grid structure multi-objective optimization associated with integrated design and machine learning. Eng. Struct. **329**, 119827 (2025)
26. Nouri, L., Azari, K.T., Pourfouladi, M., Keramat, D., Alaghmandan, M.: Form-finding and optimization of branching columns using L-systems in early stages of design: a parametric approach. J. Build. Eng. **117**, 114817 (2025)
27. Chiozzi, A., Milani, G., Tralli, A.: A genetic algorithm NURBS-based new approach for fast kinematic limit analysis of masonry vaults. Comput. Struct. **182**, 187–204 (2016)
28. Tiberti, S., Grillanda, N., Mallardo, V., Milani, G.: A genetic algorithm adaptive homogeneous approach for evaluating settlement-induced cracks in masonry walls. Eng. Struct. **221**, 111073 (2020)

Funicular Analysis of a Non-symmetric Sail Vault

Danila Aita[1(✉)], Matteo Bruggi[1], Enrico Malavolta[2], and Alberto Taliercio[1]

[1] Department of Civil and Environmental Engineering, Politecnico di Milano, 20133 Milan, Italy
danila.aita@polimi.it

[2] School of Civil, Environmental and Land Management Engineering, Politecnico di Milano, 20133 Milan, Italy

Abstract. This work is part of a research project aimed at exploring the applicability of a computational funicular method to masonry structures with non-trivial geometries, with the aim of adequately describing the flow of compressive forces. As a case study, a non-symmetric vault was selected, namely a sail vault in the Fortezza Vecchia (Old Fortress) in Livorno, Italy, which covers a trapezoidal room and is characterised by an octagonal *oculus*. The study of the mechanical response of the vault is conducted by means of a funicular approach based on a mathematical programming formulation within the framework of the static theorem of limit analysis. The proposed investigation considers simplified assumptions regarding the mechanical behaviour of masonry, namely zero tensile strength, infinite compressive strength, and infinite friction. The objective function was specifically implemented to identify minimum thrust solutions. The results are discussed and compared with those obtained from a finite element analysis performed in Abaqus CAE.

Keywords: Masonry · Sail Vault · Funicular Network Analysis · Limit Analysis

1 Introduction

Modelling masonry vaults is a complex challenge, given the non-homogeneous and anisotropic nature of this material, characterized by low tensile strength and high compressive strength [1]. According to [2], the very definition of the concept of 'masonry' is a challenging task because it includes a variety of materials depending on the components used (stone, bricks, etc.), the types of blocks, the assembly method, the presence or absence of mortar and the construction technique adopted. Without claiming completeness, some contributions aim to create realistic models capable of faithfully representing the structural response of masonry structures (or masonry elements), by using homogenization techniques [3], or by proposing non-linear finite element analyses adopting different modelling strategies. Among other examples, [4] homogeneously models a masonry structure with a complex geometry, discretizing it through macro-blocks obeying a Mohr-Coulomb failure criterion; [5] proposes a discretization of the mortar in

O. Gervasi et al. (Eds.): ICCSA 2026 Workshops, LNCS 16758, pp. 499–514, 2027.
https://doi.org/10.1007/978-3-032-30497-1_30

masonry walls subjected to in-plane loads. However, the high degree of uncertainty surrounding the material properties constitutes a disadvantage that makes it difficult to select the appropriate mechanical parameters. Observing that finite element analyses are often complex, mesh-dependent and require the application of ad hoc constitutive laws to capture the intricacy of the mechanical response of masonry structures, some studies aim to bridge the gap between sophisticated modelling and real-world implementation; see for example [6], where a simple nonlinear truss model is proposed to assess the stability of curved masonry structures. Additionally, one of the most notable characteristics of masonry is its uncertain tensile strength, which is often significantly lower than its compressive strength. In this complex context, a simplified approach based on Heyman's assumptions [7] is commonly followed, even in the most recent scientific literature [8], to evaluate the structural response of masonry structures. According to these assumptions, masonry can transmit only compressive forces; the compressive strength is assumed to be infinite, while the tensile strength is zero; furthermore, sliding between blocks is assumed to be prevented by an ideally infinite friction. Heyman's hypotheses allow the problem to be rigorously treated within the framework of the theorems of limit analysis.

In this context, Heyman's assumptions are adopted to find purely compressive load paths; see for example [9], where masonry is described as a no-tension solid continuum, or [10], where purely compressed shells are identified by exploiting the Airy stress function. Several studies have revisited the historical contributions on the thrust line method for masonry arches and vaults or the inverted catenary concept; see for example [11]. Advances in graphical statics and the development of computer-aided techniques have made it possible to design the funicular polygon corresponding to the actual loads for the safety assessment of masonry structures with complex geometry. One of the techniques arising from this background is the thrust network approach [12, 13].

The purpose of the research here presented is to investigate whether a computational funicular method can be applied to masonry structures with complex or non-symmetric geometries to accurately describe the flow of compressive forces under service conditions. The approach, in which Heyman's hypotheses are adopted regarding the mechanical behaviour of masonry, is based on the mathematical programming formulation suggested in [14]. The procedure begins with the construction of a spatial network with a specified planar geometry and considering an independent set of force densities. The load path in the vault is found by formulating an optimization problem in terms of the vertical coordinates of the constrained nodes. Depending on the goal, different objective functions can be chosen. To identify anti-funicular networks (in equilibrium with the loads) that are located within the vault's shape, restrictions are imposed on the height of the nodes and the sign of the force densities. The method, implemented in MATLAB, has been already successfully applied to the study of symmetric and non-symmetric masonry vaults subjected to their self-weight [15]. Furthermore, some applications have been provided for the study of arches and vaults subjected to seismic loads [14, 16]; recent developments of the method are able to take into account strength requirements and stereotomy [17].

This research aims to examine a significant case study of a non-symmetric vault, a sail vault in the Fortezza Vecchia in Livorno, Italy, which covers a trapezoidal room and is distinguished by an octagonal *oculus* [18]. The geometry of the sail vault was reconstructed from the results of an accurate terrestrial laser scanner survey of the entire fortress, available as a point cloud.

The funicular method is used to investigate networks that represent paths of compressive force flow in equilibrium with prescribed loads. In this regard, it should be remembered that this method fits into the context of limit analysis. It is based on Heyman's safe theorem [7], which states that the structural stability of masonry structures is guaranteed if at least one statically admissible compressive load path can be found within the geometry of the structure. It is therefore necessary to identify the most plausible equilibrium state among the infinite admissible ones. To this end, the "principle of least pressure", proposed by Moseley in 1833 [19] and originally conceived for masonry arches, is applied; according to this principle, the "true" thrust line is that which minimizes the horizontal component of the thrust itself. In light of the above, in the funicular method the concept of "thrust" is extended to three dimensions and the generalized horizontal "thrust" is minimized. Because only low tensile stresses are expected to develop in the vault, this choice ensures a meaningful comparison with the results of the linear elastic finite element analyses performed in Abaqus CAE, despite being based on a different modelling of the masonry material. This comparison allows one to verify the reliability of the minimum thrust funicular solution.

2 The Sail Vault of the Fortezza Vecchia in Livorno: History and Previous Structural Analyses

The history of the fortress, described in detail in [18], begins in the 16th century, when the Medici family took control of Livorno and began significantly modifying the existing buildings. Under the guidance of his brother Giuliano, Antonio da Sangallo the Elder developed the *Fortezza* plans. With the help of numerous expert engineers, its construction took place between 1519 and 1533. The structure has irregular and unique architectural lines with three imposing bastions. Inside the Canaviglia bastion, there is a characteristic trapezoidal room (Fig. 1a) covered by a sail vault with an octagonal ventilation opening (*oculus*) at the centre (Fig. 1b).

The entire fortress, including the vault, is an example of Renaissance architecture of great value, which testifies to the impact of Filippo Brunelleschi's innovations on the building panorama of the time (such as the *opus spicatum* as a construction technique for vaults) and the technical expertise of Antonio da Sangallo the Elder.

Some previous research on the structural behaviour of the vault was performed by [20–24] within a research project of the University of Pisa (programme PRA 2017, project *"Architetture toscane rinascimentali: casi studio fra indagine storica, rilievo e analisi strutturale"*). These works provided some preliminary results - within the context of the safe theorem of limit analysis - related to the behaviour of the vault subjected to vertical loads, by seeking statically admissible solutions. Assuming either Heyman's hypotheses [7, 22], or a limited compressive strength [20, 23], and simplifying the vault's geometry by adopting an analytical expression for the intrados surface, these studies were conducted both by reviewing Durand-Claye method [21–23, 25] and by considering the vault as a thin shell. For simplicity, the analyses were limited to axisymmetric stress distributions. From these studies, the vault was found to be safe under vertical loads.

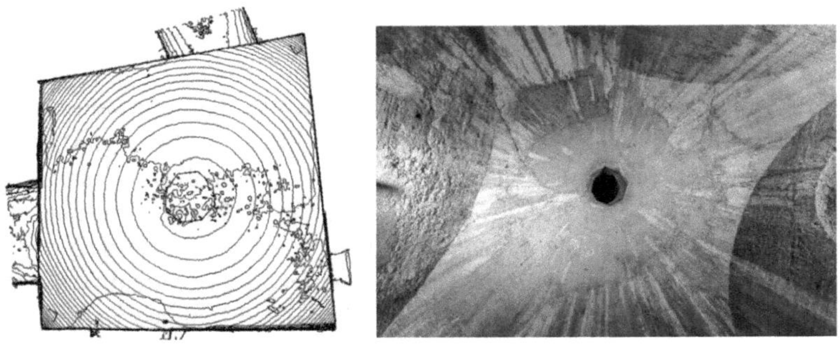

(*a*) (*b*)

Fig. 1. The sail vault in the Canaviglia bastion of the Fortezza Vecchia in Livorno. (*a*) Trapezoidal shape of the plan with the contour lines describing the geometric irregularities (courtesy of Prof. Andrea Piemonte, University of Pisa). (*b*) view from the inside, with the central octagonal *oculus*.

3 From the Survey to the Structural Analysis

As part of a collaboration with the University of Pisa [18], the administrative bodies (*Autorità di Sistema Portuale del Mar Tirreno Settentrionale* - North Tyrrhenian Sea Port Authority) have made available the data collected from a terrestrial laser scanner survey (both internal and external) of the entire fortress. The *status quo* geometrical survey is described in [24].

The geometries required for the structural analysis were extracted from the survey, accessible as a point cloud provided in Autodesk ReCap format, with a density of approximately three points per square centimetre. The region that corresponded to the vault was separated from the remainder of the fortress, by operating with the CloudCompare software. The resulting model was exported in the .pts format, making it compatible with three-dimensional modelling software like AutoCAD and Rhino (Fig. 2).

The Rhino graphics software was used to create a solid surface from the point cloud of the vault through the *Patch* command. This procedure enabled reproduction of the intrados surface with sufficient precision, including its irregularities. Furthermore, the vault's intrados was chosen as the reference surface for building the model of the extrados surface (which is inaccessible for direct surveying due to the fill layers and flooring). To this end, the *OffsetSrf* command in Rhino was used, by assuming a constant average vault thickness of 0.5 m, based on previous research and results of an experimental campaign, as described in [23].

The 3D survey and the previous contributions on the structural response of the sail vault cited in Sect. 2 constitute the starting point for further investigation, developed in [26]. As will be described in Sects. 4 and 5, the research here proposed – using both the funicular method and finite element analyses – aims to fully understand the three-dimensional behaviour of the vault under service conditions, exploring the effects of non-symmetry on the equilibrium solutions.

Once the 3D model definition was completed, it was exported in .sat format and integrated into the Abaqus CAE structural calculation software, with the aim to perform

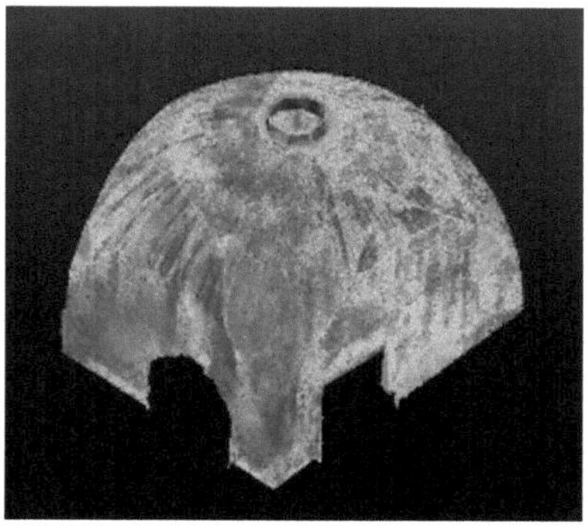

Fig. 2. Point cloud of the sail vault, with the side walls, extracted using the CloudCompare software.

FEM analyses to benchmark the results obtained via the funicular approach, as will be illustrated in Sect. 5.

To perform the funicular analysis of the vault under gravitational loads, it was necessary to define the network nodes through geometric processing operating in Rhino. In order to derive a network with a fixed projection on the horizontal plane, a planar grid was obtained by subdividing the opposite sides of the trapezoidal base perimeter into a number of equal segments (through the command *Divide*) and connecting the points belonging to opposite sides, as shown in Fig. 3a. In the present study, a 16 × 16 subdivision was adopted. After extracting the intersection points of the planar grid (using the commands *Explode* and *ExtractPoints*), vertical lines were conducted from each base point. By means of the *Trim* command, using the vault surfaces as the cutting object, and, again, the *ExtractPoint* command, the intersection points between the vertical lines and the intrados and extrados vault's surfaces were obtained.

The *EvaluatePt* command, an internal Rhino function, is used to extract the x, y, z^{min} and z^{max} coordinates, with z^{min} (respectively, z^{max}) derived from the intrados (resp., extrados) surface.

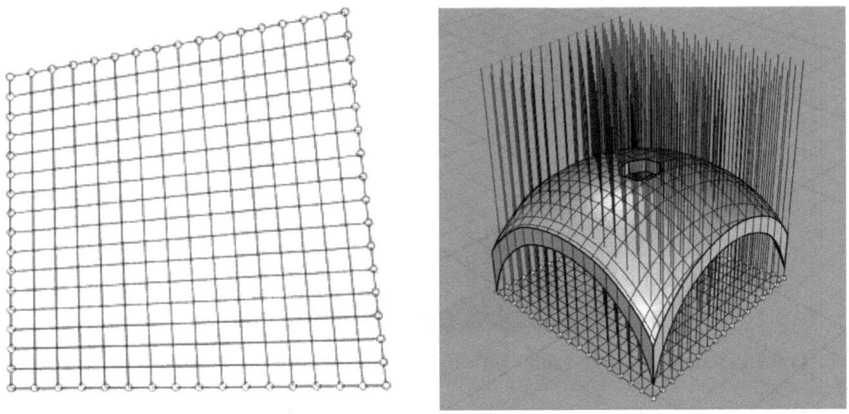

(*a*) (*b*)

Fig. 3. Procedure for obtaining a network with fixed projection on the horizontal plane. (*a*) Planar grid (16 × 16 subdivision). (*b*) The intrados and extrados points are derived by intersecting the vertical lines drawn starting from the planar grid with the intrados and extrados surfaces.

4 Funicular Analysis of the Sail Vault

4.1 The Force Density Method

The method adopted here [14] builds upon the concept of force density, as presented by H. J. Schek [27]. The Force Density Method is used to determine the geometric static equilibrium configurations of spatial structures subjected to external loads relying on linear equations. Through this approach, it is possible to manage the equilibrium of anti-funicular networks consisting of $n_s = n + n_f$ nodes (where n and n_f are the number of unrestrained and restrained nodes, respectively) which connect m branches.

In the applications, masonry vaults are modelled as statically indeterminate networks subjected only to compressive stresses and in equilibrium with the loads applied at the nodes. It is recalled that, according to Heyman's safe theorem [7], a masonry arch is in equilibrium if there exists a thrust line contained within the arch. This theorem implicitly refers to the concept of 'line of resistance' [28], related to the centre of pressure of internal reaction inside any joint, whereas anti-funicular polygons correspond to the concept of 'line of pressure' [28], see also the discussion in [29]. In this contribution joints are disregarded. An appropriate set of enforcements is formulated to prescribe lower and upper bounds for the vertical coordinates z of the nodes, to ensure that the retrieved anti-funicular networks remain within the vault's thickness, i.e., $z^{min} \leq z \leq z^{max}$, for the assigned loads. These constraints provide a good approximation of the conditions arising from the safe theorem in order to guarantee the equilibrium of the vault.

The introduction of the force densities vector, **q**, collecting the force-to-length ratio in each branch of the network, allows formulating the equilibrium of the n unrestrained nodes as a set of linear equations. Furthermore, the condition $\mathbf{q}_j \leq 0, For j = 1, ..., m$, allows for enforcing that the branches are subjected to compression, ensuring a no-tension behaviour.

For the details on the procedure here applied, the interested reader is referred to [14], where the optimization problem is conveniently formulated in terms of the reduced set of independent density forces, $\overline{\mathbf{q}}$, calculated via a preliminary Gauss-Jordan elimination, and solved by using sequential convex programming techniques, such as the Method of Moving Asymptotes [30].

For the purposes of this contribution, it is sufficient to recall that the required input data are the planimetric coordinates of the nodes (x, y), the vertical limits for the height of the nodes, z^{min} and z^{max}, the nodal loads, and the connectivity between the elements.

The optimization algorithm searches for the anti-funicular network that, respecting the limits described above, corresponds to the minimum thrust based on the objective functions defined below:

$$f(\mathbf{q}) = \sum_{h}^{n_f} \sqrt{R_{xh}^2 + R_{yh}^2}, \tag{1}$$

where R_{xh} and R_{yh} are the reactions along the x and y direction. Equation (1) is intended to be an extension of thrust concept, commonly used for the equilibrium of masonry arches, to three-dimensional vaults. As regards the minimization of the horizontal thrust, this choice is based on the suggestions provided in [19] and on the discussion proposed in [31].

4.2 Definition of the Nodal Loads

To assign loads to each node in the network, we proceed by constructing a secondary planar grid, as shown in Fig. 4a, dividing each segment of the original grid in Fig. 3a in half. The three-dimensional model of the vault (in Rhino) is then sectioned using vertical planes drawn from the lines belonging to this new planar grid; in this way, irregular blocks with a quadrangular base are obtained, see Fig. 4b. It is thus possible to compute, after some processing in Rhino, the volume of each block. The centre of gravity of each block lies on a straight vertical line that passes approximately through each of the primary grid nodes, see the white dots in Fig. 4a.

The procedure just described allows us to evaluate the nodal load corresponding to the self-weight, by multiplying the volume of each block by the unit weight of masonry, assumed to be equal to 18 kN/m^3. For brevity, the procedure for evaluating the nodal load corresponding to the infill between the vault's extrados and the upper floor level is omitted. It is sufficient to remember that a specific weight of 17 kN/m^3 is assumed for the infill, consistent with both previous studies on the vault's structural behaviour and the technical documentation available [18, 20–24]. The nodal loads are then obtained by adding the weights of masonry and infill.

4.3 Different Configurations of the Network

The vault analyses were conducted considering different configurations of the funicular network of increasing complexity. The starting point was a network with relatively low computational complexity, according to a quadrilateral grid scheme like the one shown in Fig. 5a ($n_s = 256$; $m = 472$). A second configuration is obtained by adding connectivity

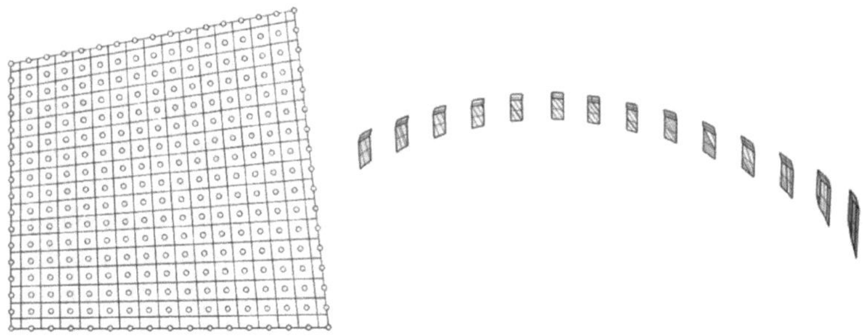

(*a*) (*b*)

Fig. 4. Procedure for assigning loads to each node. (*a*) Secondary planar grid (straight lines) and intersection points of the primary grid (white dots). (*b*) Blocks are obtained by sectioning the 3D model of the vault with vertical planes passing through the secondary grid lines (discretization of an arch belonging to the vault).

restrictions between nodes located along the diagonals of the trapezoidal plan; see Fig. 5b ($n_s = 256$; $m = 499$).

Increasing the degree of redundancy, additional branches are added along lines parallel to the main diagonals of the trapezoidal plan and starting from the vertices of the *oculus* (Fig. 5c): the asymmetry of the ensuing grid is clearly visible ($n_s = 256$; $m = 549$).

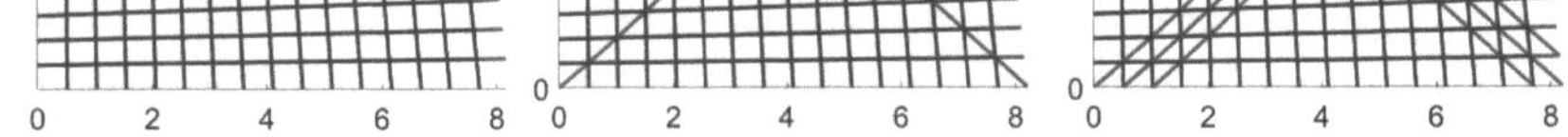

(*a*) (*b*) (*c*)

Fig. 5. Different configurations of the anti-funicular networks for the analysis of the sail vault. Branches where independent force densities act are marked in red. (*a*) Base configuration. (*b*) Addition of branches corresponding to the diagonals of the trapezoidal plan. (*c*) Addition of further branches starting from the vertices of the *oculus*.

To identify any significant compressive flows inside the dome, a fourth configuration adds branches concentric to the octagonal *oculus*, so as to simulate circumferential stresses; see Fig. 6a ($n_s = 256$; $m = 693$).

By adding branches corresponding to the diagonals of each quadrangular module (Fig. 6b), a network of greater complexity is obtained, characterized by an increase in the

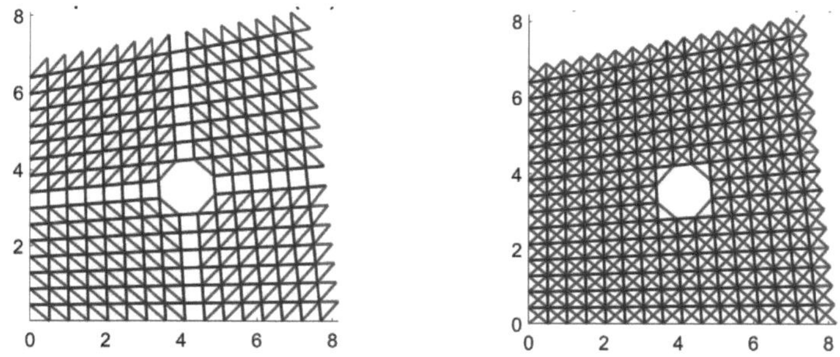

(*a*) (*b*)

Fig. 6. Different configurations of the anti-funicular networks for the analysis of the sail vault. Branches where independent force densities act are marked in red. (*a*) Addition of branches concentric to the octagonal *oculus*. (*b*) Addition of branches corresponding to the diagonals of each quadrangular module.

degree of static indeterminacy ($n_s = 256$; $m = 996$). This configuration was designed to capture more general compression flows.

4.4 Anti-Funicular Networks of Minimum Thrust

The results of the equilibrium analyses conducted using the network configurations defined in Sect. 4.3 will be now illustrated.

For the simplest network, corresponding to Fig. 5a, the anti-funicular network of minimum thrust is shown in Fig. 7a (plan) and Fig. 7b (axonometric view). In this case, the computation time required for the complete analysis was less than 1 min; CPU times referred to a processor Intel(R) Core(TM) i5-8250U CPU @ 1.60GHz (1.80 GHz).

Longer computation times are required as the degree of static indeterminacy (see the number of network elements) increases. For the second configuration, where additional branches corresponding to the diagonals of the trapezoidal plan were added (Figs. 5b and 8), the time required for the complete analysis was 1 h 45 min 27 s; for the third one, with additional branches starting from the vertices of the octagonal *oculus* (Fig. 5c and Fig. 9), it was 3 h 47 min 24 s.

Given the simplified nature of the networks, the first three scenarios just described constitute a first validation phase of the method, with particular attention to the reliability of the results (i.e., the attainment of convergence to a solution that is fully admissible with respect to the prescribed constraints) rather than their capability of reproducing the actual behaviour of the vault.

Despite a considerable increase in computation time, the more complex networks, corresponding to the configurations depicted in Figs. 6a and 6b, are the most suitable for capturing the three-dimensional behaviour of the dome, as will be clarified comparing the results deriving from the funicular method with the analyses conducted with Abaqus CAE in Sect. 5.

For the configuration with additional concentric branches (Fig. 6a), the minimum-thrust anti-funicular network is shown in Fig. 10. The computation time is 5 h 42 min

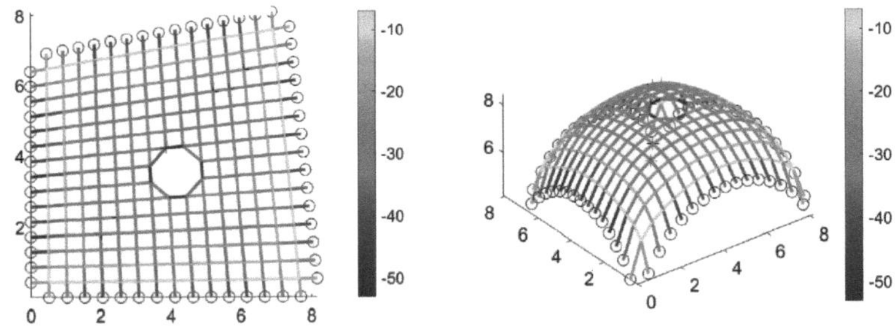

(a) (b)

Fig. 7. Anti-funicular network of minimum thrust corresponding to the simplest configuration (Fig. 5a): (*a*) plan view; (*b*) axonometric view. Forces are in kN.

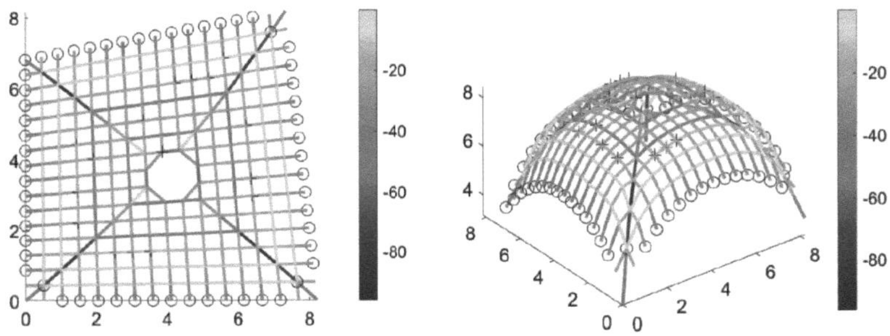

(a) (b)

Fig. 8. Anti-funicular network of minimum thrust corresponding to the configuration with additional branches along the diagonals of the trapezoidal plan (Fig. 5b): (*a*) plan view; (*b*) axonometric view. Forces are in kN.

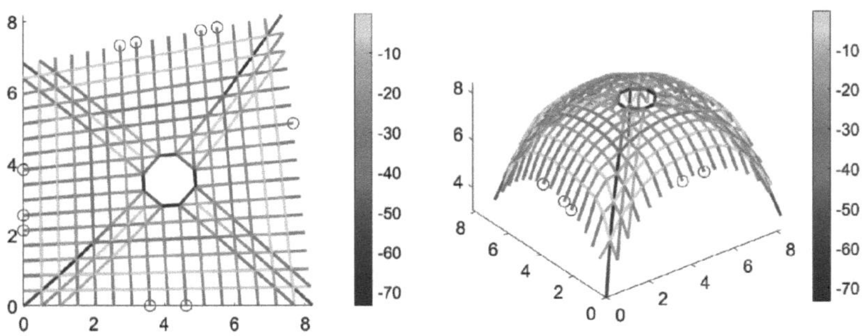

(a) (b)

Fig. 9. Anti-funicular network of minimum thrust corresponding to the configuration with additional diagonal branches starting from the vertices of the octagonal *oculus* (Fig. 5c): (*a*) plan view; (*b*) axonometric view. Forces are in kN.

39 s. For the most complex case, i.e., the network with branches along the diagonals of each quadrangular module (Fig. 6b), it increases further and reaches 21 h 12 min 16 s. The related anti-funicular network is shown in Fig. 11.

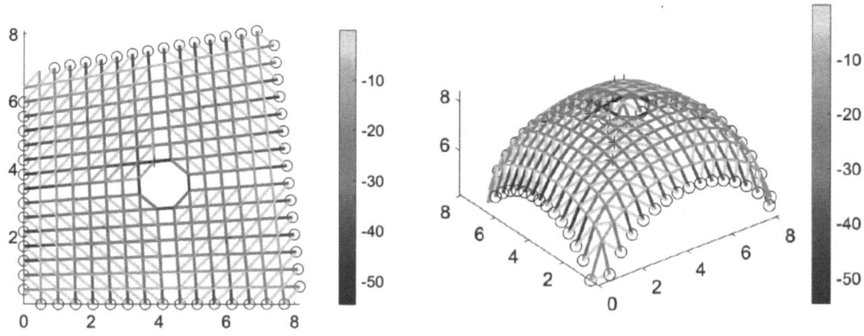

(*a*) (*b*)

Fig. 10. Anti-funicular network of minimum thrust corresponding to the configuration with the addition of concentric branches (Fig. 6a): (*a*) plan view; (*b*) axonometric view. Forces are in kN.

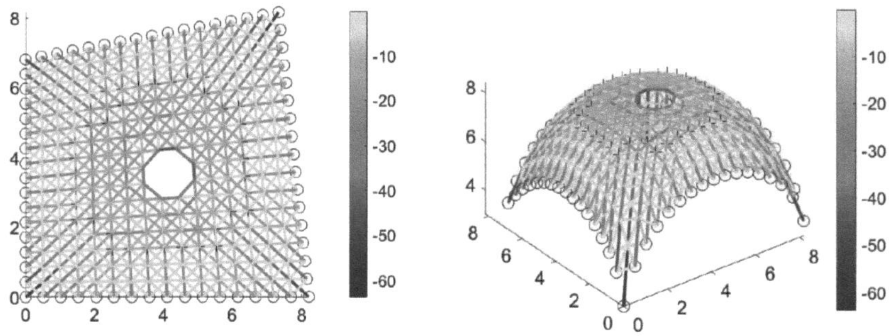

(*a*) (*b*)

Fig. 11. Anti-funicular network of minimum thrust corresponding to the configuration with additional branches along the diagonals of each quadrangular module (Fig. 6b): (*a*) plan view; (*b*) axonometric view. Forces are in kN.

From Figs. 10 and 11, the dome's portion near the octagonal *oculus* is visibly subjected to compressive stresses; the shape of the compressed cap is consistent with quasi-circumferential forces. In Fig. 10, the compressive forces increase near the side walls, as indicated by the blue branches; the corners appear to be less stressed. In Fig. 11 a different response is observed, as an increase in compressive forces can be seen along the main diagonals from top to bottom (corresponding to meridional forces). According to the comparison with the finite element results presented in Sect. 5, the most suitable configuration is found to be that shown in Fig. 10 (see also Fig. 6a).

5 A Comparison Between Minimum Thrust Funicular Solutions and Finite Element Analyses with Abaqus CAE

To compare the results obtained with the funicular method (Sect. 4) with those of a more standardized approach, a simplified analysis of the structural response of the vault under gravitational loads was carried out using the Finite Element Abaqus CAE software, modelling masonry as an isotropic linear elastic material.

To represent the confinement exerted by the perimeter walls, kinematic constraints were imposed (pinned boundary condition), in which the displacements in all three directions were blocked (Fig. 12a).

The self-weight of the vault was applied through the *Gravity* command. The load from the infill was modelled as a vertical *Surface traction* acting on the extrados of the vault. The FE mesh consists of solid tetrahedral elements, considering that the dome is not thin enough to use shell elements (Fig. 12b). A quadratic interpolation was chosen to achieve a clearer representation of the stress variation along the vault's thickness. The vault was discretized into 3,730 quadratic tetrahedral finite elements, resulting in 111,900 degrees of freedom.

To facilitate the comparison of the stresses obtained with the two methods, a spherical reference system was adopted in the FE analysis.

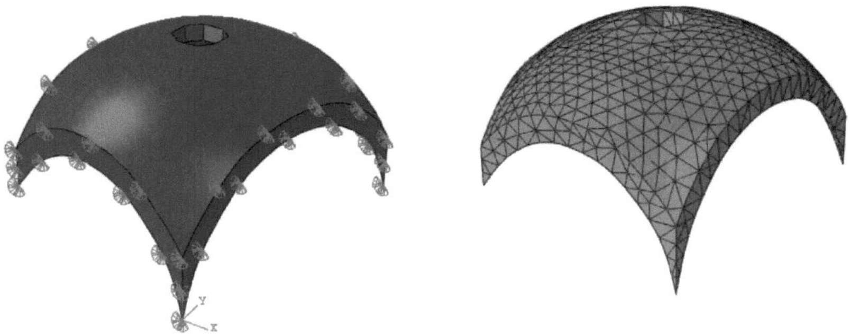

(*a*) (*b*)

Fig. 12. Finite element analyses with Abaqus CAE: (*a*) pinned boundary conditions; (*b*) FE mesh of the sail vault.

The results obtained from the linear elastic analysis of the vault are presented below. Specifically, for subsequent comparison with the funicular model, the values, expressed in Pa, of the minimum principal stresses (Fig. 13), of the circumferential stresses (S22, Fig. 14), and of the meridional stresses (S33, Fig. 15) are reported.

From the analyses in Abaqus CAE it is observed that the upper portion of the dome is subjected to circumferential compression (Figs. 13a, 14a), while asymmetries in the stress distribution are evident.

The internal forces acting along the branches of the funicular network and their orientation with respect to the spherical coordinate system adopted in the FE analyses are also evaluated. The procedure, omitted here for brevity, calculates the ratio of

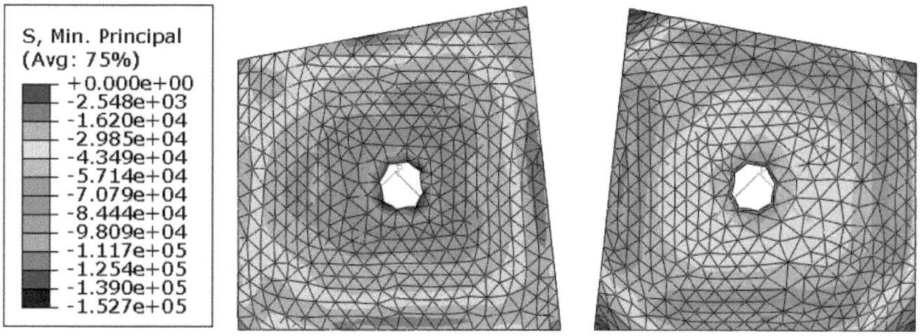

(*a*) (*b*)

Fig. 13. Finite element analyses with Abaqus CAE: minimum principal stresses (*a*) extrados; (*b*) intrados. Stresses are measured in Pa.

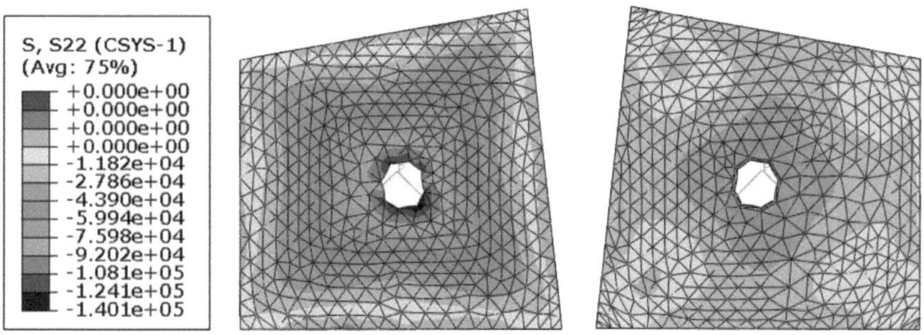

(*a*) (*b*)

Fig. 14. Finite element analyses with Abaqus CAE: circumferential stresses, S22 (*a*) extrados; (*b*) intrados. Stresses are measured in Pa.

the internal forces to the corresponding cross-section of the vault, with some geometric simplifications. The network of Fig. 10 is found to better capture the mechanical response of the vault: the presence of a compressed cap is confirmed, and the circumferential stresses obtained from the funicular model substantially match those derived from the finite element model. Furthermore, both Fig. 15b, which reports the intrados meridional stresses obtained with the finite element analyses, and Fig. 10, where the most compressed branches are highlighted in blue, are consistent with an increase in the meridional compressive stresses towards the central portion of the sides of the trapezoidal plan, while the corners are less loaded.

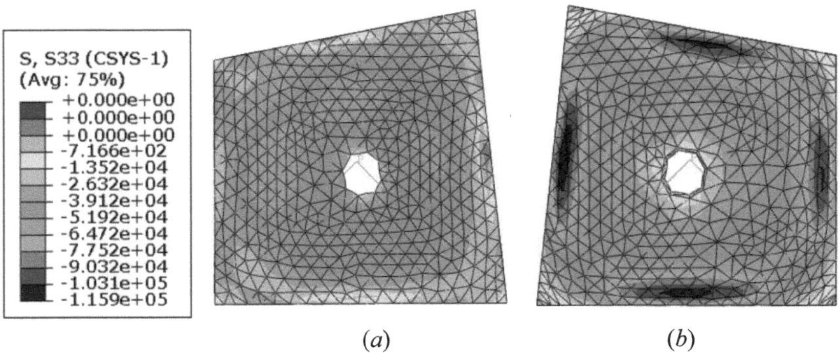

Fig. 15. Finite element analyses with Abaqus CAE: meridional stresses, S33 (*a*) extrados; (*b*) intrados. Stresses are measured in Pa.

6 Concluding Remarks

In this research, the analysis of the sail vault of the *Fortezza Vecchia* in Livorno is conducted by adopting a funicular method exploiting both the concept of force density and a mathematical programming formulation [14].

The objective function was specifically implemented to identify minimum thrust solutions. As a first step, the vault was modelled using a network with relatively low computational complexity, connecting each node to its adjacent ones so as to obtain a network composed of quadrilaterals. Subsequently, increasingly complex network configurations were considered, introducing diagonal branches, which allow some features of the structural response to be captured more accurately.

To benchmark the results thus obtained, simplified finite element analyses were performed in Abaqus CAE by modelling masonry as a linear elastic isotropic material.

Although the two methods - funicular analysis and finite element analysis - belong to different theoretical frameworks (limit analysis and elastic analysis), the minimum thrust solutions derived from the funicular network were shown to be compatible with the results obtained with Abaqus CAE, in particular with reference to circumferential stresses.

Further investigations are needed to fully interpret the real crack pattern observed in the vault: in this regard, the simplified results just obtained seem to highlight the importance of considering a limited compressive strength to describe masonry (observing both meridional and circumferential cracks). Future developments will consider the presence of ground settlements, and seismic loading conditions. Furthermore, in finite element analyses with Abaqus CAE, both the consideration of masonry plasticity and the adoption of a concrete damaged plasticity model can be crucial to capture cracking, crushing and stiffness degradation. In this context, a further development of this research could be the determination of a geometric safety factor, i.e. the ratio between the current thickness and the limit thickness (obtained by progressively reducing the thickness of the vault until collapse) considering different modelling strategies and material properties.

Acknowledgments. The authors wish to express their gratitude to Prof. Andrea Piemonte (University of Pisa) for the valuable collaboration.

Disclosure of Interests. The authors have no competing interests.

References

1. Castellazzi, G., Taliercio, A.: Principles and Analysis of Historical Masonry Structures: The Strength of the Past, 1st edn. Cambridge Scholars Publishing, Newcastle upon Tyne (UK) (2025)
2. Angelillo, M., Lourenço, P.B., Milani, G.: Masonry behaviour and modelling. In: Angelillo, M. (ed.) Mechanics of Masonry Structures. CISM international centre for mechanical sciences, vol. 551, pp. 1–26. Springer, Vienna (2014)
3. Milani, G., Taliercio, A.: Chapter 12 – homogenization limit analysis. In: Ghiassi, B., Milani, G. (eds.) Numerical modeling of masonry and historical structures, pp. 423–467. Woodhead Publishing Series in Civil and Structural Engineering, Woodhead Publishing, Sawston (2019)
4. Meloni, G., Pourfouladi, M., Pingaro, N.: Parametric modelling and nonlinear FE analysis of trepponti bridge subjected to differential settlements. Buildings **16**, 47 (2026)
5. Pingaro, N., Milani, G.: Simple interface element equipped with thickness for the non-linear static heterogeneous analysis of masonry walls in-plane loaded: implementation and validation. Eng. Struct. **351**, 122056 (2026)
6. Pingaro, N., Buzzetti, M., Gandolfi, A.: A numerical strategy to assess the stability of curved masonry structures using a simple nonlinear truss model. Buildings **15**, 2226 (2025)
7. Heyman, J.: The stone skeleton. Int. J. Solids Struct. **2**(2), 249–279 (1966)
8. Maia Avelino, R., Yang, W., Weichbrodt, A., Ochsendorf, J., Flatt, R.J.: Augmented reality for structural inspection of historic monuments: the case of lausanne cathedral. Int. J. Architect. Heritage (2025)
9. Angelillo, M., Iannuzzo, A., Montanino, A.: Discretised continuum approaches: from continuum to dis-continuum. In: Bagi, K., Angelillo, M. (eds.) Discrete Computational Mechanics of Masonry Structures, pp 95–163. CISM International Centre for Mechanical Sciences, vol. 609. Springer, Cham (2023). https://doi.org/10.1007/978-3-031-32476-5_3
10. Olivieri, C., Cocking, S., Fabbrocino, F., Iannuzzo, A., Placidi, L., Adriaenssens, S.: Seismic capacity of purely compressed shells based on Airy stress function. Continuum Mech. Thermodyn. **37**, 21 (2025)
11. Alexakis, H., Makris, N.: Limit equilibrium analysis of masonry arches. Arch. Appl. Mech. **85**(9–10), 1363–1381 (2015)
12. Block, P., Ochsendorf, J.: Thrust network analysis: a new methodology for three dimensional equilibrium. J. Int. Assoc. Shell Spat. Struct. **48**(155), 167–173 (2007)
13. Maia Avelino, R., Iannuzzo, A., Van Mele, T., Block, P.: Assessing the safety of vaulted masonry structures using thrust network analysis. Comput. Struct. **257**, 106647 (2021)
14. Bruggi, M.: A constrained force density method for the funicular analysis and design of arches, domes and vaults. Int. J. Solids Struct. **193–194**, 251–269 (2020)
15. Bruggi, M., Lógó, B.A., Deák, Z.: Funicular analysis of ribbed masonry vaults: a case study. Int. J. Architect. Heritage **16**(12), 1809–1823 (2022)
16. Bruggi, M., Taliercio, A.: Funicular analysis of masonry vaults under general loading conditions through a constrained force density method. In: Proceedings of the 9th Euro-American Congress on Construction Pathology, Rehabilitation Technology and Heritage Management, (2022)

17. Aita, D., Bruggi, M., Taliercio, A.: Limit analysis of masonry arches and domes with finite strength: funicular analysis versus stability area method. Meccanica **60**, 601–620 (2025)
18. Ulivieri, D.: Fortezza Vecchia in Livorno. Nexus Netw. J. **16**, 675–697 (2014)
19. Moseley, H.: On a new principle in statics, called the principle of least pressure. London Edinburgh Dublin Philosoph. Magaz. J. Sci. **3**(16), 285–288 (1833)
20. Barsi, F., Barsotti, R. and Bennati, S.: Equilibrium of masonry sail vaults: the case study of a subterranean vault by Antonio da Sangallo the Elder in the "Fortezza Vecchia" in Livorno. In: Carcaterra, A., Paolone, A., Graziani, G. (eds.) Proceedings of XXIV AIMETA Conference 2019. AIMETA 2019, pp. 2094–2103, LNME. Springer, Cham (2019). https://doi.org/10.1007/978-3-030-41057-5_166
21. Aita, D., Barsotti, R., Bennati, S.: Equilibrium analysis of a sail vault in Livorno's Fortezza Vecchia through a modern re-edition of the stability area method. In: Carcaterra, A., Paolone, A., Graziani, G. (eds.) Proceedings of XXIV AIMETA Conference 2019. AIMETA 2019, pp. 989–998, LNME. Springer, Cham. (2019). https://doi.org/10.1007/978-3-030-41057-5_81
22. Bennati, S., et al.: A trapezoidal plan sail vault by Antonio da Sangallo the Elder in the Livorno Fortezza Vecchia: from historical investigations to an analysis of its structural behaviour. In: Barros, H., Ferreira, C., Adam, J.M., Delatte N. (eds.) 3rd International Conference on Recent Advances in Nonlinear Design Resilience and Rehabilitation of Structures, CoRASS 2019 – Proceedings, pp. 244–253 (2019)
23. Barsi, F., Aita, D., Barsotti, R., Ulivieri, D., Bennati, S.: Studying a masonry sail vault by Antonio da Sangallo the Elder in the Fortezza Vecchia in Livorno. In: Roca, P., Pelà, L., Molins, C. (eds.) 12th International Conference on Structural Analysis of Historical Constructions (SAHC 2021), pp. 1338–1345. CIMNE, Barcelona (2021)
24. Bevilacqua, M.G., Caroti, G., Piemonte, A., Ulivieri, D.: Reconstruction of lost architectural volumes by integration of photogrammetry from archive imagery with 3-D models of the status quo. Int. Arch. Photogramm. Remote Sens. Spatial Inf. Sci. **XLII-2**(W9), 119–125 (2019)
25. Durand-Claye, A.: Vérification de la stabilité des voûtes et des arcs. Applications aux voûtes sphériques. Ann. des Ponts et Chaussées **19**(I sem.), 416–440 (1880)
26. Malavolta, E.: Thrust Network Analysis for non-symmetrical vaults: the case of Livorno's fortress, Master's Thesis in Civil Engineering - Ingegneria Civile. Advisor: Prof. Alberto Taliercio, Co-advisors: Prof. Danila Aita, Prof. Matteo Bruggi. Politecnico di Milano. Academic Year: 2024–2025
27. Schek, H.J.: The force density method for form finding and computation of general networks. Comput. Meth. Appl. Mech. Eng. **3**(1), 115–134 (1974)
28. Moseley, H.: The Mechanical Principles of Engineering and Architecture. Longman, Brown, Green, and Longmans, London (1843)
29. Aita, D.: Masonry arches: thrust line and strength. Encyclopedia **6**(3), 57 (2026)
30. Svanberg, K.: Method of moving asymptotes - a new method for structural optimization. Int. J. Numer. Meth. Eng. **24**, 359–373 (1987)
31. Heyman, J.: The Stone Skeleton: Structural Engineering of Masonry Architecture. Cambridge University Press, Cambridge (1995)

Limit Analysis of Irregular Masonry with Rigid and Deformable Blocks

Yahroun Fei Long Hermans[1,2](✉), Yiwei Hua[2], Karim Ehab Moustafa Kamel[1], Thierry Jacques Massart[1], and Gabriele Milani[2]

[1] Université libre de Bruxelles, Brussels 1050, Belgium
yahroun.fei.hermans@ulb.be
[2] Politecnico di Milano, Milan 20133, Italy

Abstract. The mechanical behavior of masonry assemblies is strongly influenced by the geometry and connectivity of the mortar joint network. While mesoscale modeling approaches are commonly developed for regular bond patterns, the analysis of irregular masonry systems remains comparatively less explored. In particular, the application of deformable element kinematic limit analysis to irregular masonry geometries has received limited attention. In this contribution, irregular masonry patterns are taken directly from an image of real irregular masonry. The geometry is subsequently processed into an interface-based description in which joints are lumped onto zero-thickness interfaces separating adjacent blocks. The resulting assemblies are analyzed using kinematic limit analysis. Both rigid and deformable block formulations are considered, allowing the influence of block deformability on the predicted structural response to be assessed. In the rigid formulation, energy dissipation is confined to the interfaces, whereas in the deformable formulation, dissipation occurs both at the interfaces and within the blocks through in-element plastic deformation. Interfaces between blocks are described using a Mohr–Coulomb failure criterion with a compression cap and tensile cut-off. Collapse loads are computed under combined loading conditions defined by biaxial unequal compression and biaxial unequal compression combined with shear. The resulting solutions provide insight into the collapse mechanisms and structural response of irregular masonry assemblies.

Keywords: Irregular Masonry · Engineering Homogenization · Kinematic Limit Analysis · Deformable Elements · Linear Programming · Second Order Cone Programming

1 Introduction

Masonry structures constitute a large portion of the existing building stock and remain widely used in construction practice. Their mechanical behavior is governed by the interaction between blocks and mortar joints, of which the

O. Gervasi et al. (Eds.): ICCSA 2026 Workshops, LNCS 16758, pp. 515–532, 2027.
https://doi.org/10.1007/978-3-032-30497-1_31

arrangement strongly influences the global strength and failure mechanisms of the assembly [1–3]. Due to the presence of interfaces and the limited tensile strength of mortar joints, masonry typically exhibits a highly nonlinear and anisotropic mechanical response [4]. Consequently, the geometry and connectivity of the joint network play a fundamental role in determining the macroscopic behavior of masonry systems, particularly in the case of irregular masonry.

Various modeling approaches have been proposed to capture the mechanical behavior of masonry assemblies. At the structural scale, continuum models employing anisotropic constitutive laws are often used to describe the global response of masonry structures [5,6,22,23]. While computationally efficient, these approaches rely on phenomenological parameters that are not always directly linked to the underlying block–joint microstructure. To address this limitation, mesoscale modeling strategies explicitly represent the discrete nature of masonry by modeling blocks and mortar joints separately, allowing failure mechanisms to be described in terms of sliding and separation along interfaces [7]. In this context, joints are commonly represented as zero-thickness interfaces between adjacent blocks, providing an effective compromise between computational efficiency and an accurate representation of joint mechanics [8–10]. These approaches have proven particularly effective for analyzing collapse mechanisms and strength limits while retaining a clear connection to the underlying masonry topology [11,12].

Within the framework of limit analysis, alternative kinematic formulations have also been proposed, such as the Piecewise Rigid Displacement (PRD) method [24], which enables the automatic detection of collapse mechanisms based on dual energy criteria. More recently, limit analysis approaches have been extended toward engineering applications, including the seismic assessment of masonry façades [25]. In parallel, continuum approaches based on advanced constitutive modeling, such as multilaminate formulations [26], provide an alternative macroscopic description of masonry behavior.

However, many historical masonry structures exhibit strongly irregular block geometries and highly heterogeneous joint networks. Accurately capturing their behavior therefore requires modeling strategies capable of representing irregular masonry stackings. Several approaches have been proposed to generate masonry geometries for mechanical analysis. Image-based techniques allow the extraction of block geometries directly from photographs or scans of existing masonry assemblies, enabling realistic representations of irregular block arrangements [2,3]. Alternatively, synthetic geometry generation procedures may be used to construct masonry-like computational geometries with controlled morphological characteristics [13,14].

Limit analysis methods provide an efficient framework for investigating the collapse behavior of masonry systems [23]. In particular, kinematic limit analysis has been widely used to determine collapse mechanisms and failure envelopes of block assemblies interacting through frictional interfaces. In many formulations, masonry blocks are assumed to behave as rigid bodies, leading to efficient numerical procedures in which energy dissipation is concentrated exclusively at the interfaces between blocks [2,3,10,15]. While this assumption is often justified by the relatively high stiffness of masonry units compared to mortar joints, it neglects the possibility of deformation and dissipation within the blocks themselves.

Recent developments have therefore introduced deformable element formulations of limit analysis [16], in which blocks are allowed to undergo internal deformation while still interacting through frictional interfaces. Unlike rigid-block formulations, where all energy dissipation is confined to interfaces, these approaches allow dissipation to occur both at the joints and within the blocks. This is achieved by constructing a suitable velocity interpolation and plastic constitutive behavior for the element, such that in-element plastic strains generate additional dissipation. Consequently, block deformability is not merely kinematic but also energetically active, contributing directly to the overall collapse mechanism and potentially influencing both failure modes and strength predictions.

Despite these developments, the role of block deformability in the limit analysis of masonry assemblies with complex geometries remains insufficiently understood. Most existing studies rely on idealized geometries or rigid-block formulations [2,3], and the combined effect of irregular block shapes and block deformability and dissipation on the predicted structural response has not been thoroughly investigated.

In this contribution, the limit analysis of irregular masonry assemblies is investigated using kinematic formulations. The geometrical input is directly taken from [18] and subsequently processed into two interface-based representations. The resulting geometries are analyzed using both rigid and deformable element kinematic limit analysis formulations. The influence of block deformability on the predicted collapse mechanisms and pressure is assessed under two loading conditions: (i) a combined compressive state defined by the loading direction $(\sigma_{xx}, \sigma_{yy}, \sigma_{xy}) = (-0.3\Gamma, -\Gamma, 0)$, and (ii) a combined compression-shear state defined by the loading direction $(\sigma_{xx}, \sigma_{yy}, \sigma_{xy}) = (-0.3\Gamma, -\Gamma, 0.6\Gamma)$ (as detailed in Sect. 4.2). By comparing rigid and deformable formulations on image-based masonry geometries, the present work aims to clarify the role of block deformability in the structural response of irregular masonry systems.

2 Lumped Joint Geometry Generation

The mechanical behavior of masonry assemblies is strongly influenced by the stacking arrangement of blocks. Accurately describing this geometry is therefore essential for reliable mechanical analysis. In the context of mesoscale modeling and the analysis of irregular masonry, however, constructing representative masonry geometries (RVEs) remains a challenging task. Existing approaches either rely on virtual generation techniques that aim to reproduce the morphological characteristics of masonry through synthetic procedures [13,14], or on image acquisition and segmentation methods, in which real or experimentally obtained geometries are transformed into computational models suitable for structural analysis [2,3,18]. In the present work, the point of departure is a RVE extracted from the bitmap data presented in [18].

2.1 Distance Field-Based Tessellation Procedure

The tessellation procedure relies on the computation of distance fields associated with the blocks. A distance field, denoted by DN_k, is defined over the entire RVE domain and represents the Euclidean distance from a point of the domain to the boundary of the k-th nearest block. As detailed in [2,3,13,14], the field DN_1 is defined as a signed distance field, taking positive values outside the inclusion and negative values inside.

Fig. 1. Top left: Irregular masonry used in [18]. Top right: First nearest distance map. Bottom left: Second nearest distance map. Bottom right: The O_V function defined by Eq. (1). In the distance-based fields (top right and bottom subfigures), solid white lines indicate the block outlines.

The distance maps associated with the nearest neighboring blocks (Fig. 1) can be used to modify the spatial configuration of the block assembly. In particular, the distance functions DN_1 and DN_2, corresponding to the distances to the closest and second closest blocks at any point of the RVE, allow constructing a scalar field O_V the zero level set of which identifies the locus of points equidistant from these two blocks [13]:

$$O_V = DN_1(\mathbf{x}) - DN_2(\mathbf{x}) \tag{1}$$

This locus approximates the medial axis of the mortar joint network and therefore naturally delineates the boundaries between adjacent blocks, effectively lumping the joint.

For the kinematic limit analysis procedure, the scalar field O_V must be converted into a discrete representation of the mortar joint network composed of vertices and edges.

The adopted extraction procedure is based on the medial axis of the assembly. In the present context, only the outer medial axis is required, as it corresponds to the mortar joints separating adjacent blocks. The extraction is carried out in two stages, as defined in [2]: (i) The triple junctions are identified. These junctions are connected, and (ii) progressively refined to follow the zero-level of the O_V.

Let (k,l,m) denote three neighboring blocks. For each pair of blocks, a pairwise Voronoi-like function is introduced as

$$O_{V_{ij}}(\mathbf{x}) = DN_i(\mathbf{x}) - DN_j(\mathbf{x}), \qquad (i,j) \in \{(k,l),(l,m),(k,m)\}, \tag{2}$$

so that the triple junction $\mathbf{x}^*$ is defined by the simultaneous conditions

$$O_{V_{kl}}(\mathbf{x}^*) = 0, \qquad O_{V_{lm}}(\mathbf{x}^*) = 0, \qquad O_{V_{km}}(\mathbf{x}^*) = 0. \tag{3}$$

As described in [3], starting from an initial guess located in the vicinity of the junction, the point is iteratively displaced using the values of the functions $O_{V_{ij}}$ and their gradients $\nabla O_{V_{ij}}$ until the conditions in Eq. (3) are satisfied within a prescribed tolerance.

Once the triple junctions have been determined, neighboring junctions are connected using straight segments, yielding a simplified polygonal representation of the mortar joint network. This representation already provides a lumped geometry suitable for mechanical analysis. In a second stage, additional points are introduced along these segments and displaced toward the zero level sets of the corresponding pairwise functions $O_{V_{ij}}$. Repeating this procedure recursively yields a refined curved representation of the medial axis.

Algorithm (1) therefore provides two distinct geometric representations. The first one, $\mathcal{G}^{\text{simp}}$, is obtained by directly connecting the identified triple junctions and corresponds to a simplified straight-segment approximation of the mortar joint network. The second one, $\mathcal{G}^{\text{curv}}$, is obtained after recursive insertion and projection of intermediate edge points, resulting in a curved representation that follows the medial axis more closely. In both cases (Fig. 2), the extracted joint network is used to define the interface geometry required by the limit analysis formulation.

3 Kinematic Limit Analysis

The mechanical response of the masonry assemblies is analyzed using kinematic limit analysis. According to the kinematic theorem of limit analysis, collapse occurs when the external work associated with a kinematically admissible velocity field is equal to the internal energy dissipation within the system.

Algorithm 1: Extraction of simplified and curved lumped geometries

Input: Pairwise functions $O_{V_{ij}}(\mathbf{x})$; gradients $\nabla O_{V_{ij}}(\mathbf{x})$; tolerances ε and $\ell_{\max}$
Output: Simplified geometry $\mathcal{G}^{\text{simp}}$; Curved geometry $\mathcal{G}^{\text{curv}}$
$\mathcal{T} \leftarrow \emptyset$;
foreach *triplet of neighboring blocks* (k, l, m) **do**
  Choose an initial point $\mathbf{x}_0$ near the junction;
  $n \leftarrow 0$;
  while $\max(|O_{V_{kl}}(\mathbf{x}_n)|, |O_{V_{lm}}(\mathbf{x}_n)|, |O_{V_{km}}(\mathbf{x}_n)|) > \varepsilon$ **do**
    $\mathbf{x}_{n+1} = \mathbf{x}_n - \alpha\left(O_{V_{kl}}(\mathbf{x}_n)\nabla O_{V_{kl}}(\mathbf{x}_n) + O_{V_{lm}}(\mathbf{x}_n)\nabla O_{V_{lm}}(\mathbf{x}_n) + O_{V_{km}}(\mathbf{x}_n)\nabla O_{V_{km}}(\mathbf{x}_n)\right)$;
    $n \leftarrow n + 1$;
  $\mathcal{T} \leftarrow \mathcal{T} \cup \{\mathbf{x}_n\}$;
$\mathcal{G}^{\text{simp}} \leftarrow$ connect neighboring points of $\mathcal{T}$ with straight segments;
$\mathcal{G}^{\text{curv}} \leftarrow \mathcal{G}^{\text{simp}}$;
foreach *edge e in* $\mathcal{G}^{\text{curv}}$ **do**
  while *segment length* $> \ell_{\max}$ **do**
    insert midpoint $\mathbf{p}$ on segment;
    find neighboring blocks (i, j) of $\mathbf{p}$;
    while $|O_{V_{ij}}(\mathbf{p})| > \varepsilon$ **do**
      $\mathbf{p} \leftarrow \mathbf{p} - \dfrac{O_{V_{ij}}(\mathbf{p})}{\|\nabla O_{V_{ij}}(\mathbf{p})\|^2}\nabla O_{V_{ij}}(\mathbf{p})$;
return $\mathcal{G}^{\text{simp}}, \mathcal{G}^{\text{curv}}$;

In rigid block formulations, energy dissipation is exclusively concentrated at the interfaces, as the blocks are assumed to remain undeformed. In contrast, when block deformability is introduced, an additional dissipation mechanism can be activated within the blocks through the assignment of a continuum-type constitutive behavior, allowing in-element plastic deformation to contribute directly to the total dissipation alongside the interfacial contribution. In this work, both formulations are considered: (i) the rigid block formulation and (ii) the deformable/dissipating block formulation.

3.1 Rigid Block Formulation

As discussed in [3], masonry units are assumed in this case to behave both as infinitely stiff and infinitely strong in the rigid block formulation. Consequently, deformation and failure cannot occur within the blocks themselves and are confined to the interfaces separating adjacent blocks, corresponding to the mortar joints. Relative normal and tangential displacements may therefore develop only along these interfaces.

The mechanical behavior of the joints is described using a perfect rigidplastic constitutive model governed by a yield criterion. According to the classical assumptions of limit analysis [11], plastic flow follows an associated flow rule. In

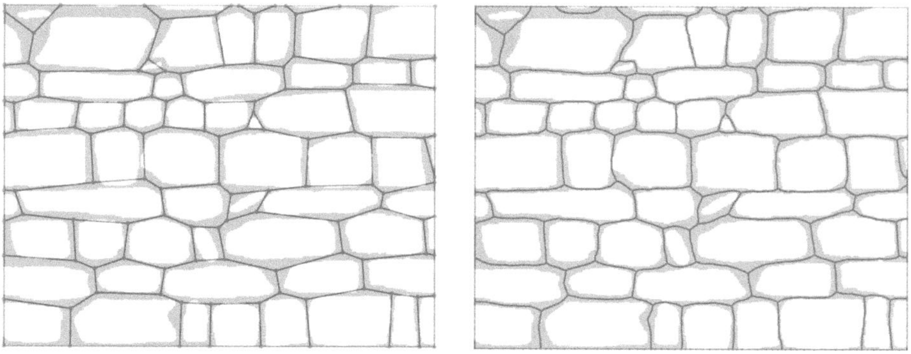

Fig. 2. Left: Geometry after lumping joints resulting from connecting triple junctions. Right: Lumped joint geometry after further joint delineation.

the present formulation, interface failure is governed by a Mohr–Coulomb criterion with compression cap and tensile cut-off (see [21] for more details), hereafter referred to as the modified Mohr–Coulomb criterion. Furthermore, small displacement rates are assumed, allowing the block kinematics to be linearized.

Under these assumptions, collapse mechanisms are described by discontinuous velocity fields characterized by relative velocity jumps across the interfaces. The corresponding collapse load is obtained by enforcing the Principle of Virtual Powers, which equates the external work of the applied loads to the internal rate of dissipation along the interfaces.

Constitutive Equations. The velocity jump across an interface, expressed in the local reference frame, follows the associated flow rule:

$$\Delta\tilde{\dot{\mathbf{u}}} = \dot{\boldsymbol{\lambda}}\frac{\partial f(\boldsymbol{\sigma})}{\partial \boldsymbol{\sigma}} \tag{4}$$

where $f(\boldsymbol{\sigma})$ denotes the yield surface, here defined by a modified Mohr–Coulomb criterion, and $\dot{\boldsymbol{\lambda}}$ represents the non-negative plastic multiplier rates.

To solve the problem as a linear programming problem, the yield surface is linearized. Equation (4) can therefore be expressed as

$$\dot{\boldsymbol{\lambda}}\frac{\partial f(\boldsymbol{\sigma})}{\partial \boldsymbol{\sigma}} = \sum_{e=1}^{N_p} \dot{\lambda}_e \frac{\partial f(\boldsymbol{\sigma})_e}{\partial \boldsymbol{\sigma}} \tag{5}$$

where N_p denotes the number of branches used to approximate the linearized failure criterion. The plastic multipliers satisfy the standard Kuhn-Tucker conditions [17].

The velocity jump expressed in the local coordinate system is related to the global reference frame through the rotation matrix $\mathbf{R}$:

$$\Delta\tilde{\dot{\mathbf{u}}} = \mathbf{R}\Delta\dot{\mathbf{u}} \tag{6}$$

Due to the rigid-block assumption and small displacement rates, the velocity of any point P belonging to a block with centroid G can be written as

$$\dot{\mathbf{u}}_P = \mathbf{A}_G^P \dot{\mathbf{x}}_{k,j}, \qquad \mathbf{A}_G^P = \begin{bmatrix} 1 & 0 & -(y^P - y^G) \\ 0 & 1 & (x^P - x^G) \end{bmatrix} \tag{7}$$

where $\mathbf{A}_G^P$ is the kinematic matrix and $\dot{\mathbf{x}}_{k,j}$ is the vector of degrees of freedom associated with the centroid of the jth block. Under the rigid-body assumption, the block kinematics are defined by two translational and one rotational velocity:

$$\dot{\mathbf{x}}_{k,j} = \left[\dot{u}_x,\ \dot{u}_y,\ \dot{\phi}_z\right]^\top, \qquad j = 1, \ldots, N_B \tag{8}$$

where N_B denotes the number of blocks in the assembly.

Combining Eqs. (6) and (7), the velocity jump at a discretization point P_i located on the interface between blocks j and $j+1$ can be expressed as

$$\Delta\tilde{\dot{\mathbf{u}}}_{P_i} = \mathbf{R}\left(\mathbf{A}_{G,j+1}^{P_i}\dot{\mathbf{x}}_{k,j+1} - \mathbf{A}_{G,j}^{P_i}\dot{\mathbf{x}}_{k,j}\right) \tag{9}$$

Substituting Eq. (5) and (9) into Eq. (4) yields the compatibility condition for a discretized interface point:

$$\mathbf{R}\left(\mathbf{A}_{G,j+1}^{P_i}\dot{\mathbf{x}}_{k,j+1} - \mathbf{A}_{G,j}^{P_i}\dot{\mathbf{x}}_{k,j}\right) - \sum_{e=1}^{N_p} \dot{\lambda}_e \frac{\partial f(\boldsymbol{\sigma})_e}{\partial \boldsymbol{\sigma}} = 0 \tag{10}$$

Virtual Power. Since dissipation occurs only along the interfaces, the collapse load multiplier Γ is obtained by enforcing the Principle of Virtual Powers:

$$\Gamma P_{ext,unit} = P_{in} \qquad \Longleftrightarrow \qquad \Gamma = \frac{P_{in}}{P_{ext,unit}} = \frac{\mathbf{c}^\top \mathbf{x}}{P_{ext,unit}} \tag{11}$$

where P_{in} denotes the internal dissipation power and $P_{ext,unit}$ the externally applied unit load. The vector $\mathbf{c}$ collects the coefficients such that $P_{in} = \mathbf{c}^\top \mathbf{x}$. The vector of unknowns is defined as

$$\mathbf{x} = \left[\dot{\mathbf{x}}_k, \dot{\boldsymbol{\lambda}}\right],$$

which gathers the kinematic variables and the plastic multiplier rates.

Canonical Form. The resulting problem can be formulated as a linear programming minimization problem:

$$\begin{aligned} &\text{minimize } \Gamma = \mathbf{c}^\top \mathbf{x} \\ &\text{subject to } \mathbf{A}^* \mathbf{x} = \mathbf{b} \\ &\qquad \dot{\boldsymbol{\lambda}} \geq \mathbf{0} \end{aligned} \tag{12}$$

where $\mathbf{A}^*$ and $\mathbf{b}$ define the equality constraints resulting from the constitutive relations and the normalization of the externally applied power.

3.2 Deformable Polygon Blocks

Starting from the rigid block formulation presented in Sect. 3.1, the extension to deformable polygonal elements requires only minor modifications. This follows directly from the interface-based framework, where interfacial discontinuities are already explicitly represented.

From a kinematic standpoint, the main modification consists in enriching the matrix $\mathbf{A}_G^P$ used to describe the velocity field within each element. In addition to rigid body motion, three additional modes are introduced to account for constant-strain deformation within the polygonal elements, corresponding to axial deformation in the x- and y-directions and in-plane xy shear.

Accordingly, the vector of unknowns $\dot{\mathbf{x}}_k$ associated with each block j is extended to include three additional degrees of freedom, representing the constant strain-rate components $\dot{\varepsilon}_x$, $\dot{\varepsilon}_y$, and $\dot{\varepsilon}_{xy}$. The resulting kinematic description is expressed as

$$\begin{gathered}\mathbf{A}_G^P = \begin{bmatrix} 1 & 0 & -(y^P - y^G) & (x^P - x^G) & 0 & (y^P - y^G) \\ 0 & 1 & (x^P - x^G) & 0 & (y^P - y^G) & (x^P - x^G) \end{bmatrix} \\ \dot{\mathbf{x}}_{k,j} = \begin{bmatrix} \dot{u}_x, & \dot{u}_y, & \dot{\phi}_z, & \dot{\varepsilon}_x, & \dot{\varepsilon}_y, & \dot{\varepsilon}_{xy} \end{bmatrix}^\top\end{gathered} \tag{13}$$

Substituting this enriched kinematic operator into the formulation, the velocity jumps at the interfaces can be computed in a manner consistent with the rigid block case (Eq. (9)).

The introduction of element deformation requires a constitutive model to constrain the additional strain-rate variables. Here, a continuum plasticity model is adopted, combining a Mohr–Coulomb criterion (Eq. (14)) with a compression cap defined in principal stress space (Eq. (15)). Both criteria can be expressed in a conic quadratic form, allowing their incorporation into a convex optimization framework.

$$F_{\mathrm{MC}}(\boldsymbol{\sigma}) = (\sigma_x - \sigma_y)^2 + (2\tau_{xy})^2 - (2c\cos\varphi - (\sigma_x + \sigma_y)\sin\varphi)^2 \tag{14}$$

$$F_{\mathrm{C}}(\boldsymbol{\sigma}) = (\sigma_x - \sigma_y)^2 + (2\tau_{xy})^2 - (2\sigma_c + (\sigma_x + \sigma_y))^2 \tag{15}$$

Within the kinematic formulation, plastic flow is governed by an associated flow rule. For each conic surface, three plastic multipliers are introduced to describe the corresponding plastic flow. As a consequence of associativity, these multipliers are constrained to lie within the second-order cones that are dual to the constitutive one. The compatibility condition for the deformable elements can thus be written as:

$$\begin{gathered}\mathbf{B}_j \dot{\mathbf{x}}_{k,j} = \sum_{e=1}^{3} \dot{\lambda}_e^{\mathrm{MC}} \frac{\partial F_{\mathrm{MC}}(\boldsymbol{\sigma})_e}{\partial \boldsymbol{\sigma}} + \sum_{e=1}^{3} \dot{\lambda}_e^{\mathrm{C}} \frac{\partial F_{\mathrm{C}}(\boldsymbol{\sigma})_e}{\partial \boldsymbol{\sigma}} \\ \mathbf{B}_j = [\mathbf{O}_{3\times 3}\ \mathbf{I}_{3\times 3}], \quad \dot{\lambda}_e^{\mathrm{MC}}, \dot{\lambda}_e^{\mathrm{C}} \in \mathcal{Q}^3 := \{\mathbf{x} : x_1 \geq \|(x_2, x_3)\|_2\}\end{gathered} \tag{16}$$

where the matrix $\mathbf{B}_j$ extracts the deformation-related components from the global vector of unknowns [16].

As a result of these modifications, the kinematic limit analysis problem for deformable elements can be formulated as a Second-Order Cone Programming (SOCP) problem:

$$\begin{aligned} &\text{minimise } \Gamma = \mathbf{c}^\top \mathbf{x} \\ &\text{subject to } \mathbf{A}^* \mathbf{x} = \mathbf{b} \\ &\qquad\qquad \dot{\boldsymbol{\lambda}} \geq \mathbf{0},\, \dot{\boldsymbol{\lambda}}_1 \in \mathcal{Q}_1^3 \times \mathcal{Q}_2^3 \times \cdots \times \mathcal{Q}_l^3 \end{aligned} \tag{17}$$

where l refers to the number of non-interface (deformable) elements, and $\mathcal{Q}^3$ denotes a three-dimensional second-order cone. For each element, three plastic multiplier components are introduced, corresponding to the adopted yield criteria (Mohr–Coulomb, compression cap, and tensile cut-off).

Compared to the rigid block formulation, additional constraints associated with the element deformation (Eq. (16)) must be introduced, and the vector of unknowns is extended as

$$\mathbf{x} = \left[\dot{\mathbf{x}}_k, \dot{\boldsymbol{\lambda}}, \dot{\boldsymbol{\lambda}}_1\right],$$

where $\dot{\boldsymbol{\lambda}}_1$ denotes the plastic multipliers associated with the in-element constitutive model (i.e. $\dot{\lambda}_e^{\mathrm{C}}$ or $\dot{\lambda}_e^{\mathrm{MC}}$ depending on the active criterion in the block).

In contrast to the rigid case, energy dissipation now arises both from interfacial mechanisms and from plastic deformation within the elements. The corresponding dissipation is incorporated into the objective function, which retains the form $\mathbf{c}^\top \mathbf{x}$. A detailed derivation of the formulation can be found in [16].

4 Results and Discussions

The kinematic limit analysis framework is used to investigate the mechanical response of the RVEs considered in Sect. 2. The aim is to assess the influence of block deformability by comparing the predictions from the rigid and deformable formulations.

The differences are expected to be more pronounced under compressive loading. Two loading scenarios are therefore considered: (i) biaxial compression and (ii) biaxial compression combined with shear. Both $\mathcal{G}^{\text{curv}}$ and $\mathcal{G}^{\text{simp}}$ are analyzed, allowing the combined effects of geometry and block deformability to be evaluated.

4.1 Representative Volume Element

The RVE has fixed dimensions of 869 mm in width and 684 mm in height (Fig. 3). As described in Sec. (2), two geometric representations are considered: (i) the curved geometry $\mathcal{G}^{\text{curv}}$ and simplified geometry $\mathcal{G}^{\text{simp}}$ respectively.

Based on the rigid and deformable element formulations, two modeling approaches are considered for the RVE: (i) the inclusions are treated as rigid

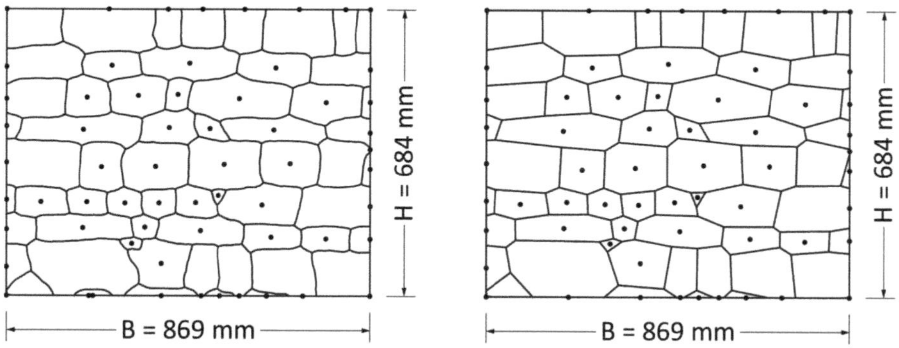

Fig. 3. Left: Curved interface-based geometry $\mathcal{G}^{\text{curv}}$ considered in the analysis. Right: Simplified interface-based geometry $\mathcal{G}^{\text{simp}}$ considered in the analysis.

blocks, and all dissipation is confined to the interfaces. Interface behavior is governed by a Mohr–Coulomb criterion supplemented with a compression cap and tensile cut-off to account for crushing and tensile failure; (ii) block deformability is introduced, allowing plastic deformation to develop within the polygonal inclusions. In this last case, in-element plasticity is described by a Mohr–Coulomb criterion combined with a compression cap.

Table 1. Material properties assumed for the interfaces and inclusions.

Interface		Element	
Cohesion	c	Cohesion	$5c$
Compression strength	$40c$	Compression strength	$40c$
Tension cutoff	$c/1.4$		

The interfacial cohesion is set to 50 kPa. The remaining strength parameters for both interfaces and inclusions are defined proportionally to this value for comparison purposes (Table 1). The friction angle φ is taken equal to 22° for both interfaces and elements, in accordance with the design code Italian Annex [19]. The slope of the compression cap for the interfaces is set to 45°.

The material parameters reported in Table 1 are selected to provide a consistent and controlled comparison between the rigid and deformable formulations. In particular, the interfacial cohesion is taken as a reference value, and the remaining strength parameters are defined proportionally in order to preserve realistic strength ratios between mortar joints and masonry units. The higher cohesion assigned to the elements reflects the typical mechanical contrast between blocks and mortar, where units exhibit significantly larger compressive and shear strength. The compression cap is introduced to account for crushing under high compressive stress states, which is particularly relevant under the loading conditions considered. These assumptions are not intended to represent a specific material but rather to provide a representative parameter set suitable for comparative analysis.

4.2 Loads and Boundary Conditions

For each boundary, an additional node is introduced to impose a multi-point constraint (MPC) on the velocities of the boundary nodes (Fig. 4a). The four boundary segments of the RVE are denoted by $i \in \{\partial X^-, \partial X^+, \partial Y^-, \partial Y^+\}$, corresponding to the left, right, bottom, and top boundaries, respectively. Each of these nodes possesses two degrees of freedom in the global Cartesian system, associated with the averaged boundary velocities U_x^i and U_y^i in the corresponding directions (Eq. (18)).

For a given boundary segment i, the index $j \in i$ refers to the set of boundary edges belonging to that segment. Each edge j is defined by its end nodes A and B, with associated nodal velocities $u_x^{j,A}$, $u_x^{j,B}$ (and similarly for u_y), and length l_j. The averaged boundary velocities U_x^i and U_y^i are computed as weighted averages over these edges.

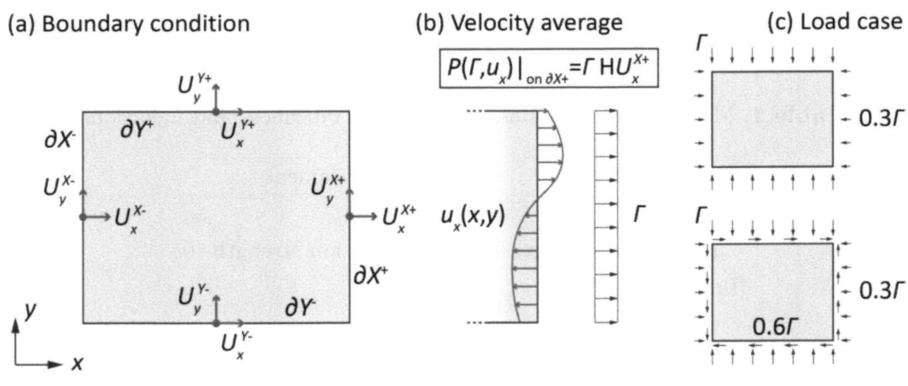

Fig. 4. Loading and boundary condition considered for RVE.

This formulation enforces an average boundary velocity based on the Principle of Virtual Work. The work of a uniform stress field acting on the boundary velocity distribution is taken to be equivalent to the work of the corresponding resultant acting on the MPC node (see Fig. 4b). The MPC conditions for the four boundaries can thus be expressed in matrix form as Eq. (19), where $\bar{\mathbf{U}}$ collects the averaged boundary velocities, and $\mathbf{L}_u$ is the matrix relating the global velocity vector $\dot{\mathbf{x}}$ to these averaged quantities.

$$U_x^i = \frac{1}{2}\frac{\sum_{j\in i}\left(u_x^{j,A}+u_x^{j,B}\right)l_j}{\sum l_j}, \quad U_y^i = \frac{1}{2}\frac{\sum_{j\in i}\left(u_y^{j,A}+u_y^{j,B}\right)l_j}{\sum l_j}, \quad i = \partial X^-, \partial X^+, \partial Y^-, \partial Y^+ \tag{18}$$

$$\mathbf{L}_u\dot{\mathbf{x}} = \bar{\mathbf{U}}, \quad \bar{\mathbf{U}} = \left[U_x^{X^-}\; U_y^{X^-}\; \cdots\; U_x^{Y^+}\; U_y^{Y^+}\right]^\top \tag{19}$$

The biaxial compression case (Case A) is defined by Eq. (20), with the compression predominantly applied in the vertical direction. In the compression-shear case (Case B), an additional shear component is superimposed onto the same biaxial compression state (Fig. 4c).

The prescribed uniform stress field is applied along each boundary by computing the corresponding resultant force and assigning it to the associated MPC node. The corresponding external power can therefore be expressed in terms of the averaged boundary velocities (Eq. (21)), where the vector $\mathbf{q}$ collects the resultant forces associated with the prescribed stress field acting on each boundary segment.

Following the positive work condition [20], the external work is normalized to unity, such that the internal dissipation is directly equal to the collapse multiplier Γ.

$$\begin{aligned}&\text{Case A}: \sigma_{xx} = -0.3\Gamma,\ \sigma_{yy} = -\Gamma,\ \sigma_{xy} = 0\\ &\text{Case B}: \sigma_{xx} = -0.3\Gamma,\ \sigma_{yy} = -\Gamma,\ \sigma_{xy} = 0.6\Gamma\end{aligned} \tag{20}$$

$$P_{ext,unit} = \mathbf{q}^\top\bar{\mathbf{U}} = 1 \tag{21}$$

Including boundary MPC velocities also allows a convenient suppression of rigid body motion. To avoid rigid body translation, the averaged velocities on opposite boundaries are constrained to sum to zero (Eq. (22)). In addition, the averaged rotational rate of the RVE is enforced to be zero to suppress rigid body rotation (Eq. (23)). Using Green's theorem, this rotational term can be computed from the integral of the boundary velocity field, and is ultimately expressed as a linear combination of the MPC velocities. The periodic boundary conditions can thus be written in matrix form as Eq. (24), where Ω denotes the RVE domain, with area $|\Omega|$, width B, and height H.

Finally, the rotational rate of the boundary elements is constrained to zero in order to further reduce zero-dissipation deformation modes.

$$\begin{aligned}U_x^{X^+} + U_x^{X^-} = 0, \quad U_x^{Y^+} + U_x^{Y^-} = 0\\ U_y^{X^+} + U_y^{X^-} = 0, \quad U_y^{Y^+} + U_y^{Y^-} = 0\end{aligned} \tag{22}$$

$$\begin{aligned}\bar{W} := \frac{1}{2|\Omega|}\int_\Omega\left(\frac{\partial u_y}{\partial x} - \frac{\partial u_x}{\partial y}\right)\mathrm{d}\Omega = \frac{1}{2|\Omega|}\oint_{\partial\Omega} u_x\mathrm{d}y + u_y\mathrm{d}x\\ = \frac{H}{|\Omega|}\left(U_y^{X^+} - U_y^{X^-}\right) + \frac{B}{|\Omega|}\left(U_x^{Y^+} - U_x^{Y^-}\right) = 0\end{aligned} \tag{23}$$

$$\mathbf{L}_m \bar{\mathbf{U}} = \mathbf{0} \tag{24}$$

where $\mathbf{L}_m$ is there constraint matrix for the periodic boundary conditions. All the aforementioned load and boundary conditions are incorporated into the equality constraints of the problem, i.e., within the matrix $\mathbf{A}^*$ and vector $\mathbf{b}$. The canonical formulations for the rigid and deformable cases remain unchanged (Eqs. (12) and (17)).

In the following, the collapse results obtained for both $\mathcal{G}^{\text{simp}}$ and $\mathcal{G}^{\text{curv}}$, under different element modeling assumptions, are presented. The computed collapse stresses are normalized with respect to the interfacial cohesion c.

5 Results

5.1 Collapse Results

Under biaxial compression, the use of rigid and deformable elements leads to different collapse mechanisms. In the rigid formulation, the macroscopic deformation is accommodated through interfacial mechanisms. The compressive response is characterized by the formation of extended horizontal crushing bands, accompanied by localized sliding along adjacent vertical joints (Fig. 5). Energy dissipation is therefore concentrated along interfaces aligned with the dominant stress direction. Boundary units, particularly smaller blocks, show pronounced relative motion, resulting in significant interface penetration. Failure of vertical joints is more pronounced for $\mathcal{G}^{\text{curv}}$ than for $\mathcal{G}^{\text{simp}}$, likely due to increased interlocking effects attributed to the geometrical roughness.

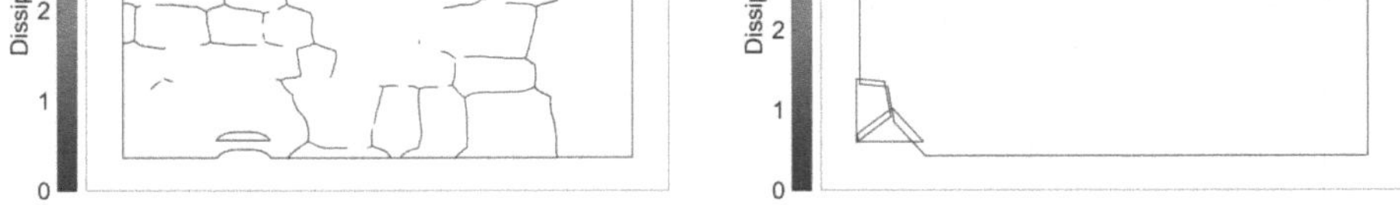

Fig. 5. Collapse mechanism of RVE under biaxial compression load, rigid units; left: $\mathcal{G}^{\text{curv}}$ - right: $\mathcal{G}^{\text{simp}}$.

In contrast, in the deformable formulation, the predicted deformation field is nearly uniform for both $\mathcal{G}^{\text{curv}}$ and $\mathcal{G}^{\text{simp}}$ (Fig. 6), with only minor localization observed in small boundary units. In this case, dissipation is no longer confined to the interfaces but develops within the block interiors, leading to a more distributed deformation pattern. The resulting stress magnitude in the dominant compression direction is consistent with the prescribed compressive strength of the blocks.

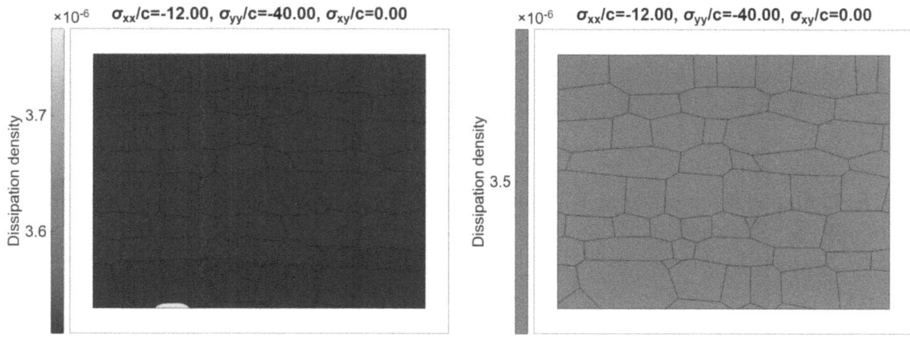

Fig. 6. Collapse mechanism of RVE under biaxial compression load, deformable units; left: $\mathcal{G}^{\mathrm{curv}}$ - right: $\mathcal{G}^{\mathrm{simp}}$.

The superimposed shear stress significantly alters the collapse behavior. The combined loading induces tensile effects along the diagonal of the RVE, partially counteracting the compressive state. As a result, in the rigid formulation, the horizontal crushing bands disappear and are replaced by pronounced interfacial separation and sliding (Fig. 7). Crushing is limited and primarily observed near boundary regions. Due to geometric interlocking, large portions of $\mathcal{G}^{\mathrm{curv}}$ exhibit limited interfacial activity, resulting in a slightly higher collapse load compared to $\mathcal{G}^{\mathrm{simp}}$.

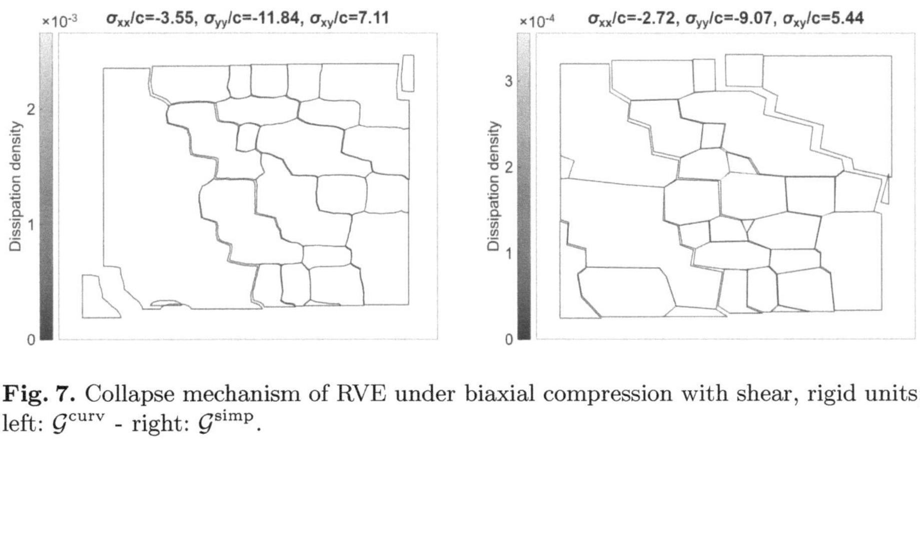

Fig. 7. Collapse mechanism of RVE under biaxial compression with shear, rigid units; left: $\mathcal{G}^{\mathrm{curv}}$ - right: $\mathcal{G}^{\mathrm{simp}}$.

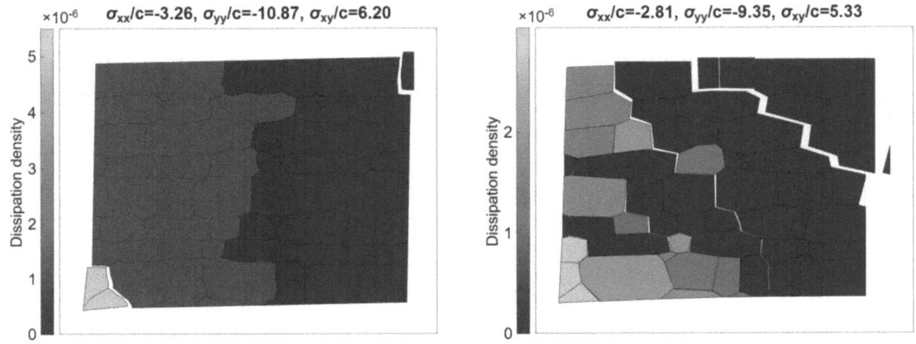

Fig. 8. Collapse mechanism of RVE under biaxial compression with shear, deformable units; left: $\mathcal{G}^{\text{curv}}$ - right: $\mathcal{G}^{\text{simp}}$.

A similar trend is observed in the results of the deformable formulation (Fig. 8). In $\mathcal{G}^{\text{curv}}$, the deformation field remains relatively continuous, reflecting a typical shear-dominated response, with dissipation concentrated in regions influenced by interlocking. In contrast, $\mathcal{G}^{\text{simp}}$ exhibits more pronounced interfacial separation, particularly near the boundaries, leading to a reduction in the predicted collapse load. Compared to the rigid-unit predictions, localized interfacial cracking is partially replaced by distributed in-element dissipation, resulting in a smearing of the failure pattern. Despite these differences, the locations of large cracks remain consistent between rigid and deformable formulations.

Overall, under combined compression-shear loading, the differences between rigid and deformable formulations are less pronounced. Both approaches provide consistent predictions in terms of collapse mechanisms and load levels.

5.2 Discussions

Despite the advantages of employing deformable elements, certain theoretical limitations must be acknowledged. In particular, constant-strain polygonal elements are prone to an internal locking phenomenon, as discussed in [16]. This issue arises from the constant-strain assumption, which is insufficient to fully represent the kinematics of polygonal blocks. As a result, additional constraints are introduced at the block level, leading to an overestimation of the collapse load. Several strategies may be adopted to alleviate this issue, including the use of piecewise-constant elements or the subdivision of polygonal blocks into triangular elements. The severity of the locking effect is expected to increase in the presence of high deformation gradients. However, in the context of RVE analysis under uniform stress fields, this effect is likely to remain limited, although this assumption requires further verification through dedicated comparative studies.

The present results nevertheless highlight the importance of accounting for block deformability when predicting the mechanical response of RVEs. Although the material parameters considered in this study are selected for comparative purposes, the proposed framework allows the use of experimentally calibrated properties for realistic material characterization.

Furthermore, the proposed formulation can be extended to construct the homogenized failure surface of RVEs through an iterative procedure, which will be investigated in future work.

Acknowledgments. The first author gratefully acknowledges the support of the Fonds de la Recherche Scientifique FNRS Communauté française de Belgique through the funding of a FRIA grant under grant number 40021962.

Disclosure of Interests. The authors declare that they have no known competing financial interests or personal relationships that could have appeared to influence the work reported in this paper. The third author gratefully acknowledges the support of the Fonds de la Recherche Scientifique FNRS Communaut franaise de Belgique through the funding of a Postdoctoral Researcher (CR) mandate under grant number 40010864, and the support of Innoviris under project reference 2023-RDIR-49

References

1. Senthivel, R., Lourenço, P.B.: Finite element modelling of deformation characteristics of historical stone masonry shear walls. Eng. Struct. **31**(9), 1930–1943 (2009)
2. Hermans, Y., Grillanda, N., Ehab Moustafa Kamel, K., Milani, G., Massart, T.J.: Efficient image-based homogenized limit analysis for irregular masonry with lumped mortar joints representation. Eng. Struct. **318**, 118688 (2024)
3. Hermans, Y., Ehab Moustafa Kamel, K., Debeir, O., Milani, G., Massart, T.J.: Image-based structural kinematic limit analysis for historical masonry structures. Meccanica **60**, 2107–2124 (2025)
4. D'Altri, A.M., et al.: Modeling strategies for the computational analysis of unreinforced masonry structures: review and classification. Arch. Comput. Meth. Eng. **27**, 1153–1185 (2020)
5. Lourenço, P.B., de Borst, R., Rots, J.G.: A plane stress softening plasticity model for orthotropic materials. Int. J. Numer. Meth. Eng. **40**, 4033–4057 (1997)
6. Gatta, C., Addessi, D.: Orthotropic multisurface model with damage for macromechanical analysis of masonry structures. Eur. J. Mech. A. Solids **102**, 105077 (2023)
7. Wang, Q., Dos Santos, K.R.M.., Beyer, K.: Micro modeling of irregular stone masonry walls using mathematical programming. In: Endo, Y., Hanazato, T. (eds.) Structural Analysis of Historical Constructions, SAHC 2023. RILEM Bookseries, vol. 46, pp. 591–602. Springer, Cham (2023). https://doi.org/10.1007/978-3-031-39450-8_49
8. Lotfi, H.R., Shing, P.B.: Interface model applied to fracture of masonry structures. J. Struct. Eng. **120**(1), 63–80 (1994)
9. Alfano, G., Sacco, E.: Combining interface damage and friction in a cohesive-zone model. Int. J. Numer. Meth. Eng. **68**, 542–582 (2006)
10. Portioli, F., Casapulla, C., Gilbert, M., Cascini, L.: Limit analysis of 3D masonry block structures with non-associative frictional joints using cone programming. Comput. Struct. **143**, 108–121 (2014)
11. de Buhan, P., de Felice, G.: A homogenization approach to the ultimate strength of brick masonry. J. Mech. Phys. Solids **45**(7), 1085–1104 (1997)

12. Sacco, E.: A nonlinear homogenization procedure for periodic masonry. Eur. J. Mech. A. Solids **28**(2), 209–222 (2009)
13. Sonon, B., François, B., Massart, T.J.: A unified level set based methodology for fast generation of complex microstructural multi-phase RVEs. Comput. Meth. Appl. Mech. Eng. **30**(1), 116–136 (2012)
14. Kamel, K.E.M., Massart, T.J.: Towards automated image-based cohesive zone modeling of cracking in irregular masonry. Math. Mech. Solids **30**(1), 116–136 (2024)
15. Gilbert, M., Casapulla, C., Ahmed, H.M.: Limit analysis of masonry block structures with non-associative frictional joints using linear programming. Comput. Struct. **84**(13–14), 873–887 (2006)
16. Hua, Y., Milani, G.: New deformable element with arbitrary polygon shape for continuous modeling of limit analysis. Int. J. Solids Struct. **326**, 113745 (2026)
17. Simo, J.C.: Numerical analysis and simulation of plasticity. In: Handbook of Numerical Analysis, vol. 6, pp. 183–499 (1998)
18. Tiberti, S., Milani, G.: 2D pixel homogenized limit analysis of non-periodic masonry walls. Comput. Struct. **219**, 16–57 (2019)
19. Ministero delle Infrastrutture e dei Trasporti: Istruzioni per l'applicazione dell'aggiornamento delle Norme Tecniche per le Costruzioni di cui al Decreto Ministeriale 17 gennaio 2018. Gazzetta Ufficiale della Repubblica Italiana (2019)
20. Maier, G., Nappi, A.: A theory of no-tension discretized structural systems. Eng. Struct. **12**, 227–5234 (1990)
21. Milani, G., Lourenço, P.B., Tralli, A.: Homogenised limit analysis of masonry walls, part I: failure surfaces. Comput. Struct. **84**(3–4), 166–180 (2006)
22. Mascolo, I., Gesualdo, A., Olivieri, C., Fortunato, A.: On blocks detection in unilateral masonry-like structures: a rigid-elastic displacement approach. Int. J. Masonry Res. Innov. **7**(4), 395–405 (2022)
23. Olivieri, C., Cocking, S., Fabbrocino, F., Iannuzzo, A., Placidi, L., Adriaenssens, S.: Seismic capacity of purely compressed shells based on airy stress function. Continuum Mech. Thermodyn. **37**(2), 21 (2025)
24. Iannuzzo, A., Van Mele, T., Block, P.: Piecewise rigid displacement (PRD) method: a limit analysis-based approach to detect mechanisms and internal forces through two dual energy criteria. Mech. Res. Commun. **107**, 103557 (2020)
25. Iannuzzo, A., Montanino, A.: A limit analysis-based CASS approach for the in-plane seismic capacity of masonry façades. Int. J. Solids Struct. **289**, 112633 (2024)
26. Sangirardi, M., Di Santo, G., Amorosi, A.: An enriched and phenomenologically sound multilaminate model for masonry: JMM-E. Eng. Struct. **352**, 122113 (2026)

Stability Analysis of Masonry Domes and Crack Interpretation Through a 3D-Rigid-Block Model with Concentrated Deformability

Stefano Galassi[1,2(✉)] and Giacomo Tempesta[1]

[1] Department of Architecture, University of Florence, Florence, Italy
stefano.galassi@unifi.it
[2] Department of Mediterranean Architecture Research Center, Faculty of Applied Sciences, Catholic University "Our Lady of Good Counsel" of Tiranë, Tiranë, Albania

Abstract. The preservation of buildings belonging to architectural heritage is a topic that is very close to society's heart. They are mainly constructed of load-bearing masonry and feature typical architectural and structural components such as arches, colonnades, vaults and domes. These components often have cracks and, in some cases, an extensive crack pattern can even be observed. Cracking is a common occurrence in masonry structures, given the very low tensile strength of the mortar joints used to bind the masonry units. What really matters is determining the causes to prevent local or global collapse and to design appropriate reinforcement measures. To this purpose, structural analyses must be performed. Therefore, targeted mechanical models and analysis methods must be developed. This paper focuses especially on domes, for the analysis of which methods based on graphic statics were developed in the past. According to them, a dome was analyzed as a series of meridian slices acting as individual arches and the stability was assessed using the thrust line method. The advent of elasticity theory in the 19th century introduced new methods of analysis, such as the membrane theory; however, this theory is not particularly suitable for the study of masonry domes because, to satisfy the equilibrium conditions, it also considers tensile stresses along the lower parallels. In this paper, a 3D-Rigid-block model with concentrated deformability is presented. The deformability is concentrated in the joints, to which a no-tension behavior or a low threshold strength can be assigned. This model can predict the occurrence of cracks in joints and, consequently, interpret their cause. Its reliability is demonstrated by the analysis of a well-known and much-debated case study.

Keywords: Domes · Masonry · No-Tension · Nonlinear Analysis · Stability · Crack Interpretation

1 Introduction

Every country has historic buildings that tell the story of its origins. Italy is the country with the highest concentration of historical and architectural heritage in the world [1]. Most of the historic building stock consists of masonry buildings, some of which are

O. Gervasi et al. (Eds.): ICCSA 2026 Workshops, LNCS 16758, pp. 533–550, 2027.
https://doi.org/10.1007/978-3-032-30497-1_32

in ruins and others merely damaged; they are characterized by typical architectural and structural elements, such as arches, vaults, domes, spiral stairs, etc. We must preserve these architectural structures as a tribute to our past. To preserve them, we need to assess their stability based on reliable analysis methods [2–20].

As regards to masonry domes – the subject of this paper – the first significant analysis methods based on equilibrium date back to the 18th century, with the publication of numerous memoirs by the Royal Academy of Sciences in Paris. We denote the set of this 18th century memoirs as the "first school of thought", to distinguish it from the changed way of thinking that emerged in the 19th century.

We can identify Pierre Bouguer [21] as the leading figure of this early school of thought, which interprets the behavior of a dome as a set of independent, arch-shaped structural elements. According to this theory, the stability of a dome is assessed by analyzing the stability of these one-dimensional elements, which can be done by identifying a line of thrust that lies entirely within their profile using the principles of graphic statics. It is worth noting that this interpretation of the mechanical behavior of a dome corresponds to that of Poleni [22] who analyzed in 1734 the stability of San Peter's dome in Rome as an assemblage of "solid sectors". Even the analysis of a dome divided into a series of "orange slices" – which Heyman [23] proposed in the 1960s in the context of limit analysis and which assumes the absence of forces along the dome's parallels, i.e. of interactions between these arched elements – can also be traced back to these earlier interpretations.

Bouguer's studies cover both the design of a new dome and the structural analysis of an existing dome. In his memoir, the first subject is referred to as the "first question" and concerns determining the best shape for a dome capable of supporting its own weight. He was the first to propose the equation of the funicular meridian as the solution to this problem: the best shape for the dome is achieved by modelling the curve of the meridian so that it coincides with the funicular curve of the own weight of a slice of the dome. The second subject, instead, is called the "second question" and concerns the stability analysis of an existing dome. Even if he did not provide the mathematical solution to this problem, he realized that the stress state inside a dome is two-dimensional and, consequently, introduced the topic of two-dimensional behavior.

The subject of the two-dimensional behavior of the dome was developed in depth in the 19th century, with the advent of the theory of elasticity. The most famous method developed in this period and in this context is the one called "membrane theory", devised by E. Beltrami [24]. Even if this method was originally conceived to analyze membranes, it was also applied from the very beginning to the analysis of masonry domes despite the latter do not behave like membranes. In fact, according to this theory, the internal forces in a dome are axial compressive forces along the meridians, with values increasing from the crown to the base, and axial forces along the parallels which have different signs: they are compressive on the upper parallels and tension on the lower ones. The position of the parallel that marks the transition from compression to the tension forces, referred to as the neutral parallel, depends only on the shape of the dome.

This scenario of internal forces is generally not consistent with the one that a masonry dome can withstand, because it is not as thin as a membrane and has a very low tensile strength. Tensile forces cause the development of cracks along the meridians, the internal forces are no longer located in the middle surface of the dome and the position of the neutral parallel is variable and depends on these aspects. Based on this reasoning, H. T. Eddy in 1878 [25] and M. Lévy [26] in 1888 proposed, independently of each other, two very similar graphical methods to assess the stability of a masonry dome based on the assumption that the dome has a double behavior: the portion above the neutral axis has a two-dimensional behavior, characterized by compressive forces both along the meridians and the parallels; instead, below the neutral parallel the dome splits into a series of meridian arches caused by the tensile forces along the lower meridians and, therefore, the lower portion of the dome behaves as a set of independent one-dimensional structures. These graphical methods allow one to identify the position of the neutral parallel and draw the thrust line at the bottom [27].

All these methods have a common feature: they are based only on equilibrium because, as is known, masonry structures collapse due to lack of stability, which is determined by the geometric shape of the structure and the unilateral no-tension nature of the material, rather than to the material's failure due to exceeding its strength thresholds. Accordingly, thrust line methods, originally formalized by Gerstener [28], have been extended to the analysis of three-dimensional masonry structures, such as vaults and domes, using thrust networks. Thrust network analysis, based on Heyman's assumptions, was originally developed by O'Dwyer [29], fully developed by Block and Ochsendorf [30] and then reformulated and extended by Marmo and Rosati [31]. It consists in identifying a network of only compressive forces within the boundary of masonry to ensure stability. However, it does not give any additional information about the level of stability. To compute the level of stability, this method has further been extended in [32] exploiting the concept of geometrical factor of safety proposed by Heyman.

However, this approach, which is framed in the context of limit analysis under Heyman's assumptions, can lead to overestimate the load-bearing capacity. To overcome this issue, many authors proposed methods to account for a finite compressive strength and stereotomy [33, 34], and the most recent paper found in the literature is that of Aita [35, 36], who uses a numerical approach based on the force density method.

In this paper, instead, to analyze the stability of masonry domes a three-dimensional rigid-block model with deformability concentrated at joints is proposed. Joints along the parallels and the meridians are modelled as discrete devices consisting of a set of axial and shear links, the former are arranged orthogonally to the middle plane of the joints and the latter are arranged within it along the meridians and parallels. Material nonlinearity is considered by incorporating failure criteria for the axial compressive and tensile links as well as for the shear links. The nonlinear numerical procedure that handles the static and elastic-kinematic analysis of this model uses Somigliana distortions to satisfy the failure criteria. The failure of the links that do not meet the failure criteria allows one to detect the occurrence of cracks in the joints and to draw the deformed configuration of the structure. The reliability of the proposed procedure is demonstrated by the stability analysis of the dome of Santa Maria del Fiore in Florence (Italy) and by the comparison between the numerically predicted crack pattern and the one observed in the existing dome. The computer program *BrickWORK 2.0* has been developed to create the structural model of the dome and automatically perform the analysis.

2 Numerical Approach

2.1 Mechanical Model

The model of the masonry dome consists of a set of rigid blocks, cut out between two adjacent meridians and parallels. Except for specific cases, these are mainly rigid hexahedral elements. They are connected to one other by meridian and parallel joints, which act as thin elastic layers. By doing so, this structural model is defined as "rigid block model with concentrated elasticity" and, accordingly, it is governed by equilibrium equations of blocks and congruency equations of joints. Let n and m denote the overall number of blocks and joints, respectively (Fig. 1).

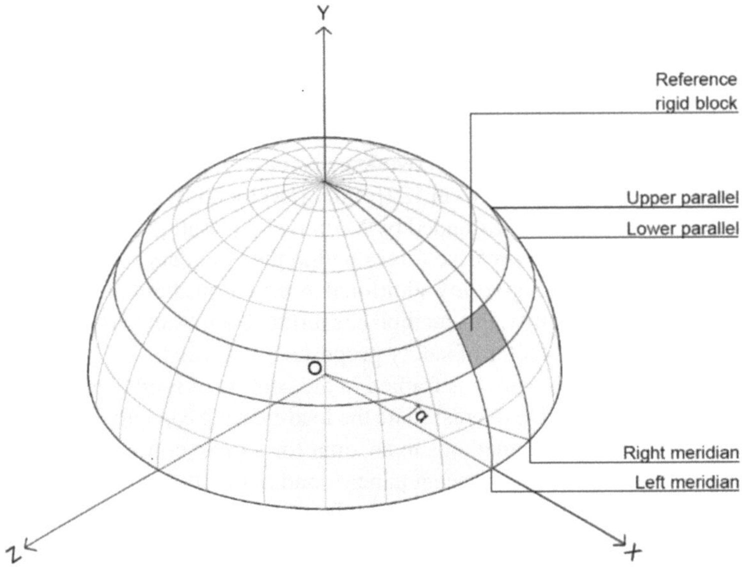

Fig. 1. Discrete model of the dome.

According to Drucker, joints are modelled through a discrete device consisting of a set of links orthogonal to the middle plane of the joint, to transfer the axial force between the blocks, and a set of links lying on it to transfer the shear force (Fig. 2). The greater the number of axial and shear links, the more refined the model and the more accurate the results, particularly with regard to the calculation of cracks. It is worth noting that the number of shear links is twice that of the axial links. We denote the number of axial links by k. The reason for it is that every point i of the joint (with $1 \leq i \leq k$) connecting two adjacent blocks must transfer three internal forces to prevent internal instability: the axial force and two shear forces acting along two different directions within the middle plane of the joint. Accordingly, the simplest device of the joint consists of four axial links, at the four vertices of the middle plane of the joint to connect two adjacent blocks, two shearing links along the upper and lower parallel and two shearing links along the

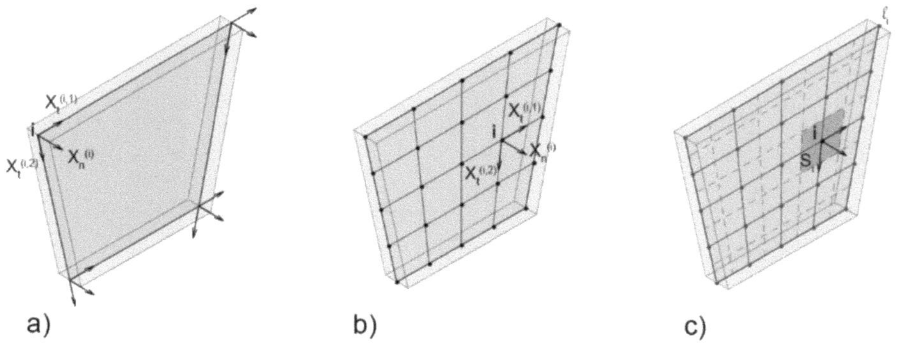

Fig. 2. Discrete model of the joint device: in a) the simplest device; in b) a more refined device; in c) cross-sectional area and length of the i-th link.

left and right meridian. In Fig. 2a, which shows this device, the links are replaced by the internal forces associated with them.

In Fig. 2b, instead, a more refined joint device is shown. This is achieved by further discretizing the simple device shown in Fig. 2a, by subdividing the four edges of the middle plane of the joint into three equal segments which identify four nodes on each edge. By connecting these, a network of 16 nodes is created. At each node there is an axial and two shear links. The axial link passing through the node is perpendicular to the middle plane. The directions of the shear links are those of the parallel and the meridian passing through the node.

2.2 Behavior of the Joints

Joints are designed as thin, elastic layers inserted between the rigid blocks that make up the structure. However, a distinction must be made between compression and tensile deformation in order to accurately reproduce the actual properties of the masonry. Accordingly, different strength criteria are assigned to the axial and shear links of the joint device.

Axial links may be assigned either an infinite compression strength if a linear-elastic behavior is assumed (Fig. 3a) or a limit threshold strength corresponding to the crushing of masonry if a linear-elastic-perfectly plastic behavior is adopted (Fig. 3b). With regard to tension, a no-tension material may be adopted but a limit threshold strength can also be considered that causes the failure of the link and the occurrence of a crack if a linear elastic-rigid behavior is assumed under tension (Fig. 3a,b). Shear links, instead, may be assigned either an infinite shear strength to prevent sliding if a linear-elastic behavior is assumed (Fig. 3c) or a limit threshold strength which can result in two different effects: the failure of that link if a linear-elastic-brittle behavior is adopted (Fig. 3d); its yielding in case of a linear-elastic-perfectly plastic behavior (Fig. 3e).

It is worth noting that the tensile failure of an axial link involves also the failure of the two shear-links associated with it in order for the crack to occur, but not vice versa. In this way, sliding occurs without dilatancy because the axial link maintains its axial force.

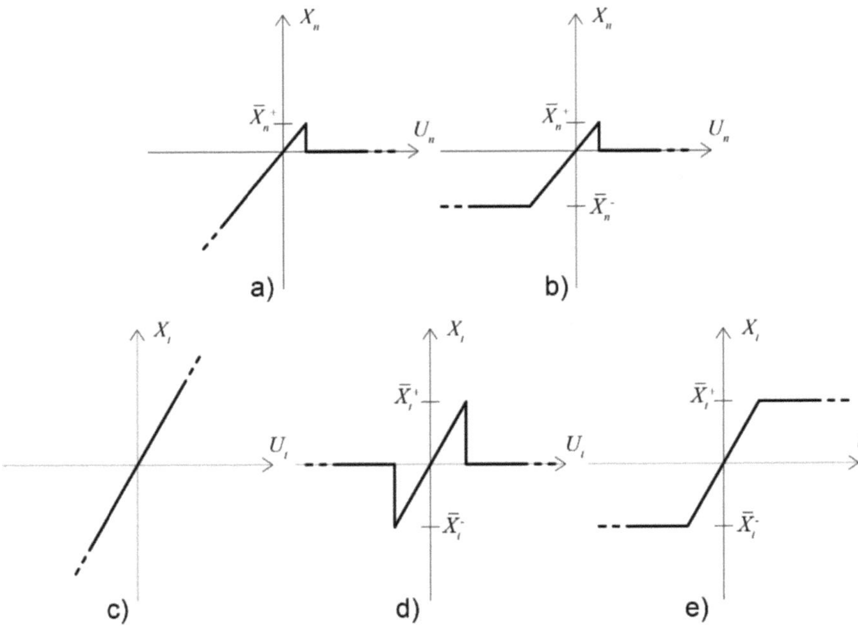

Fig. 3. Mechanical behavior of the joint axial links with finite tensile strength and infinite (a) or finite (b) compressive strength; joint shear links with (c) infinite strength or a threshold strength value causing the failure (d) or its yielding (e).

2.3 Problem Setting

To analyze the discrete model of the dome shown in Fig. 1 and Fig. 2, the equilibrium equations of rigid blocks and the elastic-kinematic equations of joints are formulated. The overall system of linear equations that is obtained is written in matrix form in Eq. 1:

$$\begin{cases} AX + F = 0 \\ \tilde{A}U + KX = \Delta \end{cases} \tag{1}$$

In the first equation, that describes the equilibrium condition, F is the load vector, X is the vector of the axial and shear forces within the links of the joint device to be calculated and A is the matrix of its coefficients.

In the second equation, $\tilde{A}$ is the kinematic matrix and it is the transpose of the equilibrium matrix A according to the static-kinematic duality, U is the vector of the displacements of the block centroids and its entries are the horizontal displacements along the x and z axes, the vertical displacement along the y axis and the three rotations about the x, y and z axes. Matrix K is a square diagonal matrix and its entries $k_{i,i} = \frac{\ell_i}{E \cdot S_i}$ are the deformability coefficients of the joint links. In detail, ℓ_i is the length of the i-th link of the joint device, S_i its sectional area and E the Young's modulus of the joint (Fig. 2c). Finally, vector Δ is denoted as "distortion vector" and its purpose is twofold in the numerical procedure:

- to ensure that the axial and shear forces in the links meet the specified failure criteria;

- to ensure compatibility even when some links fail and cracks develop.

Therefore, vector Δ is partitioned into the sub-vector Δ^* to address the first issue and the sub-vector Δ^{**} to address the second.

For the purposes of the analysis, the failure criteria described in Sect. 2.2 and associated with the specific behaviour of the axial and shear links shown in Fig. 3, are formulated in Eq. 2:

$$\begin{cases} \overline{X}_n^{-(i)} \leq X_n^{(i)} \leq \overline{X}_n^{+(i)} \\ \left|X_t^{(i)}\right| \leq \left|\overline{X}_t^{(i)}\right| = |c| + \mu \cdot \left|X_n^{(i)}\right| \end{cases} \tag{2}$$

where the vector of internal forces is partitioned into the sub-vector X_n of the axial forces and the sub-vector X_t of the shear forces to properly handle the relevant failure criteria.

The first inequality of Eq. 2 sets the threshold compressive strength $\overline{X}_n^{-(i)}$ and the threshold tensile strength $\overline{X}_n^{+(i)}$ for the axial force $X_n^{(i)}$ of the i-th link. It goes without saying that to define a no-tension material, one simply sets $\overline{X}_n^{+(i)} = 0$ and to define a marerial with infinite compression strength one sets $\overline{X}_n^{-(i)} = -\infty$.

The second inequality describes the frictional behavior of the joint with non-associated flow rule. According to the Coulomb strength criterion, the shear force $X_t^{(i)}$ of the i-th link, computed as the vector sum of the shear force $X_t^{(i,1)}$ along the parallel and the shear force $X_t^{(i,2)}$ along the meridian passing through point i, must not exceed the threshold value, given by the sum of the friction force $\mu \cdot X_n^{(i)}$ and the cohesion c to prevent sliding. In the second inequality of Eq. 2, μ is the friction factor of the joint and $X_n^{(i)}$ is the axial force acting at point i. Refer to Fig. 2 for the nomenclature.

These failure criteria imply nonlinear behaviour of the masonry dome. Accordingly, a nonlinear numerical procedure, that works as follows, is developed:

- First, the vector of internal forces X, corresponding to the linear-elastic static solution of the problem, is calculated by solving Eq. 1. We denote this vector X_0. Therefore, at the starting point of the analysis, we have $X = X_0$;

- Then, this vector is partioned into the sub-vectors X_n and X_t to check if the axial and shear forces meet the corresponding failure criteria set in Eq. 2. If some entries do not meet them, distoritons Δ^* are introduced, iteratively, in the link where the internal force exceeds its threshold value the most. Therefore, this is an iterative procedure.

Specifically, referring to Fig. 3a and Fig. 3b, the distortion introduced in an axial link subjected to a tensile force exceeding the tensile threshold value $\overline{X}_n^+$, nullifies the internal force and causes the failure of that link and the associated shear links along the parallel and meridian, as well as the development of a crack. Furthermore, referring to Fig. 3b, the distortion introduced in an axial link subjected to a compression force exceeding the compression threshold value $\overline{X}_n^-$, sets the internal forces to that value and causes the yielding of that link.

Figures 3d and 3e show, instead, the effect of distortions on the shear links along the parallels and meridians. In detail, if the shear behavior in Fig. 3d is adopted, the distortion introduced in a shear link subjected to a shear force exceeding the threshold value $\overline{X}_t$, nullifies the internal force and causes the failure of that link. Convesely, if we consider the shear behavior shown in Fig. 3e, the distortion sets the internal forces to the threshold value and causes the yielding of that link. In both cases, sliding occurs. It is worth noting that if the behavior shown in Fig. 3c is assumed, distortions are never introduced in the shear links and sliding is prevented.

In the forthcoming sections of the paper, the numerical procedure is described in detail, discussing first the static analysis, then the elastic-kinematic analysis.

2.4 Calculation of Internal Forces

By solving Eq. 1 in accordance with the failure criteria expressed by Eq. 2, we obtain the vector X of the internal forces within the axial and shear links of the joint device:

$$X = -K^{-1}\tilde{A}R^{-1}F + K^{-1}\left(I - K^{-1}\tilde{A}R^{-1}A\right)\Delta^* \tag{3}$$

It can be noticed that this vector is given by the sum of two vectors, respectively shown in Eq. 4 and Eq. 5:

$$X_0 = -K^{-1}\tilde{A}R^{-1}F \tag{4}$$

$$X_\perp = K^{-1}\left(I - K^{-1}\tilde{A}R^{-1}A\right)\Delta^* \tag{5}$$

In Eqs. 3 to 5, matrix $R = AK^{-1}\tilde{A}$ is the stiffness matrix of the structure.

The vector X_0 is the linear-elastic solution obtained by setting $\Delta^* = 0$ and solving Eq. 1. The vector $X_\perp$, on the other hand, is the solution of Eq. 1 that can be obtained by setting vector $F = 0$, assuming that there are two separate static problems: the dome subject only to the dead loads F and the dome subject only to the distortions Δ^*. However, the two problems are closely linked, as the distortions are aimed at meeting the failure criteria in Eq. 2. For this reason, it is observed that it is not possible to calculate the distortion vector Δ^* before calculating the static solution vector X, but also the latter is a function of the former (see Eq. 3). It is like a dog biting its own tail. To get around this trouble, a numerical workaround has been devised, as illustrated in the equations below.

By defining the distortion matrix D as follows:

$$D = K^{-1}\left(I - K^{-1}\tilde{A}R^{-1}A\right) \tag{6}$$

Equation 5 is re-written, in a more concise way, in the form of Eq. 7:

$$X = X_0 + D\Delta^* \tag{7}$$

Next, matrix D and vectors X, X_0 and Δ^* are partitioned in such a way as to separate entries that meet the failure criteria from those that do not. We denote the former by the subscript b and the latter by the subscript c. With this in mind, Eq. 7 is partitioned as follows:

$$\begin{bmatrix} X_b \\ T \end{bmatrix} = \begin{bmatrix} X_{0b} \\ X_{0c} \end{bmatrix} + \begin{bmatrix} D_b & B \\ \tilde{B} & D_c \end{bmatrix} \cdot \begin{bmatrix} 0 \\ \Delta_c^* \end{bmatrix} \tag{8}$$

In Eq. 8, the final static solution vector X is composed of two sub-vectors: the sub-vector T that is populated by the axial and shear forces modified by the distortions introduced to meet the failure criteria, whilst the sub-vector X_b consists of the internal forces that do not require distortions to satisfy the criteria.

Entries of sub-vector T are defined in Eq. 9, depending on the failure critera adopted for the i-th axial or shear link:

$$t_i = \begin{cases} \overline{X}_n^{+(i)} \\ \overline{X}_n^{-(i)} \\ \overline{X}_t^{(i)} = 0 \\ \overline{X}_t^{(i)} = c + \mu \cdot X_n^{(i)} \end{cases} \tag{9}$$

The first and the second terms of Eq. 9 relate to the first failure criterion in Eq. 2 for the axial links. In particular, the first one refers to a no-tension axial link (Fig. 3a and Fig. 3b) and the second one to the yielding of an axial compressed link (Fig. 3b).

The third and the fourth terms of Eq. 9 relate to the second failure criterion in Eq. 2 for the shear links. Specifically, the third one refers to the elastic-rigid behavior shown in Fig. 3d whilst the fourth refers to the elastic-plastic behavior shown in Fig. 3e.

The solution to Eq. 8 provides precisely the sub-vector Δ_c^* (Eq. 10), consisting of the non-zero entries of the distortion vector Δ^* aimed at satisfying the failure criteria and, subsequently, the sub-vector X_b (Eq. 11), consisting of the entries of vector X that have been indirectly influenced by the distorsions introduced in other links:

$$\Delta_c^* = D_c^{-1}(T - X_{0c}) \tag{10}$$

$$X_b = X_{0b} + \mathrm{B}D_c^{-1}(T - X_{0c}) \tag{11}$$

We refer to the sub-vector Δ_c^* as the "vector of effective distortions".

2.5 Displacements and Crack Pattern

The second phase of the analysis involves calculating the displacement of the blocks, as well as the deformation and propagation of cracks along the joints.

To draw the displaced configuration of the dome, it is necessary to calculate the displacements of the eight vertices of the blocks. They are computed in function of the displacements of the block centroids.

The latter could be computed by directly solving Eq. 1 only if the internal forces do not exceed their threshold values expressed by the failure conditions in Eq. 2. In this specific case the vector of the displacement of block centroids corresponds to the linear-elastic solution and is expressed by Eq. 12:

$$U = \mathrm{R}^{-1}\left(F + \mathrm{A}K^{-1}\Delta\right) \tag{12}$$

However, Eq. 12 does not hold when some of the links in the joint device fail or yield plastically, resulting in cracks or slippage. To take these occurrences into account, we apply the same numerical workaround to the elastic-kinematic equation as we used previously for the equilibrium equation. In this case, distortions Δ^{**} are introduced to restore the compatibility that has been altered by the cracks and slippage. Consequently, the second of Eq. 1 is partitioned to distinguish between entries that have been directly altered by the distortions Δ^{**} introcuced and those that have been changed only as a result:

$$\begin{bmatrix} \tilde{A}_b & K_b & 0 \\ \tilde{A}_c & 0 & K_c \end{bmatrix} \begin{bmatrix} \overline{U} \\ X_b \\ 0 \end{bmatrix} = \begin{bmatrix} 0 \\ \Delta_c^{**} \end{bmatrix} \tag{13}$$

The solution to Eq. 13 provides precisely the vector $\overline{U}$ of effective displacements of block centroids and, consequently, the sub-vector Δ_c^{**}, consisting of the non-zero entries of the distortion vector Δ^{**} aimed at restoring compatibility.

$$\overline{U} = -A_b(\tilde{A}_b A_b)^{-1}(K_b X_b) \tag{14}$$

$$\Delta_c^{**} = \tilde{A}_c \overline{U} \tag{15}$$

Note that vector $\overline{U} \neq U$ and entries of vector Δ_c^{**} represent the width of cracks at the joint links and, therefore, allow the crack pattern to be determined.

Finally, the new coordinates of the block vertices can be determined based on the six displacements of the block centroids stored in the vector $\overline{U}$.

Considering the j-th vertex P of the i-th block (denoted by $P_j^{(i)}$, with $1 \le j \le 8$, $1 \le i \le n$), the six displacements of the block centroid are referred as $u_{xG}^{(i)}$, $u_{yG}^{(i)}$, $u_{zG}^{(i)}$, $\varphi_{G,x}^{(i)}$, $\varphi_{G,y}^{(i)}$, $\varphi_{G,z}^{(i)}$ and the new coordinates of the displaced position of the vertex $P_j'^{(i)}$ are calculated, according the rules of finite kinematics, using the matrix Eq. (16):

$$\begin{Bmatrix} x'^{(i)}_{P_j} \\ y'^{(i)}_{P_j} \\ z'^{(i)}_{P_j} \end{Bmatrix} = \begin{Bmatrix} u_{xG}^{(i)} \\ u_{yG}^{(i)} \\ u_{zG}^{(i)} \end{Bmatrix} + \begin{bmatrix} 1 & 0 & 0 \\ 0 & cos\varphi_{G,x}^{(i)} & -sin\varphi_{G,x}^{(i)} \\ 0 & sin\varphi_{G,x}^{(i)} & cos\varphi_{G,x}^{(i)} \end{bmatrix} \cdot \begin{bmatrix} cos\varphi_{G,y}^{(i)} & 0 & sin\varphi_{G,y}^{(i)} \\ 0 & 1 & 0 \\ -sin\varphi_{G,y}^{(i)} & 0 & cos\varphi_{G,y}^{(i)} \end{bmatrix} \cdot \begin{bmatrix} cos\varphi_{G,z}^{(i)} & -sin\varphi_{G,z}^{(i)} & 0 \\ sin\varphi_{G,z}^{(i)} & cos\varphi_{G,z}^{(i)} & 0 \\ 0 & 0 & 1 \end{bmatrix} \cdot \begin{Bmatrix} x^{(i)}_{P_j} \\ y^{(i)}_{P_j} \\ z^{(i)}_{P_j} \end{Bmatrix} \tag{16}$$

This equation can also be written in a shorter, more compact form using Eq. 17:

$$P\prime = \overline{U}_i + \left(R_x R_y R_z\right) P \tag{17}$$

In Eq. 16 and Eq. 17, R_x, R_y and R_z are the rotation matrices about the x, y and z axes calculated from the angles $\varphi_{G,x}^{(i)}$, $\varphi_{G,y}^{(i)}$, $\varphi_{G,z}^{(i)}$, respectively, and entries of the sub-vector $\overline{U}_i = \left\{ u_{xG}^{(i)}\ u_{yG}^{(i)}\ u_{zG}^{(i)} \right\}$. of vector $\overline{U}$ are the displacements along the x, y and z axes of the centroid G of the i-th block.

2.6 *BrickWORK* Software-Aided Modelling

To analyze 3D-structures made of rigid blocks with deformability concentrated at joints, the computer program *BrickWORK* [37–40] has been extended. With this new release,

BrickWORK 2.0 is equipped with a graphical user interface (GUI) that allows one to easy create 3D-models obtained by the extrusion of a plane profile along a straight or a circular line.

To create a dome model, a series of rigid blocks, positioned at the spacing of the radial joints (those that will form the joints along the dome's parallels), is constructed along the directrix curve of the reference meridian in the Cartesian x, y plane. These rigid blocks can be drawn as closed polylines in a CAD environment and imported into *BrickWORK* as DXF vector file.

Next, using the "Joints" tool available in the software, the radial joints between the blocks and those at the base of the meridian are defined. The plane joint device is modelled as a set of links orthogonal to the bisector of the joint, to transfer the axial force between blocks, and a set of links along the bisector to transfer the shear force. The number of shear links is equal to the number of axial links. The simplest device of the joint consists of two axial links located at the upper and lower vertices of the middle plane of the joint (i.e. the bisector of the joint) connecting two adjacent blocks, and two shear links connecting the same points on the model (Fig. 4a). A more refined joint device (Fig. 4b) is obtained by dividing the joint's bisector into three equal segments which define four nodes. At each node there is one axial and one shear link. The latter device is particularly useful when the analysis aims to identify the crack pattern at the joints.

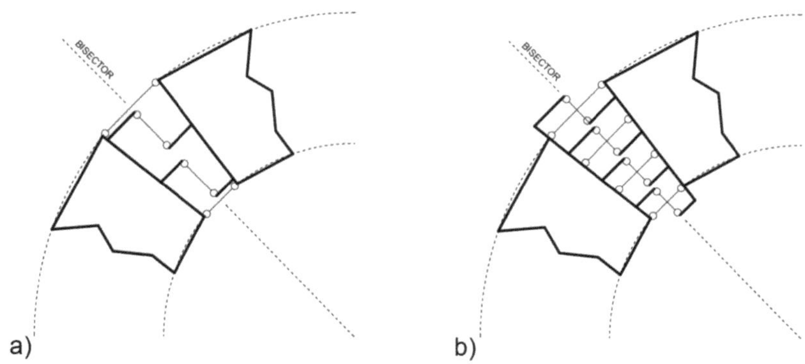

Fig. 4. Discrete model of the 2D-joint device: in a) the simplest device; in b) a more refined device.

This two-dimensional model is then extruded along a circular generatrix (Fig. 5) to form a full dome or a half-dome, such as that used to cover the apses of churches. To do this, *BrickWORK* provides a specific tool called "Create 3D model". This procedure requires the input of three parameters: the number s of meridian slices to be created, the angular amplitude β of the meridian joints between them and the angular amplitude α of the meridian slices measured along the circular generatrix (longitude), which comprises half the amplitude of the left and right meridian joints. It is worth noting that for a complete dome to form, $s \cdot \alpha$ must equal 2π. Furthermore, it is also possible to divide the meridian slices into a series of sectors in order to refine the mesh of the rigid blocks, but also to create geometric models differing from the axially symmetric domes.

The extrusion algorithm transforms the plane rigid blocks into three-dimensional rigid blocks and the plane device that forms the radial joints shown in Fig. 4 into the three-dimensional device that forms the parallel joints shown in Fig. 2. At the same time, three-dimensional devices of the meridian joints are also being produced, of the same type as the devices arranged along the parallels.

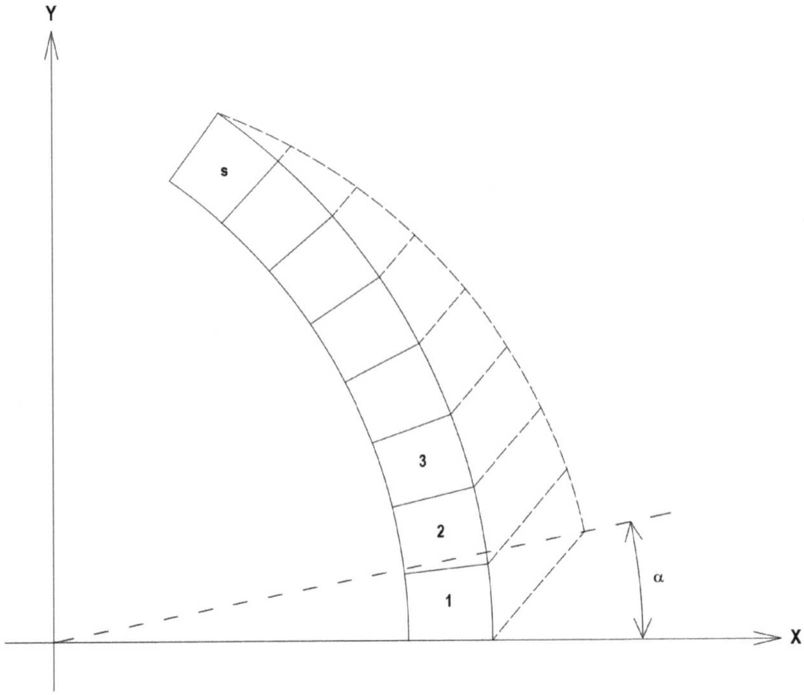

Fig. 5. Extrusion of the plane meridian profile to obtain the meridian slices that make up the three-dimensional model of the dome.

2.7 A Relevant Case Study

The numerical procedure presented in this paper has been used to analyze the stability of the Dome of Santa Maria del Fiore in Florence (Italy). *BrickWORK* 2.0 has been used to create the mechanical model of the dome and to perform the structural analysis.

The dome of Santa Maria del Fiore is an unusually shaped dome. Unlike typical axially symmetrical masonry domes, this is a polygonal dome built on an octagonal drum and crowned by an octagonal lantern (Fig. 6).

It was built between 1420 and 1436 by Filippo Brunelleschi, who won the competition for the dome of Santa Maria del Fiore, which was launched in 1418 in Florence by the Arte della Lana to resolve the issue of the cathedral's roof, which had remained unfinished.

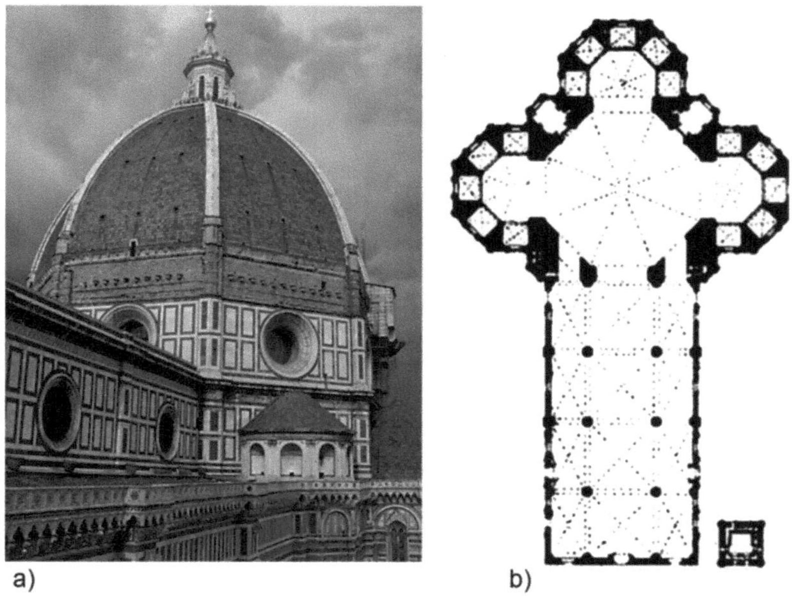

Fig. 6. Dome of Santa Maria del Fiore in Florence: a) picture; b) schematic plan.

The dome consists of two shells, one inner and one outer, separated by a cavity approximately 1.2 m wide that hosts the staircases leading to the lantern, and is composed of eight lunes that are segments of elliptical cylinders. The two shells are joined by a system of 24 meridian ribs (eight at the corners of the octagonal plan plus two per lune) and 10 parallel ribs.

The geometrical data used to create the mechanical model were derived from the pioneering studies by Salvatore di Pasquale published in 1977 [41] and they are shown in Fig. 7 together with the geometrical construction. This figure shows the octagonal plan of the dome (Fig. 7a), the cross sections of the dome drawn along the diagonal of the octagon (Fig. 7b) and at the middle of the octagon's sides (Fig. 7c). Please note that the shape has been regularized, as it is, in fact, an irregular octagon.

The profile of the diagonal rib of the inner shell is a circular curve whose radius, measuring 36 m, is 4/5 the inner diameter of the base. The inner and outer diameter are 45 and 54 m long, respectively; consequently, the overall thickness of the inner shell, the outer shell and the cavity between them is 4.5 m. Furthermore, the average thickness of the inner and the outer shell, taken at the middle of the lunes, is 2.20 and 0.90 m, respectively. Brunelleschi designed this pointed arch profile to give the dome greater height and make it more visible from the city.

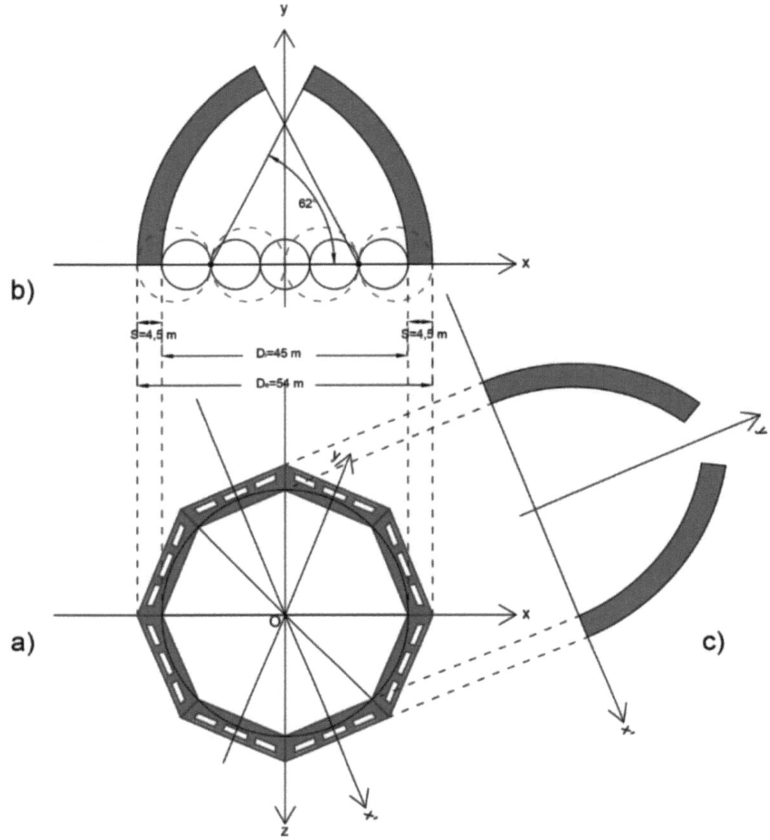

Fig. 7. Geometry: construction rules.

The three-dimensional mechanical model of the dome (Fig. 8) was constructed based on the shape of the meridian, which forms the circular rib. This consists of two parallel rows of 14 rigid blocks, the upper ones of which form the base of the lantern. For the assembly of the blocks, radial and meridian joints of minimum thickness were incorporated, consisting of devices comprising four axial and four shear links. The plane meridian was then extruded along a circular generatrix eight times at 45-degree intervals, so as to form a complete octagonal dome consisting of eight lunes. Each lune was also divided into eight sectors and, to create the eight corner ribs and the two ribs for each lune, some of the rigid blocks forming the outer structure were removed from the model. Finally, vertical point forces were applied to the upper blocks to simulate the weight of the lantern.

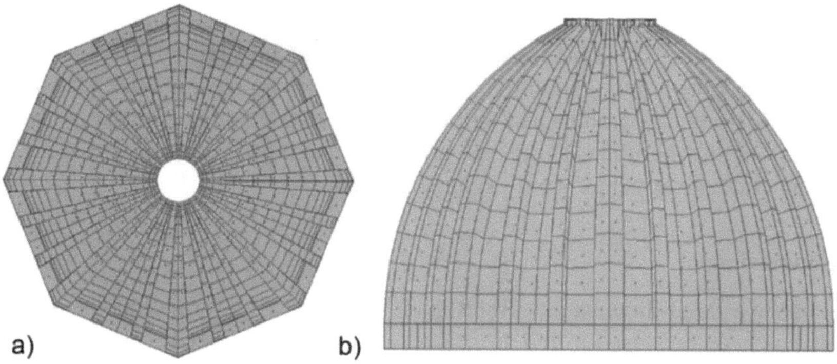

Fig. 8. Three-dimensional rigid block model of the dome of Santa Maria del Fiore: a) plan view; b) elevation view.

The analysis was carried out taking into account the axial behavior shown in Fig. 3a with a no-tension material and the shear behavior shown in Fig. 3c, thereby following Heyman's assumptions.

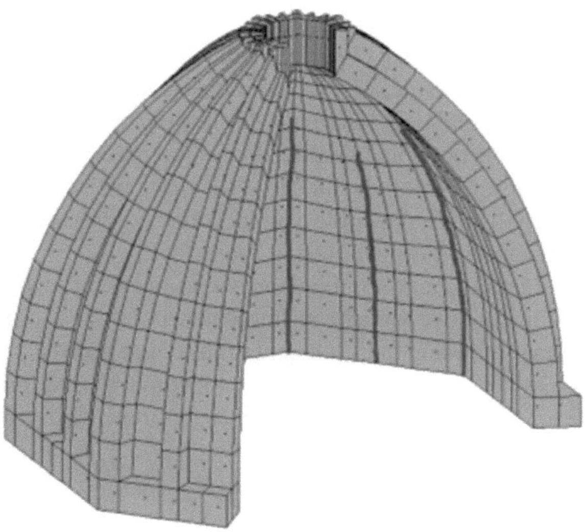

Fig. 9. Crack pattern predicted by the numerical procedure.

From the analysis, the dome is stable under the damage conditions illustrated in Fig. 9. The crack pattern, consisting of main meridional cracks along the big corner ribs and minor meridional cracks at the middle of the lunes, corresponds to that actually observed on the dome.

Furthermore, the compressive stresses are relatively low. At the base of the dome the predicted maximum compressive stress is 0.79 MPa at the major corner ribs, 0.78 MPa at the medium ribs and 0.47 MPa at the center of the lunes. These compression stresses ensure that the strength criteria used in the analysis are consistent, as the crushing of the masonry can be disregarded.

It should also be noted that, unlike axially symmetric domes, in which shear forces are zero both along all parallels and meridians, in the case at hand the shear forces are zero only along the meridians at the big corner ribs and those at the middle of the lunes, which constitute the structure's only symmetry planes.

2.8 Conclusions

In this paper a three-dimensional rigid-block model with deformability concentrated at joints has been proposed to model masonry structures obtained using the extrusion procedure included in the software *BrickWORK 2.0*. The specific case of masonry domes was considered. Joints are represented by a discrete device consisting of links orthogonal to the middle plane of the joints, designed to transfer the axial force, and links lying within that plane, designed to transfer the shear force. For such links appropriate laws are formulated that describe the mechanical behavior together with the failure criteria. To address these criteria involving material nonlinearity, a nonlinear numerical procedure for stability analysis has been proposed, which uses Somigliana distortions to satisfy the failure criteria. The analysis of a significant case study, the dome of Santa Maria del Fiore in Florence (Italy), demonstrated the reliability of the proposed mechanical model and the numerical procedure to assess the stability of the structure and predict the crack pattern, which is consistent with that observed in the dome.

The extrusion procedure and the software developed enable the automatic modelling of structures that can be obtained by extruding a discrete planar model along a circular or straight line. Therefore, it is possible to model domes (complete, with hole and lantern, or on a drum), church apses, barrel and cloister vaults that include load-bearing walls. Further improvements will make it possible to model other types of structures that cannot be produced using extrusion processes, such as cross vaults.

Furthermore, the employment of Somigliana distortions offers a significant alternative to the traditional methods of variable stiffness matrix or linear programming, as it addresses nonlinear analysis using tools inherent to structural analysis rather than purely mathematical ones. On the contrary, as an iterative method is used, the computational cost can be significant. To reduce processing times, a single-step procedure is being developed to replace the current iterative procedure.

References

1. Meloni, G., Pourfouladi, M., Pingaro, N.: Parametric modelling and nonlinear FE analysis of Trepponti bridge subjected to differential settlements. Buildings **16**(47), 1–20 (2026)
2. Pingaro, N., Buzzetti, M., Gandolfi, A.: A numerical strategy to assess the stability of curved masonry structures using a simple nonlinear truss model. Buildings **15**, 1–21 (2025)
3. Pingaro, N., Milani, G.: Simple interface element equipped with thickness for the non-linear static heterogeneous analysis of masonry walls in-plane loaded: implementation and validation. Eng. Struct. **351**, 122056 (2026)
4. Pingaro, N., Milani, G.: Simple non-linear numerical modelling of masonry arches reinforced with SRG using elasto-fragile and elasto-ductile truss finite elements. Eng. Struct. **293**, 116637 (2023)

5. Gandolfi, A., Pingaro, N., Milani, G.: Simple nonlinear numerical modeling for unreinforced and FRP-reinforced masonry domes. Buildings **14**(166), 1–21 (2024)
6. Gandolfi, A., Pingaro, N., Milani, G.: Elastic Body Spring Method (EBSM) for the stability analysis of the Global Vipassana Pagoda in Mumbai, India. Buildings **15**(653), 1–17 (2025)
7. Hua, Y., Buzzetti, M., Pingaro, N., da Silva, L.C.M., Milani, G.: A computerized tool for the kinematic limit analysis of 2D masonry structures failing on a tilting table. SoftwareX **30**, 102180 (2025)
8. Pingaro, N., Buzzetti, M., Milani, G.: Advanced FE nonlinear numerical modeling to predict historical masonry vaults failure: assessment of risk collapse for a long span cloister vault heavily loaded at the crown by means of a general-purpose numerical protocol. Eng. Fail. Anal. **167**, 109070 (2025)
9. Galassi, S., Tempesta, G.: Safety assessment of masonry undamaged and damaged arches subjected to gravitational loads and horizontal forces: a numeric procedure to identify the optimal thrust line. Int. J. Solids Struct. **301**, 112943 (2024)
10. Galassi, S.: An alternative approach for limit analysis of masonry arches on moving supports in finite small displacements. Eng. Fail. Anal. **145**, 107004 (2023)
11. Galassi, S., et al.: A numerical tool for assessing the effect of foundation settlements on the stability of masonry walls. In: Gusella, V., et al. (eds.) AID Monuments 2025 – Modello, interpretazione, Progetto. Lecture Notes in Civil Engineering, vol. 806, pp. 498–509. Springer, Cham (2026)
12. Cascini, L., Gagliardo, R., Portioli, F.: LiABlock_3D: a software tool for collapse mechanism analysis of historic masonry structures. Int. J. Archit. Herit. **14**(1), 75–94 (2020)
13. Paris, V., Gobbin, F., Nannei, V.M., Resmini, M., Mirabella Roberti, G.: Distinct element method analyses for damage assessment: the Northern Spur of Valverde Bulwark in the Venetian Fortress of Bergamo. Int. J. Archit. Herit. **19**(5), 687–701 (2025)
14. Iannuzzo, A., Mallardo, V.: A novel approach to model differential settlements and crack patterns in masonry structures. Eng. Struct. **323**, 119220 (2025)
15. Iannuzzo, A., Musone, V., Ruocco, E.: A neural network-based automated methodology to identify the crack causes in masonry structures. Comput. Aided Civ. Inf. **39**(24), 3769–3785 (2024)
16. Olivieri, C., Iannuzzo, A., Fortunato, A., DeJong, M.J.: The effect of concentrated loads on open-well masonry spiral stairs. Eng. Struct. **272**, 114952 (2022)
17. Iannuzzo, A., Gesualdo, A., Olivieri, C., Montanino, A.: 3D exploration of internal stresses due to lateral loads and foundation movements in a semicircular arch. In: M. Papadrakakis, M. Fragiadakis (eds.) 9th ECCOMAS Thematic Conference on Computational Methods in Structural Dynamics and Earthquake Engineering, pp. 2476–2491. Eccomas Procedia (2023)
18. Iannuzzo, A., Montanino, A.: A limit analysis-based CASS approach for the in-plane seismic capacity of masonry façades. Int. J. Solids Struct. **289**, 112633 (2024)
19. Cusano, C., Montanino, A., Olivieri, C., Paris, V., Cennamo, C.: Graphical and analytical quantitative comparison in the domes assessment: the case of San Francesco di Paola. Appl. Sci. **11**(8), 3622 (2021)
20. Cusano, C., Angjeliu, G., Montanino, A., Zuccaro, G., Cennamo, C.: Considerations about the static response of masonry domes: a comparison between limit analysis and finite element method. Int. J. Mason. Res. Innov. **6**(4), 502–528 (2021)
21. Bouguer, P.: Sur les lignes courbes qui sont propres à former les voûtes en dôme. Académie royale des sciences, Paris, pp. 149–66 (1734)
22. Poleni, J.: Memorie istoriche della gran cvpola del tempio vaticano e de' danni de essa, e de' ristoramenti loro, divise in libri cinqve, alla santità di nostro Signore papa Benedetto XIV. Nella Stamperia del Seminario, Padova (1748)
23. Heyman, J.: On shell solution for masonry domes. Int. J. Solids Struct. **3**(2), 227–241 (1967)

24. Beltrami, E.: Sull'equilibrio delle superfici flessibili ed inestensibili. Memorie dell'Accademia delle Scienze dell'Istituto di Bologna **4**(3), 217–265 (1882)
25. Eddy, H.T.: Researches in Graphical Statics. Van Noostrand, New York (1878)
26. Levy, M.: La statique graphique et ses applications aux constructions. Gauthier-Villars Imprimeur-Librarie, Paris (1888)
27. Galassi, S., Misseri, G., Rovero, L., Tempesta, G.: Equilibrium analysis of masonry domes: on the analytical interpretation of the Eddy-Lévy graphical method. Int. J. Archit. Herit. **11**(8), 1195–1211 (2017)
28. Gerstener, F.: Handbuch der mechanik. Spurny, Prague (1831–1834)
29. O'Dwyer, D.: Funicular analysis of masonry vaults. Comput. Struct. **73**(1), 187–197 (1999)
30. Block, P., Ochsendorf, J.: Thrust network analysis: a new methodology for three-dimensional equilibrium. J. Int. Assoc. Shell Spatial Struct. **48**(155), 167–173 (2007)
31. Marmo, F., Rosati, L.: Reformulation and extension of the thrust network analysis. Comput. Struct. **182**, 104–118 (2017)
32. Avelino, R.M., Iannuzzo, A., Van Mele, T., Block, P.: Assessing the safety of vaulted masonry structures using thrust network analysis. Comput. Struct. **257**, 106647 (2021)
33. Pourfouladi, M., Pingaro, N., Valente, M.: PoliBrick plugin as a parametric tool for digital stereotomy modelling. Comput. Struct. **311**, 107722 (2025)
34. Paris, V., Olivieri, C., Adriaenssens, S.: The impact of construction on the structural design of a complex masonry curved shell. Int. J. Space Struct. **40**(2–3), 180–194 (2025)
35. Aita, D., Bruggi, M., Taliercio, A.: Limit analysis of masonry arches and domes with finite strength: funicular analysis versus stability area method. Meccanica **60**, 601–620 (2025)
36. Aita, D., Bruggi, M., Taliercio, A.: Thrust network analysis of masonry arches and domes of any stereotomy with finite compressive strength: multi-constrained minimization problem versus stability area method. In: Gabriele, S., Manuello Bertetto, A., Marmo, F., Micheletti, A. (eds.) Shell and Spatial Structures (IWSS 2023). Lecture Notes in Civil Engineering, vol. 437, pp. 150–160. Springer, Cham (2024)
37. Galassi, S., Ruggieri, N., Tempesta, G.: Ruins and archaeological artifacts: vulnerabilities analysis for their conservation through the original computer program BrickWORK. In: Aguilar, R., Torrealva, D., Moreira, S., Pando, M., Ramos, L.F. (eds.) Structural Analysis of Historical Constructions – An interdisciplinary approach, Proceedings of 11th International Conference on structural analysis of historical constructions (SAHC2018), RILEM bookseries 18, pp. 1839–1848. Springer International Publishing (2019)
38. Galassi, S., Ruggieri, N., Tempesta, G.: A novel numerical tool for seismic vulnerability analysis of ruins in archaeological sites. Int. J. Archit. Herit. **14**(1), 1–22 (2020)
39. Galassi, S., et al.: Digital survey and structural investigation on the triumphal arch of Caracalla in the archaeological site of volubilis in Morocco: retracing the timeline of collapses occurred during the 18th century earthquake. Int. J. Archit. Herit. **16**(6), 940–955 (2022)
40. Galassi, S., Zampieri, P.: A new automatic procedure for nonlinear analysis of masonry arches subjected to large support movements. Eng. Struct. **276**, 115359 (2023)
41. Di Pasquale, S.: Primo rapporto sulla Cupola di Santa Maria del Fiore. CLUSF, Firenze (1977)

Structural Stability for AR Guided Construction

Vittorio Paris(✉) and Davide Prati

Department of Engineering and Applied Sciences, University of Bergamo, Via G. Marconi 3, Dalmine, BG, Italy
vittorio.paris@unibg.it

Abstract. Numerous installations, i.e., Armadillo project, Angelus Novus, or InnixAR, demonstrate a renewed interest in masonry constructions. Despite efforts, the application of arches, vaults, and domes in current construction practices remains limited. High construction costs and limited knowledge in construction are among the reasons for their limited contemporary use. The study and the application of the scaffold-free vaulting techniques highlight even more complications. Several investigations focus on combining the potential of digital tools, such as AR technologies, with innovative design approaches to overcome existing challenges. AR could facilitate complex tasks, impact the learning curve, and provide a relevant aid in tracing operations. The research investigation focuses on demonstrating that deep control over structural investigation could support design choices and provide valuable information for using AR.

Keywords: Distinct Element Method · Augmented reality · Thin tile vaulting

1 Introduction

1.1 Research Context

The Architecture, Engineering, and Construction (AEC) sector has undergone a profound transformation since the late twentieth century, characterised by increasing specialisation of roles and progressive mechanisation of construction processes [15]. While these developments have improved efficiency in contemporary building processes, they have also resulted in a highly fragmented production chain, where coordination and management have become critical yet complex tasks [4].

The transition towards digitalisation, accelerated by the introduction of Building Information Modelling (BIM) standards such as the ISO 19650 series, has further increased the level of process integration required across design and construction phases. Within this evolving framework, the reconstruction and construction of masonry arches and vaults reveal criticalities. Unlike contemporary structural systems based on reinforced concrete or steel, masonry vaults are governed by geometry-dependent equilibrium conditions [12], requiring a high level of craftsmanship and an implicit understanding of structural behaviour [5]. These limitations are exacerbated in renovation and heritage contexts, where interventions must account for the non-standard geometry of

O. Gervasi et al. (Eds.): ICCSA 2026 Workshops, LNCS 16758, pp. 551–563, 2027.
https://doi.org/10.1007/978-3-032-30497-1_33

historical buildings, are subject to limited accessibility, and are characterised by high uncertainty.

A further critical issue is the erosion of traditional construction knowledge, particularly in highly skilled roles [7]. In the case of historical scaffold-free vaulting techniques,e.g., Thin-Tile (TT) vaulting [10], the shortage of skilled labour [7] severely hinders the development of a new generation of masons capable of applying such advanced construction techniques. Indeed, all scaffold-free vaulting methods, such as herringbone or TT vaulting, require many years of apprenticeship, during which the mason learns the secrets of these construction techniques through practice. A lack of knowledge of how to apply scaffold-free vaulting methods affects quality and productivity. It directly affects structural safety during construction, as geometric deviations can significantly alter load paths and stability, necessitating external temporary supports (Fig. 1).

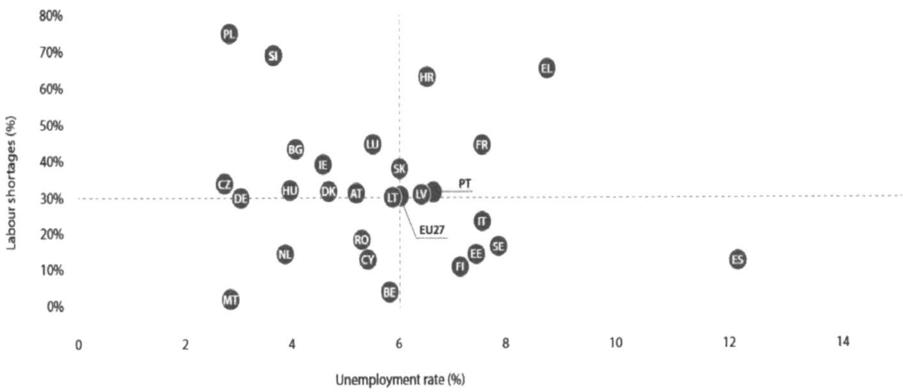

Source: Eurostat [ei_bsin_q_r2; ei_bsbu_m_r2; ei_bsse_q_r2; une_rt_m]

Fig. 1. Resume of labour shortage vs unemployment rate in the AEC sector for European countries [7].

1.2 Notes on AR as a Tool for Supporting the Construction Phase

Digital technologies, such as robotics and additive manufacturing, although promising, are not yet integrated into on-site processes; they cannot replace human behaviour in on-site construction. Many operations are still performed without digital support, leading to inefficiencies, information loss, and increased variability in execution. Among emerging technologies capable of bridging the gap between design and construction phases, unmanned aerial vehicles and Augmented Reality (AR) have attracted increasing attention. Unmanned aerial vehicles are widely used nowadays for surveying and monitoring, and provide valuable support in open environments or during the preliminary phase of design.

AR has the potential to integrate digital information directly into the physical construction environment. It enables the superimposition of georeferenced digital content onto real-world contexts, offering new possibilities for supporting on-site decision-making, geometric control, and workflow coordination. Several studies have predominantly focused on the use of AR in construction management, addressing issues related to supervision [3], performance monitoring, and safety [1]. The construction phase is the most critical yet least efficient stage of the process, as it entails the direct materialisation of the design through the coordinated actions of multiple actors, including engineers, architects, and skilled workers. In this context, AR has demonstrated potential in improving communication, coordination, and quality control. By leveraging Building information models, AR systems enable real-time design review, clash detection, and visualisation of construction sequences, thereby enhancing the understanding of complex assemblies. AR can assist in tracing geometries, controlling the positioning of individual elements, and ensuring adherence to predefined construction logic. Furthermore, AR-based systems can enhance safety by identifying potential hazards and communicating risk information directly to workers through wearable devices, thus enabling proactive risk management.

Despite the promising capabilities, the application of AR within the AEC sector remains limited. AR technologies are still evolving; the absence of shared standards limits their maturity, as well as the availability of consolidated methodological frameworks and hardware.

1.3 Technology Application of Augmented Reality for REnovation Work (TAARReW) Research

The paper reports the design methodology for defining the case study, and the partial findings of the construction approach adopted in the Technology Application of Augmented Reality for REnovation Work (TAARReW) project. TAARReW aims to assess the potential impact of AR in the construction of complex masonry structures. The research proposes a preliminary methodology for designing the assembly process that accounts for structural considerations. In the research, a specific technique was investigated: the TT vaulting, a historical, scaffold-free technique that utilises gypsum-based mortar and lightweight, thin tiles [10]. TT vaults are environmentally sustainable, light, and stiff structures [2]. Like all shells, they can withstand tremendous loads with a modest amount of material [2]. Unlike other curved structures, their construction does not require temporary supports, avoiding the need to build centering and reducing waste [11]. However, mastering the TT vaulting technique requires several years of training, and, due to the lack of trained labour, only a few master masons can apply it properly nowadays. The preservation of techniques such as TT is essential for safeguarding historical masonry shells. One of the most challenging tasks in TT techniques is tracing curved geometry in the air. To this end, the AR supported tracing by projecting the shell geometry at the exact position and providing step-by-step guidance and real-time instructions, thereby facilitating on-site construction operations.

2 Methodology

2.1 Design of the Case Study

To evaluate the design of the assembly process, a TT Lowered Vault (LV) was geometrically designed as a case study. The LV measures 1.4 × 1.4 m, with a rectangular base and is composed of more than 50 thin tiles forming the patterning shown in Fig. 2. The vault rise is about 15 cm, i.e., the ratio of rise to span is about 0.11. The adopted tile dimensions are approximately 3.5 × 12 × 25 cm, and it weighs 1.4 kg, while the mortar joints are approximately 1 cm thick.

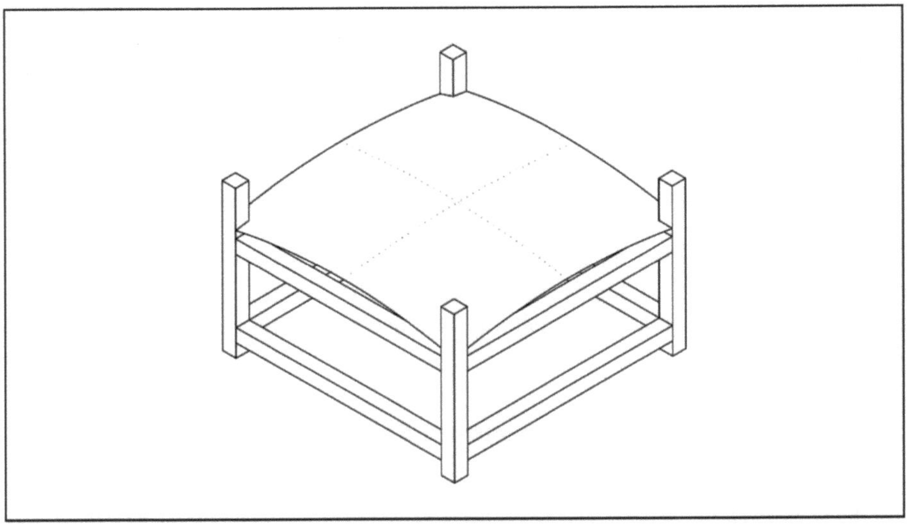

Fig. 2. Design of the lowered vault.

The overall LV design was defined, taking into account the existing literature [14], practical experience, and interviews with master masons, and aimed to highlight the characteristics of the TT technique. Two patterns (A) and (B) were evaluated. As depicted in Fig. 3, the (A) tiling pattern is a spiral, with tiles arranged to start from the center toward the edges of the shells. The tiles of the (B) were placed parallel to one another, forming several arches with the same span and different rises, see Fig. 4. For both, the structural state during construction was evaluated to assess the feasibility of safe construction.

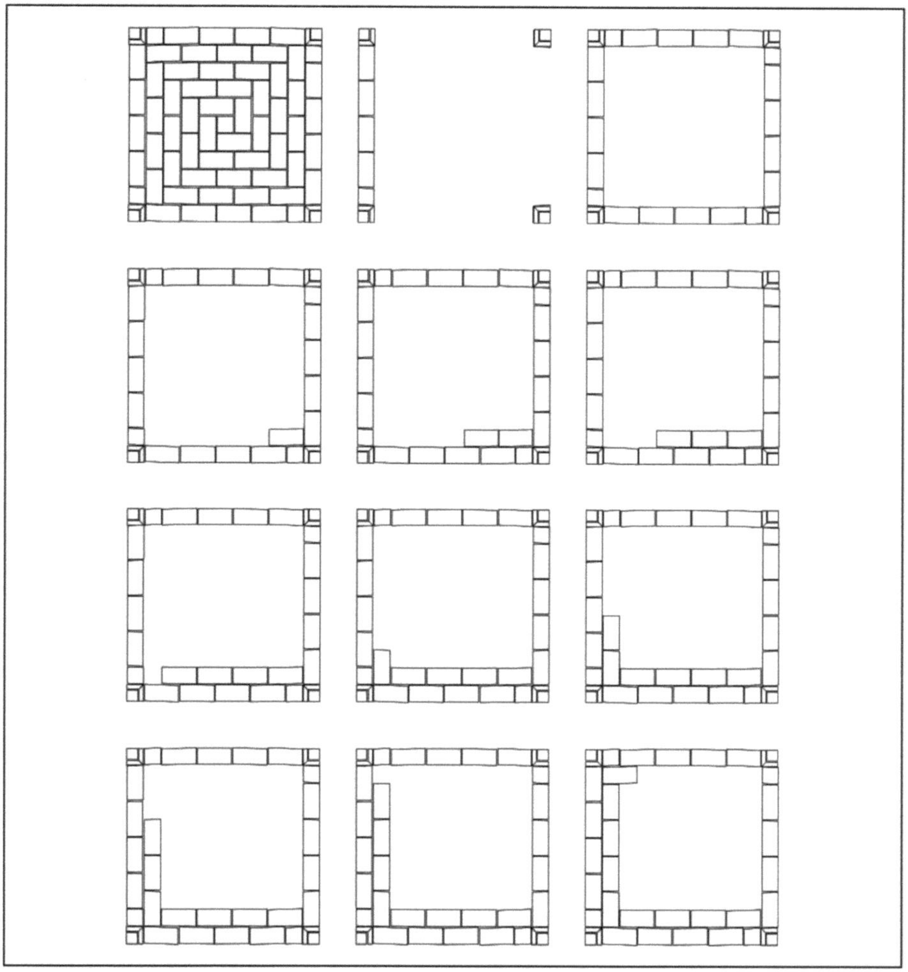

Fig. 3. Top view of the (A) pattern of the LV (Top-left). Scheme of the construction sequence (from top to bottom).

The construction sequences accounted for (A) consisted of following the spiral geometry and laying the 61 tiles to build 20 arches sequentially. These arches are classified as sub-structures. The first four arches built are the ones near the edge of the LV with maximum span, while the last tile corresponds to the central element positioned at t the crown of the vault. The arches present decreasing spans; the first four arches laid have a thickness-above-span ratio of 0.025, while the inner arches have a ratio of 0.095. The average thickness-above-span ratio is 0.048.

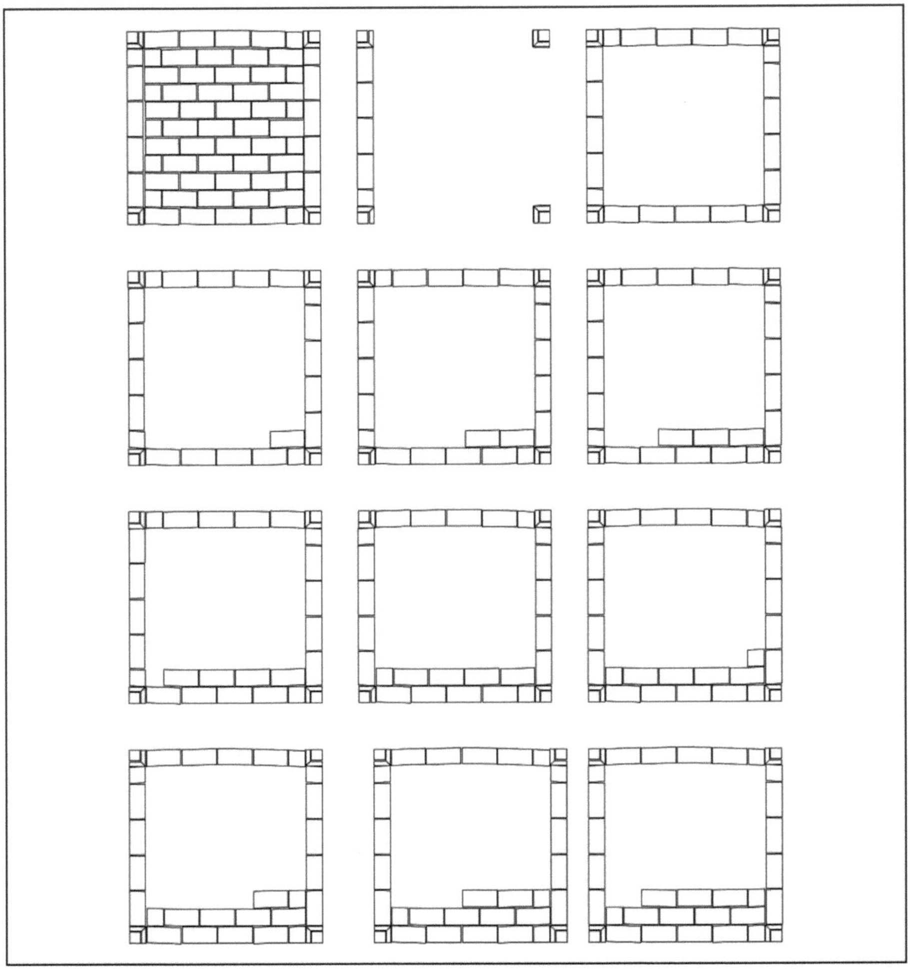

Fig. 4. Top view of the (B) pattern of the LV (Top-left). Scheme of the construction sequence (from top to bottom).

The (B) pattern instead presents arches with a constant span with a thickness-above-span ratio of 0.025. Here, the simulated construction sequence consists of laying the four external arches as shown in Fig. 4, and then placing the tiles to create parallel arches. For both patterns, the four external arches were built using centering; hence, the structural state was simulated once closed. For both LV patterns, the mortar joints were designed to be 0.5–1.0 cm thick, and no on-site tile cutting was allowed.

The (A) pattern was designed based on the TT traditional pattern, while the (B) pattern is not commonly used.

2.2 The Numerical Model

Two sets of structural analyses were performed: one assuming a Construction with Centering (CC) and the other simulating the Construction adopting the TT (CTT) techniques (b). The CC was conducted to evaluate the overall state of both patterns (A) and (B). Once the overall structural state was established, the CTT aimed to highlight the feasibility and impact of construction techniques on structural behaviour. Both CC and CTT analyses were carried out using numerical simulations with the Distinct Element Method (DEM) [6] in 3DEC 9.0 (Itasca, Minneapolis, MN, USA) [8].

The LV was described as a system of rigid bodies, in which each body is a thin tile, and, unlike other numerical methods [9], the bodies can slide, rotate, collide, or even detach from one another. The evolution of the system of rigid bodies is carried out by the explicit integration of Newton's laws of motion.

Deformable joints are modelled at the interfaces between bodies. The interfaces, tile-mortar-tile, were modelled using a spring system governed by the Mohr-Coulomb friction model with a tensile cutoff. The normal (jK_N) and the shear (jK_S) stiffness of the springs are defined by (1) and (2) [13]:

$$jK_N = \frac{E_m E_t}{l_m E_t + l_t E_m} \tag{1}$$

$$jK_s = jK_N 10^{-1} \tag{2}$$

where E denotes the Young modulus, l corresponds to the characteristic dimension of the brick, and the subscripts t and m indicate the tile and mortar, respectively. Deformations and displacements of the actual structures are lumped at the interfaces.

The values of Em and Et were obtained from the datasheet and the literature [x], accounting for the setting phenomena in Em estimation. The adopted Et value is about 3.4·1010 Pa, while Em is about 2·109 Pa after mortar hardening (i.e., for the CC analyses). For CTT simulations, the value was determined through physical testing. The jKN values range from 8·1010 Pa/m to 1.94·1011 Pa/m for CCT and CC, respectively.

Precisely as for jKN and jKS, the values of j_{ten} and j_{coh} were evaluated at different curing ages, assuming a tensile cut-off equal to the cohesion value for safety. For CTT numerical analyses, $j_{ten} = 2.5 \cdot 10^{10}$ Pa and j_{coh} $2.5 \cdot 10^{10}$ Pa [11]. The friction angle is equal to 33°. All numerical analyses were performed under self-weight only, assuming fixed blocks at the corners.

3 Results

3.1 CC Simulations

The CC numerical analyses carried out on LV (A) and (B) underline the similar behaviour. The maximum displacement is $2.35 \cdot 10^{-2}$ mm recorded in (B), while (A) displays a maximum of $2.13 \cdot 10^{-2}$ mm. The displacement maps shown in Fig. 5 indicate negligible differences attributable to TT patterns. (A) LV shows a wider area with displacement above $2.00 \cdot 10^{-2}$ mm. Due to the modest dimension of the LV, the stresses are extremely low.

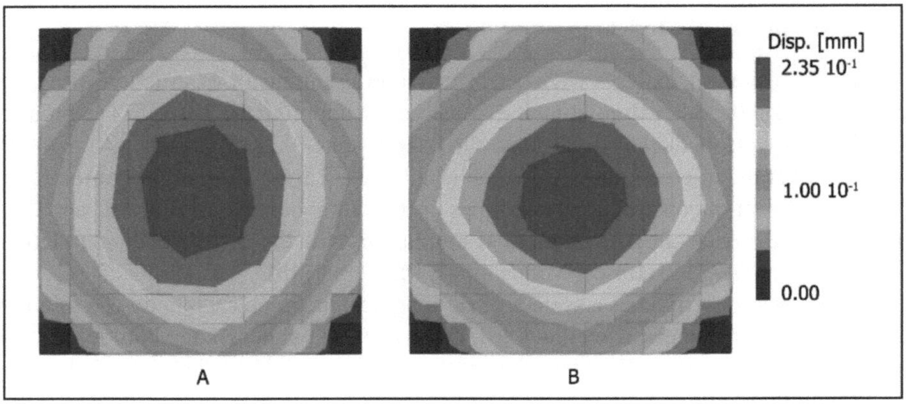

Fig. 5. Top view of the displacement map of (A) and (B) LV, CC simulations.

3.2 CTT Simulations

As mentioned in Sect. 2, CTT was carried out by investigating the possibility of building without the need for centering adopting the TT vaulting technique. The construction was divided into sequential steps, and for each step, the structural evaluation was executed. The first four steps correspond to the construction of the four external arches, because they had to be built with centering. After those for each tile, a new step was implemented, and the structural state was numerically assessed. For both LV (A and B), the displacement of the X checkpoints was recorded to observe the local response of the vault. In practice, the equilibrium of the tile during laying depends on the mortar's material properties: traditionally, Gypsum mortar is used, and the maximum weight of each tile should be less than 1.4 kg. Each thin tile weighs 1.2 kg.

The LV characterised by (A) pattern is stable, with no collapse or local failure. The displacement map changes drastically compared with the CC analyses. During the construction of the four external arches, the maximum displacements are about 0.1 mm, located near the central portion of each arch. The CCT simulations show that, once built, the arches remain stable until the inner tiles are laid. Then, the vertical displacements increase. Upon completion of construction, the maximum displacements of the external arches reach about 0.4 mm.

The CCT simulation highlighted the impact of constructing without temporary supports. During construction, the completed arches already in place provide the resources to avoid collapse, balancing the out-of-plane loads from the new inner tiles being laid. This out-of-plane displacement is visible in the displacement map shown in Fig. 6 for the (A) pattern. On the other hand, the numerical simulation of the (B) pattern shows the role of the tiling pattern and substructures in structural stability. The numerical simulation associated with (B) was conducted using the same approach as in (A). The external arches were built with external support, then the vaulting sequence continued as depicted in Fig. 4. The simulation underscores the instability of such a construction sequence. During the first steps, the behaviour of the first four arches is the same as in the (A) case, then when the second inner arch is laid, collapse occurs, see Fig. 7.

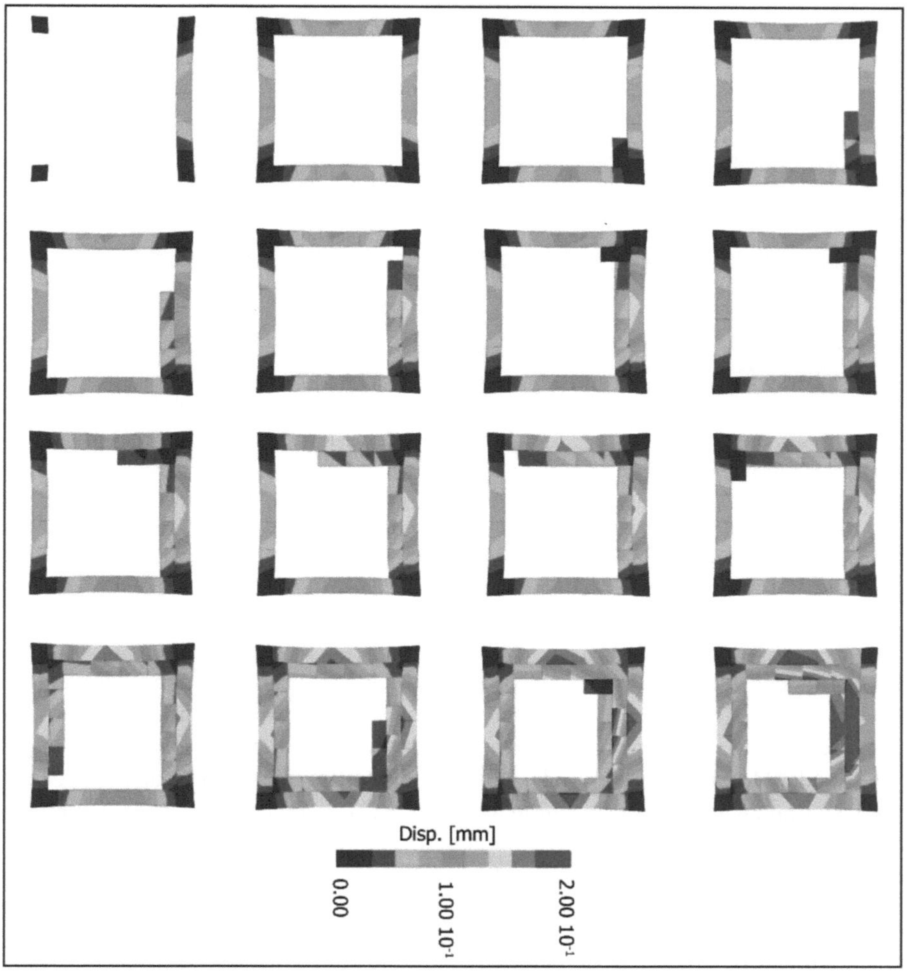

Fig. 6. Top view of displacement maps of (A) LV, CTT simulations. Starting from the top left and moving toward the bottom right, each row shows the variation in displacement according to the traditional construction sequence.

The different construction sequence affects the structural stability, drastically impacting the equilibrium. The numerical analyses show slipping at the interface between the second and third inner arches due to tensile failure. Regarding the (B) pattern, further investigation was conducted to account for the sensitivity of j_{ten} and j_{coh}. The equilibrated state was found when j_{ten} and j_{coh} were assumed equal to $6 \cdot 10^{10}$ Pa.

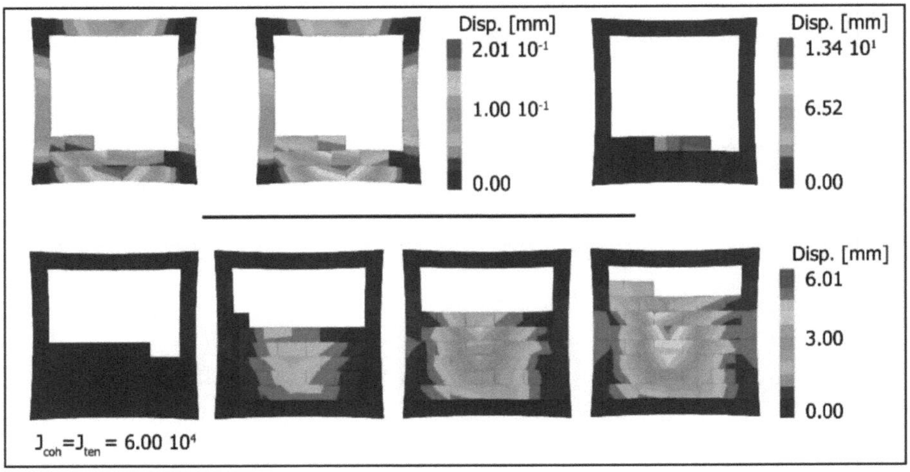

Fig. 7. Top view of displacement maps of (B) LV, CTT simulations. In the top row j_{ten} and j_{coh} equal to CCT simulation for (A) pattern. In the bottom row, the values of jten and jcoh were assumed to be more than 2 times the CCT simulation values for the (A) pattern.

3.3 The Physical Tests

The (A) model was built by a team of masons with no prior experience in vaulting, aided by AR systems. The AR supports the mason with the tracing operation. The team attended a 2-h workshop on AR and was trained in the TT vaulting technique, using standard training. i.e., tutorials, videos, audio testimonies, and manuals. The team tested the framework developed within the TAARReW. It aimed to integrate AR into the construction process as an operative system for real-time guidance and control, explicitly grounded in structural stability criteria. The approach departs from conventional AR applications limited to visualisation, and instead defines a process-driven workflow in which digital projections are generated according to both geometric and structural requirements. The very same construction sequence modelled for numerical analyses was implemented to enrich with information related to the construction sequence, which is treated as a critical parameter for the knowledge transfer.

Unlike traditional approaches, which verify stability primarily in the completed structure, this methodology explicitly accounts for the evolution of stability during construction. Based on the decomposition performed for CTT simulations, the AR system is configured to project tracing lines and positioning guides from the digital model. During the on-site construction phase, operators use AR devices (e.g., head-mounted displays or handheld devices) to visualise the projected tracing lines directly within the physical environment. Each element is manually positioned according to these projections, which indicate not only its location but also its orientation, its relation to adjacent units, and the correct sequence of construction.

Upon completion, a geometric validation was conducted by comparing the as-built structure with the original design model. This enables assessment of deviations and evaluation of the effectiveness of the AR-guided process in maintaining structural fidelity.

Overall, the proposed methodology establishes a deep relationship among design, construction, and structural behaviour, with AR serving as an interface between digital information and manual execution. The workflow enables the construction of complex geometries with enhanced accuracy, reduced reliance on formwork, and improved stability control throughout the entire building process.

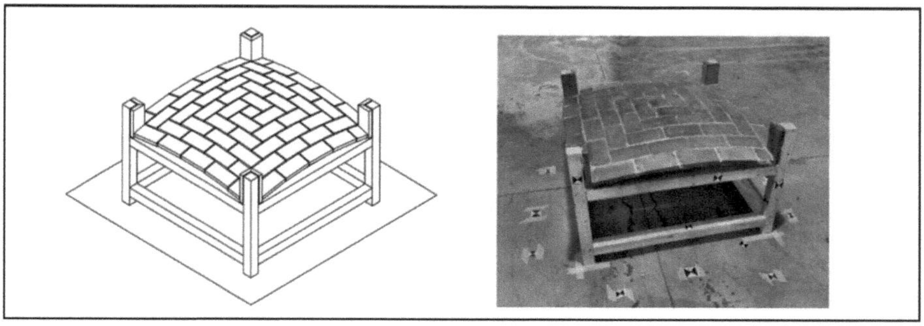

Fig. 8. Lowered vault built by T2, employing AR.

A survey using a laser scanner was conducted to assess the vault's accuracy in comparison to the digital model. The parameters were selected to ensure a survey with sufficient accuracy and precision, enabling evaluation of geometric deviations from the designed model. The scanning was performed with a resolution of 3 mm at distances beyond 10 m, a quality setting of 3X, and a reduced field of view ranging from 60° to 0° in the vertical plane and from 140° to 240° in the horizontal plane. The scan duration was reduced to 8 min and 34 s, enabling detection of both the RGB channel and the reflectance threshold. Back-office alignment was performed using both sets of markers, with those placed on each vault, to obtain accurate alignments. Mean errors on targets were also confirmed by evaluating scan statistics on individual points. Overall, based on approximately 48 million points surveyed, the average error was 1.4 mm, with a maximum of 1.7 mm and a minimum scan overlap of 32.6%.

The comparison between the point clouds and the designed geometry was carried out using Cloud Compare software, and it reveals the geometrical discrepancies. Indeed, the colour map of the geometrical discrepancy shown in Fig. 8 displays a range of -1.4 to $+3.0$ cm. Positive values in the range indicate that the measured points lie above the designed geometry, whereas negative values indicate points below it (Fig. 9).

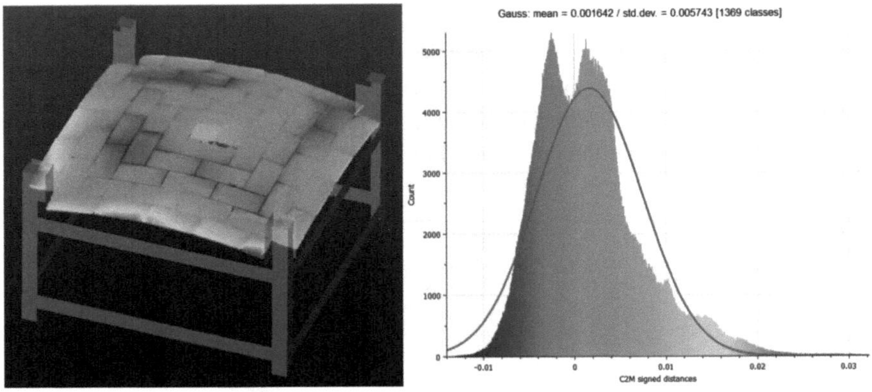

Fig. 9. Comparison of built model vs designed geometry. Left: geometrical discrepancy colour map. Right: distribution of geometrical discrepancies

4 Discussion

The research explored the integration of AR, parametric design, and historically grounded self-balanced construction principles to support the preservation of efficient scaffold- free vaulting techniques. The study uses AR-assisted guidance to execute geometrically complex tasks, thereby improving spatial accuracy and reducing dependence on highly specialised craftsmanship.

The numerical results indicate that the proposed workflow for DEM simulation has the potential to address several critical limitations that currently hinder the adoption of masonry vaulting systems. By incorporating the construction sequence into structural assessment and integrating it with AR tools, it is possible to overcome a lack of practical knowledge.

However, the present study represents an initial step within a broader experimental framework. Future work will focus on extending the validation of the proposed methodology through additional empirical testing. In particular, further analyses will be conducted to validate the CCT simulation associated with the(B) pattern. Moreover, additional tests will be completed to deepen the evaluation of performance metrics, including geometric accuracy, construction time, cognitive load, and overall process efficiency.

These forthcoming investigations will help consolidate the methodological framework and define operational best practices for implementing AR-assisted masonry construction in both experimental and real-world applications.

Funding. The project was supported by the Young Independent Research Group – CUP F55F21002580006: Technology Application of Augmented Reality for Renovation work (TAAReW) fund.

References

1. Abraham, M., Annunziata, M.: Augmented Reality is already improving worker performance (2017). https://hbr.org/2017/03/augmented-reality-is-already-improving-worker-performance

2. Adriaenssens, S., et al. (eds): Shell structures for architecture: form finding and optimisation. Routledge/Taylor & Francis Group, London ; New York (2014)
3. Alkan, I.B., Basaga, H.B.: Augmented reality technologies in construction project assembly phases. Autom. Constr. **156**, 105107 (2023). https://doi.org/10.1016/j.autcon.2023.105107
4. Barbosa, F. et al.: Reinventing Construction: A Route of Higher Productivity. McKinsey Global Institute (2017)
5. Collins, G.R.: The transfer of thin masonry vaulting from Spain to America. J. Soc. Archit. Hist. **27**(3), 176–201 (1968). https://doi.org/10.2307/988501
6. Cundall, P.A.: Formulation of a three-dimensional distinct element model—Part I. A scheme to detect and represent contacts in a system composed of many polyhedral blocks. Int. J. Rock Mech. Min. Sci. Geomech. Abstracts **25**(3), 107–116 (1988). https://doi.org/10.1016/0148-9062(88)92293-0
7. European Construction Observatory: Analytical report on skills: European Construction Observatory. European Commission (2026)
8. Itasca Consulting Group Inc.: 3DEC (2016). https://www.itascacg.com/software/3dec
9. Meloni, G., et al.: Parametric modelling and nonlinear FE analysis of trepponti bridge subjected to differential settlements. Buildings **16**(1), 47 (2025)
10. Ochsendorf, J.A.: Guastavino Vaulting: The Art of Structural Tile. Princeton Architectural Press, New York (2013)
11. Paris, V., et al.: The impact of construction on the structural design of a complex masonry curved shell. Int. J. Space Struct. **40**(2–3), 180–194 (2025). https://doi.org/10.1177/09560599251381901
12. Pingaro, N., et al.: A numerical strategy to assess the stability of curved masonry structures using a simple nonlinear truss model. Buildings **15**(13), 2226 (2025)
13. Simon, J., Bagi, K.: Discrete element analysis of the minimum thickness of oval masonry domes. Int. J. Arch. Heritage **10**(4), 457–475 (2016). https://doi.org/10.1080/15583058.2014.996921
14. Tablet, M.D.P.: Bóvedas extremeñas y alentejanas de rosca y sin cimbra
15. OECD Skills Outlook 2025: Building the Skills of the 21st Century for All. OECD Publishing, Paris (2025). https://doi.org/10.1787/26163cd3-en

VEDEM+: Enhancing Engineering Assessment of Complex Stereotomic Structures via 3DEC-to-CAD Post-Processing Workflows

Lino Cusano[1(✉)] and Antonino Iannuzzo[2]

[1] University of Sannio, Benevento, Italy
l.cusano@studenti.unisannio.it

[2] Department of Engineering, University of Sannio, Piazza Roma, 28, 82100 Benevento, Italy
aniannuzzo@unisannio.it

Abstract. The use of Distinct Element Methods such as 3DEC by Itasca is now widespread, not only for geotechnical analyses of discontinuous materials but also, in the last two decades, for the study of masonry structures. In recent years, DEM-based approaches have been successfully applied to block-based assemblies, including historical constructions and newly designed structures assembled with dry joints. In this context, while distinct element software enables the simulation of complex mechanical scenarios, it still lacks features that facilitate rapid engineering assessment and interpretation of results. This paper presents VEDEM+ (*Visualisation Environment for Distinct Element Method*), a dedicated post-processing plugin for Rhinoceros 8 developed by the authors, which enables in-depth interpretation of 3DEC results within a CAD environment. A stereotomic flat vault with complex geometry is used as a reference structural system to demonstrate how the proposed workflow enables a rapid and effective engineering assessment of structural response, with particular attention to contact force visualisation, interface failure tracking, and gap/penetration mapping across incremental loading steps.

Keywords: 3DEC · Distinct element modelling · Masonry · Flat vault · Stereotomy · Non-convex blocks · Rigid blocks · Force path · VEDEM+

1 Introduction

The construction industry is one of the main causes of global resource consumption and CO_2 emissions. For decades, attention has been placed primarily on reducing operational energy, obtaining remarkable results, while embodied emissions now represent the central environmental challenge. To address this, the Reduce-Reuse-Recycle methodology provides a rigorous framework: reuse of

O. Gervasi et al. (Eds.): ICCSA 2026 Workshops, LNCS 16758, pp. 564–580, 2027.
https://doi.org/10.1007/978-3-032-30497-1_34

structural components alone can reduce embodied carbon by 40–70% compared to recycling [7,16].

Floor systems are a primary target: in medium-to-high-rise buildings, floors account for over 40% of total structural mass and embodied emissions [6,58]. The widespread use of the reinforced concrete flat slab is both materially inefficient and incompatible with circularity, since the steel-concrete composite bond prevents component reuse or clean material recovery.

Compression-based structural systems offer an efficient alternative. Recently built examples confirm their viability: the *Striatus* footbridge and its second iteration *Phoenix* [4,17], developed at ETH Zurich, demonstrated that dry-assembled unreinforced concrete voussoirs can be fully disassembled and their material reused or recovered. Applied to floor systems, the Rippmann Floor System (RFS) [6,59] showed that compression-based funicular geometries can reduce concrete mass by 67–75% and reinforcement steel by approximately 90% compared to conventional reinforced concrete flat slabs of equivalent span. In this logic, the stereotomic flat vault system represents a historically grounded extension, combining compression-only load transfer with the inherent disassemblability of dry-assembled masonry, directly addressing circularity imperatives. Their structural behaviour, however, is considerably more complex than double-curved shells: large horizontal thrusts, sensitivity to joint geometry, and vulnerability to support displacements make numerical assessment essential [30,39,42,45]. Cracks can appear, drastically redirecting the internal flow of forces and significantly changing the thrusts exerted on the supports. However, since the seminal work of Heyman [26], it has been understood that cracks are not a structural concern [46], as arched structures can experience significant deformation until collapse, as demonstrated in experimental tests [15,20–22,25].

Several methods have been developed to assess the stability of masonry structures, using revised versions of graphic statics [12–14,49], rigid block approaches [23,24,27,44,57], continuous approaches [19,34,41], and finite element approaches based on limit analysis [8,55,56]. Flat vaults are particularly sensitive to support displacements, and several 2D and 3D models have been developed to investigate the mechanical response of masonry systems to boundary conditions [20,21,25,29,31–33]. Optimisation-based methods have also been developed to capture the 3D mechanical response in terms of internal forces, including discontinuous approaches such as Thrust Network Analysis [2,43] and continuous methods such as Membrane Equilibrium Analysis [1,40,47–49].

In general, masonry can be modelled using two main strategies [37,38]. Equivalent continuum (macro) models treat masonry as a homogeneous material with smeared properties, suitable for large-scale assessments but unable to capture local joint behaviour. Discontinuum (micro) models represent joints explicitly, as interface elements in the Finite Element Method (FEM) or contacts in the Distinct Element Method (DEM), providing accurate simulation of fracture, sliding, and opening at a higher computational cost. A numerical technique qualifies as a Distinct Element Method if it satisfies three assumptions [9]: (i) the model is composed of distinct finite elements that can be either rigid or deformable;

(ii) large displacements are permitted; (iii) contact topology is automatically tracked and updated, allowing the formation of new contacts between blocks. These features are well-suited for masonry structures, with nonlinearity concentrated in the contacts [3,37,38], and in particular for stereotomic flat vaults, whose structural behaviour is governed entirely by joint geometry and mechanics. Moreover, the limited number of blocks (order of tens) makes a full DEM micro-model computationally tractable [18].

The application of DEM to masonry structures has a well-established research lineage. Among the earliest contributions were nonlinear seismic analyses of drum columns at the Temple of Apollo at Bassae [52], subsequently validated against shaking table tests on a 1:3 marble model of a Parthenon column [51]. Masonry arches were an early focus of DEM studies: Pagnoni and Vanzi [50] and Lemos [36] investigated arch behaviour under various loading and support conditions. Subsequent work extended DEM to barrel vaults, groin vaults, and doubly-curved shells [18,39,53,54,61].

Several software environments implement the DEM for the analysis of masonry structures. 3DEC [35] is the three-dimensional extension of UDEC and is today one of the most widely used commercial platforms for structural masonry analysis. It models elements as convex polyhedra or assemblies of convex sub-blocks, treated as either rigid or deformable, with contacts automatically detected and discretised into sub-contacts at nodal intersection points. Discontinuous Deformation Analysis (DDA), introduced by [63], uses an implicit time integration strategy and models blocks with a uniform strain field, offering greater numerical stability at the cost of potential convergence difficulties in problems with frequently changing contact topologies.

This paper presents the potential offered by VEDEM+, an in-house developed plugin for Rhinoceros 8 that provides a dedicated post-processing environment for analyses carried out with 3DEC 9.0 by Itasca. The plugin addresses a series of practical limitations that users typically face when working in DEM software, particularly for the analysis of block-based structures with attention to early-stage design and engineering interpretation.

2 3DEC Software Features

As detailed above, in general, as other DEM solvers, 3DEC is selected as the modelling environment for three reasons: its three-dimensional formulation for capturing the structural response; the flexibility in assigning material properties to match the physical characteristics of real and 3D-printed specimens; and the ability to extract data and develop custom post-processing routines.

2.1 Block Modelling Options

3DEC offers three ways to model blocks based on how rigidity and internal deformation are handled.

Perfectly rigid blocks treat each block as a rigid body with six degrees of freedom. All forces are reduced to the centroid, generating resultant force and moment vectors; the equations of motion directly yield translational and rotational accelerations at each time step. This formulation requires minimal material property input, is computationally efficient, and is physically accurate whenever joint compliance vastly exceeds block compliance, as is the case for strong stone masonry or hard 3D-printed blocks.

Deformable blocks are modelled by subdividing each polyhedral block into an internal mesh of tetrahedral finite elements with uniform strain [11]. Nodal translations are the kinematic unknowns; the equations of motion are applied to nodal accelerations, allowing evaluation of internal stress distributions. For most masonry analyses, deformable blocks are treated as elastic, since nonlinear behaviour is primarily associated with joint interactions; however, elasto-plastic or damage constitutive laws can also be assigned, and user-defined models are supported through FISH.

Joined block groups are generated by merging adjacent blocks into a single kinematic unit via the `block join` command [35]. The interface between joined blocks permits no relative displacement, slip, or separation, and generates no force contribution to the equations of motion. Joining is the primary mechanism for creating non-convex geometries in 3DEC: a non-convex voussoir is decomposed into convex sub-blocks, which are then joined to behave as a single unit (Fig. 4). In the present study, deformable blocks are modelled without internal plasticity; structural nonlinearity is therefore exclusively concentrated at the un-joined dry joints.

2.2 Contact Representation and Constitutive Models

In 3DEC, contacts are modelled using the point contact approach [37], with the common plane concept used to handle contact detection efficiently [10]. Once two blocks are identified as being in contact, 3DEC defines specific sub-contacts based on the geometry of the interaction. The mechanical behaviour at each sub-contact is governed by a joint constitutive model; the most widely adopted is the Mohr-Coulomb model with tension cut-off, requiring normal stiffness k_n, shear stiffness k_s, friction angle, cohesion, and tensile strength as input parameters. Contact stiffness is a critical parameter: an excessively low normal stiffness leads to unrealistic block interpenetration, governed by:

$$\Delta\sigma_n = k_n \, \Delta u_n \tag{1}$$

3 VEDEM+: a 3DEC-to-CAD Post-Processing Plugin

Despite the widespread use of DEM tools, a practical gap remains between numerical analysis and the engineering interpretation of results. A typical displacement capacity analysis involves a sequence of tens to hundreds of incremental steps, each producing outputs such as block positions, velocities, and interface forces. Assembling these data into readable force paths, force-displacement curves, and joint-level Mohr-Coulomb failure checks, as well as visualising deformed geometries and comparing results across loading steps, requires significant manual effort that is difficult to automate within the 3DEC scripting environment alone. Moreover, the built-in visualisation tools of 3DEC offer limited parametric flexibility compared to dedicated CAD environments such as Blender [5] or Rhino [60], where extensive Python libraries are readily available.

3.1 Architecture and Data Exchange

VEDEM+ is written in C# targeting the .NET 7.0 runtime, the standard managed environment for Rhino 8 on Windows, using the RhinoCommon SDK and the Eto.Forms a cross-platform UI framework. The choice of a compiled language over Python-based scripting was deliberate: parsing large JSON files encoding the full block geometry, displacement, and contact state of models with dozens of blocks and hundreds of sub-contacts requires the performance and type safety of C#.

Communication between 3DEC and the plugin is mediated by JSON files generated at the end of each loading step by FISH scripts executed within the solver. Three categories of files are produced per step:

- **Block export**: vertex coordinates and face connectivity in the deformed configuration, together with centroid scalar quantities (displacement, velocity, applied and unbalanced forces, mass, volume).
- **Subcontact export**: for each contact pair, the list of active sub-contacts with position, area, normal and shear forces, normal and shear displacements, slip state, and gap value.
- **Penetration export**: normal gap at each sub-contact, enriched with the contact normal vector and tributary area, used to drive the oriented-disc visualisation described below.

This three-tier structure separates block-level quantities, contact-level state, and gap/penetration data, each loaded independently by the plugin. All imported steps are organised under a named layer hierarchy in Rhino (`3DEC::step_N`), enabling direct visual comparison between steps by toggling layer visibility.

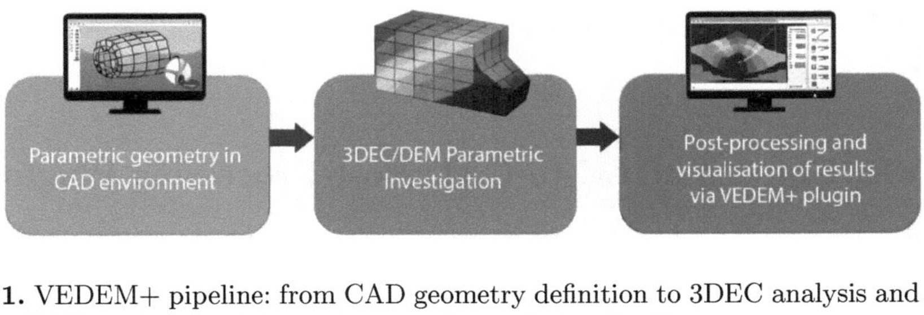

Fig. 1. VEDEM+ pipeline: from CAD geometry definition to 3DEC analysis and back to the CAD environment for post-processing and visualisation.

3.2 Modelling Workflow

The computational pipeline used to model and analyse the flat vault consists of three stages, summarised in Fig. 1. The vault geometry is defined parametrically in a CAD environment, modelling voussoirs, supporting abutments, and connection elements. Non-convex voussoirs are decomposed into convex sub-blocks for compatibility with 3DEC's contact detection (Fig. 4); once imported, sub-blocks are rejoined via the `block join` command to reconstruct the original non-convex shapes (Fig. 3a). Analyses are performed directly in 3DEC, including incremental displacement capacity, load-bearing or dynamic tests (Fig. 3b). This sequence of results is then exported back to Rhino, where VEDEM+ is used to visualise and interpret the structural response (Fig. 5).

Fig. 2. A non-convex block reconstructed by joining two convex sub-blocks. When blocks are modelled as rigid, the red interface is locked and no forces can be derived from the 3DEC calculation. (Color figure online)

3.3 Visualisation Features

VEDEM+ provides four main visualisation modules, each addressing a specific analytical need.

Block Scalar Heatmaps. Each block is rendered as a triangulated mesh and coloured according to any scalar field available in the data model: displacement components and magnitude, velocity, unbalanced force, applied force, mass, or volume. A sequential five-stop palette (blue to red) is applied, normalised to the observed range within the current step, with min/max values displayed in the legend panel (Fig. 3b).

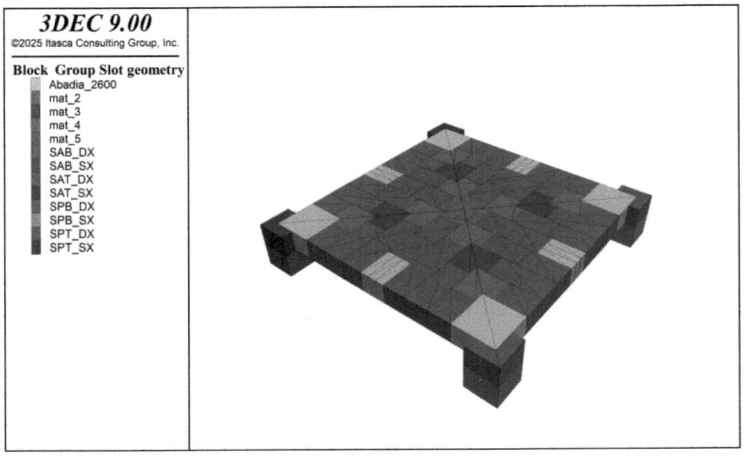

(a)

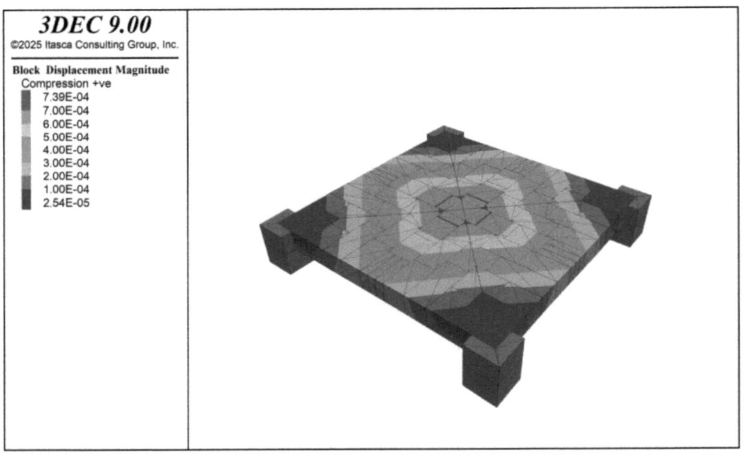

(b)

Fig. 3. (a) Non-convex block geometry reconstructed in 3DEC by joining convex sub-blocks via the `block join` command, with each block family identified by a distinct colour; (b) typical 3DEC displacement heatmap at a given loading step: while the solver output is complete, extracting engineering-relevant quantities requires significant additional effort.

Contact and Subcontact Force Visualisation. At the contact level, the plugin draws the resultant normal force N, tangential force T, and total resultant R as scaled line segments anchored at the centre of pressure of each interface. The sign convention follows 3DEC's native convention: positive normal force indicates compression. Normal components are shown in blue, tangential components in red, providing an immediate visual assessment of load paths through the joint network (Fig. 5). At the subcontact level, forces are rendered as coloured spheres or oriented flat discs, with colour encoding the chosen scalar quantity through the same sequential heatmap.

Gap and Penetration Mapping. For each sub-contact, the normal gap g is defined as:

$$g = a_{\text{ini}} + u_n \quad (2)$$

where a_{ini} is the initial mechanical aperture and u_n is the accumulated normal displacement (positive in tension). A negative gap indicates interpenetration (closed, loaded contact); a positive gap indicates joint opening. Each sub-contact is rendered as a flat circular disc oriented with its axis parallel to the contact normal, with radius computed as $r = \sqrt{A_{\text{sc}}/\pi}$, ensuring that adjacent discs tessellate the joint surface without overlap. A divergent colour scheme encodes the gap value: penetrating contacts use a blue-to-red heatmap; opening contacts are rendered in blue tones (Fig. 7). This visualisation proved particularly effective for tracking the progressive detachment of joint faces as support displacement was incremented.

Interface Force History and Mohr-Coulomb Tracking. The Interfaces tab constitutes the primary analytical module for investigating per-contact force histories across the loading sequence. Interactive handles, represented by polygon hulls projected onto each contact plane, are generated at the centre of pressure of each

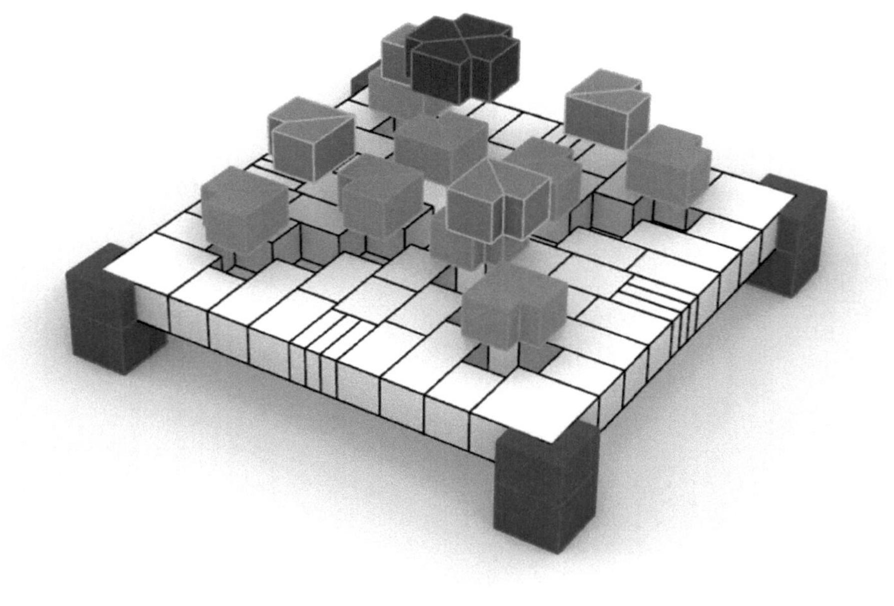

Fig. 4. A 3D view of the four non-convex block families, each identified by a distinct colour.

interface. Selecting a handle opens an Interface detail dialog displaying real-time metrics for the active step: resultant forces ($|N|$, $|T|$, $|R|$), the T/N ratio, torque, and the centre of pressure coordinates.

The Charts tab provides four synchronised plots visualising the evolution of N, T, R, and the T/N friction ratio across all loaded steps (Fig. 6). The friction ratio chart includes a dashed red line representing the Mohr-Coulomb failure threshold $\tan\phi$, where ϕ is automatically extracted from the sub-contact data but can be manually overridden to trigger an immediate re-rendering. An interactive crosshair tooltip snaps to the nearest data point and displays exact values at each step, removing the need to export data to a spreadsheet for inspection. A batch export function iterates automatically over every contact in the model, producing four PNG charts and one structured CSV file per interface, eliminating the need to open each dialog individually.

4 Application to the Flat Vault

The flat vault used as a structural case study to demonstrate the capabilities of VEDEM+ is a simplified digital model (Fig. 4) of a real structure built in Spain by the construction company Mass Piedra [62] and designed by Prof. Enrique Rabasa of the Politecnica de Madrid. As part of an ongoing collaboration, the research group at the University of Sannio was invited to assess the structural response of the vault in situ. A dedicated paper presenting the full-scale analysis on the real model and structural behaviour is forthcoming. In the present work, the geometry serves exclusively as a reference application to demonstrate how VEDEM+ can provide engineering-relevant insight in a real-case scenario. The

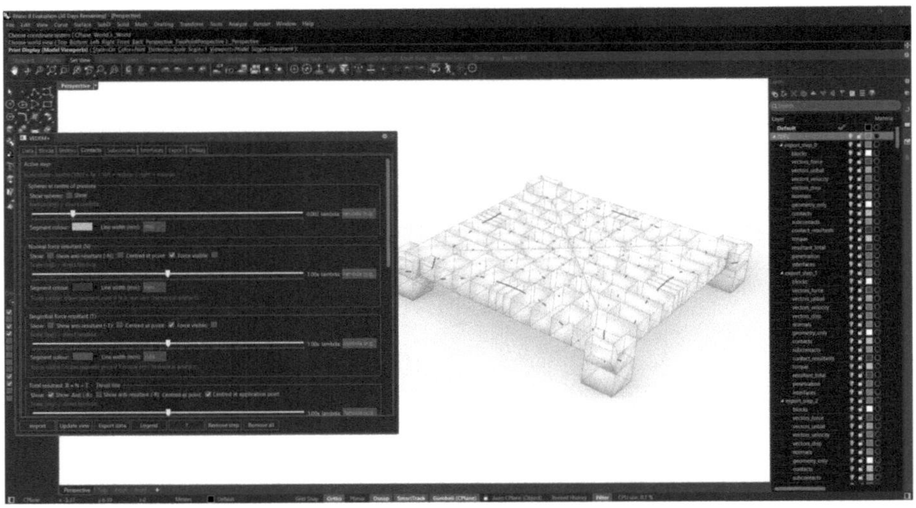

Fig. 5. VEDEM+ visualisation of contact interface resultant forces: arching behaviour visible from top and lateral views, unavailable in the native 3DEC environment.

four families of non-convex blocks are identified by distinct colours in Fig. 4; the model is imported into 3DEC, where dedicated scripts automatically join the convex sub-blocks and set up the analysis (Fig. 3).

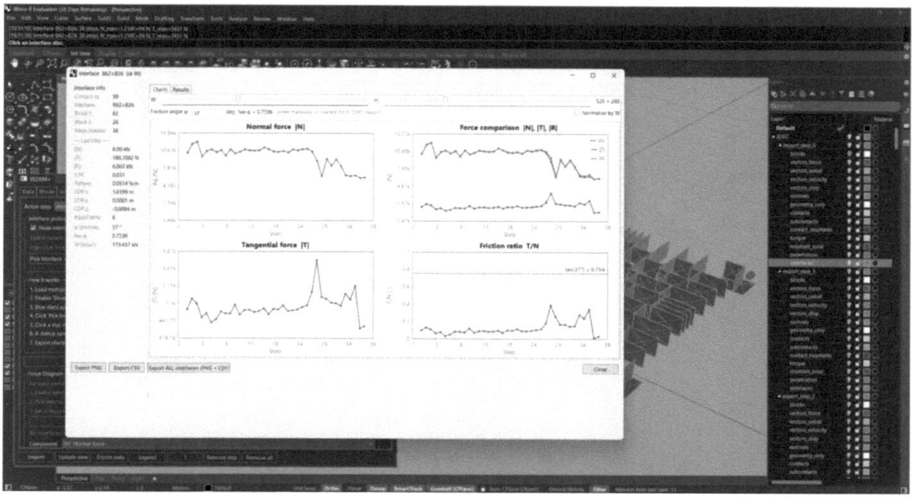

Fig. 6. VEDEM+ interface force history for a user-selected contact: evolution of N, T, R, and T/N across loading steps, with the Mohr-Coulomb threshold ($\tan\phi$) shown as a dashed red line. (Color figure online)

Four structural characteristics make the DEM analysis of flat vaults more demanding than other standard masonry typologies and motivate the use of a dedicated post-processing workflow.

Sensitivity to Joint Geometry: the stereotomy is designed to activate internal force paths orthogonal to the joints. Small deviations from the designed geometry, due to fabrication tolerances or assembly imperfections, can significantly alter the internal force distribution and structural stability [26,28].

Large Horizontal Thrusts: flat vaults generate very large horizontal thrusts relative to their vertical load-carrying capacity. The thrust-to-weight ratio is substantially higher than that of a typical semicircular arch of the same span, making stability highly sensitive to the stiffness and displacement of the lateral supports.

Coupled Sliding and Hinging Mechanisms: flat vault collapse typically involves a combination of sliding and hinging at block interfaces. The relative contribution of each mechanism depends on the joint friction angle and contact stiffnesses.

Sensitivity to Support Displacements: even small outward movements of the abutments can trigger collapse, requiring careful tracking of interface force evolution throughout the loading sequence.

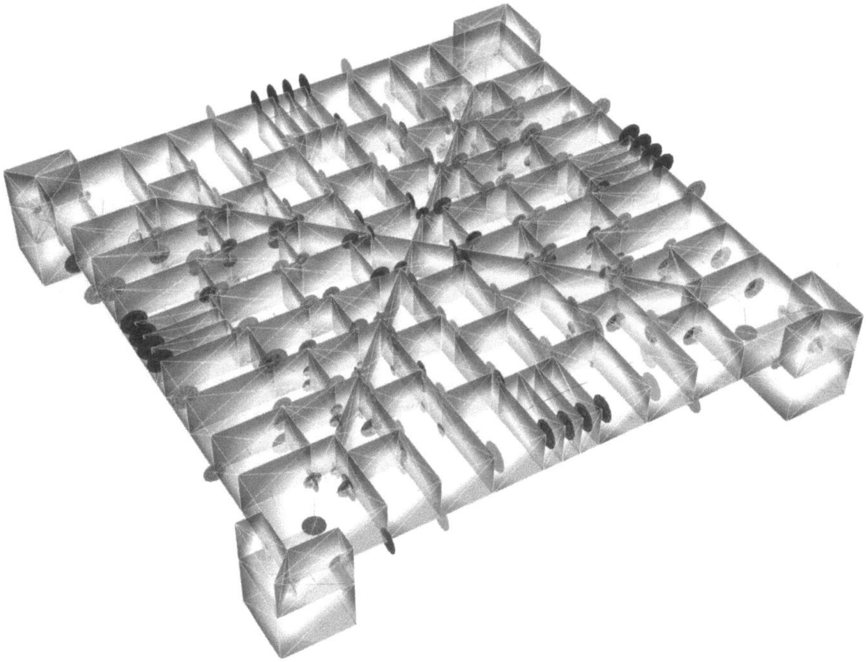

Fig. 7. VEDEM+ gap and penetration mapping: oriented discs are placed at subcontact positions where block interpenetration exceeds a user-defined threshold, encoding contact force magnitude via a blue-to-red colour scale, with warmer tones indicating higher compressive forces; joint opening is identified on the opposite face regions. (Color figure online)

VEDEM+ was used systematically throughout the analysis. The block geometry export allowed the deformed shape of the assembly to be visualised at each settlement increment alongside the original CAD model, providing an intuitive check of physical consistency. The subcontact force visualisation was used to track the evolution of the internal force distribution as support displacement was incremented; the normal force heatmap on joint faces provided a spatial reading of compression trajectories, whose progressive concentration at the extrados and intrados of selected joints is the signature of hinge formation Fig. 8. The gap and penetration maps were instrumental in identifying the sequence of joint openings, allowing the redistribution of internal forces to be followed step by step and correlated with the displacement histories exported by 3DEC (Fig. 7). The interface force history charts enabled direct verification of whether the T/N ratio at each joint remained within the Mohr-Coulomb cone throughout the loading sequence, providing a rigorous, step-resolved picture of the sliding-to-hinging transition.

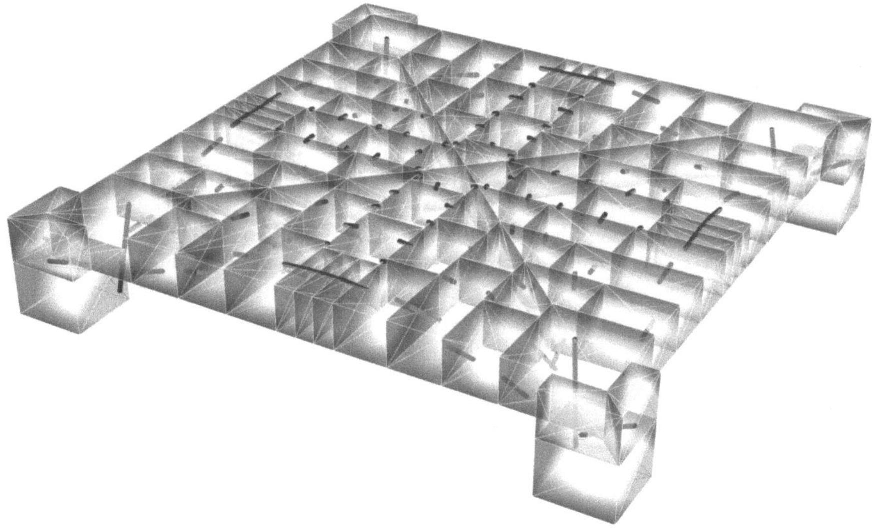

Fig. 8. VEDEM+ visualisation of contact resultant forces across the flat vault assembly.

5 Conclusions

This paper has presented VEDEM+, a post-processing plugin for Rhinoceros 8 developed to bridge the output of the 3DEC solver with a fully controllable CAD environment. The plugin addresses a practical gap in existing DEM workflows: while 3DEC is a mature and capable solver, its native visualisation tools are not well suited to the engineering interpretation of incremental analyses of block-based masonry structures. The plugin provides four main capabilities: block scalar heatmaps for deformed geometry inspection; contact and subcontact force visualisation with resultant diagrams; gap and penetration mapping via oriented discs; and per-interface force history tracking with integrated Mohr-Coulomb failure assessment. Applied to the analysis of a stereotomic flat vault, VEDEM+ enabled a step-resolved interpretation of the sliding-to-hinging transition, the progressive formation of hinges, and the redistribution of internal forces in response to support displacement. Current limitations include the absence of zone-level stress visualisation for deformable blocks, per-step colour normalisation rather than global normalisation across the loading sequence, and a file-based data exchange that introduces overhead for large models. Future developments will address these limitations through zone data export, global heatmap normalisation, and a live connection between 3DEC and Rhino via a shared memory buffer or local socket. A further planned development is a standalone viewer, independent of any specific CAD environment, allowing engineers to inspect and interrogate DEM results.

Acknowledgments. The authors warmly thank Prof. Enrique Rabasa and Catalina Sànchez Robles of Mass Piedra for generously sharing the geometry of the flat vault and for their kind collaboration. The real-scale experience on the vault at Caravaca de la Cruz, Spain, motivated the intensive development of VEDEM+ as a tool for detailed engineering assessment of structural response; both the features implemented and those planned for future releases were directly inspired by the practical needs encountered during that experience, which was therefore adopted as the reference case study given its geometric complexity. This research is funded by the Italian Ministry of University and Research through the Programme "Rita Levi Montalcini for Young Researchers" (FFO 2020). The authors gratefully acknowledge Itasca for providing the 3DEC software under the Educational Discount Agreement.

References

1. Angelillo, M., Iannuzzo, A., Montanino, A.: Discretised continuum approaches: from continuum to dis-continuum. In: Discrete Computational Mechanics of Masonry Structures, pp. 95–163. Springer (2023). https://doi.org/10.1007/978-3-031-32476-5_3
2. Avelino, R.M., Iannuzzo, A., Van Mele, T., Block, P.: Assessing the safety of vaulted masonry structures using thrust network analysis. Comput. Struct. **257**, 106647 (2021). https://doi.org/10.1016/j.compstruc.2021.106647
3. Bagi, K., Angelillo, M.: Discrete Computational Mechanics of Masonry Structures, vol. 609. Springer Nature (2023). https://doi.org/10.1007/978-3-031-32476-5
4. Bhooshan, S., Dell'Endice, A., Ranaudo, F., Van Mele, T., Block, P.: Unreinforced concrete masonry for circular construction. Architectural Intelligence **3**(1), 7 (2024). https://doi.org/10.1007/s44223-023-00043-y
5. Blender Foundation: Blender - a 3D modelling and rendering package. Blender Foundation, Amsterdam (2024). http://www.blender.org
6. Block, P.: Strength through geometry and material effectivenes, pp. 72–78. (2022). no open-access link available
7. Brütting, J., De Wolf, C., Fivet, C.: The reuse of load-bearing components. In: IOP Conference Series: Earth and Environmental Science. vol. 323, p. 012025 (2019). https://doi.org/10.1088/1755-1315/323/1/012025,
8. Buzzetti, M., Pingaro, N., Milani, G.: Automatic detection of local collapse mechanisms in historical masonry buildings: Fast and robust fe upper bound limit analysis. Eng. Fail. Anal. **170**, 109310 (2025). https://doi.org/10.1016/j.engfailanal.2025.109310
9. Cundall, P.A.: A computer model for simulating progressive, large-scale movements in blocky rock systems. In: Proceedings of the Symposium of the International Society of Rock Mechanics. vol. 1, pp. II–8. Nancy, France (1971). https://www.researchgate.net/publication/285299738
10. Cundall, P.A.: Formulation of a three-dimensional distinct element model – Part I: A scheme to detect and represent contacts in a system composed of many polyhedral blocks. Int. J. Rock Mech. Mining Sci. Geomech. Abstracts **25**(3), 107–116 (1988). https://doi.org/10.1016/0148-9062(88)92293-0
11. Cundall, P.A., Strack, O.: A discrete numerical model for granular assemblies. Géotechnique **29**(1), 47–65 (1979). https://doi.org/10.1680/geot.1979.29.1.47

12. Cusano, C., Angjeliu, G., Montanino, A., Zuccaro, G., Cennamo, C.: Considerations about the static response of masonry domes: A comparison between limit analysis and finite element method. Int. J. Masonry Res. Innov **6**(4), 502–528 (2021). https://doi.org/10.1504/IJMRI.2021.118835
13. Cusano, C., Montanino, A., Cennamo, C., Zuccaro, G., Angelillo, M.: Geometry and stability of a double-shell dome in four building phases: the case study of Santa Maria Alla Sanità in Naples. Int. J. Architectural Heritage **17**(2), 362–388 (2023). https://doi.org/10.1080/15583058.2021.1922954
14. Cusano, C., Montanino, A., Olivieri, C., Paris, V., Cennamo, C.: Graphical and analytical quantitative comparison in the Domes assessment: The case of San Francesco di Paola. Appl. Sci. **11**(8), 3622 (2021). https://doi.org/10.3390/app11083622
15. Daponte, P., De Vito, L., Iannuzzo, A., Monaco, M., Neyestani, A., Picariello, F.: Low-cost marked tracking monitoring system for 3D-scaled masonry models. In: 2024 IEEE International Workshop on Metrology for Living Environment (MetroLivEnv), pp. 172–177. IEEE (2024). https://doi.org/10.1109/MetroLivEnv60384.2024.10615826
16. De Wolf, C., Hoxha, E., Fivet, C.: Comparison of environmental assessment methods when reusing building components: A case study. Sustain. Cities Soc. **61**, 102322 (2020). https://doi.org/10.1016/j.scs.2020.102322
17. Dell'Endice, A., Bouten, S., Van Mele, T., Block, P.: Structural design and engineering of striatus, an unreinforced 3d-concrete-printed masonry arch bridge. Eng. Struct. **292**, 116534 (2023). https://doi.org/10.1016/j.engstruct.2023.116534
18. Dell'Endice, A., Iannuzzo, A., DeJong, M.J., Van Mele, T., Block, P.: Modelling imperfections in unreinforced masonry structures: Discrete element simulations and scale model experiments of a pavilion vault. Eng. Struct. **228**, 111499 (2021). https://doi.org/10.1016/j.engstruct.2020.111499
19. Fortunato, A., Gesualdo, A., Mascolo, I., Monaco, M.: P-Bézier energy optimisation for elastic solutions of masonry-like panels. Int. J. Masonry Res. Innov. **7**(1–2), 113–125 (2022). https://doi.org/10.1504/IJMRI.2022.119857
20. Galassi, S.: An alternative approach for limit analysis of masonry arches on moving supports in finite small displacements. Eng. Fail. Anal. **145**, 107004 (2023). https://doi.org/10.1016/j.engfailanal.2022.107004
21. Galassi, S., Misseri, G., Rovero, L.: Capacity assessment of masonry arches on moving supports in large displacements: Numerical model and experimental validation. Eng. Fail. Anal. **129**, 105700 (2021). https://doi.org/10.1016/j.engfailanal.2021.105700
22. Galassi, S., Misseri, G., Rovero, L., Tempesta, G.: Failure modes prediction of masonry voussoir arches on moving supports. Eng. Struct. **173**, 706–717 (2018). https://doi.org/10.1016/j.engstruct.2018.07.015
23. Galassi, S., et al.: A numerical tool for assessing the effect of foundation settlements on the stability of masonry walls. In: International Conference of Architecture, Engineering, and Design for Monuments Safeguarding, pp. 498–509. Springer (2025). https://doi.org/10.1007/978-3-032-15387-6_34
24. Galassi, S., Tempesta, G.: Safety assessment of masonry undamaged and damaged arches subjected to gravitational loads and horizontal forces. a numeric procedure to identify the optimal thrust line. Int. J. Solids Struct. **301**, 112943 (2024). https://doi.org/10.1016/j.ijsolstr.2024.112943
25. Galassi, S., Zampieri, P.: A new automatic procedure for nonlinear analysis of masonry arches subjected to large support movements. Eng. Struct. **276**, 115359 (2023). https://doi.org/10.1016/j.engstruct.2022.115359

26. Heyman, J.: The stone skeleton. Int. J. Solids Struct. **2**(2), 249–279 (1966). https://doi.org/10.1016/0020-7683(66)90018-7
27. Hua, Y., Buzzetti, M., Pingaro, N., da Silva, L.C., Milani, G.: A computerized tool for the kinematic limit analysis of 2d masonry structures failing on a tilting table. SoftwareX **30**, 102180 (2025). https://doi.org/10.1016/j.softx.2025.102180
28. Huerta, S.: Wedges and Plate Bandes Mechanical Theories After De La Hire En L Architrave Le Plancher La Plate Forme Nouvelle Histoire De La Construction Pag 405 435 Presses Polytechniques Et Universitaires Romandes (2012). Wedges and plate-bandes: mechanical theories after de la hire
29. Iannuzzo, A., Musone, V., Ruocco, E.: A neural network-based automated methodology to identify the crack causes in masonry structures. Comput.-Aided Civil Infrastructure Eng. **39**(24), 3769–3785 (2024). https://doi.org/10.1111/mice.13311
30. Iannuzzo, A., Bagi, K., Herczeg, M., Mousavian, E.: Equilibrium analysis of 2d complex discrete assemblies modelled using cracking blocks with non-dilatant interfaces. In: Proceedings of the Fifteenth International Conference on Computational Structures Technology, pp. 1–14. Civil-Comp Press (2024)
31. Iannuzzo, A., Gesualdo, A., Olivieri, C., Montanino, A.: 3d exploration of internal stresses due to lateral loads and foundation movements in a semi-circular arch. In: COMPDYN Proceedings, pp. 2476–2491 (2023). https://www.scopus.com/inward/record.uri?eid=2-s2.0-85175847244&partnerID=40&md5=8edeef8ffd0b5e72961ce432ffed7a61
32. Iannuzzo, A., Mallardo, V.: A novel approach to model differential settlements and crack patterns in masonry structures. Eng. Struct. **323**, 119220 (2025). https://doi.org/10.1016/j.engstruct.2024.119220
33. Iannuzzo, A., Mele, T.V., Block, P.: Stability and load-bearing capacity assessment of a deformed multi-span masonry bridge using the PRD method. Int. J. Masonry Res. Innov. **6**(4), 422–445 (2021). https://doi.org/10.1504/IJMRI.2021.118842
34. Iannuzzo, A., Montanino, A.: A limit analysis-based CASS approach for the in-plane seismic capacity of masonry façades. Int. J. Solids Struct. **289**, 112633 (2024). https://doi.org/10.1016/j.ijsolstr.2023.112633
35. Itasca Consulting Group: 3DEC — Three-Dimensional Distinct Element Code, Version 7.0. Itasca Consulting Group, Minneapolis, Minnesota (2020). https://www.itascacg.com/software/3dec
36. Lemos, J.V.: Assessment of the ultimate load of a masonry arch using discrete elements. Computer Methods in Structural Masonry **3**, 294–302 (1995). no open-access link available
37. Lemos, J.V.: Discrete element modeling of masonry structures. Int. J. Architectural Heritage **1**(2), 190–213 (2007). https://doi.org/10.1080/15583050601176868
38. Lourenço, P.B.: Computations on historic masonry structures. Prog. Struct. Mat. Eng. **4**(3), 301–319 (2002). https://doi.org/10.1002/pse.120
39. McInerney, J., DeJong, M.J.: Discrete element modelling of groin vault displacement capacity. Int. J. Architectural Heritage **9**(8), 1037–1049 (2015). https://doi.org/10.1080/15583058.2014.923953
40. Montanino, A., Iannuzzo, A.: A quadrilateral plate-type finite element to model stress singularities in no-tension materials. Comput. Methods Appl. Mech. Eng. **432**, 117433 (2024). https://doi.org/10.1016/j.cma.2024.117433
41. Montanino, A., Olivieri, C., Zuccaro, G., Angelillo, M.: From stress to shape: Equilibrium of cloister and cross vaults. Appl. Sci. **11**(9), 3846 (2021). https://doi.org/10.3390/app11093846

42. Mousavian, E., Kibriya, G., Bagi, K., Iannuzzo, A.: Multi-surface plasticity model for analysis of complex interlocking assemblies. In: Structures and Architecture, pp. 893–900. CRC Press (2025)
43. Nodargi, N.A., Bisegna, P.: Thrust line analysis revisited and applied to optimization of masonry arches. Int. J. Mech. Sci. **179**, 105690 (2020). https://doi.org/10.1016/j.ijmecsci.2020.105690
44. Nodargi, N.A., Bisegna, P.: A unifying computational approach for the lower-bound limit analysis of systems of masonry arches and buttresses. Eng. Struct. **221**, 110999 (2020). https://doi.org/10.1016/j.engstruct.2020.110999
45. Ochsendorf, J.A.: The masonry arch on spreading supports. Struct. Eng. **84**(2), 29–35 (2006). https://www.istructe.org/journal/volumes/volume-84-(2006)/issue-2/the-masonry-arch-on-spreading-supports/
46. Ochsendorf, J.A.: Collapse of masonry structures (2002). Ph.D. thesis
47. Olivieri, C.: FORMERLY-Math: Constrained form-finding through membrane equilibrium analysis in Mathematica. Softw. Impacts **16**, 100512 (2023). https://doi.org/10.1016/j.simpa.2023.100512
48. Olivieri, C., Cocking, S., Fabbrocino, F., Iannuzzo, A., Placidi, L., Adriaenssens, S.: Seismic capacity of purely compressed shells based on airy stress function. Continuum Mech. Thermodyn. **37**(2), 21 (2025). https://doi.org/10.1007/s00161-024-01350-z
49. Olivieri, C., Fortunato, A., DeJong, M.: A new membrane equilibrium solution for masonry railway bridges: the case study of Marsh Lane Bridge. Int. J. Masonry Res. Innov. **6**(4), 446–471 (2021). https://doi.org/10.1504/IJMRI.2021.118831
50. Pagnoni, T., Vanzi, I.: Experimental and numerical study of the seismic response of block structures (1995). no open-access link available
51. Papantonopoulos, C., Psycharis, I., Papastamatiou, D., Lemos, J., Mouzakis, H.: Numerical prediction of the earthquake response of classical columns using the distinct element method. Earthquake Eng. Struct. Dyn. **31**(9), 1699–1717 (2002). https://doi.org/10.1002/eqe.185
52. Papastamatiou, D., Psycharis, I.: Seismic response of unbraced multidrum columns. Earthquake Eng. Struct. Dyn. **22**(10), 857–872 (1993). https://doi.org/10.1002/eqe.4290221004
53. Paris, V., Gobbin, F., Nannei, V., Resmini, M., Mirabella Roberti, G.: Distinct element method analyses for damage assessment: The northern spur of valverde bulwark in the venetian fortress of bergamo. Int. J. Archit. Heritage **19**(5), 687–701 (2025). https://doi.org/10.1080/15583058.2024.2345701. cited by: 3
54. Paris, V., Olivieri, C., Adriaenssens, S.: The impact of construction on the structural design of a complex masonry curved shell. Int. J. Space Struct. **40**(2–3), 180–194 (2025). https://doi.org/10.1177/09560599251381901. cited by: 3; All Open Access, Hybrid Gold Open Access
55. Pingaro, N., Buzzetti, M., Milani, G.: Advanced FE nonlinear numerical modeling to predict historical masonry vaults failure: Assessment of risk collapse for a long span cloister vault heavily loaded at the crown by means of a general-purpose numerical protocol. Eng. Fail. Anal. **167**, 109070 (2025). https://doi.org/10.1016/j.engfailanal.2024.109070
56. Pingaro, N., Cardani, G., Coronelli, D., Milani, G.: On the stability of masonry arches through limit analysis and a nonlinear finite element-based method. In: International Conference on Protection of Historical Constructions, pp. 201–208. Springer (2025). https://doi.org/10.1007/978-3-031-87316-4_25

57. Pourfouladi, M., Pingaro, N., Valente, M.: Polibrick plugin as a parametric tool for digital stereotomy modelling. Comput. Struct. **311**, 107722 (2025). https://doi.org/10.1016/j.compstruc.2025.107722
58. Ranaudo, F., Van Mele, T., Block, P.: A low-carbon, funicular concrete floor system: Design and engineering of the HiLo floors. Tech. rep., ETH Zurich, Block Research Group (2021). https://doi.org/10.2749/ghent.2021.2016, https://www.research-collection.ethz.ch/handle/20.500.11850/479967
59. Rippmann, M., Liew, A., Van Mele, T., Block, P.: Design, fabrication and testing of discrete 3D sand-printed floor prototypes. Mater. Today Commun. **15**, 254–259 (2018). https://doi.org/10.1016/j.mtcomm.2018.08.002
60. Robert McNeel & Associates: Rhinoceros 3D. Robert McNeel & Associates, Seattle, WA (2023). https://www.rhino3d.com
61. Roberti, G.M., Ruscica, G., Paris, V.: From the herringbone dome by sangallo to the serlio floor of emy (and beyond). Curved Layered Struct. **8**(1), 259–270 (2021). https://doi.org/10.1515/cls-2021-0023. cited by: 3; All Open Access, Gold Open Access, Green Open Access
62. Sánchez Robles, C.: Mass piedra — coordinadora. https://masspiedra.org/ (2025). Accessed 2025
63. Shi, G.H.: Discontinuous Deformation Analysis: A New Numerical Model for the Statics and Dynamics of Deformable Block Structures. Ph.D. thesis, University of California, Berkeley (1992). https://escholarship.org/uc/item/3027n5vk

Nonlinear Analysis of Arches: A Comparison Among Three Recent Methodologies Applied to a Multi-ring Model

Gandolfi Alessandro[1(✉)], Hua Yiwei[1], Pingaro Natalia[1,2], and Milani Gabriele[1]

[1] Department of Architecture, Built Environment and Construction Engineering, Politecnico di Milano, Piazza Leonardo da Vinci 32, Milan, Italy
alessandro.gandolfi@polimi.it

[2] European Centre for Training and Research in Earthquake Engineering (EUCENTRE Foundation), 27100 Pavia, Italy

Abstract. The structural assessment of masonry arches is challenging due to their heterogeneous composition and highly nonlinear response. This is particularly relevant in for multi-ring arches where inter-ring joints and interlocking govern the sliding, hinging, and ring separation mechanisms that simplified homogeneous approaches cannot capture. This paper compares three recent heterogeneous strategies for the nonlinear analysis of a representative multi-ring masonry arch. First, a heterogeneous Limit Analysis approach with a non-associated flow rule is employed to estimate collapse loads while avoiding artificial dilatancy effects. Second, an automated Ruled Explicit Meshing (REM) workflow is used to generate Elastic Body and Spring Models compatible with commercial FE software. Starting from a simplified geometric input, the routine produces block–interface representations with limited user intervention, reducing modelling time and modelling inconsistencies. The third approach, the FEMANOLA code, is adopted to simulate the full nonlinear response, including damage evolution and interaction between failure modes, though requiring deeper calibration. The comparison highlights the advantages and limitations of each approach in terms of ultimate capacity, damage evolution, computational effort, and practical applicability.

Keywords: Multi-ring arches · Heterogeneous Modelling · Elastic Body and Spring Method (EBSM) · Ruled Explicit Meshing (REM) · Limit Analysis (LA) · FEMANOLA

1 Introduction

The structural assessment of masonry arches is inherently complex due to the heterogeneous nature of the material and its nonlinear and asymmetric behaviour [1, 2]. These challenges are further amplified in multi-ring arches, even though they constitute a small fraction of existing masonry structures. The presence of ring interfaces introduces additional planes of weakness, making ring separation, sliding, and interlocking effects dominant mechanisms governing the structural response [3].

O. Gervasi et al. (Eds.): ICCSA 2026 Workshops, LNCS 16758, pp. 581–599, 2027.
https://doi.org/10.1007/978-3-032-30497-1_35

Experimental and numerical studies proved that the mechanics of masonry structures is strongly affected by geometry and unit arrangement [4–6]. In particular, multi-ring arches exhibit significantly different behaviour compared to single-ring ones, with failure often controlled by ring sliding and separation rather than purely rotational mechanisms [7]. Such mechanisms are controlled by ring staggering and blocks interlocking. Therefore, simplified homogeneous approaches may lead to inaccurate predictions, often overestimating the structural capacity by neglecting the discrete nature of the rings and their interaction.

To address these issues, comparable modelling strategies can be found in the literature [8–10]. Among them, three approaches are considered in this work and treated as complementary tools for the assessment of masonry arches.

A first approach is represented by heterogeneous Limit Analysis formulations, where masonry is idealised as an assemblage of rigid blocks connected by frictional interfaces. This method provides direct estimation of collapse loads and mechanisms with relatively low computational cost [11–13]. However, when non-associated flow rules are introduced to better represent frictional behaviour, the problem becomes non-linear and non-convex, leading to potential non-uniqueness of the solution and increased computational complexity.

The second approach consists of heterogeneous Finite Element (FE) modelling based on block–interface representations. Within this framework, the REM (Ruled Explicit Meshing) procedure enables the automatic generation of models starting from simplified geometric inputs. Compared to previous versions [14, 15], this strategy significantly reduces preprocessing effort and user dependency, while maintaining the ability to capture localised damage. Nevertheless, the accuracy of the results still depends on mesh assumptions and interface idealisations, and convergence issues typical of nonlinear FE analyses may arise.

Finally, FEMANOLA code represents a dedicated FE-based tool specifically developed for masonry structures. By adopting an explicit iterative strategy with progressive stiffness degradation at Gauss points, it is capable of reproducing complex nonlinear phenomena such as crack initiation, propagation, and failure modes combination. This enables a detailed description of the structural behaviour with a computational cost reduced by approximately 90% compared to REM, although it requires a more careful calibration of the mechanical parameters.

In this context, the present work proposes an automated REM-based workflow and evaluates its performance through a comparative analysis with heterogeneous Limit Analysis and FEMANOLA. The objective is to highlight the potentialities and limitations of each method when applied to multi-ring masonry arches, providing a consistent framework for their combined use in structural assessment.

1.1 The Case Study Analysed

The effectiveness of the three methodologies is demonstrated through one methodological benchmark. Although the geometry is inspired by an existing pedestrian bridge arch, the heterogeneous model and the boundary conditions are intentionally idealised to provide a repeatable comparison among the three numerical approaches. The arch in Fig. 1 spans 8271 mm, has a radial thickness of 930 mm and an out of plane depth of

660 mm. The aim is not to provide a full validation against an experimental campaign, but to compare the predictions of three independently developed methodologies under the same geometric, mechanical and loading assumptions.

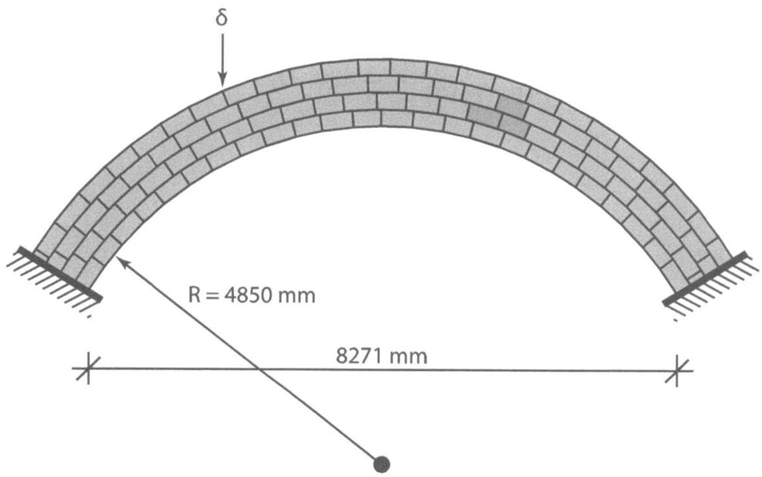

Fig. 1. Geometrical description of the multi-ring arch analysed

2 Heterogeneous Limit Analysis

In this section, a Limit Analysis (LA) formulation is used to compute the collapse load of the abovementioned structure. The arch bricks are simulated through rigid elements, with the plasticity reduced only at the interfaces. The interface constitutive model follows the classic Mohr-Coulomb friction with tension cutoff, considering both associated and non-associated flow rules. The LA formulation is constructed from a kinematic view.

2.1 Recall of Associated Limit Analysis Formulation

Determining the kinematics of the rigid units is quite straightforward. The velocity field of the rigid element with arbitrary polygonal shapes can be expressed as in Eq. (1). $\mathbf{u}^i$ contains the three rigid-body velocity components in 2D, and the mapping matrix $\mathbf{H}_{\mathcal{R}}(\mathbf{r})$ correspondingly collects in columns three 2D rigid-body basis modes (given in Eq. (2)).

$$\mathbf{u}^i(\mathbf{r}) = \mathbf{H}_{\mathcal{R}}(\mathbf{r})\mathbf{u}^i. \tag{1}$$

$$\mathbf{u}^i = \begin{bmatrix} u_x^i \; u_y^i \; \omega_{xy}^i \end{bmatrix}^T, \; \mathbf{H}_{\mathcal{R}}(\mathbf{r}) = \begin{bmatrix} 1 & & -\mathbf{r}_{(2)} \\ & 1 & \mathbf{r}_{(1)} \end{bmatrix}. \tag{2}$$

Identifying the element velocity field enables further calculation of the velocity jumps at the interfaces, which can be implemented as in Eq. (3). Four degrees of freedom are assigned to each contact to describe the velocity discontinuities at the two nodes. These discontinuities can be computed from the subtraction of the adjacent element velocities, with additional projection onto the local *n*-*s* frame (Fig. 2a).

$$\mathbf{q}_j = \left[\, \Delta u^j_{\mathrm{n},1}\ \Delta u^j_{\mathrm{t},1}\ \Delta u^j_{\mathrm{n},2}\ \Delta u^j_{\mathrm{t},2} \right]^T = \left[-\left(\mathbf{A}^a_j\right)^T \left(\mathbf{A}^b_j\right)^T \right] \begin{bmatrix} \mathbf{u}^a \\ \mathbf{u}^b \end{bmatrix}$$
$$\mathbf{A}^i_j = \begin{bmatrix} \mathbf{Q}_j \mathbf{H}^i_{\mathcal{R}}\left(\mathbf{r}^i_1\right) \\ \mathbf{Q}_j \mathbf{H}^i_{\mathcal{R}}\left(\mathbf{r}^i_2\right) \end{bmatrix}^T,\ i = a, b,\ \mathbf{Q}_j = \left[\mathbf{e}^j_{\mathrm{n}}\ \mathbf{e}^j_{\mathrm{t}} \right]^T. \tag{3}$$

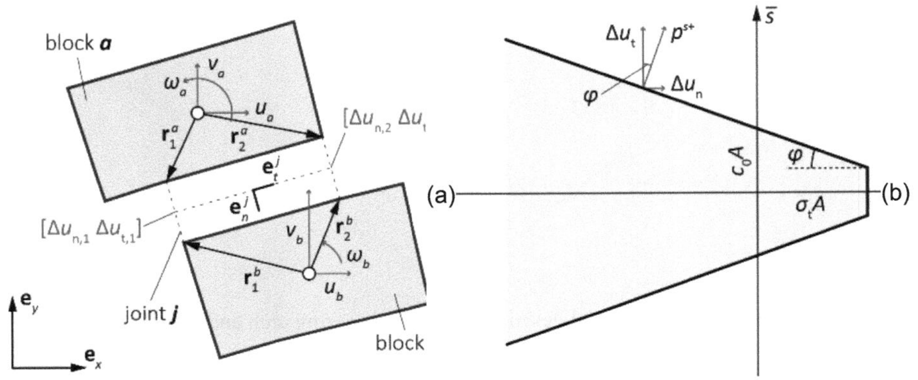

Fig. 2. 2D rigid block limit analysis: (a) computation of interfacial velocity jump; (b) interfacial constitutive model, Mohr-Coulomb friction with tension cut-off.

Assembling the relations over all the interfaces, the global constraint on element velocities and interfacial discontinuities can be written as a linear equality, known as the compatibility condition (Eq. (4)):

$$\mathbf{A}^T\mathbf{u} = \mathbf{q}. \tag{4}$$

The constitutive model for the interface is based on the 2D Mohr-Coulomb friction (Fig. 2b). Given the consideration of the tensile limit of mortar in the following FEM-based modelling, a tension cut-off is also superposed for the consistency (Eq. (5)). As a result, the matrix form of the constitutive model can be written as in Eq. (6), where the components of the constitutive operator **N** and cohesion vector $\mathbf{c}_0$ for a specific joint *j* have been given in Eq. (7). **x** collects the interfacial forces corresponding to the discontinuity unknowns assigned at the kinematic side.

$$F_{\mathrm{MC}}(\overline{n}, \overline{s}) = \overline{n}\sin\varphi + |\overline{s}|\cos\varphi - \frac{1}{2}c_0 A\cos\varphi$$
$$F_{\mathrm{t}}(\overline{n}, \overline{s}) = \overline{n} - \frac{1}{2}\sigma_{\mathrm{t}}A. \tag{5}$$

$$\mathbf{N}\mathbf{x} - \mathbf{c}_0 = \mathbf{z}_0,\ \mathbf{z}_0 \leq 0. \tag{6}$$

$$\mathbf{N}_{j,1} = \mathbf{N}_{j,2} = \begin{bmatrix} \sin\varphi & \sin\varphi & 1 \\ \cos\varphi & -\cos\varphi & 0 \end{bmatrix}^T, \ \mathbf{N}_j = \begin{bmatrix} \mathbf{N}_{j,1} & \\ & \mathbf{N}_{j,2} \end{bmatrix}$$
$$\mathbf{c}_{j,1} = \mathbf{c}_{j,2} = \frac{1}{2}\left[c_0 A \cos\varphi \ c_0 A \cos\varphi \ \sigma_t A \right], \ \mathbf{c}_j = \left[\mathbf{c}_{j,1} \ \mathbf{c}_{j,2} \right]^T. \tag{7}$$

Assuming an associated flow rule, namely the direction of the plastic flow is always orthogonal to the constitutive limit surface, the plastic flow constraint for the kinematic side can conveniently be represented as a conjugate matrix form that associates the vector of plastic multiplier $\mathbf{p}$ and interfacial velocity jumps $\mathbf{q}$. The flow operator is the transpose of the constitutive one. The dissipation on the interfaces can be computed as an inner product of the cohesion vector and the plastic multiplier vector. More mathematical deduction can be found in the literature [12].

$$\mathbf{q} = \mathbf{N}^T\mathbf{p}, \ \mathbf{p} \geq 0. \tag{8}$$

$$P_D^C = \mathbf{c}_0^T\mathbf{p}. \tag{9}$$

If the associativity holds, the upper-bound and lower-bound LA formulations (Eqs. (10) and (11)) produce consistent predictions, which are actually a pair of dual Linear Programming (LP) problems, in terms of mathematical optimization, so that the uniqueness of the solution is guaranteed. A couple of solvers is already available and can tackle these sorts of optimizations and quickly search for the solution in a single step.

$$\begin{aligned} &\min. \ -\mathbf{f}_D^T\mathbf{u} + \mathbf{c}_0^T\mathbf{p} \\ &\text{s.t.} \ \ \mathbf{f}_L^T\mathbf{u} = 1 \\ &\qquad \mathbf{A}^T\mathbf{u} = \mathbf{N}^T\mathbf{p}, \ \mathbf{p} \geq 0. \end{aligned} \tag{10}$$

$$\begin{aligned} &\max \ \alpha \\ &\text{s.t.} \ \ \mathbf{A}\mathbf{x} = \alpha\mathbf{f}_L + \mathbf{f}_D \\ &\qquad \mathbf{N}\mathbf{x} - \mathbf{c}_0 = \mathbf{z}_0, \ \mathbf{z}_0 \leq 0. \end{aligned} \tag{11}$$

2.2 Solution for Non-Associated Sliding

Nevertheless, the associated flow rule will bring about a spurious dilation at the interfaces, which should not be expected in a rational collapse mechanism. This assumption will even overestimate the predicted load multiplier [16]. A more realistic modeling for the interaction between bricks is the non-associated flow with zero dilation. In this case, we have to modify the plastic flow constraint by substituting the constitutive operator $\mathbf{N}$ with the flow operator $\mathbf{V}$ that constitutes the real dilation angle for the interface (Eq. (12)). The lower-bound and upper-bound formulations are therefore uncoupled, and the uniqueness of the solution is lost.

We utilise the Sequential Linear Programming (SLP) procedure, proposed by Gilbert et al. [11, 17], to search for the solution of the arch collapse with a non-associated flow rule. The iteration procedure can be expressed as sequentially solving the pair of associated problems below (Eqs. (13) and (14)), where in each iteration, the friction angle and cohesion are updated based on the solution from the previous step. The initial solution for the iteration is taken from the associated formulation.

$$\mathbf{q} = \mathbf{V}^T\mathbf{p},\ \mathbf{p} \geq 0$$
$$\mathbf{V}_{j,1} = \mathbf{V}_{j,2} = \begin{bmatrix} \sin\psi & \sin\psi & 1 \\ \cos\psi & -\cos\psi & 0 \end{bmatrix}^T,\ \mathbf{V}_j = \begin{bmatrix} \mathbf{V}_{j,1} & \\ & \mathbf{V}_{j,2} \end{bmatrix}. \tag{12}$$

$$\begin{aligned} &\max\ \alpha_{[k]} \\ &\text{s.t.}\ \ \mathbf{A}\mathbf{x}_{[k]} = \alpha_{[k]}\mathbf{f}_L + \mathbf{f}_D \\ &\qquad \mathbf{N}_{[k]}\mathbf{x}_{[k]} - \mathbf{c}_{[k]} = \mathbf{z}_{[k]},\ \mathbf{z}_{[k]} \leq 0. \end{aligned} \tag{13}$$

$$\begin{aligned} &\min.\ -\mathbf{f}_D^T\mathbf{u}_{[k]} + \mathbf{c}_{[k]}^T\mathbf{p}_{[k]} \\ &\text{s.t.}\ \ \mathbf{f}_L^T\mathbf{u}_{[k]} = 1 \\ &\qquad \mathbf{A}^T\mathbf{u}_{[k]} = \mathbf{N}_{[k]}^T\mathbf{p}_{[k]},\ \mathbf{p}_{[k]} \geq 0 \end{aligned} \tag{14}$$

At every iteration the friction angle is updated in the constitutive (flow) operator $\mathbf{N}$ through $\xi_{[k]}$ (Eqs. (15) and (16)), which is a monotonically decreasing parameter bounded by $\xi_{\min}$. This sequence gradually brings the friction angle to the dilation angle so that the real dilation of the interface can be reproduced. When ψ is equal to zero, the sliding dilation thereby vanishes in the converged solution. Remark that approaching the target dilation angle starts from the negative side to guarantee the conservative property of the searched multiplier. The interfacial cohesion is accordingly adjusted, aligned with the decrease of the frictional angle (Eq. (17)).

$$\mathbf{N}_{j,1}^{[k]} = \mathbf{N}_{j,2}^{[k]} = \begin{bmatrix} \sin\varphi_{[k]} & \sin\varphi_{[k]} & 1 \\ \cos\varphi_{[k]} & -\cos\varphi_{[k]} & 0 \end{bmatrix}^T,\ \mathbf{N}_j^{[k]} = \begin{bmatrix} \mathbf{N}_{j,1}^{[k]} & \\ & \mathbf{N}_{j,1}^{[k]} \end{bmatrix} \tag{15}$$

$$\tan\varphi_{[k]} = -\xi_{[k]}\tan\varphi + \left(1 + \xi_{[k]}\right)\tan\psi,\ \xi_{[k]} \leftarrow \max\left\{\frac{\xi_{[k-1]}}{2}, \xi_{\min}\right\} \tag{16}$$

$$\mathbf{c}_{[k]} = c_* + \mathbf{c}_0 - \left(1 + \xi_{[k]}\right)(\mathbf{N} - \mathbf{V})\mathbf{x}_{[k-1]} \tag{17}$$

Figure 3 illustrates in a more intuitive manner the physical meaning of these updates in each iteration. Actually, the updated constitutive (flow) operator and cohesion vector construct for each interface a new limit surface that passes the joint force state obtained from the previous step. These interfacial resultants are then pulled back onto the original Mohr-Coulomb limit surface, implicitly obeying the constitutive model. Consequently, the solution of the kinematic formulation will present a precise interfacial separation defined by the dilation angle when ξ decreases, whereas the Mohr-Coulomb frictional condition still holds on the static side.

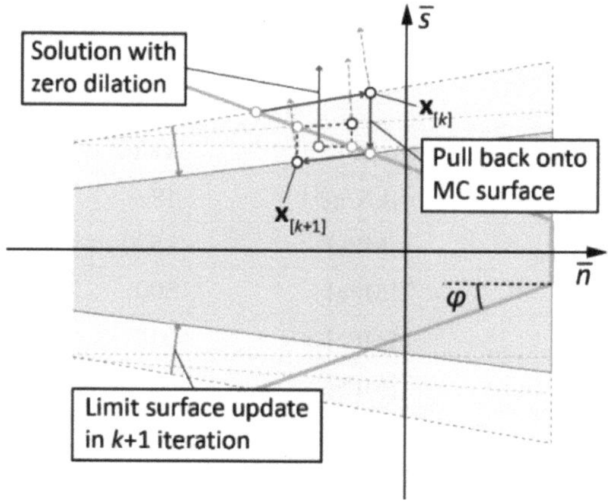

Fig. 3. Adjustment of the limit surfaces during the SLP iterations, zero-dilation case.

To improve convergence, the procedure also features a stabilisation technique to avoid the underlying fluctuation of the normal resultants at some joint nodes (Eq. (18)). The resultant solutions used to construct the new limit surface are the average of the solutions predicted in the present and the previous steps, proportioned by a suitable parameter β. A spurious cohesion term $c*$ is additionally inserted into the cohesion update (Eq. (17)) at the initial stage to suppress the instability that is more likely to appear in the cohesionless case. The procedure will quit when the error of the two sequential multipliers predicted reaches an assigned limit.

$$\mathbf{x}_s = \beta \mathbf{x}_{[k]} + (1 - \beta)\mathbf{x}_{[k-1]} \quad (18)$$

3 Finite Element Analysis with Ruled Explicit Meshing (REM)

In this section, the arch is modelled according to the Elastic Body and Spring Method (EBSM), developed by three of the authors for masonry structures [18]. Hyperelastic blocks (plate elements in this 2D case) are joined by special unidimensional elements available in the Strand7® library, namely Point Contacts (PC). In this case, tension PC have been used to simulate the behaviour of unilateral frictional contact. They behave as nonlinear trusses with infinite compressive and limited tensile strength. Further details are provided in the following subsection. (§3.1).

To speed up the analysis and make it easily repeatable minimising user errors, the mesh preparation is automated by a MATLAB® routine (REM) created and recently updated by some of the authors [14, 15]. By inputting a few mechanical parameters (listed in Table 1), the code prepares the data and saves a *.txt file.

Table 1. Mechanical parameters set for the REM + FEM analysis.

Property	u.m	Value
ρ	[kN/m^2]	18
E_{blocks}	[MPa]	1500
E_{joint}	[MPa]	500
f_t	[MPa]	0.05
f_c	[MPa]	∞

The file, read by Strand7, gives the data for producing the mesh of Fig. 1, a portion of which is detailed in Fig. 4, with a scheme for PC elements [19].

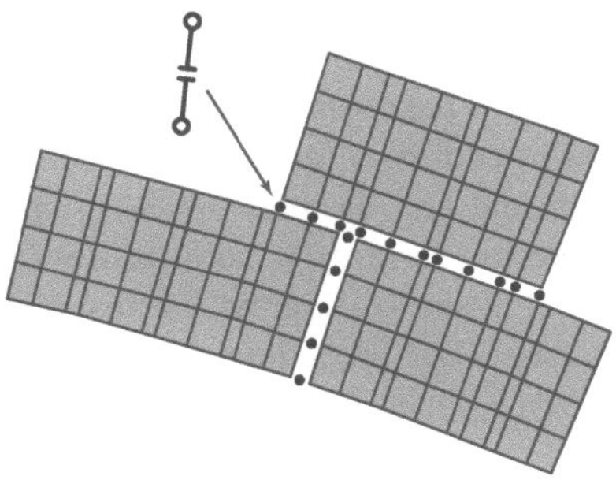

Fig. 4. Zoom of the highlighted bricks of Fig. 1. The reader can see how the mesh is formed to comply with the joint size and a visual representation of the Point Contact elements.

3.1 Point Contact Elements in Strand7

Point Contact (PC) elements connect pairs of nodes to represent interfaces. They become active or inactive depending on the relative axial displacement between the faces of objects (bricks) in contact. Therefore, this type of element is inherently nonlinear.

Three distinct interaction states are possible: the nodes may be separating (open state), approaching or in full contact without relative sliding (closed state), or in contact with mutual sliding (sliding state).

Among the four formulations of PC available in Strand7 [19], the present study employs the *Tension* formulation, which is always active in compression (no separation condition, $\Delta L < 0$) and transmits axial forces (F_{ax}) in tension and lateral forces ($F_{lat,i}$), according to Eq. (19), up to a defined threshold. Once the tensile force reaches the limit, the element is automatically released and ceases to contribute to the global stiffness matrix (Eq. (20)). No frictional behaviour is accounted for, and axial and lateral stiffness are equal. This makes the Tension formulation well-suited to interfaces whose tensile capacity is limited, such as lightly bonded construction joints of historical masonry structures.

$$F_{ax} = k_{ax}\Delta L and F_{lat,i} = k_{lat,i}D_{lat,i} with k_{lat,i} = k_{ax} \tag{19}$$

$$F_{ax} = 0 and F_{lat,i} = 0 \tag{20}$$

Being k_{ax} and $k_{lat,i}$ the axial and lateral stiffness respectively, ΔL is the axial change in length and $D_{lat,i}$ the lateral relative displacement in direction $i = 1, 2$.

Table 2 proves that shear transfer is preserved only while the element remains active (there is contact); after axial failure, no residual tangential resistance is retained for the PC elements (no friction with null contact): when $F_{ax} = 0$, , then no shear force is accounted for anymore ($F_{lat,2} = 0$) [19].

Table 2. Summary of PC element behaviour in elastic phase and at failure with k_{ax} set as in Eq. (22) and $D_{lat,i}$ deduced from the FEM results.

# PC	d [mm] (@step)	F_{ax} [kN]	F_2 [kN]	state
1034 (ring joint)	10 (0)	0.0761	−0.1248	elastic
	10.9 (432)	−2.084	28.7670	elastic
	15 (540)	0	0	failed
1177 (radial joint)	10 (0)	−2.3582	0.2356	elastic
	10.9 (432)	0	0	failed
	15 (540)	0	0	failed

Only two input parameters are required for the analysis: the axial stiffness, calculated with the classic expression in Eq. (21), and the maximum tension of Eq. (22), filled with the data of Table 1.

$$k_{ax} = \frac{EA}{l} = \frac{E_{joint} \cdot A_{inf}}{th_{joint} \cdot 1000}\left[\frac{kN}{mm}\right] \tag{21}$$

$$F_{T,max} = \frac{A_{inf} \cdot f_t}{1000}[kN] \tag{22}$$

4 FEMANOLA

FEMANOLA [20, 21] is a Finite Element–based numerical methodology, implemented by two of the authors, specifically developed for the nonlinear analysis of masonry structures through a heterogeneous block–interface representation. Blocks are modelled as elastic plate elements, while interfaces (thick or thin for mortar and dry joint, respectively) are discretised with four-node isoparametric elements. A key feature of the joint formulation is that the elastic stiffness matrix is diagonal, with the normal component along the joint direction set to zero, thereby suppressing spurious normal stress transfer across the interface. The stiffness matrix $\mathbf{D}_i$ of the ith element, assuming zero elastic stiffness in the normal joint direction, is given by:

$$\mathbf{D}_i = \begin{bmatrix} 0 & 0 & 0 \\ 0 & E_{k,i} & 0 \\ 0 & 0 & G_{k,i} \end{bmatrix} \tag{23}$$

where $E_{k,i}$ and $G_{k,i}$ the degraded elastic and shear moduli at the ith Gauss point at k^{th} load step.

The element stiffness is computed via standard Gaussian integration of four points in a local reference frame aligned with each joint, then rotated into the global system. Nonlinearity is handled through an iterative elastic scheme: at each loading increment, the stiffness of Gauss points that have exceeded their strength threshold is progressively reduced according to a return-to-limit-surface algorithm. The procedure is fully explicit; thus, it doesn't require sub-iterations for adequately small increments. Analyses are typically conducted under displacement control. A comprehensive description of FEMANOLA and the treatment of nonlinearity is described in detail in [20, 21], where the reader is referred for further details.

4.1 Constitutive Behaviour

The mechanical response of the interfaces follows a cohesive–frictional model with softening, coupling normal and shear behaviour. The joint constitutive model distinguishes three failure modes:

- *Tension*: an initial linear elastic response up to the tensile strength, followed by exponential softening governed by fracture energy.
- *Compression*: defined point-by-point to capture hardening and subsequent softening.
- *Shear*: a cohesive-frictional law couples tangential and normal stress. Peak and residual shear strengths vary linearly with the applied normal stress through a friction angle and zero-confinement strength parameters. Post-peak softening follows a linear-exponential decay toward the residual strength, with the Mode II fracture energy itself depending on the current normal stress level through a dimensionless scaling factor that varies parabolically under compression and linearly under tension.

All mechanical parameters have a direct physical interpretation and are defined through a preprocessing spreadsheet interface. The parameters used in this case are listed in Table 3.

Table 3. Mechanical parameters set for FEMANOLA.

Property	u.m	Value
ρ	[kN/m^2]	18
E_{blocks}	[MPa]	1500
E_{joint}	[MPa]	500

(continued)

Table 3. (*continued*)

Property	u.m	Value
G_{joint}	[MPa]	250
f_t	[MPa]	0.05
f_c	[MPa]	10

5 Structural Analysis

5.1 Heterogeneous LA

In the LA model, only the arrangement of brick units is considered, whereas the thickness of the mortar joints is collapsed into a zero-thickness interface. The dimension of the units is therefore correspondingly expanded to take over the space of the mortar thickness. The geometric model of the arch is sketched in AutoCAD® and then imported into MATLAB for limit analysis computation.

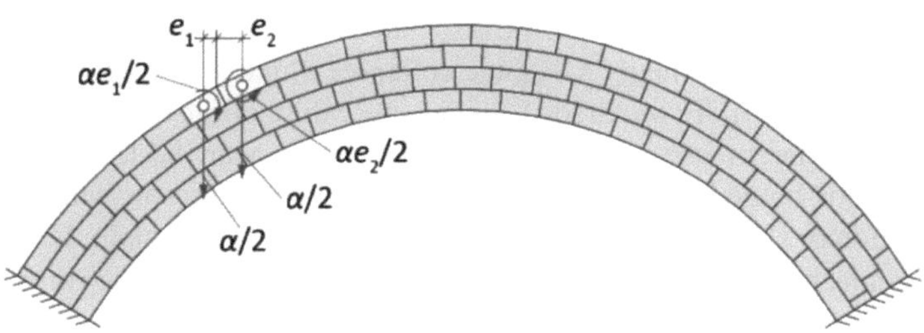

Fig. 5. Limit analysis of the main arch of the Treponti Bridge: geometry, load, and boundary conditions.

Table 4. Mechanical parameter set for the heterogeneous LA.

Parameter	u.m	Value
ρ	[kN/m³]	18
c	[MPa]	0.05
φ	[°]	30

Table 5. Parameter setting for the non-associated procedure.

Parameter	Value
ξ_0	0.3
ξ_{min}	10^{-6}
β	0.6
tol	10^{-3}
$c*$	$10^{-6}\max(\mathbf{x}_{[0]})$

As displayed in Fig. 5, the concentrated load is equivalently imposed onto two neighbouring blocks. The boundary conditions at the springing are all cohesive-frictional contact, in line with the feature of the mortar interfaces. The Limit Analysis (LA) considers interfacial modelling of both the associated flow rule and the non-associated flow rule with zero dilation (i.e., $\psi = 0$). The material properties of the brick units and the interfaces are listed in Table 4. Table 5 lists the additional parameters that are required to control the SLP procedure when considering the non-associated sliding, which follows the ones employed in [11].

The collapse results predicted from the associated formulation are illustrated in Fig. 6. The mechanism presents virtually a 4-hinge collapse, which is a typical 2D collapse of a bridge arch (see [22]). Two extrados hinges are exhibited at the loading point and right springing, whereas one intrados hinge takes place near the left springer of the arch. The intrados hinge at the right quarter span is not significant, which is smeared by the separation or sliding movement among the bricks in this domain. Unlike the thin arch collapse mechanism, a considerable sliding happens between the rings, causing a noticeable spurious dilation.

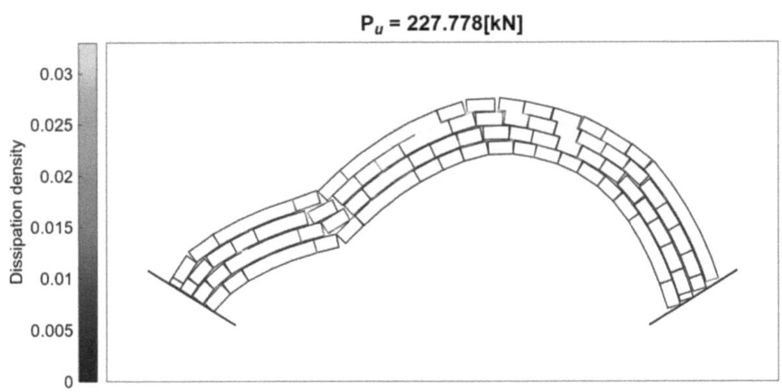

Fig. 6. Collapse of the modelled arch, limit analysis prediction with associated flow rule.

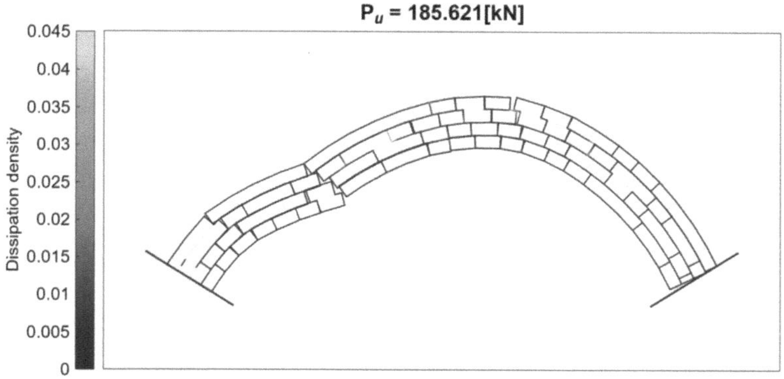

Fig. 7. Collapse of the modelled arch, limit analysis prediction with non-associated flow rule.

As expected, the non-associated formulation brings about a more conservative load prediction (Fig. 7), which is more consistent with the peak load of the FEM-based solutions. The sliding among the ring layers still appears, but the separations in normal significantly reduce, thereby exhibiting a more reasonable mechanism prediction. The presentation of the four hinges is more remarkable, in line with the indication of the FEM solutions. Due to a negative proximity to the real dilatancy on the limit surface, some penetrations take place among the brick units between the layers, although these local inaccuracies do not affect the precision of the global mechanism prediction. It should be concluded that when analysing the collapse of a thick multi-ring arch, the employment of the non-associated flow rule for the interfaces is quite necessary.

5.2 REM + FEM

The results of the arch modelled with the REM + FEM procedure are reported in Fig. 8. As can be noted, the deformed configuration at 10.9 mm displacement lines up with the ones deduced through the LA formulation. A four-hinge mechanism forms with good agreement on the location of damage.

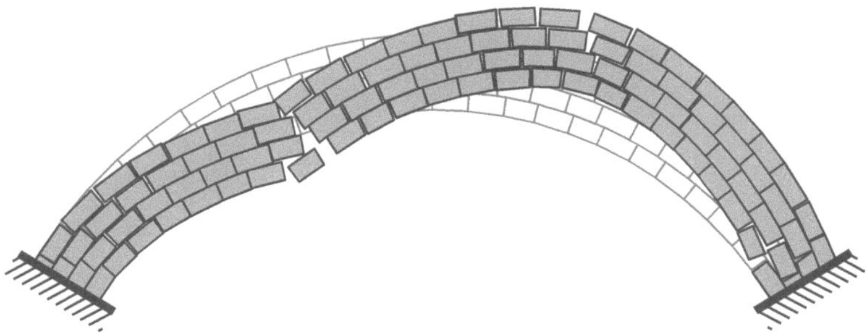

Fig. 8. Deformed configuration of the arch deduced from FEM analysis (d = 10.9 mm)

The most careful reader may note that at this stage of the analysis, one block starts detaching from the structure, initiating a mechanism that goes out of the FEM range of operability. This required the addition of some elements with a negligible elastic modulus to enhance convergence.

5.3 FEMANOLA

In this section, the results obtained by analysing the arch with FEMANOLA are gathered for two cases: one assuming infinite shear strength (Fig. 9) and the other considering finite shear strength (Fig. 10). Moreover, the output lets the user check the progressive state of damage, thus the deformed configurations are reported for the step 25 (half) and 50 (end) of the analysis.

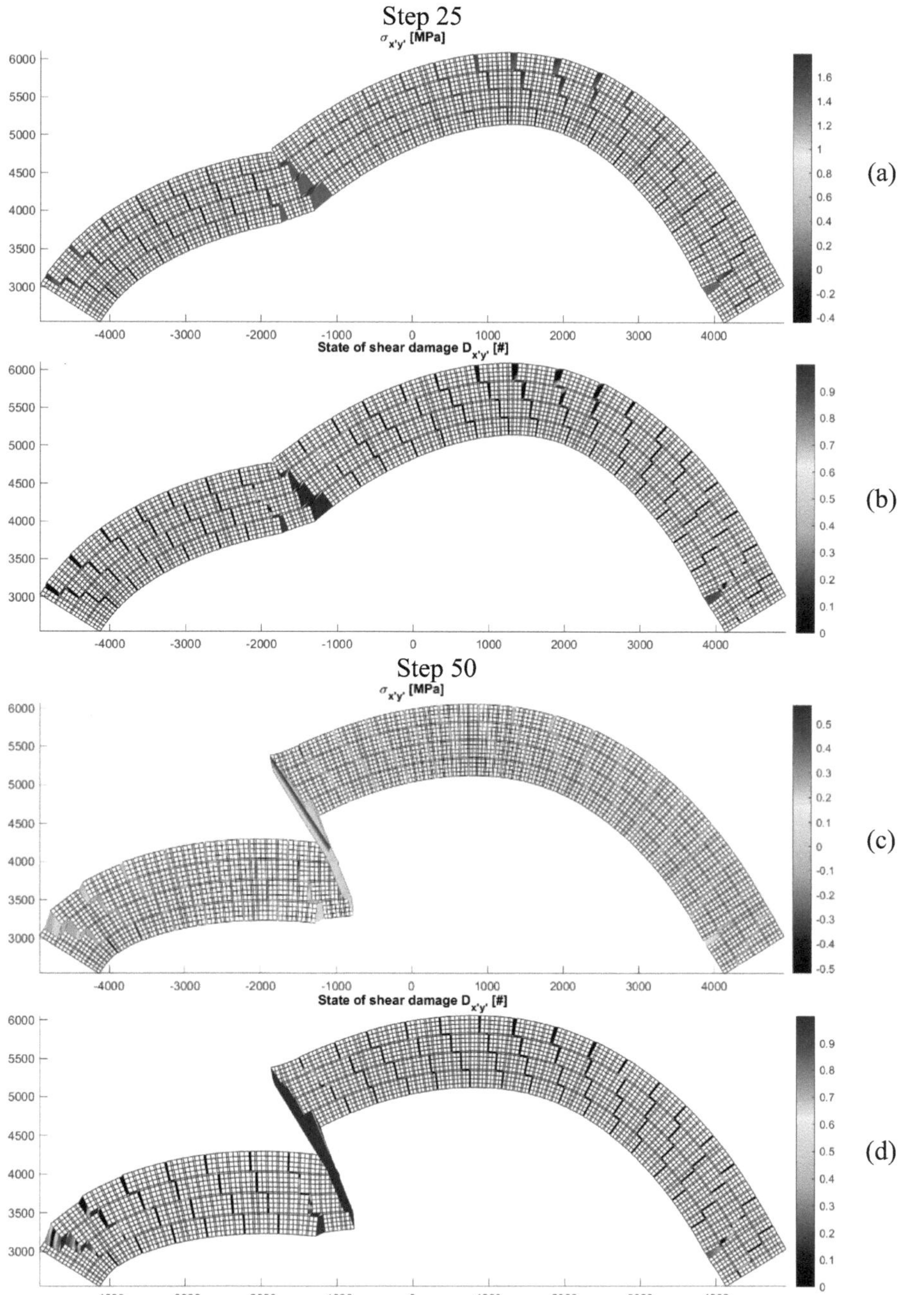

Fig. 9. Stress (a, c) and damage (b, d) states for steps 25 and 50 of FEMANOLA under the associated flow rule.

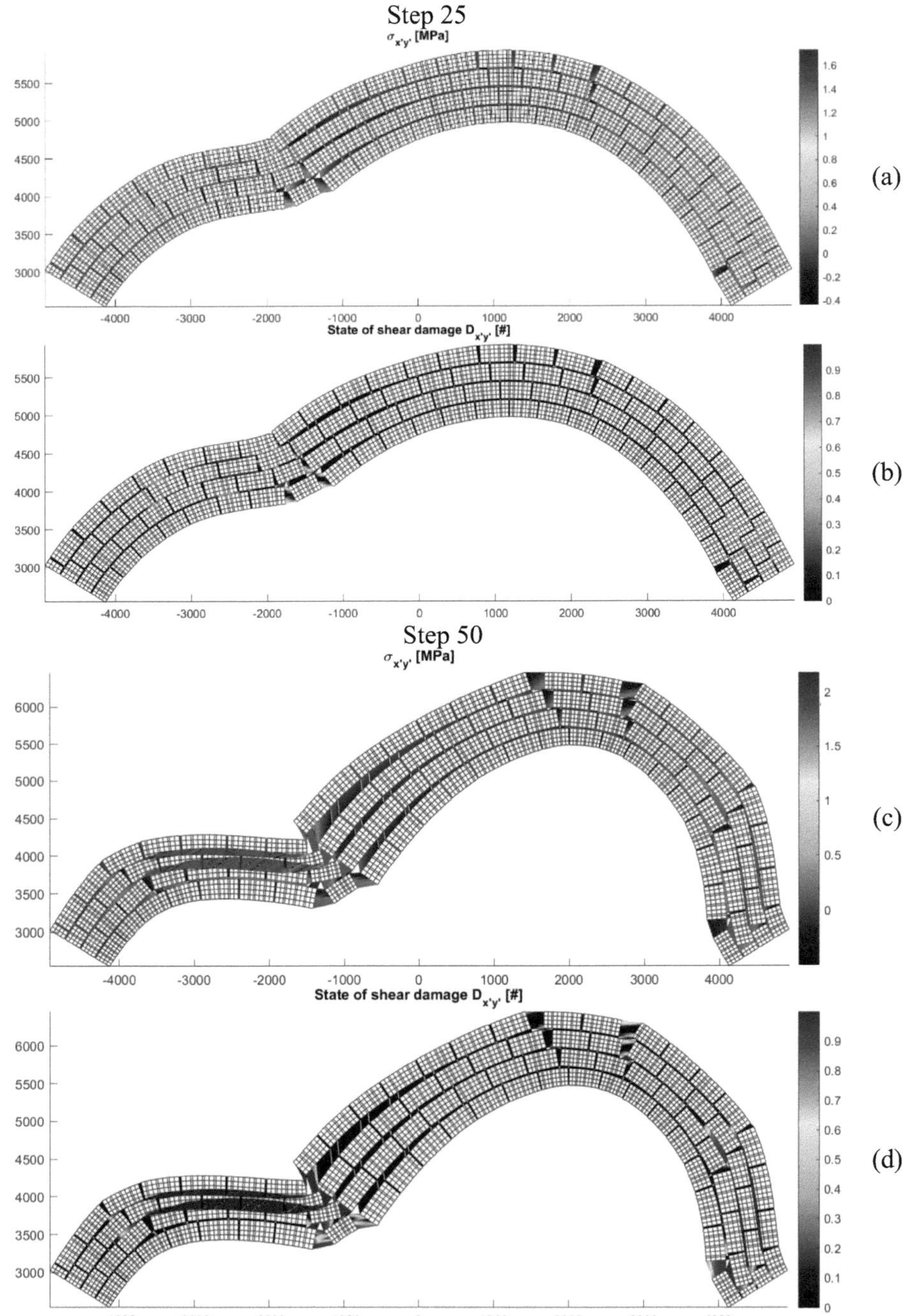

Fig. 10. Stress (a, c) and damage (b, d) states for steps 25 and 50 of FEMANOLA under the non-associated flow rule.

6 Discussion

The chart in Fig. 11 compares the capacities obtained with the three methodologies reported. The results are very satisfactory, with a good mutual agreement among them. Concerning the associated flow rule result, it indicates an underlying overestimation of the load prediction with reference to the FEM solutions. Indeed, both the predictions from the proposed REM + FEM and FEMANOLA are more conservative.

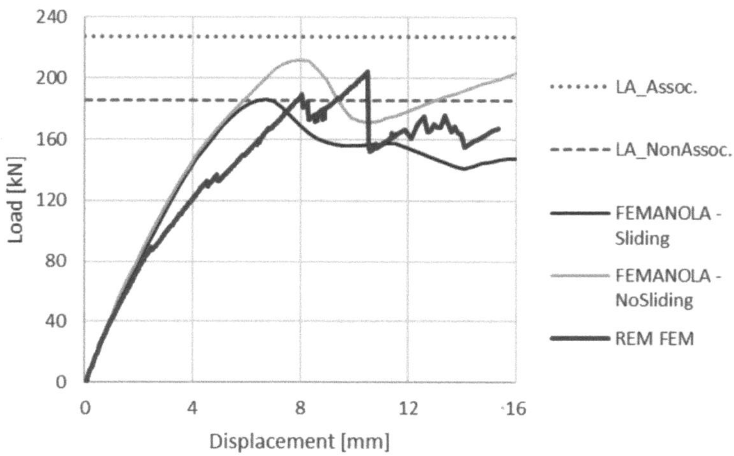

Fig. 11. Heterogeneous LA, REM + FEM, and FEMANOLA collapse load results in comparison.

The REM + FEM procedure proved to be in between the other two methods, giving more conservative results than LA while being conceptually simpler than FEMANOLA. Because of what is stated in §3.1, while the shear component is accounted in the elastic phase of interface Point Contact elements, no shear resistance is ensured after the element reaches its axial elastic limit. This may explain why the capacity curve lies between the two FEMANOLA curves of infinite and finite shear strength.

Eventually, to prove the efficiency of these analyses, Table 6 gathers some information on the time needed to run the analysis depending on the machines exploited.

Table 6. Comparison between the three methodologies and analysis time based on software environment and hardware capacity.

	U. Load [kN]	Sw. Used	Time [min]	Processor	Base freq. [GHz]
Non-associated LA	185.62	MATLAB®	< 0.03	Intel Core Ultra 9 275HX	2.70
REM + FEM	167.28	Strand7®	~ 38	Intel Core i9-14900KF	3.20
FEMANOLA	147.59	MATLAB®	~ 4	Apple M3 Max	4.05 (P-cores)

From the engineering point of view, heterogeneous Limit Analysis is particularly suitable for rapid screening of the ultimate capacity and – with non-associated flow rule – the collapse mechanisms. FEMANOLA is preferable when a detailed progressive evolution of local damage and interface stresses is of primary interest. The REM + FEM workflow provides an intermediate solution, useful when models must be generated efficiently and analysed within commercial FE environments, which are economically and theoretically more accessible.

Acknowledgments. The work has been partially carried out within the MAECI-TUBITAK Bilateral Cooperation Project 2026–2028 "ENFCorMas" Seismic Corner Collapse Mechanisms in Masonry Structures through Experimental, Numerical, and Field Studies across Italy and Turkey: From Lab to Field (Italian PI: Prof. Gabriele Milani). The Italian Ministry for Foreign affairs is gratefully acknowledged. Furthermore, the study was partially developed within the research activities carried out in the framework agreement 2024–2028 of ReLUIS Project – WP10 masonry structures (Coordinator – Prof. Guido Magenes), specifically by means of the research carried out in Task 1.1 local mechanisms and Task 2 complex systems (Task Coordinators – respectively Prof. Serena Cattari-and Prof. Sergio Lagomarsino with Dr. Gabriele Guerrini), and ReLUIS is gratefully acknowledged.

Disclosure of Interests. The authors have no competing interests to declare that are relevant to the content of this article.

References

1. Pingaro, N., Buzzetti, M., Gandolfi, A.: A numerical strategy to assess the stability of curved masonry structures using a simple nonlinear truss model. Buildings **15**, 226 (2025). https://doi.org/10.3390/buildings15132226
2. Meloni, G., Pourfouladi, M., Pingaro, N.: Parametric modelling and nonlinear FE analysis of trepponti bridge subjected to differential settlements. Buildings **16**, 47 (2025). https://doi.org/10.3390/BUILDINGS16010047
3. Nela, B., Pingaro, M., Trovalusci, P., Pasca, M.: Limit analysis of multi-ring masonry arches: a parametric study on the effects of friction angle, geometry, interlocking, and ring number. Front. Built. Environ. **9**, 1309696 (2023). https://doi.org/10.3389/fbuil.2023.1309696
4. Paris, V., Olivieri, C., Adriaenssens, S.: The impact of construction on the structural design of a complex masonry curved shell. Int. J. Space Struct. **40**, 180–194 (2025). https://doi.org/10.1177/09560599251381901;PAGEGROUP:STRING:PUBLICATION
5. Paris, V., Gobbin, F., Nannei, V.M., et al.: Distinct element method analyses for damage assessment: the northern spur of valverde bulwark in the venetian fortress of bergamo. Int. J. Arch. Heritage **19**, 687–701 (2025). https://doi.org/10.1080/15583058.2024.2345701
6. Iannuzzo, A., Block, P., Angelillo, M., Gesualdo, A.: A continuous energy-based numerical approach to predict fracture mechanisms in masonry structures: CDF method. Comput. Struct. **257**, 106645 (2021). https://doi.org/10.1016/J.COMPSTRUC.2021.106645
7. Gilbert, M., Melbourne, C.: Analysis of multi-ring brickwork arch bridges (1995)
8. Galassi, S.: An alternative approach for limit analysis of masonry arches on moving supports in finite small displacements. Eng. Fail. Anal. **145**, 107004 (2023). https://doi.org/10.1016/J.ENGFAILANAL.2022.107004
9. Galassi, S., Zampieri, P.: A new automatic procedure for nonlinear analysis of masonry arches subjected to large support movements. Eng. Struct. **276**, 115359 (2023). https://doi.org/10.1016/J.ENGSTRUCT.2022.115359

10. Galassi, S., Tempesta, G.: Safety assessment of masonry undamaged and damaged arches subjected to gravitational loads and horizontal forces: a numeric procedure to identify the optimal thrust line. Int. J. Solids Struct. **301**, 112943 (2024). https://doi.org/10.1016/J.IJSOLSTR.2024.112943
11. Gilbert, M., Casapulla, C., Ahmed, H.M.: Limit analysis of masonry block structures with non-associative frictional joints using linear programming. Comput. Struct. **84**, 873–887 (2006). https://doi.org/10.1016/j.compstruc.2006.02.005
12. Hua, Y., Milani, G.: Rigid block limit analysis of masonry arches with associated and non-associated slides. In: Research for Development. Springer Science and Business Media Deutschland GmbH, pp. 169–203 (2022)
13. Iannuzzo, A., Montanino, A.: A limit analysis-based CASS approach for the in-plane seismic capacity of masonry façades. Int. J. Solids Struct. **289**, 112633 (2024). https://doi.org/10.1016/J.IJSOLSTR.2023.112633
14. Buzzetti, M., Gandolfi, A., Pingaro, N., Milani, G.: A new advanced and simple procedure for the nonlinear static analysis of curved masonry structures. In: Protection of Historical Constructions: Proceedings of PROHITECH 2025, pp 176–183. Springer Nature, Naples (2025)
15. Gandolfi, A., Pingaro, N., Buzzetti, M., Milani, G.: An automatic procedure to simplify nonlinear static analysis of curved masonry structures. In: 14th International Conference on Structural Analysis of Historical Constructions, Lausanne (2025)
16. Livesley, R.K.: Limit analysis of structures formed from rigid blocks. Int. J. Numer. Methods Eng. **12**, 1853–1871 (1978). https://doi.org/10.1002/nme.1620121207
17. Nodargi, N.A., Intrigila, C., Bisegna, P.: A variational-based fixed-point algorithm for the limit analysis of dry-masonry block structures with non-associative Coulomb friction. Int. J. Mech. Sci. **161–162**, 105078 (2019). https://doi.org/10.1016/j.ijmecsci.2019.105078
18. Gandolfi, A., Pingaro, N., Milani, G.: Elastic body spring method (EBSM) for the stability analysis of the global vipassana pagoda in Mumbai, India. Buildings **15**, 653 (2025). https://doi.org/10.3390/buildings15050653
19. Strand7 Pty Ltd. Theoretical Manual. Theoretical backgrund to the Straus7 finite element analysis system (2004)
20. Pingaro, N., Milani, G.: Simple interface element equipped with thickness for the non-linear static heterogeneous analysis of masonry walls in-plane loaded: Implementation and validation. Eng. Struct. **351**, 122056 (2026). https://doi.org/10.1016/j.engstruct.2025.122056
21. Pingaro, N., Milani, G.: FEMANOLA v3.0 as a tool to predict settlement-induced cracks in masonry walls. In: Lecture Notes in Computer Science, pp 396–409. Springer Science and Business Media Deutschland GmbH (2026)
22. Hua, Y., Milani, G.: Novel block element with axial-only deformation for limit analysis of masonry arch bridges. Comput. Struct. **298**, 107361 (2024). https://doi.org/10.1016/j.compstruc.2024.107361

Artificialization of land, Urban Transformation, and Territorial Resilience in a changing Climate (AUTTREC 2026)

Circular Infrastructure for a Regenerative Wool Economy: Revitalizing the Italian Sheep Wool Supply Chain in the Mediterranean

Celestina Fazia[1(✉)], Salvatore Bognanno[2], Salvatore Bordonaro[2], Kh. Md. Nahiduzzaman[3], and Matteo Bognanno[4]

[1] Department Engineering and Architecture, University Kore of Enna, Cittadella Universitaria, 94100 Enna, Italy
celestina.fazia@unikore.it
[2] Department of Agriculture, Food and Environment, University of Catania, S. Sofia 100, 95123 Catania, Italy
[3] Citinnov for Integrated Territorial Planning and Smart Cities, Mohammed VI Polytechnic University (UM6P), 11103 Rabat, Morocco
[4] Department of Agraria, Mediterranea University of Reggio Calabria, Feo di Vito, 89122 Reggio Calabria, Italy

Abstract. To rebuild the wool supply chain in Italy, understand the critical issues, and study the possibilities for its use, we must start from a certain fact: the wool from approximately 6 million sheep, raised more for dairy and meat production than for weaving, is virtually unused. Farmers do not know how to use the 'dirty' wool that has just been sheared and still needs to be washed, due to the lack of washing facilities for small and medium quantities. Some try to store it, while others are forced to dispose of it and pay to do so. The legislation considers dirty wool to be special waste and without the availability of a washing plant, the 'virtuous' cycle of wool management is therefore interrupted. Yet, once washed, dirty wool has important strengths: it has good technical characteristics, and its use would enable a fully traceable supply chain across the country. Sicily alone has 700,000 sheep that produce around 1,330,000 kg of wool. This figure is very important and requires greater scientific attention. The complexity of the issue indicates the need to define a model to resolve certain critical issues and restart the Italian wool sector. The promotion of 100% Italian sheep's wool is the goal that many Italian regions, in synergy with some local communities, are pursuing through various solutions with zero environmental impact.

Keywords: Regenerative wool · Economy · Development

1 Introduction: Wool in the Mediterranean and New Frontiers for Recovery

Since prehistoric times, the Mediterranean basin has always been the cradle of small ruminant farming (sheep and goats). The mild springs are associated with the production of spontaneous and cultivated vegetative biomass, which determines farmers' decisions

O. Gervasi et al. (Eds.): ICCSA 2026 Workshops, LNCS 16758, pp. 603–614, 2027.
https://doi.org/10.1007/978-3-032-30497-1_36

to graze sheep and production milk[1]. The productive aptitudes of sheep are in order: milk, meat, and woo[l]. The mild climate has, therefore, led farmers to focus on milk production, which begins in the early autumn months and ends in summer. As a result, the sheep population is used for milk production, with wool as a secondary by-product.

Wool is the result of shearing, which is carried out at the beginning of summer, allowing the animals to cope with the high summer temperatures without the woolly coat that has accompanied and protected them from the cold during the winter. The main sheep breeds raised in Sicily with a predominantly milk-producing aptitude are defined as open-fleece type, and the wool obtained from their shearing is of lower quality than that obtained from animals specialized in this production. Therefore, its use in yarns has been replaced by wool produced by specialized farms located in the southern hemisphere i.e., Australia, New Zealand, South Africa, and Argentina. The use of wool from dairy farms is beginning to present critical issues related to its use in yarn production, thus becoming a product that can be used and regenerated in other production cycles.

In recent years, which was mainly used for mattress fillings, has ceased to be considered a source of income due to the lack of a market [1, 2]. Wool has become a form of "special waste" because, if left in the open air, it is difficult to decompose and, as such, must be treated, with the costs of disposal borne by farmers. There are still traders who sporadically purchase small batches of dirty wool, but they offer very low prices (€0.10–0.20 per kg). In this context, many who see their hard work devalued tend to bury, abandon, or even burn the wool to save on disposal costs [1]. It is clear how wrong it is for farmers not to dispose of wool properly and for institutions not to adequately compensate them for the costs they incur. The process of purifying dirty wool involves sterilization at over 130 °C, wasting considerable amounts of energy and water, not to mention the problem of purifying the water used in washing. In this tug-of-war between the understandable and the wrong, there is a need to find alternatives, and to do so, initiatives are emerging in Sicily, where grazing land is of particular importance (see Fig. 1).

Section 2 presents the results and best practices already implemented in national and international contexts. The transformation of sheep's wool into materials for use in construction and bio-architecture represents a very promising market sector, with significant positive impacts on the economic, social, and environmental spheres. In Sect. 6, the results of the study suggest that the proposed method could be easily implemented, with significant positive impacts on the landscape and the local area.

1.1 Characteristics of Wool

Wool is a modification of the hair covering of mammals, with the primary function of protecting the animal from adverse weather conditions [1, 2]. It is obtained by shearing the live animal, either by hand or with the aid of mechanical shears, in late spring. The fleece can be divided into an outer layer and an inner layer. The former is coarser, while the latter, known as the undercoat, is finer and more valuable. The fiber structure has a keratin base consisting mainly of 50% carbon, 22–24% oxygen, 7% hydrogen, 17%

[1] This § is part of: Bognanno S, "Sustainability of the sheep farming industry in Sicily: tradition and innovation", Degree Thesis, University of Catania, 2023.

nitrogen, and 3–4% sulfur. The protein that forms the fibrous structure of wool has a common structure that differs between genetic types in length and diameter. The quality of wool differs precisely in this last aspect, from which the product types are derived: - Textile wool, less than 25 MICRON - Croisee wool, between 25 and 30 MICRON - Mattress wool, from 35 to 60 MICRON The quantity and quality of wool produced by an animal vary according to age, sex, environmental conditions and, above all, breed.

Fig. 1. Sicilian sheep grazing, Photo credit: Matteo Bognanno

Wool is no longer considered a source of income due to the absence of a market that uses it and has become a problem for farmers. In the past, it was the most widely used textile fiber, as evidenced by examples from ancient cultures such as the Sumerians, Babylonians, Assyrians, and Chinese. Over the centuries, the breeding of specialized wool breeds has led to wool production being concentrated in New Zealand, Argentina, and Australia.

2 State of the Art: The Sicilian Wool District

The Sicilian wool district was founded in Cammarata (AG) in the heart of the Sicani Mountains and is responsible for promoting wool from Sicilian farms. The aim of the district is to support sheep farms by creating a genuine supply chain. The wool produced by Sicilian farms is reintroduced into production cycles far removed from animal husbandry, thus improving not only its economic value but also its environmental value, and in this way the beneficiary is none other than the regional territory [1]. The idea behind the district is to transform raw wool into liquid fertilizer through a process of hydrolysis. Applied research and the process of introducing technological innovation are moving along two lines of action. The first concerns the use of wool derivatives in agriculture. Wool, in fact, when subjected to thermal and chemical treatment, can be used as 'biochar' (a stable carbon product derived from by-products, waste, or biomass of plant and/or animal origin), but also as a soil conditioner for sustainable agriculture. The starting point for the implementation of the hydrolysis process is the Greenwoolf project 'Recycling wool waste into protein hydrolysates for organic farming'. The fertilizer obtained can be liquid or solid, in pellet form, and is currently being tested in the field on vineyards and small fruits. It would therefore be capable of nourishing extensive crops such as vines in a completely natural and cost-effective way. This is not a small-scale "niche" recycling project, but a method capable of relieving sheep farmers of the cost of wool that cannot be used for textiles, reviving industrial production of machinery for the Italian and foreign markets, and spreading good organic farming practices.

Wool, like hair and nails, is mostly composed of keratin, a protein [1, 2]. Breaking it down to make its substances available is common practice. The dirty wool is placed in a reactor with water at around 170 °C for one hour. The reactor rotates around an axis that allows the water to penetrate the entire surface and inside the wool using saturated steam produced by a boiler. Controlled hydrolysis with superheated water breaks down keratin into simpler compounds. Due to its characteristics, wool, when treated, is an exceptional soil conditioner because it provides carbon, nitrogen, and sulfur, the main nutrients for plants. However, its use in its raw state is not recommended because infections can occur due to the very slow biodegradation process. In fact, wool is classified as a category 3 by-product, the disposal of which is regulated by EU Regulation 142 of 2011. The novelty of the district's project lies in the fact that, after the process, the wool returns to the animal through grazing, thanks to agricultural practices. This disposal system offers several advantages: - environmental: the sulfide bonds in wool, which make it dangerous when burned, are useful in this case because the sulfur added to the fields acts as a fertilizer and fungicide 40 - agronomic: soil structure is improved through the absorption of excess water (water retention). Economically, the costs of synthetic fertilizers are reduced. The profits of sheep farms are increased [3].

3 Wool Products

The other strand concerns the use of wool in traditional crafts which, thanks to the rediscovery of ancient manual skills, can produce true works of art. In central Sicily, unused wool can be put to further use that should not be overlooked [1, 2]. Felt is a "non-woven fabric" obtained through a process called felting. In this process, the wool fibers are intertwined, arranged in a single direction, and pressed manually with the aid of hot water and soap. Clearly, this is a process that does not require any special tools, is completely natural, and does not require the addition of chemicals. The result is an elastic fabric that is perfect for creating clothing, furnishing fabrics, and much more.

It also has remarkable thermal insulation properties against both heat and cold, due to the air trapped inside the wool during processing. Another strength of this product is its hygroscopicity. Felt is capable of storing 20–25% water when wet and 50% when dripping. The production of felt in Sicily offers opportunities not only to make use of a resource that would otherwise be wasted, but also to revive small historic production businesses whose ancient art deserves further exploration.

4 Current Practices

Some local communities have developed the "Tramando s'innova" project in collaboration with other specialized entities such as the Agenzia Lane d'Italia, which, with "Woolscape" is promoting a virtuous relationship between textile production and cultural and landscape heritage, while also mapping the wool industry region by region, reconstructing the identity of Italian wool, which can provide ideas for potential applications.

One need only observe nature to grasp its suggestions. Sheep's wool, for example, can be used to insulate our homes. The panels that make up the insulation have characteristics that allow them to compete very well with traditional building materials. Among the successful experiences in relation to its use in the construction sector, Edilana is worth mentioning. The Edilana company was founded in Sardinia with the aim of creating wool products using wool from Sardinian farms as its raw material. This company manufactures innovative products for use not only in agriculture but also in construction and furniture. The company immediately committed itself to promoting not only raw material but also respect for environmental issues. In the construction sector, the company decided to invest in the creation of a panel made from wool from native Sardinian sheep. The panel exploits the extraordinary properties of wool fibers, which, thanks to their high keratin content, are able to bind and eliminate many toxic substances. This interesting depolluting capacity allows it to absorb and neutralize smog, fine dust, heavy metals, and many substances harmful to health used in the construction industry. It can be used not only to create healthy living spaces but also to renovate and remediate buildings constructed in the past with materials that release harmful gases. Edilana panels, in combination with fir strips and sheep's wool, are used in PRONTOMAT for their acoustic and thermal insulation properties.

Edilana Design, on the other hand, manufactures padded garments: pillows for neck and back pain, postpartum pillows, therapeutic duvets and jackets, and garments that limit excessive sweating. In addition to saving over 60% of water, they strengthen, nourish, and protect the soil. The products do not need to be disposed of, they degrade slowly into the soil, increasing their fertility, and they reduce $CO2$, making them particularly environmentally friendly. In Friuli-Venezia Giulia, the start-up Agrivello, in collaboration with the University of Udine, the Friuli Centrale University Health Authority, and the Friuli Foundation, has led to the creation of the experimental project "Agrilana in pellet."

Among the companies operating in the field of wool application in the environmental and naturalistic sectors are the Pro Patrimonio Montano PatriMont network, Brebey, a Sardinian cooperative founded in 2012 that produces sheep wool-based panels, the

Sicilian Wool Production District based in Cammarata (AG) in the heart of the Sicani Mountains, as well as Mariantonia Urru Tessuti e Tappeti Sardi and the Valcamonica Wool Tail Association. With specific reference to the use of wool in naturalistic engineering projects, we can look to Turkey, where sheep's wool is used to combat erosion of agricultural land. In Turkey's hilly landscapes, farmers have long faced a crucial challenge: soil erosion and rapid rainwater runoff. These phenomena, exacerbated by climate change and intensive land use, reduce soil fertility and jeopardize agricultural productivity.

In Italy, according to Istat data from 2017, 8,200 tons of raw wool are produced each year from the shearing of six million sheep [2, 3]. As mentioned, wool can be used as it is, mixed with soil to retain moisture and slowly nourish plants, or transformed into pellets that release nutrients (nitrogen) and are ideal for vegetable gardens, orchards, and pots. It is an ecological alternative to chemical fertilizers, improves soil structure, and reduces environmental impact.

5 Methods: Nature-Based Engineering and Potential Applications of Wool

Nature-based engineering, as is well known, studies how living plant components (plants or parts thereof) can be used as building materials in combination with non-cementitious aggregates such as stone, earth, wood, and steel, as well as in combination with mats made of plant or synthetic fibers, mainly for hydrogeological stabilization projects related to soil consolidation in areas subject to erosion. The use of living materials for various purposes is a fairly ancient practice, but a strong impetus for the development of naturalistic engineering began in the 1990s in response to the need to simultaneously secure areas at risk of hydrogeological instability and protect the environment by minimizing the environmental impact of soil protection works. It is a cross-disciplinary science that, due to its many possible applications, requires technicians to have a basic knowledge of several scientific disciplines, which are integrated depending on the complexity of the context of intervention. Naturalistic engineering techniques [2–4] perform multiple functions and involve the use of different natural materials. Processed wool-in the form of bricks, geomats, or biomats[2] can be combined with plants and wood material.

Plants play a fundamental role in preventing hydrogeological instability by stabilizing slopes and banks from both a hydrological and mechanical point of view. In the first case, by intercepting rain, they protect the soil from splash detachment and increase evapotranspiration; in the second case, through their roots, they perform a cohesive action on the soil, protecting it from erosion linked to the surface flow of runoff water. When natural engineering techniques are applied to riverbank protection in river environments, they offer additional benefits by reducing the lateral expansion of watercourses and promoting the re-naturalization and strengthening of the ecological role of the river corridor through the development of favorable conditions (shading, reduction of sediment input,

[2] They are generally classified according to whether they are natural, made from plant fibers such as wood, coconut, and straw (e.g., bio-mats), or industrial, made from synthetic materials (e.g., geomats). They perform a variety of tasks, including erosion prevention, vegetation support, drainage, and soil waterproofing.

removal of pollutants, etc.) Finally, the vegetation component plays a role in mitigating environmental impact and has strong aesthetic and landscape value. For this reason, natural engineering works often fall into the broader category of nature-based solutions [5, 6].

Plant material includes seeds, cuttings, stakes, branches, and turf, which are used in different ways depending on site characteristics and the purpose of the intervention (erosion reduction, surface stabilization, etc.). There are precise rules governing their use and requirements necessary for the success of the interventions, including being native species and having a fast regenerative capacity, good technical characteristics, and a deep root system. Among the most suitable species are willows, poplars, alders, and tamarisks [5–7]. Wool bricks, geomats, or wool biomats can be associated with plants in naturalistic engineering works.

Wooden material essentially performs a supporting function, especially in the phase immediately following the completion of the intervention when the plant component is not yet sufficiently developed and able to perform all its functions. Mainly logs of various sizes belonging to tree species with good characteristics in terms of density, durability, and resistance (e.g., chestnut, fir, larch) are used. If large, it is used for support and consolidation purposes, otherwise as filling material, for example in gabions and pilings [6, 7].

In river environments, in particular, it provides suitable solutions for protecting the foot of the banks from erosion – thanks to its high resistance to the forces exerted by currents, as well as for the construction of structures directly in the riverbed with ecological functions, such as fish ladders. Wool bricks for filling gabions, geomats, or biomats can be combined with other wood materials in naturalistic engineering works.

6 Results: Characteristics and Applications of Wool

Sheep's wool is a renewable product because it grows back on animals every year. It has excellent thermal and sound insulation properties, is breathable, hygroscopic, and self-extinguishing because it does not burn or distribute heat. The natural function of wool is to protect animals from the elements and insulate them from heat and cold. Sheep's wool is often considered a waste product of farming and underutilized, but in reality, wool is a valuable material: it is breathable and retains water, is completely biodegradable, enriches the soil by decomposing slowly and releasing nitrogen and nutrients, and acts as a natural barrier against erosion. To address this problem, the idea was born to use bricks made from compressed sheep's wool to build sloping flower beds and agricultural terraces [8]. Wool is used as thermal and acoustic insulation in wall cavities, in internal and external cladding exposed to wind, in false ceilings, in partition walls, and as acoustic insulation panels. In addition to its various uses, it also offers a range of interesting application methods, as it can be used loose, in rolls, or in panels ranging from 20 to 80 mm for the following applications:

- Filling wool, which is used in cracks or frames as insulation.
- Insulating rolls that can be cut and worked with extreme ease. They offer uniform mechanical resistance and can be used in walls, counter walls, and roofs.

– Insulating panels, specifically for thermal and acoustic insulation of wooden and continuous floors.

Once sheared, the wool is washed, rinsed with sodium bicarbonate, and treated with boron salts, which not only make it more fire-resistant but also moth-proof. Carding is used to obtain the desired thicknesses, which can be reinforced with polypropylene fiber. To be used as a building material, the wool must be properly treated because, in the presence of moisture, the boron salts are washed away, making it susceptible to pests again. It can be seen that wool, considered a waste product, has all the right qualities to be valued and used in a myriad of different ways, each of which respects the environment. Given the abundance of the product and its easy availability, especially in western Sicily, we can conclude that not exploiting its potential is not only an economic waste but also a moral one. Its great abundance, the simplicity of the production processes it undergoes, and the wide range of uses can succeed in giving value and utility to this product from our sheep.

7 Proposal Model: Areas of Application and Sustainability

The project aims to develop a virtuous model for the recovery and application of wool in the form of a material that is useful for protecting the land and respecting the environment [9–11][3].

Wool Bricks
The blocks are densely packed and molded into interlocking structures. Placed on slopes, they create layered platforms that stabilize the soil, retain moisture, reduce surface runoff, and promote crop growth without chemical additives.

Biomatts and Geomatts
Biomatts can be used for surface erosion control and covering (grass planting, biomatts, and geomatts), surface stabilization (together with piling, wattle fencing, and fascines), support/consolidation (combined with gabions and breakwaters), and rockfall protection.

In addition to this, there are also indirect environmental functions (Fig. 2) that are useful for:

– river and ecological redevelopment,
– restoration and re-naturalization,
– mitigation of environmental impacts.

Thanks to their versatility, they can be used in various contexts: on the banks of rivers, streams, and canals or directly in their beds, on unstable slopes, on railway embankments or road embankments, in abandoned areas and quarries, and in coastal and lagoon areas.

Here are some examples of the most common types of natural engineering works and techniques used in Italy, according to the methods of implementation and construction:

[3] ISPRA, Tipologia di opere e tecniche di ingegneria naturalistica https://www.isprambiente.gov.it/contentfiles/00000400/431-tb-battistella3.pdf (Available in Febrary 2026).

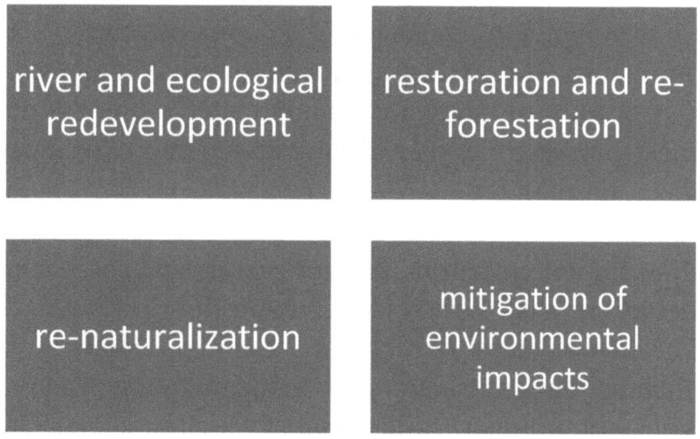

Fig. 2. Indirect environmental functions, credit: Celestina Fazia

stone gabions, box gabions, reinforced green terramesh, hydraulic riverbank stabilisation (riverbank gabions) and slope stabilisation (wickerwork, terraces and live cordonata, live grating, simple palisade, trellis, double-walled piling, reinforced and/or reinforced earth) [10, 11]. These techniques are used to secure slopes, restore riverbeds, stabilize coastal dunes, reinforce road embankments, and reclaim quarries. Compared to traditional techniques, they have a lower environmental impact and blend in better with the landscape.

7.1 Externalities of a Project for the Use of Wool in the Sicily Region

The innovation that a project for the reuse of wool in naturalistic engineering works aims to introduce concerns the transformation process: the production of bricks made from compressed sheep's wool to build sloping flower beds and agricultural terraces, but also the production of other materials, panels or geo-mats for naturalistic engineering, becomes an innovative process when wool is successfully transformed - from shearing to processing - into a low-impact green product. Sicily is the leading region in Italy in terms of UAA (Utilised Agricultural Area), with 1.342 million hectares, and ranks second in terms of the number of active farms, with 142,416. It is the Italian region with the largest area of organic farming (338,000 ha). In order to mitigate the socio-economic decline of inland areas, it is necessary to develop rural entrepreneurship. Section 2 of the CSR (Complemento di programmazione per lo Sviluppo Rurale, or Rural Development Programme Supplement) for Sicily refers to the need to promote transition, research and technological innovation [12]. The tourism objective is closely linked to the rural landscape of historical interest, agricultural practices and traditional knowledge [12, 13].

UNESCO recently recognised the dry stone walls found in Sicily. They play a fundamental role in the landscape, the environment and the defence of the territory, helping to prevent landslides and flooding. The presence of dry stone walls helps to combat erosion, desertification and soil salinisation. They are advantageous because the materials can be sourced locally, but they are not always suitable for containing clayey embankments, requiring commitment and skill to build.

The idea is consistent with the provisions of the EIP, European Innovation Partnership (Reg. (EU) 2021/2115), as the use of low-impact green materials places it in the virtuous cycle of sustainable development, increasing the competitiveness of farms in both the short and long term, thanks to a gradual approach to research and technology transfer. Furthermore, through the use of circular economy materials, it will be easier and more effective to intervene to preserve the soil and habitats and improve the ecosystem services closely linked to sheep farming [3].

The Sicilian wool district is responsible for promoting wool. Wool is renewable, has thermal and sound insulation properties, is hygroscopic and self-extinguishing, retains water, is biodegradable, enriches the soil by decomposing slowly and releasing nitrogen and nutrients, and acts as a natural barrier against erosion. However, its use in its raw state is not recommended due to its very slow biodegradation process. In fact, wool is classified as a category 3 by-product, the disposal of which is regulated by EU Regulation 142/2011 [11–13].

The use of wool for different purposes, which allows it to be sanitised without costly and environmentally harmful processes, specifically for bricks or wool-based products used to contain embankments or slopes in natural engineering works and to delimit cultivated areas, is in line with CSR objectives [12, 13].

8 Conclusion: Agricultural and Environmental Benefits

Farmers can use beds made from wool bricks to plant vegetables, herbs, and even fruit bushes. Every drop of rain is absorbed and stored in the soil instead of running off [10]. The slow release of nutrients from the decomposition of wool supports healthy and vigorous plant growth, reducing the need for synthetic fertilizers. The effects on the environment are noteworthy. This practice not only transforms waste material into a resource, but is also a concrete example of regenerative agriculture:

- it reduces waste and costs,
- improves soil fertility,
- combats erosion and desertification,
- supports rural communities with low environmental impact solutions.

It is a demonstration of how innovation can arise from respect for nature and the intuition to make the most of existing resources [5]. The use of wool helps to halt and reverse the process of biodiversity loss, strengthen ecosystem services, and preserve habitats and landscapes. Wool is an economic resource, but it also carries values and culture. Reviving wool means supporting the territories and those who care for them, first and foremost the shepherds. But that's not all.

Many Italian landscapes have unique features that must be preserved even when it is necessary to intervene to protect embankments and slopes. The field of naturalistic engineering, created to introduce effective intervention methods with low environmental impact, is one of the possible contexts in which this material can be used. Through the use of wool bricks, for example, it will help to preserve the historical elements of the rural landscape while improving the integration of defensive structures into the landscape.

It is important to emphasize that the research findings are consistent with Specific Objective 5 of the PAC (Common Agricultural Policy of the European Union) "to promote sustainable development and the efficient management of natural resources such as water, soil, and air, including by reducing reliance on chemicals," as it is based on the recovery of sheep's wool through a sustainable process that involves low use of energy, environmental resources, and chemicals. Furthermore, it contributes to halting and reversing the loss of biodiversity, strengthening ecosystem services, and preserving habitats and the landscape. Wool is an economic resource but also carries cultural and symbolic value. Revitalizing wool means supporting local communities and those who care for them, first and foremost the shepherds. But that's not all. Many Italian landscapes possess unique characteristics that must be preserved even when intervention is necessary to protect embankments and slopes. The field of naturalistic engineering, which emerged with the goal of introducing intervention methods that are effective and have minimal environmental impact, is one potential context for the material's use. It will help, through the use of materials such as wool bricks, to preserve the historical and cultural elements of the rural landscape while improving the integration of protective structures into the landscape.

It would be both possible and desirable to identify the network of businesses that use the new product—the result of circular economies arising from the transformation of a local product— since, through the use of low-impact green materials, the company that uses "processed" wool for eco-friendly materials positions itself within the virtuous cycle of sustainable development, increasing the competitiveness of agricultural businesses—both in the short and long term—thanks to a gradual shift toward research and technology transfer.

Acknowledgments. All authors contributed to the drafting of this paper, offering their specific expertise. We would like to thank Dr. Sebastiano Tosto, president of the Sicilian Wool Production District Cammarata (AG), for his suggestions and the information he provided.

Disclosure of Interests. The authors have no competing interests to declare that are relevant to the content of this article.

References

1. Ibn-Elhaj, S., Mounir, S., Khabbazi, A., Sarghini, H.: Effect of clay's multilayer composites material on the energy efficiency of buildings. J. Compos. Sci. **6**(5), 151 (2022)
2. Bognanno, S.: Sustainability of the sheep farming industry in Sicily: tradition and innovation. Degree Thesis, University of Catania (2023)
3. International Renewable Energy Agency: Off-Grid Renewable Energy Statistics 2022. International Renewable Energy Agency, Abu Dhabi (2022)
4. Rohit, K., Dixit, S.: A review – future aspect of natural fiber reinforced composite. Polym. Renew. Resour. **7**(2), 43–60 (2016)
5. Kozłowski, R.: Handbook of Natural Fibres, Volume 1: Types, Properties and Factors Affecting Breeding and Cultivation. Woodhead Publishing in Association with the Textile Institute, Series in Textiles No. 118, Oxford, Cambridge, Philadelphia, New Delhi (2012)
6. Zhang, H.: Building Materials in Civil Engineering. Ed. Woodhead Publishing in Materials, Oxford, Cambridge, Philadelphia, New Delhi (2011). ISBN: 978-1-84569-955-0
7. AAVV: Sicilia agricoltura. Accessed 01 Feb 2026
8. Carus, M.: The European hemp industry: cultivation, processing and applications for fibres, shivs, seeds and flowers. In: European Industrial Hemp Association (EIHA), Hürth (Germany), pp. 1–9 (2017)

9. Schiechtl Meinhard, H.: Ingegneria Naturalistica, Steti (2016)
10. Fazia, C., Nahiduzzaman, K.M., Al-Ramadan, B., Aldosary, A., Moraci, F.: Counteract soil consumption through ecosystem services and landscape restoration for an efficient urban regeneration. Land **13**(323) (2024)
11. ISPRA: Tipologia di opere e tecniche di ingegneria naturalistica. Accessed 01 Feb 2026
12. Assessorato regionale dell'Agricoltura, dello sviluppo rurale e della pesca mediterranea, Piano strategico della PCA 2023-2027. https://sviluppoprurale.regione.sicilia.it/storage/2023/10/MASAF_2023_0198160_Allegato_CSR_PSP2023_27Sicilia_MARZO_2023-1.pdf
13. EUR-LEX, Regolamento (UE) 2021/2115 del Parlamento europeo e del Consiglio del 2 dicembre 2021 recante norme sul sostegno ai piani strategici che gli Stati membri devono redigere nell'ambito della politica agricola comune (piani strategici della PAC) e finanziati dal Fondo europeo agricolo di garanzia (FEAGA) e dal Fondo europeo agricolo per lo sviluppo rurale (FEASR) e che abroga i regolamenti (UE) n. 1305/2013 e (UE) n. 1307/2013. https://eur-lex.europa.eu/legal-content/IT/ALL/?uri=CELEX%3A32021R2115

Bridging Land Use Planning, Resilience and AI for Flood-Induced Urban Management

Soulaf Ata, Kh. Md. Nahiduzzaman, and Hassan Radoine(✉)

Mohammed VI Polytechnic University, Rabat, Morocco
{Soulaf.ATA,KhMd.NAHIDUZZAMAN,Hassan.RADOINE}@um6p.ma

Abstract. Natural hazards are becoming more frequent and severe due to climate change, laying bare the limitations of conventional land use planning and risk management approaches. For instance, events like floods and other disruptions highlight the importance of developing adaptive and resilient strategies that can respond to diverse hazards, especially in rapidly urbanizing regions. In existing studies, land use, infrastructure, and risk assessment are treated separately. Moreover, planning processes do not integrate local knowledge and AI-based predictive tools, particularly in developing countries.

This paper aims to bridge this gap by proposing a conceptual framework that connects all the previously mentioned elements. Using a multi-scalar approach that funnels from global experiences to the Moroccan context, it identifies relevant challenges and opportunities. In this context, the paper advances three research pillars: (1) adaptive land use planning and multi-hazard resilient infrastructure, (2) integration of local knowledge with science-driven solutions, and (3) AI-driven predictive modeling for multi-disruption scenario planning.

Keywords: Adaptive land use planning · multi-hazard resilience · climate change adaptation · AI-driven prediction · local knowledge · urban resilience

1 Introduction

1.1 Global Climate Risk Context and the Inadequacy of Traditional Planning

Across the globe, climate change has deeply spread its roots, burgeoning into intense natural hazards such as floods, droughts, heatwaves, and earthquakes, which place a huge pressure on urban systems (IPCC 2021). When combining their repercussions with already existing vulnerabilities, human settlements are now more than ever in need of coping with and withstanding the consequences of past interventions in the natural environment.

As climate change increases both the frequency and intensity of hazards, existing vulnerabilities are exacerbated, particularly in rapidly urbanizing areas where development often expands into high-risk zones. This dynamic raises critical questions about the relationship between risk management, climate adaptation, and spatial planning (Farinós-Dasí et al. 2025). In this context, planning becomes a form of governance

O. Gervasi et al. (Eds.): ICCSA 2026 Workshops, LNCS 16758, pp. 615–630, 2027.
https://doi.org/10.1007/978-3-032-30497-1_37

arena for disaster risk management where governance can metaphorically be seen as the controlling strings. It converts scientific knowledge into tangible actions and mediates between all the actors and sectoral policies.

1.2 From Traditional Disaster Management to Disaster Risk Management

The transition from traditional disaster management to disaster risk management (DRM) shows a fundamental shift in perspective. Conventional disaster management focuses on addressing disasters after they occur, whereas DRM prioritizes anticipating their impact through proactive risk assessment. The first approach treated disasters as isolated events. The latter, however, highlights that climate change has altered hazard patterns, exacerbating their intensity and frequency. As a result, risks are no longer static but evolving, which requires constant assessment and adaptation (Farinós-Dasí et al. 2025).

Furthermore, the Hyogo Framework for Action (2005–2015) and its successor, the Sendai Framework (2015–2030), formalized this transition. They emphasized that climate change adaptation can be established through risk and hazard mapping and vertical coordination between all stakeholders. As such, climate change adaptation can be understood as the process of adjusting to current and future effects of climate change using spatial planning as a key means to implement it.

1.3 The Planning Implementation Gap: Lessons from the International Practices

However, even if climate adaptation and resilience plans widely exist in large cities worldwide, they remain ineffective. Olazabal et al. (2021) justify this weakness by a planning-implementation disconnection. In essence, climate adaptation plans are often non-binding, poorly financed, and weakly connected to land-use regulation (Olazabal et al. 2021). Thus, these plans frequently exist as standalone policy documents without integration into legally binding planning instruments that govern development decisions (Olazabal et al. 2021).

In many African cities, including Moroccan urban centers, local adaptation planning is minimal or absent. This reveals significant regional disparities in the institutionalization and operationalization of climate adaptation. Therefore, the challenge lies in how to bridge risk knowledge and enforceable planning action.

1.4 The Role of Communities, Data, and Artificial Intelligence

Beyond technical and institutional dimensions, recent literature emphasizes the importance of communities in resilience. Farinós-Dasí et al. (2025) underscore the importance of the local community participation and knowledge as well as the active involvement of stakeholders. These insights pinpoint the importance of multi-level and data-informed planning that can predict risk and improve decision-making.

Simultaneously, the rise of artificial intelligence AI-driven tools for extreme event modeling and impact assessment presents a revolutionary opportunity (Camps-Valls et al. 2024). Through leveraging AI, planners can enhance detection, prediction, and scenario analysis, which will highly support anticipatory strategies.

1.5 Research Problem and Objectives

Despite the increasing importance of climate risks and the availability of technical tools, the impacts of disasters in Morocco are devastating in terms of human and material losses. The limited integration of risk prevention in land-use planning tools is to blame. In fact, current planning instruments in Morocco remain largely reactive and lack the integration of hazard mapping and indigenous knowledge into planning documents (The N.S.D.R.M, Morocco 2020). In fact, the disconnection between the comprehension of risks and the implementation of planning regulations exacerbates vulnerability. Indeed, this is mainly true in rapidly urbanizing areas where development pressures overlook safety considerations.

This paper addresses this critical gap through three primary objectives: (1) to examine international practices in adaptive land use planning and identify transferable lessons. (2) Analyze the Moroccan context, and (3) conceptualize a framework grounded in three pillars: adaptive land use strategies, hybrid knowledge integration, and AI-driven planning.

1.6 From International Examples to the Moroccan Context: A Funnel Approach

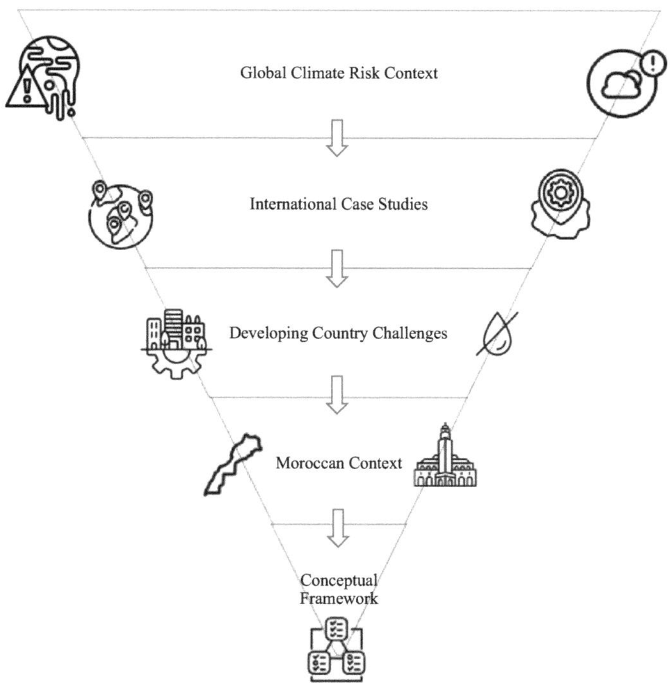

Fig. 1. The Funnel Approach: From Global Climate Risk Context to a Context-Specific Adaptive Land-Use Framework for Morocco. Source: Developed by Author

Thus, this chapter seeks to explore adaptive land use, resilient strategies, hybrid knowledge, and AI-driven planning. The analysis unfolds through a funnel approach, beginning with global perspectives on adaptive planning and resilience, narrowing progressively to the context of developing nations. These countries share challenges (e.g. rapid urbanization, governance fragmentation, and limited resources) with Morocco, facilitating a smooth transition to the Moroccan case. This progression allows us to identify transferable lessons while taking context-specific limitations into consideration (Fig. 1).

2 Global Overview: Adaptive Land Use and Resilient Strategies

2.1 Evolution of Urban Planning Under Climate Risk: Transitioning from Hazard-Centric to Resilience-Oriented Strategies

Over the past decades, urban and territorial planning systems all around the world have faced a lot of natural hazards whose intensity is drastically increasing. In essence, floods, heatwaves, droughts, and all of their compound effects have unearthed deficiencies in land-use planning approaches that were initially designed to tackle hazards separately. In fact, traditional planning paradigms treated natural hazards as independent events requiring distinct sectoral responses. Therefore, this siloed approach overlooks the interconnected nature of urban systems and the cascading effects of multiple hazards.

In response, planning has progressively shifted towards resilience-based approaches that orbit around systemic thinking and long-term adaptability. Instead of treating hazards in isolation, resilience thinking tends to conceptualize cities as interconnected socio-ecological systems where infrastructure, ecosystems, and human communities interact through dynamic feedback loops (Magoni 2017). Moreover, resilience thinking in spatial planning is linked to the city's ability to change, adapt, and transform while facing outside disturbances rather than bouncing back to its initial state (Udovyk et al. 2025). Taken together, this shift reflects a broader transformation in planning philosophy, from reactive hazard control toward an anticipatory governance of risk.

2.2 Resilience Frameworks: Ecological, Social and Urban

Urban climate adaptation is closely linked to three resilience paradigms: ecological, social, and urban resilience. They have evolved in separate disciplines, yet they converge in practice.

Ecological resilience refers to a system's capacity to absorb disturbances while maintaining its core functions (Holling 1973). Social resilience extends this perspective to human communities, emphasizing their capacity to anticipate, respond to, and recover from these disturbances while maintaining social cohesion (Wannewitz et al. 2024). It also highlights that vulnerability is unevenly distributed and is shaped by socio-economic and political factors.

Accordingly, urban resilience integrates these dimensions within the city through frameworks such as the socio-ecological-technological systems (SETS), where social, ecological, and technological components interact in disaster management (Lee & Hong 2024). However, empirical applications often reveal imbalances due to emphasizing technical solutions over ecological and spatial ones.

2.3 International Case Studies: Operationalizing Adaptive Planning

The following international case studies illustrate diverse approaches to adaptive land use planning. They demonstrate the integration of technical innovation, local knowledge, and governance reform.

Case Study 1: Rotterdam Netherlands: Resilience Through Placemaking
Rotterdam, located in the Rhine-Meuse delta in the Netherlands, mainly faces multiple flooding hazards due to its low-lying geography. While the city relies on extensive flood protection infrastructure, climate change projections suggest that "hard" measures alone are insufficient. (Peinhardt 2021).

Katherine Peinhardt (2021) examines the Rotterdam case study in the Netherlands, where climate adaptation is integrated into spatial planning by transforming public squares into multifunctional flood risk infrastructure. In essence, the Waterplein Benthemplein water square serves two finalities: providing a well-kept public space while absorbing the excess storm water. Decision makers opted for reshaping the current square rather than designing an invisible technical amenity underground, which would have provided no additional benefits.

However, despite its potential, several barriers may hinder its implementation. At the municipal level, limited staff expertise regarding climate adaptation, insufficient data, and financial constraints are problematic. Other barriers can also emerge, namely political obstacles and poor coordination between departments. These barriers are particularly relevant for the Moroccan context, where municipal capacity, interdepartmental coordination, and dedicated climate adaptation funding are often limited.

Case Study 2: Peruvian Amazon: Integrating Indigenous Knowledge
In the Peruvian Amazon, indigenous communities have developed detailed knowledge of environmental risks, seasonal cycles, and ecosystem dynamics. However, formal planning processes have often overlooked this knowledge in favor of external technical expertise.

Furthermore, adaptive land-use planning has shown improvement when local knowledge is integrated with scientific tools such as satellite imagery and hydrological modeling. According to Rodriguez et al., this hybrid approach enhances the contextual understanding and supports effective planning decisions. Nevertheless, challenges remain, especially in scaling knowledge co-production within formal governance systems as well as overcoming institutional rigidity. In fact, these challenges are highly relevant for Morocco, where local and traditional knowledge exists. However, these precious assets are rarely integrated into formal planning instruments. In this context, the Peruvian case illustrates both the value of knowledge integration and the institutional reforms needed to enable it.

Ultimately, both the Rotterdam and Peruvian Amazon cases reveal two complementary dimensions of adaptive planning. On one hand, Rotterdam illustrates spatial integration of infrastructure within a high-capacity governance system. On the other hand, the Peruvian example emphasizes community co-production in a more context-sensitive environment. Even if their institutional conditions differ, both cases show that resilience emerges when planning moves beyond siloed technical solutions toward multi-actor governance structures. Nevertheless, their contrasting institutional capacities reveal that adaptive planning models cannot be directly transplanted across contexts. Thus, it is imperative to consider governance frameworks and cultural contexts.

2.4 Emerging Knowledge Integration: Connecting Scientific and Local Knowledge

The integration of local knowledge with scientific approaches has emerged as a critical frontier in climate adaptation. Olazabal et al. (2021) argue that subaltern knowledge can be an important source of innovation and can further enhance adaptation solutions. The article discusses the disconnect between climate adaptation planning and its tangible implementation. This is due to overreliance on technical knowledge, namely, scientific data and models. They often fail to consider local contexts and social inequalities.

Overall, the article concluded that we urgently need to move away from purely technocratic approaches in order to ensure an inclusive and adaptive environment. Ultimately, integrating indigenous knowledge is more about empowering local communities and involving them in shaping their own future in the face of climate change.

2.5 AI-Driven Predictive Tools: Opportunities and Challenges

Artificial intelligence and machine learning have rapidly emerged as transformative tools for urban planning and climate risk assessment. In this work, Kesavan et al. (2024) focuses on using AI to assess risk precisely and address flooding risks. The research introduces AI for the resilient cities model and applies it in the vulnerable area of Penthakata in the coastal city of Puri, Odisha. The study leverages cutting-edge geospatial technology, deep learning, and multi-parameter analysis to evaluate flood vulnerabilities.

Furthermore, the paper emphasizes integrating technology with community volunteers and local knowledge, whose role was mainly to assist in data collection and implement mitigation measures. Therefore, AI complements rather than replaces human knowledge.

3 Developing Countries Context

3.1 Developing Countries' Challenges

Developing nations are more exposed to climate change impacts and have less adaptive capacity. Tarhule (2012) discusses the NAPA (National Adaptation Programs of Action), which is a mechanism under the UNFCC (United Nations Framework Convention on Climate Change). It aims to help developing countries to reach climate adaptation and, more importantly, provide funding in order to ensure its implementation (Tarhule 2012).

Initially, more attention was directed towards mitigation, which aims to reduce greenhouse emissions, in other words, preventing the situation from getting worse. Later, there was a realization that even if we stopped greenhouse gas emissions completely, the effects of past emissions will still be felt for decades to come. Unfortunately, developing countries will bear the heavier consequences due to their vulnerability. Vulnerability can be defined as a function of exposure, sensitivity, and adaptive capacity (IPCC). This framing shows that vulnerability is not solely environmental but structurally embedded within socio-economic and institutional systems, especially in rapidly urbanizing contexts.

3.2 Rapid Urbanization and Informal Settlements as Amplifiers of Climate Risks

Rentschler et al. (2022) provides systematic evidence that countries are involuntarily increasing their exposure to flooding. As a matter of fact, settlements in flood-prone areas have expanded faster than those in safer zones since 1985, especially in low- and middle-income countries. These trends show that urban expansion patterns actively shape exposure, stressing the fact that land-use governance is central to disaster risk reduction.

Furthermore, disaster losses are constantly climbing. This is mainly due to the fact that informal settlements often emerge in marginal lands such as floodplains, steep slopes, and coastal edges, where land is affordable but hazardous. In such areas, disaster losses are not only driven by intensifying hazards but also by planning decisions that allowed such risky expansion.

Overall, in areas with high flood exposure, it is crucial to invest in disaster preparedness. On the other hand, in areas where exposure is still low but increasing rapidly, it is essential to revise land-use and urbanization plans as well as building codes and infrastructure master plans.

3.3 Governance Gaps and Institutional Weaknesses in Climate Adaptation

Termeer et al. (2017) argue that adaptation to climate change is primarily a governance issue and is not only limited to technical solutions. It is about the interaction between public and private actors aiming to solve societal problems related to climate change. However, climate adaptation faces several challenges on the governance level.

First, institutional fragmentation undermines coordination, while unclear mandates blur responsibility. The second challenge is uncertainty. No one knows for sure future climate impacts, so it is difficult to plan effective policies. The third challenge concerns the long-term horizon of climate impacts. Decisions should be made in the present, but their repercussions should be felt years later. Balancing short-term economic interests with long-term climate risks is hard. Unlike mitigation, adaptation is new on the policy agenda, so responsibilities, procedures, and solutions are weakly defined.

Therefore, effective governance arrangements require multi-level coordination, alignment of sectoral boundaries, and clear policy instruments. Overall, the paper suggests that the development of governance arrangements for climate adaptation is both context and time specific. There is no one-size-fits-all solution since it depends on existing institutions. In that sense, governance is a continuous process of adaptation and learning rather than a fixed institutional design.

3.4 Infrastructure Deficiencies and Cascading Vulnerabilities

Kiunsi (2013) discusses in his article the complexities of dealing with climate change in a rapidly developing urban environment. Through the example of Dar Es Salaam, a major city in Tanzania, the author highlights the challenges it faces and their role as stressors in worsening climate change impacts. It shows how inadequate drainage, sanitation, and waste management exacerbate flood impacts. Hence, the city's top priority is to address these challenges before tackling climate adaptability. Moreover, informal settlements are particularly vulnerable due to the absence of foundational infrastructure, especially those located in low-lying areas. Consequently, this reveals that adaptation cannot be effectively implemented where basic services are lacking.

More importantly, the case of Dar Es Salaam illustrates that climate adaptation in developing cities must be integrated into every aspect of urban development, from infrastructure planning to community engagement. In this sense, this case study reflects structural issues observed in other developing contexts, such as informal urbanization and fragmented governance.

3.5 Social Vulnerabilities and Environmental Injustice

Climate risk is socially differentiated. Andersen et al. (2023) examine the health risk of climate change in Mukuru informal settlement, Nairobi, Kenya. The case study was chosen because Mukuru lacks basic services and its residents are particularly vulnerable to climate change, which makes it a critical area to study. The study aims to investigate what the local residents know and think and how they act in regard to climate change and climate change-mediated health risks.

The study deduced that there is a strong awareness foundation that can be leveraged for action. The collected findings are useful for policymakers, planners, and researchers to work locally on adaptive and mitigation strategies. For example, intervention can focus on improving housing, sanitation, and access to clean water, which will in turn reduce vulnerability to climate-related health risks. Overall, this suggests that knowledge alone is insufficient without institutional and infrastructural support. Additionally, the study also reflects that vulnerability is not only spatial but also socio-economic and cultural. Therefore, resilience planning should not focus solely on technical solutions, but it also needs to take social equity into consideration.

3.6 Opportunities and Lessons: Hybrid Strategies from Similar Regions

In his article on urban development and governance in Nigeria, Awuah (2018) unveils the opportunities hidden behind several urban weaknesses. In fact, the literature enumerates many weaknesses, such as rapid urban growth and rising urban poverty, which created opportunities for large-scale urban development. In other words, these conditions show that even a flawed system can offer meaningful opportunities if its potential is recognized. In the end understanding the perspectives of key stakeholders is crucial.

On another note, the author explains pluralistic social steering, which means that urban planning and governance can succeed through diverse sources of social inputs and directions. It is not just top-down; it involves various actors working together. To sum up, the combination of innovative approaches, stakeholder involvement, as well as strong government support is required to step forward since it provides the infrastructure, the very foundation of urban development. It is about recognizing both the challenges and the opportunities and working collaboratively to build a better urban environment.

4 Moroccan Context: Need for Context-Specific Adaptive Strategies

4.1 Climate Hazards in Morocco: A Multi-hazard Landscape

Morocco's diverse geography and variable climate expose it to major natural hazards such as floods, droughts, earthquakes, and tsunamis in addition to forest fires, heat waves, cold snaps, storms, submergence, landslides, locust infestations, and blizzards. The first four natural hazards have a significant impact on the human and economic level, which is why they need serious and urgent attention (OECD 2024). Throughout modern history, Morocco has been marked by several key natural catastrophes whose effects were disastrous. The tsunami of 1755 was a direct result of the Great Lisbon Earthquake, the 1960 Agadir earthquake, and the 2004 Al Hoceima earthquake. During the end of 2025 and the beginning of 2026, due to intense and sudden rainfall, Morocco faced one of the deadliest flooding events ever witnessed in the past decade, which occurred in Safi, with an important number of human casualties (Al-Jazeera 2025). Moreover, other cities across the countries suffered from the excess of rain but with fewer human losses, such as Ksar Lekbir, where prevention measures have been carefully enforced (Africa Climate Reports 2026).

4.2 Urban Expansion and Peri-Urban Growth Pressures

Tribak & El Amrani (2018) explain that the Great Nador agglomeration faces critical climate hazards, primarily floods, which are exacerbated by rapid and unplanned urban expansion. Thus, this dynamic creates considerable pressure on land use and increases vulnerability within the region. In short, the article highlights how human interventions and rapid urban expansion worsen those hazards.

In this context, the rapid urbanization in the Great Nador territory is characterized by excessive spatial growth that encroaches upon sensitive and risky areas. The study also answers the following question: What are the factors that drive sprawl into risk areas? First, strong land pressure reduces the effectiveness of development plans for urban agglomeration. Moreover, technical errors, such as overlooking non-buildable zones (ZNA) in the absence of hydrological studies, lead to the construction of buildings in high-risk areas.

This dynamic is driven by a notable imbalance between land supply and demand, which has caused land prices to triple in the recent decades. Consequently, affordable and accessible building lands are rare, which will force the low-income population to settle in marginal and dangerous areas of the agglomeration. Additionally, the authors state that the population is strongly attached to their place of residence and relatives. This leads to buildings being constructed in areas frequently threatened by natural hazards, despite official urbanization policies.

Over time, the spatial dispersion of urbanization and the occupation of flood-prone areas created fragmented urban fabric. Therefore, flood risk management became a priority, especially in highly populated and dangerous areas. Historically, areas near main rivers in Great Nador were free of construction until the late 1950s. The plains were solely reserved for agriculture and fishing. However, over the past 50 years, urbanization expanded into flood zones, and human settlements developed in marshy and floodable areas, significantly increasing vulnerability. This transformation illustrates how spatial planning decisions can "formalize" long-term vulnerability when they are misaligned with environmental realities.

4.3 Infrastructure Gaps and Socio-Economic Vulnerabilities

Morocco has faced severe droughts leading to water scarcity. Water infrastructure deficits represent critical vulnerabilities across Morocco's urban systems. Despite the government's efforts to build over 153 dams exceeding 19 billion cubic meters of storage capacity and target 51% renewable energy by 2030, severe challenges persist in improving drinking water infrastructure, especially in low-income districts (Dahchour et al. 2025).

At the same time, vulnerability is not only infrastructural but socio-economic. The case of Tetouan illustrates how rapid urbanization along with landscape characteristics, increases flood exposure (Salhi et al. 2024). Moreover, risk perception and response may vary according to gender, education and socio-economic conditions, therefore shaping how communities anticipate and cope with flood risks.

While awareness exists, it does not always translate into effective action due to structural constraints. This highlights that vulnerability is both spatial and social. Thus, it is crucial to have integrated approaches that combine infrastructure development with social, institutional along with measures centered around communities.

4.4 Vulnerability of Housing

The late Haouz earthquake that occurred in 2023 marked the region's history as the most devastating natural hazard in over a decade. Ait Zamzami et al. (2024). Discusses the housing vulnerability in the western High Atlas of Morocco, namely traditional dwellings. These structures are built with natural materials such as earth, stone and wood, reflect local knowledge and resource availability but remain structurally vulnerable to seismic risks (Ait Zamzami et al. 2024). Beyond emergency reconstruction, integrating disaster risk into rural planning frameworks is essential for sustainable territorial planning in Morocco (Amini Alaoui et al. 2024).

The aim of the reconstruction process is to create a balance between strengthening the existing building method and introducing more resilient materials while respecting the cultural heritage of the region. Simply put, the local identity should be preserved while ensuring the safety of residents. Additionally, understanding the seismic risks and adapting practices are very essential for protecting these communities from future disasters.

4.5 Local Knowledge and Community Practices

Morocco has a rich heritage of traditional water management systems. It has sustained communities in arid and semi-arid environments for centuries. For instance, the khettarat system of Marrakech illustrates this indigenous socio-technical heritage. They are underground systems of wells and channels for sustainable water delivery and have met Marrakech's drinking water needs until the early 1990s. This demonstrates their effectiveness in oasis environments (Messous 2025). Although their use has declined due to institutional and economic changes, they remain relevant as models for contemporary adaptation strategies.

Similarly, vernacular architecture in Morocco has evolved over centuries, shaped by adaptation to local conditions and material availability as well as cultural preferences. Traditional construction practices in mountain villages use natural materials such as earth, stone, and wood, which reflect knowledge of local resources and environmental constraints (Ait Zamzami et al. 2024). However, these practices face challenges from a durability and resistance perspective, especially in the face of earthquakes.

Conversely, reconstruction efforts reveal tensions between traditional knowledge and modern building regulations. In essence, the states introduce administrative regulations into vernacular construction processes, which challenges local builders' credibility (Belahnech 2025). Overall, the challenge is to develop eco-construction approaches that take into account vernacular building culture while addressing contemporary safety and performance requirements. Simply put, we should recognize that traditional practices embody valuable climate adaptation knowledge. For instance, thermal mass for temperature regulation, natural ventilation strategies, and water-sensitive design should not be replaced by modern construction methods.

On another note, community-based adaptation strategies further illustrate the importance of local knowledge. Practices developed by farmers and livestock breeders vary across regions and respond to specific environmental and socio-economic conditions (Snaibi 2020). At the same time, there are differences between local priorities and external planning approaches which stresses the need for participatory and context-sensitive strategies (Olazabal et al. 2021).

Urban contexts present different community adaptation challenges. Research in Tetouan emphasizes that solely relying on structural engineering for risk management is inadequate. Instead, we should advocate for tailored awareness campaigns, educational initiatives, and capacity-building programs that enhance social engagement and resilience (Salhi et al. 2024). Therefore, the psychosocial dimensions of risk and resilience are acknowledged.

4.6 Synthesis: Why Morocco Requires Context-Specific Research

To summarize, Morocco's position at the intersection of Mediterranean, Atlantic, and Saharan climate zones creates exceptional variability in precipitation and temperature (Ongoma et al. 2024). Moreover, the semi-arid to arid climate generates fundamental water scarcity constraints with uneven rainfall distribution, which necessitate context-specific management systems (Hafyani et al. 2020; Dahchour et al. 2025). Furthermore, coastal areas face sea level rise (Chtioui et al. 2024), mountainous regions face flash floods (Sallak 2019). All of these demand different adaptation strategies depending on their unique context.

On the other hand, the colonial-era transformations created a path full of vulnerabilit**ies** with contemporary high-risk zones connected to areas transformed under the protectorate (Bolca 2025). Additionally, cultural practices influence settlement patterns and risk perceptions (Tribak et al. 2018) and gender as well as education differences affect risk awareness (Salhi et al. 2024). Traditional systems such as khettarat are still relevant (Messous 2025) but integrating vernacular practices with contemporary requirements requires negotiation between state systems and local knowledge networks (Belahnech 2025).

Despite the existence of progressive frameworks like Water Law 36–15 (Grijsen et al. 2017), implementation challenges persist. For example, Bouaakkaz et al. (2018) show that the Souss watershed has insufficient institutional frameworks and inadequate flood management. Moreover, national strategies face implementation delays while flood risk integration into urban planning remains inadequate (Tribak et al. 2018). Therefore, Morocco requires solutions specific to its own institutional structures and capacity constraints.

5 Critical Gaps in Literature

Despite growing attention to climate adaptation and resilience, there are still gaps in the literature, especially in the developing country context. This section synthesizes four key gaps that this research addresses.

Existing literature often treats land use planning and infrastructure development as separate domains, with limited attention to their interdependencies (Ahern 2011). In fact, resilience strategies focus on either spatial planning or infrastructure without adequately addressing how they interact. For example, flood risk management may emphasize drainage infrastructure without considering how land-use patterns may contribute to flood risks (Balvanera et al. 2013). This is clearly illustrated through impervious surfaces and loss of green space.

Ultimately, this research addresses this gap by developing integrated approaches that link land use strategies with infrastructure resilience. Therefore, it recognizes that sustainable adaptation requires coordinated interventions across multiple domains (Biggs et al. 2012).

Moreover, combining scientific and local knowledge is still difficult even if its value has been widely recognized. The reason lies in the fact that much of the literature discusses the importance of local knowledge vaguely without providing concrete methods on merging both.

On the other hand, even if AI is advancing rapidly, its implementation in urban planning and DRM remains quite limited, especially in developing countries. Existing research often focuses on technical capabilities without addressing implementation challenges, ethical considerations, or integration with participatory processes.

Additionally, much of the resilience literature emphasizes technical and environmental dimensions while neglecting social equity, cultural values, and governance structures. Adaptation strategies that fail to address inequalities will exacerbate existing vulnerabilities and create new forms of marginalization. On another note, ignoring cultural values and governance contexts can lead to solutions that are technically correct but socially unacceptable or even institutionally infeasible. Therefore, there is a need for an integrated, context-sensitive, and governance-aware adaptive land-use framework for multi-hazard contexts such as Morocco.

6 Conclusion: From Context to Framework

This paper attempted to trace a funnel from global climate risks and international practices to the specific context of Morocco. Rotterdam's multifunctional infrastructure and the Peruvian Amazon's hybrid knowledge integration offer valuable lessons in multifunctionality, nature-based solutions, knowledge integration, and participatory processes. However, the analysis reveals that Morocco's unique combination of multi-hazard exposure, rapid urbanization, governance challenges, and rich traditional knowledge demands context-specific approaches. Therefore, the direct transplantation of these models is insufficient.

In light of the above, effective climate-responsive spatial planning in Morocco requires the following elements (Table 1).

Table 1. Key Requirements for Effective Climate-Responsive Spatial Planning in Morocco

Dimension	Requirements	Intended Outcome
Risk Assessment	Develop context-adapted multi-hazard protocols	Prioritized and feasible climate risk management
Knowledge Systems	Institutionalize local knowledge integration	Inclusive and context-sensitive planning
Planning Instruments	Strengthen and enforce existing regulatory tools	Reduced Implementation gap
Governance	Reform coordination and accountability mechanisms	Improved institutional coherence
Management Approach	Embed adaptive and learning-based processes	Long-term resilience and flexibility

The path forwards requires learning from global experiences while developing distinctly Moroccan approaches. Morocco is exposed to a variety of natural hazards and it is worsening because of climate change and the already deeply embedded vulnerabilities related to rapid urbanization. Yet, the kingdom possesses numerous assets such as policy commitment, rich traditional knowledge as well as growing technical capacity. If the country develops a framework adapted to its context it can pave a path towards climate-responsive spatial planning. More importantly, this framework should integrate scientific rigor with local knowledge, and address governance challenges pragmatically as well as prioritizes equity and participation. Therefore, it can serve as a model for other countries facing similar challenges. Overall, this chapter outlined a framework that provides a theoretical foundation that will serve as a basis for more detailed and focused future research.

References

Wisner, B., Blaikie, P., Cannon, T., Davis, I.: At Risk: Natural Hazards, People's Vulnerability and Disasters, 2nd edn. Routledge (2003)

Kingdom of Morocco, Ministry of Interior, General Directorate of Civil Protection: National strategy for disaster risk management (2020)

Camps-Valls, G., et al.: AI for extreme event modeling and understanding: methodologies and challenges. arXiv. http://arxiv.org/abs/2406.20080 (2024)

Peinhardt, K.: Resilience through placemaking: public spaces in Rotterdam's climate adaptation approach (2021)

Rodríguez, L.O., Cisneros, E., Pequeño, T., Fuentes, M.T., Zinngrebe, Y.: Building adaptive capacity in changing social-ecological systems: integrating knowledge in communal land-use planning in the Peruvian Amazon. Sustainability **10**(2), 511 (2018). https://doi.org/10.3390/su10020511

Mayar, K., Carmichael, D.G., Shen, X.: Resilience and systems—a review. Sustainability **14**(14), 8327 (2022). https://doi.org/10.3390/su14148327

Wisner, B., Blaikie, P., Cannon, T., Davis, I.: At Risk: Natural Hazards, People's Vulnerability and Disasters. Routledge (1994)

Lee, Y., Hong, C.-Y.: Unraveling urban disaster management: a deep dive into SETS implications through a case study of Toyama City, Japan. Land (2024). https://doi.org/10.3390/land13050679

Olazabal, M., Chu, E., Castán Broto, V., Patterson, J.: Subaltern forms of knowledge are required to boost local adaptation. One Earth **4**(6), 828–838 (2021). https://doi.org/10.1016/j.oneear.2021.05.006

Tarhule, A.: Climate change adaptation in developing countries: beyond rhetoric. InTech (2012). https://doi.org/10.5772/29482

Global evidence of rapid urban growth in flood zones since 1985 (2022). https://doi.org/10.21203/rs.3.rs-1460344/v1

Kiunsi, R.B.: The constraints on climate change adaptation in a city with a large development deficit: the case of Dar es Salaam. Environ. Urban. **25**(2), 321–337 (2013). https://doi.org/10.1177/0956247813489617

Andersen, J.G., Kallestrup, P., Karekezi, C.W., Yonga, G., Kraef, C.: Climate change and health risks in Mukuru informal settlement in Nairobi, Kenya: knowledge, attitudes and practices among residents. BMC Public Health **23**(1) (2023). https://doi.org/10.1186/s12889-023-15281-y

Awuah, K.G.B.: Urban development and governance in Nigeria: challenges, opportunities and policy direction. Int. Dev. Plan. Rev. **40**(1), 27–49 (2018). https://doi.org/10.3828/idpr.2018.1

Tribak, A., El Amrani, H.: Urban occupancy of areas with flood risk and territorial dynamics: the case of the Great Nador agglomerations (Morocco). Revista de Estudios Andaluces **36**, 55–71 (2018). https://doi.org/10.12795/REA.2018.I36.03

Ait Zamzami, H., Elaanzouli, M., Saidi, J., Boumeaza, T.: Resilience and vulnerability: the Haouz earthquake's effect on housing in the Western High Atlas of Morocco. Int. J. Disaster Dev. Interface (2024). https://doi.org/10.53824/ijddi.v4i1.64

Flooding in semi-unformal urban areas in North Africa: Environmental and psychosocial drivers, Adil Salhi a, Ihsan Larifi a, Hamza Salhi a, Essam Heggy (2024). https://doi.org/10.1016/j.scitotenv.2024.172486

Al Jazeera: Dozens dead after flash floods hit Moroccan city of Safi. Al Jazeera, 15 December 2025. https://www.aljazeera.com/news/2025/12/15/dozens-dead-after-flash-floods-hit-moroccan-city-of-safi

Africa Climate Reports article (Ksar El-Kébir flood evacuation), February 2026. https://africaclimatereports.org/2026/02/morocco-evacuates-50000-as-flooding-threatens-city-after-weeks-of-heavy-rain/

Bolca, P.: Postcolonial resilience in Casablanca: colonial legacies and climate vulnerability. Sustainability **17**, 8656 (2025). https://doi.org/10.3390/su17198656

Balvanera, P., et al.: Linking biodiversity and ecosystem services: current uncertainties and the necessary next steps. BioScience **64**(1), 49–57 (2013). https://doi.org/10.1093/biosci/bit003

Ahern, J.: From fail-safe to safe-to-fail: sustainability and resilience in the new urban world. Landsc. Urban Plan. **100**(4), 341–343 (2011). https://doi.org/10.1016/j.landurbplan.2011.02.021

Biggs, R., Schluter, M., Biggs, D., Bohensky, E.L., BurnSilver, S., Cundill, G.: Toward principles for enhancing the resilience of ecosystem services. Annu. Rev. Environ. Resour. **37**, 421–448 (2012). https://doi.org/10.1146/annurev-environ-051211-123836

Dahchour, A., El Hajjaji, S., Labjar, N.: Environmental challenges and management of vital resources in urban Moroccan cities. IntechOpen (2025). https://doi.org/10.5772/intechopen.1008182

Chtioui, H., Khalfaoui, S., Benmoussa, T., Nachite, D., Anfuso, G.: Assessing coastal flood risk under extreme events and sea level rise in the Casablanca-Mohammedia coastline (Morocco). Nat. Hazards **120**, 11547–11571 (2024). https://doi.org/10.1007/s11069-024-06624-y

Farinos-Dasí, J., Pinazo-Dallenbach, P., Peiró Sánchez-Manjavacas, E., Rodríguez-Bernal, D.C.: Disaster risk management, climate change adaptation and the role of spatial and urban planning: evidence from European case studies. Nat. Hazards **121**, 23479–23512 (2025). https://doi.org/10.1007/s11069-024-06448-w

Grijsen, J., et al.: Managing Urban Water Scarcity in Morocco: Summary Report. World Bank Group (2017)

Hafyani, M.E., Essahlaoui, A., Oualai, A.E., Hmaidi, A.E., Ouali, A.E.: Assessing regional scale water balances through remote sensing techniques: a case study of Boufakrane River Watershed, Meknes Region, Morocco. Water **12**(2), 320 (2020). https://doi.org/10.3390/W12020320

Messous, S.: Hydraulic networks and vernacular architecture: ingenuity and sustainable management of a vital resource. Mater. Res. Proc. **47**, 347–354 (2025). https://doi.org/10.21741/9781644903391-40

Magoni, M.: Resilience thinking and urban metabolism in spatial planning: which possible integrations. City Territory Archit. **4**, 19 (2017). https://doi.org/10.1186/s40410-017-0074-0

Ongoma, V., et al.: Morocco's climate change impacts, adaptation and mitigation—a stocktake. Reg. Environ. Change **24**, 16 (2024). https://doi.org/10.1007/s10113-023-02176-2

Salhi, A., et al.: Flooding in semi-uniform urban areas in North Africa: environmental and psychosocial drivers. Sci. Total. Environ. **927**, 172486 (2024). https://doi.org/10.1016/j.scitotenv.2024.172486

Sallak, M.: Les risques hydrologiques d'inondations et la problématique d'aménagement des territoires de piémont : cas du "dir" de Taghzirt à Zaouit Echeikh, Province de Béni Mellal, Maroc [Doctoral dissertation]. Morocco. In: Contemporary Urban Design Thinking, pp. 93–108. Springer (2019). https://doi.org/10.1007/978-3-031-77347-7_7

Belahnech, H.: Developing eco-construction at the risk of vernacular building cultures Case of Moroccan mountain villages in post-earthquake context. Mater. Res. Proc. **47**, 53–60 (2025). https://doi.org/10.21741/9781644903391-7

Bouaakkaz, B., Bouchaou, L., Bouimoussa, H., Ouatiki, H., Chehbouni, A.: Flood risk management in the Souss watershed. E3S Web Conf. **37**, 04005 (2018). https://doi.org/10.1051/e3sconf/20183704005

Udovyk, O., et al.: From "build back the same" to transformative recovery: enablers and barriers for climate-focused pathways in post-disaster case studies across Europe. Front. Sustain. Cities **7**, 1656725 (2025). https://doi.org/10.3389/frsc.2025.1656725

Amini Alaoui, K., Radoine, H., Nahiduzzaman, K.M.: Rural planning evaluation and sustainable development potential in rural communes of Rehamna province (Morocco). J. Urban Manag. **13**, 624–638 (2024). https://doi.org/10.1016/j.jum.2024.07.002

Kesavan, H., Choudhary, S., Khan, S., Samhita, R., Sharma, A.: AI based urban resilience planning: opportunities and challenges (2024). https://doi.org/10.30564/jees.v6i2.6681

Intergovernmental Panel on Climate Change: Climate change 2021: The physical science basis. Contribution of Working Group I to the Sixth Assessment Report of the Intergovernmental Panel on Climate Change. Cambridge University Press (2021). https://doi.org/10.1017/9781009157896

Wannewitz, M., et al.: Progress and gaps in climate change adaptation in coastal cities across the globe. Nat. Cities (2024). https://doi.org/10.1038/s44284-024-00106-9

Territorial Transformation in the Digital Age: Remote Work, E-Commerce, and Resilience Implications

Halima Ennaciri(✉), Kh. Md. Nahiduzzaman, and Hassan Radoine

Mohammed VI Polytechnic University, Rabat Campus – Rocade Rabat-Salé, Rabat, Morocco
Halima.ENNACIRI@um6p.ma

Abstract. Covid-19 played the role of one of the biggest territorial disruptors in modern history, since it changed our lifestyles through changes in housing choices, shopping behaviours, and our working routines. Precisely following the preventive lockdowns that forced the mass adoption of remote working and e-commerce to ensure the continuity of economies and provide for our needs, we then witnessed an acceleration of the virtualization process, even after the pandemic period, provoking a butterfly effect on commercial activity, real estate, territorial flows and consequently land use. It is not just an acceleration of existing digital trends, but an intrinsic metamorphosis of territorial dynamics and organization. Therefore, there is an important need to develop an integrated framework encompassing all the aspects related to these territorial dynamics, especially housing choices, property prices, logistics land, commercial real estate and land use, across different global contexts, in order to develop the most adapted and adaptable resilience framework capable of addressing these changes and making territories more agile and better equipped to benefit from this new territorial configuration. Our research work aims at developing this new resilience framework to assist policymakers in this context of these new territorial transformational dynamics. This paper serves as a theoretical foundation for upcoming subsequent research papers where each aspect will be addressed in detail.

Keywords: Covid-19 · e-commerce · remote work · housing · real estate · land use · territorial resilience

1 Introduction

The pandemic the world witnessed in late 2019 caused a profound shock across different aspects of human life: health, the economy, lifestyle, and territory. After a few weeks of its emergence in early 2020, around 90 countries resorted to lockdowns to limit its spread [1]. This new condition generated a rapid global decrease in most activities requiring human presence. Consequently, two important alternatives emerged and have persisted to this day: e-commerce and remote or hybrid working. None of them was new, but Covid-19 compressed years of their gradual adoption into a few months of lockdown, which had a profound impact on territories.

O. Gervasi et al. (Eds.): ICCSA 2026 Workshops, LNCS 16758, pp. 631–644, 2027.
https://doi.org/10.1007/978-3-032-30497-1_38

The spatial dimension is what makes this disruption different from previous shocks. The crises the world has undergone throughout history, whether financial downturns or industrial recessions, have mainly changed economic geographies through employment losses, investment withdrawal, and similar effects. Unlike these, the pandemic simultaneously altered not only the organization of work, businesses, and consumer behavior, but also impacted physical dynamics within territories, such as residential patterns, work locations, and transit.

We should not only focus on the negative side of these shifts; they should also be perceived as an opportunity for a new territorial redistribution, where goods, services, activity demand, value, and investment move back and forth between suburbs and cities, creating more balanced and equitable dynamics. However, this challenge requires a better understanding of new data through a systemic analytical perspective (Fig. 1).

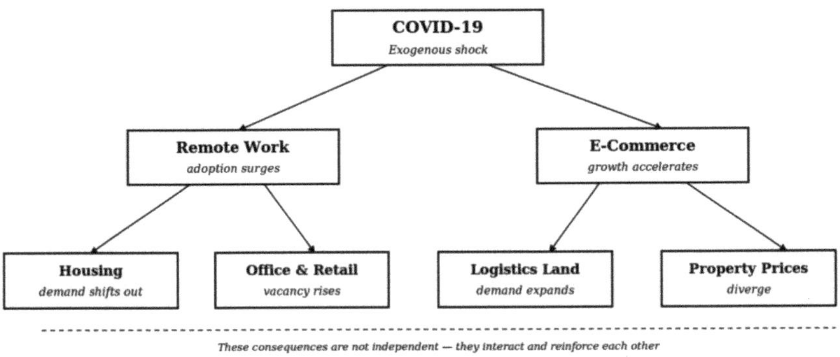

Fig. 1. COVID-19 and its territorial consequences

During the lockdown, physical retail experienced a significant decline, while e-commerce saw rapid and exponential growth. Projections indicate that it will exceed $8 trillion by 2027, representing a 39% increase from 2023 [3]. This growth did not only change consumer behavior, but also the territorial and physical organization of urban areas and territories in general: an increase in demand for urban logistics land, the intensification of last-mile delivery, a rise in the number of delivery agents, and commercial real estate vacancies across traditional commercial strips [6] Research projects a 60% increase in carbon emissions, resulting from a global rise in last-mile delivery vehicles, estimated at 61% [3]. These consequences go beyond logistical impacts; they are affecting the entire territory, as the spatial dynamics of consumption are being reorganized on a large scale. For example, every parcel delivered to a home represents a trip that once brought a consumer to a physical store. Multiplying this pattern across billions of transactions each year makes this shift a fundamental transformation of urban mobility, land use, and economic geography.

The size and capacity of the logistics infrastructure required to support this transformation should not be underestimated. The real estate and land reserves needed for the different components of this logistical chain, whether warehouses, sorting facilities, last-mile depots, or urban consolidation centres, now form a new layer of urban land use and compete directly with residential, commercial, and institutional uses. The demand for logistics land is increasingly shifting toward peri-urban areas, which are simultaneously attracting more residents from core urban areas. This creates a form of collision between two powerful dynamics, generating pressure on the same land at the same time. It is a tension that existing planning frameworks are not equipped to handle, as they were designed for slower, more separable sectoral systems rather than integrated and mixed territorial dynamics (Fig. 2).

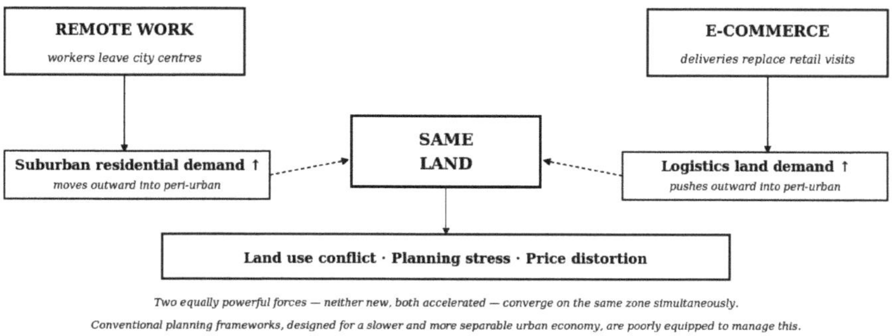

Fig. 2. The peri-urban collision: two forces, one zone

The second consequence of the lockdown, namely remote work, experienced a similar transformation to e-commerce, with the share of home working days increasing from around 5% before the pandemic to 60% in 2020, and then stabilizing at 28–30% by 2023–2024 [2]. By the end of 2023, 12.7% of workers remained fully remote, while the majority adopted a hybrid work model [1]. According to researchers, this shift is no longer considered a temporary adjustment but a structural change in where and how we work [1]. The new flexibility of work patterns is pushing cities that once depended on the daily concentration of workers to adapt to this new reality, as offices, originally designed and built for full weekly occupancy, are now vacant most of the time, raising many questions about their use and efficiency.

The consequences of this shift go beyond the office real estate market. A worker moving from daily commuting to remote working several days a week impacts all layers and systems of territories. Public transport use declines, and commercial activity in core urban areas loses the consistent daily flow of customers on which its economic model relies. With the convenience of remote work, co-location is no longer an obligation, so households begin to reevaluate their residential choices, placing greater emphasis on space, access to outdoor areas, quiet environments, home accommodations, and overall better living conditions rather than proximity to the workplace. As a result, suburban and peri-urban areas with lower land prices are becoming more attractive to urban households, creating a disruption of the pre-pandemic territorial equilibrium based on commuting patterns and housing costs.

These transformations cause rapid and significant spatial impacts: housing demand has shifted from city centers to peripheral fringes and surrounding territories, as workers are no longer dependent on daily commuting and have begun prioritizing the comfort offered by peripheral areas [4]. This had a direct impact on the real estate market. For example, housing prices in the United States increased by 24% between 2019 and 2021, with remote work contributing more than 60% of this increase [14] Meanwhile, office markets experienced a drastic decline, with vacancy rates reaching 20.1% in 50 large U.S. cities by mid-2024, the highest level since 1979, equivalent to a loss of $556.8 billion in real estate value [5]. Cities were therefore confronted with multiple pressures occurring simultaneously: declining demand for office and retail space, increasing demand for logistics land, and rising housing prices in suburban areas, all without governance frameworks or analytical tools adapted to managing these combined dynamics.

What makes this moment analytically difficult is that these trends do not operate independently, but are closely interconnected. A worker relocating from a city centre to a suburb becomes, at the same time, a former office occupier, a generator of suburban housing demand, a daily logistics customer, and a contributor to changing retail footfall. Each of these roles feeds into property markets, land use patterns, infrastructure systems, and fiscal revenues. Examining any single dimension in isolation therefore produces a partial, and potentially misleading, interpretation. A city focusing only on the office vacancy dimension of remote work may prioritise the conversion of empty buildings into housing, without fully accounting for the fact that these same remote workers are also increasing e-commerce delivery pressures that compete with residential uses for surrounding land. Policies developed in silos are unlikely to be effective in a system that functions as an integrated whole.

This paper serves as the conceptual foundation of the research. Its purpose is to develop an integrated resilience framework linking all these factors—e-commerce, remote work, housing choices, property prices, and land use change—as an interconnected system.

2 Global Cases

As part of establishing the conceptual foundation of this study, tracking case studies from different global contexts helps us understand virtualization trends and their territorial impacts. None of these dynamics is specific to a single country, but their intensity and pace vary depending on the context, including local economies, housing market conditions, the quality of digital and physical infrastructure, and planning governance and tools. As a result, these redistribution processes are more pronounced in knowledge-intensive, digitally enabled countries:

2.1 North America

The United States represents one of the most documented cases of these transformations. In San Francisco, office vacancy rates increased from around 2% before the pandemic to nearly 30%, while in New York City, office real estate lost an estimated $90.3 billion in value between 2019 and 2023 [5, 8]. Cities with a strong concentration of knowledge-economy activities experienced the most significant disruptions, as their workforces were among the most capable of shifting to remote work. San Francisco is a particularly illustrative case, as its economic model was largely based on the co-location of tech talent, which became difficult to sustain once the need for physical proximity weakened.

These changes have also generated important fiscal impacts, as the decline in commercial real estate values has reduced property tax revenues, creating structural budget pressures that are not easily absorbed.

Suburban housing prices increased significantly as households relocated toward peripheral areas in search of more space and lower costs [4]. However, this pattern was not uniform across the country. Metropolitan areas with a large supply of affordable suburban housing experienced the strongest in-migration, while cities facing supply constraints saw price increases across both urban and suburban markets. This variation reflects underlying supply-side limitations that were revealed, rather than created, by the expansion of remote work. In areas where housing supply was more flexible, remote work allowed households to relocate toward preferred residential environments. In contrast, where supply was constrained, similar demand pressures resulted mainly in rising prices across all locations, without necessarily improving living conditions.

In Pittsburgh, the city responded to e-commerce delivery pressures by deploying AI-powered smart loading zones that increased curb turnover by 40% and cut CO_2 emissions by 12 tonnes per year, [3] an early example of adaptive logistics governance. This case illustrates the potential for technology-enabled urban management to moderate the negative externalities of logistics intensification without prohibiting the e-commerce activity that generates it. It also illustrates the governance gap: most cities lack the institutional capacity, data infrastructure, and regulatory flexibility to implement such adaptive systems at scale.

The Congressional Research Service confirmed that while some secondary cities attracted in-migrants with purchasing power, many rural and peripheral areas remained unable to capture these flows due to inadequate broadband infrastructure and constrained housing supply [5]. The geography of remote work benefit is uneven even within a single country. Location flexibility benefits those who already have the most options. Workers in sectors that cannot be performed remotely, logistics, care, hospitality, construction, do not have access to this flexibility, and in many cases bear the costs of the spatial redistribution that their more advantaged counterparts generate: higher housing costs in receiving suburbs, reduced service intensity in abandoned urban cores.

2.2 Europe

Responses across Europe were more heterogeneous. US suburban price gradients continued to flatten in 2021–2022, while comparable gradients in Denmark, France, and the UK remained relatively stable, reflecting wealthier, better-serviced American suburbs being more attractive to relocating workers [9]. This divergence points to an important structural difference: European cities typically offer stronger public transport, denser service provision, and more mixed-use suburban environments than their American counterparts. The relative attractiveness of urban living is higher in many European contexts, which moderated the suburbanisation impulse that was so pronounced in North America.

London house prices fell post-lockdown while surrounding counties gained; office take-up in London's Q1 2023 was 19% below the five-year average [8, 16].

Paris showed a certain level of resilience, supported by its economic diversity, strong public transport system, and continued demand for co-working spaces [8]. This case suggests that cities with more diversified economies, not relying on a single dominant sector, are better able to absorb these disruptions. At the same time, the quality of public infrastructure plays an important role in maintaining urban attractiveness, even with increased spatial flexibility. Cities that offer strong amenity value, rather than depending mainly on employment concentration, are therefore more able to retain both population and economic activity.

In Italy, the rise of remote work has increased residential mobility, especially among families, with pressures similar to gentrification appearing in secondary cities [13]. Cities such as Bologna, Turin, and Florence, which were attractive but not primary destinations, are now attracting households leaving Milan in search of more space and lower costs, while still offering urban amenities. This creates a double effect: these cities benefit from new purchasing power, but at the same time face increasing affordability pressures for lower-income residents who do not have the same ability to relocate. At the same time, urban congestion has increased in some contexts. For example, congestion in Dublin rose from 45% to 66% between 2018 and 2023, and in Milan from 30% to 45%, partly linked to the growth of delivery activity [3]. This shows a form of urban pressure that is often overlooked, as the reduction in commuting is offset by the increase in delivery traffic, which keeps congestion levels the same or even higher.

In Portugal and Spain, digital nomad visa schemes were introduced to attract high-income remote workers, supporting local economic activity while at the same time contributing to rising housing prices for local residents [7]. This dynamic creates a clear tension between economic benefits and affordability pressures, reflecting a structural trade-off that territorial strategies need to address. On one side, attracting these workers generates tax revenues, supports local businesses, and increases the international attractiveness of these territories, while on the other side it creates additional pressure on housing markets, particularly where local incomes cannot compete with stronger foreign purchasing power.

This dynamic is further reinforced by digital geo-arbitrage, where workers earn salaries from northern Europe or North America while living in lower-cost southern European contexts, intensifying these pressures and highlighting the limits of existing governance tools, which remain insufficient to manage these effects.

2.3 Asia and Australia

In Japan, cellular network data revealed a clear spatial redistribution pattern, where populations in office districts declined significantly while residential areas experienced corresponding increases, directly reflecting the adoption of remote work [12]. This approach, based on near real-time tracking of population movements, represents an important advancement in the analysis of territorial dynamics, offering a level of precision and immediacy that traditional survey-based methods are not able to capture. Although Japan, along with Italy, recorded some of the lowest sustained levels of remote work globally, largely influenced by cultural factors and the structure of their economic systems [8], the spatial impacts of these shifts remained clearly observable. This is particularly significant, as it suggests that even limited changes in work organization are sufficient to generate measurable transformations in urban form, population distribution, and property markets, indicating that the threshold required to trigger territorial change may be lower than previously assumed.

China represents the largest e-commerce market globally, with online retail surpassing $2.17 trillion in 2023, which reshaped not only urban logistics systems but also rural settlement patterns and agricultural supply chains [17]. The Chinese case is particularly interesting in the extent to which e-commerce has penetrated rural areas, where platforms such as Alibaba's Taobao Villages allow rural entrepreneurs to access national and international markets without the need for physical relocation, reducing the importance of distance and enabling new territorial dynamics.

Australian city centres saw weekday pedestrian counts remain 35% below 2019 levels through 2024 while weekend counts fully recovered, indicating a reorganisation of urban rhythms rather than simple urban decline [20]. City centres are shifting from places of weekday obligation to places of weekend choice. That distinction has direct consequences for which businesses are viable and how public space should be managed and programmed. Businesses oriented toward Monday-to-Friday office workers, sandwich shops, dry cleaners, business hotels, face structural demand reduction that cannot be recovered by weekend visitors who have different needs and spending patterns. Meanwhile, businesses oriented toward leisure, culture, and hospitality may find that the shift to weekend urbanity creates genuine opportunity.

In Istanbul, professional workers expressed significant intentions to leave the city if remote work became permanent, seeking space and lower costs in peripheral areas [21]. This finding from a middle-income, rapidly urbanising context underscores that the spatial consequences of remote work are not confined to wealthy, post-industrial cities. Even in cities where urban-suburban price differentials are smaller and where the middle class is still investing in urban living, the spatial logic of remote work generates centrifugal pressure.

These dynamics suggest that territorial planners across different income contexts, not only in advanced economies, need to engage with these emerging spatial shifts, as these transformations are not limited to specific regions but are reshaping territorial organization more broadly.

2.4 Cross-Regional Patterns

Across regions, three main patterns can be identified. Cities with more diversified economies tended to be more resilient than those concentrated in a single sector [8]. Urban economies dominated by specific activities, such as technology (San Francisco), finance (parts of London), or government functions (some national capitals), were more vulnerable, as they lacked the capacity to absorb shifts in demand within a single sector. At the same time, flexible land use governance played an important role, allowing faster adaptation compared to rigid single-use zoning systems [11]. Cities and regions with planning frameworks that enabled the conversion of commercial to residential uses, or industrial to logistics uses, were better able to respond to these changes.

However, the spatial benefits of digitalisation were not equally distributed, as they tended to favour higher-income and higher-skill populations, raising equity issues across different contexts [9]. What differs between regions is mainly the speed and the scale of these transformations, rather than the nature of the dynamics themselves.

3 Discussion

A significant amount of research has examined different dimensions of this transformation, particularly in relation to housing and commercial real estate dynamics. In the housing literature, Mondragon and Wieland [4] and Van Nieuwerburgh [10] quantified the causal contribution of remote work to residential price increases, showing through econometric analysis that housing price growth during the pandemic was largely driven by the decoupling of residence from workplace location, rather than by income growth or demographic shifts. In parallel, research in the field of commercial real estate, notably by the Congressional Research Service [5] and Penn IUR [11], documented the scale of the disruption affecting office markets and its fiscal implications, estimating losses that represent one of the largest declines in real estate value in American urban history. On e-commerce logistics, NAIOP [6] and the Center for Transportation Research [15] analysed how logistic infrastructure is reshaping urban industrial land, documenting the competitive pressure on scarce urban land that logistics demand generates. On resilience, Yang and Li [22] grounded the conceptual link between urban transformation and inclusive adaptive capacity, arguing that resilience is not merely about absorbing shocks but about ensuring that adaptation does not reproduce or deepen existing inequalities.

The gap in this literature, however, is that each of these bodies of work studies its dimension in isolation. Research on housing markets does not systematically account for what e-commerce logistics is simultaneously doing to industrial land use. Studies of commercial real estate decline rarely engage with the e-commerce dynamics that are partially driving it, consumers who shop online rather than in physical stores are not simply choosing convenience; they are generating logistics infrastructure that competes for the same urban land that commercial real estate once dominated. Resilience scholarship has engaged only marginally with digital economic transformation as a driver of territorial stress, tending instead to focus on environmental shocks, industrial decline, or demographic change as the primary stressors requiring resilience response.

What remains limited is an integrated analytical framework that considers remote work and e-commerce simultaneously as joint drivers of territorial change, without accounting for the interdependencies between these outcomes and their collective implications for territorial resilience. This gap is particularly significant for developing countries, where the combined effects of these transitions may be most consequential and least understood. Middle-income urban economies that are simultaneously expanding their digital infrastructure, absorbing rapid urbanisation, and managing informality in housing and labour markets face a particularly complex version of the challenges documented in wealthy-country contexts, without the institutional capacity, data systems, or fiscal resources that have supported adaptation in those contexts.

The contribution of this research lies in directly addressing this fragmentation. So far no study has simultaneously and systematically examined remote work, e-commerce, housing, commercial real estate, logistics land use, and territorial resilience within a single integrated framework. This approach considers these dimensions as components of a unified spatial system, where elements are causally interconnected: remote work influences residential relocation, [2, 4] which in turn affects commercial real estate outcomes, [11] while interacting with the expansion of e-commerce logistics, [6, 15] and together shaping how effectively a territory adapts [22]. Analysing any one of these elements in isolation leads to an incomplete and potentially misleading understanding.

These dynamics generate feedback effects that cannot be understood through single-dimension analyses, as changes in one component directly influence others within the territorial system. The increase in suburban housing demand driven by the arrival of remote workers leads to rising land values in these areas, which then increases the cost of logistics land, creating direct competition between residential development and logistics functions for the same space. As these costs increase, logistics activities are pushed further toward peripheral locations, increasing the distance between warehouses and delivery points, which results in higher vehicle kilometres, increased emissions, and additional congestion along the main corridors connecting these areas to urban centers.

These effects then reshape the way households, firms, and governments respond to these changes, as households relocating to peripheral areas may face the same congestion they initially sought to avoid, firms are required to integrate these constraints into their location and investment strategies, and governments are confronted with infrastructure and fiscal pressures resulting from spatial changes they did not anticipate. As a result, the system evolves through interconnected dynamics that cannot be explained through isolated or single-variable approaches.

The practical implications of these dynamics are significant, as interventions addressing one dimension without considering others may generate new tensions instead of resolving existing ones. For example, converting vacant office buildings into housing without taking into account the logistics pressures generated by e-commerce in nearby industrial areas may lead to new forms of spatial conflict rather than balanced territorial outcomes [11]. While such conversions may reduce one pressure, namely excess commercial vacancy, they can also intensify competition between residential and logistics uses over the same urban land. Residents in converted buildings are likely to expect quiet and clean environments, whereas logistics activities in adjacent zones generate noise, traffic, and air quality impacts. The governance challenge therefore extends beyond enabling conversion, and requires managing the interface between these competing uses in ways that are both economically viable and socially acceptable.

A city attracting remote workers through visa schemes without managing housing affordability risks displacing existing residents [7]. The digital nomad who occupies a rental property in Lisbon or Barcelona at a price determined by northern European earnings is not doing anything individually unreasonable, but the aggregate effect of many such decisions is to price local workers out of the housing markets of their own cities. Territorial resilience cannot be designed dimension by dimension. It requires simultaneous management of economic attraction, housing supply, and distributional consequence.

Short-run and long-run effects also differ in ways that complicate policy design. While vacancy and price shocks were acute in 2020–2022, long-run equilibrium depends on how housing supply, infrastructure investment, and planning adapt to the new spatial configuration [18]. A city that responds to office vacancy by rapidly facilitating conversion may destroy stock just before hybrid work norms restabilise demand and occupancy recovers to a new, lower but stable equilibrium. A suburb that absorbs remote worker in-migrants without building complementary services and infrastructure imports purchasing power while creating congestion, school crowding, and infrastructure deficits that erode the quality of life that attracted in-migrants in the first place. Only a longitudinal, integrated framework can track these dynamics with the temporal resolution that good policy requires, one that can distinguish between the acute phase of a shock and its structural long-run implications, and that can model how policy interventions at one point in time will shape the system's trajectory over subsequent years.

The equity dimension of this transformation deserves particular emphasis. The spatial benefits of the post-pandemic digital economy, location flexibility, access to space, exposure to lower-cost housing markets, reduced commuting time and cost, are distributed highly unequally. They accrue primarily to knowledge workers in digitally-enabled occupations who already tend to be higher-earning, better-educated, and more asset-wealthy than average. Workers in sectors that cannot be performed remotely, logistics, care, hospitality, construction, not only lack access to these benefits but often bear the costs of the spatial redistribution that higher-income remote workers generate. They face higher housing costs in suburban receiving areas, reduced urban service intensity as commercial activity shifts away from cores, and increased traffic as delivery vehicles multiply. A territorial resilience framework that does not attend to these distributional dynamics will design adaptation strategies that serve some residents well while leaving others more exposed (Fig. 3).

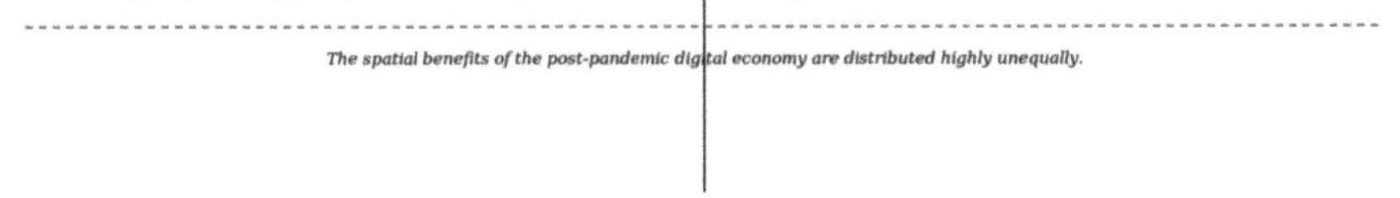

Fig. 3. The equity divide: who benefits and who bears the costs

4 Conclusion

Remote work and e-commerce are not simply economic trends. They function as spatial forces that are reshaping residential patterns, urban functioning, and the relative performance of territories. Across North America, Europe, Asia, and Australia, the same dynamics appear: housing demand is moving away from city centers, commercial real estate remains under pressure, logistics land is expanding at the urban fringe, and outcomes differ depending on infrastructure, governance, and economic structures. These changes are not temporary, and cities are not going back to their pre-2019 situation, but are evolving toward a new spatial organization. It is a structural reconfiguration that has established a new baseline around which future urban development will be organised.

Territorial resilience in this context means more than bouncing back. It means converting obsolete office stock into productive uses, managing suburban growth pressure, decarbonising logistics, and ensuring that the benefits of the digital economy are broadly shared rather than concentrated among the already-privileged [22]. This requires active governance, not merely passive adaptation. The difference between a territory that capitalises on the new spatial economy and one that is damaged by it is not primarily a function of location or endowment, it is a function of institutional capacity, governance flexibility, and the political will to make distributional choices explicit and to pursue equity as a policy objective (Fig. 4).

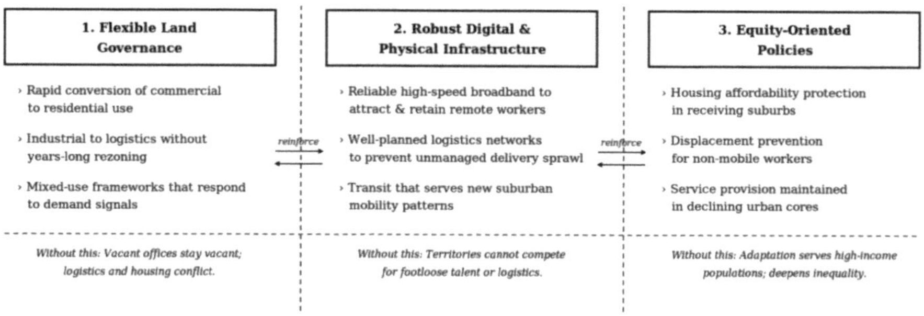

Fig. 4. Three conditions for territorial resilience

Three enabling conditions consistently distinguish more resilient territories across the evidence base. Flexible, mixed-use land governance that allows adaptive reuse [11] is the first: the ability to convert commercial to residential, industrial to logistics, or retail to community use in response to changing demand signals, without the years-long delays that conventional rezoning processes impose. Robust digital and physical infrastructure that enables both remote work and logistics [19] is the second: territories that lack reliable high-speed broadband cannot attract or retain remote workers, and territories that lack well-planned logistics infrastructure will experience unmanaged delivery intensification that degrades quality of life.

Equity also becomes an important condition in this context, as the distributional effects of these spatial changes cannot be ignored [9]. Without addressing housing affordability, displacement risks, and access to services for less mobile workers, adaptation strategies that mainly benefit higher-income populations may reinforce and deepen existing inequalities.

When these conditions are present together, the post-pandemic digital economy can create real opportunities for territorial transformation. Suburban areas can attract higher-value activities without necessarily losing their existing character, while city centers can shift toward more mixed uses such as leisure, culture, and services instead of relying mainly on office activities. At the same time, smaller cities and even rural areas with good connectivity can start attracting mobile workers, which was not possible before when proximity to major employers was essential.

However, when these conditions are not present, the same dynamics tend to reinforce existing inequalities. Cities may lose part of their economic base without finding alternatives, suburban areas absorb population growth without adequate services, and lower-income populations face increasing pressure between rising costs in the areas they move to and declining opportunities in the areas they leave.

The difference between these two outcomes is not accidental, but reflects deliberate policy choices related to land governance, infrastructure investment, and the groups that territorial adaptation is intended to benefit. Resilience should not be understood as an inherent characteristic that territories either possess or lack; rather, it is shaped through institutional design, fiscal commitment, and political decisions. The analytical work of identifying the mechanisms through which spatial change generates inequality or opportunity is inseparable from the normative work of deciding whose resilience matters and what kind of territorial future is worth building toward.

This chapter is the starting point for our research work. The integrated framework established here will underpin a series of subsequent papers that examine specific aspects of this transformation in empirical depth: the effects of remote work on housing affordability and residential mobility across different urban typologies; the logistics land use implications of e-commerce growth in peri-urban areas; the adaptive reuse of vacant commercial real estate and its governance conditions; and comparative territorial resilience across regions at different levels of digital development. Each of these future papers will draw on the conceptual structure developed here, testing and refining it through empirical investigation across diverse geographical contexts. The framework is designed to be generative, not a closed system but an open analytical scaffold that successive empirical studies will populate, challenge, and revise.

The holistic perspective is not an academic preference. It is a necessity. The post-pandemic digital economy is restructuring urban and territorial space as a system. Understanding it, and building resilient responses to it, requires an equally systemic approach. Fragmented analysis produces fragmented policy, and fragmented policy produces adaptation that solves one problem while creating another. The integrated framework developed here is an attempt to provide the analytical foundation that systemic governance requires.

The dynamics described in this chapter are already reshaping cities and territories in ways that are measurable, consequential, and in many cases irreversible. They are also deeply uneven: the same forces that generate opportunity for some territories and populations create stress and exclusion for others. This raises a question that is both analytical and normative, one that drives all the empirical work that follows:

What is the future equilibrium resulting from these dynamics? And what resilience framework can make it sustainable, integrated, and equitable?

Answering this question requires understanding not just how territories absorb shocks, but how they can proactively shape the new equilibrium: determining who benefits, who is protected, what land is converted and to what use, and how the infrastructure of the digital economy is governed in the public interest.

Territorial resilience, in this context, should not be seen only as a reactive response. It is rather a way to anticipate and manage these transformations, taking into account the structural role of digitalisation, remote work, and e-commerce. The objective is to understand how institutions, investments, and policies can guide these dynamics toward more balanced, sustainable, and productive territorial outcomes. This is the perspective adopted in the following analysis.

Acknowledgments. The author has no specific funding to acknowledge.

Disclosure of Interests. The author has no competing interests to declare that are relevant to the content of this article.

References

1. Kellerman, A.: Global trends in work location, before, during, and after COVID-19: office, home, hybrid, and nomad. Urban Plan. Transp. Res. 2025
2. Ramani, A., Alcedo, J., Bloom, N.: How working from home reshapes cities. Proc. Natl. Acad. Sci. **121**(45), e2408930121 (2024)
3. World Economic Forum/Accenture: Sustainable deliveries: how cities and companies can lead on logistics (2024)
4. Mondragon, J.A., Wieland, J.: Housing demand and remote work. NBER Working Paper No. 30041 (2022)
5. Congressional Research Service: Economic development implications of remote work in the post-pandemic environment. CRS Report R48528 (2025)
6. Aderneck, E., Whitehead, R.: How e-commerce affects urban industrial lands and transportation systems. NAIOP Commer. Real Estate Dev. Mag. (2022)
7. Pacheco, F.: Digital geoarbitrage, workation, and remote work: new spatial mobility regimes and urban consequences. Int. J. Adv. Res. **13**(7), 546–559 (2025)
8. Chernick, H., Copeland, D.: How is remote work changing the urban landscape post pandemic? OECD Cogito Blog, 28 July 2023
9. Biljanovska, N., Dell'Ariccia, G.: Reshaping the housing market: the enduring effects of the pandemic. CEPR VoxEU (2023)
10. Van Nieuwerburgh, S.: The remote work revolution: Impact on real estate values and the urban environment. Real Estate Econ. (2023)
11. Penn Institute for Urban Research: Expert voices 2024: Remote Work - Its Impact on Cities (2024)
12. Akatsuka, H., Toyoda, M.: Analysis of the relationship between urban dynamics and prevalence of remote work based on population data generated from cellular networks. Sci. Rep. **13**, 20139 (2023)
13. Jansen, T., Ascani, A., Faggian, A., Palma, A.: Remote work and location preferences: a study of post-pandemic trends in Italy. Ann. Reg. Sci. **73**(3), 897–944 (2024)
14. Kmetz, A., Mondragon, J., Wieland, J.: Remote work and housing demand. Fed Reserve Bank San Francisco Econ Lett. (2022). [Reported in: BLS Monthly Labor Review, April 2023]
15. Center for Transportation Research, University of Texas at Austin. Evaluate Logistics Sprawl's Impacts on E-commerce Travel. CTR Technical Report 0-7165-1
16. Penn Institute for Urban Research: Policy Brief: How Remote Work is Affecting Real Estate Markets, December 2022
17. Li, F., Gan, Y.: Research on the sustainable development capability of Chinese rural e-commerce based on multidimensional perspective. Sci. Rep. **15**, 11547 (2025)

18. Howard, G., Liebersohn, J., Ozimek, A.: The short- and long-run effects of remote work on U.S. housing markets. J. Financ. Econ. **150**(1), 166–184 (2023). https://doi.org/10.1016/j.jfineco.2023.103705
19. Schoenberg, A.M., Bartholomae, F.W., Göschl, M.-L.: Mobile working vs. labour mobility: conceptual exploration of substitution and urban change. Int. J. Urban Sci. (2025). https://doi.org/10.1080/12265934.2025.2559794
20. Lim, S.J., Burke, M., Lim, C.: City use patterns post COVID-19: reflections of resilience or adaptation. Reg. Stud. Reg. Sci. (2025)
21. Pakoz, M.Z., Kaya, N.: Personal adaptations to remote working in the post-pandemic city: the case of Istanbul. Transp. Res. Rec. (2023)
22. Yang, C., Li, H.: Editorial: urban resilience and inclusive development. Front. Sustain. Cities (2026)

Spatial Heat Resilience Mapping Using Graph Neural Networks

Sonia Alnajjar(✉), Antonio García-Martínez, and Victoria Patricia López-Cabeza

Instituto Universitario de Arquitectura y Ciencias de la Construcción IUACC, Escuela Técnica Superior de Arquitectura, Universidad de Sevilla, Sevilla, Spain
sonalnfay@alum.us.es

Abstract. Urban heat is intensifying across Mediterranean cities due to dense urban morphology and increasing climate extremes. While machine learning is widely used to assess urban heat, most spatial regression approaches treat data points as independent observations and aggregate data into broad administrative neighbourhoods, inherently failing to capture localized, micro-climatic interactions. This study proposes a novel, micro-scale Graph Neural Network (GNN) framework to assess and predict Urban Heat Vulnerability at the individual building level in Seville, Spain. A spatial graph was constructed wherein 29,542 individual buildings operate as nodes, with edges computationally defining physical adjacency to capture thermodynamic neighbourhood spillover effects. Node features strictly integrate satellite-derived Land Surface Temperature (LST) and the Normalized Difference Vegetation Index (NDVI) acquired during an extreme heatwave in 2025, alongside architectural compactness and Euclidean distance to major parks. A composite Urban Heat Vulnerability Index (UHVI) was formulated as the supervised learning target. Deploying a Graph Convolutional Network (GCN) via a message-passing architecture, the model successfully captured non-linear spatial interactions, achieving exceptional predictive accuracy (Mean Absolute Error of 2.81 on a 100-point scale). Subsequent feature importance analysis revealed that extreme micro-scale vulnerability is primarily driven by a building's spatial isolation from major green infrastructure, substantially outweighing localized deficits in street-level vegetation. By shifting from macro-scale approximations to building-level topological deep learning, this study advances computational urban climatology and provides a highly precise, actionable framework for targeted climate adaptation planning in Mediterranean cities.

Keywords: Graph Neural Networks · Urban Heat Resilience · Mediterranean Districts · Urban Heat Vulnerability · Spatial Deep Learning · Climate Adaptation

1 Introduction

The accelerating pace of urbanisation in the Mediterranean region has produced cities characterised by high building densities, expansive impervious surfaces, and pronounced disparities in green infrastructure provision [1] The phenomenon of urban overheating is

O. Gervasi et al. (Eds.): ICCSA 2026 Workshops, LNCS 16758, pp. 645–661, 2027.
https://doi.org/10.1007/978-3-032-30497-1_39

receiving increasing attention in the Mediterranean basin, where rapid urban growth has intensified impervious surface cover—a key driver of land surface temperature elevation and urban heat island intensification [1–3]. These structural conditions, combined with escalating climate extremes driven by anthropogenic warming [4], have elevated urban heat from a seasonal inconvenience into a persistent public health and territorial justice concern. The IPCC Sixth Assessment Report identifies the Mediterranean as a major climate change hotspot: temperature extremes and heatwaves have increased in intensity, frequency, and duration in recent decades, and are projected to continue intensifying with high confidence under all Shared Socioeconomic Pathways through the twenty-first century [5]. Under SSP2-4.5 and SSP5-8.5 scenarios, urban heatwave exposure risk is projected to increase by 619% and 1,740% respectively by 2100, with elderly urban populations facing disproportionately elevated exposure—rising between 1,642% and 5,529% [6]. Seville exemplifies this compounding vulnerability. Its dense historic core, expansive peri-urban residential belts developed during rapid post-war urbanisation, and spatially uneven distribution of parks and street trees create sharp intra-urban thermal gradients. The broader Mediterranean basin and south-eastern European regions are already emerging as major hotspots for climate-related health impacts, with a substantial rise in heat-related mortality projected throughout the twenty-first century [7]. Heatwave mortality statistics consistently identify elderly residents, low-income households, and neighbourhoods with limited green infrastructure as disproportionately exposed populations. Existing evidence confirms that groups most vulnerable to heatwave health impacts include the elderly, low-income populations, outdoor workers, and individuals living alone, vulnerabilities that compound significantly when green space access is constrained [8]. In Mediterranean dry climates in particular, the scarcity of green-blue infrastructure is especially consequential, as limited vegetation cover reduces the cooling benefits that green space provides in more temperate urban environments [9, 10]. Yet policy responses have remained largely reactive, targeting individual buildings or isolated green interventions rather than the systemic spatial configuration that underpins resilience, or its absence.

The application of machine learning to urban climate analysis has proliferated over the past decade. Convolutional neural networks (CNNs), random forests, and support vector machines have been deployed to downscale land surface temperature (LST) retrievals, predict thermal comfort indices, and classify urban heat island intensity. However, these methods share a critical structural limitation: they treat spatial observation units, like census tracts, planning districts, grid cells, as statistically independent entities. This assumption ignores the well-established phenomenon of spatial autocorrelation, wherein proximate places tend to exhibit more similar attributes than distant ones, and more importantly, it cannot represent the spatial spillover of heat stress and adaptive capacity deficits across neighbourhood boundaries. Graph Neural Networks (GNNs) offer a principled alternative; by encoding spatial units as nodes in a graph and their adjacency relationships as edges, GNN architectures can learn representations that explicitly incorporate the influence of spatial neighbours. Recent applications in urban remote sensing [11], traffic forecasting [12], building and civil infrastructure operation and maintenance [13], building attribute and energy predictions [14, 15], have proved the effectiveness and good results of such methods.

Traditional approaches also tend to treat buildings as isolated data points, ignoring the complex topological reality of urban environments where a building's thermal performance is heavily influenced by the shading, density, and environmental context of its immediate neighbours. To bridge this critical research gap, this study introduces a novel, micro-scale predictive framework leveraging GNN's ability to model complex spatial relationships that shape the city's urban heat distribution [16].

The novelty of this approach lies in the deployment of a Graph Convolutional Network (GCN) to mathematically simulate how physical proximity, architectural compactness, and local environmental deficits compounded heat stress during the extreme 2025 heatwave. By predicting a composite Urban Heat Vulnerability Index (UHVI) at the individual building level, this methodology provides a transition from urban heat mitigation from neighbourhood-level generalizations to building-specific interventions.

1.1 Research Objectives

The primary aim of this study is to develop and validate a spatially aware deep learning model capable of evaluating urban heat vulnerability at the individual building scale. To achieve this, the research is guided by the following specific objectives:

- **To formulate a micro-scale Urban Heat Vulnerability Index (UHVI):** To construct a comprehensive composite metric that integrates satellite-derived thermal exposure (LST), micro-level vegetation presence (NDVI), architectural heat-trapping potential (Building Compactness), and infrastructural isolation (Distance to Parks) for over 29,000 individual structures.
- **To develop a topological deep learning architecture:** To design and train a Graph Convolutional Network (GCN) that successfully maps the spatial relationships between buildings, allowing the model to learn the contextual, neighbourhood-level drivers of heat vulnerability.
- **To evaluate predictive performance and spatial error:** To assess the accuracy of the GNN against ground-truth index calculations and map spatial prediction errors to identify geometric or geographic anomalies within the urban fabric.
- **To identify primary drivers of micro-scale vulnerability:** To conduct a feature importance analysis on the model's highest-risk predictions, isolating whether architectural geometry, lack of vegetation, or distance to cooling infrastructure acts as the primary catalyst for severe, localized urban heat stress.

2 Study Area

The study focuses on the metropolitan area of Seville, Andalusia, southern Spain (37.39°N, 5.99°W). Seville exhibits pronounced intra-urban heterogeneity in morphology, socio-economic structure, and green infrastructure provision—conditions widely documented as primary drivers of differential heat exposure across Mediterranean cities [1, 17]. The historic centre (*Casco Antiguo*) is characterised by compact morphology, enclosed courtyards, limited street canopy, and a predominantly elderly population; its high building density makes heat mitigation interventions particularly difficult to implement and amplifies nocturnal urban heat island intensity.

Seville's Köppen–Geiger *Csa* classification [18], produces some of the highest summer temperatures in continental Europe, with multiple heatwave episodes recorded in a single season and heat stress disproportionately concentrated in dense, low-vegetation urban zones [17, 19]. Heatwave mortality risk is the highest of any major Spanish city, with excess mortality at the 99th temperature percentile reaching a relative risk of 2.73 (95% CI: 2.34–3.18) [20].

Under high-emissions trajectories, and its climatic, morphological, and socio-demographic conditions, Seville would make an exemplary and scientifically compelling case for building-level heat resilience research.

3 Methodology

This study proposes a spatially aware, deep learning framework to assess and predict Urban Heat Vulnerability at the building level. The methodology is divided into four primary stages: data acquisition and feature engineering, formulation of the vulnerability index, spatial graph construction, and the design and training of a Graph Convolutional Network (GCN). Unlike traditional studies that aggregate data into arbitrary administrative neighbourhood units (*barrios*), the spatial extent of this analysis is defined strictly at the micro-scale, utilizing individual buildings as the fundamental units (nodes) of observation. The study area encompasses 29,542 distinct building geometries across the urban extent of Seville, extracted via OpenStreetMap (OSM).

By conceptualizing the city as a topological spatial graph, where each building acts as a discrete node connected to its immediate physical neighbours, this high-resolution approach bypasses the modifiable areal unit problem (MAUP) inherent to rigid census boundaries [21]. This extreme level of granularity ensures that highly localized environmental and structural indicators are captured with precise spatial accuracy, rather than being artificially averaged out across heterogeneous areas ranging from dense historic cores to sprawling peri-urban growth zones. The research is divided into five primary phases that encompass data acquisition, spatial graph construction, and GNN-based vulnerability assessment, Fig. 1.

3.1 Data Acquisition

Remote Sensing Inputs During the 2025 Extreme Heatwave

To capture the thermal and biophysical properties of the urban environment under severe climate stress, remote sensing data were exclusively acquired during the extreme heatwave of 2025. Land Surface Temperature (LST) retrievals were extracted to quantify localised, building-level heat exposure across the city. Concurrently, the Normalized Difference Vegetation Index (NDVI) was computed to measure the density of micro-level vegetation and green canopy presence immediately surrounding each structure. These two metrics served as environmental inputs for assessing localized heat risk and natural cooling capacity.

Urban Morphology and Green Space Proximity

To model the physical urban form and its potential to trap or exacerbate heat, building compactness was calculated for every individual structure in the dataset.

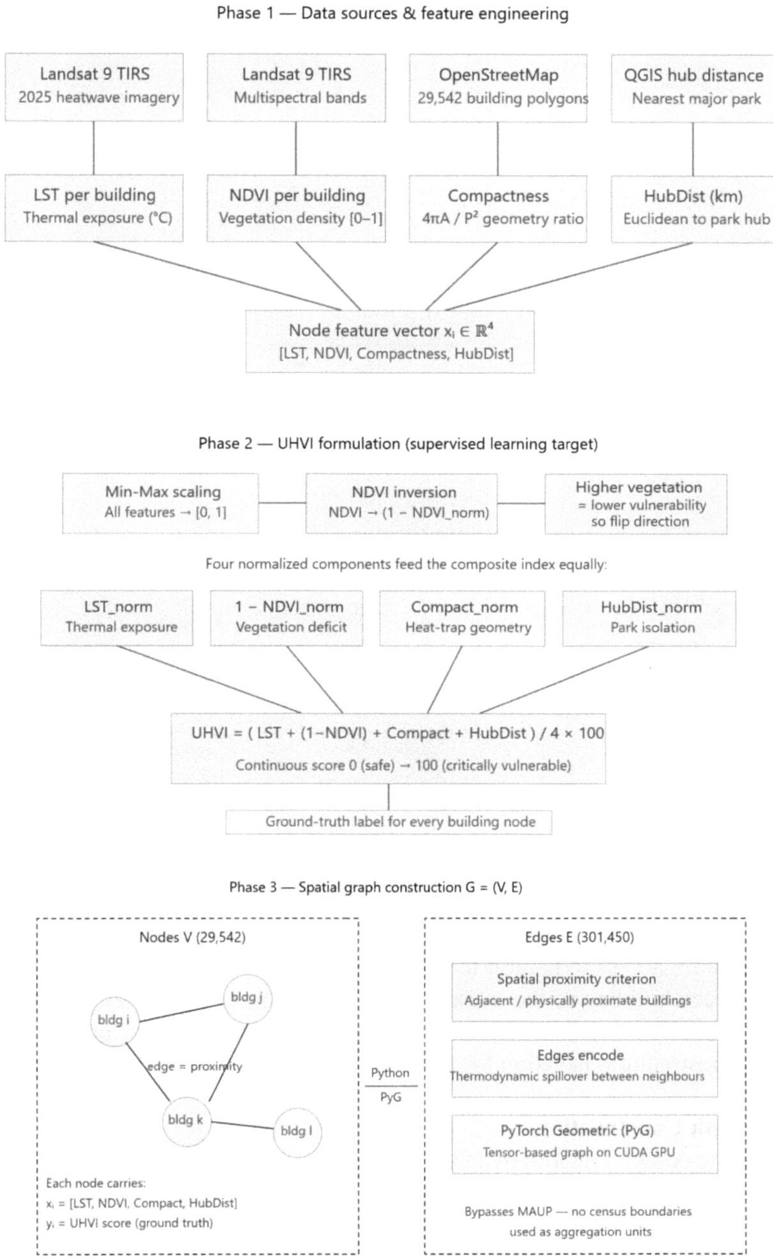

Fig. 1. Proposed study workflow, illustrating the integration of spatial data, graph construction, and GNN-based vulnerability assessment.

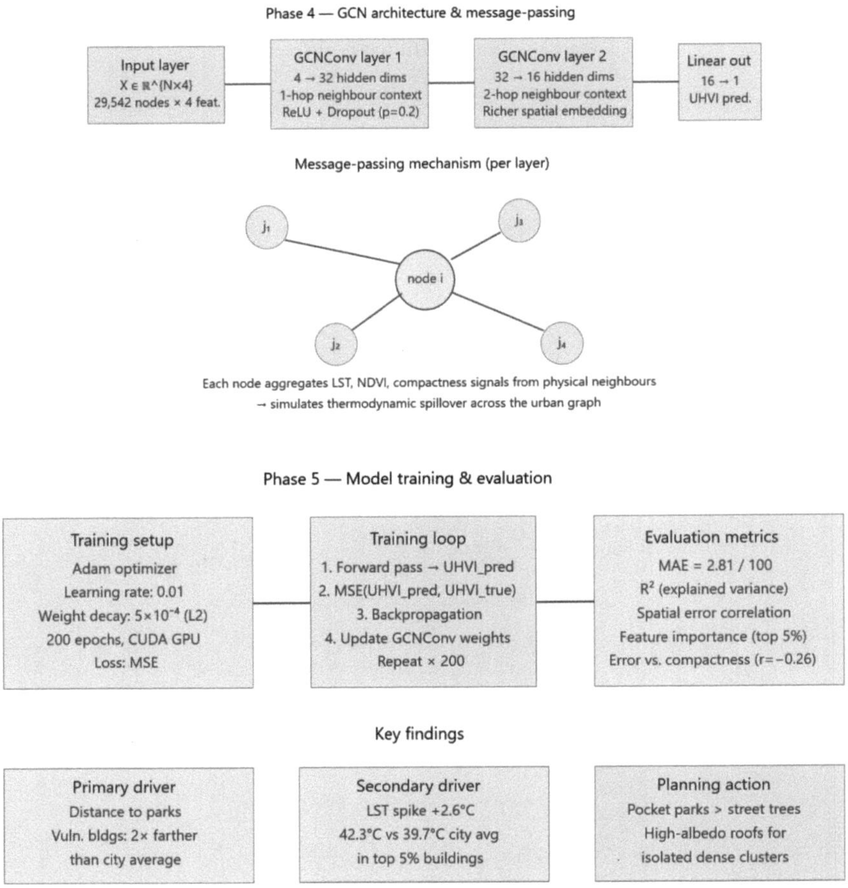

Fig. 1. *(continued)*

Furthermore, access to natural thermal relief was quantified by measuring the distance from each building to the nearest major green space. The distance to parks was calculated spatially using QGIS (Quantum GIS), providing a highly accurate, continuous metric of infrastructural isolation for every building in the study area.

Spatial Graph Construction

To capture the complex thermodynamic interactions between neighbouring structures, the dataset was modelled as a spatial graph utilizing a micro-scale topological approach where:

Nodes (Vertices): Individual buildings were designated as the fundamental nodes of the graph. Each node was attributed with a strict four-dimensional feature vector consisting of: LST, NDVI, Compactness, and Distance to Parks.

Edges (Relations): The spatial relationships between the buildings were defined computationally using Python. Edges were generated to connect adjacent and physically proximate buildings, allowing the model to simulate how heat and cooling effects diffuse through localised urban clusters. Table 1 summarizes the node features used in the GNN framework, including their data sources, processing methods, and their alignment with the Exposure–Sensitivity–Adaptive Capacity (ESAC) dimensions of vulnerability.

Table 1. Summary of node features used in the GNN framework.

Feature	Description	Source	Processing Software/Method	ESAC Dimension
Land Surface Temperature (LST)	Thermal exposure during the 2025 extreme heatwave	Landsat 9 TIRS	Remote Sensing Extraction	Exposure
Vegetation Index (NDVI)	Green canopy density and vegetation presence	Landsat 9 TIRS	Remote Sensing Extraction	Adaptive Capacity
Compactness	Morphological metric of heat-trapping potential, computed as $4\pi A/P^2$	OSM	Spatial geometry calculation in QGIS/Python	Sensitivity
Distance to Parks (HubDist)	Euclidean distance from each building centroid to the nearest major green space or cooling hub	OSM	Calculated in QGIS	Adaptive Capacity

Distance to Parks (HubDist): The Euclidean distance to the nearest major green space or cooling hub was used as a proxy for accessibility to natural thermal relief. This metric captures the spatial availability of urban cooling infrastructure, reflecting the extent to which buildings can benefit from the mitigating effects of vegetation and shaded environments [22]. Proximity to parks has been widely associated with reduced land surface temperatures, improved microclimatic conditions, and enhanced thermal comfort, particularly during extreme heat events. Moreover, accessibility to green infrastructure is increasingly recognised as a critical component of adaptive capacity within urban heat vulnerability frameworks [23], as limited access to cooling spaces disproportionately affects vulnerable populations. These thresholds, Table 2, are informed by empirical studies on the spatial influence of urban green spaces, which indicate that the cooling effects of vegetation typically diminish with distance, often within a few hundred meters from the source. Distances exceeding 1 km are therefore considered indicative of limited access to effective cooling infrastructure, contributing to heightened exposure and reduced adaptive capacity.

Table 2. Interpretation of distance to parks (adapted from literature)

Distance	Meaning
0–0.2 km	Excellent access (strong cooling benefit)
0.2–0.5 km	Good access
0.5–1 km	Moderate access
>1 km	Poor access (increased heat vulnerability)

3.2 Formulation of the Urban Heat Vulnerability Index (UHVI)

To generate a target variable for the predictive model, a composite Urban Heat Vulnerability Index (UHVI) was formulated. Because the input variables operate on entirely different mathematical scales, a Min-Max scaling technique was applied to normalize all features to a standard range of [0, 1].

Since higher vegetation corresponds to lower vulnerability, the normalized NDVI values were inverted. The UHVI for each building *i* was then computed as the unweighted average of the four standardized components:

$$UHVI_i = \frac{LST_{norm} + Compactness_{norm} + (1 - NDVI_{norm}) + HubDist_{norm}}{4} \times 100 \quad (1)$$

This formulation yields a continuous vulnerability score ranging from 0 (lowest vulnerability) to 100 (highest vulnerability), representing a balanced integration of thermal exposure, morphology, and accessibility to cooling resources.

This produced a ground-truth vulnerability score for every building in the dataset, ranging from 0 (minimal risk) to 100 (severe risk).

3.3 Spatial Graph Construction and GNN Architecture

To explicitly model spatial interdependencies, the dataset was represented as a graph:

$$G = (V, E)$$

The Vertices (V): each building is represented as a node with a feature matrix $X \in R^{NxF}$ which contains N = 29,542 nodes (individual buildings) and F = 4 features (LST, NDVI, Compactness, and Distance to Parks) extracted during the 2025 extreme heatwave. All features were normalized to a [0, 1] scale using Min-Max scaling. Edges (E): connections were established based on spatial proximity, resulting in 301,450 edges capturing neighbourhood relationships.

This graph structure, Fig. 2, enables the modelling of spatial spillover effects, where thermal conditions and urban form are influenced by adjacent buildings.

The graph was implemented using the PyTorch Geometric (PyG) framework, allowing efficient tensor-based processing and integration with deep learning architectures.

To predict the UHVI of buildings while accounting for neighbourhood context, a Graph Convolutional Network (GCN) was deployed. The GCN architecture leverages a message-passing mechanism to capture thermodynamic spatial spillovers between adjacent buildings. The model utilizes two GCNConv layers. The first layer maps the 4 input features to a hidden dimension of 32 to capture immediate neighbourhood effects, followed by a Rectified Linear Unit (ReLU) activation function and a Dropout layer $P = 0.2$ for regularization. A second GCNConv layer compresses the embeddings to a 16-dimensional space, followed by a final linear output layer projecting to the continuous scalar UHVI prediction.

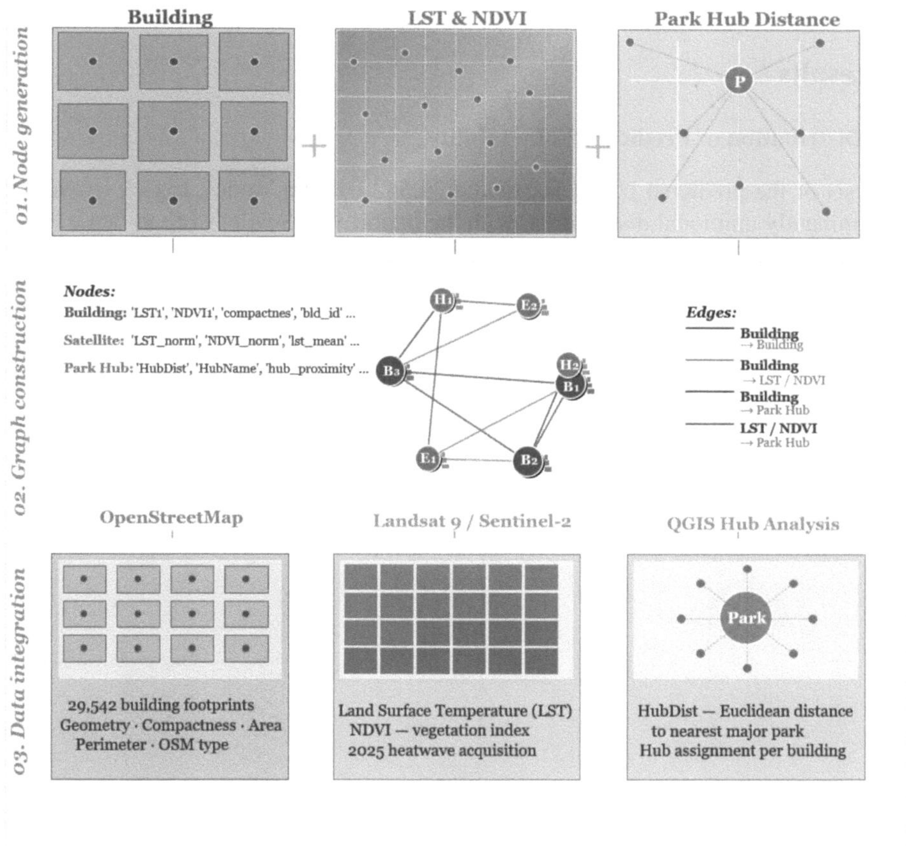

Fig. 2. Schematic of the three-stage GNN graph construction pipeline for Seville

3.4 Model Training and Evaluation

The model was trained to perform node-level regression. The dataset was loaded onto a CUDA-enabled GPU for accelerated processing. Training was executed over 200 epochs using the Adam optimizer with a learning rate of (0.01) and a weight decay of 5×10^{-4} for L2 regularization.

The loss function was defined as Mean Squared Error (MSE):

$$MSE = \frac{1}{n}\sum_{i=1}^{n}(Y_i - \widehat{Y}_i)^2 \tag{2}$$

Where Y_i denotes the ground-truth UHVI and $\widehat{Y}_i$ the predicted value.

Model performance was evaluated using Mean Absolute Error (MAE): for interpretability of prediction error, and Coefficient of Determination (R^2): to assess explained variance.

4 Results

4.1 Distribution of Predicted Vulnerability

Analysis of the predicted UHVI across the 29,542 building nodes, Fig. 3, revealed a predominantly unimodal distribution, with the majority of Seville's urban fabric registering moderate vulnerability scores between 40 and 60 on a 100-point scale. Notably, the distribution exhibited a pronounced right skew, isolating the top 5% of buildings that face critical exposure (scores $\geq$75). Spatial visualization of these high-risk predictions highlighted intense micro-scale clustering, demonstrating that severe urban heat vulnerability is not a diffuse, district-wide phenomenon, but is instead acutely localized within specific high-density blocks.

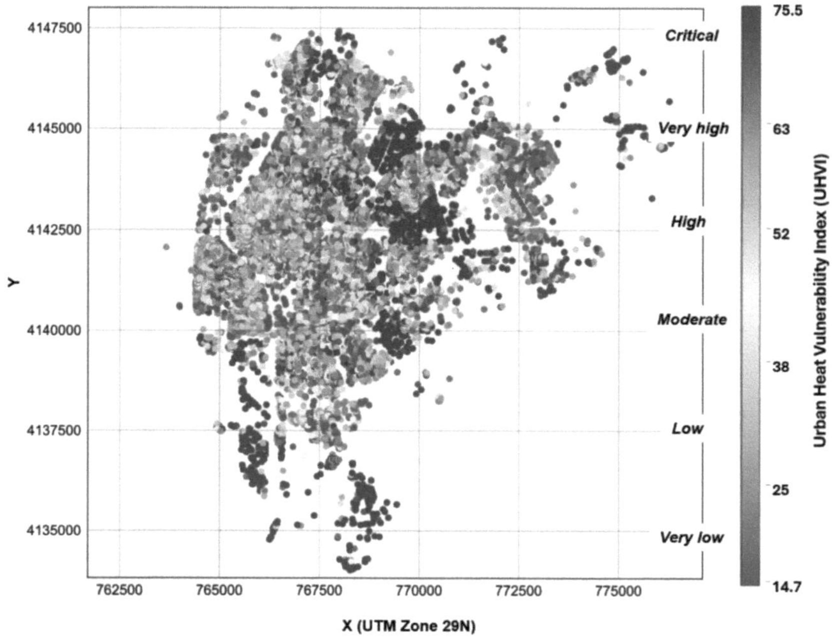

Fig. 3. Urban Heat Vulnerability distribution.

4.2 Feature Importance in High-Risk Zones

A contrastive feature analysis comparing the top 5% most vulnerable buildings against the city-wide baseline, Figs. 4 and 5, identified the primary structural and environmental drivers of extreme heat stress. The most discriminating feature was building compactness, with the highest-risk buildings recording a mean normalised value of 0.74 compared to the city average of 0.57 ($\Delta = +0.17$), indicating that geometrically compact, heat-trapping morphologies are the strongest predictor of severe localised vulnerability.

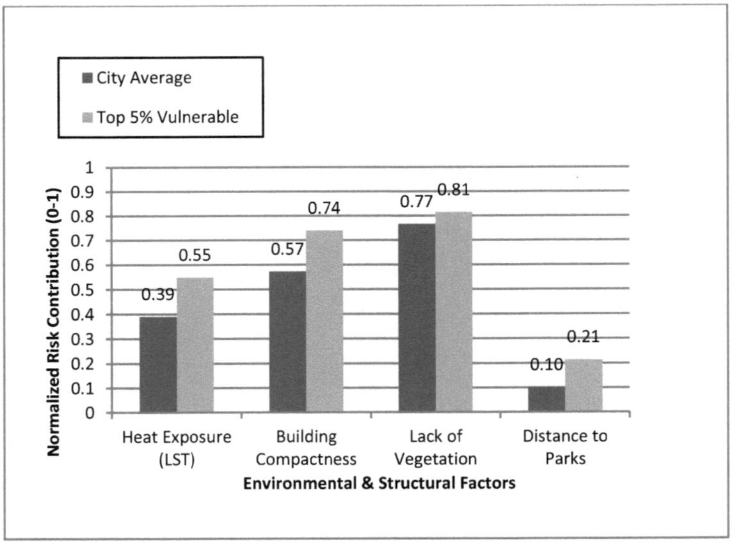

Fig. 4. Contrastive feature analysis of GCN-predicted vulnerability. Compares mean normalised risk factors (0 = minimal risk, 1 = maximum penalty) of the urban baseline (N = 29,542) against the top 5% highest-risk buildings.

Thermal exposure (LST) emerged as the second most critical driver, with the top 5% of buildings recording a mean surface temperature of 42.28 °C against the city average of 39.72 °C—a statistically meaningful gap of 2.56 °C (Δ = +0.16 normalised). Distance to parks contributed a moderate differential (city average: 0.595 km; top 5%: 1.249 km—more than double), confirming that structural isolation from major green cooling infrastructure compounds vulnerability, though its normalised contribution (Δ = +0.11) was smaller than compactness and thermal exposure. Notably, vegetation deficit (NDVI) showed the weakest discriminating power (Δ = +0.05), indicating that localised differences in street-level greening between the most exposed buildings and the city average are marginal, and that building geometry and direct thermal loading are the principal catalysts of micro-scale heat stress in Seville's urban fabric.

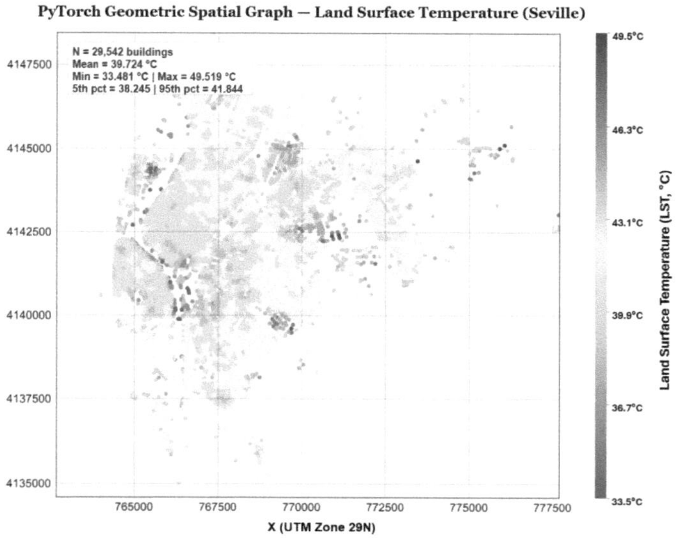

(a)

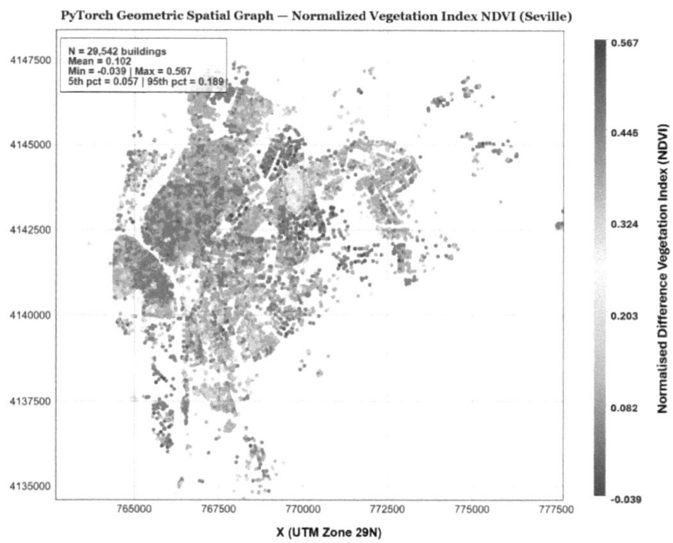

(b)

Fig. 5. Spatial distribution of the four GNN node features across 29,542 building nodes in Seville. (a) Land Surface Temperature (LST, °C), (b) Normalized Difference Vegetation Index (NDVI), (c) Distance to nearest park (HubDist, km), (d) Building compactness, indicating dense, heat-trapping morphologies typical of traditional Mediterranean urban blocks.

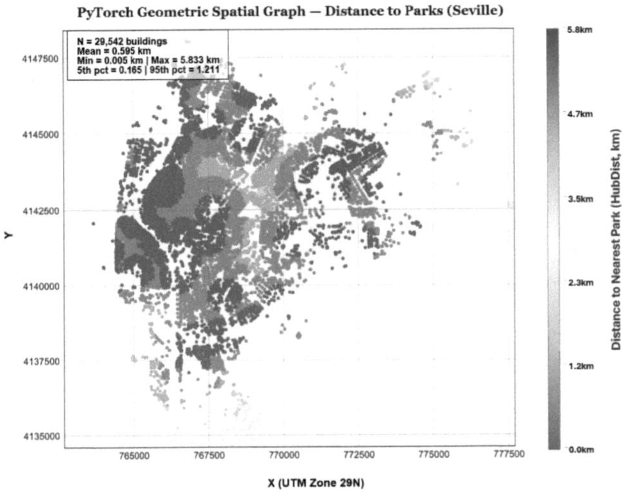

(c)

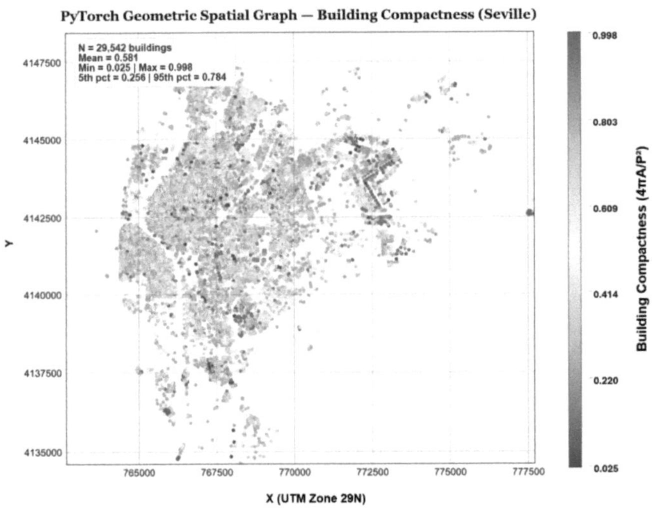

(d)

Fig. 5. *(continued)*

4.3 Predictive Performance

The trained GCN achieved high predictive accuracy at the building level, producing an average Mean Absolute Error (MAE) of just 2.81 points (out of 100). This minimal error margin confirms that the message-passing architecture successfully learned the nonlinear spatial interactions between building geometry and environmental exposure. The network accurately simulated how localized heat (LST) and cooling sources (NDVI) diffuse across physical adjacency edges, providing predictive information far beyond what standard, attribute-only linear regressions could achieve.

5 Discussion

This This study advances urban heat research along two principal methodological axes. First, by operationalising a micro-scale building-level graph of 29,542 individual nodes, it structurally bypasses the MAUP that systematically distorts vulnerability assessments conducted at the census-tract or administrative-district level Second, the application of a Graph Convolutional Network to extreme heatwave data acquired during the 2025 event embeds urban thermodynamic spillover directly into the learning architecture: each graph edge encodes the physical adjacency through which the heat-trapping geometry of one building propagates thermal stress to its immediate neighbours—a spatial dependency that conventional regression and grid-based deep learning models cannot represent. The finding that building compactness is the dominant predictor of micro-scale heat vulnerability, followed closely by direct thermal exposure (LST), carries concrete implications for climate adaptation planning in Seville and analogous Mediterranean cities. The data indicate that for the most critically exposed buildings—characterised by dense, geometrically compact morphologies and elevated surface temperatures—localised street-tree planting will yield only marginal risk reduction, given that vegetation deficit (NDVI) showed the weakest discriminating power between high-risk and baseline structures. Municipal interventions for identified hotspots should instead prioritise morphological and material upgrades: mandatory installation of high-albedo roofing systems to reduce direct solar absorption, and the targeted conversion of impervious surfaces within compact clusters into pocket parks or permeable green corridors that interrupt heat accumulation at source.

The primary limitation of this study lies in the two-dimensional nature of its input feature set. Although the spatial graph successfully captured plan-view physical proximity and building footprint compactness, it lacked three-dimensional architectural context—specifically, building height, street canyon aspect ratio, vertical shading patterns, and roof material properties. These volumetric characteristics govern wind flow channelling, shortwave radiation trapping, and nocturnal longwave emission; their absence directly accounts for the model's moderately elevated error margins in the most compact urban zones. Future iterations of this framework should incorporate 3D node features derived from LiDAR point clouds or urban digital twins to fully resolve the thermodynamic complexity of dense Seville street canyons.

6 Conclusion

As urban heat stress intensifies across Mediterranean cities under accelerating climate change, mitigation strategies must transition from macro-scale generalisation to precise, building-level intervention. This study presented a novel micro-scale GCN framework to map and predict Urban Heat Vulnerability across 29,542 individual buildings in Seville during the extreme 2025 heatwave—operationalising the city not as a collection of administrative districts, but as a continuous topological fabric of thermodynamic relationships.

By encoding buildings as interconnected graph nodes and physical adjacency as edges, the GCN successfully captured the spatial diffusion of heat stress across the urban fabric, achieving a Mean Absolute Error of 2.81 on a 100-point vulnerability index. Contrastive feature analysis of the highest-risk buildings revealed that building compactness is the primary structural driver of extreme localised vulnerability, followed by direct thermal exposure (LST), with vegetation deficit (NDVI) and park distance contributing comparatively smaller differentials. These findings reframe the dominant narrative in urban heat adaptation: geometric morphology—not green infrastructure scarcity alone—is the critical determinant of micro-scale heat risk in Seville's densest urban zones. The resulting building-level vulnerability surface provides municipal planners with a spatially precise, actionable framework for deploying cooling interventions where topological and environmental risk factors compound most severely. Future research should prioritise three principal extensions: the integration of 3D architectural features—including building height, street canyon aspect ratios, and roof albedo—into the graph node feature set; the incorporation of socio-demographic vulnerability indicators to construct a composite climate justice index; and the temporal extension of the model across multiple heatwave events to assess inter-annual stability of the identified risk patterns.

Disclosure of Interests. The authors declare no competing interests.

References

1. Ncir, N.B.H., Rejeb, A., Claramunt, C.: Urbanization and thermal vulnerability: spatio-temporal assessment in a Mediterranean city. Sustain. Cities Soc., 107311 (2026). https://doi.org/10.1016/j.scs.2026.107311
2. Bahi, H., Rhinane, H., Bensalmia, A., Fehrenbach, U., Scherer, D.: Effects of urbanization and seasonal cycle on the surface urban heat island patterns in the coastal growing cities: a case study of Casablanca, Morocco. Remote Sens. **8** (2016). https://doi.org/10.3390/rs8100829
3. Zhou, Z., Liu, Y.: Surface urban heat island disparities and the role of urban form across the urban-rural gradient. Environ. Impact Assess. Rev. **116**, 108144 (2026). https://doi.org/10.1016/j.eiar.2025.108144
4. Drobinski, P., et al.: How warmer and drier will the Mediterranean region be at the end of the twenty-first century? Reg. Environ. Change **20**, 78 (2020). https://doi.org/10.1007/s10113-020-01659-w
5. IPCC: Technical summary. In: Climate Change 2022 – Impacts, Adaptation and Vulnerability, pp. 37–118. Cambridge University Press (2022). https://doi.org/10.1017/9781009325844.002
6. Chen, M., et al.: Rising vulnerability of compound risk inequality to ageing and extreme heatwave exposure in global cities. npj Urban Sustain. **3**, 38 (2023). https://doi.org/10.1038/s42949-023-00118-9
7. Janoš, T., et al.: Heat-related mortality in Europe during 2024 and health emergency forecasting to reduce preventable deaths. Nat. Med. **31**, 4065–4074 (2025). https://doi.org/10.1038/s41591-025-03954-7
8. Kang, Y., Park, J., Jang, D.-H.: Compound impact of heatwaves on vulnerable groups considering age, income, and disability. Sci. Rep. **14**, 24732 (2024). https://doi.org/10.1038/s41598-024-75224-4
9. Liu, Q., Hang, T., Wan, M., Song, Y.: Advancing climate justice for vulnerable groups: optimizing spatial configuration of urban blue–green infrastructure to mitigate heat risks leveraging explainable machine learning. Sustain. Cities Soc. **140**, 107228 (2026). https://doi.org/10.1016/j.scs.2026.107228

10. Kumar, P., et al.: Urban heat mitigation by green and blue infrastructure: drivers, effectiveness, and future needs. Innovation **5**, 100588 (2024). https://doi.org/10.1016/j.xinn.2024.100588
11. Zhang, T., et al.: Classifying urban functional zones via a multilevel graph neural network and multimodal geospatial data. IEEE J. Sel. Top. Appl. Earth Obs. Remote Sens. **18**, 23210–23227 (2025). https://doi.org/10.1109/JSTARS.2025.3603189
12. Ahmed, S.F., et al.: Enhancement of traffic forecasting through graph neural network-based information fusion techniques. Inf. Fus. **110**, 102466 (2024). https://doi.org/10.1016/j.inffus.2024.102466
13. Wettewa, S., Hou, L., Zhang, G.: Graph Neural Networks for building and civil infrastructure operation and maintenance enhancement. Adv. Eng. Inform. **62**, 102868 (2024). https://doi.org/10.1016/j.aei.2024.102868
14. Hu, Y., Cheng, X., Wang, S., Chen, J., Zhao, T., Dai, E.: Times series forecasting for urban building energy consumption based on graph convolutional network. Appl. Energy **307**, 118231 (2022). https://doi.org/10.1016/j.apenergy.2021.118231
15. Liang, X., Yap, W., Biljecki, F.: Heterogeneous graph neural networks for building attribute prediction from hierarchical urban features and cross-view imagery. ISPRS J. Photogramm. Remote Sens. **234**, 185–204 (2026). https://doi.org/10.1016/j.isprsjprs.2026.02.016
16. Bormudoi, A., Hinge, G., Nagai, M., Barman, P.: A novel framework for urban heat analysis combining thermal roughness and temporal dynamics in Delhi with Graph Neural Networks. Urban Clim. **65**, 102804 (2026). https://doi.org/10.1016/j.uclim.2026.102804
17. Hidalgo-García, D., Rezapouraghdam, H.: Variability of heat stress using the UrbClim climate model in the city of Seville (Spain): mitigation proposal. Environ. Monit. Assess. **195**, 1164 (2023). https://doi.org/10.1007/s10661-023-11768-8
18. Andrade, C., Contente, J.: Köppen's climate classification projections for the Iberian Peninsula. Clim. Res. **81**, 71–89 (2020). https://doi.org/10.3354/cr01604
19. Alnajjar, S., García-Martínez, A., López-Cabeza, V.P., Al-Azhari, W.: A multidimensional approach to mapping urban heat vulnerability: integrating remote sensing and spatial configuration. Smart Cities **8**, 137 (2025). https://doi.org/10.3390/smartcities8040137
20. Royé, D., Codesido, R., Tobías, A., Taracido, M.: Heat wave intensity and daily mortality in four of the largest cities of Spain. Environ. Res. **182**, 109027 (2020). https://doi.org/10.1016/j.envres.2019.109027
21. Meng, L.: The modifiable areal unit problem (MAUP) and spatial accessibility assessments of urban parks: empirical evidence from Nanjing's central urban area, China. Urban For. Urban Green. **113**, 129027 (2025). https://doi.org/10.1016/j.ufug.2025.129027
22. Molla, A., Lamer, K., Sailor, D.J.: Citizen science coupled with machine learning to quantify green-blue infrastructure cooling potential in Maricopa County, Arizona. Sustain. Cities Soc. **139**, 107211 (2026). https://doi.org/10.1016/j.scs.2026.107211
23. Stumpe, B., Stuhrmann, N., Marschner, B.: Variability of cooling distances and intensities of urban green spaces over six hot summer days affects their relevance for UHI mitigation in Berlin, Germany. Sustain. Cities Soc. **137**, 107139 (2026). https://doi.org/10.1016/j.scs.2026.107139

Author Index

O. Gervasi et al. (Eds.): ICCSA 2026 Workshops, LNCS 16758, pp. 663–664, 2027.
https://doi.org/10.1007/978-3-032-30497-1

MIX
Papier aus verantwortungsvollen Quellen
Paper from responsible sources
FSC® C105338

If you have any concerns about our products,
you can contact us on
ProductSafety@springernature.com

In case Publisher is established outside the EU,
the EU authorized representative is:
Springer Nature Customer Service Center GmbH
Europaplatz 3, 69115 Heidelberg, Germany

Printed by Libri Plureos GmbH
in Hamburg, Germany